Discovering
Molecular
Genetics

Jeffrey H. Miller

DEPARTMENT OF MICROBIOLOGY
AND MOLECULAR GENETICS
AND MOLECULAR BIOLOGY INSTITUTE
UNIVERSITY OF CALIFORNIA LOS ANGELES

Discovering Molecular Genetics

A CASE STUDY COURSE WITH PROBLEMS & SCENARIOS

Cold Spring Harbor Laboratory Press 1996

Illustration Credits

Front cover: Original black and white drawing by Margaret L. Kowalczyk based on an idea suggested to the author by Anthony J.F. Griffiths.

Back cover: *lac* repressor–DNA complex from *Escherichia coli* with two operator sequences. (*Courtesy of University of Pennsylvania*)

xix, (*top, middle, bottom right*) Cold Spring Harbor Laboratory Archives, (*bottom left*) Courtesy of Igor Gamow

xx, (*top, middle right, bottom*) Cold Spring Harbor Laboratory Archives, (*middle left*) Courtesy of Karl Maramorosch

xxi, (*top left*) Courtesy of Barbara Beckwith, (*top right, bottom*) Cold Spring Harbor Laboratory Archives

xxii–xxiii, Cold Spring Harbor Laboratory Archives

13, Cold Spring Harbor Laboratory Archives

16, Modified from *Introduction to Biostatistics* by R.R. Sokal and F.J. Rohlf. ©1973 W.H. Freeman and Company

59, Cold Spring Harbor Laboratory Archives

95, Courtesy of Scripps Clinic and Research Foundation

113, Cold Spring Harbor Laboratory Archives

135, Cold Spring Harbor Laboratory Archives by permission of Dr. Norton Zinder

183, 185, Cold Spring Harbor Laboratory Archives

235, (*top*) Courtesy of Barbara Beckwith, (*bottom*) Cold Spring Harbor Laboratory Archives

287, Cold Spring Harbor Laboratory Archives

320, Redrawn from M.L. Michaels and J.H. Miller. 1992. *Journal of Bacteriology 174:* 6322

599–603, M.W. Ebert Graphics

604, UPI/Bettmann

605, The Bettmann Archive

607, MONOPOLY®, the distinctive design of the game board, the four corner squares, as well as each of the distinctive elements of the board and the playing pieces are trademarks of Tonka Corporation for its real estate trading game and game equipment. © 1935, 1936, 1947, 1951, 1952, 1954, 1961, 1973, 1994 Parker Brothers, Division of Tonka Corporation, Beverly, Massachuestts 01915

609, (*top right*) UPI/Bettmann, (*top left*) Springer/Bettmann Film Archive, (*bottom*) The Bettmann Archive

610, The Bettmann Archive

613, Line drawing ©1971 John Lawrence from *The Hollow Crown* published by Hamish Hamilton Ltd., London. ©1971 John Barton and Joy Law

615, The Empire Strikes Back™ TM & © Lucasfilm Ltd. (LFL) 1980. All Rights Reserved.

616, (*top*) Return of the Jedi™ TM & © Lucasfilm Ltd. (LFL) 1983. All Rights Reserved. (*bottom*) The Empire Strikes Back™ TM & © Lucasfilm Ltd. (LFL) 1980. All Rights Reserved.

617–620, The Bettmann Archive

623, Redrawn from *The Hollow Crown* published by Hamish Hamilton Ltd., London. ©1971 John Barton and Joy Law

625, (*top*) Reprinted from *The Solution of Codes and Ciphers* by Louis C.S. Mansfield. Alexander Maclehose and Co., London (1936), (*bottom*) The Bettmann Archive

630, Courtesy Cell Press, Cambridge, Massachusetts 02138

631, (*top*) The Bettmann Archive, (*bottom*) M.W. Ebert Graphics

639–641, 643–648, M.W. Ebert Graphics

649, Masterprints™ Silver Surfer™ TM & © Marvel Entertainment Group, Inc. All Rights Reserved. Produced and distributed exclusively by Fleer Corp.

650, 652, 654, 656, 658, M.W. Ebert Graphics

Quotations

13, 183, 184, *The Statue Within* by François Jacob ©1988 Basic Books, Inc.

Discovering Molecular Genetics

A CASE STUDY COURSE
WITH PROBLEMS
& SCENARIOS

©1996 by Cold Spring Harbor Laboratory Press
All Rights Reserved.
Design by Emily Harste

Library of Congress Cataloging-in-Publication Data

Miller, Jeffrey H.
    Discovering molecular genetics / Jeffrey H. Miller.
      p.   cm.
    Includes bibliographical references and index.
    ISBN 0-87969-475-0 (alk. paper)
    1. Molecular genetics.
    QH442.M545   1996
    574.87'328--dc20   95-49965
                        CIP

All Cold Spring Harbor Laboratory Press publications may be ordered directly from Cold Spring Harbor Laboratory Press, 10 Skyline Drive, Plainview, New York 11803-2500. Phone: 1-800-843-4388 in Continental U.S. and Canada. All other locations: (516) 349-1930. FAX: (516) 349-1946.

To my parents
Irma Miller and
in memory, Jerome S. Miller

Contents

Contents

Unit 5 / Conjugation and Genetic Recombination 133

Unit 6 / Genetic Regulatory Mechanisms 181

Section II

Updated Papers

Unit 10 / Transposable Elements   431

Section III

Questions, Answers, Problems, & Scenarios

Scenarios 599

A Paradigm 659

The Purloined Letter
by Edgar Allen Poe

Appendix 671

The Gold Bug
by Edgar Allen Poe

Preface

When I was a biochemistry and molecular biology graduate student in the late 1960s, my fellow students and I used to muse over how anyone could have conceived of doing serious molecular biology research before the structure of DNA had been elucidated. We had been brought into the research scene after the DNA structure was taken for granted, and we simply couldn't fathom how so many researchers could function 15–20 years before. We listened, unconvinced, as our advisors described the excitement in genetic research that took place in the 1940s with the work of Beadle, Tatum, Lederberg, Delbrück, Hershey, and others. Then we went out into the world and started our own laboratories, and today we find our students sitting and wondering how we could have attempted serious molecular biology research without being able to clone and sequence DNA! (Not to mention without monoclonal antibodies, Southerns, and PCR.) When we try to explain to them the thrill and excitement of the work of Crick, Brenner, Jacob, Monod, Yanofsky, Signer, Beckwith, Perutz, and their colleagues, we are met with the same scepticism that we ourselves once expressed to our advisors. "Genetics without site-directed mutagenesis? Impossible!" we are told. "Mapping a gene in vivo without using restriction enzymes? Inconceivable!" "Analyzing mutations in a gene without just sequencing the entire gene by automated methods? No way!"

The above thoughts and sentiments underscore one of the main reasons I have written this text. The major portion of this book seeks to describe molecular genetics research before DNA sequencing. However, it is not intended as an historical record, but rather as a celebration of some of the most brilliant papers ever written in molecular biology. The period covered in the classical section represents the high point of pure molecular genetics. Most of the papers were written in a 10-year period from the late 1950s to the late 1960s. The year 1961 alone saw the publication of Benzer's classic analysis of the fine structure of the gene; the elucidation of the triplet nature of the genetic code by Crick, Brenner, and their co-workers; and the treatise on genetic regulation by Jacob and Monod. Toward the end of this period, we see the imaginative genetics of Jon Beckwith and Ethan Signer, who ushered in the era of in vivo genetic engineering and influenced people to appreciate the advantages of cloning. In many ways, the elaborate cloning methodologies that were developed from the mid-1970s on were inspired by their work. We also see the putting together of genetics and biochemistry, as exemplified by Max Perutz's work on human hemoglobin variants.

No less interesting than the work chronicled here are the scientists themselves. Fortunately, several of these investigators have published autobiographies that are highly recommended. François Jacob's *The Statue Within* chronicles many of his experiences during World War II and follows his early career at the Pasteur Institute. This is a touching and candid memoir, which was a best-seller in France. In *What Mad Pursuit*, Francis Crick reviews much of his scientific career. Crick displayed a brilliant insight into the workings of the cell, as documented by his achievements. Sydney Brenner demonstrated this same type of intuition.

This intuition invites comparisons of Crick and Brenner with the detective created by Edgar Alan Poe, C. August Dupin, who was, in fact, the prototype of Arthur Conan Doyle's character Sherlock Holmes. Dupin could solve mysteries merely from the newspaper accounts. He is introduced to us in "Murders in the Rue Morgue," where simply by reading the accounts of a series of gruesome murders he is able to determine what had really happened. In the more complex story "Mystery of Marie Roget," Poe transposed a true murder, that of Marie Rogers in New York, to Paris and simply from the newspaper accounts of the actual case was able to suggest who the murderer might be. The following year, the New York police arrested the murderer predicted by Dupin in the story. However, it is in "The Purloined Letter" that we meet Dupin at his finest. In this story, reprinted at the end of this book, the police inspector asks to see Dupin for advice concerning a matter of the utmost urgency and discretion. A female member of the royal family has had an indiscrete letter, dealing with an affair, stolen by a minister who is blackmailing her. In his absence, the police have searched his lodgings in the most detailed manner, but they can find nothing. Dupin tells the inspector to look again. Several weeks later, the inspector returns in dismay and says that the reward for the return of the letter has tripled, and he would personally give a large sum to secure possession of the letter for the Crown. Dupin asks if he is serious and then says, "Write me a check for the amount and I will give you the letter." Astonished, the inspector writes a check and Dupin opens a drawer, hands him the letter, and takes the check. The inspector staggers out, unbelieving. Dupin then confides to his friend that the inspector had failed to understand the level of sophistication of his opponent. He had been looking too deeply to see the solution which was much simpler than he imagined. He had searched where he would have hidden the letter. Since the thief understood this, the inspector was doomed to failure.

In fact, many schoolboys could reason better. For example, as pointed out by Dupin, there is a game played by schoolboys that is called even-odd. There are two marbles, and the game is for one person to guess whether there is an even or an odd number of marbles in the second person's hand. The person who usually won this game to become school champion was not necessarily the smartest student. It was simply the student who could best guess the astuteness of his opponents. Suppose our boy has a dope for an opponent. Our boy guesses odd and loses, but then he wins because he knows that the dope will say to himself, "This time I will do the opposite." Now suppose instead that our boy's opponent is one level higher than a dope. He realizes that our boy has guessed odd when it really was even. He is tempted to switch to odd, but that is too simple, so he keeps even. Our boy realizes that this boy is one step up from a dope, so he guesses even. The key is for the reasoner to identify with the intellect of his opponent. Because the thief knew that the inspector would search in out-of-the-way places, he was driven to simplicity. Therefore, he placed the letter, in only slightly disguised form, in an open rack hanging from the mantelpiece, right in front of everyone's noses.

I myself encountered this same mentality when I was in high school and pledged for a fraternity. On the last day of pledging (or hazing), we were treated to "hell day." After being subjected to minor tortures, we were blindfolded and dropped off 50–100 miles from home. We then had to get back on our own. Since this was known in advance, the goal was to hide at least a dime somewhere, since at that time a coin deposit was required even to make a collect call home to have our parents come and pick us up. I spent hours beforehand taking apart the heel of my sneaker to hide a dime and then sewing it up. To placate those searching our clothing for money, I Scotch-taped a second dime just under the tongue of the sneaker, so that they could easily find this and feel that they had found my secret phone money. During the search of our clothing, just before transporting us to some unknown destination, I was crestfallen when they discovered the dime I had so arduously hidden in the sneaker heel. When they dropped me off later and I untied the blindfold, I was in a bull field in upstate New York, 60 miles from my suburban home outside New York City. Imagine my surprise when I reached down and found that the dime I had taped under the tongue of the sneaker was still there, untouched! Just as in "The Purloined Letter," the searchers had overlooked the obvious and only searched where they would have hidden a dime.

Another example of failing to see the obvious, also recounted by Poe, is the game of maps. One selects, say, the map of Egypt and picks a name on the map, and the other person must guess the name by asking a series of questions. Of course, if the name EGYPT, which runs across the whole face of the map, is picked, then the second person never finds it, since he is looking for too much detail. Crick and Brenner succeeded more often than not because they did not overlook the obvious and were not always captured by all of the small details of a problem.

For further descriptions of these scientists and others, I recommend Horace Freeland Judson's book, *The Eighth Day of Creation.* This volume is an excellent source of biographical information on Jacques Monod, who stayed in Paris during the German occupation in World War II, working with the French Resistance. Despite the danger of possibly being caught by the Nazis, Monod still had the courage and determination to secretly slip into the Pasteur Institute at night to do experiments in bacterial genetics. And we, today, have the nerve to complain about our research support and facilities? Another heroic personage was Max Perutz, whose book, *Is Science Necessary?*, chronicles his experiences as an internee in Canada before being enlisted into a secret project for the British War Office.

The above brief descriptions point out the second reason for this book, namely, to honor the scientists who created the field of molecular genetics as we know it today and who set an example for the next generation of biologists. Countless investigators have been inspired by the work of Crick, Brenner, Jacob, Monod, and their colleagues, who have given so much to molecular biology.

Finally, the book comprises a syllabus for a course that I have given at UCLA during the past seven years, and in an abbreviated form at Scripps Research Institute in La Jolla in 1993 with Sydney Brenner. The course uses a "case study" approach in which the students read original papers and discuss the lives of the scientists along with the emergence of the research. Following the section on classical papers is a section containing more recent papers concentrating on aspects of mutagenesis and transposition. Each unit is introduced with a discussion of key concepts required to understand the featured paper(s) and to answer the questions from the reading(s), which can be used for take-home exams. Because understanding concepts, rather than simple memorization, is encouraged, all exams are either take-home or open-book. For the take-home exams, students are allowed to work together in preassigned groups of five or six students. This allows for more penetrating problems than could normally be assigned. Many of the Unit Problems and Scenarios provided at the back of the book are taken from just such exams that I have given. Different historical or science fiction themes are included to make the exams more colorful. The more searching take-home problems are assigned for two-week periods, with variations of the problems given to different groups. These problems and scenarios provide a "workbook" throughout the course, so that the sit-down exams are just asking students to reapply concepts they have already worked out. I hope that you will have as much fun working out some of these problems as I and my students (so I am told) have had.

I am indebted to Nancy Ford for the time and effort she has put into making this book a reality. I would also like to express my sincere appreciation to Jim Watson and the Cold Spring Harbor Laboratory Press for supporting so many scientific publications such as this one. I am grateful to my many colleagues who have read different problem scenarios and offered encouragement, and especially to Sydney Brenner, Francis Crick, Jon Beckwith, Charles Yanofsky, and Max Perutz for sharing with me their remembrances of both the research and personalities involved in much of the work chronicled here. Finally, I would like to thank my wife, Kim Anh Miller, for tolerance and support during the writing of this manuscript.

July 1995

Jeffrey H. Miller
University of California
Los Angeles

J.D. Watson and F.H.C. Crick
1993 40th Anniversary of the Double Helix

S. Brenner, F. Jacob, and S. Benzer
1985 Cold Spring Harbor Symposium

J.D. Watson
ca. 1956
Wearing RNA Tie
Club tie

G. Gamow
ca. 1954 With model of a nucleic acid structure

C. Yanofsky
1966 Cold Spring Harbor Symposium

E.-L. Wollman
ca. 1950s

J. Monod
1969 Cold Spring Harbor
Lactose Operon Meeting

W. Hayes
1953 Cold Spring Harbor Symposium

A.B. Pardee
1984 Cold Spring Harbor Cancer Cells Meeting

J.R. Beckwith
1991

M.E. Gottesman
1974 Advanced Bacterial Genetics Workshop

R.A. Weisberg
1984 Cold Spring Harbor Symposium

M.F. Perutz
1987 Cold Spring Harbor Symposium

G.R. Fink and F. Sherman
1979 Cold Spring Harbor Yeast Meeting

F. Sherman
1979 Cold Spring Harbor Yeast Course

B.N. Ames
1966 Cold Spring Harbor Symposium

J.H. Miller
ca. 1973 Cold Spring Harbor

A.I. Bukhari and E. Ljungquist
1982 Cold Spring Harbor Phage Meeting

M. Faelen
1980 Cold Spring Harbor Symposium

A. Toussaint
1978 Cold Spring Harbor
Symposium

J.A. Shapiro
1984 Cold Spring Harbor

N. Datta
1980 Cold Spring Harbor Symposium

D. Botstein
1976 Cold Spring Harbor

Section I

Classical Papers

Introduction

When we look back on the emergence of molecular biology as a field, we can see that it chronicles the progression of ideas and concepts along with technical advances, but it is also the story of people, for it is their history, too. Appreciating the interplay of ideas, technology, and people gives us a better perspective on the past and present and provides a foundation for the future.

Looking at some of the key molecular biologists whose work we will be studying, it is interesting to note that many of their lives were greatly influenced by World War II. They were young men at the time, and some of them were caught up in the conflict in one way or another. For example, Francis Crick helped design mines that were used to sink enemy ships in the North Sea; Seymour Benzer worked on radar detection devices; and Charles Yanofsky fought in the Battle of the Bulge in the Ardennes in Belgium. François Jacob left France during the German occupation and served with the Free French forces; he was seriously wounded shortly after the invasion of Normandy. Jacques Monod was a leader of the French underground resistance in Paris. Max Perutz was interned as an enemy alien and incarcerated in Canada before being released to serve with the British War Office on a secret project. After the war, these scientists continued their research and in the 1950s and 1960s carried out brilliant studies that we will read about. We'll meet them and take a glimpse at their lives through their own words in autobiographies and through interviews. Their work and that of their colleagues formed the basis of molecular biology as we know it today.

HISTORICAL PERSPECTIVE

Before we begin analyzing some of the key papers reprinted in this section, most of which were published over a 10-year period beginning in 1959, let's step back and get an historical perspective on where the field was when Brenner, Crick, Benzer, Yanofsky, Perutz, and their colleagues were engaged in their studies. The research carried out during the 1940s and at the beginning of the 1950s had established the following:

1. The genetic material is DNA. Avery and co-workers showed in the 1940s that the transforming principle discovered by Griffiths in 1928 was DNA. This fact was confirmed in a more influential experiment by Hershey and Chase in 1952.

2. Genes code for proteins. Beadle and Tatum's one gene–one enzyme hypothesis in the 1940s described the fact that the genetic material controlled the structure of proteins.

3. Gene transfer could occur in bacteria. Lederberg and Tatum's discovery of conjugation and Lederberg and Zinder's finding of transduction opened the door for genetic experiments in bacteria.

4. Mutations in bacteria produced stable mutants and these were shown by Luria and Delbrück to arise spontaneously in growing bacterial cultures.

5. Bacteriophage could be analyzed genetically. The work of Luria, Delbrück, and Hershey, among others, demonstrated that viruses could be dissected by genetic means. Mutants could be detected and the corresponding mutations crossed with one another to yield recombinants.

6. Protein structure was just beginning to be understood. It was realized that proteins had a primary structure, which consisted of a linear sequence of amino acids, and secondary structure units, such as the α helix, were identified.

The Structure of DNA

In 1953, Watson and Crick elucidated the structure of DNA, as recorded in the papers reprinted here on pages 6–9. This signaled an end to the "classical" period of bacterial genetics. The Watson-Crick structure enabled investigators to see the genetic material in terms of a molecular structure, and thus began the era of molecular genetics. The structure of DNA had several important implications:

- It indicated that a linear code existed to convert the sequence of nucleotides in the DNA into the sequence of amino acids in a protein.

- Because the individual bases were elements that could be changed, or mutated, the gene should have a fine structure. In other words, mutations within a gene should be able to recombine with one another.

- The pairing properties of the bases suggested several mechanisms of mutagenesis.

- The pairing properties of the bases also suggested how the genetic material could be self-replicating.

REFERENCES

Beadle, G.W. 1945. Biochemical genetics. *Chem. Rev.* **37:** 15–96.

Delbrück, M. and W.T. Bailey. 1946. Induced mutations in bacteriophage. *Cold Spring Harbor Symp. Quant. Biol.* **11:** 33–50.

Hershey, A.D. 1946. Spontaneous mutations in bacterial viruses. *Cold Spring Harbor Symp. Quant. Biol.* **11:** 67–77.

Hershey, A.D. and M. Chase. 1952. Independent functions of viral proteins and nucleic acid in growth of bacteriophage. *J. Gen. Physiol.* **36:** 39–56.

Lederberg, J. and E.L. Tatum. 1946a. Gene recombination in *Escherichia coli. Nature* **158:** 558.

Lederberg, J. and E.L. Tatum. 1946b. Novel genotypes in mixed cultures of biochemical mutants of bacteria. *Cold Spring Harbor Symp. Quant. Biol.* **11:** 113–114.

Luria, S.E. 1947. Recent advances in bacterial genetics. *Bacteriol. Rev.* **11:** 1–40.

Luria, S.E. and M. Delbrück. 1943. Mutations of bacteria from virus sensitivity to virus resistance. *Genetics* **28:** 491–511.

Zinder, N.D. and J. Lederberg. 1952. Genetic exchange in *Salmonella. J. Bacteriol.* **64:** 679–699.

SUGGESTED READING

Brock, Thomas D. 1990. *The Emergence of Bacterial Genetics.* Cold Spring Harbor Laboratory Press, Cold Spring Harbor, New York. pp. 346. An exceptional account of the history of bacterial genetics that traces many of the themes and concepts of this branch of science to their early origins.

Reprinted with permission from
Nature, Vol. 171, No. 4356, April 25, 1953
pp. 737–738.

MOLECULAR STRUCTURE OF NUCLEIC ACIDS

A Structure for Deoxyribose Nucleic Acid

WE wish to suggest a structure for the salt of deoxyribose nucleic acid (D.N.A.). This structure has novel features which are of considerable biological interest.

A structure for nucleic acid has already been proposed by Pauling and Corey[1]. They kindly made their manuscript available to us in advance of publication. Their model consists of three intertwined chains, with the phosphates near the fibre axis, and the bases on the outside. In our opinion, this structure is unsatisfactory for two reasons: (1) We believe that the material which gives the X-ray diagrams is the salt, not the free acid. Without the acidic hydrogen atoms it is not clear what forces would hold the structure together, especially as the negatively charged phosphates near the axis will repel each other. (2) Some of the van der Waals distances appear to be too small.

Another three-chain structure has also been suggested by Fraser (in the press). In his model the phosphates are on the outside and the bases on the inside, linked together by hydrogen bonds. This structure as described is rather ill-defined, and for this reason we shall not comment on it.

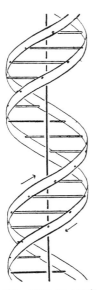

This figure is purely diagrammatic. The two ribbons symbolize the two phosphate—sugar chains, and the horizontal rods the pairs of bases holding the chains together. The vertical line marks the fibre axis

We wish to put forward a radically different structure for the salt of deoxyribose nucleic acid. This structure has two helical chains each coiled round the same axis (see diagram). We have made the usual chemical assumptions, namely, that each chain consists of phosphate diester groups joining β-D-deoxyribofuranose residues with 3′,5′ linkages. The two chains (but not their bases) are related by a dyad perpendicular to the fibre axis. Both chains follow right-handed helices, but owing to the dyad the sequences of the atoms in the two chains run in opposite directions. Each chain loosely resembles Furberg's[2] model No. 1; that is, the bases are on the inside of the helix and the phosphates on the outside. The configuration of the sugar and the atoms near it is close to Furberg's 'standard configuration', the sugar being roughly perpendicular to the attached base. There is a residue on each chain every 3·4 A. in the z-direction. We have assumed an angle of 36° between adjacent residues in the same chain, so that the structure repeats after 10 residues on each chain, that is, after 34 A. The distance of a phosphorus atom from the fibre axis is 10 A. As the phosphates are on the outside, cations have easy access to them.

The structure is an open one, and its water content is rather high. At lower water contents we would expect the bases to tilt so that the structure could become more compact.

The novel feature of the structure is the manner in which the two chains are held together by the purine and pyrimidine bases. The planes of the bases are perpendicular to the fibre axis. They are joined together in pairs, a single base from one chain being hydrogen-bonded to a single base from the other chain, so that the two lie side by side with identical z-co-ordinates. One of the pair must be a purine and the other a pyrimidine for bonding to occur. The hydrogen bonds are made as follows : purine position 1 to pyrimidine position 1 ; purine position 6 to pyrimidine position 6.

If it is assumed that the bases only occur in the structure in the most plausible tautomeric forms (that is, with the keto rather than the enol configurations) it is found that only specific pairs of bases can bond together. These pairs are : adenine (purine) with thymine (pyrimidine), and guanine (purine) with cytosine (pyrimidine).

In other words, if an adenine forms one member of a pair, on either chain, then on these assumptions the other member must be thymine ; similarly for guanine and cytosine. The sequence of bases on a single chain does not appear to be restricted in any way. However, if only specific pairs of bases can be formed, it follows that if the sequence of bases on one chain is given, then the sequence on the other chain is automatically determined.

It has been found experimentally[3,4] that the ratio of the amounts of adenine to thymine, and the ratio of guanine to cytosine, are always very close to unity for deoxyribose nucleic acid.

It is probably impossible to build this structure with a ribose sugar in place of the deoxyribose, as the extra oxygen atom would make too close a van der Waals contact.

The previously published X-ray data[5,6] on deoxyribose nucleic acid are insufficient for a rigorous test of our structure. So far as we can tell, it is roughly compatible with the experimental data, but it must be regarded as unproved until it has been checked against more exact results. Some of these are given in the following communications. We were not aware of the details of the results presented there when we devised our structure, which rests mainly though not entirely on published experimental data and stereochemical arguments.

It has not escaped our notice that the specific pairing we have postulated immediately suggests a possible copying mechanism for the genetic material.

Full details of the structure, including the conditions assumed in building it, together with a set of co-ordinates for the atoms, will be published elsewhere.

We are much indebted to Dr. Jerry Donohue for constant advice and criticism, especially on interatomic distances. We have also been stimulated by a knowledge of the general nature of the unpublished experimental results and ideas of Dr. M. H. F. Wilkins, Dr. R. E. Franklin and their co-workers at

King's College, London. One of us (J. D. W.) has been aided by a fellowship from the National Foundation for Infantile Paralysis.

J. D. WATSON
F. H. C. CRICK
Medical Research Council Unit for the
Study of the Molecular Structure of
Biological Systems,
Cavendish Laboratory, Cambridge.
April 2.

[1] Pauling, L., and Corey, R. B., *Nature*, **171**, 346 (1953) ; *Proc. U.S. Nat. Acad. Sci.*, **39**, 84 (1953).
[2] Furberg, S., *Acta Chem. Scand.*, **6**, 634 (1952).
[3] Chargaff, E., for references see Zamenhof, S., Brawerman, G. and Chargaff, E., *Biochim. et Biophys. Acta*, **9**, 402 (1952).
[4] Wyatt. G. R., *J. Gen. Physiol.*, **36**, 201 (1952).
[5] Astbury, W. T., Symp. Soc. Exp. Biol. 1, Nucleic Acid, 66 (Camb. Univ. Press, 1947).
[6] Wilkins, M. H. F., and Randall, J. T., *Biochim. et Biophys. Acta*, **10**, 192 (1953).

GENETICAL IMPLICATIONS OF THE STRUCTURE OF DEOXYRIBONUCLEIC ACID

By J. D. WATSON and F. H. C. CRICK

Medical Research Council Unit for the Study of the Molecular Structure of Biological Systems, Cavendish Laboratory, Cambridge

Reprinted with permission from
Nature, Vol. 171, No. 4361, May 30, 1953
pp. 964–967.

THE importance of deoxyribonucleic acid (DNA) within living cells is undisputed. It is found in all dividing cells, largely if not entirely in the nucleus, where it is an essential constituent of the chromosomes. Many lines of evidence indicate that it is the carrier of a part of (if not all) the genetic specificity of the chromosomes and thus of the gene itself.

Until now, however, no evidence has been presented to show how it might carry out the essential operation required of a genetic material, that of exact self-duplication.

We have recently proposed a structure[1] for the salt of deoxyribonucleic acid which, if correct, immediately suggests a mechanism for its self-duplication. X-ray evidence obtained by the workers at King's College, London[2], and presented at the same time, gives qualitative support to our structure and is incompatible with all previously proposed structures[3]. Though the structure will not be completely proved until a more extensive comparison has been made with the X-ray data, we now feel sufficient confidence in its general correctness to discuss its genetical implications. In doing so we are assuming that fibres of the salt of deoxyribonucleic acid are not artefacts arising in the method of preparation, since it has been shown by Wilkins and his co-workers that similar X-ray patterns are obtained from both the isolated fibres and certain intact biological materials such as sperm head and bacteriophage particles[2,4].

The chemical formula of deoxyribonucleic acid is now well established. The molecule is a very long chain, the backbone of which consists of a regular alternation of sugar and phosphate groups, as shown in Fig. 1. To each sugar is attached a nitrogenous base, which can be of four different types. (We have considered 5-methyl cytosine to be equivalent to cytosine, since either can fit equally well into our structure.) Two of the possible bases—adenine and guanine—are purines, and the other two—thymine and cytosine—are pyrimidines. So far as is known, the sequence of bases along the chain is irregular. The monomer unit, consisting of phosphate, sugar and base, is known as a nucleotide.

The first feature of our structure which is of biological interest is that it consists not of one chain, but of two. These two chains are both coiled around

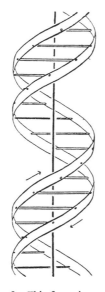

D.N.A.

Fig. 1. Chemical formula of a single chain of deoxyribonucleic acid

Fig. 2. This figure is purely diagrammatic. The two ribbons symbolize the two phosphate-sugar chains, and the horizontal rods the pairs of bases holding the chains together. The vertical line marks the fibre axis

a common fibre axis, as is shown diagrammatically in Fig. 2. It has often been assumed that since there was only one chain in the chemical formula there would only be one in the structural unit. However, the density, taken with the X-ray evidence[2], suggests very strongly that there are two.

The other biologically important feature is the manner in which the two chains are held together. This is done by hydrogen bonds between the bases, as shown schematically in Fig. 3. The bases are joined together in pairs, a single base from one chain being hydrogen-bonded to a single base from the other. The important point is that only certain pairs of bases will fit into the structure. One member of a pair must be a purine and the other a pyrimidine in order to bridge between the two chains. If a pair consisted of two purines, for example, there would not be room for it.

We believe that the bases will be present almost entirely in their most probable tautomeric forms. If this is true, the conditions for forming hydrogen bonds are more restrictive, and the only pairs of bases possible are :

adenine with thymine ;
guanine with cytosine.

The way in which these are joined together is shown in Figs. 4 and 5. A given pair can be either way-round. Adenine, for example, can occur on either chain ; but when it does, its partner on the other chain must always be thymine.

This pairing is strongly supported by the recent analytical results[5], which show that for all sources of deoxyribonucleic acid examined the amount of adenine is close to the amount of thymine, and the amount of guanine close to the amount of cytosine, although the cross-ratio (the ratio of adenine to guanine) can vary from one source to another. Indeed, if the sequence of bases on one chain is irregular, it is difficult to explain these analytical results except by the sort of pairing we have suggested.

The phosphate-sugar backbone of our model is completely regular, but any sequence of the pairs of bases can fit into the structure. It follows that in a long molecule many different permutations are possible, and it therefore seems likely that the precise sequence of the bases is the code which carries the genetical information. If the actual order of the

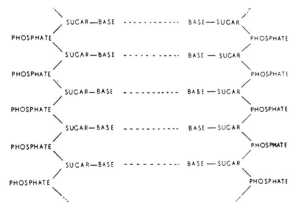

Fig. 3. Chemical formula of a pair of deoxyribonucleic acid chains. The hydrogen bonding is symbolized by dotted lines

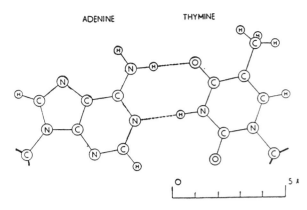

Fig. 4. Pairing of adenine and thymine. Hydrogen bonds are shown dotted. One carbon atom of each sugar is shown

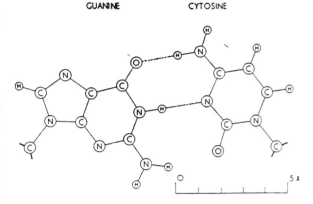

Fig. 5. Pairing of guanine and cytosine. Hydrogen bonds are shown dotted. One carbon atom of each sugar is shown

bases on one of the pair of chains were given, one could write down the exact order of the bases on the other one, because of the specific pairing. Thus one chain is, as it were, the complement of the other, and it is this feature which suggests how the deoxyribonucleic acid molecule might duplicate itself.

Previous discussions of self-duplication have usually involved the concept of a template, or mould. Either the template was supposed to copy itself directly or it was to produce a 'negative', which in its turn was to act as a template and produce the original 'positive' once again. In no case has it been explained in detail how it would do this in terms of atoms and molecules.

Now our model for deoxyribonucleic acid is, in effect, a *pair* of templates, each of which is complementary to the other. We imagine that prior to duplication the hydrogen bonds are broken, and the two chains unwind and separate. Each chain then acts as a template for the formation on to itself of a new companion chain, so that eventually we shall have *two* pairs of chains, where we only had one before. Moreover, the sequence of the pairs of bases will have been duplicated exactly.

A study of our model suggests that this duplication could be done most simply if the single chain (or the relevant portion of it) takes up the helical configuration. We imagine that at this stage in the life of the cell, free nucleotides, strictly polynucleotide precursors, are available in quantity. From time to time the base of a free nucleotide will join up by hydrogen bonds to one of the bases on the chain already formed. We now postulate that the polymerization of these monomers to form a new chain is only possible if the resulting chain can form the proposed structure. This is plausible, because steric reasons would not allow nucleotides 'crystallized' on to the first chain to approach one another in such a way that they could be joined together into a new chain, unless they were those nucleotides which were necessary to form our structure. Whether a special enzyme is required to carry out the polymerization, or whether the single helical chain already formed acts effectively as an enzyme, remains to be seen.

Since the two chains in our model are intertwined, it is essential for them to untwist if they are to separate. As they make one complete turn around each other in 34 A., there will be about 150 turns per million molecular weight, so that whatever the precise structure of the chromosome a considerable amount of uncoiling would be necessary. It is well known from microscopic observation that much coiling and uncoiling occurs during mitosis, and though this is on a much larger scale it probably reflects similar processes on a molecular level. Although it is difficult at the moment to see how these processes occur without everything getting tangled, we do not feel that this objection will be insuperable.

Our structure, as described[1], is an open one. There is room between the pair of polynucleotide chains (see Fig. 2) for a polypeptide chain to wind around the same helical axis. It may be significant that the distance between adjacent phosphorus atoms, 7·1 A., is close to the repeat of a fully extended polypeptide chain. We think it probable that in the sperm head, and in artificial nucleoproteins, the polypeptide chain occupies this position. The relative weakness of the second layer-line in the published X-ray pictures[3a,4] is crudely compatible with such an idea. The function of the protein might well be to control the coiling and uncoiling, to assist in holding a single polynucleotide chain in a helical configuration, or some other non-specific function.

Our model suggests possible explanations for a number of other phenomena. For example, spontaneous mutation may be due to a base occasionally occurring in one of its less likely tautomeric forms. Again, the pairing between homologous chromosomes at meiosis may depend on pairing between specific bases. We shall discuss these ideas in detail elsewhere.

For the moment, the general scheme we have proposed for the reproduction of deoxyribonucleic acid must be regarded as speculative. Even if it is correct, it is clear from what we have said that much remains to be discovered before the picture of genetic duplication can be described in detail. What are the polynucleotide precursors ? What makes the pair of chains unwind and separate ? What is the precise role of the protein ? Is the chromosome one long pair of deoxyribonucleic acid chains, or does it consist of patches of the acid joined together by protein ?

Despite these uncertainties we feel that our proposed structure for deoxyribonucleic acid may help to solve one of the fundamental biological problems—the molecular basis of the template needed for genetic replication. The hypothesis we are suggesting is that the template is the pattern of bases formed by one chain of the deoxyribonucleic acid and that the gene contains a complementary pair of such templates.

One of us (J.D.W.) has been aided by a fellowship from the National Foundation for Infantile Paralysis (U.S.A.).

[1] Watson, J. D., and Crick, F. H. C., *Nature*, **171**, 737 (1953).

[2] Wilkins, M. H. F., Stokes, A. R., and Wilson, H. R., *Nature*, **171**, 738 (1953). Franklin, R. E., and Gosling, R. G., *Nature*, **171**, 740 (1953).

[3] (a) Astbury, W. T., Symp. No. 1 Soc. Exp. Biol., 66 (1947). (b) Furberg, S., *Acta Chem. Scand.*, **6**, 634 (1952). (c) Pauling, L., and Corey, R. B., *Nature*, **171**, 346 (1953) ; *Proc. U.S. Nat. Acad. Sci.*, **39**, 84 (1953). (d) Fraser, R. D. B. (in preparation).

[4] Wilkins, M. H. F., and Randall, J. T., *Biochim. et Biophys. Acta*, **10**, 192 (1953).

[5] Chargaff, E., for references see Zamenhof, S., Brawerman, G., and Chargaff, E., *Biochim. et Biophys. Acta*, **9**, 402 (1952). Wyatt, G. R., *J. Gen. Physiol.*, **36**, 201 (1952).

Unit 1

The Fine Structure
of the Gene

In this unit, we will review Seymour Benzer's heroic study of the fine structure of the gene. It should be remembered that at the time Benzer began his classic work, the concept of the gene was different from what it is today. Genes were thought to be indivisible and to be the smallest units of recombination, mutation, and function. Genes could have different allelic states, but these alleles represented the whole gene, not parts of it. Earlier, apparent examples of alleles within the same gene were even called "pseudo alleles." However, the Watson-Crick structure of DNA clearly pointed to individual base pairs as being points for mutation. Benzer's work bridged the gap between the classical view of the gene as an indivisible unit and the Watson-Crick structure. In his paper "On the Topology of the Genetic Fine Structure," Benzer showed that the gene consisted of a linear array of subelements that could be mutated and could recombine with one another. Later, these subelements could be correlated with the base pairs as the smallest units of mutation and recombination. Benzer also examined the substructure of the gene in his paper "On the Topography of the Genetic Fine Structure." Here, he showed that the subelements, rather than having identical properties, displayed widely differing mutabilities. Let's consider some aspects of Benzer's career and examine the main concepts underlying his work before considering these papers.

Seymour Benzer

Seymour Benzer initially studied solid state physics, earning his Ph.D. at Purdue in 1947. He accepted an assistant professorship in physics at Purdue but took time off to pursue research in biology. He took the Phage Course at Cold Spring Harbor in 1948, spent a year at Oak Ridge, and then worked with Max Delbrück at Caltech from 1949 to 1951. This was followed by a year in André Lwoff's laboratory at the Pasteur Institute in Paris, where he worked with François Jacob.

In his autobiography, *The Statue Within,* Jacob, writing on the American's freedom of manner, noted: "When Seymour Benzer asked for a key to the Pasteur Institute library so he could work there at night, the librarian almost had an epileptic fit." Jacob also notes, "Seymour Benzer and I shared my laboratory for all of the year 1951–1952. During the first months, there were few exchanges between us. We did not keep the same hours. I arrived at nine in the morning; he, around one in the afternoon. As he came in, he would throw out a resounding 'Hi,' and then, after lunch, immerse himself in the inspection of his cultures. During the afternoon he would belch once or twice. Around seven o'clock in the evening, I would bid him goodnight and leave him to his nocturnal experiments. . . . Of average height, balding, with a fleshy face and a stoutish body, Seymour hid behind an impassive mask much charm and warmth."

Benzer made a strong impression on Jacob not only because of his scientific prowess, but also because of his interest in exotic foods. According to Jacob, "[Benzer] loved exotic foods. Every day, at lunch, he brought some unusual dish—cow's udder, bull's testicles, crocodile tail, filet of snake—which he had unearthed on the other side of Paris and which he simmered on his Bunsen burner." (I myself realized how deeply into weird dishes Benzer was when I described to him an exotic banquet I attended to celebrate a course I gave in Ho Chi Minh City, formerly Saigon, where we were served roast giant lizard, together with eels and blood oysters.

His eyes lit up as I described each dish, which at the time had made me totally nauseous.) As Jacob continues, "And, with all this, a pronounced taste for good jokes. When an American colleague, a football fan, was in Paris and wanted to know where he could find out about football in France, Seymour suggested he try André Lwoff. When the American asked Lwoff which match he would recommend for the following Sunday, the bewildered André at first took him for a madman before answering, 'I have never, sir, set foot in a football stadium.' When Jacques Monod was invited to lecture at the university where Seymour taught, the latter introduced him as follows: 'This is Doctor Monod. He says that in his youth he hesitated between two careers: biologist or musician. Having played music with him, I can tell you that he was right to choose biology.' Monod did not appreciate this one bit."

We should note that several of the people who Benzer studied under or worked with (Delbrück, Lwoff, Jacob) later won the Nobel prize. Benzer headed a laboratory at Purdue from 1953 until he moved to Caltech in 1975. After working on bacteriophage T4, Benzer's interests changed and he has since carried out research in neurobiology.

BENZER'S STUDY
OF THE FINE STRUCTURE
OF THE GENE

Key Concepts

Before we examine Seymour Benzer's original papers, let's look at some of the concepts underlying his work. First, we should ask why Benzer and others chose to use microorganisms. The key concept underlying this choice was the ability to **select** for recombinants in a cross. Instead of having to examine many different progeny from a cross for the rare recombinants, one could plate bacteria on selective medium and observe the growth of recombinants under conditions where the parental types did not grow. This allowed the detection of events that took place as infrequently as one per million (10^{-6}) or less; even rare revertants of mutations could be detected. (Can you imagine the work involved in trying to find one recombinant per million progeny in a cross of *Drosophila*?) In addition, one could apply selection not only to bacterial crosses, but also to crosses among different phage mutants. This leads to the second key concept exploited by Benzer, that of **conditional mutants.** Such mutants can grow under one set of **permissive** conditions but not under another, or **restrictive,** set of conditions. Some examples of conditional mutants are given below.

- Temperature-sensitive mutants will grow at one temperature, for example 30°C, but not at a second temperature, such as 42°C.

- Mutants carrying chain-terminating nonsense mutations will not grow in the absence of a nonsense suppressor but will grow in the presence of such a suppressor.

- Certain mutants that cannot grow in normal medium will grow in the presence of high (0.5 M) KCl.

- T4 *r*II mutants can grow on *Escherichia coli* B but not on *E. coli* K12 (λ).

It is the last example, discovered by Benzer, that made his work possible, and we will return to this topic in the discussion of the *r*II system.

The third key concept is the difference between **complementation** and **recombination**. Recombination involves the generation of new combinations of genes through the physical rearrangement of the chromosome. Complementation occurs by the mixing of gene products in the cytoplasm.

A fourth concept essential to Benzer's work was the use of the **Poisson distribution** to analyze mutational data. It is important to understand the Poisson distribution and how Benzer applied it, and we will consider the Poisson distribution in detail in the discussion of Benzer's study of topography.

The *r*II System

Before examining the papers, it is also important to understand some of the aspects of bacteriophage that Benzer and others exploited.

Life Cycle. Bacteriophage infect bacteria and undergo a life cycle that involves injection of the DNA into the cell, synthesis of viral proteins, replication of the viral DNA, packaging of the DNA into phage heads, lysis of the bacteria, and release of the phage progeny into the medium, where new cycles of infection and replication can begin.

Host Range. Bacteriophage infect and replicate in certain hosts but not in others. This "host range" allowed investigators to type different viruses. Phages were termed T1, T2, T3, T4, etc. The phage T4 was the subject of frequent study during the 1950s and 1960s.

Plaque Morphology. When dilutions of a phage suspension are adsorbed to a suspension of bacteria and plated on agar plates with tryptone medium, each phage becomes an infective center, giving rise to a clearing that results from the successive rounds of infection and lysis of neighboring bacteria. This clearing, or **plaque**, is the visible marker of the virus. Different plaque morphologies could be detected in different mutants. The "*r*" mutants, which were originally detected by Hershey, produce large plaques on *E. coli* B. The larger plaque size is due to *rapid* lysis, thus the name "*r*" mutants. Benzer discovered that some of the *r* mutants, the *r*II class, could not grow on *E. coli* K12 carrying λ as a prophage, *E. coli* K12 (λ), which is abbreviated here as *E. coli* K. Therefore, one can say that the host range of *r*II mutants is different from that of the wild type and that they are conditional mutants, since they can grow on one strain of *E. coli* but not on another. It is important to master this relationship for *r*II mutants in order to understand Benzer's subsequent analysis.

| Phage | Strain | |
	E. coli B	*E. coli* K
T4 wild type	Small plaques	Small plaques
T4 *r*II	Large plaques	No growth/plaques

Recombination and Selection. Phage crosses could be carried out in which two different *r*II mutants are used to simultaneously infect the same *E. coli* B bacterial cell. Because *r*II mutants cannot grow on *E. coli* K, it is necessary to use *E. coli* B to allow replication of the phage. During replication, recombination takes place, and the resulting lysate contains, in addition to the parental *r*II mutant phage, recombinant phage that are wild-type. When samples of this lysate are then plated on *E. coli* K, only the wild-type recombinants can grow. The K indicator selects the wild-type phage. The fraction of the total phage progeny (which form plaques on B) that form plaques on K allows one to calculate the recombination frequency.

Topology—Deletion Mapping

Benzer's paper on topology serves as a background for the main paper of this unit, his study of topography. In the topology study, Benzer wanted to ask about the substructure of the gene and how the parts interconnect. Two essential concepts used in this study are important for all of Benzer's work. The first involves the use of deletions for mapping. **Deletions** are mutations that eliminate segments of the DNA. They have great advantages for mapping experiments. First, these mutations never revert. Therefore, one never has to contend with background reversion interfering with the interpretation of results. Benzer found 145 such nonreverting mutations out of a collection of 2000 spontaneous mutations. Second, deletion mapping removes the tedium of comparing exact recombination frequencies, since the entire mapping is done with a set of "yes–no" tests. If a deletion removed the region containing the wild-type allele of a mutation, then no recombination was observed. If a deletion did not remove the wild-type region, then significant recombination was observed. The results of Benzer's topology study showed that the gene consists of a linear structure of subelements.

The second concept in the topology paper is the use of the ***cis-trans* test** to demonstrate functional units. This complementation test, shown in Figure 8 on page 50, looks for the mixing of gene products and does not involve the reassortment of genes on the chromosome. All of the *r*II mutations fit into one of two functional units, or cistrons, which were termed A and B. The mutations that fell into the A group mapped in one portion of the *r*II region and those that fell into the B cistron mapped in the other portion of the *r*II region. Thus, the *r*II region is really split into two apparently adjacent genes or cistrons.

Topography

In his study of topography, Benzer first isolated several thousand *r*II mutants and determined which ones reverted at low, but nonzero, rates. His next task was to divide these into groups on the basis of whether they were at the same or different sites in the gene. If one were to attempt to do this by pairwise crosses of each point mutation against each other point mutation, it would represent a prohibitive amount of work. Here, Benzer could take advantage of his characterized deletion mutations, which subdivided the gene into 47 segments as shown in Figure 3 on page 21. The methodology for his simple deletion tests is shown in Figure 2 on page 20. He first mapped each of the mutations against a set of 7 deletions and then applied an additional set of 3–10 deletions that defined subintervals within each main deletion interval. Thus, with a limited set of crosses, Benzer could place each mutation into one of 47 intervals. Then he could do pairwise crosses with representatives of the mutations within each subinterval. A comparison of the ordering of mutations by deletions versus ordering them via conventional point mutation × point mutation crosses, gives a perfect correlation with respect to the order (see Figure 5, page 23).

Mutations within the same small segment that recombine with one another are certainly part of different sites and those that do not recombine are defined as being at the same site. Since the latter result is based on negative evidence, it is not as certain as the former result. In any case, repeat occurrences at the same site are defined in this manner; namely, as revertible mutations that fail to recombine with one another. Figure 6 on page 25 shows how the mutations were distributed in the *r*II genes. Over 1600 mutations were included in this diagram. The key point of Figure 6 can best be described in Benzer's own words: "That the distribution is not random leaps to the eye." Over 500 mutations were observed at just one site! Sites that were much more mutable than expected at random were termed **hotspots**.

The Poisson Distribution. To determine whether certain sites were really hotspots, Benzer compared the distribution of mutations with that expected from a Poisson distribution. It is essential to understand what a Poisson distribution is and how it can be applied in order to appreciate how Benzer used it in Figure 7 on page 26. The Poisson distribution describes the distribution of *random* events. In the general formula for Poisson distribution given below, P = the probability, or fraction, of events that occur n times and m = the mean number of events per interval.

$$P_n = \frac{m^n e^{-m}}{n!}$$

Lets's look at an example. Suppose there are 40 students sitting equally spaced in a classroom and that someone drops a bucket of jelly beans on the heads of the students. Let's assume that the jelly beans fall randomly, so that each jelly bean has an equal probability of hitting each student on the head. In this case, the Poisson distribution will apply. Now suppose there are 200 jelly beans. What is the distribution of jelly beans hitting the students' heads? The average, or mean, is clearly 200/40 or $m = 5$. Thus, on average, 5 jelly beans fall on the head of each student. Does this mean that each student will be hit by exactly 5 jelly beans? No, of course not. We know that although many of the students will be hit by 5 jelly beans, others will be hit by 4, and others by 6, and probably a few will be hit by 3 or 7, and maybe an occasional student will be hit by only 1 or 2 or as many as 8 or 9. We can use the Poisson distribution to calculate the fraction of students hit by any number of jelly beans. Using the formula for the Poisson distribution given on page 15, let's expand the distribution for values of n from 0 to 10.

$$P_0 = e^{-m} = 0.0067$$

$$P_1 = me^{-m} = 0.034$$

$$P_2 = m^2 e^{-m}/2! = 0.084$$

$$P_3 = m^3 e^{-m}/3! = 0.140$$

$$P_4 = m^4 e^{-m}/4! = 0.175$$

$$P_5 = m^5 e^{-m}/5! = 0.175$$

$$P_6 = m^6 e^{-m}/6! = 0.146$$

$$P_7 = m^7 e^{-m}/7! = 0.104$$

$$P_8 = m^8 e^{-m}/8! = 0.065$$

$$P_9 = m^9 e^{-m}/9! = 0.036$$

$$P_{10} = m^{10} e^{-m}/10! = 0.018$$

We can now see the fraction of students hit by 0, 1, 2, 3, etc., jelly beans. For example, the fraction of students hit by exactly 5 jelly beans is 0.175. Note again that the distribution deals with probabilities, or fractions. The sum of all the probabilities, or fractions, equals 1.0. If we want to know the number of students in the class hit by any number of jelly beans, then we must multiply the fraction by the total number of students in the class. In this case, the total number of students is 40, so each fraction must be multiplied by 40 to find the desired number of students. For example, if we want to know the number of students hit by 5 jelly beans, then we multiply the fraction of students hit by 5 jelly beans (0.175) by the total number of students (40) to yield 7 students hit

by 5 jelly beans each. It is important when using the Poisson distribution to be able to distinguish between fractions (or probabilities) and expected number of events. To find the expected number of events, we must multiply the fraction by the total number of events, just as we did here for the total number of students. The best way to become familiar with the use of the Poisson distribution is to work out sample problems. A number of these are given in Section III (see pages 535–539, 599–603, and 639-640). A plot of Poisson distributions for several different values of m is given below:

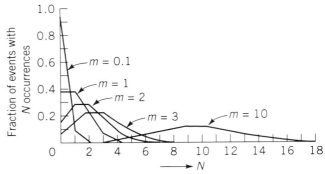

Poisson distributions for five different mean values: m is the mean number of events per interval, and N is the actual number of events per interval.

Hotspots. As mentioned above, Benzer needed to determine in his topography study whether sites that appeared to be very mutable were really exceptional or instead had a large number of recurrences of mutations simply by chance. To do this, he used the Poisson distribution. The problem can be envisioned as trying to find the expected random distribution of a large number of mutations (in this case 1612) among a set number of mutational sites in the rII region. Benzer's problem was that he did not know the total number of sites available, since it was presumed that there were many sites of 0 occurrence of a mutation in this collection. In other words, just as there were many sites with 1 or 2 occurrences of a mutation in this collection, there was also a set of sites with equivalent mutability to the sites with 1 or 2 occurrences at which no mutations were found this time. Thus, he could not determine the fraction in any case. Despite this, Benzer was able to calculate the expected Poisson distribution, which is shown in Figure 7 on page 26. See if you can determine how he solved this problem and what assumptions he made. (The solution is given in the answer to Question 11 in Section III, page 534.)

It can be seen from the distribution that Benzer plotted (Figure 7) that there were at least 129 sites that were not observed (the 0 occurrence sites). In addition, any sites with 5 or more occurrences were "hot" relative to sites that had 0, 1, or 2 occurrences. There were at least 60 sites that were more mutable than the average site. Clearly, as he noted, each of the two hottest sites had special properties. Benzer also examined the spectrum of induced mutations and found that there were hotspots for each mutagen and these hotspots differed from mutagen to mutagen.

CONCLUSIONS

Benzer's work changed our notion of the concept of the gene by demonstrating that the gene had a fine structure consisting of a linear array of subelements. Each subelement could be mutated and could recombine. Therefore, different mutations (alleles) could occur within the same gene and could recombine with one another. Later work showed that the smallest unit of mutation and recombination was indeed a single base pair. Benzer's topography study revealed that different parts of the gene had different properties. Specifically, mutability varied greatly from one site to another. Some sites with higher than normal rates of mutation could be identified and these were termed "hotspots." Later work, described in Unit 9 in Section II, determined the identity of several different types of hotspots.

ON THE TOPOGRAPHY OF THE GENETIC FINE STRUCTURE

By Seymour Benzer

DEPARTMENT OF BIOLOGICAL SCIENCES, PURDUE UNIVERSITY

Read before the Academy, April 27, 1960*

In an earlier paper,[1] a detailed examination was made of the structure of a small portion of the genetic map of phage T4, the *r*II region. This region, which controls the ability of the phage to grow in *Escherichia coli* strain K, consists of two adjacent cistrons, or functional units. Various *r*II mutants, unable to grow in strain K, have mutations affecting various parts of either or both of these cistrons. The topology of the region; i.e., the manner in which its parts are interconnected, was intensively tested and it was found that the active structure can be described as a string of subelements, a mutation constituting an alteration of a point or segment of the linear array.

This paper is a sequel in which inquiry is made into the topography of the structure, i.e., local differences in the properties of its parts. Specifically, are all the subelements equally mutable? If so, mutations should occur at random throughout the structure and the topography would be trivial. On the other hand, sites or regions of unusually high or low mutability would be interesting topographic features.

The preceding investigation of topology was done by choosing mutants showing no detectable tendency to revert. This avoided any possible confusion between recombination and reverse mutation, so that a qualitative (yes-or-no) test for recombination was possible. The class of non-reverting mutants automatically included those marked by relatively large alterations, which will be referred to as "deletions." Such a mutant is defined for the present purposes as one which inter-

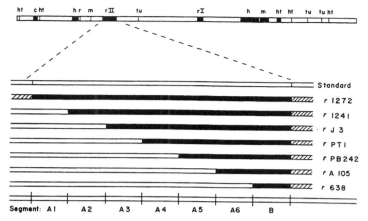

FIG. 1a.—At the top, the *r*II region is shown compared with the entire genetic map of the phage. This map is a composite[15] of markers mapped in T4 and the related phage T2. Seven segments of the *r*II region are defined by a set of "deletions" beginning at different points and extending to the right-hand end (and possibly beyond, as indicated by shading).

sects (fails to give recombination with) two or more mutants that do recombine with each other. Deletions provided overlaps of the sort needed to test the topology and to divide the map into segments.

The present investigation of topography, however, is concerned with differentiation of the various points in the structure. For this purpose mutants which do revert are of the greater interest, since they are most likely to contain small alter-

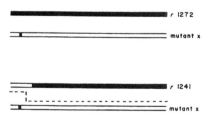

FIG. 1b.—Mapping a mutation by use of the reference deletions. If mutant x has a mutation in segment 1, it is overlapped by *r*1272, but not by *r*1241. Therefore, standard-type recombinants (as indicated by the dotted line) can only arise when x is crossed with *r*1241.

ations. As a rule (there are exceptions) an *r*II mutant that reverts behaves as if its alteration were localized to a point. That is to say, mutants that intersect with the same mutant also intersect with each other. In a cross, recombination can be scored only if it is clearly detectable above the spontaneous reversion noise of the mutants involved. Therefore, the precision with which a mutation can be mapped is limited by its reversion rate. The detailed analysis of topography can best be done with mutants having low, non-zero reversion rates.

Some thousands of such *r*II mutants, both spontaneous and induced, have been analyzed and the resultant topographic map is presented here.

Assignment of Mutations to Segments.—To test thousands of mutants against one another for recombination in all possible pairs would require millions of crosses. This task may be greatly reduced by making use of deletions. Each mutant is first tested against a few key deletions. The recombination test gives a negative result if a deletion overlaps the mutation in question and a positive result if it does not overlap. These results quickly locate a mutation within a particular segment of the map. It is then necessary to test against each other only the group of mutants having mutations within each segment, so that the number of tests needed is much smaller. In addition, if the order of the segments is known, the entire set of point mutations becomes ordered to a high degree, making use of only qualitative tests.

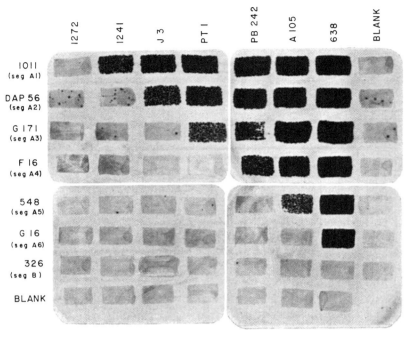

Fig. 2.—Crosses for mapping rII mutations. The photograph is a composite of four plates. Each row shows a given mutant tested against the reference deletions of Figure 1a. Plaques appearing in the blanks are due to revertants present in the mutant stock. The results show each of these mutations to be located in a different segment.

Procedure for crosses—The broth medium is 1% Difco bacto-tryptone plus 0.5% NaCl. For plating, broth is solidified with 1.2% agar for the bottom layer and 0.7% for the top layer. Stocks are grown in broth using *E. coli* BB which does not discriminate between rII mutants and the standard type. To cross two mutants, one drop of each at a titer of about 10^9 phage particles/ml is placed in a tube and cells of *E. coli* B are added (roughly 0.5 ml of a 1-hour broth culture containing about 2×10^8 cells/ml). The rII mutants are all able to grow on strain B and have an opportunity to undergo genetic recombination. After allowing a few minutes for adsorption, a droplet of the mixture is spotted (using a sterile paper strip) on a plate previously seeded with *E. coli* K. If the mutants recombine to produce standard type progeny, plaques appear on K. A negative result signifies that the proportion of recombinants is less than about 10^{-3}% of the progeny.

Within any one segment, however, the order of the various sites remains undetermined. This order can still be determined, if desired, by quantitative measurements of recombination frequencies.

In order to facilitate this project many more deletions have been mapped than were described in the previous paper. These suffice to carve up the structure into 47 distinct segments. By virtue of the proper overlaps, the order of almost all of these segments is established.   Observe first the seven large mutations in Figure 1a. These are of a kind which begin at a particular point and extend all the way to one end.   Thus, they serve to divide the structure into the seven major segments shown.

Consider a small mutation located in the segment Al, as indicated in Figure 1b. It is overlapped by r1272 and therefore when crossed with it cannot give rise to standard type recombinants.   It will, however, give a positive result with r1241 or any of the others, since, with them, recombinants can form as indicated by the

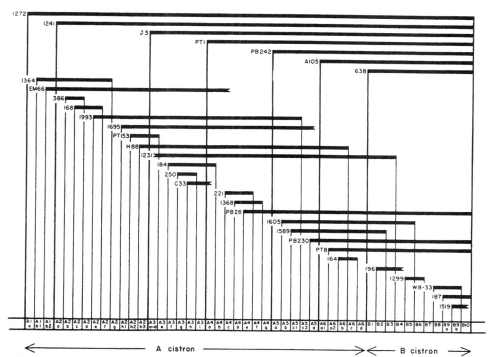

Fig. 3.—Deletions used to divide the main segments of Figure 1 into 47 smaller segments. (Some ends have not been used to define a segment, and are drawn fluted.)   The A and B cistrons, which are defined by an independent functional test, coincide with the indicated portions of the recombination map.   Most of the mutants are of spontaneous origin.   Possible exceptions are EM66, which was found in a stock treated with ethyl methane sulfonate, and the PT and PB mutants, which were obtained from stocks treated with heat at low pH.   The PT mutants were contributed by Dr. E. Freese.

dotted line.   A point mutation located in the second segment will give zero with mutants r1272 and r1241 but not with the rest, and so on.   Thus, if any point mutant is tested against the set of seven reference mutants in order, the segment in which its mutation belongs is established simply by counting the number of zeros. Figure 2 shows photographs of the test plates for seven mutants, each having its mutation located in a different segment.

Only these seven patterns, with an uninterrupted row of zeros beginning from the left, have ever been observed for thousands of mutants tested against these seven deletions.   The complete exclusion of the other 121 possible patterns confirms the linear order of the segments.

Now a given segment can be further subdivided by means of other mutations having suitable starting or ending points. Figure 3 shows the set used in this study and the designation of each segment. Each mutant is first tested against the seven which have been chosen to define main segments. Once the main segment is known,

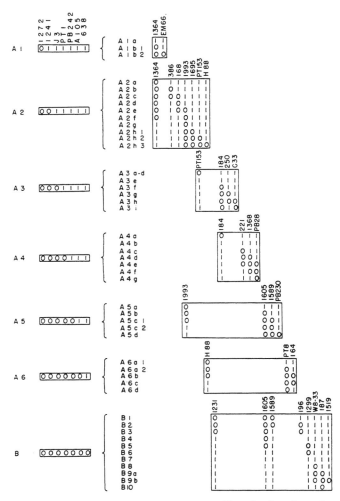

Fig. 4.—The test pattern which identifies the location of a point mutation in each of the segments of Figure 3. The test is done in two stages. An unknown mutant is first crossed with the "big seven" of Figure 1 in order. *Zero* signifies no detectable recombination and *one* signifies some, and the number of zeros defines the major segment. Once this is known, the mutant is crossed with the pertinent selected group of deletions to determine the small segment to which it belongs.

the mutant is tested against the appropriate secondary set. Figure 4 shows the pattern which identifies the location of a point mutation within each of the small segments. Thus, in two steps, a point mutation is mapped into one of the 47 segments.

The order of the first 42 segments, Ala through B6, is uniquely defined. Unfortunately, there remains a gap between *r*1299 and *r*W8-33. Therefore the order of segments B8 through B10, although fixed among themselves, could possibly be the reverse of that shown.[17] Also if there exists space to the right of segment B10, a mutation in that segment might map as if it were in segment B7, so that the latter segment must be tentatively regarded as a composite.

In the previous topology paper, the possibility that the structure contains branches was not eliminated. As pointed out by Delbrück, the existence of a branch would not lead to any contradiction with a linear topology if loss of a segment containing the branch point automatically led to loss of the entire branch.

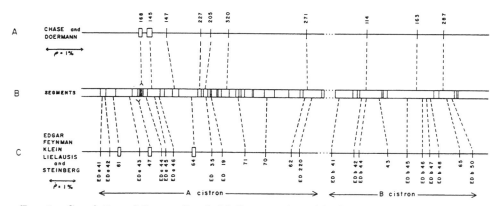

FIG. 5.—Correlation of the results of deletion mapping with the conventional method. *A:* The map constructed by Chase and Doermann[2] for ten *r*II mutants of phage T4B, using quantitative measurements of recombination frequency. The interval between adjacent mutations is drawn proportional to the frequency of recombination in a cross between the two. *C:* The map constructed in similar fashion by Edgar *et al.* (personal communication) with *r*II mutants of the very closely related phage T4D. The procedure used by Edgar *et al.* gives higher recombination frequencies. Therefore, the scales of the two maps are adjusted in the figure to produce a good over-all fit. Some of the mutations cover several sites and are drawn as having a corresponding length. A gap is left between the two cistrons because crosses between mutations in different cistrons give abnormally high frequencies due to the role of heterozygotes[16].

All of these mutations have also been mapped by the deletion method, and dotted lines indicate their locations in the various segments (*B*). The length of each segment is drawn in proportion to the number of distinct sites that have been found within it.

To show that a given segment is *not* a branch, it is required to find a mutation which penetrates it partially. From the mutations shown in Figure 3, it can be concluded that no branch exists that contains more than one of the 47 segments.

Comparison of Deletion Mapping by Recombination Frequencies.—The conventional method of genetic mapping makes use of recombination frequency as a measure of the distance between two mutations and requires careful quantitative measurements of the percentage of recombinant type progeny in each cross. By the method of overlapping deletions the order of mutations can be determined entirely by qualitative yes-or-no spot tests. Maps obtained independently by the two methods are compared in Figure 5. The upper part of the figure (*A*) shows the order obtained by Chase and Doermann[2] for a set of ten mutants, the distance between adjacent mutations being drawn proportional to the percentage of standard-type recombinants occurring among the progeny of a cross between the two. The central part of the figure (*B*) shows the *r*II region divided into the segments of

Figure 3, with the size of each segment drawn in proportion to the number of distinct sites which have been discovered within it (see below). As indicated by the dotted lines, there is perfect correlation in the order. In the lower part of the figure, a similar comparison is made for a set of *r*II mutations in the closely related phage strain T4D, which have been mapped, using recombination frequencies, by Edgar, Feynman, Klein, Lielausis, and Steinberg. Again the order agrees perfectly with that obtained by the use of deletions.

Topography for Spontaneous Mutations.—We now proceed to map reverting mutants of T4B which have arisen independently and spontaneously. The procedure is exactly as in Figure 4: first localizing into main segments, then into smaller segments. Finally mutants of the same small segment are tested against each other. Any which show recombination are said to define different sites. If two or more reverting mutants are found to show no detectable recombination with each other, they are considered to be repeats and one of them is chosen to represent the site in further tests. A set of distinct sites is thus obtained, each with its own group of repeats.

This procedure is based on the assumption that revertibility implies a point mutation. While this is a good working rule for *r*II mutants, a few exceptions have been found which appear to revert (i.e., give rise to some progeny which can produce detectable plaques on stain K) yet fail to give recombination with two or more mutants that do recombine with each other. If a mutant chosen to represent a "site" happens to be of this kind, mutations it overlaps will appear to be at the same site. Therefore, a group of "repeats" remains subject to splitting into different groups when they are tested against each other. This has not yet been done for all of the sites described here. It is, of course, in the nature of the recombination test that it is meaningful to say that two mutations are at different sites, while the converse conclusion is always tentative.

Figure 6 shows the map obtained for spontaneous mutants, with each occurrence of a mutation at a site indicated by a square. Within each segment the sites are drawn in arbitrary order. Other known sites are also indicated even though no occurrences were observed among this set of spontaneous mutants.

That the distribution is non-random leaps to the eye. More than 500 mutations have been observed at the most prominent "hotspot," while, at the other extreme, there are many sites at which only a single occurrence, or none, has so far been found.

To decide whether a given number of recurrences is significantly greater than random, the data may be compared with the expectation from a Poisson distribution. Figure 7 shows a distribution calculated to fit the least hot of the observed spontaneous sites, i.e., those at which one or two mutations have occurred, on the assumption that these sites belong to a uniform class of sites of low mutability. Comparing the observations with this curve, it would seem that if a site has four occurrences, there is a two-thirds probability that it is truly hotter than the class of sites of low mutability. Those having five or more are almost certainly hot. It can be concluded that at least sixty sites belong in a more mutable class than the coolest spots. Whether the hot sites can be divided into smaller homogeneous groups, assuming a Poisson distribution within each class, is difficult to say. Each of the two hottest sites is obviously unique.

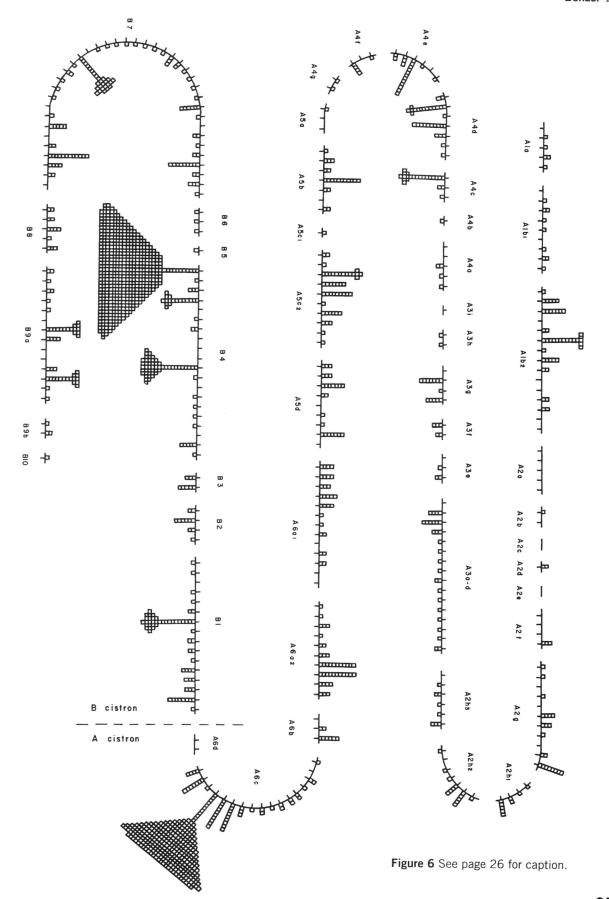

Figure 6 See page 26 for caption.

From the distribution it can be predicted that there must exist at least 129 spontaneous sites not observed in this set of mutants. This is a minimum estimate since it is calculated on the assumption that the 2-occurrence sites are no more mutable than the 1-occurrence sites. If this is not correct, the predicted number of

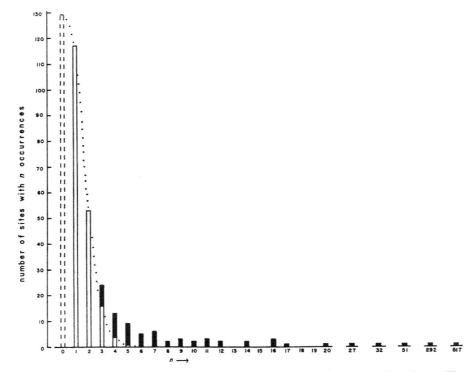

Fig. 7.—Distribution of occurrences of spontaneous mutations at various sites. The dotted line indicates a Poisson distribution fitted to the numbers of sites having one and two occurrences. This predicts a minimum estimate for the number of sites of comparable mutability that have zero occurrences due to chance (dashed column at n = 0). Solid bars indicate the minimum numbers of sites which have mutation rates significantly higher than the one- and two-occurrence class.

0-occurrence sites will be larger. Also, of course, there could exist a vast class of sites of much lower mutability. With 251 spontaneous sites identified and at least 129 more to be found, the degree of saturation of the map achieved with this set of 1,612 spontaneous mutants can be no greater than 66 per cent.

←

Fig. 6.—Topographic map of the rII region for spontaneous mutations. Each square represents one occurrence observed at the indicated site. Sites with no occurrences indicated are known to exist from induced mutations and from a few other selected spontaneous ones. The order of the segments is known for A1a through B7, but is only tentative for B7 through B10.[17] The arrangement of sites within each segment is arbitrary.

Each mutant arose independently in a plaque of either standard-type T4B or, in somewhat less than half of the cases, revertants of various rII mutants. All revertants (except F) gave results very similar to T4B. The pattern for rII mutants isolated from revertant F differs noticeably only in a reduced rate at the hotspot 117 (the site of its original rII mutation) and therefore does not significantly alter the topography. All the data for mutants isolated from standard type and from revertants are pooled in this figure.

Topography for Induced Mutations.—By the use of specific mutagens, new topographic features are revealed. This has been shown for *r*II mutants induced during reproduction of the phage inside the bacterial host cell with 5-bromouracil (Benzer and Freese[3]), proflavine (Brenner, Barnett, and Benzer[4]), and 2-aminopurine (Freese[5]). Other effective mutagens are 2,6-diaminopurine (Freese[5]) and 5-bromodeoxycytidine (Gregory, personal communication). Mutations may also be induced *in vitro*, i.e., in extracellular phase particles, by ethyl methane sulfonate (Loveless[6]) and nitrous acid (Vielmetter and Wieder;[7] Freese;[8] Tessman[9]).

*r*II mutants induced by all of these mutagens have now been mapped with respect to each other and spontaneous ones, and the results are given in Figure 8 (facing page 416) which shows the locations of over 2,400 induced and spontaneous mutations. Only *r*II mutants that have low reversion rates and are not too "leaky" on K have been included.

Each "spectrum" differs obviously from the spontaneous one. While the specificities of the various mutagens overlap in many respects, each differs significantly from the others at specific points. In making the comparison it must be borne in mind that the total number of mutants mapped is not the same for each mutagen and also that each induced set inevitably includes some proportion of spontaneous mutants. (An upper limit to this background can be set from the number of occurrences at the hottest spontaneous sites.) Also, none of the spectra are "saturated." Therefore, even if two mutagens act similarly upon a given site, it is possible, due to chance, that a few occurrences would be observed in one spectrum and not the other. Within these limitations, the map shows the comparative response at each site to each mutagen as well as the locations of various kinds of hotspots in various segments of the *r*II region.

The study of the induced mutations has added 53 new sites to the 251 identified by the spontaneous set alone, bringing the total to 304. (Four sites more are shown in Figure 8, but they come from a selected group of mutants outside this study.) Thus, a closer approach toward saturation of all the possible sites must have been made. By lumping together all the data, both spontaneous and induced, one can again make an estimate of the number of sites which must be detectable if one were to continue mapping mutants in the same proportion for the same mutagens. The result is that there must exist still a minimum of 120 sites not yet discovered. This appears discouragingly similar to the estimate based on spontaneous mutations alone. However, it need not be surprising if the use of mutagens brings into view some sites which have extremely low spontaneous mutability. With 308 sites identified and at least 120 yet to be found, the maximum degree of saturation of the map is 72 per cent.

Discussion.—One topographic feature, non-random mutability at the various sites, is obvious. Another question is whether mutable sites are distributed at random, or whether there exist portions of the map that are unusually crowded with or devoid of sites. The mapping technique used here defines only the order of sites from one segment to another (but not within a given segment). The distance between sites remains unspecified. However, all mutations in a segment more distal to a given point must be farther away than those in a more proximal segment. If the number of sites in a segment is used as a measure of its length, as in Figure 5, it can be seen that there is no major discrepancy between these distances and those defined in terms of another measure of distance, recombination frequency. On a gross scale, therefore, there is no evidence for any large portion of the rII region that is unusually crowded or roomy with respect to sites. This does not necessarily mean that some other measure of distance would not reveal such regions, since it is at least conceivable that mutable sites coincide with points highly susceptible to recombination. The distribution of sites on a finer scale, within a small segment, remains to be investigated.

The number of points at which mutations can wreck the activity of a cistron is very large. This would be expected if a cistron dictates the formation of a polypeptide chain and "nonsense" mutations[10] are possible which interrupt the completion of the chain. Such mutations would be effective at any point of the structure, whereas ones which lead to "missense," i.e., the substitution of one amino acid for another, might be effective at relatively special points or regions which are crucial in affecting the active site or folding.

It would be of interest to compare the number of genetic sites to the material embodiment of the rII region in terms of nucleotides. Unfortunately, the size of the latter is not well known. Estimates based upon its length, in units of recombination frequency compared to the length of the entire genetic structure, are uncertain. A more direct attempt has been made using equilibrium sedimentation in a cesium chloride gradient and looking for a change in density of mutants known by genetic evidence to have portions of the rII region deleted (Nomura, Champe, and Benzer, unpublished). This technique has been successful in characterizing defective mutants of phage λ (Weigle, Meselson, and Paigen[11]) and is sufficiently sensitive to detect a decrease of 1 per cent in the amount of DNA per phage particle, but has so far failed with rII mutants. Although other explanations are possible, this result may suggest that the physical structure corresponding to the rII region represents less than 1 per cent of the total DNA of the phage particle, or less than 2,000 nucleotide pairs. If this is so, the number of possible sites would be of the order of at least one-fifth of the number of nucleotide pairs.

The data show that, if each site is characterized by its spontaneous mutability and response to various mutagens, the sites are of many different kinds. Some response patterns are represented only once in the entire structure. According to the Watson-Crick model[12] for DNA, the structure consists of only two types of elements, adenine-thymine (AT) pairs and guanine-hydroxymethylcytosine (GC) pairs. This does not mean, however, that there can only be two kinds of mutable sites, even if a site corresponds to a single base pair. Considering only base pair substitutions, a given AT pair can undergo three kinds of change: AT can be replaced by GC, CG, or TA. Certain of these changes may lead to a mutant phenotype, but some may not. The frequency of observable mutations at a particular AT pair will be determined by the sum of the probabilities for each type of change, each multiplied by a coefficient (either one or zero) according to whether that specific alteration at that particular pair does or does not represent a mutant type. Thus, if the probability that a base pair will be substituted is independent of its neighbors, the various AT sites may have seven different mutation rates. Similarly, there are seven rates possible for the various GC sites, so that it would be possible to account for fourteen classes by this mechanism. Some of these may have (total) spontaneous mutation rates that are similar. If a mutagen induces only certain substitutions, it will facilitate further discriminations between sites but there should still be no more than fourteen classes.

If one allows for interactions between neighbors, the number of possible classes increases enormously. Such interactions are to be expected. As an example, consider the fact that AT pairs are held together much less strongly than are GC pairs.[13] If several AT pairs occur in succession, this segment of the DNA chain will be relatively loose, making it easier to consummate an illicit base pairing during replication. Thus, guanine and adenine, which make a very satisfactory pair of hydrogen bonds but require a larger than normal separation between the backbones, could be more readily accommodated. This would lead, in the next replication, to a replica in which one of the AT pairs has been substituted by a CG pair, with the orientation of purine and pyrimidine reversed. Thus, a region rich in AT pairs will tend to be more subject to substitution. If the same (standard-type) phenotype can be achieved by alternative sequences, the ones containing long stretches of AT pairs would tend to be lost because of their high mutability. In other words, cistrons ought to have evolved in such a way as to eliminate hotspots. The spontaneous hotspots that are observed would be remnants of an incomplete ironing-out process. In fact, a map of the rII region of the related phage T6 (Benzer, unpublished) also shows hotspots at locations corresponding to r131 and r117. However, while the first of these has a mutability similar to that in T4, the second is lower by a factor of four.

This point is emphasized by the data on reverse mutations. It is not uncommon for an rII mutant to have a reverse mutation rate that is greater than the total forward rate observed for the composite of at least 400 sites. That some of these high-rate reverse mutations represent true reversion (and not "suppressor" mutations) has been established in several cases by the most stringent criteria, including the demonstration that the revertant has exactly the same forward mutation rate at the same site as did the original standard type (Benzer, unpublished). It would therefore appear that certain kinds of highly mutable configurations are systematically excluded from the standard form of the rII genetic structure, and a mutation may recreate one of these banned sequences.

In the attempt to translate the genetic map into a nucleotide sequence, the detection of the various sites by forward mutation is necessarily the first step. By studies on the specificity of induction of reverse mutations,[14] one site at a time can be analyzed in the hope of identifying the specific bases involved.

Summary.—A small portion of the genetic map of phage T4, the two cistrons of the rII region, has been dissected by overlapping "deletions" into 47 segments. If any branch exists, it cannot be larger than one of these segments. The overlapping deletions are used to map point mutations and the map order established by this method is consistent with the order established by the conventional method that makes use of recombination frequencies. Further dissection has led to the identification of 308 distinct sites of widely varied spontaneous and induced mutability. The distributions throughout the region for spontaneous mutations and those induced by various chemical mutagens are compared. Data are included for nitrous acid and ethyl methane sulfonate acting *in vitro*, and 2-aminopurine, 2,6-diaminopurine, 5-bromouracil, 5-bromodeoxycytidine, and proflavine acting *in vivo*. The characteristic hotspots reveal a striking topography.

It is a pleasure to thank Mrs. Karen Sue Supple, Mrs. Joan Reynolds, and Mrs. Lynne Bryant for their indefatigable assistance in mapping mutants and bookkeeping. I am indebted to Dr. Robert S. Edgar and his associates for permission to make use of their unpublished data in Figure 5 and to Dr. Ernst Freese for several deletions as well as mutants induced with 2-aminopurine and 5-bromodeoxyuridine. This research was supported by grants from the National Science Foundation and the National Institutes of Health.

* Given by invitation of the Committee on Arrangements for the Annual Meeting as part of a Symposium on Genetic Determination of Protein Structure, Robley C. Williams, Chairman.

[1] Benzer, S., these PROCEEDINGS, 45, 1607 (1959).

[2] Chase, M., and A. H. Doermann, *Genetics*, 43, 332 (1958).

[3] Benzer, S., and E. Freese, these PROCEEDINGS, 44, 112 (1958).

[4] Brenner, S., L. Barnett, and S. Benzer, *Nature*, 182, 983 (1958).

[5] Freese, E., *J. Molec. Biol.*, 1, 87 (1959).

[6] Loveless, A., *Nature*, 181, 1212 (1958).

[7] Vielmetter, W., and C. M. Wieder, *Z. Naturforsch*, 14b, 312 (1959).

[8] Freese, E., *Brookhaven Symposia in Biol.*, 12, 63 (1959).

[9] Tessman, I., *Virology*, 9, 375 (1959).

[10] Crick, F. H. C., J. S. Griffith, and L. E. Orgel, these PROCEEDINGS, 43, 416 (1957).

[11] Weigle, J., M. Meselson, and K. Paigen, *J. Molec. Biol.*, 1, 379 (1959).

[12] Watson, J. D., and F. Crick, *Cold Spring Harbor Symposia Quant. Biol.*, 18, 123 (1953).

[13] Doty, P., J. Marmur, and N. Sueoka, *Brookhaven Symposia in Biol.*, 12, 1 (1959).

[14] Freese, E., these PROCEEDINGS, 45, 622 (1959).

[15] Brenner, S., in *Advances in Virus Research* (New York: Academic Press, 1959), pp. 137–158.

[16] Edgar, R. S., *Genetics*, 43, 235 (1958).

[17] The terms topology and topography are used here in the following senses (Webster's New Collegiate Dictionary, 1959)—*topology:* the doctrine of those properties of a figure unaffected by any deformation without tearing or joining; *topography:* the art or practice of graphic and exact delineation in minute detail, usually on maps or charts, of the physical features of any place or region.

[18] *Note added in proof.* Recent data have established that the orientation shown for segments B8 through B10 is the correct one.

Note: Figure 8 on the following pages was originally published as a pull out chart. The caption is reprinted below.

Fig. 8.—Topographic map of the *r*II region for mutations arising spontaneously and induced by various mutagens. In each case, only *r*II mutants have been used that have low reversion rates and are not very leaky.

Spontaneous mutants: See legend to Figure 6.

Nitrous acid (NT) mutants: Standard type T4B was diluted in M-9 buffer plus 1.8 M NaNO$_2$, pH around 6.5, and incubated at 37°C for 80 minutes. The fraction of phage particles surviving was 2×10^{-2} and included 0.4% of *r* type and mottled plaques. Four fifths of the mutants were isolated from this stock and the rest from a second stock exposed under similar conditions for 20 minutes to give 0.3% mutants. For nitrous acid, as for the other mutagens below, mutants were picked from both *r* type and mottled plaques. Spontaneous mutants in the untreated stock have also been mapped (not shown here) and confirm that most of the NT hotspots cannot be due to large clones previously present.

Ethyl methane sulfonate (EM) mutants: A broth stock of T4B was diluted in M-9 buffer plus 0.12 M ethyl methane sulfonate (gift of Dr. A. Loveless) and incubated at 37°C for 75 minutes. The survival was 70% and the proportion of *r* and mottled plaques among survivors was 1.0%.

2-aminopurine (AP) mutants: These mutants, isolated by Dr. E. Freese, were obtained by growing *E. coli* B infected with phage T4B in a medium containing 2-aminopurine. See Freese.[5]

2,6-diaminopurine (DAP) mutants: *E. coli* B infected with T4B at low multiplicity were diluted into broth containing 2.5 mg/ml. of 2,6-diaminopurine (Sigma Chemical Co.) at 37°C. After 60 minutes the culture was treated with chloroform. The average yield of phage particles per infected cell was 90 and the proportion of *r* and mottled plaques was about 1.9%. The DAP mutants were isolated from platings of a single stock, so that they did not necessarily arise independently. However, only a small fraction of the mutants present in the stock was used, so that the probability that two were derived from the same burst was small.

5-bromouracil (N) mutants: These include the mutants of Benzer and Freese[3], which were induced by growth of T4B on *E. coli* B in synthetic medium containing sulfanilamide plus 5-bromouracil. Added to these are the data for mutants isolated in the presence of 5-bromodeoxyuridine and thymidine (Freese[5]). Dr. Freese contributed mutants representing sites not found in the first set.

5-bromodeoxycytidine (BC)mutants: The effectiveness of this mutagen on phage was discovered by Dr. J. Gregory, who kindly supplied a sample synthesized by Dr. D. W. Visser. The procedure used was the same as for the DAP mutants except that the mutagen was 5-bromodeoxycytidine at a concentration of 5×10^{-4} M. The average yield was 80 and the proportion of *r* and mottled plaques was 0.8%.

Proflavine (P) mutants: These are the mutants, described by Brenner, Barnett, and Benzer[4], induced by proflavine during the growth of T4B on *E. coli* B. Each mutant was isolated from an independent burst.

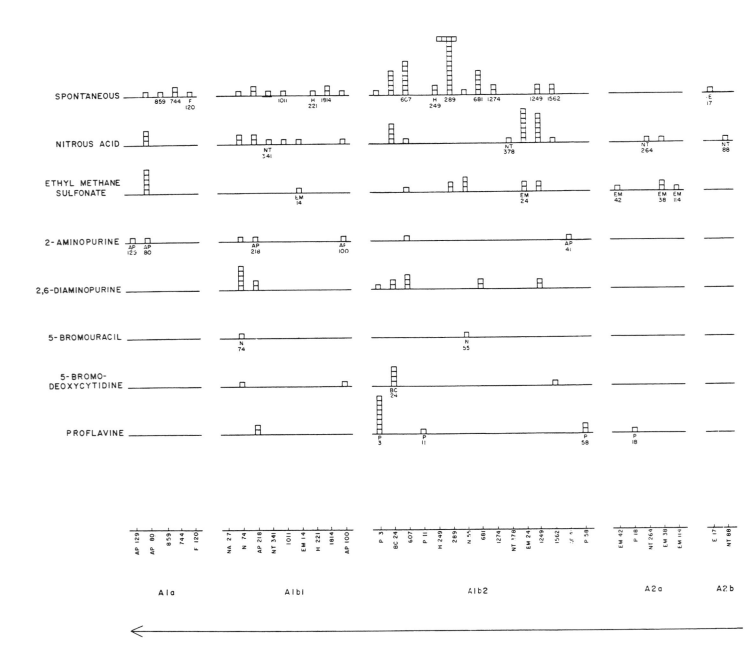

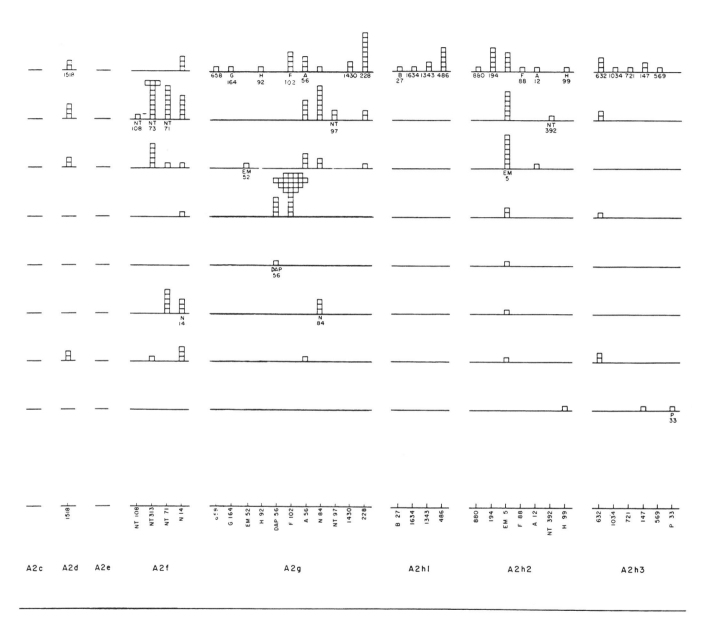

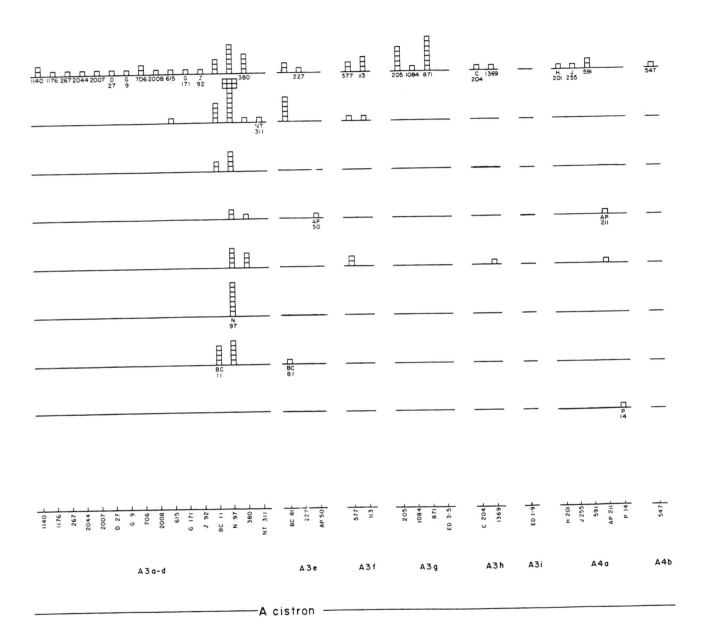

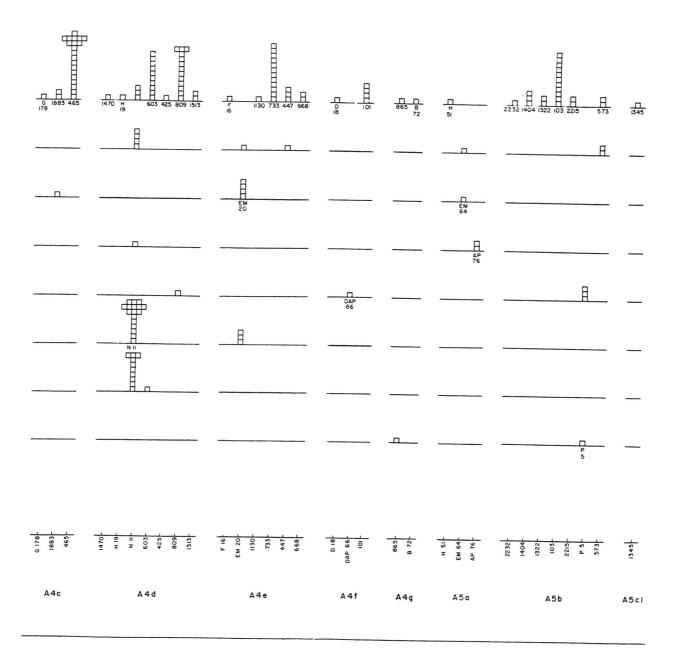

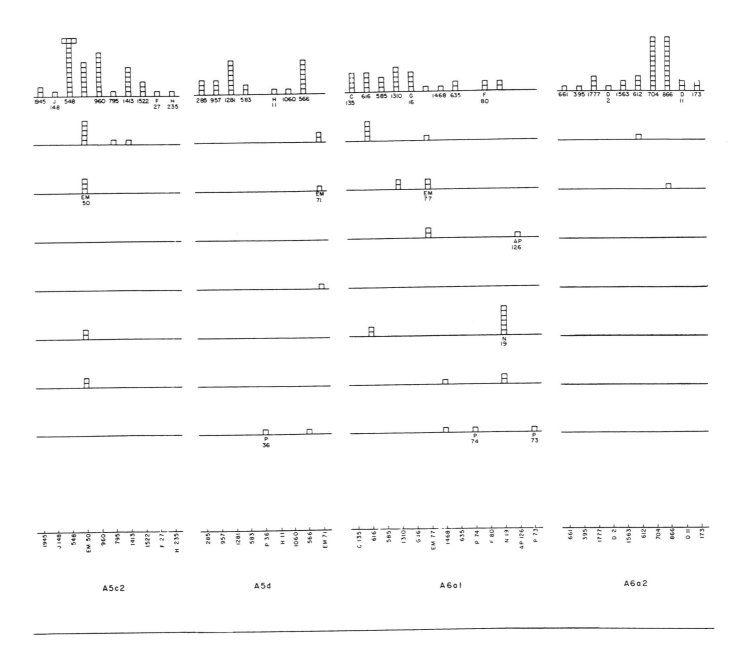

A5c2

A5d

A6a1

A6a2

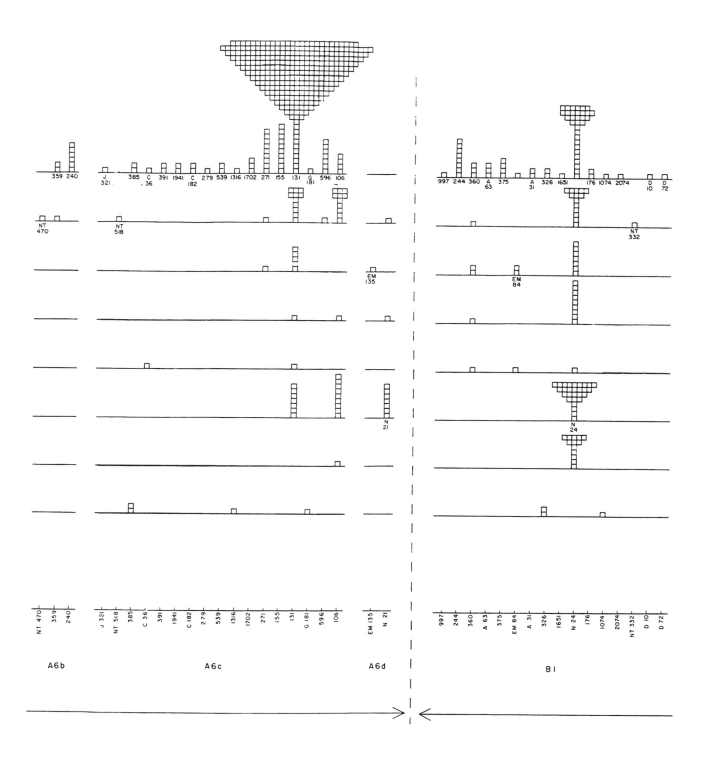

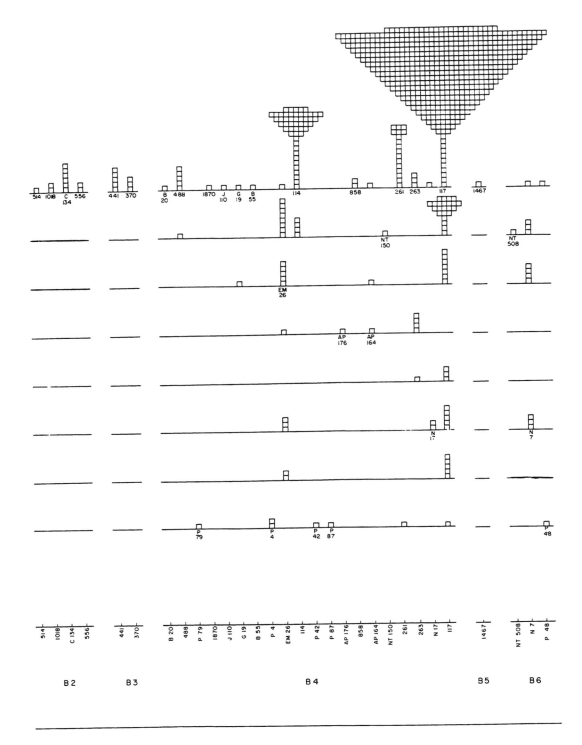

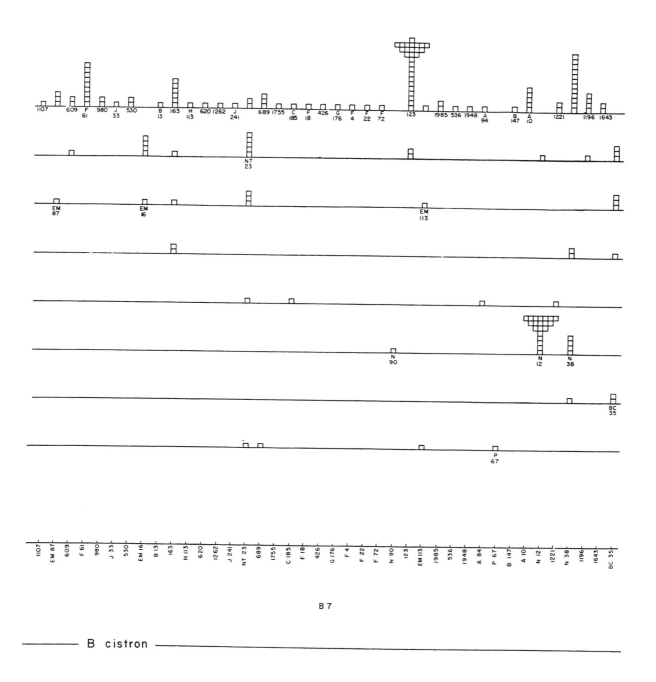

B 7

B cistron

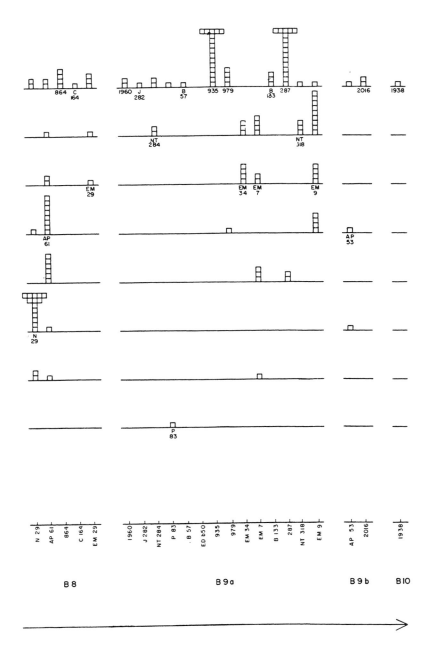

ON THE TOPOLOGY OF THE GENETIC FINE STRUCTURE

By Seymour Benzer

DEPARTMENT OF BIOLOGICAL SCIENCES, PURDUE UNIVERSITY

Communicated by M. Delbrück, September 8, 1959

From the classical researches of Morgan and his school,[1] the chromosome is known as a linear arrangement of hereditary elements, the "genes." These elements must have an internal structure of their own. At this finer level, within the "gene" the question arises again: what is the arrangement of the *sub*-elements? Specifically, are *they* linked together in a linear order analogous to the higher level of integration of the genes in the chromosome?

Until recently, the sensitivity of genetic analysis has been insufficient to answer this question. Mapping of a genetic structure is done by observing the recombination of its parts, and recombination involving parts of the structure that are very close together is a rare event. Observation of such rare events requires very many offspring and a selective trick for detecting the few individuals in which the event is recorded. It is for this reason that microorganism are the material of choice for studies of genetic fine structure, and have made it feasible to extend the fineness of genetic mapping by orders of magnitude. In favorable systems, the attainable resolution reaches the level of the molecular subunits of the hereditary material, and experimental testing of the linear arrangement of the finest structural details is therefore possible.

A number of cases have been investigated on this level.[2] As a rule, closely linked mutations affecting the same characteristic can be seriated in an unambiguous way, suggesting a linear model. However, the "distances" (i.e., recombination frequencies) between mutations are not always strictly additive, and certain complexities ("negative interference" effects[3, 4]) make quantitative analysis difficult. As pointed out by Muller[5] in regard to similar difficulties encountered in mapping on the chromosomal level, strict additivity of "distances" should not be taken as the criterion for the linear character of an array. A crucial examination of the question should be made from the point of view of *topology*, since it is a matter of how the parts of the structure are *connected* to each other, rather than of the distances between them. Experiments to explore the topology should ask *qualitative* questions (e.g., do two parts of the structure touch each other or not?) rather than *quantitative* ones (how far apart are they?).

In what follows, such an investigation is attempted for a small portion of the genetic structure of a virus, the "*rII*" region of phage T4. Using only qualitative tests, an examination is made of the topology of this structure at the molecular level.

The Material and the Method.—The methods for studying *rII* mutants of phage T4 have been described in detail elsewhere.[6,7] Briefly, T4 phage of the "standard" form can multiply normally in either of two bacterial host strains, B or K. From the standard form of T4, *rII* mutants occasionally arise (detectable by their plaque morphology on B) that are defective in growth on K. An *rII* mutant *can* grow normally on K if the cell is simultaneously infected with a particle of the standard type phage. Thus, the standard type is able to perform some necessary function which the mutant cannot. Our interest is in the genetic structure that controls this particular function of the phage. The controlling structure has been traced to a small portion of the genetic map of the phage, the "*rII*" region, and various *rII* mutants can be shown to contain different blemished versions of the structure, as distinguished by certain criteria.

One criterion is the recombination test, in which two mutants are allowed to multiply within the same host cell, thereby providing an opportunity for the production of progeny which obtain parts of their genetic information from each parent. By *recombination* of the unblemished portions of the two mutant versions, some standard (i.e., non-mutant) individuals may be regenerated. To perform the recombination test with *rII* mutants, one can infect cells of strain B (in which the mutants are able to multiply) with the two mutants in question and examine the progeny for the appearance of standard type individuals by plating on cells of strain K, on which only the standard type can grow. Such recombinants will occur only if the two mutants do not contain blemishes affecting the same part of the structure. The sensitivity of the test is sufficient to resolve mutations separated by the smallest conceivable distance, i.e., that corresponding to the spacing between nucleotides in the DNA.[6]

Thus, a simple experiment gives a qualitative yes or no answer to the question of whether or not two mutations overlap. This provides a key to the study of the topology of the structure.

The postulates upon which the procedure is based may be stated as follows:

(1) A hereditary structure in the phage determines its activity (i.e., ability to multiply in K). *The standard structure consists of a set of elements, alteration of one or more of which produces a mutant (inactive) form.* The subset of altered elements in any particular mutant is assumed to be continuous and not to enclose an unaltered region within its boundaries.

(2) When two or more phage particles infect the same cell, *genetic recombination* may occur: *each element of the hereditary structure in a progeny phage particle is derived from the corresponding element in one or the other of the parental phages.* The nature of the recombination mechanism, (e.g., whether involving material transfer of parental parts or a partial copying mechanism) is immaterial.

Given these postulates, the recombination test, applied to two *rII* mutants, reveals whether their mutations overlap or do not. By applying this test to many mutants, it should be possible to determine the manner in which the various parts or the structure are interconnected.

Effect of the topological nature of the structure: A few illustrations for model structures of different sorts may be helpful in clarifying this approach. Consider an example of an unconnected structure: a pack of cards. A complete pack of 52 subunits constitutes an active (standard) structure. The individual cards are interrelated as members of a set, but are not connected in any fixed order. A simple alteration, such as the damage or loss of one of the cards, renders the pack inactive (mutant). However, given *two* mutant packs, it is possible to produce a standard pack by recombination, *but only if the two mutations do not intersect,* i.e., the same card must not be altered in both cases. If such a test were extended to an unlimited number of mutant packs, comparing them two-by-two and in each case recording only whether a good pack *could* or *could not* be produced, the mutants would fall into fifty-two categories. Thus, the data would reveal that the standard structure consists of fifty-two distinct parts and there would be no indication of any connections between the parts.

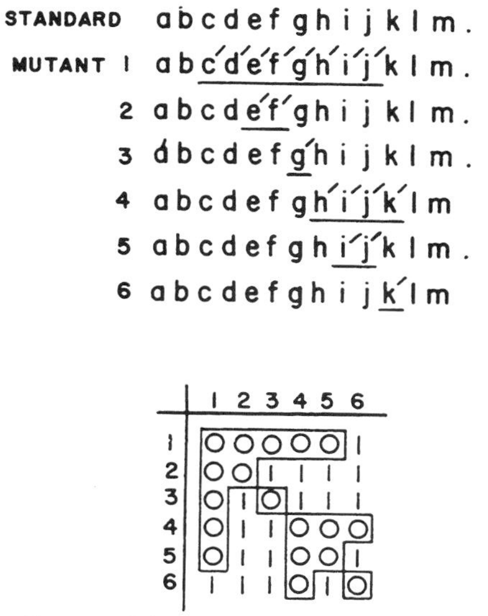

Consider now a connected standard structure of linear topology without branches or loops: a perfect tape recording of a piece of music. Such a structure can be rendered unacceptable by a blemish—one false note, perhaps, or a blank interval (due to a jump of the tape, say). Given two independent "mutant" versions, it may be possible to fabricate a standard one by recombination, but only if the two blemishes do not overlap. The exact mechanism is immaterial—either reciprocal exchange of parts (scissors and paste) or copy-choice (partial playback) will do. Now if various mutant versions are tried, two-by-two, in each case noting only whether or not successful recombination is possible, a new sort of result may be found with this connected structure that was not possible with an unconnected pack of cards. A blemish in the recording can involve a *segment* of the structure (and still be "simple" according to the restriction in the first postulate). It may therefore occur that one mutation intersects two others that do not themselves intersect. Given enough defective versions, the yes-or-no results of recombination experiments would enable one to construct a linear map showing the various defects in their relative positions within the standard structure.

A linear topology places certain restrictions on the pattern of results. Representing the standard structure as a sequence of elements *a b c d* .... the structure becomes mutant upon alteration of one element or a continuous series of them.

STANDARD a b c d e f g h i j k l m .

MUTANT 1 a b c d e f g h i j k l m .

2 a b c d e f g h i j k l m .

3 d b c d e f g h i j k l m .

4 a b c d e f g h i j k l m .

5 a b c d e f g h i j k l m .

6 a b c d e f g h i j k l m

FIG. 1.—(*a*) A linear standard structure is indicated as a series of elements. Alteration of any element or continuous group of elements produces a "mutant" structure. Six examples are given, arranged in dictionary order.

(*b*) The recombination matrix for these six mutants. A one indicates that standard type can be produced by recombination, a zero that it cannot.

A collection of such mutants can be arranged in *dictionary order* according to the first altered element, as in Figure 1a. If the six mutants shown are *crossed* (i.e., subjected to the recombination test) in all possible pairs, the pattern shown in Figure 1b is obtained. A zero indicates that standard type cannot arise by recombination, while a one indicates that it can. Diagonal values (i.e., for crosses of mutants with themselves) are, of course, always zero, and non-diagonal values are zero or one according to whether or not the two mutations in question overlap. The matrix has a characteristic feature which is a necessary consequence of the fact that the mutants have been arranged in dictionary order. By starting from a point on the diagonal, and moving to the right (or down), one reads off the results of crossing a particular mutant with successive ones on the list. Once the *first* non-intersecting mutant is reached, there must be *no further* intersecting ones. (If there were, they would belong higher up on the list.) Therefore, the zeros in any row or column (starting from the diagonal and moving to the right or down) must form a series unbroken by ones.

Conversely, given the data obtained on a set of mutants, *if the mutants can be listed in an order such that the matrix satisfies this criterion, their mutations can be represented as segments of a simple linear structure.*

This is by no means possible for any set of data. A two-dimensional structure, for example, can give quite different results. In two dimensions it would be possible for four mutations to intersect as shown in Figure 2, where mutation 4 inter-

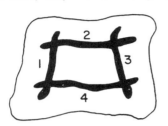

Fig. 2.—(a) A two-dimensional structure is shown, with four "mutations" mapped on it.
(b) The three possible arrangements of the recombination matrix for these "mutants."

sects with 1 and 3 *without* intersecting with 2. Such a situation would be impossible in a linear structure. Pairwise crosses of the four mutants would give the results shown. By listing the mutants in various ways, three different patterns may be obtained, but in no case is it possible to persuade all the zeros to form uninterrupted rows and columns.

And so on for three dimensions, branched structures, etc., each of which, if explored with a sufficient number of mutants, would give characteristic results impossible to represent in one dimension. For example, if crosses of six mutants were to give the results shown in Figure 3b, a branched structure as in Figure 3a would be required to account for them. Note that a single occurrence of a one where a zero should be is sufficient to force this conclusion. It would be an interesting mathematical problem to derive the characteristic feature of the matrix for each kind of topological space.

Experimental.—Our objective is to examine the topology of the structure in phage T4 that controls its ability to multiply in K, and specifically to make a rigorous test of the notion that the structure is linear.

The experiment consists of starting with a single particle of standard type T4 phage and isolating from it many independent, spontaneously-arising rII mutants, each of which may contain an alteration in a different part of the structure. These mutants are to be crossed with each other, noting in each case whether standard type recombinants do or do not appear. It is then to be determined what sort of structure is required to account for the results.

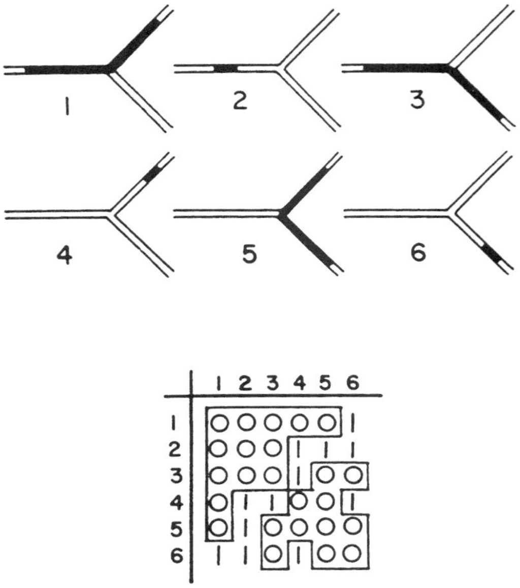

Choice of non-reverting mutants: Most rII mutants have some tendency to revert spontaneously to standard type. This is a serious limitation since, when such a mutant is used in a cross, one cannot readily distinguish standard type particles arising by recombination from those due to reversion. To circumvent this difficulty in the present experiment, only those mutants are used *for which reversion has not been detected.* About one in fifteen spontaneous rII mutants is extremely stable against reversion. The reversion test is most stringent, since revertants would be readily detectable on K in a proportion as low as 10^{-8}.

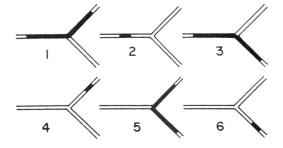

Fig. 3.—(a) Six possible "mutations" are shown in a branched structure. (b) A recombination matrix for these six "mutants."

Another advantage in choosing non-reverting mutants is that they are, *a priori*, most likely to include the ones in which *large* alterations have occurred, thereby giving a set rich in intersections.

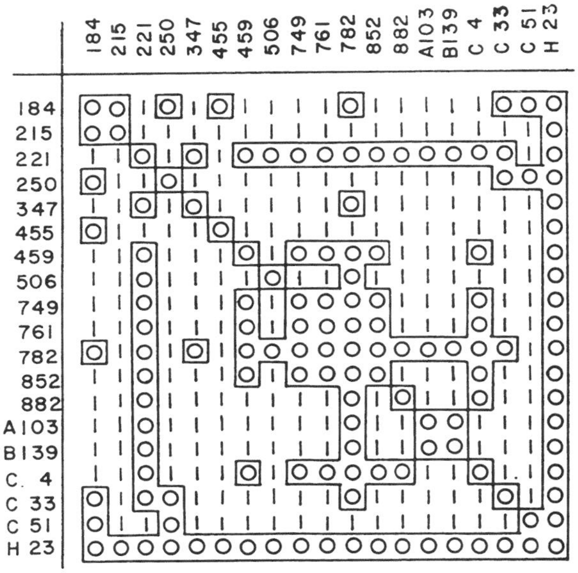

The 145 non-reverting rII mutants used in the present study were chosen by screening some 2,000 spontaneous r mutants[8] of T4 and rejecting any that were not of the rII type, or were seriously "leaky" (i.e., able to grow partially on K), or reverted detectably. The chosen mutants were crossed in many pairs, in each case testing for the appearance of standard

Fig. 4.—Recombination matrix for 19 rII mutants of phage T4, arranged in arbitrary order.

	H23	184	215	455	C51	250	C33	782	221	A103	B139	506	C4	459	749	761	852	882	347
H 23	0	0	0	0	0	0	0	0	0	0	0	0	0	0	0	0	0	0	0
184	0	0	0	0	0	0	0	0	1	1	1	1	1	1	1	1	1	1	1
215	0	0	0	1	1	1	1	1	1	1	1	1	1	1	1	1	1	1	1
455	0	0	1	0	1	1	1	1	1	1	1	1	1	1	1	1	1	1	1
C 51	0	0	1	1	0	0	1	1	1	1	1	1	1	1	1	1	1	1	1
250	0	0	1	1	0	0	0	1	1	1	1	1	1	1	1	1	1	1	1
C 33	0	0	1	1	1	0	0	0	0	1	1	1	1	1	1	1	1	1	1
782	0	0	1	1	1	1	0	0	0	0	0	0	0	0	0	0	0	0	0
221	0	1	1	1	1	1	0	0	0	0	0	0	0	0	0	0	0	0	0
A 103	0	1	1	1	1	1	1	0	0	0	0	1	1	1	1	1	1	1	1
B 139	0	1	1	1	1	1	1	0	0	0	0	1	1	1	1	1	1	1	1
506	0	1	1	1	1	1	1	0	0	1	1	0	1	1	1	1	1	1	1
C 4	0	1	1	1	1	1	1	0	0	1	1	1	0	0	0	0	0	1	1
459	0	1	1	1	1	1	1	0	0	1	1	1	0	0	0	0	0	1	1
749	0	1	1	1	1	1	1	0	0	1	1	1	0	0	0	0	0	1	1
761	0	1	1	1	1	1	1	0	0	1	1	1	0	0	0	0	0	1	1
852	0	1	1	1	1	1	1	0	0	1	1	1	0	0	0	0	0	1	1
882	0	1	1	1	1	1	1	0	0	1	1	1	1	1	1	1	0	0	1
347	0	1	1	1	1	1	1	0	0	1	1	1	1	1	1	1	1	1	0

FIG. 5.—Recombination matrix for the mutants of Figure 4, rearranged in "dictionary order."

type progeny. With the procedure used (a simple spot test[7]), the result *zero* for a cross indicates that, among the progeny from cells infected with the two mutants in question, standard type particles are fewer than one in about 10⁴.

Results: Figure 4 gives the results for a family of nineteen mutants related to each other by intersections. These have been crossed in all possible pairs and are listed in the order in which the mutants were isolated.

Are these data consistent with a linear structure? This can be decided by attempting to rearrange the mutants in an order which brings the zeros together into unbroken series. At first glance this might appear to be a formidable undertaking (the number of permutations of 19 mutants is greater than 10^{17}), but in practice it can be readily accomplished. In Figure 5 the mutants have been successfully rearranged. Thus, all the mutations can be represented as portions of a linear space, as shown in Figure 6

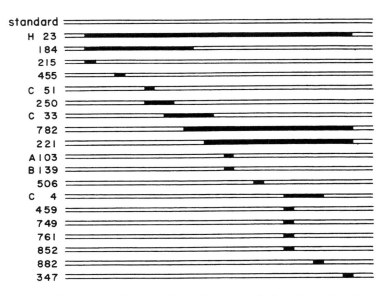

FIG. 6.—Relative positions of the mutations, as deduced from the data of Figure 5.

These results *rule out* an unconnected (pack of cards) structure, *are compatible with* a linear structure, and *do not require* any higher order of dimensionality.

The order shown in Figure 6 is not the only possible satisfactory one, since certain groups can be freely permuted without making any difference (e.g., *r*215. *r*184, *r*C51, *r*250, *r*C33, *r*782, *r*221, and *r*347). The number of uniquely ordered individuals increases as more mutants are brought into play.

In Figure 7 data are given for 145 non-reverting mutants, the mutants having been arranged in a satisfactory order, although not all the possible pairs have been crossed. All the results can be represented on a map in one dimension, as shown in Figure 8.

Functional units· The recombination test has shown that the hereditary structure controlling the ability of the phage to multiply in K consists of many parts. While alteration of any one of these leads to the same apparent physiological defect, it does not necessarily follow that all of the *r*II mutations block the same unitary function. For instance, growth in K could require a series of reactions, absence of any one of which would suffice to block the end result. It is therefore of interest to see whether the *r*II region can be subdivided in a functional sense.

It will be recalled that the needed function can be supplied to a mutant by simultaneous infection of the cell with standard type phage. Suppose that K is infected with two mutants simultaneously, as illustrated in Figure 9 (*trans* arrangement). If the two defects concern independent functional processes, the system should be active, since each mutant is intact with respect to the function affected in the other. However, if both mutants are defective in the same unitary function, the combination should still be inactive.

A proper control for this experiment is provided by testing the same genetic material in the *cis* arrangement (Fig. 9), i.e., with both mutations in one of the phages, the second phage being standard type. (In order to perform this test, the double mutant must be previously obtained by recombination.) The physiological activity of the *trans* arrangement is to be compared with that of the *cis*. If the *trans* is relatively inactive, a functional affiliation is indicated.

As applied to *r*II mutants, the *cis* test has invariably given an *active* system, as is to be expected when the standard type is present. The *trans* test divides the mutants into two clear-cut groups. Any mutant of group A can complement any one of group B, giving activity similar to that obtained in the *cis* configuration. Among mutants of the same group, however, the *trans* configuration is essentially inactive. Thus, the mutations can affect either of two distinct functional units, as defined by the *cis-trans* test. A functional unit so defined has been called[5] a "cistron."

When two mutants affected in different cistrons are tested for recombination by the usual spot test, their complementary action in lysing K leads to a massive response qualitatively different from that obtained due to recombination between mutants of the same cistron.[7] Such a massive response is indicated in Figure 7 by a two. A few *r*II mutants are defective in *both* functions, that is to say, complement *neither* A *nor* B group mutants, and therefore have defects affecting *both* cistrons.

It is important to point out that functional complementation, when it occurs, is not due to the formation of standard type recombinants inside K; full comple-

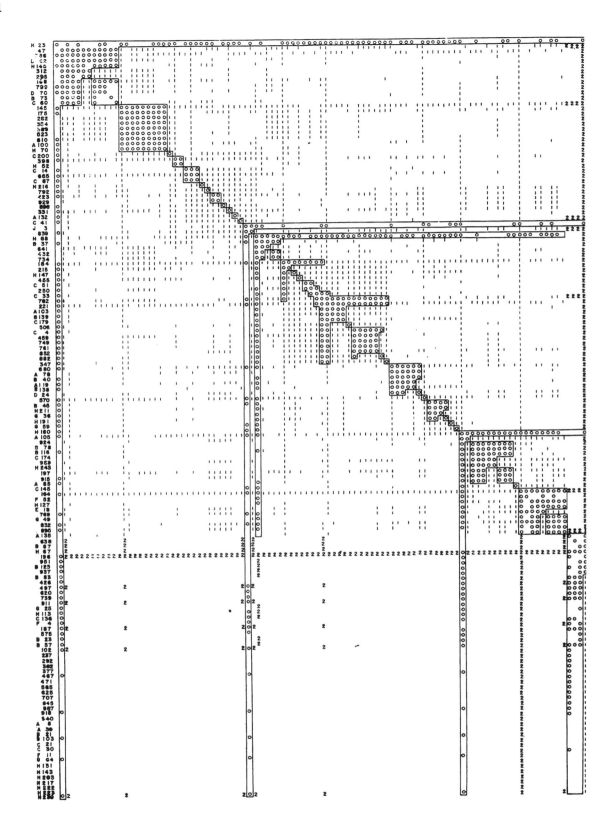

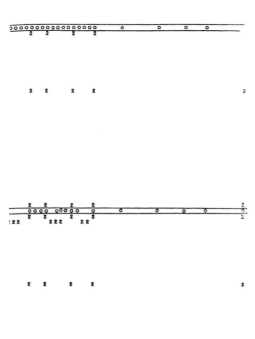

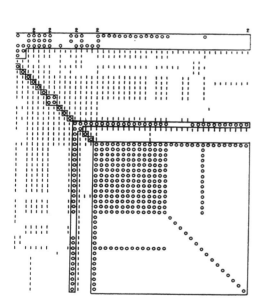

FIG. 7.—Recombination matrix for 145 *r*II mutants of phage T4. A two indicates a massive response, as occurs in crosses between mutants affected in different cistrons.

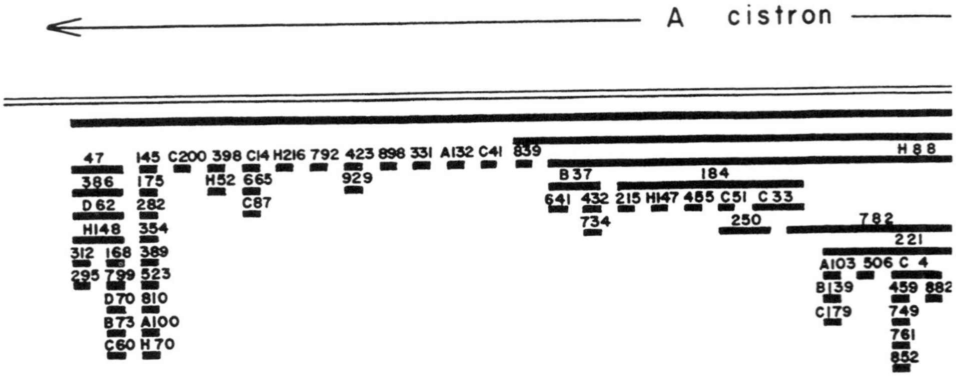

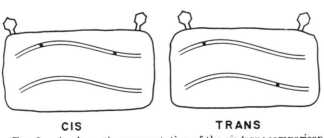

A cistron

FIG. 8.—A genetic map deduced from the recombination data of Figure 7. Each cistron represents a separate functional unit as defined by the *cis-trans* test.

mentation may occur even with mutants giving very little recombination. Thus, if K is mixedly infected with *r*164 and *r*638, whose mutations lie very close together, the cells lyse nicely even though very few of them liberate any standard type particles. Conversely, if K is infected with *r*164 and *r*168, practically none of the cells lyse, even though these mutants are capable (in growth on B) of producing standard type recombinants in most of the mixedly infected cells.

CIS **TRANS**

FIG. 9.—A schematic representation of the *cis-trans* comparison for testing the functional affiliation of two mutations. In the *trans* case each infecting phage carries a single mutation while in the *cis* one of the phages carries both.

Correlation of recombination and function tests: How does the assignment of mutations into cistrons by the *functional* test correlate with their locations on the map derived from the independent *recombination* test? It turns out that the map may be split into two portions by the divide indicated in Figure 8 as a vertical broken line. All mutants assigned to group A by the functional test have mutations located to the *left* of the divide on the basis of recombination. All mutations causing functional defect B lie to the *right* of the divide. Those few mutants which are defective in both functions have mutations extending to both sides.

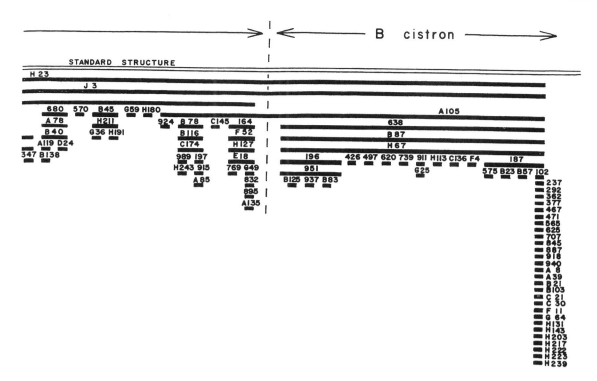

Thus, each cistron corresponds to a sharply limited segment of the linear structure.

Discussion.—In genetic mapping, mutation and recombination are both necessary, but emphasis can be placed upon one or the other. The conventional map is made by using mutations merely as "markers," the structure being surveyed by measurements of the frequency of recombination between markers. The mapping method we have used here is a complementary one, in which the frequency of recombination is unimportant, but, in effect, mutations have been used to explore the structure.

The particular mutants used in the present work represent a special class of the spontaneously-arising *r*II mutants, having been chosen for their non-reverting and non-leaky character. Mutants containing large structural alterations would naturally be found in this group, and such large mutations are necessary for overlaps of the sort needed to test the topology of the structure. In fact, *r*II mutants that show any tendency to revert behave as though their mutations are localized to points and would have been useless in this approach. The omission of leaky mutants is perhaps part of the reason why partial complementation effects did not cause difficulty in the assignment of the mutants to clean-cut cistronic groups. This difficulty, which has occurred in some other systems,[2] has also been encountered with some leaky *r*II mutants.

The postulates on which the analysis is based are, of course, idealizations when applied to an experimental system. The standard structure is not necessarily unique. There are many examples in genetics where the observable effect of a mutation may be compensated for by a "suppressor" mutation at a different location. Thus, when two rII mutants are crossed, the double mutant formed by recombination could have the standard phenotype, thereby causing an apparent doubling of the number of standard recombinants. However, this would have no bearing on the method of mapping that has been used here, which is independent of the frequency of recombination.

One of the postulates includes the assumption that each mutation is topologically "simple." In a linear structure this would mean that a mutant should not contain two or more alterations separated by an unchanged segment. Such double mutants are, of course, possible, but were rare enough not to cause complications in this study. A stock of standard type T4 typically contains a proportion of about 2×10^{-4} of spontaneous rII mutants. Therefore, on the assumption that each mutation occurs as an independent event, the proportion of the mutants containing a second mutation would be expected to be of the order of one in several thousand. Such double rII mutants would almost certainly not revert detectably. Among the roughly 2,000 mutants screened to select the 145 non-reverting mutants used in this study, one instance of a double mutant was in fact detected having a point defect in each of the two cistrons. When this mutant was crossed to standard type, two single mutant segregants were obtained, an A cistron one and a B cistron one. (This result does not occur for true large mutations, such as rH23.) The mutant (r928) has therefore been omitted from Figures 7 and 8. Note that the use of mutagens to raise the mutation rate is undesirable, as it would increase the proportion of double mutants.

Has the foregoing test of a one-dimensional scheme been sufficiently exhaustive? Even a set of nonsense data might happen to be compatible with a linear representation. Suppose one were to construct a matrix by tossing a coin to determine whether each "cross" gives zero or one. What is the probability that the "mutants" of such a random pattern would satisfy the criterion for a linear topology? For n "mutants," the number of matrix elements to be determined is $n(n-1)/2$. Each element is either zero or one, so there exist $2^{n(n-1)/2}$ different patterns, all equally probable. Some patterns will fit the criterion for linearity, namely those in which the zeros in each row form an unbroken series, starting from the diagonal. The first row, for instance, will be satisfactory if it contains no non-diagonal zeros, or a zero adjacent to the diagonal, or two zeros adjacent to the diagonal, etc. Thus, the first row can be satisfactory in n ways, the second row in $n-1$ ways, and so forth. Altogether, there are $n!$ satisfactory patterns, and the probability of obtaining one of these at the first go is $n!/2^{n(n-1)/2}$.

It may be, however, that an unsatisfactory pattern can be converted into a satisfactory one by rearrangement of the rows (and columns), and any given set of data may be subjected to $n!$ such arrangements. Although many of these will give redundant patterns, multiplying by this factor gives a *maximum* estimate for the chance that random data would be compatible with a linear scheme.

For $n = 19$, as for the data of Figure 4, this maximum estimate is approximately 10^{-17}. Considering the much larger set of data for Figure 7, the possibility of a fortuitous fit with a linear topology all but vanishes.

Therefore, the observed data are manifestly not random. However, this estimate does not really apply with the same force to the question of whether the structure is linear. The problem really is: given a topological space which is other than linear, what is the probability that this will not make itself felt (in terms of exceptions) when a given number of mutants is studied? The answer depends upon the assumptions made as to the nature of the space and the distribution of mutations within it. In the case presented above, the assumption that the matrix elements are random amounts to assuming a very complex space indeed and a distribution of mutations such that intersections are very common. This leads to a particularly low probability that the results will be compatible with a linear order.

Of particular interest is the question of branches. No case was experimentally observed of six mutants with the relationship shown in Figure 3b, which would require a branched map. However, it has been assumed that mutations have no effect upon the unaltered parts of the structure. Suppose instead that a loss along the main line which includes a branch point also necessarily leads to the loss of the whole branch. This means that in Figure 3a loss No. 1 is impossible (if the lower right arm is taken to be the branch). The remaining mutants can then be arranged in a simple line, in the order 3, 2, 5, 6, 4. More generally, if *many* deficiencies relating to the branch were available, one would find an apparent linear structure all along this line, with a section along the line (the portion which in reality is the branch) which is well ordered inside, but has *no* deletions reaching into it from the outside and stopping somewhere inside. Therefore, to eliminate the possibility that a given segment constitutes such a branch, it must be subdivided by a mutation reaching into it. This occurs for two mutants with respect to the A cistron (J3 and A105), but there are none that have this property with respect to the B cistron. While this can hardly be taken as suggesting that the B cistron is a branch, it is also true that a more exhaustive study will be necessary to rule out such a possibility.[9]

It is in the nature of the present analysis that the existence of complex situations cannot be disproved. However, the fact of the matter is that a simple linear model suffices to account for the data.

In confining this investigation to *r*II mutants of T4, attention has been focused upon a tiny bit of hereditary material constituting only a few per cent of the genetic structure of a virus and representing altogether some thousand nucleotide links in a DNA chain.[6] It would seem, therefore, that the fine structure of the hereditary material, even down to its smallest molecular components, may indeed be analogous to the linear order in which the genes are integrated in the chromosome.

Summary. -- The topology of the fine structure of a region of the genetic map of phage T4 is investigated by determining whether various mutations do or do not overlap. The results permit representation of the mutations as alterations in a linear structure in which the functional units defined by the *cis-trans* test correspond to unique segments. The possibility of branches within the structure is not necessarily excluded.

I am indebted to Mrs. Marion Sjodin for assistance in the isolation of many of the mutants, to Dr. Leslie Orgel of Cambridge University for suggesting the "dictionary order" analogy, and to Dr. Max Delbrück for suggestions regarding the possibility of branches and for his usual moderating influence. This work was assisted by grants from the National Science Foundation and the National Institutes of Health.

[1] Morgan, T. H., *The Theory of the Gene* (New Haven: Yale University Press, 1926), or any textbook on genetics.

[2] For an excellent review of this subject, see Pontecorvo, G., *Trends in Genetic Analysis* (New York: Columbia University Press, 1958).

[3] Chase, M., and A. H. Doermann, *Genetics*, **43**, 332–353 (1958).

[4] Pritchard, R. H., *Heredity*, **9**, 343–371 (1955).

[5] Muller, H. J., *American Naturalist*, **54**, 97–121 (1920).

[6] Benzer, S., these PROCEEDINGS, **41**, 344–354 (1955).

[7] Benzer, S., "The Elementary Units of Heredity," in *The Chemical Basis of Heredity*, ed. W. D. McElroy and B. Glass, (Baltimore: The Johns Hopkins Press, 1957).

[8] Mutants herein designated with a simple arabic number were derived directly from the T4 B standard type strain. Some mutants, obtained in connection with another study, were not derived directly from the original standard type, but from revertants of various (revertible) rII mutants, and are designated with a roman letter prefix.

[9] *Note added in proof:* Further studies of still more mutants have now turned up three instances of partial penetration into the B cistron, as well as three more cases for the A cistron.

Unit 1 / The Fine Structure of the Gene

Benzer 1961

1. Explain the *r*II system and the host range of *r*II mutants compared to wild-type T4 phage.

2. What does Benzer mean by topology and topography?

3. What is the concept behind deletion mapping?

4. What does Benzer mean when he says: "It is more meaningful to say that a mutation does recombine with a deletion or another mutation than to say that it does not."?

5. Why did Benzer choose mutations that reverted at very low levels (versus ones that did not revert at all) for his topography study?

6. Explain Figure 2 on page 20. Exactly how did Benzer perform this test? (You will have to understand the host range of *r*II mutants in order to answer this question.)

7. What exactly is Benzer trying to show in Figure 5 on page 23?

8. Explain how the diagram in Figure 6 on page 25 was constructed. What does each square mean? What is the overall purpose of making this diagram?

9. What is a Poisson distribution? Give its formula and explain what each symbol means and when this formula is applicable.

10. How did Benzer use the Poisson distribution to determine hotspots?

11. Describe specifically how Benzer calculated the number of sites in the *r*II region with 0 occurrence of mutations. (Be careful, this is a little tricky.) Find the total number of sites that are part of the Poisson distribution.

12. How does Benzer, in the discussion, arrive at 14 different rates for base substitutions without even taking into account the effects of neighboring base pairs?

Unit 2

The Nature
of the Genetic Code

In this unit, we will consider in depth a brilliant paper by Francis Crick, Sydney Brenner, and co-workers that determined the triplet nature of the genetic code by a fascinating series of genetic experiments. While solving the structure of DNA, Watson and Crick realized that the linear sequence of bases coded for the linear sequence of amino acids. However, there was a significant amount of trial and error involved in finding the true code. Following the publication of the DNA structure, George Gamow, the physicist who was involved in the big bang theory and the understanding of background radiation in the universe, wrote a key letter to Watson and Crick in 1953. In this letter, he detailed his idea for a genetic code in which the DNA served as a template for the assembly of amino acids into a protein. Actually, the distances were about right, and this made the code palatable to Gamow. Although Gamow's code, often referred to as the "diamond code," was soon shown to be implausible, the letter did make Crick aware that one could view the coding problem as an abstract problem. By then, one assumed that the messenger was RNA, even though it took a number of years to prove this experimentally. Since there were 20 amino acids and only 4 nucleotides, the problem was how to encode the amino acids with the different bases. Gamow's code (see page 72) had this property but it was an overlapping code (see diagram page 60), which placed significant restrictions on the amino acid sequences possible and predicted that single mutations would lead to multiple amino acid changes. The number of dipeptides already detected by 1953 could disprove his code, as well as all overlapping triplet codes, as shown by Brenner (see pages 73–80). Two other codes also had the property of allowing 4 bases to encode 20 amino acids. Gamow, Rich, and Yčas proposed a "combination code" in which a triplet code was used and the order of bases did not matter, only the composition. As it turned out, there are only 20 combinations of 4 things taken 3 at a time. Thus, AAA, AAB, AAC, AAD, ABC, ABD, ADC, ABB, ACC, ADD, BBB, BBC, BCC, BDD, BDC, BBD, CCC, CCD, CDD, DDD. Of course, this code proved to be false.

At the outset, it was also unclear whether or not the code had commas. For example, perhaps every fourth base was a comma. However, Crick, Griffith, and Orgel devised a code without commas. In this code (see pages 81–86), all overlapping triplets must be nonsense. They asked, "What is the maximum number of amino acids that can be encoded in this fashion?" Tantalizingly, the maximum number is 20. The authors could give at least one unique solution. Once again, this type of code proved to be incorrect. However, the incisive study by Crick, Brenner, and co-workers featured in this unit firmly established that the code was nonoverlapping, had no commas, was read from a fixed starting point, and used three bases to code for one amino acid. Before we consider this paper in detail, let's take a brief glimpse at Francis Crick's career.

Francis Crick

Francis Crick was born in 1916 and attended University College in London, from which he graduated at 21 with a degree in physics. He started research at University College studying the viscosity of water under pressure at 100°C–150°C. He felt that problem was dull. World War II started in 1939, and the following year he was given a civilian job at the Admiralty. He married and had a son, and then transferred to the mine design department on the south coast of England. He designed magnetic and acoustic mines (noncontact). These were dropped by planes into relatively shallow water in shipping channels in the Baltic and North Seas. The trick was to design mines that could distinguish between a real ship and a mine sweeper, which attempted to detonate the mines with signals. His efforts were very successful.

After the war, he applied for a permanent position as a scientific civil servant. He then realized that he wanted to do fundamental research, and he had two interests: the "borderline" between the living and the nonliving, in other words, the molecules of life, and the brain. He decided initially to work on the former, and he became a student at Cambridge in the MRC unit that had just been established, initially to study proteins, under Max Perutz and Lawrence Bragg. Of course, the rest is history, since by now all of us are familiar with the story of how he and Jim Watson solved the structure of DNA, for which they shared the Nobel prize in 1962 with Maurice Wilkins.

Following the elucidation of the structure of DNA, Crick applied himself to solving the coding problem, as outlined above and described in the paper analyzed in this unit. Around this time, George Gamow had instituted a select club called the "RNA Tie Club," which was limited to 20 of the top molecular biologists of the era. Each person was designated by an amino acid and received a specially designed tie. Crick was tyrosine. The

members of the Tie Club would exchange ideas in writing, usually speculative papers. One of Crick's extraordinary theories was contained in such a communication entitled "On Degenerate Templates and the Adaptor Hypothesis" in which the existence of tRNAs was predicted based solely on theoretical considerations. Never published in a leading journal in its original form, this was nonetheless a very influential paper. Shortly afterwards, the tRNAs themselves were first demonstrated in the laboratory.

In 1976, Crick went to the Salk Institute in La Jolla, California, first as part of a sabbatical leave, and then accepting a permanent position there. He has been Head of the Salk Institute since 1994. Although he still published some papers in molecular biology, such as a thought-provoking paper on "Selfish DNA" with Leslie Orgel, Crick's interests have focused on the workings of the brain and in 1994 he published the book *The Astonishing Hypothesis: The Scientific Search for the Soul*. He has concentrated on the visual system and aspects of consciousness. In his own words, "It is essential to understand our brain in some detail if we are to assess correctly our place in this vast and complicated universe we see all around us."

GENERAL NATURE OF THE GENETIC CODE FOR PROTEINS

Crick, Brenner, and co-workers examined the coding problem in their classic paper entitled "General Nature of the Genetic Code for Proteins." They asked, "How do 4 bases code for 20 amino acids, and what is the nature of the code?" Their reasoning took the following steps.

1. They first concluded that the code is not overlapping. What exactly do we mean by overlapping and nonoverlapping? The diagram below shows the difference between an overlapping and a nonoverlapping code.

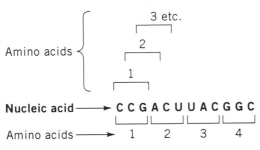

Overlapping Code

Nonoverlapping Code

Crick and co-workers distinguished between these two types of codes by the following line of reasoning.

a. Two groups, Wittmann, and Tsugita and Fraenkel-Conrat, had sequenced mutants of the tobacco mosaic virus coat protein produced by nitrous acid and found that only one amino acid at a time was altered. In an overlapping code, one would expect two or three amino acid changes to result frequently from a single mutation.

b. All of the altered hemoglobins show only one amino acid alteration at a time.

c. Brenner had demonstrated that if the code was universal, then all overlapping triplet codes were ruled out (see pages 73–80). He did this by looking at sequenced dipeptides. Note that in an overlapping triplet code there are 64 triplets and therefore a maximum of 256 dipeptides instead of 400 (from 20 × 20). Thus, if one could find more than 256 dipeptides among the sequenced proteins, then one could rule out overlapping triplet codes. Unfortunately, not enough sequences were known at the time. However, Brenner approached it in a different

fashion. Let's look at each codon in a triplet code. On the left side, one of four bases could occur, meaning that four dipeptides could be encoded for each base appearing on the left. To encode a fifth dipeptide, a new triplet is required. Therefore, you could divide the number of each type of dipeptide by four and get the minimum number of codons. For example, there were 18 dipeptides of the type X-lys. This would require a minimum of five triplets to encode all of the X-lys dipeptides, since each triplet could encode only four X-lys dipeptides. When Brenner added up the minimum number of codons to account for the known dipeptides, the number came out to 72. Since this is greater than the 64 possible codons in an overlapping triplet code, it was clear that the triplet code could not be overlapping.

2. How does the cell select the correct codons along the continuous sequence of bases? Perhaps every fourth base is a comma or perhaps only some triplets make sense, as in the commaless codes described above. Another alternative was that there is a fixed starting point from which one continues for each three or four, etc., bases at a time. This last explanation was the favored one and was later proven by the work in the paper by Crick, Brenner, and co-workers reprinted here on pages 64–71.

3. To carry out their work, Crick and his colleagues first had to develop their own theory of mutagenesis. This was because Freese had originally postulated that since acridines such as proflavin produced a different spectrum than base analogs, then base analogs produced transitions and proflavin produced transversions. (Recall that a **transition** involves the substitution of a pyrimidine for a pyrimidine or a purine for a purine, whereas a **transversion** involves the change from a purine to a pyrimidine or a pyrimidine to a purine.) However, Brenner, Crick, and co-workers correctly argued in a separate paper (provided here on pages 87–90 as Supplementary Reading) that the Freese hypothesis was false and that proflavin produced the addition or deletion of base pairs. Their reasoning was based on the following:

a. When one examined the distribution of mutations induced by both acridines and by base analogs, there were no common sites. One would not expect this in the Freese hypothesis, since transversions should occur at the same sites where transitions occurred.

b. The *o* locus of phage T4 (resistance to osmotic shock) probably encodes a head protein. Although base analog mutagens can induce *o* mutants, none had been found after treatment with acridine. In other words, the finished protein is required, and this is not produced by acridines.

c. The *h* locus in T21 phage controls a finished protein in the tail fiber. Again, it is very difficult to produce *h*[+] mutants with proflavin but it is easy with the base analog 5-bromouracil. All spontaneous *h*[+] mutants reverted with 5-bromouracil. However, one can induce mutants with proflavin in the *r*II locus, a locus that is not needed in *E. coli* B.

d. Acridine mutants are seldom leaky; they seem to destroy function completely.

Provided with the above precepts as starting points, Crick, Brenner, and co-workers proceeded to analyze the revertants of a nonleaky, proflavin-induced mutation in the B1 segment of *r*IIB, which, for the reasons elaborated above, was presumed to represent an addition or deletion rather than a base substitution. Their findings are listed below:

1. They found that *FC0* reverted by a second mutation nearby—a **suppressor** in the same gene. Here we should note that a suppressor is a mutation that overcomes the effects of another mutation. Operationally, a suppressor mutation can be separated from the original mutation to restore the mutant phenotype. There are many different types of suppressors. They detected 18 different suppressors, which are mapped in Figure 2 on page 66. The mapping of the suppressors was very important in the evolution of their ideas, since initially they had entertained the notion that the suppressible mutations might be located in regions of secondary structure of the corresponding mRNA, as shown in the diagram below.

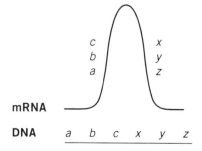

For example, if a hairpin loop were involved, then one could envision that a mutation (*a*) could be corrected by having a corresponding mutation (*z*) in the opposite portion of the hairpin, which would compensate for the original mutation. This idea predicted that the suppressor mutations would map in defined places, as can be seen in the diagram. However, when the suppressors were mapped, their positions did not conform to these predictions. The suppressors of any specific mutation mapped in numerous positions. Therefore, the secondary structure idea was disproved. The understanding of the insertion and deletion mechanism for acridines then led to the correct explanation.

2. They could separate the suppressor mutation from the original *FC0* mutation. This was done by first doing a backcross with wild-type T4 phage and then plating on *E. coli* B so that *r*II plaques could be recognized. These were then test-crossed against *FC0* to determine whether they were *FC0* or a different *r*II mutation that recombined with *FC0* to give wild-type phage. Thus, at this point, it was already clear that two different *r*II mutations could combine to yield a wild-type phage.

3. They could isolate suppressors of the suppressors. This was done by taking a suppressor that had been separated out from *FC0* and using it to find revertants that could be shown to be due to the occurrence of a suppressor mutation at yet another site. Again, each new suppressor could be shown to be a nonleaky *r* mutation that mapped in the B segment of *r*II. They could even isolate suppressors of suppressors of suppressors. All of these suppressors arose spontaneously.

4. Some of the double mutants resulting from suppression of the starting mutation have pseudo wild-type phenotypes, meaning that they could be distinguished from the wild type by their somewhat slower growth.

5. It was clear that one was not dealing with complementation, since the mutations must be together on the same chromosome or phage, in other words in **cis**. If the experiment were carried out in **trans** and *E. coli* K was simultaneously infected with each mutant, then no suppression occurred.

The explanation for these results is that the sequence is read from a fixed starting point without any commas. Thus, an addition or deletion would shift the bases in each codon from that point on, and the suppressor of such a mutation represents the deletion or addition of a base that restores the correct phase.

Only the codons in the space in between will be altered. Suppose we designate FC0 as plus (+) by convention. The suppressors are therefore minus (−), and the suppressors of these suppressors are plus (+), and so forth.

The explanation can be verified by making different combinations of double mutants. The prediction is that all combinations of + and + or of − and − will be r mutants. Crick and co-workers made 14 such pairs and found that all of them were r mutants. (How did they make the pairs? They crossed the two r mutants in E. coli B and test-crossed all of the r progeny with each of the two original r mutants. Only the double mutant would fail to recombine with each starting mutant to produce wild-type phage, but it would yield single r mutants after a backcross with wild type.)

In addition, as expected, many combinations of + and − yielded wild type or pseudo wild type, but there were exceptions. The brilliance of the authors is demonstrated by their understanding of these exceptions, since they realized that in some cases, nonsense mutations were generated in the incorrect reading frame. They expected that in, say, a triplet code, nonsense mutations would be produced in different places in the + reading frame than in the − reading frame. We can see from Figure 4 on page 68 that the + reading frame is unacceptable in several regions where the − reading frame is acceptable. (Figure 3, page 67, introduces the arrow convention, where the head of the arrow represents the + shift and the tail the − shift, based on the convention of naming FC0 as a + shift.) The unacceptable points were termed **barriers**. The fact that Crick and co-workers could predict that these barriers existed, define where they were, predict how different pairs would react to them (see Table 2, page 68), and understand that they were nonsense mutations represents extraordinarily penetrating deductions on their part.

The authors also made six triple mutants of the type + + + or − − −. (See if you can figure out how they constructed them. The answer is provided in Section III, page 545). In all cases, the triple mutants were wild-type or pseudo wild-type! Let's take a step back and look at this absolutely amazing result. Here, three mutations, each resulting in an r mutant, were used. Any combination of two of them still resulted in an r mutant, but the combination of three resulted in wild type! This fascinating result proved that the coding ratio is three or a multiple of three.

It is fortunate that Crick and co-workers were able to use a portion of the rIIB gene that could be altered without greatly damaging protein function. Independent proof that this region of the gene and corresponding protein was not necessary came from use of a deletion in rII, the 1589 deletion, which was described by Benzer and Champe. This deletion apparently fused the beginning of the rIIB gene to the rIIA gene, as shown in Figure 5 on page 69. Even though the resulting hybrid gene is missing part of the B gene, it still registers as A⁻B⁺ in complementation tests. The rII mutants employed by Crick, Brenner, and co-workers fell into the region of B missing in the 1589 deletion. The authors employed this deletion to show that proflavin-induced mutations in A, which normally never affect B function, did in fact destroy B function in the 1589 deletion. They reasoned that the A portion of the fusion was only required to maintain the proper reading frame in B. Once the reading frame in A was altered, then the reading frame in B was also altered and B function abolished. In addition, two different frameshift mutations in A could be combined in a double mutant, and although each alone results in no B function in the fusion, each suppresses the other when placed in combination.

CONCLUSIONS

By employing elegant genetic methods Crick, Brenner, and co-workers demonstrated that the genetic code was read from a fixed starting point, had no commas, and used either three bases, or a multiple of three bases, such as six, to encode one amino acid. They correctly reasoned that three bases was almost certainly the case, since other mutagens in addition to proflavin, such as acridine yellow, gave the same type of suppressible mutations, and mutations induced by proflavin could in fact be suppressed by those induced by other mutagens. Unless each of these mutagens caused the addition and deletion of exactly two, three, or four base pairs, then this cross-suppression could not have been observed. The assumption that each mutagen deleted or added a single base pair was the most likely and proved to be correct. In addition, the code would be very complicated if six or nine bases were used to encode each amino acid.

In addition to working out the form of the genetic code, the authors demonstrated the existence of frameshift mutations and, in so doing, showed that the published explanation of proflavin mutations was incorrect. They also correctly interpreted the "barriers" as nonsense mutations and understood and employed gene fusions for the first time. Finally, they were able to deduce that the code was highly degenerate, in that several codons could be used for each amino acid. This was because with 64 triplet codons and 20 amino acids, either the code was degenerate or there were many nonsense codons. If the latter were true, however, then they would not be able to translate open reading frames for any length after a frame shift, since nonsense codons would be encountered rapidly in any incorrect reading frame. All in all, the Crick et al. 1961 paper represents a remarkable mastery of phage genetics to explain molecular events.

At the very end of the paper, the authors refer to the breakthrough by Nirenberg and Matthaei (which was announced at the Biochemical Congress in Moscow) in which polyuracil was shown to generate polyphenylalanine in a cell-free system, leading to the conclusion that UUU was a codon for phenylalanine. Additional code words were filled in rapidly, and the final genetic code is shown below. The next unit deals with the deciphering of two of the nonsense codons that signal termination of the polypeptide chain.

The Genetic Code

Second letter

First letter		U	C	A	G	Third letter
U		UUU ⎫ Phe UUC ⎬ UUA ⎫ Leu UUG ⎭	UCU ⎫ UCC ⎬ Ser UCA ⎪ UCG ⎭	UAU ⎫ Tyr UAC ⎬ UAA Stop UAG Stop	UGU ⎫ Cys UGC ⎬ UGA Stop UGG Trp	U C A G
C		CUU ⎫ CUC ⎬ Leu CUA ⎪ CUG ⎭	CCU ⎫ CCC ⎬ Pro CCA ⎪ CCG ⎭	CAU ⎫ His CAC ⎬ CAA ⎫ Gln CAG ⎭	CGU ⎫ CGC ⎬ Arg CGA ⎪ CGG ⎭	U C A G
A		AUU ⎫ AUC ⎬ Ile AUA ⎭ AUG Met	ACU ⎫ ACC ⎬ Thr ACA ⎪ ACG ⎭	AAU ⎫ Asn AAC ⎬ AAA ⎫ Lys AAG ⎭	AGU ⎫ Ser AGC ⎬ AGA ⎫ Arg AGG ⎭	U C A G
G		GUU ⎫ GUC ⎬ Val GUA ⎪ GUG ⎭	GCU ⎫ GCC ⎬ Ala GCA ⎪ GCG ⎭	GAU ⎫ Asp GAC ⎬ GAA ⎫ Glu GAG ⎭	GGU ⎫ GGC ⎬ Gly GGA ⎪ GGG ⎭	U C A G

GENERAL NATURE OF THE GENETIC CODE FOR PROTEINS

By Dr. F. H. C. CRICK, F.R.S., LESLIE BARNETT,
Dr. S. BRENNER and Dr. R. J. WATTS-TOBIN

Medical Research Council Unit for Molecular Biology,
Cavendish Laboratory, Cambridge

THERE is now a mass of indirect evidence which suggests that the amino-acid sequence along the polypeptide chain of a protein is determined by the sequence of the bases along some particular part of the nucleic acid of the genetic material. Since there are twenty common amino-acids found throughout Nature, but only four common bases, it has often been surmised that the sequence of the four bases is in some way a code for the sequence of the amino-acids. In this article we report genetic experiments which, together with the work of others, suggest that the genetic code is of the following general type:

(a) A group of three bases (or, less likely, a multiple of three bases) codes one amino-acid.

(b) The code is not of the overlapping type (see Fig. 1).

(c) The sequence of the bases is read from a fixed starting point. This determines how the long sequences of bases are to be correctly read off as triplets. There are no special 'commas' to show how to select the right triplets. If the starting point is displaced by one base, then the reading into triplets is displaced, and thus becomes incorrect.

(d) The code is probably 'degenerate'; that is, in general, one particular amino-acid can be coded by one of several triplets of bases.

The Reading of the Code

The evidence that the genetic code is not overlapping (see Fig. 1) does not come from our work, but from that of Wittmann[1] and of Tsugita and Fraenkel-Conrat[2] on the mutants of tobacco mosaic virus produced by nitrous acid. In an overlapping triplet code, an alteration to one base will in general change three adjacent amino-acids in the polypeptide chain. Their work on the alterations produced in the protein of the virus show that usually only one amino-acid at a time is changed as a result of treating the ribonucleic acid (RNA) of the virus with nitrous acid. In the rarer cases where two amino-acids are altered (owing presumably to two separate deaminations by the nitrous acid on one piece of RNA), the altered amino-acids are not in adjacent positions in the polypeptide chain.

Brenner[3] had previously shown that, if the code were universal (that is, the same throughout Nature), then all overlapping triplet codes were impossible. Moreover, all the abnormal human hæmoglobins studied in detail[4] show only single amino-acid changes. The newer experimental results essentially rule out all simple codes of the overlapping type.

If the code is not overlapping, then there must be some arrangement to show how to select the correct triplets (or quadruplets, or whatever it may be) along the continuous sequence of bases. One obvious suggestion is that, say, every fourth base is a 'comma'. Another idea is that certain triplets make 'sense', whereas others make 'nonsense', as in the comma-free codes of Crick, Griffith and Orgel[5]. Alternatively, the correct choice may be made by starting at a fixed point and working along the sequence of bases three (or four, or whatever) at a time. It is this possibility which we now favour.

Experimental Results

Our genetic experiments have been carried out on the B cistron of the r_{II} region of the bacteriophage $T4$, which attacks strains of *Escherichia coli*. This is the system so brilliantly exploited by Benzer[6,7]. The r_{II} region consists of two adjacent genes, or 'cistrons', called cistron A and cistron B. The wild-type phage will grow on both *E. coli B* (here called B) and on *E. coli K12* (λ) (here called K), but a phage which has lost the function of either gene will not grow on K. Such a phage produces an r plaque on B. Many point mutations of the genes are known which behave in this way. Deletions of part of the region are also found. Other mutations, known as 'leaky', show partial function; that is, they will grow on K but their plaque-type on B is not truly wild. We report here our work on the mutant $P\,13$ (now re-named $FC\,0$) in the $B1$ segment of the B cistron. This mutant was originally produced by the action of proflavin[8].

We[9] have previously argued that acridines such as proflavin act as mutagens because they add or delete a base or bases. The most striking evidence in favour of this is that mutants produced by acridines are seldom 'leaky'; they are almost always completely lacking in the function of the gene. Since our note was published, experimental data from two sources have been added to our previous evidence: (1) we have examined a set of 126 r_{II} mutants made with

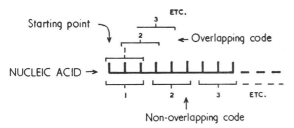

Fig. 1. To show the difference between an overlapping code and a non-overlapping code. The short vertical lines represent the bases of the nucleic acid. The case illustrated is for a triplet code

acridine yellow; of these only 6 are leaky (typically about half the mutants made with base analogues are leaky); (2) Streisinger[10] has found that whereas mutants of the lysozyme of phage $T4$ produced by base-analogues are usually leaky, all lysozyme mutants produced by proflavin are negative, that is, the function is completely lacking.

If an acridine mutant is produced by, say, adding a base, it should revert to 'wild-type' by deleting a base. Our work on revertants of $FC\ 0$ shows that it usually reverts not by reversing the original mutation but by producing a second mutation at a nearby point on the genetic map. That is, by a 'suppressor' in the same gene. In one case (or possibly two cases) it may have reverted back to true wild, but in at least 18 other cases the 'wild type' produced was really a double mutant with a 'wild' phenotype. Other workers[11] have found a similar phenomenon with r_{II} mutants, and Jinks[12] has made a detailed analysis of suppressors in the h_{III} gene.

The genetic map of these 18 suppressors of $FC\ 0$ is shown in Fig. 2, line a. It will be seen that they all fall in the $B1$ segment of the gene, though not all of them are very close to $FC\ 0$. They scatter over a region about, say, one-tenth the size of the B cistron. Not all are at different sites. We have found eight sites in all, but most of them fall into or near two close clusters of sites.

In all cases the suppressor was a non-leaky r. That is, it gave an r plaque on B and would not grow on K. This is the phenotype shown by a complete deletion of the gene, and shows that the function is lacking. The only possible exception was one case where the suppressor appeared to back-mutate so fast that we could not study it.

Each suppressor, as we have said, fails to grow on K. Reversion of each can therefore be studied by the same procedure used for $FC\ 0$. In a few cases these mutants apparently revert to the original wild-type, but usually they revert by forming a double mutant. Fig. 2, lines b–g, shows the mutants produced as suppressors of these suppressors. Again all these new suppressors are non-leaky r mutants, and all map within the $B1$ segment for one site in the $B2$ segment.

Once again we have repeated the process on two of the new suppressors, with the same general results, as shown in Fig. 2, lines i and j.

All these mutants, except the original $FC\ 0$, occurred spontaneously. We have, however, produced one set (as suppressors of $FC\ 7$) using acridine yellow as a mutagen. The spectrum of suppressors we get (see Fig. 2, line h) is crudely similar to the spontaneous spectrum, and all the mutants are non-leaky r's. We have also tested a (small) selection of all our mutants and shown that their reversion-rates are increased by acridine yellow.

Thus in all we have about eighty independent r mutants, all suppressors of $FC\ 0$, or suppressors of suppressors, or suppressors of suppressors of suppressors. They all fall within a limited region of the gene and they are all non-leaky r mutants.

The double mutants (which contain a mutation plus its suppressor) which plate on K have a variety of plaque types on B. Some are indistinguishable from wild, some can be distinguished from wild with difficulty, while others are easily distinguishable and produce plaques rather like r.

We have checked in a few cases that the phenomenon is quite distinct from 'complementation', since the two mutants which separately are phenotypically r, and together are wild or pseudo-wild, must be put together in the same piece of genetic material. A simultaneous infection of K by the two mutants in separate viruses will not do.

The Explanation in Outline

Our explanation of all these facts is based on the theory set out at the beginning of this article. Although we have no direct evidence that the B cistron produces a polypeptide chain (probably through an RNA intermediate), in what follows we shall assume this to be so. To fix ideas, we imagine that the string of nucleotide bases is read, triplet by triplet, from a starting point on the left of the B cistron. We now suppose that, for example, the mutant $FC\ 0$ was produced by the insertion of an additional base in the wild-type sequence. Then this addition of a base at the $FC\ 0$ site will mean that the reading of all the triplets to the right of $FC\ 0$ will be shifted along one base, and will therefore be incorrect. Thus the amino-acid sequence of the protein

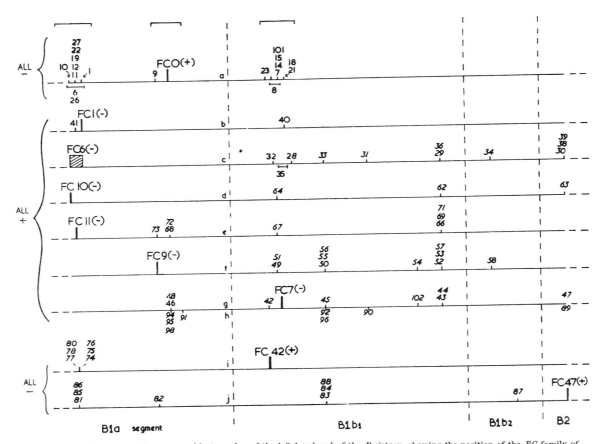

Fig. 2. A tentative map—only very roughly to scale—of the left-hand end of the *B* cistron, showing the position of the *FC* family of mutants. The order of sites within the regions covered by brackets (at the top of the figure) is not known. Mutants in italics have only been located approximately. Each line represents the suppressors picked up from one mutant, namely, that marked on the line in bold figures

which the B cistron is presumed to produce will be completely altered from that point onwards. This explains why the function of the gene is lacking. To simplify the explanation, we now postulate that a suppressor of FC 0 (for example, FC 1) is formed by deleting a base. Thus when the FC 1 mutation is present by itself, all triplets to the right of FC 1 will be read incorrectly and thus the function will be absent. However, when both mutations are present in the same piece of DNA, as in the pseudo-wild double mutant FC (0 + 1), then although the reading of triplets between FC 0 and FC 1 will be altered, the original reading will be restored to the rest of the gene. This could explain why such double mutants do not always have a true wild phenotype but are often pseudo-wild, since on our theory a small length of their amino-acid sequence is different from that of the wild-type.

For convenience we have designated our original mutant FC 0 by the symbol + (this choice is a pure convention at this stage) which we have so far considered as the addition of a single base. The suppressors of FC 0 have therefore been designated − . The suppressors of these suppressors have in the same way been labelled as + , and the suppressors of these last sets have again been labelled − (see Fig. 2).

Double Mutants

We can now ask : What is the character of any double mutant we like to form by putting together in the same gene any pair of mutants from our set of about eighty ? Obviously, in some cases we already know the answer, since some combinations of a + with a − were formed in order to isolate the mutants. But, by definition, no pair consisting of one + with another + has been obtained in this way, and there are many combinations of + with − not so far tested.

Now our theory clearly predicts that all combinations of the type + with + (or − with −) should give an r phenotype and not plate on K. We have put together 14 such pairs of mutants in the cases listed in Table 1 and found this prediction confirmed.

At first sight one would expect that all combinations of the type (+ with −) would be wild or pseudo-wild, but the situation is a little more intricate than that, and must be considered more closely. This springs

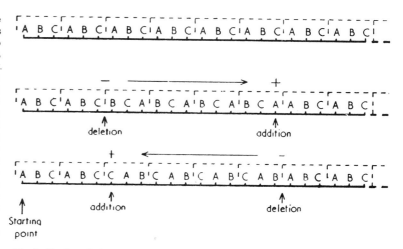

Fig. 3. To show that our convention for arrows is consistent. The letters, A, B and C each represent a different base of the nucleic acid. For simplicity a repeating sequence of bases, ABC, is shown. (This would code for a polypeptide for which every amino-acid was the same.) A triplet code is assumed. The dotted lines represent the imaginary 'reading frame' implying that the sequence is read in sets of three starting on the left

from the obvious fact that if the code is made of triplets, any long sequence of bases can be read correctly in one way, but incorrectly (by starting at the wrong point) in two different ways, depending whether the 'reading frame' is shifted one place to the right or one place to the left.

If we symbolize a shift, by one place, of the reading frame in one direction by → and in the opposite direction by ←, then we can establish the convention that our + is always at the head of the arrow, and our − at the tail. This is illustrated in Fig. 3.

We must now ask : Why do our suppressors not extend over the whole of the gene? The simplest postulate to make is that the shift of the reading frame produces some triplets the reading of which is 'unacceptable'; for example, they may be 'nonsense', or stand for 'end the chain', or be unacceptable in some other way due to the complications of protein structure. This means that a suppressor of, say, FC 0 must be within a region such that no 'unacceptable' triplet is produced by the shift in the reading frame between FC 0 and its suppressor. But, clearly, since for any sequence there are *two* possible misreadings, we might expect that the 'unacceptable' triplets produced by a → shift would occur in different places on the map from those produced by a ← shift.

Examination of the spectra of suppressors (in each

Table 1. DOUBLE MUTANTS HAVING THE r PHENOTYPE

− With −	+ With +	
FC (1 + 21)	FC (0 + 58)	FC (40 + 57)
FC (23 + 21)	FC (0 + 38)	FC (40 + 58)
FC (1 + 23)	FC (0 + 40)	FC (40 + 55)
FC (1 + 9)	FC (0 + 55)	FC (40 + 54)
	FC (0 + 54)	FC (40 + 38)

case putting in the arrows → or ←) suggests that while the → shift is acceptable anywhere within our region (though not outside it) the shift ←, starting from points near *FC* 0, is acceptable over only a more limited stretch. This is shown in Fig. 4. Somewhere in the left part of our region, between *FC* 0 or *FC* 9 and the *FC* 1 group, there must be one or more unacceptable triplets when a ← shift is made; similarly for the region to the right of the *FC* 21 cluster.

Thus we predict that a combination of a + with a − will be wild or pseudo-wild if it involves a → shift, but that such pairs involving a ← shift will be phenotypically *r* if the arrow crosses one or more of the forbidden places, since then an unacceptable triplet will be produced.

Table 2. Double Mutants of the Type (+ with −)

\\+	*FC* 41	*FC* 0	*FC* 40	*FC* 42	*FC* 58*	*FC* 63	*FC* 38
FC 1	*W*	*W*	*W*		*W*		*W*
FC 86		*W*	*W*	*W*	*W*	*W*	
FC 9	*r*	*W*	*W*	*W*	*W*		*W*
FC 82	*r*		*W*	*W*	*W*	*W*	
FC 21	*r*	*W*			*W*		*W*
FC 88	*r*	*r*			*W*	*W*	
FC 87	*r*	*r*	*r*	*r*			*W*

W, wild or pseudo-wild phenotype; *W*, wild or pseudo-wild combination used to isolate the suppressor; *r*, *r* phenotype.
* Double mutants formed with *FC* 58 (or with *FC* 34) give sharp plaques on *K*.

We have tested this prediction in the 28 cases shown in Table 2. We expected 19 of these to be wild, or pseudo-wild, and 9 of them to have the *r* phenotype. In all cases our prediction was correct. We regard this as a striking confirmation of our theory. It may be of interest that the theory was constructed before these particular experimental results were obtained.

Rigorous Statement of the Theory

So far we have spoken as if the evidence supported a triplet code, but this was simply for illustration. Exactly the same results would be obtained if the code operated with groups of, say, 5 bases. Moreover, our symbols + and − must not be taken to mean literally the addition or subtraction of a single base.

It is easy to see that our symbolism is more exactly as follows:

$$+ \text{ represents } + m, \text{ modulo } n$$
$$− \text{ represents } − m, \text{ modulo } n$$

where n (a positive integer) is the coding ratio (that is, the number of bases which code one amino-acid) and m is any integral number of bases, positive or negative.

It can also be seen that our choice of reading direction is arbitrary, and that the same results (to a first approximation) would be obtained in whichever direction the genetic material was read, that is, whether the starting point is on the right or the left of the gene, as conventionally drawn.

Triple Mutants and the Coding Ratio

The somewhat abstract description given above is necessary for generality, but fortunately we have convincing evidence that the coding ratio is in fact 3 or a multiple of 3.

This we have obtained by constructing triple mutants of the form (+ with + with +) or (− with − with −). One must be careful not to make shifts

Table 3. Triple Mutants having a Wild or Pseudo-Wild Phenotype

$$FC\,(0 + 40 + 38)$$
$$FC\,(0 + 40 + 58)$$
$$FC\,(0 + 40 + 57)$$
$$FC\,(0 + 40 + 54)$$
$$FC\,(0 + 40 + 55)$$
$$FC\,(1 + 21 + 23)$$

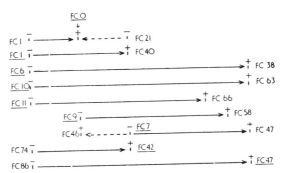

Fig. 4. A simplified version of the genetic map of Fig. 2. Each line corresponds to the suppressor from one mutant, here underlined. The arrows show the range over which suppressors have so far been found, the extreme mutants being named on the map. Arrows to the right are shown solid, arrows to the left dotted

across the 'unacceptable' regions for the ← shifts, but these we can avoid by a proper choice of mutants.

We have so far examined the six cases listed in Table 3 and in all cases the triples are wild or pseudo-wild.

The rather striking nature of this result can be

seen by considering one of them, for example, the triple (*FC* 0 with *FC* 40 with *FC* 38). These three mutants are, by themselves, all of like type (+). We can say this not merely from the way in which they were obtained, but because each of them, when combined with our mutant *FC* 9 (−), gives the wild, or pseudo-wild phenotype. However, either singly or together in pairs they have an *r* phenotype, and will not grow on *K*. That is, the function of the gene is absent. Nevertheless, the combination of all three in the same gene partly restores the function and produces a pseudo-wild phage which grows on *K*.

This is exactly what one would expect, in favourable cases, if the coding ratio were 3 or a multiple of 3.

Our ability to find the coding ratio thus depends on the fact that, in at least one of our composite mutants which are 'wild', at least one amino-acid must have been added to or deleted from the polypeptide chain without disturbing the function of the gene-product too greatly.

This is a very fortunate situation. The fact that we can make these changes and can study so large a region probably comes about because this part of the protein is not essential for its function. That this is so has already been suggested by Champe and Benzer[13] in their work on complementation in the *r*$_{II}$ region. By a special test (combined infection on *K*, followed by plating on *B*) it is possible to examine the function of the *A* cistron and the *B* cistron separately. A particular deletion, 1589 (see Fig. 5) covers the right-hand end of the *A* cistron and part of the left-hand end of the *B* cistron. Although 1589 abolishes the *A* function, they showed that it allows the *B* function to be expressed to a considerable extent. The region of the *B* cistron deleted by 1589 is that into which all our *FC* mutants fall.

Joining two Genes Together

We have used this deletion to reinforce our idea that the sequence is read in groups from a fixed starting point. Normally, an alteration confined to the *A* cistron (be it a deletion, an acridine mutant, or any other mutant) does not prevent the expression of the *B* cistron. Conversely, no alteration within the *B* cistron prevents the function of the *A* cistron. This implies that there may be a region between the two cistrons which separates them and allows their functions to be expressed individually.

We argued that the deletion 1589 will have lost this separating region and that therefore the two (partly damaged) cistrons should have been joined together. Experiments show this to be the case,

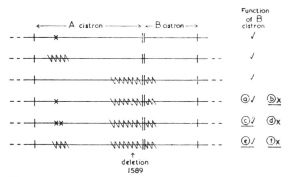

Fig. 5. Summary of the results with deletion 1589. The first two lines show that without 1589 a mutation or a deletion in the *A* cistron does not prevent the *B* cistron from functioning. Deletion 1589 (line 3) also allows the *B* cistron to function. The other cases, in some of which an alteration in the *A* cistron prevents the function of the *B* cistron (when 1589 is also present), are discussed in the text. They have been labelled (*a*), (*b*), etc., for convenience of reference, although cases (*a*) and (*d*) are not discussed in this paper. √ implies function; × implies no function

for now an alteration to the left-hand end of the *A* cistron, if combined with deletion 1589, can prevent the *B* function from appearing. This is shown in Fig. 5. Either the mutant *P*43 or *X*142 (both of which revert strongly with acridines) will prevent the *B* function when the two cistrons are joined, although both of these mutants are in the *A* cistron. This is also true of *X*142 *S*1, a suppressor of *X* 142 (Fig. 5, case *b*). However, the double mutant (*X*142 with *X*142 *S*1), of the type (+ with −), which by itself is pseudo-wild, still has the *B* function when combined with 1589 (Fig. 5, case *c*). We have also tested in this way the 10 deletions listed by Benzer[7], which fall wholly to the left of 1589. Of these, three (386, 168 and 221) prevent the *B* function (Fig. 5, case *f*), whereas the other seven show it (Fig. 5, case *e*). We surmise that each of these seven has lost a number of bases which is a multiple of 3. There are theoretical reasons for expecting that deletions may not be random in length, but will more often have lost a number of bases equal to an integral multiple of the coding ratio.

It would not surprise us if it were eventually shown that deletion 1589 produces a protein which consists of part of the protein from the *A* cistron and part of that from the *B* cistron, joined together in the same polypeptide chain, and having to some extent the function of the undamaged *B* protein.

Is the Coding Ratio 3 or 6?

It remains to show that the coding ratio is probably 3, rather than a multiple of 3. Previous rather rough estimates[10,14] of the coding ratio (which are admittedly very unreliable) might suggest that the coding ratio is not far from 6. This would imply, on our theory, that the alteration in $FC\ 0$ was not to one base, but to two bases (or, more correctly, to an even number of bases).

We have some additional evidence which suggests that this is unlikely. First, in our set of 126 mutants produced by acridine yellow (referred to earlier) we have four independent mutants which fall at or

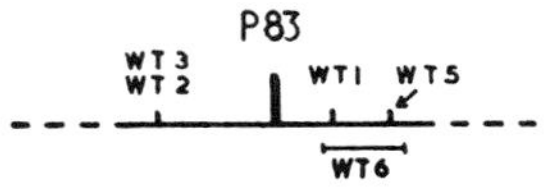

Fig. 6. Genetic map of $P\ 83$ and its suppressors, $WT\ 1$, etc. The region falls within segment $B\ 9a$ near the right-hand end of the B cistron. It is not yet known which way round the map is in relation to the other figures

close to the $FC\ 9$ site. By a suitable choice of partners, we have been able to show that two are $+$ and two are $-$. Secondly, we have two mutants ($X146$ and $X225$), produced by hydrazine[15], which fall on or near the site $FC\ 30$. These we have been able to show are both of type $-$.

Thus unless both acridines and hydrazine usually delete (or add) an even number of bases, this evidence supports a coding ratio of 3. However, as the action of these mutagens is not understood in detail, we cannot be certain that the coding ratio is not 6, although 3 seems more likely.

We have preliminary results which show that other acridine mutants often revert by means of close suppressors, but it is too sketchy to report here. A tentative map of some suppressors of $P\ 83$, a mutant at the other end of the B cistron, in segment $B\ 9a$, is shown in Fig. 6. They occur within a shorter region than the suppressors of $FC\ 0$, covering a distance of about one-twentieth of the B cistron. The double mutant $WT\ (2 + 5)$ has the r phenotype, as expected.

Is the Code Degenerate?

If the code is a triplet code, there are 64 ($4 \times 4 \times 4$) possible triplets. Our results suggest that it is unlikely that only 20 of these represent the 20 amino-acids and that the remaining 44 are nonsense. If this were the case, the region over which suppressors of the $FC\ 0$ family occur (perhaps a quarter of the B cistron) should be very much smaller than we observe, since a shift of frame should then, by chance, pro-

duce a nonsense reading at a much closer distance. This argument depends on the size of the protein which we have assumed the B cistron to produce. We do not know this, but the length of the cistron suggests that the protein may contain about 200 amino-acids. Thus the code is probably 'degenerate', that is, in general more than one triplet codes for each amino-acid. It is well known that if this were so, one could also account for the major dilemma of the coding problem, namely, that while the base composition of the DNA can be very different in different micro-organisms, the amino-acid composition of their proteins only changes by a moderate amount[16]. However, exactly how many triplets code amino-acids and how many have other functions we are unable to say.

Future Developments

Our theory leads to one very clear prediction. Suppose one could examine the amino-acid sequence of the 'pseudo-wild' protein produced by one of our double mutants of the ($+$ with $-$) type. Conventional theory suggests that since the gene is only altered in two places, only two amino-acids would be changed. Our theory, on the other hand, predicts that a string of amino-acids would be altered, covering the region of the polypeptide chain corresponding to the region on the gene between the two mutants. A good protein on which to test this hypothesis is the lysozyme of the phage, at present being studied chemically by Dreyer[17] and genetically by Streisinger[10].

At the recent Biochemical Congress at Moscow, the audience of Symposium I was startled by the announcement of Nirenberg that he and Matthaei[18] had produced polyphenylalanine (that is, a polypeptide all the residues of which are phenylalanine) by adding polyuridylic acid (that is, an RNA the bases of which are all uracil) to a cell-free system which can synthesize protein. This implies that a sequence of uracils codes for phenylalanine, and our work suggests that it is probably a triplet of uracils.

It is possible by various devices, either chemical or enzymatic, to synthesize polyribonucleotides with defined or partly defined sequences. If these, too, will produce specific polypeptides, the coding problem is wide open for experimental attack, and in fact many laboratories, including our own, are already working on the problem. If the coding ratio is indeed 3, as our results suggest, and if the code is the same throughout Nature, then the genetic code may well be solved within a year.

We thank Dr. Alice Orgel for certain mutants and for the use of data from her thesis, Dr. Leslie Orgel for many useful discussions, and Dr. Seymour Benzer for supplying us with certain deletions. We are particularly grateful to Prof. C. F. A. Pantin for allowing us to use a room in the Zoological Museum, Cambridge, in which the bulk of this work was done.

[1] Wittman, H. G., Symp. 1, Fifth Intern. Cong. Biochem., 1961, for refs. (in the press).

[2] Tsugita, A., and Fraenkel-Conrat, H., *Proc. U.S. Nat. Acad. Sci.*, **46**, 636 (1960); *J. Mol. Biol.* (in the press).

[3] Brenner, S., *Proc. U.S. Nat. Acad. Sci.*, **43**, 687 (1957).

[4] For refs. see Watson, H. C., and Kendrew, J. C., *Nature*, **190**, 670 (1961).

[5] Crick, F. H. C., Griffith, J. S., and Orgel, L. E., *Proc. U.S. Nat. Acad. Sci.*, **43**, 416 (1957).

[6] Benzer, S., *Proc. U.S. Nat. Acad. Sci.*, **45**, 1607 (1959), for refs. to earlier papers.

[7] Benzer, S., *Proc. U.S. Nat. Acad. Sci.*, **47**, 403 (1961); see his Fig. 3.

[8] Brenner, S., Benzer, S., and Barnett, L., *Nature*, **182**, 983 (1958).

[9] Brenner, S., Barnett, L., Crick, F. H. C., and Orgel, A., *J. Mol. Biol.*, **3**, 121 (1961).

[10] Streisinger, G. (personal communication and in the press).

[11] Feynman, R. P.; Benzer, S.; Freese, E. (all personal communications).

[12] Jinks, J. L., *Heredity*, **16**, 153, 241 (1961).

[13] Champe, S., and Benzer, S. (personal communication and in preparation).

[14] Jacob, F., and Wollman, E. L., *Sexuality and the Genetics of Bacteria* (Academic Press, New York, 1961). [Levinthal, C. (personal communication).

[15] Orgel, A., and Brenner, S. (in preparation).

[16] Sueoka, N., *Cold Spring Harb. Symp. Quant. Biol.* (in the press).

[17] Dreyer, W. J., Symp. 1, Fifth Intern. Cong. Biochem., 1961 (in the press).

[18] Nirenberg, M. W., and Matthaei, J. H., *Proc. U.S. Nat. Acad. Sci.*, **47**, 1588 (1961).

Possible Relation between Deoxyribonucleic Acid and Protein Structures

IN a communication in *Nature* of May 30, p. 964, J. D. Watson and F. H. C. Crick showed that the molecule of deoxyribonucleic acid, which can be considered as a chromosome fibre, consists of two parallel chains formed by only four different kinds of nucleotides. These are either (1) adenine, or (2) thymine, or (3) guanine, or (4) cytosine with sugar and phosphate molecules attached to them. Thus the hereditary properties of any given organism could be characterized by a long number written in a four-digital system. On the other hand, the enzymes (proteins), the composition of which must be completely determined by the deoxyribonucleic acid

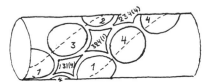

Fig. 1

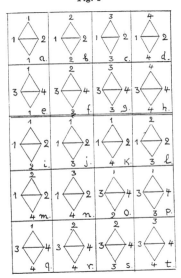

Fig. 2

molecule, are long peptide chains formed by about twenty different kinds of amino-acids, and can be considered as long 'words' based on a 20-letter alphabet. Thus the question arises about the way in which four-digital numbers can be translated into such 'words'.

It seems to me that such translation procedure can be easily established by considering the 'key-and-lock' relation between various amino-acids, and the rhomb-shaped 'holes' formed by various nucleotides in the deoxyribonucleic acid chain. Fig. 1 shows schematically the structure of the deoxyribonucleic acid molecule as derived by Watson and Crick. We see that each 'hole' is defined by only three of the four nucleotides forming it since, indeed, two nucleotides located across the axis of the cylinder are related by $1 \longleftrightarrow 2$ and $3 \longleftrightarrow 4$ binding conditions. It can easily be seen that there are twenty different types of such 'holes', as shown in Fig. 2. The first eight of them are simple, while each of the remaining twelve can exist either in right-handed or left-handed modification. It is inviting to associate these 'holes' with twenty different amino-acids essential for living organisms.

One can speculate that free amino-acids from the surrounding medium get caught into the 'holes' of deoxyribonucleic acid molecules, and thus unite into the corresponding peptide chains. If this is true, there must exist a partial correlation between the neighbouring amino-acids in protein molecules, since the neighbouring holes have two common nucleotides. There must also exist a correlation between adenine-to-guanine ratios in different organisms, and the relative amount of various amino-acids in the corresponding proteins. The detailed account of the proposed theory will appear in *Kong. Dan. Vid. Selsk.*

G. GAMOW

George Washington University,
Washington, D.C. Oct. 22.

ON THE IMPOSSIBILITY OF ALL OVERLAPPING TRIPLET CODES IN INFORMATION TRANSFER FROM NUCLEIC ACID TO PROTEINS

By S. Brenner

MEDICAL RESEARCH COUNCIL UNIT FOR THE STUDY OF THE MOLECULAR STRUCTURE OF BIOLOGICAL SYSTEMS, CAVENDISH LABORATORY, CAMBRIDGE, ENGLAND

Communicated by G. Gamow, June 10, 1957

It is a generally accepted view that nucleic acids control the synthesis of proteins, and it has been proposed more specifically that the sequence of amino acids in a polypeptide chain is determined by the order of nucleotides in ribo- or deoxyribonucleic acid. The problem of how this determination is effected has come to be known as the "coding" problem. The formal aspects of this problem can be investigated theoretically, and most of the work done in this field has recently been reviewed by Gamow, Rich, and Yčas.[1]

Since there are only four different nucleotides in RNA or DNA to determine twenty different amino acids, it is clear that more than one nucleotide must be used to code for each amino acid. Most codes have been constructed on the basis that each amino acid is determined by a set of three nucleotides. Such triplet codes, however, have an excess of information, since there are sixty-four different triplets for the twenty amino acids. In Gamow's original diamond code,[2] several triplets, chosen in a particular way, coded for any given amino acid; the code was therefore "degenerate." This code was also of the overlapping type—that is, the number of nucleotides in the nucleic acid was equal to the number of amino acids in the polypeptide chain. Gamow's diamond code does not, in fact, code for known sequences, and the same is true for the major-minor code, another overlapping triplet code, invented by L. Orgel.[1] These are, however, only two examples of a large number of possible codes of this type which can be obtained by choosing different ways of degenerating the triplets. To test all of these systematically is clearly impossible, and hence it is necessary to have some general theorem about such codes.

The general overlapping triplet code has the following properties.

(i) The coding triplets are chosen from four nucleotides, A, B, C, and D, giving sixty-four different triplets.

(ii) Coding is overlapping, each triplet sharing two nucleotides with the succeeding triplet in a sequence. Thus the sequence $ABCDA$ codes for three amino acids: ABC for the first, BCD for the second, and CDA for the third.

(iii) An amino acid may be represented by more than one triplet; that is, the sixty-four triplets are degenerated into twenty sets.

Since any dipeptide sequence is represented by a sequence of four nucleotides, there cannot be more than 256 different dipeptides. On the other hand, if all dipeptide sequences were possible, 400 would be expected. Thus overlapping codes introduce restrictions in amino acid sequences. The number of dipeptide sequences known is less than 256, and, although statistical studies have suggested that all dipeptides are likely to be found, the significance of this result has been difficult to assess.[1] The sample of proteins studied is highly selected, a large number of sequences are fragmentary, and the methods used to study sequences further bias the data.

However, sufficient sequences are known to prove that it is impossible to code them with overlapping triplets. The proof is simple and does not depend on any special way of degenerating the triplets. It consists in the demonstration that sixty-four triplets are insufficient to code the known sequences.

Proof: Since successive triplets share two nucleotides in common, any given triplet can be preceded by only four different triplets and succeeded by only four different triplets. In an amino acid sequence $j.k.l.$, we call j an N-neighbor, and l a C-neighbor, of k. For every four different N-neighbors (or C-neighbors) or part thereof, k must have one triplet assigned to it. Thus the *minimum* number of triplet representations for each amino acid can be counted from a table of neighbors.

The available sequences are given in the Appendix. From these sequences a grid is constructed and the different neighbors counted for each amino acid. The number of triplets assigned to each amino acid is based on the larger number of its neighbors. These data are given in Table 1, from which it can be seen that seventy

TABLE 1

Amino Acid	C-Neighbors	N-Neighbors	Minimum No. of Triplets Required	Amino Acid	C-Neighbors	N-Neighbors	Minimum No. of Triplets Required
Lys	18	17	5	Pro	13	12	4
Ser	17	13	5	Tyr	12	10	3
Gly	15	15	4	Glu	11	11	3
Leu	15	15	4	Glun	12	9	3
Cys	15	14	4	Asp	10	11	3
Arg	14	16	4	Asn	9	10	3
Ala	14	15	4	Ileu	9	9	3
Val	14	12	4	His	6	9	3
Thr	13	14	4	Met	5	7	2
Phe	13	14	4	Try	3	3	1
						Total	70

triplets would be required to code the sequences. We conclude, then, that all overlapping triplet codes are impossible.

This result has one important physical implication. The original formulation of overlapping codes was based on the similarity of the internucleotide distance in DNA to the spacing between amino acid residues in an extended polypeptide chain. It was supposed that each amino acid was spatially related in a one-to-one way with each nucleotide on a nucleic acid template. The present result shows that this cannot be so and that each amino acid is stereochemically related to at least two, if not three, nucleotides, depending on whether coding is partially overlapping or nonoverlapping. The difficulties raised by this can easily be overcome by assuming that the polypeptide sequence is in contact with the nucleic acid template only at the growing point, and detailed schemes can be readily proposed.

As far as the coding problem is concerned, it now appears that all amino sequences are likely to be found and that it will not be possible to effect a "decoding" by discovering restrictions in sequences. The nonoverlapping of triplets implies that there must be some way of determining which triplets in a sequence are coding triplets and which are not, and a very interesting code has recently been proposed by Crick, Griffith, and Orgel,[3] in which this problem is dealt with in a novel manner.

APPENDIX

Amino Acid Sequences

In writing the sequences, the same conventions used by Gamow et al.[1] have been followed. Wherever doubt exists as to whether glutamic acid is present as such (glu) or as the amide (glun), it has been assigned as "glux," and the same rule has been followed for aspartic acid and asparagine. All the longer lysozyme sequences suggested by Thompson (*Biochem. J.*, **60**, 507; **61**, 253, 1955) have been omitted, since some of these appear to be incorrect when compared with those established by the French workers. Sequences established by carboxypeptidase digestions alone are given at the end of the list but are omitted from the grid. The same applies to the pepsin sequence of Williamson and Passmann (*J. Biol. Chem.*, **222**, 151, 1956), as there are conflicting reports about the N-terminal group (Van Vunakis and Herriott, *Biochim. et Biophys. Acta*, **23**, 60, 1957).

The grid (Table 2) shows the number of times dipeptide sequences are found. Identical sequences from the closely related proteins vasopressin and oxytocin and corticotrophin and melanophore-stimulating hormone are only recorded once. Dipeptide sequences from lysozyme are not recorded if the same sequence is found in a longer peptide. When both glu and glun are absent, glux is counted as a neighbor, and the same rule is followed for asp, asn, and ax.

SEQUENCES USED IN THE GRID*

-thr. gly. ileu[c]-

-thr. ser. ileu[c, d]-

-ala. gly. val[b]-

Insulin A: Gly. ileu. val. glu. glun. cys. cys. ala. ser. val[a]. cys. ser. leu. tyr. glun. leu. glu. asn. tyr. cys. asn.[4-6]

Insulin B: Phe. val. asn. glun. his. leu. cys. gly. ser. his. leu. val. glu. ala. leu. tyr. leu. val. cys. gly. glu. arg. gly. phe. phe. tyr. thr. pro. lys. ala.[4, 5]

Oxytocin: Cys. tyr. ileu. glun. asn. cys. pro. leu. gly. NH₂.[7]

-arg[a]-

Vasopressin: Cys. tyr. phe. glun. asn. cys. pro. lys[b]. gly. NH₂.[8]

Corticotrophin: Ser. tyr. ser. met. glu. his. phe. arg. try. gly. lys. pro. val. gly. lys. lys. arg-arg. pro. val. lys. val. tyr. pro. *asp. gly. ala. glu.*[9] asp. glun. leu. ala[b]. glu. ala. phe. pro. leu-

-glux. ala. ser[c]-

glu. phe.[10-13]

Glucagon: His. ser. glun. gly. thr. phe. thr. ser. asp. thr. ser. lys. tyr. leu. asp. ser. arg. arg. ala. glun. asp. phe. val. glun. try. leu. met. asn. thr.[14]

-ser[a]-

Melanophore-stimulating hormone: Asp. glu[b]. gly. pro. tyr. lys. met. glu. his. phe. arg. try. gly. ser. pro. pro. lys. asp.[15-17]

* [a] Cattle. [b] Pig. [c] Sheep. [d] Whale. [e] Horse. [f] Salmon. [g] Chicken. [h] Man.

TABLE 2

GRID SHOWING NUMBERS OF N- AND C- NEIGHBORS

N-Neighbor \ C-Neighbor	Lys	Ser	Gly	Leu	Cys	Arg	Ala	Val	Thr	Phe	Pro	Tyr	Glu	Glun	Glux	Asp	Asn	Asx	Ileu	His	Met	Try
Try	·	·	1	1	·	1	1	·	·	·	·	·	·	·	·	·	·	·	·	·	·	1
Met	2	·	·	·	·	·	·	1	·	·	·	·	·	·	·	1	1	·	1	1	·	1
His	1	1	3	·	·	1	1	·	·	·	·	1	·	·	·	·	·	·	·	·	·	·
Ileu	·	·	1	1	1	·	1	·	4	·	·	·	·	·	·	·	·	·	1	·	·	·
Asx	1	·	1	·	2	·	2	·	·	·	·	·	·	·	·	2	·	1	·	3	·	·
Asn	·	1	·	1	2	3	·	2	·	·	1	·	·	·	3	·	·	·	·	·	·	·
Asp	·	3	1	·	·	3	1	·	1	1	·	2	·	1	·	3	·	·	·	·	·	·
Glux	·	1	·	·	·	·	·	·	·	·	·	·	·	·	·	·	·	·	1	·	·	·
Glun	1	1	·	·	3	2	·	·	·	·	·	·	·	·	2	·	·	·	·	1	1	·
Glu	1	2	·	·	4	·	·	1	·	1	·	1	·	·	1	·	·	·	·	·	·	·
Tyr	2	1	·	2	2	2	·	1	·	2	2	·	2	·	·	2	·	·	·	3	·	·
Pro	4	1	2	·	1	·	3	·	·	1	·	·	1	·	·	1	·	1	·	·	1	·
Phe	2	·	·	1	·	2	·	1	·	1	·	·	2	·	2	·	2	·	1	·	·	·
Thr	2	5	2	1	·	2	·	·	·	·	4	·	·	1	·	·	2	·	·	·	·	·
Val	2	1	2	2	5	·	3	·	·	1	·	2	3	3	1	·	3	·	1	·	·	·
Ala	4	3	2	3	2	·	4	·	2	·	1	·	2	2	1	·	·	·	·	·	1	1
Arg	1	·	4	2	2	1	·	·	1	·	2	·	·	·	1	·	·	·	·	·	1	1
Cys	2	·	4	1	·	4	1	·	1	·	2	·	1	·	3	2	·	1	·	·	·	·
Leu	1	2	1	2	·	2	4	1	·	2	2	·	·	1	·	·	·	·	1	·	·	·
Gly	3	4	3	2	1	·	2	·	2	·	·	·	·	·	2	·	·	·	2	·	1	·
Ser	1	4	3	1	5	2	3	2	·	3	2	·	2	1	·	·	2	1	1	1	·	·
Lys	1	1	3	2	1	3	1	2	1	2	2	1	·	·	2	2	1	1	1	1	·	·

Hypertensin: Asp. arg. val. tyr. val[a]. his. pro. phe. his. leu.[18, 19]

$$-\text{ileu}^{\epsilon}-$$

Cytochrome c: -val. glun. lys. cys. ala[a, b, e, f]. glun. cys. his. thr. val. glu. lys-[20, 21]

$$-\text{ser}^{g}-$$

Trypsinogen: Val. asp. asp. asp. asp. lys. ileu. val. gly-[22, 23]

Ribonuclease: Lys. glu. thr. ala. ala. ala. lys. phe. glun. arg. glu-[24–26]

-tyr. cys. asn. glun. met. met. lys. ser. arg. asn. leu. thr. lys. asp. arg. cys.[24–27]

-lys. asn. val. ala. cys. lys. asn. thr-[26, 27]

-cys. asn. arg. glu. ser. thr. ser. gly. lys. tyr. pro. asn. ala. cys. tyr. lys. thr. thr. asn. glun. ala. lys. his-[26, 27]

-tyr. glun. ser. tyr-[24]

-phe. asp. ala. ser. val.[24, 28, 29]

Lysozyme: -lys. asx-[30]

-arg. his. lys-[31]

Lys. val. phe. gly. arg-

-ala. lys. phe. glux-

-asx. tyr. arg. gly-

-arg. gly. tyr. ileu. leu-

-asn. ala. tyr. gly. ser. leu. asn-

-thr. pro-

-leu. pro-[32]

-asn. arg-

-ileu. arg-

-thr. pro. gly. ser. arg-

-val. ala. try. arg-[33]

-gly. cys. arg. leu.

-phe. glu. ser. phe. asp. glu. ala. thr. asp. arg-

-cys. glu. ala. leu. ala. ala. met. lys. arg-[34]

-ala. ala-	-asx. ileu-	-ileu. arg-	-ser. ala-
-ala. leu-	-asx. leu-	-ileu. asx-	-ser. arg-
-ala. lys-	-cys. ala-	-ileu. val-	-ser. asx-
-ala. met-	-cys. arg-	-leu. ala-	-ser. leu-
-arg. asx-	-cys. asx-	-leu. cys-	-ser. val-
-arg. cys-	-cys. glux-	-leu. leu-	-thr. ala-
-arg. gly-	-cys. ileu-	-lys. gly-	-thr. asx-
-arg. leu-	-cys. lys-	-met. asx-	-thr. gly-
-asx. ala-	-gly. leu-	-met. lys-	-thr. glux-
-asx. arg-	-gly. met-	-phe. asx-	-thr. pro-
-asx. asx-	-glux. ala-	-phe. glux	-val. ala-
-asx. gly-	-glux. leu-		-val. asx-
			-val. cys-
			-val. glux-[35]

Ovalbumin: -ala. gly. val. asx. ala. ala-[36]

-asx. ser. glux. ileu. ala-

-glux. ser. ala-[37]

-cys. ala-	-thr. cys-	-cys. phe-
-cys. gly-	-val. cys-	-gly. cys-
-cys. val-	-cys. glux-	-asx. cys-[38]
-ser. cys-	-phe. cys-	
	-val. ser. pro.[28]	

Papain: Ileu. pro. glux-[39]
      -ser. asx-   -cys. asx-   -val. cys-[40]
      -asx. cys-   -cys. gly. asx-

Hemoglobin: Val. glun. leu-
      Val. leu-[41]
      -lys. arg-   -arg. leu-   -val. lys-
      -lys. leu-   -phe. lys-   -arg. lys-
      -ser. arg-   -arg. phe-   -tyr. arg-
      -ala. arg-   -leu. arg-   -phe. arg-[42]

Myoglobin: Gly. leu-[43, 44]

γ-Globulin: Ala. leu. val. asx. glux-[45, 46]

β-Lactoglobulin: -val. glux-   -thr. lys-   -ala. lys-
      -val. leu-   -lys. gly-   -leu. lys-
      -asx. lys-   -pro. lys-   -phe. lys-[47]
      -glux. lys-   -lys. pro-

Carboxypeptidase: Asn. ser-
      -ser. thr-[48]

      -thr[h]-
Serum albumin: Asx. ala[a]-[49]

Lactogenic hormone: Thr. pro. val. thr. pro-[50]

Tobacco mosaic virus: -thr. ser. gly. pro. ala. thr.[51]
      Pro. ileu. glux-[52]

Casein: Lys. leu. val. ala. glux. asx-[53]
      -leu. gly-   -ser. pro-   -ser. leu-[47]

Chymotrypsinogen: -gly. leu. ser. arg. ileu. val-[54, 55]
      -tyr. thr. asn. ala-[56]
      -gly. asp. ser. gly-[57]

SEQUENCES NOT USED IN THE GRID

Serum albumin: -gly. val. ala. leu[h].[58]
      -ser. val. thr. leu. ala. ala[a].[58]

Actin: -his. ileu. phe.[59]

Tropomyosin: -ala. ileu. met. thr. ser. ileu.[59]

Pepsin: Leu. gly. asp. asp. his. glu-[60] (cf.[61])

[1] G. Gamow, A. Rich, and M. Yčas, *Advances in Biol. and Med. Physics*, Vol. **4** (New York, Academic Press, Inc., 1955).

[2] G. Gamow, *Nature*, **173**, 318, 1954; *Kgl. Danske Videnskab. Selskab Biol. Medd.*, **22**, 3, 1954.

[3] F. H. C. Crick, J. S. Griffith, and L. E. Orgel, these PROCEEDINGS, **43**, 416, 1957.

[4] A. P. Ryle, F. Sanger, L. F. Smith, and R. Kitai, *Biochem. J.*, **60**, 541, 1955.

[5] H. Brown, F. Sanger, and R. Kitai, *Biochem. J.*, **60**, 556, 1955.

[6] J. I. Harris, F. Sanger, and M. A. Naughton, *Arch. Biochem. and Biophys.*, **65**, 427, 1956.

[7] V. Du Vigneaud, C. Ressler, and S. Trippett, *J. Biol. Chem.*, **205**, 949, 1953.

[8] E. A. Popenoe and V. Du Vigneaud, *J. Biol. Chem.*, **207**, 563, 1954.

[9] Different sequences for the italicized amino acids have been reported by White and Land-

mann and Li *et al.* (see nn. 12–13 below) in pig and sheep corticotrophin, but these are doubtful (see Howard *et al.* [n. 11 below]).

[10] P. H. Bell, *J. Am. Chem. Soc.*, **76**, 5566, 1954.

[11] K. S. Howard, R. G. Shepherd, E. A. Eigner, D. S. Davies, and P. H. Bell, *J. Am. Chem. Soc.*, **77**, 3420, 1955.

[12] W. F. White and W. A. Landmann, *J. Am. Chem. Soc.*, **77**, 1712, 1955.

[13] C. H. Li, I. I. Geschwind, R. D. Cole, D. Raacke, J. I. Harris, and J. S. Dixon, *Nature*, **176**, 687, 1955.

[14] W. W. Bromer, L. G. Sinn, A. Straub, and O. K. Behreus, *J. Am. Chem. Soc.*, **78**, 3858, 1956.

[15] J. I. Harris and P. Roos, *Nature*, **177**, 527, 1956.

[16] I. I. Geschwind, C. H. Li, and L. Barnafi, *J. Am. Chem. Soc.*, **78**, 4494, 1956.

[17] I. I. Geschwind, C. H. Li, and L. Barnafi, *J. Am. Chem. Soc.*, **79**, 1003, 1957.

[18] D. F. Elliott and W. S. Peart, *Nature*, **177**, 527, 1956.

[19] L. T. Skeggs, K. E. Lentz, J. R. Kahn, N. P. Shumway, and K. Woods, *J. Exptl. Med.*, **104**, 193, 1956.

[20] H. Tuppy and G. Bodo, *Monatsh.*, **85**, 1024, 1954.

[21] H. Tuppy and S. Paleus, *Acta Chem. Scand.*, **9**, 353, 1955.

[22] E. W. Davie and H. Neurath, *J. Biol. Chem.*, **212**, 515, 1955.

[23] P. Desnuelle and C. Fabre, *Biochim. et Biophys. Acta*, **18**, 49, 1955.

[24] C. H. W. Hirs, W. H. Stein, and S. Moore, *J. Biol. Chem.*, **221**, 151, 1956.

[25] R. R. Redfield and C. B. Anfinsen, *J. Biol. Chem.*, **221**, 385, 1956.

[26] C. H. W. Hirs, *Federation Proc.*, **16**, 196, 1957.

[27] C. B. Anfinsen and R. R. Redfield, *Advances in Protein Chem.*, **11**, 1, 1956.

[28] C. B. Anfinsen, *J. Biol. Chem.*, **221**, 405, 1956.

[29] C.-I. Niu and H. Fraenkel-Conrat, *J. Am. Chem. Soc.*, **77**, 5882, 1955.

[30] R. Acher, M. Justisz, and C. Fromageot, *Biochim. et Biophys. Acta*, **8**, 442, 1952.

[31] R. Acher, J. Thaureaux, C. Crocker, M. Justisz, and C. Fromageot, *Biochem. et Biophys. Acta*, **9**, 339, 1952.

[32] R. Acher, U.-R. Laurila, and C. Fromageot, *Biochim. et Biophys. Acta*, **19**, 97, 1956.

[33] J. Thaureaux and R. Acher, *Biochim. et Biophys. Acta*, **20**, 559, 1956.

[34] J. Thaureaux and P. Jolles, *Compt. rend. Acad. Sci.*, **243**, 1926, 1956.

[35] A. R. Thompson, *Biochem. J.*, **60**, 507; **61**, 253, 1955.

[36] M. Ottessen and A. Wollenberg, *Compt. rend. trav. Lab. Carlsberg.*, *Ser. chim.*, **28**, 463, 1953.

[37] M. Flavin, *J. Biol. Chem.*, **210**, 771, 1954.

[38] M. Flavin and C. B. Anfinsen, *J. Biol. Chem.*, **211**, 375, 1954.

[39] E. O. P. Thompson, *J. Biol. Chem.*, **207**, 863, 1954.

[40] J. R. Kimmel, E. O. P. Thompson, and E. G. Smith, *J. Biol. Chem.*, **217**, 151, 1955.

[41] R. R. Porter and F. Sanger, *Haemoglobin*, ed. F. J. W. Roughton and J. C. Kendrew (London: Butterworth & Co., Ltd.), 1949.

[42] P. Mäsiar, B. Keil, and F. Sorm, *Chem. Listy*, **51**, 352, 1957.

[43] H. Fraenkel-Conrat, *J. Am. Chem. Soc.*, **76**, 3606, 1954.

[44] V. M. Ingram, *Biochim. et Biophys. Acta*, **16**, 599, 1956.

[45] R. R. Porter, *Biochem. J.*, **46**, 473, 1950.

[46] M. L. McFadden and E. L. Smith, *J. Biol. Chem.*, **214**, 185, 1955.

[47] B. A. Askonas, P. N. Campbell, C. Godin, and T. S. Work, *Biochem. J.*, **61**, 105, 1955.

[48] E. O. P. Thompson, *Biochim. et Biophys. Acta*, **10**, 633, 1953.

[49] E. O. P. Thompson, *J. Biol. Chem.*, **208**, 565, 1954.

[50] R. D. Cole, I. I. Geschwind, and C. H. Li, *J. Biol. Chem.*, **224**, 399, 1957.

[51] C.-I. Niu and H. Fraenkel-Conrat, *Arch. Biochem. and Biophys.*, **59**, 538, 1955.

[52] G. Braunitzer, *Naturwissenschaften*, **42**, 371, 1955.

[53] N. Seno, K. Murai, and K. Shimura, *J. Biochem. (Japan)*, **42**, 699, 1955.

[54] W. J. Dreyer and H. Neurath, *J. Biol. Chem.*, **217**, 527, 1955.

[55] M. Rovery, M. Poilroux, A. Curnier, and P. Desnuelle, *Biochim. et Biophys. Acta*, **17**, 565, 1955.

[56] M. Rovery, M. Poilroux, A. Yoshida, and P. Desnuelle, *Biochim. et Biophys. Acta*, **23**, 608, 1957.

[57] N. K. Schaffer, L. Simet, S. Harshman, R. R. Engle, and R. W. Driske, *J. Biol. Chem.*, **225**, 197, 1957.

[58] W. F. White, J. Shields, and K. S. Robbins, *J. Am. Chem. Soc.*, **77**, 1267, 1955.

[59] R. H. Locker, *Biochim. et Biophys. Acta*, **14**, 533, 1954.

[60] M. B. Williamson and J. M. Passmann, *J. Biol. Chem.*, **222**, 151, 1956.

[61] H. Van Vunakis and R. M. Herriott, *Biochim. et Biophys. Acta*, **23**, 60, 1957.

CODES WITHOUT COMMAS

By F. H. C. Crick, J. S. Griffith, and L. E. Orgel

MEDICAL RESEARCH COUNCIL UNIT, CAVENDISH LABORATORY, AND DEPARTMENT OF THEORETICAL CHEMISTRY, CAMBRIDGE, ENGLAND

Communicated by G. Gamow, February 11, 1957

This paper deals with a mathematical problem which arose in connection with protein synthesis. We present the solution here because it gives the "magic number" 20, so that our answer may perhaps be of biological significance. To make this clear, we sketch in the biochemical background first.

It is assumed in one of the more popular theories of protein synthesis that amino acids are ordered on a nucleic acid strand (see, for example, Dounce[1]) and that the order of the amino acids is determined by the order of the nucleotides of the nucleic acid. There are some twenty naturally occurring amino acids commonly found in proteins, but (usually) only four different nucleotides. The problem of how a sequence of four things (nucleotides) can determine a sequence of twenty things (amino acids) is known as the "coding" problem.

This problem is a formal one. In essence, it is not concerned with either the chemical steps or the details of the stereochemistry. It is not even essential to specify whether RNA or DNA is the nucleic acid being considered. Naturally, all these points are of the greatest interest, but they are only indirectly involved in the formal problem of coding.

The first definite proposal was made by Gamow.[2] His code, which was suggested by the structure of DNA, was of the "overlapping" type. The meaning of this is illustrated in Figure 1. Gamow's code was also "degenerate"—that is, several sets of three letters (picked in a special way) stood for a particular amino acid. However, all the 64 ($4 \times 4 \times 4$) possible sets of three letters stood for one amino acid or another, so that any sequence whatever of the four letters stood for a definite sequence of amino acids.

It is easy to see that codes of the overlapping type impose severe restrictions on the allowed amino acid sequences. Unfortunately, no such restrictions have been found, although considerable (unpublished) efforts have been made, by a number of workers, to find them. Part of this work has been reviewed by Gamow, Rich, and Yčas.[3]   However, the amino acid sequences so far determined experimentally are of limited extent, and it is possible that there may be restrictions on the neighbors of the rarer amino acids, such as tryptophan.   Thus, while overlapping codes seem highly unlikely, partial overlapping is not impossible.   At the moment, however, nonoverlapping codes seem the most probable, and these are the only ones we shall consider here.

	B C A C D D A B A B D C

Overlapping code	B C A
	  C A C
	    A C D
	      C D D

Partial overlapping code	B C A
	    A C D
	        D D A
	           A B A

Nonoverlapping code	B C A
	      C D D
	          A B A
	              B D C

Fig. 1.—The letters A, B, C, and D stand for the four bases of the four common nucleotides. The top row of letters represents an imaginary sequence of them.   In the codes illustrated here each set of three letters represents an amino acid.   The diagram shows how the first four amino acids of a sequence are coded in the three classes of codes.

If each amino acid were coded by *two* bases (rather than the three shown in Fig. 1), we should only be able to code $4 \times 4 = 16$ amino acids.   It is natural, therefore, to consider nonoverlapping codes in which *three* bases code each amino acid. This confronts us with two difficulties: (1) Since there are $4 \times 4 \times 4 = 64$ different triplets of four nucleotides, why are there not 64 kinds of amino acids?   (2) In reading the code, how does one know how to choose the groups of three?   This difficulty is illustrated in Figure 2.   The second difficulty could be overcome by reading off from one end of the string of letters, but for reasons we shall explain later we consider an alternative method here.

$$\ldots, \quad B \ C \ A, \quad C \ D \ D, \quad A \ B \ A, \quad B \ D \ C, \quad \ldots$$
or
$$\ldots \ldots \ B, \quad C \ A \ C, \quad D \ D \ A, \quad B \ A \ B, \quad D \ C \quad \ldots$$

Fig. 2.—The commas divide the string of letters into groups of three, each representing one amino acid.   If the ends of the string of letters are not available, this can be done in more than one way, as illustrated.   The problem is how to read the code if the commas are rubbed out, i.e., a comma-less code.

We shall assume that there are certain sequences of three nucleotides with which an amino acid can be associated and certain others for which this is not possible. Using the metaphors of coding, we say that some of the 64 triplets make sense and some make nonsense. We further assume that all possible sequences of the *amino acids* may occur (that is, can be coded) and that at every point in the string of letters one can only read "sense" in the correct way. This is illustrated in Figure 3. In other words, any two triplets which make sense can be put side by side, and yet the overlapping triplets so formed must always be nonsense.

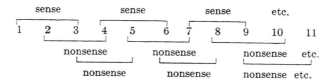

Fig. 3.—The numbers represent the positions occupied by the four letters *A*, *B*, *C*, and *D*. It is shown which triplets make sense and which nonsense.

It is obvious that with these restrictions one will be unable to code 64 different amino acids. The mathematical problem is to find the maximum number that can be coded. We shall show (1) that the maximum number cannot be greater than 20 and (2) that a solution for 20 can be given.

To prove the first point, we consider for the moment the restrictions imposed by placing each amino acid next to itself. Then, clearly, the triplet *AAA* must be nonsense, since, if it corresponded to an amino acid, α, then $\alpha\alpha$ would be *AAAAAA*, and this sequence can be misinterpreted by associating α with the second to fourth, or third to fifth, letters. We can thus reject *AAA*, *BBB*, *CCC*, and *DDD*.

It is easy to see that the 60 remaining triplets can be grouped into 20 sets of three, each set of three being cyclic permutations of one another. Consider as an example *ABC* and its cyclic permutations *BCA* and *CAB*. It is clear that we can choose any one of these, but not more than one. For suppose that we let *BCA* stand for the amino acid β; then $\beta\beta$ is *BCABCA*, and so *CAB* and *ABC* must, by our rules, be nonsense. Since we can choose at the most one triplet from each cyclic set, we cannot choose more than 20. No solution is possible, therefore, which codes more than 20 different amino acids.

We have so far not considered the effects of putting unlike amino acids together, to give pairs of the form $\alpha\beta$ and $\beta\alpha$. It might be thought that this would still further reduce the possible number of amino acids, but this turns out not to be so, since we can write down a construction which obeys all our rules and yet codes 20 different amino acids. One possible solution is

$$A \quad B \quad {A \atop B} \qquad {A \atop B} \quad C \quad {A \atop {B \atop C}} \qquad {A \atop {B \atop C}} \quad D \quad {A \atop {B \atop {C \atop D}}}$$

where $A\,B\,{A \atop B}$ means *ABA* and *ABB*, etc. It is easy to see, by systematic enumeration, that one can place any two triplets of this set next to each other without producing overlapping triplets which belong to the set.

The solution given above is not unique. Another satisfactory choice of 20 allowed sequences is

$$B \quad A \quad A$$

$$\begin{array}{c} A \\ B \end{array} \quad C \quad \begin{array}{c} A \\ B \\ C \end{array} \qquad \begin{array}{c} A \\ B \\ C \end{array} \quad D \quad \begin{array}{c} A \\ B \\ C \\ D \end{array}$$

$$A \quad B \quad B$$

If we exclude trivial variations, such as permuting letters (e.g., A into C and C into A) or writing the code backwards, there are at least 8 different solutions. These can be obtained by taking one or the other of the two solutions given above and reversing either the entire second set of triplets, or the entire third set, or both. For example, if we reverse the second set of triplets in the first solution given above, we obtain the solution

$$A \quad B \quad \begin{array}{c} A \\ B \end{array} \qquad \begin{array}{c} A \\ B \\ C \end{array} \quad C \quad \begin{array}{c} A \\ B \end{array} \qquad \begin{array}{c} A \\ B \\ C \end{array} \quad D \quad \begin{array}{c} A \\ B \\ C \\ D \end{array}$$

If we enumerate *all* solutions we have been able to find, including the variations produced by interchanging letters and reversing the direction of the code, we obtain a total of 288 solutions (192 from variants of the first solution above and 96 from variants of the second one).

The problem we have considered is a special case of the more general situation in which one Greek letter is determined by n Roman letters selected from a total of m different Roman letters. One can obtain an upper limit for the number of possible Greek letters by the methods we have used, but it is not in general easy to see whether this upper limit can be achieved. One can easily see by trial that the upper limit of six, corresponding to $n = 2$, $m = 4$, cannot be achieved, only five Greek letters being possible; hence the upper limit cannot be achieved for $n = 2$, $m > 4$, either. The solution for $n = 3$ and arbitrary m is

$$A \quad B \quad \begin{array}{c} A \\ B \end{array} \qquad \begin{array}{c} A \\ B \end{array} \quad C \quad \begin{array}{c} A \\ B \\ C \end{array} \ldots \ldots \ldots \ldots \quad \begin{array}{c} A \\ B \\ C \\ \cdot \\ L \end{array} \quad K \quad \begin{array}{c} A \\ B \\ C \\ \cdot \\ \cdot \\ L \\ M \end{array}$$

or, more concisely, writing $A_1 A_2 \ldots A_m$ for the nucleotides, then a solution which attains the upper limit is the set of triplets $A_i A_j A_k$ for all $i, j, k = 1, 2, \ldots, m$, satisfying $k \leqslant j, i < j$. We have not solved the general problem.

A Physical Interpretation.—To fix ideas, we shall describe a simple model to illustrate the advantages of such a code. Imagine that a single chain of RNA, held in a regular configuration, is the template. Let the intermediates in protein synthesis be 20 distinct molecules, each consisting of a trinucleotide chemically attached to one amino acid. The bases of each trinucleotide are chosen according to the code given above. Let these intermediate molecules combine, by hydrogen bonding between bases, with the RNA template and there await polymerization. Now imagine that such an amino acid–trinucleotide were to diffuse into an incorrect place on the template, such that *two* of its bases were hydrogen-bonded, though not the third. We postulate that this incomplete attachment will only retain the intermediate for a very brief time (for example, less than 1 millisecond) before the latter breaks loose and diffuses elsewhere. However, when it eventually diffuses to the correct place, it will be held by hydrogen bonds to all three bases and will thus be retained, on the average, for a much longer time (say, seconds or minutes). Now the code we have described insures that this more lengthy attachment can occur only at the points where the intermediate is needed. If one of the 20 intermediates could stay for a long time on one of the false positions, it would effectively block the two positions it was straddling and hold up the polymerization process. Our code makes this impossible. This scheme, therefore, allows the intermediates to accumulate at the *correct* positions on the template without ever blocking the process by settling, except momentarily, in the wrong place. It is this feature which gives it an advantage over schemes in which the intermediates are compelled to combine with the template one after the other in the correct order.

The example given here is only for illustration, but it brings out the physical idea behind the concept of a comma-less code.

In passing, it should be mentioned that while the idea of making three nonoverlapping nucleotides code for one amino acid at first sight entails certain stereochemical difficulties, these are not insuperable if it is assumed that the polypeptide chain, *when polymerized*, does not remain attached to the template. A detailed scheme along these lines has been described to us by Dr. S. Brenner (personal communication).

General Remarks.—The arguments and assumptions which we have had to employ to deduce this code are too precarious for us to feel much confidence in it on purely theoretical grounds. We put it forward because it gives the magic number—20—in a neat manner and from reasonable physical postulates. It should be noted, however, that other codes can be derived which restrict the amino acids to 20, in particular the "combination code" of Gamow and Yčas,[4] though we regard the physical assumption underlying their code as implausible. Some direct experimental support is therefore required before our idea can be regarded as anything more than a tentative hypothesis.

Summary.—The problem of how, in protein synthesis, a sequence of four things (nucleotides) determines a sequence of many more things (amino acids) is known as the coding problem. We consider codes involving nonoverlapping triplets of nucleotides, each triplet coding for one amino acid. We show that to allow all possible amino acid sequences without giving false readings of the code (due to reading the last part of one triplet and the first part of the next), we must limit the number of kinds of amino acids which the code can handle. We prove that an upper bound is 20 and show that a code for 20 can in fact be written down. It is well known that 20 is the number found experimentally.   The physical ideas behind such a code are briefly discussed.

[1] A. L. Dounce, *Enzymologia*, **15**, 251, 1952.

[2] G. Gamow, *Nature*, **173**, 318, 1954; *Kgl. Danske Videnskab. Selskab Biol. Medd.*, **22**, 3, 1954.

[3] G. Gamow, A. Rich, and M. Yčas, *Advances in Biol. and Med. Physics*, Vol. **4** (New York: Academic Press Inc., 1955).

[4] G. Gamow and M. Yčas, these PROCEEDINGS, **41**, 1011, 1955.

The Theory of Mutagenesis

In this preliminary note we wish to express our doubts about the detailed theory of mutagenesis put forward by Freese (1959b), and to suggest an alternative.

Freese (1959b) has produced evidence that shows that for the r_{II} locus of phage T4 there are two mutually exclusive classes of mutation and we have confirmed and extended his work (Orgel & Brenner, in manuscript). The technique used is to start with a standard wild type and make a series of mutants from it with a particular mutagen. Each mutant is then tested with various mutagens to see which of them will back-mutate it to wild type.

It is found that the mutations fall into two classes. The first, which we shall call the base analogue class, is typically produced by 5-bromodeoxyuridine (BD) and the second, which we shall call the acridine class, is typically produced by proflavin (PF). In general a mutant made with BD can be reverted by BD, and a mutant made with PF can be reverted by PF. A few of the PF mutants do not appear to revert with either mutagen, but the strong result is that no mutant has been found which reverts identically with both classes of mutagens, and that (with a few possible exceptions) mutants produced by one class cannot be reverted by the other.

Freese also showed that 2-aminopurine falls into the base analogue class, and that most (85%) spontaneous mutants at the r_{II} locus were not of the base analogue type. We have confirmed this and shown that they are in fact revertible by acridines. We have also shown that a number of other acridines, and in particular 5-aminoacridine, act like proflavin (Orgel & Brenner, in manuscript).

Freese has produced an ingenious explanation of these results, which should be consulted in the original for fuller details. In brief he postulated that the base analogue class of mutagens act by altering an A—T base-pair on the DNA (A = adenine, T = thymine) into a G—C pair, or *vice versa* (G = guanine, C = cytosine, or, in the T even phages, hydroxymethylcytosine). The fact that BD, which replaces thymine, could act both ways (from A—T to G—C or from G—C to A—T) was accounted for (Freese, 1959a) by assuming that in the latter case there was an error in pairing of the BD (such that it accidentally paired with guanine) while *entering* the DNA, and in the former case after it was already in the DNA.

Such alterations only change a purine into another purine, or a pyrimidine into another pyrimidine. Freese (1959b) has called these "transitions." He suggested that other conceivable changes, which he called "transversions" (such as, for example, from A—T to C—G) which change a purine into a pyrimidine and *vice versa*, occurred during mutagenesis by proflavin. This would neatly account for the two mutually exclusive classes of mutagens, since it is easy to see that a transition cannot be reversed by a transversion, and *vice versa*.

We have been led to doubt this explanation for the following reasons.

Our suspicions were first aroused by the curious fact that a comparison between the *sites* of mutation for one set of mutants made with BD and another set made with PF (Brenner, Benzer & Barnett, 1958) showed there were no sites in the r_{II} gene, among the samples studied, common to both groups.

Now this result alone need not be incompatible with Freese's theory of mutagenesis, since we have no good explanation for "hot spots" and this confuses quantitative argument. However it led us to the following hypothesis:

that acridines act as mutagens because they cause the insertion or the deletion of a base-pair.

This idea springs rather naturally from the views of Lerman (1960) and Luzzati (in preparation) that acridines are bound to DNA by sliding *between* adjacent base-pairs, thus forcing them 6·8 Å apart, rather than 3·4 Å. If this occasionally happened between the bases on *one* chain of the DNA, but not the other, during replication, it might easily lead to the addition or subtraction of a base.

Such a possible mechanism leads to a prediction. We know practically nothing about coding (Crick, 1959) but on most theories (except overlapping codes which are discredited because of criticism by Brenner (1957)) the deletion or the addition of a base-pair is likely to cause not the substitution of just one amino acid for another, but a much more substantial alteration, such as a break in the polypeptide chain, a considerable alteration of the amino acid sequence, or the production of no protein at all.

Thus one would not be surprised to find on these ideas that mutants produced by acridines were not capable of producing a slightly modified protein, but usually produced either no protein at all or a grossly altered one.

Somewhat to our surprise we find we already have data from two separate genes supporting this hypothesis.

(1) The *o* locus of phage T4 (resistance to osmotic shock) is believed to control a protein of the finished phage, possibly the head protein, because it shows phenotypic mixing (Brenner, unpublished). Using various base analogues we have produced mutants of this gene, though these map at only a small number of sites. We have failed on several occasions to produce any *o* mutants with proflavin. On another occasion two mutants were produced; one never reverted to wild type, while the other corresponded in position and spontaneous reversion rate to a base analogue site. We suspect therefore that these two mutants were not really produced by proflavin, but were the rarer sort of spontaneous mutant (Brenner & Barnett, unpublished).

(2) We have also studied mutation at the *h* locus in T2L, which controls a protein of the finished phage concerned with attachment to the host (Streisinger & Franklin, 1956).

Of the six different spontaneous h^+ mutants tested, all were easily induced to revert to h with 5-bromouracil (BU)†. This is especially significant when it is recalled that 85% of the spontaneous r_{II} mutants could not be reverted with base analogues (Freese, 1959*b*).

We have also shown (Brenner & Barnett, unpublished) that it is difficult to produce h^+ mutants from h by proflavin, though relatively easy with BU. The production of r mutants was used as a control.

It can be seen from Table 1 that if the production of h^+ mutants by BU and proflavin were similar to the production of r mutants we would expect to have obtained $\frac{57 \times 26}{108} = 13 h^+$ mutants with proflavin, whereas in fact we only found 1, and this may be spontaneous background.

---

† (Added in proof.) Five of these have now been tested and have been shown not to revert with proflavin.

Let us underline the difference between the *r* loci and the *o* and *h* loci. The former appear to produce proteins which are probably *not* part of the finished phage. For both the *o* and the *h* locus, however, the protein concerned forms part of the finished phage, which presumably would not be viable without it, so that a mutant can be picked up only if it forms an *altered* protein. A mutant which deleted the protein could not be studied.

TABLE 1

	r	*h*⁺
BU	108	57
Proflavin	26	1

It is clear that further work must be done before our generalization—that acridine mutants usually give no protein, rather than a slightly modified one—can be accepted. But if it turns out to be true it would support our hypothesis of the mutagenic action of the acridines, and this may have serious consequences for the naïve theory of mutagenesis, for the following reason.

It has always been a theoretical possibility that the reversions to wild type were not true reversions but were due to the action of "suppressors" (within the gene), possibly very closely linked suppressors. The most telling evidence against this was the existence of the two mutually exclusive classes of mutagens, together with Freese's explanation.

For clearly if the forward mutation could be made at one base-pair and the reverse one at a different base-pair, we should expect, on Freese's hypothesis, exceptions to the rule about the two classes of mutagens. Since these were not found it was concluded that even close suppressors were very rare.

Unfortunately our new hypothesis for the action of acridines destroys this argument. Under this new theory an alteration of a base-pair at one place *could* be reversed by an alteration at a different base-pair, and indeed from what we know (or guess) of the structure of proteins and the dependence of structure on amino acid sequence, we should be surprised if this did not occur.

It is all too easy to conceive, for example, that at a certain point on the polypeptide chain at which there is a glutamic residue in the wild type, and at which the mutation substituted a proline, a further mutation might alter the proline to aspartic acid and that this might appear to restore the wild phenotype, at least as far as could be judged by the rather crude biological tests available. If several base-pairs are needed to code for one amino acid the reverse mutation might occur at a base-pair close to but not identical with the one originally changed.

On our hypothesis this could happen, and yet one would still obtain the two classes of mutagens. The one, typified by base analogues, would produce the substitution of one base for another, and the other, typically produced by acridines, would lead to the addition or subtraction of a base-pair. Consequently the mutants produced by one class could not be easily reversed by the mutagens of the other class.

Thus our new hypothesis reopens in an acute form the question: which back-mutations to wild type are truly to the original wild type, and which only appear to be so? And on the answers to this question depend our interpretation of all experiments on back-mutation.

We suspect that this problem can most easily be approached by work on systems for which the amino acid sequence of the protein can be studied, such as the phage lysozyme of Dreyer, Anfinsen & Streisinger (personal communications) or the phosphatase from *E. coli* of Levinthal, Garen & Rothman (Garen, 1960). Meanwhile we are continuing our genetic studies to fill out and extend the preliminary results reported here.

Medical Research Council Unit   S. BRENNER
for Molecular Biology   LESLIE BARNETT
Cavendish Laboratory   F. H. C. CRICK

Pathology Laboratory   ALICE ORGEL
both of Cambridge University
England

Received 16 December 1960

REFERENCES

Brenner, S. (1957). *Proc. Nat. Acad. Sci., Wash.* **43**, 687.
Brenner, S., Benzer, S. & Barnett, L. (1958). *Nature*, **182**, 983.
Crick, F. H. C. (1959). In *Brookhaven Symposia in Biology*, **12**, 35.
Freese, E. (1959a). *J. Mol. Biol.* **1**, 87.
Freese, E. (1959b). *Proc. Nat. Acad. Sci., Wash.* **45**, 622.
Garen, A. (1960). 10th Symposium *Soc. Gen. Microbiol.*, London, 239.
Lerman, L. (1961). *J. Mol. Biol.* **3**, 18.
Streisinger, G. & Franklin, N. C. (1956). In *Cold Spr. Harb. Sym. Quant. Biol.* **21**, 103.

Unit 2 / The Nature of the Genetic Code

Crick et al. 1961

1. What is the difference between an overlapping and a nonoverlapping code?

2. What are the consequences of an overlapping code that can be tested by experiments and which experiments cited by the authors tested each prediction?

3. What evidence led the authors to believe that acridines act as mutagens by adding or deleting a base?

4. What is a suppressor? How many different types of suppressors can you imagine?

5. The authors selected suppressors of a mutation, *FC0*, and then found that "in all cases the suppressor was a nonleaky *r*." What does this mean? How could they determine this?

6. Describe the sequence of experiments portrayed in Figure 2 on page 66.

7. What is "complementation" as mentioned in the second column of the paper on page 65? How could the authors test that a given pair of mutations was not exhibiting complementation?

8. Explain how the following combinations of mutations could be constructed and tested: a + + or a − −.

9. Explain the concept of "barriers" that prevented certain + − and − + combinations from producing the wild-type phenotype.

10. Which experiment of the authors demonstrated best that the coding ratio was three or a multiple of three? How might they have constructed the mutant involved?

11. Which argument was used to say that the code was a triplet code, rather than one involving six or nine nucleotides to encode an amino acid?

12. Explain the use of the 1589 deletion.

13. What is meant by a degenerate code and how did the authors reason that the triplet code was likely to be degenerate?

14. What direct experiment did the authors suggest to test their theory of frameshifts in the *r*II region?

Unit 3

Decoding the *amber* and *ochre* Triplets

Brenner et al. 1965
Genetic Code: The 'Nonsense' Triplets for Chain Termination
and Their Suppression
Reprinted with permission from *Nature 206:* 994–998

101

Evidence for the existence of chain-terminating codons began to accumulate from several sources, including the work on "barriers" resulting from frameshifts in the *r*II region, as mentioned in the previous discussion of the paper by Crick, Brenner, and co-workers in Unit 2. As the race to identify different code words in the genetic code heated up, it became very important to identify the punctuation marks in the code; namely, the start and stop points. Brenner and co-workers published a paper in 1965 that elucidated two of the chain-terminating nonsense triplets almost completely by genetic methods. This ingenious study involves a masterful exploitation of nonsense suppressors and mutagenic specificity and demonstrates how powerful bacterial and phage genetics can be.

Before examining the paper, let's take a brief look at one of the principal scientists involved in these experiments, Sydney Brenner.

Sydney Brenner

Sydney Brenner was born in 1927 in a small town in South Africa, his parents having emigrated from Latvia and Lithuania. As a child, he was introduced to science by the book *The Young Chemist* by Sherwood Taylor, and he even began setting up elementary experiments. He developed a keen interest in biology and decided to become a research biologist. His intellect was recognized at an early age, and in 1942, at the age of 15, he entered the University of the Witwatersrand in Johannesburg. To obtain a fellowship, however, he had to study medicine. Since the program took six years, he would have finished before he was 22, the required age for certification as a doctor, so he took time off to do a B.Sc. in Medical Science and a Masters in Anatomy, which he obtained in 1946. He spent the next several years teaching, starting a research program in cytogenics, and completing his medical degree. He published his first research paper in 1947, which involved carrying out cytochemical tests on liver sections that had been treated in an air turbine ultracentrifuge which he had built himself!

After completing his medical degree, he went to Oxford in 1952 to work towards a doctorate in the Department of Physical Chemistry with Sir Cyril Hinshelwood. Brenner's interests were in the emerging area of cell physiology, which we now call molecular biology. Unfortunately, his thesis advisor did not believe in the concept of mutation, instead attributing altered phenotypes to "adaptive" changes. Therefore, when Brenner began work on bacteriophage, he had to convince Hinshelwood that bacterial phage resistance was indeed due to mutation. Fortunately, he met an increasing group of stimulating people such as Leslie Orgel, with whom he regularly discussed the structure of the gene and how proteins might be synthesized. Thus, in 1953, he traveled to Cambridge, where he met Jim Watson and Francis Crick and saw the new structure of DNA. During this period he married and he and his wife had their first child.

When his doctorate was completed in 1954, he briefly returned to South Africa before spending several months in the United States, including some time at Cold Spring Harbor in the laboratory of Milislav Demerec. He also traveled to Woods

Hole and Caltech, where he met Seymour Benzer, Max Delbrück, and again Watson and Crick. He also spent some time in Günther Stent's lab in Berkeley carrying out experiments on protoplasts. Once, when passing through Washington D.C., he encountered George Gamow, who had published one of the first genetic codes (the "diamond code" mentioned in Unit 2). Brenner showed Gamow his dipeptide occurrence chart, which disproved all overlapping triplet codes (also discussed in Unit 2). Sydney later communicated these results to the RNA Tie Club.

After two years in Johannesburg, he went to work in Cambridge at the MRC Unit for the Study of the Molecular Structure of Biological Systems and established a laboratory for genetics research. The goal of his laboratory was to crack the genetic code by demonstrating colinearity of the gene and protein (see Unit 4) and by deciphering different triplets with the aid of chemical mutagens (as described in this unit). In 1960, during a three-week stretch, he carried out a set of experiments in collaboration with François Jacob at Caltech that proved the existence of messenger RNA, later copublishing these findings with a group at Harvard. In 1962, Brenner's interests began to turn toward higher cells, although he still continued to work in the molecular genetics of phage and bacteria. However, starting in 1964, he began to develop the techniques required to study the anatomy of nematodes. Subsequently, his work on the nematode *C. elegans* attracted many aspiring young molecular biologists, and now this organism is one of the leading systems for the study of development.

In 1979, Sydney Brenner was appointed Director of the MRC Laboratory of Molecular Biology. However, he was seriously injured in a motorcycle accident the week before, which left him partially disabled. Despite this, he has maintained a vigor and zest for attacking new problems in molecular biology, such as genome mapping, and expanding the arsenal of powerful cloning techniques. His travel schedule and energy level are much greater than those of most of his significantly younger colleagues. This is evidenced by his initiation of a new laboratory in Cambridge, the MRC Unit of Molecular Genetics, and his association with Scripps Research Institute in LaJolla, California, where, until recently, he spent part of each year.

Brenner's most recent outlook is best summarized in his own words: "I think that there is an area of biology which is based not on problem solving by experiment but on discovery, that is, it is less like physics and more like astronomy. What I am trying to do now is to make better telescopes to see more of our biological heaven."

THE NATURE
OF NONSENSE CODONS

Suppressor mutations were a crucial part of the genetic analysis which led to the elucidation of the triplet nature of the genetic code by Crick, Brenner, and co-workers (see Unit 2). As noted before, there are many different types of suppressor mutations, since a **suppressor** can be defined as any mutation that counteracts the effects of a separate mutation. Crick and co-workers studied frameshift mutations that suppressed other frameshift mutations in the same gene. Other suppressors that were external (or outside the gene that contained the mutation) were discovered in different systems in several laboratories. In the paper by Brenner and co-workers discussed in this unit, the authors first define two classes of suppressible mutations and argue that they are nonsense mutations resulting in chain termination. They then use chemical mutagens to determine the composition of each codon, and by examining the biochemical evidence available at the time, assign each to a specific triplet.

Nonsense mutations represent a type of conditional mutation, just as *rII* mutations are conditional. In the case of *rII* mutations, the permissive conditions are provided by *E. coli* B and the restrictive conditions are provided by *E. coli* K. Likewise, nonsense mutations can grow in certain strains but not in others. The permissive strains contain suppressor mutations, which act like genetic markers and can be mapped, and the restrictive strains do not contain suppressors. Thus, the mutations are recognized as sense in one strain and nonsense in another. This ambiguity was recognized initially, and the mutations were sometimes labeled as "ambivalent." The first step in the paper by Brenner and co-workers was to recognize that nonsense mutations found in many different systems could be assigned to one of two groups on the basis of their response to different suppressors. Thus, one set of mutations could be suppressed by one group of suppressors. Included in this set was the **amber** mutation, which gets its name from the translation of the German word Bernstein (the family name of one of the original discoverers). A second set of mutations found in different systems responded to a second set of suppressors, and these have been termed **ochre** mutations. The following two points should be noted:

1. Whereas **amber suppressors** can only suppress *amber* mutations, **ochre suppressors** can suppress both *amber* and *ochre* mutations. Therefore, *amber* mutations can be defined as mutations that respond to both *amber* and *ochre* suppressors) and *ochre* muta-

tions can be defined as those that respond to *ochre* suppressors but not to *amber* suppressors. This can be seen in the table below.

Suppressor	Nonsense Mutation	
	amber	*ochre*
amber	+	−
ochre	+	+

2. Some *amber* mutations are suppressed only by certain *amber* suppressors. This **pattern of suppression** is characteristic of each *amber* mutation.

Table 1 on page 103 shows the suppression patterns of different nonsense mutations in the *rII* region. Note how none of the *ochre* mutations are suppressed by any of the *amber* suppressors, whereas all of the *amber* mutations are suppressed by at least one *ochre* suppressor. In addition, most of the *amber* mutations are suppressed by all of the *amber* suppressors. An exception is mutation *S116*, which responds only to su^+_{III}. This is because each suppressor inserts a specific amino acid. Clearly, the corresponding site in the protein is sensitive to certain amino acid substitutions, so only the amino acid inserted by the suppressor su^+_{III} is acceptable at that position.

The following combination of results led Brenner and co-workers to conclude that *amber* and *ochre* mutations are nonsense and result in chain termination during protein synthesis.

1. *Amber* mutations in the gene encoding alkaline phosphatase produced no immunologically identifiable material. The presense of some cross-reacting material (CRM) is common for mutants resulting from base-analog treatment.

2. Benzer and Champe found that in combination with the 1589 fusion deletion in *rII*, *amber* mutations disrupted the function of the *rIIB* cistron in a strain lacking a suppressor (su^-). (Recall how this fusion was used by Crick et al. [see page 62] to help determine the action of frameshifts.) However, in the presence of a suppressor, the activity of B was restored.

3. As shown in Figure 1 on page 102, when *amber* mutants of the T4 phage head protein are analyzed, each mutant produces a characteristic fragment of the protein chain in su^- bacteria, but in su^+ bacteria, the full-length protein is restored and the amino acid inserted at the previous termina-

tion point is characteristic of the suppressor used. Although *ochre* suppression is too weak to allow the same analysis of *ochre* suppressors, the assumption was that they operate in the same manner as *amber* suppressors, namely, by inserting an amino acid at the site corresponding to an *ochre* codon.

DECIPHERING *AMBER* AND *OCHRE* TRIPLETS

Brenner and his colleagues attempted to use information from the specificity of mutagens to decode the *amber* and *ochre* triplets. This work is in two parts. Initially, they examined the reversion of *amber* and *ochre* triplets, and their interconversion, with known mutagens. This provided some information that led to their most revealing experiment, which involved inducing *amber* and *ochre* mutations from the wild type. The combined results allowed them to deduce the composition of the *amber* and *ochre* codons.

This work was made possible because of the properties of hydroxylamine and the unique aspects of the *r*II system in phage T4. When used to treat DNA or phage particles in vitro, hydroxylamine is very specific, altering cytosine residues to a form that pairs exactly like uracil. We now know that this is due to the formation of *N*-4-hydroxycytosine, although in the paper it is referred to as U'. The alteration of cytosine by hydroxylamine will cause a mutation at the next round of replication, since it will pair with adenine instead of guanine. Interestingly, if the C is on the **sense strand** (see Note on page 100), then the effects of the change will have immediate consequences, since the altered C will direct an A at that point in the mRNA. However, if the C is on the **antisense strand**, then the mRNA would still be synthesized off of the wild-type sense strand and would not be affected. This only holds for the period of time between the alteration and DNA replication, since after replication both strands will contain either the wild-type or the mutated base pair. (These consequences of changes on the sense and antisense strands are shown in Figure 2 on page 102.) This is very important because the nature of the *r*II defect allows one to exploit the sense–antisense phenomenon. Recall that *r*II mutants can grow in *E. coli* B but not in *E. coli* K. Moreover, *r*II mutants cannot even replicate in *E. coli* K, since the defect occurs in a step prior to DNA synthesis. Therefore, when treated with hydroxylamine, *r*II mutants will express the wild-type mRNA in *E. coli* K if the *r*II mutation is on the sense strand but they will not if the mutation is on the antisense strand.

Reversion to Wild Type

Previous studies had shown that neither *amber* nor *ochre* mutations could be reverted to wild type with hydroxylamine. Strictly speaking, that would say that there were no G·C pairs in either the *amber* or *ochre* codon that could be converted to a wild-type codon via a G·C→A·T change. However, the original experiments done by Benzer and Champe involved plating on *E. coli* K directly after mutagenesis. We now realize (from Figure 2) that only sense-strand changes would register. Therefore, Brenner and co-workers retested the reversion properties by first passaging the hydroxylamine-mutagenized phage through *E. coli* B, to allow all phage to replicate, before plating on *E. coli* K. This would allow the detection of antisense-strand changes that generated revertants. Their results are shown in Table 2 on page 104. It can be seen that even when the treated phage are allowed to grow first on *E. coli* B, hydroxylamine does not stimulate the reversion of *amber* or *ochre* codons. Therefore, it was clear that neither the *amber* nor *ochre* codon contained a G·C base pair unless it was connected to another nonsense codon by a G·C→A·T change. However, both *amber* and *ochre* could be induced from wild type. Thus, each codon must have at least one A·T base pair.

Conversion of One Nonsense Mutation to Another Nonsense Mutation

One could test whether one nonsense mutation could be converted to another nonsense mutation by starting with an *ochre* mutation and attempting to convert it to an *amber* mutation. Since *ochre* mutations are not suppressed by *amber* suppressors, one could select for growth on *E. coli* K *su*+. Note that the reverse selection cannot be carried out because *amber* mutations are suppressed by both *amber* and *ochre* suppressors. Here, 2-aminopurine (2AP) was used, since this base-analog mutagen can make either the G·C→A·T or the A·T→G·C change. *E. coli* B growing in 2AP was infected with different *ochre* mutants, and after lysis, the progeny were plated on *E. coli* K *su*+. Some of the phage that form plaques on this strain could be *amber* mutants, but others could simply be wild-type revertants. Therefore, a sample of phage (about 50) from each experiment had to be tested on *E. coli* K *su*− to determine the percentage of phage that were true conversions to *amber* and the percentage that were wild-type revertants. Table 3 on page 104 depicts the results, which show that *ochre* mutations can readily be converted to *amber* mutations. This result shows that the *amber* and *ochre* codons are identical at two of the three positions (since a single base change can convert one to the other). In addition, they are related at the third position by a G·C→A·T change.

The next step was to determine which codon, the *amber* or *ochre*, has the G·C base pair at the position involved in the 2AP conversion. To answer this, Brenner and co-workers looked at the ability of hydroxylamine to stimulate the same *ochre* to *amber* conversion. As can be seen from Table 4 on page 104, in contrast to 2AP, hydroxylamine cannot stimulate this conversion. Therefore, the *ochre* codon must have an A·T base pair that is converted by 2AP (but not hydroxylamine) to a G·C base pair when the *ochre* is converted to an *amber*.

To summarize up to this point, both the *ochre* and *amber* codons have two base bairs in common (because they are connected to each other by a single base change), and at least one of these base pairs is an A·T base pair (because they can be induced from wild type but not reverted to wild type by hydroxylamine). In addition, the base pair that is not in common is a G·C base pair in the *amber* and an A·T base pair in the *ochre* (because of the conversion of *ochre* to *amber* by 2AP but not by hydroxylamine). Although this may seem like fragmentary data, it did represent an important beginning.

Induction of *amber* and *ochre* Mutations

Brenner and co-workers next carried out a fascinating experiment on a par with the fine structure analysis of *rII* by Benzer (see Unit 1). To best understand this experiment, we should return to Figure 2 (page 102), which we discussed earlier, and recall the consequences of sense- and antisense-strand changes. We should also note that here we are changing the direction of the experiment. Until now, we have discussed reversion of *amber* and *ochre* mutations to wild type, whereas for this experiment we will be discussing going from wild type to *amber* or *ochre*. Let's consider a wild-type codon in *rII* in the context of Figure 2. When phage are treated with hydroxylamine and then passaged immediately through *E. coli* K, *rII* mutations that result from a change on the sense strand will immediately express the *rII* mRNA and fail to grow. However, *rII* mutations that result from a change on the antisense strand will make the wild-type mRNA before replication, and the required functions will be expressed, thus allowing replication and survival of the mutant. Therefore, some *rII* mutants will grow and others will fail to grow depending on whether the sense or antisense strand is affected. However, if following treatment with hydroxylamine the phage are first passaged through *E. coli* B instead

of *E. coli* K, then all *rII* mutants will grow, since the *rII* function is not required in *E. coli* B.

The concepts discussed above set up the following experiment aimed at determining whether one could detect two different classes of *rII* nonsense mutations—those arising from sense-strand changes and those arising from antisense-strand changes. After mutagenesis with hydroxylamine, the treated phage were separated into two fractions. One fraction, called set K, was first passaged through *E. coli* K prior to plating on *E. coli* B to look for *rII* mutants. The second fraction, called set B, was first passaged through *E. coli* B before plating on *E. coli* B to look for *rII* mutants. A large number of *rII* mutants were collected from each set, and these were tested with *amber* and *ochre* suppressors to detect those mutants carrying *amber* and *ochre* mutations. These were then mapped and tested for their patterns of suppression so that they could be assigned to one of the known *amber* or *ochre* sites in *rII* that had been identified previously through intensive analysis. This involved an extraordinary amount of work, as can be seen from Table 5A on page 105, which shows that more than 7000 mutations were characterized to yield 319 *ambers* from set B and 121 *ambers* from set K. We should also appreciate that to find an *rII* mutant, large plaques on *E. coli* B are found and then tested for growth on *E. coli* K, and that to find 7000 *r* mutants, close to 700,000 phage plaques had to be screened!

Let's look at Table 5B on page 105, which shows the results of this elaborate genetic experiment. The goal is to see whether there are two classes of *rII amber* sites. One class, resulting from sense-strand changes, would only be recovered in set B (passaged first through *E. coli* B) and not in set K, since when passaged first through *E. coli* K the change on the sense strand would immediately program an *rII* mRNA that would result in failure to replicate. This class was found, as evidenced by the mutations *N97, S116, S24, N34, X237,* and *HB232* in Table 5B. The second class, resulting from antisense-strand changes, would be recovered in both sets, since even when passaged through *E. coli* K, wild-type mRNA would initially be synthesized. This class was also detected, as represented by the mutations *HB118, HB129, S99, N19, EM84,* and *AP164* in Table 5B.

CONCLUSIONS

Finding two classes of sites with set B and only one with set K was a brilliant verification of the theory of the experiment and it also established that the two bases in common for the *amber* and *ochre* codons were A·T base pairs with opposite orientations. This is because the authors had already shown that one base pair is a G·C in the *amber* and an A·T in the *ochre*, so the other two base pairs are the A·T and T·A base pairs for the *amber* (and thus also for the *ochre*). Therefore, the composition of the *amber* codon, without regard to order, was (UAG or UAC) and of the *ochre* codon (UAA or UAU). The ambiguity was resolved by determining which codons the *amber* triplet was connected to by a single transition mutation. In addition to the *ochre* triplet, (UAG) could be converted by a transition to (CAG) and (UGG), whereas (UAC) could be converted to (CAC) and (UGC). From biochemical work referred to on pages 105–106, it was evident that the *amber* triplet is connected to both glutamine and tryptophan via a transition. Since the composition of a glutamine codon had been established to be (CAG) and not (CAC), and since (UGG) had been assigned to tryptophan, it was clear that the composition of the *amber* triplet was (UAG).

Finally, the orientation of bases in the triplet could be ascertained as being UAG on the basis of the specific assignment of CAG to glutamine by Nirenberg and co-workers and on the assignment of other codons connected by a single transversion to *amber*.

NOTE

The designations "sense strand" and "antisense strand" for the DNA are those used by the authors in the original paper. Although some textbooks have now reversed these designations, in the original literature the "sense strand" is the strand off of which the mRNA is synthesized. As a consequence, the mRNA is complementary to the sense strand and has the same sequence as the "antisense strand." To avoid confusion, some texts now simply refer to the DNA strand off of which the mRNA is made as the "template strand" and the complementary DNA strand as the "non-template strand."

GENETIC CODE: THE 'NONSENSE' TRIPLETS FOR CHAIN TERMINATION AND THEIR SUPPRESSION

By Dr. S. BRENNER, F.R.S., Dr. A. O. W. STRETTON and Dr. S. KAPLAN

Medical Research Council, Laboratory of Molecular Biology, Cambridge, England

THE nucleotide sequence of messenger RNA is a code determining the amino-acid sequences of proteins. Although the biochemical apparatus which translates the code is elaborate, it is likely that the code itself is simple and consists of non-overlapping nucleotide triplets. In general, each amino-acid has more than one triplet corresponding to it, but it is not known how many of the sixty-four triplets are used to code for the twenty amino-acids. Triplets which do not correspond to amino-acids have been loosely referred to as 'nonsense' triplets, but it is not known whether these triplets have an information content which is strictly null or whether they serve some special function in information transfer.

The evidence that there are nonsense triplets is mainly genetic and will be reviewed later in this article. A remarkable property of nonsense mutants in bacteria and bacteriophages is that they are suppressible; wild-type function can be restored to such mutants by certain strains of bacteria carrying suppressor genes. It was realized early that this implies an ambiguity in the genetic code in the sense that a codon which is nonsense in one strain can be recognized as sense in another. The problem of nonsense triplets has become inextricably connected with the problem of suppression and, in particular, it has proved difficult to construct a theory of suppression without knowing the function of the nonsense triplet.

In this article we report experiments which allow us to deduce the structure of two nonsense codons as UAG and UAA. We suggest that these codons are the normal recognition signals in messenger RNA for chain termination and, on this basis, propose a theory of their suppression.

Nonsense mutants and their suppressors. One class of suppressible nonsense mutants which has been widely examined includes the subset I ambivalent rII mutants[1], the suppressible mutants of alkaline phosphatase[2], the *hd* or *sus* mutants of phage λ[3], and many of the *amber* mutants of bacteriophage T4 (ref. 4). These mutants have been isolated in various ways and the permissive (*su+*) and non-permissive (*su-*) strains used have been different. When isogenic bacterial strains, differing only in the *su* locus, are constructed, it can be shown that all these mutants respond to the same set of suppressors. They are therefore of the same class and we propose that all these mutants should be called *amber* mutants.

We may now consider the evidence that these mutants contain nonsense codons. Garen and Siddiqi[2] originally noted that *amber* mutants of the alkaline phosphatase of *E. coli* contained no protein related immunologically to the enzyme. Benzer and Champe[1] also showed that the mutants exert drastic effects and suggested that *amber* mutants of the rII gene interrupt the reading of the genetic message. In the rII genes, a deletion, r1589, joins part of the A cistron to part of the B cistron; complementation tests show that this mutant still possesses B activity although it lacks the A function. It may therefore be used to test the effects of mutants in the A cistron on the activity of the B. Double mutants, composed of an A *amber* mutant together with r1589 did not have B activity on the *su-* strain; this effect is suppressed by the *su+* strain which restores B activity. This result is explained by our finding that each *amber* mutant of the head protein produces a characteristic fragment of the polypeptide chain in *su-* bacteria[6]. More recently we have shown that the polarity of the fragment is such that it can only be produced by the termination of the growing polypeptide chain at the site of the mutation[6]. In *su+* strains, both the fragment and a completed chain are produced, and the efficiency of propagation depends on which of the suppressors is carried by the strain. In *su+I*, the efficiency of propagation is about 65 per cent[7], and the completed chain contains a serine at a position occupied by a glutamine in the wild type[6] as shown in Fig. 1.

In addition to the *amber* mutants, there are other mutants, called *ochre* mutants, which are suppressed by a different set of suppressors[8]. *Ochre* mutants of the A cistron of rII abolish the B activity of r1589. This effect is not suppressed by *amber* suppressors, which shows that the *ochre* mutants are intrinsically different from the *amber* mutants.

Thus, nonsense mutants may be divided into two types, *amber* and *ochre* mutants, depending on their pattern of suppression. In Table 1, which is abstracted from a larger set of results[8], it can be seen that strains, carrying the *amber* suppressors *su+I*, *su+II*, *su+III* and *su+IV*, suppress different but overlapping sets of *amber* mutants, but do not suppress any *ochre* mutants. This is the feature which distinguishes the two classes of mutants from each other. Table 1 also shows that *ochre* mutants are suppressed by one or more of the strains carrying the *ochre* suppressors *su+B*, *su+C*, *su+D* and *su+E*. These suppressors are also active on various *amber* mutants, and we have not yet been able to isolate suppressors specific for *ochre* mutants.

Wild Type   Ala.Gly.(Val,Phe)Asp.Phe.Gln.Asp.Pro.Ile.Asp.Ile.Arg...

H 36 on   Ala.Gly.Val.Phe.Asp.Phe.

su⁻

H 36 on   Ala.Gly.Val.Phe.Asp.Phe.

su⁺ I   and

                   Ala.Gly.Val.Phe.Asp.Phe.Ser.Asp.Pro.Ile.Asp.Ile.Arg...

Fig. 1.   Amino-acid sequences of the relevant region of the head protein in wild-type *T4D* and in the *amber* mutant *H*36 on *su⁻* and *su⁺₁* strains

A

antisense	——————— G ———————		antisense	——————— C ———————
sense	——————— C ———————		sense	——————— G ———————
m RNA	——————— G ———————		m RNA	——————— C ———————

B

antisense	——————— G ———————		antisense	——————— U′ ———————
sense	——————— U′———————		sense	——————— G ———————
m RNA	——————— A ———————		m RNA	——————— C ———————

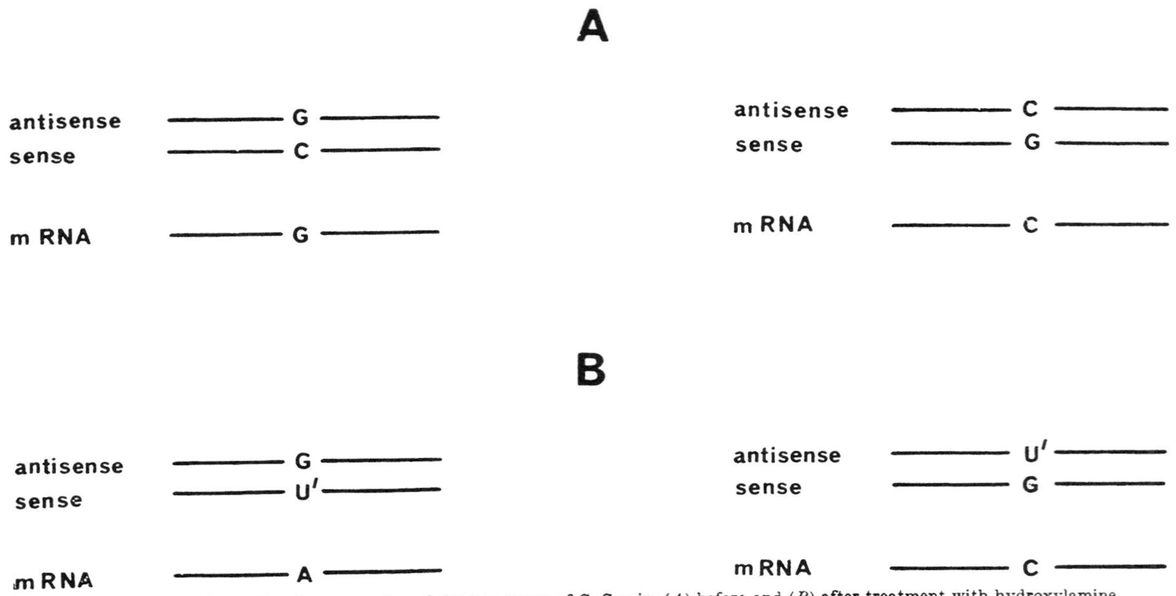

Fig. 2.   Diagram illustrating the expression of the two types of G–C pairs (*A*) before and (*B*) after treatment with hydroxylamine

Table 1. SUPPRESSION OF rII MUTANTS BY su+ STRAINS OF E. coli Hfr H(λ)

Amber mutants		Amber suppressors				Ochre suppressors			
		su+I	su+II	su+III	su+IV	su+B	su+C	su+D	su+E
rIIA	HD120	+	+	+	+	+	0	+	0
	N97	+	poor	+	0	poor	poor	+	0
	S116	0	0	+	0	0	+	+	0
	N19	+	poor	+	0	poor	0	+	0
	N34	+	+	+	0	+	+	+	0
rIIB	HE122	+	+	+	0	poor	0	+	0
	HB74	+	+	+	+	+	+	+	+
	X237	+	poor	+	0	0	+	+	0
	HB232	+	+	+	+	0	+	0	+
	X417	+	+	+	+	0	poor	+	0
Ochre mutants									
rIIA	HD147	0	0	0	0	+	+	+	+
	N55	0	0	0	0	+	+	+	0
	X20	0	0	0	0	+	0	+	0
	N21	0	0	0	0	+	0	+	0
rIIB	UV375	0	0	0	0	+	0	0	+
	360	0	0	0	0	+	0	+	+
	375	0	0	0	0	+	0	+	+
	HF208	0	0	0	0	+	0	0.	+
	N29	0	0	0	0	0	0	+	0

Table 1 also shows that the suppressor strains can be differentiated by the set of mutants they suppress.

Unlike some of the *amber* suppressors, all the *ochre* suppressors are weak[7,8]. This has made the isolation of *ochre* mutants of the head protein impossible. We therefore do not know the molecular consequences of *ochre* mutants, but we shall assume that, like the *amber* mutants, they too result in chain termination.

If we accept that both types of nonsense mutants result in termination of the polypeptide chain, we have to ask: at which level of information transfer is this effect exerted ? We have recently shown that it is likely that chain termination occurs as part of protein synthesis, since both types of mutants vanish when the phase of reading of the genetic message is altered[9]. This leads us to conclude that *amber* and *ochre* mutants produce different triplets which have to be read in the correct phase and which are recognized as signals for chain termination.

Decoding of amber and ochre triplets. We have done two types of experiments which allow us to deduce the structures of the *amber* and *ochre* triplets. First, we studied the production and reversion of rII *amber* and *ochre* mutants using chemical mutagens. We show that the two triplets are connected to each other and that we can define their possible nucleotide compositions. Next, we investigated head protein *amber* mutants, to define the amino-acids connected to the *amber* triplet. Comparison of these results with known amino-acid codons allows us to deduce the structures of the *amber* and *ochre* triplets.

The experiments with rII mutants depend on the specificity of the mutagenic agent, hydroxylamine. This reacts only with cytosine in DNA, and although the exact structure of the product has not yet been defined, the altered base (called U') appears to act like T with high efficiency, producing base-pair transitions of the G—C → A—T type[10]. Hence, response of any particular site of the DNA to hydroxylamine is evidence for the existence of a G—C pair at that site. Usually, phage particles are treated with hydroxylamine and, since these contain double-stranded DNA, the alteration of C occurs on only one of the strands. In any given gene, only one of the strands is transcribed into messenger RNA (ref. 11). This is the *sense* strand; it carries the genetic information proper and contains a nucleotide sequence which is the inverse complement of the sequence of the messenger RNA. The other strand, the *antisense* strand, has the same sequence as the messenger. In a phage, treated with hydroxylamine, the altered base, U', could be on either the sense or the antisense strand of the DNA. Since the rII genes express their functions before the onset of DNA replication[12], only sense strand changes will register a phenotypic effect in the first cycle of growth; changes on the antisense strand, while still yielding altered DNA progeny, will go unexpressed (Fig. 2).

We can now examine the reversion properties of *amber* and *ochre* mutants. Champe and Benzer[12] studied reversion of a large number of rII mutants using different mutagens. They noted that no *amber* mutant was induced to revert by hydroxylamine. Some of the mutants they studied can now be identified as *ochre* mutants, and their results show that *ochre* mutants are equally insensitive to hydroxylamine. However, in their experiments, the treated mutant phages were plated directly on the bacterial strain which restricts the growth of rII mutants. They could therefore detect *sense* strand changes only, and any mutation on the antisense strand would not have been expressed. Strictly speaking, then, their results tell us that neither the *amber* nor the *ochre* triplet contains a C on the sense strand of the DNA, or, if any one does, it is connected by a C → U change to another nonsense codon. To extend this result and to recover all possible mutational changes, we grow the mutagenized phages in *E. coli B*, in which the rII functions are unnecessary, and then plated the progeny on strain *K* to measure reversion frequency. Table 2 shows that *amber* and *ochre* mutants are not induced to revert by hydroxylamine, and we conclude that in neither mutant, does the triplet in the DNA contain G—C pairs, or, if a G—C pair is present, that triplet is connected by a G—C → A—T transition to another nonsense codon. In other words, subject to the last important reservation, we can conclude that the codons on the messenger RNA contain neither G nor C.

However, we next discovered that *ochre* mutants can be converted into *amber* mutants by mutation. Since *ochre* mutants are not suppressed by *amber* suppressors, plating on strains carrying such suppressors selects for *amber* revertants. Wild-type revertants also grow, but the two can be distinguished by testing revertant plaques on the *su−* strain. Twenty-six rII *ochre* mutants have been

Table 2. REVERSION OF AMBER AND OCHRE MUTANTS AFTER ALLOWING DNA REPLICATION

		Reversion index × 10⁻⁷	
		Control	NH₂OH
amber mutants	S116	0·04	0·03
	HD26	0·1	0·2
	S24	0·4	0·9
	S99	0·1	0·1
	N19	0·15	0·13
	HD59	0·0	0·05
	HB232	0·1	0·4
ochre mutants	UV375	0·8	2·0
	360	0·6	0·8
	X27	0·3	0·5
	375	0·8	0·9
	X511	0·2	0·3
	UV256	1·0	230

Phages were incubated in a solution of M NH₂OH in 2 M NaCl and 0·05 M sodium phosphate (pH 7·5) for 2 h at 37°. The reaction was terminated by dilution into acetone broth. About 10⁵ phage particles were used to infect a culture of *E. coli* B which was grown to lysis, and the progeny assayed on *E. coli* B and *E. coli* K12(λ). The reversion index is the *K/B* ratio. The control was treated in the same way except that hydroxylamine was omitted. The mutant *UV256*, which is not an *ochre* or an *amber* mutant, was used to check the efficacy of the mutagenic treatment.

studied and, of these, 25 have been converted into *amber* mutants. A sample of the results is given in Table 3, which shows that the mutation is strongly induced by 2-aminopurine, as strongly as the reversion of the *ochre* mutant to wild type. Other experiments, not reported here, show that the mutations of *ochre* mutants both to the *amber* and to the wild type are also induced by 5-bromouracil, but the induction is weaker than with 2-aminopurine. These results prove that the *amber* and *ochre* triplets differ from each other by only one nucleotide base, and must have the other two bases in common. 2-Aminopurine is a base analogue mutagen inducing the transition A—T ⇌ G—C in both directions[13]. This tells us that one of the triplets has a G—C pair in the DNA. The experiment reported in Table 4 shows that *ochre* mutants cannot be induced to mutate to *amber* mutants with hydroxylamine, even after the treated phages have been grown in *E. coli* B. This shows that it is the *amber* triplet which has the G—C pair and the *ochre* which contains the A—T pair.

Table 3. MUTATION OF ochre MUTANTS TO amber MUTANTS

	Spontaneous	2-Aminopurine	
	Reversion index × 10⁻⁷		
rIIA cistron	(wild type + ambers)	wild type	amber
N55	0·5	830	280
X20	0·05	100	2,100
X372	0·1	300	2,100
X352	0·06	340	1,500
HD147	0·3	370	50
rIIB cistron			
X511	0·2	710	65
N17	0·2	610	80
SD160	0·6	380	390
N29	1·0	3,900	330
AP53	0·7	350	15

Cultures of *E. coli* B in minimal medium with and without 2-aminopurine (600 μg/ml.) were inoculated with about 100 phages and grown to lysis. These were plated on *E. coli* B and on *E. coli* K12(λ) su⁺. About 50 induced revertants were tested on *E. coli* K12(λ) su⁻ to measure the relative frequencies of *amber* revertants.

Table 4. INDUCTION OF THE ochre→amber MUTATION

		Reversion index × 10⁻⁷	
		r⁺	amber
360	Control	0·6	0·2
	Hydroxylamine	0·8	0·3
	2AP	200	1,200
UV375	Control	0·8	0·4
	Hydroxylamine	2·0	1·0
	2AP	660	140
X27	Control	0·3	< 0·1
	Hydroxylamine	1·0	0·5
	2AP	7·0	73
375	Control	0·8	0·4
	Hydroxylamine	2·0	1·0
	2AP	1,400	1,700

Hydroxylamine treatment and growth of the mutagenized phages, and 2-aminopurine induction, were carried out as described in Tables 2 and 3.

Although the insensitivity of the mutants to reversion induction by hydroxylamine might suggest that they contain A—T base pairs only, the conversion of *ochre* mutants to *amber* mutants shows that, in one position, the *amber* mutant contains a G—C pair. The other two bases must be common to both triplets, but we cannot conclude that both are A—T pairs. In fact, both could be G—C pairs and the triplets may be connected to other nonsense triplets by G—C → A—T changes. However, we know that *amber* and *ochre* mutants can be induced by hydroxylamine from wild type. This proves that both triplets have at least one common A—T pair.

We now present an experiment which shows that the *amber* triplet has two A—T base pairs, and which also establishes the orientation of the pairs with respect to the two strands of DNA. Let us suppose that the *amber* triplet in the messenger RNA contains a U. This corresponds to an A in the sense strand of DNA of the *amber* mutant, implying that the wild-type DNA contains a G in this strand and a C in the antisense strand. When the wild-type DNA is treated with hydroxylamine to alter this C the change is not effective and normal messenger is still made (Fig. 2, right). On the other hand, if the *amber* triplet in the messenger contains an A, the mutant will be induced by the action of hydroxylamine on a C in the sense strand of the wild-type phage DNA, and provided that the U′ produced acts identically to U in messenger synthesis, mutant messenger will be made. This argument has been tested by the following experiment. Wild-type *T4r⁺* phages were treated with hydroxylamine to induce *r* mutants to a frequency of 1 per cent. In set B, the phages were then grown on *E. coli* B, in which the *rII* functions are not required, to recover all mutants. In set K, the phages were grown through *E. coli* K12(λ) su⁻, to eliminate from the population all phages with an immediate mutant expression. *Amber* and *ochre* mutants were then selected and mapped. Table 5 summarizes the results. About the same number of *rI* mutants were recorded in each set, and since these mutants show no difference in growth on the two bacterial strains, this shows that the results may be compared directly. It will be seen that *amber* mutants at the sites, N97, S116, S24, N34, X237 and HB232, recur many times in set B, but are absent or rarely found in set K. At other *amber* sites, such as HB118, HB129, EM84 and AP164, mutants occur with approximately equal frequency in both sets. The first class fulfils the expectation for a C → U change on the sense strand, while the second class must arise by C → U changes on the antisense strand. This shows that the *amber* triplet in the messenger contains both an A and a U. The same should be true of the *ochre* mutants. However, as shown in Table 5, *ochre* mutants are not as strongly induced by hydroxylamine as are *amber* mutants, and we cannot separate the two classes with the same degree of confidence. Nevertheless, since we have already shown that the mutants are connected, it follows that the *ochre* triplet must also contain an A and a U. We conclude

Table 5. HYDROXYLAMINE INDUCTION OF *amber* AND *ochre* MUTANTS

A. No. of mutants isolated

	Set B	Set K
rI	2,010	1,823
Leaky or high reverting rII	720	508
non-suppressible rII	1,144	433
amber	319	121
ochre	83	82
Total	4,276	2,967

B. Recurrences found at different sites

Amber mutants No. found at each site			*Ochre* mutants No. found at each site		
Site	Set B	Set K	Site	Set B	Set K
A cistron			A cistron		
HB118	27	15	HD147	2	0
C204	1	0	HF220	1	0
N97	44	1	HF240	1	0
S116	31	2	N55	19	19
N11	3	3	X20	9	8
S172	9	5	HF219	1	0
S24	44	3	HF245	1	0
HB129	14	25	N31	3	5
S99	12	16	HM127	0	1
N19	15	9	N21	2	2
N34	8	0			
B cistron			B cistron		
HE122	1	0	360	11	10
EM84	20	21	UV375	2	0
HB74	16	5	N24	6	4
X237	14	2	375	2	5
AP164	28	12	N17	5	3
HB232	21	1	HF208	1	2
X417	1	0	N7	4	12
HD231	1	1	N12	5	7
			X234	0	2
			X191	1	0
			HE267	5	0
			AP53	2	2

T4Br+ was treated with M hydroxylamine (see Table 2) for 2 h at 37° C. Survival was 50 per cent, and the frequency of r and mottled plaques, 1 per cent. 1·2 × 10⁷ phage particles were adsorbed to 10⁹ cells of *E. coli* B (set B) and to *E. coli* K12(λ) su⁻ (set K). After 8 min, the infected bacteria were diluted a thousand-fold into 2 litres of broth, incubated for 35′ and lysed with CHCl₃. The burst sizes in both sets were 60. r mutants were isolated from each set using less than 2 ml. to ensure that the mutants selected had mostly arisen from independent events. These were picked and stabbed into B and K, and rI mutants and leaky mutants discarded. The rII mutants were then screened on su⁺III and su⁺B to select for *amber* and *ochre* mutants which were then located by genetic mapping.

that the *amber* and *ochre* triplets are, respectively, either (UAG) and (UAA), or (UAC) and (UAU). If we had a strain which suppressed *ochre* mutants only, we could specify the third base by studying the induction of the *amber* → *ochre* change with hydroxylamine.

Fortunately, we can resolve the ambiguity by determining the amino-acids to which the *amber* triplet is connected by mutation. In particular, we note that it should be connected to two and only two amino-acid codons by transitions, corresponding, in fact, to the two types of origin of the mutants described here. The third codon to which it is connected by a transition is the *ochre* triplet. As mentioned earlier, the head *amber* mutant H36 has arisen from glutamine (Fig. 1). This mutant was induced with hydroxylamine. We have evidence that two other mutants, E161 and B278 induced by 2-aminopurine and 5-bromouracil respectively, have arisen from tryptophan. In a recent study of two *amber* mutants of the alkaline phosphatase, Garen and Weigert[14] found one mutant to arise from glutamine and the other from tryptophan; and Notani et al.[15] have found an *amber* mutant to arise from glutamine in the RNA phage f2. In addition, we have examined 2-aminopurine induced revertants of 10 different head *amber* mutants. Ten to 12 independently induced revertants of each of the mutants have been screened for tryptophan containing peptides by examining the ¹⁴C-tryptophan labelled protein. Among a total of 115 revertants, 62 are to tryptophan. Determination of glutamine involves sequence analysis and takes more time. So far, among the remaining 53 revertants, glutamine has been identified in one revertant of H36. These results suggest that the two amino-acids connected to the *amber* triplet are glutamine and tryptophan. If the *amber* triplet is (UAC), then one of these must be (CAC) and the other (UGC); if it is (UAG), then the corresponding codons are (CAG) and (UGG). Nirenberg et al.[16] have shown that poly AC does not code for tryptophan, but does for glutamine. However, they find that the triplet for glutamine clearly has the composition (CAA) and is definitely not (CAC). Since this latter triplet corresponds neither to glutamine nor to tryptophan we can eliminate the first alternative. We note with satisfaction that (UGG) is the composition of a codon assigned to tryptophan[16,17], and this assignment of (UAG) to the *amber* triplet suggests that glutamine is (CAG).

We can also make a reasonable assignment of the order of the bases in the triplet. Our original argument was based on deductions from a few known triplets and from amino-acid replacement data; it will not be given here. The order of the bases follows directly from a recent demonstration by Nirenberg et al.[18] that the triplet CAG does, in fact, correspond to glutamine. The *amber* triplet is therefore UAG and the *ochre* triplet UAA. This assignment is supported by the following additional evidence. We have found a tyrosine replacement in 21 independent spontaneous mutants of the head *amber* mutant, *H36* (ref. 19). This change must be due to a transversion because we have already accounted for all the transitions of the *amber* triplet. In support of this, we find that the change is not induced by 2-aminopurine. There are six possible transversions of the *amber* triplet, namely, AAG, GAG, UUG, UCG, UAU and UAC. It has recently been shown that both UAU and UAC correspond to tyrosine[20] which confirms the order. The spontaneous revertants of the *amber* mutants to leucine, serine and glutamic acid found by Weigert and Garen[21] are further evidence for the assignment. UUG, a transversion of the *amber* triplet, does in fact code for leucine[22], and reasonable allocations for serine and glutamic acid are UCG and GAG, respectively. Weigert and Garen[21] also find revertants of an *amber* mutant to either lysine or arginine. This may be the final transversion expected since AAG is a codeword for lysine[20].

It should be noted that in the foregoing discussion it has been tacitly assumed that the *amber* and *ochre* signals are triplets. Examination of revertants of *amber* mutants has supported this assumption, since in 41 independent revertants of *H36* the amino-acid replaced is always at the site of mutation, and never in adjacent positions. The 21 revertants that Weigert and Garen[21] isolated reinforce this conclusion.

Function of amber and ochre triplets and the mechanism of suppression. According to present-day ideas of protein synthesis, it is expected that the termination of the growth of the polypeptide chain should involve a special mechanism. Since the terminal carboxyl group of the growing peptide chain is esterified to an *sRNA* (ref. 23), chain termination must involve not only the cessation of growth, but also the cleavage of this bond. Since the *amber* mutants have been shown to result in efficient termination of polypeptide chain synthesis, it is reasonable to suppose that this special mechanism may be provided by the *amber* and *ochre* triplets.

We postulate that the chain-terminating triplets UAA and UAG are recognized by specific *sRNAs*, just like other codons. These *sRNAs* do not carry amino-acids but a special compound which results in termination of the growing polypeptide chain. There are many possible ways of formulating the mechanism in detail, but all are speculative and will not be considered here. The essential feature of this hypothesis is to make the process of chain termination exactly congruent with that of chain extension.

In suppressing strains, a mechanism is provided for competing with chain termination; it is easy to visualize this process as being due to two ways of recognizing the nonsense codon—one by the chain-terminating *sRNA*, and the other by an *sRNA* carrying an amino-acid. Mechanisms of suppression can be classified according to which *sRNA* carries the amino-acid to the nonsense codon.

Alteration in the recognition of the chain-terminating *sRNA* might allow the attachment of an amino-acid to this *sRNA*. This could be brought about either by modifying normal activating enzymes so as to widen their specificity, or by changing the chain terminating *sRNAs* to allow them to be recognized by activating enzymes.

Another possibility is that the region of an amino-acyl *sRNA* used for triplet recognition is modified so that it can recognize the nonsense triplet. Clearly, this alteration must not affect the normal recognition of its own codon by the amino acyl *sRNA* because such a change would be lethal. Either there must be more than one gene for the given *sRNA*, or else the change must produce an ambiguity in the recognition site so that it can read both its own codon and the nonsense codon. Such ambiguity could result not only from mutation in the *sRNA* gene but also by enzymatic modification of one of the bases in the recognition site. The ambiguity, however, must be narrowly restricted to prevent the suppression from affecting codons other than the *amber* and *ochre* triplets. Moreover, the amino-acids which are inserted by the *amber* suppressors must be those the codons of which are connected to UAG. It should be noted that this condition is fulfilled by su^+_I which inserts serine, since serine has been found as a reversion of an *amber* mutant. This theory does not easily explain the *ochre* suppressors. Since these recognize both *amber* and *ochre* mutants the *sRNA* must possess this ambiguity as well.

Another quite different possibility for suppression that has been considered is that the suppressors alter a component of the ribosomes to permit errors to occur in the reading of the messenger RNA (ref. 24). This is probably the explanation of streptomycin suppression[25], but suppression of *amber* and *ochre* mutants cannot be readily explained by this theory. It is scarcely likely that such a mechanism could be specific for only one or two triplets, and for this reason it might be expected to give us suppression of mutants which are not nonsense, but missense, and this has not been found[1,8]. Moreover, the efficiency of *amber* suppression argues strongly against such a mechanism. It is unlikely that a generalized error in reading nucleotides could produce the 60 per cent efficiency of suppression found for su^+_I without seriously affecting the viability of the cell.

It is a consequence of our theory that normal chain termination could also be suppressed in these strains. Since the *amber* suppressors are efficient we have to introduce the *ad hoc* hypothesis that the UAG codon is rarely used for chain termination in *Escherichia coli* and bacteriophage *T4* and that UAA is the common codon. This is supported by the fact that all *ochre* suppressors thus far isolated are weak[7,8]. Another possibility is that neither is the common chain terminating triplet. We cannot exclude the existence of other chain terminating triplets which are not suppressible.

To summarize: we show that the triplets of the *amber* and *ochre* mutants are UAG and UAA, respectively. We suggest that the 'nonsense' codons should be more properly considered to be the codons for chain termination. In essence, this means that the number of elements to be coded for is not 20 but more likely 21. We propose that the recognition of the chain-terminating codons is carried out by two special *s*RNAs.

We thank our colleagues for their advice, and Dr. M. Nirenberg for allowing us to quote his unpublished results.

[1] Benzer, S., and Champe, S. P., *Proc. U.S. Nat. Acad. Sci.*, **47**, 1025 (1961); **48**, 1114 (1962).

[2] Garen, A., and Siddiqi, O., *Proc. U.S. Nat. Acad. Sci.*, **48**, 1121 (1962).

[3] Campbell, A., *Virology*, **14**, 22 (1961).

[4] Epstein, R. H., Bolle, A., Steinberg, C. M., Kellenberger, E., Boy de la Tour, E., Chevalley, R., Edgar, R. S., Susman, M., Denhardt, G. H., and Lielausis, A., *Cold Spring Harbour Symp. Quant. Biol.*, **28**, 375 (1963).

[5] Sarabhai, A., Stretton, A. O. W., Brenner, S., and Bolle, A., *Nature*, **201**, 13 (1964).

[6] Stretton, A. O. W., and Brenner, S., *J. Mol. Biol.* (in the press).

[7] Kaplan, S., Stretton A. O. W., and Brenner, S. (in preparation).

[8] Brenner, S., and Beckwith, J. R. (in preparation).

[9] Brenner, S., and Stretton, A. O. W. (in preparation).

[10] Brown, D. M., and Schell, P., *J. Mol. Biol.*, **3**, 709 (1961). Freese, E., Bautz-Freese, E., and Bautz, E., *J. Mol. Biol.*, **3**, 133 (1961). Schuster, H., *J. Mol. Biol.*, **3**, 447 (1961). Freese, E., Bautz, E., and Freese, E. B., *Proc. U.S. Nat. Acad. Sci.*, **47**, 845 (1961).

[11] Tocchini-Valentini, G. P., Stodolsky, M., Aurisicchio, A., Sarnat, M., Graziosi, F., Weiss, S. B., and Geiduschek, E. P., *Proc. U.S. Nat. Acad. Sci.*, **50**, 935 (1963). Hayashi, M., Hayashi, M. N., and Spiegelman, S., *Proc. U.S. Nat. Acad. Sci.*, **50**, 664 (1963). Marmur, J., Greenspan, C. M., Palacek, E., Kahan, F. M., Levene, J., and Mandel, M., *Cold Spring Harbor Symp. Quant. Biol.*, **28**, 191 (1963). Bautz, E. K. F., *Cold Spring Harbor Symp. Quant. Biol.*, **28**, 205 (1963). Hall, B. D., Green, M., Nygaard, A. P., and Boezi, J., *Cold Spring Harbor Symp. Quant. Biol.*, **28**, 201 (1963).

[12] Champe, S. P., and Benzer, S., *Proc. U.S. Nat. Acad. Sci.*, **48**, 532 (1962). Tessman, I., Poddar, R. K., and Kumar, S., *J. Mol. Biol.*, **9**, 352 (1964).

[13] Freese, E., *J. Mol. Biol.*, **1**, 87 (1959). Freese, E., *Proc. U.S. Nat. Acad. Sci.*, **45**, 622 (1959). Howard, B. D., and Tessman, I., *J. Mol. Biol.*, **9**, 372 (1964).

[14] Garen, A., and Weigert, M. G., *J. Mol. Biol.* (in the press).

[15] Notani, G. W., Engelhardt, D. L., Konigsberg, W., and Zinder, N., *J. Mol. Biol.* (in the press).

[16] Nirenberg, M., Jones, O. W., Leder, P., Clark, B. F. C., Sly, W. S., and Pestke, S., *Cold Spring Harbor Symp. Quant. Biol.*, **28**, 549 (1963).

[17] Speyer, J. F., Lengyel, P., Basilio, C., Wahba, A. J., Gardner, R. S., and Ochoa, S., *Cold Spring Harbor Symp. Quant. Biol.*, **28**, 559 (1963).

[18] Nirenberg, M., Leder, P., Bernfield, M., Brimacombe, R., Trupin, J., and Rottman, F., *Proc. U.S. Nat. Acad. Sci.* (in the press).

[19] Stretton, A. O. W., and Brenner, S. (in preparation).

[20] Trupin, J., Rottman, F., Brimacombe, R., Leder, P., Bernfield, M., and Nirenberg, M., *Proc. U.S. Nat. Acad. Sci.* (in the press). Clark, B. F. C., presented before the French Biochemical Society, February, 1965.

[21] Weigert, M. G., and Garen, A., *Nature* (preceding communication).

[22] Leder, P., and Nirenberg, M. W., *Proc. U.S. Nat. Acad. Sci.*, **52**, 1521 (1964).

[23] Gilbert, W., *J. Mol. Biol.*, **6**, 389 (1963). Bretscher, M. S., *J. Mol. Biol.*, **7**, 446 (1963).

[24] Davies, J., Gilbert, W., and Gorini, L., *Proc. U.S. Nat. Acad. Sci.*, **51**, 883 (1964).

[25] Gorini, L., and Kataja, E., *Proc. U.S. Nat. Acad. Sci.*, **51**, 487 (1964).

Unit 3 / Decoding the *amber* and *ochre* Triplets

Brenner et al. 1965

1. What property allowed mutants from different systems to be classified as *amber*?

2. What is the evidence that *amber* mutants contain nonsense codons?

3. How are *ochre* mutants different from *amber* mutants?

4. On which mutations can *amber* and *ochre* suppressors act?

5. What evidence shows that chain termination occurs as part of protein synthesis?

6. Show why only sense-strand changes created by hydroxylamine will result in phenotypic change before DNA replication.

7. Describe the experiment reported in Table 2 on page 104 and indicate how Table 2 was constructed.

8. Describe the experiment that led to Table 3 on page 104 and indicate how Table 3 was compiled.

9. What does Table 4 on page 104 show?

10. Describe the experiment reported in Table 5 on page 105 and explain what each entry in Table 5 means.

11. How does the experiment reported in Table 5 on page 105, together with previous experiments, establish the compositions of the *amber* and *ochre* codons?

12. How could the authors determine whether the composition of the *amber* codon was (UAC) or (UAG)?

13. How did the authors assign the order of bases in the *amber* triplet?

14. What was the authors' proposed mechanism of chain termination and how accurate was their guess based on what we know today? What about their proposed mechanism of suppression?

Unit 4

The Search for Colinearity

After the basic outlines of the genetic code became clear, a major concern was the **colinearity problem:** The test of the concept that the linear sequence of nucleotides in a segment of DNA (a gene) becomes translated into the linear sequence of amino acids in the corresponding polypeptide. The obvious way to do this was to show that mutations mapped in the same linear order as the altered amino acids in the corresponding proteins. There was intense competition. Yanofsky was attempting to demonstrate colinearity in the *Escherichia coli* tryptophan synthetase (*trpA*) system; Benzer was trying to use the T4 rII system for this purpose; Allan Garen and Cy Levinthal were developing alkaline phosphatase; Sydney Brenner was using the T4 head protein; and George Streisinger was using phage T4 lysozyme.

The two groups that succeeded ended up using different approaches. Yanofsky and co-workers showed that mutations in the *trpA* gene mapped in the same order as the amino acid changes in the tryptophan synthetase α subunit; and Sarabhai, Brenner, and co-workers showed that the size of T4 head protein fragments produced by chain termination corresponded to the order of the nonsense mutations in the gene.

Charles Yanofsky

When Charley Yanofsky arrived at Yale in 1948 to begin his graduate work, it was only shortly after the demonstration by Beadle and Tatum that genes specify enzymes, which then control biochemical pathways. This work stimulated the search for the precise relationship between genes and proteins and for an understanding of protein structure. The students of Beadle and Tatum, including David Bonner at Yale, followed up on their studies of pathways in *Neurospora* by examining different *Neurospora* enzymes. Each of Bonner's students selected a different *Neurospora* enzyme. For example, one student picked β-galactosidase, another selected kyureninase, and Charley Yanofsky selected tryptophan synthetase. Yanofsky's graduate studies centered around the synthesis of niacin in *Neurospora*, which is synthesized from tryptophan, so it seemed natural to study the biosynthesis of tryptophan. In addition, an enzyme activity had been identified, and a mutant lacking that activity could not synthesize tryptophan. Yanofsky first isolated numerous mutants that were blocked in the conversion of indole to tryptophan. Each mutant lacked the enzyme activity then called tryptophan desmolase, which is now termed tryptophan synthetase. All of the mutations mapped at the same locus. In fact, this was the first time that it was demonstrated that many independent mutations eliminating a single enzyme occurred at a single genetic locus. (In this context, locus was used to indicate a gene.)

Yanofsky was greatly influenced by a course he took at Yale in 1950 given by Louis Stadler. The course dealt with the question: Are mutational changes at a single locus genetically separable? The requirement of the course was to write a paper on an unexplained genetic phenomenon. Yanofsky chose "Genetic Suppression" and offered explanations involving the repair of damaged, inactive, mutant proteins. This stimulated Yanofsky to work on suppressors of tryptophan synthetase mutants. He found that some of the mutants reverted via second-site suppressor mutations. Then, working with Sig Suskind, he tested different mutants to see whether they synthesized immunologically cross-reacting material (CRM). The suppressible mutants

synthesized CRM, whereas the nonsuppressible ones did not. Thus, Yanofsky and Suskind could distinguish different types of mutations, and they also found that suppressors were rather specific. They argued that there was a substructure in the genetic locus for tryptophan synthetase and that different subunits of the locus were damaged in the distinguishable mutants.

In 1954, Yanofsky moved to Case Western Reserve, and the following year he presented his findings at a meeting in Denver, where he met Seymour Benzer for the first time. Benzer's studies on the fine structure of the gene were already underway. They discussed possible explanations for the suppressible mutants. Recall that the DNA structure had only been published two years before. Yanofsky realized that to do more-detailed studies, it would be prudent to switch to *Escherichia coli*, particularly since generalized transduction had just been discovered. Together with Ed Lennox, Yanofsky showed that fine structure analysis could be performed with phage P1 in the *trp* region of *E. coli*. During the mid-1950s, Yanofsky and his students defined the tryptophan biosynthetic pathway in *E. coli*. At the same time, Milislav Demerec and his group were working on the *Salmonella typhimurium* tryptophan biosynthetic pathway at Cold Spring Harbor. Sydney Brenner worked with Demerec at Cold Spring Harbor for a brief period, and Yanofsky met Brenner there during this period. It was evident that the tryptophan biosynthetic enzymes were regulated, and this was first worked out by Georges Cohen and François Jacob (see Unit 6 for studies of gene regulation).

In 1958, Yanofsky moved to Stanford. It took some time to understand that the active, complete tryptophan synthetase consisted of two different subunits, each encoded by a different gene. At this point, Yanofsky's interests turned to the colinearity problem. The first step was to determine the amino acid changes in the tryptophan synthetase α subunit in a number of TrpA mutants. Vernon Ingram's newly developed two-dimensional fingerprinting was put to good use here by Ulf Henning and Don Helinski in Yanofsky's group. Together with Virginia Horn, Yanofsky began to construct a fine structure genetic map of the trpA locus. As can be seen in the paper reprinted here on pages 124–126, the linear order of mutations on the fine structure genetic map of trpA corresponded exactly with the order of amino acid changes in the tryptophan synthetase α peptide. In addition, the genetic map distances correlated roughly with distances in the protein. Their initial findings were described at the Cold Spring Harbor Symposium of 1963. Brenner reported the results of his group's work with phage T4 head protein mutants at about the same time.

During the past 37 years at Stanford, Charley Yanofsky has established the trp system as one of the best understood gene control systems. His group is still very active in this area.

ON THE COLINEARITY OF GENE STRUCTURE AND PROTEIN STRUCTURE

The Tryptophan System

Tryptophan synthetase from *E. coli* consists of two α subunits and two β subunits, which together catalyze the reaction of indole-3-glycerol phosphate with serine to form tryptophan. The separated subunits catalyze partial reactions.

The 1964 paper by Yanofsky et al. (reprinted here on pages 117–123) shows the map positions of 16 mutations and the corresponding changes in the primary sequence of the protein. Figure 1 on page 118 shows the order of the mutational sites. Note that this map was based on three types of experiments: Two-factor-cross recombination frequencies, deletion mapping, and ordering by three-factor crosses. The last method is instrumental in ordering mutations that are within the same gene when deletions are not available to separate them. Therefore, let's examine the concept behind a three-factor cross and examine Yanofsky's actual data.

A three-factor cross is simply a cross in which three different mutations are scored. A careful look at the notes to Table 2 on page 120 shows that in addition to two different *trp* mutations, here designated as x and y, the outside marker *anth* was used. This marker maps outside the *trp* region. The idea here is to force a crossover between two very close mutations within the *trpA* gene and then to see whether the resulting Trp⁺ recombinant is Anth⁺ or Anth⁻. The diagram below depicts the cross.

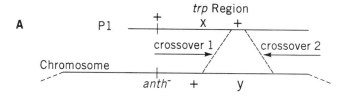

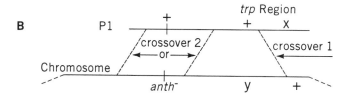

The recipient chromosome carries the *anth* mutation and one of the two *trp* mutations (y), and the incoming P1 transducing particle carries the wild-type *anth* gene and the second *trp* mutation (x). Recall that two crossovers are needed to recombine a segment of the P1 particle onto the chromosome. One of the cross-

overs must be in between the two *trp* mutations and the other crossover must be to one side or the other of the mutations to produce a Trp⁺ recombinant. We can see in diagram A above that if the order of *trp* mutations is as shown (*anth*, x, y), then the second crossover must be to the right of the *trp* mutations in order to generate a Trp⁺. Therefore, in most cases, the recipient chromosome will retain the *anth* mutation. Indeed, it was found that in about 80% of such cases, the Trp⁺ recombinant was Anth⁻. However, if the order of x and y are reversed, then, as shown in diagram B, the second crossover will be to the left of the *trp* region. Some of these crossovers will be between the *trp* region and the *anth* mutation and some will be to the left of the *anth* mutation. In practice, one finds that about 50% of the Trp⁺ recombinants are Anth⁻ if the order of mutations is as shown in diagram B.

Let's look at some of the entries in Table 2 on page 120. The first cross has *trp34* on the P1 phage and *trp223* on the chromosome. Here, 34 = x in diagram A and 223 = y. We can see from the results that only 18% of the Trp⁺ recombinants are Anth⁺ (82% Anth⁻). This is exactly what we expect if the order is *anth-34-223* as in diagram A. We note that this is the assigned order in Table 2. The second cross has *trp46* on the P1 and again *trp223* on the chromosome. This time 48% of the recombinants are Anth⁺, which is what we expect if the order is like that shown in diagram B. Thus, we would assign the order *anth-223-46*, as did the authors in Table 2.

The data in Figure 1 and Tables 1 and 2 (pages 118, 119, and 120, respectively) clearly show that the positions of the amino acid replacements in the A protein are in the same order as the corresponding mutations in the *trpA* gene, thus demonstrating colinearity. Table 3 on page 122 also shows that there is a reasonable correspondence between the genetic map distances and the separation of altered residues in the protein. This correlation is not perfect and varies over a fivefold range, but the majority of separations give a very similar result, as a careful inspection of Table 3 will show. A more complete summary of the data, including the complete amino acid sequence of the TrpA protein, is given in the 1967 paper by Yanofsky et al. reprinted here on pages 124–126.

Colinearity in the T4 Head Protein

Sarabhai, Brenner, and co-workers demonstrated colinearity using a completely different method than that used by the Yanofsky group. First, they demonstrated that the molecular consequence of suppressible *amber* mutations affecting the T4 head protein was the production of a fragment of the head protein in strains not carrying a suppressor. The size of the fragment depended on the position of the nonsense mutation. They used tryptic peptide maps to show the length of the fragment in each case. They also mapped the nonsense mutations with a series of two- and three-factor crosses. The order of mutations on the genetic map (shown in Table 1 on page 130) corresponded to the order of sizes of T4 head protein fragments. This proved that the gene was colinear with the polypeptide chain.

What is so extraordinary about this study is the rapidity with which it was done. This was possible because the authors could take advantage of several aspects of T4 infection. First, late during infection, about 50% of the protein synthesized is head protein. Thus, by adding labeled amino acids late in infection, the authors could follow the production of head protein fragments without any purification. Second, the infection by T4 phage inhibits cellular breakdown of protein fragments, which would otherwise have made this approach difficult or even impossible.

CONCLUSIONS

Both studies presented here showed that the gene and the polypeptide chain are colinear: The order of bases in the DNA is the same as the respective encoded amino acids in the polypeptide chain.

ON THE COLINEARITY OF GENE STRUCTURE AND PROTEIN STRUCTURE*

BY C. YANOFSKY, B. C. CARLTON,† J. R. GUEST,‡ D. R. HELINSKI,†
AND U. HENNING†

DEPARTMENT OF BIOLOGICAL SCIENCES, STANFORD UNIVERSITY

Communicated by Victor Twitty, December 18, 1963

The pioneering studies of Beadle and Tatum with *Neurospora crassa*[1] led to the concept that there is a 1:1 relationship between gene and enzyme. Subsequent studies on the structure of proteins[2] and genetic material[3] permitted a restatement of this relationship in molecular terms;[4] the linear sequence of nucleotides in a gene specifies the linear sequence of amino acids in a protein.

Several years ago studies were initiated with the A gene–A protein system of the tryptophan synthetase of *Escherichia coli* with the intention of examining this concept of a colinear relationship between gene structure and protein structure. A large number of mutant strains which produced altered A proteins were isolated, and genetic and protein primary structure studies were performed with these strains to locate the positions of the alterations within the A gene and the A protein.[5-10] It was hoped that with information of this type it would be possible to determine whether a genetic map and the primary structure of the corresponding protein were colinear. Recently, Kaiser[11] has demonstrated the correspondence of the genetic map with the sequence of blocks of nucleotides in DNA. Thus if a colinear relationship could be established between a genetic map and the primary structure of a protein, it would be reasonable to conclude that this relationship extends to the nucleotide sequence corresponding to the genetic map.

In previous reports on studies with the tryptophan synthetase A protein, conclusive evidence was presented for the colinearity of a segment of the A gene and a segment of the A protein.[12, 13] The present communication deals with more extensive data with 16 mutants with mutational alterations in one segment of the A gene and the A protein.

Materials and Methods.—*Mutant strains:* Of the A-protein mutants examined in detail in this paper, strains A23, A27, A28, A36, A46, A58, A78, A90, A94, A95, A169, A178, and A187 were isolated following ultraviolet irradiation of the K-12 wild-type strain of *E. coli*, and strain A223 was isolated following treatment of the wild-type strain with ethylmethanesulfonate. Mutant A446 (previously designated PR8)[14] and mutant A487 were initially isolated as spontaneous second-site reversions and subsequently were separated from the original A mutants with which they had been associated. Strains $anth_1{}^-$ and $anth_2{}^-$ are blocked prior to anthranilic acid in the tryptophan pathway and respond to anthranilic acid, indole, or tryptophan. $V_1{}^R$ and $V_1{}^R$ $tryp^-$ deletion mutants were isolated by treatment of T1-sensitive populations of the various mutants with phage T1h+. All of the $V_1{}^R$ mutations mentioned are very closely linked to the A gene, and the $V_1{}^R$ $tryp^-$ deletions include the $V_1{}^R$ locus and some segment of the A gene.[15] A stock of unrestricted T1 phage (uT1)[16] was kindly supplied by J. R. Christensen.

Protein studies: The altered A proteins were isolated and examined for primary structure changes as described previously.[6, 7, 9] The ordering of the tryptic peptides mentioned in the paper will be described in detail elsewhere.[17, 18]

Genetic studies: Recombination experiments were performed with the temperate-transducing phage P1kc.[19] Recombination distances between A mutants were obtained by determining the frequency of appearance of $tryp^+$ transductants. Transduction from $his^- \rightarrow his^+$ was scored in each experiment for internal reference, and the ratio of $tryp^+/his^+$ transductants calculated.[20]

Each value was halved to correct for the difference in relative frequency of transduction in the *his* and *tryp* regions.[20] In transduction experiments with leaky mutants (A169, A223, A446, and A487) the plating medium was supplemented with 0.1 μg/ml DL-5-methyltryptophan to suppress growth of the leaky mutants. This supplement has little or no effect on the growth of wild-type recombinants and does not appear to affect the recombination values obtained with nonleaky mutants. In spite of the presence of 5-methyltryptophan, it was frequently difficult to score recombination in experiments with leaky mutants. Anthranilic acid requirement was scored either by picking and streaking or by replication to appropriate test media. Resistance to phage T1 (V₁ᴿ) was scored by picking, streaking, and spot testing with phage uT1. As shown by Drexler and Christensen,[16] P1 lysogeny does not prevent the multiplication of uT1.

Results and Discussion.—Relative order of mutational alterations in the A gene: The genetic map based on recombination frequencies, deletion mapping, and three-point crosses is shown in Figure 1.

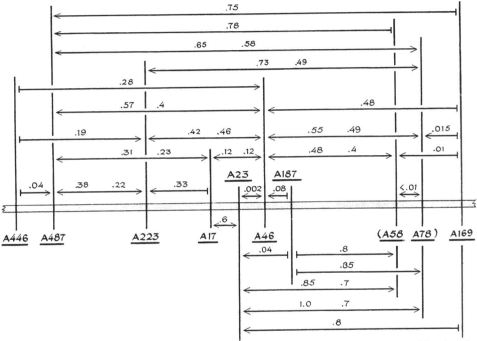

Fig. 1.—The order of mutationally altered sites in the A gene based on recombination frequencies, deletion mapping, and three-point genetic tests. The head of each arrow points to the recipient in each transduction cross. If two values are given, the cross was performed in both directions. In such cases each value is placed near the recipient in the cross.

Recombination frequency data: Recombination frequency data alone establishes close linkage of three groups of mutants: (1) A446 and A487; (2) A46, A23, and A187; and (3) A58, A78, and A169. The recombination values obtained also suggest that the order of these groups is as indicated in the figure, but they do not permit ordering within any of the groups.[21] In most cases recombination experiments were performed in both directions, i.e., each strain served as donor and recipient, and fair agreement was observed between the two values. However, it is evident from the data in Figure 1 that there were some exceptions. The exceptions generally involved leaky mutants, and it is possible that the scoring difficulties encountered with these strains were responsible.

Two of the mutants examined, A23 and A187, gave recombination values considerably higher than those obtained with mutant A46. Other mutants which were independent isolates resembling A23 (A27, A28, A36) and A46 (A95, A178) exhibited the same recombination behavior as the strain they resembled. Extensive mapping experiments with other A mutants and the strains mentioned above indicate that the A23 and A187 recombination values are probably exceptionally high rather than the A46 values exceptionally low. Since the mutational alterations in strains of the A23 and A46 type were probably single nucleotide changes,[22] it would appear that differences of single nucleotide pairs between donor DNA and recipient DNA can influence the frequency of recombinational events. An alternative explanation, that all A23 and A187 double mutants are prototrophic, seems very unlikely on the basis of numerous tests with recombinants from crosses involving A23 and A187.

Recombinants were not obtained in crosses of A23 × A27, A28, cr A36; A46 × A95 or A178; or A58 × A90 or A94. On the basis of these tests and the primary structure studies to be described, it was concluded that each of these groups consists of members which arose by repeat identical mutations at the same site. Mutants A58 and A78 are clearly different, but they do not give recombinants at the 0.01 per cent level.

Deletion mapping: Information on the order of the mutational alterations in the relevant mutant strains was obtained in transduction experiments with a series of $V_1{}^R$-*tryp*$^-$ deletion mutants (Table 1). These latter strains had regions of the A gene deleted, including, in each case, the V_1 locus which is situated at one end of the A gene.[15] Thus all the deletions extended into the A gene from the same side, and are overlapping, but may have different end points in the A gene. The recovery of tryptophan-independent recombinants from a transduction cross between any A mutant and a deletion mutant would indicate that the mutationally altered site in the A mutant was outside the region of the A gene that was missing in the deletion mutant. Recombination values were determined in transduction crosses with some of the deletion mutants to approximate the relative distance from a mutationally altered site in an A mutant to the end point of a deletion.

It is clear from the crosses with T$^-$70 and T$^-$689 that the altered sites in mutants A23, A46, A187, A58, A78, and A169—but not those in A446, A487, and A223—are within the region of the A gene that is missing in these deletion mutants. The rela-

TABLE 1

RECOMBINATION TESTS WITH VARIOUS TRYP$^-$ DELETION MUTANTS

Donor	*his*$^-$ $V_1{}^R$ *tryp*$^-$ Deletion Mutant Recipient					
	T$^-$201	T$^-$5	T$^-$70	T$^-$689	T$^-$211	T$^-$226
A446	0	0	0.08‡	0.08‡		
A487	0	0	0.19*	0.5		
A223	0	0	0.17	0.06	+	+
A23	0	0	0	0	1.3	+
A46	0	0	0	0	0.86	0.77
A187	0	0	0		1.3	+
A58	0	0	0	0	0.09	0.1
A78	0	0	0		0.1	0.1
A169			0		0.1	0.1
A38	+	+	+	+	+	+

+, 0 = recombinants or no recombinants, respectively, in qualitative transduction experiments.
* = each recombination value represents the uncorrected observed ratio of *tryp*$^+$ to *his*$^+$ transductants.
‡ A446 gives unusually low recombination values in all experiments.

tive order of the altered sites in mutants A446, A487, and A223 could not be established by quantitative transduction experiments with the same deletion mutants. The quantitative transduction experiments with deletion mutants $T^{-}211$ and $T^{-}226$ divide the other mutants into two groups: (A46, A23, and A187) and (A58, A78, and A169). The combined results presented suggest the following order of altered sites: A38......(A446, A487, A223)......(A46, A23, A187)......(A58, A78, A169)......V_1.

Three-point genetic tests: Genetic tests employing outside markers were performed to determine relative order within each group of closely linked mutants. These tests are summarized in Table 2. The results obtained support the conclusions concerning group order that were arrived at by the previous methods and indicate relative orders within each closely linked group. Crosses 1–7 establish the order anth......A34......A446......A487......A223......A46, crosses 8 and 9 the order anth......A46......A78......A169, and crosses 10 and 11 the order anth......(A23, A46)......A187. The order anth......A23-A46 had tentatively been assigned on the basis of other data.[22] Crosses 12–15 confirm orders established by other methods. The combined genetic analyses with the mutants examined suggest the sequence of mutational alterations shown in Figure 1—A446-A487-A223-A23-A46-A187-(A58, A78)-A169.

TABLE 2

OUTSIDE-MARKER ORDERING OF MUTATIONALLY ALTERED SITES

	Transduction cross	Nonselective markers	Recombinants detected*		$anth^+$ (%)	Order
(1)	34 → $anth_2^{-}$-223	$anth_2$	72 $anth^+$;	332 $anth^-$	18	$anth$-34-223
(2)	46 → $anth_2^{-}$-223	$anth_2$	180 $anth^+$;	196 $anth^-$	48	$anth$-223-46
(3)	446 → $anth_2^{-}$-223	$anth_2$	14 $anth^+$;	112 $anth^-$	11	$anth$-446-223
(4)	487 → $anth_2^{-}$-223	$anth_2$	29 $anth^+$;	118 $anth^-$	20	$anth$-487-223
(5)	34 → $anth_2^{-}$-487	$anth_2$	86 $anth^+$;	368 $anth^-$	19	$anth$-34-487
(6)	46 → $anth_2^{-}$-487	$anth_2$	27 $anth^+$;	28 $anth^-$	49	$anth$-487-46
(7)	446 → $anth_2^{-}$-487	$anth_2$	7 $anth^+$;	31 $anth^-$	23	$anth$-446-487
(8)	46 → $anth_2^{-}$-78	$anth_2$	52 $anth^+$;	220 $anth^-$	19	$anth$-46-78
(9)	169 → $anth_2^{-}$-78	$anth_2$	22 $anth^+$;	24 $anth^-$	48	$anth$-78-169
(10)	187 → $anth_1^{-}$-23	$anth_1$	9 $anth^-$;	42 $anth^+$	83	$anth$-23-187
(11)	187 → $anth_1^{-}$-46	$anth_1$	14 $anth^-$;	116 $anth^+$	89	$anth$-46-187
(12)	46 V_1^R→ $anth_1^{-}$-58 V_1^S	$anth_1$; V_1	22 $anth^-$ V_1^R;	1 $anth^+$ V_1^R	4	$anth$-46-58-V_1
(13)	58 V_1^R→ $anth_1^{-}$-46 V_1^S	$anth_1$; V_1	10 $anth^+$ V_1^S;	1 $anth^+$ V_1^R; 73 4 $anth^-$ V_1^s		$anth$-46-58-V_1
(14)	169 V_1^R→ $anth_1^{-}$-46 V_1^S	$anth_1$; V_1	6 $anth^+$ V_1^S;	1 $anth^-$ V_1^S	90	$anth$-46-169-V_1
(15)	446 → $anth_1^{-}$-46	$anth_1$	81 $anth^-$; 20 $anth^-$-446-46;	22 $anth^+$ 65 $anth^+$ 446$^-$-46	21 76	$anth$-446-46

Order of markers: $anth$-A34 .... (A446, etc.) - - - V_1R.
* In crosses with the outside marker $anth_2$ the percentage of $anth^+$ recombinants is approximately 20% if the order is $\dfrac{+\qquad x}{anth^-\quad y}$ and approximately 50% if the order of x and y is reversed. With the marker $anth_1$ different values are obtained but the order of x and y relative to $anth$ can be clearly established. The explanation for the different values obtained with the two outside markers is not known.

Primary Structure Studies.—Amino acid substitutions have been detected in primary structure studies with each of the 16 A mutants.[6, 7, 14, 17, 18] The substitutions observed and the peptides in which they are present are shown in Figure 2. The conclusions from the genetics studies are also included in the figure (i.e., order of alterations and approximation of recombination distances between alterations). It is apparent that mutants with alterations extremely close to one another in the A gene have amino acid substitutions close to one another in the A protein. Primary structure studies with the A protein[17, 18] have established the linear sequence

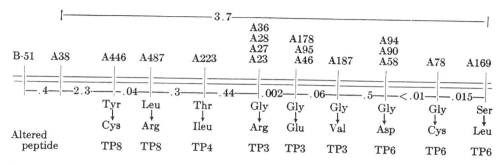

Fig. 2.—Amino acid substitutions in the A proteins of various mutants.[6],[7],[14],[17],[18] The A58, A78, A90, A94, and A169 substitutions will be described in detail elsewhere.[18]

of peptides TP-11, TP-8, TP-4, TP-18, TP-3, and TP-6, constituting a 75-residue segment of the A protein. This sequence and the sequence of the amino acids of most of these peptides are presented in Figure 3. This segment accounts for approximately one fourth of the residues in the A protein and is not at the amino or car-

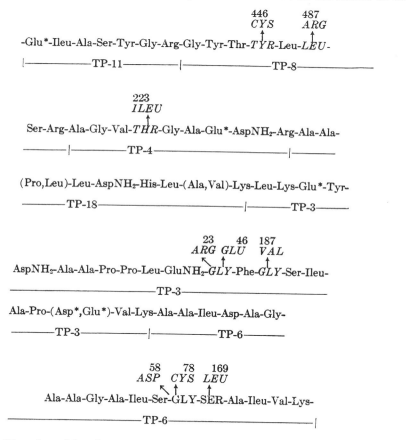

Fig. 3.—Peptide and partial amino acid sequence of a segment of the A protein. The positions of amino acid substitutions in the A proteins of the various mutants are indicated. Based on the studies by Carlton and Yanofsky[17] and Guest and Yanofsky.[18] (* = not known whether present as acid or amide.)

boxyl end of the protein. The positions of the amino acid replacements in the A proteins of the various mutants are also shown. It is clear that the positions of the amino acid replacements in the segment of the A protein are in the same relative order as the order of the mutationally altered sites of the corresponding mutants in the A gene. These findings convincingly demonstrate a colinear relationship between gene structure and protein structure.

The relationship between the map and residue distances observed is also of interest and can be seen most clearly from the representative values summarized in Table 3. Although the map distance/residue distance ratio varies between 0.01 and 0.05, in most cases this value is approximately 0.02. It would appear, therefore, that distances on the genetic map are representative of distances between amino acid residues in the corresponding protein.

TABLE 3
RELATIONSHIP BETWEEN MAP DISTANCES AND RESIDUE DISTANCES

Mutant pair	Map distance	Amino acid residue distance	$\dfrac{\text{Map distance}}{\text{Residue distance}}$
A58-A78	<0.01	0	—
A46-A23	0.002	0	—
A58-A169	0.01	1	0.01
A78-A169	0.015	1	0.015
A46-A187	0.08	2	0.04
A23-A187	0.04	2	0.02
A446-A487	0.04	2	0.02
A487-A223	0.3	6	0.05
A446-A223	0.19	8	0.02
A46-A58	0.44	23	0.02
A46-A78	0.52	23	0.02
A23-A58	0.78	23	0.03
A23-A78	0.85	23	0.04
A46-A169	0.48	24	0.02
A23-A169	0.8	24	0.03
A223-A46	0.44	28	0.02
A487-A46	0.48	34	0.01
A446-A46	0.28	36	0 01
A78-A223	0.61	51	0.01
A169-A487	0.75	58	0.01

Summary.—The concept of colinearity of gene structure and protein structure was examined with 16 mutants with alterations in one segment of the A gene and the A protein of tryptophan synthetase. The results obtained demonstrate a linear correspondence between the two structures and further show that genetic recombination values are representative of the distances between amino acid residues in the corresponding protein.

Note added in proof: Dr. Francis Crick has recently forwarded a manuscript which deals with a study of colinearity in another system (Sarabhai *et al., Nature,* in press).

The authors are indebted to Virginia Horn for performing the genetic analyses described in this paper. They are also indebted to Deanna Thorpe, Patricia Schroeder, Donald Vinicor, and John Horan for their excellent technical assistance.

* This investigation was supported by grants from the National Science Foundation and the U.S. Public Health Service.

† Present address: B. C. Carlton, Department of Biology, Yale University, New Haven, Connecticut; D. R. Helinski, Department of Biology, Princeton University, Princeton, New Jersey; U. Henning, Max-Planck Institut für Zellchemie, Munich, Germany.

‡ Guinness Research Fellow, on leave from Department of Biochemistry, Oxford, England.

[1] Beadle, G. W., and E. L. Tatum, these PROCEEDINGS, **27**, 499 (1941).

[2] Sanger, F., and H. Tuppy, *Biochem. J.*, **49**, 481 (1951).

[3] Watson, J. D., and F. H. C. Crick, in *Viruses*, Cold Spring Harbor Symposia on Quantitative Biology, vol. 18 (1953), p. 123.

[4] Crick, F. H. C., *Symp. Soc. Exptl. Biol.*, **12**, 138 (1958).

[5] Yanofsky, C., D. R. Helinski, and B. D. Maling, in *Cellular Regulatory Mechanisms*, Cold Spring Harbor Symposia on Quantitative Biology, vol. 26 (1961), p. 11.

[6] Helinski, D. R., and C. Yanofsky, these PROCEEDINGS, **48**, 173 (1962).

[7] Henning, U., and C. Yanofsky, these PROCEEDINGS, **48**, 183 (1962).

[8] *Ibid.*, 1497 (1962).

[9] Helinski, D. R., and C. Yanofsky, *Biochim. Biophys. Acta*, **63**, 10 (1962).

[10] Carlton, B. C., and C. Yanofsky, *J. Biol. Chem.*, **238**, 2390 (1963).

[11] Kaiser, A. D., *J. Mol. Biol.*, **4**, 275 (1962).

[12] Yanofsky, C., in *Synthesis and Structure of Macromolecules*, Cold Spring Harbor Symposia on Quantitative Biology, vol. 28 (1963), in press.

[13] Yanofsky, C., in *The Bacteria*, ed. I. C. Gunsalus and R. Y. Stanier (Academic Press), vol. 5, in press.

[14] Helinski, D. R., and C. Yanofsky, *J. Biol. Chem.*, **238**, 1043 (1963).

[15] Somerville, R., and C. Yanofsky, unpublished observations.

[16] Drexler, H., and J. R. Christensen, *Virology*, **13**, 31 (1961).

[17] Carlton, B. C., and C. Yanofsky, in preparation.

[18] Guest, J., and C. Yanofsky, in preparation.

[19] Lennox, E. S., *Virology*, **1**, 190 (1955).

[20] Yanofsky, C., and E. S. Lennox, *Virology*, **8**, 425 (1959).

[21] On the basis of preliminary two-point mapping data with mutant A2, it earlier had tentatively been concluded that the alterations in mutants A58, A78, A90, and A94 were to the left of the alterations in A17 and A46.[5] The more extensive data presented in Figure 1 and the deletion and three-point data indicate that the correct order is as shown in Figure 1.

[22] Yanofsky, C., in *Synthesis and Structure of Macromolecules*, Cold Spring Harbor Symposia on Quantitative Biology, vol. 28 (1963), in press.

THE COMPLETE AMINO ACID SEQUENCE OF THE TRYPTOPHAN SYNTHETASE A PROTEIN (α SUBUNIT) AND ITS COLINEAR RELATIONSHIP WITH THE GENETIC MAP OF THE A GENE*

BY CHARLES YANOFSKY, GABRIEL R. DRAPEAU,† JOHN R. GUEST,† AND BRUCE C. CARLTON†

DEPARTMENT OF BIOLOGICAL SCIENCES, STANFORD UNIVERSITY

Communicated December 19, 1966

Previously we presented findings demonstrating the existence of a colinear relationship between gene structure (the genetic map) and protein structure.[1,2] The altered tryptophan synthetase A proteins produced by a group of mutants of *Escherichia coli* were examined for primary structure changes and each mutant protein was found to differ from the wild-type protein by a change of a single amino acid.[3-6] The colinear relationship was then established by showing that the order of the positions at which these single amino acid changes occurred in the A protein was the same as the order of the respective mutational sites on the genetic map.[1,2] It was also observed in these investigations that distance on the genetic map was reasonably representative of distance in the polypeptide chain.[1,2] Colinearity of gene structure and protein structure has also been convincingly demonstrated as a result of studies with very different experimental material, viz., nonsense mutants[7,8] and frame-shift mutants.[9]

Recently the complete sequence of the 267 amino acid residues in the tryptophan synthetase A protein has been determined,[10] and consequently the relationship between the genetic map of the A gene and the changes in mutationally altered A proteins can be reconsidered in terms of the primary structure of the entire protein. The purpose of this report is to re-examine this relationship.

Results and Discussion.—The amino acid sequence of the A protein, shown in Figure 1, was determined by analysis of fragments derived by treating the protein with various proteolytic enzymes or with cyanogen bromide. The details of the sequence studies will be described elsewhere.[10]

The genetic map of the relevant mutationally altered sites in the A gene is presented in Figure 2. Mutants A38 and A96 do not produce detectable altered A proteins; the map locations of their alterations are included because these sites presently represent the most distant sites in the A gene. The A38 site maps closest to the B gene and to the·operator end of the tryptophan operon.[11,12] The other altered sites on the map are the genetic locations of mutational alterations which lead to the single amino acid substitutions in the A protein that are indicated. Of these altered sites, the positions of the A3 and A33 changes are closest to the A38 site. As can be seen in Figure 2, the A3 and A33 mutational alterations lead to amino acid changes at position 48 in the protein, the closest position to the amino-terminal end of the protein at which amino acid changes are observed. The other mutationally altered sites shown correspond to amino acid changes at positions in the protein which are in the same relative order as the respective altered sites on the genetic map, as reported previously.[1,2] The A169 mutational alteration is closest to the A96 site on the genetic map and the affected position in the protein is

Met-Gln-Arg-Tyr-Glu-Ser-Leu-Phe-Ala-Gln-Leu-Lys-Glu-Arg-Lys-Glu-Gly-Ala-Phe-Val-
                                              10   20

Pro-Phe-Val-Thr-Leu-Gly-Asp-Pro-Gly-Ile-Glu-Gln-Ser-Leu-Lys-Ile-Asp-Thr-Leu-Ile-
                                  30   40

Glu-Ala-Gly-Ala-Asp-Ala-Leu-<u>Glu</u>-Leu-Gly-Ile-Pro-Phe-Ser-Asp-Pro-Leu-Ala-Asp-Gly-
                                      50   60

Pro-Thr-Ile-Gln-Asn-Ala-Thr-Leu-Arg-Ala-Phe-Ala-Ala-Gly-Val-Thr-Pro-Ala-Gln-Cys-
                          70   80

Phe-Glu-Met-Leu-Ala-Leu-Ile-Arg-Gln-Lys-His-Pro-Thr-Ile-Pro-Ile-Gly-Leu-Leu-Met-
                              90   100

Tyr-Ala-Asn-Leu-Val-Phe-Asn-Lys-Gly-Ile-Asp-Glu-Phe-Tyr-Ala-Gln-Cys-Glu-Lys-Val-
                              110   120

Gly-Val-Asp-Ser-Val-Leu-Val-Ala-Asp-Val-Pro-Val-Gln-Glu-Ser-Ala-Pro-Phe-Arg-Gln-
                              130   140

Ala-Ala-Leu-Arg-His-Asn-Val-Ala-Pro-Ile-Phe-Ile-Cys-Pro-Pro-Asn-Ala-Asp-Asp-Asp-
                              150   160

Leu-Leu-Arg-Gln-Ile-Ala-Ser-Tyr-Gly-Arg-Gly-Tyr-Thr-<u>Tyr</u>-Leu-<u>Leu</u>-Ser-Arg-Ala-Gly-
                              170   180

Val-<u>Thr</u>-Gly-Ala-Glu-Asn-Arg-Ala-Ala-Leu-Pro-Leu-Asn-His-Leu-Val-Ala-Lys-Leu-Lys-
                      190   200

Glu-Tyr-Asn-Ala-Ala-Pro-Pro-Leu-Gln-<u>Gly</u>-Phe-<u>Gly</u>-Ile-Ser-Ala-Pro-Asp-Gln-Val-Lys-
                                  210   220

Ala-Ala-Ile-Asp-Ala-Gly-Ala-Ala-Gly-Ala-Ile-Ser-<u>Gly</u>-<u>Ser</u>-Ala-Ile-Val-Lys-Ile-Ile-
                              230   240

Glu-Gln-His-Asn-Ile-Glu-Pro-Glu-Lys-Met-Leu-Ala-Ala-Leu-Lys-Val-Phe-Val-Gln-Pro-
                              250   260

Met-Lys-Ala-Ala-Thr-Arg-Ser

FIG. 1.—Amino acid sequence of the tryptophan synthetase A protein of *E. coli.*[10] The under-lined residues are at the positions in the protein at which amino acid changes have occurred in mutants.

only 33 residues from the carboxy-terminus of the protein. Thus, for almost the entire length of the map of the A gene, the existing evidence indicates that it is colinear with the structure of the A protein. The established orientation of the A protein relative to the A gene and consequently to the operator region of the operon, in conjunction with the orientation of the operon on the *E. coli* chromosome,[14] permits the orientation of the amino acid sequence of the A protein relative to the chromosome. The nucleotide sequence corresponding to the A protein runs in a clockwise direction from the region specifying the COOH-terminal end; i.e., the order is *thr-gal*—A gene region specifying the COOH-terminal end of the A protein—A gene region specifying the amino-terminal end of the A protein—*his*.

A representative value relating distance on the genetic map to distance in the polypeptide chain can be calculated by dividing the map distance separating the A3 and A169 sites by the number of amino acid residues in between the positions of the

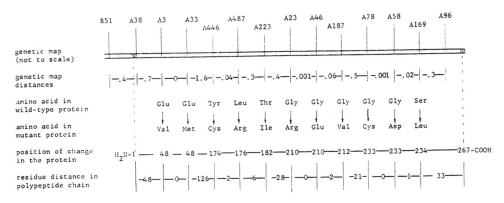

FIG. 2.—Genetic map of the A gene and the corresponding amino acid changes in the A protein. The positions of these changes in the amino acid sequence are also indicated. Mutants A3 and A33, and their amino acid replacements, will be described in detail elsewhere.[13]

corresponding amino acid changes. The value so obtained is about 0.015 map units per amino acid residue. Using this value we can estimate that the genetic map of the A gene should extend some 0.7 units to the left of the A3 site and about 0.5 units beyond the A169 site. This would give a total length of approximately 4.2 map units for the A gene, and would place the A38 site at or very near the beginning of the A gene.

The authors are pleased to acknowledge the assistance of Virginia Horn, Donald Vinicor, Deanna Thorpe, and George Pegelow at various stages of this investigation.

* These investigations were supported by grants from the U.S. Public Health Service and the National Science Foundation.

† Present addresses: G. R. D., Department of Microbiology, University of Montreal, Montreal, Quebec, Canada; J. R. G., Department of Microbiology, Sheffield University, Sheffield, England; B. C. C., Department of Biology, Yale University, New Haven, Connecticut.

[1] Yanofsky, C., in *Cold Spring Harbor Symposia on Quantitative Biology*, vol. 28 (1963), p. 296.

[2] Yanofsky, C., B. C. Carlton, J. R. Guest, D. R. Helinski, and U. Henning, these PROCEEDINGS, **51**, 266 (1964).

[3] Helinski, D. R., and C. Yanofsky, these PROCEEDINGS, **48**, 173 (1962).

[4] Henning, U., and C. Yanofsky, these PROCEEDINGS, **48**, 183 (1962).

[5] Guest, J. R., and C. Yanofsky, *J. Biol. Chem.*, **240**, 679 (1965).

[6] Carlton, B. C., and C. Yanofsky, *J. Biol. Chem.*, **240**, 690 (1965).

[7] Sarabhai, A. S., A. O. W. Stretton, S. Brenner and A. Bolle, *Nature*, **201**, 13 (1964).

[8] Fowler, A. V., and I. Zabin, *Science*, **154**, 1027 (1966).

[9] Streisinger, G., Y. Okada, J. Emrich, J. Newton, A. Tsugita, E. Terzaghi, and M. Inouye, in *Cold Spring Harbor Symposia on Quantitative Biology*, vol. 31, in press.

[10] Guest, J. R., B. C. Carlton, and C. Yanofsky, in preparation; Carlton, B. C., J. R. Guest, and C. Yanofsky, in preparation; Drapeau, G., and C. Yanofsky, in preparation; and Yanofsky, C., J. R. Guest, G. Drapeau, and B. C. Carlton, in preparation.

[11] Guest, J. R., and C. Yanofsky, *Nature*, **210**, 799 (1966).

[12] Matsushiro, A., K. Sato, S. Ito, S. Kida, and F. Imamoto, *J. Mol. Biol.*, **11**, 54 (1965).

[13] Drapeau, G., W. Brammar, and C. Yanofsky, in preparation.

[14] Signer, E. R., J. R. Beckwith, and S. Brenner, *J. Mol. Biol.*, **14**, 153 (1965).

CO-LINEARITY OF THE GENE WITH THE POLYPEPTIDE CHAIN

By Dr. A. S. SARABHAI, Dr. A. O. W. STRETTON and Dr. S. BRENNER

Medical Research Council, Laboratory of Molecular Biology, Cambridge

AND

Dr. A. BOLLÉ

Institut de Biologie Moleculaire, Université de Genève

THE 'sequence hypothesis' states that the amino-acid sequence of a protein is specified by the nucleotide sequence of the gene determining that protein[1]. It has always been assumed that a simple congruence exists between these two sequences such that the order of the codons in the gene is the same as the order of the corresponding amino-acids in the polypeptide chain. There is no direct evidence for this co-linearity; but it is known that mutations close together in the gene affect the same amino-acid in the protein[2]. In this article we show that a class of suppressible mutations affecting the head protein of bacteriophage T4D produce fragments of the polypeptide chain. This property allows us to prove that the gene is co-linear with the polypeptide chain. Dr. C. Yanofsky of Stanford University has informed us that he has shown co-linearity in an examination of the tryptophan synthetase of E. coli.

Suppressible Mutants

Benzer and Champe[3] have found that certain strains of Escherichia coli permit the growth of some phage mutants which do not grow on other strains. Bacteria with this permissive property are said to suppress the effect of the mutation. These suppressible mutants could be divided into different classes depending on the permissive host strain used. Benzer and Champe[4] later showed that one class of these mutants (subset 1), when grown in non-permissive bacteria, appeared to prevent the reading of the genetic message. They suggested that these mutants contained a nonsense codon and that permissive hosts could translate this codon into an amino-acid.

Mutations have been found in other genes in bacteria and bacteriophages which are suppressed by strains suppressing subset 1 mutants[5]. In particular, a large number of suppressible mutants of this class, called amber mutants, have been isolated in bacteriophage T4D (ref. 6). These are distributed throughout the genetic map of the phage, and it appears that any gene is susceptible to this type of mutation.

In order to characterize the molecular consequences of these suppressible mutations and their mechanism of suppression, we have examined amber mutants affecting the head protein of the bacteriophage. About 90 per cent of the protein of the phage particle is head protein[7], and Koch and Hershey[8] have shown that 60–70 per cent of the proteins synthesized late during infection are ultimately incorporated into mature phage particles. Thus more than one-half of the late protein synthesis of the infected cell is devoted to the manufacture of head protein; this has allowed us to detect fragments of the head polypeptide chain without any prior purification.

Isolation and Genetic Mapping of Amber Mutants

A previous examination of the amber mutants of bacteriophage T4D suggested that seven cistrons might be involved in the synthesis of the head protein[6]. We first proved that the cistron characterized by one of these (am B17) controlled the head protein. This was done by a special complementation test between am B17 and a known peptide difference[9] in the head protein.

Fourteen mutants, induced in phage T4D by base analogue mutagens (5-bromouracil, 2-aminopurine and hydroxylamine) were located in the head protein cistron by their failure to complement am B17 on the non-permissive strain (E. coli B). Some of these were shown to be recurrences by spot test crosses. In all, ten different sites were found, and one representative of each site was chosen. Double mutants were constructed by crossing two mutants and were tested by back-crossing progeny to the two parents. In most cases, the double mutants are less well suppressed by the permissive strain (E. coli CR63) than are the parents.

Standard crosses were carried out, and the frequency of wild-type recombinants was measured by plating on E. coli B. This was multiplied by 2 to give the recombination frequency. The results are summarized in

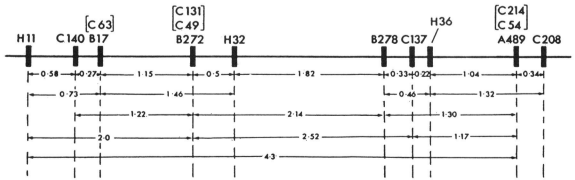

Fig. 1. Genetic map of amber mutants of the head protein gene. In many cases the recombination frequencies represent the average of several experiments and may differ slightly from those shown in Table 1

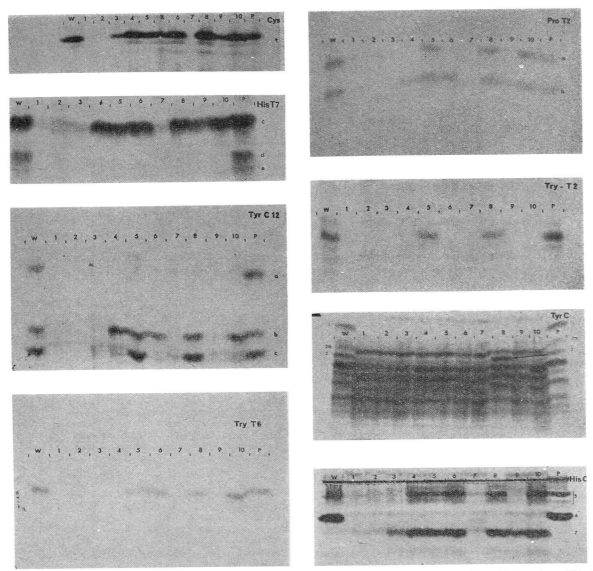

Fig. 2. Autoradiographs of tryptic (T) and chymotryptic (C) peptides, labelled with radioactive amino-acids. P is wild-type phage, W (and X in one case) is wild-type infected cells, 1–10 are *amber* mutant infected cells, as follows: 1 = H11, 2 = B17, 3 = B272, 4 = B278, 5 = A489, 6 = C137, 7 = C140, 8 = C208, 9 = H32, and 10 = H36.

10 ml. cultures of *E. coli* B (5 × 10³ cells/ml.) in minimal medium were infected with phage (multiplicity = 5) and, 5 min later, superinfected to produce lysis inhibition. For labelling with sulphur-35 the minimal medium used contained no sulphur at the time of infection. 10 min after the initial infection, 5 μc. of carbon-14-labelled amino-acid, or 50 μc. of ³⁵SO₄⁻, was added. After 1–1·5 h protein synthesis was terminated by the addition of chloramphenicol (50 μg/ml.). The cells were removed by centrifugation, suspended in water, and heated at 100° C for 10 min. Lysozyme (50 μg/ml.), DNase (10 μg/ml.) and RNase (10 μg/ml.) were added, and, after digestion for 14 h at 37° C, the suspensions were dialysed against 2,500 volumes of distilled water for 18 h. Each preparation was made 1 per cent in ammonium bicarbonate and divided into two parts, one part was digested with chymotrypsin (10 μg/ml.), the other with trypsin (10 μg/ml.). After 14 h, digestion was stopped by the addition of acetic acid. For each radioactive amino-acid, all ten *amber* mutants and a wild-type were treated in parallel as described here. At the same time, labelled wild-type phage was prepared by allowing 20 ml. cultures of *T4D*-infected cells to assimilate radioactive amino-acid for 4 h. After lysis with chloroform, the phage was purified by differential centrifugation. Suspensions were heated, the released DNA digested with DNase, and the denatured ghosts removed by centrifugation. These were washed, suspended in 1 per cent ammonium bicarbonate, and proteolytic digestion and subsequent treatment carried out as described here.

The same amount of radioactivity of each digest was applied to Whatman 3 MM paper, and after high-voltage ionophoresis at *p*H 6·4 the peptide zones located by autoradiography. Selected zones were purified by ionophoresis at *p*H 3·6

Fig. 1 in the form of a genetic map of the region, showing relevant 2-factor recombination frequencies. The additivity of recombination frequencies is good, but we have not relied on this to establish the order of the mutants. This has been done by 3-factor crosses (Table 1), and although such crosses are complicated by high negative interference[10] they uniquely determine the genetic order shown in Fig. 1.

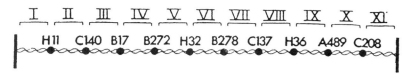

Head Protein Peptides in *Amber* Mutants

The proteins being synthesized in the phage-infected cells were labelled with radioactive amino-acids. The cells were then lysed, the nucleic acid removed and without further purification the mixture was digested with either trypsin or chymotrypsin. The peptides thus produced were characterized by high-voltage ionophoresis on paper, their position being located by autoradiography. Labelled proteins from purified wild-type phage were also examined in the same way. The technical details are given in the legend to Fig. 2.

The peptides characteristic of the head protein of the phage can easily be recognized in digests of cells infected with the wild-type phage. This shows that the contamination introduced by other proteins synthesized in the infected cells is not serious. We have only scored peptides present in digests of both wild-type phage and the wild-type infected cells. The first general result is that while some of the peptides of the head protein are present in cells infected with a given *amber* mutant, others are absent, and the pattern differs for each *amber* mutant. Hence peptides can be classified as to whether or not they are included in the polypeptide synthesized by an *amber* mutant.

For example, in Fig. 2 it can be seen that the Cys peptide is clearly absent in cells infected with the mutants H11, C140 and B17 but is present in all other cases. This suggests that the mutants produce fragments of the head polypeptide chain such that some of the fragments include the Cys peptide while others do not. The peptide His T7c is synthesized in cells infected with H32, B278, C137, H36, A489 and C208 but not in cells infected with H11, C140, B17 and B272. This peptide would therefore be absent in the fragments made by the last four mutants. These two peptides distinguish the fragment made by B272 from the other fragments, since only in this case is the Cys peptide present and the His T7c peptide absent. By extension of the experimental data it should be possible to characterize each fragment uniquely in this way. Some 96 tryptic and chymotryptic peptides, detected by separate labelling experiments with ^{14}C-tyrosine, phenylalanine, histidine, tryptophan, proline and arginine, and [35]SO$_4$-- (methionine + cysteine), have been scored, and examples are given in Fig. 2.

The number of peptides found in any one mutant is a measure of the length of the fragment produced. It is therefore possible to arrange the fragments in order of increasing size: each fragment should include all the peptides present in smaller fragments, together with extra ones. The difference between two fragments defines a segment of the polypeptide chain, and the arrangement of the fragments by increasing size orders these segments. If the gene and the polypeptide chain are co-linear, then the order of the polypeptide segments should be identical with the order of the segments into which the genetic map is divided by the mutants.

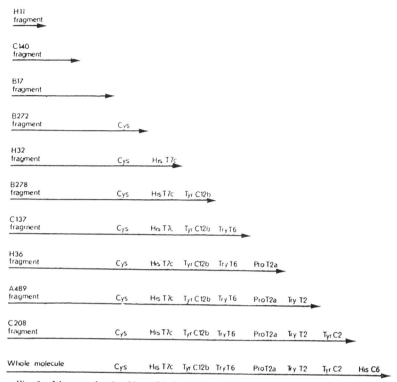

Fig. 3. Diagram showing hierarchical ordering of the fragments and the correlation of the segments with the genetic map. The peptides are those shown in Fig. 2

The hierarchical order of the peptides is shown in Table 2 and in Fig. 3. No peptides scored as head protein peptides have been found to distinguish H11, C140 and B17 from each other. Thus only nine of the eleven segments can be defined. However, we note that since peptides defining segment I are present in all *amber* mutants, there is no internal evidence that they are peptides of the head protein. This difficulty could be resolved by extensive purification, but until this is carried out we have chosen to leave segment I out of account. The order deduced from the fragments is therefore: (H11, C140, B17) B272, H32, B278, C137, H36, A489, C208 with eight segments uniquely defined. The order is the same as the genetic order (compare Fig. 1) and hence to a high degree of confidence these experiments show that the two structures are co-linear.

No exception to this order has been found for peptides which are present in the wild-type phage and absent from at least one *amber* mutant. However, peptides are found in some *amber* mutants which are not present in the wild-type phage. We might expect such peptides for two reasons:

(1) The point of termination of a fragment may cut a wild-type peptide, and thus produce a new peptide which occurs in that *amber* mutant only. We appear to have found an example of this in one case.

(2) Some wild-type peptides never show on the paper because they form part of the insoluble 'core'. However, when fragments of the protein are digested such peptides may become soluble, either because they have become accessible to the proteolytic enzyme or because the region of the protein which co-precipitated them is now absent.

129

Table 1. ORDERING OF MUTANTS BY 3-FACTOR CROSSES

E. coli CR63, at a concentration of 2×10^4 cells/ml. in buffer, was infected with a mixture of the parental phages, each at a multiplicity of 5. After 8 min at 37° C to allow adsorption, the complexes were diluted 1 : 200 into tryptone broth and lysed with chloroform after 1 h at 37° C. Appropriate dilutions were plated by preadsorption on *E. coli* CR63 to measure total progeny yield and on *E. coli* B to measure wild-type recombinants

Cross	Recombination (per cent)	Order deduced					
B17 × H11	0·80						
B17 × H11 + B278	0·14	H11		B17		B278	
B278 × A489	1·30						
B278 × B17 + A489	0·34		B17		B278		A489
B272 × B278	2·20						
B272 × H11 + B278	0·32	H11		B272		B278	
B272 × B17	1·30						
B272 × B17 + A489	0·24		B17	B272			A489
C140 × B17	0·27						
C140 × H11 + B17	0·04						
C140 × B17 + B272	0·20	H11	C140	B17	B272		
H32 × B272	0·5						
H32 × B17 + B272	0·36						
H32 × B272 + B278	0·05		B17	B272	H32	B278	
C137 × B278	0·33						
C137 × B272 + B278	0·28						
C137 × B278 + A489	0·06						
H36 × B278	0·46						
H36 × B272 + B278	0·40						
H36 × B278 + A489	0·06		B272	B278	(C137	H36)	A489
H36 × C137	0·22						
H36 × C137 + A489	0·05						
C137 × H36 + A489	0·20				C137	H36	A489
C208 × A489	0·34						
C208 × B17	4·0						
C208 × B17 + A489	0·33						
C208 × B278 + A489	0·29		B17		B278	A489	C208
Order:		H11 C140 B17 B272 H32 B278 C137 H36 A489 C208					

Table 2. DISTRIBUTION OF PEPTIDES IN AMBER-INFECTED CELLS

Segment	H11	C140	B17	B272	H32	B278	C137	H36	A489	C208	Wild	Chymotryptic	Tryptic	Example (see Fig. 2)
I	+	+	+	−	−	−	−	+	−	−	+	13	11	—
II	−	+	+	−	−	−	+	+	+	−	+	0	0	—
III	−	−	+	−	−	+	+	+	−	−	+	0	0	—
IV	−	−	−	+	−	+	+	−	−	−	+	8	3	Cys
V	−	−	−	−	+	+	+	+	+	−	+	0	1	His T7c
VI	−	−	−	−	+	+	+	+	−	−	+	10	2	Tyr C12b
VII	−	−	−	−	−	+	+	+	+	−	+	2	2	Try T6
VIII	−	−	−	−	−	+	+	+	−	+	+	5	1	Pro T2a
IX	−	−	−	−	−	−	+	+	−	+	+	8	11	Try T2
X	−	−	−	−	−	−	−	+	+	+	+	1	1	Tyr C2
XI	−	−	−	−	−	−	−	−	+	+	+	7	10	His C6

Note: The number of peptides found in a segment is not a measure of the length of the segment, since in some cases the same peptide sequence may be scored more than once, either because of being labelled by two different amino-acids, or because of partial enzymatic degradation products.

Such peptides can also be assigned to segments. We have been able to score ten of these peptides. They agree with the order of segments previously found and in addition there is one peptide which defines segment II; that is, it is present in all *amber* mutants except H11.

The remarkable property of the *amber* mutations of the head protein cistron and, by inference, of all other suppressible mutations of this class, is that they lead to the synthesis of a fragment of the polypeptide chain. Qualitatively, fragments appear to be produced in amounts comparable with that of the wild-type protein. Although we do not as yet have any direct evidence, it is likely that the fragments include the N-terminus of the head protein, since proteins are synthesized sequentially from their N-terminal ends[11]. If this is so, then the nonsense codon introduced by the *amber* mutation results in polypeptide chain termination, without permitting re-initiation of synthesis beyond that point. The exact details of this mechanism are unknown, as indeed is the mechanism of suppression itself. However, it is hoped that further analysis of the *amber* mutants should throw more light on these problems.

To summarize: we have shown that suppressible *amber* mutations of the head protein lead to the production of fragments of the polypeptide chain. Analysis of the fragments allows us to define eight segments of the polypeptide chain which are in the same order as the segments defined on a genetic map. We conclude that the gene is co-linear with the polypeptide chain.

We thank Dr. R. H. Epstein for providing some of the mutants used, and Dr. F. H. C. Crick for interesting discussions. We also thank Mrs. R. M. Fishpool, Miss M. I. Wigby and Mr. P. A. Wright for their assistance.

[1] Crick, F. H. C., *Symp. Soc. Exp. Biol.*, 12, 138 (1958).

[2] Henning, U., and Yanofsky, C., *Proc. U.S. Nat. Acad. Sci.*, 48, 1497 (1962). See also Rothman, F., *Cold Spring Harbor Symp. Quant. Biol.*, 26, 23 (1961).

[3] Benzer, S., and Champe, S. P., *Proc. U.S. Nat. Acad. Sci.*, 47, 1025 (1961).

[4] Benzer, S., and Champe, S. P., *Proc. U.S. Nat. Acad. Sci.*, 47, 1114 (1962).

[5] Campbell, A., *Virology*, 14, 22 (1961). Garen, A., and Siddiqi, O., *Proc. U.S. Nat. Acad. Sci.*, 48, 1121 (1962).

[6] Epstein, R. H., Bolle, A., Steinberg, C. M., Kellenberger, E., Boy de la Tour, E., Chevalley, R., Edgar, R. S., Susman, M., Denhardt, G. H., and Lielausis, A., *Cold Spring Harbor Symp. Quant. Biol.*, 28 (in the press).

[7] Van Vunakis, H., Baker, W. H., and Brown, R. K., *Virology*, 5, 327 (1958). Brenner, S., Streisinger, G., Horne, R. W., Champe, S. P., Barnett, L., Benzer, S., and Rees, M. W., *J. Mol. Biol.*, 1, 281 (1959).

[8] Koch, G., and Hershey, A. D., *J. Mol. Biol.*, 1, 260 (1959).

[9] Brenner, S., and Barnett, L., *Brookhaven Symp. Biol.*, 12, 86 (1959).

[10] Chase, M., and Doermann, A. H., *Genetics*, 43, 332 (1958).

[11] Dintzis, H. M., *Proc. U.S. Nat. Acad. Sci.*, 47, 247 (1961). Goldstein, A. and Brown, B. J., *Biochim. Biophys. Acta*, 53, 438 (1961).

Unit 4 / The Search for Colinearity

Yanofsky et al. 1964

1. How were the A-protein mutants isolated?

2. Describe the life cycle of P1 phage and show how generalized transduction occurs.

3. How were the recombination experiments performed? How were recombination distances determined?

4. Show how the mutations were ordered. Explain Table 2 on page 120.

Yanofsky et al. 1967

5. Using the genetic code (see page 63), show the nucleotide changes that produced the altered proteins indicated in Figure 2 on page 126.

6. What is odd about mutant A33 in Figure 2 on page 126? Do you have any ideas about how it was created?

Sarabhai et al. 1964

7. What gene were the authors working with and what is its protein product?

8. How did the authors order mutations? Explain Table 1 on page 130.

9. Explain what complementation tests with T4 phage are.

10. How did the authors produce the patterns shown in Figure 3 on page 129?

11. Can you imagine any alternative explanations for the phenomenon described by the authors other than that they were seeing fragments produced during termination of polypeptide synthesis?

Unit 5

Conjugation and Genetic Recombination

After the discovery of gene transfer and recombination in *Escherichia coli* by Lederberg and Tatum (see Introduction to Section I and references therein), numerous studies were carried out to elucidate the mechanisms involved in bacterial mating and recombination. Many of the observations were confusing, and different speculative theories were put forth. For example, Joshua Lederberg proposed that the fusion of two bacterial cells led to chromosome mixing and the segregation and loss of certain genetic markers. It was the work of William Hayes that provided a clear understanding of the phenomenon of bacterial conjugation. His model, described in 1952, showed how conjugation involved the ordered transfer of parts of the chromosome from a donor cell to a recipient cell and that the partners were not equal. His subsequent work on the properties of the F factor and that of Elie Wollman and François Jacob are nicely summarized in the 1956 review article reprinted here.

William Hayes

Bill Hayes studied in Ireland before serving as a British medical officer in India during World War II. He initiated experiments in bacterial research there, despite meager facilities—incubators had to be cooled by fans! Hayes received an appointment to Trinity College in Dublin after the war's end and later in London became a senior lecturer at the Royal Postgraduate Medical School, where he pursued his interest in bacterial genetics.

Hayes, aided by strains from Luca Cavalli-Sforza, opened the door to understanding bacterial conjugation with his presentation at a meeting in Pallanza, Italy, in September 1952, in which he relayed his recently published results on the unidirectional transfer of genetic markers from a donor to a recipient. This ran counter to the Lederberg model of cellular fusion. Wollman and Jacob, at the Pasteur Institute, soon began a collaboration with Hayes, studying the kinetics of gene transfer.

Hayes also discovered the fertility factor F, as did Lederberg independently, which confers the ability to act as a donor in conjugational crosses. In 1953, Hayes reported the discovery of an Hfr strain, still termed Hfr Hayes. (Cavalli had previously reported a strain with similar properties.)

Hayes headed a British MRC Microbial Genetics Research Unit founded for him in 1957 at Hammersmith Hospital and attracted young students and postdoctoral researchers, including Jon Beckwith, Paul Broda, Simon Silver, Jim Shapiro, John Scaife, Roy Clowes, Neville Symonds, Julian Gross, and many others, who later became important figures in the field.

In addition to his research accomplishments and his encouragement of scientific careers, Bill Hayes wrote the most important bacterial genetics book of its era, *The Genetics of Bacteria and Their Viruses*,

which was published in 1964, with a second edition in 1968. This volume has been the definitive work in the field ever since.

Hayes' unit moved to Edinburgh in 1968, where he helped establish a molecular biology department in the university. The MRC unit flourished in Edinburgh as it had in London. In 1974, Bill Hayes accepted the Chair of Genetics at the Australian National University in Canberra, officially retiring in 1978. Thereafter, he spent a year at Caltech with Max Delbrück and then returned to the Australian National University. Suffering from progressive Alzheimer's disease, he died in January 1994 of coronary failure.

Bill Hayes left behind not only a legacy of scientific writings, but also a contingent of students who have attempted to maintain his standards in teaching bacterial genetics to yet another generation of students.

NATURE OF GENE TRANSFER IN BACTERIAL CONJUGATION

Let's begin by examining some of the milestones in the unraveling of the mystery of gene transfer, which are discussed in detail in the paper by Wollman, Jacob, and Hayes reprinted here on pages 138–159.

The Transfer of Chromosomal Markers Is Unidirectional

A key starting point was the demonstration in 1952 by Hayes that the genetic transfer of chromosomal markers was unidirectional, with one strain serving as the donor and the second as the recipient. To prove this, Hayes used the bactericidal agent streptomycin, which lyses growing cells after a period of time. He carried out variations of the standard cross used to demonstrate recombination in bacteria, employing two strains with different auxotrophic markers. However, he had isolated a streptomycin-resistant derivative of one of the strains (W677), whereas the other strain (58-161) remained sensitive to the antibiotic. It was expected that addition of streptomycin would prevent the emergence of recombinants from a cross of these two strains. Surprisingly, the presence of streptomycin at different times of plating did not affect the number of recombinants observed!

Another variation of the experiment involved treating the 58-161 strain with streptomycin and then washing it out before mixing the treated strain with the streptomycin-resistant version of W677. Again, recombinants occurred. However, when the situation was reversed and a streptomycin-resistant derivative of 58-161 was used with a sensitive version of W677, then pretreatment of W677 with streptomycin blocked the formation of recombinants.

Hayes interpreted these experiments as indicating that the streptomycin-treated (and no longer viable) cells of 58-161 served mainly as a passive carrier for genetic elements. After they are expelled, the cell is no longer needed. The only explanation for the inability of the streptomycin-treated W677 cells to yield recombinants was that W677 was the acceptor and needed to incorporate the genetic element genes from 58-161 into its own genome. Thus, Hayes correctly understood at this point that both partners in bacterial conjugation did not contribute equally. Although he speculated in his 1952 paper that the one way genetic transfer might be mediated was through a virus, later work amended that interpretation. (The 1952 paper is reprinted here as Supplemental Reading, see page 160.)

The F Factor

Subsequent work by Hayes in 1953 (also reprinted here as Supplemental Reading, see pages 161–177) showed that the ability to transfer genetic markers was conveyed by a cytoplasmic element, termed F, which itself could be transferred from one strain to another. He had first found that the donor strain 58-161 had lost the ability to donate genetic markers after storage, although it could now function efficiently as a recipient. Hayes adopted the terms F+ and F− (first used by the Lederbergs) to describe the donor and recipient states, respectively. He observed that:

1. Growing an F− strain together with an F+ strain resulted in the conversion of as much as 75% of the F− cells to the F+ state.

2. None of the other markers in the F− strain had changed, meaning that recombination apparently had not occurred.

3. The F+ agent could be transmitted in series from one F− strain to another and could not be filtered.

4. In crosses where recombinants arose, most of the unselected marker characters had the phenotype of the F− parent.

These findings led Hayes to propose "that F+ is a non-lytic infectious agent, harboured by F+ cells and absent from F− cells, which becomes effectively associated with a part (or parts) of the chromosomes of a smaller proportion of the cells it inhabits. The F+ agent thus acts as a gene carrier in the transfer of genetic material from F+ to F− cells."

Hfr Strains

The isolation of Hfr strains, which resulted in a *h*igh *f*requency of *r*ecombinants when used as donors in conjugation experiments, was a major breakthrough. These strains gave a 20,000-fold increase in recombinant frequency for some markers but not for others. It was recognized that Hfr strains resulted from the integration of the F factor into the chromosome. In a population of cells carrying F in the cytoplasm, only a small percentage of cells have F integrated into the chromosome. These cells can transfer chromosomal markers at a high rate, although the population of cells as a whole transfers only at a low rate. When these rare Hfr cells in the population are isolated, clones derived from them generate a population of cells in which each member is an Hfr, thus leading to a very high frequency of transfer for the entire population.

Zygotic Induction

Zygotic induction allowed the immediate detection of transfer of the λ prophage during Hfr × F⁻ crosses. Work by Wollman and Jacob is pictured in Figure 2 on page 142, which shows the effects of zygotic induction. In Figure 2A, they score the inheritance of *T⁺L⁺* and *Gal⁺* in a cross where both the donor Hfr and the recipient have λ (or both do not have λ). Figure 2B shows the same cross, but this time the donor carries λ and the recipient does not. Here, the entry of λ into the recipient, which does not have λ immunity in the cytoplasm, results in phage production and lysis, which can be measured by scoring the titer of λ infectious centers (IC). The diagram below depicts the concept involved in comparing the two crosses. Note that the inheritance of markers that enter before λ, such as *T⁺L⁺*, is virtually unaffected, whereas the inheritance of markers entering very close to or after λ, for example *Gal⁺* in Figure 2B, is severely reduced.

This is because the random breakage of the entering chromosome results in many mating pairs that have received the *T⁺L⁺* markers but not the λ prophage.

Interrupted Mating

The kinetics of mating could be studied by interrupting Hfr × F⁻ crosses at different intervals and monitoring the number of resulting recombinants. This demonstrated that Hfr strains transfer from a fixed point, or origin, in a single direction. Figure 4 on page 144 presents a good picture of the time sequence of transfer of different characters.

Gradient of Marker Transfer

Because only a fragment of the donor chromosome is transferred during conjugation, a gradient of transfer of markers results, with markers donated earliest being the most frequently transferred and inherited.

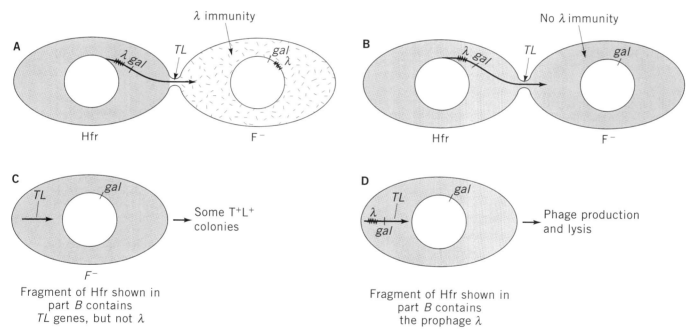

Zygotic Induction When an Hfr carrying λ is crossed with a recipient that also carries λ, as in *A* above, the immunity in the cytoplasm prevents the incoming λ from going into the virulent cycle and lysing the bacteria. The inheritance of all markers is essentially the same as for a cross in which the Hfr does not carry λ. However, if the recipient does not carry λ, then when the Hfr depicted in *A* transfers the λ prophage, it will enter a cell without immunity, as in *B*. This is similar to infection of a sensitive, nonimmune cell by λ, and phage production and lysis of the bacteria results. During such crosses, donor chromosomes break off, leaving fragments of the chromosome in the recipient. If such a fragment carries markers donated before λ, but not λ itself, such as depicted in *C*, then the inheritance of these earlier markers is as normal. However, if the markers are very tightly linked to λ, such as *gal*, or enter after λ, then the situation shown in *D* prevails. Here, each cell that receives the *gal* gene also receives λ. These cells lyse, and virtually no Gal⁺ recombinants are recovered.

Conjugation and Genetic Recombination in *Escherichia coli* K-12

E.-L. Wollman, F. Jacob and W. Hayes

Institut Pasteur, Paris, France and The Postgraduate Medical School of London, London, England

"... it is also a good rule not to put overmuch confidence in the observational results that are put forward *until they have been confirmed by theory.*"

—Sir Arthur Eddington, "New Pathways in Science."

It is just ten years since the first report of genetic recombination in *Escherichia coli* K-12 was made to this Symposium by Lederberg and Tatum. Since then a great deal of work has been devoted to study of the genetics of recombination but, in general, such studies have tended to stress the complexity of the genetic process by bringing to light the anomalies inherent in it rather than to elucidate its mechanism. We do not intend to summarise all this work here since it has already been covered by recent reviews (Lederberg, Lederberg, Zinder and Lively, 1951; Hayes, 1953b; Lederberg, 1955; Cavalli and Jinks, 1956) but only to recall such facts as are strictly relevant to our present purpose. The object of this paper is to define the different steps involved in the processes of conjugation and recombination in *E. coli* K-12, to offer a systematic analysis of what we know about these steps, based primarily on work done in the authors' laboratories in Paris and London, and from this analysis to construct a simple model of the mating process. While we are very conscious that many gaps remain in our knowledge of this subject and that alternative hypotheses may be advanced to explain some of the experimental results, we propose to adopt a rather didactic approach in order to clarify the presentation of this work.

I. The Nature of the System

Since Lederberg and Tatum's discovery, most of the work on genetic recombination in *E. coli* has involved crosses in which the observed frequency of appearance of recombinants was only 10^{-5} to 10^{-6} that of the parental population. This necessitated the use of the original experimental design of Lederberg and Tatum in which a mixture of two doubly auxotrophic mutants of the K-12 strain of *E. coli* was plated on a minimal medium on which only prototrophs, that is, bacteria in which the nutritional deficiencies of both parents had been eliminated by recombination, could grow. Under such conditions it is impossible directly to investigate events occurring at the cellular level, while interpretation of genetic results is difficult since selection permits the recovery of only one class of the progeny of numerous mating events.

When the auxotrophic parental strains were further marked by a series of differential characters which were not selected by the minimal medium used for prototroph detection, these unselected markers were found to have undergone reassortment among the prototrophic progeny of the cross. Analysis of such reassortments revealed linkage of many of the unselected markers to one another as well as to the nutritional selective markers, and four groups of clearly linked genes were revealed. However, although all the characters studied appeared to show some degree of interdependence in their inheritance, they could not be mapped on a single chromosome. Difficulties were even encountered in the analysis of recombination data between clearly linked genes, while the results of back-crosses between recombinants and parental strains frequently diverged grossly from those anticipated by genetical theory. It seemed likely that pure genetic analysis would lead only to increasing complication, rather than to clarification, of the picture and that further progress awaited the discovery of some fundamental aspect of the mating process which had not hitherto been taken into account.

A. One-Way Genetic Transfer and F Polarity

It was first demonstrated that the two parental strains of a fertile cross played different roles in mating. Although both strains were equally sensitive to streptomycin, treatment of one of them with this drug invariably resulted in sterility of the cross, whereas treatment of the other did not have this effect although the fertility of the cross was often greatly reduced. It therefore appeared that while the role of one parent was transient and independent of the capacity for further multiplication, the continued viability of the other parent was vital. The function of the first parent or gene donor was simply to fertilise the other parent or gene recipient, which thus became the zygote cell (Hayes, 1952a). In the light of subsequent work it is now believed that this differential effect was revealed because the bactericidal action of streptomycin was sufficiently slow to allow the donor population, or a moiety of it, to initiate and complete its fertilising function although further cell division was suppressed.

Another difference between the two strains is that irradiation of donor strains with small doses of ultraviolet light markedly enhances the fertility of crosses while similar irradiation of recipient strains does not (Hayes, 1952b).

This functional distinction between the two strains was independently confirmed, at the same time, by the observation that crosses between recipient strains were always sterile. Donor strains were called F⁺ (for fertility) and recipient strains F⁻ (Lederberg, Cavalli and Lederberg, 1952). It was further shown that F⁻ cells could be converted to F⁺ by contact with F⁺ cells, with an efficiency about 10⁵ times higher than that of recombination. The F⁺ character acquired in this way by an F⁻ cell is inheritable and very stable in cultures, but a chromosomal locus for it could not be determined (Lederberg et al., 1952; Cavalli, Lederberg and Lederberg, 1953; Hayes, 1953a, b).

B. Partial Transfer of Genetic Material

Comparison of the results of crosses of reciprocal F polarity between the same parental strains showed that the majority of the unselected markers present among recombinants were those of the F⁻ (recipient) bacteria, irrespective of the cross or of the selection employed. The hypothesis was therefore made (Hayes, 1953a) that only a part of the donor chromosome was transferred to the recipient cell to form an incomplete zygote. An alternative hypothesis, based on results obtained with diploid heterozygotes (Lederberg, 1949), was that a complete zygote was formed but that part of the genetic material, usually contributed by the donor cell, was subsequently eliminated after crossing-over (see Lederberg, 1955). Evidence strongly favouring the hypothesis of partial transfer will be presented later.

C. Hfr Systems

The usual frequency of recombinants arising from F⁺ × F⁻ crosses is about 10^{-5} to 10^{-6} of the parental population. Two mutant strains of the same F⁺ strain were independently isolated which showed a very much higher frequency of recombination in crosses with F⁻ strains. Such strains were called Hfr (high frequency of recombination). One of these strains (HfrC) was isolated after treatment of the parent F⁺ culture with nitrogen mustard (Cavalli, 1950); the other (HfrH) arose spontaneously (Hayes, 1953b). It is this latter strain, HfrH, or Hfr derivatives from it, which has predominantly been employed in the work to be described.

Hfr strains behave as typical donor strains but differ strikingly from F⁺ strains in several important respects:

1. When crossed with F⁻ strains under the conditions generally used throughout this work, the frequency of recombinants is about 2×10^4 times higher than in the equivalent F⁺ × F⁻ cross (Hayes, 1957).

2. Hfr behaviour is only manifest when selection is made for inheritance of an Hfr marker or markers (T^+L^+ or Lac^+) situated on a particular linkage group. Selection for markers on other linkage groups (M, B_1 or S, Mal) yields only a low frequency of recombinants (Lfr) comparable to that found in F⁺ × F⁻ crosses (Hayes, 1953b). Since only a single group of linked characters is therefore transmitted at high frequency to the recombinants, this system offers more dramatic evidence for the hypothesis, suggested by the results of F⁺ × F⁻ crosses, that only this group of characters is usually transferred from the Hfr to the F⁻ cell to form a partial zygote. The Hfr chromosome can thus provisionally be visualised (Fig. 1) as having a preferential region of rupture, such that only characters located on region A will be transferred at high frequency. It is evident that the terms "high" or "low" frequency of recombination have meaning only when the selective conditions of the cross are defined. As will be seen later, there are other conditions which can profoundly influence the productivity of a cross.

3. Hfr strains, unlike F⁺, do not convert F⁻ strains to either F⁺ or Hfr at high frequency, nor is the F⁺ character inherited by recombinants from Hfr × F⁻ crosses. Recombinants from such crosses are F⁻ when markers on region A (Fig. 1) are selected, but when markers on region B are selected they are either F⁻ or Hfr depending on the particular selection employed. Nevertheless Hfr strains can revert at a low rate to an F⁺ state indistinguishable from that of the parent F⁺ strain.

4. Irradiation of Hfr strains, unlike that of F⁺ strains, does not increase the frequency of recombinants when markers on region A are selected, but markedly enhances Hfr fertility at low frequency when selection is made for markers on region B.

The use of Hfr strains has provided proof of one-way transfer in this system. For example when exconjugants from visually observed pairs of Hfr and F⁻ cells are isolated with a micromanipulator and cultured, only the F⁻ partners yield recombinants (Lederberg, 1955). Furthermore, the discovery of zygotic induction, now to be recounted, offers not only independent proof of one-way transfer but also strong evidence in support of partial transfer as well.

$$\overbrace{\text{T L Az T}_1 \text{ Lac}_1 \text{ T}_6 \text{ Gal}}^{A} : \overbrace{\text{S Mal Xyl}_1 \text{ Mtl M B}_1}^{B}$$

FIGURE 1. The *E. coli* K-12 linkage group (after Cavalli and Jinks, 1956). Symbols refer to threonine (*T*), leucine (*L*), methionine (*M*) and thiamine (*B₁*) synthesis; resistance to sodium azide (*Az*), bacteriophage T1, bacteriophage T6, streptomycin (*S*); fermentation of lactose (*Lac*), galactose (*Gal*), maltose (*Mal*), xylose (*Xyl*) and mannitol (*Mtl*).

D. Zygotic Induction

The wild-type strain of *E. coli* K-12 and most of its derivatives are lysogenic for the temperate phage λ, but non-lysogenic strains have been isolated from it (E. Lederberg, 1951) and can be obtained at will. In crosses between lysogenic and non-lysogenic strains, lysogeny segregates and is linked to certain galactose markers (Lederberg and Lederberg, 1953; Wollman, 1953). Reciprocal crosses between lysogenic (*ly*+) and non-lysogenic (*ly*−) bacteria do not give symmetrical results, however, so far as inheritance of lysogeny is concerned (Wollman, 1953; Appleyard, 1954). In a cross between non-lysogenic HfrH and a lysogenic F− strain, lysogeny segregates among the recombinants and can thus be shown to occupy a genetic locus on the chromosome near to the *Gal* locus. Similarly when HfrH and F− parental strains, each of which is lysogenic for a different mutant of λ phage, are crossed, the two prophages segregate among recombinants in precisely the same way as did lysogeny and non-lysogeny in the previous cross, thus demonstrating that it is the prophage which is the genetic determinant of lysogeny (Wollman and Jacob, 1954, 1957).

On the other hand when the Hfr parent is characterised by lysogeny and the F− parent by non-lysogeny, the outcome of the cross is quite different, for lysogeny is no longer found to be inherited by any recombinant. Instead, the transfer of λ prophage is invariably followed by the *immediate* induction of its development within the fertilised F− cells with consequent lysis of the zygotes and liberation of λ phage. When the F− strain used is one which imposes a phenotypic modification on λ phage, this modification is found to characterise the liberated phage (Jacob and Wollman, 1954, 1956b). This is a clear example of the one-way transfer of genetic characters in Hfr × F− crosses.

Lambda prophage is therefore a genetic character whose *transfer to the F− cell is immediately expressed* by zygotic induction, before genetic recombination has taken place. The fact that some recombinants are formed in HfrH(*ly*)+ × F−(*ly*)− crosses but that these recombinants do not contain λ prophage, indicates that in these cases λ prophage has not been transferred to the F− recipient cells. This demonstrates that the genetic locus, λ prophage, at least, is not transferred to many zygotes which yield recombinants, that is that these zygotes are not complete. This method of approach to the problem of whether the partial inheritance of Hfr characters among recombinants is entirely due to partial transfer from donor to recipient cells will be amplified later in this paper.

E. The Presumptive Stages of Mating

Despite the restriction that only a limited group of Hfr genetic characters are inherited, the proportion of recombinants issuing from Hfr × F− crosses is sufficiently high to allow a quantitative study of the mating process. When Hfr and F− cells are mixed one can, *a priori*, distinguish the following presumptive stages of mating:

1. Conjugation. This stage is synonymous with that of zygote formation and includes the entire sequence of events from the first encounter between donor and recipient cells to the completion of genetic transfer. It can be divided into the following substages:

(a) *Collision.* This is obviously the essential first step and is a process determined by chance.

(b) *Effective contact.* This step follows collision and involves a specific attachment between a donor and a recipient cell which probably depends on the surface properties of the two cells.

(c) *Genetic transfer.* The genome, or part of the genome, of the donor cell is transferred to the recipient cell which thus becomes the zygote. When transfer is accomplished the donor cell has discharged its function and is no longer necessary.

2. Formation of recombinants. This process comprises two important steps:

(a) *Integration.* The process at the genetic level whereby the chromosome of the recombinant cell is evolved in the zygote from the chromosomal contributions of the two parents.

(b) *Expression of the recombinants.* This stage comprises *segregation* of the haploid recombinant cell from the zygote cell and the *phenotypic expression* of the new recombinant chromosome in the cell which inherits it.

Before presenting an experimental analysis of these stages by means of Hfr × F− crosses, we must first examine the methodology of such crosses and the kind of information which can be derived from them.

F. Methods of Approach to Hfr × F− Crosses

Until recently the occurrence of mating could be measured only by the formation of recombinants. Since recombinants are the end-products of the reaction between mating cells, so that their number and constitution can potentially be modified at any stage of the process, the analytical information which they can yield is limited. What is needed in analysis is to measure the different available expressions of recombination so that information concerning different stages of the process is obtained which can then be evaluated and equated. The phenomenon of zygotic induction answers this need by giving a direct indication of the extent of genetic transfer from the Hfr cells to the zygotes, since ultraviolet-inducible prophages, located on the chromosome segment transferred at high frequency by HfrH, are expressed immediately upon transfer to the recipient cell, *before* the formation of recombinants, by the liberation of phage. Thus comparison of the results of zygotic induction and of recombination from the same cross has yielded valuable information about the nature of both transfer and integration (Jacob and Wollman, 1955a; Wollman and Jacob, 1957).

Conditions of mating: For comparative quantitative studies, crosses are made under the following basic conditions. Exponentially growing cultures of the Hfr and F⁻ strains are mixed in liquid medium and aerated, the population density of one of the strains, usually the F⁻ recipient, generally being in 20-fold excess in order to increase the efficiency of specific collisions. The frequency of the effect to be measured is then expressed as a percentage of the number of minority parental cells initially present. Samples of the mixture are removed at suitable times, diluted to prevent further contacts, and plated either on a selective minimal medium if recombination is being studied or, in the case of zygotic induction, with a phage-sensitive indicator strain on nutrient agar. It is clear that lysogenic Hfr parental cells, if present, will interfere with results by themselves producing infectious centres if they are permitted to grow on the latter medium. Moreover, in many recombination experiments a prototrophic Hfr strain, capable of growth on minimal agar, was used. It is therefore necessary either to prevent further growth of the Hfr parent after plating, or to eliminate it from the mixture, once genetic transfer has been effected and it is no longer required. When the Hfr parent is streptomycin-sensitive and the F⁻ parent resistant, the simplest and most efficient way of inhibiting Hfr growth is to incorporate streptomycin in the agar on which the mixture is plated. As one might expect from the fact that streptomycin sensitivity from strain HfrH is never inherited among recombinants formed at high frequency, the use of streptomycin in this way has no effect on the outcome of the cross (Hayes, 1953b).

Elimination of Hfr cells is achieved by treating the undiluted mixture with a high-titre preparation of virulent phage T6 to which only the Hfr parent is susceptible. After subsequent dilution, the concentration of phage on the plate is not such as to affect the frequency of appearance of recombinants inheriting sensitivity to the phage from the Hfr parent: the use of anti-phage serum is, therefore, unnecessary. In most of the recombination experiments in which the phage technique was used, the Hfr strain was auxotrophic and streptomycin-resistant so that streptomycin was not added to the minimal agar (Hayes, 1957).

Expressions of mating. 1. Formation of recombinants. Selection of recombinants from an Hfr × F⁻ cross means that selection is made for inheritance by the F⁻ cells of characters derived from the Hfr donor cells (Hayes, 1953b). Accordingly, Hfr and F⁻ strains are chosen which differ in as many as possible of those markers which are

inherited at high frequency by the F⁻ cells (Fig. 1). The F⁻ recipient strain is marked by the minus alleles of those characters which can be used for selection, for example threonine⁻, leucine⁻, lactose⁻, galactose⁻ ($T^-L^-Lac^-Gal^-$), and is resistant to streptomycin (S^r). The Hfr strain has the wild alleles of these characters and is sensitive to streptomycin ($T^+L^+Lac^+Gal^+S^s$). In addition, the two strains can be made to differ in markers such as resistance or sensitivity to sodium azide (Az^r, Az^s) or to virulent phages ($T1^r$, $T1^s$) which are not usually used for selection. Thus by the use of suitable selective media one can select for different recombinant classes issuing from the same cross. For instance in a cross between Hfr·$T^+L^+Az^sT1^sLac_1^+Gal_b^+S^s$ and F⁻·$T^-L^-Az^r$-$T1^rLac_1^-Gal_b^-S^r$, $T^+L^+S^r$ or Gal^+S^r recombinants can be specifically selected and the inheritance of the other, unselected, markers among them studied. Two kinds of information can be obtained from such crosses:

(a) *The frequency of recombination:* the number of recombinants of any type (*e.g.*, $T^+L^+S^r$ or Gal^+S^r) per 100 initial Hfr cells.

(b) *The genetic constitution* of these recombinants, that is, the distribution among them of unselected Hfr markers.

2. Formation of infectious centres. What is looked for here is the proportion of lysogenic Hfr cells which, on mating with non-lysogenic F⁻ cells, transfer their prophage to the recipient F⁻ cells which thereby liberate phage as a result of zygotic induction. The cross is therefore made between Hfr$(ly)^+S^s$ and F⁻$(ly)^-S^r$ parental strains and the mixture plated for infectious centres with a streptomycin-resistant, phage-sensitive indicator strain, on streptomycin-agar. Results are expressed as the *frequency of induction* which is the number of infectious centres (plaques) per 100 initial Hfr cells.

In the following two sections the various stages of mating in Hfr × F⁻ crosses will be discussed in detail against the background of our present knowledge. Our immediate aim is not to offer a definitive answer to the many questions which can be posed about the problem but rather to report the facts as we know them in the light of our own experience. These facts relate mainly to the experimental definition of each stage and substage, and to the analysis of some of them in kinetic terms by means of the methods we have already outlined.

II. Conjugation in Hfr × F⁻ Crosses

Conjugation connotes the sequence of events from the initial collision to the completion of fertilisation of the F⁻ cell, that is up to the time at which further participation of the Hfr donor cell is no longer necessary.

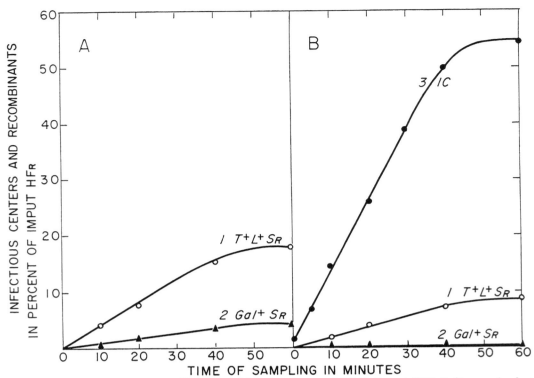

FIGURE 2. The kinetics of conjugation. Exponential broth cultures of HfrH S^s and P678 F^-S^r are mixed at time 0 (1 to 2.10^7 Hfr/ml and 2 to 5.10^8 F^-/ml) and aerated in broth. The differential characters of the two strains are: HfrH $S^sT^+L^+Az^sT1^sLac_1^+Gal_b^+$ (for symbols see Fig. 1) and: P678 $F^-S^rT^-L^-Az^rT1^rLac_1^-Gal_b^-$. At different intervals of time samples are immediately plated, either for recombinants on glucose minimal medium + streptomycin ($T^+L^+S^r$ recombinants, curves 1) and on galactose minimal medium + threonine (T), leucine (L), and streptomycin (Gal^+S^r recombinants, curves 2), or for infectious centers on nutrient agar + streptomycin resistant indicator bacteria for phage λ (curve 3). The numbers of recombinants or of infectious centers obtained are expressed as a percentage of the number of initial Hfr cells. 2 A, cross between HfrH S^s (λ)$^+$ and P678 F^-S^r (λ)$^+$, both lysogenic (λ)$^+$ for phage λ. 2 B cross between HfrH S^s (λ)$^+$ and P678 F^-S^r(λ)$^-$. (From Wollman and Jacob, 1957).

A. The Kinetics of Conjugation

1. Effective contacts. A standard cross is made between an Hfr·S^s and an F^-·S^r strain, both strains being either lysogenic or non-lysogenic. At intervals after mixing in broth, samples are removed, diluted and plated for recombinants. Selection is made for inheritance of either T^+L^+ or of Gal^+ from the Hfr parent, these being the most widely separated of the known selective markers on that part of the Hfr chromosome which is inherited at high frequency (Wollman and Jacob, 1955, 1957; Jacob and Wollman, 1954, 1956b). The results of such an experiment are shown in Figure 2A.

Figure 2B shows the results obtained under the same conditions when the Hfr strain is lysogenic for λ prophage and the F^- strain is non-lysogenic, so that zygotic induction occurs, the samples being plated for infectious centres as well as for $T^+L^+S^r$ and Gal^+S^r recombinants.

Inspection of Figures 2A and 2B shows: 1. In all cases the curves start from the origin (*i.e.* from the time of mixing) and then continue to rise until a plateau is reached, irrespective of whether the curves express the formation of recombinants or of infectious centres. 2. All the curves reach their plateaux at about the same time although the maximum levels represented by the plateaux vary from 58 per cent for frequency of induction (Fig. 2B) to 5 per cent for frequency of Gal^+S^r recombination (Fig. 2A). Since the slope of each curve, from its inception to its maximum, represents the same rate of increase (about 2.5 % per minute), all must be an expression of the same phenomenon, the conjugation of Hfr and F^- cells. The fact that all the plateaux are attained at about the same time indicates that at this time the maximum frequency of conjugation has been achieved.

2. Zygote formation. Crosses are made in the same manner as before but the samples, instead of being plated directly, are treated with a high titre preparation of phage T6, to which only the Hfr cells are susceptible, before dilution and plating (Hayes, 1957). The results of such an experiment are shown in Figure 6A (first curve).

The striking difference between curve 1 of Figure 2A and the first curve of Figure 6A is that whereas, in the first case, the number of T^+L^+ recombinants begins to rise from the time of mixing, when the samples are treated with phage there is a lag of eight minutes before recombinants begin to appear. This difference is explained in the following way. The curves constructed from untreated samples represent the kinetics of those contacts between Hfr and F⁻ cells which survive dilution and plating and can therefore continue through the succeeding steps leading to formation of recombinants or infectious centres on the plate; they thus express the *kinetics of the formation of effective contacts*. On the other hand, the curves constructed from samples treated with phage indicate the rate of development of mating pairs in which the markers T^+L^+ have already been transferred from donor to recipient cell at the time of treatment, so that the Hfr cell is no longer needed to form T^+L^+ recombinants: that is, the *kinetics of zygote formation*. From this two inerences can be drawn:

1. Effective contacts are formed very quickly, since the kinetic curve arises from the zero point of the time axis.
2. Transfer of the markers T^+L^+ from the Hfr to the F⁻ parent occupies about eight minutes from the time of contact.

B. Genetic Transfer

1. The kinetics of transfer. In an attempt to distinguish actual genetic transfer from conjugation as a whole, samples removed at intervals after mixing the Hfr and F⁻ cells were either plated directly as before, or subjected to violent agitation in a Waring blendor before dilution and plating in order to separate bacteria in the act of conjugation (Wollman and Jacob, 1955, 1957). Treatment in a blendor affects neither the viability of bacterial cells (Anderson, 1949) or recombinants, nor the ability of phage-infected cells

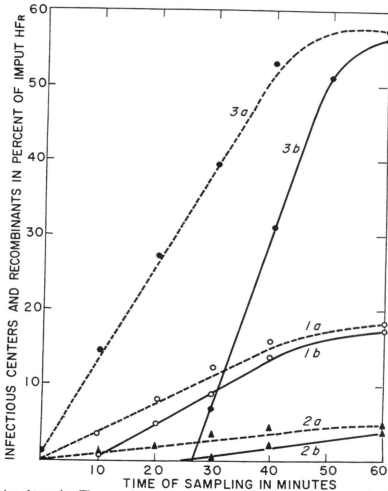

FIGURE 3. The kinetics of transfer. The experiments are the same as illustrated on Figure 2. At different time intervals samples of the mating mixtures are either plated directly on indicator media (dotted lines) or treated for 2 minutes in a Waring blendor and then immediately plated (solid lines). Curves 1 and 2 refer to the kinetics of formation of $T^+L^+S^r$ recombinants (curves 1 a and 1 b) and of Gal^+S^r recombinants (curves 2 a and 2 b) in a cross between Hfr(λ)⁺ × F⁻(λ)⁺. Curves 3 a and 3 b represent the kinetics of formation of infectious centers in a cross between Hfr(λ)⁺ × F⁻(λ)⁻. (From Wollman and Jacob, 1957).

to form plaques (Hershey and Chase, 1952). The results of two experiments of this kind are given in Figure 3. Curves 1a and 2a represent the kinetics of the formation of T^+L^+ and Gal^+ recombinants respectively in an Hfr × F⁻ cross in which both parents are lysogenic for λ phage, samples being diluted and plated without treatment. Curves 1b and 2b are derived from equivalent samples after treatment in the blendor. Similarly, curves 3a and 3b express the formation of infectious centres, without treatment and after treatment respectively, in an Hfr × F⁻ cross in which the Hfr parent is lysogenic for λ phage and the F⁻ parent non-lysogenic.

It will be seen that while the curves obtained from the untreated samples all arise from the origin and reach a plateau at about 50 minutes, as in Figure 2A and 2B, the corresponding curves obtained after treatment do *not* pass through the origin but nevertheless reach the same plateaux at about the same time. Moreover the times at which the various genetic markers appear to enter the zygote vary widely. For instance, T^+L^+ recombinants begin to appear at about nine minutes, as after phage treatment, while the appearance of Gal^+ recombinants and λ infectious centres

is delayed until 25 minutes. Since the time of appearance of markers widely separated on the chromosome, such as T^+L^+ on the one hand and Gal_b^+ on the other, is very different whereas closely linked markers like Gal_b and λ prophage appear at the same time despite the great disparity in their mode of expression, the conclusion is inescapable that *there exists a definite relationship between the time at which a given marker is transferred from the Hfr to the F⁻ cell and the location of that marker on the Hfr chromosome.*

2. Transfer as an oriented process. If this point of view is correct, then the frequency distribution among T^+L^+ recombinants of markers situated between TL and Gal_b on the Hfr chromosome should vary widely according to the time after mixing at which samples are treated in the blendor. T^+L^+ recombinants from untreated samples (Figure 3, curve 1a) and from treated samples (Figure 3, curve 1b) were therefore analysed for inheritance of unselected markers as a function of the time of sampling. The genetic constitution of T^+L^+ recombinants derived from untreated samples is constant irrespective of the time of sampling and, therefore, of the proportion of the population that have formed effective contacts.

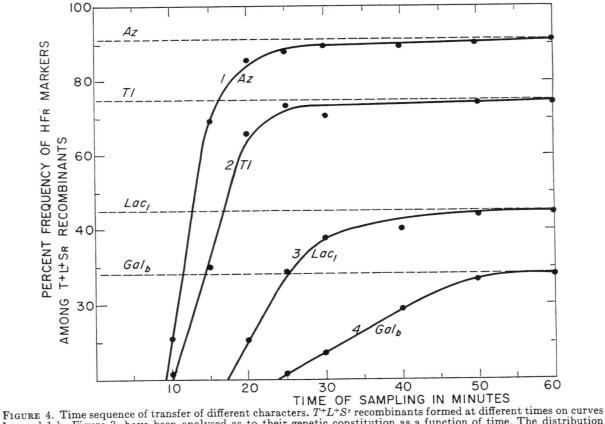

FIGURE 4. Time sequence of transfer of different characters. $T^+L^+S^r$ recombinants formed at different times on curves 1 a and 1 b, Figure 3, have been analysed as to their genetic constitution as a function of time. The distribution among $T^+L^+S^r$ recombinants of characters originating from the Hfr donor is represented as a percentage of the $T^+L^+S^r$ recombinants arising from the same sample. In dotted lines: from untreated samples. In solid lines: from treated samples. (From Wollman and Jacob, 1954 and 1957).

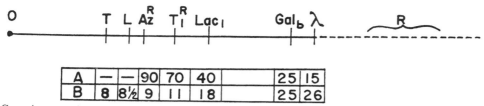

FIGURE 5. Genetic map of the OR chromosomal segment of Hfr H. The location of the different characters as measured in HfrH × P678 F⁻ crosses by A: the percentage of $T^+L^+S^r$ recombinants which have inherited the different Hfr alleles; B: the time at which individual Hfr characters start penetrating into the F⁻ recipient cells in a Waring blendor experiment. (From Wollman and Jacob, 1957).

As can be seen from the table and Figure 4, the percentage of various Hfr markers found among $T^+L^+S^r$ recombinants is approximately: Az^s 90 per cent, $T1^s$ 75 per cent, Lac^+ 45 per cent and Gal_b^+ 28 per cent. On the contrary, the frequency of inheritance of these same markers among $T^+L^+S^r$ recombinants stemming from the *treated* samples varies in a striking way according to the time of sampling, as the curves in Figure 4 show. The time at which any given character begins to appear among T^+L^+ recombinants is directly related to its distance from TL on the chromosome map (Fig. 5), the further the distance the greater being the delay in its appearance. Once a character begins to be found among T^+L^+ recombinants, the frequency of its inheritance increases rapidly as a function of time until its normal level is attained. Thus Az first appears at about nine minutes, $T1$ at ten minutes, Lac at 18 minutes and Gal at 25 minutes. At 50 minutes after mixing, all the markers transferred from the Hfr to the F⁻ cell have reached their normal frequency of inheritance. It is therefore clear that the Hfr chromosome penetrates the F⁻ cell in a specifically orientated way. The extremity, O (for "origin") enters first, to be followed by T^+L^+ eight to nine minutes later, and then by the other markers in the order of their arrangement on the chromosome and at intervals of time proportional to the distance between them until, at about 35 minutes after contact, the whole segment $O—R$ has been transferred (Fig. 5). The effect of treatment in the blendor thus seems to cut this chromosome segment during transfer and thus to determine the length of segment which enters the zygote and the markers which will be available for subsequent incorporation into recombinants (Wollman and Jacob, 1955, 1957).

Two kinds of evidence indicate that the agitation intervenes in *transfer* rather than in subsequent stages:

1. The very closely linked markers Gal_b and λ prophage appear at about the same time (25 minutes) after mixing despite the fact that transfer of prophage to the zygote is expressed immediately after transfer while the Gal_b marker is involved in the process of recombination.

2. Results similar to those obtained with the blendor are given by treatment of samples from a mating mixture with virulent phage to which only the Hfr cells are susceptible (see Fig. 6). Destruction of the Hfr parent in this way allows an analysis of events occurring solely within the F⁻ cells which are unaffected by the phage (Hayes, 1957).

C. Physiology of Conjugation

1. Nutritional requirements. Zygote formation does not occur at a significant rate if parental cultures grown aerobically in broth are washed and mixed in buffer. This is especially the case if the parental suspensions are starved by aeration in buffer before mixing. Addition to the buffer of both glucose and sodium aspartate, but neither alone, allows zygote formation to proceed at a rate comparable to that found in broth. Krebs cycle dicarboxylic acids and glutamic acid, but no other dicarboxylic or amino acids, can replace aspartic acid in promoting the formation of zygotes while such metabolic inhibitors as fluoracetic acid, malonic acid, and cyanide, as well as 2:4 dinitrophenol (DNP), inhibit the process. Zygote formation does not occur in buffer + glucose + sodium aspartate under anaerobic conditions. It thus appears that energy liberated by the Krebs cycle is required (Fisher, 1957a). Moreover, differential starvation experiments show that only the Hfr parent requires energy, the F⁻ cells playing an entirely passive part until the completion of genetic transfer.

For what purposes do the Hfr cells require their energy? If a series of identical mixtures of Hfr and F⁻ cells, previously grown aerobically in broth, are made under anaerobic conditions and, at different intervals after mixing, oxygen is then admitted to each mixture in turn, it is found that, in each case, zygote formation (*i.e.*, transfer of T^+L^+ from the Hfr to the F⁻ cells) begins at eight minutes after the commencement of oxygenation and then progresses at precisely the same rate *irrespective of the duration of the preceding anaerobiosis*. This shows that, under anaerobic conditions, nothing happens which affects the efficiency of subsequent conjugation although the probability of chance contacts is the same as in the presence of oxygen. Thus the establishment of effective contacts between parental cells is an energy-requiring act performed by the donor cells (Fisher, 1957b).

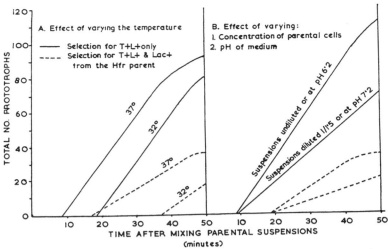

FIGURE 6. The kinetics of zygote formation, using phage T6 to eliminate the Hfr parental cells. Cultures of HfrH M⁻T6ˢ and F⁻TLB₁⁻T6ʳ were washed, resuspended in buffer + glucose + sodium aspartate at the appropriate temperature, mixed and aerated at the same temperature. At intervals samples were treated with phage T6, diluted and plated on: a. minimal agar + B₁ + glucose (selection for inheritance of T^+L^+ only from the Hfr parent); b. minimal agar + B₁ + lactose (selection for inheritance of T^+L^+ and Lac^+). A shows the effect of varying the temperature at which zygote formation occurs. B shows the effect of varying the concentration of the parental cells or the pH of the medium. (From Hayes, 1957, J. Gen. Microbiol., in press).

The kinetics of genetic transfer, as demonstrated by the use of the Waring blendor, can be reproduced with great precision by arresting the transfer of the chromosome with DNP and then killing the Hfr cells with virulent phage. The use of DNP alone does not kill the parental cells so that transfer is resumed when the effective concentration of the drug is reduced by dilution. Similarly, if an Hfr × F⁻ mixture at 37°, in which chromosome transfer is proceeding, is diluted to prevent further contacts at about 20 minutes after mixing and then rapidly cooled to 4°, analysis of subsequent samples reveals no change in the inheritance of the Hfr marker Lac^+ among T^+L^+ recombinants, showing that chromosome transfer has been arrested. When, however, the diluted mixture is warmed again to 37°, the inheritance of Lac^+, which had only begun to enter at the time of cooling, immediately commences to rise again at its initial rate until its normal frequency is attained. Since the formation of new contacts was prevented by dilution, the secondary increase in Lac^+ inheritance among T^+L^+ recombinants must have been due to subsequent entry of this locus into cells which had previously acquired T^+L^+. Such experiments not only confirm the continuity of chromosomal movement into the F⁻ cell but show that energy is required throughout the period of chromosome transfer. However, energy is not needed to hold mating cells together once effective contacts have been established (Fisher, 1957b).

2. The effect of temperature. As might be expected from the fact that the Hfr cells require energy for chromosomal transfer, the efficiency of zygote formation falls rapidly as the temperature

diverges from the optimal at 37°. Thus at 44° the number of F⁻ cells which have received the T^+L^+ markers from the Hfr parent in a given time is only 25 per cent, and at 25° only 6 per cent that at 37° (Hayes, 1956). Figure 6A shows what happens when the kinetics of chromosome transfer are studied in identical Hfr × F⁻ crosses in buffer + glucose + sodium aspartate, at 37° and at 32°. The reduction of temperature will lower the overall capacity of the Hfr cells to produce energy by carbohydrate oxidation. At 37° the T^+L^+ markers (continuous line) begin to enter the F⁻ cells at eight minutes and the marker Lac^+ (interrupted line) at 17 minutes after mixing, so that transfer from *TL* to *Lac* occupies nine minutes at this temperature. At 32°, on the other hand, T^+L^+ enters at 18 minutes and Lac^+ at 38 minutes so that transfer of the same piece of chromosome takes 20 minutes, that is about twice as long, at the lower temperature. It has been mentioned that since the curve expressing the kinetics of formation of effective contacts commences at zero time, effective contacts must be made very quickly so that it may be assumed that transfer of the O——*TL* segment occupies virtually the whole of the lag period preceding entry of T^+L^+ into the F⁻ cell. Thus at 37°, transfer of O——*TL* takes eight minutes and of O——*TL*——*Lac* 17 minutes, while at 32° transfer of these same segments takes 18 and 38 minutes respectively. The proportionality between these times strongly suggests that that part of the chromosome from *O* to *Lac*, at least, enters the F⁻ cell at a uniform rate which depends upon the available energy, so that measurement of the relative distances between chromosomal markers in terms of time is a valid procedure (Hayes, 1957).

The fact that the curves shown in Figure 6A are parallel, although displaced on the time axis, indicates that the only effect of this degree of limitation of energy, in so far as conjugation is concerned, is to slow the rate of chromosome transfer.

3. *The effect of population density.* When the frequency with which chance contacts occur in Hfr × F⁻ mixtures is altered by mixing the same number of cells of each parent in a different volume of fluid, the relationship of the resulting curves (shown in Fig. 6B) is quite different from that characterising alterations in temperature. It will be seen that the time of entry of various markers into the F⁻ cells remains unchanged when the population density of the parental cells is reduced; the curves arise from the same point on the time axis but their slopes differ (Hayes, 1957). This same effect of population density is observed whether the manifestation studied is formation of recombinants or infectious centres. It is thus evident that the *slope* of the curves expressing the rate of zygote formation is a simple function of the frequency of chance contacts between Hfr and F⁻ cells, within a certain population range.

4. *The effect of pH.* The rate of zygote formation in buffer + glucose + sodium aspartate is doubled when the pH is reduced from 7.2 to 6.2. Since this effect is also apparent when the cross is made in unsupplemented buffer it must be unrelated to energy requirements, because, under these conditions, the Hfr cells are limited to their endogenous resources (Fisher, 1957b). The effect is not found, or is not marked, when crosses are made in broth. When the kinetics of chromosomal transfer are compared for identical Hfr × F⁻ crosses in buffer + glucose + sodium aspartate at pH 7.2 and at pH 6.2, the same result is obtained as when the population density is varied, as Figure 6B demonstrates (Hayes, 1957). The effect of lowering the pH must therefore be ascribed to physical action on the cell surfaces which facilitates the intimacy of chance contacts so that a higher proportion of such contacts can become effective in a given time. This is in keeping with the surface differences, probably attributable to differences of charge, between F⁺ and F⁻ cells which have previously been described (Maccacaro, 1955).

A difference between the surface antigenic properties of donor and recipient strains is suggested by the results of preliminary experiments by L. and S. Le Minor at the Pasteur Institute.

D. The Frequency of Conjugation

When Hfr cells are mixed in broth at 37° with an excess of F⁻ cells, what proportion of the Hfr cells have conjugated at about 50 minutes after mixing, when the curves defining the kinetics of effective contact formation have reached their plateaux (Fig. 2)? If one were to examine only one expression of conjugation, such as the frequency of T^+L^+ recombinants, no absolute answer could be given to this question since the proportion of zygotes which do not yield recombinants of this class is not known. Since the frequency of T^+L^+ recombinants in Hfr (λ)⁺ × F⁻ (λ)⁺ crosses is about 20 per cent of the Hfr cells initially present, it could only be asserted that not less than 20 per cent of the Hfr cells must have conjugated. By correlating the frequency of recombination with that of zygotic induction, however, it can be estimated that approximately 100 per cent of the Hfr population conjugate (Jacob and Wollman, 1955a; Wollman and Jacob, 1957).

As has been said, in the cross Hfr (λ)⁺ × F⁻ (λ)⁺, 20 per cent of the Hfr cells form zygotes which yield T^+L^+ recombinants (Fig. 2A). When the same Hfr (λ)⁺ strain is crossed under the same conditions with F⁻ (λ)⁻, about 50 per cent of the Hfr cells transmit λ prophage to the F⁻ cells with the result that about 50 per cent of the maximum number of possible zygotes is destroyed by zygotic induction. But, as reference to Figure 2B will show, this destruction of zygotes only reduces the frequency of T^+L^+ recombinants by a factor of 2, from 20 per cent to 10 per cent. If it is assumed that those zygotes which yield T^+L^+ recombinants in Hfr (λ)⁺ × F⁻ (λ)⁻ crosses did not inherit λ prophage, then since only half of the potential T^+L^+ recombinants are removed when 50 per cent of the total possible zygotes are destroyed, the total number of zygotes formed must account for 100 per cent of the Hfr cells present.

When Hfr × F⁻ cells are mixed together and the mixture examined at intervals under a light microscope, an increasing number of pairs is observed which remain in contact for long periods. Such pairs are particularly noticeable when the two parental strains differ morphologically as in the case of HfrH and F⁻ *E. coli* strain C (Lieb, Weigle and Kellenberger, 1955). Electron microphotographs obtained by Dr. T. F. Anderson (Anderson, Wollman and Jacob, 1957) are presented in Figure 7. The top picture shows conjugation between HfrH and the F⁻ strain P678 which has been used in most of our studies. HfrH has long flagella whereas P678 is covered with bristles. As an additional distinguishing feature, HfrH has had ultraviolet-killed λc phage adsorbed to its surface: P678 is resistant to this phage. The middle picture demonstrates conjugation between HfrH and *E. coli* C. In this case the two strains are so different in their morphology that additional labelling is not required. In both crosses the conjugating bacteria appear to be united by a cellular bridge.

E. The Evidence for Partial Genetic Transfer

The experiments reported above demonstrate that, by use of the blendor or the phage technique, it is possible to regulate at will the length of chromosome segment transferred from the Hfr to the F⁻ cell. The partial zygote thus formed is perfectly operative and recombinants will be formed in exactly the same fashion as when transfer is allowed to proceed normally. Interruption of the mating process at about 50 minutes after mixing when Gal_b, the last known biochemical marker on the O——R segment, has been transferred (Fig. 5), has no effect either on the number or on the genetic constitution of the recombinants formed.

It can be shown that in a normal cross, where only those characters situated on the O——R segment *appear* to be transferred from donor to recipient cells, the whole of this segment is not, in fact, transferred to every zygote (Jacob and Wollman, 1955a; Wollman and Jacob, 1957). As the leading locus, O, followed in order by the other loci, penetrates the F⁻ cell, spontaneous breakages may occur in certain cases. The occurrence of zygotic induction in certain crosses makes it possible to estimate some of these breakages. Penetration of λ prophage into a non-lysogenic recipient cell leads to destruction of the zygote. If λ prophage entered every zygote no recombinants would ever be formed: an Hfr (λ)⁺ × F⁻ (λ)⁻ cross would be sterile. This, however, is not the case since half the usual number of T^+L^+ recombinants (10 % instead of 20 %) is recovered while only about one half the number of possible zygotes are scored as infectious centres (see *The Frequency of Conjugation*, above). These results are readily interpretable in the light of the mechanism of transfer which has been described. About half the zygotes inherit the Hfr segment O——Gal——λ and are thus destroyed by zygotic induction. The other half receives a segment *shorter* than O——Gal and will not be destroyed, so that about 20 per cent of them will yield T^+L^+ recombinants. These T^+L^+ recombinants constitute a special group in so far as they are derived from zygotes which have been selected by acquiring a shorter normal piece of Hfr chromosome. Thus, if the theory is right, they should show a lower frequency of inheritance of those unselected markers least linked to TL than does the *whole* group of T^+L^+ recombinants from a cross in which zygotic induction does not occur (Wollman and Jacob, 1954, 1957). That this is indeed so can be seen by comparing the results of crosses 3 and 4 in the table.

In the case of zygotic induction (cross 4) the frequency among T^+L^+ recombinants of those markers located close to λ prophage is greatly reduced, the closer the linkage to λ the greater being the reduction. In particular, the marker Gal_b, which is most closely linked to λ, is almost absent as can also be inferred from the $T^+L^+:Gal^+$ ratios in the table. On the other hand there is no significant difference in the inheritance of unselected markers between crosses 3 and 4 (table) when Gal^+ is selected instead of T^+L^+, showing that if Gal^+ enters the zygote and the zygote

survives, the outcome of the cross is the same irrespective of the lysogenic relationships. As a matter of fact the orientated nature of chromosomal transfer from the Hfr to the F⁻ cell can be deduced directly from comparison of the data of Figures 2A and 2B and of the table. The blendor experiment is only a direct demonstration of its reality.

It can also be shown by the study of a series of inducible prophages (Jacob and Wollman, 1955a, 1956b) that the probability of chromosomal rupture increases rapidly as R is approached. All these prophages are located on the O——R segment between Gal_b and R. The frequency of zygotic induction which they evoke is a measure of the frequency of their transfer from Hfr(ly)⁺ to F⁻(ly)⁻. For the seven different prophages studied, this ranges from 65 per cent to 5 per cent. When this information is correlated with the order of arrangement of these prophages on the chromosome, established by genetic analysis of Hfr(ly)⁻ × F⁻(ly)⁺ crosses in which there is no zygotic induction, it is found that the further a prophage is located from Gal_b the lower is the frequency of prophage transfer. The relative positions of these prophages can also be assessed by the blender technique, their times of entry ranging from 25 to 33 minutes.

The point of rupture, R, beyond which no markers enter the F⁻ cell can formally be considered as genetically equivalent, although conceptually opposed, to the elimination locus, E, which Cavalli and Jinks (1956), working with F⁺ × F⁻ systems, have located at, or very close to, the λ locus.

III. The Formation of Recombinants

As a result of conjugation a zygote is formed. The experiments recounted in the previous sections indicate unambiguously that the mechanisms involved in bacterial conjugation are quite different from what is found in other organisms. The two main differences are the following:

1. Bacterial conjugation involves a one-way transfer of genetic material from a donor to a recipient strain.

2. This transfer is partial since only a piece of the Hfr chromosome of variable size is injected into the recipient cell. The resulting zygote is therefore a rather peculiar one for which the term *merozygote* has been proposed (Wollman and Jacob, 1957).

Once the merozygote is formed, a series of processes is initiated which ultimately result in the appearance of a recombinant bacterium. It is unlikely that these processes differ fundamentally from those which mediate the expression of other kinds of partial genetic transfer among bacteria, such as transformation and transduction. In all three cases a recombinant chromosome is evolved which is essentially that of the recipient parent

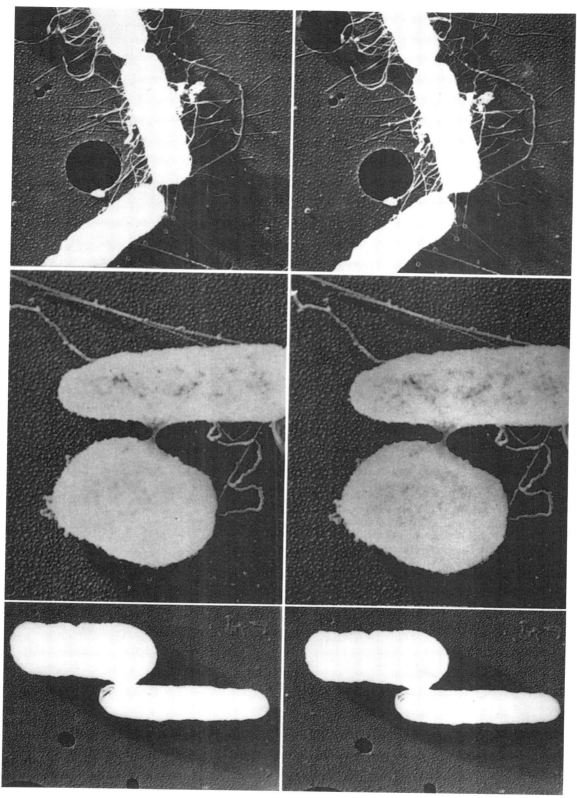

FIGURE 7.

TABLE 1. GENETIC ANALYSIS OF $T^+L^+S^r$ AND Gal^+Sr RECOMBINANTS OBTAINED IN VARIOUS CROSSES BETWEEN HfrH·S^s AND P678 F⁻·S^r

The strains used are, as in Figure 2, HfrH·$S^s T^+ L^+ Az^s T_1^s Lac_1^+ Gal_b^+$ and P678 F⁻$S^r T^- L^- Az^r T1^r Lac^- Gal_b^-$ (for symbols see Figure 1).

In column 1 are the different crosses reported (for details see text).

In column 2 the ratio of the numbers of $T^+L^+S^r$ to Gal^+S^r recombinants obtained.

In column 3 the distribution of the different alleles contributed by the Hfr donor to $T^+L^+S^r$ recombinants on one side, to Gal^+S^r recombinants on the other side, as a percentage of recombinants having inherited those characters. (From Wollman and Jacob, 1957.)

No.	Crosses	Ratio $T^+L^+S^r$/Gal^+S^r	Genetic constitution of recombinants									
			$T^+L^+S^r$					Gal^+S^r				
			Az	$T1$	Lac	Gal_b	(λ)	TL	Az	$T1$	Lac	(λ)
1	Hfr$(\lambda)^-$ × F⁻$(\lambda)^-$	4.2	91	72	48	27	—	83	78	79	81	—
2	Hfr$(\lambda)^-$ × F⁻$(\lambda)^+$	3.7	92	73	49	31	15	75	75	74	74	84
3	Hfr$(\lambda)^+$ × F⁻$(\lambda)^+$	4.2	90	70	47	29	14	80	78	78	82	82
4	Hfr$(\lambda)^+$ × F⁻$(\lambda)^-$	54	86	60	21	2.5	<0.1	82	79	78	74	1
5	Hfr$(\lambda)^-$U.V. × F⁻$(\lambda)^-$	4.5	50	32	9	1	—	17	24	29	41	—

save that a segment or segments of variable size have been replaced by homologous fragments of the donor genome. Once this integration has been achieved, the recombinant cell will emerge through segregation and phenotypic expression of the character or characters contributed by the donor parent.

We will now discuss in turn the available information relating to each of these steps.

A. Chromosomal Integration

There is at present little understanding of the processes which lead to the formation of a recombinant chromosome from the two parental constituents of a merozygote. Since there is insufficient evidence on which to base a definite hypothesis we will simply examine briefly the facts that are known to us.

1. Genetic patterns of integration. The segment of Hfr chromosome which enters the zygote may or may not be incorporated into a new recombinant chromosome. When, however, integration does occur, the asymmetry of the chromosomal contributions from the two parents may be ex-

pected to impose certain patterns of recombination.

(a) Efficiency of integration. It is possible to calculate the probability that a character derived from the donor parent will appear in recombinants, and this probability is found to be very constant for any given cross. It has already been shown, by comparison of the frequency of recombination with that of zygotic induction, that whereas the Hfr markers T^+L^+ are transferred to about 100 per cent of zygotes, only some 20 per cent of these zygotes yield T^+L^+ recombinants. Thus the efficiency of integration of these markers together is about $\frac{1}{5}$. Similarly we know that the Gal_b marker is transferred to about 60 per cent of zygotes but is only found among recombinants issuing from five per cent of the total zygotes, so that it is integrated with an efficiency of about $\frac{1}{12}$. There is thus rather a small probability of integration for an Hfr gene which has entered the zygote, and this probability varies with the location of the gene on the chromosome (Jacob and Wollman, 1955a; Wollman and Jacob, 1957).

(b) Polarity of integration. From the example

FIGURE 7. Stereoscopic electron micrographs showing connections between cells of opposite mating type. Top. Mixture of *E. coli* K-12 Hfr and K-12 F⁻/λ. Bacteriophage λc (which had previously been killed with ultraviolet light) was adsorbed on the Hfr cells to identify them. The F⁻/λ which failed to adsorb the phage could also be recognized by their numerous "bristles." In this view, a bridge 1500 Å wide can be seen connecting the end of a dividing F⁻ bacterium with the end of a Hfr bacterium to which bacteriophage particles are attached. EMG 5.IV.56 Bl, 2. × 21,000. Middle. Mixture of *E. coli* K-12 Hfr and *E. coli* CF⁻. At the top is a typically long and narrow K-12 Hfr cell connected by a 500 Å bridge to a typically short and plump CF⁻ cell. EMG 20.IV.56 C 3, 4. × 40,000. Bottom. Mixture of *E. coli* K-12 F⁺ and *E. coli* CF⁻. Here the plump CF⁻ cell at the top is in intimate contact with the narrow K-12 F⁺ cell in the lower part of the picture. EMG 3.V.56 D, 4, 5. ×20,000. It seems probable that during conjugation the genetic material from Hfr or F⁺ donor cells passes to F⁻ recipient cells through connections like the ones shown here.

Twenty minutes after mixing, specimens were fixed in the vapor over 2% OsO₄ and then dried by the critical point method to conserve the three dimensional structure of the specimen. Specimens were lightly shadowed with a An-Pd mixture and coated with 10 Å of carbon to reduce charging effects in the electron microscope. (From Anderson, Wollman and Jacob, 1957).

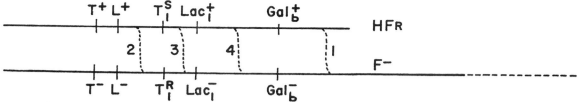

FIGURE 8. Patterns of integration among Gal^+S^r recombinants in a cross between HfrH S^s and P678 F$^-S^r$. Different classes observed, expressed as a percentage of total Gal^+S^r recombinants

Percent	Alleles from Hfr donor					Crossing over in region
68	T	L	T1	Lac	Gal	1
5			T1	Lac	Gal	1 and 2
1.7				Lac	Gal	1 and 3
11.6					Gal	1 and 4
7.5	TL			Lac	Gal	1, 2 and 3
2.5	TL		T1		Gal	1, 3 and 4
1.7	TL				Gal	1, 2 and 4
2			T1		Gal	1, 2, 3 and 4

just given it would appear that the closer a gene is situated to O the greater is its chance of integration. The O——R segment therefore seems to be characterized by an integration gradient as well as by a gradient of transfer. These two gradients are exemplified by comparison of the genetic constitution of $T^+L^+S^r$ and Gal^+S^r recombinants from crosses 1, 2 and 3 in the table. While the frequency of inheritance of markers among T^+L^+ recombinants is strongly dependent on their distances from O, in the Gal^+ recombinants all the unselected markers on the O——R region appear with the same high frequency (Jacob and Wollman, 1955a; Wollman and Jacob, 1957). Figure 8 illustrates the types of recombinants observed in the Gal^+S^r class, which have issued from zygotes which certainly received the whole of the O——Gal_b segment from the Hfr parent. It will be seen that almost 70 per cent have inherited the TL——Gal_b segment as a whole. If O represents the extremity of the chromosome, as seems reasonable, these recombinants would result from a single crossover in position 1. The other recombinants would be the result of two or more crossings-over. A certain amount of negative interference is therefore apparent.

The table clearly shows that the combined effect of a gradient of integration as well as of transfer is to facilitate mapping of the *order* of unselected markers when characters close to O (such as T^+L^+) are selected but to render this mapping almost impossible when selection is made for characters (such as Gal_b) situated close to R since, in this latter case, all the unselected markers appear with the same high frequency among the recombinants. The possibility of simple genetic mapping is precluded even following T^+L^+ selection, since the genetic outcome also depends in part on variations in transfer. Thus the only reliable way of mapping the *distances* between genes as well as their order is to measure their relative times of appearance in the F$^-$ cell by means of the blendor or some equivalent technique. The only assumption which must be made

to establish the validity of this mode of measurement is that injection of the Hfr chromosome into the F$^-$ cell proceeds at a constant speed, and evidence has been provided that this is so as long as the available energy is kept constant. The value of the blendor technique is well shown by attempts to map some of the inducible prophages located on the Gal——R segment. Whereas some of the phages situated farthest from Gal can scarcely be located by analysis of a cross between lysogenic and non-lysogenic cells, the blendor technique allows an accurate determination of the time at which the prophage enters the F$^-$ cell (Wollman and Jacob, 1957).

2. The process of integration. The following experiments may throw some light on how integration is accomplished.

(a) The effect of ultraviolet light on integration. If, in a non-lysogenic system, the Hfr parent is exposed to small doses of ultraviolet light prior to mating, the genetic constitution of recombinants is drastically modified although their total number is only slightly decreased, irrespective of whether T^+L^+ or Gal^+ is selected (Jacob and Wollman, 1955a and unpub.). The table (cross 5) reveals that the frequency with which unselected markers are found among both $T^+L^+S^r$ and Gal^+S^r recombinants is strikingly reduced by ultraviolet treatment. This means that radiation results in a loosening of the linkage observed among the markers lying between TL and Gal or, to put it another way, that the probability of a crossover occurring between two markers is increased. Since the frequency of recombination is decreased proportionately for both classes, it seems likely that radiation affects the processes of integration within the merozygote rather than genetic transfer from Hfr to F$^-$ cell.

If a mating mixture is diluted in nutrient broth at 37° 15 minutes after mixing, in order to prevent further collisions, and samples are thereafter irradiated with ultraviolet at intervals, it is observed that irradiation affects the genetic constitution of recombinants up to 70 minutes after the time of mixing. Thus ultraviolet irradiation evokes the same genetic outcome whether the Hfr cells alone or the formed zygotes are treated. After 70 minutes the effect diminishes until, at 120 minutes, it is no longer found. This suggests that the processes involved in the formation of the recombinant chromosome begin to be completed at about 70 minutes and are complete by 120 minutes.

This action of ultraviolet light on bacterial recombination recalls the similar effect which the same ultraviolet doses exert on recombination in λ phage (Jacob and Wollman, 1955b) which was thought to be best interpreted according to Levinthal's hypothesis of replication and recombination (Levinthal, 1954). According to this view recombination does not take place by breakage and reunion of already formed vegetative particles, but through partial replicas commenced on one phage type and finished on another. In an elementary act of recombination, only one recombinant type would therefore by formed. Small doses of ultraviolet light would interfere with the process of replication so that the replicas formed would be smaller. The same interpretation could account for the results found with bacteria, recombination in them, too, resulting from the integration of replicas formed along the transferred chromosome segment during replication of the recipient's chromosome.

(b) Labelling of the Hfr parent with P³². Another way of studying both the kinetics and the mechanism of integration is to label the DNA of the Hfr parental cells with P^{32}. After conjugation with a non-radioactive F^- strain, the behaviour of the radioactive material transferred to the zygote can then be followed in a relatively simple manner, since it is known that bacteria containing a high specific radioactivity lose their ability to multiply as a function of P^{32} decay (Fuerst and Stent, 1956). Once the Hfr cells have injected their radioactive genetic material into the non-radioactive F^- cells, it is possible to arrest the functions of the zygotes by freezing them at various intervals thereafter, and then subsequently to measure the survival of various classes of recombinants as a function of time (Fuerst, Jacob and Wollman, in preparation). Results so far obtained have provided two kinds of information. First of all, when the mating process is stopped early (40 minutes after mixing) the final rate of inactivation observed among the recombinants varies according to the selection. $T^+L^+Gal^+$ recombinants, on which inheritance of both T^+L^+ *and* Gal^+ from the Hfr parent has been imposed, are inactivated at a faster rate than are T^+L^+ recombinants. At first approximation the rate of inactivation appears to be correlated with the length of the segment selected for (O———TL or O———TL———Gal), as estimated by the blendor technique and recombination data. The second point is that, for each class of recombinants, the

rate of inactivation decreases between 40 and 80 minutes after mixing and is no longer measurable after 100 minutes. Whatever the mechanism of this stabilisation may be, it implies that after 100 minutes the genetic information of the Hfr fragment has been transmitted to material which is not susceptible to P^{32} decay.

B. Expression of Recombinants

This is the final stage in the sequence of events which follows fertilisation of the F^- cell. The recombinant chromosome has been formed within the zygote. The process whereby it attains an autonomous position within a haploid cell is known as *segregation*. Each bacterial cell normally possesses 2 to 4 chromatinic bodies which are justifiably regarded as nuclear analogues. The fact that recombinants are usually clonal indicates that only one of the nuclei of either donor or recipient cell normally participates in zygote formation. Thus after conjugation the recipient cell (zygote) will contain at least one haploid F^- nucleus and one heterozygous or hemizygous diploid nucleus. It therefore resembles a heterokaryon rather than a simple zygote so that segregation will yield at least one F^- cell in addition to the products of the heterozygote itself. On the other hand, partial transfer would exclude the appearance of the Hfr parental type among the progeny of the zygote cell. This has been shown to be the case in the HfrH × F^- cross (Hayes, 1957).

For one reason or another all the characters inherited from the donor parent may not be able to operate functionally at the time of segregation, that is, their *phenotypic expression* may be delayed. The time required for expression will depend not only on whether a gene is a dominant or recessive allele but also on whether the particular character a gene controls manifests itself directly, for example through synthesis of an enzyme, or requires reorganization of some complex structure such as the cell wall. In this section some facts concerning the kinetics of segregation and phenotypic expression will be discussed.

1. The kinetics of segregation. The time at which the recombinant segregant cells undergo their first division, either on minimal agar or in broth, is easily assessed. The first step is to allow zygotes to form for about 30 minutes in an Hfr × F^- cross in broth and then to eliminate the Hfr parent by treatment with phage so that only zygotes and F^- cells remain. To assess the time of segregation on minimal agar, the zygotes are spread on a series of plates selective for T^+L^+ recombinants and, at intervals thereafter, plates are removed in turn and their surfaces vigorously rubbed with distilled water by means of a glass spreader. This separates the progeny of any T^+L^+ recombinants that have already divided so that the subsequent colony count is doubled for each generation (Hayes, 1957). An example of the results obtained

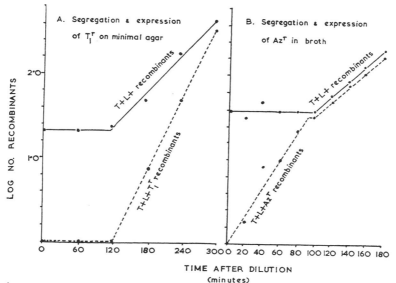

FIGURE 9. The kinetics of segregation and phenotypic expression. A. On minimal agar (+B₁). Young broth cultures of HfrH $M^-Az^rT1^rT6^s$ and F⁻ $TLB_1^-Az^sT1^sT6^r$ were mixed and aerated at 37° for 30 minutes. The mixture was then treated with phage T6 for 10 minutes to eliminate the Hfr cells, diluted and plated on each of two series of warm plates of minimal agar + B₁, and incubated. At intervals thereafter the surfaces of the plates of one series were rubbed in turn with distilled water to separate the progeny of T^+L^+ recombinants; plates of the other series were similarly rubbed with a washed, high titre T1 suspension so as to select only T^+L^+ recombinants in which $T1^r$ had become phenotypically expressed. B. *In nutrient broth*. After treatment with phage T6 as above, the mixture was diluted into fresh broth at 37° and aerated at 37°. At intervals thereafter samples were further diluted and plated on: 1. minimal agar + B₁, for T^+L^+ recombinants; 2. minimal agar + B₁ + sodium azide (M/1500) for T^+L^+ recombinants in which Az^r had become phenotypically expressed. (From Hayes, 1957, J. Gen. Microbiol, in press).

by this kind of experiment is illustrated by the curve (continuous line) in Figure 9A. The T^+L^+ recombinants begin to divide about 120 minutes after plating and thereafter multiply with a generation time of about 60 minutes.

To follow segregation in broth, the zygotes are diluted into fresh broth. Samples are then removed as a function of time, appropriately diluted and plated on minimal agar for T^+L^+ recombinants (Hayes, 1957). A representative result is given by the curve (continuous line) in Figure 9B. The recombinants begin to divide at about 100 minutes after dilution (*i.e.* about 140 minutes after mixing the parental cultures) with a generation time of 20 minutes.

Assuming that timing starts when the parental cultures are mixed, it may be profitable to discuss a very tentative correlation of our findings if only to indicate the potentialities of the kinetic approach in analysis.

There are three sets of data. The first in order of timing is the stabilisation of the inactivation of zygotes due to decay of P³² introduced in the donor chromosome fragment: this becomes complete about 100 minutes after mixing. It suggests that, at this time, a P³²-free replica or template of the donor genetic contribution has been formed in all the zygotes. Secondly, ultraviolet irradiation ceases to have any effect on the genetic constitution of recombinants at about 120 minutes implying that the process of integration has by then been completed in all the zygotes. Twenty min-

utes later (*i.e.*, the generation time of both parental and recombinant cells), at 140 minutes after mixing, the first division of the recombinant segregants is initiated.

2. The kinetics of phenotypic expression. The Hfr genes determining resistance or sensitivity to sodium azide and to phage T1 are linked to the selective markers T^+L^+ and are inherited respectively by about 90 per cent and 75 per cent of T^+L^+ recombinants (Fig. 5). For this reason, and because they manifest their functions in quite different ways, these two markers are admirably suited to the study of phenotypic expression. Only the expression of *resistance* to sodium azide (Az^r) and phage T1 ($T1^r$), inherited from the Hfr parent, has so far been examined (Hayes, 1957).

The experiments are conducted in parallel with those for determining the kinetics of segregation either on minimal agar or in nutrient broth. In the cross Hfr·Az^rT1^r × F⁻·Az^sT1^s selection is made for $T^+L^+Az^r$ or $T^+L^+T1^r$ recombinants, as a function of time, as well as for the whole T^+L^+ recombinant class. The kinetics of expression, in terms of generation time, are about the same whether assessed on minimal agar, nutrient agar or in broth. Figure 9A correlates the kinetics of segregation (continuous line) and expression of the character T1ʳ (interrupted line) on minimal agar. In Figure 9B, segregation in broth (continuous line) is similarly related to phenotypic expression of the character Az^r (interrupted line). The patterns of expression of the two markers inherited from the Hfr parent are quite different. Expression of the character Az^r commences at the time of dilution (or of plating) of the zygotes and then rises exponentially to become complete just before the segregants which inherit it start to divide (Figure 9B). In contrast, the character $T1^r$ does not begin to be expressed until *after* segregation while full expression (i.e. in 75 % of all T^+L^+ recombinants) is delayed until the fourth generation (Figure 9A).

The gene $T1^r$ has been reported, from work on *E. coli* diploids, to be recessive to $T1^s$ (Lederberg, 1949) so that its expression is not to be expected until after segregation; the further extension of its phenotypic lag is a natural consequence of the dependence of the development of phage resistance on structural alterations of the cell wall. Since expression of the character Az^r rises rapidly during a period when both alleles must be present together in the diploid merozygote, it follows that Az^r is dominant to Az^s; this is an exception to the rule that wild type alleles are dominant to their mutant alleles in *E. coli*.

Knowledge of the kinetics of phenotypic expression following recombination in bacteria has a two-fold importance. Firstly it offers a normal control against which the results of mutation kinetics can be studied. Secondly, it is necessary for the rational design of recombination experiments, whether in *E. coli* or in other bacterial species. For example, the choice of selective markers which are recessive, or whose expression is normally delayed, is unlikely to yield recombinants from an otherwise fertile cross unless application of the selective agent is withheld until expression has occurred. This is well exemplified by the fact that virtually no Az^r recombinants appear if recently formed zygotes which have inherited the gene Az^r from the donor parent are plated directly on medium containing sodium azide, despite the fact that Az^r appears to be dominant and is rapidly expressed.

IV. THE RELATIONSHIP BETWEEN F+ AND Hfr SYSTEMS

The discussion so far has dealt exclusively with the features of crosses involving an Hfr donor (HfrH) and F− recipient strains. In this section we propose to examine the properties of the equivalent F+ × F− cross and hope to show that a comparative analysis of the two systems may lead to a unified interpretation of the mating process in *E. coli*. The principal points of difference between F+ and Hfr strains have already been summarized and will not be reiterated here. The main aim of this analysis is to attempt to equate the two systems. It will be found that some of the paradoxes which seem to exist are resolved as the analysis proceeds: others remain and will be discussed in their proper context.

In the light of the results of analysis of the Hfr system, it may be asked whether the low fre-quency of recombination found in F+ × F− crosses is due to low frequency of conjugation, of transfer, or of integration. The evidence relevant to this question will now be presented.

A. Analysis of F+ × F− Crosses

1. Conjugation. There is one character of F+ cells which is transferred to F− cells at high frequency. This is the F+ character itself, and its transfer requires cellular contact (Cavalli *et al.*, 1953; Hayes, 1953a). The kinetics of F+ transfer can be studied by the same methods as those used for the analysis of Hfr systems. A mixture of F+ and F− cells is made in broth, the F+ cells being in excess. Samples are removed at intervals and plated, both directly and after treatment in a Waring blendor, on a medium on which only the F− recipient cells can grow. The resulting F− clones are then scored for inheritance of F+ as a function of time after mixing. In the case of the untreated samples it is found that the curve expressing the proportion of F− cells which have inherited the character F+ arises from the origin and increases linearly until a plateau is reached about 50 minutes after mixing, when some 75 per cent of the F− cells have been converted. In the case of the treated samples, the F+ character begins to appear at about five minutes after mixing (Jacob and Wollman, 1955a). It thus turns out that transfer of F+ from F+ donor to F− recipient cells is very similar to the transfer of such characters as T^+L^+ from Hfr to F− cells (Fig. 3) except that F+ transfer occurs several minutes earlier than any of the hitherto known markers on the O——R segment of HfrH. It therefore seems probable that F+ is located on the F+ chromosome within a region $0'$——R' which is transferred at high frequency to the F− cell. Another kind of character which appears to be transferred at high frequency from F+ to F− cells is the ability to synthesise certain colicines such as colicine E, originally a character of *E. coli* strain K-30 (Frédéricq and Betz-Bareau, 1953). Kinetic analysis of the transfer of this ability shows that production of colicine E is transferred from a K-12 F+ strain to an F− recipient strain at about two and a half minutes after mixing. The ability to produce colicine E would therefore seem to be controlled by a locus situated between $0'$ and F+ on the F+ chromosome (Jacob and Wollman, unpub.).

One can thus conclude that conjugation between F+ and F− bacteria is no different from Hfr × F− conjugation and occurs with a frequency of the order of 100 per cent. In substantiation of this, conjoint pairs of cells, and cellular bridges uniting them, similar to those observed in Hfr × F− crosses, can also be seen in F+ × F− crosses by means of phase contrast and electron microscopy (Fig. 7, bottom picture) (Anderson, Wollman and Jacob, 1957).

2. Transfer and integration. Since the frequency of conjugation, and of transfer of certain markers, is found to be high in $F^+ \times F^-$ crosses, the question arises whether those F^+ markers which are not inherited at high frequency are absent because they are not transferred, or because they are transferred but not integrated. The most significant evidence is derived from zygotic induction. Whereas this phenomenon can be directly demonstrated in the cross HfrH $(\lambda)^+ \times F^- (\lambda)^-$, it is hardly detectable in the equivalent $F^+ (\lambda)^+ \times F^- (\lambda)^-$ cross (Jacob and Wollman, 1956b). Since the transfer of λ prophage is immediately expressed it must be concluded that prophage is not *transferred* at high frequency from an F^+ lysogenic donor to an F^- non-lysogenic recipient cell. It must therefore be assumed that the failure of at least the *Gal*—λ region of the F^+ chromosome to be inherited at high frequency is due to lack of transfer. The hypothesis can therefore be made that the two systems are similar in every respect save one; that the location of the region of preferential rupture is different. Accordingly, the chromosome of F^+ bacteria also comprises two segments separated by a new region of rupture, R', such that the segment O'—R', carrying the markers colicine E and F^+, is transferred at high frequency. The other known genetic markers are all located on the other segment which is not transferred at high frequency.

B. The Mechanism of Low Frequency of Recombination

HfrH cells can only transfer, at high frequency, markers located on the O—R segment of the chromosome. In the case of the equivalent F^+ cells, only markers on the chromosome segment O'—R' can similarly be transferred to F^- cells. Let us consider how, in either case, a marker situated on neither of these segments may be transferred at low frequency. There are two possible hypotheses; either each Hfr or F^+ cell has a small but equal probability of transferring a chromosome segment on which the marker is located, or else there exists in each Hfr or F^+ population a small fraction of mutant cells which can transfer the marker with high efficiency. In this latter event the number of recombinants formed by independent cultures of the same F^+ strain should be extremely variable as compared with those formed by samples of the same culture. The results of such fluctuation tests (Luria and Delbrück, 1943) in which the F^+ population was standardised so as to contain only a few presumptive mutant clones in each independent culture, are in agreement with this prediction (Jacob and Wollman, 1956a). Genetic analysis of recombinants isolated from fluctuation tests of this kind affords striking confirmation of the mutation hypothesis. When the genetic patterns of the progeny of different independent cultures are compared they are found to vary widely between cultures, both in the characters of the F^+ parent

which are transferred and the proportion of these characters found among recombinants. On the other hand, the genetic constitution of recombinants arising from different samples of the same culture is very homogeneous.

It is therefore probable that most, if not all, of the recombinants formed in an $F^+ \times F^-$ cross must be due to preexisting Hfr mutants in the F^+ population. By means of the method of indirect selection known as "replica plating" (Lederberg and Lederberg, 1952), it is in fact possible to isolate different types of Hfr strains from F^+ cultures. When the means of selection are adequate, the efficiency of isolation of Hfr mutants responsible for particular recombinant colonies is close to 100 per cent. By selecting for recombinants which have inherited different markers from the F^+ parent it is possible, by the replica plating method, to isolate a variety of different Hfr strains capable of transmitting the selected marker to recombinants at high frequency. These Hfr strains differ from one another not only in the characters they can transfer to the zygote but also in the *sequence* in which these characters are transferred (Jacob and Wollman, 1956a). Each of the known markers of *E. coli* K-12 can be transferred at high frequency by one or another Hfr strain but no single Hfr strain has so far been isolated which alone can transfer all these markers. That low frequency of appearance of a given character among recombinants is indeed due to the fact that the locus determining it is not situated on the chromosome segment transferred at high frequency, is demonstrated by the fact that zygotic induction is not observed in crosses between strains of Hfr$(\lambda)^+$ which do not transmit the Gal$_b$ character, and non-lysogenic F^- strains. This situation is found in crosses involving HfrC. This strain has been otherwise shown by Skaar and Garen (personal communication) to transfer the TL—Lac segment in a sequence which is the reverse of that exhibited by HfrH.

The hypothesis therefore appears well substantiated that characters transmitted to recombinants at low frequency, either in $F^+ \times F^-$ or in Hfr $\times F^-$ crosses, are transferred by spontaneous Hfr mutants. Among the Hfr strains isolated there seem to exist certain preferential patterns of transfer but the possibility has not yet been excluded that this is due to a bias introduced by the use of streptomycin as a contra-selective agent. The properties of these different Hfr strains is still under investigation.

Despite the low frequency with which recombinants are found, $F^+ \times F^-$ mixtures in broth can be analysed kinetically by the use of virulent phage to eliminate the F^+ parent, in the same way as the Waring blendor has been used for analysis of Hfr $\times F^-$ crosses (Hayes, 1957). In comparative experiments of this kind the cross HfrH $\times F^-$ is found to be about 2×10^4 times more productive of T^+L^+ recombinants than the equivalent $F^+ \times$

F^- cross. When selection is made for the T^+L^+, $T^+L^+Lac^+$ or $T^+L^+B_1^+$ markers of the F^+ parent (see Fig. 1), it is found that the transfer of T^+L^+ starts at about eight minutes and of Lac^+ at 18 minutes after mixing, exactly as in the equivalent Hfr × F^- cross. Unlike the Hfr × F^- cross, however, the F^+ marker B_1^+ is transferred at about 45 minutes after mixing. No recombinants inheriting the xylose, maltose or streptomycin markers of the F^+ parent are found up to 90 minutes after mixing when selection is made for them. This implies that among those Hfr mutants which can transfer T^+L^+ at high frequency, the most common types are broadly similar to HfrH. The late transfer of the F^+ marker B_1^+, and its appearance among T^+L^+ recombinants with a frequency of five per cent, indicates, however, that at least five per cent of these Hfr mutants can transfer at high frequency a different chromosome segment.

V. DISCUSSION

A. Sexual Differentiation

Sexual conjugation in *E. coli* takes place between cells of opposite mating type which can, for convenience, be referred to as *donor* and *recipient* since, after cellular contact, genetic material is transferred from the former to the latter. At the present time these two mating types can only be defined in terms of the properties expressed by the donor. These properties comprise a surface configuration which enables effective contact with the recipient cell's surface to be established, the ability to inject a chromosomal segment, O——R, which differs from donor to donor and finally, the capacity to mutate from one donor type to another. Upon high frequency transfer of a small chromosome segment from an F^+ donor to an F^- recipient, the recipient is thereby converted into an F^+ donor in which these three properties are simultaneously expressed. It is not known, however, whether these properties are all expressions of the same genetic factor or whether they may exist independently.

The distinction between F^+ and Hfr donor strains is more artificial than real since the frequency of recombination observed in practice will depend only upon whether the selective markers used happen to lie on the O——R segment or beyond it. Since the low frequency of recombination found in the latter case appears to be mediated by different Hfr mutants preexisting in the donor culture, use of the terms "Hfr" and "F^+" to denote a fundamental distinction in the capacity of the two strains to yield recombinants loses its validity. The term "F^+ strain" has also been used to imply the ability of the strain to transmit the donor state to F^+ cells at high frequency. In contrast, neither of the Hfr strains hitherto isolated could transmit either the F^+ or Hfr donor state at high frequency. However, when selection is made for certain markers of either HfrH or HfrC, the Hfr donor state is inherited by a high proportion of recombinants and, in the case of HfrC at least, appears to be controlled by a specific locus closely linked to one of the *Gal* loci (Hayes, 1953b; Cavalli and Jinks, 1956).

In its transmissibility and inheritance, F^+ displays the properties of a gene. In strain HfrH, F^+ is no longer found as such but appears to be replaced by a new locus determining the donor state, situated distal to a new region of rupture. Since this strain can revert to the original F^+ donor state, the most likely hypothesis is that the *position* of F^+ determines the region of preferential rupture and that mutation to Hfr is a function of the shift of F^+ to a new position on the chromosome. If, in a Hfr strain, F^+ happened to be located on the O——R segment proximal to the region of rupture it determined, then the donor state would be transferred at high frequency to F^- cells as in the case of F^+ strains. The range of Hfr strains which have now been isolated has not yet been investigated from this point of view. It should be pointed out, however, that in F^+ × F^- crosses all, or nearly all, the recombinants may be F^+ even when the cross is made in broth and the F^+ parent is eliminated by phage to prevent secondary transfer of the F^+ character to the recombinant cells after plating. If, as is supposed, these recombinants result from Hfr mutants one would expect them to inherit either the Hfr or the F^- character, not the F^+ (Hayes, 1957).

Different donor strains differ in the chromosomal location of the region of rupture, R, which determines the length of chromosome they are able to transfer. Any donor type apparently possesses the potentiality to mutate to other donor types, with a consequent shift in the position of R ($F^+ \rightleftharpoons Hfr_1 \rightleftharpoons Hfr_2$ etc.), as well as to the recipient type (Lederberg *et al.*, 1952; Hayes, 1953a). When a recipient F^- cell inherits that region of a donor chromosome controlling the donor properties of the cell (F^+ or Hfr) it also inherits the capacity to mutate to other donor types. Thus it has been possible to obtain F^+ and various Hfr derivatives of *E. coli* strain C which was originally F^- (Jacob and Wollman, unpub.). The occurrence of mutation from the recipient to the donor state has not yet been reported.

A population of donor cells is therefore heterogeneous and contains, in addition to a majority of the original type which, on conjugation, can transfer a particular chromosomal segment, a variety of other donor types which are responsible for the recombinants formed at low frequency. Recombinants obtained by crossing an F^+ population of this kind with an F^- population would be formed by different Hfr mutants transferring a different range of characters. Their number and genetic make-up would depend on the relative frequencies of the different Hfr types present in the donor population. Moreover it may be expected that the results of crosses involving the same F⁻ strain but F⁺ strains of different origin will not be the same but will differ according to the "Hfr mutability pattern" of the F⁺ strain employed. The difficulties encountered in the genetic analysis of $F^+ \times F^-$ crosses are readily understandable in such a model (Jacob and Wollman, 1956a).

The mechanism of the mutation from one donor type to another is still a matter for speculation. It may be an example of chromosomal mutation since it seems to involve breakage and rearrangement within the chromosome which can only be expressed when the donor character is present. Such mutation appears to be associated with a change in the location of the donor character although it is not known whether the alterations in position are the cause or the effect of the rearrangements. This behaviour is reminiscent of the phenomena found in maize by McClintock (1956). The "donor character" could be conceived as being a "controlling element" whose location commands, in an unknown fashion, the region of chromosome breakage, R, as well as the pattern of chromosome rearrangements. Whether or not the "donor character" will be transferred on conjugation will depend on whether it is located between O and R or distal to R.

B. Meromixis

Once the genetic contribution of the donor cell has been transferred to the recipient cell a partial zygote or *merozygote* is formed which comprises the entire genome of the recipient cell together with a chromosomal segment of variable size from the donor cell. Thus a comparable situation is attained in transformation, transduction and conjugation, the three varieties of genetic transfer found among bacteria, for in each only a fragment of the genome of a donor cell is transferred to a recipient cell. The difference between them lies in the method whereby genetic transfer is accomplished, transformation being effected by the DNA extracts of donor cells, transduction by a phage vector and conjugation by direct injection of a chromosomal segment into the recipient cell by the donor cell. In some strains like *E. coli* K-12 transfer of genetic material can be performed by either conjugation or transduction (Lennox, 1955; Jacob, 1955). We therefore propose to unite, under the name of *meromixis*, these three known processes which are characterised by partial genetic transfer.

As to the mechanisms whereby characters transferred from the donor cell are integrated into a recombinant chromosome, the same problems are clearly raised by the three types of meromixis, and have already been considered in the case of transformation (Ephrussi-Taylor, 1955; Hotchkiss, 1955) and transduction (Demerec and Demerec, 1955; Lederberg, 1955). In conjugation it is evident that a segment of donor chromosome, although present in a merozygote, does not always

participate in the formation of a recombinant chromosome and, when it does, that it is not necessarily incorporated as a whole. A mechanism analogous to crossing over must therefore be assumed although its physical basis is likely to differ from one of simple breakage and reunion in view of the asymmetry of the parental components, one of which may be very small. The question therefore arises whether the transferred fragment itself enters into the constitution of the recombinant chromosome, or whether some mechanism in which replication and recombination are combined, such as that proposed by Levinthal for recombination in phage, is not more likely. The experiments briefly reported here on the effects of ultraviolet light on recombination, as well as those involving the transfer of a radioactive chromosome segment to the merozygote, favour such an hypothesis although their interpretation cannot yet be regarded as unequivocal.

Recombination of genetic characters in bacteria is thus accomplished by means of mechanisms very different from those known in other organisms, since chromosomal fragments of variable size are transferred from one bacterium to another. Of the three known processes by which this transfer is accomplished, that of conjugation in *E. coli* is the most highly developed and most closely resembles a sexual mechanism with sex differentiation, the donor's chromosome segment playing the role of an incomplete male gamete while the recipient cell is analogous to a female gamete which contributes both its intact genome and its cytoplasm to the zygote.

SUMMARY

1. When Hfr and F⁻ bacteria are mixed, effective pairing between donor and recipient cells follows chance collisions. The efficiency of this pairing is modifiable by environmental influences such as pH, and is an energy requiring process. An actual bridge of cellular material can be seen to join the paired cells in electron microphotographs. Under optimal conditions, 100 per cent of Hfr cells conjugate.

2. Effective contact is immediately followed by the orientated transfer of a segment of Hfr chromosome, O——R, to the F⁻ cell which thus becomes a partial zygote. Loci situated on this segment always penetrate the F⁻ cell in the same order as their arrangement on the chromosome. Transfer of the whole O——R segment takes about 35 minutes in broth at 37°. Markers located beyond R do not enter the F⁻ cell at all and are therefore not inherited among recombinants.

3. During chromosome transfer spontaneous breaks occur and the probability of breaking increases towards its distal end. This distal end, R, is therefore thought to be a region of increasing fragility rather than a well defined locus.

4. Chromosome transfer is an energy-requiring process carried out solely by the Hfr cell. The

speed at which the chromosome proceeds appears to be constant at any given temperature but can be modified by changes in the energy supply.

5. The O——R segment of chromosome can be ruptured at will during transfer, either by mechanical separation of the mating bacteria or by selectively killing the donor parent with phage. Only those Hfr markers which have already entered the F⁻ cell at the time of treatment will participate in recombination.

6. Hfr markers which have entered the zygote have a probability of being integrated into the recombinant chromosome which becomes less the further the marker is situated from O on the O——R segment, as might be deduced from the partial nature of the zygote if it is assumed that O is an extremity of the donor chromosome.

7. The time at which a marker inherited from the donor cell is phenotypically expressed in the recombinant segregant cell or its progeny depends on whether it is dominant or recessive, as well as on its manner of expression. Expression of the Hfr gene determining resistance to sodium azide commences in the zygote and is complete before the segregants begin to divide: resistance to phage T1 is not expressed until after segregation and requires four generations for completion.

8. F⁺ × F⁻ crosses show a high frequency of conjugation and of F⁺ transfer. The kinetics of F⁺ transfer are compatible with the view that F⁺ donor cells transfer a segment of chromosome O'——R', on which F⁺ is located, to F⁻ cells. F⁺ markers situated distal to R' are not transferred.

9. Transfer of any particular marker situated distal to R on the Hfr chromosome, or to R' on the F⁺ chromosome, is mediated by Hfr mutants in the donor population which can transfer the marker to F⁻ cells at high frequency. These Hfr mutants are very heterogeneous both in the range of markers they can transfer and in the order of transference.

10. The mechanisms by which donor strains may mutate from one type to another are discussed.

REFERENCES

ANDERSON, T. F., 1949, The reactions of bacterial viruses with their host cells. Bot. Rev. 15: 477.

ANDERSON, T. F., WOLLMAN, E. L., and JACOB, F., 1957, Sur les processus de conjugaison et de recombinaison génétique chez *E. coli*. III. Aspects morphologiques en microscopie électronique. Ann. Inst. Pasteur (in press).

APPLEYARD, R. K., 1954, Segregation of λ lysogenicity during bacterial recombination in *Escherichia coli* K-12. Genetics 39: 429–439.

CAVALLI, L. L., 1950, La sessualita nei batteri. Boll. Ist. sierotera. Milano 29: 1–9.

CAVALLI-SFORZA, L. L., and JINKS, J. L., 1956, Studies on the genetic system of *Escherichia coli* K-12. J. Genet. 54: 87–112.

CAVALLI, L. L., LEDERBERG, J., and LEDERBERG, E. M., 1953, An infective factor controlling sex compatibility in *Bacterium coli*. J. Gen. Microbiol. 8: 89–103.

DEMEREC, M., and DEMEREC, Z. E., 1955, Analysis of linkage relationships in *Salmonella* by transduction techniques. Brookhaven Symp. Biol. 8: 75–87.

EDDINGTON, A., 1935, New Pathways in Science. Cambridge, England, Cambridge Univ. Press.

EPHRUSSI-TAYLOR, H., 1955, Current status of bacterial transformations. Adv. Virus Res. 275–307.

FISHER, K., 1957a, The role of the Krebs cycle in conjugation in *Escherichia coli* K-12. J. Gen. Microbiol. 16: No. 1 (in press).

1957b, The nature of the endergonic processes in conjugation in *Escherichia coli* K-12. J. Gen. Microbiol. 16: No. 1 (in press).

FREDERICQ, P., and BETZ-BAREAU, M., 1953, Transfert génétique de la propriété colicinogène en rapport avec la polarité F des parents. C. R. Soc. Biol. 147: 2043–2045.

FUERST, C. R., and STENT, G. S., 1956, Inactivation of bacteria by decay of incorporated radioactive phosphorus. J. Gen. Physiol. 40: 73–90.

FUERST, C. R., JACOB, F., and WOLLMAN, E. L. 1957, Sur les processus de conjugaison et de recombinaison génétique chez *E. coli*. Etude de la recombinaison à l'aide du phosphore radioactif (in preparation).

HAYES, W., 1952a, Recombination in *Bact. coli* K-12: unidirectional transfer of genetic material. Nature, Lond. 169: 118–119.

1952b, Genetic recombination in *Bact. coli* K-12: analysis of the stimulating effect of ultraviolet light. Nature, Lond. 169: 1017–1018.

1953a, Observations on a transmissible agent determining sexual differentiation in *Bact. coli*. J. Gen. Microbiol. 8: 72–88.

1953b, The mechanism of genetic recombination in *Escherichia coli*. Cold Spring Harb. Symp. Quant. Biol. 18: 75–93.

1957, The kinetics of the mating process in *Escherichia coli*. J. Gen. Microb. 16: No. 1 (in press).

HERSHEY, A. D., and CHASE, M., 1952, Independent functions of viral protein and nucleic acid in growth of bacteriophage. J. Gen. Physiol. 36: 39–56.

HOTCHKISS, R. D., 1955, Bacterial transformation. J. Cell. Comp. Physiol. 45, suppl. 2: 1–22.

JACOB, F., 1955, Transduction of lysogeny in *Escherichia coli*. Virology 1: 207–220.

JACOB, F., and WOLLMAN, E. L., 1954, Induction spontanée du développement du bactériophage λ au cours de la recombinaison génétique chez *E. coli* K-12. C. R. Acad. Sci. 239: 317–319.

1955a, Etapes de la recombinaison génétique chez *E. coli* K12. C. R. Acad. Sci. 240: 2566–2568.

1955b, Etude génétique d'un bactériophage tempéré d'*E. coli*. III Effet du rayonnement ultraviolet sur la recombinaison génétique. Ann. Inst. Pasteur 88: 724–749.

1956a, Recombinaison génétique et mutants de fertilité. C. R. Acad. Sci., 242: 303–306.

1956b, Sur les processus de conjugaison et de recombinaison génétique chez *E. coli*. I. L'induction par conjugaison ou induction zygotique. Ann. Inst. Pasteur 91: 486–510.

LEDERBERG, E. M., 1951, Lysogenicity in *E. coli* K-12. Genetics 36: 560.

LEDERBERG, E. M., and LEDERBERG, J., 1953, Genetic studies of lysogenicity in *E. coli*. Genetics 38: 51–64.

LEDERBERG, J., 1947, Gene recombination and linked segregations in *E. coli*. Genetics 32: 505–525.

1949, Aberrant heterozygotes in *Escherichia coli*. Proc. Nat. Acad. Sci. Wash. 35: 178–184.

1955, Recombination mechanisms in bacteria. J. Cell. Comp. Physiol. 45, suppl. 2: 75–107.

LEDERBERG, J., and LEDERBERG E. M., 1952, Replica plating and indirect selection of bacterial mutants. J. Bact. 63: 399–406.

LEDERBERG, J., LEDERBERG, E. M., ZINDER, N. D., and LIVELY, E. R., 1951, Recombination analysis of bacterial heredity. Cold Spring Harb. Symp. Quant. Biol. 16: 413–441.

LEDERBERG, J., and TATUM, E. L., 1946, Novel genotypes in mixed cultures of biochemical mutants of bacteria. Cold Spring Harb. Symp. Quant. Biol. *11:* 113–114.

LENNOX, E. S., 1955, Transduction of linked genetic characters of the host by bacteriophage P₁. Virology *1:* 190–206.

LEVINTHAL, C., 1954, Recombination in phage T2: its relationship to heterozygosis and growth. Genetics *39:* 169–184.

LIEB, M., WEIGLE, J. J. and KELLENBERGER, E., 1955, A study of hybrids between two strains of *E. coli*. J. Bact. *69:* 468–471.

MACCACARO, G. A., 1955, Cell surface and fertility in *E. coli*. Nature, Lond. *176:* 125–126.

MCCLINTOCK, B., 1956, Controlling elements and the gene. Cold Spring Harb. Symp. Quant. Biol. *21:* 197–216.

NEWCOMBE, M. B., and NYHOLM, M. H., 1950, Anomalous segregation in crosses of *E. coli*. Amer. Nat. *84:* 457–465.

ROTHFELS, K. H., 1952, Gene linearity and negative interference in crosses of *E. coli*. Genetics *37:* 297–311.

WOLLMAN, E. L., 1953, Sur le determinisme génétique de la lysogénie. Ann. Inst. Pasteur *84:* 281–293.

WOLLMAN, E. L., and JACOB, F., 1954, Lysogénie et recombinaison génétique chez *E. coli* K-12. C. R. Acad. Sci. *239:* 455–456.

1955, Sur le mécanisme du transfert de matériel génétique au cours de la recombinaison chez *E. coli* K-12. C. R. Acad. Sci. *240:* 2449–2451.

1957, Sur les processus de conjugaison et de recombinaison génétique chez *E. coli*. II. Polarité du transfert et de la recombinaison génétique. Ann. Inst. Pasteur (in press).

Recombination in *Bact. coli K* 12: Unidirectional Transfer of Genetic Material

THE development of nutritionally independent prototroph colonies from mixed cultures of doubly dependent mutant strains of *Bact. coli K* 12 was first demonstrated in 1946[1]. Back mutation to prototrophism did not occur when the mutants were cultured separately. Since the pattern of unselected marker characters in prototrophs was usually different from that in either mutant, the phenomenon was clearly due to genetic recombination. The incompetence in recombination of culture filtrates (unlike type transformation in *Pneumococcus*), and recent evidence for the occasional occurrence of diploid heterozygous prototrophs[2], strongly support the current theory that the genetic transfer is mediated by sexual conjugation. Attempts to reproduce the phenomenon in other strains and species have failed, though successful out-crossing of *K* 12 mutants with a strain of *Bact. acidi lactici* has been reported[3].

In the following experiments, *K* 12 mutants 58–161, requiring biotin and methionine, and *W* 677, requiring leucine, threonine and aneurin, were employed. An attempt was made to investigate the dynamics of recombination by adding streptomycin at intervals to a series of plates of basal medium (plus aneurin) seeded with a mixture of 58–161 and a streptomycin-resistant mutant of *W* 677 (*W* 677/S^r). It was anticipated that the streptomycin would rapidly block the recombination mechanism by inactivating 58–161, while allowing resistant prototroph cells formed prior to its addition to develop into colonies. In practice, the number of prototroph colonies did not differ greatly whether streptomycin was incorporated in the basal medium before plating or was added up to four hours later. Since similar results were obtained when the mutants were mixed for the first time during plating, the occurrence of recombination in mixtures before contact with streptomycin was excluded. Either prototrophs arose before the action of streptomycin on the sensitive mutant became effective, or else those functions of the cell affected by streptomycin were not involved in recombination.

Logarithmic-phase broth cultures of 58–161 were treated with either 1,000 or 2,000 μgm./ml. streptomycin for periods up to 18 hr., under conditions optimal for bactericidal effect. Washed saline concentrates of treated cultures (58–161/S^t), although frequently sterile, invariably stimulated prototroph formation when mixed with *W* 677/S^r on basal medium containing 200 μgm./ml. streptomycin. Whenever streptomycin treatment failed to produce sterility, control reconstruction experiments showed that at least a thousand times as many untreated 58–161 cells as those which had survived treatment were necessary for prototroph formation under similar conditions.

Mixtures of streptomycin-treated *W* 677 (*W* 677/S^t) and 58–161/S^r, on the other hand, invariably failed to produce prototrophs, although comparable recombination-rates were given by the mixtures (*W* 677/S^r + 58–161) and (58–161/S^r + *W* 677). In these experiments streptomycin was not incorporated in the basal medium, since previous analysis of proved prototrophs had shown that about 95 per cent carried the S^r or S^s character of *W* 677. The clear-cut distinction between 58–161/S^t and *W* 677/S^t in ability to participate in recombination was shown to be independent both of the presence of the S^r character in the complementary mutant and of the basal medium environment. Thus (58–161/S^t + *W* 677) produced prototroph colonies on every occasion, whether cultured directly on basal medium or initially on nutrient agar. The mixture (*W* 677/S^t + 58–161), however, failed to do so repeatedly on basal medium and, in a single experiment, when seeded on nutrient agar.

It is unlikely that sensitive cells which have been acted upon for 18 hr. by very high concentrations of streptomycin can still participate in cytoplasmic fusion in the continued presence of the drug. Moreover, if conjugation under these conditions was possible for 58–161/S^t, it might also be assumed for *W* 677/S^t. Yet suspensions of the latter are inactive in recombination. It is more probable that recombination is mediated by genetic elements, extruded by the viable cell, which adhere to the cell wall and which, like viruses, are unaffected by streptomycin. Thus, the dead cell could serve merely as a passive carrier for its genetic elements after their expulsion. The incompetence of *W* 677/S^t becomes intelligible only if we suppose that the role of *W* 677 is primarily the vital one of accepting genes and incorporating them into its genetic structure.

It is known that symbiotic bacterial viruses can transfer hereditary characters to heterologous strains[4], and that *K* 12 harbours a virus which can be liberated by small doses of ultra-violet light[5]. The known facts of recombination and especially its marked enhancement by small sub-mutagenic doses of ultra-violet light[6] and the presumptive one-way transfer of the genetic agent from 58–161 to *W* 677, suggest the possibility that this agent may be a virus. The existence of a latent virus in 58–161 has been unmasked by X-radiation (personal observation).

W. HAYES

Department of Bacteriology,
Postgraduate Medical School of London,
Ducane Road, W.12.
Nov. 6.

[1] Lederberg, J., and Tatum, E. L., *Nature*, **158**, 558 (1946).
[2] Lederberg, J., *Proc. U.S. Nat. Acad. Sci.*, **35**, 178 (1949).
[3] Cavalli, L. L., and Heslot, H., *Nature*, **164**, 1057 (1949).
[4] Felix, A., and Anderson, E. S., *Nature*, **167**, 603 (1951).
[5] Weigle, J. J., and Delbrück, M., *J. Bact.*, **62**, 301 (1951).
[6] Haas, F., Wyss, O., and Stone, W. S., *Proc. U.S. Nat. Acad. Sci.*, **34**, 229 (1948).

Observations on a Transmissible Agent Determining Sexual Differentiation in *Bacterium coli*

BY W. HAYES

Department of Bacteriology, Postgraduate Medical School of London,
Ducane Road, London W. 12

SUMMARY: Analysis of a pair of *Bacterium coli* K-12 mutants which had ceased to show genetic recombination after storage, implicated mutant 58-161, which had previously behaved as a gene donor strain, as the infertile parent. Infertile 58-161 failed to display recombination when crossed with a gene acceptor strain (W-677) but was able to mate successfully with wild-type K-12 and prototrophic recombinant donor strains, i.e. it had become a gene acceptor. The terms 'F +' and 'F −' have been adopted (after Lederberg, Cavalli & Lederberg, 1952) to denote donor and acceptor strains respectively. Growth of either 58-161/F − or W-677/F − in mixed broth culture with 58-161/F + resulted in the conversion to F + of up to 75 % of re-isolated colonies of the initially F − strain. F − strains converted to F + by strains of dissimilar genotype showed no phenotypic alteration and, therefore, were not recombinants. Washed, mixed cultures on minimal agar yielded an F + conversion rate of only 3·6 %, while 100 % recombinants were F + under the same conditions. The F + agent could be transmitted serially through F − strains and was not filterable. While F − × F − crosses were sterile, F + × F − crosses showed maximum fertility. F + × F + crosses were *c.* 10–20 times less productive than F + × F −. The F + agent had a determining effect on the phenotype of recombinants. Thus, when the F + F − relationship was reversed in F + × F − crosses between the same pair of mutants, almost all recombinants which did not show new patterns of unselected marker characters had the phenotype of the F − parent. Among recombinants from F + × F + crosses, the phenotypes of both parents were represented though not always equally. This effect of F + on the phenotype of segregants invalidates much of the evidence for genetic linkage in K-12. Reversal of F + potential in otherwise similar crosses also had a marked effect on the efficiency of prototroph formation on minimal agar supplemented with various growth factors required by one of the parent auxotrophs. A tentative theory of the mechanism of recombination is presented on the basis of this and previous work. This supposes that F + is a non-lytic infectious agent, harboured by F + cells and absent from F − cells, which becomes effectively associated with a part (or parts) of the chromosomes of a small proportion of the cells it inhabits. The F + agent thus acts as a gene carrier in the transfer of genetic material from F + to F − cells.

Genetic recombination in bacteria was first demonstrated in the K-12 strain of *Bacterium coli* (Lederberg & Tatum, 1946; Tatum & Lederberg, 1947) and its occurrence in this strain has since been confirmed by many workers. Lederberg, Cavalli & Lederberg (1952) have recently reported some forty strains of *Bact. coli* from over 2000 separate isolates which either out-cross with K-12 mutants or show inter-fertility, so that genetic recombination may be considered a not uncommon feature of this species when such potential incompatibility factors as colicine production and lysogenicity are taken into account (Lederberg, 1951).

When irradiation-induced mutants of K-12, having two or more complementary nutritional dependencies, were grown together in a complete medium and the mixed culture washed free of nutrients and plated in minimal agar, one colony developed for every 10^6–10^7 cells seeded (Lederberg & Tatum, 1946). The cells of these colonies were prototrophic, i.e. they resembled the wild-type strain in having acquired the inheritable capacity to synthesize all the growth factors upon which the mutant strains were dependent. The mutant strains did not show mutational reversion to prototrophism when cultured separately in minimal agar. By a further series of mutational steps the auxotrophic 'parent' mutants were labelled with a number of complementary differences in characters, such as fermentative capacity and phage resistance or sensitivity, which were not selected by growth in minimal medium. Analysis revealed that the patterns of these unselected marker characters in prototrophs frequently differed from that in either mutant, while their distribution afforded plausible evidence of linkage (Lederberg, 1947). Since culture filtrates of either mutant were incompetent in recombination (Davis, 1950) it seemed reasonable to assume as a working hypothesis that the genetic rearrangements found in prototroph clones were the outcome of a more or less orthodox sexual mechanism involving zygote formation, crossing over and meiosis. The validity of this assumption was strengthened when Lederberg (1949; Zelle & Lederberg, 1951) described the occurrence of prototroph strains which behaved like heterozygous diploids in continually segregating out different but stable recombination types. As a result of these findings, most published work on recombination in K-12 has been concerned with the elaboration of linkage behaviour and the application of the phenomenon to analysis of such problems as the genetic basis of resistance to antibiotics (e.g. Cavalli & Maccacaro, 1950; Newcombe & Nyholm, 1950 *a*, *b*), while further investigation of the mechanism of recombination itself has been somewhat neglected.

The first indication of sexual differentiation among K-12 mutants was the observation by Hayes (1952*a*) that streptomycin destroyed the fertility of only one of the two equally sensitive mutants with which he worked. He interpreted this differential action of streptomycin as providing evidence against the occurrence of conjugation and as suggesting the uni-directional transfer of genetic material from a 'gene donor' to a 'gene acceptor' cell. He postulated that the living donor cell extruded genetic elements which adhered to its surface so that the cell could continue to function as a gene carrier despite its subsequent 'killing' by streptomycin. On the other hand, the role of the acceptor cell was the vital one of taking up genes from the donor cell and incorporating them into its genetic structure. Hayes (1952*b*) later showed that exposure of his donor strain to small doses of ultraviolet light increased its fertility fivefold or more, while similar treatment of the acceptor strain reduced fertility *pari passu* with the viable count. Moreover, the conditions necessary for ultraviolet enhancement of donor cell fertility closely paralleled those described by Lwoff and others (Lwoff, Siminovitch & Kjelgaard, 1950*a*, *b*; Lwoff, 1951) for the maturation of prophage and subsequent liberation of lytic phage from lysogenic bacteria. Since both K-12 mutants carried λ phage (Weigle & Delbrück, 1951), which has been excluded as a possible agent of recombination (Lederberg, personal correspondence; Lederberg *et al.* 1952), it was undecided whether the effect of ultraviolet irradiation on donor cell fertility was primary or merely secondary to λ release, as suggested to the author by Lederberg.

Confirmation of sexual differentiation between K-12 mutants has been reported by Lederberg *et al.* (1952), whose findings are essentially similar to those described below. This paper concerns an investigation into the cause of infertility arising spontaneously in a pair of K-12 mutants which had previously shown normal recombination.

MATERIALS AND METHODS

Bacterial strains

(*a*) K-12 (wild-type strain). This strain is prototrophic and grows well in unsupplemented minimal medium.

(*b*) 58-161. A methionine-requiring (M −) mutant of K-12 which ferments lactose, maltose, mannitol, galactose, xylose and arabinose, is sensitive to coliphage T_1 and resistant to T_3 (Lac + Mal + Mann + Gal + Xyl + Arab + $T_1{}^sT_3{}^r$). This mutant was originally described as biotin-dependent as well as M − (Lederberg, 1947). Since, however, it grows optimally in minimal medium + methionine alone, and in which glucose is substituted by an acid hydrolysate of pure sucrose (kindly supplied by Thomas Kerfoot and Co., Vale of Bardsley, Lancashire) it must be presumed not to require biotin now. Despite this, its rate of back-mutation to prototrophism is, fortunately, extremely low, and the development of M + colonies has never been observed from control platings on minimal agar under the conditions employed in recombination tests.

(*c*) W-677. A mutant of K-12 requiring threonine, leucine and thiamine (vitamin B_1) (TLB$_1$ −). Its marker characters are complementary to those of 58-161 (i.e. Lac − Mal − Mann − Gal − Xyl − Arab − $T_1{}^rT_3{}^s$).

(*d*) Streptomycin (SM)-resistant mutants (58-161/S^r, W-677/S^r etc.) were selected by plating very large inocula of each strain on nutrient agar containing 200–250 μg. SM/ml. The largest and most rapidly growing colonies were picked, purified by replating on SM-agar and tested for growth on agar without SM. Only one S^r mutant of each strain was used throughout this work. The nutritional and marker characters of these S^r mutants were identical with those of their parent strains.

Stock cultures were maintained on Dorset's egg medium at 4° whence subcultures were made to nutrient broth as required.

Media. The constitution of minimal agar (MA) was that recommended by Tatum & Lederberg (1947) except that asparagine was omitted. Except when otherwise stated, this medium was supplemented with thiamine (MA + B$_1$) in a final concentration of 0·0005 % (w/v). The term 'prototroph' should properly be reserved for those recombinants having the nutritional independence of the wild-type. Although the majority of recombinants arising on MA + B$_1$ are

$B_1 -$, the word 'prototroph' will, for convenience, still be applied to all colonies developing on this medium.

Nutrient broth and *nutrient agar* were those routinely employed by this department and were prepared from a tryptic digest of beef. Whenever possible, the same batch of medium was used over long periods and always throughout one experiment.

Technique of recombination tests

(1) *Standard technique.* Bottles of nutrient broth at 37° were seeded separately with 1/10 vol. overnight broth culture of each of the two strains to be mated. After 3–5 hr. growth at 37°, 5 ml. of each culture were mixed, centrifuged at once, and the deposit washed in three changes of 0·9 % (w/v) NaCl buffered at pH 7·2 (hereafter referred to as saline) and resuspended in 1·0 ml. saline. A standard loopful (i.e. a fully charged 2 mm. diameter welded platinum loop = c. 0·01 ml.) of this suspension was transferred to the surface of $MA + B_1$ in 3 cm. diameter plates and uniformly distributed with a small glass spreader. Tests involving counts of prototroph colonies were always duplicated or triplicated and the counts made after 40–45 hr. at 37°. Using this technique, the usual 58-161 × W-677 mating yielded 20–80 prototroph colonies per plate, depending on the age of the broth cultures employed. With less efficient mating systems the mixture, after washing, was resuspended in appropriate smaller volumes of saline.

(2) *Simplified screening technique.* Later in this work the need arose for a technique whereby large numbers of colonies could be tested rapidly for capacity to show recombination with a gene acceptor (indicator) strain. A portion of each colony to be tested was picked with a platinum loop and rubbed over an area c. 0·75 cm. diameter on the surface of a nutrient agar plate. About thirty such areas could be accommodated on a 9 cm. diameter plate. After 1–1·5 hr. at 37° the plate was exposed to a standard dose of ultraviolet light and reincubated for 1 hr. The growth on each area was then thoroughly rubbed up in a standard (2 mm.) loopful of a young broth culture of the indicator strain and the plate reincubated at 37° overnight. The mixed growth from each area was suspended in 0·5 ml. saline and a standard loopful of this suspension spread over an area of similar size on $MA + B_1$. Recombination was assessed by the presence or absence of colonies after c. 42 hr. at 37°. The small amount of nutrient material in the dense saline suspensions usually initiated considerable confluent syntrophic growth but this did not seriously interfere with the reading of results. When the colonies to be tested were S^s, an S^r indicator strain was employed and SM incorporated in the $MA + B_1$. This effectively abolished syntrophic growth without affecting the development of prototroph colonies. Falsely positive results do not arise with this screening technique, while false negatives never exceeded 10 % and were usually considerably lower. Cultures of all colonies showing aberrant or unexpected results were checked by the standard technique after exposure to ultraviolet irradiation.

Total viable counts. A $1/10^5$ (or other appropriate) dilution of each broth culture was made just before mixing, and standard (2 mm.) loopfuls spread on nutrient agar in triplicate. Colonies were counted after 16–18 hr. at 30°. Since the strains of bacteria used were 'rough' (with one exception mentioned below), loss of cells during washing was negligible, so that results of viable counts indicated fairly accurately the actual numbers of cells of each mutant participating in recombination.

Technique for determining marker characters of prototrophs

The surfaces of prototroph colonies on $MA + B_1$ were touched with a sterile wire which was then rubbed over nutrient agar slants in such a way as to yield isolated colonies. After incubation a well separated colony of each isolate was picked and suspended in a small volume of saline to yield a faint turbidity. Using a straight wire, a very small inoculum from these suspensions was spotted to points on the surface of a series of solid indicator media in 9 cm. diameter plates positioned over a template. The following media were used:

(1) *Fermentative capacity.* Peptone water-agar containing 1·0 % (w/v) of the carbohydrate + neutral red as indicator.

(2) *Phage resistance or sensitivity.* Nutrient agar plates flooded with undiluted phage suspension containing not less than 10^9 particles/ml., the excess fluid being withdrawn and the plates dried.

(3) *Streptomycin sensitivity or resistance.* Nutrient agar containing 200–250 μg./ml. streptomycin (SM). A plate of $MA + B_1$ was always included in the series as a check on prototrophism.

In some later experiments involving the testing of considerable numbers of prototrophs for fermentative and SM characters only, prototroph colonies were touched with a sterile wire and spotted directly to a series of plates of $MA + B_1$ containing the test carbohydrates in place of glucose (growth indicating fermentation), and of $MA + B_1 + glucose + SM$ (200 μg./ml.).

RESULTS

A strain of each of the K-12 mutants 58-161 and W-677 which had ceased to yield prototroph colonies in mixed culture after storage for a year on inspissated egg in the refrigerator, were kindly supplied by Dr C. C. Spicer. These strains, which will be referred to initially as 58-161/*sp* and W-677/*sp*, were shown to be identical in their nutritional and marker characters to the fertile strains of the same designation described above.

Analysis of the infertile 58-161/sp × W-677/sp mating

Each strain was crossed with the heterologous fertile mutant. The mating 58-161 × W-677/*sp* yielded about the same number of prototrophs as 58-161 × W-677, while the 58-161/*sp* × W-677 and 58-161/*sp* × W-677/*sp* matings were sterile. The inference that 58-161/*sp* was the defective partner of the infertile combination was confirmed for fifteen colonies from a plating of this strain. In order to demonstrate, in so far as was possible, that the infertility of 58-161/*sp* was complete and not merely minimal, a culture of one of these colonies was tested for recombination with W-677 after ultraviolet irradiation under optimal conditions. No recombination was observed. Following irradiation, however, strain 58-161/*sp* (like 58-161 and W-677) liberated λ phage so that its infertility was not due to failure of some genetic mechanism potentiated by the lysis accompanying phage release.

Behaviour of infertile 58-161/sp *as a gene acceptor*

These findings had been predicted by the hypothesis that gene donor cells (58-161) differed from gene acceptor cells (W-677) only in the possession of an agency whereby genes, or groups of genes, could be transferred outside the cell and thence, by contact, to an acceptor cell. For the sake of simple exposition the term 'carrier' will be used to denote this agency without any implications as to its nature or function. It seemed, therefore, that the most likely cause of infertility in a previously fertile combination was loss by the donor partner of its carrier. The cells of such a strain would be similar to acceptor cells so far as their potential for recombination was concerned, and should therefore be capable of mating and forming prototrophs with a donor strain of dissimilar genotype.

A streptomycin-resistant mutant of 58-161/*sp* was selected (58-161/*sp*/S^r) and tested in comparison with W-677/S^r for ability to show recombination with K-12 (wild-type) and with ten prototroph strains derived from a 58–161 × W-677 cross. The 'SRP' (streptomycin-resistant prototroph) method described by Lederberg (1951) was used, in which a mixture of an S^r mutant of a nutritionally dependent strain (e.g. W-677/S^r) and an S^s prototrophic strain is seeded to MA + SM which prevents growth of both parent strains but allows S^r prototrophic recombinants to develop into colonies. Since the rate of mutation to S^r is about one/10^{10} cell generations in *Bact. coli* (Newcombe & Hawirko, 1949) the ratio of mutant to recombinant colonies is insignificant. In the present series of tests, control platings of double inocula of each strain on MA + B$_1$ + SM yielded no mutant colonies. Strain 58-161/*sp*/S^r proved fertile when mated with K-12 and yielded about the same number of recombinant colonies as the K-12 × W-677/S^r cross. Similarly, 58-161/*sp*/S^r was successfully mated with nine of the ten prototroph recombinant strains tested, the one strain which did not form recombinants failing to do so with W-677/S^r also. The findings described above are summarized in Table 1. It was evident from this analysis that 58-161/*sp* had lost its donor properties and had in consequence become an acceptor strain displaying the same degree of fertility as W-677 in matings with K-12 and other prototroph donors.

Lederberg *et al.* (1952), in an independent and closely parallel investigation, have suggested the symbol 'F −' to denote strains which are completely infertile on mating together, and 'F +' to denote strains which form fertile matings with F − as well as with other F + strains. Since it has become quite clear that the term 'donor' is synonymous with 'F +' and 'acceptor' with 'F −', this convenient terminology will be used henceforth in this paper. Thus 58-161 is F +, and W-677 and 58-161/*sp* are F −.

Restoration of 58-161/F − fertility

Working on the assumption that the alteration of 58-161/*sp* from F + to F − was due to loss of a gene carrier, it seemed possible that this strain might be able to reacquire its carrier by infection from an F + strain of similar genotype, and thus be restored to the F + state, in much the same way that lysogenic bacteria which have lost their phage can reacquire it by infection.

Table 1. *Summary of results of various matings relating to fertility analysis of the sterile pair of K-12 mutants 58-161/sp and W-677/sp*

Object of matings	Matings	No. prototroph colonies (Average of duplicates)
Initial analysis	58-161/*sp* × W-677/*sp*	0
	58-161/*sp* × W-677	0
	58-161 × W-677/*sp*	109
	58-161 × W-677	71
Confirmation by sensitive ultra-violet technique	58-161/*sp*/UV × W-677	0
	58-161 × W-677	52
	58-161/UV × W-677	365
Behaviour of infertile 'donor' strain as a gene acceptor	K-12 × 58-161/*sp*/S^r	144
	K-12 × W-677/S^r	180
Prototrophs (S^s): nos. 1, 2, 3, 4, 6, 7, 8, 9, 10	× 58-161/*sp*/S^r	Numerous, not counted
	× W-677/S^r	Numerous, not counted
Prototroph (S^s): no. 5	× 58-161/*sp*/S^r	0
	× W-677/S^r	0

58-161 and W-677 = mutants of fertile combination.
58-161/*sp* and W-677/*sp* = mutants of sterile combination obtained from Dr C. C. Spicer.
/UV = exposed to standard dosage ultraviolet light, followed by incubation in nutrient broth for 60 min. prior to mixing with W-677 culture and washing.
/S^r = streptomycin-resistant mutant.
S^s prototrophs derived from a 58-161 × W-677 mating.

Strain 58-161/S^r/F − was marked by resistance to 0·002 M-sodium azide (Az^r) so that it could be selected from mixed culture with a doubly sensitive strain and identified with certainty. To a young broth culture of 58-161/F +, 1/20 vol. of a similar culture of 58-161/S^{r}Az^r/F − was added and the mixture incubated overnight at 37°. A loopful was plated on nutrient agar + SM. After incubation, twenty-five well isolated colonies were picked, purified by replating on SM-agar and checked for azide resistance. Each of the twenty-five recovered strains was then tested by the screening technique for recombination with W-677/F −. In two separate experiments, 8/25 and 10/25 recovered strains (i.e. an average of 36 %) yielded prototroph colonies and had, therefore, become F +.

F + transfer between strains of dissimilar genotype

The uniquely high rate of F − to F + transformation in 58-161/F − suggested that 58-161/F + might transfer its F + factor to W-677/F − with equal efficiency. An S^{r}Az^r mutant of W-677/F − was grown in mixed culture

167

with 58-161/F + under the same conditions as in the previous experiments. Recovered W-677/S^{r}Az^r isolates showed a 75% conversion rate to F + as shown by the ability of the isolates to yield prototrophs with 58-161/F −. Repeated experiments using the same technique, or simply employing fermentation capacity as a marker when the originally F − strain was S^{s}Az^s, have never shown a conversion rate of less than 40% after overnight mixed culture in nutrient broth.

It was realized that the concept upon which these experiments had been planned, i.e. that the agent responsible for F + transfer and the carrier concerned in recombination were the same, now seemed to lead to the paradox that the real recombination rate was about a million times greater than the rate demonstrable by the usual technique of prototroph selection. If this was indeed the case, frequent rearrangements of marker and nutritional characters would be expected among F + isolates from an F − strain converted by an F + strain of complementary genotype. Twenty-five W-677/F + isolates, from two separate mixed cultures of W-677/F − and 58-161/F +, were tested for alteration in each of ten characters which distinguish W-677 from 58-161. All the isolates conformed to W-677 phenotype.

Properties of the F + agent

For technical reasons only a small number of experiments on the character of the F + agent have as yet been performed. The results of certain of these experiments are sufficiently clear-cut, however, to warrant reporting.

Transmissibility and stability. The F + agent appears to be indefinitely transmissible through a series of F − strains. For example, in the course of preparing various F + stocks, the following series of transfers was effected without apparent loss in efficiency of transmission:

$$58\text{-}161/F + \; \rightarrow \; W\text{-}677/S^rAz^r/F - \; \rightarrow \; 58\text{-}161/F - \; \rightarrow W\text{-}677/F - \; \rightarrow$$
$$58\text{-}161/S^rAz^r/F -.$$

Stocks of F + strains obtained in this way have proved stable on subculture and on storage for several months on Dorset's egg medium at 4°.

Filterability. The F + agent appears to be held back by a collodion membrane of $0.74\,\mu$. A.P.D. In three experiments, overnight growth of W-677/F − in filtrates of young broth cultures of 58-161/F + failed to yield any recombinants or any F + isolates from a total of 115 colonies tested. Even if only a very small number of F + agents had passed the filter, a disproportionately large number of conversions would be expected from autoinfection during overnight incubation.

F + transfer in relation to prototroph development on MA. Since all except one of a considerable number of recombinant prototrophs from F + × F − crosses had proved to be F +, it was decided to determine whether the high efficiency of F − to F + conversion in nutrient broth obtained also under actual conditions of recombination on MA + B$_1$. A washed suspension of a mixture of 58-161/F + and W-677/F − was prepared under standard conditions and three drops (c. 0.06 ml.) spread evenly over the surface of MA + B$_1$

in a 9 cm. diameter plate. After 24 hr. at 37° developing prototroph colonies were clearly discernible with a hand-lens. Sweeps were made with a wire loop from four areas on the plate (taking care to avoid prototroph colonies), the organisms suspended in saline and then plated on lactose indicator medium. After incubation, 60 W-677 (non-lactose-fermenting) colonies were picked and tested for recombination with 58-161/F −. Only 2/60 isolates had become F +. On the other hand, when sixty of 102 prototroph colonies which had arisen on the original plate were picked, purified and tested for recombination with 58-161/F − by precisely the same technique as before, 55/60 were found to be F +. The remaining five strains which appeared F − proved to be F + also when re-tested by the standard technique following ultraviolet irradiation. Thus, when tested under similar conditions, the F + conversion rate of non-recombinant F − cells under the actual conditions of the recombination test was only 3·6 %, while that of recombinants was 100 %.

The relative efficiency of F + × F − and F + × F + crosses

The obvious relevance of the F + agent to the recombination process, as shown by the sterility of F − × F − matings, implied that fertility depended either on both mating cells being F +, or on one being F + and the other F −. If possession of F + by each of two cells is necessary for mating, then clearly an F + × F + cross should be more efficient than an F + × F − one since in the former all the cells are compatible from the start, while in the latter, mating must occur in two stages—first the transference of F + to the F − partner (which was shown above to be inefficient under recombination conditions on MA) and, secondly, the actual mating between the now compatible F + cells. On the other hand, if an F + cell is merely one which possesses a carrier (i.e. is a gene donor) which can only be taken up by a carrier-free F − cell, then an F + × F − cross should be much the more productive. The details of one of several such comparative experiments are given in Table 2.

Table 2. *Relative efficiency of F + × F − and F + × F + matings*

Standard recombination technique employed

Matings	No. prototroph colonies				Av.	Total viable counts (av. of triplicates)	
						Strain	Organisms per ml.
58-161/F + × W-677/F −	92	105	108	82	97	58-161/F +	945×10^6
						58-161/F −	828×10^6
58-161/F + × W-677/F +	5	2	4	5	4	W-677/F +	477×10^6
58-161/F − × W-677/F +	39	59	nt	nt	49	W-677/F −	450×10^6

Strain 58-161/F + = original F + strain; strain 58-161/F − = 58-161/*sp.*; strain W-677/F + = W-677/F − converted to F + by 58-161/F +.
nt = no test performed.

It will be seen that the 58-161/F + × W-677/F − cross yielded *c.* 20 times as many prototrophs as 58-161/F + × W-677/F +. That this result was not due to some abnormality of W-677/F +, apart from its acquisition of F +, is shown by the 12-fold rise in recombination rate when this strain was crossed with 58-161/F −. Strain 112-12, a non-lysogenic cystine- and histidine-requiring F + mutant of K-12 (kindly supplied by Dr A. Lwoff and Dr E. Wollman), was similarly tested against F + and F − strains of 58-161 and W-677. In each case the F + × F − cross was 15–30 times more productive than F + × F +.

Strain 58-161/F − is relatively 'smooth' and therefore slower to sediment on centrifugation than the other strains used, so that loss during washing tends to become appreciable. When steps were taken to decrease this loss to a minimum, the matings 58-161/F + × W-677/F − and 58-161/F − × W-677/F + produced the same number of prototrophs on $MA + B_1$. When, however, samples of these same two mixtures were plated, under the same conditions, on MA alone and on $MA + B_1 + T$, the relative efficiency of the two matings varied widely, as Table 3 shows. These findings have been confirmed and offer

Table 3. *The effect of growth factor supplements on the relative efficiency of* $58\text{-}161/F + \times W\text{-}677/F -$ *and* $58\text{-}161/F - \times W\text{-}677/F +$ *matings*

Standard recombination technique employed

Matings	Medium		
	MA	$MA + B_1$	$MA + B_1 + T$
	No. of prototroph colonies (triplicate counts)		
58-161/F + × W-677/F −	3–2–5 (3)	51–57–54 (54)	113–114–107 (111)
58-161/F − × W-677/F +	32–35–28 (32)	64–56–58 (59)	22–18–21 (20)
Controls:			
58-161 alone (F + and F −)	(0)	(0)	(0)
W-677 alone (F + and F −)	(0)	(0)	(0)

MA = minimal agar; B_1 = thiamine 0·0005 % (w/v); T = threonine 0·0025 % (w/v); strain 58-161 = $M - T + L + B_1 +$; strain W-677 = $M + T - L - B_1 -$; () = average of triplicate counts.

some additional evidence for one-way transfer of genetic material from the F + to the F − strain. Thus when W-677, requiring three growth factors (T, L, B_1), is F −, the addition of each successive supplement to MA should reduce the number of genetic deficiencies to be made good by transfer from 58-161/F + in order to allow growth, and should therefore increase the apparent recombination rate. This in fact occurs. On the other hand, 58-161 is M − only, so that the efficiency of the W-677/F + × 58-161/F − cross should be unaffected by B_1 and T supplements, except insofar as these supplements might encourage syntrophic growth. Why the addition of threonine decreases the efficiency of this mating is not known, although it may possibly act as a methionine inhibitor. Teas, Horowitz & Fling (1948), working with a doubly deficient *Neurospora* mutant, implicated homoserine as the precursor of both threonine and methionine in this strain and reported inhibition of growth in the presence of excess methionine which was reversed by increasing the threonine concentration.

The relationship of the F + agent to the phenotype of recombinants

Previous analysis of 404 prototroph colonies from sixteen separate 58-161/F + × W-677/F − crosses had shown that, while 279 had a pattern of unselected marker characters (Lac, Mann, T_1 and T_3) different from that of either parent, 103 showed the phenotype of W-677 and only four that of 58-161. Moreover, the four prototrophs displaying the 58-161 phenotype all arose among thirty prototrophs from two consecutive matings. If these two aberrant matings are excluded, then of 374 prototrophs from fourteen separate matings, ninety-seven had the phenotype of W-677 and none that of 58-161. If the two fermentative reactions (Lac, Mann) alone are considered, 62 % of prototrophs had the W-677 phenotype of unselected markers. Discovery of the F + factor suggested that this gross bias of recombinants towards the phenotype of the F − (or gene acceptor) strain might be reversed by transposing the F potential of the mating partners. The effect of F + transposition on the phenotype of recombinants is clearly demonstrated by the results of the two experiments presented in Table 4. The number of prototrophs tested is small but the results are clear-cut and reproducible, although

Table 4. *The effect of F + transposition on the phenotype of prototrophs from otherwise similar crosses*

	No. of protroph colonies having the phenotype of			
Matings	58-161	W-677	New combinations	Total
Exp. 1. Marker characters = Lac, Mann, Mal, Gal, SM				
58-161/S^r/F+ × W-677/F −	0	11	4	15
58-161/S^r/F − × W-677/F +	11	0	3	14
58-161/S^r/F+ × W-677/F +	4	6	4	14
Exp. 2. Marker characters = Lac, Mann, phages T_1, T_3				
58-161/F+ × W-677/F −	0	8	2	10
58-161/F − × W-677/F +	13	0	7	20
58-161/F+ × W-677/F +	8	7	5	20

Strain 58-161 = Lac + Mann + Mal + Gal + phages $T_1{}^s T_3{}^r$
Strain W-677 = Lac − Mann − Mal − Gal − phages $T_1{}^r T_3{}^s$

the proportion of prototrophs having new combinations of unselected markers to those having the F − phenotype seems to vary widely from one experiment to another irrespective of the marker pattern used for analysis. Since all these recombinants were obtained by prototroph selection, it was pertinent to determine whether recombinants selected by some other method showed bias of their nutritional requirements towards those of the F − partner. Strain 58-161/F + was mated with W-677/S^r/F − on MA + Lac + SM, supplemented with all the growth factors required by both strains (M, T, L, B_1). Since 58-161 is Lac + S^s and W-677 is Lac − S^r, only Lac + S^r recombinants can develop on this medium. Control experiments showed that no colonies arose from back-mutation when each strain was plated separately. Of forty-eight recombinant colonies selected in this way, all grew on $MA + TLB_1$ and only one on $MA + M$ (this isolate also grew on MA alone). Analysis of these strains was restricted by contamination of the available amino-acid preparations by thiamine. However, eleven of twenty-four of these recombinants were found to require $T + L$ for growth and since $c.$ 90 % of prototrophs from similar crosses on $MA + B_1$ are B_1-dependent (Lederberg, 1947) it may be assumed that nearly all of these were $TLB_1 -$ and, therefore, of $W-677/F -$ phenotype. The converse of this experiment after $F +$ transposition has not yet proved possible due to difficulty in obtaining a stable Lac $-$ mutant of $58-161/S^r/F -$. It is clear that this dependence of phenotype on the $F +$ relationships of a mating invalidates the evidence for at least a proportion of genetic linkages previously postulated for K-12. For instance, Newcombe & Nyholm (1950 a, b) tentatively suggested linkage between S^r and the biotin and methionine loci as the result of reversed crosses in which S^r was introduced alternately into each parent as in matings 1 and 2 in Table 5. Moreover, using 58-161 and W-677, they observed evidence of linkage between S^r and fermentation of the sugars Gal, Mal, Xyl, Arab but not of Lac. Reference to Table 5 shows that when the same reverse crosses are carried out after $F +$ transposition (matings 3 and 4) the apparent linkage of S^r is the opposite of that implied by matings 1 and 2, indicating that S^r is not linked with methionine. When the sugar

Table 5. *The effect of F + transposition on the inheritance of streptomycin resistance in reversed crosses*

	No. of prototrophs		
Matings	S^r	S^s	No. examined
1. $58-161/S^r/F + \times W-677/F -$	3	149	152
2. $58-161/F + \times W-677/S^r/F -$	146	5	151
3. $58-161/S^r/F - \times W-677/F +$	56	8	64
4. $58-161/F - \times W-677/S^r/F +$	6	54	60

fermentations of prototrophs from these $S^s \times S^r$ crosses are examined the same contrary results are obtained, matings 1 and 2, for example, suggesting positive linkage and matings 3 and 4 negative linkage between S^r and Mal $+$. Thus the evidence of Tables 4 and 5 invalidates the evidence for the postulated linkages between loci for growth requirements and sugar fermentations, streptomycin and phage susceptibility, and between loci for streptomycin and sugar fermentations.

DISCUSSION

Since all the salient findings described above have been independently discovered and reported by Lederberg *et al.* (1952), and by Cavalli, Lederberg & Lederberg (1953), there can be little doubt as to the validity of the results themselves. Their interpretation, however, is controversial. The chief point at issue, from which any ultimate concept of the physiological and genetic basis of recombination in *Bact. coli* must stem, is whether the phenomenon is fundamentally one of zygote formation followed by crossing-over and segregation in which the full chromosomal content of each partner participates more or less equally but in which the phenotypic expression of segregants may be profoundly modified by elimination of chromosomal segments introduced by the F + partner (Lederberg, 1949; Lederberg *et al.* 1952), or whether there is a one-way transfer of restricted groups of genes from the F + to the F − parent, possibly followed by crossing-over and meiosis limited to the immigrant genes and their alleles, so that the genotype of the progeny remains basically that of the F − parent (see Hayes, 1952 *a, b* and the following discussion).

The concept of one-way gene transfer arose from the observation that SM destroyed the fertility of F − but not of F + cells. The essential validity of this observation was confirmed by Lederberg (personal correspondence) who found that while S^{s}F + × S^{r}F − crosses were productive on SM − minimal agar, the fertility of S^{r}F + × S^{s}F − crosses was negligible. Moreover F − cells which have been converted to F + behave as 'natural' F + cells in relation to SM, irrespective of their genotype. There is thus little doubt that SM exerts a differential effect on F + and F − cells. Since both types of cell are equally sensitive to the lethal action of the drug it is logical to conclude that F + cells must possess an agent, intimately associated with fertility and at least relatively resistant to the action of SM, which is absent from F − cells.

The effect of ultraviolet light in stimulating the fertility of F +, but not of F −, cells (Hayes, 1952 *b*) confirmed the possession by the former of an additional function related to the recombination process. The similarity of the conditions under which exposure of F + cells to ultraviolet became effective, to those required for maturation of prophage in lysogenic bacteria suggested that some agency of the nature of virus or prophage might be the instrument of gene transfer (Lwoff *et al.* 1950 *a, b*; Lwoff, 1951). This ultraviolet work has now been in part repeated with each of two non-lysogenic, F + mutants of K-12 (kindly supplied by Dr A. Lwoff and Dr E. Wollman, and by Dr J. Lederberg) with the same results, so that the effect of ultraviolet on the recombination potential of F + cells is a primary one and not secondary to release of λ phage. Recent work on the action of ultraviolet in inducing synthesis of new substances such as pyocines and colicines (as well as of phage) for which the cells have a covert propensity (Jacob, Siminovitch & Wollman, 1951; Lwoff, 1953), enlarges the field of speculation as to the mechanism of fertility enhancement of F + strains of K-12. It was thought not improbable that the agent of genetic transfer, while clearly not λ phage (Lederberg *et al.* 1952), or other potentially lytic phage, might be a non-pathogenic virus whose only overt function was to act as a genetic carrier. The discovery of the F + factor with its high efficiency of transfer to F − cells, its replication within them and its essential role in recombination, appeared to offer strong vindication of this theory. The fact that the great majority of F − cells, infected with F + factor derived from cells of complementary genotype, showed no phenotypic alteration did not exclude F + as a genetic carrier, since effective association of such a carrier with genes from the cell it inhabits might well occur only under exceptional physiological conditions. This interpretation appeared the more plausible in view of the difficulty of accounting for the low rate of recombination among the cells of potentially fertile bacterial clones by more orthodox sexual mechanisms.

The factual relationship of the F + factor to recombination is not in dispute: F − × F − matings are completely sterile; maximum fertility is shown by F + × F − matings, while the fertility of F + × F + matings is much lower. Lederberg *et al.* (1952) tentatively suggest that this is compatible with a concept of relative sexuality, whereby the fertility of different crosses would be proportional to the F + differential between the partners. Thus there would exist different grades of F +, F − having a grade of zero, so that the highest recombination rate would be given by F 4 + × F − crosses and progressively lower rates by the series of crosses F 3 + × F −, F 2 + × F − or F 4 + × F 2 +, F 4 + × F 3 + and so on. In support of this they show that the ratio of efficiency of F + × F + : F + × F − crosses may vary widely when various combinations of different auxotrophic mutants are tested. On the other hand, Table 3 of the present paper shows that the relative efficiency of 58-161/F + × W-677/F − and 58-161/F − × W-677/F + crosses can vary from 1:10 to 5:1 depending on the addition to, or withdrawal from, the minimal medium of growth factor supplements. It is simpler to suppose that fertility depends on the presence of a gene carrier in F + cells and its absence from F − cells. The greater productivity of F + × F − over F + × F + crosses is thus explained since in the former every contact between an F + and an F − cell is a potentially fertile mate. The occurrence of limited fertility in F + × F + crosses requires the assumption that a proportion of F + cells from each parental population becomes effectively F −. It is evident that many F + cells must extrude or otherwise liberate their F + agent, in order to account for its transmissibility to F − cells, so that such cells might become effectively F − until reinfected by F + agent from either homologous or heterologous cells. In the latter case a small proportion of reinfected cells would become recombinants. Since in F + × F + crosses the majority of contacts would be between F + cells which form potentially infertile mates, a low degree of fertility would be expected. Direct evidence for the presence of F − cells in F + populations is lacking and would be difficult to obtain since their existence must be transitory due to the efficiency of the F + conversion process. All of 140 colonies tested from the plating of a 58-161/F + clone were F +. There is, however, some significant indirect evidence. For instance, Table 4 demonstrates that in F + × F − matings the majority of prototrophs carry the phenotype of the F − parent and none that of the F + parent. In prototrophs from F + × F + crosses, however, the phenotypes of both parents are more or less equally represented, while the proportion of prototrophs showing new combinations of characters is the same as before. If a proportion of the cells of an F + clone are transiently F −, then treatment of an F + culture with SM should destroy the fertility of these F − cells. Provided that mating can occur only between F + and F − cells, it follows that if only one F + parent culture in an F + × F + cross is treated with SM, then the treated parent should behave as pure F + and the untreated parent as pure F − as judged by analysis of the unselected marker patterns of the resulting prototrophs. This has recently been demonstrated experimentally, irrespective of which F+ parent in the cross was subjected to SM treatment. When both F+ parents were treated with SM, the cross was sterile. Again, if either F+ parent in an F+ ×F+ cross is treated with ultraviolet light the prototroph yield increases markedly while the phenotype of prototrophs shifts markedly towards that of the unirradiated strain, i.e. the irradiated parent behaves as if its 'F+ grade' had been increased. The theory of relative sexuality would therefore predict that if both F+ parents were irradiated, the prototroph count should fall to its former level from restoration of the relative F+ grades on both sides of the cross. In fact, when both F+ parents are irradiated the prototroph count rises to a higher level than when either parent alone is treated with ultraviolet.

The parental phenotypes are not always equally distributed among prototrophs from various F+ ×F+ crosses, but since in most of these experiments the same F+ agent was harboured by both parents (as a result of previous direct or serial transmission from one to the other) the variable results would point to different degrees of stability of F+ in different strains rather than to any qualitative grades of fertility involving all the cells of a strain.

Aberrant linkage behaviour in K-12 has been noted by several workers (Lederberg, 1949, 1950; Newcombe & Nyholm, 1950 a–c). The attention of Lederberg himself was drawn to these aberrations by the apparent elimination of certain chromosomal segments, involving especially the SM and Mal loci, from persistent K-12 diploids which consequently appeared hemizygous for these characters. It was then found that the segment subject to elimination was that contributed by the F+ parent. Lederberg et al. (1952) therefore tentatively explained the bias of recombinants towards the F− phenotype by the elimination of segments of the F+ chromosome after zygote formation. Some of the experimental results recorded here would seem to require elimination of large parts of the F+ chromosome, or of different parts of it under different environmental conditions of recombination, while the role of F+ in the matter remains obscure. A more economical hypothesis is that only part of the F+ chromosome is transmitted to the F− parent in the first place. If it is supposed, in addition, that the F+ agent is the genetic carrier, then the determining role of this factor on fertility and phenotype falls neatly into place.

F+ has many of the characters of a non-lytic infective agent. Since it is hardly to be supposed that its high efficiency of transfer is mediated by cytoplasmic fusion it must presumably leave the cell and, since it is not present in filtrates, remain adsorbed to the cell surface until taken up by an F− cell. These latter are two of the properties attributed to a hypothetical gene carrier as a result of previous work before the F+ agent was discovered (Hayes, 1952 a, b). It was first shown by Cavalli (personal communication) and has been confirmed here and by Lederberg et al. (1952) that all recombinant prototrophs (with the single exception mentioned above) are F+; there is also evidence that F+ ×F− combinations alone are fertile (so far as individual cells are concerned) and that the direction of gene transfer is from the

F + to the F − parent. Under the actual conditions of recombination in an F + × F − cross on minimal agar, however, the efficiency of transfer of the F + agent is only 3–4 %. Assuming the premises are valid, there is thus a high degree of probability that the transfer of genes and of F + agent are correlated. Against this may be placed the results of a single experiment which seems to show fairly clearly (1) that while treatment of the F + parent of a cross with ultraviolet light greatly increases the recombination rate, the efficiency of F + transmission is concurrently depressed and (2) that the action of SM on S^sF+ reduces the F + conversion rate markedly in disproportion to the prototroph count when the treated suspension is mixed with an S^rF- strain. Substantiation of the first of these findings would not invalidate the theory suggested here, for while the F + agent is favoured as the most likely carrier of the genetic elements, the two are regarded as distinct entities. If, for example, one of the effects of ultraviolet light was to increase 20-fold the proportion of F + agents effectively associated with parts of the bacterial chromosome, a concomitant 50 % reduction in the efficiency of F + transfer (approximately that actually observed) would still allow a tenfold enhancement of recombination rate. While discussion of the differential action of SM on the transfer of genes and F + agent is, perhaps, premature, it is possible that an explanation may be found in different degrees of stability of complexes of SM with F + agent alone and with F + agent associated with chromosomal segments, such as have been described for coliphage T_2 and T_4, with and without an external coating of deoxyribonucleic acid, by Cohen (1947 a, b).

The main aim of this discussion has been to present a theory of recombination which is sufficiently plausible to serve as a useful working hypothesis. It is possible that its substantiation in principle might reveal recombination in *Bact. coli* as a key stage in the evolution of mature sexual processes from simple genetic transformations. The speculative nature of the theory is fully admitted, however, and it is clear that a generally acceptable concept of the intimate mechanism of recombination must await the results of further experimental work.

I wish to express my indebtedness to Dr L. L. Cavalli and Dr J. Lederberg, not only for gifts of cultures but especially for the stimulus which the free exchange of views and experimental results with them has offered me; and to Dr D. A. Mitchison for the benefit of many discussions with him on this subject.

REFERENCES

CAVALLI, L. L., LEDERBERG, J. & LEDERBERG, E. M. (1953). An infective factor controlling sex compatibility in *Bacterium coli. J. gen. Microbiol.* 8, 89.

CAVALLI, L. L. & MACCACARO, G. A. (1950). Chloromycetin resistance in *E. coli*, a case of quantitative inheritance in bacteria. *Nature, Lond.* 166, 991.

COHEN, S. S. (1947a). Streptomycin and desoxyribonuclease in the study of variations in the properties of a bacterial virus. *J. biol. Chem.* 168, 511.

COHEN, S. S. (1947b). The synthesis of bacterial viruses in infected cells. *Cold Spr. Harb. Symp. quant. Biol.* 12, 35.

DAVIS, B. D. (1950). Nonfiltrability of the agents of genetic recombination in *Escherichia coli*. *J. Bact.* **60**, 507.

HAYES, W. (1952a). Recombination in *Bact. coli* K-12: uni-directional transfer of genetic material. *Nature, Lond.* **169**, 118.

HAYES, W. (1952b). Genetic recombination in *Bact. coli* K-12: analysis of the stimulating effect of ultra-violet light. *Nature, Lond.* **169**, 1017.

JACOB, F., SIMINOVITCH, L. & WOLLMAN, E. (1951). Induction de la production d'une colicine par la rayonnement ultraviolet. *C.R. Acad. Sci., Paris*, **233**, 1500.

LEDERBERG, J. (1947). Gene recombination and linked segregations in *Escherichia coli*. *Genetics*, **32**, 505.

LEDERBERG, J. (1949). Aberrant heterozygotes in *Escherichia coli*. *Proc. Nat. Acad. Sci., Wash.* **35**, 178.

LEDERBERG, J. (1950). Segregation in *Escherichia coli*. *Genetics*, **35**, 119 (Abstract).

LEDERBERG, J. (1951). Prevalence of *Escherichia coli* strains exhibiting genetic recombination. *Science*, **114**, 68.

LEDERBERG, J., CAVALLI, L. L. & LEDERBERG, E. M. (1952). Sex compatibility in *Escherichia coli*. *Genetics*, **37**, 720.

LEDERBERG, J. & TATUM, E. L. (1946). Gene recombination in *Escherichia coli*. *Nature, Lond.* **158**, 558.

LWOFF, A. (1951). Conditions de l'efficacité inductrice du rayonnement ultraviolet chez une bactérie lysogène. *Ann. Inst. Pasteur*, **81**, 370.

LWOFF, A. (1953). The nature of phage reproduction. Contribution to Symposium on *The Nature of Virus Multiplication*. *Soc. gen. Microbiol. Symp.* Cambridge University Press. (In the Press.)

LWOFF, A., SIMINOVITCH, L. & KJELGAARD, N. (1950a). Induction de la lyse bactériophagique de la totalité d'une population microbienne lysogène. *C.R. Acad. Sci., Paris*, **231**, 190.

LWOFF, A., SIMINOVITCH, L. & KJELGAARD, N. (1950b). Induction de la production de bacteriophages chez une bacterié lysogène. *Ann. Inst. Pasteur*, **79**, 815.

NEWCOMBE, H. B. & HAWIRKO, R. (1949). Spontaneous mutation to streptomycin resistance and dependence in *Escherichia coli*. *J. Bact.* **57**, 565.

NEWCOMBE, H. B. & NYHOLM, M. H. (1950a). Crosses with streptomycin resistant and dependent mutants of *Escherichia coli*. *Genetics*, **35**, 126 (Abstract).

NEWCOMBE, H. B. & NYHOLM, M. H. (1950b). The inheritance of streptomycin resistance and dependence in crosses of *Escherichia coli*. *Genetics*, **35**, 603.

NEWCOMBE, H. B.. & NYHOLM, M. H. (1950c). Anomalous segregation in crosses of *Escherichia coli*. *Amer. Nat.* **84**, 457.

TATUM, E. L. & LEDERBERG, J. (1947). Gene recombination in the bacterium *Escherichia coli*. *J. Bact.* **53**, 673.

TEAS, H. J., HOROWITZ, N. H. & FLING, M. (1948). Homoserine as a precursor of threonine and methionine in *Neurospora*. *J. biol. Chem.* **172**, 651.

WEIGLE, J. J. & DELBRÜCK, M. (1951). Mutual exclusion between an infecting phage and a carried phage. *J. Bact.* **62**, 301.

ZELLE, M. R. & LEDERBERG, J. (1951). Single cell isolations of diploid heterozygous *Escherichia coli*. *J. Bact.* **61**, 351.

(*Received 7 July* 1952)

Wollman et al. 1956

1. Why do Hfr strains display a higher rate of transfer and recombination of chromosomal markers in a cross with an F⁻ strain than an F⁺ strain does in a cross with an F⁻ strain?

2. What is the mechanism of transfer of chromosomal markers from an F⁺ strain to an F⁻ strain?

3. Describe the experiments pictured in Figure 2 on page 142.

4. Describe the experiments pictured in Figures 3 and 4 on pages 143 and 144, respectively, and explain how they differ from the experiments pictured in Figure 2 on page 142.

5. Explain the experiment pictured in Figure 8 on page 151.

6. What is meant by "segregation" and "phenotypic expression"?

Unit 6

Genetic
Regulatory
Mechanisms

Jacob and Monod 1961
Genetic Regulatory Mechanisms in the Synthesis
of Proteins   **192**

Reprinted with permission from *Journal of Molecular Biology 3:* 318–356

In 1961, François Jacob and Jacques Monod published a series of reviews on their work and that of their colleagues at the Pasteur Institute in Paris that described the extensive experiments that allowed them to formulate the Operon Model of gene regulation. This paradigm reshaped thinking in biology, and all of the incisive work on gene control in both prokaryotes and eukaryotes emanates from their original, brilliant work for which they, together with André Lwoff, were awarded the Nobel prize in medicine in 1965. Their treatise in the *Journal of Molecular Biology*, reprinted here on pages 192–230, is a fascinating paper to dissect, for it shows a style of science that influenced many students and future investigators.

The lives of both Jacob and Monod were greatly affected by the events of World War II, since France was overrun by the Nazis in 1940 and occupied until the summer of 1944. Before analyzing their work, let's review the biographies of these two scientists.

François Jacob

François Jacob's autobiography, *The Statue Within*, in which he bares his soul in reliving his early life and wartime experiences and elaborating on the impressions they made on him, is essential reading for anyone wishing to become acquainted with this extraordinary person. A sample of his writing follows:

> Thus, I carry within a kind of inner statue, a statue sculpted since childhood, that gives my life a continuity and is the most intimate part of me, the hardest kernal of my character. I have been shaping this statue all my life. I have been constantly retouching, polishing, refining it. Here, the chisel and the gouge are made of encounters and interactions; of discordant rhythms; of stray pages from one chapter that slip into another in the almanac of the emotions; terrors induced by what is all sweetness; a need for infinity erupting in bursts of music; a delight surging up at the sight of a stern gaze; an exaltation born from an association of words; all the sensations and constraints, marks left by some people and by others, by the reality of life and by the dream. Thus, I harbor not just one ideal person with whom I continually compare myself. I carry a whole train of moral figures, with utterly contradictory qualities, who in my imagination are always ready to act as my fellow players in situations and dialogues imprinted in my head since childhood or adolescence. For every role in this repertory of the possible, for all the activities that surround me and involve me directly, I thus hold actors ready to respond to cues in comedies and tragedies inscribed in me long ago. Not a gesture, not a word, but has been imposed by the statue within.

Jacob was born in 1920 and grew up against a darkening background in Europe. He was 15 when civil war broke out in Spain, 16 when Germany rearmed and occupied the Rhineland, 17 when the Germans annexed Austria, and 18 when they marched into Czechoslovakia. At this point, he took his university exam and enrolled in medical school.

Jacob initially wanted to be a surgeon, but he notes that during his first year he had hospital training, and when he had to do anesthesia for an operation, he almost killed the patient. This was a difficult time for the young Jacob since his mother was dying of an abdominal tumor. She passed away in June 1940, as the Germans were approaching Paris. When the Germans entered Paris, Jacob, who

was Jewish, fled to Bordeaux with several medical students. He bitterly resented the loss of his country. He was able to sneak onto a boat carrying Polish refugees that was leaving for England. There he joined the Free French forces under Charles de Gaulle. Jacob joined the artillery, where he was assigned to the Medical Corps, since he had had two years of medical school training.

Jacob went with the Free French forces to Africa, stopping in Freetown (Sierra Leone) and Dakar. He served in Gabon and in 1942 in Chad, in the city of Mao, where, under oppressive heat, he performed some surgery and traveled by camel to get to his patients. Once during a minor outbreak of meningitis, Jacob was called to the house of the local sultan to inoculate the sultan and his wives. Jacob looked forward with great anticipation to seeing the sultan's harem. However, on the appointed day, Jacob was led to a room where there was a curtain with a hole in it. As each wife's turn came to be inoculated, an arm would appear through the hole—hardly the view of the mysterious harem that Jacob had expected. It was around this time that Jacob learned of the death of his closest comrade, who was killed some fifty miles from where Jacob was stationed by a spear thrown during an ambush by local tribesmen. Later, Jacob's unit traveled over 1000 miles of desert to reach Libya in the beginning of 1943. In March 1943, they faced Hitler's Africa Korps in Tunisia, and in April 1944, his unit sailed from Casablanca to England.

On August 1, 1944, less than two months after D-Day, Jacob landed at Normandy with General LeClerc's forces. One week later, they moved out toward Le Mans during the night, but they were attacked by German bombers. They evacuated their truck and took cover in a ditch during the raid. After the first assault, Jacob attended to a lieutenant who was seriously wounded. At this point, a second wave of German Junkers approached. Although everyone raced for cover, Jacob, sympathetic to the pleas of the wounded lieutenant, stayed with his comrade. A fragmentation bomb exploded nearby. Jacob felt a shock in his shoulder, and when he tried to move he passed out. He had been severely wounded, with more than 100 pieces of shrapnel in his right side. He was in a large cast and in traction for six months, and he later returned to the hospital for numerous operations to have shrapnel removed. He slowly regained his health, although his wounds trouble him intermittently to this day.

After completing most of his medical studies, Jacob still needed to complete a research thesis to get his medical degree. With antibiotics beginning to revolutionize medicine in the postwar period, Jacob decided to work on tyrothricin, an antibiotic used to treat local infections. Since he had no laboratory experience, his initial efforts to purify the drug from bacteria producing it (which were supplied by an American laboratory) were full of frustration. "Charlie Chaplin goes to the lab," as Jacob phrased it. In time, he gained considerable expertise in this area and soon purified enough material to use in clinical trials at hospitals. The antibiotic was very effective in treating boils, anthrax, and throat ailments. Thus, able to write a thesis, Jacob received his medical degree in the spring of 1947. Subsequently, Jacob married and decided to go into research as a career. In 1949, he received a research fellowship to work at the Pasteur Institute. However, he had to find a place to work. He applied several times to work in André Lwoff's lab, since it was the only lab in the Pasteur doing research that was close to Jacob's emerging interest. He was finally accepted on the day that Lwoff discovered induction of the prophage. Jacob was assigned to work on this project beginning in September 1950. It was in Lwoff's lab that Jacob met Jacques Monod, and sometime later they forged their historic collaboration. Jacob also met many of the top researchers of the day at the Pasteur, and they made the following deep impressions on him:

The Englishman Martin Pollock: "who always, when speaking to you, kept his handsome, insolently aristocratic face fixed on the horizon above your head..."

The Canadian Roger Stanier: "a debonair giant with a wild grin, his eyes crinkling with mischief behind his glasses..."

Sol Spiegelman: "Short, stocky, broken-nosed, looking like a featherweight boxer .... His gestures abrupt and precise. His sentences short and choppy.... Fine little bull this Spiegelman, very excitable, very combative."

Jacques Monod: "Short, with black hair, a handsome face, a determined chin, and high cheekbones, he looked like a cross between a Roman emperor and a Hollywood movie star."

Seymour Benzer: "Of average height, balding, with a fleshy face and a stoutish body, Seymour hid behind an impassive mask much charm and warmth."

Jim Watson: "At the time, to a French student who had not yet been inside an American university or seen its denizens, Jim Watson was an amazing character. Tall, gawky, scraggly, he had an inimitable style. Inimitable in his dress: shirttails flying, knees in the air, socks down around his ankles. Inimitable in his bewildered manner, his mannerisms: his eyes always bulging, his mouth always open, he uttered short, choppy sentences punctuated by 'Ah! Ah!' Inimitable also in his way of entering a room, cocking his head like a rooster looking for the finest hen, to locate the most important scientist present and charging over to his side. A surprising mixture of awkwardness and shrewdness."

Max Delbrück: "A formidable character.... The very conscience of the Phage Group.... Delbrück's rigor, his frankness, his way of going to the heart of a problem were combined with his surprising youthfulness, of mind as of body."

In May 1954, Jacob defended his doctoral thesis. Subsequently, he carried out important experiments with Elie Wollman on conjugation (as reviewed earlier in Unit 5) and worked on the λ and *lac* control systems, as reviewed in this unit. At the end of the 1960s, Jacob shifted his work toward mammalian cells and cancer and he is still active in these areas.

Jacques Monod

Jacques Monod was born in Paris in 1910 to an American mother and a French father. His father was severely afflicted with infantile paralysis, which Monod also contracted as an infant, rendering him lame in one leg. From his youth, Monod was interested in music, and he played the cello throughout his life. In 1928, Monod enrolled at the Sorbonne in Paris, but he was not impressed with the level of teaching there. Several years later, a stay at a Marine Biology Station put him in contact with biologists such as Lwoff and Ephrussi, reinforcing his interest in genetics, which was not emphasized in France. In 1935, Ephrussi invited Monod to come with him to Caltech, where Monod was funded by a Rockefeller fellowship. During this time, he met and was influenced by some of the top geneticists of the era, such as Sturtevant, Beadle, and McClintock. While in the United States, Monod was also greatly influenced by the American style of free discussions.

At Caltech, Monod continued to follow his interest in music, organizing a Bach society that gave public performances. (He had previously formed a Bach choral group in Paris.) He was even offered a position to teach music appreciation at Caltech. Monod's priorities were of course in science.

After returning to Paris in 1937, Monod started work on his thesis, selecting *E. coli* growth as his topic. He initiated a series of experiments measuring the growth rate of *E. coli* on different sugars. The following year he got married, and the year after that he was the father of twins. When war broke out in Europe in 1939, Monod served briefly with the Army, even though he had been exempted from military service because of his leg. After the Nazi occupation of Paris, Monod still maintained a laboratory at the Sorbonne and carried out experiments on bacterial growth.

In 1940, Monod discovered diauxic growth. This phenomenon occurs when bacteria are presented with two sugars. At first, the bacteria grow rapidly on one carbon source until it is exhausted, and then, after a lag time, they grow on the second, although at a slower rate. It was thought by many, including Lwoff, that this was a case of so-called enzymatic adaptation in which the bacteria developed the capacity to synthesize the enzyme to metabolize the second sugar. Monod received his Ph.D. at the end of 1940.

Also in 1940, Monod sent his Jewish wife to the south of France to escape persecution and joined the Resistance movement. He also joined the Communist Party, since this was a prerequisite to having influence in the most effective armed resistance group. Because members of the Resistance were constantly being exposed and arrested, he was often on the run, sleeping in different houses on different nights. Possibly wanted by the Nazis, he could no longer return to his lab at the Sorbonne, where on one occasion he had hidden secret papers in the hollow leg bones of a giraffe skeleton. However, Lwoff let him work in his lab at the Pasteur Institute.

To explain the apparent enzymatic adaptation he had observed, Monod temporarily embraced a model in which enzymes were formed from precursors, something one could only envision in vague terms. The substrate allowed the precursors to form around it, thus molding the catalytic center. We should recall that at that time neither the structure of a protein nor the mechanism of its synthesis had been elucidated.

In 1944, Monod completed an extraordinary study with Alice Audureau. Working with a naturally occurring Lac⁻ strain that could revert to Lac⁺, which Monod termed *E. coli mutabile,* he detected the Lac⁺ revertants as papillae. The number of papillae was not uniform, which independently showed the partly random origin of spontaneous mutations. (Several months later he read the Luria and Delbrück paper on the same topic.) He focused on the diauxic phenomenon in the Lac⁺ bacteria, in which the ability to metabolize lactose appeared when the cells were exposed to lactose after a lag (the "induction effect").

Monod rose to the post of Chief of Staff of Operations in the Resistance in the Paris area and helped to coordinate Allied parachute drops of materials and arms prior to the Normandy invasion by communicating through Switzerland. After the war ended, Monod split with the Communist Party over the infamous Lysenko affair. Lysenko, who had been an obscure minister, rose to fame in Communist Russia by denouncing Western ideas about genetics and inheritance. He insisted that acquired characteristics could be inherited. People who disagreed with him were purged from the Party and even imprisoned. Under Stalin, he rose to head the agricultural research program, and by 1948 he had forced Russian biologists to denounce the chromosomal theory of inheritance. For them, genes did not exist! Many members of the Communist Party abroad broke with the Party. When Monod wrote articles objectively attacking Lysenko's ideas as nonsense, he was villified by other Communists in France, who never forgave him. However, he was supported by the French author Albert Camus. This episode, together with Monod's war experiences, demonstrate that the courage of Monod as a scientist equaled his courage as a person.

By 1947, Monod was focused on the lactose induction problem, trying to purify the enzyme responsible for breaking down lactose. In 1950, Jacob came to Lwoff's lab, and the ensuing collaborative work with Monod led to an historic understanding of gene control. Monod's group at the Pasteur, together with that of Jacob, was the place to be in the late 1950s and the 1960s. Many of today's top molecular geneticists spent time there as postdocs or visiting faculty. Monod served as the head of the Pasteur Institute until his death in 1976.

GENETIC REGULATORY MECHANISMS IN THE SYNTHESIS OF PROTEINS

The phenomenon that sparked much of the work described in the 1961 treatise by Jacob and Monod reprinted here was termed "enzyme induction" and had been known for many years, sometimes under the term "enzyme adaptation." In short, in a number of cases, bacterial enzymes were found only in the presence of their specific substrates. For example, in the case of β-galactosidase, which cleaves lactose and certain other β-galactosides, one can easily demonstrate that there is greater than 1000-fold more enzyme present when *E. coli* cells are grown in the presence of a galactoside "inducer" than when these cells are grown simply in glucose or glycerol. Labeling experiments demonstrated that new enzyme molecules are synthesized during the induction process.

The lactose metabolism system required not only the enzyme β-galactosidase, but also a permease, which was needed to transport lactose into the cell. A third activity, apparently associated with the permease, was also detected. At the time, it was thought that this activity was displayed by the permease itself, but it was subsequently shown to be due to a third enzyme, thiogalactoside transacetylase.

After demonstrating that induction involved the synthesis of new enzyme molecules, Monod and his collaborators looked at the kinetics of induction and found that the rapid onset of enzyme synthesis upon the addition of inducers (certain galactosides in this system) and the rapid cessation of synthesis after removal of the inducers ruled out one possibility, namely, that an inducer activates the production of a stable intermediate that can accumulate in the cell.

The Specificity of Induction

One of the really nice experiments in the 1961 review concerns the specificity of induction. This experiment is presented in its entirety in Table 1 on page 198, which compiles a rather extensive set of data. Here, different compounds were tested for their ability to induce both β-galactosidase and galactoside transacetylase, and their affinities and reaction velocities were measured for the respective enzymes. Several things are evident from a careful perusal of Table 1. First, both β-galactosidase and galactoside transacetylase respond identically to all compounds. What the authors did was to take the highest induction level seen, which occurred in the case of isopropyl-β-

D-thiogalactoside (IPTG), and place this value at 100. They then expressed the level of enzyme seen with the other inducers relative to that value of 100. This makes it easy to see that β-galactosidase and galactoside transacetylase have similar levels for each inducer.

Second, it is clear that there is little correlation between compounds that are good inducers and those that have high affinity for β-galactosidase or are good substrates for the enzyme. Phenylethyl-β-D-thiogalactoside has a very high affinity for the enzyme but is a poor inducer, whereas IPTG has a low affinity for the enzyme, and is not even a substrate, but is a very efficient inducer. In addition, phenyl-β-D-galactoside is an excellent substrate but a weak inducer, and melibiose, an α-D-galactoside is a good inducer but has no affinity for the enzyme and is not cleaved by β-galactosidase. However, all of the inducers of the lactose enzymes and all of the substrates for β-galactosidase are galactosides. Therefore, it is apparent that the recognition element for the inducer has a distinct stereospecificity that is different from the stereospecific recognition by β-galactosidase for its substrate. This is really an extraordinary observation, since the similar yet different stereospecificity might have fooled many people. These results are confirmed by other experiments mentioned by the authors in which an inactive β-galactosidase can be recognized by its immunological cross-reaction to antibodies made against wild-type enzyme. The altered enzyme is induced by galactosides even though it cannot recognize its substrate.

The most logical conclusion from these experiments is that an additional protein acts as a receptor for the inducer and that this protein is different from either β-galactosidase or acetylase.

Regulator Genes

Mutations affecting both β-galactosidase and permease were found and mapped to two closely linked, but separate, genes. Those that affected β-galactosidase mapped in a locus termed the *Z* gene and those that affected permease mapped in a locus termed the *Y* gene. A third group of mutations that resulted in the loss of inducibility was characterized. Cells harboring these mutations had a high, or "constitutive," level of β-galactosidase and acetylase even in the absence of inducer. These **constitutive** mutants resulted from mutations at a locus termed the *I* gene (for inducibility). (Note that the current convention calls for the use of capital letters for gene designations of this type; at that time, however, lowercase letters were used.) The definition of the *I* gene was of great importance because it represented the first gene shown to be involved in the **regulation** of an enzyme, or in this case a set of enzymes.

Complementation. Examining the complementation relationships of the different *lac* mutations provided the next important clues to the nature of the regulatory element. Initially, it was not possible to construct stable diploids, and Hfr conjugation was used to create "transient diploids." We will discuss these experiments later. However, the discovery of F′ factors carrying the *lac* genes allowed the construction of stable strains carrying parts of the chromosome as a diploid. These partial diploids (or "merodiploids") were invaluable in determining complementation results. As expected, the combination of Z^+/Z^- resulted in the Z^+ phenotype and the combination of Y^+/Y^- resulted in the Y^+ phenotype, since the presence of one good copy of the *Z* or *Y* gene resulted in an active enzyme. The key test was the introduction of both an I^+ and an I^- copy into the same cell. Table 2 on page 205 shows the results of this test in lines 4 and 5. Here it can be seen that in a diploid that is I^+/I^-, the synthesis of both β-galactosidase and galactoside transacetylase is inducible, going from less than 1 unit in the absence of inducer to values ranging from 120 to 280 in the presence of inducer. This experiment argued very strongly that the *I* gene synthesized a cytoplasmic product that could act in *trans* to prevent induction of β-galactosidase and permease/transacetylase. It also indicated that the I^+ form of the gene was the active form. Jacob and Monod offered two interpretations of the data:

- **Model 1:** The I^+ gene determines the synthesis of a repressor that is inactive or absent in the I^- alleles.

- **Model 2:** The I^+ gene determines the synthesis of an enzyme that destroys an inducer produced by an independent pathway.

Note that the inducer in the second hypothesis should not be confused with externally added galactoside inducers such as IPTG. It refers to an internally synthesized inducer required for expression of the lactose genes. In both models, IPTG would inactivate the *I* gene product.

Several lines of argument are presented in the Jacob and Monod paper to prove the first theory and disprove the second. A diagram of the two theories is given below. Clearly, the first theory is the simplest.

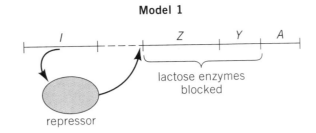

Model 1

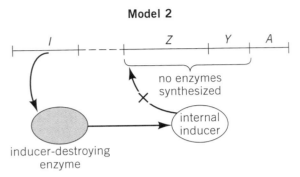

Model 2

Although the authors did choose the correct model, in hindsight the arguments presented are not really airtight. Let's examine them. First, a mutant, I^s, was characterized that fails to synthesize both galactosidase and permease even in the presence of inducer (see Table 2, line 8, page 205). The mutation responsible for this phenotype maps in the *I* gene. In diploids of the type I^s/I^+, the I^s mutation is dominant (seen Table 2, line 9). The obvious explanation is that this mutation alters the structure of the repressor so that it can no longer be affected by the external galactoside inducers. This explanation was reinforced by the finding that Lac$^+$ revertants of I^s mutants are often I^- mutants. In other words, the I^s gene must be inactivated to allow expression of the *lac* genes. The authors then argue: "The properties of this remarkable mutant could evidently not be understood under the assumption that the *I* gene governs the synthesis of an inducer-destroying enzyme."

However, in the second model, the I^s mutation could also alter the *I* gene product so that it can no longer be affected by external galactoside inducers such as IPTG. If the *I* gene product is really an enzyme that destroys an internally generated inducer, then the I^s protein will continue to destroy this inducer even in the presence of IPTG. In addition, in a diploid of the type I^s/I^+, the I^s product, unaffected by IPTG, will continue to destroy the internally generated inducer and thus still prevent the synthesis of the *lac* enzymes even in the presence of the normal I^+ gene product. Therefore, like the first model, the second model could be consistent with the I^s data.

The PaJaMo Experiment. Other evidence arguing against the second model involves experiments aimed at determining the chemical nature of the cytoplasmic product of the *I* gene. Figure 4 on page 206, originally published in 1959, recaps a fascinating experiment by Pardee, Jacob, and Monod. (This experiment is often called the PaJaMo experiment after the first two letters of each author's name.) Before the advent of F'*lac* episomes, the only way to study complementation for the *lac* region was to construct transient partial diploids by carrying out matings with Hfr strains that donated the *lac* genes early. The donated *lac* genes could function in the recipient F$^-$ cell for a number of hours, during which time experiments could be performed. In the experiment pictured in Figure 4, an Hfr was used to donate an I^+Z^+ *lac* region to an F$^-$ that was I^-Z^-. After killing the male cells with T6 phage and preventing protein synthesis in the male cells with streptomycin (the F$^-$ cells were resistant to both agents), the levels of β-galactosidase were measured. It can be seen that in the absence of added inducer, β-galactosidase is synthesized at its maximal rate for the first 60–80 minutes and then stops being synthesized, although if inducer is added at this point, then the synthesis can continue. The interpretation of this experiment was that since the cytoplasm of the F$^-$ contained no *I* gene product, then there was nothing to block the synthesis of β-galactosidase. However, after the entry of the I^+ gene, the *I* gene product could build up in the cytoplasm until a sufficient concentration was reached to block β-galactosidase synthesis.

At the time the PaJaMo experiment was first published, it had a great influence on the molecular biology community and clearly pointed to a cytoplasmic repressor. The interpretation of this experiment by Jacob and Monod was another brilliant insight, particularly since this experiment does not represent a true *cis-trans* test in that there is no real *trans* complementation occurring. Thus, the *I* gene product might have been a *cis*-acting protein (several examples of which are now known) or even an mRNA molecule that folds back and blocks the operator in *cis*. The slow time to exhibit this effect might have been attributed to a weaker promoter, slower transcription or translation of the *I* gene relative to the *Z* gene, or a combination of these factors. Shortly thereafter, the introduction of F'*lac* episomes and the ability to study a true *trans* effect, the complementation of I^-Z^+ by I^+Z^- (see Table 2 on page 205), allowed Jacob and Monod to demonstrate the cytoplasmic nature of the *I* gene product in a definitive fashion.

One could employ the PaJaMo experiment to ascertain the chemical nature of the *I* gene product. Pardee and Prestidge used 5-methyltryptophan, a protein synthesis inhibitor, to see whether repressor could still accumulate during the 60-minute period before the blockage of β-galactosidase synthesis. The argument was that if the *I* gene product was a protein, then by adding a protein synthesis inhibitor during the first 60 minutes after entry of the *lac* region, no repressor synthesis could occur. Thus, when the inhibitor was washed out, one should see 60 minutes of uncontrolled β-galactosidase synthesis followed by the shutting off of the synthesis. However, if the repressor was not a protein but was instead, say, an RNA molecule, then it would be able to accumulate during the exposure to 5-methyltryptophan. In this case, when the inhibitor was removed, β-galactosidase synthesis would be blocked.

The results of the above experiment showed that the *I* gene product does appear to accumulate during the exposure to 5-methyltryptophan. Therefore, one could conclude that the *I* gene product was not a protein. However, if the *I* gene product was not a protein, then it could not be an enzyme, and thus the second model was ruled out, since it postulated that the *I* gene product was an enzyme that destroyed an internal inducer. Similar results, quoted in the Jacob and Monod paper, were obtained using chloramphenicol, another protein synthesis inhibitor. These two results led to the assumption that the repressor was an RNA molecule, and part of the paper discusses the dilemma of trying to understand how the stereospecific binding to inducer could be exhibited by an RNA molecule. Of course, we now know that the repressor is indeed a protein. The leakiness of the inhibitors probably compromised the experiments.

In all fairness, it should be pointed out that the basic simplicity of the repressor model was instrumental in its acceptance. With the increasing number of gene control systems in bacteria and bacteriophage that behaved in the same manner as *lac*, one would have had to postulate an additional gene and protein to accommodate the second model in every system. This seemed very unlikely. In addition, one failed to find mutants with defects in the synthesis of the internal inducer, which would have been Lac$^-$, but not involving the *lacZ* or *lacY* genes. This argued strongly against the second model. Therefore, the favoring of the simpler model certainly proved correct in this case and is a tribute to the judgment of the authors.

The Operator

One of the most piercing insights of the Jacob and Monod work was the definition of the operator. Having established that enzyme synthesis was blocked by a repressor molecule, they presumed that a site that interacts with the repressor must exist on the DNA. They looked for mutations in this "operator" site that would result in constitutive synthesis of β-galactosidase even in the presence of repressor. They did this by selecting for constitutive mutants, starting with a strain that was diploid for the *lac* region. With two copies of the *I* gene present, one would expect that typical *I* mutations would not appear. As Table 3 on page 216 shows, the mutations that were found, which mapped between *I* and *Z*, were partly constitutive in the presence of a normal *I* gene. In addition, the O^c mutations are dominant in the *cis*, but not the *trans*, position (note lines 4–5 and 7–8 in Table 3). This is precisely what is expected of a mutation in a recognition site on the DNA. In other words, only the *Z* and *Y* genes that are linked and on the same DNA segment as the operator mutation will be affected by it.

Immunity in Temperate Phage Systems

Initially, Monod had studied the *lac* system and Jacob had worked on the temperate phage λ. Soon it became clear that these two systems shared a common strategy for control. When λ is in the prophage state, its genes are turned off, although they can be induced by ultraviolet light. It is also immune to superinfection from homologous phage, which enter the lysogenic cells but cannot express their genes. Studies of diploids showed that immunity is dominant over nonimmunity and is therefore conferred via a cytoplasmic particle. A key experiment was the interpretation of the phenomenon of **zygotic induction** (discussed in Unit 5), which results from the induction of λ after transfer into an F⁻ cell that is not lysogenic for λ. Here, Jacob and Monod recognized the analogy between this experiment and the PaJaMo experiment described above. Clearly, the cytoplasm of the F⁻ recipient determines whether or not λ genes will be expressed. Again, the same two hypotheses can be put forward: Either λ encodes a repressor or it encodes an enzyme that destroys a metabolite required for the vegetative multiplication of the phage. As referred to above, since so many phages with differing immunities were known, it would appear unlikely that each would have its own cellular metabolite specific for that phage.

Detailed genetic studies of the λ immunity region identified three loci (*cI*, *cII*, and *cIII*) involved in immunity, with *cI* being the most important and encoding the λ repressor. In addition, operator mutations were detected that behaved like the operator mutations in the *lac* system. These mutations conferred virulence even in the presence of immunity functions. One study even found mutations in the λ *cI* gene that were analogous to the *I*ˢ mutations in *lac*. These *ind⁻* mutations were impervious to the inducer, in this case ultraviolet light, and *ind⁻* was dominant to *ind⁺*.

The Operon Model of Jacob and Monod is pictured in Figure 6 on page 218. Model I represents the outline of the basic model for gene control that emanated from their experiments. Note how relevant it is even today.

The Discovery of Messenger RNA

In 1960, when the Operon Model was fully formulated, it was still believed that ribosomes contained the information for the synthesis of proteins and that each gene had its own ribosome. However, the finding that β-galactosidase synthesis began very shortly after introduction of *lac* genes into the cytoplasm of cells containing no repressor (the PaJaMo experiment) was inconsistent with this idea because ribosomes were very stable entities. In addition, the idea of an interaction on the DNA between the repressor and the operator could not be reconciled with the version of protein synthesis that held that the ribosome contained the specific information for the synthesis of each protein. The most likely explanation was to hypothesize the existence of an unstable intermediate molecule, presumably RNA, that carried the information for each protein to be synthesized. Jacob labeled this intermediate "X" but had difficulty in convincing the scientific community of the validity of this model. However, when Jacob reported the results of an experiment by Arthur Pardee and Monica Riley to Francis Crick and Sydney Brenner, they were excited by the findings. Pardee and Riley had used ³²P-labeled male strains and then transferred *lac* to an unlabeled recipient. This was a version of the PaJaMo experiment, but now the *lac* genes were destroyed by ³²P decay after a period of time. The ability to synthesize β-galactosidase was then lost as a function of the amount of decay. Clearly, the integrity of the transferred gene was required in order to synthesize β-galactosidase. Thus, the information was not transferred from the gene in the form of a stable molecule. Brenner and Crick immediately linked these results to a recent experiment of Elliot Volkin and Lazarus Astrachan, who had shown that when T2 phage infect *E. coli*, they block the synthesis of new ribosomes, and the only RNA synthesized had the same base composition as the phage DNA and was unstable. Jacob and Brenner immediately planned to carry out experiments at Caltech (where they were both scheduled to spend a month) to detect this unstable RNA species using the new CsCl gradient technique developed by Messelson at Caltech.

Their published results, reviewed in the Jacob and Monod paper, were as follows: Cells were first grown in heavy nitrogen, ^{15}N, and then suspended in ^{14}N medium, infected with phage, and exposed to pulses of ^{32}P or ^{35}S. The ribosomes were examined in CsCl density gradients. The labeled mRNA synthesized after infection was associated with unlabeled ribosomes synthesized before infection, and newly formed labeled protein was found associated with the ribosomes before appearing in the soluble protein fraction. In other words, the phage protein was synthesized on bacterial ribosomes and associated with phage mRNA. Thus, the information for the proteins had to be provided by the phage mRNA rather than by the bacterial ribosomes.

CONCLUSIONS

Gene control is mediated by cytoplasmic intermediates. In the first cases analyzed by Jacob and Monod, these intermediates were repressor molecules that exerted negative control. Normally, they bind to specific sequences on the DNA and thus block transcription of the linked genes. The repressor becomes inactivated in response to the presence or absence of certain small molecules, inducers in the lactose system, and falls off the DNA, allowing enzyme synthesis to occur. Systems studied later utilize positive control, in which the activation of a protein is required in order to allow transcription of the genes under control. Modifications of this latter type of control have been found to be prevalent in many eukaryotic transcription systems.

REVIEW ARTICLE

Genetic Regulatory Mechanisms in the Synthesis of Proteins †

FRANÇOIS JACOB AND JACQUES MONOD

Services de Génétique Microbienne et de Biochimie Cellulaire,
Institut Pasteur, Paris

(*Received 28 December 1960*)

The synthesis of enzymes in bacteria follows a double genetic control. The so-called structural genes determine the molecular organization of the proteins. Other, functionally specialized, genetic determinants, called regulator and operator genes, control the rate of protein synthesis through the intermediacy of cytoplasmic components or repressors. The repressors can be either inactivated (induction) or activated (repression) by certain specific metabolites. This system of regulation appears to operate directly at the level of the synthesis by the gene of a short-lived intermediate, or messenger, which becomes associated with the ribosomes where protein synthesis takes place.

1. Introduction

According to its most widely accepted modern connotation, the word "gene" designates a DNA molecule whose specific self-replicating structure can, through mechanisms unknown, become translated into the specific structure of a polypeptide chain.

This concept of the "structural gene" accounts for the multiplicity, specificity and genetic stability of protein structures, and it implies that such structures are not controlled by environmental conditions or agents. It has been known for a long time, however, that the synthesis of individual proteins may be provoked or suppressed within a cell, under the influence of specific external agents, and more generally that the relative rates at which different proteins are synthesized may be profoundly altered, depending on external conditions. Moreover, it is evident from the study of many such effects that their operation is absolutely essential to the survival of the cell.

It has been suggested in the past that these effects might result from, and testify to, complementary contributions of genes on the one hand, and some chemical factors on the other in determining the final structure of proteins. This view, which contradicts at least partially the "structural gene" hypothesis, has found as yet no experimental support, and in the present paper we shall have occasion to consider briefly some of this negative evidence. Taking, at least provisionally, the structural gene hypothesis in its strictest form, let us assume that the DNA message contained within a gene is both necessary and sufficient to define the structure of a protein. The elective effects of agents other than the structural gene itself in promoting or suppressing the synthesis of a protein must then be described as operations which control the rate of transfer of structural information from gene to protein. Since it seems to be established

† This work has been aided by grants from the National Science Foundation, the Jane Coffin Childs Memorial Fund for Medical Research and the Commissariat à l'Energie Atomique.

that proteins are synthesized in the cytoplasm, rather than directly at the genetic level, this transfer of structural information must involve a chemical intermediate synthesized by the genes. This hypothetical intermediate we shall call the structural messenger. The rate of information transfer, i.e. of protein synthesis, may then depend either upon the activity of the gene in synthesizing the messenger, or upon the activity of the messenger in synthesizing the protein. This simple picture helps to state the two problems with which we shall be concerned in the present paper. If a given agent specifically alters, positively or negatively, the rate of synthesis of a protein, we must ask:

(a) Whether the agent acts at the cytoplasmic level, by controlling the activity of the messenger, or at the genetic level, by controlling the synthesis of the messenger.

(b) Whether the specificity of the effect depends upon some feature of the information transferred from structural gene to protein, or upon some specialized controlling element, not represented in the structure of the protein, gene or messenger.

The first question is easy to state, if difficult to answer. The second may not appear so straightforward. It may be stated in a more general way, by asking whether the genome is composed exclusively of structural genes, or whether it also involves determinants which may control the rates of synthesis of proteins according to a given set of conditions, without determining the structure of any individual protein. Again it may not be evident that these two statements are equivalent. We hope to make their meaning clear and to show that they are indeed equivalent, when we consider experimental examples.

The best defined systems wherein the synthesis of a protein is seen to be controlled by specific agents are examples of enzymatic adaptation, this term being taken here to cover both enzyme induction, i.e. the formation of enzyme electively provoked by a substrate, and enzyme repression, i.e. the specific inhibition of enzyme formation brought about by a metabolite. Only a few inducible and repressible systems have been identified both biochemically and genetically to an extent which allows discussion of the questions in which we are interested here. In attempting to generalize, we will have to extrapolate from these few systems. Such generalization is greatly encouraged, however, by the fact that lysogenic systems, where phage protein synthesis might be presumed to obey entirely different rules, turn out to be analysable in closely similar terms. We shall therefore consider in succession certain inducible and repressible enzyme systems and lysogenic systems.

It might be best to state at the outset some of the main conclusions which we shall arrive at. These are:

(a) That the mechanisms of control in all these systems are negative, in the sense that they operate by inhibition rather than activation of protein synthesis.

(b) That in addition to the classical structural genes, these systems involve two other types of genetic determinants (regulator and operator) fulfilling specific functions in the control mechanisms.

(c) That the control mechanisms operate at the genetic level, i.e. by regulating the activity of structural genes.

2. Inducible and Repressible Enzyme Systems

(a) *The phenomenon of enzyme induction. General remarks*

It has been known for over 60 years (Duclaux, 1899; Dienert, 1900; Went, 1901) that certain enzymes of micro-organisms are formed only in the presence of their specific substrate. This effect, later named "enzymatic adaptation" by Karstrom (1938), has been the subject of a great deal of experimentation and speculation. For a long time, "enzymatic adaptation" was not clearly distinguished from the selection of spontaneous variants in growing populations, or it was suggested that enzymatic adaptation and selection represented *alternative* mechanisms for the acquisition of a "new" enzymatic property. Not until 1946 were adaptive enzyme systems shown to be controlled in bacteria by discrete, specific, stable, i.e. genetic, determinants (Monod & Audureau, 1946). A large number of inducible systems has been discovered and studied in bacteria. In fact, enzymes which attack exogeneous substrates are, as a general rule, inducible in these organisms. The phenomenon is far more difficult to study in tissues or cells of higher organisms, but its existence has been established quite clearly in many instances. Very often, if not again as a rule, the presence of a substrate induces the formation not of a single but of several enzymes, sequentially involved in its metabolism (Stanier, 1951).

Most of the fundamental characteristics of the induction effect have been established in the study of the "lactose" system of *Escherichia coli* (Monod & Cohn, 1952; Cohn, 1957; Monod, 1959) and may be summarized in a brief discussion of this system from the biochemical and physiological point of view. We shall return later to the genetic analysis of this system.

(b) *The lactose system of* Escherichia coli

Lactose and other β-galactosides are metabolized in *E. coli* (and certain other enteric bacteria) by the hydrolytic transglucosylase β-galactosidase. This enzyme was isolated from *E. coli* and later crystallized. Its specificity, activation by ions and transglucosylase *vs* hydrolase activity have been studied in great detail (*cf.* Cohn, 1957). We need only mention the properties that are significant for the present discussion. The enzyme is active exclusively on β-galactosides unsubstituted on the galactose ring. Activity and affinity are influenced by the nature of the aglycone moiety both being maximum when this radical is a relatively large, hydrophobic group. Substitution of sulfur for oxygen in the galactosidic linkage of the substrate abolishes hydrolytic activity completely, but the thiogalactosides retain about the same affinity for the enzyme site as the homologous oxygen compounds.

As isolated by present methods, β-galactosidase appears to form various polymers (mostly hexamers) of a fundamental unit with a molecular weight of 135,000. There is one end group (threonine) and also one enzyme site (as determined by equilibrium dialysis against thiogalactosides) per unit. It is uncertain whether the monomer is active as such, or exists *in vivo*. The hexameric molecule has a turnover number of 240,000 mol $\times$ min^{-1} at 28°C, pH 7·0 with *o*-nitrophenyl-β-D-galactoside as substrate and Na$^+$ (0·01 M) as activator.

There seems to exist only a single homogeneous β-galactosidase in *E. coli*, and this organism apparently cannot form any other enzyme capable of metabolizing lactose, as indicated by the fact that mutants that have lost β-galactosidase activity cannot grow on lactose as sole carbon source.

However, the possession of β-galactosidase activity is not sufficient to allow utilization of lactose by *intact E. coli* cells. Another component, distinct from β-galactosidase, is required to allow penetration of the substrate into the cell (Monod, 1956; Rickenberg, Cohen, Buttin & Monod, 1956; Cohen & Monod, 1957; Pardee, 1957; Képès, 1960). The presence and activity of this component is determined by measuring the rate of entry and/or the level of accumulation of radioactive thiogalactosides into intact cells. Analysis of this active permeation process shows that it obeys classical enzyme kinetics allowing determination of K_m and V_{max}. The specificity is high since the system is active only with galactosides (β or α), or thiogalactosides. The spectrum of apparent affinities ($1/K_m$) is very different from that of β-galactosidase. Since the permeation system, like β-galactosidase, is inducible (see below) its formation can be studied *in vivo*, and shown to be invariably associated with protein synthesis. By these criteria, there appears to be little doubt that this specific permeation system involves a specific protein (or proteins), formed upon induction, which has been called galactoside-permease. That this protein is distinct from and independent of β-galactosidase is shown by the fact that mutants that have lost β-galactosidase retain the capacity to concentrate galactosides, while mutants that have lost this capacity retain the power to synthesize galactosidase. The latter mutants (called cryptic) cannot however use lactose, since the intracellular galactosidase is apparently accessible exclusively *via* the specific permeation system.

Until quite recently, it had not proved possible to identify *in vitro* the inducible protein (or proteins) presumably responsible for galactoside-permease activity. During the past year, a protein characterized by the ability to carry out the reaction:

Ac. Coenzyme A + Thiogalactoside → 6-Acetylthiogalactoside + Coenzyme A

has been identified, and extensively purified from extracts of *E. coli* grown in presence of galactosides (Zabin, Képès & Monod, 1959). The function of this enzyme in the system is far from clear, since formation of a free covalent acetyl-compound is almost certainly not involved in the permeation process *in vivo*. On the other hand:

(a) mutants that have lost β-galactosidase and retained galactoside-permease, retain galactoside-acetylase;

(b) most mutants that have lost permease cannot form acetylase;

(c) permeaseless acetylaseless mutants which revert to the permease-positive condition simultaneously regain the ability to form acetylase.

These correlations strongly suggest that galactoside-acetylase is somehow involved in the permeation process, although its function *in vivo* is obscure, and it seems almost certain that other proteins (specific or not for this system) are involved. In any case, we are interested here not in the mechanisms of permeation, but in the control mechanisms which operate with β-galactosidase, galactoside-permease and galactoside-acetylase. The important point therefore is that, as we shall see, galactoside-acetylase invariably obeys the same controls as galactosidase.†

(c) *Enzyme induction and protein synthesis*

Wild type *E. coli* cells grown in the absence of a galactoside contain about 1 to 10 units of galactosidase per mg dry weight, that is, an average of 0·5 to 5 active molecules

† For reasons which will become apparent later it is important to consider whether there is any justification for the assumption that galactosidase and acetylase activities might be associated with the same fundamental protein unit. We should therefore point to the following observations:

(a) There are mutants which form galactosidase and no acetylase, and *vice versa*.

(b) Purified acetylase is devoid of any detectable galactosidase activity.

(c) The specificity of the two enzymes is very different.

(d) The two enzymes are easily and completely separated by fractional precipitation.

(e) Acetylase is highly heat-resistant, under conditions where galactosidase is very labile.

(f) Anti-galactosidase serum does not precipitate acetylase; nor does anti-acetylase serum precipitate galactosidase.

There is therefore no ground for the contention that galactosidase and acetylase activities are associated with the same protein.

per cell or 0·15 to 1·5 molecules per nucleus. Bacteria grown in the presence of a suitable inducer contain an average of 10,000 units per mg dry weight. This is the induction effect.

A primary problem, to which much experimental work has been devoted, is whether this considerable increase in specific activity corresponds to the synthesis of entirely "new" enzyme molecules, or to the activation or conversion of pre-existing protein precursors. It has been established by a combination of immunological and isotopic methods that the enzyme formed upon induction:

(a) is distinct, as an antigen, from all the proteins present in uninduced cells (Cohn & Torriani, 1952);

(b) does not derive any significant fraction of its sulfur (Monod & Cohn, 1953; Hogness, Cohn & Monod, 1955) or carbon (Rotman & Spiegelman, 1954) from pre-existing proteins.

The inducer, therefore, brings about the complete *de novo* synthesis of enzyme molecules which are new by their specific structure as well as by the origin of their elements. The study of several other induced systems has fully confirmed this conclusion, which may by now be considered as part of the *definition* of the effect. We will use the term "induction" here as meaning "activation by inducer of enzyme-protein synthesis."

(d) *Kinetics of induction*

Accepting (still provisionally) the structural gene hypothesis, we may therefore consider that the inducer somehow accelerates the rate of information transfer from gene to protein. This it could do either by provoking the synthesis of the messenger or by activating the messenger. If the messenger were a *stable* structure, functioning as a catalytic template in protein synthesis, one would expect different kinetics of induction, depending on whether the inducer acted at the genetic or at the cytoplasmic level.

The kinetics of galactosidase induction turn out to be remarkably simple when determined under proper experimental conditions (Monod, Pappenheimer & Cohen-Bazire, 1952; Herzenberg, 1959). Upon addition of a suitable inducer to a growing culture, enzyme activity increases at a rate proportional to the increase in total protein within the culture; i.e. a linear relation is obtained (Fig. 1) when total enzyme activity is plotted against mass of the culture. The slope of this line:

$$P = \frac{\Delta z}{\Delta M}$$

is the "differential rate of synthesis," which is taken by definition as the measure of the effect. Extrapolation to the origin indicates that enzyme formation begins about three minutes (at 37 °C) after addition of inducer (Pardee & Prestidge, 1961). Removal of the inducer (or addition of a specific anti-inducer, see below) results in cessation of enzyme synthesis within the same short time. The differential rate of synthesis varies with the concentration of inducer reaching a different saturation value for different inducers. The inducer therefore acts in a manner which is (kinetically) similar to that of a dissociable activator in an enzyme system: activation and inactivation follow very rapidly upon addition or removal of the activator.

The conclusion which can be drawn from these kinetics is a negative one: the inducer does not appear to activate the synthesis of a stable intermediate able to accumulate in the cell (Monod, 1956).

Similar kinetics of induction have been observed with most or all other systems which have been adequately studied (Halvorson, 1960) with the exception of penicillinase of *Bacillus cereus*. The well-known work of Pollock has shown that the synthesis of this enzyme continues for a long time, at a decreasing rate, after removal of inducer (penicillin) from the medium. This effect is apparently related to the fact that minute amounts of penicillin are retained irreversibly by the cells after transient exposure to the drug (Pollock, 1950). The unique behavior of this system therefore does not contradict the rule that induced synthesis stops when the inducer is removed from the cells. Using this system, Pollock & Perret (1951) were able to show that the inducer acts catalytically, in the sense that a cell may synthesize many more enzyme molecules than it has retained inducer molecules.

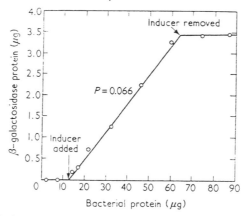

Fig. 1. Kinetics of induced enzyme synthesis. Differential plot expressing accumulation of β-galactosidase as a function of increase of mass of cells in a growing culture of *E. coli*. Since abscissa and ordinates are expressed in the same units (micrograms of protein) the slope of the straight line gives galactosidase as the fraction (P) of total protein synthesized in the presence of inducer. (After Cohn, 1957.)

(e) *Specificity of induction*

One of the most conspicuous features of the induction effect is its extreme specificity. As a general rule, only the substrate of an enzyme, or substances very closely allied to the normal substrate, are endowed with inducer activity towards this enzyme. This evidently suggests that a correlation between the molecular structure of the inducer and the structure of the catalytic center on the enzymes is *inherently* involved in the mechanism of induction. Two main types of hypotheses have been proposed to account for this correlation, and thereby for the mechanism of action of the inducer:

(a) The inducer serves as "partial template" in enzyme synthesis, molding as it were the catalytic center.

(b) The inducer acts by combining specifically with preformed enzyme (or "pre-enzyme"), thereby somehow accelerating the synthesis of further enzyme molecules.

It is not necessary to discuss these "classical" hypotheses in detail, because it seems to be established now that the correlation in question is in fact *not* inherent to the mechanism of induction.

Table 1 lists a number of compounds tested as inducers of galactosidase, and as substrates (or specific inhibitors) of the enzyme. It will be noted that:

(a) no compound that does not possess an intact unsubstituted galactosidic residue induces;

TABLE 1

Induction of galactosidase and galactoside-transacetylase by various galactosides

Compound	Concentrations		β-galactosidase			Galactoside-transacetylase	
			Induction value	V	$1/K_m$	Induction value	V/K_m
β-D-thiogalactosides							
(isopropyl)	10^{-4} M		100	0	140	100	80
(methyl)	10^{-4} M		78	0	7	74	30
	10^{-5} M		7·5	—	—	10	—
(phenyl)	10^{-3} M		<0·1	0	100	<1	100
(phenylethyl)	10^{-3} M		5	0	10,000	3	—
β-D-galactosides							
(lactose)	10^{-3} M		17	30	14	12	35
(phenyl)	10^{-3} M		15	100	100	11	—
α-D-galactoside							
(melibiose)	10^{-3} M		35	0	<0·1	37	<1
β-D-glucoside							
(phenyl)	10^{-3} M		<0·1	0	0	<1	50
(galactose)	10^{-3} M		<0·1	—	4	<1	<1
Methyl-β-D-thiogalactoside (10^{-4} M) + phenyl-β-D-thiogalactoside (10^{-3} M)			52	—	—	63	—

Columns "induction value" refer to specific activities developed by cultures of wild type *E. coli* K12 grown on glycerol as carbon source with each galactoside added at molar concentration stated. Values are given in percent of values obtained with *iso*propyl-thiogalactoside at 10^{-4} M (for which actual units were about 7,500 units of β-galactosidase and 300 units of galactoside-transacetylase per mg of bacteria). Column V refers to maximal substrate activity of each compound with respect to galactosidase. Values are given in percent of activity obtained with phenyl-galactoside. Column $1/K_m$ expresses affinity of each compound with respect to galactosidase. Values are given in percent of that observed with phenylgalactoside. In case of galactoside-transacetylase, only the relative values V/K_m are given since low affinity of this enzyme prevents independent determination of the constants. (Computed from Monod & Cohn, 1952; Monod *et al.*, 1952; Buttin, 1956; Zabin *et al.*, 1959; Képès *et al.*, unpublished results.)

(b) many compounds which are not substrates (such as the thiogalactosides) are excellent inducers (for instance *iso*propyl thiogalactoside);

(c) there is no correlation between affinity for the enzyme and capacity to induce (*cf*. thiophenylgalactoside and melibiose).

The possibility that the enzyme formed in response to different inducers may have somewhat different specific properties should also be considered, and has been rather thoroughly tested, with entirely negative results (Monod & Cohn, 1952).

There is therefore no quantitative correlation whatever between inducing capacity and the substrate activity or affinity parameters of the various galactosides tested. The fact remains, however, that only galactosides will induce galactosidase, whose binding site is complementary for the galactose ring-structure. The possibility that this correlation is a necessary requisite, or consequence, of the induction mechanism was therefore not completely excluded by the former results.

As we shall see later, certain mutants of the galactosidase structural gene (z) have been found to synthesize, in place of the normal enzyme, a protein which is identical to it by its immunological properties, while being completely devoid of any enzymatic activity. When tested by equilibrium dialysis, this inactive protein proved to have no measurable affinity for galactosides. In other words, it has lost the specific binding site. In diploids carrying both the normal and the mutated gene, both normal galactosidase and the inactive protein are formed, to a quantitatively similar extent, in the presence of different concentrations of inducer (Perrin, Jacob & Monod, 1960).

This finding, added to the sum of the preceding observations, appears to prove beyond reasonable doubt that the mechanism of induction does not imply any inherent correlation between the molecular structure of the inducer and the structure of the binding site of the enzyme.

On the other hand, there is complete correlation in the induction of galactosidase and acetylase. This is illustrated by Table 1 which shows not only that the same compounds are active or inactive as inducers of either enzyme, but that the relative amounts of galactosidase and acetylase synthesized in the presence of different inducers or at different concentrations of the same inducer are constant, even though the absolute amounts vary greatly. The remarkable qualitative and quantitative correlation in the induction of these two widely different enzyme proteins strongly suggests that the synthesis of both is directly governed by a common controlling element with which the inducer interacts. This interaction must, at some point, involve stereospecific binding of the inducer, since induction is sterically specific, and since certain galactosides which are devoid of any inducing activity act as competitive inhibitors of induction in the presence of active inducers (Monod, 1956; Herzenberg, 1959). This suggests that an enzyme, or some other protein, distinct from either galactosidase or acetylase, acts as "receptor" of the inducer. We shall return later to the difficult problem raised by the identification of this "induction receptor."

(f) *Enzyme repression*

While positive enzymatic adaptation, i.e. induction, has been known for over sixty years, negative adaptation, i.e. specific inhibition of enzyme synthesis, was discovered only in 1953, when it was found that the formation of the enzyme tryptophan-synthetase was inhibited selectively by tryptophan and certain tryptophan analogs (Monod & Cohen-Bazire, 1953). Soon afterwards, other examples of this effect were observed (Cohn, Cohen & Monod, 1953; Adelberg & Umbarger, 1953; Wijesundera &

Woods, 1953), and several systems were studied in detail in subsequent years (Gorini & Maas, 1957; Vogel, 1957a,b; Yates & Pardee, 1957; Magasanik, Magasanik & Neidhardt, 1959). These studies have revealed that the "repression" effect, as it was later named by Vogel (1957a,b), is very closely analogous, albeit symmetrically opposed, to the induction effect.

Enzyme repression, like induction, generally involves not a single but a sequence of enzymes active in successive metabolic steps. While inducibility is the rule for catabolic enzyme sequences responsible for the degradation of exogeneous substances, repressibility is the rule for anabolic enzymes, involved in the synthesis of essential metabolites such as amino acids or nucleotides.† Repression, like induction, is highly specific, but while inducers generally are substrates (or analogs of substrates) of the sequence, the repressing metabolites generally are the product (or analogs of the product) of the sequence.

That the effect involves inhibition of enzyme *synthesis*, and not inhibition (directly or indirectly) of enzyme *activity* was apparent already in the first example studied (Monod & Cohen-Bazire, 1953), and has been proved conclusively by isotope incorporation experiments (Yates & Pardee, 1957). It is important to emphasize this point, because enzyme repression must not be confused with another effect variously called "feedback inhibition" or "retro-inhibition" which is equally frequent, and may occur in the same systems. This last effect, discovered by Novick & Szilard (in Novick, 1955), involves the inhibition of activity of an early enzyme in an anabolic sequence, by the ultimate product of the sequence (Yates & Pardee, 1956; Umbarger, 1956). We shall use "repression" exclusively to designate specific inhibition of enzyme *synthesis*.‡

(g) *Kinetics and specificity of repression*

The kinetics of enzyme synthesis provoked by "de-repression" are identical to the kinetics of induction (see Fig. 2). When wild type *E. coli* is grown in the presence of arginine, only traces of ornithine-carbamyltransferase are formed. As soon as arginine is removed from the growth medium, the differential rate of enzyme synthesis increases about 1,000 times and remains constant, until arginine is added again, when it immediately falls back to the repressed level. The repressing metabolite here acts (kinetically) as would a dissociable inhibitor in an enzyme system.

The specificity of repression poses some particularly significant problems. As a rule, the repressing metabolite of an anabolic sequence is the ultimate product of this sequence. For instance, L-arginine, to the exclusion of any other amino acid, represses the enzymes of the sequence involved in the biosynthesis of arginine. Arginine shows no specific affinity for the early enzymes in the sequence, such as, in particular, ornithine-carbamyltransferase. In this sense, arginine is a "gratuitous" repressing metabolite for this protein, just as galactosides are "gratuitous inducers" for the mutated (inactive) galactosidase. The possibility must be considered however that arginine may be converted back, through the sequence itself, to an intermediate product

---

† Certain enzymes which attack exogeneous substrates are controlled by repression. Alkaline phosphatase (*E. coli*) is not induced by phosphate esters, but it is repressed by orthophosphate. Urease (*Pseudomonas*) is repressed by ammonia.

‡ We should perhaps recall the well-known fact that glucose and other carbohydrates inhibit the synthesis of many *inducible* enzymes, attacking a variety of substrates (Dienert, 1900; Gale, 1943; Monod, 1942; Cohn & Horibata, 1959). It is probable that this non-specific "glucose effect" bears some relation to the repressive effect of specific metabolites, but the relationship is not clear (Neidhardt & Magasanik, 1956a,b). We shall not discuss the glucose effect in this paper.

or substrate of the enzyme. This has been excluded by Gorini & Maas (1957) who showed that, in mutants lacking one of the enzymes involved in later steps of the sequence, ornithine transcarbamylase is repressed by arginine to the same extent as in the wild type. Moreover, neither ornithine nor any other intermediate of the sequence is endowed with repressing activity in mutants which cannot convert the intermediate into arginine. It is quite clear therefore that the specificity of action of the repressing metabolite does not depend upon the specific configuration of the enzyme site.

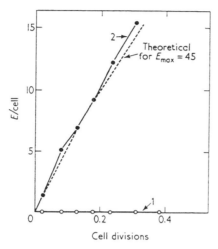

FIG. 2. Repression of ornithine-transcarbamylase by arginine. *E. coli* requiring both histidine and arginine were grown in a chemostat with 1 μg/ml. histidine + 6 μg/ml. arginine (curve 1) or with 10 μg/ml. histidine + 5 μg/ml. arginine (curve 2). Cultures are inoculated with washed cells taken from cultures growing exponentially in excess of arginine. The theoretical curve was calculated from the constant enzyme/cell value reached after 4 cell divisions. (After Gorini & Maas, 1958.)

The same conclusion is applicable to the enzymes of the histidine synthesizing pathway which are repressed in the presence of histidine, both in the wild type and in different mutants lacking one of the enzymes. The work of Ames & Garry (1959) has shown that the rates of synthesis of different enzymes in this sequence vary in *quantitatively* constant ratios under any set of medium conditions, and that the ratios are the same in various mutants lacking one of the enzymes and in the wild type. Here again, as in the case of the lactose system, the synthesis of widely different, albeit functionally related, enzymes appears to be controlled by a single common mechanism, with which the repressing metabolite specifically interacts.

In summary, repression and induction appear as closely similar effects, even if opposed in their results. Both control the rate of synthesis of enzyme proteins. Both are highly specific, but in neither case is the specificity related to the specificity of action (or binding) of the controlled enzyme. The kinetics of induction and repression are the same. Different functionally related enzymes are frequently co-induced or co-repressed, quantitatively to the same extent, by a single substrate or metabolite.

The remarkable similarity of induction and repression suggests that the two effects represent different manifestations of fundamentally similar mechanisms (Cohn & Monod, 1953; Monod, 1955; Vogel, 1957a, b; Pardee, Jacob & Monod, 1959; Szilard,

1960). This would imply either that in inducible systems the inducer acts as an antagonist of an internal repressor or that in repressible systems the repressing metabolite acts as an antagonist of an internal inducer. This is not an esoteric dilemma since it poses a very pertinent question, namely what would happen in an adaptive system of either type, when *both* the inducer and the repressor were eliminated? This, in fact, is the main question which we shall try to answer in the next section.

3. Regulator Genes

Since the specificity of induction or repression is not related to the structural specificity of the controlled enzymes, and since the rate of synthesis of different enzymes appears to be governed by a common element, this element is presumably not controlled or represented by the structural genes themselves. This inference, as we shall now see, is confirmed by the study of certain mutations which convert inducible or repressible systems into constitutive systems.

(a) *Phenotypes and genotypes in the lactose systems*

If this inference is correct, mutations which affect the controlling system should not behave as alleles of the structural genes. In order to test this prediction, the structural genes themselves must be identified. The most thoroughly investigated case is the lactose system of *E. coli*, to which we shall now return. Six phenotypically different classes of mutants have been observed in this system. For the time being, we shall consider only three of them which will be symbolized and defined as follows:

(1) Galactosidase mutations: $z^+ \rightleftharpoons z^-$ expressed as the loss of the capacity to synthesize active galactosidase (with or without induction).

(2) Permease mutations: $y^+ \rightleftharpoons y^-$ expressed as the loss of the capacity to form galactoside-permease. Most, but not all, mutants of this class simultaneously lose the capacity to synthesize active acetylase. We shall confine our discussion to the acetylaseless subclass.

(3) Constitutive mutations: $i^+ \rightleftharpoons i^-$ expressed as the ability to synthesize large amounts of galactosidase *and* acetylase in the absence of inducer (Monod, 1956; Rickenberg *et al.*, 1956; Pardee *et al.*, 1959).

The first two classes are specific for either galactosidase or acetylase: the galactosidaseless mutants form normal amounts of acetylase; conversely the acetylaseless mutants form normal amounts of galactosidase. In contrast, the constitutive mutations, of which over one hundred recurrences have been observed, invariably affect both the galactosidase and the permease (acetylase).† There are eight possible combinations of these phenotypes, and they have all been observed both in *E. coli* ML and K12.

The loci corresponding to a number of recurrences of each of the three mutant types have been mapped by recombination in *E. coli* K12. The map (Fig. 3) also

† The significance of this finding could be questioned since, in order to isolate constitutive mutants, one must of course use selective media, and this procedure might be supposed to favour double mutants, where the constitutivity of galactosidase and permease had arisen independently. It is possible, however, to select for $i^+ \rightarrow i^-$ mutants in organisms of type $i^+z^+y^-$, i.e. permeaseless. Fifty such mutants were isolated, giving rise to "constitutive cryptic" types $i^-z^+y^-$ from which, by reversion of y^-, fifty clones of constitutive $i^-z^+y^+$ were obtained. It was verified that in each of these fifty clones the permease was constitutive.

indicates the location of certain other mutations (*o* mutations) which will be discussed later. As may be seen, all these loci are confined to a very small segment of the chromosome, the *Lac* region. The extreme proximity of all these mutations raises the question whether they belong to a single or to several independent functional units. Such functional analysis requires that the biochemical expression of the various genetic structures be studied in heterozygous diploids. Until quite recently, only transient diploids were available in *E. coli*; the recent discovery of a new type of gene transfer in these bacteria (sexduction) has opened the possibility of obtaining stable clones which are diploid (or polyploid) for different small segments of the chromosome.

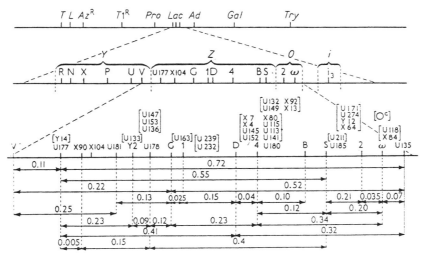

FIG. 3. Diagrammatic map of the lactose region of *E. coli* K12. The upper line represents the position of the *Lac* region with respect to other known markers. The middle line represents an enlargement of the *Lac* region with the four loci *y*, *z*, *o* and *i*. The lower line represents an enlargement of the *z* and *o* loci. Recombination frequencies (given at the bottom) are obtained in two factor crosses of the type *Hfr Lac$_A^-$ad$^+$S^s × F$^-$Lac$_B^-$ad$^-$S^r*, from the ratios "recombinants *Lac$^+$ad$^+$S^r*/ recombinants *ad$^+$S^r*." The total length of the *z* gene may be estimated to be 0·7 map units, i.e. about 3,500 nucleotide pairs for about 1,000 amino acids in the monomer of β-galactosidase.

In this process, small fragments of the bacterial chromosome are incorporated into the sex factor, *F*. This new unit of replication is transmissible by conjugation, and is then added to the normal genome of the recipient bacterium which becomes diploid for the small chromosomal fragment. Among the units thus isolated, one carries the whole *Lac* region (Jacob & Adelberg, 1959; Jacob, Perrin, Sanchez & Monod, 1960). To symbolize the genetic structure of these diploids, the chromosomal alleles are written in the usual manner, while the alleles attached to the sex factor are preceded by the letter *F*.

Turning our attention to the behaviour of *z* and *y* mutant types, we may first note that diploids of structure *z$^+$y$^-$/Fz$^-$y$^+$* or *z$^-$y$^+$/Fz$^+$y$^-$* are wild type, being able to ferment lactose, and forming normal amounts of both galactosidase and acetylase. This complete complementation between *z$^-$* and *y$^-$* mutants indicates that they belong to independent cistrons. Conversely, no complementation is observed between different *y$^-$* mutants, indicating that they all belong to a single cistron. No complementation is observed between most *z$^-$* mutants. Certain diploids of structure *z$_a^-$z$_b^+$/Fz$_a^+$z$_b^-$* synthesize galactosidase in reduced amounts, but pairs of mutually non-complementing mutants overlap mutually complementing mutants, suggesting again that a single cistron is involved, as one might expect, since the monomer of galactosidase has a single N-terminal group. It should be recalled that intracistronic partial complementation has been observed in several cases (Giles, 1958), and has (tentatively) been explained as related to a polymeric state of the protein.

Mutations in the z gene affect the structure of galactosidase. This is shown by the fact that most of the z^- mutants synthesize, in place of active enzyme, a protein which is able to displace authentic (wild type) galactosidase from its combination with specific antibody (Perrin, Bussard & Monod, 1959). Among proteins synthesized by different z^- mutants (symbolized Cz_1, Cz_2, etc.) some give complete cross reactions (i.e. precipitate 100% of the specific antigalactosidase antibodies) with the serum used, while others give incomplete reactions. The different Cz proteins differ therefore, not only from wild type galactosidase, but also one from the other. Finally, as we already mentioned, diploids of constitution z^+/z_1^- synthesize wild type galactosidase and the modified protein simultaneously, and at similar rates (Perrin *et al.*, 1960). These observations justify the conclusions that the z region or cistron contains the structural information for β-galactosidase. Proof that mutations in the y region not only suppress but may in some cases modify the structure of acetylase has not been obtained as yet, but the assumption that the y region does represent, in part at least, the structural gene for the acetylase protein appears quite safe in view of the properties of the y mutants.

(b) *The* i+ *gene and its cytoplasmic product*

We now turn our attention to the constitutive (i^-) mutations. The most significant feature of these mutations is that they invariably affect simultaneously two different enzyme-proteins, each independently determined, as we have just seen, by different structural genes. In fact, most i^- mutants synthesize more galactosidase and acetylase than induced wild type cells, but it is quite remarkable that the *ratio* of galactosidase to acetylase is the same in the constitutive cells as in the induced wild type, strongly suggesting that the mechanism controlled by the i gene is the same as that with which the inducer interacts.

The study of double heterozygotes of structures: i^+z^-/Fi^-z^+ or i^-y^+/Fi^+y^- shows (Table 2, lines 4 and 5) that the inducible i^+ allele is dominant over the constitutive and that it is active in the *trans* position, with respect to both y^+ and z^+.

Therefore the i mutations belong to an independent cistron, governing the expression of y and z *via* a cytoplasmic component. The dominance of the inducible over the constitutive allele means that the former corresponds to the active form of the i gene. This is confirmed by the fact that strains carrying a *deletion* of the izy region behave like i^- in diploids (Table 2, line 7). However, two different interpretations of the function of the i^+ gene must be considered.

(a) The i^+ gene determines the synthesis of a repressor, inactive or absent in the i^- alleles.

(b) The i^+ gene determines the synthesis of an enzyme which destroys an inducer, produced by an independent pathway.

The first interpretation is the most straightforward, and it presents the great interest of implying that the fundamental mechanisms of control may be the same in inducible and repressible systems. Several lines of evidence indicate that it is the correct interpretation.

First, we may mention the fact that constitutive synthesis of β-galactosidase by $i^-z^+y^+$ types is not inhibited by thiophenyl-galactoside which has been shown (Cohn & Monod, 1953) to be a competitive inhibitor of induction by exogenous galactosides (see p. 325).

TABLE 2

Synthesis of galactosidase and galactoside-transacetylase by haploids and heterozygous diploids of regulator mutants

Strain No.	Genotype	Galactosidase		Galactoside-transacetylase	
		Non-induced	Induced	Non-induced	Induced
1	$i^+z^+y^+$	<0·1	100	<1	100
2	$i_6^-z^+y^+$	100	100	90	90
3	$i_3^-z^+y^+$	140	130	130	120
4	$i^+z_1^-y^+/Fi_3^-z^+y^+$	<1	240	1	270
5	$i_3^-z_1^-y^+/Fi^+z^+y_U^-$	<1	280	<1	120
6	$i_3^-z_1^-y^+/Fi^-z^+y^+$	195	190	200	180
7	$\Delta_{izy}/Fi^-z^+y^+$	130	150	150	170
8	$i^sz^+y^+$	<0·1	<1	<1	<1
9	$i^sz^+y^+/Fi^+z^+y^+$	<0·1	2	<1	3

Bacteria are grown in glycerol as carbon source and induced, when stated, by *iso*propyl-thio-galactoside, 10^{-4} M. Values are given as a percentage of those observed with induced wild type (for absolute values, see legend of Table 1). Δ_{izy} refers to a deletion of the whole *Lac* region. It will be noted that organisms carrying the wild allele of one of the structural genes (z or y) on the F factor form more of the corresponding enzyme than the haploid. This is presumably due to the fact that several copies of the *F-Lac* unit are present per chromosome. In i^+/i^- heterozygotes, values observed with uninduced cells are sometimes higher than in the haploid control. This is due to the presence of a significant fraction of i^-/i^- homozygous recombinants in the population.

A direct and specific argument comes from the study of one particular mutant of the lactose system. This mutant (i^s) has lost the capacity to synthesize *both* galactosidase and permease. It is not a deletion because it recombines, giving *Lac*$^+$ types, with all the z^- and y^- mutants. In crosses with z^-i^- organisms the progeny is *exclusively* i^- while in crosses with z^-i^+ it is *exclusively* i^+, indicating exceedingly close linkage of this mutation with the i region. Finally, in diploids of constitution i^s/i^+, i^s turns out to be *dominant*: the diploids cannot synthesize either galactosidase or acetylase (see Table 2, lines 8 and 9).

These unique properties appear exceedingly difficult to account for, except by the admittedly very specific hypothesis that mutant i^s is an allele of i where the *structure* of the repressor is such that it cannot be antagonized by the inducer any more. If this hypothesis is correct, one would expect that the i^s mutant could regain the ability to metabolize lactose, not only by reversion to wild type ($i^s \rightarrow i^+$) but also, and probably more frequently, by inactivation of the i gene, that is to say by achieving the constitutive condition ($i^s \rightarrow i^-$). Actually, Lac^+ "revertants" are very frequent in populations of mutant i^s, and 50% of these "revertants" are indeed constitutives of the i^- (recessive) type. (The other revertants are also constitutives, but of the o^c class which we shall mention later.) The properties of this remarkable mutant could evidently not be understood under the assumption that the i gene governs the synthesis of an inducer-destroying enzyme (Willson, Perrin, Jacob & Monod, 1961).

Accepting tentatively the conclusion that the i^+ gene governs the synthesis of an intracellular repressor, we may now consider the question of the presence of this substance in the cytoplasm, and of its chemical nature.

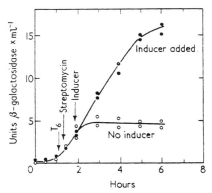

Fig. 4. Synthesis of β-galactosidase by merozygotes formed by conjugation between inducible, galactosidase-positive males and constitutive, galactosidase-negative females. Male ($Hfr\ i^+z^+T6^sS^s$) and female ($F^-\ i^-z^-T6^rS^r$) bacteria grown in a synthetic medium containing glycerol as carbon source are mixed in the same medium (time 0) in the absence of inducer. In such a cross, the first zygotes which receive the Lac region from the males are formed from the 20th min. The rate of enzyme synthesis is determined from enzyme activity measurement on the whole population, to which streptomycin and phage T6 are added at times indicated by arrows to block further formation of recombinants and induction of the male parents. It may be seen that in the absence of inducer enzyme synthesis stops about 60 to 80 min after penetration of the first z^+i^+ segment but is resumed by addition of inducer (From Pardee *et al*, 1959).

Important indications on this question have been obtained by studying the kinetics and conditions of expression of the i^+ and z^+ genes when they are introduced into the cytoplasm of cells bearing the inactive (z^- and i^-) alleles. The sexual transfer of the Lac segment from male to female cells provides an adequate experimental system for such studies. It should be recalled that conjugation in *E. coli* involves essentially the transfer of a male chromosome (or chromosome segment) to the female cell. This transfer is oriented, always beginning at one extremity of the chromosome, and it is progressive, each chromosome segment entering into the recipient cell at a fairly precise time following inception of conjugation in a given mating pair (Wollman & Jacob, 1959). The conjugation does not appear to involve any significant cytoplasmic mixing, so that the zygotes inherit virtually all their cytoplasm from the female cell, receiving only a chromosome or chromosome segment from the male. In order to study galactosidase synthesis by the zygotes, conditions must be set up such that the unmated parents cannot form the enzymes. This is the case when mating between inducible galactosidase-positive, streptomycin-sensitive males ($\male\ z^+i^+Sm^s$) and constitutive, galactosidase-negative, streptomycin-resistant females ($\female z^-i^-Sm^r$) is performed in presence of streptomycin (Sm), since: (i) the male cells which are sensitive to Sm cannot synthesize enzyme in its presence; (ii) the female cells are genetically incompetent; (iii) the vast majority of the zygotes which receive the z^+ gene. do not become streptomycin sensitive (because the Sm^s gene is transferred only to a small proportion of them, and at a very late time). The results of such an experiment, performed in the absence of inducer, are shown in Fig. 4. It is seen that galactosidase synthesis starts almost immediately following actual entry of the z^+ gene. We shall return later to a more precise analysis of the expression of the z^+ gene. The important point to be stressed here is that during this initial period the zygotes behave like *constitutive* cells, synthesizing enzyme in the *absence* of inducer. Approximately sixty minutes later, however, the rate of galactosidase synthesis falls off to zero. If at that time inducer is added, the maximum rate of enzyme synthesis is resumed. We are, in other words, witnessing the conversion of the originally i^- phenotype of the zygote cell, into an i^+ phenotype. And this experiment clearly shows that the "inducible" state is associated with the presence, at a sufficient level, of a *cytoplasmic* substance synthesized under the control of the i^+ gene. (It may be pointed out that the use of a female strain carrying a *deletion* of the *Lac* region instead of the i^-z^- alleles gives the same results (Pardee *et al.*, 1959).)

If now 5-methyltryptophan is added to the mated cells a few minutes before entry of the z^+ gene, no galactosidase is formed because, as is well known, this compound inhibits tryptophan synthesis by retro-inhibition, and therefore blocks protein synthesis. If the repressor is a protein, or if it is formed by a specific enzyme, the synthesis of which is governed by the i^+ gene, its accumulation should also be blocked. If on the other hand the repressor is not a protein, and if its synthesis does not require the preliminary synthesis of a specific enzyme controlled by the i^+ gene, it may accumulate in presence of 5-methyltryptophan which is known (Gros, unpublished results) *not* to inhibit energy transfer or the synthesis of nucleic acids.

The results of Pardee & Prestidge (1959) show that the repressor *does* accumulate under these conditions, since the addition of tryptophan 60 min after 5-methyl-tryptophan allows immediate and complete resumption of enzyme synthesis, *but only in the presence of inducer*; in other words, the cytoplasm of the zygote cells has been converted from the constitutive to the inducible state during the time that protein synthesis was blocked. This result has also been obtained using chloramphenicol as the agent for blocking protein synthesis, and it has been repeated using another system of gene transfer (Luria *et al.*, unpublished results).

This experiment leads to the conclusion that the repressor is not a protein, and this again excludes the hypothesis that the i^+ gene controls an inducer-destroying enzyme. We should like to stress the point that this conclusion does not imply that no enzyme is involved in the synthesis of the repressor, but that the enzymes which may be involved are *not* controlled by the i^+ gene. The experiments are negative, as far as the chemical nature of the repressor itself is concerned, since they only eliminate protein as a candidate. They do, however, invite the speculation that the repressor may be the primary product of the i^+ gene, and the further speculation that such a primary product may be a polyribonucleotide.

Before concluding this section, it should be pointed out that constitutive mutations have been found in several inducible systems; in fact wherever they have been searched for by adequate selective techniques (amylomaltase of *E. coli* (Cohen-Bazire & Jolit, 1953), penicillinase of *B. cereus* (Kogut, Pollock & Tridgell, 1956), glucuronidase of *E. coli* (F. Stoeber, unpublished results), galactokinase and galactose-transferase (Buttin, unpublished results)). That *any* inducible system should be potentially capable of giving rise to constitutive mutants, strongly indicates that such mutations occur, or at least can always occur, by a loss of function. In the case of the "galactose" system of *E. coli*, it has been found that the constitutive mutation is pleiotropic, affecting a sequence of three different enzymes (galactokinase, galactose-transferase, UDP-galactose epimerase), and occurs at a locus distinct from that of the corresponding structural genes (Buttin, unpublished results).

The main conclusions from the observations reviewed in this section may be summarized as defining a new type of gene, which we shall call a "regulator gene" (Jacob & Monod, 1959). A regulator gene does not contribute structural information to the proteins which it controls. The specific product of a regulator gene is a cytoplasmic substance, which inhibits information transfer from a structural gene (or genes) to protein. In contrast to the classical structural gene, a regulator gene may control the synthesis of several different proteins: the one-gene one-protein rule does not apply to it.

We have already pointed out the profound similarities between induction and repression which suggest that the two effects represent different manifestations of the same fundamental mechanism. If this is true, and if the above conclusions are valid, one expects to find that the genetic control of repressible systems also involves regulator genes.

(c) *Regulator genes in repressible systems*

The identification of constitutive or "de-repressed" mutants of several repressible systems has fulfilled this expectation. For the selection of such mutants, certain analogs of the normal repressing metabolite may be used as specific selective agents, because they cannot substitute for the metabolite, except as repressing metabolites. For instance, 5-methyltryptophan does not substitute for tryptophan in protein synthesis (Munier, unpublished results), but it represses the enzymes of the tryptophan-synthesizing sequence (Monod & Cohen-Bazire, 1953). Normal wild type *E. coli* does not grow in the presence of 5-methyltryptophan. Fully resistant stable mutants arise, however, a large fraction of which turn out to be constitutive for the tryptophan system.† The properties of these organisms indicate that they arise by mutation of a regulator gene R_T (Cohen & Jacob, 1959). In these mutants tryptophan-synthetase as well as at least two of the enzymes involved in previous steps in the sequence are formed at the same rate irrespective of the presence of tryptophan, while in the wild type all these enzymes are strongly repressed. Actually the mutants form more of the enzymes in the presence of tryptophan, than does the wild type in its absence (just as i^-z^+ mutants form more galactosidase in the absence of inducer than the wild type does at saturating concentration of inducer). The capacity of the mutants to concentrate tryptophan from the medium is not impaired, nor is their tryptophanase activity increased. The loss of sensitivity to tryptophan as repressing metabolite cannot therefore be attributed to its destruction by, or exclusion from, the cells, and can only reflect the breakdown of the control system itself. Several recurrences of the R_T mutation have been mapped. They are all located in the same small section of the chromosome, at a large distance from the cluster of genes which was shown by Yanofsky & Lennox (1959) to synthesize the different enzymes of the sequence. One of these genes (comprising two cistrons) has been very clearly identified by the work of Yanofsky (1960) as the structural gene for tryptophan synthetase, and it is a safe assumption that the other genes in this cluster determine the structure of the preceding

† Resistance to 5-methyltryptophan may also arise by other mechanisms in which we are not interested here.

enzymes in the sequence. The R_T gene therefore controls the rate of synthesis of several different proteins without, however, determining their structure. It can only do so *via* a cytoplasmic intermediate, since it is located quite far from the structural genes. To complete its characterization as a regulator gene, it should be verified that the constitutive (R_T^-) allele corresponds to the inactive state of the gene (or gene product), i.e. is recessive. Stable heterozygotes have not been available in this case, but the transient (sexual) heterozygotes of a cross $\male\ R_T^- \times \female R_T^+$ are sensitive to 5-methyltryptophan, indicating that the repressible allele is dominant (Cohen & Jacob, 1959).

In the arginine-synthesizing sequence there are some seven enzymes, simultaneously repressible by arginine (Vogel, 1957*a,b*; Gorini & Maas, 1958). The specific (i.e. probably structural) genes which control these enzymes are dispersed at various loci on the chromosome. Mutants resistant to canavanine have been obtained, in which several (perhaps all) of these enzymes are simultaneously de-repressed. These mutations occur at a locus (near Sm^r) which is widely separated from the loci corresponding (probably) to the structural genes. The dominance relationships have not been analysed (Gorini, unpublished results; Maas, Lavallé, Wiame & Jacob, unpublished results).

The case of alkaline phosphatase is particularly interesting because the structural gene corresponding to this protein is well identified by the demonstration that various mutations at this locus result in the synthesis of altered phosphatase (Levinthal, 1959). The synthesis of this enzyme is repressed by orthophosphate (Torriani, 1960). Constitutive mutants which synthesize large amounts of enzyme in the presence of orthophosphate have been isolated. They occur at two loci, neither of which is allelic to the structural gene, and the constitutive enzyme is identical, by all tests, to the wild type (repressible) enzyme. The constitutive alleles for both of the two loci have been shown to be recessive with respect to wild type. Conversely, mutations in the structural (P) gene do not affect the regulatory mechanism, since the altered (inactive) enzyme formed by mutants of the P gene is repressed in the presence of orthophosphate to the same extent as the wild type enzyme (Echols, Garen, Garen & Torriani, 1961).

(d) *The interaction of repressors, inducers and co-repressors*

The sum of these observations leaves little doubt that repression, like induction, is controlled by specialized regulator genes, which operate by a basically similar mechanism in both types of systems, namely by governing the synthesis of an intracellular substance which inhibits information transfer from structural genes to protein.

It is evident therefore that the metabolites (such as tryptophan, arginine, orthophosphate) which inhibit enzyme synthesis in repressible systems are not active by themselves, but only by virtue of an interaction with a repressor synthesized under the control of a regulator gene. Their action is best described as an activation of the genetically controlled repression system. In order to avoid confusion of words, we shall speak of repressing metabolites as "co-repressors" reserving the name "repressors" (or apo-repressors) for the cytoplasmic products of the regulator genes.

The nature of the interaction between repressor and co-repressor (in repressible systems) or inducer (in inducible systems) poses a particularly difficult problem. As a purely formal description, one may think of inducers as antagonists, and of co-repressors as activators, of the repressor. A variety of chemical models can be imagined to account for such antagonistic or activating interactions. We shall not go into these speculations since there is at present no evidence to support or eliminate any particular model. But it must be pointed out that, in any model, the structural specificity of inducers or co-repressors must be accounted for, and can be accounted for, only by the assumption that a stereospecific receptor is involved in the interaction. The fact that the repressor is apparently not a protein then raises a serious difficulty since the capacity to form stereospecific complexes with small molecules appears to be a privilege of proteins. If a protein, perhaps an enzyme, is responsible for the specificity, the structure of this protein is presumably determined by a structal gene and muta-tion in this gene would result in loss of the capacity to be induced (or repressed). Such mutants, which would have precisely predictable properties (they would be pleio-tropic, recessive, and they would be complemented by mutants of the other structural genes) have not been encountered in the lactose system, while the possibility that the controlled enzymes themselves (galactosidase or acetylase) play the role of "induction enzyme" is excluded.

It is conceivable that, in the repressible systems which synthesize amino acids, this role is played by enzymes simultaneously responsible for essential functions (e.g. the activating enzymes) whose loss would be lethal, but this seems hardly conceivable in the case of most inducible systems. One possibility which is not excluded by these observations is that the repressor itself synthesizes the "induction protein" and remains thereafter associated with it. Genetic inactivation of the induction enzyme would then be associated with structural alterations of the repressor itself and would generally be expressed as constitutive mutations of the regulator gene.† This possibility is mentioned here only as an illustration of the dilemma which we have briefly analysed, and whose solution will depend upon the chemical identification of the repressor.

(e) *Regulator genes and immunity in temperate phage systems*

One of the most conspicuous examples of the fact that certain genes may be either allowed to express their potentialities, or specifically prohibited from doing so, is the phenomenon of immunity in temperate phage systems (*cf.* Lwoff, 1953; Jacob, 1954; Jacob & Wollman, 1957; Bertani, 1958; Jacob, 1960).

The genetic material of the so-called temperate phages can exist in one of two states within the host cell:

(1) In the *vegetative state*, the phage genome multiplies autonomously. This process, during which all the phage components are synthesized, culminates in the production of infectious phage particles which are released by lysis of the host cell.

(2) In the *prophage state*, the genetic material of the phage is attached to a specific site of the bacterial chromosome in such a way that both genetic elements replicate as a single unit. The host cell is said to be "lysogenic." As long as the phage genome remains in the prophage state, phage particles are not produced. For lysogenic bacteria to produce phage, the genetic material of the phage must undergo a transition from the prophage to the vegetative state. During normal growth of lysogenic bacteria, this event is exceedingly rare. With certain types of prophages, however, the transition can be induced in the whole population by exposure of the culture to u.v. light,

---

† Such a model could account for the properties of the i^s (dominant) mutant of the regulator gene in the lactose system, by the assumption that in this mutant the repressor remains active, while having lost the capacity to form its associated induction protein.

X-rays or various compounds known to alter DNA metabolism (Lwoff, Siminovitch & Kjeldgaard, 1950; Lwoff, 1953; Jacob, 1954).

The study of "defective" phage genomes, in which a mutation has altered one of the steps required for the production of phage particles, indicates the existence of at least two distinct groups of viral functions, both of which are related to the capacity of synthesizing specific proteins (Jacob, Fuerst & Wollman, 1957). Some "early" functions appear as a pre-requisite for the vegetative multiplication of the phage genome and, at least in virulent phages of the T-even series, it is now known that they correspond to the synthesis of a series of new enzymes (Flaks & Cohen, 1959; Kornberg, Zimmerman, Kornberg & Josse, 1959). A group of "late" functions correspond to the synthesis of the structural proteins which constitute the phage coat. The expression of these different viral functions appears to be in some way co-ordinated by a sequential process, since defective mutations affecting some of the early functions may also result in the loss of the capacity to perform several later steps of phage multiplication (Jacob *et al.*, 1957).

In contrast, the viral functions are not expressed in the prophage state and the protein constituents of the phage coat cannot be detected within lysogenic bacteria. In addition, lysogenic bacteria exhibit the remarkable property of being specifically *immune* to the very type of phage particles whose genome is already present in the cell as prophage. When lysogenic cells are infected with homologous phage particles, these particles absorb onto the cells and inject their genetic material, but the cell survives. The injected genetic material does not express its viral functions: it is unable to initiate the synthesis of the protein components of the coat and to multiply vegetatively. It remains inert and is diluted out in the course of bacterial multiplication (Bertani, 1953; Jacob, 1954).

The inhibition of phage-gene functions in lysogenic bacteria therefore applies not only to the prophage, but also to additional homologous phage genomes. It depends only upon the presence of the prophage (and not upon a permanent alteration, provoked by the prophage, of bacterial genes) since loss of the prophage is both necessary and sufficient to make the bacteria sensitive again.

Two kinds of interpretation may be considered to account for these "immunity" relationships:

(a) The prophage occupies and blocks a *chromosomal* site of the host, specifically required in some way for the vegetative multiplication of the homologous phage.

(b) The prophage produces a *cytoplasmic* inhibitor preventing the completion of some reactions (presumably the synthesis of a particular protein) necessary for the initiation of vegetative multiplication.

A decision between these alternative hypotheses may be reached through the study of persister[+] diploids, heterozygous for the character lysogeny. A sex factor has been isolated which has incorporated a segment of the bacterial chromosome carrying the genes which control galactose fermentation, *Gal*, and the site of attachment of prophage, λ. Diploid heterozygotes with the structure *Gal*⁻ λ⁻/*F Gal*⁺ λ⁺ or *Gal*⁻ λ⁺/ *F Gal*⁺ λ⁻ are immune against superinfection with phage λ, a result which shows that "immunity" is dominant over "non-immunity" and has a cytoplasmic expression (Jacob, Schaeffer & Wollman, 1960).

The study of transient zygotes formed during conjugation between lysogenic (λ⁺) and non-lysogenic (λ⁻) cells leads to the same conclusion. In crosses ♂λ⁺ × ♀λ⁻, the transfer of the prophage carried by the male chromosome into the non-immune recipient results in transition to the vegetative state: multiplication of the phage occurs in the zygotes, which are lysed and release phage particles. This phenomenon is known as "zygotic induction" (Jacob & Wollman, 1956). In the *reverse* cross $\male \lambda^- \times \female \lambda^+$, however, *no zygotic induction occurs*. The transfer of the "non-lysogenic" character carried by the male chromosome into the immune recipient does not bring about the development of the prophage and the zygotes are immune against super-infection with phage λ.

The opposite results obtained in reciprocal crosses of lysogenic by non-lysogenic male and female cells are entirely analogous to the observations made with the lactose system in reciprocal crosses of inducible by non-inducible cells. In both cases, it is evident that the decisive factor is the origin of the *cytoplasm* of the zygote, and the conclusion is inescapable, that the immunity of lysogenic bacteria is due to a cyto-plasmic constituent, in the presence of which the viral genes cannot become expressed (Jacob, 1960).

The same two hypotheses which we have already considered for the interpretation of the product of the regulator gene in the lactose system, apply to the cytoplasmic inhibitor insuring immunity in lysogenic bacteria.

(a) The inhibitor is a specific repressor which prevents the synthesis of some early protein(s) required for the initiation of vegetative multiplication.

(b) The inhibitor is an enzyme which destroys a metabolite, normally synthesized by the non-lysogenic cell and specifically required for the vegetative multiplication of the phage.

Several lines of evidence argue against the second hypothesis (Jacob & Campbell, 1959; Jacob, 1960). First, for a given strain of bacteria, many temperate phages are known, each of which exhibits a different immunity pattern. According to the second hypothesis, each of these phages would specifically require for vegetative multiplica-tion a different metabolite normally produced by the non-lysogenic cells, an assump-tion which appears extremely unlikely. The second argument stems from the fact that, like the repressor of the lactose system, the inhibitor responsible for immunity is synthesized in the presence of chloramphenicol, i.e. in the absence of protein synthesis: when crosses $\male \lambda^+ \times \female \lambda^-$ are performed in the presence of chloramphenicol, no zygotic induction occurs and the prophage is found to segregate normally among recombinants.

In order to explain immunity in lysogenic bacteria, we are led therefore to the same type of interpretation as in the case of adaptive enzyme systems. According to this interpretation, the prophage controls a cytoplasmic repressor, which inhibits specific-ally the synthesis of one (or several) protein(s) necessary for the initiation of vegetative multiplication. In this model, the introduction of the genetic material of the phage into a non-lysogenic cell, whether by infection or by conjugation, results in a "race" between the synthesis of the specific repressor and that of the early proteins required for vegetative multiplication. The fate of the host-cell, survival with lysogenization or lysis as a result of phage multiplication, depends upon whether the synthesis of the repressor or that of the protein is favoured. Changes in the cultural conditions favoring the synthesis of the repressor such as infection at low temperature, or in the presence of chloramphenicol, would favor lysogenization and *vice versa*. The pheno-menon of induction by u.v. light could then be understood, for instance, in the follow-ing way: exposure of inducible lysogenic bacteria to u.v. light or X-rays would transiently disturb the regulation system, for example by preventing further synthesis of the repressor. If the repressor is unstable, its concentration inside the cell would decrease and reach a level low enough to allow the synthesis of the early proteins. Thus the vegetative multiplication would be irreversibly initiated.

The similarity between lysogenic systems and adaptive systems is further strengthened by the genetic analysis of immunity. Schematically, the genome of phage λ appears to involve two parts (see Fig. 5): a small central segment, the C region, contains a few determinants which control various functions involved in lysogenization (Kaiser, 1957); the rest of the linkage group contains determinants which govern the "viral functions," i.e. presumably the structural genes corresponding to the different phage proteins. Certain strains of temperate phages which exhibit different immunity patterns are able nevertheless to undergo genetic recombination. The specific immunity pattern segregates in such crosses, proving to be controlled by a small segment "im" of the C region (Kaiser & Jacob, 1957). In other words, a prophage contains in its C region a small segment "im" which controls the synthesis of a specific repressor, active on the phage genome carrying a homologous "im" segment.

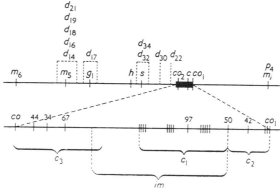

FIG. 5. Diagrammatic representation of the linkage group of the temperate bacteriophage λ. The upper diagram represents the linear arrangement of markers. Symbols refer to various plaque size, plaque type and host-range markers. Symbols d refer to various defective mutations. The C region represented by a thicker line is enlarged in the lower diagram. The figures correspond to various C mutations. The C region can be subdivided into three functional units, C_1, C_2 and C_3; the segment controlling immunity is designated im.

In the "im" region, two types of mutations arise, whose properties are extremely similar to those of the different mutations affecting the regulator genes of adaptive enzyme systems.

(1) Some mutations ($C_I^+ \to C_I$) result in the complete loss of the capacity for lysogenization in single infection. All the C_I mutations are located in a cluster, in a small part of the "im" segment, and they behave as belonging to a single cistron in complementation tests.

In mixed infections with both C_I and C_I^+ phages, double lysogenic clones carrying both C_I and C_I^+ prophages can be recovered. In such clones, single lysogenic cells segregate, which carry the C^+ type alone but never the C_I type alone. These findings indicate that the wild allele is dominant over the mutant C_I alleles and is cytoplasmically expressed, repressing the mutant genome into the prophage state. The properties of the C_I mutations are therefore similar to those of the recessive constitutive mutations of adaptive systems. The evidence suggests that the C_I locus controls the synthesis of the repressor responsible for immunity, and that the C_I mutations correspond to inactivation of this locus, or of its product.

(2) A mutation ($ind^+\rightarrow ind^-$) has been found which results in the loss of the inducible property of the prophage, i.e. of its capacity to multiply vegetatively upon exposure of lysogenic bacteria to u.v. light, X-rays or chemical inducers. This mutation is located in the C_I segment. The mutant allele ind^- is dominant over the wild allele ind^+ since double lysogenic $\lambda ind^+/\lambda ind^-$ or diploid heterozygotes of structure $Gal^-\lambda ind^+/F\ Gal^+\lambda ind^-$ or $Gal^-\lambda ind^-/F\ Gal^+\lambda ind^+$ are all non-inducible. In addition, the mutant λind^- exhibits a unique property. If lysogenic bacteria K12 (λ^+) carrying a wild type prophage are exposed to u.v. light, the whole population lyses and releases phage. Infection of such cells with λind^- mutants, either before or immediately after irradiation, completely inhibits phage production and lysis.

The properties of the ind^- mutant appear in every respect similar to those of the previously described mutant i^s of the lactose system. The unique properties of the ind^- mutants can be explained only by the same type of hypothesis, namely that the mutation ind^- affects, quantitatively or qualitatively, the synthesis of the repressor in such a way that more repressor or a more efficient repressor is produced. If this assumption as well as the hypothesis that the C_I mutation results in the loss of the capacity to produce an active repressor, are correct, the double mutants $C_I ind^-$ should have lost the capacity of inhibiting phage multiplication upon infection of wild type lysogenic cells. This is actually what is observed. It is evident that the properties of the ind^- mutant cannot be accounted for by the assumption that the C_I locus controls the synthesis of a metabolite-destroying enzyme (Jacob & Campbell, 1959).

In summary, the analysis of lysogenic systems reveals that the expression of the viral genes in these systems is controlled by a cytoplasmic repressor substance, whose synthesis is governed by one particular "regulator" gene, belonging to the viral genome. The identity of the proteins whose synthesis is thus repressed is not established, but it seems highly probable that they are "early" enzymes which initiate the whole process of vegetative multiplication. With the (important) limitation that they are sensitive to entirely different types of inducing conditions, the phage repression systems appear entirely comparable to the systems involved in enzymatic adaptation.

4. The Operator and the Operon

(a) *The operator as site of action of the repressor*

In the preceding section we have discussed the evidence which shows that the transfer of information from structural genes to protein is controlled by specific repressors synthesized by specialized regulator genes. We must now consider the next problem, which is the site and mode of action of the repressor.

In regard to this problem, the most important property of the repressor is its characteristic pleiotropic specificity of action. In the lactose system of *E. coli*, the repressor is both *highly specific* since mutations of the *i* gene do not affect any other system, and *pleiotropic* since both galactosidase and acetylase are affected simultaneously and quantitatively to the same extent, by such mutations.

The specificity of operation of the repressor implies that it acts by forming a stereo-specific combination with a constituent of the system possessing the proper (complementary) molecular configuration. Furthermore, it must be assumed that the flow of information from gene to protein is interrupted when this element is combined with the repressor. This controlling element we shall call the *"operator"* (Jacob & Monod, 1959). We should perhaps call attention to the fact that, once the existence of a specific repressor is considered as established, the existence of an operator element defined as above follows necessarily. Our problem, therefore, is not whether an operator exists, but where (and how) it intervenes in the system of information transfer.

An important prediction follows immediately from the preceding considerations. Under any hypothesis concerning the nature of the operator, its specific complementary configuration must be genetically determined; therefore it could be affected by mutations which would alter or abolish its specific affinity for the repressor, without necessarily impairing its activity as initiator of information-transfer. Such mutations would result in *constitutive* synthesis of the protein or proteins. These mutations would define an "operator locus" which should be genetically distinct from the regulator gene (i.e. its mutations should not behave as alleles of the regulator); the most distinctive predictable property of such mutants would be that the constitutive allele should be *dominant* over the wild type since, again under virtually any hypothesis, the presence in a diploid cell of repressor-sensitive operators would not prevent the operation of repressor-insensitive operators.

(b) *Constitutive operator mutations*

Constitutive mutants possessing the properties predicted above have so far been found in two repressor-controlled systems, namely the phage λ and *Lac* system of *E. coli.*

In the case of phage λ, these mutants are characterized, and can be easily selected, by the fact that they develop vegetatively in immune bacteria, lysogenic for the wild type. This characteristic property means that these mutants (v) are *insensitive* to the repressor present in lysogenic cells. When, in fact, lysogenic cells are infected with these mutant particles, the development of the wild type prophage is induced, and the resulting phage population is a mixture of v and v^+ particles. This is expected, since presumably the initiation of prophage development depends only on the formation of one or a few "early" enzyme-proteins, which are supplied by the virulent particle (Jacob & Wollman, 1953).

In the *Lac* system, dominant constitutive (o^c) mutants have been isolated by selecting for constitutivity in cells diploid for the *Lac* region, thus virtually eliminating the recessive (i^-) constitutive mutants (Jacob *et al.*, 1960a). By recombination, the o^c mutations can be mapped in the *Lac* region, between the i and the z loci, the order being (*Pro*) *yzoi* (*Ad*) (see Fig. 3). Some of the properties of these mutants are summarized in Table 3. To begin with, let us consider only the effects of this mutation on galactosidase synthesis. It will be noted that in the absence of inducer, these organisms synthesize 10 to 20% of the amount of galactosidase synthesized by i^- mutants, i.e. about 100 to 200 times more than uninduced wild type cells (Table 3, lines 3 and 7). In the presence of inducer, they synthesize maximal amounts of enzyme. They are therefore only partially constitutive (except however under conditions of starvation, when they form maximum amounts of galactosidase in the absence of inducer (Brown, unpublished results)). The essential point however is that the enzyme is synthesized constitutively by diploid cells of constitution o^c/o^+ (see Table 3). The o^c allele therefore is "dominant."

If the constitutivity of the o^c mutant results from a loss of sensitivity of the operator to the repressor, the o^c organisms should also be insensitive to the presence of the altered repressor synthesized by the i^s (dominant) allele of the i^+ gene (see page 331). That this is indeed the case, as shown by the constitutive behavior of diploids with the constitution i^so^+/Fi^+o^c (see Table 3, line 12), is a very strong confirmation of the interpretation of the effects of *both* mutations (i^s and o^c). In addition, and as one would expect according to this interpretation, o^c mutants frequently arise as lactose positive "revertants" in populations of i^s cells (see p. 332).

TABLE 3

Synthesis of galactosidase, cross-reacting material (CRM), and galactoside-transacetylase by haploid and heterozygous diploid operator mutants

Strain No.	Genotype	Galactosidase		Cross-reacting material	
		Non-induced	Induced	Non-induced	Induced
1	o^+z^+	<0·1	100	—	—
2	$o^+z^+/Fo^+z_1^-$	<0·1	105	<1	310
3	o^cz^+	15	90	—	—
4	o^+z^+/Fo^cz_1	<0·1	90	30	180
5	$o^+z_1^-/Fo^cz^+$	90	250	<1	85

Strain No.	Genotype	Galactosidase		Galactoside-transacetylase	
		Non-Induced	Induced	Non-induced	Induced
6	$o^+z^+y^+$	<0·1	100	<1	100
7	$o^cz^+y^+$	25	95	15	110
8	$o^+z^+y_U^-/Fo^cz^+y^+$	70	220	50	160
9	$o^+z_1^-y^+/Fo^cz^+y_U^-$	180	440	<1	220
10	$i^+o_{84}^oz^+y^+$	<0·1	<0·1	<1	<1
11	$i^+o_{84}^oz^+y^+/Fi^-o^+z^+y^+$	1	260	2	240
12	$i^so^+z^+y^+/Fi^+o^cz^+y^+$	190	210	150	200

Bacteria are grown in glycerol as carbon source and induced when stated, with *isopropyl-thiogalactoside*, 10^{-4} M. Values of galactosidase and acetylase are given as a percentage of those observed with induced wild type. Values of CRM are expressed as antigenic equivalents of galactosidase. Note that the proteins corresponding to the alleles carried by the sex factor are often produced in greater amount than that observed with induced haploid wild type. This is presumably due to the existence of several copies of the *F-Lac* factor per chromosome. In o^c mutants, haploid or diploid, the absolute values of enzymes produced, especially in the non-induced cultures varies greatly from day to day depending on the conditions of the cultures.

We therefore conclude that the $o^+\rightarrow o^c$ mutations correspond to a modification of the specific, repressor-accepting, structure of the operator. This identifies the operator locus, i.e. the genetic segment responsible for the structure of the operator, but not the operator itself.

(c) *The operon*

Turning now to this problem, we note that the o^c mutation (like the i^- mutation) is pleiotropic: it affects simultaneously and quantitatively to the same extent, the synthesis of galactosidase and acetylase (see Table 3, lines 7 and 8). The structure of the operator, or operators, which controls the synthesis of the two proteins, therefore, is controlled by a single determinant.†

Two alternative interpretations of this situation must be considered:

(a) A single operator controls an *integral* property of the z-y genetic segment, or of its cytoplasmic product.

(b) The specific product of the operator locus is able to associate in the cytoplasm, with the products of the z and y cistrons, and thereby governs the expression of both structural genes.

The second interpretation implies that mutations of the operator locus should behave as belonging to a cistron *independent* of both the z and y cistrons. The first interpretation requires, on the contrary, that these mutations behave functionally as if they *belonged to both cistrons simultaneously*. These alternative interpretations can therefore be distinguished without reference to any particular physical model of operator action by testing for the *trans* effect of o alleles, that is to say for the constitutive *vs* inducible expression of the two structural genes in o^+/o^c diploids, heterozygous for one or both of these structural genes.

The results obtained with diploids of various structures are shown in Table 3. We may first note that in diploids of constitution $o^+z^+/F o^c z_1^-$ or $o^+z_1^-/F o^c z^+$ (lines 4 and 5), both the normal galactosidase produced by the z^+ allele and the altered protein (CRM) produced by the z_1^- allele are formed in the presence of inducer, while in the *absence of* inducer, *only the protein corresponding to the* z *allele in position cis to the* o^c *is produced.* The o^c therefore has no effect on the z allele in position *trans*. Or putting it otherwise: the expression of the z allele attached to an o^+ remains fully repressor-sensitive even in the presence of an o^c in position *trans*. The o locus might be said to behave as belonging to the same cistron as the z markers. But as we know already, the o^c mutation is equally effective towards the acetylase which belongs to a cistron independent of z, and not adjacent to the operator locus. The results shown in Table 3, lines 8 and 9, confirm that the $o \rightarrow y$ relationship is the same as the $o \rightarrow z$ relationship, that is, the effect of the o^c allele extends *exclusively* to the y allele in the *cis* position. For instance, in the diploid $o^+z^-y^+/F o^c z^+y_U^-$ the galactosidase is constitutive and the acetylase is inducible, while in the diploid $o^+z^+y_U^-/F o^c z^+y^+$ both enzymes are constitutive.

These observations, predicted by the first interpretation, are incompatible with the second and lead to the conclusion that the operator governs an integral property of the genetic segment *ozy*, or of its cytoplasmic product (Jacob *et al.*, 1960*a*; Képès, Monod & Jacob, 1961).

This leads to another prediction. Certain mutations of the o segment could modify the operator in such a way as to inactivate the whole *ozy* segment resulting in the loss of the capacity to synthesize *both* galactosidase and permease.

These "o^o" mutants would be *recessive* to o^+ or o^c, and they would *not* be complemented either by $o^+z^+y^-$ or by $o^+z^-y^+$ mutants. Several point-mutants, possessing

---

† Let us recall again that no *non-pleiotropic* constitutive mutants of any type have been isolated in this system, in spite of systematic screening for such mutants.

precisely these properties, have been isolated (Jacob *et al.*, 1960a). They all map very closely to o^c, as expected (see Fig. 3). It is interesting to note that in these mutants the i^+ gene is functional (Table 3, line 11), which shows clearly, not only that the i and o mutants are not alleles, but that the o segment, while governing the expression of the z and y genes, does not affect the expression of the regulator gene.

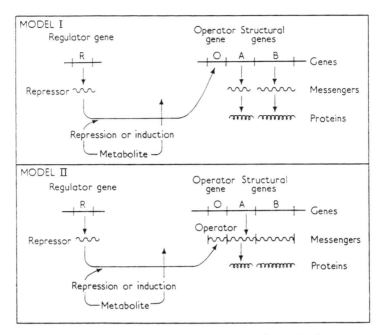

FIG. 6. Models of the regulation of protein synthesis.

In conclusion, the integral or *co-ordinate* expression of the *ozy* genetic segment signifies that the operator, which controls this expression, is and remains attached (see Fig. 6):

(a) either to the genes themselves (Fig. 6, I),

(b) or to the cytoplasmic messenger of the linked z and y genes which must then be assumed to form a single, integral, particle corresponding to the structure of the whole *ozy* segment, and functioning as a whole (Fig. 6, II).

In the former case, *the operator would in fact be identical with the o locus and it would govern directly the activity of the genes*, i.e. the synthesis of the structural messengers.

Both of these models are compatible with the observations which we have discussed so far. We shall return in the next section to the question whether the operator, i.e. the site of specific interaction with the repressor, is genetic or cytoplasmic. In either case, the *ozy* segment, although containing at least two independent structural genes, governing two independent proteins, behaves as a *unit* in the transfer of information. This *genetic unit of co-ordinate expression* we shall call the *"operon"* (Jacob *et al.*, 1960a).

The existence of such a unit of genetic expression is proved so far only in the case of the *Lac* segment. As we have already seen, the *v* mutants of phage λ, while illustrating the existence of an operator in this system, do not define an operon (because the number and the functions of the structural genes controlled by this operator are unknown). However, many observations hitherto unexplained by or even conflicting with classical genetic theory, are immediately accounted for by the operon theory. It is well known that, in bacteria, the genes governing the synthesis of different enzymes sequentially involved in a metabolic pathway are often found to be extremely closely linked, forming a cluster (Demerec, 1956). Various not very convincing speculations have been advanced to account for this obvious correlation of genetic structure and biochemical function (see Pontecorvo, 1958). Since it is now established that simultaneous induction or repression also generally prevails in such metabolic sequences, it seems very likely that the gene clusters represent units of co-ordinate expression, i.e. operons.

We have already mentioned the fact that two inducible enzymes sequentially involved in the metabolism of galactose by *E. coli*, galactokinase and UDP-galactose-transferase, are simultaneously induced by galactose, or by the gratuitous inducer D-fucose (Buttin, 1961). The genes which control specifically the synthesis of these enzymes, i.e. presumably the structural genes, are closely linked, forming a cluster on the *E. coli* chromosome. (Kalckar, Kurahashi & Jordan, 1959; Lederberg, 1960; Yarmolinsky & Wiesmeyer, 1960; Adler, unpublished results.) Certain point-mutations which occur in this chromosome segment abolish the capacity to synthesize both enzymes. These pleiotropic loss mutations are not complemented by any one of the specific (structural) loss mutations, an observation which is in apparent direct conflict with the one-gene one-enzyme hypothesis. These relationships are explained and the conflict is resolved if it is assumed that the linked structural genes constitute an operon controlled by a single operator and that the pleiotropic mutations are mutations of the operator locus.

We have also already discussed the system of simultaneous repression which controls the synthesis of the enzymes involved in histidine synthesis in *Salmonella*. This system involves eight or nine reaction steps. The enzymes which catalyse five of these reactions have been identified. The genes which individually determine these enzymes form a closely linked cluster on the *Salmonella* chromosome. Mutations in each of these genes result in a loss of capacity to synthesize a single enzyme; however, certain mutations at one end of the cluster abolish the capacity to synthesize all the enzymes simultaneously, and these mutations are not complemented by any one of the specific mutations (Ames, Garry & Herzenberg, 1960; Hartman, Loper & Serman, 1960). It will be recalled that the relative rates of synthesis of different enzymes in this sequence are constant under any set of conditions (see p. 327). All these remarkable findings are explained if it is assumed that this cluster of genes constitutes an operon, controlled by an operator associated with the *g* cistron.

The rule that genes controlling metabolically sequential enzymes constitute genetic clusters does not apply, in general, to organisms other than bacteria (Pontecorvo, 1958). Nor does it apply to all bacterial systems, even where simultaneous repression is known to occur and to be controlled by a single regulator gene, as is apparently the case for the enzymes of arginine biosynthesis. In such cases, it must be supposed that several identical or similar operator loci are responsible for sensitivity to repressor of each of the independent information-transfer systems.

It is clear that when an operator controls the expression of only a single structural cistron, the concept of the operon does not apply, and in fact there are no conceivable genetic-biochemical tests which could identify the operator-controlling genetic segment as distinct from the structural cistron itself.† One may therefore wonder whether it will be possible experimentally to extend this concept to dispersed (as opposed to clustered) genetic systems. It should be remarked at this point that many enzyme proteins are apparently made up of two (or more) different polypeptide chains. It is tempting to predict that such proteins will often be found to be controlled by two (or more) adjacent and co-ordinated structural cistrons, forming an operon.

5. The Kinetics of Expression of Structural Genes, and the Nature of the Structural Message

The problem we want to discuss in this section is whether the repressor-operator system functions at the genetic level by governing the *synthesis* of the structural message or at the cytoplasmic level, by controlling the protein-synthesizing *activity* of the messenger (see Fig. 6). These two conceivable models we shall designate respectively as the "genetic operator model" and the "cytoplasmic operator model."

The existence of units of co-ordinate expression involving several structural genes appears in fact difficult to reconcile with the cytoplasmic operator model, if only because of the size that the cytoplasmic unit would have to attain. If we assume that the message is a polyribonucleotide and take a coding ratio of 3, the "unit message" corresponding to an operon governing the synthesis of three proteins of average (monomeric) molecular weight 60,000 would have a molecular weight about $1\cdot8\times10^6$; we have seen that operons including up to 8 structural cistrons may in fact exist. On the other hand, RNA fractions of *E. coli* and other cells do not appear to include polyribonucleotide molecules of molecular weight exceeding 10^6.

This difficulty is probably not insuperable; and this type of argument, given the present state of our knowledge, cannot be considered to eliminate the cytoplasmic operator model, even less to establish the validity of the genetic model. However, it seems more profitable tentatively to adopt the genetic model and to see whether some of the more specific predictions which it implies are experimentally verified.

The most immediate and also perhaps the most striking of these implications is that the structural message must be carried by a very short-lived intermediate both rapidly formed and rapidly destroyed during the process of information transfer. This is required by the kinetics of induction. As we have seen, the addition of inducer, or the removal of co-repressor, provokes the synthesis of enzyme at maximum rate within a matter of a few minutes, while the removal of inducer, or the addition of co-repressor interrupts the synthesis within an equally short time. Such kinetics are incompatible with the assumption that the repressor-operator interaction controls the rate of synthesis of *stable* enzyme-forming templates (Monod, 1956, 1958). Therefore, if the genetic operator model is valid, one should expect the kinetics of structural gene expression to be *essentially the same* as the kinetics of induction: injection of a "new" gene into an otherwise competent cell should result in virtually immediate synthesis of the corresponding protein at maximum rate; while removal of the gene should be attended by concomitant cessation of synthesis.

† It should be pointed out that the operational distinction between the operator locus and the structural cistron to which it is directly adjacent rests exclusively on the fact that the operator mutations affect the synthesis of several proteins governed by linked cistrons. This does not exclude the possibility that the operator locus is actually *part* of the structural cistron to which it is "adjacent." If it were so, one might expect certain constitutive operator mutations to involve an alteration of the structure of the protein governed by the "adjacent" cistron. The evidence available at present is insufficient to confirm or eliminate this assumption.

(a) *Kinetics of expression of the galactosidase structural gene*

Additions and removals of genes to and from cells are somewhat more difficult to perform than additions or removals of inducer. However, it can be done. Gene injection without cytoplasmic mixing occurs in the conjugation of *Hfr* male and *F⁻* female *E. coli*. In a mixed male and female population the individual pairs do not all mate at the same time, but the distribution of times of injection of a *given* gene can be rather accurately determined by proper genetic methods. The injection of the z^+ (galactosidase) gene from male cells into galactosidase-negative (z^-) female cells is rapidly followed by enzyme synthesis within zygotes (cf. p. 332). When the rate of enzyme synthesis in the population is expressed as a function of time, taking into

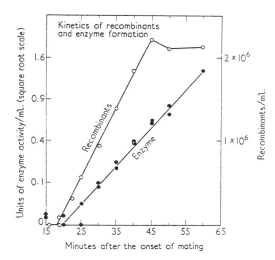

FIG. 7. Kinetics of enzyme production by merozygotes formed by conjugation between inducible galactosidase-positive males and constitutive galactosidase-negative females. Conditions are such that only the zygotes can form enzyme. Increase in the number of z^+ containing zygotes is determined by counting recombinants on adequate selective medium. Formation of enzyme is followed by enzyme activity measurements on the total population. It is seen that the enzyme increases linearly with the square of time. Since the zygote population increases linearly with time, it is apparent that the rate of enzyme synthesis per zygote is constant from the time of penetration of the z^+ gene. (From Riley *et al.*, 1960.)

account the increase with time of the number of z^+ containing zygotes, it is found (see Fig. 7):

(1) that enzyme synthesis begins within two minutes of the penetration of the z^+ gene;

(2) that the rate per zygote is constant and maximum over at least the first 40 min following penetration (Riley, Pardee, Jacob & Monod, 1960).

These observations indicate that the structural messenger is very rapidly formed by the z^+ gene, and does not accumulate. This could be interpreted in one of two ways:

(a) the structural messenger is a short-lived intermediate;

(b) the structural messenger is stable, but the gene rapidly forms a limited number of messenger molecules, and thereafter stops functioning.

If the second assumption is correct, removal of the gene after the inception of enzyme synthesis should not prevent the synthesis from continuing. This possibility is tested by the "removal" experiment, which is performed by loading the male chromosome with ^{32}P before injection. Following injection (into unlabelled female cells), ample time (25 min) is allowed for expression of the z^+ gene, before the zygotes are frozen to allow ^{32}P decay for various lengths of time. The rate of galactosidase synthesis by the population is determined immediately after thawing. It is found to decrease sharply as a function of the fraction of ^{32}P atoms decayed. If a longer period of time (110 min) is allowed for expression before freezing, no decrease in either enzyme-forming capacity or in viability of the z^+ marker are observed. This is to be expected, since by that time most of the z^+ genes would have replicated, and this observation provides an internal control showing that no indirect effects of ^{32}P disintegrations are involved.

This experiment therefore indicates that even after the z^+ gene has become expressed its integrity is required for enzyme synthesis to continue, as expected if the messenger molecule is a short-lived intermediate (Riley *et al.*, 1960).

The interpretation of both the injection and the removal experiment rests on the assumption that the observed effects are not due to (stable) cytoplasmic messenger molecules introduced with the genetic material, during conjugation. As we have already noted, there is strong evidence that no cytoplasmic transfer, even of small molecules, occurs during conjugation. Furthermore, if the assumption were made that enzyme synthesis in the zygotes is due to pre-formed messenger molecules rather than to the activity of the gene, it would be exceedingly difficult to account for both (a) the very precise coincidence in time between inception of enzyme synthesis and entry of the gene (in the injection experiment) and (b) the parallel behaviour of enzyme-forming capacity and genetic viability of the z^+ gene (in the removal experiment).

These experiments therefore appear to show that the kinetics of expression of a structural gene are entirely similar to the kinetics of induction-repression, as expected if the operator controls the activity of the gene in the synthesis of a short-lived messenger, rather than the activity of a ready-made (stable) messenger molecule in synthesizing protein.

It is interesting at this point to recall the fact that infection of *E. coli* with virulent (ϕII, T2, T4) phage is attended within 2 to 4 minutes by inhibition of *bacterial* protein synthesis, including in particular β-galactosidase (Cohen, 1949; Monod & Wollman, 1947; Benzer, 1953). It is known on the other hand that phage-infection results in rapid visible lysis of bacterial nuclei, while no major destruction of pre-formed bacterial RNA appears to occur (Luria & Human, 1950). It seems very probable that the inhibition of specific bacterial protein synthesis by virulent phage is due essentially to the depolymerization of bacterial DNA, and this conclusion also implies that the integrity of bacterial genes is required for continued synthesis of bacterial protein. In confirmation of this interpretation, it may be noted that infection of *E. coli* by phage λ, which does not result in destruction of bacterial nuclei, allows β-galactosidase synthesis to continue almost to the time of lysis (Siminovitch & Jacob, 1952).

(b) *Structural effects of base analogs*

An entirely different type of experiment also leads to the conclusion that the structural messenger is a short-lived intermediate and suggests, furthermore, that this intermediate is a ribonucleotide. It is known that certain purine and pyrimidine analogs are incorporated by bacterial cells into ribo- and deoxyribonucleotides, and it has been found that the synthesis of protein, or of some proteins, may be inhibited in the presence of certain of these analogs. One of the mechanisms by which these effects could be explained may be that certain analogs are incorporated into the structural messenger. If so, one might hope to observe that the molecular structure of specific proteins formed in the presence of an analog is modified. It has in fact been found that the molecular properties of β-galactosidase and of alkaline phosphatase synthesized by *E. coli* in the presence of 5-fluorouracil (5FU) are strikingly altered. In the case of β-galactosidase, the ratio of enzyme activity to antigenic valency is decreased by 80%. In the case of alkaline phosphatase, the rate of thermal inactivation (of this normally highly heat-resistant protein) is greatly increased (Naono & Gros, 1960*a,b*; Bussard, Naono, Gros & Monod, 1960).

It can safely be assumed that such an effect cannot result from the mere presence of 5FU in the cells, and must reflect incorporation of the analog into a constituent involved in some way in the information transfer system. Whatever the identity of this constituent may be, the kinetics of the effect must in turn reflect the kinetics of 5FU incorporation into this constituent. The most remarkable feature of the 5FU effect is that it is almost immediate, in the sense that abnormal enzyme is synthesized almost from the time of addition of the analog, and that the degree of abnormality of the molecular population thereafter synthesized does not increase with time. For instance, in the case of galactosidase abnormal enzyme is synthesized within 5 min of addition of the analog, and the ratio of enzyme activity to antigenic valency remains constant thereafter. In the case of alkaline phosphatase, the thermal inactivation curve of the abnormal protein synthesized in the presence of 5FU is monomolecular, showing the molecular population to be *homogeneously* abnormal rather than made up of a mixture of normal and abnormal molecules. It is clear that if the constituent responsible for this effect were stable, one would expect the population of molecules made in the presence of 5FU to be heterogeneous, and the fraction of abnormal molecules to increase progressively. It follows that the responsible constituent must be formed, and also must decay, very rapidly.

Now it should be noted that, besides the structural gene-synthesized messenger, the information transfer system probably involves other constituents responsible for the correct translation of the message, such as for instance the RNA fractions involved in amino acid transfer. The 5FU effect could be due to incorporation into one of these fractions rather than to incorporation into the messenger itself. However, the convergence of the results of the different experiments discussed above strongly suggests that the 5FU effect does reflect a high rate of turnover of the messenger itself.

(c) *Messenger RNA*

Accepting tentatively these conclusions, let us then consider what properties would be required of a cellular constituent, to allow its identification with the structural messenger. These qualifications based on general assumptions, and on the results discussed above, would be as follows:

(1) The "candidate" should be a polynucleotide.

(2) The fraction would presumably be very heterogeneous with respect to molecular weight. However, assuming a coding ratio of 3, the average molecular weight would not be lower than 5×10^5.

(3) It should have a base composition reflecting the base composition of DNA.

(4) It should, at least temporarily or under certain conditions, be found associated with ribosomes, since there are good reasons to believe that ribosomes are the seat of protein synthesis.

(5) It should have a very high rate of turnover and in particular it should saturate with 5FU within less than about 3 min.

It is immediately evident that none of the more classically recognized cellular RNA fractions meets these very restrictive qualifications. Ribosomal RNA, frequently assumed to represent the "template" in protein synthesis, is remarkably homogeneous in molecular weight. Its base composition is similar in different species, and does not reflect the variations in base ratios found in DNA. Moreover it appears to be entirely stable in growing cells (Davern & Meselson, 1960). It incorporates 5FU only in proportion to net increase.

Transfer RNA, or (sRNA) does not reflect DNA in base composition. Its average molecular weight is much lower than the 5×10^5 required for the messenger. Except perhaps for the terminal adenine and cytidine, its rate of incorporation of bases, including in particular 5FU, is not higher than that of ribosomal RNA.

However, a small fraction of RNA, first observed by Volkin & Astrachan (1957) in phage infected *E. coli*, and recently found to exist also in normal yeasts (Yčas & Vincent, 1960) and coli (Gros, *et al.*, 1961), does seem to meet all the qualifications listed above.

This fraction (which we shall designate "messenger RNA" or M-RNA) amounts to only about 3% of the total RNA; it can be separated from other RNA fractions by column fractionation or sedimentation (Fig. 8). Its average sedimentation velocity coefficient is 13, corresponding to a minimum molecular weight of 3×10^5, but since the molecules are presumably far from spherical, the molecular weight is probably much higher. The rate of incorporation of ^{32}P, uracil or 5FU into this fraction is extremely rapid: half saturation is observed in less than 30 sec, indicating a rate of synthesis several hundred times faster than any other RNA fraction. Its half life is also very short, as shown by the disappearance of radioactivity from this fraction in pre-labelled cells. At high concentrations of Mg^{2+} (0·005 M) the fraction tends to associate with the 70s ribosomal particles, while at lower Mg^{2+} concentrations it sediments independently of the ribosomal particles (Gros *et al.*, 1961).

The striking fact, discovered by Volkin & Astrachan, that the base-composition of this fraction in T2-infected cells reflects the base composition of *phage* (rather than bacterial) DNA, had led to the suggestion that it served as a precursor of phage DNA. The agreement between the properties of this fraction and the properties of a short-lived structural messenger suggests that, in phage infected cells as well as in normal cells, this fraction served in fact in the transfer of genetic information from phage DNA to the protein synthesizing centers. This assumption implies that the same protein-forming centers which, in uninfected cells, synthesize bacterial protein, also serve in infected cells to synthesize phage protein according to the new structural information provided by phage DNA, *via* M-RNA. This interpretation is strongly supported by recent observations made with T4 infected *E. coli*. (Brenner, Jacob & Meselson, 1961).

Uninfected cells of *E. coli* were grown in the presence of ^{15}N. They were then infected and resuspended in ^{14}N medium. Following infection, they were exposed to short pulses of ^{32}P or ^{35}S, and the ribosomes were analysed in density gradients. It was found:

(1) that no detectable amounts of ribosomal RNA were synthesized after infection;

(2) labelled M-RNA formed *after* infection became associated with unlabelled ribosomal particles formed *before* infection;

(3) newly formed (i.e. phage-determined) protein, identified by its ^{35}S content, was found associated with the 70s particles before it appeared in the soluble protein fraction.

These observations strongly suggest that phage protein is synthesized by *bacterial* ribosomes formed before infection and associated with *phage-determined* M-RNA. Since the structural information for phage protein could not reside in the bacterial ribosomes, it must be provided by the M-RNA fraction.

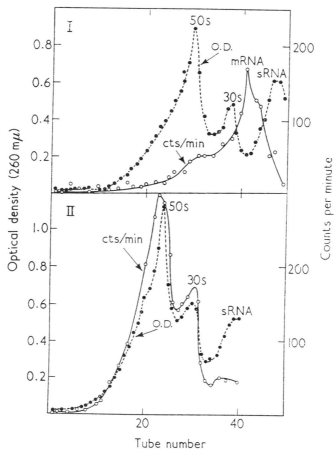

FIG. 8. Incorporation and turnover of uracil in messenger RNA. *E. coli* growing exponentially in broth were incubated for 5 sec with [^{14}C]-uracil. The bacteria were centrifuged, washed and resuspended in the original volume of the same medium containing 100-fold excess of [^{12}C]-uracil. Half the bacteria were then harvested and frozen (I) and the remainder were incubated for 15 min at 37°C (II) prior to harvesting and freezing. The frozen samples were ground with alumina and extracted with tris buffer (2-amino-2 hydroxymethylpropane-1:3-diol) containing 10^{-4}M-Mg, treated with DNase and applied to a sucrose gradient. After 3 hr, sequential samples were taken for determination of radioactivity and absorption at 260 mμ. It may be seen (part I) that after 5 sec, M-RNA is the only labelled fraction, and that subsequently (part II) uracil incorporated into M-RNA is entirely renewed. (From Gros *et al.*, 1961.)

Finally, the recent experiments of Lamfrom (1961) independently repeated by Kruh, Rosa, Dreyfus & Schapira (1961) have shown directly that species specificity in the synthesis of haemoglobin is determined by a "soluble" RNA-containing fraction rather than by the ribosomal fraction. Lamfrom used reconstructed systems, containing ribosomes from one species (rabbit) and soluble fractions from another (sheep) and found that the haemoglobin formed *in vitro* by these systems belonged in part to the type characteristic of the species used to prepare the *soluble* fraction. It is not, of course, positively proved that *inter-specific* differences in haemoglobin structure are gene-determined rather than cytoplasmic, but the assumption seems safe enough. In any case, Lamfrom's experiment proves beyond doubt that the ribosomes cannot be considered to determine entirely (if at all) the specific structure of proteins.

We had stated the problem to be discussed in this section as the choice between the genetic operator model and the cytoplasmic operator model. The adoption of the genetic operator model implies, as we have seen, some very distinctive and specific predictions concerning the behaviour of the intermediate responsible for the transfer of information from gene to protein. These predictions appear to be borne out by a considerable body of evidence which leads actually to a tentative identification of the intermediate in question with one particular RNA fraction. Even if this identification is confirmed by direct experiments, it will remain to be proved, also by direct experiments, that the synthesis of this "M-RNA" fraction is controlled at the genetic level by the repressor-operator interaction.

6. Conclusion

A convenient method of summarizing the conclusions derived in the preceding sections of this paper will be to organize them into a model designed to embody the main elements which we were led to recognize as playing a specific role in the control of protein synthesis; namely, the structural, regulator and operator genes, the operon, and the cytoplasmic repressor. Such a model could be as follows:

The molecular structure of proteins is determined by specific elements, the *structural genes*. These act by forming a cytoplasmic "transcript" of themselves, the structural messenger, which in turn synthesizes the protein. The synthesis of the messenger by the structural gene is a sequential replicative process, which can be initiated only at certain points on the DNA strand, and the cytoplasmic transcription of several, linked, structural genes may depend upon a single initiating point or *operator*. The genes whose activity is thus co-ordinated form an *operon*.

The operator tends to combine (by virtue of possessing a particular base sequence) specifically and reversibly with a certain (RNA) fraction possessing the proper (complementary) sequence. This combination blocks the initiation of cytoplasmic transcription and therefore the formation of the messenger by the structural genes in the whole operon. The specific "repressor" (RNA?), acting with a given operator, is synthesized by a *regulator gene*.

The repressor in certain systems (inducible enzyme systems) tends to combine specifically with certain specific small molecules. The combined repressor has no affinity for the operator, and the combination therefore results in *activation of the operon*.

In other systems (repressible enzyme systems) the repressor by itself is inactive (i.e. it has no affinity for the operator) and is activated only by combining with certain specific small molecules. The combination therefore leads to *inhibition of the operon*.

The structural messenger is an unstable molecule, which is destroyed in the process of information transfer. The rate of messenger synthesis, therefore, in turn controls the rate of protein synthesis.

This model was meant to summarize and express conveniently the properties of the different factors which play a specific role in the control of protein synthesis. In order concretely to represent the functions of these different factors, we have had to introduce some purely speculative assumptions. Let us clearly discriminate the experimentally established conclusions from the speculations:

(1) The most firmly grounded of these conclusions is the existence of *regulator* genes, which control the rate of information-transfer from *structural* genes to proteins, without contributing any information to the proteins themselves. Let us briefly recall the evidence on this point: mutations in the structural gene, which are reflected as alterations of the protein, do not alter the regulatory mechanism. Mutations that alter the regulatory mechanism do not alter the protein and do not map in the structural genes. Structural genes obey the one-gene one-protein principle, while regulator genes may affect the synthesis of several different proteins.

(2) That the regulator gene acts *via* a specific cytoplasmic substance whose effect is to *inhibit* the expression of the structural genes, is equally clearly established by the *trans* effect of the gene, by the different properties exhibited by genetically identical zygotes depending upon the origin of their cytoplasm, and by the fact that absence of the regulator gene, or of its product, results in uncontrolled synthesis of the protein at maximum rates.

(3) That the product of the regulator gene acts directly as a *repressor* (rather than indirectly, as antagonist of an endogenous inducer or other activator) is proved in the case of the *Lac* system (and of the λ lysogenic systems) by the properties of the dominant mutants of the regulator.

(4) The chemical identification of the repressor as an RNA fraction is a logical assumption based only on the *negative* evidence which indicates that it is not a protein.

(5) The existence of an operator, defined as the site of action of the repressor, is deduced from the existence and specificity of action of the repressor. The identification of the operator with the genetic segment which controls sensitivity to the repressor, is strongly suggested by the observation that a *single* operator gene may control the expression of *several adjacent structural genes*, that is to say, by the demonstration of the *operon* as a co-ordinated unit of genetic expression.

The assumption that the operator represents an initiating point for the cytoplasmic transcription of several structural genes is a pure speculation, meant only as an illustration of the fact that the operator controls an integral property of the group of linked genes which form an operon. There is at present no evidence on which to base any assumption on the molecular mechanisms of the operator.

(6) The assumptions made regarding the interaction of the repressor with inducers or co-repressors are among the weakest and vaguest in the model. The idea that specific coupling of inducers to the repressor could result in inactivation of the repressor appears reasonable enough, but it raises a difficulty which we have already pointed out. Since this reaction between repressor and inducer must be stereospecific (for both) it should presumably require a specific enzyme; yet no evidence, genetic or biochemical, has been found for such an enzyme.

(7) The property attributed to the structural messenger of being an unstable intermediate is one of the most specific and novel implications of this scheme; it is required, let us recall, by the kinetics of induction, once the assumption is made that the control systems operate at the genetic level. This leads to a new concept of the mechanism of information transfer, where the protein synthesizing centers (ribosomes) play the role of non-specific constituents which can synthesize different proteins, according to specific instructions which they receive from the genes through M-RNA. The already fairly impressive body of evidence, kinetic and analytical, which supports

this new interpretation of information transfer, is of great interest in itself, even if some of the other assumptions included in the scheme turn out to be incorrect.

These conclusions apply strictly to the bacterial systems from which they were derived; but the fact that adaptive enzyme systems of both types (inducible and repressible) and phage systems appear to obey the same fundamental mechanisms of control, involving the same essential elements, argues strongly for the generality of what may be called "repressive genetic regulation" of protein synthesis.

One is led to wonder whether all or most structural genes (i.e. the synthesis of most proteins) are submitted to repressive regulation. In bacteria, virtually all the enzyme systems which have been adequately studied have proved sensitive to inductive or repressive effects. The old idea that such effects are characteristic only of "non-essential" enzymes is certainly incorrect (although, of course, these effects can be detected only under conditions, natural or artificial, such that the system under study is at least partially non-essential (gratuitous). The results of mutations which abolish the control (such as constitutive mutations) illustrate its physiological importance. Constitutive mutants of the lactose system synthesize 6 to 7% of all their proteins as β-galactosidase. In constitutive mutants of the phosphatase system, 5 to 6% of the total protein is phosphatase. Similar figures have been obtained with other constitutive mutants. It is clear that the cells could not survive the breakdown of more than two or three of the control systems which keep in pace the synthesis of enzyme proteins.

The occurrence of inductive and repressive effects in tissues of higher organisms has been observed in many instances, although it has not proved possible so far to analyse any of these systems in detail (the main difficulty being the creation of controlled conditions of gratuity). It has repeatedly been pointed out that enzymatic adaptation, as studied in micro-organisms, offers a valuable model for the interpretation of biochemical co-ordination within tissues and between organs in higher organisms. The demonstration that adaptive effects in micro-organisms are primarily negative (repressive), that they are controlled by functionally specialized genes and operate at the genetic level, would seem greatly to widen the possibilities of interpretation. The fundamental problem of chemical physiology and of embryology is to understand why tissue cells do not all express, all the time, all the potentialities inherent in their genome. The survival of the organism requires that many, and, in some tissues most, of these potentialities be unexpressed, that is to say *repressed*. Malignancy is adequately described as a breakdown of one or several growth controlling systems, and the genetic origin of this breakdown can hardly be doubted.

According to the strictly structural concept, the genome is considered as a mosaic of independent molecular blue-prints for the building of individual cellular constituents. In the execution of these plans, however, co-ordination is evidently of absolute survival value. The discovery of regulator and operator genes, and of repressive regulation of the activity of structural genes, reveals that the genome contains not only a series of blue-prints, but a co-ordinated program of protein synthesis and the means of controlling its execution.

REFERENCES

Adelberg, E. A. & Umbarger, H. E. (1953). *J. Biol. Chem.* **205**, 475.
Ames, B. N. & Garry, B. (1959). *Proc. Nat. Acad. Sci., Wash.* **45**, 1453.
Ames, B. N., Garry, B. & Herzenberg, L. A. (1960). *J. Gen. Microbiol.* **22**, 369.
Benzer, S. (1953). *Biochim. biophys. Acta,* **11**, 383.
Bertani, G. (1953). *Cold. Spr. Harb. Symp. Quant. Biol.* **18**, 65.

Bertani, G. (1958). *Advanc. Virus Res.* **5**, 151.

Brenner, S., Jacob, F. & Meselson, M. (1961). *Nature*, **190**, 576.

Bussard, A., Naono, S., Gros, F. & Monod, J. (1960). *C. R. Acad. Sci., Paris*, **250**, 4049.

Buttin, G. (1956). Diplôme Et. Sup., Paris.

Buttin, G. (1961). *C. R. Acad. Sci., Paris*, in the press.

Cohen, G. N. & Jacob, F. (1959). *C. R. Acad. Sci., Paris*, **248**, 3490.

Cohen, G. N. & Monod, J. (1957). *Bact. Rev.* **21**, 169.

Cohen, S. S. (1949). *Bact. Rev.* **13**, 1.

Cohen-Bazire, G. & Jolit, M. (1953). *Ann. Inst. Pasteur*, **84**, 1.

Cohn, M. (1957). *Bact. Rev.* **21**, 140.

Cohn, M., Cohen, G. N. & Monod, J. (1953). *C. R. Acad. Sci., Paris*, **236**, 746.

Cohn, M. & Horibata, K. (1959). *J. Bact.* **78**, 624.

Cohn, M. & Monod, J. (1953). In *Adaptation in Micro-organisms*, p. 132. Cambridge University Press.

Cohn, M. & Torriani, A. M. (1952). *J. Immunol.* **69**, 471.

Davern, C. I. & Meselson, M. (1960). *J. Mol. Biol.* **2**, 153.

Demerec, M. (1956). *Cold Spr. Harb. Symp. Quant. Biol.* **21**, 113.

Dienert, F. (1900). *Ann. Inst. Pasteur*, **14**, 139.

Duclaux, E. (1899). *Traité de Microbiologie*. Paris: Masson et Cie.

Echols, H., Garen, A., Garen, S. & Torriani, A. M. (1961). *J. Mol. Biol.*, in the press.

Flaks, J. G. & Cohen, S. S. (1959). *J. Biol. Chem.* **234**, 1501.

Gale, E. F. (1943). *Bact. Rev.* **7**, 139.

Giles, N. H. (1958). *Proc. Xth Intern. Cong. Genetics*, Montreal, **1**, 261.

Gorini, L. & Maas, W. K. (1957). *Biochim. biophys. Acta*, **25**, 208.

Gorini, L. & Maas, W. K. (1958). In *The Chemical Basis of Development*, p. 469. Baltimore: Johns Hopkins Press.

Gros, F., Hiatt, H., Gilbert, W., Kurland, C. G., Risebrough, R. W. & Watson, J. D. (1961). *Nature*, **190**, 581.

Halvorson, H. O. (1960). *Advanc. Enzymol.* in the press.

Hartman, P. E., Loper, J. C. & Serman, D. (1960). *J. Gen. Microbiol.* **22**, 323.

Herzenberg, L. (1959). *Biochim. biophys. Acta*, **31**, 525.

Hogness, D. S., Cohn, M. & Monod, J. (1955). *Biochim. biophys. Acta*, **16**, 99.

Jacob, F. (1954). *Les Bactéries Lysogènes et la Notion de Provirus*. Paris: Masson et Cie.

Jacob, F. (1960). *Harvey Lectures*, 1958–1959, series **54**, 1.

Jacob, F. & Adelberg, E. A. (1959). *C.R. Acad. Sci., Paris*, **249**, 189.

Jacob, F. & Campbell, A. (1959). *C.R. Acad. Sci., Paris*, **248**, 3219.

Jacob, F., Fuerst, C. R. & Wollman, E. L. (1957). *Ann. Inst. Pasteur*, **93**, 724.

Jacob, F. & Monod, J. (1959). *C.R. Acad. Sci., Paris*, **249**, 1282.

Jacob, F., Perrin, D., Sanchez, C. & Monod, J. (1960a). *C.R. Acad. Sci., Paris*, **250**, 1727.

Jacob, F., Schaeffer, P. & Wollman, E. L. (1960b). In *Microbial Genetics*, Xth Symposium of the Society for General Microbiology, p. 67.

Jacob, F. & Wollman, E. L. (1953). *Cold Spr. Harb. Symp. Quant. Biol.* **18**, 101.

Jacob, F. & Wollman, E. L. (1956). *Ann. Inst. Pasteur*, **91**, 486.

Jacob, F. & Wollman, E. L. (1957). In *The Chemical Basis of Heredity*, p. 468. Baltimore: Johns Hopkins Press.

Kaiser, A. D. (1957). *Virology*, **3**, 42.

Kaiser, A. D. & Jacob, F. (1957). *Virology*, **4**, 509.

Kalckar, H. M., Kurahashi, K. & Jordan, E. (1959). *Proc. Nat. Acad. Sci., Wash.* **45**, 1776.

Karstrom, H. (1938). *Ergebn. Enzymforsch.* **7**, 350.

Képès, A. (1960). *Biochim. biophys. Acta*, **40**, 70.

Képès, A., Monod, J. & Jacob, F. (1961). In preparation.

Kogut, M., Pollock, M. & Tridgell, E. J. (1956). *Biochem. J.* **62**, 391.

Kornberg, A., Zimmerman, S. B., Kornberg, S. R. & Josse, J. (1959). *Proc. Nat. Acad. Sci., Wash.* **45**, 772.

Kruh, J., Rosa, J., Dreyfus, J.-C. & Schapira, G. (1961). *Biochim. biophys. Acta*, in the press.

Lamfrom, H. (1961). *J. Mol. Biol.* **3**, 241.

Lederberg, E. (1960). In *Microbial Genetics*, The Xth Symposium of the Society of General Microbiology, p. 115.

Levinthal, C. (1959). In *Structure and Function of Genetic Elements*, Brookhaven Symposia in Biology, p. 76.

Luria, S. E. & Human, M. L. (1950). *J. Bact.* **59**, 551.

Lwoff, A. (1953). *Bact. Rev.* **17**, 269.

Lwoff, A., Siminovitch, L. & Kjeldgaard, N. (1950). *Ann. Inst: Pasteur*, **79**, 815.

Magasanik, B., Magasanik, A. K. & Neidhardt, F. C. (1959). In *A Ciba Symposium on the Regulation of Cell Metabolism*, p. 334. London: Churchill.

Monod, J. (1942). *Recherches sur la Croissance des Cultures Bactériennes*. Paris: Hermann.

Monod, J. (1955). *Exp. Ann. Biochim. Méd.* série XVII, p. 195. Paris: Masson et Cie.

Monod, J. (1956). In *Units of Biological Structure and Function*, p. 7. New York: Academic Press.

Monod, J. (1958). *Rec. Trav. Chim. des Pays-Bas*, **77**, 569.

Monod, J. (1959). *Angew. Chem.* **71**, 685.

Monod, J. & Audureau, A. (1946). *Ann. Inst. Pasteur*, **72**, 868.

Monod, J. & Cohen-Bazire, G. (1953). *C.R. Acad. Sci., Paris*, **236**, 530.

Monod, J. & Cohn, M. (1952). *Advanc. Enzymol.* **13**, 67.

Monod, J. & Cohn, M. (1953). In *Symposium on Microbial Metabolism*. VIth Intern. Cong. of Microbiol., Rome, p. 42.

Monod, J., Pappenheimer, A. M. & Cohen-Bazire, G. (1952), *Biochim. biophys. Acta*, **9**, 648.

Monod, J. & Wollman, E. L. (1947). *Ann. Inst. Pasteur*, **73**, 937.

Naono, S. & Gros, F. (1960a). *C.R. Acad. Sci., Paris*, **250**, 3527.

Naono, S. & Gros, F. (1960b). *C.R. Acad. Sci., Paris*, **250**, 3889.

Neidhardt, F. C. & Magasanik, B. (1956a). *Nature*, **178**, 801.

Neidhardt, F. C. & Magasanik, B. (1956b). *Biochim. biophys. Acta*, **21**, 324.

Novick, A. & Szilard, L., in Novick, A. (1955). *Ann. Rev. Microbiol.* **9**, 97.

Pardee, A. B. (1957). *J. Bact.* **73**, 376.

Pardee, A. B., Jacob, F. & Monod, J. (1959). *J. Mol. Biol.* **1**, 165.

Pardee, A. B. & Prestidge, L. S. (1959). *Biochim. biophys. Acta*, **36**, 545.

Pardee, A. B. & Prestidge, L. S. (1961). In preparation.

Perrin, D., Bussard, A. & Monod, J. (1959). *C.R. Acad. Sci., Paris*, **249**, 778.

Perrin, D., Jacob, F. & Monod, J. (1960). *C.R. Acad. Sci., Paris*, **250**, 155.

Pollock, M. (1950). *Brit. J. Exp. Pathol.* **4**, 739.

Pollock, M. & Perret, J. C. (1951). *Brit. J. Exp. Pathol.* **5**, 387.

Pontecorvo, G. (1958). *Trends in Genetic Analysis*. New York: Columbia University Press.

Rickenberg, H. V., Cohen, G. N., Buttin, G. & Monod, J. (1956). *Ann. Inst. Pasteur*, **91**, 829.

Riley, M., Pardee, A. B., Jacob, F. & Monod, J. (1960). *J. Mol. Biol.* **2**, 216.

Rotman, B. & Spiegelman, S. (1954). *J. Bact.* **68**, 419.

Siminovitch, L. & Jacob, F. (1952). *Ann. Inst. Pasteur*, **83**, 745.

Stanier, R. Y. (1951). *Ann. Rev. Microbiol.* **5**, 35.

Szilard, L. (1960). *Proc. Nat. Acad. Sci., Wash.* **46**, 277.

Torriani, A. M. (1960). *Biochim. biophys. Acta*, **38**, 460.

Umbarger, H. E. (1956). *Science*, **123**, 848.

Vogel, H. J. (1957a). *Proc. Nat. Acad. Sci., Wash.* **43**, 491.

Vogel, H. J. (1957b). In *The Chemical Basis of Heredity*, p. 276. Baltimore: Johns Hopkins Press.

Volkin, E. & Astrachan, L. (1957). In *The Chemical Basis of Heredity*, p. 686. Baltimore: Johns Hopkins Press.

Went, F. C. (1901). *J. Wiss. Bot.* **36**, 611.

Wijesundera, S. & Woods, D. D. (1953). *Biochem. J.* **55**, viii.

Willson, C., Perrin, D., Jacob, F. & Monod, J. (1961). In preparation.

Wollman, E. L. & Jacob, F. (1959). *La Sexualité des Bactéries*. Paris: Masson et Cie.

Yanofsky, C. (1960). *Bact. Rev.* **24**, 221.

Yanofsky, C. & Lennox, E. S. (1959). *Virology*, **8**, 425.

Yarmolinsky, M. B. & Wiesmeyer, H. (1960). *Proc. Nat. Acad. Sci., Wash.* in the press.

Yates, R. A. & Pardee, A. B. (1956). *J. Biol. Chem.* **221**, 757.

Yates, R. A. & Pardee, A. B. (1957). *J. Biol. Chem.* **227**, 677.

Yčas, M. & Vincent, W. S. (1960). *Proc. Nat. Acad. Sci., Wash.* **46**, 804.

Zabin, I., Képès, A. & Monod, J. (1959). *Biochem. Biophys. Res. Comm.* **1**, 289.

Unit 6 / Genetic Regulatory Mechanisms

Jacob and Monod 1961

1. Distinguish between "structural" and "regulatory" genes.

2. What is "enzymatic adaptation"?

3. What was known about the induction phenomenon in the lactose system of *E. coli* at the start of the work described in the 1961 Jacob and Monod paper? What was known about the enzymology of the system?

4. What was meant by negative control?

5. What were cryptic mutants?

6. What was the evidence that galactosidase and acetylase activities were different proteins and not the same protein?

7. Which experiments showed that "induction" caused the synthesis of new enzyme molecules?

8. What conclusion could be drawn from studying the kinetics of induction? How was this conclusion reached?

9. Describe the studies on the specificity of induction reported in Table 1 on page 198. What did they demonstrate?

10. What is the distinction between the "induction" effect and the "repression" effect? What is "derepression"? Give an example.

11. What are Z^-, Y^-, and I^- mutants? What are "constitutive" mutants?

12. Explain how stable partial diploids are formed and used.

13. Explain the complementation relationship between Z, Y, and I mutations as shown in Table 2 on page 205. What do the numbers indicate?

14. What experiment determined that the I gene synthesized a cytoplasmic product? What are two interpretations of the result, and how did Jacob and Monod distinguish between them?

15. Explain the experiment shown in Figure 4 on page 206. How was it carried out, and what was the interpretation of the experiment? Can you imagine any alternative explanation?

16. It is now known that there are I^- mutations that are dominant to I^+ mutations. Can you provide an explanation for this?

17. Which experiment mentioned by Jacob and Monod showed that the repressor was not a protein? What might the investigators have done wrong in this experiment?

18. Describe the phage immunity system and point out the similarities between it and the *lac* system.

19. Describe "zygotic induction" and provide an explanation for this phenomenon.

20. What are O^c mutants? How were they isolated?

21. What does Table 3 on page 216 show? What were the key experiments, and what were the conclusions from these experiments?

22. Briefly outline the Operon Model. Define "operon."

Unit 7

In Vivo Genetic Engineering

In the mid-1960s, when Jon Beckwith and Ethan Signer began their collaborative work, the methods for cloning genes onto small vectors, the cornerstone of what we now call genetic engineering, were quite limited. Although certain genes could be incorporated into specialized transducing phage, this was restricted to genes that happened to be next to the attachment sites of the few temperate phage known to be able to act as specialized transducing phage. For example, phage λ could incorporate the *gal* or *bio* genes into its chromosome, and phage φ80 could incorporate the *trp* genes or the *supF* gene (Su3) into its chromosome, because all of these genes were located very close to the respective phage attachment regions. However, there was no way to clone or incorporate other genes, such as *lac*, *leu*, or *pro,* into a small genome that could be amplified because these genes were not adjacent to known attachment sites for temperate phage.

In this unit, we examine the studies that opened the door to cloning virtually any gene in *Escherichia coli* by in vivo genetic manipulations. The pioneering work was carried out by Jon Beckwith and Ethan Signer, who developed a method for transposing genes to different locations on the *E. coli* chromosome and who also perfected a technique for selecting for the transposition of genes to certain specific places, including near the attachment sites for temperate phage such as φ80 and later λ. This allowed the construction of φ80 and λ phages carrying the transposed genes.

In the first two papers under study here, we will follow the transposition of the *lac* genes and the isolation of a φ80*lac* transducing phage, effectively cloning the *lac* genes. Subsequent work by several different groups demonstrated the utility of these phages. In my opinion, this work was really the beginning of genetic engineering, since it stimulated a search for many different transducing phages, and for different ways of obtaining them, and put the spotlight on the advantages of cloning genes. The third paper in this unit describes an independent method of obtaining new specialized transducing phage by eliminating the normal λ attachment site and selecting for the integration of λ into new, secondary, attachment sites. Many of these new sites were near genes of interest, and methods were developed for selecting for the integration of λ near certain genes of choice. This work by Shimada, Weisberg, and Gottesman was published in 1972. Several years later, in vitro methods were introduced for cloning genes onto λ vectors and plasmids, and the era of genetic engineering was in full swing.

Jonathan Beckwith and Ethan Signer

Jon Beckwith (*photo top right*) received his undergraduate degree in chemistry at Harvard and also a Ph.D. in biochemistry there working with Lowell Hager. He was inspired by the work from the Pasteur Institute and applied to work in Jacob's lab. However, places were difficult to secure in this now fashionable lab, so he first did postdoctoral research with Arthur Pardee at Berkeley and Bill Hayes in London. He then did a short stint with Sydney Brenner in Cambridge to work on the *ochre* suppressors that he (Beckwith) had recently discovered. There he met Ethan Signer (*photo bottom right*), another American who had migrated to Europe. Signer had received his degree at MIT, working with Cyrus Levinthal, before coming to Brenner's lab as a postdoc. At the time they met, Beckwith had been working with the *lac* system and Signer was carrying out experiments with phage λ. In 1964, Beckwith went to the Pasteur Institute to work with François Jacob. There he flourished in the atmosphere of the Pasteur, which at the time was a Mecca for geneticists. Signer arrived in Jacob's lab at around the same time.

Beckwith was intrigued by experiments done at the Pasteur by Jacob and a graduate student, François Cuzin, in which a temperature-sensitive F'*lac* was introduced into a strain deleted for *lac* and that contained no homology for the episome. At high temperature, the only cells that could replicate had the F'*lac* integrated into the chromosome, and this occurred at different places in different strains. Beckwith set about mapping some of the integration points, which would also be the point to which *lac* had been transposed. When he noticed that one strain placed *lac* near the attachment site for φ80, he discussed this with Signer, who had carried out experiments on creating different specialized transducing phage, including those from φ80. They decided to see whether a specialized transducing phage carrying the *lac* genes could be isolated from the transposition strain. When they found that it could be, this launched a fruitful collaboration and began the era of designing specific transducing phage. The description of their experiments, including those exploiting the use of *trp-lac* fusions, is given in the papers reprinted here on pages 241–261 and discussed in detail in this unit. This work led to the construction of many additional transducing phages and, as mentioned above, launched the era of genetic engineering.

In 1965, Jon Beckwith moved to Harvard Medical School, where he founded and continues to lead a research group that has continued to make important contributions in understanding, among other things, control elements in the *lac* system, the utilization and generation of genetic fusions, and protein transport. He has also devoted considerable energy to ethical issues in science.

Ethan Signer set up a laboratory at MIT in 1966, where he studied site-specific recombination and, more recently, the genetics of *Rhizobium*.

TRANSPOSITION OF THE *lac* GENES

The starting point for the transposition of the *lac* genes was provided by initial experiments carried out by Cuzin and Jacob, who used a strain carrying a deletion of the *lac* region. The particular deletion used also deleted the *proA,B* genes. An episome carrying the *lac* genes was introduced into this strain. The episome also carried a mutation, *114*, that rendered the F' factor unable to replicate at 42°C, although it could replicate at 30°C. This meant that at 42°C, the F factor carrying the *lac* genes would not replicate and would be lost from the cell unless it integrated into the host chromosome, whose replication was not temperature-sensitive. If the *lac* genes were at the normal locus, then the *lac* genes on the episome would offer a nice region of homology for the reciprocal recombination event required for integration of the episome into the chromosome. However, the *lacpro* deletion on the chromosome removed all homology between bacterial genes carried on the episome and the chromosome. Any integration events would have to involve sites other than the *lac* region. It was reasoned that these events might be at a significantly lower frequency than the normal recombination events, so some type of selection would need to be employed.

If the strain (termed EC0) that carries the *lacpro* deletion and the F'$_{ts}$*114* episome is plated at 42°C, then only those cells in which the F'$_{ts}$*lac* episome had integrated into the chromosome will be Lac$^+$. These Lac$^+$ colonies can be recognized on lactose indicator plates. Thus, by selecting for Lac$^+$ at 42°C, we ensure that the *lac* region has been transposed to a different region of the chromosome. The integration of the F'$_{ts}$*lac* should actually generate an Hfr strain (see previous discussion in Unit 6) with its origin at the point of integration of the F'. Beckwith and Signer tested a series of Lac$^+$ temperature-resistant strains derived from EC0 to determine whether they were Hfr strains and where their points of origin were. They were able to show that each was indeed an Hfr strain and that their points of origin were scattered around the chromosome (see Figure 2, page 254). Although some sites were favored points of integration, as evidenced by repeated occurrences of certain Hfr points of origin, they could identify 12 different integration points in the first 30 strains tested. Both directions of transfer were found. In other words, the F'$_{ts}$*lac* could be integrated in either orientation.

The Hfr strains derived from EC0 were labeled EC1, EC2, EC3, etc. In one of these strains, EC8, F'$_{ts}$*lac* was integrated near the attachment site for phage φ80, as shown in Figure 1 on page 243. The data for this assignment is given in Table 1 on page 243. Here, EC8 can be seen to transfer Su_c, but not att_{80}, as an early gene. It is clear from Figure 1 that the *lac* region in EC8 may be near enough to att_{80} to allow the construction of a transducing phage derived from φ80 that carries the *lac* genes. Clearly, the finding of EC8 was fortuitous, and it took a lot of work to characterize the set of Hfr strains to find one in which integration had occurred near an attachment site. As a means of positioning genes next to attachment sites, this method could be very laborious and does not really represent a general method. Therefore, Beckwith and Signer attempted to modify the method to allow direct selection for transpositions that were near specific attachment sites.

Selection for Integration into Specific Genes

When F'$_{ts}$*lac* integrates into a gene, the gene is disrupted and its function is destroyed. Therefore, if in addition to selecting for Lac$^+$ at high temperature, a simultaneous selection for the disruption of a specific gene is applied, then one should be able to find Hfr strains with their points of origin within the desired gene. Beckwith and Signer tested this method by using the T6*rec* (now called *tsx*) locus, since this locus encodes the phage receptors that allow infection by the virulent phage T6. If this gene is inactivated, the cell will become resistant to phage T6. Thus, T6-resistant Lac$^+$ cells at 42°C should have the F'$_{ts}$*lac* integrated into the T6*rec* locus. Beckwith and Signer were in fact able to isolate the strain EC102 by using such a simultaneous selection, and they found it to be an Hfr that transfers chromosomal markers in the manner expected for a strain with the origin of transfer at or near the T6*rec* locus.

The same method can be applied to find transpositions near the φ80 attachment site, since, fortunately, the T1*rec* locus (now called *tonB*) lies very near att_{80} (see Figure 1 on page 243). Therefore, the authors selected for Lac$^+$ at high temperature and simultaneously selected for T1 phage resistance. A careful reading of their paper will show that they did not actually apply a sample of a lysate of T1 phage on a plate but instead used a mixture of two different lysates, one containing both colicin V and colicin B and the other containing φ80 virulent phage. This may seem confusing at first, but there are several good reasons for doing this. First, one never uses phage T1 itself in a bacterial genetics lab, since this phage is air-stable and can devastate bacterial cultures for weeks after its use. Instead, one uses other phage or phagelike particles that employ the same T1rec receptor. Virulent derivatives of φ80 (φ80vir) are fine for this purpose. However, the φ80 receptor site requires the functional product of two genes, T1rec (tonB) and tonA. If only φ80vir was used, then many of the survivors would be TonA mutants and not the desired T1rec mutants. However, the proteinaceous infectious agents colicin V and B also use a receptor site that requires the product of the T1rec gene together with a different second gene. When the combination of φ80vir and colicin V and B is used, the only survivors will have mutations inactivating the T1rec (tonB) locus. When Beckwith and Signer carried out this experiment, they detected one Lac+ colony out of seven survivors of the treatment at high temperature. This strain, EC15, indeed turned out to be an Hfr with an origin in the T1rec locus, as judged by its early donation of try (now termed trp) but not of att$_{80}$ or purB. Figure 1 on page 243 shows the map position of EC15, and Table 1 on page 243 and Figure 2 on page 244 display the Hfr transfer data.

Isolation of Specialized Transducing Phage Carrying lac

Because the lac region in both EC8 and EC15 is positioned near the φ80 attachment site, it should be possible to isolate φ80 transducing phage from each strain that carries the lac genes. The first step involves infecting each strain with a wild-type φ80 phage. (You might note that since the strains have been made T1rec and thus resistant to infection with φ80, some technical trick must be used to permit infection of EC8 and EC15 with φ80. See if you can work out how Beckwith and Signer did this. The answer is provided in Section III, page 571.) After infection, the lysogens are induced with ultraviolet (UV) light, and the resulting lysate is used to infect a Trp$^-$ strain. Table 2 on page 245 shows that lac can indeed be transduced by φ80 phage derived from the lysogens of EC8 and EC15. As expected, Beckwith and Signer could not find simultaneous transduction of both try (trp) and lac, since the intervening segment of the F' episome prevents these two markers from being carried on the same transducing particle.

Table 3 on page 246 presents data from experiments aimed at determining whether the φ80lac transducing phage derived in the manner described above carry a recognizable portion of the F factor. To demonstrate that these phage carry some functional F genes, Beckwith and Signer looked for complementation of a partially defective F factor, which has sharply reduced transfer frequency. The data in Table 3 show that each φ80lac phage can complement these defective F factors and result in transfer from an origin located within the integrated transducing phage. The direction of transfer is the same as the strain from which the transducing phage is derived (EC8 or EC15).

The Orientation of the lac Region

Several genetic experiments were used to prove that the orientation of the lac region in each of the two original Hfr strains, EC8 and EC15, was different and that the origin in the resulting transducing phage was different after integration into the φ80 attachment site of a recipient host.

By referring to Figure 1 on page 243, it can be seen that for each of the two Hfr strains, the lacZ gene is nearest the φ80 attachment site, whereas the lacY gene is farther away. Thus, from each starting Hfr, one should be able to isolate φ80 transducing phage carrying the entire intact lacZ gene but only a fragment of the lacY gene. Such transducing phage would behave as though they carried a deletion of the latter part of the lacY gene. However, one should not be able to detect phage that carry an intact portion of lacY and only a fragment of lacZ. In other words, Z^+Y^- phage are predicted but not Z^-Y^+ phage. To screen for the Z^+Y^- phage, the authors ingeniously made use of a newly discovered **operon fusion** that placed the lacY gene under the control of the purE operon by means of a deletion that eliminated a portion of the purE operon and also a portion of the lacZ gene. In this case, the lacY gene product, the lac permease, is synthesized in response to low adenine and is shut off in the presence of high adenine. Therefore, strains deleted for the lac genes and containing this fusion on an episome are phenotypically Z^-Y^+ in the absence of external adenine and phenotypically Z^-Y^- in the presence of high external adenine. Why would the authors go to all of this trouble? To detect a Z^+Y^- transducing phage, it is first necessary to find phage that confer the Z^+ phenotype and then to examine them to see whether they also confer the Y^+ phenotype. One way of doing this would be to utilize a Z^-Y^+ strain, transduce it to Lac+, and then test each Lac+ transductant by making a new lysate from it and transducing a second strain that is Y^- to determine whether the phage derived from the transductant can confer the Y^+ phenotype or not. This would be very laborious, especially when one considers that the Z^+Y^- phage would be relatively rare compared with the frequency of Z^+Y^+ phage. However, by using a **conditionally** expressed Y gene, one could first transduce under conditions (low adenine) where the recipient strain was Z⁻Y⁺ and select for Lac⁺ colonies and then simply transfer these colonies to medium with high adenine, which prevents synthesis of the Y gene product from the fusion on the episome. Thus, the recipient cell is now effectively Y⁻ unless the transducing phage carries a functional Y gene. When Beckwith and Signer did this experiment, they found that of 383 phage derived from EC8 that conferred the Lac⁺ phenotype in the absence of adenine, 3 were Lac⁻ in the presence of adenine. Likewise, 4 of 181 phage derived from EC15 had these same properties. When the respective phage were purified and tested, they were indeed found to carry the *lacZ* gene and a portion of the *lacY* gene. Recombination tests with different point mutations in *lacY* allowed Beckwith and Signer to map the extent of the remaining portion of *lacY*, as shown in Figure 3 on page 247.

If the orientations of the phage derived from EC8 and EC15 are as expected (consult Figure 1 on page 243), then not only would we be able to find Z⁺Y⁻ phage, but also we should fail to find Z⁻Y⁺ phage. This is because the Z gene is closer to the φ80 attachment site in both EC8 and EC15 and the formation of specialized transducing phage should occasionally result in the aberrant excision joint ending in Y, still leaving Z intact. However, if the joint ended in Z, then no part of the Y gene would end up within the transducing particle. To test for the possible presence of Z⁻Y⁺ transducing phage, Beckwith and Signer transduced a strain carrying a deletion of the *lac* region and selected for growth on the sugar melibiose at 42°C. This α-galactoside requires the *lacY* permease for transport into the cell at high temperature. The selection is therefore a Y⁺ selection, which is independent of the Z gene. The Mel⁺ transductants could then be tested for Lac⁺ to see whether the transducing phage also contained the Z gene. In all cases, 412 from EC8 and 360 from EC15, the transductants selected for only Y⁺ were also Z⁺. Thus, no Z⁻Y⁺ transducing phage were found.

The most elegant experiment to ascertain the orientation of the *lac* region in transducing phages obtained from the transposed *lac* regions employed Hfr strains formed by the integration of the episome carrying the *purB-lac* fusion into the *lac* region carried by the φ80*lac* transducing phage. This is a complicated experiment and it requires some thought to appreciate its power. Figure 4 on page 248 shows how the pairing of the fusion episome with the integrated φ80d*lac* phage derived from EC8 and EC15 occurs. Because the *lacY* end is missing from the integrated transducing phage and the *lacZ* end is missing from the episome, the only region of homology between the two *lac* elements is in the beginning of the Y gene

and the end of the Z gene. Since the two transducing phage were derived from strains in which the *lac* operon was oriented in different directions (see Figure 1 on page 243), then the integration of these transducing phage into the φ80 attachment site should regenerate the same opposing orientations, as depicted in Figure 4. Thus, when Hfr strains are formed via the reciprocal recombination event that integrates the fusion episome into the *lac* region of the transducing phage, the directions of transfer of the two Hfr strains will be different. You may need to diagram this, based on Figure 4, to convince yourself that this is so. The integration event depicted in Figure 4 was actually selected for by looking for Lac⁺ colonies in the presence of adenine. Recall that adenine will shut off the *purB-lacY* fusions, making the cell Y⁻ (and thus Lac⁻). Only those cells in which an intact Y gene had been reconstituted through the recombination event shown in Figure 4 could be Y⁺ in the presence of adenine and grow on melibiose at 42°C (recall that the *lac* permease is required to transport melibiose into the cell at high temperature). Figure 5 and Table 4 (both on page 249) depict the results of experiments that show the direction of transfer of the Hfr strains derived by selecting for Y⁺ in the presence of adenine. It can be seen that the Hfr strain resulting from integration of the fusion episome into the φ80*lac* derived from EC8 transfers *purB* but not *try* (*trp*), whereas the parallel Hfr emanating from the φ80*lac* originating in EC15 transfers *try* but not *purB*.

Operon Fusions

The positioning of the *lac* operon near the *trp* (previously *try*) operon in strains transduced with φ80*lac* phage allowed the construction of strains in which the *lac* and *trp* genes were fused via a deletion of the intervening material. Figure 6 in the paper by Beckwith et al. (see page 258) depicts some of the classes of deletions possible and the resulting fusions. Recall that the first genetic fusion was the 1589 deletion which fused the *r*IIA and *r*IIB genes. Initially characterized by Benzer and Champe, this fusion was exploited by Crick, Brenner, and co-workers in their genetic study of the triplet nature of the genetic code (see previous discussion in Unit 2). Later, Jacob and co-workers described the fusion of the *lac* permease to the *purB* operon. In each case, a rare deletion arose that had each endpoint within one of the genes being fused. The advantage offered by the *trp-lac* system was that the T1rec (*tonB*) locus was situated between *trp* and *lac*, as shown in Figure 6. This greatly facilitated the isolation of strains carrying fusions of *trp* and *lac*, since T1 resistance could be selected for directly and most of the resistant mutants had deletions of the *tonB* (T1*rec*) locus. Thus, T1-resistant survivors of a virulent phage treatment could be plated on Lac indicator plates and examined for their Lac phenotype and then replicated onto minimal medium with and without tryptophan to score for the Trp phenotype. By using the TonB (T1rec) selection to enrich for deletions between *trp* and *lac*, exceedingly rare fusion deletions could still be detected. Beckwith and his students exploited genetic fusions during the next 20 years.

PROPHAGE LAMBDA AT UNUSUAL CHROMOSOMAL LOCATIONS

After the success of the Beckwith and Signer method for generating specialized transducing phage for different genes in *E. coli*, attempts were made to find additional methods for cloning genes in vivo. The most effective technique devised during that period was described by Shimada, Weisberg, and Gottesman in 1972. Unlike the Beckwith and Signer method of transposing genes from one chromosomal location to another near the attachment site for a temperate phage, this method involved isolating strains in which λ integrated at different sites in the chromosome.

Understanding the basics of λ integration and excision is important for appreciating the work in the Shimada et al. paper. The integration of λ into its attachment sites occurs as a site-specific recombination event catalyzed by the λ-encoded *int* gene product, λ integrase. The site-specific reaction occurs between the phage integration site, represented by the adjacent assymetric elements P and P' in Figure 1 on page 263, and the assymetric integration site on the bacterial chromosome, BB'. The recombination event results in the integration of λ into the bacterial chromosome and the generation of the two hybrid half-integration sites BP' and PB', as shown in the bottom portion of Figure 1. Excision is the exact reverse of the integration event except that in addition to the λ integrase, a second protein, encoded by the λ *xis* gene, is required.

The λ attachment site is located between *gal* and *bio* on the bacterial chromosome. Until this work, λ had never been observed at other sites on the chromosome. However, the authors employed a strain, a derivative of HfrH, that was deleted for the normal λ attachment site. They then asked the following questions:

1. Could one detect integration of λ at other sites in the bacterial chromosome when the normal attachment site was deleted and, if so, at what frequency?

2. If integration at secondary sites was found, was the integration *int*-dependent?

3. What was the distribution of secondary sites in the bacterial chromosome? Were they random or were there favored sites?

4. Would excision from secondary sites be *int*- and *xis*-dependent?

5. Could one isolate specialized transducing phage carrying genes near the λ phage integrated at different sites?

To select for λ integration in the strain deleted for the λ attachment site, a heat-inducible λ phage was used to infect the cells at low temperature. (This property of heat-inducibility would greatly facilitate the making of lysates later.) The cells were then challenged with a phage, such as λ*b2C*, that had no immunity and could not integrate into the chromosome. Strains that had integrated the heat-inducible λ had immunity, which prevented killing by the challenge phage. Since strains that were resistant to λ infection due to altered receptor sites for λ adsorption could also survive the selection, the surviving colonies were also tested against a virulent λ, λ*vir*, which was not subject to λ repressor. Those cells that were still sensitive to infection and killing by λ*vir* and that could grow at 33°C but not at 42°C were lysogens containing the heat-inducible λ, λ*cI857*, at some site in the chromosome. Table 4 on page 268 shows that there is a 200-fold drop in the normal frequency of forming lysogens when the attachment site is deleted. However, the integration into other sites is indeed *int*-dependent. What this argues is that the λ integration system is catalyzing λ integration at secondary sites rather than that recombination into the chromosome is occurring by some other recombination system.

The integration of λ into secondary sites could be verified by other evidence. For example, some of the resulting lysogens were auxotrophs, such as Leu⁻ or Pro⁻. When the auxotrophs were reverted back to wild type, 8 out of 8 Pro⁺ revertants and 20 out of 20 Leu⁺ revertants had lost the integrated λ, as shown by the fact that they were now heat-resistant and sensitive to superinfection by the challenge phage. Clearly, the λ had integrated into the *pro* or *leu* genes in these cases. The authors also demonstrated this by curing the integrated phage via heteroimmune superinfection. This involves spotting a drop of a lysate of λ*imm²¹* onto the lysogen. The integration and excision proteins specific for λ are made, since the hybrid phage cannot be shut off by the lysogen's λ immunity. Bacteria growing in the spot are usually lysogens for the superinfecting phage, about half of which have lost the original phage. When Pro⁻ auxotrophs resulting from λ integration were cured in this manner, 63 out of 63 that had lost the λ had also become Pro⁺!

Shimada et al. were able to map the sites of prophage insertion by several methods. As stated above, sometimes the prophage inserted into known genes and created auxotrophs, such as Pro⁻ strains. The *pro* insertion site could be easily mapped. In addition, zygotic induction (discussed in Unit 5) was used to map the location of prophage insertion, since the time of entry of the source of phage infective centers could be plotted. A third method exploited the fact that survivors of heat induction of the prophage often carry deletions of nearby genes, since these spontaneous deletion mutants, present in the population before the heat shift, had eliminated some of the prophage genes involved in heat-induced cell killing. Sometimes the deletions result in recognizable defects, such as auxotrophy, and the auxotrophic markers could be mapped. The deletions themselves could be used to map the order of inserted prophage genes by looking for marker rescue of different defective λ phage. The resulting prophage map, shown in Table 6 on page 273, was the same as the normal λ prophage map, again arguing that the insertion into secondary attachment sites was by the same pathway as normal λ integration.

Using the strains with λ integrated at secondary attachment sites, it was easy to isolate new transducing phage by simply heat-inducing and transducing a strain carrying the appropriate markers. Lambda phage carrying *leu, proB, proA, purE, cys, lysA, galR,*

thyA, recC, and *metC* were initially detected. Subsequently, other investigators isolated additional transducing phage that proved important to studies of gene regulation. Shimada et al. found that the distribution of insertions was not random, since some of the secondary sites were clearly preferred over other sites. However, even though some sites were never found, they could be selected for, since they were able to select for integration into the *tsx* locus, which encodes phage T6 resistance. In this experiment, phage were challenged by both λ clear mutants and by T6 phage. The only single event allowing resistance to both phage would be an integration of λ into the *tsx* locus. Such integrations were found and verified. Thus, as with the Beckwith and Signer method, one could select for the insertion of a replicating element, in this case λ, into a specific locus.

CONCLUSIONS

Elegant genetic experiments allowed the cloning of many bacterial genes before restriction enzymes were utilized for this purpose. Beckwith and Signer developed a method for transposing genes carried on an F′ episome to a locus near the attachment site of a lambdoid phage. This made possible the isolation of specialized transducing phage carrying the gene of interest. Initially, genes were transposed near the φ80 attachment site, but later it was possible to select for the transposition of genes near the λ attachment site. Shimada et al. subsequently employed a method for selecting λ integrations at different positions in the *E. coli* chromosome. When the integrations occurred near a gene of interest, a specialized transducing derivative of λ carrying that gene could be isolated. Integration near certain genes could be selected for directly.

Transposition of the *Lac* Region of *Escherichia coli*

I. Inversion of the *Lac* Operon and Transduction of *Lac* by φ80

Jonathan R. Beckwith† and Ethan R. Signer‡

Service de Genetique Microbienne, Institut Pasteur
Paris, France

(*Received 11 March 1966*)

We describe a technique for isolating transpositions of *lac* to specific regions of the *Escherichia coli* chromosome. From two strains, EC8 and EC15, in which *lac* is transposed, we have isolated φ80*lac* transducing particles which also carry a part of the sex factor, F. We have shown that in EC8 and EC15 the *lac* operons are inverted relative to one another. In addition, we discuss and present evidence in support of a model for the origin of such Hfr's.

1. Introduction

Gene transposition in bacteria is a rare event (see, for example, Jacob & Wollman, 1961). Recently however, methods of selecting transpositions of chromosomal genes carried by the F-factor in *Escherichia coli* have been described (Cuzin & Jacob, 1964; Scaife & Pekhov, 1964; Scaife, 1966).

In this paper we describe experiments in which the transposition of the *lac*§ region to different sites on the *E. coli* chromosome suggests new ways of studying the expression of the *lac* operon. We find that it is possible in certain cases to obtain transpositions of the *lac* genes to a region of the chromosome chosen in advance. This technique makes it feasible to isolate Hfr's the origins of which lie in regions where they may be useful, and to move the *lac* region and F-factor into positions on the chromosome where different aspects of their functions may be studied. In particular, we are able to obtain specialized transduction of both the *lac* region and a portion of the F-factor by the phage φ80 in some of the transposed strains.

Transduction of *lac* by φ80 has permitted several novel experimental approaches to *lac* operon expression and to the nature of specialized transduction. In further communications we shall describe deletions joining the *lac* and *try* operons; studies on the expression of the *lac* operon after induction of, or infection by, the transducing phage; properties of transducing phages; and experiments on the determination of specificity in lysogeny.

† Present address: Department of Bacteriology and Immunology, Harvard Medical School, Boston, Mass., U.S.A.

‡ Present address: Department of Biology, Massachusetts Institute of Technology, Cambridge, Mass., U.S.A.

§ Abbreviations used: *lac*, utilization of lactose; *pro, try, pur, pyr*, requirement for proline, tryptophan, purine, pyrimidine; *T1rec, T6rec*, synthesis of receptor for phage T1, phage T6; *T1ʳ, T1,5ʳ*, resistance to phage T1, phages T1 and T5; *att₈₀*, attachment site for phage φ80; *Su*, suppressor; *Smˢ, Smʳ*, sensitive and resistant to streptomycin; *col* colicin; HFT, high-frequency transducing lysate; φ80*lac*, φ80 transducing phage carrying the *lac* region.

The technique used may, of course, be extended to markers other than *lac* in suitable systems (Scaife & Pekhov, 1964; Scaife, 1966).

2. Materials and Methods

Methods are those of Signer, Beckwith & Brenner (1965) for bacterial genetics and of Signer (1966) for $\phi 80$.

Media are those of Signer *et al.* (1965), except that minimal medium was medium 63 of Pardee, Jacob & Monod (1959). We recall that, on LZ agar, isolated *lac*$^+$ colonies are white, and isolated *lac*$^-$ colonies are red.

In addition to strains described previously (Signer *et al.*, 1965), we have used the following *lac* mutants:

deletion: X74, deletion of the entire *lac* operon, from Dr F. Jacob;
X111, deletion of *pro*B and *lac*, from Dr F. Jacob;

z$^-$: X90, *ochre* mutant (Newton, Beckwith, Zipser & Brenner, 1965);

y$^-$: NG328, *amber* mutant, from Dr D. Zipser;
NG707, *amber* mutant, from Dr D. Zipser;
R, from Dr F. Jacob;
U8202, from Dr J. Scaife.

Strain EC0 is $(proB\ lac)_{X111}$$^-$$Sm^s$ carrying $F_{TS-114}lac^+$, which is an F-linked episome unable to replicate autonomously at high temperature (Cuzin & Jacob, 1964). Temperature-resistant *lac*$^+$ Hfr's were isolated by plating EC0 on LZ agar at 42°C and picking white colonies.

Strain EZ0 is $lac_{X74}$$^-$$Sm^s$ carrying F-*lac* z^-y^+-*pur*E-d25$(F'$-*ad*-$z^-y^+)$; the episomal *lac* z^-y^+ is linked to *pur*E by a deletion which places the *y* gene under purine control (Jacob, Ullman & Monod, 1965).

F_{def} is a defective F$^+$ episome (Signer & Beckwith, unpublished experiments) isolated in F$^-$ $(proB\ lac)_{X111}$$^-$$Sm^s$ after crossing with Hfr P10 by Dr F. Cuzin.

Flac$^+$*pro C*$^+$ was isolated by Dr F. Jacob.

Male-specific phage F2 (Loeb & Zinder, 1961) and female-specific phage ϕII (Cuzin, 1965) were obtained from Dr F. Jacob.

Colicin lysates were prepared from a strain carrying F *col V col B* (P. Fredericq, personal communication; see Signer *et al.*, 1965) and $\phi 80$. Induction of $\phi 80$ led to lysates having high colicin titre as judged from killing of $T1,5^r$ strains. $\phi 80$-virulent (Signer, 1966) was added to the lysates for mutant selection (see text).

3. Results

Jacob, Brenner & Cuzin (1963) have isolated an F-*lac* episome the replication of which is temperature-sensitive (F_{TS}-*lac*). In strains carrying this episome and a *lac*$^-$ mutation on the host chromosome, they selected for integration of F_{TS}-*lac* into the chromosome by selecting rare derivatives which remained *lac*$^+$ at high temperature. Such derivatives were Hfr donors as a result of integration of the episome into the *lac* region. When the host chromosome carried an extensive deletion of the *lac* region, the episome integrated not in the *lac* region, but at several different chromosomal sites, resulting in transposition of the *lac* genes (Cuzin & Jacob, 1964).

We have isolated a series of Hfr's (to be described in a subsequent paper) using the technique of Cuzin & Jacob (1964). To isolate temperature-resistant *lac*$^+$ Hfr's, we have used EC0, a strain carrying an F_{TS}-*lac* (114) and a deletion, X111, of the *lac* and *pro*B markers (Cuzin & Jacob, 1964). In one Hfr, EC8, F_{TS}-*lac* has integrated between the attachment site for $\phi 80$ (att_{80}) and an *ochre* suppressor locus, Su_c (Signer *et al.*, 1965). EC8 transfers Su_c^-, but not att_{80} as an early marker (Table 1 and Fig. 1). The *lac* region is transferred as the terminal marker, indicating the order, Su_c^- F-factor origin-*lac*-att_{80}. We have used EC8 in experiments described below.

TABLE 1

Transfer of markers by EC8 and EC15 in 60-min blendor experiments

Time of mating (min)	Number of recombinants/ml. ($\times 10^{-3}$)						
	EC8	EC15	EC8	EC8	EC15	EC8	EC15
	*pur*B		*Su*$_c$$^-$		*att*$_{80}$		*try*
0	0	0	0	–	–	0	0
60	300	0	300	0	0	0	500

Transfer of Su_c^- was determined in a cross of EC8 with a strain carrying a *lac*$^-$ *ochre* mutant (*lac*$^-$$_2$) (Brenner & Beckwith, 1965) and Su_c^+. The strain is phenotypically *lac*$^+$. Su_c^- (*lac*$^-$) colonies were scored on LZ agar (Signer *et al.*, 1965). To determine transfer of *att*$_{80}$, both EC8, lysogenic for λ*h*80 (Signer, 1964), and EC15 were crossed with an F$^-$ strain which was lysogenic for the temperature-inducible phage λ*i*$_{857}$*h*80 and which was *pur*B$^-$ and *try*$^-$. The transfer of *att*$_{80}$ was determined by examining for the loss of temperature sensitivity among 100 *pur*B$^+$ recombinants (EC8) and 50 *try*$^+$ recombinants (EC15). In the case of EC8, the cross was also allowed to proceed for 6 hr, after which we found that 12 of 25 *try*$^+$ recombinants were temperature-insensitive, indicating transfer of *att*$_{80}$ as a terminal marker with *try*.

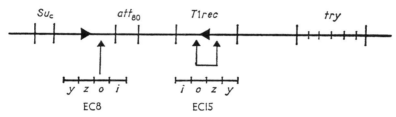

FIG. 1. The orientations of Hfr EC8 and Hfr EC15. See Signer *et al.* (1965) for a detailed map of this region of the chromosome. The double arrow for the *lac* region of EC15 indicates that the position of *lac* relative to the Hfr origin is not known. *Lac* is normally located far from this region.

(a) *The integration of* F$_{TS}$-lac *into genes*

If the integration of F_{TS}-*lac* into the chromosome is due to recombination between episome and chromosome in regions of weak homology, it may be possible, occasionally, that this homology lies within a gene on the chromosome. If the integration of the F_{TS}-*lac* into this gene occurs by a single reciprocal cross-over (Campbell, 1962), the gene would be split by the cross-over and the two resultant fragments of the gene separated by the length of the F_{TS}-*lac*. The gene should thus be inactivated. We have isolated three different Hfr's in which the F_{TS}-*lac* appears to have integrated into a gene resulting in the loss of gene function. The first, Hfr EC11, is an Hfr derived from EC0, which grows on nutrient but not on synthetic medium. The integration of the F_{TS}-*lac* appears to have resulted in auxotrophy for a requirement, as yet uncharacterized.

In the other two examples, in order to isolate strains in which the F_{TS}-*lac* is integrated into a specific locus, we have simultaneously selected for temperature-independent

lac^+ and resistance to a bacteriophage. In this way we have isolated a $T6^r$, lac^+ temperature-resistant Hfr, EC102, which transfers its chromosome as though it were in or very close to the $T6rec$ gene near purE (Jacob & Beckwith, unpublished results). In order to obtain another Hfr in which lac is integrated near $\phi80$, as in EC8, we selected for integration of the F_{TS}-lac into the $T1rec$ locus adjacent to att_{80}. A culture of EC0 was spread on LZ agar at 42°C, together with a lysate containing $\phi80$-virulent (Signer, 1964), colicin V and colicin B; mutants resistant to all three of these agents should arise only at the $T1rec$ locus adjacent to att_{80} (Gratia, 1964). Of seven colonies which appeared, one (EC15) was lac^+. Since the normal frequency of integration of F_{TS}-lac in EC0 is approximately 10^{-4}, it appears likely that a single event is responsible for the mutation to $T1^r$ and the integration of F_{TS}-lac. EC15 is an Hfr which transfers its chromosome with an origin very close to $T1rec$ (Fig. 1). It donates try but neither att_{80} nor purB as an early marker (Fig. 2 and Table 1). These results indicate that the $T1^r$ phenotype is caused by the integration of F_{TS}-lac into $T1rec$. Due to the high frequency of reversion of this strain to the autonomous F_{TS}-lac condition, we have not been able to determine whether lac is donated as the first or last marker.

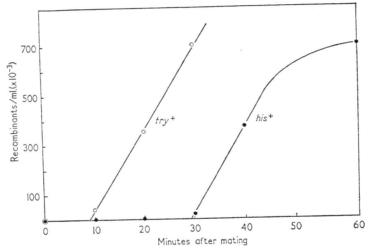

FIG. 2. Kinetics of marker transfer in interrupted mating experiments. Donor EC15, recipient try^-his^-.

(b) Specialized transduction of lac by φ80

We have isolated two Hfr's, EC8 and EC15, in which lac is located very close to att_{80}, and we should like to know whether $\phi80$ can transduce lac from lysogens of these strains. This seems possible, since in both strains F_{TS}-lac is integrated between $\phi80$ and a transducible marker: Su_c (Signer, 1966) in the case of EC8, and try (Matsushiro, 1963) in the case of EC15. Table 2 shows that lac is indeed transducible by $\phi80$ in both cases. Since $\phi80$ never transduces lac from wild-type strains (Matsushiro, 1963), this strongly indicates that specialized transduction of a marker is a consequence only of its location next to the prophage on the donor chromosome (for a discussion of this point, see Signer, 1966). Transduction of lac by $\phi80$ closely resembles that of other markers by $\phi80$ (Matsushiro, 1963; Signer, 1966) and of gal by λ (Morse, Leder-

TABLE 2

Low-frequency transduction by φ80 induced from lysogens of EC8

φ80 induced from lysogen of	Transductants per active phage for		
	lac^+	try^+	lac^+try^+
EC8	8×10^{-7}	3×10^{-7}	$<1 \times 10^{-10}$
EC15	3×10^{-9}	see text	$<1 \times 10^{-10}$

Since EC15 is TI^r its lysogen was made by phenotypic mixing (Signer, 1966); use of the host range mutant φ80*h* (obtained from Dr B. Hall) gave similar frequencies. The transduction recipient was Hfr $lac^-_{X74}try^-_{X25}$; similar frequencies were obtained with lac^- point mutants and with F⁻ strains.

berg & Lederberg, 1956). Further details of the system will be described elsewhere (Signer & Beckwith, manuscript in preparation).

We have also tried to determine the effect of the integrated *Flac* in EC8 and EC15 on low-frequency transduction of other markers by φ80. Signer (1966) has shown that the transduction frequency of a marker is increased when the marker is moved closer to the prophage by deletion of intervening genes. Analogously, we should expect that integration of F_{TS}-*lac* between a given marker and att_{80} would decrease the transduction frequency of that marker by φ80. That is, we expect the transduction of Su_c to be reduced in EC8, and that of *try* to be reduced in EC15 (see Fig. 1). However, since both strains are Su_c^- we could not score transduction of this marker. In the case of EC8, tranduction of *try* occurs at the normal frequency (Table 2), as expected from the fact that it is on the opposite side of att_{80} from the integrated F_{TS}-*lac*. In the case of EC15, the high reversion to autonomous F_{TS}-*lac* meant that any *try* transductants observed might have originated from cells which had already lost F_{TS}-*lac* from the chromosome before induction of the prophage. Nevertheless, the absence of simultaneous tranduction of *try* and *lac* (Table 2) is consistent with our expectation.

(c) *Specialized transduction of the F-factor by φ80*

In order to see whether φ80 can also transduce the F-factor from EC8 and EC15, we have screened one φ80 *lac* transducing phage derived from each strain. The following results show that both transducing phages carry a portion of the F-factor in addition to the *lac* genes. The F-factor carries loci responsible for sensitivity to the male-specific phage F2 (Loeb & Zinder, 1961) and resistance to the female-specific phage φII (Cuzin, 1965). Standard male (F2^{s}φII^r) and female (F2^{r}φII^s) strains, and recombinant strains F2^{s}φII^s and F2^{r}φII^r, do not change their response to F2 or φII, demonstrating that neither φ80*lac* carries these two loci. Standard female strains carrying either φ80*lac* do not donate markers to other females in mating. However, lysogenization with either φ80*lac* at att_{80} modifies the mating behaviour of a strain carrying a defective episomal F-factor (F2^{s}φII^s), as shown in Table 3. The presence of φ80*lac* increases the transfer of certain markers several hundredfold: in each case the transducing phage confers upon the strain an origin and a direction corresponding to those of the strain from which it was derived, EC8 or EC15 (compare with Table 1 and Fig. 2). This might be due to complementation by the defective F-factor of an origin present in $\phi80lac$, or to chromosome mobilization (Scaife & Gross, 1963) by the defective F-factor through some other portion of F present in the transducing phage. Since replacement of the defective F-factor by an active *Flac pro C* results in only a slight increase in transfer frequency (Table 3), the former explanation would require that the complementing function be much more active in *cis* than in *trans* position. In any event, it is clear that both transducing phages carry in addition to the *lac* genes some but not all of the F-factor.

TABLE 3

Transfer in 60-min blendor experiments

Experiment	Episomal F-factor	$\phi80lac$ derived from	Transfer frequency ($\times 10^5$) per donor cell for			
			*pur*B	(*lac*)	*try*C	*pyr*F
1	—	—	<0.1	<0.1	<0.1	<0.1
	F_{def}	—	5	<0.1	4	8
	F_{def}	EC8	100	13	11	14
	F_{def}	EC15	5	5	130	160
2	F_{def}	EC8	13	<0.1		2
	Flac⁺pro C⁺	EC8	32	32,000		<0.3
	F_{def}	EC15	<0.3	<0.3		16
	Flac⁺pro C⁺	EC15	<0.6	16,000		28

Donors: F^- (*pro*B *lac*)$_{X111}$⁻ carrying F_{def} or *Flac pro C* and $\phi80lac$ derived from EC8 or EC15 located at att_{80}. Recipient: F^- *lac* z_x^- *pur*B *try*C⁻ *pyr*F⁻ S^r ($\phi80$). Similar results are obtained when the donors are additionally lysogenic for $\phi80$.

(d) *The opposite orientation of* lac *in EC8 and EC15*

The Hfr's, EC8 and EC15, transfer their chromosomes in opposite directions. It seems likely that this is due to the insertion of the F-factor into the chromosomes of these two strains in opposite orientations. Since the autonomous $F_{TS}lac$ is presumed to be a single molecule of DNA, it is then possible that integration has resulted in the *lac* operon as well being in opposite orientations in EC8 and EC15, as indicated in Fig. 1. We shall now show that this is the case. In Fig. 1 the *lac* operator region is closest to att_{80} and the *y* gene farthest from it in both Hfr's. If the $\phi80$ transducing particles obtained in these strains arise by the single reciprocal cross-over event suggested by Campbell (1962), then those particles which carry a marker near att_{80} may not always carry a more distant marker. However, a transducing particle which carries one of the more distant markers of a group would always carry the markers between att_{80} and that marker. These predictions of the Campbell model have been confirmed for $\phi80$ by the studies of Matsushiro (1963) and Signer (1966), and for λ by Adler & Templeton (1963). We shall assume that these hold true as well for transduction of *lac* by $\phi80$. In order to determine the orientation of the *lac* operons in these strains, we have studied the kinds of $\phi80lac$ transducing particles that can be obtained from these strains.

Since we propose that in both Hfr's EC8 and EC15 the z gene is closer to att_{80} than the y gene, we predict that from these strains occasional $\phi 80$ transducing particles could be obtained which carry an intact z gene and only part of the y gene. In contrast, it should not be possible to obtain from these strains $\phi 80 lac\, z^- y^+$ transducing particles. We have devised a simple method for screening for such transducing phages which are $z^+ y^-$. The principle of this isolation is to obtain lac^+ transductants in a recipient strain which carries a conditionally expressed y gene. In such a strain, those trans-ductants which carry $\phi 80 lac\, z^+ y^+$ will be lac^+ whether or not the y gene of the recipient is expressed; in contrast, those transductants which carry $\phi 80 lac\, z^+ y^-$ will be lac^+ only when the y gene of the recipient is expressed. In this way, the two types of transducing phages can be distinguished. Jacob *et al.* (1965) have isolated strains in which the *lac* permease gene is connected to the *pur*E operon and is thus under purine control. Permease production is, therefore, repressed in the presence of adenine. The hybrid operon, which has a partially deleted z gene, is carried on an F′ episome. One of these strains, EZ0, was used to screen for $\phi 80 lac\, z^+ y^-$ transducing phages.

Using low-frequency transducing lysates made from lysogens of EC8 and EC15, transductants of EZ0, which were lac^+ in the absence of adenine, were isolated on lactose–synthetic agar plates. Under these conditions, the permease of EZ0 is made. The lac^+ transductants were then partially purified by picking on to the same selective plates and then replicated on to lactose synthetic medium with and without adenine. From lysates of *both* strains, we have found lac^+ transductants of EZ0 which are lac^- in the presence of adenine (9/383 from EC8 and 4/181 from EC15). These transductants were then further purified and lysates of high-frequency transducing titre (HFT) were made. All HFT lysates were tested on a series of lac^- strains to confirm their $z^+ y^-$ character. None of the lysates could transduce to lac^+ a strain carrying a complete deletion of the *lac* region, X74, but all could transduce a $z^- y^+$ strain, X90. Furthermore, different HFT transducing phages were shown by their recombination patterns with various y^- mutants to carry different sized deletions of the y end of the operon (Fig. 3). Thus we have obtained $\phi 80 lac\, z^+ y^-$ phages from both EC8 and EC15. We have also screened for $\phi 80 lac\, z^- y^+$ transducing particles by selecting for y^+ transductants of a *lac*-deletion strain, X74, and then scoring the z character. It is possible to select only for y function by selecting for growth on melibiose as sole

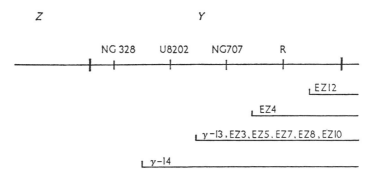

Fig. 3. Extent of y deletions in $\phi 80 lac\, z^+ y^-$ inferred from recombination as determined by spotting HFT lysates on streaks of the appropriate *lac* mutants. EZ7, 8 and 10 are derived ulti-mately from EC15 and the rest from EC8.

carbon source (Pardee, 1957; Beckwith, 1963). We have not obtained $\phi 80 lac\ z^- y^+$ transducing particles from either EC8 (0/412) or EC15 (0/360). These results provide substantial evidence that the orientation of the *lac* operons relative to att_{80} in EC8 and EC15 is as indicated in Fig. 1.

(e) *Further evidence for inversion*

The Campbell model predicts that the orientation of a transduced gene located in a transducing phage lysogenized at the phage attachment site be the same as in the strain from which it was derived. We have already shown above that the direction of marker transfer conferred upon an appropriate strain by $\phi 80 lac$ is the same as that of the Hfr from which it was derived. Therefore, in cases where $\phi 80 lac\ z^+ y^-$ has integrated at att_{80}, the partial *lac* operons should have the same orientation as in the original Hfr's. The *lac* operon in transductants of EZ0 deriving from EC8 should be oriented in the opposite direction from those deriving from EC15. The following experiment demonstrates that this is in fact the case. In these tranductants of EZ0 there exists a small degree of genetic homology between the *lac* regions of the F' episome and of the integrated phage (Fig. 4). It should be possible to isolate, from these

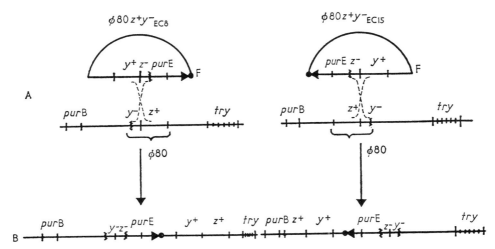

FIG. 4. Integration of $F'-ad-z^- y^+$ into 2 chromosomes lysogenic for $\phi 80 lac\ z^+ y^-$ phages with opposite orientations. Part A shows synapsis between the homologous regions of the $F'-ad-lac$ episome (the closed line) and the chromosome (straight line) carrying either of the integrated transducing phages. The dotted lines represent a reciprocal cross-over event within the region of homology. Part B shows the products of these cross-overs, Hfr's the direction of transfer of which depends upon the orientation of the chromosomal *lac* region in part A.

strains, recombinants in which the permease is no longer under the control of adenine and which are, therefore, lac^+ even in the presence of adenine. When the recombination event is due to a single reciprocal cross-over in the *lac* region, the integration of the episome into the chromosome should result in an Hfr in which the direction of chromosome transfer is dependent upon the orientation of the *lac* operon in the transducing phage (Fig. 4). We have isolated recombinants which are lac^+ in the presence of adenine from three transductants of EZ0, two of which derive from EC15 and one from EC8. These recombinants are Hfr's with direction of chromosome transfer the same as the Hfr from which the transducing phage is derived (Table 4 and Fig. 5).

TABLE 4

Transfer of markers by Hfr's derived from the integration of F'-ad-z⁻y⁺ in strains lysogenic for φ80 z⁺y⁻_EC8 and φ80 z⁺y⁻_EC15 in 60-min blendor experiments

	Number of recombinants/ml. ($\times 10^{-3}$)			
	$purB^+$		try^+	
	0 min	60 min	0 min	60 min
EZ103_EC8	0	400	0	2
EZ104_EC15	0	5	0	100
EZ105_EC15	0	4	0	150

Strain EZ103 was isolated from a derivative of EZ0, which is lysogenic for a φ80 z⁺y⁻ phage derived originally from EC8. EZ104 and EZ105 are similar strains, except that the transducing phages are derived originally from EC15. All 3 strains were picked up as rare *lac⁺* colonies on LZ agar, where most of the colonies were *lac⁻* due to the repression of the permease by the adenine in the nutrient medium. The Hfr's were crossed with a recipient F⁻ strain, *purB⁻*, *try⁻* and lysogenic for φ80 to avoid the complication of zygotic induction.

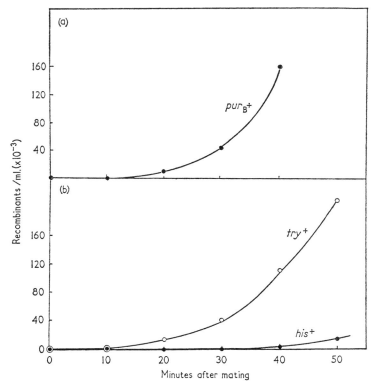

Fig. 5. Kinetics of marker transfer in interrupted mating experiments. (a) Donor EZ103, recipient *purB⁻*. (b) Donor EZ104, recipient *try⁻his⁻*.

4. Discussion

(a) *Isolation of Hfr's*

The evidence presented here strongly suggests that the Hfr EC15 arose from the integration of the F_{TS}-*lac* into the *T1rec* gene, since the origin of the Hfr is in the very short region (Signer *et al.*, 1965) between att_{80} and *try*, where the *T1rec* gene lies, and since this Hfr occurred at a high frequency amongst $T1^r$ derivatives of the parental strain. The inactivation of the *T1rec* gene would result from its splitting into two fragments as a consequence of the integration of the F_{TS}-*lac*. We cannot exclude the possibility that integration of the episome in close proximity to a gene could inactivate it; however, no examples of this type of position effect have been described in *E. coli*. We propose the same type of event to account for the auxotrophic Hfr, EC11, and for the $T6^r$ temperature-resistant *lac*+ Hfr, EC102.

(b) *A model for inversion of* lac *resulting from integration*

The Hfr's EC8 and EC15 donate their chromosomes in opposite directions. One explanation for the formation of Hfr's which donate in opposite directions is presented in Fig. 6. Evidence for the role of homology in the integration of episomes into the chromosome has already been presented by other workers (Scaife & Gross, 1963; Jacob *et al.*, 1963). These workers found that integration of *F-lac* into the chromosome

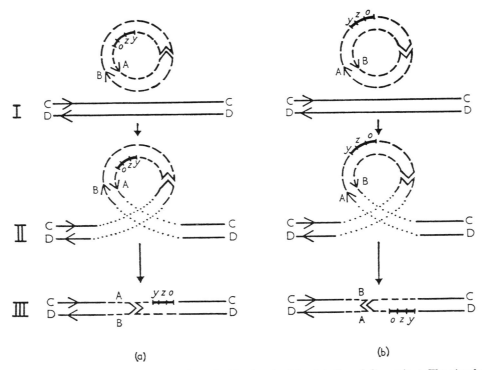

(a)   (b)

FIG. 6. Origin of Hfr's with opposite polarities (see text for details and discussion). The circular broken lines represent the *F-lac* episomes, and the continuous straight lines the chromosome. The arrows on complementary strands indicate their antiparallel nature. The directions of transfer of the episomes and of the resultant Hfr's are indicated by the dovetailing segments.

In part II, the dotted lines represent the cross-over between episome and chromosome.

of *point lac* mutants occurred preferentially in the *lac* region. Cuzin & Jacob (1964) proposed that the integration which is found at other sites of the chromosomes of strains carrying large deletions, such as that discussed in this paper, is due to the presence at such points of regions of weak homology with the episome. We, therefore, present the following detailed model. We assume that the integration of the F_{TS}-*lac* episome into the chromosome by a single reciprocal cross-over results in the formation of an Hfr (Campbell, 1962). Both episome and chromosome are DNA double helices. We assume that the direction of transfer determined by the F-factor in bacterial crosses is constant with respect to the orientation of its (antiparallel) strands. We also assume that only one strand of the operon carries the information for synthesis of the *lac* proteins.

The stages of integration of the episome involve first the pairing between homologous regions of the episome and chromosome. If the homology is to lead to integration, we must define homology to mean that not only are there similar nucleotide sequences, but also the chemical directions of these sequences are the same. In case (a) (Fig. 6) a region of strand A of the episome is homologous with one on strand C of the chromosome, and similarly on the complementary strands B and D (I). A single reciprocal cross-over in this region (II) will lead to an Hfr (III) with the polarity of transfer indicated in Fig. 6(a). Strand A of the episome, including the *lac* informational strand, becomes continuous with strand C of the chromosome, as does strand B with strand D (III).

In contrast, in case (b) (Fig. 6), in a different region of the chromosome, the homology may be between nucleotide sequences on strand A of the episome and strand D of the chromosome, and similarly between the complementary strands B and C (I). For the integration of episome into chromosome as a result of this homology, the episome must be inverted relative to the chromosome compared to case (a), in order that the homologous strands do, indeed, have the same chemical direction. The result of subsequent integration of the episome (II) is an Hfr (III) the polarity of transfer of which is opposite to that derived in case (a). Now strand A of the episome, again including the *lac* informational strand, is continuous with strand D of the chromosome, and strand B with strand C. Thus, in the two cases, not only do the two Hfr's donate in opposite directions, but also the *lac* operons in the two strains are opposite in orientation and furthermore are on different strands of the host chromosome DNA duplex.

According to the Campbell model, integration results in the presence at each end of the integrated episome of a complete copy of the homology region through which pairing and recombination have taken place. However, if this homology region is only a short segment of a functional gene, then clearly integration of the episome will lead to the separation of the gene into two inactive fragments, in spite of the duplication of the homology segment at each end of the integrated episome. This will account for the formation of EC11 and EC15.

(c) *Experimental verification of inversion*

We have been able to test the prediction that in two Hfr's with opposite polarities of transfer derived from an F_{TS}^--*lac*, the *lac* operons will be oriented in opposite directions. From our information on the Hfr origins of EC8 and EC15, we know that the *lac* operons are on opposite sides of att_{80} on the chromosomes of the two Hfr's (Fig. 1). Since we have been able to obtain $\phi 80lac\ z^+y^-$ transducing phages from *both* Hfr's, it seems very likely that the order of the *lac* genes relative to att_{80} is as indicated in Fig. 1. This conclusion is based on the evidence, from other systems, that specialized transducing phages can transduce a near marker without necessarily transducing a more distant marker, but not *vice versa*.

Further evidence supporting the scheme presented in Fig. 6 comes from studies on the Hfr's derived from recombination between the *lac* regions of the $F\text{-}ad\text{-}z^-y^+$ episome and different $\phi 80lac\ z^+y^-$ phages integrated in the chromosome. When Hfr's are obtained in this way from two such strains which carry $\phi 80lac\ z^+y^-$ phages having *lac* regions in opposite orientations, the direction of transfer of the resultant Hfr's corresponds to the *lac* orientation.

We have thus shown that in EC8 and EC15 the *lac* operons are pointing in opposite directions. It follows from the model presented in Fig. 6, that the informational *lac* strand relative to the rest of the chromosome is different in the two Hfr's. Studies on the expression of *lac* operon on different strands indicate that it functions equally well on both strands. These studies will be presented and discussed in a subsequent paper (Beckwith & Signer, in preparation).

We thank Dr Francois Jacob and Dr Francois Cuzin for many useful discussions during the course of this work and Dr Jacob and Dr John Scaife for invaluable suggestions in the preparation of the manuscript. We are grateful to Dr Jacob for the use of his laboratory. We were both Fellows of the Jane Coffin Childs Memorial Fund for Medical Research. This investigation was supported in part by grants from the National Science Foundation and the Délégation Générale à la Recherche Scientifique et Technique to Dr F. Jacob.

REFERENCES

Adler, J. & Templeton, B. (1963). *J. Mol. Biol.* **7**, 710.

Beckwith, J. R. (1963). *Biochim. biophys. Acta,* **76**, 162.

Brenner, S. & Beckwith, J. R. (1965). *J. Mol. Biol.* **13**, 629.

Campbell, A. (1962). *Advanc. Genetics,* **11**, 101.

Cuzin, F. (1965). *C.R. Acad. Sci. Paris,* **260**, 6482.

Cuzin, F. & Jacob, F. (1964). *C.R. Acad. Sci., Paris,* **258**, 1350.

Gratia, J. P. (1964). *Ann. Inst. Pasteur,* **107**, 132.

Jacob, F., Brenner, S. & Cuzin, F. (1963). *Cold Spr. Harb. Symp. Quant. Biol.* **28**, 329.

Jacob, F., Ullman, A. & Monod, J. (1965). *J. Mol. Biol.* **13**, 704.

Jacob, F. & Wollman, E. L. (1961). In *Sexuality and the Genetics of Bacteria,* pp. 164–167. New York: Academic Press.

Loeb, T. & Zinder, N. D. (1961). *Proc. Nat. Acad. Sci., Wash.* **47**, 282.

Matsushiro, A. (1963). *Virology,* **19**, 475.

Morse, M. L., Lederberg, E. & Lederberg, J. (1956). *Genetics,* **41**, 758.

Newton, W. A., Beckwith, J. R., Zipser, D. & Brenner, S. (1965). *J. Mol. Biol.* **14**, 290.

Pardee, A. B. (1957). *J. Bact.* **73**, 376.

Pardee, A. B., Jacob, F. & Monod, J. (1959). *J. Mol. Biol.* **1**, 165.

Scaife, J. (1966). *Genet. Res., Camb.* in the press.

Scaife, J. & Gross, J. (1963). *Genet. Res., Camb.* **4**, 328.

Scaife, J. & Pekhov, A. (1964). *Genet. Res., Camb.* **5**, 495.

Signer, E. R. (1964). *Virology,* **22**, 650.

Signer, E. R. (1966). *J. Mol. Biol.* **15**, 243.

Signer, E. R., Beckwith, J. R. & Brenner, S. (1965). *J. Mol. Biol.* **14**, 153.

Transposition of the *Lac* Region of *E. coli*

Jonathan R. Beckwith,[1,2]* Ethan R. Signer,[1]* and Wolfgang Epstein[3,4]*

[1] *Service de Genetique Microbienne, Institut Pasteur, Paris, France*
[2] *Department of Bacteriology and Immunology, Harvard Medical School, Boston, Massachusetts*
[3] *Service de Biochemie Cellulaire, Institut Pasteur, Paris, France*
[4] *Biophysical Laboratory, Harvard Medical School, Boston, Massachusetts*

It has recently become possible to isolate strains of *Escherichia coli* in which certain genes are transposed to new locations on the bacterial chromosome (Cuzin and Jacob, 1964; Scaife and Pekhov, 1964). Such strains are of particular interest because, in certain cases, transposition of genes allows new experimental approaches to the study of gene function. These approaches may not

experiments designed to provide information on the control of the expression of the *lac* operon.

ISOLATION OF TRANSPOSITIONS

The method of Cuzin and Jacob (1964) for isolating *lac* transpositions is illustrated in Fig. 1. It involves the use of a thermosensitive episome,

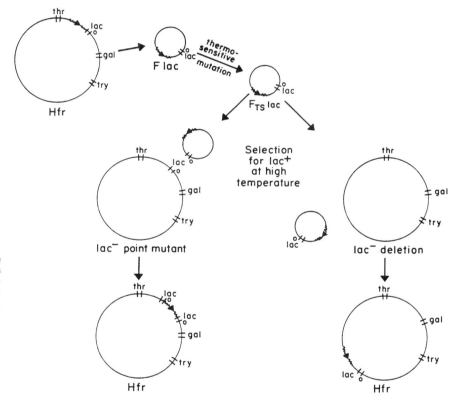

FIGURE 1. The origin of $F_{TS}lac$ and its properties in strains carrying *lac* mutation. Abbreviations for Figs. 1 and 2: thr, pro, pur, pyr, try, his, tyr, arg—requirement for threonine, proline, purine, pyrimidine, tryptophan, histidine, tyrosine, arginine; gal—inability to ferment galactose; Sm—streptomycin resistance locus; att_{80}—attachment site for bacteriophage $\phi80$.

be possible with the genes at their normal chromosomal location.

In this paper we wish to summarize studies on the transposed *lac* operon of *E. coli*. The properties of several transposed strains have been exploited in

*Present addresses: J. R. B.—Dept. of Bacteriology and Immunology, Harvard Medical School, Boston, Mass.; E. R. S.—Dept. of Biology, Massachusetts Institute of Technology, Cambridge, Mass.; W. E.—Biophysical Laboratory, Harvard Medical School, Boston, Mass.

$F_{TS}lac^+$, which can replicate autonomously in the cell cytoplasm at low but not at high temperature, and which carries the *lac* operon. When a growing culture of a strain which carries a *lac*⁻ point mutation on the chromosome and also the episome $F_{TS}lac^+$ (i.e., diploid *lac*⁻/$F_{TS}lac^+$) is shifted from low to high temperature, it rapidly becomes haploid *lac*⁻ as the episome stops replicating and is diluted out of the population. Rare colonies

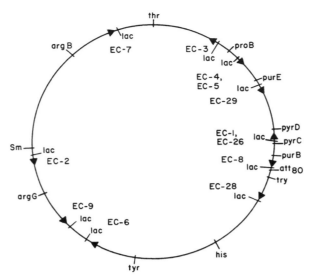

FIGURE 2. *Hfr* strains derived from the integration of $F_{TS}lac$.

(about 1 in 10^2) which remain *lac+* at high temperature can be isolated from such a culture. They are due to integration of the episome into the chromosome as a result of recombination between the homologous *lac* regions, thus placing the episome under the replicative control of the chromosome. If the chromosomal *lac−* allele is an extensive deletion of the *lac* region, this homology is no longer present. Nevertheless, cells which are *lac+* at high temperatures can still be isolated from the appropriate diploid, although at a lower frequency (about 1 in 10^4) than in the case of a point *lac−* mutant. Such cells are found to have integrated $F_{TS}lac+$ at one of a number of different points on the chromosome, possibly as a result of weak homology. Thus, the *lac* region in these strains is transposed.

The chromosomal location of the transposed *lac* region in such strains can be readily determined, since integration of the *F*-factor converts the cell to an *Hfr* male which transfers its chromosome with an origin at the site of integration. Figure 2 shows the location of *lac* in a series of transposition *Hfrs* isolated in this way. As previously found by

Cuzin and Jacob (1964), *Hfrs* are obtained which transfer the chromosome either clockwise or counterclockwise, and with *lac* as either the first or the last marker. The *Hfr* type presumably depends upon where on the episome the crossing-over has taken place. Although *Hfrs* with *lac* at a relatively large number of different sites have been isolated, certain sites do appear to be favored. For example, about 20% of the independently isolated *Hfrs* appear to be identical with EC-1 and EC-26.

DIRECTED TRANSPOSITIONS

The integrated $F_{TS}lac+$ is presumed to be inserted into the continuity of the bacterial chromosome. Clearly, if integration of the episome should occur *within* a gene, that gene would be inactivated. This might explain why one of the *Hfrs* isolated by the procedure outlined above was found to have acquired an as yet unidentified auxotrophic requirement. In certain cases, it is possible to select directly for the inactivated state of a gene. For example, mutation to phage resistance results from inactivation of the phage receptor locus. In such cases, simultaneous selection for *lac+* at high temperature *and* for the inactivated state of a given gene should result in the isolation of strains in which $F_{TS}lac+$ has integrated within that gene.

This technique has been used successfully to isolate a series of *Hfrs* which behave as though $F_{TS}lac+$ has integrated within the *T6-rec* (T6-receptor) (Jacob and Beckwith, unpubl.), *T1-rec*, or *T1, 5-rec* loci (Fig. 3), by simultaneous selection for phage resistance and *lac+* at high temperature. Although such *Hfrs* are rather frequent among phage resistant mutants (as high as 15%), their frequency in the total population is only about 1 in 10^9; nevertheless, they have been found in nearly every instance in which they were sought.

This method thus makes possible the isolation of strains in which *lac* is transposed to regions of the chromosome chosen in advance. An example illustrating the usefulness of these directed transpositions will be discussed below.

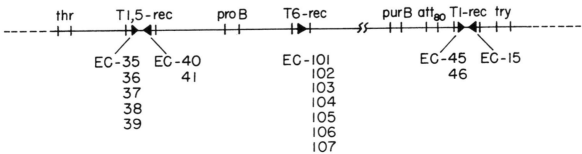

FIGURE 3. Directed transposition *Hfrs*.

Directed transpositions may be useful as a technique for determining the essentiality of a gene product. Since the gene in which the integration event takes place is presumably split into two fragments as a result, this type of mutation should completely abolish gene function. In any case in which it is possible to integrate the episome into a gene without lethal effects, it can be tentatively concluded that the product of that gene is not essential to the cell.

STABILITY OF TRANSPOSITION *Hfr*s

The integrated $F_{TS}lac^+$ reverts to the autonomous state at frequencies which vary widely among the set of *Hfr*s. In the auxotrophic *Hfr* referred to above, and in the three *Hfr*s integrated within the *T1-rec* locus (Fig. 3), reversion to the wild phenotype (prototrophy or sensitivity to T1) was also studied. (T1^r strains will not grow on minimal agar plates, thus allowing selection of reversion to the T1^s state by selecting for growth on such plates.) In all cases the transition of $F_{TS}lac^+$ from the integrated to the autonomous state failed to restore the wild-type phenotype, and in direct screening no reversion to wild-type was detected (less than 1 in 10^9). It thus appears that the event of integration is reversible with regard to $F_{TS}lac^+$, but not with regard to the alteration of the gene in which it has integrated.

TRANSDUCTION OF *LAC* BY ϕ80

The *lac* region in the transposition *Hfr* EC-8 (Fig. 2) lies very close to the attachment site (att_{80}) of the temperate phage ϕ80. Since this phage can carry out specialized transduction of neighboring markers, ϕ80 lysates induced from a lysogen of EC-8 were screened for transduction of *lac*. ϕ80 was found to transduce *lac* and a part of the *F*-factor from EC-8 (Beckwith and Signer, 1966).

In view of this result, the directed transposition technique described above was used to isolate EC-15, in which $F_{TS}lac^+$ appears to have integrated within the *T1-rec* locus adjacent to att_{80} (Fig. 3). As in the case of EC-8, ϕ80 was found to transduce *lac* and a part of the *F*-factor from EC-15 (Beckwith and Signer, 1966).

The ϕ80*lac* transduction system has proved to be a powerful analytical tool. In the remaining sections, several experiments in which this system is used to investigate the control of *lac* operon expression are presented.

INVERSION OF THE *LAC* OPERON

The direction of transfer by a given *Hfr* is presumably a structural property of the *F*-factor.

The isolation of both clockwise and counterclockwise transposition *Hfr*s would then seem to indicate that the *F*-factor of $F_{TS}lac^+$ can be inserted into the chromosome in both possible orientations. The $F_{TS}lac^+$ is thought to be a single molecule of DNA. Therefore, unless insertion involves a physical rearrangement of the episome, the *lac* operon should also be in opposite orientation in the two types of *Hfr*. This can be seen in Fig. 1, in the right half of which is an example illustrating inversion of *lac*. The ϕ80 transduction system has permitted a demonstration that this is indeed the case for the two *Hfr*s, EC-8 (counterclockwise; see Fig. 2) and EC-15 (clockwise; see Fig. 3), which yield ϕ80*lac* transducing phages.

Since the $F_{TS}lac^+$ was originally derived from a counterclockwise *Hfr* (F. Jacob, pers. commun.), the *lac* operon is expected to be in the wild-type orientation in counterclockwise *Hfr*s such as EC-8, but inverted in clockwise *Hfr*s such as EC-15, as shown in Fig. 4. In both cases the z (β-galactosidase) cistron would lie closer to att_{80} than the y (galactoside-permease) and a (thiogalactoside-transacetylase) cistrons. It has been shown both for ϕ80 (Matsushiro, 1963; Signer, 1966) and the related phage λ (Adler and Templeton, 1963), that in specialized transduction, a tranducing phage which carries a given marker will always, in addition, carry markers which are closer to the phage attachment site, but not necessarily markers which are further away. Therefore, if the orientation shown in Fig. 4 is correct, both EC-8 and EC-15 may yield ϕ80*lac* phages which transduce z without transducing y and a, but all ϕ80*lac* which transduce y and a will transduce z as well.

Lysates were screened for ϕ80*lac* z^+y^- using as recipient a strain which is conditionally y^+a^+. This strain is z^-, and expresses its own y and a cistrons only in the absence of purine (Jacob, Ullman, and Monod, 1965). Thus *lac*$^+$ transductants isolated in the *absence* of adenine which are *lac*$^-$ in the *presence* of adenine must carry ϕ80*lac* z^+y^-. To screen for ϕ80*lac* $z^-y^+a^+$, a *lac*$^-$ deletion strain was used as recipient; transductants were isolated on media containing as carbon source the α-galactoside melibiose. Selection for melibiose$^+$ transductants requires only the presence of an intact permease gene (y) (Pardee, 1957; Beckwith, 1963). Any melibiose$^+$ transductants which nevertheless remain *lac*$^-$ should carry ϕ80*lac* $z^-y^+a^+$.

Table 1 shows that lysates derived from both EC-8 and EC-15 contain ϕ80*lac* $z^+y^-a^-$, but not ϕ80*lac* $z^-y^+a^+$. This and other evidence (Beckwith and Signer, 1966) confirm that *lac* is in the wild-type orientation in EC-8 but inverted in EC-15, as shown in Fig. 4. It seems reasonable to generalize this finding to the other transposition *Hfr*s. Those

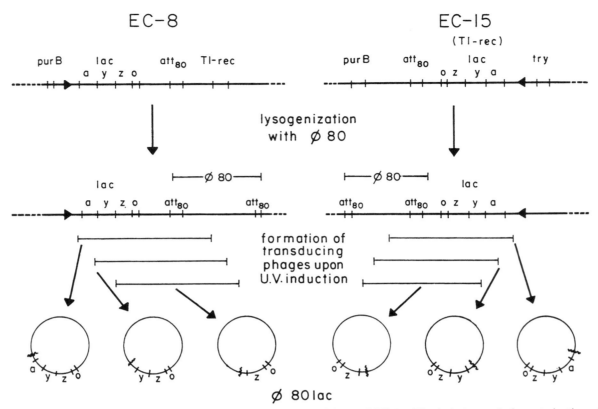

FIGURE 4. The formation of $\phi80lac$ transducing particles from EC-8 and EC-15. The isolation and characterization of EC-8 and EC-15 are described in detail in Signer, Beckwith, and Brenner (1965) (EC-8) and Beckwith and Signer (1966) (EC-8 and EC-15).

Hfrs which transfer counterclockwise would have the *lac* operon in the wild-type orientation, while in the clockwise *Hfrs, lac* would be inverted.

The orientation of the *lac* operon presumably indicates which strand of the DNA carries the *lac* informational complement. (By informational complement we mean that strand of the operon in the DNA duplex which is complementary to the messenger-RNA copied from the operon. We make no assumptions as to whether both strands might be *necessary* for transcription.) There are at least 2 reasons for believing that in transposition strains having the *lac* operon in opposite orientations the *lac* informational complement is on different strands of the chromosomal DNA duplex. First, a model for the integration of F-lac, based on the

Campbell model for episome integration (Campbell, 1962), predicts this result (Beckwith and Signer, 1966). Secondly, it seems very likely that the *lac* operon has a unique direction of transcription (e.g. $5'-3'$ and $\xrightarrow{ozya}$). In view of the antiparallel chemical nature of the 2 strands of a DNA duplex, operons with opposite orientations on the chromosome, in order to be transcribed, must have their informational complements on opposite strands of the DNA. Thus in the counterclockwise *Hfrs* the *lac* informational complement will be on the same strand as in the wild type, while in the clockwise *Hfrs* it will be on the *opposite* strand, with respect to the rest of the bacterial chromosome.

EXPRESSION OF THE INVERTED *LAC* OPERON

Table 2 shows the basal and induced levels of β-galactosidase in 5 clockwise *Hfrs* and 6 counterclockwise *Hfrs*. Although there is some variation among the different strains, there does not appear to be any correlation with the direction of transfer of the *Hfr*, and therefore (considering the results of the preceding section) with the orientation of the *lac* operon. The operon thus seems to be

TABLE 1. THE FREQUENCY OF PARTIAL $\phi80lac$
AMONG $\phi80lac$ TRANSDUCING PHAGES

$\phi80lac$ type	Derived from	
	EC-8	EC-15
$z^+y^-a^-$	9/383	4/181
$z^-y^+a^+$	0/412	0/360

Screening of lysates of $\phi80$ derived from EC-8 and EC-15 for $\phi80lac\ z^-y^+a^+$ and $\phi80lac\ z^+y^-a^-$, as described in text.

TABLE 2. LEVELS OF β-GALACTOSIDASE IN
TRANSPOSITION *Hfrs*

Direction of *Hfr*	Strain	Location of *lac* relative to *Hfr* origin	Levels of β-galactosidase	
			Induced	Uninduced
Clockwise:	EC-1 EC-26	proximal	0.47 ± 0.03	—
	EC-2	proximal	0.82 ± 0.07	0.0012
	EC-3	proximal	0.83 ± 0.04	0.0014
	EC-9	distal	0.63 ± 0.04	0.0010
Counter-clockwise:	EC-4	proximal	0.78 ± 0.07	0.0014
	EC-5	proximal	0.77 ± 0.05	0.0015
	EC-6	distal	0.62 ± 0.03	0.0011
	EC-7	distal	0.67 ± 0.03	0.0011
	EC-28	distal	0.85 ± 0.05	—
	EC-29	proximal	0.67 ± 0.07	—

None of the *Hfrs* reverted to the autonomous F-*lac* state
at higher than 0.5% frequency. β-galactosidase was
assayed by the hydrolysis of *o*-nitrophenyl-β-D-galactoside
and measurement of the *o*-nitrophenol at 420 mμ according
to the method of Pardee, Jacob, and Monod (1959). Units
are calculated as follows: (OD$_{420m\mu}$ − 1.75 × OD$_{550m\mu}$)/
OD$_{600m\mu}$ of the culture/minute. Cultures in Tables 2 and 3
were grown in glucose-M63 synthetic medium with IPTG
(1.5 × 10⁻³ M) for induction. Average errors are based on
4 to 8 independent assays of each strain.

expressed equally well no matter which strand of the
bacterial chromosome carries the *lac* informational
complement. Comparison of Table 2 and Fig. 2
also shows that there is no consistent variation
which can be attributed to the position of *lac* on the
chromosome or to its situation (proximal or distal)
relative to the *Hfr* origin. We have not been able
to measure accurately the levels of β-galactosidase
in EC-8 and EC-15 since they revert to the episomal
condition at high frequency. However, they both
appear as strong *lac*⁺s on *lac*-tetrazolium plates,
indicating high enzyme levels.

In two cases, *T1-rec* and *T1, 5-rec* (Fig. 3),
transpositions have been isolated within a single
gene with both possible orientations. This strongly
suggests that there is no strand-selective restriction
on transcription in any given segment of the
chromosome.

EXPRESSION OF THE TERMINALLY DELETED *LAC* OPERON

The isolation of ϕ80*lac* $z^+y^-a^-$ transducing phages
has been described above (Table 1). Such phages
have been shown by genetic recombination to be
missing the terminal part (i.e., furthest from the
operator) of the *lac* operon, including in each case
more or less of the *y* cistron (Beckwith and Signer,
1966).

A second class of phages carrying terminal
deletions of the *lac* operon has been isolated in
collaboration with Dr. C. F. Fox (Fox, Beckwith,

Epstein, and Signer, 1966). As in the case of ϕ80*lac*
$z^+y^-a^-$, they were obtained by transduction of the
conditional y^+a^+ strain described above. Transductants isolated in the *absence* of adenine (host
y^+a^+ expressed) were screened in the *presence* of
adenine (host y^+a^+ repressed) for their ability to
synthesize thiogalactoside-transacetylase. This procedure revealed transductants carrying ϕ80*lac*
$z^+y^-a^-$, which were phenotypically *lac*⁻ in the
presence of adenine. In addition, a second class of
transductants was found which synthesized no
acetylase, yet remained *lac*⁺ in the *presence* of
adenine. *Lac*⁻ deletion strains carrying the transducing phages from these transductants synthesize
no acetylase, but are indistinguishable from wild
type with respect to synthesis of β-galactosidase;
transport and accumulation of galactosides; synthesis of *M*-protein, which appears to be the
product of the *y* cistron (Fox and Kennedy, 1965);
and growth on lactose. Such phages should then
be ϕ80*lac* $z^+y^+a^-$. Thiogalactoside-transacetylase
seems therefore to have no identifiable role in the
metabolism of lactose.

Since terminal deletion of the *lac* operon will
remove any control elements situated at the *a*
end, the levels of β-galactosidase were measured
in transductants of both the $z^+y^-a^-$ and the
$z^+y^+a^-$ types. Table 3 shows that deletion of the
terminal part of the operon has no effect on
the expression of the remaining segment.

Terminal deletion must lead to fusion of the
remaining *lac* segment with some part of the ϕ80
genome (see Fig. 4). The present results agree well
with those of Sato and Matsushiro (1965), who
showed that initial but not terminal deletion of the
try (tryptophan) operon in ϕ80*try* may place the
remaining *try* cistrons under the control of phage
immunity.

TABLE 3. LEVELS OF β-GALACTOSIDASE IN
DISTALLY DELETED OPERONS

Nature of transducing phage	− inducer	+ inducer
ϕ80*lac* $z^+y^+a^+$	0.0010	0.81 ± 0.03
ϕ80*lac* $z^+y^+a^-_{\overline{EZ-15}}$	0.0010	0.80
ϕ80*lac* $z^+y^+a^-_{\overline{EZ-16}}$	0.0010	0.78
ϕ80*lac* $z^+y^-a^-_{\overline{y-14}}$	0.0013	0.82 ± 0.03
ϕ80*lac* $z^+y^-a^-_{\overline{EZ-12}}$	0.0012	0.73 ± 0.08
ϕ80*lac* $z^+y^-a^-_{\overline{EZ-4}}$	0.0018	0.84 ± 0.05
ϕ80*lac* $z^+y^-a^-_{\overline{EZ-5}}$	0.0019	0.84 ± 0.02

Units as in Table 2.
A *lac*-deletion strain, 2000-XIII, was lysogenized with
the phages indicated. All assays of induced strains were
done on four separate colony isolates of each strain except
for the $z^+y^+a^-$ strains. The frequency of segregation of the
phages in each strain was measured by plating out for
single colonies on Mackonkey Agar with IPTG. The segregants were white, and transductants red. The levels of
β-galactosidase were corrected for amount of segregation.

FIGURE 5. Deletions of the *lac* operon. See text for discussion.

In addition, these results indicate that there are no control elements at the *a* end of the *lac* operon.

EXPRESSION OF THE INITIALLY DELETED *LAC* OPERON

Jacob and Monod (1961) have presented a detailed hypothesis of operon function. Operon expression is controlled by the action of a cytoplasmic repressor (in the case of *lac*, the product of the *i* gene) upon an operator (*o*) located at one end of the operon. In a subsequent paper (Jacob, Ullman, and Monod, 1964), an additional element called the promoter (*p*) was postulated as being located between *o* and the operon it controls, and as being necessary for the absolute expression of the operon; it is viewed as subject to control by the interaction of the *i*-product with *o*. The evidence for *p* rests primarily on the fact that no deletions have been found which cover *o* and the initial part of *z* (presumably deleting *p*), without also extending past *i* (Fig. 5).

The φ80*lac* transduction system permits a deletion analysis of the control elements located at the operator end of *lac*. It is known from the work of Franklin, Dove, and Yanofsky (1965) that bacterial mutations to resistance to phage T1 include deletions covering *T1-rec*, some of which may extend into the *try* operon on one side and prophage φ80 on the other. In a strain carrying prophage φ80*lac* located at *att*$_{80}$, such deletions should extend into the *lac* operon. In particular, in the case of φ80*lac* derived from EC-8, in which *lac* is in the wild-type orientation, the four classes of deletion shown in Fig. 6 should be generated.

The analysis of *T1-rec* deletions is still in a preliminary stage. Several of class I have been isolated; they occur spontaneously at frequencies of less than 1 in 10^{10} cells. In these strains the *y* and *a* cistrons appear to be controlled by the *try* operator, since at least the *y* gene (as measured by growth on melibiose) is expressed only in the absence of tryptophan (in an *F try* merodiploid) or when the repressor-constitutive mutation R^-_{try} (Cohen and Jacob, 1959) is present in the cell as well. Analogous deletions fusing the *lac* and *purE*

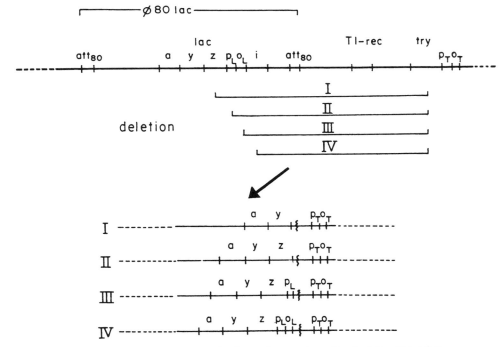

FIGURE 6. Deletions fusing the *lac* and *try* regions. See text for discussion.

(purine) operons have been described by Jacob, Ullman, and Monod (1965). Deletions of this type show that an operator controls all cistrons physically connected to it, regardless of the function of the proteins for which they code.

Deletions of classes II, III, and IV have also been sought. Although one spontaneous deletion of class IV was isolated, the spontaneous frequency of these classes seems to be less than 1 in 10^{11} cells. Mutagenesis with nitrous acid considerably increases the frequency of class IV deletions. Such mutants synthesize the *lac* enzymes constitutively even in the presence of tryptophan. In *F lac i⁺* diploids the *ϕ80lac* enzymes are repressed in the absence of inducer, indicating that the *lac* operator is intact, and confirming the map order *z–o–i* (Jacob and Monod, 1965).

Deletions of classes II and III have not yet been isolated. It is clear that their isolation would provide strong evidence for the promoter postulate. This postulate suggests that fusion of *lac* and *try* by a deletion covering *o* but not *p* (class III) will lead to operator-type constitutivity of the *lac* enzymes even in the presence of tryptophan, whereas deletion of *p* as well (class II) would result in control of the *lac* operon by tryptophan as in the case of class I.

Further experiments in progress are directed at isolating deletions fusing *lac* and *try* from a strain carrying *ϕ80lac* derived from EC-15, in which *lac* is in the inverted orientation. Such deletions would be expected to result in a fused operon having the remaining segments of the *lac* and *try* informational complements on different DNA strands, and one operator at each end.

EXPRESSION OF THE *LAC* OPERON IN *ϕ80lac*

We have used *ϕ80lac* to study the changes in expression of the *lac* operon resulting from induction of a *ϕ80lac* prophage. We find that there is a partial escape from repression of the *lac* operon under these conditions. A similar escape from repression was found by Revel, Luria, and Young (1961) in experiments with *P1dl*, and Buttin (1963) and Yarmolinsky (1963) in experiments with *λ dg*. The experiments reported below give further support to the hypothesis (Revel and Luria, 1963) that escape is due to a rapid increase in the number of *lac* operator sites per cell without a concomitant increase in the number of repressor molecules.

Figure 7 shows that ultraviolet (UV) induction of a strain lysogenic for both *ϕ80* and *ϕ80lac* results in a change in the expression of the *lac* operon. None of these effects are seen in a *lac⁺*

strain lysogenic for *ϕ80* alone (Epstein, Signer, and Beckwith, in prep.). The top part of the figure shows the IPTG (isopropylthio-β-D-galactoside)-induced β-galactosidase synthesis. After a lag of one hour (after UV), this synthesis increases to a high rate, which remains linear with time until lysis. The differential rate of β-galactosidase synthesis (measured with reference to the incorporation of C^{14} l-isoleucine) during this linear phase is 6–10 times the rate during normal growth of the same strain, and a nearly parallel increase occurs in the rate of synthesis of thiogalactoside-transacetylase. This marked increase in the rate of synthesis of *lac* enzymes presumably reflects the increase in the number of *lac* genes per cell due to the induction of the replication of *ϕ80lac* by UV. We are thus able to enrich for synthesis of *lac*-specific enzymes.

At about the time that the IPTG-induced rate of β-galactosidase synthesis begins to increase rapidly, there is also a large transient increase in the *basal* rate of β-galactosidase synthesis (middle

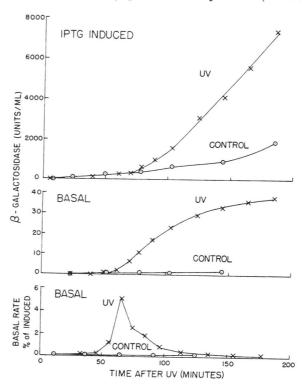

FIGURE 7. A *pro⁻lac⁻* (*i⁻z⁻y⁻* deletion) strain lysogenic for *ϕ80* and *ϕ80lac* was grown with shaking at 37° in medium 63 (Pardee, Jacob, and Monod, 1959) containing glycerol, thiamine, and proline. At time zero, half of the culture was irradiated with ultraviolet light (UV), the other half serving as control. *Top:* β-galactosidase activity in the presence of an inducer of the *lac* operon (IPTG, 3 × 10⁻⁴ M). *Middle:* β-galactosidase activity in the absence of IPTG (basal synthesis). *Bottom:* Basal synthesis *during each interval* expressed as a per cent of the IPTG-induced synthesis *during that interval.*

of Fig. 7). In the bottom part of Fig. 7, the basal rate for each time interval has been plotted as a percentage of the IPTG-induced rate for that interval. The escape from repression is seen to be maximal at the time of acceleration of the IPTG-induced rate. Such kinetics suggest that it is replication of the *lac* operon which causes escape. This escape from repression is manifested not only by *lac* genes carried on the phage. Figure 8 shows an experiment with a strain in which the chromosomal *lac* genes are $i^+z^+y^-$, while those carried on the $\phi80lac$ prophage are $i^-z^-y^+$. As expected, the IPTG-induced rate of β-galactosidase synthesis does not rise, since the gene that replicates does not make functional enzyme. However, the basal rate of synthesis *does* rise at about the same time as in the experiment of Fig. 7, showing that replication of $\phi80lac$ can cause escape of the *chromosomally* located *lac* genes.

The experiment of Fig. 8 shows that escape is not due to the location of the *lac* genes on $\phi80$ nor to the high rate of their replication. We presume that escape is a result of the replication of *lac* operator sites. Since each operator site binds a certain amount of repressor, a multiplication of operators could depress the cell pool of repressor and lead to less effective repression. This hypothesis is supported by the observation that doubling the number of i^+ genes present initially (by use of a strain that carries an i^+ gene on the chromosome in addition to that on the prophage) results in a 10-fold decrease in the

maximal rate of escape synthesis (Epstein, Signer, and Beckwith, in prep.). Also consistent with this hypothesis is the finding that escape is a transient phenomenon in the experiment of Fig. 7, while it persists to lysis in the experiment of Fig. 8. In the former case replication of $\phi80lac$ leads to an increase in the number of i^+ genes; these in time build up a high pool of repressor and reinstitute effective repression, analogous to the late appearance of repression in the mating experiments of Pardee, Jacob, and Monod (1959) and Revel (1965). In the experiment of Fig. 8 the $\phi80lac$ carries an i^- gene so replication does not lead to an increase in i^+ genes, and the cell pool of repressor does not rise to match the increase in number of operators.

SUMMARY AND CONCLUSIONS

The experiments described here indicate some of the advantages provided by the study of gene transposition. The method for isolating directed transpositions is particularly useful, since in this way transposition to a previously chosen chromosomal site can be obtained.

The following conclusions regarding the expression of the *lac* operon can be drawn from these experiments:

1. Expression of the *lac* operon is invariant with respect to inversion; the operon is expressed in the same way when its informational complement is on either DNA strand of the *E. coli* chromosome. This follows from the demonstration, using $\phi80lac$, that *lac* is inverted in clockwise transposition *Hfr*s, and from the comparison of enzyme levels in clockwise and counterclockwise *Hfr*s.

2. All of the *lac* control elements are located at the *o* end of the operon, as suggested by Jacob and Monod (1961); none are located at the *a* end. This is shown by the fact that deletion of the *a* end does not affect the expression of *lac*, whereas deletion of the *o* end and fusion of *lac* with *try* places the remaining *lac* cistrons under control of the *try* operator. Furthermore, deletion of *a* but not *y* does not detectably alter the *lac*+ phenotype, suggesting that thiogalactoside-transacetylase has no role in the metabolism of lactose.

3. The *lac* repressor (i.e., the product of the *i* gene) is present in the cell as a pool which can be depleted by an increase in the number of operator sites. This is suggested by measurements of the basal rate of β-galactosidase synthesis after UV induction of $\phi80lac$.

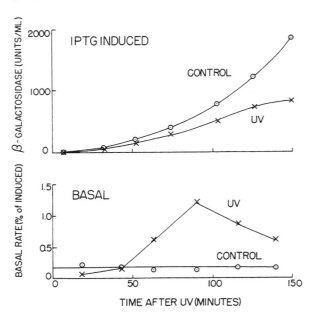

FIGURE 8. Effect of prophage induction on *lac* expression in a strain carrying $i^+z^+y^-$ genes on the chromosome and lysogenic for $\phi80$ and a $\phi80lac$ carrying $i^-z^-y^+$. Experimental details are as described for Fig. 7.

ACKNOWLEDGMENTS

We should like to thank Dr. Francois Jacob and Dr. Francois Cuzin for many useful discussions during the course of this work. We should also like to thank Dr. F. Jacob, Dr. J. Monod, and Dr. A. Képès for the hospitality shown us during our stay at the Institut Pasteur. Two of us (J. R. B. and E. R. S.) were fellows of the Jane Coffin Childs Memorial Fund during part of this work. One of us (W. E.) is a training Fellow of the Basic Science Research Training Program, United States Public Health Service (2G-466) of the Department of Medicine, New York University Medical Center and is, at present, on leave from that institution.

This investigation was supported in part by grants from the National Science Foundation and the Délégation Générale à la Recherche Scientifique et Technique to Dr. F. Jacob, in part by grants from the National Institutes of Health, Jane Coffin Childs Memorial Fund, National Science Foundation, Délégation Générale à la Recherche Scientifique et Technique and the Commissariat à l'Énergie Atomique to Dr. J. Monod and Dr. A. Képès, and in part by Grant #GM-13017 from the National Institute of General Medical Sciences to Dr. Beckwith. One of us (J. R. B.) would like to acknowledge the excellent technical assistance of Miss Mickey Gillmor.

REFERENCES

ADLER, J., and B. TEMPLETON. 1963. The amount of galactose genetic material in λdg bacteriophage with different densities. J. Mol. Biol. 7: 710–720.

BECKWITH, J. R. 1963. Restoration of operon activity by suppressors. Biochim. Biophys. Acta 76: 162–164.

BECKWITH, J. R., and E. R. SIGNER. 1966. Transposition of the lac region of E. coli I. Inversion of the lac operon and transduction of lac by φ80. J. Mol. Biol. 19: 254–265.

BUTTIN, G. 1963. Mecanismes regulateurs dans la biosynthèse des enzymes du metabolisme du galactose chez Escherichia coli K12. III. L' "éffet de dérépression" provoqué par le développement du phage. J. Mol. Biol. 7: 610–631.

CAMPBELL, A. 1962. Episomes. Adv. Genetics 11: 101–145.

COHEN, G. N., and F. JACOB. 1959. Sur la repression de la synthèse des enzymes intervenant dans la formation du tryptophane chez E. coli. C.R. Acad. Sci. 248: 3490–3492.

CUZIN, F., and F. JACOB. 1964. Délétions chromosomiques et intégration d'un episome sexuel F-lac+ chez Escherichia coli K12. C. R. Acad. Sci. 258: 1350–1352.

FOX, C. F., J. R. BECKWITH, W. EPSTEIN, and E. R. SIGNER. 1966. Transposition of the lac region of E. coli II. On the role of thiogalactoside transacetylase in lactose metabolism. J. Mol. Biol. 19: 576–579.

FOX, C. F., and E. P. KENNEDY. 1965. Specific labeling and partial purification of the M protein, a component of the β-galactoside transport system of E. coli. Proc. Natl. Acad. Sci. 54: 891-899.

FRANKLIN, N. C., W. F. DOVE, and C. YANOFSKY. 1965. The linear insertion of a prophage into the chromosome of E. coli shown by deletion mapping. Biochem. Biophys. Res. Commun. 18: 910–923.

JACOB, F., and J. MONOD. 1961. On the regulation of gene activity. Cold Spring Harbor Symp. Quant. Biol. 26: 193–211.

——, ——. 1965. Genetic mapping of the elements of the lactose region in Escherichia coli. Biochem. Biophys. Res. Commun. 18: 693–701.

JACOB, F., A. ULLMAN, and J. MONOD. 1964. Le promoteur, élément génétique nécessaire a l'expression d'un opéron. C.R. Acad. Sci. 258: 3125–3128.

——, ——, ——. 1965. Délétions fusionnant l'opéron lactose et un opéron purine chez Escherichia coli. J. Mol. Biol. 13: 704–719.

MATSUSHIRO, A. 1963. Specialized transduction of tryptophan markers in Escherichia coli K12 by bacteriophage φ80. Virology 19: 475–482.

PARDEE, A. B. 1957. An inducible mechanism for accumulation of melibiose in Escherichia coli. J. Bact. 73: 376–385.

PARDEE, A. B., F. JACOB, and J. MONOD. 1959. The genetic control and cytoplasmic expression of "inducibility" in the synthesis of β-galactosidase by E. coli. J. Mol. Biol. 1: 165–178.

REVEL, H. R. 1965. Synthesis of β-D-galactosidase after F-duction of lac genes into Escherichia coli. J. Mol. Biol. 11: 23–34.

REVEL, H. R., and S. E. LURIA. 1963. On the mechanism of unrepressed galactosidase synthesis controlled by a transducing phage. Cold Spring Harbor Symp. Quant. Biol. 28: 403–407.

REVEL, H. R., S. E. LURIA, and N. L. YOUNG. 1961. Derepression of β-D-galactosidase synthesis following induction of phage development in lysogenic bacteria. Proc. Natl. Acad. Sci. 47: 1974–1980.

SATO, K., and A. MATSUSHIRO. 1965. The tryptophan operon regulated by phage immunity. J. Mol. Biol. 14: 608–610.

SCAIFE, J. G., and A. P. PEKHOV. 1964. Deletion of chromosomal markers in association with F-prime factor formation in Escherichia coli K12. Genet. Res. 5: 495–498.

SIGNER, E. R. 1966. Interaction of prophages at the att80 site with the chromosome of Escherichia coli. J. Mol. Biol. 15: 243–255.

SIGNER, E. R., J. R. BECKWITH, and S. BRENNER. 1965. Mapping of suppressor loci in Escherichia coli. J. Mol. Biol. 14: 153–166.

YARMOLINSKY, M. B. 1963. Influence of phages on the synthesis of host enzymes of bacteria, p. 151-172. In Viruses, nucleic acids, and cancer. The Williams and Wilkins Co., Baltimore.

Prophage Lambda at Unusual Chromosomal Locations

I. Location of the Secondary Attachment Sites and the Properties of the Lysogens

Kazunori Shimada, Robert A. Weisberg

Laboratory of Molecular Genetics
National Institute of Child Health and Human Development
National Institutes of Health, Bethesda, Md. 20014, U.S.A.

AND

Max E. Gottesman

Section on Biochemical Genetics
Laboratory of Molecular Biology
National Cancer Institute
National Institutes of Health
Bethesda, Md. 20014, U.S.A.

(*Received 21 June 1971*)

The integration frequency of phage λ into a mutant host deleted for the normal prophage insertion site is reduced about 200-fold relative to integration into wild-type *Escherichia coli*. This residual integration, like normal integration, requires the *int* gene of the phage and occurs by a cross-over at the normal attachment site on the phage chromosome. Analysis of the resulting abnormal lysogens indicates that there are certain sites on the mutant bacterial chromosome which are preferentially utilized for prophage insertion. In addition, lysogens in which λ has inserted into or near a specific gene, thereby inactivating its function, may be obtained by the appropriate selection technique. When a bacterial gene has been inactivated by prophage integration, prophage excision can restore its function.

Prophage excision from the abnormal sites is inefficient but, like excision from the normal site, it requires two phage genes: *int* and *xis*. In this respect the abnormal bacterial attachment sites resemble the normal bacterial attachment site rather than a phage or a hybrid attachment site.

The abnormal lysogens are of value for deletion mapping of various portions of the *E. coli* chromosome and for the production of novel types of transducing phages.

1. Introduction

Phage λ integrates into *Escherichia coli* by recombination between the prophage and bacterial chromosomes at specific sites in each DNA which are called *att*'s (for attachment sites; Campbell, 1962). There is one *att* on the phage chromosome (*att* P.P') and another on the bacterial chromosome (*att* B.B'); efficient integration does not occur if either *att* is missing or altered (Campbell, 1965; Adhya, Cleary & Campbell, 1968). Integration also requires a protein (Int) which is encoded by the *int* gene of the phage (Zissler, 1967; Gingery & Echols, 1967; Gottesman & Yarmolinsky, 1968a) and which specifically promotes recombination at the *att*'s (Weil & Signer, 1968; Echols, Gingery & Moore, 1968).

As shown in Figure 1, the Int-promoted recombination *att* P.P' × *att* B.B' inserts the phage chromosome into the bacterial chromosome and thus generates two new *att*'s, *att* B.P' at the left prophage end and *att* P.B' at the right prophage end. Prophage excision occurs by the recombination *att* B.P' × *att* P.B' and is a reversal of insertion in all respects but one: the product of another phage gene, the *xis* gene, is required for *att* B.P' × *att* P.B' but not for *att* P.P' × *att* B.B' recombination (Guarneros & Echols, 1970; Kaiser & Masuda, 1970).

Wild-type λ has never been found inserted into a site other than *att* B.B'. However, we suspected that other insertion sites in the bacterial chromosome might be found if insertion at *att* B.B' were eliminated. Accordingly, using a selection method to detect rare lysogens, we studied the integration of λ into a host deleted for *att* B.B'. We found that λ integration into the deletion strain is reduced about 200-fold but still requires Int. Analysis of the resulting lysogens indicates that certain sites on the *att* B.B'-deleted chromosome are frequently used for λ insertion. In addition, there

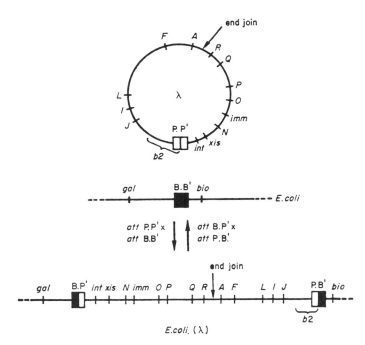

FIG. 1. Insertion and excision of the λ chromosome (after Campbell, 1962 and Guerrini, 1969). The lines represent a circularized phage chromosome and a short portion of the bacterial chromosome. The open square represents the chromosome segment corresponding to *att* P.P', the filled square that corresponding to *att* B.B'. Insertion is thought to occur by breakage and reciprocal exchange of the two participating chromosomes at a specific crossover locus within each attachment site. This locus is denoted by the dot. The squares labeled P.B' and B.P' represent the recombinant attachment sites which bracket the inserted prophage. Circularization of the phage chromosome is accomplished by joining the ends of the linear infecting DNA at the site marked "end join". (Reviewed in Gottesman & Weisberg, 1971, and Yarmolinsky, 1971). Genes *A*, *F*, *L*, *I*, *J*, *b2*, *int*, *xis*, *N*, *imm*, *O*, *P*, *Q*, and *R* are phage markers used in this work and genes *gal* and *bio* are bacterial markers near *att* B.B'.

probably exists a large number of rarely utilized sites. Prophage excision is inefficient in these lysogens but, as in normal lysogens, requires Int and Xis. The secondary-site lysogens are of value for deletion mapping of portions of the *E. coli* chromosome and for the production of novel types of specialized transducing phages.

2. Materials and Methods

(a) *Phage strains*

The λ strains used in this work are listed in Table 1.

TABLE 1

Phage strains

Phage	Source or reference
λcI857	F. Jacob: Sussman & Jacob (1962)
λb2	See Gottesman & Yarmolinsky (1968*a*)
λb2c	See Gottesman & Yarmolinsky (1968*a*)
λch80⁺del9	u.v.-induced clear plaque mutant of λh80⁺del9 which is deleted for *int80* (N. Franklin, personal communication).
λvir	L. Pereira da Silva; Jacob & Wollman (1954)
λint6	Gottesman & Yarmolinsky (1968*a*)
λint6c	Gottesman & Yarmolinsky (1968*a*)
λint29	J. Zissler
λxis1·susJ6	Guarneros & Echols (1970)
λimm²¹sus12	Derived from 21hy5 of Liedke-Kulke & Kaiser (1967)
λimm²¹int6	See Gottesman & Yarmolinsky (1968*a*)
λimm²¹int29	J. Zissler
λimm²¹xis6	Guarneros & Echols (1970)
λcI90c17	W. Sly
λsusN7 N53	E. Signer
λsus 029	W. Sly
λsus P80	W. Sly
λsus Q73 Q51	I. Herskowitz
λsus R5	J. Weil
λsus A11	A. Campbell
λsus F96	F. Stahl
λsus L63	F. Stahl
λsus I2	F. Stahl
λsus J418	R. Huskey

All phages whose immunity is not given carry *imm*λ and, except for λb2c, λcI90c17, λvir, λsusR, λsusF and λsusI, all *imm*λ phages carry the *cI857* temperature-sensitive *cI* mutation.

(b) *Bacterial strains*

Table 2 lists the bacterial strains employed in this study. Selection methods for isolating *att* B.B′-deleted *E. coli* strains are described below.

(c) *Media*

Tryptone broth was used for bacterial growth, and Luria broth was used in bacterial crosses. Tryptone broth agar was used for phage and bacterial assays, and EMBO agar for measuring integration frequencies. These media are described in Gottesman & Yarmolinsky (1968*a*). MacConkey-lactose or galactose agar is described in the Difco Manual (Difco Laboratory, Detroit, Mich.). The minimal agar medium containing (per liter) 6 g Na_2HPO_4, 3 g KH_2PO_4, 0·5 g NaCl, 1 g NH_4Cl, 0·25 g $MgSO_4 \cdot 7H_2O$, 0·015 g $CaCl_2 \cdot 2H_2O$, and 16 g agar was supplemented with 1 μg vitamin B_1/ml., 0·1 μg biotin/ml., 1·0% glucose or arabinose and, when required, 20 μg of each of the appropriate amino

TABLE 2

Bacterial strains

Strain	Relevant genotype†	Source
594	λ^s sup^-str^r	J. Weigle
C600	λ^s $supE^+$	R. Appleyard
AB1157	λ^s thr leu $proA$ his $argE$ ara str^r	P. Howard-Flanders
AB1157λ^r		M. Gottesman
AB1157λ^r ($\lambda cI857$ $int6$)		M. Gottesman
HfrH	λ^s sup^-str^s	W. Hayes
HfrH Δatt B.B′	λ^s $sup^-(gal\text{-}uvrB)^\Delta$ str^s	This work
KL16-99	Hfr λ^s sup^-recA str^s	B. Low
KL16-99 Δatt B.B′	Hfr λ^s sup^-recA $(gal\text{-}uvrB)^\Delta$ str^s	This work
W3102 ($\lambda cI857$)$_n$	Multiple λ lysogen	M. Gottesman
W3102 ($\lambda cI857$)	Single λ lysogen	M. Gottesman

† Abbreviations used: sus = sensitive to amber suppressors, sup = inability to support the growth of λ sus mutants, att = attachment site, str^s, str^r = sensitivity or resistance to streptomycin, T^r = ability to grow at 41°C, Δ = deletion, λ^s, λ^r = sensitivity or resistance to λ phage, Int = product of int gene, Xis = product of xis gene. The other genetic symbols are those used by Taylor (1970).

acids/ml. Tris–magnesium–gelatin solution, containing 0·01 M-MgSO$_4$, 0·01 M-Tris, pH 7·4, and 0·01% gelatin was used as a non-nutrient diluent for phage and bacteria.

(d) *Phage assays and phage stocks*

Assays of free phage and infective centers and infection with phage were performed as described in Gottesman & Yarmolinsky (1968a). Phage stocks were made by the plate method (Adams, 1959).

(e) *Isolation of att B.B′-deleted E. coli*

E. coli gal^+ bio^+ $uvrB^+$ sup^- strains, lysogenic for the thermoinducible excision-defective $\lambda cI857$ $xis1$ $sus J6$, were plated on MacConkey-galactose plates at 41°C. A fraction of the survivors formed gal^- (white) colonies. These were tested for growth in the absence of biotin by streaking on minimal agar and for u.v. sensitivity by streaking on Tryptone broth agar plates and irradiating the plate with light from a GE germicidal lamp (G8T5). (The energy output of the lamp was determined with a YSI model 65 radiometer and a YSI model 6551 radiometer probe. No correction was made for absorption. The u.v. dose was varied by changing the time of exposure and/or the lamp-to-plate distance.) Some of the gal^- colonies were found to require biotin, were sensitive to u.v., and showed a reduced ability to support λ-integration (see Table 3 and Results). Therefore, we believe the chromosome segment $gal–uvrB$ which includes bio and att B.B′ (see Taylor, 1970) has been deleted in these strains.

(f) *Measurement of lysogenization frequency*

Overnight cultures, starved by incubation in 0·01 M-MgSO$_4$ for 1 hr, were infected with $\lambda cI857$ at a multiplicity of about 10 and then spread on EMBO plates seeded with about 10^9 $\lambda b2$ c, $\lambda int6$ c, or $\lambda h80^+$ $del9$ c. Both lysogens and λ-resistant bacteria survive this selection procedure and appear as pink-staining colonies after about 20 hr of incubation at 33°C. To eliminate the λ-resistant clones, the colonies were cross-streaked against λvir at 33°C or 41°C on tryptone broth plates; clones which were resistant to λvir or which grew at 41°C were discarded.

(g) *Measurement of curing frequency*

(i) *Spontaneous curing*

To measure spontaneous curing, λvir-resistant derivatives were constructed from each lysogen. Exponentially growing cultures of these derivatives were appropriately diluted

TABLE 3

Ultraviolet-resistance of strains used in this work

| Strain | Ultraviolet dose to plate (ergs mm^{-2})† | | |
	approx. 100	approx. 40	approx. 10
HfrH	+‡	+	+
HfrH *ΔattB.B'*	−	+	+
KL16-99	−	−	+
KL16-99 *ΔattB.B'*	−	−	−

Individual colonies of cultures to be tested were streaked on half of a TB plate and a known u.v.-resistant strain was streaked on the other half. A sector of the plate was then exposed to a u.v. lamp in such a way that half of each streak received the indicated dose. The other half served as an unirradiated control. The plate was incubated at 33°C for 12 to 24 hr and read.

† See Materials and Methods for determination of u.v. dose.

‡ + Means no apparent reduction in the number of colonies on the exposed sector; − means no growth on the exposed sector.

and plated on Tryptone broth plates at 33°C or 41°C. The ratio of the bacterial titer at 41°C to that at 33°C is defined as the curing frequency.

(ii) *Heat-pulse curing*

Exponentially growing λ*vir*-resistant derivatives of λ*cI857* lysogens at 33°C were diluted 100-fold into fresh Tryptone broth at 41°C. After 6 minutes they were again diluted 100-fold into Tryptone broth at 33°C, were grown for 4 to 6 hr at 33°C and then plated at 33°C and 41°C on Tryptone broth plates to determine the curing frequency.

(iii) *Superinfection curing*

Cells were grown at 33°C in Tryptone broth supplemented with 0·2% maltose and 0·01 M-MgSO$_4$. The culture, at a density of 1 to 2×10^8 cells/ml. was mixed with 5 to 10 heteroimmune phage particles/bacterium. After 20 min adsorption, the cells were diluted in Tryptone broth at 33°C, incubated for 4 to 6 hr and the curing frequency determined as described above. Phage adsorption was essentially complete under these conditions.

(h) *Measurement of phage-release by the various lysogens*

Exponentially growing λ*vir*-resistant derivatives were diluted 1000-fold into fresh Tryptone broth, supplemented with 0·01 M-MgSO$_4$, at 40°C and then incubated for 2 hr. Phage titer was determined after treatment of the culture with chloroform. Burst-sizes are expressed as phage titer after 2 hr incubation at 40°C divided by the colony count at 33°C just before the temperature shift.

(i) *Detection of residual phage markers*

The presence of a given λ marker in a prophage deletion mutant was determined by spotting 10^6 to 10^7 particles of a λ*sus* mutant or a λ*sus*$^+$ control on a Tryptone broth agar plate containing approx. 10^7 cells from an exponential culture of the bacterial deletion mutant. HfrH, the lysogenic host, is *sup*$^-$ and will not permit the growth of λ*sus* mutants. The presence of a given allele in a particular deletion mutant generally resulted in confluent lysis at the location of the phage spot. An exponential culture of non-lysogenic HfrH was always used as a negative, and AB1157 (*sup*$^+$) as a positive control.

(j) *Bacterial crosses*

(i) *HfrH (λcI857) × F$^-$ AB1157 λ^r matings*

To determine the time of prophage entry into the F$^-$, overnight cultures of the strains to be crossed were diluted at least 20-fold into fresh Luria broth, grown to approximately 10^9 cells/ml. at 33°C with gentle agitation, and then mixed in a ratio of approximately 5 F$^-$ to 1 Hfr. This mixture was then incubated at 33°C in a flat-bottomed flask without agitation. Chromosome transfer was interrupted at 10-min intervals by diluting the mixture 100-fold in Tris–magnesium–gelatin solution and violently agitating for 30 sec on a vortex mixer. Infective centers, arising as a result of zygotic induction (Jacob & Wollman, 1961), were measured by plating the vortexed mixture on Tryptone broth plates supplemented with 200 μg of streptomycin/ml.; strain 594 (str^r) was used as an indicator. Since the prophage carried the ind^- mutation and the Hfr donor was str^s, the background of plaques not resulting from zygotic induction was negligible. The efficiency of transfer was measured by determining the frequency of $proA^+$ str^r recombinants on appropriately supplemented minimal plates. The time of entry of the $proA^+$ gene at 33°C was 15 to 20 min (see Fig. 2). We usually found about 0·05 to 0·1 $proA^+$ str^r recombinants per input Hfr after 50 min of mating.

(ii) $Hfr \times Hfr$ matings

In order to measure recombination between two different Hfr strains, we converted one of them to an F^- phenotype by overnight aeration of a saturated culture (Brinton, Gemski & Carnahan, 1964). The mating technique was otherwise similar to the one described above.

(k) Determination of the number of prophages

The repressor level in a lysogen is proportional to the number of prophages it carries (Merril & Gottesman, manuscript in preparation). The degree of resistance of a lysogen to the virulent mutant $\lambda cI90c17$ depends on the intracellular concentration of repressor (W. Sly, personal communication). It has been found that single lysogens are sensitive but multiple lysogens are immune to this mutant (Merril & Gottesman, manuscript in preparation). Lysogens were tested for their sensitivity to $\lambda cI90c17$ by cross-streaking exponential cultures on Tryptone broth or EMBO plates against $\lambda cI90c17$ at 10^7/ml. Lysis at the intersection after 12 hr of incubation indicates that the lysogen is single; multiple lysogens show no lysis. Exponential cultures of a known multiple lysogen and single lysogen (see Table 2) were always used as controls.

(l) Measurement of EDTA-sensitivity of λ phage

A portion of each phage solution was diluted at least 20-fold into 0·01 M-EDTA, 0·01 M-Tris · HCl buffer, pH 7·4, and held at 33°C for about 10 min. The solutions were then chilled, and 0·05 vol. of 1 M-MgSO$_4$ was added. The EDTA treated and untreated lysates were assayed for phage titer on C600.

3. Results

(a) The frequency of integration of λ into E. coli deleted for att B.B'

The frequency of integration of $\lambda cI857$ into the att B.B'-deleted strain was measured by titering the number of immune survivors after infection (see Materials & Methods). These results (Table 4) indicate that deletion of the bacterial attachment site reduces the efficiency of integration to 0·5% that obtained with a non-deleted host. The frequency of integration of $\lambda cI857$ $int6$ into a deleted host is at least 100-fold less than that of an int^+ phage; this suggests that Int still promotes insertion into the att B.B'-deleted chromosome. The frequency of integration of $\lambda cI857$ $xis1$ $susJ6$ into a deleted host was approximately the same as that of λxis^+ (data not shown). We also found that the frequency of λ integration into a deleted host is reduced several-fold when the host carries a mutation in the $recA$ gene.

(b) Prophage locations in the att B.B'-deleted lysogens

(i) Auxotrophic lysogens

We found that three out of 65 independently isolated lysogens were converted into auxotrophs: two became leu and one pro. The following results show that these new

TABLE 4

Integration frequency of λ into B.B'-deleted E. coli

Host	Frequency of integration	
	λint$^+$	*λint6*
HfrH	0·88	*ca.* 0·00005
HfrH *ΔattB.B'*	0·0043	*ca.* 0·00001
KL16-99 *recA*	0·40	NT†
KL16-99 *recA ΔattB.B'*	*ca.* 0·00033	NT

The frequency of integration was measured as described in Materials and Methods, section (f).
† NT = not tested.

nutritional requirements are a direct consequence of prophage insertion. First, eight out of eight spontaneous *pro*$^+$ revertants from the *pro* lysogen, and 20 out of 20 spontaneous *leu*$^+$ revertants (selected from both *leu* lysogens) were found to be heat resistant and sensitive to superinfection by λ. At least two of the *pro*$^+$ and four of the *leu*$^+$ revertants were of independent origin. (The growth of the original lysogens was temperature-sensitive because the λc*I*857 prophage synthesizes a repressor the activity of which is heat-labile (Sussman & Jacob, 1962).) Second, the *pro* lysogen can be cured of its prophage by heteroimmune superinfection (see Table 8). Of 63 such cured colonies tested, all proved to be *pro*$^+$; most of these colonies were of independent origin. Neither *leu* lysogen was tested in this way.

These facts are consistent with the hypothesis that the inserted prophages disrupt the continuity of genes required for the biosynthesis of proline or leucine. If so we can fix the site of prophage insertion in the leucine-requiring lysogens at 1 minute on the *E. coli* map (see Taylor, 1970), since all known *leu* genes are found at this location. This determination of location is consistent with the results of deletion mapping and transduction experiments (see below).

The site of prophage insertion in the proline requiring lysogen was located as follows. Three genes, *proA*, *proB*, and *proC*, are known to be required for proline biosynthesis (see Taylor, 1970). When a culture of the *pro* lysogen was cross-streaked on minimal agar against cultures of known *proA*, *proB*, and *proC* mutants, growth occurred, presumably due to cross-feeding, at the intersection with the *proC* but not with the *proA* or *proB* cultures. This result suggests that the site of prophage insertion is in either the *proA* or the *proB* genes (Curtiss, 1965). The results of deletion mapping and transduction experiments (see below) are consistent with a site in the *proB* gene (located at 9 to 10 min).

(ii) *Mapping by zygotic induction*

To locate the other prophages, we purified 14 independently isolated prototrophic lysogens of *att* B.B'-deleted HfrH. These lysogens were mated at 33°C with a non-lysogenic λ^{r}F$^-$. Prophage locations were determined by the time of appearance of infective centers; these were produced by zygotic induction (see Materials and Methods). These results (see Table 5, column 3 and Fig. 2) enabled us to group the 14 lysogens into five groups, A, B, C, D and E-I, which are ordered according to increasing time of prophage entry into the non-lysogenic recipient. The group showing the latest

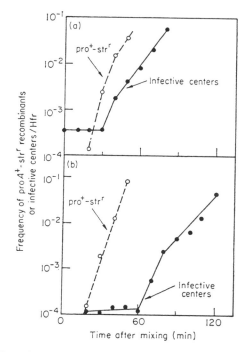

Fig. 2. Kinetics of *proA* and λ prophage transfer in interrupted mating experiments.
(a) Donor: HfrH (λ*cI*857); recipient: AB1157λ^r.
(b) Donor: HfrH Δ*att*B.B′ (λ*cI*857) = strain 46; recipient: AB1157λ^r.
The mating mixture, after agitation at the indicated times, was plated on streptomycin-containing plates in order to select against donor colonies. The other experimental procedures were described in Materials and Methods.

entry time, group E-I, was later subdivided into five new groups as a result of deletion mapping studies. Since we have not studied the effect of temperature on the kinetics of chromosome transfer, the times of prophage entry obtained by matings performed at 33°C cannot be used directly to position the abnormally located prophages on the standard (37°C) map of *E. coli*.

(iii) Deletion mapping

Most cells of a λ*cI*857-lysogenic culture die at high temperature (41°C) because phage functions lethal to the host are induced. The rare heat-resistant survivors often derive from cells in which the phage genes specifying or controlling the lethal functions have been deleted (Shapiro & Adhya, 1969; Neubauer & Calef, 1970). The deletion may extend into adjacent bacterial regions (Shapiro & Adhya, 1969). The determination of the nutritional requirement(s) (if any) of these deletion mutants can give a more precise prophage location than that obtained by measuring zygotic induction.

The results of deletion mapping are summarized in Table 5, columns 4, 5 and 6. Auxotrophic heat-resistant survivors could be selected from most of the lysogenic strains. The determination of the requirement in conjunction with the time-of-entry data provided a precise prophage location in several cases.

Leu and Pro groups. Heat-resistant cells were selected from cultures of the *leu* and *pro* lysogens described in Results section (b) (i). In the case of both *leu* lysogens, such

TABLE 5

Mapping of prophage sites

Group	Strain	Time† of entry (min)	Tʳ survivors:‡ auxotrophs / total	Nutritional requirements of Tʳ derivatives	Probable location	Map position (min)
Leu	73	—	4/4	Leucine	leuA,B	1
	75	—	12/12	Leucine	leuA,B	1
Pro	47	—	31/138	Proline	proB	9–10
A	69	10	1/ca. 2,000	Pyrimidine		
B	81	20	2/65, 2/126	Purine	near purE	13
C	76	40	1/ca. 2,000	Pyrimidine		
	80	40	1/ca. 2,000	Pyrimidine		
D	46	60	1/ca. 2,000	Pyrimidine		
E	60	90	7/204, 1/63, 1/42	Histidine	near his	38–39
	4	90	1/137, 3/26, 3/39	Histidine, Tryptophan, Ferric ion		
F	99	90	1/280	Phenylalanine	near pheA	(50)
G	10	90	3/207	Cysteine	near cys H,P,Q	53
	90	90	8/60	Cysteine	near cys H,P,Q	53
	62	90	1/179	Cysteine	near cys H,P,Q	53
	66	90	2/64, 3/81	Cysteine	near cys H,P,Q	53
H	72	90	2/64, 6/77	Lysine	near lysA	54–55
I	58	90	1/ca. 1,000	Methionine	near metC	60

† Time of entry was measured as described in Materials and Methods. (Estimates of time of entry are very inaccurate beyond 60 min.)

‡ 10⁸ to 10⁹ stationary phase lysogens were spread on warmed Tryptone broth plates and incubated at 40°C for 24 hr. Survivors were replica plated to 1·0% glucose + vitamin B₁ + biotin supplemented minimal plates. Survivors which failed to grow on these plates were further analyzed.

spontaneously arising heat-resistant lines almost always retained their leucine requirement. In addition about 0·1 to 0·5% of the heat-resistant lines were unable to utilize the sugar arabinose; this is presumably a consequence of a deletion which extends from the prophage into the *ara* operon. The existence of *leu–ara* deletions not otherwise affecting the cell phenotype has been reported in *E. coli* B/r (Kessler & Englesberg, 1969) and supports our proposed prophage location (1 min) for this strain. In contrast to these results, 78% of the spontaneously arising heat-resistant cells selected from cultures of the *pro* lysogen became *pro⁺*. This finding suggests that in this strain Tʳ cells usually arise by prophage excision which restores the integrity of the *pro⁺* gene (see Results section (b) (i)). About 0·1% of the heat-resistant colonies retained their proline requirement and in addition were unable to utilize the sugar lactose. This phenotype is presumably a consequence of a single deletion extending from *pro* to *lac*. We believe that the prophage is probably located in the *proB* rather than the *proA* gene since *proA–lac* deletions are expected to be λ^r and T7^r (R. Curtiss, 1965 and personal communication), whereas the *pro lac* heat-resistant lines isolated here were λ^s and T7^s. However, since the location of the gene which determines sensitivity to these phages has not been precisely determined, a site in the *proA* gene is not excluded.

B group. Purine requiring auxotrophs isolated from the sole lysogen of this group (strain no. 81) were characterized as *purE* mutants (located at 10 min on the Taylor (1970) map) because lysates of this strain contained particles capable of transducing a known *purE* strain to *pur*$^+$.

E group. From strain no. 60, we isolated several independent *his* auxotrophs. One of the *his* auxotrophs (strain no. 60-10, see Table 6) was further characterized and shown to lack gluconate-6-phosphate dehydrogenase (*gnd*) and TDP-glucose oxidoreductase (*som*) while retaining a normal level of methylgalactoside permease (*mgl* P) (M. Levinthal, personal communication). On the basis of this evidence we conclude that the λ genome in strain no. 60 is inserted within the 38- to 40-minute segment of the *E. coli* map (see Taylor, 1970).

Strain no. 4 was tentatively classified within the E group from the results of the time-of-entry experiment and other properties of the lysogen (see Table 7). From this strain, we isolated three different kinds of auxotrophs. The requirements of these three auxotrophic classes are (1) His, (2) Trp and (3) ferric ion, respectively. This lysogen may contain multiple prophages inserted at different sites, and this may account for the peculiar characteristics of the T^r survivors.

G group. Four independently-isolated group G lysogens transfer their prophages late in bacterial crosses and generate heat-resistant *cys* auxotrophs. In order to determine which of the many scattered *cys* genes was linked to the prophage, we used *str*^{r} derivatives of the heat-resistant *cys* auxotrophs as recipients (see Materials and Methods) in crosses with Hfr KL16-99 *str*^{s} which transfers the *cys* H, P, Q region early (Low, 1968). After 25 minutes of mating at 37°C, we obtained about 2 *cys*$^+$ *str*^{r} recombinants per 100 input males. Moreover, all of these independently isolated *cys* strains lacked sulfite reductase and adenosine 3′-phosphate 5′-sulfatophosphate reductase activities while retaining normal levels of serine transacetylase, O-acetyl-serine sulfhydrylase, ATP sulfurylase, and adenosine 5′-sulfatophosphate kinase (N. Kredich, personal communication). These results suggest that the prophage is located near *cys* H, P, Q (52 to 53 min) in class G lysogens.

H group. From strain no. 72, we isolated several lysine requiring strains. Some of these strains are also deleted for the *galR* gene. Although all of the *lys* strains were *thy*$^+$, λ *thyA* transducing phages which did not carry *lys*$^+$ could be isolated from this lysogen. From these results, we conclude that in this strain the prophage is inserted between the *lysA* and *thyA* genes.

I group. From strain no. 58, we isolated one heat-resistant methionine-requiring auxotroph. This auxotroph can grow on a homocysteine-supplemented minimal plate. These results suggest that the methionine requirement is due to deletion of *metA*, *metB*, or *metC* (Smith & Childs, 1966). Lysates of a heat-induced culture of strain no. 58 contain particles which can transduce the *met* auxotroph; this suggests that the heat-resistant methionine-requiring phenotype is the result of a single deletion. The particles will also transduce a known *metC* mutant, indicating a prophage location near *metC* (59 min).

Other groups. Selection of heat-resistant cells from cultures of the group F lysogen (no. 99) yielded one phenylalanine requiring auxotroph. To determine the location of the mutation, we mated this auxotroph with a *his⁻ str^r* female (AB1157) and, after 45 minutes of mating at 37°C, selected *his⁺ str^r* recombinants. 18 out of 19 of these recombinants were still *phe⁻*. These results suggested that the mutant *phe* gene was located distal to the *his* gene. We then used a *str^r* derivative of the *phe⁻* auxotroph as a recipient in crosses with HfrKL16-99 *str^s* which transfers the *pheA* gene early. After 20 minutes of mating at 37°C, we obtained about 0·13 *phe⁺ str^r* recombinants per 100 input males. This result suggests that this *phe* requirement is probably *pheA* (50 min). We have isolated pyrimidine-requiring auxotrophs from group A, C and D lysogens. Further characterization of these auxotrophs is in progress. It should be noted that, in cases where only a single auxotrophic heat-resistant clone has been obtained, and where transducing phage have not yet been isolated, the possibility remains that the heat-resistance and the auxotrophy are unrelated.

(c) *Prophage gene order*

As we mentioned above (section (a)), it is likely that prophage insertion into an *att* B.B′-deleted host is Int-promoted. In normal hosts, Int-promoted insertion breaks the phage chromosome at *att* P.P′ thereby generating a characteristic prophage map which differs from the phage map by a cyclic permutation of the markers (Franklin, Dove & Yanofsky, 1965; Rothman, 1965; Adhya *et al.*, 1968) (see Fig. 1). Since Int promotes recombination specifically at *att* P.P′ (Weil & Signer, 1968; Echols *et al.*, 1968), we expected that a similar permutation of markers would have occurred in the prophages at abnormal bacterial sites. This appears to be the case.

Prophage maps have been constructed by testing survivors of thermal induction for residual phage markers (see Materials and Methods section (i)). If we assume that the prophage genes responsible for cell killing are deleted in a single continuous block, analysis of the remaining prophage markers in a set of independent deletion lines gives the prophage map (Franklin *et al.*, 1965). If the partial prophage deletion has also removed an adjacent bacterial gene, the orientation of the prophage with respect to that gene can also be determined. As may be seen in Table 6, the prophage map of the secondary-site lysogens is, for those lysogens thus far examined, the same as that of normal lysogens. This is consistent with our hypothesis of Int-promoted insertion at *att* P.P′. In the H group, the orientation of the prophage genome with respect to the bacterial chromosome is the reverse of that determined for normal lysogens.

In the case of the deletion strain 73-4-2A [(N-R)^d (A-J)⁺] (see Table 6), which derives from a Leu-group lysogen, the presence of the *b2⁺* region was established. In normal lysogens, the *b2⁺* region is located between gene *J* and the right prophage end (Fischer-Fantuzzi, 1967; see Fig. 1). Therefore, we expected that line 73-4-2A, which had retained genes *A* through *J* of the original prophage, would be able to donate *b2⁺* to λ *b2*. This prediction was confirmed by the following experiment. We constructed 73-4-2A (λcI857 *b2*) by selecting immune survivors of infection with λcI857 *b2*. Upon induction, this lysogen liberated, per cell, about 40 phages; nearly all of these were λ*b2⁺* as judged by the following criteria. (1) At least 95% of the phage particles in the lysate integrate efficiently into a non-lysogenic recipient strain

TABLE 6

Prophage deletion mapping

Group	Strain no.	N	O	P	Q	R	A	F	L	I	J	Genotype
Leu	73-4	−	−	−	+	+	+	+	+	+	+	*leu*
	73-4-2A	−	−	−	−	−	+	+	+	+	+	*leu*
	73-3-2	−	−	−	−	−	−	+	+	+	+	*leu*
	73-4-2B	−	−	−	−	−	−	−	−	−	−	*leu*
	75-1-1	−	−	−	−	−	−	+	+	+	+	*leu & ara*
	75-1-2	−	−	−	−	−	−	−	−	−	−	*leu*
Pro	47-30	−	+	+	+	+	+	+	+	+	+	*pro*
	47-57	−	−	−	+	+	+	+	+	+	+	*pro*
	47-38	−	−	−	−	−	−	+	+	+	+	*pro*
	47-54	−	−	−	−	−	−	−	−	−	−	*pro & lac*
C	76-6-8	−	−	−	−	−	−	−	−	−	+	+
	76-6-30	−	−	−	−	−	−	−	−	−	−	*pyr*
	80-14-9	−	−	−	−	−	+	+	+	+	+	+
	80-15-1	−	−	−	−	−	−	−	−	−	−	*pyr*
E	60-10-23	−	+	+	+	+	+	+	+	+	+	+
	60-8	−	−	−	+	+	+	+	+	+	+	+
	60-18-3	−	−	−	−	−	+	+	+	+	+	*his*
	60-10	−	−	−	−	−	+	−	+	+	+	*his, gnd & som*
	60-11	−	−	−	−	−	−	+	+	+	+	+
	60-16	−	−	−	−	−	−	−	−	−	−	+
	4-15-1	−	−	+	+	+	+	+	+	+	+	+
	4-3-10	−	−	−	+	+	+	+	+	+	+	*ferric ion*
	4-12	−	−	−	−	−	−	+	+	+	+	+
	4-13-10	−	−	−	−	−	−	−	−	−	−	*his*
	4-13-8	−	−	−	−	−	−	−	−	−	−	*trp*
H	72-1-12	−	−	−	−	−	−	+	+	+	+	*lys & galR*
	72-2-38	−	−	−	−	−	−	−	−	−	+	*lys & galR*
	72-2-28	−	−	−	−	−	−	−	−	−	−	*lys*

Survivors were scored for phage markers and nutritional requirements as described in Materials and Methods. The number before the first hyphen refers to the strain from which the heat-resistant strains were obtained; thus 73-4 derives from strain no. 73 etc.

(strain 594), whereas λb2 does not (Kellenberger, Zichichi & Weigle, 1961); and (2) the phage were inactivated to a survival of about 10^{-4} by treatment with EDTA (see Materials and Methods, section (1)) whereas λb2 is resistant to EDTA (Parkinson & Huskey, 1971). If we assume that no secondary rearrangement of prophage genes occurred in strain 73-4-2A, the finding that the $b2^+$ region can be rescued indicates that it is located between gene J and the right prophage end in the original Leu-group lysogen. We have also established the presence of the $b2^+$ region in derivatives of strain 47 (group Pro) which had sustained deletions of the left prophage end. Since the $b2^+$ region includes the *att* element P and ends at the Int-specific crossover locus (Davis & Parkinson, 1971; see Fig. 1), we conclude that prophage insertion must have occurred at a point between the *att* element P and gene N (the leftmost prophage gene known to be missing in strain 73-4-2A), most likely at the crossover locus. The fact that strain 73-4-2A (λ *cI857 b2*) liberated mainly λ *b2*$^+$ can be reasonably explained by assuming that λ *b2* integrated by Int-promoted recombination at the remaining attachment site of the deleted prophage and that excision occurred by end-cutting or by generalized recombination (Gottesman & Yarmolinsky, 1968*b*; Mousset & Thomas, 1969; Howe, as cited by Signer, 1968). Such excision would generate only *b2*$^+$ chromosomes.

(d) *The formation of transducing phage lines*

Induction of a λ lysogen results in the occasional liberation of phage particles which contain bacterial DNA (transducing phage) (see Franklin, 1971). The incorporation of a given segment of the bacterial chromosome into a transducing phage particle depends on the proximity of that segment to the prophage (Signer & Beckwith, 1966); it is likely that any bacterial marker which is within roughly 0·5 λ-length of either prophage end can potentially appear in a transducing phage particle (Kayajanian & Campbell, 1966). We therefore expected that λ transducing phage for new bacterial markers could be obtained from abnormally located prophages.

Several lines of transducing phage-carrying bacterial markers thought to be near the prophage on the basis of time-of-entry and deletion analysis have been obtained. There are λ*leu* (group Leu), λ*proB* and λ*proA proB* (group Pro), λ*purE* (group B), λ*cys* (group G) λ*lysA galR*, λ*thyA*, λ*thyA recC* (group H) and λ*metC* (group I). The properties of these transducing phage will be the subject of a subsequent communication.

(e) *The distribution of prophages among secondary sites*

Groups Leu, C, G and E contain more than one independently isolated lysogenic strain. The results of deletion mapping experiments with lysogens of these groups (Results section (b) and Table 5) are consistent with the hypothesis that there is only one or a small number of closely linked prophage insertion sites for each group (see below). This non-random distribution of prophage locations on the bacterial chromosome is strikingly illustrated by the limited kinds of auxotrophy which result from lysogenization of an *att* B.B'-deleted host. Thus far only two leucine-requiring and six proline-requiring strains have been found among about 1000 independent lysogens tested. Since the efficiency of our procedure for isolating lysogens (selection of immune cells) should not vary with prophage location, we conclude that certain sites or regions of the *att* B.B'-deleted chromosome are especially favored for prophage insertion. Because of the limited number of lysogens which have been mapped, we are unable to say how many frequently utilized secondary sites there are or whether the sites thus far identified are uniform with respect to the efficiency of prophage insertion.

We attempted to test directly whether prophage insertion in the two independently isolated leucine-requiring lysogens (see Table 4) occurred at the same chromosomal site. For this purpose, we used a *lac str*^{r} derivative of the *leu* lysogen no. 73 as a recipient in a mating with lysogen no. 75 (HfrH *leu lac*$^+$ *str*^{s}). If the two prophages had inserted at different sites, such a cross could produce *leu*$^+$ recombinants. In fact, we found that the number of *leu*$^+$ recombinants was less than 0·001% of the number of *lac*$^+$ *str*^{r} recombinants. Although this result is consistent with the idea that both prophages have inserted at the same site, other interpretations are not ruled out. For example, recombination in an interval between two differently located but very closely linked prophages might be impeded by the extensive regions of non-homology bracketing the interval.

The fact that prophage insertion into an *att* B.B'-deleted chromosome is Int-promoted suggests an explanation for our finding that the distribution of prophage locations is non-random. There is good reason to believe that specific nucleotide sequences in *att* B.B' are required for efficient Int-promoted recombination at this site (Signer & Beckwith, 1966; Signor, 1968*a*). Thus prophage insertion in *att* B.B'-deleted hosts may occur most frequently at sites where the nucleotide sequence closely resembles that of *att* B.B'. (This point will be taken up again in the Discussion.) It is important to mention, however, that there are secondary insertion sites which are rarely utilized and are thus not detected by selection for λ-immune cells *per se*. This is shown by the finding that a new secondary site of λ insertion could be detected by selecting for inactivation of a specific gene function. The gene chosen was *tsx*, since prophage insertion into this gene is expected to lead to the easily selectable T6^r phenotype (Lederberg, 1949; Beckwith, Signer & Epstein, 1966). We infected an *att* B.B'-deleted host with λ*cI857* as described (see Materials and Methods) and then diluted the infected cells into fresh medium to permit segregation of T6^r clones. After 5 to 7 doublings in liquid medium, the infected cells were spread on EMBO plates together with about 2×10^{10} T6 and about 2×10^9 λ*c*. Three T6^r λ-immune clones were purified by restreaking and studied further. After a heat-pulse (see Materials and Methods), two of these clones segregated cured cells which were also T6^s. We conclude that the T6^r phenotype of these two clones is a consequence of λ lysogeny. Most likely it results directly from prophage insertion into the *tsx* gene, the only gene known to be altered in T6^r mutants (see Taylor, 1970). Such insertion is rare because if λ-infected *att* B.B'-deleted cells are selected for T6-resistance and then tested for immunity, only about 2% prove to be immune to λ. Thus, the frequency of prophage insertion into the *tsx* gene is considerably smaller than the frequency of spontaneously occurring T6^r mutants. Although we have no direct evidence that prophage insertion into gene *tsx* is Int-promoted, we have shown that prophage excision from that site requires Int and Xis (see Results section (f) (iii)). Therefore, insertion into gene *tsx* may be fundamentally similar to insertion into more frequently utilized sites.

The location of the secondary attachment sites for λ phage, thus far determined, is summarized in Figure 3.

(f) *Other properties of the lysogens*

(i) *Polylysogeny*

Nine of 17 lysogens were resistant to λ*cIc17* and were therefore multiple (Table 7, column 3). The frequency of polylysogeny in normal hosts is 40% at a multiplicity of infection of 3, 35% at a multiplicity of infection of 10 and 57% at a multiplicity of infection of 40 (Freifelder & Kirshner, 1971). In several cases (for strains 4, 47, 58, 60, 66, 69, 72, 76 and 81), we were able to convert the polylysogens to single lysogens by a heat-pulse (see Methods and Materials).

The number of phage particles liberated after heat induction depended mainly on whether the lysogens were single or multiple; no single lysogen released more than about 3 phages per cell while multiple lysogens released 20 to 200 phage per cell (Table 7, column 6). We assume that efficient phage production by the polylysogens is a consequence of excision by end cutting (Gottesman & Yarmolinsky, 1968*b*; Mousset & Thomas, 1969). The less efficient phage release by the single lysogens presumably reflects a structural excision defect similar to but frequently less severe

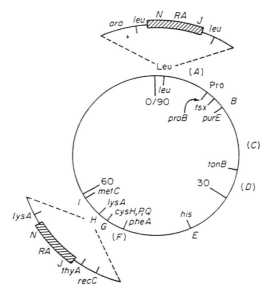

FIG. 3. Partial genetic map of *E. coli* (after Taylor, 1970) showing secondary λ attachment sites.

The position of the symbol for each lysogenic group represents the prophage map location for that group. Parentheses have been placed around groups whose locations are known mainly from time-of-entry data. These locations are less certain than those based on deletion mapping and transduction experiments (see text). The expanded segments show the orientation of the inserted prophages with respect to the bacterial chromosome.

than that seen in normally located λ*b*2 lysogens (Gottesman & Yarmolinsky, 1968*b*) (see below). The burst sizes of the single lysogens ranged from less than 0·01 to 3 phage per cell (Table 7).

(ii) *Heat-pulse curing*

Normal λ*cI*857 lysogens are efficiently cured by a brief heat pulse (Weisberg & Gallant, 1967; see Materials and Methods). The frequency of heat-pulse curing of a series of secondary-site lysogens is shown in Table 7, column 4. Although no secondary-site lysogen was cured with full efficiency, the curing frequencies covered a broad range: from below 10^{-5} (strain no. 73) to $8\cdot1\times10^{-2}$ (strain no. 10). The frequencies seem to be reasonably constant among lysogens of the same group. Likewise, the frequencies show no apparent dependence on the number of prophages carried by the lysogens. These findings suggest that the efficiency of curing at a given chromosomal site reflects the efficiency of recombination at the *att*'s which bracket the prophage(s).

(iii) *Requirement for Int and Xis*

Two phage functions, Int and Xis, are normally required for prophage excision (see the Introduction). These functions are also required for prophage excision from secondary sites in the three abnormal lysogens that were tested: strain no. 47 (group Pro), strain no. 10 (group G), and strain 363 (group Tsx; see Results section (e)). To show this, we superinfected the abnormal lysogens as well as a normal lysogen with λ*imm*[21], λ*imm*[21] *int*[-], or λ*imm*[21] *xis*[-] (Table 8). We found that mutation either in *int* or *xis* reduced the curing frequency about 25-fold in a normal lysogen and from 17 to more

TABLE 7

Other properties of the lysogens

Group	Strain no.	Sensitivity to $\lambda cIcl7$	Frequency of: Spontaneous curing	Heat-pulse curing	Superinfection curing	Burst size (phage/cell)
Leu	73	s†	$<10^{-5}$	$<3{\cdot}2\times10^{-6}$	$2{\cdot}0\times10^{-4}$	$<0{\cdot}01$
	75	s	$<10^{-5}$	$2{\cdot}5\times10^{-5}$	$1{\cdot}4\times10^{-4}$	$<0{\cdot}01$
Pro	47	r	$<10^{-5}$	$4{\cdot}7\times10^{-2}$	$1{\cdot}6\times10^{-1}$	52
A	69	r	63×10^{-5}	$6{\cdot}7\times10^{-3}$	$4{\cdot}8\times10^{-4}$	20
B	81	r	$<10^{-5}$	$1{\cdot}3\times10^{-3}$	$5{\cdot}0\times10^{-3}$	73
C	76	r	$<10^{-5}$	$2{\cdot}3\times10^{-4}$	$2{\cdot}1\times10^{-2}$	42
	80	s	$<10^{-5}$	$4{\cdot}3\times10^{-4}$	$2{\cdot}7\times10^{-2}$	$0{\cdot}12$
D	46	s	$<10^{-5}$	$4{\cdot}0\times10^{-3}$	$1{\cdot}8\times10^{-2}$	$0{\cdot}22$
E	60	r	$<10^{-5}$	$3{\cdot}7\times10^{-5}$	$6{\cdot}7\times10^{-3}$	62
	4	r	$<10^{-5}$	$9{\cdot}8\times10^{-5}$	$4{\cdot}7\times10^{-3}$	49
F	99	s	$<10^{-5}$	$4{\cdot}6\times10^{-3}$	$1{\cdot}0\times10^{-2}$	$0{\cdot}97$
G	10	s	34×10^{-5}	$8{\cdot}1\times10^{-2}$	$3{\cdot}6\times10^{-1}$	$0{\cdot}31$
	90	s	16×10^{-5}	$1{\cdot}1\times10^{-2}$	$2{\cdot}8\times10^{-1}$	$0{\cdot}07$
	62	s	$<10^{-5}$	$4{\cdot}4\times10^{-2}$	$5{\cdot}0\times10^{-1}$	$0{\cdot}39$
	66	r	$<10^{-5}$	$3{\cdot}9\times10^{-2}$	$4{\cdot}1\times10^{-1}$	91
H	72	r	19×10^{-5}	$6{\cdot}8\times10^{-3}$	$4{\cdot}0\times10^{-3}$	200
I	58	r	$<10^{-5}$	$2{\cdot}0\times10^{-3}$	$6{\cdot}4\times10^{-3}$	160
Normal lysogen		s	$4{\cdot}8\times10^{-5}$	$3{\cdot}2\times10^{-1}$	$5{\cdot}2\times10^{-1}$	110

Sensitivity to $\lambda cI90cl7$, curing frequencies and burst size were determined as described in Materials and Methods.

† s = sensitive; r = resistant.

TABLE 8

Requirement for Int and Xis

Host	Superinfecting phage λimm^{21}	$\lambda imm^{21}int^-$	$\lambda imm^{21}xis^-$	None
HfrH (λ)	$5{\cdot}4\times10^{-1}$	210×10^{-4}	220×10^{-4}	$0{\cdot}5\times10^{-5}$
47 (= Pro group)	$1{\cdot}9\times10^{-1}$	$4{\cdot}1\times10^{-4}$	$3{\cdot}6\times10^{-4}$	$0{\cdot}3\times10^{-5}$
10 (= G group)	$2{\cdot}0\times10^{-1}$	11×10^{-4}	$3{\cdot}4\times10^{-4}$	$3{\cdot}0\times10^{-5}$
363 (= Tsx group)	$0{\cdot}034\times10^{-1}$	$2{\cdot}0\times10^{-4}$	$1{\cdot}0\times10^{-4}$	$<0{\cdot}1\times10^{-5}$

Superinfection curing frequencies were determined as described in Materials and Methods. Lambda $imm^{21}sus\ int29$ was the int^- phage used for HfrH (λ), 47 and 10; $\lambda imm^{21}int6$ for 363. Lambda $imm^{21}\ susI2$ and $\lambda imm^{21}\ sus\ xis6$ was used for the experiments of columns 1 and 3, respectively.

than 500-fold in the abnormal lysogens. The residual levels of prophage excision observed after superinfection with the mutant phage lines may be a consequence of low level expression of the prophage int^+ gene (Kaiser & Masuda, 1970; Signer, 1970; Weisberg, 1970) or of Xis-independent modes of prophage excision (for example, insertion of the superinfecting $\lambda imm^{21} xis^-$ to form a tandem double lysogen followed by Xis-independent excision of the prophage). As we mentioned above (section (b) (i)), the cured cells deriving from the *pro* lysogen reverted to *pro*$^+$ presumably because Int-Xis-promoted prophage excision restored a functional *proB* gene. Likewise, the T6^r strain usually reverted to T6^s after superinfection curing.

We also measured the curing frequencies of other secondary-site lysogens after heteroimmune superinfection (Table 7, column 5). These curing frequencies were always less than that of a normal lysogen and ranged from about 0·1 to 200 times those found after a heat-pulse of the same strain. We are not certain why the frequencies of the two types of curing seem to vary independently. One possible explanation is that in some of the lysogens superinfection curing proceeds by substitution of the superinfecting phage for the prophage.

4. Discussion

Deletion of the normal bacterial attachment site for bacteriophage λ reduces but does not eliminate phage integration. The residual integration does not appear to be random, but instead occurs preferentially at certain loci in the host chromosome. We believe that these loci resemble normal attachment sites.

(1) The integration is *int*-dependent. Normally Int only promotes recombination at the phage and the bacterial attachment sites, or at hybrids of the two (Weil & Signer, 1968; Echols *et al.*, 1968; Gottesman & Yarmolinsky, 1968a). We have, in fact, shown by analysis of the prophage gene order in the secondary site lysogens that this phage integration had occurred by recombination at the normal attachment site on the phage chromosome (*att* P.P').

(2) Prophage excision from the secondary integration sites is *int*- and *xis*-dependent. This suggests that these sites do not contain the elements of the phage attachment site (P or P') as might be the case if the host carried a number of cryptic λ prophages. Xis is known to be required for the recombination involved in normal prophage excision (*att* B.P' $\times$ *att* P.B') but does not promote the recombinations *att* P.P $\times$ *att* P.P', *att* P.P' $\times$ *att* P.B' or *att* P.P' $\times$ *att* B.P' (Guarneros & Echols, 1970; Echols, 1970). If integration had occurred at loci containing phage *att* elements, excision would involve one of these latter recombinations and would therefore be *xis*-independent.

We have also demonstrated that insertion of λ into specific loci can be achieved by the appropriate selection technique. Thus, simultaneous selection for T6^r and λ-immunity after infection of an *att* B.B'-deleted host yields some lysogens in which the prophage has probably inserted into gene *tsx*. Similarly, insertion into a *ton* gene can be detected by selecting for resistance to phage ϕ80 and immunity to λ (unpublished experiments). As in the case of the *leu* and *pro* lysogens, cured cells reacquire the parental phenotype: T6 or ϕ80 sensitivity. The *tsx* and *ton* sites are utilized rarely since they cannot be detected by selecting for λ-immunity alone. We have not, as yet, demonstrated directly that insertion into these rarely utilized sites involves the Int-pathway. Nevertheless, it seems likely that this is the case because excision from the *tsx* (and also from the *ton*) site requires Int and Xis.

The curing frequencies of the secondary-site lysogens, listed in Table 7, vary over a 3000-fold range (see column 5). The frequencies of insertion in these experiments clearly are not free to vary to the same extent since integration at the poorest sites would not have been detected by selecting for λ-immunity alone. Although insertion and excision efficiencies need not, therefore, vary co-ordinately with changes in *att* B.B', no secondary site was as efficient for insertion or excision as the normal site. Thus, changes in this *att* affecting one reaction affect the other as well. It has previously been found that both insertion and excision defects can result from an alteration of *att* P.P' (Gottesman & Yarmolinsky, 1968*b*; Weisberg & Gottesman, 1969).

The yield of phage after induction of single secondary-site lysogens was always lower than phage yields from normal lysogens, and varied over a greater than 300-fold range (Table 7, column 7). Surprisingly, the phage yields of the single lysogens did not always vary in parallel with their curing frequencies (compare columns 5 and 7 of Table 7); both parameters should reflect the efficiency of recombination at the *att*'s which bracket the prophage. We tested the possibility that an alternate pathway of excision not involving the *att*'s could account for a high phage yield when the curing frequency is low, by determining the density of the phage in the lysate. We found the density of phage in lysates of strains no. 46, 80 and 99 to be that of wild-type λ, suggesting that they arise by recombination at the *att*'s. We do not have an alternative explanation.

We have shown that, in cases where prophage insertion has inactivated a bacterial gene (*pro*, *leu*, *tsx* and *ton*), excision can restore gene function. If these insertions occurred within nucleotide sequences which specify amino acids, we can conclude that excision probably restores the original sequence of nucleotides as well. However, we cannot exclude the possibility that these insertions have inactivated these genes indirectly as a polar effect of operon disruption. In this event, it is possible that gene function could be restored even if the original sequence of nucleotides were not. If we assume that the first model is correct, it is likely that a cycle of insertion and excision at *att* B.B' also preserves the original sequence of nucleotides. It is already known that such a cycle at *att* B.B' does not alter the function of that *att* (Signer, 1968).

Insertion of λ at secondary sites may be analogous to the Int-dependent formation of phage deletions (Parkinson, 1971; Davis & Parkinson, 1971). These authors observed that rare deletion mutants could be isolated from stocks of vegetatively grown *int*⁺ phage. The mutants were of two classes: in one the left end point of the deletion was within *att* and in the other, the right end point was within *att*. A simple model which accounts for Int-promoted deletion formation (Davis & Parkinson, 1971) is shown diagramatically in Figure 4. We assume that the bacterial chromosome, like the phage chromosome, has a number of sites which are secondary substrates for Int-promoted recombination. These are designated *att* Δ.Δ', where the nucleotide sequences represented by the Δ's are assumed to differ from the P and B counterparts. Recombination between or within phage chromosomes involving one of these sites and *att* P.P' creates deletion mutants which carry either *att* P.Δ' or *att* Δ.P'. In an analogous way, λ insertion into an *att* Δ.Δ' on the bacterial chromosome will generate a secondary-site prophage with *att* Δ.P' at its left-hand terminus and *att* P.Δ' at its right-hand terminus.

In support of this model, we have found that the *att* Δ.P' of λ*b*2 (Davis & Parkinson, 1971) resembles the left-hand attachment site of a secondary-site prophage: Xis is required for efficient Int-promoted recombination with the right-hand attachment site of secondary-site prophages (unpublished experiments). Further, the right-hand

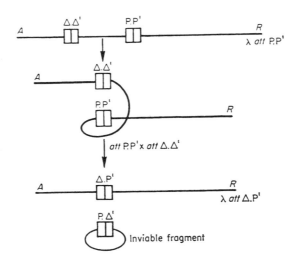

FIG. 4. Int-dependent formation of a phage deletion.

P.P′ stands for the normal λ phage attachment site. Δ.Δ′ stands for one of the postulated secondary Int-specific sites on the phage chromosome. Genes *A* and *R* are included as reference points. Deletions are generated by *att* P.P′ × *att* Δ.Δ′ recombination. The resulting deletion mutant carries *att* Δ.P′ instead of *att* P.P′.

attachment site of secondary-site prophages is not *att* P.B′, because λ*gal* (*att* B.P′) forms stable lysogens with high frequency in hosts carrying the former but not the latter attachment site (unpublished experiments, and Guerrini, 1969). We have argued above that the secondary *att* on the bacterial chromosome cannot contain either P or P′. Therefore, we conclude that the secondary attachment sites in the bacterial chromosome are either *att* B.Δ′ or *att* Δ.Δ′.

Rao & Smith (1968) working with phage P22 have described a phenomenon which is similar in some respects to λ insertion in *att* B.B′-deleted hosts. P22 integrates with low frequency into cells deleted for the normal P22 *att*. Both integration into and excision from these hosts requires Int. Unlike the analogous λ lysogens, all P22 lysogens showed very efficient excision.

The integration of phage P2 in a wild-type host also resembles the integration of λ into *att*-deleted cells. Integration, which requires the *int* gene of P2, occurs efficiently at two chromosomal sites and less frequently at a large number of others (see G. Bertani, 1968). Prophage excision is always inefficient in P2 lysogens because the P2 *int* gene is not expressed after induction (Bertani, 1968, 1970).

The *int*-gene products of λ, P22 and P2 have in common the ability to promote recombination at specific sites on DNA molecules (Weil & Signer, 1968; Echols *et al.*, 1968; Botstein & Matz, 1970; Lindahl, 1969). None of these systems appears to show absolute specificity, since all promote recombination at a number of different sites. In this context, it is relevant to note that a selection for point mutants of phage λ in *att* has yielded mutants with a reduced but still significant ability to participate in Int-promoted recombination (Shulman & Gottesman, 1971). This is consistent with the hypothesis that the Int pathway can still function after small changes in the nucleotide composition of *att*.

Finally, the use of secondary-site lysogens provides a method of obtaining novel transducing phages which can supplement those techniques already described (Gottesman & Beckwith, 1969; Press *et al.*, 1971). In addition these lysogens furnish us with a technique not previously available for deletion mapping of the bacterial chromosome.

We are indebted to Drs N. Kredich and M. Levinthal for enzyme assays, to Dr L. Caro for advice, and to Drs B. J. Bachmann, A. J. Clark, R. Curtiss III, R. C. Greene, M. Mortimer-Jones, and A. L. Taylor for sending us mutants.

REFERENCES

Adams, M. (1959). *Bacteriophages*. New York: Interscience.

Adhya, S., Cleary, P. & Campbell, A. (1968). *Proc. Nat. Acad. Sci., Wash.* **61**, 956.

Beckwith, J. R., Signer, E. R. & Epstein, W. (1966). *Cold Spr. Harb. Symp. Quant. Biol.* **31**, 393.

Bertani, G. (1968). *Molecular Genetics*, p. 180. Springer Verlag: Berlin, Heidelberg, New York.

Bertani, L. E. (1968). *Virology*, **36**, 87.

Bertani, L. E. (1970). *Proc. Nat. Acad. Sci., Wash.* **65**, 331.

Botstein, D. & Matz, M. J. (1970). *J. Mol. Biol.* **54**, 417.

Brinton, C. C. Jr., Gemski, P. & Carnahan, J. (1964). *Proc. Nat. Acad. Sci., Wash.* **52**, 776.

Campbell, A. (1962). *Advanc. Genetics*, **11**, 101.

Campbell, A. (1965). *Virology*, **27**, 340.

Curtiss, R. (1965). *J. Bact.* **89**, 28.

Davis, R. W. & Parkinson, J. S. (1971). *J. Mol. Biol.* **56**, 403.

Echols, H. (1970). *J. Mol. Biol.* **47**, 575.

Echols, H., Gingery, R. & Moore, L. (1968). *J. Mol. Biol.* **34**, 251.

Fischer-Fantuzzi, L. (1967). *Virology*, **32**, 18.

Franklin, N. C. (1971). Illegitimate Recombination in *The Bacteriophage Lambda*, ed. by A. D. Hershey, p. 175. New York: Cold Spring Harbor Press.

Franklin, N. C., Dove, W. F. & Yanofsky, C. (1965). *Biochem. Biophys. Res. Comm.* **18**, 910.

Freifelder, D. & Kirshner, I. (1971). *Virology*, **44**, 633.

Gingery, R. & Echols, H. (1967). *Proc. Nat. Acad. Sci., Wash.* **58**, 1507.

Gottesman, M. E. & Yarmolinsky, M. B. (1968*a*). *J. Mol. Biol.* **31**, 487.

Gottesman, M. E. & Yarmolinsky, M. B. (1968*b*). *Cold Spr. Harb. Symp. Quant. Biol.* **33**, 735.

Gottesman, S. & Beckwith, J. R. (1969). *J. Mol. Biol.* **44**, 117.

Gottesman, M. E. & Weisberg, R. A. (1971). Prophage Insertion and Excision. In *The Bacteriophage Lambda*, ed. by A. D. Hershey, p. 113. New York: Cold Spring Harbor Press.

Guarneros, G. & Echols, H. (1970). *J. Mol. Biol.* **47**, 565.

Guerrini, F. (1969). *J. Mol. Biol.* **46**, 523.

Jacob, F. & Wollman, E. (1954). *Ann. Inst. Pasteur*, **87**, 653.

Jacob, F. & Wollman, E. (1961). *Sexuality and the Genetics of Bacteria*, New York: Academic Press.

Kaiser, A. D. & Masuda, T. (1970). *J. Mol. Biol.* **47**, 557.

Kayajanian, G. & Campbell, A. (1966). *Virology*, **30**, 482.

Kellenberger, G., Zichichi, M. L. & Weigle, J. (1961). *J. Mol. Biol.* **3**, 39.

Kessler, D. P. & Englesberg, E. (1969). *J. Bact.* **98**, 1159.

Lederberg, J. (1949). *Proc. Nat. Acad. Sci., Wash.* **35**, 178.

Liedke-Kulke, M. & Kaiser, A. (1967). *Virology*, **32**, 465.

Lindahl, G. (1969). *Virology*, **39**, 861.

Low, B. (1968). *Proc. Nat. Acad. Sci., Wash.* **60**, 160.

Mousset, S. & Thomas, R. (1969). *Nature*, **221**, 241.

Neubauer, Z. & Calef, E. (1970). *J. Mol. Biol.* **51**, 1.

Parkinson, J. S. (1971). *J. Mol. Biol.* **56**, 385.

Parkinson, J. S. & Huskey, R. J. (1971). *J. Mol. Biol.* **56**, 369.

Press, R., Glansdorff, N., Miner, P., DeVries, J., Kadner, R. & Maas, W. K. (1971). *Proc. Nat. Acad. Sci., Wash.* **68**, 795.

Rao, R. N. & Smith, H. O. (1968). *Virology*, **36**, 328.

Rothman, J. (1965). *J. Mol. Biol.* **12**, 892.

Shapiro, J. & Adhya, S. (1969). *Genetics*, **62**, 249.

Shulman, M. & Gottesman, M. E. (1971). In *The Bacteriophage Lambda*, ed. by A. D. Hershey, p. 477. New York: Cold Spring Harbor Press.

Signer, E. R. (1968*a*). *Ann. Rev. Microbiol.* **22**, 451.

Signer, E. R. (1968*b*). *Cold Spr. Harb. Symp. Quant. Biol.* **33**, 754.

Signer, E. R. (1970). *Viroloqy*, **40**, 624.

Signer, E. R. & Beckwith, J. R. (1966). *J. Mol. Biol.* **22**, 33.

Smith, D. A. & Childs, J. D. (1966). *Heredity*, **21**, 265.

Sussman, R. & Jacob, F. (1962). *C. R. Acad. Sci., Paris*, **254**, 1517.

Taylor, A. L. (1970). *Bact. Rev.* **34**, 155.

Weil, J. & Signer, E. R. (1968). *J. Mol. Biol.* **34**, 273.

Weisberg, R. A. & Gallant, J. A. (1967). *J. Mol. Biol.* **25**, 537.

Weisberg, R. A. & Gottesman, M. E. (1969). *J. Mol. Biol.* **46**, 565.

Weisberg, R. A. (1970). *Virology*, **41**, 195.

Yarmolinsky, M. B. (1971). Making and Joining DNA Ends. In *The Bacteriophage Lambda*, ed. by A. D. Hershey, p. 97. New York: Cold Spring Harbor Press.

Zissler, J. (1967). *Virology*, **31**, 189.

Unit 7 / In Vivo Genetic Engineering

Beckwith and Signer 1966

1. Explain the difference between specialized and generalized transduction.

2. Describe the steps used to isolate the strain EC15.

3. Why were φ80*vir* and colicin V and B used to select for T1rec mutants, and how do these lysates select for T1rec mutants?

4. Describe the properties of strains EC8 and EC15.

5. Describe the steps in making a φ80d*lac* phage after the *lac* region has been transposed near the φ80 attachment site.

6. Since EC15 has the F'*lac* integrated into the T1*rec* locus, how could the authors infect EC15 with φ80 (see Question 5) to create a lysogen? The T1*rec* (*tonB*) locus is required for φ80 infection. (The answer to this is not actually given in the paper. See if you can work out a method for doing this. There are several possible ways.)

7. Explain Table 2 on page 245.

8. What were the experiments reported in Table 3 on page 246 trying to show?

9. How were φ80d*lacZ*+*Y*− phage obtained?

10. Explain Figure 3 on page 247.

11. Explain Table 4 and Figure 5 on page 249.

Beckwith et al. 1966

12. How were fusions of the *lac* and *trp* (previously called *try*) operons isolated?

13. What are the properties of the *trp* (*try*)-*lac* fusions?

Shimada et al. 1972

14. Describe the normal integration process of phage λ. Which genes and DNA segments are required?

15. How are the requirements for excision different from those for integration?

16. How did the authors isolate lysogens with λ integrated at different sites?

17. Compare the frequency of λ integration at the normal attachment site with that at secondary sites.

18. Is integration into secondary sites dependent on *int*? How do we know?

19. Explain auxotrophic lysogens and the experiments that characterized them.

20. How were most of the prophage mapped? Describe these experiments in detail.

21. Explain how deletion mapping helps in finding prophage integration sites.

22. How was prophage gene order determined?

23. Describe how new transducing phage were obtained. Compare the strategy of Shimada et al. with that described by Beckwith and Signer.

24. What is the distribution of prophage among secondary sites?

25. How often did multiple lysogens occur?

Unit 8

Structure-Function Relationships in Proteins

The analysis of protein structure by Max Perutz and his colleagues in the mid-1960s represents one of the landmarks in molecular genetics. We can categorize this work as molecular genetics because the study by Perutz and Lehmann, "Molecular Pathology of Human Haemoglobin," relies on the use of many different hemoglobin variants found in the population. Although this paper appeared in 1968, if it were first published today it would still be regarded as a brilliant and contemporary piece of work. In this unit, we will focus on two complementary studies. The first, by Perutz et al., compares the structures of hemoglobins and myoglobins from different species. The second, referred to above, examines hemoglobin variants. Together, the information revealed by these two analyses provides powerful insights into the structure–function relationships in globular proteins.

Max Perutz

Max Perutz was born in 1914 in Vienna. As a student, he was trained in organic chemistry and worked on the structure of alkaloids in a classic Austrian laboratory. He found alkaloids boring and thought that biochemistry was somewhat backward in Vienna. When in 1934, at the age of 20, he attended a lecture on biological compounds, he realized that was where his interests lay. His goal was to go to Cambridge to study the structure of vitamins. When he arrived there in 1936, it was to work in Bernal's laboratory, which was pioneering the use of X-ray crystallography. The following year, he started to work on hemoglobin and succeeded in obtaining high-quality crystals of horse hemoglobin. One should appreciate that at this point in time, one of the great questions in the field was the structure of proteins. The next year, the Nazis invaded his native Austria.

After the Germans invaded the low countries in the spring of 1940, the English, panicked about a possible invasion of their shores, rounded up and interned all aliens of German, Austrian, and Italian descent living south of a certain line, an area which included Cambridge. This mindless persecution of refugees, many of whom were Jews who had fled Hitler's Germany, was something akin to the internment of Japanese Americans in California by the United States. Max Perutz was caught up in this web. In his own words, "It was a cloudless Sunday morning in May of 1940. The policeman who came to arrest me said that I would be gone for only a few days, but I packed for a long journey. I said good-bye to my parents."

After being shuffled from one camp to another, he was interned on the Isle of Man, in the Irish Sea, and then transported to Canada in July, where he was confined in the Citadel, high above Quebec, along with several hundred other prisoners.

The conditions aboard the transport ship were terrible. Ironically, a group of German prisoners of war were transported in a different section of the same ship and they received far better treatment and rations than the internees. It was a harrowing experience, particularly considering that a sister troop ship had been sunk the week before with the loss of 600 internees. Perutz was embittered. "Having first been rejected as a Jew by my native Austria, which I loved, I now found myself rejected as a German by my adopted country."

When Perutz realized how many other scientists were also interned with him, he organized a sort of camp "University" in which different "faculty" members gave lectures in their favorite disciplines. Several of his teaching staff became famous. Hermann Bondi lectured on mathematics. He later was knighted and helped formulate one of the leading cosmological theories of the time, the steady-state theory of the creation of the universe. Klaus Fuchs lectured on theoretical physics. He subsequently worked on the Manhattan Project and created a sensation in 1950 when he confessed to being a Russian spy.

After almost six months in Canada, Perutz was allowed to return to England. However, in 1942, he was enlisted by the British government on a secret project code-named "Habakkuk." Initially, Perutz was not even informed of the goal of the project, which involved producing reinforced ice by mixing small quantities of wood pulp with water prior to freezing. Perutz had taken part in an expedition to the Swiss Alps in 1938 to study aspects of glacier formation, and this "expertise" later attracted sponsors of Project Habakkuk to him. As it turned out, the goal of the project was to build an island of ice in the mid-Atlantic to serve as a landing and refueling area for planes enroute from the U.S. to

England. The project was championed by none other than Louis Mountbatten, then Chief of Combined Operations. Some aspects of the project seemed like science fiction. For example, the final designs gave the "bergship," as it was called, a displacement of 2.2 million tons, or 26 times that of the Queen Elizabeth, which was then the largest ship afloat. Turboelectric steam generators were to supply 33,000 horse power to 26 electric motors! The civilian originator of the project had even more ludicrous ideas, such as using the floating ice stations to attack enemy ports, using massive blasts of supercooled water to petrify enemy ships, and building a gigantic tube from Burma into China to allow troops to be jettisoned in by compressed air. The project was presented to Roosevelt and Churchill at a summit meeting in Quebec in 1943 and it was given the highest priority. The planning center of the project was shifted to Washington. Interestingly, when Perutz applied for a visa at the U.S. embassy in London to join the British team, he was denied entry into the U.S. because he had been classified an enemy alien. So the British, who had initially interned him, now issued him a British passport within one day! After several months in limbo, it was realized that the project was technically not feasible. In addition, the main supporter of the project, Mountbatten, had left combined operations and had become chief of the Allied forces in Southeast Asia. So, finally, Perutz returned to research in Cambridge in 1944.

Max Perutz has spent more than 50 years studying the intricacies of the hemoglobin molecule and of similar proteins. His appreciation for the fine-tuned aspects of enzyme structure–function relationships are best-expressed in his own words: "Evolution is a brilliant chemist." Perutz spent many years as director of the MRC Unit for Molecular Biology in Cambridge and has received many honors, including the Royal Medal of the Royal Society, the Copley Medal of the Royal Society, the Companion of Honour, and the Order of Merit. In 1962, he received the Nobel prize in Chemistry.

STUDIES OF HEMOGLOBIN

Hemoglobin (Hb) carries O_2 from arteries to tissues and helps carry back CO_2. There are 280 million Hb molecules in one red blood cell. Each molecule contains 10,000 atoms. When Perutz began working on hemoglobin, the largest molecule whose structure had been determined by X-ray crystallography contained only 58 atoms. Hemoglobin is composed of four subunits, consisting of two copies of an α chain and two copies of a β chain. The oxygen is carried by the **heme prosthetic group,** which is bound to the protein via an iron atom. In this way, Hb increases the oxygen-carrying capacity of blood 70-fold. Each iron atom takes up one O_2 molecule in a reaction that is reversible as a function of the oxygen pressure. The iron atom must be in the ferrous, Fe^{++}, state to bind O_2.

Let's look at the paper by Perutz et al. on the "Structure and Function of Haemoglobin." Here, the authors compared the structures of hemoglobins and myoglobins from different vertebrates. The question they wanted to ask arose from the fact that the basic configuration of the polypeptide chain was identical in all of the myoglobins and hemoglobins analyzed, even though the amino acid sequence was not the same. Therefore, what aspects of the amino acid sequence were responsible for maintaining this very similar structure? In other words, what features of the sequence did each of these proteins have in common and which ones were important in determining the ultimate three-dimensional structure? Interestingly, of the 140 sites in a single globin chain, only 9 sites are **invariant,** or occupied by the same residue in each case. Clearly, these 9 sites are not sufficient to determine the structure for the entire chain. The authors found that the most important feature was a set of sites at which only nonpolar residues were found. Most of these sites are in the interior of the protein. If we look at Table 4 on page 295, it can be seen that there are 33 sites that are completely buried, in that they have no contact with water. All but three of these sites (B9, C4, and G16) are occupied by nonpolar residues, which are probably hydrogen-bonded internally. However, in many cases, a variety of different nonpolar residues are allowed. For example, in Table 4 look at H8 at which Leu, Phe, Met, Trp, and Tyr have been found. However, if we look at sites that are at the surface or in surface crevices, we find that only 10 of 44 remain consistently nonpolar. Moreover, 7 of these 10 have special functions. Thus, most of the surface residues can be freely exchanged for both polar and nonpolar amino acids. For example, look at positions A7, A9, and A13 in Table 5 on page 296, where 8, 7, and 6 different residues, respectively, have been found. Although several residues had been thought to be antihelical, only proline was found to limit the length of helices, and this was much more prominent in hemoglobin than in myoglobin. Table 6 on page 297 summarizes all of the replacement data of sperm whale myoglobin based on the sequences of different myoglobins and hemoglobins.

The main finding of the Perutz et al. paper is best expressed in the authors' own words: "The most striking feature common to all globin chains is the almost complete exclusion of polar residues from interior sites." The results suggest that the pattern of nonpolar side chains is the crucial determinant of the configuration of the polypeptide chain. Interestingly, the authors predicted the value of future hydropathy plots when they stated, "Proteins of similar structure might be recognized by the pattern of consistently nonpolar side chains which their sequences have in common." In addition, they could project the basic findings for mutational studies, since they postulated that replacing an interior nonpolar residue with a polar one would lead to a destruction of function.

In their paper on the "Molecular Pathology of Human Haemoglobin," Perutz and Lehmann present a wonderful catalog of altered hemoglobins detected either by random electrophoretic screening of the population or by examining the hemoglobins from patients with clinical symptoms. They then illustrated the positions of the altered residues in stereoscopic diagrams. The results confirm the conclusions drawn from the previous study. Thus, many of the sites at which only nonpolar residues occur are at contact points with the heme group. Mutations that weaken this contact would be expected to lead to impairment of function and to severe anemia. This is indeed the case for a number of altered hemoglobins, including the following:

- **Hb Torino:** The Phe to Val change results in the removal of two —CH groups that touch the heme molecule. This leaves a gap that makes the protein unstable, resulting in inclusion body anemia.

- **Hb Sydney** and **Hb Santa Ana:** The Val to Ala and Leu to Pro changes result in the removal of two methyl groups that are normally in contact with heme, which causes it to drop out, resulting in hemolytic anemia.

- **Hb Hammersmith:** The Phe to Ser change loses two —CH groups and introduces the polar hydroxyl group of serine into the interior. Water enters the pocket and the heme group drops out. This results in a severe inclusion body anemia and cyanosis.

- **Hb M Milwaukee:** Here, an internal valine is replaced by glutamic acid. The carboxyl group forms an ionic link with the iron atom, stabilizing it in the ferric form, which leads to cyanosis and methemoglobin anemia. As mentioned above, it is crucial to keep the iron atom in the ferrous state to allow the reversible association with oxygen.

The importance of maintaining the nonpolar environment in the interior of the protein is evidenced by Hb Wien, in which an internal polar group is introduced via a Tyr to Asp change. To accommodate this, the protein undergoes a large conformational change to create an extra positive charge internally, which neutralizes the negative charge. The defective protein results in hemolytic anemia even in heterozygotes.

CONCLUSIONS

The interior of a globular protein is made up almost exclusively of nonpolar amino acids. The positions of the critical nonpolar residues that form the internal core are instrumental in determining the basic configuration of the polypeptide chain. Some interior substitutions of other nonpolar residues are permitted, but substituting a polar residue for a nonpolar residue in the interior of the protein will destabilize the structure. Polar and nonpolar residues on the exterior of the protein can often be freely substituted without affecting the activity or stability of the protein, unless they involve sites that are involved in intersubunit contacts or in ligand binding sites, for example, the catalytic center. The latter site is often in a crevice of the protein. Proline is an exception, since it breaks up α-helical regions and can destabilize the protein when introduced at certain positions even on the exterior of the protein.

Structure and Function of Haemoglobin

II. Some Relations between Polypeptide Chain Configuration and Amino Acid Sequence

M. F. Perutz, J. C. Kendrew and H. C. Watson

Medical Research Council Laboratory of Molecular Biology
Hills Road, Cambridge, England

(*Received 18 June 1965*)

X-Ray data suggest that the globin chain has the same configuration in the myoglobins and haemoglobins of all vertebrates. Sequence data, on the other hand, show that only 9 out of more than 140 sites are occupied by the same amino acid residue in all the globin chains analysed so far. The different globins do not have any marked pattern of ionized or of polar residues in common. The most prominent common feature is the almost total exclusion of polar residues from the interior of the globin chains; this expresses itself in a pattern of 30 sites where only non-polar residues occur. Along α-helical segments these invariant non-polar sites tend to repeat on the average at regular intervals of about 3·6 residues, making the interior face of the helix non-polar.

At most sites at the surface or in surface crevices, on the other hand, replacements of many different kinds seem to occur without affecting the tertiary structure: these include replacement of non-polar by polar residues and *vice versa*.

Prolines are confined to the ends of helices or to non-helical regions; otherwise their incidence in the globins of different species is largely random. If all the proline sites observed are plotted along the sequence, they are seen to place limits on the possible lengths of helical regions. In many instances, serine, threonine, aspartic acid or asparagine occupies the first site at the amino end of the helix, followed by a proline at the second site.

In a protein of unknown structure, a regular periodicity of invariant non-polar sites might serve to recognize helical regions, and the incidence of prolines to define their lengths. A common pattern of non-polar sites might also help to identify structurally similar proteins with different enzymic function.

1. Introduction

With minor variations, the configuration of the polypeptide chain first discovered in sperm whale myoglobin (Bodo, Dintzis, Kendrew & Wyckoff, 1959; Kendrew *et al.*, 1960) is probably characteristic of the myoglobins and haemoglobins of all vertebrates (Kendrew, 1963; Perutz, 1963). Both genetic and physico-chemical evidence shows that the configuration of myoglobin and other proteins is not determined by an outside template, but is taken up spontaneously as the most stable configuration for the given amino acid sequence (Harrison & Blout, 1965; for other references, see Perutz, 1962). It seemed of interest, therefore, to ask what features the amino acid sequences of different types of globin chain have in common and which of these features might be important in determining the secondary and tertiary structures. Identical residues occupying structurally corresponding sites in all globin chains number only 9—too few to be decisive in determining the structure. The most prominent common feature is found to be a pattern of sites where only non-polar residues occur. Most of these are located in the interior of the globin chain, away from contact with water. As a result, long α-helical segments exhibit a regular periodicity of invariant non-polar sites. Prolines are restricted to sites at the ends of helices or to non-helical regions. With one exception, the occurrence of prolines at various corners or non-helical regions of various globins is random. However, if the total incidence of prolines is plotted along the chain, it is found to define the lengths of nearly all the helical segments.

Table 1 lists the species of myoglobin and haemoglobin the amino acid sequences of which are either fully or partially known. The most recently published summary of sequences is in a review by Braunitzer, Hilse, Rudloff & Hilschmann (1964).

TABLE 1

Sources of information on amino acid sequences in myoglobin and haemoglobin

Myoglobin	Sperm whale	C	Edmundson, 1965
	Human	P	Hill, 1965 (U)
Haemoglobin	Human α and β	C	Braunitzer *et al.*, 1961
			Konigsberg, Guidotti & Hill, 1961
			Goldstein, Konigsberg & Hill, 1963
	γ	C	Schroeder, Shelton, Shelton & Cormick, 1963
	Lemur fulvus α and β	C	Hill, 1965 (U)
	Propithecus verreauxi	P	Hill (1965)
	Horse α	C	Braunitzer & Matsuda, 1961
	β	P	Smith, 1964
	Pig α and β	P	Braunitzer & Köhler, 1965 (U)
	Rabbit α and β	P	Naughton & Dintzis, 1962
			Braunitzer & Schrank, 1965 (U)
	Lama α and β	P	Braunitzer & Hilschmann, 1965 (U)
	Carp α	P	Braunitzer & Hilse, 1965 (U)
	Lamprey	P	Braunitzer & Rudloff, 1965 (U)

C, Complete sequence; P, partial sequences of tryptic and other peptides; U, unpublished data communicated to the authors.

In cases where only the composition of tryptic peptides but not the sequence of residues along them was known, a tentative sequence was drawn up by using homologies with the most closely related chain of known sequence. This led to uncertainties in some of the very long peptides, but these hardly affect the present argument. The notation of sites adopted here follows that of Watson & Kendrew (1961) given in the preceding paper (Perutz, 1965†, Fig. 1 and Table 1). Sequential residue numbers of any site can be found by reference to Table 1 in paper I of this series, p. 650.

2. Invariant Residues (Table 2)

Residues are defined here as invariant when they occur at structurally identical sites in all the normal myoglobins and haemoglobins so far investigated. Abnormal haemoglobins have been excluded, because some of their abnormalities interfere with the oxygen-combining function, so that the protein can no longer be regarded as a haemoglobin.

† Perutz (1965) will be referred to as paper I of this series.

It might be thought that polypeptide chains which adopt a similar tertiary structure have many invariant residues in common. This holds for the family of cytochrome c's, in which half the residues are invariant (Margoliash & Smith, 1964), but not for the family of globins, where the number of invariant residues has now shrunk to 9. These include the two haem-linked histidine residues E7 and F8. Two other residues which may form an essential part of the environment of the haem group are phenylalanine CD1 (see paper I, Fig. 6(b)) and leucine F4. In addition, there are four residues which

TABLE 2

The 9 invariant residues

B 6	Gly	Close contact with Gly or Ala E8
C 2	Pro	BC corner
C 4	Thr	BC corner and haem contact
CD 1	Phe	Haem contact
E 7	His	Distal haem link; absent in Hb of marine worm? (*Aplysia*†)
F 4	Leu	Haem contact
F 8	His	Haem linked
H10*	Lys	External. No visible function
H23*	Tyr	Internal H-bond with CO in FG corner

Present in primates, horse, pig, rabbit, lama, carp α and lamprey haemoglobins and sperm whale and human myoglobin, except:
A14, B6, GH5 and H10* unknown in lamprey. GH5 and H10* unknown in carp α and rabbit β.

The numbering of the residues in helix H adopted here differs from that used in earlier publications: Hn (Watson & Kendrew, 1961) = H(n + 1)* (present paper).

† Wittenberg, Briehl & Wittenberg (1965).

may be important in determining the tertiary structure of the polypeptide chain: glycine B6 brings helix B into close contact with helix E at the site of glycine or alanine E8; proline C2 and threonine C4 form the BC corner; and tyrosine H23* forms an internal hydrogen bond with the α-carbonyl of residue FG5. Lysine H10* is external and has no obvious function. (For a discussion of these and other side-chains, see Watson & Kendrew, 1961; Kendrew, 1962.)

This list clearly shows that the invariant residues can have only a limited role in determining the secondary and tertiary structure of the globin chain.

3. Common Residues ionized at Neutral pH (Table 3)

It might be thought that the pattern of electric charges formed by the ionized side-chains helps to determine the structure of the globin chain. However, Table 3 shows only three sites which consistently carry basic side-chains ionized at neutral pH (histidines are not counted, since they are not necessarily ionized at neutral pH). Only two sites carry acidic side-chains and only one carries either acidic or basic ones. Seeing that the total number of ionized groups on the surface of sperm whale myoglobin is 43, it seems unlikely that the few sites listed in Table 3 are of decisive importance.

TABLE 3

Common residues ionized at neutral pH

Consistently basic		Consistently acidic	
		A4	Asp, Glu
B12	Arg, Lys	B8	Asp, Glu
E 5	Arg, Lys		
H10*	Lys	*Consistently either*	
		acidic or basic	
(G19	Arg, Lys, His)	G6	Arg, Lys, Glu
(H24*	Arg, Lys, His)		

Present in primates, horse, pig, rabbit, lama and lamprey haemoglobin; also sperm whale and human myoglobin, except:

residues A14, B8 and H10* unknown in lamprey; H24* absent in lamprey.

4. Other Polar Residues

How many sites are consistently occupied by polar, though not necessarily by ionized, residues? There are only 17 such sites and 11 of these are connected with special functions: two haem-linked histidines, two lysines probably linked to the propionic acid side-chains of haem in haemoglobin, and seven polar residues occupying positions one and four in α-helices, as described below. Among the remaining six invariably polar sites no special function can be discerned at present.

5. Anti-helical Residues

If residues forming part of an α-helix are defined as having their α-carbonyl, or their α-imino groups or both, hydrogen-bonded within the helix, then model building shows that proline can occur in sites 1, 2, 3 or $n + 1$ of an α-helix containing n residues. Prolines are in fact observed in all these positions. A combination frequently found in haemoglobin consists of serine, threonine, aspartic acid or asparagine in position 1 followed by proline in position 2 of the helix. Kendrew & Watson have shown that in this situation the oxygen of the OH or COO$^-$ group can be hydrogen-bonded to the α-NH group of residue 4 of the helix. An alternative combination, first found by Kendrew & Watson in the BC corner of myoglobin, consists of proline in position 2 with an internally hydrogen-bonded threonine in position 4. In one instance prolines actually occur in both positions 2 and 3 of an α-helix (helix Hβ of human haemoglobin).

Synthetic polypeptides consisting of serine, threonine, valine, isoleucine or cysteine do not form α-helices, but random coils or β-structures (Blout, de Lozé, Bloom & Fasmann, 1960; Blout, 1962). It might be expected, therefore, that these residues occur preferentially in non-helical regions. In fact, however, all the cysteines in haemoglobin lie in α-helical regions, and the other so-called "anti-helical" residues are found equally in helical and non-helical ones. The non-helical region EF in sperm whale myoglobin contains no anti-helical residue, and the neighbourhood of the AB corner in the α-chain of horse haemoglobin only one valine. On the other hand, it is true that, in sperm whale myoglobin, helix E is bent at a position where four out of five residues are of the anti-helical kind. Nevertheless, the absence of any consistent correlation implies that there must be other features of the amino acid sequence not yet considered which are powerful in determining the secondary structure.

6. Non-polar Residues (Tables 4 and 5)

These include glycine, alanine, valine, leucine, isoleucine, phenylalanine, proline, cysteine and methionine. In addition, the behaviour of tryptophan and tyrosine seems to be dominated by their non-polar aromatic rings rather than their polar groups, at least in the proteins considered here, and they will be classified as non-polar (Tanford, 1962).

TABLE 4

Replacements among the 33 internal sites

Residue	Observed	Residue	Observed
A 8	Val, Ile, Leu	E 15	Val, Leu, Phe
11	Ala, Val, Leu	18	Gly, Ala, Ile
12	Trp, Phe	19	Val, Leu, Ile
15	Val, Leu, Ile		
		F 1	Leu, Ile, Phe, Tyr
B 6	Gly		
9	Ala, Ile, *Ser, Thr*	FG 5	Val, Ile
10	Leu, Ile		
13	Met, Leu, Phe	G 5	Phe, Leu
14	Leu, Phe	8	Val, Leu, Ile
		11	Ala, Val, Cys.H
C 4	*Thr*	12	Leu, Ile
		16	Leu, Val, Ser
CD 1	Phe		
4	Phe, Trp		
		H 8*	Leu, Phe, Met, Trp, Tyr
D 5	Val, Leu, Ile, Met	11*	Ala, Val, Phe
		12*	Val, Leu, Phe
E 4	Val, Leu, Phe	15*	Val, Phe
8	Gly, Ala	19*	Leu, Ile, Met
11	Val, Ile	23*	Tyr
12	Ala, Leu, Ile		

Invariably non-polar, except where indicated, in primates, horse, pig, rabbit, lama, carp α and lamprey haemoglobin; sperm whale and human myoglobin.

Not yet known:
A11, 15; B6, 9, 10; F1; G8, 11, 12, 16; GH5; H8*, 11*, 12*, 15* in lamprey (15 residues).
A8; G8, 11, 12, 16; GH5; H8*, 11*, 12*, 15*, 19* in carp α (11 residues).
G8, 11, 12, 16; GH5; H8*, 11*, 12*, 15*, 19* in rabbit β (10 residues).
H11*, 12*, 15*, 19* in lama α.
H15*, 19* in pig α.
G5, 11, 12, 16 in human myoglobin.
D5 absent in α-chains.

Examination of the models of myoglobin and haemoglobin shows that there are 33 sites which are interior in the sense that they are cut off from contact with the surrounding water. These are listed in Table 4. With three exceptions, they are invariably occupied by non-polar residues. The exceptions are threonine C4 mentioned previously, serine and threonine B9, and serine G16, which are probably also hydrogen-bonded internally. A wide variety of replacements seems to be open among the non-polar residues at many of the sites.

TABLE 5

Replacements among 44 non-polar residues at the surface or in surface crevices

Residue	Observed	Residue	Observed
NA 2	Gly, Val, Asp, His, Leu	EF 3	Gly, Asp
3	Leu, Phe	7	Gly, Ala, Asn, Lys
A 3	Gly, Ala, Asp, Glu	F 3	Ala, Ser, Thr, Asp, Gln, Lys, Pro
5	Trp, Lys, Asp	4	Leu
7	Gly, Ala, Leu, Thr, Asp, Asn, Lys, His	5	Ala, Ser
9	Gly, Leu, Thr, Asp, Asn, Lys, Arg	9	Ala, Cys.H
13	Gly, Ala, Ser, Thr, Asp, Lys	G 1	Asp, Pro
AB 1	Ala, Gly, Ser	2	Ile, Pro
		4	Tyr, Asn, Asp
B 2	Ala, Val, Glu	7	Leu, Ile, Phe
3	Gly, Ala, Asp, Glu, Lys	13	Ala, Val, Ile, Leu
4	Gly, Ala, Asp, Glu, Lys	15	Val, Thr, Glu
11	Gly, Ile, Glu	GH 2	Gly, Pro
C 2	Pro	3	Gly, Ala, Asp, Lys, His
5	Leu, Gln, Lys, Arg	5	Phe, Lys
		H 1*	Gly, Ser, Thr, Asp
CD 7	Leu, Ile, Met	2*	Ala, Pro
		4*	Val, Leu, Ala, Phe
D 3	Ala, Ser, Asp, Glu	6*	Gly, Ala
7	Gly, Ala, Lys	7*	Ala, Ser
		14*	Gly, Leu, Ser, Thr, Ala
E 9	Val, Ser, Glu, Lys	20*	Ala, Ser, Thr, Arg?
14	Gly, Ala, Ser, Glu, Asp	21*	Ala, Ser, His
16	Gly, Ser, Thr, Asp		
17	Ala, Leu, Asp, Asn, Glu, Lys		

All residues are exchanged for polar ones in one or other haemoglobin except:

NA 3 Surface crevice, holds NA segment in place.
C 2 At BC corner.
CD 7 Surface crevice, holds CD and D together.
F 4 Haem contact.
F 9 Reactive SH-group.
G 2 At FG corner.
G 7 Surface crevice.
G13 $\alpha-\beta$ contact.
H 4* Surface crevice.
H 6* Surface.

By constrast, there are only 10 sites at the surface or in surface crevices which remain consistently non-polar (Table 5). Seven of these non-polar residues have special functions. Sperm whale myoglobin contains 34 other non-polar residues at sites on or near the surface, but all these are replaced by polar residues in some of the other globin chains. The great variety of different residues which is permissible at many of the superficial sites is surprising.

Table 6 summarizes the replacements among the internal and superficial sites of sperm whale myoglobin observed in other globins.

TABLE 6

Summary of replacements of sperm whale myoglobin sites in different myoglobins and haemoglobins

		Site in sperm whale myoglobin			
		Polar		*Non-polar*	
(a)	33 internal sites	Threonine C4	1	Always non-polar	30
				Replaced by polar	2
					32
(b)	120 sites on surface or in surface crevices.	Haem-linked histidines	2	Always non-polar	
		Always basic	3	special function	7
		Always acidic	2	no visible function	3
		Always acidic or basic	1	Replaced by polar	34
		Always polar	17		
		Replaced by non-polar	45		
		Deleted	2	Deleted	4
			72		48
	Totals of (a) and (b)		73		80

Note: Replaced by polar, or non-polar, here means that such a replacement has been observed at least once.

7. Distinguishing Features of Sequences along Helical and Non-helical Regions

The only major consistent feature found here is the pattern of non-polar residues in the interior of the globin chains. In a long α-helical region, offering a regular alternation of external and internal sites, consistently non-polar residues at internal sites should recur on the average at intervals of about 3·6 residues. In Fig. 1 the secondary structure of the globin chain is summarized by representing the helical segments as sine waves and the non-helical ones as straight lines; the site of each residue is marked by a circle or cross. Black circles mark sites consistently occupied by non-polar residues, white circles those occupied by any kind of residue. Crosses mark the incidence of prolines or combinations of serines and threonines with prolines. The top of each sine wave points towards the inside of the globin chain or subunit, the bottom faces the surface.

A regular periodicity of sites occupied by non-polar residues is apparent along each of the longer α-helical regions A, B, E, G and H. There are three inconsistencies: the external sites G7, G13 and H6* are invariably non-polar; G13 probably because it lies at the αβ boundary in haemoglobin; G7 and H6* may prove to be not consistently non-polar. Segments G and H are those where least is known as yet about the sequences of many of the species included in this survey.

The structure of the globin chain is such that all non-helical regions lie at the surface, so that any of their side-chains could be exterior. Non-helical regions should therefore be

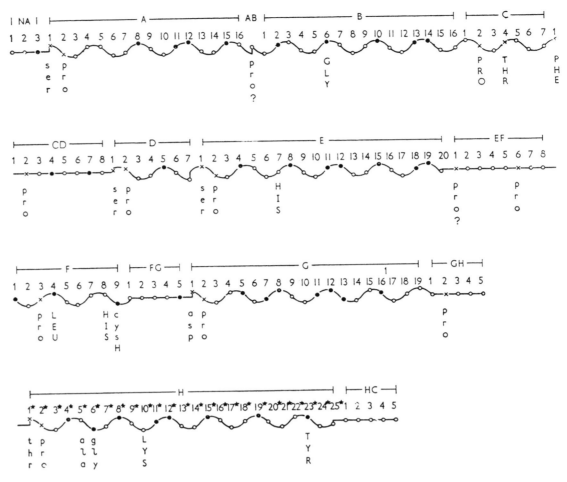

FIG. 1. Secondary structure of globin. α-Helical segments are represented as sine waves, non-helical ones as straight lines. Segments are marked as in paper I, Fig. 1 and Table 1. Black circles mark sites where only non-polar residues occur; crosses where prolines or combination of prolines with serine, threonine, aspartic acid or asparagine occur. All other sites are marked by blank circles. Residues in capital letters mark homologies, those in small letters mark other residues of special interest, such as the reactive cysteine of the β-chain which must be on the surface of the chain. Note that this diagram shows the total incidence of prolines in all species analysed so far. No single species contains prolines at all the points indicated here. Pro GH2 occurs in position $n + 1$ of helix G, since refinement of the structure of sperm whale myoglobin has shown GH1 to be the C-terminal residue of that helix. The sine waves are drawn so that the top of each wave points to the *inside* of the globin chain.

distinguished by the occasional occurrence of polar residues in all the sites. This is true of the regions EF and GH and, with one exception, of FG, but CD has two invariant non-polar sites at intervals of three; these are in fact connected by one helical turn of three residues.

With the exception of the C-termini of helices F and H, prolines mark the boundaries of all helical regions. The amino ends of six of the eight helical regions are exactly defined by the occurrence of serine, threonine, aspartic acid, or asparagine in position 1, followed by proline in position 2. It is interesting that the boundary between the helices A and B is the site of a phase shift of 90° in the regular periodicity of non-polar residues.

8. Discussion

The most striking feature common to all globin chains is the almost complete exclusion of polar residues from interior sites. This is a remarkable vindication of the predictions by Kauzmann (1959) discussed in paper I. By contrast, only a small minority of sites at or near the surface are occupied consistently by any particular type of residue, non-polar, acidic, basic or dipolar. Only 9 out of more than 140 sites are occupied by the same residue throughout the range of globins studied, and this list may well shrink further. Prolines play a prominent part in limiting the length of the helical regions in human haemoglobin, but a less important one in myoglobin. Other so-called anti-helical residues are randomly distributed over helical and non-helical regions. Some of the corners or points of transition from helical to non-helical regions are devoid of any residues specifically designed to terminate helices.

These findings suggest that the pattern of invariantly non-polar side-chains, together with the non-polar parts of the porphyrin ring, may be decisive in determining the configuration of the globin chain. Proteins of similar structure might be recognized by the pattern of consistently non-polar side-chains which their sequences have in common. Mutations which lead to the replacement of a non-polar by a polar residue at an interior site are probably lethal. It is significant that no such replacements have been observed in any of the abnormal human haemoglobins.

The only other protein system for which a comparable amount of chemical information has been collected is cytochrome c (Margoliash & Smith, 1964). Here, however, the situation is quite different. Among cytochrome c's of the mammalian type, half the residues are invariant. Among the variable sites a set of consistently non-polar ones is found, but a search for a regular periodicity in the incidence of such sites proved fruitless. It looks as though cytochrome c is devoid of long helical regions, which is consistent with the low helical content (27 to 39%) observed by optical methods (Urry & Doty, 1965).

We thank Dr G. Braunitzer and Dr R. L. Hill for letting us see the unpublished sequences of various myoglobins and haemoglobins, and for permission to use these data for Tables 2 to 6.

Note added in proof. Since this paper was written, Dr A. V. Guzzo, of the University of Chicago, has sent us a statistical analysis of the distribution of different amino-acid residues in the middle of helical regions, near the ends of helices and in non-helical regions in myoglobin and haemoglobin. His results suggest that the presence of histidine, glutamic acid or aspartic acid is a necessary, though not a sufficient, condition for the formation of corners or non-helical regions. We have had access to the amino-acid sequences of some species which were not available to Guzzo. Examination of these sequences confirms that histidine, glutamic acid or aspartic acid is indeed a constituent of every corner or of its immediate neighbourhood and of every non-helical region.

REFERENCES

Blout, E. R. (1962). In *Polyamino Acids, Polypeptides and Proteins*, ed. by M. A. Stahmann, p. 275. Madison, Wisconsin: University of Wisconsin Press.

Blout, E. R., de Lozé, C., Bloom, S. M. & Fasmann, G. D. (1960). *J. Amer. Chem. Soc.* **82**, 3787.

Bodo, G., Dintzis, H. M., Kendrew, J. C. & Wyckoff, H. W. (1959). *Proc. Roy. Soc.* A, **253**, 70.

Braunitzer, G., Gehring-Müller, R., Hilschmann, N., Hilse, K., Hobom, G., Rudloff, V. & Wittmann-Liebold, B. (1961). *Hoppe-Seyl. Z.* **325**, 283.

Braunitzer, G., Hilse, K., Rudloff, V. & Hilschmann, N. (1964). *Advanc. Protein Chem.* **19**, 1.

Braunitzer, G. & Matsuda, G. (1961). *Hoppe Seyl. Z.* **324**, 91.

Edmundson, A. B. (1965). *Nature*, **205**, 883.

Goldstein, J., Konigsberg, W. & Hill, R. J. (1963). *J. Biol. Chem.* **238**, 2016.

Harrison, S. C. & Blout, E. R. (1965). *J. Biol. Chem.* **240**, 299.

Kauzmann, W. (1959). *Advanc. Protein Chem.* **14**, 1.

Kendrew, J. C. (1962). *Brookhaven Symp. Biol.* **15**, 216.

Kendrew, J. C. (1963). *Science*, **139**, 1259.

Kendrew, J. C., Dickerson, R. E., Strandberg, B. E., Hart, R. G., Davies, D. R., Phillips, D. C. & Shore, V. C. (1960). *Nature*, **185**, 422.

Konigsberg, W., Guidotti, G. & Hill, R. J. (1961). *J. Biol. Chem.* **236**, PC 55.

Margoliash, E. & Smith, E. L. (1964). Rutgers Univ. Symposium on *Evolving Genes and Proteins*, ed. by H. Vogel, in the press.

Naughton, M. A. & Dintzis, H. M. (1962). *Proc. Nat. Acad. Sci., Wash.* **48**, 1822.

Perutz, M. F. (1962). In *Proteins and Nucleic Acids*, p. 51. Amsterdam: Elsevier.

Perutz, M. F. (1963). *Science*, **140**, 863.

Perutz, M. F. (1965). *J. Mol. Biol.* **13**, 646.

Schroeder, W. A., Shelton, J. R., Shelton, J. B. & Cormick, J. (1963). *Biochemistry*, **2**, 1353.

Smith, D. B. (1964). *Canad. J. Biochem.* **42**, 755.

Tanford, C. (1962). *J. Amer. Chem. Soc.* **84**, 4240.

Urry, D. W. & Doty, P. (1965). *J. Amer. Chem. Soc.* **87**, 2756.

Watson, H. C. & Kendrew, J. C. (1961). *Nature*, **190**, 663.

Wittenberg, B. A., Briehl, R. W. & Wittenberg, J. B. (1965). *Biochem. J.* **96**, 363.

Molecular Pathology of Human Haemoglobin

by

M. F. PERUTZ

MRC Laboratory of Molecular Biology,
Cambridge

H. LEHMANN

MRC Abnormal Haemoglobin Research Unit,
Department of Biochemistry,
University of Cambridge

The haemoglobin molecule is insensitive to replacements of most amino-acid residues on its surface, but extremely sensitive to even quite small alterations of internal non-polar contacts, especially those near the haems. Replacements at the contacts between α and β-subunits affect respiratory function.

THE screening of human blood samples in many parts of the world has led to the discovery of nearly a hundred different mutant haemoglobins[1,2]. The recent construction of an atomic model of the haemoglobin molecule based on an X-ray analysis of high resolution[3,4] opens the possibility of studying the stereochemical part played by the amino-acid residues which are replaced or deleted in each of these mutants. It may be objected that the model is of horse, not of human haemoglobin, but this should not matter, because the tertiary and quaternary structures of human and horse haemoglobin are indistinguishable at 5·5 Å resolution[5] and because most harmful replacements affect residues which are common to all mammalian haemoglobins of known sequence.

Comparison of the amino-acid sequences of the haemoglobins and myoglobins of different species shows that only seven out of a total of more than 140 sites are always occupied by the same residue. There is no common pattern of ionized or polar residues on the surface of the molecules, but a total exclusion of polar residues from the interior. This expresses itself in a pattern of more than thirty sites where only non-polar residues occur, suggesting that a mutation to a polar residue at any of these sites would make the tertiary structure unstable[6]. The α and β-chains of mammalian haemoglobins each have a pattern of sites which are invariably occupied by the same residues. These include nearly all haem contacts and most contacts between subunits. Mutations at these sites would be likely to affect respiratory function. These expectations are borne out by the results described here.

We have drawn up tables relating clinical symptoms and abnormal properties to the alteration in structure which each mutation is likely to produce, and have illustrated the relevant features of the haemoglobin molecule in a series of stereo-drawings.

We first noted the position of each mutant residue in the atomic model. If it was external and played no special part in the structure, we put it down as a harmless replacement. If it was in a surface crevice, or internal, we replaced the normal side chain in the model by the mutant one and noted the probable stereochemical consequences. The positions of most of the harmful mutations are illustrated in published stereo-drawings of the atomic model[4] and in the further drawings presented here. The drawings show the normal molecules; at this stage the alterations caused by the mutations can only be guessed. We also noted whether the altered residue was variable (V) or invariant (I) among the mammalian haemoglobins of known sequence and, if it was variable, whether variability was restricted to either polar (V_p) or non-polar (V_n) residues. Our notation of residues in the helical and non-helical segments is as in ref. 4.

Replacement of Residues in Contact with the Haem Groups (Table I and Figs. I and 2)

Replacements of non-polar contacts. Nearly all the sixty or so interatomic contacts between the haem groups and the globin are non-polar and invariant, suggesting that each of the contacts is essential for the functions of the haemoglobin molecule[4]. This expectation is borne out by the extreme sensitivity of the system to small stereochemical changes. For example, in haemoglobin Torino the replacement of phenylalanine CD1 by valine removes only two of the CH groups which normally touch the haem group, yet the resultant gap makes the entire α-subunit unstable. In haemoglobins Sydney and Santa Ana, the removal of two methyl groups normally in contact with the haem group actually causes it to drop out. Haemoglobin Hammersmith is a particularly severe lesion, because the removal of the two CH groups of phenylalanine CD1 is accompanied by the introduction of the polar hydroxyl group of serine; this probably facilitates the entry of water into the haem pocket which causes the haem group to drop out[21].

Haemoglobin M Milwaukee is an interesting case of an internal valine being replaced by glutamic acid, the carboxyl group of which is in a position to form an ionic link with the iron atom, thereby stabilizing it in the ferric form[22].

Replacement of histidines. Stabilization of the iron atom in the ferric form is the common feature of all haemoglobins M. In haemoglobins Boston and Saskatoon this is a result of the replacement of the distal histidine[22], and in haemoglobins Iwate and Hyde Park of the proximal histidine, by tyrosine. Insertion in the model of tyrosine in place of the distal histidine E7 shows that the phenolic oxygen comes to within 2–2·5 Å of the iron atom. The theoretical distance for an ionic link between ferric iron and oxygen is 2·04 Å, which suggests that such a link could be formed in haemoglobins Boston and Saskatoon. The short distance between the phenolic oxygen and the iron atom would leave no space for a ligand at the sixth coordination position of the iron atom. Combination of cyanide with the ferric form and of CO with the ferrous form (after reduction with dithionite) is nevertheless observed, but could take place only after the tyrosine has swung out of the way. In haemoglobins Iwate and Hyde Park the iron atoms are believed to be covalently linked to histidines E7 and to form ionic links with the phenolic oxygens of tyrosines F8; combination of the abnormal chains with ligands is not observed. The model shows that it would be more difficult for the tyrosines on the proximal side to swing out of the way in order to admit ligands. In haemoglobin Zürich reversible combination with oxygen occurs despite the replacement of the distal histidine by arginine. The arginine side chain is too big to be accommodated in the haem pocket; it must therefore protrude at the surface, leaving the haem pocket empty. This suggests that the presence of a basic residue on the distal side of the iron atom may not be necessary for reversible combination with oxygen; possibly it merely helps to keep the iron reduced.

Replacements at Contacts between Subunits

Residues at contacts between subunits are important because they may transmit the interactions on which the respiratory function of haemoglobin depends. Contacts between like subunits are tenuous and polar. Those between unlike ones are extensive and predominantly non-polar, and they are of two different kinds, named

$\alpha_1\beta_1$ and $\alpha_1\beta_2$ (Table 2 and Fig. 3 of ref. 4). In appropriate conditions the haemoglobin tetramer dissociates into dimers and also into free α- and β-chains. Chemical and crystallographic evidence suggests that dissociation into dimers takes place at the contacts $\alpha_1\beta_2$ and $\alpha_2\beta_1$, further splitting into free α- and β-chains at the contacts $\alpha_1\beta_1$ and $\alpha_2\beta_2$ (ref. 23).

The observed mutations all occur among residues which are invariant in mammalian haemoglobins and are therefore likely to be functionally important. Altered properties have been reported for seven of the twelve mutant haemoglobins listed in Table 2.

Contact $\alpha_1\beta_1$ (Figs. 4–7 of ref. 4). Haemoglobin E is an interesting case of an instability resulting from disturbance of the pattern of hydrogen bonds in the neighbourhood of the $\alpha_1\beta_1$ contact. It involves replacement of glutamic acid B8(26)β by lysine. Fig. 4 of ref. 4 shows that the glutamic acid lies in a strongly basic region and probably (in man) forms hydrogen bonds with histidines G18β and G19β (though the residue shown at G18β in the figure is arginine which replaces histidine in horse haemoglobin). There is also an arginine (B12β) which is not directly connected with the glutamic acid and which makes a hydrogen bond with the main chain carbonyl of phenylalanine GH5α. The replacement of the neutralizing carboxyl group by a positive charged amino group would disrupt the system of hydrogen bonds just described, which contributes to the stability of the contact. This explains the observed displacement of mutant β^E-chains by normal β^A-chains from $\alpha_2^A\beta_2^E$, and also suggests that haemoglobin E should show increased dissociation of $\alpha\beta$ dimers to monomers, for the splitting of dimers takes place at the contact $\alpha_1\beta_1$ (refs. 4 and 23). A similar increase in the dissociation constant of dimers to monomers might be expected in haemoglobin Tacoma in which arginine B12β is replaced by serine, and in haemoglobin New York in which a carboxyl group is introduced deep into a surface crevice near the contact $\alpha_1\beta_1$. Haemoglobin E shows normal haem–haem interaction even though its oxygen affinity is abnormally low[32]. The oxygen equilibrium curves of the other mutants at the $\alpha_1\beta_1$ contact do not seem to have been investigated as yet. It would be interesting to know whether haem–haem interaction is affected in any of them, or only in the substitutions at the $\alpha_1\beta_2$ contact described later.

No clinical symptoms or abnormal properties have been reported for haemoglobin Chiapas in which proline GH2α is replaced by arginine. This is surprising because the replacement would be expected to impair the rigidity of the GH segment, and to lessen the stability of both the α-chain and the $\alpha_1\beta_1$ contact.

In native haemoglobin A at pH 7·0, only the two cysteines F9(93)β react with paramercuribenzoate (PMB); the other four cysteines are unreactive because they are buried in the contact $\alpha_1\beta_1$, but they become reactive on treatment causing dissociation of the haemoglobin tetramer into free α- and β-chains[19]. Attachment of PMB prevents reaggregation to the tetramer. In the recently discovered haemoglobin Philly, replacement of tyrosine C1(35)β by phenylalanine causes all six cysteines to be reactive, so that after exposure for 30 min to a low concentration of PMB about half the haemoglobin obtained from a heterozygote was present in the form of free α- and β-chains (personal communication from R. F. Rieder, F. A. Oski and J. B. Clegg).

The tyrosine lies in the internal cavity of the tetramer and its hydroxyl group is hydrogen bonded to the carboxyl group of aspartic acid H9(126)α at the contact $\alpha_1\beta_1$. The side chain of the phenylalanine cannot make the hydrogen bond because it lacks the hydroxyl group, but is otherwise so similar to that of tyrosine that conformational changes are unlikely to accompany the replacement. The tipping of the equilibrium from tetramers to monomers must therefore be a result of the loss of one pair of hydrogen bonds which loosens the contacts $\alpha_1\beta_1$ and

$\alpha_2\beta_2$. It is remarkable that this should cause haemolytic anaemia by precipitation of the haemoglobin in the red cell.

Contact $\alpha_1\beta_2$ (Fig. 8 of ref. 4). Diminished haem–haem interaction has been reported for all five replacements at the contact $\alpha_1\beta_2$. Haemoglobins Chesapeake and J Capetown affect arginine FG4α which forms part of a bridge crossing from the α- to the β-chain. Haemoglobins Yakima and Kempsey affect aspartic acid G1β, the carboxyl group of which makes a hydrogen bond with the main chain imino group of glutamic acid G3β and thus stabilizes the β-chain internally. Its replacement by histidine in haemoglobin Yakima would loosen that hydrogen bond, although it could still be made by one of the imidazole nitrogens, and introduces an additional non-polar contact with the α-chain (Table 2); the replacement by asparagine in haemoglobin Kempsey would also loosen the hydrogen bond, but it could leave the local pattern of interatomic contacts almost unchanged. The stereochemical changes that may be caused by haemoglobin Kansas are described in Table 1 and discussed later. The oxygen affinity is raised in haemoglobins Chesapeake, J Capetown, Yakima and Kempsey, but lowered in haemoglobin Kansas. Despite the diminished haem–haem interaction all five haemoglobins exhibit a Bohr effect. From the point of view of respiratory function they are among the most interesting yet discovered because they offer an opportunity to study the separate factors influencing oxygen affinity, haem–haem interaction and the Bohr effect. They also demonstrate the importance of the contact $\alpha_1\beta_2$ for the transmission of haem–haem interaction.

Haemoglobin Kansas also throws light on the forces holding the subunits together, because it dissociates more easily into $\alpha\beta$ dimers. In the oxy form its dissociation constant in 0·1 M phosphate buffer at pH 7·5 and 20° C is 2×10^{-4} M compared with about $1·2 \times 10^{-6}$ M for haemoglobin A[18]. This means that in a 1·3 per cent solution of haemoglobin Kansas half the molecules would be dissociated into dimers, compared with about one thirteenth in a similar solution of haemoglobin A. In the contact $\alpha_1\beta_2$ of oxyhaemoglobin A, the hydrogen bond between asparagine G4β and aspartic acid G1α is one of more than 100 interactions, all but one or two of which are non-polar. In the mutant the hydroxyl group of threonine, which replaces the asparagine, cannot make this hydrogen bond, but instead it could make one with the main chain carbonyl of aspartic acid G1β, so that the hydrogen bond stabilizing the contact between subunits in the wild type would be replaced in the mutant by another which stabilizes the β-chain internally. At this stage the presence of conformational changes cannot be excluded, but we wonder, all the same, why the hydrogen bond in haemoglobin A should be so strong that its loss raises the dissociation constant by two orders of magnitude.

One explanation is this. In the tetramer of haemoglobin A the hydrogen bond lies in an environment from which water is largely excluded, which would raise the bond energy by lowering the local dielectric constant. On dissociation into dimers the polar groups of both asparagine and aspartic acid would be exposed to water where the dielectric constant is high, so that each of the two polar groups would form only weak hydrogen bonds with water.

Residues in General Positions (Table 3, Figs. 3 and 4)

The mutations in general positions bring out several interesting points. Positions A11 and H8 are two of the internal sites which are occupied by non-polar residues in all globins[6]. The replacement of leucine A11β by arginine in haemoglobin Sogn does not introduce an internal polar group, because the guanidinium group can protrude from the surface, but it does remove some of the non-polar contacts between segment A and segments GH and H. The appearance of free α-chains suggests that this is sufficient to make the β-chains unstable.

Table 1. RESIDUES IN CONTACT WITH HAEM GROUPS

α-Chain

Reference	Designation	Residue No.	Replacement Position	From	To	Variability	Clinical symptoms	Abnormal properties	Structural effects of replacement	Illustration
7	Torino	43	CD1	phe	val	I	Inclusion body anaemia	Unstable at 50° C	Substitution removes the contact of the haem group with Cε of phe, leaving a gap at the surface of the haem pocket. Cγ₂ of val makes a short contact with Cβ of the phe CD4(46) which would disturb the conformation of the CD segment	Fig. 1 of this article, and Fig. 2 of ref. 4
8	M Boston	58	E7	his	tyr	I	Cyanosis Methaemo-globinaemia	Difficult to reduce. α-Chains do not combine with O₂	Phenol group of tyrosine probably forms ionic links with Fe⁺, thus stabilizing it in the ferric state	,, ,, ,,
9	M Iwate	87	F8	his	tyr	I			In addition to the effects described for Hb Boston, the haem group must be displaced towards helix E. X-ray studies show that Hb Iwate has a conformation similar to normal deoxyhaemoglobin in both the reduced and oxidized states. A small conformational change occurs, but does not alter the crystal lattice*	,, ,, ,,
10	Bibba	136	H19	leu	pro	I	Inclusion body anaemia	Unstable at 50° C. Separable by electrophoresis at pH 8·6	Substitution removes contact of Cδ₂ with the haem group and leads to unfolding of residues 136–8 of helix H. Should inhibit normal function of the α-chains	Fig. 2 of ref. 4

β-Chain

Reference	Designation	Residue No.	Replacement Position	From	To	Variability	Clinical symptoms	Abnormal properties	Structural effects of replacement	Illustration
6, 21	Hammersmith	42	CD1	phe	ser	I	Inclusion body anaemia: cyanosis	Unstable at 50° C, easily oxidized, then loses haem. Lower oxygen affinity	Substitution removes the contact of the haem group with Cε and Cζ of phe, leaving a gap at the surface of the haem pocket. The presence of the hydrophilic OH opens the pocket to water	Fig. 2 of this article and Fig. 2 of ref. 4
8	M Saskatoon	63	E7	his	tyr	I	Properties similar to Hb Boston			,, ,, ,,
12, 13	Zürich	63	E7	his	arg	I	Haemolytic inclusion body anaemia on treatment with sulphonamides	Combines reversibly with O₂ but is more easily oxidized and precipitated	The arginine side chain cannot be accommodated in the haem pocket, but must protrude at the surface leaving a large cavity at the ligand site of the iron atom	,, ,, ,,
8	M Milwaukee	67	E11	val	glu	I	Properties similar to Hb Boston		COO⁻ of glu forms a salt bridge with Fe⁺ and pushes the side chain of his E7 out of the haem pocket	,, ,, ,,
14	Sydney	67	E11	val	ala	I	Haemolytic anaemia. Inclusion bodies formed on incubation of blood at 37° C	Unstable at 50° C. Easily oxidized; loss of haem on heating	Breaks contact of the haem group with 2 Cγ's of val. Loosens haem group	,, ,, ,,
*†	Santa Ana	88	F4	leu	pro	I	Haemolytic anaemia. Inclusion bodies in vivo after splenectomy	No haem in β-chain	Proline occurs at the amino-end of helix F and may not cause any change in the conformation of the main chain, but the replacement removes the contact of the haem group with Cγ and Cδ of leu. This opens a crevice on the proximal side into which water could enter	,, ,, ,,
15	M Hyde Park	92	F8	his	tyr	I	Cyanosis. Methaemoglobinaemia	Difficult to reduce. β-Chains do not combine with O₂. Unstable	See Hb M Iwate	,, ,, ,,
16, 17	Köln	98	FG5	val	met	I	Haemolytic anaemia. Inclusion bodies in vivo after splenectomy	Slightly increased + ve charge at pK 8·6, suggesting a rise in the pK of a histidine. Abnormally high oxygen affinity in red cells.	There are two possibilities. (a) The side chain of met could go into an internal position by the haem group. This would displace the haem towards the distal histidine or cause a change in conformation of the FG corner. (b) The side chain of met could be external, which could happen only at the expense of a change in conformation of the FG corner	Fig. 2 of this article and Figs. 2 and 8 of ref. 4
18	Kansas	102	G4	asn	thr	I	Cyanosis	Unstable at 50° C. Decreased oxygen affinity. Decreased Hill's constant. Large Bohr effect. High rate of autoxidation. Oxyhaemoglobin dissociates into αβ dimers	Cγ of thr probably makes short contact with vinyl and methyl of pyrrol II. This would displace either the haem or helix G. Also asn G4 of chain β₂ normally forms a hydrogen bond with asp G1 of chain α₁. This would be broken by the replacement, which should favour dissociation into αβ dimers	,, ,, ,,

* Personal communication from J. Green.
† Unpublished results of R. W. Opfell, P. A. Lorkin and H. Lehmann.

GLOSSARY FOR TABLES

Inclusion body anaemia: precipitated haemoglobin forms inclusion bodies in the red cell and shortens its life span.
Cyanosis: blue colour of skin due to deoxyhaemoglobin in the capillaries; can be due to the oxygen affinity of haemoglobin being too low.
Polycythaemia: excess of red blood cells. Can be caused by stimulation of red cell production by shortage of oxygen in the tissues; for example, if the oxygen affinity of haemoglobin is too high.
Splenomegaly: rapid destruction of red cells enlarges the spleen.
Hill's constant: a measure of the interaction between the four haem groups causing the sigmoid shape of the oxygen dissociation curve.
Bohr effect: dependence of the oxygen affinity on pH.

Table 2. RESIDUES AT CONTACTS BETWEEN SUBUNITS

α-Chain

Reference	Designation	Residue No.	Position	Replacement From	To	Variability	Clinical symptoms	Abnormal properties	Structural effects of replacement in oxyhaemoglobin	Illustration	Contact affected
24	G Chinese	30	B11	glu	gln	I	None	None	glu B11α₁ makes contact with pro H2β₁, but replacement of CO by NH₂ should not matter	Figs. 4 and 7 of ref. 4	α₁β₁
25, 26	J Capetown	92	FG4	arg	gln	I	Possibly mild polycythaemia	High oxygen affinity; diminished haem–haem interaction	arg FG4α₁ is in Van der Waals contact with arg C6β₂. In addition, its guanidinium group may make a hydrogen bond with a recipient group in β₂. Replacement may interfere with structural transition between oxy and deoxy forms	Fig. 8 of ref. 4	α₁β₂
27, 28	Chesapeake	92	FG4	arg	leu	I	Polycythaemia	High oxygen affinity; diminished haem–haem interaction; normal Bohr effect	See Hb J Capetown	,, ,,	α₁β₂
29	Chiapas	114	GH2	pro	arg	I	None	None	Would be expected to weaken GH corner and make α-chain and α₁β₁ contact less stable	Fig. 4 ref. 4	α₁β₁

β-Chain

Reference	Designation	Residue No.	Position	Replacement From	To	Variability	Clinical symptoms	Abnormal properties	Structural effects of replacement in oxyhaemoglobin	Illustration	Contact affected
30–32	E	26	B8	glu	lys	I	None in heterozygotes. Mild haemolytic anaemia in homozygotes	Diminished affinity of normal α-chains for these abnormal β-chains. Diminished oxygen affinity	Replacement of glu B8β₁ removes one of the residues designed to neutralize arg B12, introducing instead an extra + ve charge. This would disturb the hydrogen bonding between the arginine and the α₁-chain	Fig. 4 ref. 4	α₁β₁
33 *	Tacoma	30	B12	arg	ser	I	None reported	Increased oxygen affinity. Unstable at 50° C	Removes the hydrogen bond between arg B12β₁ and phe GH5α₁, thus weakening bonds between α₁ and β₁	Fig. 4 ref. 4	α₁β₁
†	Philly	35	C1	tyr	phe	I	Mild haemolytic anaemia, splenomegaly. Inclusion bodies formed on incubation of blood with brilliant cresyl blue	All six cysteines react with PMB. Unstable at 50° C	Removes the hydrogen bond between tyr C1β₁ and asp H9α₁, thus weakening bonds between α₁ and β₁		α₁β₁
34, 35	Yakima	99	G1	asp	his	I	Polycythaemia	Increased oxygen affinity; diminished haem–haem interaction; normal Bohr effect	The carboxyl group of asp G1β₂ normally forms a hydrogen bond with NH of glu G3β₁. It also touches Cγ of val G3α₁. The imidazole ring of histidine could still make the same hydrogen bond, though it would be weaker, and touch val G3α₁. In addition it would make a new contact with leu G7α₁	Fig. 8 of ref. 4	α₁β₂
36	Kempsey	99	G1	asp	asn	I	Polycythaemia; less severe than in Hb Yakima	Increased oxygen affinity; diminished haem–haem interaction; Bohr effect present	Replacement of CO⁻ by NH₂ would weaken internal hydrogen bond and alter contact with val G3α₁	Fig. 8 of ref. 4	α₁β₂
18	Kansas	102	G4	asn	thr	I	See Table 1				α₁β₂
37	New York	113	G15	val	glu	I	None reported	No increased electrophoretic mobility at pH 8·6, despite extra − ve charge	Introduces a − ve charge deep in a surface crevice. Might cause rearrangement of arg B12, glu B8 and his G19. Unchanged electrophoretic mobility might be due to a rise in pK of his G19		α₁β₁
38	K Woolwich	132	H10	lys	glu	I	None	None	Lys H10β is in a position to form a hydrogen bond with the σ-carboxyl group of histidine H24 of the opposite β-chain in oxy, but not in deoxyhaemoglobin. In deoxyhaemoglobin it may bind diphosphoglycerate. Its replacement by glutamic acid may affect the oxygen dissociation curve		β₁β₂

* And personal communication from R. T. Jones. † Personal communication from R. F. Rieder, F. A. Oski and J. B. Clegg.

Haemoglobin Wien illustrates the disastrous effect of an internal polar group. The replacement of tyrosine H8 by aspartic acid leads to haemolytic anaemia, even in the heterozygote. The absence of a change in electrophoretic mobility at pH 8·6 can hardly be a consequence of this aspartic acid residue remaining unionized, but suggests that an extra positive ion is created, accompanied by extensive conformational changes, by some mechanism such as suggested in Table 3. In haemoglobins Genova, Freiburg and Gun Hill the introduction of a proline into a helical region, or deletions of one or more residues, clearly have drastic effects on stability and function.

Prolines can be accommodated in the first three positions of an α-helix, but in all others short contacts between the pyrrolidine ring and the next turn of the helix would force conformational changes. Accordingly the introduction of a proline in position B10β must disrupt helix B. So would the deletion of valine B5 in haemoglobin Frei-burg, because it would bring glutamic acid B4, a strongly polar group, into an internal position. The deletion of five residues between positions 91 and 97 in haemoglobin Gun Hill would force drastic conformational changes in a segment which is normally in contact with the haem group, and leads to loss of haem.

External Replacements without Clinical Symptoms in Heterozygotes (Table 4)

No abnormalities have been reported for most of the external replacements, but on structural grounds some of them are likely to impair the stability of the molecule. These, together with haemoglobins S and C, have been singled out for comment at the bottom of Table 4.

Haemoglobin S has been the subject of many investigations, including X-ray analysis and electron microscopy. The unit cell dimensions and the distribution of intensities of its oxy form are identical with those of oxyhaemoglobin

Table 3. RESIDUES IN GENERAL POSITIONS

α-Chain

Refer-ence	Designation	Residue Position No.	Replacement Posi-tion	Replacement From	Replacement To	Vari-ability	Clinical symptoms	Abnormal properties	Structural effects of replacement	Illustration
39	Etobicoke	84	F5	ser	arg	I	None reported	Heat labile	In Hb A the OH of serine F5 probably forms a hydrogen bond with CO of leu H19. Substitution of arg would force a conformational change, either within helix F (short contact between Cγ(arg) and OH (ser F2)), or by pris-ing helices F and G apart	Fig. 4
	* Manitoba	102	G9	ser	arg	I	None. Present only in small proportion	Difficult to separate from Hb A by electro-phoresis at pH 8·6	In central cavity. May introduce insta-bility through excess of + ve charges in central cavity	

β-Chain

40	Tokuchi	2	NA2	his	tyr	V	None reported	Little evidence	The imidazole ring of his 2 is probably external. The phenyl ring of tyrosine is more hydrophobic and is rarely found in external positions. The replacement is likely to lead to a con-formational change in the NA segment	
41	Sogn	14	A11	leu	arg	Vn	None	Increased rate of dena-turation at 58° C. Appearance of free α-chains	Removes contact of Cδ₁ of leu A11 with Cδ + Cε of phe GH5 and of Cδ₂ with Cε of phe GH1. Also of Cδ₁ of leu A11 with Cδ₁ and Cδ₂ of leu H4. Could form salt-bridge with asp GH4	Fig. 3
42	Freiburg	23	B5	val	—	Vn	Cyanosis	High oxygen affinity	Deletion would draw the carboxyl group of glu 22 (B4) into a crevice about 4 Å below the protein surface. It would also remove the last turn of the B helix and disturb the conforma-tion of the AB corner	Fig. 4
43	Genova	28	B10	leu	pro	I	Inclusion body haemolytic an-aemia	Heat labile at 50°	Introduction of proline would disrupt helix B	
44	Gun Hill		Deletion of 5 residues between 91 and 97				Haemolytic an-aemia	No haem in β-chain	Removes section of polypeptide chain which forms essential haem contacts and contacts with α-subunits	Fig. 4 of this paper and Fig. 8 of ref. 4
	†Wien	130	H8	tyr	asp	Vn	Haemolytic an-aemia	Unstable at 50° C. No increased electropho-retic mobility at pH 8·6 despite extra neg-ative charge	In Hb A the phenyl ring of tyrosine is internal; its hydroxyl emerges in a surface crevice near helix A, probably forming a hydrogen bond with CO of val A8(11)β Its replacement by asp creates an in-ternal − ve charge which would be unstable and draw a + ve charge near it. The absence of an increased electrophoretic mobility at pH 8·6 suggests that a new + ve charge is created by a rise in pK of a previously uncharged group. This could be the imidazole of his NA2 or the α-amino group of val NA1. Either of these could be drawn in to neutralize asp H8 at the expense of a displacement of helix A	Fig. 3
45	Hope	136	H14	gly	asp	I	None	Difficult to separate from Hb A by electro-phoresis at pH 8·6	Could form salt bridge with α-amino group of val NA1 and by raising its pK produce a compensating charge	
46	Rainier	145	HC2	tyr	his	I	Polycythaemia	Increased oxygen affi-nity. Unusual resis-tance to alkali	Hb A the phenolic OH forms a hy-drogen bond with CO of val FG5, and the phenyl ring acts as a spacer be-tween helix H and the FG segment. The imidazole ring is too short to make this bond but could instead form a hydrogen bond with CO of leu H19. While the former hydrogen bond would be broken by alkali, the latter might not	Fig. 4

* Unpublished results of J. H. Crookston, J. Goldstein, H. Lehmann and D. Beale.
† Unpublished results of H. Pietschmann, P. A. Lorkin, H. Lehmann and H. Braunsteiner.

A, which excludes conformational differences between the two proteins. Deoxyhaemoglobin S crystals have been obtained, but have not yet been examined by X-rays[55]. Fig. 3 shows that the residue of glutamic acid which is replaced by valine in haemoglobin S lies at the surface of the A-helix. The insolubility of deoxyhaemoglobin S could therefore be explained without invoking con-formational differences between it and deoxyhaemo-globin A. A non-polar instead of a polar residue at a surface position would suffice to make each molecule adhere to a complementary site on a neighbouring one, that site being created by the conformational change from oxy to deoxyhaemoglobin. Its nature is still unknown, but it probably exists in both deoxyhaemo-globins S and A. Fig. 5 shows how the two-fold sym-metry axis which relates the two valines and the two complementary sites in each molecule could lead to the formation of long linear aggregates in homozygotes and how the presence of hybrid molecules in hetero-

zygotes would cut these aggregates short. Linear aggre-gates of deoxyhaemoglobin S have been observed under the electron microscope[55,56].

Table 4 includes mutations at ten "invariant" sites, but at only one of these (CD5β) does the model suggest any reason why the residue of the mutant (K Ibadan) might not serve as well as that of the wild type. Among the variable sites there is one (H4β) normally restricted to non-polar residues where the replacement of valine by glutamic acid in haemoglobin Hofu might be harmful.

Discussion

The haemoglobin molecule is a model system for study-ing the effects of somatic mutations and species variations on the structure and function of a protein molecule. It appears to be insensitive to most replacements on its surface, except those which affect the solubility of either the oxy or deoxy form, and those which disrupt some essential contact between neighbouring segments of poly-

Figs. 1–4. Stereoscopic drawings of the atomic model of horse oxyhaemoglobin. These should be viewed with a stereoviewer. (An inexpensive one is available from Stereomagniscope, Inc., 40–31 81 Street, New York. More elaborate ones are made by C. F. Casella, Ltd, Regent House, Britannia Walk, London, N1, and by the Lansing Instrument Corporation, Lansing, Michigan, USA. A pair of enlarging lenses of focal length 85 mm, mounted 70 mm apart between cardboard, is also adequate.) The main chains are drawn in bold lines and the side chains in thin lines. Broken lines indicate hydrogen bonds. Hydrogen bonds within helices have been omitted from some of the figures. Residues belonging to the α-chains are underlined; those belonging to the β-chains are not. The atomic positions in Figs. 1 and 2 are derived from photographs of the model, those of Figs. 3 and 4 from Dr R. Diamond's model building[20] and Mr T. H. Gossling's model drawing programmes, as described in ref. 4. Of the polar side chains on the surface of the β-chain in Figs. 1–4, the only ones whose conformation emerges clearly from the electron density maps are lys E3, glx B2, B3 and B8, and asx GH4. Lys E10 and GH3 and gln B4 are clear in parts. The conformation of the remaining ones has been drawn arbitrarily.

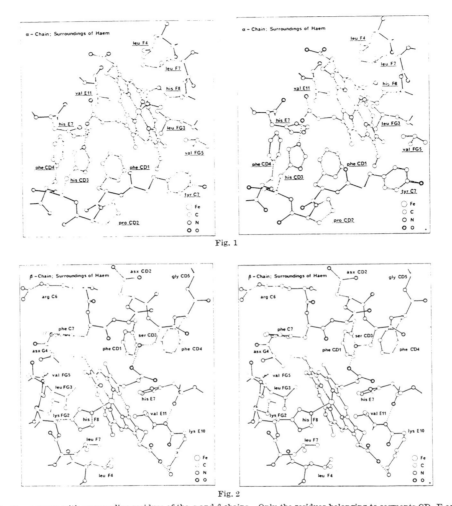

Fig. 1

Fig. 2

Figs. 1 and 2. Haem group with surrounding residues of the α and β-chains. Only the residues belonging to segments CD, E and F, which lie near the surface, are shown. The interior contacts belonging to segments G and H are omitted. Distortions of the porphyrin ring in Fig. 2 have resulted because some of the atoms were obscured in the photographs used for making the drawing, so that their positions had to be guessed. The orientation of the vinyl groups is arbitrary.

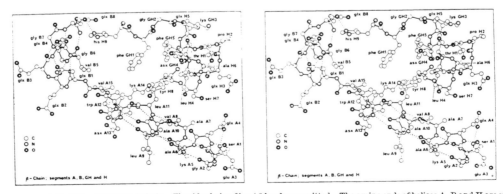

Fig. 3. Segments A, B, GH and H of the β-chain. The side chain of lys A5 has been omitted. The amino ends of helices A, B and H are stabilized by hydrogen bonds between the α-NH of residue 4 in the helix with the oxygen of serine A1, glx B1 and thr H1 respectively. Also the AB corner contains only one amide group which does not form part of either helix A or B.

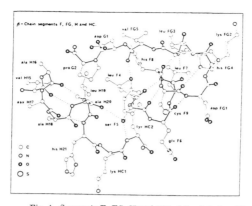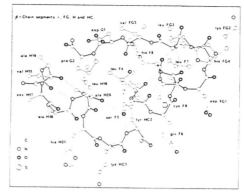

Fig. 4. Segments F, FG, H and HC of the β-chain. Note the single turn of π-helix between his F8 and his FG4.

peptide chain. Certain external positions which have no special function and are variable in normal mammalian haemoglobins show a particularly high incidence of mutations, all of which seem to be harmless in heterozygotes. On the other hand, the molecule is extremely sensitive to even quite small alterations in the pattern of non-polar contacts, especially of those near to the haem groups. Such alterations decrease its stability, leading to precipitation of the haemoglobin in the red cell, and, in some cases, to loss of haem. Similar alterations in the pattern of non-polar contacts may be the cause of instability of essential enzymes in thermosensitive microbial mutants. The haemoglobin molecule appears to react to the introduction of a negatively charged carboxyl group

into the non-polar interior of one of its subunits by a large conformational change which allows it to compensate the negative charge by a newly created positive one (haemoglobin Wien). So far, only two replacements of an internal non-polar residue by another have been reported (Köln and Sydney); there must be many others, still unknown, affecting the function and stability of the molecule.

Replacements at contacts between α and β subunits may affect the oxygen affinity, haem–haem interaction, and the equilibrium between tetramers, dimers and monomers. Changes in oxygen affinity could be brought about by alterations in the relative stabilities of the oxy and deoxy forms; increased stability of the oxy form leading to a

Table 4. EXTERNAL REPLACEMENTS WITHOUT CLINICAL SYMPTOMS IN HETEROZYGOTES

Designation	Residue Position No.	Position	Replacement From	To	Variability	Designation	Residue Position No.	Position	Replacement From	To	Variability	Designation	Residue Position No.	Position	Replacement From	To	Variability
		α-Chain						β-Chain						β-Chain			
J Toronto	5	A3	ala	asp	V	S	6	A3	glu	val	V	Hijiyama	120	GH3	lys	glu	V ›
J Paris	12	A10	ala	asp	V	C	6	A3	glu	lys	V	O Arab	121	GH4	glu	lys	V
J Oxford	15	A13	gly	asp	V	G San Jose	7	A4	glu	gly	Vp	D Punjab	121	GH4	glu	gln	V
I	16	A14	lys	glu	?	Siriraj	7	A4	glu	lys	V	Hofu	126	H4	val	glu	Vn
J Medellin	22	B3	gly	asp	V	Porto Alegre	9	A6	ser	cys	V						
Memphis	23	B4	glu	gln	V	J Baltimore	16	A13	gly	asp	V			γ-Chain			
G Audhali	23	B4	glu	val	V	D Bushman	16	A13	gly	arg	V	F Texas I	5	A2	glu	lys	V
L Ferrara	47	CD5	asp	gly	I	G Coushatta	22	B4	glu	ala	V	F Texas II	6	A3	glu	lys	V
Hasharon	47	CD5	asp	his	I	E Saskatoon	22	B4	glu	lys	V	F Alexandra	12	A9	thr	lys	V
J Sardegna	50	CD8	his	asp	I	G Taiwan-Ami	25	B7	gly	arg	Vn	F Hull	121	GH4	glu	lys	V
Russ	51	CD9	gly	arg	I	G Galveston	43	CD2	glu	ala	Vp						
Shimonoseki	54	E3	gln	arg	Vp	K Ibadan	46	CD5	gly	glu	I			δ-Chain			
Mexico	54	E3	gln	glu	Vp	G Copenhagen	47	CD6	asp	asn	Vp	A₂ Sphakia	2	NA2	his	arg	V
Norfolk	57	E6	gly	asp	V	J Bangkok	56	D7	gly	asp	V	A₂'	16	A13	gly	arg	V
G Philadelphia	68	E17	asn	lys	V	Dhofar	58	E2	pro	arg	Vn	A₂ Flatbush	22	B4	ala	glu	V
Ube II	68	E17	asn	asp	V	N Seattle	61	E5	lys	glu	I	A₂ Babinga	136	H14	gly	asp	I
Stanleyville II	78	EF7	asn	lys	V	Hikari	61	E5	lys	asn	I						
G Norfolk	85	F6	asp	asn	Vp	J Cambridge	69	E13	gly	asp	V						
Broussais	90	FG2	lys	asn	I	C Harlem	73	E17	asp	asn	V	30 variable, 6 invariant in β + γ + δ					
Dakar	112	G19	his	gln	I	J Iran	77	EF1	his	asp	Vp	Total: 45 variable, 12 invariant, 2 queries					
J Tongariki	115	GH3	ala	asp	V	G Accra	79	EF3	asp	asn	I						
O Indonesia	116	GH4	glu	lys	Vp	D Ibadan	87	F3	thr	lys	V						
						Agenogi	90	F6	glu	lys	I						
15 variable, 6 invariant						Oakridge	94	FG1	asp	asn	?						
						N	95	FG2	lys	glu	V						

Comments on some of the mutants listed above

S (sickle cell) gives rise to severe haemolytic anaemia in homozygotes, because of diminished solubility of deoxyhaemoglobin S. Substitution of a large non-polar for a polar side chain at the surface leads to filamentous aggregation of haemoglobin and to deformation of red cells in the absence of oxygen[47-49] (Fig. 3).

C, Mild haemolytic anaemia, in homozygotes, due to slightly diminished solubility of oxyhaemoglobin C. Red cells are more rigid. Splenomegaly[50-52] (Fig. 3).

I, The electron density map[3] shows the hydrocarbon chain of lysine A14α to be extended and rigid, unlike the majority of lysines which are flexible. This rigidity is probably due to both polar and non-polar contacts with aspartic acid GH4α. Replacement of the lysine by glutamic acid would be expected to make the α-chain less stable[53].

Hofu, Valine H4β lies in a surface crevice and makes non-polar contacts with leucine A11β and phenylalanine GH5β. The position H4 is occupied by non-polar residues in all mammalian haemoglobins examined so far. Its replacement by glutamic acid may make the β-chain less stable[54] (Fig. 3).

K Ibadan, Glycine CD5β probably has a conformation which is forbidden for residues with side chains. In that case its replacement by glutamic acid would entail a conformational change in the CD region, which might make the β-chains less stable[38].

Loci where more than two different mutations occur in α, β, γ and δ-chains taken together are shown below. All these loci are external, without special function, and are variable in normal mammalian haemoglobins.

Locus	No. of mutations
A3	4
A13	4
B4	5
E17	3
GH4	4

References to the abnormal haemoglobins listed here are given in refs. 1 and 2 except for those not yet published, which are mentioned by permission of the authors and include the following: Dakar (D. Labie and J. Rosa); F Alexandra (D. Loukopoulos, A. Kaltsoya and Ph. Fessas); A₂ Babinga (W. W. W. de Jong and L. F. Bernini).

307

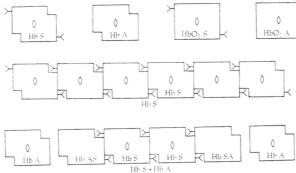

Fig. 5. Suggested scheme for linear aggregation of sickle cell haemoglobin. The top line shows from left to right: deoxyhaemoglobin S which has two valines and two sites complementary to valine; deoxyhaemoglobin A which lacks the valines but has the complementary sites; oxyhaemoglobin S which has the valines but lacks the complementary sites; and oxyhaemoglobin A which lacks both. The sign at the centre of each molecule marks the two-fold symmetry axis. The second line shows an aggregate of deoxyhaemoglobin S, made possible by two valines and two complementary sites related by a symmetry axis in each molecule. The third line shows an equimolar mixture of deoxyhaemoglobins S and A. Linear aggregates are terminated by hybrid molecules which lack the two-fold symmetry axis. Oxyhaemoglobin S cannot form aggregates because it lacks the complementary sites. The entire scheme is based on the knowledge that oxy and deoxyhaemoglobin have different quaternary structures, but it requires no conformational differences between haemoglobins A and S. The linear aggregates may, of course, take helical forms.

rise and of the deoxy form to a drop in oxygen affinity. Haemoglobins Chesapeake and J Capetown should be examples of the former and haemoglobins Kansas and E of the latter. Changes in haem–haem interaction cannot yet be interpreted, because the mechanism is still unknown, although the complete absence of haem–haem interaction usually means that the change in quaternary structure which normally accompanies the reaction with ligands is inhibited. This might be happening in haemoglobin Yakima which has a Hill constant of 1·0. Studies of the equilibrium between tetramers and dimers in haemoglobin Kansas have shown that the loss of a single pair of hydrogen bonds among a multitude of non-polar interactions at the contacts $\alpha_1\beta_2$ and $\alpha_2\beta$ may lead to a striking increase in the dissociation constant from tetramers to dimers (although the possible contribution of conformational changes cannot be excluded at this stage). Similarly the loss of a single pair of hydrogen bonds at the contacts $\alpha_1\beta_1$ and $\alpha_2\beta_2$ in haemoglobin Philly favours the dissociation of tetramers to monomers. This confirms the prediction[23] that dissociation into dimers occurs by splitting at the contacts $\alpha_1\beta_2$ and $\alpha_2\beta_1$, while splitting into monomers occurs at the contacts $\alpha_1\beta_1$ and $\alpha_2\beta_2$ (Fig. 3 of ref. 4).

The abnormal haemoglobins have been discovered either by population surveys using electrophoresis at pH 8·6 or by examination of patients with clinical symptoms. Many mutations involving neutral residues, however, might be missed by these methods, and it has been estimated that as large a fraction as one in 600 of the population may carry a mutant haemoglobin[57]. The number of different proteins in a human may be of the order of $10^5–10^6$, which makes it likely that each person carries many kinds of mutant proteins; however, the relative rarity of congenital disease suggests that deleterious mutations of most proteins are pathogenic only in homozygous but not in heterozygous form. The data presented here do not hold out any hope that the lesions in mutant protein molecules could be repaired directly; repair at the genetic level, by transduction of a wild type gene, say, is imaginable but still Utopian. A less remote possibility might be the replacement of the organ producing the abnormal protein, for example of the bone marrow to replace the red blood cells. At present the only hope lies in preventing conception of homozygotes, or even of heterozygotes carrying strongly pathogenic mutations such as haemoglobin Wien or Freiburg.

We thank Dr Hilary Muirhead for computing the views of the model shown in Figs. 3 and 4, Dr F. H. C. Crick for critical discussion, and Mr B. K. Harvey, Miss C. A. Lovett and Miss P. A. Snazle for technical assistance.

Received August 6, 1968.

[1] Wintrobe, M. M., Clinical Hematology, sixth ed., 154 (Lea and Febiger, Philadelphia, 1967).
[2] Lehmann, H., and Carrell, R. W., Brit. Med. Bull., 25, No. 1 (in the press, 1969).
[3] Perutz, M. F., Muirhead, H., Cox, J. M., Goaman, L. C. G., Mathews, F. S., McGandy E. L., and Webb, L. E., Nature, 219, 29 (1968).
[4] Perutz, M. F., Muirhead, H., Cox, J. M., and Goaman, L. C. G., Nature, 219, 139 (1968).
[5] Bolton, W., Cox, J. M., and Perutz, M. F., J. Mol. Biol., 33, 283 (1968).
[6] Perutz, M. F., Kendrew, J. C., and Watson, H. C., J. Mol. Biol., 13, 669 (1965).
[7] Beretta, A., Prato, V., Gallo, E., and Lehmann, H., Nature, 217, 1016 (1968).
[8] Gerald, P. S., and Efron, M. L., Proc. US Nat. Acad. Sci., 47, 1758 (1958).
[9] Miyaji, T., Iuchi, I., Shibata, S., Takeda, I., and Tamura, A., Acta Haematol. Jap., 26, 538 (1963).
[10] Kleihauer, E. F., Reynolds, C. A., Dozy, A. M., Wilson, J. B., Moore, R. R., Berenson, M. P., Wright, C. S., and Huisman, T. H. J., Biochim, Biophys. Acta, 154, 220 (1968).
[11] Dacie, J. V., Shinton, N. K., Gaffney, P. J., Carrell, R. W., and Lehmann, H., Nature, 216, 663 (1967).
[12] Muller, C. J., and Kingma, A., Biochim. Biophys. Acta, 50, 595 (1961).
[13] Hitzig, W. H., Frick, P. G., Betke, K., and Huisman, T. H. J., Helv. Paediat. Acta, 6, 499 (1960).
[14] Carrell, R. W., Lehmann, H., Lorkin, P. A., Raik, E., and Hunter, E., Nature, 215, 626 (1967).
[15] Heller, P., Coleman, R. D., and Yakulis, V. G., Proc. Eleventh Cong. Inter. Soc. Haematol., 427 (Government Printer, Sydney, 1966).
[16] Carrell, R. W., Lehmann, H., and Hutchison, W. D., Nature, 210, 915 (1966).
[17] Vaughan-Jones, R., Grimes, A. J., Carrell, R. W., and Lehmann, H., Brit. J. Haematol., 13, 394 (1967).
[18] Bonaventura, J., and Riggs, A., J. Biol. Chem., 243, 980 (1968).
[19] Bucci, E., and Fronticelli, C., J. Biol. Chem., 240, PC551 (1965).
[20] Diamond, R., Acta Cryst., 21, 253 (1966).
[21] Jacob, H. S., Brain, M. C., Dacie, J. V., Carrell, R. W., and Lehmann, H., Nature, 218, 1214 (1968).
[22] Watson, H. C., and Kendrew, J. C., Nature, 190, 663 (1961).
[23] Rosemeyer, M. A., and Huehns, E. R., J. Mol. Biol., 25, 253 (1967).
[24] Swenson, R. T., Hill, R. L., Lehmann, H., and Jim, R. T. S., J. Biol. Chem., 237, 1517 (1962).
[25] Botha, M. C., Beale, D., Isaacs, W. A., and Lehmann, H., Nature, 212, 792 (1966).
[26] Lines, J. G., and McIntosh, R., Nature, 215, 297 (1967).
[27] Clegg, J. B., Naughton, M. A., and Weatherall, D. J., J. Mol. Biol., 19, 91 (1966).
[28] Nagel, R. L., Gibson, Q. H., and Charache, S., Biochemistry, 6, 2395 (1967).
[29] Jones, R. T., Brimhall, B., and Lisker, R., Biochim. Biophys. Acta, 154, 488 (1968).
[30] Hunt, J. A., and Ingram, V. M., Nature, 184, 870 (1959).
[31] Tuchinda, S., Beale, D., and Lehmann, H., Humangenetik, 3, 312 (1967).
[32] Bellingham, A. J., and Huehns, E. R., Nature, 218, 924 (1968).
[33] Baur, E. W., and Motulsky, A. G., Humangenetik, 1, 621 (1965).
[34] Jones, R. T., Osgood, E. E., Brimhall, B., and Koler, R. D., J. Clin. Invest., 46, 1840 (1967).
[35] Miles, J. N., Miles, J. E., and Metcalfe, J., J. Clin. Invest., 46, 1848 (1967).
[36] Reed, C. S., Hampson, R., Gordon, S., Jones, R. T., Novy, M. J., Brimhall, B., Edwards, M. J., and Koler, R. D., Blood, 31, 623 (1968).
[37] Ranney, H. M., Jacobs, A. S., and Nagel, R. L., Nature, 213, 876 (1967).
[38] Allan, N., Beale, D., Irvine, D., and Lehmann, H., Nature, 208, 658 (1965).
[39] Crookston, J. H., Farquarson, H., Beale, D., and Lehmann, H., Canad. J. Biochem. (in the press).
[40] Shibata, S., Iuchi, I., Miyaji, T., and Takeda, I., Bull. Yamaguchi Med. School, 10, 1 (1963).
[41] Monn, E., Gaffney, P. J., and Lehmann, H., Scand. J. Haematol. (in the press).
[42] Jones, R. T., Brimhall, B., Huisman, T. H. J., Kleihauer, E. F., and Betke, K., Science, 154, 1022 (1967).
[43] Sansone, G., Carrell, R. W., and Lehmann, H., Nature, 214, 877 (1967).
[44] Bradley, T. B., Wohl, R. C., and Rieder, R. F., Science, 157, 1581 (1967).
[45] Minnich, V., Hill, R. L., Khuri, P. D., and Anderson, M. E., Blood, 25, 830 (1965).
[46] Stammatoyannopoulos, G., Adamson, J., Yoshida, A., and Heinenberg, Blood, 30, 879 (1967).
[47] Pauling, L., Itano, H. A., Singer, S. J., and Wells, I. C., Science, 110, 543 (1949).
[48] Ingram, V. M., Biochim. Biophys. Acta, 36, 402 (1959).
[49] Perutz, M. F., and Mitchison, J. M., Nature, 166, 677 (1950).
[50] Hunt, J. A., and Ingram, V. M., Nature, 184, 640 (1959).
[51] Charache, S., Conley, C. L., Waugh, D. F., Ugoretz, R. J., and Spurrell, J. R., J. Clin. Invest., 46, 1795 (1967).
[52] Kraus, A. P., and Diggs, L. W., J. Lab. Clin. Med., 47, 700 (1956).
[53] Beale, D., and Lehmann, H., Nature, 207, 259 (1965).
[54] Miyaji, T., Ohba, Y., Yamamoto, K., Shibata, S., Iuchi, I., and Takaneka, M., Nature, 217, 89 (1968).
[55] Stetson, jun., C. A., J. Exp. Med., 123, 341 (1966).
[56] Murayama, M., J. Cell Physiol., 67, Suppl., 21 (1966).
[57] Sick, K., Beale, D., Irvine, D., Lehmann, H., Goodall, P. T., and MacDougall, S., Biochim. Biophys. Acta (in the press).

Unit 8 / Structure–Function Relationships in Proteins

Perutz et al. 1965

1. What is hemoglobin? Where does it occur and what is its function?

2. What is the basic structure of hemoglobin (subunits, lengths of chains, cofactors)?

3. What is myoglobin? Where does it occur and how is it different from hemoglobin?

4. What does a comparison of myoglobins and hemoglobins from different organisms show in terms of totally conserved or invariant residues?

5. What single general rule seems to emerge from considering the structures of all of the hemoglobins and myoglobins?

6. What is the effect of proline on α helices? Where does proline usually occur in α helices?

7. What would the effect of a replacement of a nonpolar residue on the surface of the hemoglobin molecule probably be on the function of the protein? Assume that a polar residue replaces the nonpolar residue. What would happen if the same type of replacement occurred in the interior of the protein?

Perutz and Lehmann 1968

8. Find Hb Wien (the German word for Vienna) in the text and in Table 3 on page 305. Describe the change and explain why there are drastic effects.

9. Find Hb Sogn in the text and in Table 3 on page 305. Explain the changes and consequences of this variant.

10. What happens in Hb Santa Ana? Explain the effects of this mutation in terms of the replacement.

Section II

Updated Papers

Unit 9

Mutagenesis

We saw in Unit 1 how Seymour Benzer demonstrated the existence of "hotspots," sites in the DNA with high mutability. Only after the advent of DNA sequencing was the nature of some of these hotspots revealed. The first two papers in this unit, Farabaugh et al. and Albertini et al., deal with frameshift and deletion hotspots, and two additional papers, Coulondre and Miller and Coulondre et al., investigate base substitution hotspots.

Sydney Brenner and co-workers deciphered the *amber* (UAG) and *ochre* (UAA) codons, and later the *opal* (UGA) codon, by almost purely genetic means (see Unit 3). This work relied on the specificity of mutagens, in this case hydroxylamine and 2-aminopurine (2AP), and on understanding how mutagens work. There have been many advances in this area, which, for the most part, have been brought about by genetic studies that followed the lead of Benzer, Crick, Brenner, and their colleagues (see Units 1–3). The papers in this unit expand on the use of genetics to understand more about mutagenesis.

HOTSPOTS FOR DELETIONS
AND FRAMESHIFTS

The first demonstration of the sequence basis of hotspots was in the *lacI* gene, the gene first discovered by Jacob and Monod. This work, described in the paper by **Farabaugh et al.**, represented a collaboration between Jeffrey Miller's group (then at Geneva) and Walter Gilbert's group at Harvard. First, the authors used Benzer's methods to map and assort into sites a set of 140 spontaneous mutations in the *lacI* gene of *E. coli*. Figure 2 on page 324 shows this distribution. Note how similar it is in form to that found by Benzer for the *rII* genes. In the center of the gene is an enormous hotspot where 94 of the 140 mutations map into two sites distinguishable by reversion tests. In addition, 19 deletions appeared in this collection.

Representative members of each group were then sequenced, and the hotspot in the middle of the gene was found to result from a tandemly repeated sequence, CTGGCTGGCTGG, in the wild type. The three units of CTGG expand to four units in the most frequent hotspot and are reduced to two units in the second most frequent hotspot. Mutant strains with four copies of the CTGG sequence can revert back to wild type at a high rate, whereas those with two copies cannot. This property allowed the authors to easily distinguish between the two types of mutations. The high mutability of the tandemly repeated sequence can be rationalized in terms of the slipped mispairing models of Streisinger and co-workers (see Additional Readings). The hotspot, here resulting from the tandem repeat, and its expansion as a hotspot mutation can serve as a prototype for the recent findings that a number of human genetic diseases are caused by the expansion of a triplet repeat. In certain human genes, the wild type carries a triplet that is tandemly repeated 5–50 times depending on the gene involved. This can expand to a much higher copy number, which results in a defective protein and often severe symptoms. For example, in myonic dystrophy, the most common form of adult muscular dystrophy, normal individuals have the sequence CTGCTGCTGCTGCTG, or about 5 copies of the CTG triplet. This expands to 50 copies in patients with milder forms of the disease and to as many as 1000 copies in patients with severe forms of the disease (see Sutherland and Richards in Additional Readings).

The authors also determined the sequences at the endpoints of a number of deletions and showed that deletions predominate at short sequence repeats, which in the cases studied here were sometimes 5 or 8 base pairs. The two models for deletions offered by the authors involved either direct recombination between very short sequences or an extension of the Streisinger slipped mispairing model for frameshifts.

The paper by **Albertini et al.** is a continuation of the work in the Farabaugh et al. paper examining the formation of spontaneous deletions. Here, the authors wanted not only to study deletions in the *lacI* gene, whose DNA sequence was known, but also to examine deletions more than 50 base pairs in length. Therefore, they constructed a system that would select for deletions of a certain length in *lacI*. They employed a fusion deletion that fused the end of the *I* gene to the beginning of the *Z* gene. The resulting hybrid protein still retained β-galactosidase activity but depended on transcription and translation of the *lacI* gene and mRNA. The authors programmed into this fusion two widely separated frameshift mutations. In most cases, a deletion of both frameshifts was required to restore the correct reading frame in *lacI*. Thus, deletions had to be at least 700 base pairs long. However, they could not extend beyond the *lacI* promoter or into the *lacZ* gene much farther. Thus, this system ensured that the Lac⁻ to Lac⁺ revertants would all have deletions in *lacI* with lengths of 700–1000 base pairs.

The deletion endpoints were mapped and representative examples sequenced. As Figure 3 on page 340 shows, there is a prominent hotspot and several minor hotspots (see also Table 3 on page 341). Sequencing showed that the major hotspot was a deletion between the largest homologies in the system, two stretches, separated by 759 base pairs, where 14 of 17 base pairs were the same. Other recurring deletions were also between significant homologies, as were most of the other deletions. Interestingly, deletions were reduced about 20-fold in a *recA* strain, suggesting the possible involvement of recombination. However, the deletions that occurred in the *recA* strain were also at the same homologies. The importance of the homologies was underscored by an experiment in which defined mutations in *lacI* were added to the construct. (Recall that this was before the current era of site-directed mutagenesis.) Some of these mutations, shown in Figure 7 on page 342, reduced the homology at the hotspot and also lowered the deletion incidence by 20- to 40-fold (see Table 4 on page 342).

Figure 9 on page 344 presents a model for slipped mispairing as pertains to deletion formation. As mentioned above, deletions could also be generated by recombination between the short repeats.

THE SPECIFICITY OF MUTAGENS

In this section, we present a set of papers that represents the use of genetics to understand more about the relative specificity of mutagens and also spontaneous mutagenesis. We focus on some of the systems devised to monitor mutations.

The Iso-1-Cytochrome System in Yeast

The paper by Fred Sherman's group (**Prakash and Sherman**) describes a system employed in yeast that makes use of mutations in the initiation codon or in one of two early nonsense codons in the gene encoding iso-1-cytochrome c. After significant background work in this system, the authors were able to catalog each possible revertant to wild type or pseudo wild type in terms of the base change involved. This enabled them to deduce the relative specificity of each mutagen under study, at least with respect to the mutational sites examined. For example, the revertants of the mutant carrying changes at the initiation codon could have arisen either by direct reversion at the initiation codon or by the creation of a new AUG at one of several places in the gene. Their system is an artful use of genetics during a period when ambiguities in other experimental systems concerning the exact nature of the base changes responsible for different mutants or revertants produced a lot of uncertainty in the field. They could show that a number of agents, including EMS and MNNG (NTG, nitrosoguanidine), are specific for $G \cdot C \rightarrow A \cdot T$ base changes which probably result from alkylation at the O-6 position of guanine. Most of the conclusions from the work of Sherman and co-workers still hold up today.

The *his* System in *Salmonella typhimurium*

Early work from several laboratories (for example, early work from Demerec's lab and other groups) had used the reversion to wild type in response to different mutagens as a way of investigating the correlation between mutagens and carcinogens. However, the development of the histidine biosynthetic pathway genetic system in *Salmonella typhimurium* for this purpose by Ames and co-workers was responsible for the most significant advances. Initially, the correlation between mutagens and carcinogens was incomplete when one used the reversion of a His⁻ mutant to His⁺ to monitor mutagenesis. Ames and his colleagues built in a number of improvements to the existing assays, and these innovations are described in the paper by **Ames et al.** considered here. First, they employed several **different *his*⁻ mutations,** including those that reverted via a frameshift and via base substitution mutations. Second, the strains were engineered to **lack the excision repair** pathway that excises many chemical adducts from bases in the DNA. This greatly

increased the sensitivity of the assay. Third, potential mutagens were incubated with a crude preparation of mouse liver enzymes to allow **activation** of some relatively inert compounds to the active metabolite that is mutagenic in vivo. For example, benzo(a)pyrene is not active per se, but it is converted by liver enzymes to diolepoxides, which are potent mutagens and carcinogens. In addition, a mutant of *S. typhimurium* with an **altered cell wall** was employed to ensure that all of the compounds being tested could enter the cell.

The second paper by the Ames group (**McCann et al.**) reports the introduction of certain plasmids that **enhance the mutagenic response.** We now know that *Salmonella* possesses an inadequate equivalent of the *E. coli umuC,D* system, which is required for the recovery of mutants induced by certain mutagens. The plasmids employed restored a fully active counterpart of the *umuC,D* system, allowing more mutagens to be active in the His⁻ to His⁺ assay.

Taken together, the innovations employed by Ames and co-workers represent a nice use of bacterial genetics to engineer a system for a specific purpose. As the papers reprinted here show, the correlation between mutagens and carcinogens was now very high (see also McCann et al. in Additional Readings).

The *lacI* System in *Escherichia coli*

As we learned from the work of Ames and co-workers above and as we shall see in the section on the *lacZ* system below, reversion systems have many important uses and it is easy to select directly for revertants at a specific site. However, a drawback of these systems is that one is often using only one site to determine a specific base change. What if the site that is chosen is a hotspot or a coldspot for the mutation being scored? One may greatly overgeneralize from the properties of a single site or even a few sites. The other extreme is simply to look at forward mutations. One could sequence a large number of mutations in a gene after treatment with a mutagen and determine the base changes at many sites. This approach has been used often, but it represents a great deal of work. A compromise approach used in many studies starting in the late 1970s involved detecting nonsense mutations induced in the *lacI* gene and then determining the exact base change involved in each case. There are more than 80 nonsense mutations induced in the *lacI* gene via a single base change, including 72 *amber* and *ochre* mutations, and these can be recognized genetically. With many mutagens, they represent 20–30% of all of the mutations that generate the I⁻ phenotype. Could the nonsense sites be correlated with the *lacI* DNA sequence and used to build a system for determining mutagenic specificity?

The principles established by Brenner and co-workers (see Unit 3) for using mutagenic specificity to decode certain triplets were extended by Miller and co-workers to set up the *lacI* system in *E. coli* for both genetic and later sequencing analysis of mutations. First, all of the *amber* (UAG), *ochre* (UAA), and *opal* (UGA) sites that occurred in the *lacI* gene by a single base change were characterized using a combination of fine structure deletion mapping and pattern of suppression. Then, the known specificities of three mutagens were employed to mark certain deletion groups. For example, *mutT* can only induce mutations at UAU, one of the two tyrosine codons. There are eight tyrosines in the repressor, and five of the corresponding codons can be induced to mutate to *amber*. The known positions of these tyrosines in the protein sequence allowed an easy identification of the corresponding *amber* mutations on the genetic map. These marked the positions of certain deletion groups and facilitated the assignment of the 2-aminopurine (2AP)- and ethylmethanesulfonate (EMS)-induced nonsense mutations to one of the 30 possible sites corresponding to a glutamine or tryptophan codon (see Miller et al. in Additional Readings). The assignment of these mutations then further marked deletion groups and allowed the assignment of the remaining nonsense mutations (see Coulondre et al. in Additional Readings). This work was carried out just prior to the advent of DNA sequencing, which has since verified these assignments. The final result was a set of 72 *amber* and *ochre* sites that could be induced from wild type by a known single base change.

In the paper by **Coulondre and Miller** considered here, different mutagens were used to generate I^- mutations, and the *amber* and *ochre* mutations were then detected and assigned to one of the 72 known sites in the library by both deletion mapping and their response to a set of nonsense suppressors. The results were put into a chart, not by position, but by the type of base change required to induce that specific nonsense site. This system allowed the description of the relative specificity of a mutagen as a **spectrum,** since the action of the mutagen at many sites was considered. In addition, because the work is genetic, very large numbers of mutations could be analyzed, allowing statistically significant data sets to be generated. The results for the first set of mutagens analyzed by this system are detailed in the Coulondre and Miller paper. As it turned out, the analysis of ultraviolet light (UV)-induced mutations revealed that a number of new *amber* and *ochre* sites were induced, and these could be attributed to tandem double base changes. Subsequently, many different mutagens have been analyzed using this system. Figure 14 on page 404

shows the spectra for the transitions at each of 26 sites for spontaneous mutations and 5 different mutagens. This represents the distribution of over 3700 mutations and reveals a number of hotspots, particularly in the cases of spontaneous, 2AP-induced, and UV-induced mutations.

5-Methylcytosine Hotspots

The paper by **Coulondre et al.** looks at the spontaneous transition hotspots described above and shows that they are due to the presence of **5-methylcytosine** residues, which occur at the second cytosine on each strand of a CCAGG sequence. Figure 4 on page 410 shows the in vivo genetic engineering of an additional CCAGG sequence, and Figure 5 on page 410 shows that this new sequence becomes a hotspot for C→T transitions at this sequence. The 5-methylcytosine residues are hotspots for the C→T transition because deamination at 5-methylcytosines escapes repair by the enzyme uracil DNA glycosylase, which normally removes uracil (which results from deamination of cytosine) from DNA but cannot remove thymine (the deamination product of 5-methylcytosine) from DNA. As expected, *E. coli* B cells, which do not methylate cytosines, do not show hotspots for transitions in the *I* gene at CCAGG sequences. It has subsequently been found that 5-methylcytosine residues are hotspots for transitions in human cells as well. Analysis of neighboring bases at each transition site detailed in the paper allowed the determination that UV-induced mutations occur predominantly at pyrimidine-pyrimidine sequences (see Figure 7 on page 411).

The *lacZ* Reversion System

The paper by **Nghiem et al.** represents a continuation of using the *lac* system for mutational analysis. Here, both the *lacI* system described above and a reversion system in *lacZ* were employed. In order to detect new repair systems, the authors sought **mutators** (strains that have a higher than normal level of spontaneous mutagenesis), since these strains often have defects in cellular repair pathways. For example, five different loci—*dam*, *mutH*, *mutL*, *mutS*, and *uvrD*—encode components of the methyl-directed postreplication mismatch repair system. Mutations at these loci that inactivate any of these components result in potent mutator strains. Many of the known mutators increased transitions, so mutators were sought that might increase transversions. One effective way to detect mutator strains is to observe the increased level of reversion from, say, Lac⁻ to Lac⁺. On certain media with two different carbon sources, the revertants appear as small microcolonies, or papillae, growing out of the original colony. Although papillation has been used for many years, a more sensitive test was devised for this work. The medium employed contains glucose, phenyl-β-D-galactoside, and Xgal (5-bromo, 4-chloro, indolyl-β-D-galactoside). Colonies of a Lac⁻ strain grow up to a certain size before exhausting the glucose. From this point on, only Lac⁺ revertants can grow, since only they can utilize the phenylgalactoside, a substrate for β-galactosidase. They form papillae, which are then stained blue by the Xgal, a chromogenic substrate for β-galactosidase. Figure 2 on page 419 shows this blue papillation technique and how it can be used to spot mutators.

A second innovation in this paper was the construction of a set of strains that could revert back to Lac⁺ only by a specific base change. Table 2 on page 419 shows the six strains CC101–CC106, each of which contains a single base change at the coding position 461 in *lacZ*. These mutations were constructed by site-directed mutagenesis, as detailed in the paper by **Cupples and Miller** reprinted here. The wild-type amino acid glutamine is absolutely required here, and each strain can only revert back to wild type via one of the six base changes at this coding position. Therefore, by using these six strains, one can determine the ability of a mutagen or mutator to simulate each of the six possible base substitutions, at least at this one coding position. (Table 2 on page 415 shows some of these results.) In order to do this, one must be dealing with a site that can only revert by the specified route and not by suppressor mutations. In β-galactosidase, positions 461 and 503 must have glutamic acid and tyrosine, respectively. Any other amino acid will result in the Lac⁻ phenotype.

Strains carrying mutations at the coding positions 461 and 503 can also be used to detect mutator strains. As can be seen in Figure 1 on page 414, when an *amber* (UGA) mutation is used at position 503, only a transversion event (G·C→T·A or G·C→C·G) can restore the codon to the wild-type tyrosine codon. Therefore, strains carrying this *amber* mutation were mutagenized and plated on the blue papillation indicator media. Mutator colonies were detected and scored for the specificity of the increased spontaneous mutations. Several examples of a mutator specific for the G·C→T·A transversion were found. The *lacI amber* system was also used to corroborate the detailed specificity of the mutator, which was found to map near the *nupG* locus at 64 minutes.

Repair of Oxidative Damage

Subsequent work, reviewed and covered in the **Michaels et al.** paper considered here (see also

Michaels and Miller in Additional Readings), demonstrated that the *mutY* gene encodes a glycosylase that removes the A from a mispair of G and A or from a mispair of guanine oxidized at the 8 position (8-oxoG) and A. Endonuclease action and repair synthesis restores a C opposite the G. It is now clear that the *mutY* product is part of a larger repair system, called the GO system, that is aimed at eliminating the effects of **8-oxoG,** which can mispair frequently with A. A second mutator locus specific for G·C→A·T transversions, *mutM*, was detected as a follow up to the Nghiem et al. work. The MutM protein encodes a glycosylase that removes ring-opened purines and also 8-oxoG from the DNA. The 8-oxoG residues that remain can mispair with A, but then the MutY protein removes the A, allowing the MutM protein additional opportunities for repair of the damaged base. A double mutant that is defective for both *mutY* and *mutM* has an enormous mutation frequency resulting from its complete inability to deal with the 8-oxoG lesion. A third protein, the product of the *mutT* gene, hydrolyzes the triphosphate of 8-oxoG back to the monophosphate, preventing its incorporation into DNA during replication. The mispairing of the damaged guanine with A would result in A·T→C·G transversions, which are observed in strains with a defective *mutT* gene. The diagram on page 320 summarizes the action of the GO system.

CONCLUSIONS

The use of microbial genetics has resulted in the construction of systems in both yeast and bacteria that have been widely used to determine the nature of mutations induced by mutagens and by spontaneous processes. Together with biochemical studies, this large body of work has defined pathways of mutagenesis and has also elucidated many of the repair systems that act on damaged or incorrectly replicated DNA. In many cases, the inactivation of a repair system leads to a higher level of mutation and a mutator phenotype. With this background of work, it has become easier to define similar pathways and repair systems in human cells. The exciting finding of the past few years has been the realization that a number of human inherited diseases are due to pathways described for bacteria or to the deficiency of a repair function that is a counterpart to the bacterial repair system. For example, several inherited diseases (fragile X syndrome, Huntington's disease, Kennedy's disease) involve the expansion of a triplet repeat (see Sutherland and Richards in Additional Readings), which has some relation to the frameshift hotspots seen in the *E. coli lacI* gene. In addition, defects in the

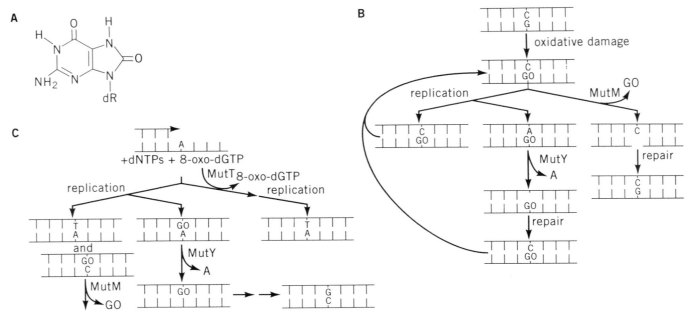

The GO System (*A*) 7,8-Dihydro-8-oxoguanine (8-hydroxyguanine). This is the structure of the predominant tautomeric form of the GO lesion. (*B*) Oxidative damage can lead to GO lesions in DNA. The GO lesions can be removed by MutM protein, and subsequent repair can restore the original G·C base pair. If the GO lesion is not removed before replication, translesion synthesis can be accurate, leading to a C/GO pair, which is a substrate for MutM protein. However, translesion synthesis by replicative DNA polymerases is frequently inaccurate, leading to the misincorporation of A opposite the GO lesion. MutY removes the misincorporated adenine from the A/GO mispairs that result from error-prone replication past the GO lesion. Repair polymerases are much less error-prone during translesion synthesis and can lead to a C/GO pair—a substrate for MutM. (*C*) Oxidative damage can also lead to 8-oxo-dGTP. MutT is active on 8-oxo-dGTP and hydrolyzes it to 8-oxo-dGMP, effectively removing the triphosphate from the deoxynucleotide pool. If MutT were not active and replication occurred with 8-oxo-dGTP in the deoxynucleotide pool, replication would be largely accurate because the polymerase preferentially inserts the correct T opposite A residues. However, inaccurate replication could result in the misincorporation of 8-oxo-dGTP opposite template A residues, leading to A/GO mispairs. MutY could be involved in the mutation process because it is active on the A/GO substrate and would remove the template A, leading to the A·T→C·G transversions that are characteristic of a *mutT* strain. The 8-oxo-dGTP could also be incorporated opposite template cytosines, resulting in a damaged C/GO pair that could be corrected by MutM.

human mismatch repair system lead to a greatly increased susceptibility to colorectal cancers (see Fishel et al. and Leach et al. in Additional Readings). The human genes corresponding to other bacterial repair genes are being investigated extensively.

ADDITIONAL READINGS

Coulondre, C. and J.H. Miller. 1977. Genetic studies of the *lac* repressor. III. Additional correlation of mutational sites with specific amino acid residues. *J. Mol. Biol.* **117:** 525–575.

Fishel, R., M.K. Lescoe, M.R.S. Rao, N.G. Copeland, N.A. Jenkins, J. Garber, M. Kane, and R. Kolodner. 1993. The human mutator gene homolog *MSH2* and its association with hereditary nonpolyposis colon cancer. *Cell* **75:** 1027–1038.

Friedberg, E.C., G.C. Walker, and W. Siede. 1995. *DNA Repair and Mutagenesis*. ASM Press, Washington D.C. pp. 697

Leach, F.S., N.C. Nicolaides, N. Papadopoulos, B. Liu (plus 31 additional authors). 1993. Mutations of a *mutS* homolog in hereditary nonpolyposis colorectal cancer. *Cell* **75:** 1215–1225.

McCann, J., E. Choi, E. Yamasaki, and B.N. Ames. 1975. Detection of carcinogens as mutagens in the *Salmonella*/microsome test: Assay of 300 chemicals. *Proc. Natl. Acad. Sci.* **72:** 5135–5139.

Michaels, M.L. and J.H. Miller. 1992. The GO system protects organisms from the mutagenic effect of the spontaneous lesion 8-hydroxyguanine (7,8-dihydro-8-oxoguanine). *J. Bact.* **174:** 6321–6325.

Miller, J.H., D. Ganem, P. Lu, and A. Schmitz. 1977. Genetic studies of the *lac* repressor. I. Correlation of mutational sites with specific amino acid residues: Construction of a colinear gene-protein map. *J. Mol. Biol.* **109:** 275–302.

Streisinger, G., Y. Okada, J. Emrich, J. Newton, A. Tsugita, E. Terzaghi, and M. Inouye. 1966. Frameshift mutations and the genetic code. *Cold Spring Harbor Symp. Quant. Biol.* **31:** 77–84.

Sutherland, G.R. and R.I. Richards. 1995. Simple tandem DNA repeats and human genetic disease. *Proc. Natl. Acad. Sci.* **92:** 3636–3641.

Genetic Studies of the *lac* Repressor

VII†. On the Molecular Nature of Spontaneous Hotspots in the *lacI* Gene of *Escherichia coli*

PHILIP J. FARABAUGH‡

Harvard University, Cambridge, Mass. U.S.A.

URSULA SCHMEISSNER§, MURIELLE HOFER

AND

JEFFREY H. MILLER

Département de Biologie, Moléculaire, Université de Genéve, Genéve, Suisse

(*Received 7 July 1978*)

140 independently occurring spontaneous mutations in the *lacI* gene of *Escherichia coli* have been examined genetically and physically. DNA sequence analysis of a genetic "hotspot" shows that the tandemly repeating sequence 5'-C-T-G-G-C-T-G-G-C-T-G-G-3' generates mutations at a high rate, either deleting or adding one unit of four nucleotides (C-T-G-G). Twelve larger deletion mutations have also been sequenced; seven of these were formed by eliminating segments between repeated sequences of five or eight nucleotides, one copy of the repeated sequence remaining after the deletion. Possible mechanisms accounting for the involvement of repeated sequences in the creation of spontaneous mutations are considered.

1. Introduction

In 1961 Seymour Benzer published a classic study of mutational sites in the *rII* cistrons of bacteriophage T4, in which he demonstrated that all sites are not equally mutable. Instead, mutability varies considerably over a range of several orders of magnitude. He termed highly mutable sites "hotspots" and suggested that some aspect of the nucleotide sequence surrounding each site might play a role in determining the rate of mutation.

Because of recent advances in DNA sequencing techniques, the molecular basis of mutational hotspots is subject to direct analysis. In this and a related study (Coulondre *et al.*, 1978) we examine the role of base sequence on mutation rate. In particular, we ask whether there are special sequences which are involved in the generation of small and large additions and deletions, and of base substitutions.

The *lacI* gene represents an ideal system for examining mutational hotspots, since the results of detailed genetic studies (Miller *et al.*, 1977; Coulondre & Miller, 1977) can be combined with the knowledge of the full nucleotide sequence (Farabaugh, 1978). Also, the recent cloning of the *I* gene onto a small plasmid (Calos, 1978) makes

† Paper VI in this series is Sommer *et al.* (1978).
‡ Present address: Cornell University, Ithaca, N.Y., U.S.A.
§ Present address: Laboratory of Molecular Biology, National Cancer Institute, Bethesda, Md, U.S.A.

possible the rapid analysis of altered sequences in the *lacI* DNA, since mutations can be crossed directly onto the plasmid by genetic techniques (see Materials and Methods). In this study we characterized a collection of 140 mutations in the *I* gene which arose spontaneously on an F'*lacproA, B* episome in an *Escherichia coli* K12 strain deleted for the *lacproB* region (GM1). The mutations were mapped and separated into distinct sites. Several different classes of mutations can be recognized, including small frameshifts, large deletions and insertions† and base substitutions.

Two very large hotspots appear in this collection. We have determined the sequence change for six representative mutations from these sites, and also for 12 deletion mutations. It is clear from the results presented in the following sections that repeated nucleotide sequences lead to a high rate of deletion and frameshift formation. In a parallel study, we show that the rates of base substitution mutations are profoundly affected by specific aspects of the DNA sequence (Coulondre *et al.*, 1978). The implications of these findings are considered in the Discussion.

2. Materials and Methods

(a) Bacterial strains

All mutations were isolated in strain GM1 (Miller *et al.*, 1977), which carries an F'*lacproB* episome with the mutations *I*q and *L8* (Müller-Hill *et al.*, 1968; Scaife & Beckwith, 1966) and harbors a deletion of the *lac* and *proB* regions on the chromosome. X7733 is Δ(*lacproB*) *galE strA thi*. The *recA*⁻ derivative of this strain (Ganem, 1972) was converted to Nal^r (Pfahl, 1972) and termed MP30.

(b) Isolation of mutants

i⁻ mutants were isolated as described by Miller *et al.* (1977).

(c) Deletion mapping

Mapping was carried out by techniques described by Schmeissner *et al.* (1977a), and by Coulondre & Miller (1977).

(d) Crossing mutations onto plasmids

Heterodiploids were constructed carrying part of the *lac* region on either the pMC1 or pMC4 plasmids (Calos, 1978) and various *I* mutations on the F'*lacproB* episome. Samples of overnight broth cultures were plated on Xgal indicator plates and deep blue colonies were picked and purified and verified for the i⁻ character. These strains were used to prepare plasmid DNA carrying the *I*⁻ mutations.

(e) DNA sequence analysis of deletion endpoints

The positions of the endpoints of the deletions analyzed here were determined by comparing the nucleotide sequence of *lacI* from the deletion strains with the wild-type sequence (Farabaugh, 1978). The position of each mutation with respect to the restriction map of *lacI*, which was approximately known from genetic mapping, was confirmed by restriction mapping. A restriction endonuclease which cleaved no more than 120 nucleotide pairs from the site of the mutation was chosen and the fragment containing the mutation isolated. The fragment was end-labeled on its two 5'-termini with [³²P]ATP and T4 polynucleotide kinase (Maxam & Gilbert, 1977). The labeled fragments were cleaved with a second restriction endonuclease and the singly labeled fragment containing the deletion subjected to the Maxam–Gilbert direct DNA sequencing procedure (Maxam & Gilbert, 1977).

† Two mutations result from the insertion of *IS*1, as determined by a physical analysis of the DNA carrying these alterations (Calos *et al.*, 1978a).

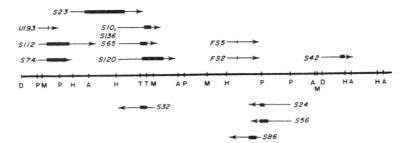

Fig. 1. A schematic diagram of the region sequenced for each mutation. The numbering system is that of Farabaugh (1978). For details see Materials and Methods.

Figure 1 is a schematic diagram of the region sequenced for each mutation. The deletions *S74*, *S112* and *U193* were sequenced from the *Hpa*II site at position −1 (the numbering system is that of Farabaugh, 1978). *S74* was sequenced from the fragment covering the region from this *Hpa*II site to the *Hae*III site at position 107. *S112* was sequenced from the fragment containing the region between the *Hpa*II site and the *Mbo*II site at position 359. *U193* was sequenced from the fragment produced by *Hpa*II cleavage at position −1 and 56 (the singly labeled fragment was produced by separation of alkali-denatured strands (Maxam & Gilbert, 1977)). The *S23* mutation is contained on a fragment extending from the *Hae*III site at position 108 to the *Mbo*II site at 359; we sequenced a fragment labeled at the *Hae*III site. Deletions *S10*, *S136*, *S65* and *S120* are all contained on the fragment extending from the *Hae*III site at position 243 to the *Hpa*II site at position 457; each was sequenced from a fragment labeled at the *Hae*III site. *S32*, a repeated occurrence of the *S65* deletion, was sequenced from a fragment labeled at the *Mbo*II site at position 358 which extended to the *Hae*III site at 243. The major hotspot deletion and insertion mutations *F32*, *FS84*, *FS5*, *FS25*, *FS45* and *FS65* are all contained on the fragment produced by cleavage at the *Hae*III site at position 589 and the *Hpa*II site at 699; each was sequenced from a fragment with the label at the *Hae*III site. *S86* is contained on the same fragment but was sequenced from the *Hpa*II site. *S24* and *S56* are contained on a fragment which extends from the *Hpa*II site at 809 to the *Hae*III site at 589; they were sequenced from a fragment labeled at the *Hpa*II site. *S42* was sequenced from a fragment labeled at the *Hind*II site at position 986 which extended to the *Alu*I site at position 979.

A complete description of the sequence of each deletion endpoint is given in Farabaugh (1977).

3. Results

(a) *Genetic characterization*

Figure 2 shows the distribution of 140 spontaneous mutations in the *lacI* gene, as determined by recombination tests with a large set of deletions (Schmeissner *et al.*, 1977*a,b*). Each mutation is of independent origin and results in an inactive repressor protein and the i⁻ phenotype (see Materials and Methods). Two hotspots† dominate the spectrum. These comprise 94 of the 140 mutations and occur at or near the same position in the middle of the gene. Although we cannot distinguish among these 94 mutations by recombination tests, we can define two classes based on the reversion rates: 78 of the mutations revert at an uncharacteristically high frequency (revertants appearing at about 10^{-5} in the population), whereas the remaining 18 mutations do not generate revertants at a detectable rate ($< 10^{-8}$). Therefore, we assume that at

† Since these mutations occur at a very high frequency relative to other mutations in the *I* gene, we define them as hotspots.

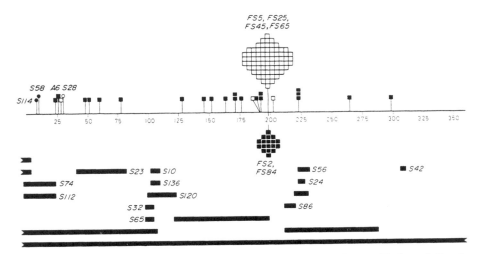

FIG. 2. The distribution of 140 spontaneous mutations in the *lacI* gene. Each mutation is of independent origin and resulted in the i⁻ phenotype. A single occurrence of an apparent point mutation is represented by a square. Filled in squares indicate mutations with very low or undetectable reversion rates, whereas open squares indicate mutations which are unstable, reverting at frequencies of 10^{-5} or greater. Deletions are shown below the line, which represents the length of the *I* gene given in terms of the position of the corresponding residue in the *lac* repressor. All mutations were mapped against the deletions used to divide the gene into 108 marked sections (Schmeissner *et al.*, 1977*a,b*). The allele numbers are given in cases where the mutational change has been sequenced. *S114* and *S58* are insertions of the transposable element *IS*1 (Calos *et al.*, 1978*b*). *S28* is an unstable duplication of 88 base-pairs (Calos *et al.*, 1978*a*). The other sequenced mutations are described in this paper.

least two different mutations are appearing at or extremely near the same point in the gene.

A number of large deletions can be identified in this collection. Most of these have both endpoints within the *I* gene and its control region. We mapped the deletions against a set of point mutations at known positions (see below). From the markers used to map the deletion endpoints it appears that in at least three cases the same or a very similar deletion recurs. Together, the deletions and the two hotspots in the middle of the gene constitute close to 80% of the spontaneous mutations detected in the *I* gene. In the following section we describe the DNA sequence analysis of these mutations. We report elsewhere the molecular nature of spontaneous base substitutions (Coulondre *et al.*, 1978), which comprise part of the remaining mutations.

(b) *DNA sequence at a hotspot*

Four mutations from the most prominent hotspot and two mutations from what appears to be a second hotspot were crossed onto the plasmid carrying the *I* gene and DNA from each of these was isolated, cut with restriction enzymes, and sequenced by procedures outlined in Materials and Methods. The results are shown in Figure 3. The wild-type sequence in this region of the gene (between bases 620 and 631) shows a striking tandem repeat of the sequence 5'-C-T-G-G-3', which occurs three times in succession. Four unstable mutations (*FS5*, *FS25*, *FS45* and *FS65*) from the major hotspot were found to contain an additional C-T-G-G sequence, thus extending the repeat to four sets of the same sequence. The high reversion at this site can then be envisioned as the subsequent loss of one C-T-G-G sequence. Two stable mutations

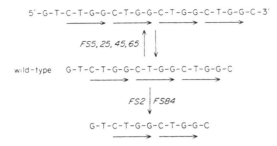

FIG. 3. The sequence change resulting from the two mutational hotspots. (See text for details.)

from the second cluster depicted in Figure 2, *FS2* and *FS84*, showed the loss of one set of the four-base sequence C-T-G-G from this same wild-type sequence. Apparently, reversion by re-addition of a C-T-G-G sequence to the two remaining sets occurs at too low a frequency (less than 10^{-8}) to be detected in this system. These results show that the same sequence is responsible for generating two different frameshift mutations both of which arise at a high rate relative to all other mutations in the *I* gene.

Figure 4 depicts the molecular consequences of each of these mutations. It can be seen that in both cases a nonsense codon is encountered soon after the shift in the reading frame. The resulting repressor fragments are 203 and 311 amino acids long, respectively, and have no activity.

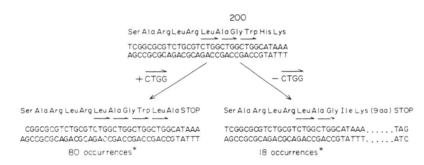

FIG. 4. The molecular consequences of the addition or deletion of 4 base-pairs resulting from each of the 2 hotspots. Hyphens omitted for clarity.

(c) DNA sequence of deletion endpoints

We crossed 12 deletions from the collection shown in Figure 2 onto the pMC1 plasmid and sequenced the relevant portion of the *I* DNA (see Materials and Methods). Figures 5 and 6 show the results. It is clear that repeated sequences are involved frequently in deletion formation, since in seven out of 12 cases (see Table 1) repeats of five or eight bases are found at each end in the wild-type sequence. The deletions remove one of the repeated sequences and all of the intervening DNA. Moreover, in three cases (*S74* and *S112*, *S10* and *S136*, *S32* and *S65*) the identical deletion has recurred independently at the same sequence! Of the deletions which did not show significant repeats none recurred in the sample, suggesting that non-repeat sites may be much less specific.

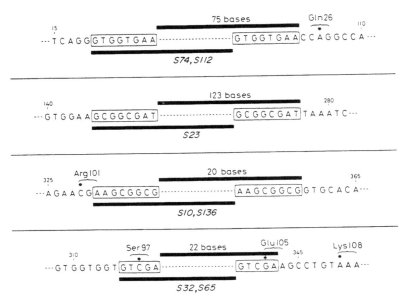

FIG. 5. The region deleted by the mutations *S74, S112, S23, S10, S136, S32* and *S65*. The repeated sequence present in the wild type before the deletion is boxed, and the deletion indicated both above and below the line. Marker rescue experiments were performed (see Table 3) using mutations at the position indicated by asterisk. The base-pair and codon numbers are also indicated to facilitate placement on the gene–protein maps. Hyphens omitted for clarity.

TABLE 1

Sequences at the endpoints of deletions

Site (no. of base-pairs)	Sequence repeat†	Bases deleted	Occurrences	
20 to 95	G-T-G-G-T-G-A-A	75	2	*S74, S112*
146 to 269	G-C-G-G-C-G-A-T	123	1	*S23*
331 to 351	A-A-G-C-G-G-C-G	20	2	*S10, S136*
316 to 338	G-T-C-G-A	22	2	*S32, S65*
694 to 707	CA	13	1	*S24*
694 to 719	CA	25	1	*S56*
943 to 956	G	13	1	*S42*
322 to 393	None	71	1	*S120*
658 to 685	None	27	1	*S86*

† This refers only to the nucleotides seen in the wild-type sequence at either end of the segment which is subsequently deleted, and does not imply that repeats of 1 or 2 bases are significant. Only the repeated sequences of 5 and 8 nucleotides are considered meaningful here.

The data shown in Figures 5 and 6 are tabulated here. The numbering system is that of Farabaugh (1978).

(d) *Additional deletions*

We also screened a collection of over 800 mutagen-induced i⁻ mutants for the presence of deletions (see Table 2). This represents an effective probe for monitoring the percentage of deletions among I^- mutations, and also the absolute frequency of induction. There is no selection involved, provided the deletions are longer than the distance between the point mutations used, or else span one of these markers (Fig. 7).

TABLE 2

Deletions among I⁻ mutations

Mutagen	Non-suppressible mutations tested	% of total	Deletions† found	% of total
2-aminopurine	334	80	9	2
Ultraviolet light	174	80	12	5·5
4-nitroquinoline-1-oxide	87	73	1	0·8
mut T	86	92	0	0
None (spontaneous)	139	99	19	14

† Excluding the frameshift mutation involving a deletion of 4 bases.

The deletions extending into *I* but not into *Z* and which are not lethal are scored here. Very small deletions, such as the frameshift caused by the removal of 4 bases depicted in Fig. 3, would not be detected by the mapping probes used (see text). The deletions appearing in the 2-amino-purine collection probably arose spontaneously in the treated cultures and were not induced by 2-aminopurine.

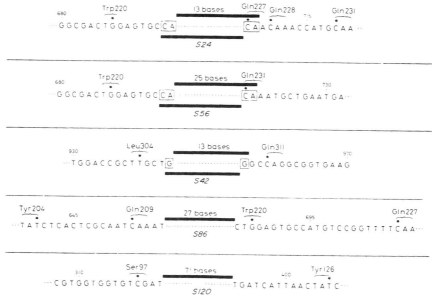

FIG. 6. The region deleted by the mutations *S24, S56, S42, S120* and *S86*. For further details see the legend to Fig. 5. Hyphens omitted for clarity.

Ultraviolet light provides a five- to tenfold stimulation of deletions of this type†, at a maximum. (u.v.-stimulated deletions have been detected in other bacterial systems (Demerec, 1960; Schwartz & Beckwith, 1969)). On the other hand, 4-nitro-quinoline-1-oxide and 2-aminopurine do not appear to stimulate deletions in this system. (The 2% deletions found after 2-aminopurine treatment probably reflect the spontaneous background, since independent tests indicate the presence of other spontaneous mutations in this collection; the spontaneous background was much lower in the u.v.-treated cells.)

† Larger deletions which would prevent episome replication are not scored here; neither are those extending into or past *lacZ*.

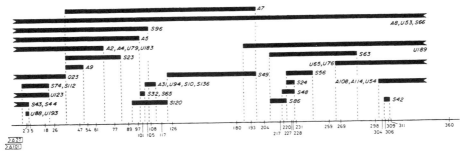

FIG. 7. The deletions found among I^- mutations. S, spontaneous; A, 2-aminopurine-induced; U, ultraviolet light-induced; Q, 4-nitroquinoline-1-oxide-induced. Some of these mutations represent the spontaneous background in the mutagenized cells (see Table 2 and text for further description).

Several deletion endpoints cluster in small regions (i.e. *A108*, *A114* and *U54*). These may represent other examples of repeated sequences. The most suggestive clustering results from the addition of *A31* and *U94* to the group already including *S10* and *S136*, since both endpoints of these deletions are mapped within short intervals, and *S10* and *S136* have already been shown to be identical (both involving a repeated sequence of eight nucleotides). Sequence analysis of these deletions should prove interesting.

(e) *Recombination tests*

Since the sequence results from the preceding sections provide us with deletions at known positions, we can test the resolution of our mapping system by utilizing point mutations at known positions. As Figures 5 and 6 indicate, the repeated sequences provide an ambiguity regarding the exact point of deletion formation. From the standpoint of "marker rescue" the bases between the markers and the deletion always include the remaining copy of the repeated sequence. Thus, in recombination tests

TABLE 3

Recombinants from crosses between deletions and point mutations

| | Frequency of recombinants ($\times 10^{-7}$) | | | | | | | | |
| | Separation from point mutations (in nucleotide pairs) | | | | | | | | |
Deletion	1	3	4	5	8	10	11	13	14
S74								50	
S112								50	
S10						20			
S136						20			
S32		1	3					60	
S65		1	4					100	
S24	< 0·2		< 0·2		10			50	
S56	< 0·2				10				
S42			40	10					
S120			10						60
S86			0·5	2					

Each approximate recombinant frequency is the average of several determinations. Crosses were carried out as described by Coulondre & Miller (1977).

between *S32* or *S65* and the mutation affecting nucleotide 318. the deletion is envisioned as removing bases 321 to 343, whereas in tests against a mutation affecting base 341, *S32* and *S65* are positioned as deleting bases 316 to 338 (see Fig. 5). With these considerations in mind we can examine Table 3 which gives the results of several recombination experiments. It is interesting to note that recombination can be detected in some cases even when the mutation is three nucleotides away from the deletion endpoint.

4. Discussion

The molecular nature of hotspots has intrigued geneticists ever since Benzer (1961) first discovered that mutations within a gene are not distributed randomly among the available sites. The work presented here demonstrates that special nucleotide sequences play an important role in determining spontaneous rates of mutation. Small frameshifts and deletions constitute two major classes of mutations occurring spontaneously, together comprising approximately 80% of the *lacI⁻* mutations. Tandemly repeated sequences, such as the C-T-G-G-T-G-G-C-T-G-G sequence found in the *I* gene, are a major source of hotspots, generating additions and deletions of the repeated unit at a high rate with respect to other mutational sites in the gene. Mutants having an additional C-T-G-G sequence at this point in the gene appear at a frequency of about 2×10^{-6}, and those having a deletion of a C-T-G-G sequence are found at approximately 0.5×10^{-6}. Larger deletions also predominate at repeated sequences as the data in Table 1 and Figure 4 demonstrate. Recurrence of identical deletions at these points serves to strengthen this conclusion.

What of the remaining 20% of the mutations? As Figure 2 shows these are scattered over numerous sites. We have crossed each of these mutations onto a plasmid and examined the size of *Hind*II restriction fragments. From this analysis two mutations (*S58* and *S114*) have now been shown to be due to the insertion of the transposable element *IS*1 (Calos *et al.*, 1978*b*). This investigation has also revealed a tandem duplication of 88 base pairs in one case (*S28*; see the accompanying paper, Calos *et al.*, 1978*a*). Both base substitutions and other small frameshift mutations should comprise many of the remaining lesions. In a separate paper we analyze base substitutions and show that these occur preferentially at 5-methylcytosines (Coulondre *et al.*, 1978). Taken in its larger perspective, spontaneous mutations predominate at special sequences, even though many different types of changes are involved.

Based on studies of altered T4 phage lysozyme sequences, Streisinger *et al.* (1966) proposed a model to account for the generation of frameshift mutations, suggesting that after breakage and digestion of a single strand, "slipped mispairing" occurs at tandemly repeated sequences. This can lead to additions and deletions adjacent to repeated sequences (Okada *et al.*, 1972). Such a model accounts for a number of characterized frameshifts in other systems (see review by Roth, 1974). The two frameshift hotspots which have been sequenced conform nicely to the predictions of the Streisinger model. Alternatively, it is possible that such events are generated by unequal crossing over in general recombination. It remains to be determined whether mutations similar to *FS2* and *FS5* (− 4 bases and + 4 bases, respectively) arise at the same frequencies in a *recA⁻* strain. However, the reversion of *FS5* to *I⁺* does occur in a *recA⁻* background (see Table 4). If sequencing experiments verify that these have indeed undergone a loss of four bases back to wild type, it would

TABLE 4

Frequency of i$^+$ revertants for the frameshift mutations FS2 and FS5

Mutation	Frequency of i$^+$ revertants ($\times 10^{-5}$) recA$^+$	recA$^-$
FS2	< 0·001	—
FS5	0·5	0·4
	1·6	0·9
	0·8	1·7
	1·4	0·7

Reversion tests were carried out in strain X7733 (*recA*$^+$) and MP30 (*recA*$^-$), as described by Coulondre & Miller (1977) (see Materials and Methods). The results of 4 different experiments are shown for *FS5*.

argue strongly against the involvement of *recA*-mediated recombination in the formation of this type of frameshift mutation. It would be of considerable interest to determine which enzymes in the cell are responsible for the generation of such frameshifts. Strains carrying fast reverting insertions such as *FS5* could conceivably be used to detect mutants which lack these enzymes by screening for the elimination of the high reversion rate. It is not unlikely that the two major hotspots reported by Benzer (1961) in the *rII* cistrons also involve repeating sets of bases, as has been suggested from reversion studies with different mutagens (S. Brenner, personal communication).

The finding that spontaneous deletions are favored at repeated sequences raises a number of interesting questions. Are deletions of all lengths also favored at repeating stretches of nucleotides? This could be answered by sequencing both termini of deletions extending over several gene lengths. Are all repeated sequences equally susceptible to deletion formation? A computer analysis of sequence repeats in *lacI* indicates that certain sequences may indeed be favored (see Appendix). The involvement of the Rec system in deletion formation should also be tested. Although general *tonB-trp* deletions have been shown to arise at approximately the same rate in *recA*$^+$ and *recA*$^-$ strains (Franklin, 1967), specific deletions have not been monitored. From Table 1 it is evident that some deletions do not occur at repeated sequences; these would not be expected to show *recA* dependence in any case. On the other hand, the deletions examined here may be formed by the same kind of "slippage" mechanism proposed for frameshifts (Streisinger *et al.*, 1966). (Previous studies with the *rII* system of phage T4 have led to predictions of the involvement of repeated sequences in the origin of spontaneous deletions; S. Brenner, personal communication.)

The recurring sequences which generate deletions should also result in the reciprocal event; namely the production of a duplication of the region between the repeats. These have not been detected in the remainder of the collection of the *I*$^-$ mutations depicted in Figure 2 in the restriction enzyme analysis of plasmids carrying these mutations (see above). The only duplication found by this method did not arise *via* a repeated sequence (Calos *et al.*, 1978*a*). (One example of this type of duplication has been detected in phage lambda; R. Maurer, unpublished results.)

In at least two systems deletions have been found in conjunction with point mutations (J. Roth, unpublished results; Barnett *et al.*, 1967). The 12 deletions analyzed here do not arise together with an additional lesion nearby, however, since the DNA sequence extending for approximately 50 bases beyond each endpoint has been shown to be identical to wild type (Farabaugh, 1977).

Experiments aimed at examining the other unstable mutations (Fig. 2) at the sequence level are currently in progress, as are attempts to determine the sequence change resulting from additional deletions found in this system.

We thank Drs S. Brenner, F. Crick, F. Stahl, W. Gilbert and J. Roth for helpful discussions. This work was supported by a grant (GM09541) from the National Institutes of Health (to W. Gilbert), and by a grant from the Swiss National Fund (F. N. 3.179.77) (to J. H. M.).

REFERENCES

Barnett, L., Brenner, S., Crick, F. H. C., Shulman, R. G. & Watts-Tobin, R. J. (1967). *Phil. Trans. Roy. Soc. ser. B*, **252**, 487–560.

Benzer, S. (1961). *Proc. Nat. Acad. Sci., U.S.A.* **46**, 1585–1594.

Calos, M. (1978). *Nature (London)*, **274**, 762–765.

Calos, M., Galas, D. & Miller, J. H. (1978a). *J. Mol. Biol.* **126**, 865–869.

Calos, M., Johnsrud, L. & Miller, J. H. (1978b). *Cell*, **13**, 411–418.

Coulondre, C. & Miller, J. H. (1977). *J. Mol. Biol.* **117**, 525–567.

Coulondre, C., Miller, J. H., Farabaugh, P. J. & Gilbert, W. (1978). *Nature, (London)*, **274**, 775–780.

Demerec, M. (1960). *Proc. Nat. Acad. Sci., U.S.A.* **46**, 1075–1079.

Farabaugh, P. J. (1977). PhD thesis, Harvard University.

Farabaugh, P. J. (1978). *Nature (London)*, **274**, 765–769.

Franklin, N. C. (1967). *Genetics*, **55**, 699–707.

Ganem, D. (1972). Honors thesis, Harvard University.

Maxam, A. & Gilbert, W. (1977). *Proc. Nat. Acad. Sci., U.S.A.* **74**, 560–564.

Miller, J. H., Ganem, D., Lu, P. & Schmitz, A. (1977). *J. Mol. Biol.* **109**, 275–302.

Müller-Hill, B., Crapo, L. & Gilbert, W. (1968). *Proc. Nat. Acad. Sci., U.S.A.* **59**, 1259–1263.

Okada, Y., Streisinger, G., Emrich, J., Newton, J., Tsugita, A. & Inouye, M. (1972). *Nature, (London)*, **236**, 338–341.

Pfahl, M. (1972). *Genetics*, **72**, 393–410.

Roth, J. R. (1974). *Annu. Rev. Genet.* **8**, 319–346.

Scaife, J. G. & Beckwith, J. R. (1966). *Cold Spring Harbor Symp. Quant. Biol.* **31**, 403–408.

Schmeissner, U., Ganem, D. & Miller, J. H. (1977a). *J. Mol. Biol.* **109**, 303–326.

Schmeissner, U., Ganem, D. & Miller, J. H. (1977b). *J. Mol. Biol.* **117**, 572–575.

Schwartz, D. & Beckwith, J. R. (1969). *Genetics*, **61**, 371–379.

Sommer, H., Schmitz, A., Schmeissner, M., Miller, J. H. & Wittmann, H. G. (1978). *J. Mol. Biol.*, **123**, 457–469.

Streisinger, G., Okada, Y., Emrich, J., Newton, J., Tsugita, A., Terzaghi, E. & Inouye, M. (1966). *Cold Spring Harbor Symp. Quant. Biol.* **31**, 77–84.

APPENDIX

An Analysis of Sequence Repeats in the
lacI Gene of Escherichia coli

DAVID J. GALAS

Département de Biologie Moléculaire, Université de Genève, Genève, Suisse

Since it is now clear that a significant fraction of non-lethal spontaneous deletions terminate in repeated sequences (see the main text), the role played by these repeats in the formation of deletions has become an important question. As a first step in the investigation of the issue, the sequence of the I gene must be analysed to establish the background of repeated sequences against which the observed deletions occurred. The possibility that a careful comparison of these observed deletions with potential sites for repeat-catalysed deletion formation may suggest or restrict hypotheses as to the processes involved is the primary motivation for such an analysis.

In this paper I present an analysis of the sequence of the I gene (Farabaugh, 1978) for direct repeats, inverted repeats, and the possibility of slipped mispairing (contiguous or overlapping repeats). This spectrum of repeats is compared with the data reported in the accompanying paper, the sequenced endpoints of deletions internal to the I gene and the frameshift mutation hotspot. It can be argued from this comparison that it is likely that the distance between repeats is an important factor, and that some sequence specificity is also involved in at least one pathway for deletion formation.

(a) Direct repeats

The sequence of the I gene was read into the computer and scanned for repeats by a program which used the following simple algorithm†. To begin, a short sequence (the first N bases) is taken for comparison with every N-base sequence in the gene. Each sequence for which the agreement is equal to, or greater than, a certain threshold, L, is printed out with its position, degree of match, and the distance between the first bases in the two N-base sequences. The next N-base sequence (shifted up one base in the gene) is then taken and the same comparisons made with the remaining sequence of the gene (one less base in the gene is used each time the N-base sequence is shifted to avoid duplicating comparisons). The parameters L and N are set as required when the program is executed. The magnitude of this process is indicated by the problem of determining the number of exact eight-base repeats. L and N are thus set to eight. The sequence scanned here is 1150 bases long, including the leader region of the transcribed DNA and 41 bases following the final sense codon. This scan then requires $(1150-8)^2/2$ pairs of eight-base sequences be compared, about 5×10^6 single base comparisons. The results of a scan for eight and nine base exact repeats are shown in Table A1.

† These calculations were performed on a Nova 840 computer. The programming was done in FORTRAN IV.

TABLE A1

Direct repeats of eight or more bases in the I gene

Repeat	Base 1	Base 2	Δ	Extent of repeat	Deletions
C-T-G-G-C-T-G-G-C	620	624	4	9	Frameshifts
G-A-A-G-C-G-G-C-G‡	143	331	188	9	—
G-C-G-C-G-T-T-G-G	814	1048	234	9	—
C-C-A-G-C-G-T-G-G	303	925	622	9	—
G-C-G-C-A-A-C-G-C	374	1113	739	9	—
A-A-G-C-G-G-C-G‡	331	351	20	8	*S10, S136*
G-T-G-G-T-G-A-A	20	95	75	8†	*S74, S112*
C-C-G-C-G-T-G-G	91	178	87	8	
T-C-T-C-G-C-G-C	281	370	89	8	
G-C-G-G-C-G-A-T	146	269	123	8	*S23*
G-C-G-A-C-T-G-G	529	681	152	8	—
A-A-G-C-G-G-C-G‡	144	351	207	8§	—
G-C-G-T-G-G-T-G	93	306	213	8§	—
G-T-G-G-A-A-G-C	140	434	294	8§	—
C-G-A-C-T-G-G-A	682	1091	403	8	—
G-G-G-C-A-A-A-C	199	917	718	8	—
G-T-T-T-C-C-C-G	86	1085	999	8	—

These repeats were found using the algorithm described in the text. Base 1 is the location, with respect to the first base of the *I* message, of the first base of the first occurrence of the repeat (with respect to the amino-terminal end of the repressor). Base 2 is the location of the first base of the second occurrence of the repeat. Δ is the number of bases between the first bases of the 2 occurrences. The deletions, designated by allele number (see the main text), are listed in the last column. The 4 notations in the next to last column indicate that the sequence is part of a larger repeat which is interrupted by one mismatch. †, indicates that 9 out of 10 bases match; ‡ indicates that there is an identical sequence; § indicates that it is part of 10 out of 11 match.

Note that the observed deletions occur only with eight-base repeat endpoints, even though there are four nine-base repeats available. Clearly the size of the repeat is not the only determining factor. As one can tell from a glance at Table A1, the nine-base repeats are spaced rather far apart; in fact, the closest of these spans a distance greater than the size of the largest deletion. It is possible that the distance between repeats reduces their probability of forming deletions sufficiently to account for the absence of nine-base repeats in this sample. That this possibility is consistent with the eight-base repeat spectrum is also clear from Table A1. It is only the closely spaced eight-base repeats that are represented here. In this sample it is entirely possible to account for the distribution by the random occurrence of deletions, at roughly the same rate, among the five most closely spaced eight-base repeats.

To illustrate this point suppose that the distance between repeats were unimportant and all eight- and nine-base repeats were equally likely as deletion sites. Then the probability that the five observed deletions would be confined to the five closest repeats, as they are in this sample, would be about 3×10^{-3}. However, the distribution of the five observed deletions among these five sites cannot be distinguished from random. If five deletions (sites) were chosen at random from a collection in which all five sites are equally represented, the probability that this sample of five would miss two sites, as in the real sample, is 0·41. Thus it is not unlikely that a random sampling would yield the observed result.

An important argument for the significance of the spacing of the repeats is encountered by considering the three repeats marked ‡ in Table A1. Since the sequences are identical the possible influence of sequence specificity is removed. The fact that the repeat spaced at 20 bases was found twice among the deletions, and that ones spaced at 207 and 187 bases are not found, argues strongly that the spacing influences the frequency of deletion formation. An examination of the seven-base repeat spectrum suggests, however, that there is more involved than the spacing between repeats. The 11 most closely spaced of these, shown in Table A2, have six among them closer than

TABLE A2

The eleven closest exact seven-base repeats in the I gene

Repeat	Base 1	Base 2	Δ
5′ 3′			
C-G-C-G-C-C-G	250	284	34
A-T-T-A-A-T-G	1063	1122	59
T-G-A-C-C-A-G	415	481	66
C-A-A-C-T-G-G	191	293	102
G-C-A-A-A-C-C	1030	1030	111
A-A-C-C-A-C-C	886	1009	123
A-T-A-T-C-T-C	637	828	191
C-C-T-G-C-A-C	244	444	200
C-A-A-A-C-C-A	710	920	210
C-T-G-G-G-C-G	533	779	246
G-G-T-G-G-T-G	21	311	290

Of the 34 exact 7-base repeats these are those with the lowest value of Δ, excepting the single overlapping repeat ($\Delta = 6$) which is entered in Table A3. The designations of the columns are defined in the legend to Table A1.

some observed deletion. It is possible that the smaller repeat unit accounts for the absence of the seven-base repeats among the deletions. However (for reasons discussed below), it seems more likely that among the deletion endpoints there is some sequence resemblance for which the process is partially specific.

Table A1 shows that there are striking similarities among the eight-base repeats for the five deletions. The *S74* and *S23* endpoints match in five out of eight bases, and if the pyrimidines are considered equivalent in seven out of eight bases. The *S10* and *S23* endpoints match in six out of eight bases with a two-base shift (G-C-G-G-C-G).

Some sort of specificity is also suggested by the deletion ending in the five-base repeat. This deletion, found twice in a sample of independently isolated deletions, is quite small (22 bases), but there are many repeats of five and six bases as close or closer together. In Figure A1 all the repeats in the *I* gene closer than 50 bases are represented. Figure A1(a), in which the repeats are displayed as a function of the length of the repeats and of their spacing, suggests that there is something notable about the particular repeats for which deletions were found, surrounded as they are by other available sites. That the deletions, *S65* and *S32*, were isolated independently and found to terminate at the same five-base repeat suggests that this site is preferred. The probability of the same deletion being found twice if all five- and six-base repeats closer than 50 bases were equally likely is about 0·03, and if all 902 five-base repeats

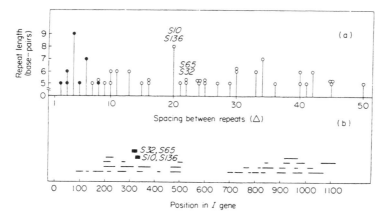

FIG. A1. The distribution of close, direct repeats in the *I* gene. Both (a) and (b) include only those repeats closer than 50 bases ($\triangle \leqslant 50$). (a) This shows the distribution with respect to the spacing between repeats, and the vertical axis indicates the length of repeat involved. Overlapping or contiguous repeats are indicated by a solid circle (●). Occurrence of more than one repeat with the same $\triangle$ is shown by multiple symbols. The deletion mutations are indicated over the repeats that are their endpoints. (b) This shows the close repeats distributed along the *I* gene. The scale is the same as in Table A1. Deletions are indicated by heavy bars and their numbers.

were equally likely, it is negligibly small. In Figure A1(b) the distribution of the close repeats near the beginning of the gene is shown. The only notable feature of this distribution is the clustering of the close repeats near the beginning and the end of the gene. Nothing can be said here of the fact that the two deletions, of roughly the same size, are located in the same region of the gene. The sample is simply too small. Only characterization of additional deletions can determine the actual specificity. In this connection it may be useful to note that subsequences of repeated deletion end-points exist elsewhere in the gene. If the specificity is even partially carried in such a subsequence, its efficacy as a deletion endpoint may be enhanced over background. An example of such a subsequence is the last entry in Table A2. This seven-base sequence matches in six out of seven bases the endpoints of deletion *S74/S112*.

There are three repeats displayed in Table A1 which have identical sequences, resulting from the triple repetition of an eight-base sequence. Such a multiple repetition is suggestive of duplication events in the evolution of the *I* gene. Other evidence supporting such an assertion will be considered in another paper.

(b) *Slipped mispairing*

The striking mutational hotspot discovered in the *I* gene has been explained as the consequence of slipped mispairings leading to the insertion or deletion of four base-pairs (see the accompanying paper). There is only one prominent hotspot in the gene, thus it may be revealing to examine the opportunities for slipped mispairing afforded by the sequence elsewhere in the *I* gene. This was done in much the same way as the repeats were analysed. We have ignored here the possibility that sequences which include mismatches can participate in slipped mispairing and have only looked for contiguous or overlapping exact repeats of five bases or more. These repeats are indicated on the left side of Figure A1(a) by the solid dots. They are also tabulated in Table A3. It can be seen immediately that the hotspot is within the stretch of DNA

TABLE A3

Opportunities for slipped mispairing in the I gene

Base 1	Base 2	Δ	Repeat	Length
			5′ 3′	
620 ⎫	624	4	C-T-G-G-C-T-G-G-C	9
620 ⎭	628	8	C-T-G-G-C	5
610	616	6	G-C-G-T-C-T-G	7
309	311	2	G-T-G-G-T-G	6
947	949	2	C-T-C-T-C	5
18	190	3	A-C-A-A-C	5
1000	1005	5	G-A-A-A-A	5

This list represents all those exact repeats of 5 or more bases which are contiguous or overlapping. The bracket marking the first 2 entries indicates that the second is a subsequence of the first. Column designations are as for Tables A1 and A2.

that can be slipped and mispaired with the maximum homology in the fashion proposed by Streisinger *et al.* (1966). Note that the same region can be slipped eight bases as well as four but at the cost of reducing the homology from nine to five bases. Only the four-base deletion and insertion events have been observed. Convincing evidence that five bases is insufficient homology for this process is provided by the observation that, having lost four bases at this point, mutants rarely revert: the hotspot is no longer hot when reduced to a five-base homology (see the accompanying paper).

There are only two other candidates in the gene for slipped mispairing, having homologies of six and seven. The situation for these sites is rather ambiguous, however, because it is not clear what effect these strand-slip-produced mutations have on the protein. The seven-base site could add or delete six bases, while the six-base site could add or delete three bases, neither resulting in a frameshift.

TABLE A4

Inverted repeats of eight or more bases in the I gene

Base 1	Base 2	Δ	Sequence	Length
			5′ 3′	
87	128	41	A-C-G-C-G-G-G-A-A-A	10
238	953	715	C-A-G-G-G-C-C-A-G	9
16	1010	994	A-C-C-A-C-C-C-T-G	9
284	605	321	T-C-G-G-C-G-C-G	8
249	606	357	C-G-G-C-G-C-G-T	8
232	683	451	G-A-C-T-G-G-A-G	8
160	655	495	A-A-T-T-C-A-G-C	8
107	621	514	T-G-G-C-T-G-G-C	8
107	625	518	T-G-G-C-T-G-G-C	8
239	954	715	A-G-G-G-C-C-A-G	8
214	973	759	C-A-A-T-C-A-G-C	8
300	1072	772	G-C-T-G-G-C-A-C	8

Column designations are as in previous Tables. However, since these are inverted repeats the 2 sequences are different and the listed sequence is that one beginning at base 2 in each case.

(c) *Inverted repeats*

To complete the picture of the structure of repeated sequences in the gene the inverted repeats have been analysed; even though no genetic events have yet been associated with them. The algorithm used here is identical to the direct repeat algorithm after a step which inverts and takes the (base-pairing) complement of the sequence of interest. The results of this scan for exact inverted repeats are shown in Table A4 for sequences of eight bases or more. The number of occurrences is in accord with the expected numbers from a random sequence.

The analysis presented here appears to support the notion that some sequence specificity is involved in deletion formation. The evidence seems rather convincing that the distance between repeat sequences is an important factor in determining the frequency of deletions with these endpoints, and that the frameshift hotspot is simply due to slipped mispairing at that site. However, the analysis is merely supportive, particularly as regards sequence specificity, and will lead to more definite conclusions as more spontaneous mutations in the *I* gene are analysed.

I thank Dr J. H. Miller for support and for reading the manuscript. This work was supported by a grant from the Swiss National Fund (F.N. 3.179.77.).

REFERENCES

Farabaugh, P. J. (1978). *Nature (London)*, **274**, 765–769.
Streisinger, G., Okada, Y., Emrich, J., Newton, J., Tsugita, A., Terzaghi, E. & Inouye, M. (1966). *Cold Spring Harbor Symp. Quant. Biol.* **31**, 77–84.

On the Formation of Spontaneous Deletions: The Importance of Short Sequence Homologies in the Generation of Large Deletions

Alessandra M. Albertini, Murielle Hofer,
Michèle P. Calos* and Jeffrey H. Miller
Département de Biologie Moléculaire
Université de Genève
Geneva, Switzerland

Summary

Using *lacI-Z* fusion strains of Escherichia coli we have devised systems that detect deletions of varying lengths. We examined deletions 700–1000 base pairs long, and genetically characterized over 250 spontaneous deletions. Of these, we analyzed 24 by direct DNA sequencing and 18 by inspection of restriction fragment patterns. Deletions of this size occur almost exclusively at short repeated sequences in both *recA*+ and *recA*− strain backgrounds, but are detected 25-fold more frequently in a *recA*+ background. The frequency of deletion formation correlates with the extent of homology between the short repeated sequences, although other factors may be involved. The largest hotspot, which accounts for 60% of the deletions detected, involves the largest homology in the system (14 of 17 base pairs). Altering a single base pair within this homology reduces deletion incidence by an order of magnitude. We discuss possible mechanisms of deletion formation and consider its relationship to the excision of transposable elements.

Introduction

Using the *lacI* system of Escherichia coli, we discovered that spontaneous deletions predominate between short homologies of as few as 5–8 base pairs (Farabaugh et al., 1978). Seven of 12 deletions sequenced were between short sequence repeats. All of the deletions examined arose in a *recA*+ background, and ranged in length from 9 to 123 base pairs. Subsequently, deletions between short repeated sequences have been demonstrated in phage T7 (Studier et al., 1979), phage T4 (Pribnow et al., 1981) and E. coli (Brake et al., 1978; Fedoroff, 1979; Ghosal and Saedler, 1979; Ross et al., 1979; Post et al., 1980; Wu et al., 1980). Deletions at repeated sequences have also been inferred in the human β-globin gene family (Marotta et al., 1977; Efstratiadis et al., 1980).

We describe the use of derivatives of a *lacI–Z* fusion strain, which allow us to study deletions more systematically than was previously possible. We have used these derivatives to investigate how frequently deletions of more than 700 base pairs occur between short homologies in both *recA*+ and *recA*− strains,

* Present address: Department of Genetics, Stanford University School of Medicine, Stanford, California 94305.

and have examined the effect of the length of the short homologies on the frequency of deletion formation. The influence of both the distance between homologies and the surrounding sequence on deletion formaton will be considered elsewhere (submitted manuscript).

Experimental Design

We have taken advantage of a deletion characterized by Müller-Hill and Kania (1974), which fuses the beginning of the Z gene to the end of the I gene. The resulting hybrid protein lacks the last four residues of the lac repressor and the first 23 residues of β-galactosidase (Brake et al., 1978; see Figure 1A). However, the β-galactosidase activity is unaffected, allowing the I gene portion of the fusion system to be used as a dispensable gene, since most mutations that do not result in the interruption of transcription or translation should not interfere with β-galactosidase activity and thus should still result in the Lac+ phenotype.

If we introduce a frameshift into the I region of the fusion depicted in Figure 1A, then the resulting strain would be Lac−, since translation could not proceed into the Z gene in the normal reading frame. Revertants to the Lac+ phenotype would result from nearby frameshifts of the opposite sign or from certain deletions. However, if we construct a strain carrying two widely separated frameshifts in the I region of the fusion, then only deletion mutations would restore the Lac+ phenotype, as shown by the example in Figure 1B. Frameshifts or small deletions can no longer restore the normal reading frame and result in Lac+ colonies, because there are too many nonsense codons in the +1 and −1 reading frames between the two frameshifts *378* (an addition of a single base pair) and *S42* (a deletion of 13 bp). Large deletions that eliminate both frameshifts and generate the normal (0) reading frame (type A, Figure 1B), can restore the Lac+ character, as can deletions that eliminate only one of the starting mutations but themselves generate a change in phase of opposite sign to the remaining frameshift mutation (type B, Figure 1B). (Deletions can leave both frameshift mutations intact provided they terminate between each respective mutation and the next out-of-phase nonsense codon. Since there are only 31 bp between *378* and the first nonsense codon in the +1 reading frame, such deletions are relatively rare.)

The minimum length of type A deletions restoring the Lac+ character is determined by the distance between the two frameshifts, which in this case is 697 bp. Since the deletions cannot go beyond the I promoter (Figure 1B) on the left end or much farther into Z on the right end, this system detects type A deletions in the size range of 700–1000 bp. Although type B deletions could be as small as 450 bp (see Figure 8), such deletions would result in an extensive length of

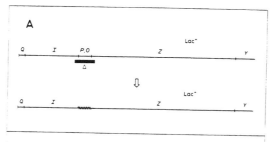

Figure 1. Fusion of *lacZ* to *I* and the Selection System Used to Detect Deletions in *lacI*

(A) The fusion deletion described by Müller-Hill and Kania, 1974 (see also Brake et al., 1978) is shown. The last four residues of repressor and the first 23 residues of β-galactosidase are missing from the resulting hybrid protein, which is synthesized under the control of the *I* promoter. (B) Two frameshift mutations, *378* and *S42*, which are separated by 697 bp have been crossed into the *lacI-Z* fusion system described in (A). Only deletions can restore the Lac⁺ character. The principal deletions detected are of type A or type B (see text).

polypeptide (up to as large as 85 amino acids) encoded by the +1 reading frame, and it is not clear how large a region of "pseudo-protein" could be tolerated by the cellular degradation systems. In practice (see below), type A deletions predominate in this system, and the few type B deletions detected are approximately 700 bp long and result in relatively small regions (less than 35 residues) of protein arising from the +1 reading frame.

The results of the application of the system pictured in Figure 1B are described below. The only Lac⁺ colonies detected result from deletions of type A or type B.

Results

Frequency in *recA*⁺ and *recA*⁻ Strains
We characterized Lac⁺ revertants resulting from the double frameshift selection pictured in Figure 1B. All of the revertants arose from deletions of between 700 and 1000 bp. As Table 1 shows, these deletions occurred 25 times more frequently (per cell per generation) in a *recA*⁺ genetic background than in a *recA*⁻ background. Controls described in Experimental Procedures argue that this result is not an artifact of the procedure used to determine mutation rates. Moreover, the experiment depicted in Figure 2 demonstrates that deletions occur more frequently in a *recA*⁺ strain. We used an *I–Z* fusion derivative containing an amber mutation (*A33*) in the *I* gene. Lac⁺

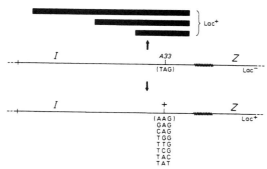

Figure 2. An Experiment to Determine the Ratio of Base Substitutions to Deletions

The amber mutation *A33* (Coulondre and Miller, 1977) affects codon 309 and results in the interruption of translation and the Lac⁻ character. Lac⁺ revertants not caused by external suppressors can result either from deletions of varying lengths (top part of figure) or from base substitutions that restore the codon at position 309 to a sense codon. Genetic mapping can distinguish between these two types of revertants (see text and Experimental Procedures).

revertants caused by mutations in the *lac* region can result either from deletions generating the normal (0) reading frame, or from point mutations at the amber site (see legend to Figure 2). Because base substitutions occur at similar rates in *recA*⁺ and *recA*⁻ strains (see Experimental Procedures), we can use the ratio of deletions to point mutations, which result in reversion of the *A33*-containing fusion derivative to Lac⁺, as a measure of the relative rates of deletion formation in *recA*⁺ and *recA*⁻ strains. Table 2 shows the results. Whereas the ratio of deletion to point mutation is 16:3 in the *recA*⁺ strain, it is 1:3 in the *recA*⁻ strain. Thus the rates of deletion formation are approximately 16-fold higher in the *recA*⁺ strain than in the *recA*⁻ strain. Similar results were obtained for 300–5000 bp deletions extending from *I* into *Z* (data not shown) when a related system was used (see Gho and Miller, 1974).

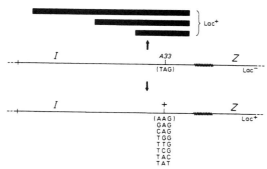

Table 1. Lac⁺ Reversion Frequencies

recA Genotype	No. Cultures	No. Cultures without Lac⁺ Colony	Average No. Cells in Culture	Lac⁺ Reversion Frequency per Cell per Generation
recA⁺	93	60	2.0×10^7	21.9×10^{-9}
recA⁻	39	17	9.8×10^8	0.85×10^{-9}

The fraction of cultures having no Lac⁺ revertants was used to calculate the reversion rate by the method of Luria and Delbrück, 1943 (see also Lea and Coulson, 1949; Moore and Sherman, 1975, and Experimental Procedures). From this fraction P_0, the average number of events m which lead to Lac⁺ revertants can be estimated from the zero term of the Poisson distribution $P_0 = e^{-m}$. Since there are no Lac⁺ revertants in the starting inocula, the rate (R) of revertants per cell division is equivalent to $R = m/N$, where N is the mean final cell count per culture.

Table 2. Relative Rates of Deletion Formation

recA Genotype	No. Deletions	No. Point Mutations	Relative Rates of Deletion Formation recA⁺:recA⁻
recA⁺	16	3	16:1
recA⁻	5	15	

Strains with episomes carrying A33, an amber mutation affecting the codon at position 309, in combination with the fusion deletion can revert via a point mutation at the amber site or via a deletion (see Figure 2 and Experimental Procedures). Independent revertants (one per culture) were mapped against a point mutation at position 298, to detect deletions longer than 25–30 bp, and also against A33 itself (selecting I⁺ recombinants) to verify revertants at the amber site A33. Lac⁺ revertants appeared about five times more frequently in the recA⁺ strain carrying A33 than in the recA⁻ strain.

Distribution of Deletions

Figure 3 depicts the distribution of deletion endpoints detected in both strain backgrounds. The left end of the deletions can be mapped easily by genetic methods, whereas positioning the right end requires biochemical analysis of the DNA (see legend to Figure 3 and Experimental Procedures). The distributions of deletion endpoints derived from recA⁺ and recA⁻ strains are strikingly similar, even though the frequency of detection of deletions in the recA⁻ background is lower.

The most prominent feature of the deletion endpoint distribution is the major hotspot, which accounts for 60% of all the deletions in both recA⁺ and recA⁻ strains. Figure 4 shows the DNA sequence change resulting from deletions in this hotspot. The deletions occur between two partially homologous sequences, termed β_I and β_{II}, which are separated by 759 bp. Of the 17 bp in these sequences, 14 are identical. The three nonidentical base pairs allow us to determine, by DNA sequence analysis, in which (or at the end of which) homologous segments, referred to here as x, y and z, the deletion event occurred. We have determined the sequence change resulting from 10 of the deletions in the hotspot (6 derived in the recA⁺ background and 4 in the recA⁻ background). Of the ten deletions, nine were identical to the example shown in Figure 4 and used subhomology x, whereas one (derived in the recA⁺ strain) used subhomology y. Another four deletions from the hotspot were characterized by restriction enzyme analysis, and these appear indistinguishable from the sequenced examples. (Deletions involving subhomology z can be distinguished from those involving subhomologies x or y by the resulting restriction patterns.) From the above results, we conclude that at least 9 of 10, and most of the 14 deletion mutations analyzed from the major hotspot depicted in Figure 4, arose by the identical event, and that therefore the vast majority of the deletions constituting the major hotspot are identical.

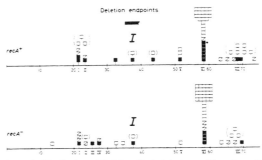

Figure 3. Distribution of Deletion Endpoints in recA⁺ and recA⁻ Strains

Each square indicates an occurrence of a deletion in the collections described in the text. The position of the left endpoint is indicated on this diagram. However, the right endpoint has been determined in many cases by analysis of restriction fragments (diagonal lines in the square) or by DNA sequencing (filled in squares). Thus the largest hotspot has 30 recurrences in the recA⁺ strain and 38 in the recA⁻ strain. The asterisk indicates one occurrence (out of ten analyzed) of a deletion with a slightly different endpoint, which can nonetheless be considered part of the same "site" (see Figure 4). The Roman numerals refer to specific deletions described in the tables and figures. Parentheses indicate a slight ambiguity in the left endpoint. See Table 3 for further details.

A SPONTANEOUS DELETION HOTSPOT

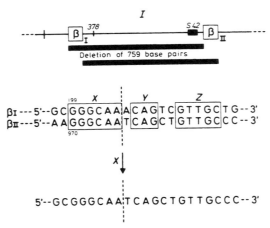

Figure 4. A Spontaneous Deletion Hotspot

The largest deletion hotspot found in this system occurs between two elements of partial homology labeled β_I and β_{II}, which are 759 bp apart. The two lines indicate that one cannot distinguish at which end of two homologous elements a deletion took place. For partial homologies, sequence determinations can reveal within which (or at the end of which) subhomology a deletion occurred. There are three subhomologies, marked x, y and z. Nine of the ten sequenced deletions occurred within subhomology x, as indicated in this diagram, and one deletion (the asterisk in Figure 3) occurred at subhomology y.

Figure 5 shows the sequence alteration resulting from other deletions depicted in Figure 3 that have been characterized at the sequence level. In these cases, the deletions appeared to have recurred several times in this collection, and the example labeled I represents a minor hotspot. In all cases but one, the deletion involves an uninterrupted sequence of 6–8 bp. Figure 6 shows the sequence change resulting from seven deletions at which no recurrences have been detected in this collection. In six of seven cases, partial homologies can be seen surrounding the deletion site. In only one case, no such partial homology can be seen.

Table 3 summarizes the data from this section. These data demonstrate that deletions predominate at short homologies in both $recA^+$ and $recA^-$ strains, and that the same hotspots are favored in both backgrounds. They do not exclude the possibility that certain deletions might occur specifically in the $recA^+$ or the $recA^-$ background, or that certain deletions do not occur at reduced rates in a $recA^-$ strain. However, such deletions could make up only a minor part of the spectrum of deletions analyzed here.

Effect of Altering the Homologies

The top part of Figure 7 shows the sequence involved in generating the most frequently detected deletion (see also Figure 4). We have previously characterized the amber mutations A9, A10 and A11 at the positions indicated (Coulondre and Miller, 1977, and references therein). The bottom portion of Figure 7 depicts the altered homology involved in the deletion hotspot resulting from strains carrying each mutation. A9 reduces the primary homology from 9 of 10 bp to 8 of 10 bp, whereas A11 breaks up the flanking 5 bp

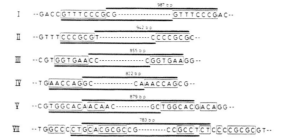

Figure 5. Other Frequent Deletions

Deletions that have been found several times in the collection analyzed are indicated in this diagram. The Roman numerals allow comparisons with Figure 4. The first five deletions occur at unbroken homologies of 6 bp or more. For these sequences we have boxed additional homologies only when they constitute 3 bp or more. For the last deletion (VII) and for the deletions in Figure 6, we have indicated lesser homologies.

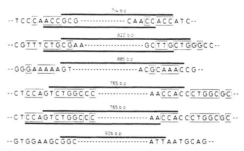

Figure 6. Additional Sequenced Deletions

The deletions indicated here (see also Table 3) occur less frequently, in general, than those indicated in Figure 5. The distance between the homologous segments takes into account the starting frameshift mutations 378 and S42.

Table 3. Summary of Deletions Analyzed

Deletion Position	Sequence Repeated	No. Bases Deleted	Occurrences (sequenced; restriction)			Overall Total Presumed from Genetic Mapping
			$recA^+$	$recA^-$	Combined	
205–975 (VI)	GGGCAA↓-CAG*↓--GTTGC	759	(6;1)7*	(4;3)7	(10;4)14	68
94–1092 (I)	GTTTCCCG	987	(2;2)4	(1;3)4	(3;5)8	8–12
189–1079 (V)	TGGCAC↓-ACA	879	(1;0)1		(1;0)1	5
96–1049 (II)	CCCGCG↓-G-TG	942	(1;1)2	(0;1)1	(1;2)3	3–4
107–927 (IV)	AACCAC	822		(1;1)2	(1;1)2	2
103–969 (III)	GGTGAA	855		(1;0)1	(1;0)1	1
247–1042 (VII)	GCC-CT↓-C-CGCGC	783	(0;1)1	(1;0)1	(1;1)2	2–3
238–1014	CCA-↓-CTGGC	765	(1;0)1		(1;0)1	1–2
237–1013	CCA↓--CTGGC	765	(1;0)1		(1;0)1	1–2
139–1038	G-AAA-↓	885	(1;0)1		(1;0)1	1
123–956	TT-CTG↓	822	(1;0)1		(1;0)1	1
180–892	C-ACC↓	714	(1;0)1		(1;0)1	1
148–1065	None	906		(1;0)1	(1;0)1	1

Twenty-four deletions were analyzed by DNA sequencing. Another 13 were mapped by the analysis of restriction fragments, which allows accurate positioning of both endpoints. All the deletions shown here were mapped genetically. (Another five alterations were characterized by restriction mapping, allowing better placement on the maps in Figure 3, but since these five alterations were not characterized by sequencing, they do not appear in this table.) The Roman numerals allow reference to Figures 3 and 5, and the base pair number in column 3 allows reference to Figure 8. An arrow in column 2 indicates a deletion point, meaning the change in sequence which would occur if the sequence were read from left to right as drawn here and in Figure 8. The asterisk indicates one deletion that uses subhomology y at site VI (see Figures 3 and 4).

homology. *A10* does not alter the homologies, but instead changes a base pair between the homologous stretches.

We have constructed double mutants carrying each amber site in combination with the short deletion *S42* and the fusion deletion del *14* (see also Figure 1). We examined the distribution of deletions in the same manner as shown in Figure 3, using genetic mapping to determine the position of the left endpoint of each deletion. This is sufficient to detect a reduction in the proportion of deletions at the hotspot site, since all deletions mapping at different positions can be clearly designated as not being at the hotspot.

Table 4 shows that altering a single base pair within the homology for the large hotspot reduces the inci-

dence of the respective deletion by an order of magnitude. Thus, in the starting strain (carrying *378,S42*), which is wild-type in this region, almost 60% of the deletions are at the hotspot. For *A10*, which does not affect the homology, a similarly high proportion (80%) of the deletions appear identical with the hotspot deletion, whereas both *A9* and *A11* reduce this proportion dramatically. When one considers the ratio (M) of deletions at the hotspot to those in other regions, it can be seen that the presence of *A9* reduces the frequency of deletions at the hotspot by a factor of 7 relative to those occurring at the hotspot in the wild-type, and by a factor of 20 relative to *A10*. Similarly, *A11* reduces the frequency by a factor of approximately 14 relative to wild-type, and by a factor of 38 relative to *A10* (see Table 4).

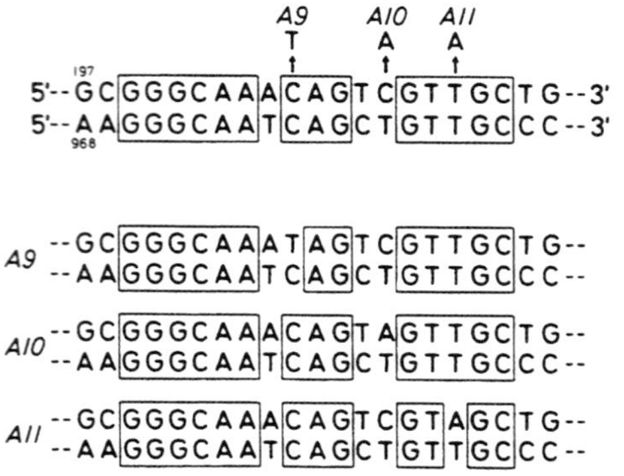

Discussion

Using a *lacI–Z* fusion system we have analyzed spontaneous deletions in the size range of 700–1000 bp. Table 3 summarizes the results, while Figure 8 shows the entire DNA sequence surrounding the endpoints of the deletions detected in this system. The vast majority of deletions of this length occur between short sequence homologies, and the deletions predominate at the largest of these homologies.

Approximately 60% of the deletions (in both $recA^+$ and $recA^-$ strains) occur at the largest homology in the system (homology A8 in Figure 8). Although one might argue that some special property of the major hotspot, apart from its large homology (14 of 17 bp) was responsible for the high incidence of deletions, these experiments demonstrate that the length of homology is important. In two cases we have used a single-base substitution, which reduces the homology to 13 of 17 bp for the major hotspot. In each example the incidence of deletions involving the main hotspot drops by an order of magnitude.

Figure 7. Mutational Alteration of the Degree of Homology at a Deletion Hotspot

The base substitution mutations *A9*, *A10* and *A11* (Coulondre and Miller, 1977) have been used to alter the homologies surrounding the largest spontaneous deletion hotspot in this system. Strains carrying double mutations (*A9*, *A10* or *A11* in combination with *S42*) were constructed and used to detect Lac⁺ revertants. The revertants were analyzed genetically to determine which deletions were involved (see Table 4 and Experimental Procedures).

Table 4. Effect of Single Base-Pair Alteration at Deletion Hotspot

	No. Deletions in Interval					Ratio (M)		
lacI Mutations	I 19–26	II 26–45	III 45–54	IV 54+	Total	(IV):(I + II + III)	$(M)_{378}/(M)$	$(M)_{A10}/(M)$
A9,S42	12	13	5	7	37	7:30	7	20
A10,S42	3	3	1	32	39	32:7		
A11,S42	17	8	8	4	37	4:33	14	38
378,S42	9	5	4	30	48	30:18		

One Lac⁺ revertant from each of 37, 39, and 37 cultures, respectively, was mapped into one of four intervals for the double mutants involving the amber mutations *A9*, *A10* and *A11*. Interval I is between mutations at coding positions 19 and 26; II between 26 and 45; III between 45 and 54, and IV just after position 54. Interval IV constitutes almost exclusively the hotspot in Figure 4, since deletions mapping after the amber used in the double selection cannot restore the Lac⁺ phenotype. For the wild-type (*378,S42*), the data are taken from Figure 3 for all of the intervals before position 62. The presence of the *A9* amber mutation would prevent the appearance of deletions involving the subhomologies y and z in Figure 4, but the vast majority of deletions at the hotspot use subhomology x, so this should not be a factor. Likewise, *A11* prevents deletions appearing at subhomology z, but few if any of the deletions at the hotspot involve z. In any case, *A10* cannot use subhomology z, and the deletions at the hotspot are still high in this example. The ratio (M) of deletions at the hotspot to those in the first three intervals for the control strains (carrying *378,S42* and *A10,S42*, respectively) can be compared with the same ratio (M) for each double mutant (see text). The $recA^+$ background was used in all cases.

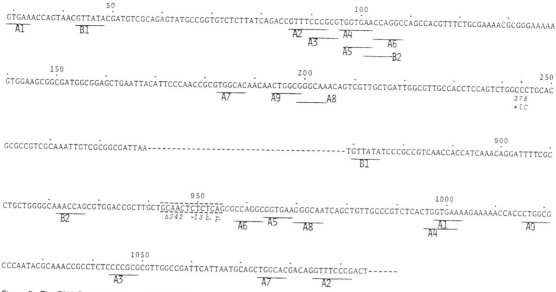

Figure 8. The DNA Sequence Surrounding the Homologies Involved in Deletion Formation in This System Derived from Farabaugh, 1978. The uninterrupted homologies of 6 bp or more are indicated for type A and type B deletions. The frameshifts generated by 378 and S42 are also shown.

The additional deletions analyzed underscore the importance of the lengths of homology. Almost half of the deletions not involving the major hotspot are generated at homologies of 6 bp or more. As Figure 8 shows, there are 11 uninterrupted homologies of 6 bp or more in this system, and six of these are represented in this collection, mostly by multiple occurrences. The largest uninterrupted homology (8 bp) results in a minor hotspot. Two other uninterrupted homologies of 6 bp are part of larger homologies of 9 of 10 bp and 9 of 11 bp, respectively (see Table 3 and Figure 5). It is likely that the sequenced deletions at these sites represent one of several occurrences. Among the larger interrupted homologies, we have characterized deletions involving the two strongest, with 8 of 10 bp and 11 of 14 bp matching (Table 3 and Figure 6). Several other occurrences of these deletions may be in this collection.

What of the less frequent deletions? Table 3 and Figure 6 show that most of the deletions which have been detected only once in the collection also involve significant homologies, although these homologies are weaker than those for the more frequent deletions.

When all of the data are considered, there is a strong correlation between the frequency of deletion formation and the length of homology between the short sequence repeats, for deletions in the same size range. It is likely that other factors, such as the distance between short repeats, the surrounding sequence and perhaps even the nature of the repeated sequence itself, also affect deletion frequency.

Mechanism of Deletion Formation

One can readily envision two classes of models to explain the generation of spontaneous deletions. The first involves single-stranded intermediates that form during DNA replication, and the second, independent recombination events mediated by enzymes that recognize short homologies.

The finding that spontaneous deletions often occur at short sequence repeats prompted the suggestion (Farabaugh et al., 1978) that "slipped mispairing" during DNA synthesis might be involved in deletion formation, as had been proposed for the generation of small frameshift mutations (Streisinger et al., 1966). Figure 9 is a schematic description of how this might occur. (A similar model has been presented by Efstratiadis et al., 1980.) Two elements of homology, labeled α_I and α_{II} in Figure 9, can slip and mispair during DNA replication (Figure 9D). It is possible that secondary structures of the type shown in Figure 9C might reduce the effective distance between α_I and α_{II} and thus increase certain slipped mispairing events (see below). Replication through intermediates such as those in Figure 9D can result in a deletion (9E and the resulting 9F), or alternatively, excision repair of the loop structure in 9D might occur before replication, as suggested by Efstratiadis et al. (1980). One would expect that the incidence of deletions generated in the above manner would depend on the length of the sequence repeats, the distance between the repeats and the sequence surrounding the repeats.

The RecA protein can promote pairing of a single

strand with duplex DNA in the absence of a free end (see Radding, 1981); therefore, the finding that deletions in the *lacI* system are reduced in a *recA⁻* strain could be reconciled with the scheme depicted in Figure 9, if one postulates that the slipped mispairing step can be catalyzed by the RecA protein. Alternatively, the *recA⁻* background might have an indirect effect on deletion formation. For example, since intermediates such as those pictured in Figure 9D might hinder replication, this replication block might be better overcome in *recA⁺* cells, which have an intact SOS repair system (see review by Witkin, 1976). Or, the RecB,C DNAase activity in *recA⁻* strains (Clark et al., 1966) might result in increased degradation of single-stranded intermediates involved in deletion formation. A lowered deletion frequency in a *recA⁻* background has not been observed in certain systems (Franklin, 1967; Ghosal and Saedler, 1979; Ross et al., 1979). Whether this discrepancy results from different *recA⁻* strain backgrounds or reflects a fundamental difference in the nature of the deletions under investigation is not clear.

The data in this paper are also consistent with models that invoke enzymes which recognize short homologies and catalyze recombination events that result in deletions. The RecA protein might be a principal enzyme involved in such events, although it is not absolutely required for deletion formation, since deletions do occur in a *recA⁻* background (at a reduced frequency). If deletions at short homologies are always enzyme-mediated, then at least one other enzyme in the cell is capable of promoting the identical events in the absence of the RecA protein. The analysis of mutants affected in spontaneous deletion formation should help pinpoint which enzymes are involved in this process.

Influence of DNA Sequence and Relation to Transposable Elements

The importance of sequence homologies in promoting high deletion frequencies is proved by the finding that mutations reducing the largest homology by even a single base pair (Figure 7) severely reduce the frequency of deletions at that site (Table 4). However, the nature of the surrounding sequence could superimpose another modulating factor on deletion incidence. Figure 10 depicts a possible secondary structure of part of the sequence surrounding the homologies β_I and β_{II} involved in the major deletion hotspot detected in this system. It is conceivable that structures of the type shown in Figure 10 might promote

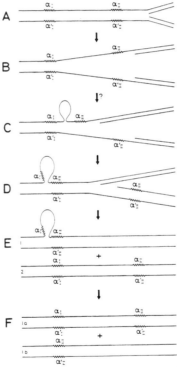

Figure 9. A Schematic Model for Deletion Formation by Slipped Mispairing

Two homologous sequences, α_I and α_{II} are indicated. During DNA replication, slipped mispairing, which might be prompted by inverted repeats interior to the two direct repeats (C), may occur, leading to deletion formation either upon either replication through the structures indicated here or by excision–repair of the looped region shown in (E1). (See also Efstratiadis et al., 1980, and text).

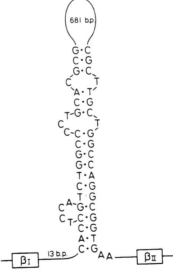

Figure 10. A Potential Secondary Structure near the Deletion Hotspot

See also Figure 4. The DNA sequence used is that for the strain carrying both *378* and *S42*.

deletion formation at nearby homologies, particularly if single-stranded intermediates, such as those depicted in Figure 9C, are involved in deletion formation. The probability of slipped mispairing between short homologies should increase as the distance between the homologies decreases, and the possibility of secondary structures forming as a result of inverted repeats internal to the short direct repeats (Figure 10) would decrease the effective distance between such short homologies. Such an arrangement of direct and inverted repeat structures is relevant to the precise excision of procaryotic transposable elements (for reviews see Calos and Miller, 1980; Starlinger, 1980), which may involve the same pathway as spontaneous deletion formation.

All known transposable elements generate a repeated sequence of characteristic length, ranging from 3 to 12 bp. In procaryotes, repeat lengths of 5 and 9 bp have been found most frequently. The elimination of transposable elements by excision resembles the type of deletions studied here, since one of the short repeats, separated by the length of the transposable element (from 768 to over 10,000 bp in procaryotes), is also removed. For Tn5 and Tn10 it has been shown that element-encoded transposition functions are not required for precise excision (Egner and Berg, 1981; Foster et al., 1981), indicating that host functions are involved. Moreover, the inverted repeats at the ends of most transposable elements might serve to reduce the effective distance between the direct repeats at the end of each integrated element, as considered above for spontaneous deletions (see also Berg, 1977). In fact, reducing the extent of the 1500 bp inverted repeats of Tn10 also reduces the frequency of Tn10 precise excision (Foster et al., 1981).

In some cases, IS1 precise excision has been reported to be reduced in a recA⁻ strain (Sommer et al., 1981), as are the spontaneous deletions described here. However, for Tn10 (Kleckner et al., 1979) and Tn9 (J. H. Miller, unpublished results), precise excision is not reduced in a recA⁻ strain and is even slightly increased. Although one might postulate that RecA protein–promoted pairing of the large homologous regions of Tn10 and Tn9 might interfere with precise excision, it is also possible that spontaneous deletion formation and precise excision of some transposable elements differ in at least one pathway.

Other deletion events associated with transposable elements are different from precise excision but also involve short homologies (Ross et al., 1979; Sommer et al., 1981). In the case of Tn10, "nearly precise excision" deletions occur independently of transposition functions and are likely to involve host pathways (Foster et al., 1981). For IS1, deletions extending into IS1 from outside the element are reduced in frequency in a recA⁻ strain (Sommer et al., 1981). Both of these

cases may represent spontaneous deletions of the type described here.

Future Applications

The lacI–Z fusion derivatives described here make it possible to assess directly the effects of different mutagens on deletion formation in a system utilizing deletions that have been characterized at the DNA sequence level. We can also analyze the influence of different repair-deficient backgrounds on deletion formation, and can exploit the Lac⁻ to Lac⁺ selection to detect additional host mutations that affect spontaneous deletion rates. This system also permits detailed comparison of deletion formation with precise excision of transposable elements.

Experimental Procedures

Strain Constructions

We constructed episomes carrying two mutations in the lacI region in combination with the I–Z fusion deletion by using phenocopy crosses. We had previously constructed F'lacproB episomes carrying one of the mutations A9-A11,S42 and 378 in combination with the fusion deletion (Calos and Miller, 1981; J. H. Miller and A. Albertini, manuscript in preparation). For crosses involving S42 and 378, both of which have a small residual β-galactosidase activity, phenocopy crosses were carried out in which a donor strain carrying the 378 episome was mated with a saturated culture of a recipient strain carrying the S42 mutation at 37°C for 1 hr, after which the cultures were diluted 1:10 in broth and grown for 2 hr and plated out on Xgal medium (Miller, 1972) with streptomycin. The donor background, P90C (Δ lacproB, ara) is streptomycin-sensitive, whereas the recipient background, S90C (Δ lacproB, ara, strA) is streptomycin-resistant. We examined several thousand colonies for those which were light blue on Xgal after 60 hr, in comparison to the starting strains, which were medium blue, as a result of residual levels of enzyme, on the same plates. Several colonies were detected, repurified and tested for reversion characteristics. The strain resulting from this cross was verified by DNA sequencing during the course of this work.

Double mutations of A9, A10 and A11 with S42 were constructed in a similar manner, except that a kanamycin-resistant derivative of the F'lacproB donor episome was used, and kanamycin was used in the Xgal medium in addition to streptomycin. This ensures that only the S90C derivatives that received the episome from the donor strain can grow. This increased the percentage of double mutants among the survivors of the cross. A9 and A10 activate reinitiation sites and have a moderate level of β-galactosidase even in S90C (in combination with the fusion deletion). A11 does not activate a reinitiation site, and therefore we used as a recipient a strain carrying an ochre suppressor (XA10C, Coulondre and Miller, 1977), since the weak suppression of A11 still results in a moderate level of β-galactosidase in the fusion derivative.

Detection of Lac⁺ Revertants

Overnight cultures were plated on lactose minimal medium (all medium is as described in Miller, 1972), and revertants were picked after 48 hr. After purification on lactose MacConkey plates and then on glucose minimal plates, the strains were used for mapping experiments. Two strain backgrounds were used for the experiments, either P90C or a recA1 derivative of this strain.

Genetic Mapping

We used a set of strains described by Coulondre and Miller, 1977, to map the deletions against chromosomal point mutations in a galE strain background selecting I⁺ recombinants. The crosses are described in Coulondre and Miller, 1977. We used nonsense mutations at positions 26, 44, 54 and 62 and missense mutations at positions 5 and 19 to map the deletions.

Reversion Frequencies

Lac$^+$ reversion frequencies were determined by the method of Luria and Delbrück, 1943, essentially as described for the determination of I$^+$ recombination frequencies (Coulondre and Miller, 1977). For the recA$^-$ strain, 0.4 ml cultures were seeded with a few hundred cells, and the cultures were grown overnight without shaking at 37°C, then aerated for 3 hr. Sample cultures were titered for viable cells, and the entire contents of the culture was spread onto lactose minimal medium and incubated for 48 hr. Lac$^+$ colonies were verified on lactose MacConkey plates. For the recA$^+$ strain, cultures were grown without shaking until a density of about 5×10^7 cells was reached. We chose this density because pilot experiments had indicated that saturated cultures of the recA$^+$ strain had 20–30 times more Lac$^+$ revertants than culture of the recA$^-$ strain. To avoid continued background growth on the lactose selection plates, which would give rise to Lac$^+$ revertants on the plate, we seeded the lactose plates with a fresh overnight culture of a scavenger for the recA$^+$ experiment. J93 (Δ lac) was used. A washed overnight culture of J93 (0.2 ml) was spread onto each lactose plate 1 hr before use. We also scored the Lac$^+$ colonies from the recA$^+$ experiment after 24 hr, to ensure that the revertants we were examining were in the culture before plating. The analysis of the fraction of cultures containing one Lac$^+$ colony, the fraction containing two Lac$^+$ colonies and the fraction containing no colonies indicates that all of the Lac$^+$ colonies found are probably part of the same Poisson distribution and were very probably in the culture before plating (see Table 1 for further details).

We also prepared recA$^+$ and recA$^-$ merodiploids carrying episomes with a Z$^-$ and Y$^-$ point mutation (the mutations were derived from strains CSH34 and CSH40, respectively; Miller, 1972). The reversion of these strains to Lac$^+$, as a result of base-substitution mutations, was similar in recA$^+$ and recA$^-$ backgrounds, arguing that background growth on the lactose selection plates was responsible for the differences in frequency of reversion of the double frameshift strain used to determine deletion frequencies.

Ratio of Deletions to Point Mutations

The strain diagrammed in Figure 2 was used to measure the ratio of deletions to point mutations in recA$^+$ and recA$^-$ backgrounds. The episome carrying the mutation A33 (Coulondre and Miller, 1977) was used in P90C and in the recA$^-$ derivative to look for Lac$^+$ revertants. After purification, the mutations were crossed into S90C to verify that the reversion event occurred in the lac region. One Lac$^+$ colony from each of 20 cultures for each background was analyzed by genetic mapping against the galE lacI$^-$ strains described above and by Coulondre and Miller, 1977. The point mutations at positions 298 and 309 were used as mapping probes to test for deletions. I$^+$ recombinants were scored.

Plasmid Construction

Heterogenotes were prepared by crossing the F'lacproB episome carrying the respective deletion mutation into a P90C derivative carrying the plasmid pMC4 (Calos et al., 1978), which carries the entire I gene and almost the entire Z gene. DNA from these heterogenotes was prepared by the method of Birnboim and Doly (1979) and used to transform an I$^-$Z$^+$ strain, in this case the tonB-trp-lacI deletion strain (Schmeissner et al., 1977) carrying deletion 196. Whereas the pMC4 plasmid renders the recipient cell I$^+$ and thus white on Xgal plates, I$^-$ recombinants that have received the I deletion render the recipient cell blue after transformation. I$^-$ recombinant strains were purified and used to prepare DNA for sequencing or for restriction digest analysis.

Plasmid Preparation

Plasmid DNA was purified following the method of Tanaka and Weisblum (1975) with a cesium chloride gradient or following the method of Birnboim and Doly (1979) adapted to larger samples (10–40 ml amplified cultures) without cesium chloride gradients.

Restriction Analysis

To define the right endpoint of each deletion, we purified from the pMC4 plasmid the Hinc II fragment bearing the lac I gene with the deletion and the lacI-Z fusion (all the examined deletions eliminate the Hinc II cutting site at the 885 bp position of the lacI gene; therefore, we could easily recognize the new Hinc II fragment). We purified the Hinc II fragment by running it in a 6% preparative acrylamide gel and then eluting it (Maxam and Gilbert, 1980). We then subjected the Hinc II fragments to analytical restriction digests, testing for the presence of Pvu II cutting sites at 980 bp and 1072 bp and the Hinf I cutting site at 1058 bp. In some cases Bst NI cutting sites at 960 bp and 1016 bp also were tested (all the cited positions are referred to as stated in Farabaugh, 1978).

Analytical digests were carried out for 3 hr with about 0.2–1 μg purified Hinc II fragment for each digestion. The restriction pattern was examined on an 8% acrylamide gel.

Sequencing

Preliminary results of the genetic map definition and of the restriction analyses showed the best strategy for sequencing. Hinc II fragment purified from 100–150 μg plasmid was digested with Hinf I or Hpa II, according to the genetic map position and restriction analysis predictions. We carried out 3'-end labeling as described previously (Calos and Miller, 1981), using approximately 0.1 unit DNA polymerase Klenow "large fragment" and 10 μl α-^{32}P-dATP or α-^{32}P-dCTP (400 or >1000 Ci/mmole; Amersham) in a 30 μl reaction volume. Labeled fragment was purified by electrophoresis on 8% acrylamide gels, and after elution a second digestion was carried out with an appropriate enzyme. The fragment to be sequenced was eluted from a new 8% acrylamide gel and subjected to the sequencing reactions and gel analysis according to the method of Maxam and Gilbert (1980), with the modifications previously described (Calos and Miller, 1981).

Acknowledgments

We would like to thank C. Combépine for expert technical assistance, and Dr. B. Müller-Hill for bacterial strains. This work was supported by grants from the Swiss National Fund and the Swiss League Against Cancer. A. Albertini was supported by a long-term fellowship from European Molecular Biology Organization.

The costs of publication of this article were defrayed in part by the payment of page charges. This article must therefore be hereby marked "advertisement" in accordance with 18 U.S.C. Section 1734 solely to indicate this fact.

Received November 25, 1981; revised March 4, 1982

References

Berg, D. E. (1977). Insertion and excision of the transposable kanamycin resistance determinant Tn5. In DNA Insertion Elements, Plasmids and Episomes, A. I. Bukhari, J. A. Shapiro and S. L. Adhya, eds. (New York: Cold Spring Harbor Laboratory), pp. 205–212.

Birnboim, H. C. and Doly, J. (1979). A rapid alkaline extraction procedure for screening recombinant plasmid DNA. Nucl. Acids Res. 7, 1513–1523.

Brake, A. J., Fowler, A. V., Zabin, I., Kania, J. and Müller-Hill, B. (1978). B-galactosidase chimeras: primary structure of a lac repressor-B-galactosidase protein. Proc. Nat. Acad. Sci. USA 75, 4824–4827.

Calos, M. P., Johnsrud, L. and Miller, J. H. (1978). DNA sequence at the integration sites of the insertion element IS1. Cell 13, 411–418.

Calos, M. P. and Miller, J. H. (1980). Transposable elements. Cell 20, 579–595.

Calos, M. P. and Miller, J. H. (1981). Genetic and sequence analysis of frameshift mutations induced by ICR-191. J. Mol. Biol. 153, 39–66.

Clark, A. J., Chamberlin, M., Boyce, R. P. and Howard-Flanders, P.

(1966). Abnormal metabolic response to ultraviolet light of a recombinant deficient mutant of *Escherichia coli* K12. J. Mol. Biol. *19*, 442–454.

Coulondre, C. and Miller, J. H. (1977). Genetic studies of the *lac* repressor III. Additional correlation of mutational sites with specific amino acid residues. J. Mol. Biol. *117*, 525–575.

Efstratiadis, A., Posakony, J. W., Maniatis, T., Lawn, R. M., O'Connell, C., Spritz, R. A., DeRiel, J. K., Forget, B. G., Weissman, S. M., Slightom, J. L., Blechl, A. E., Smithies, O., Baralle, F. E., Shoulders, C. C. and Proudfoot, N. J. (1980). The structure and evolution of the human β-globin gene family. Cell *21*, 653–668.

Egner, C. and Berg, D. E. (1981). Excision of transposon Tn5 is dependent on the inverted repeats but not on the transposase function of Tn5. Proc. Nat. Acad. Sci. USA *78*, 459–463.

Farabaugh, P. J. (1978). Sequence of the *lacI* gene. Nature *274*, 765–769.

Farabaugh, P. J., Schmeissner, U., Hofer, M. and Miller, J. H. (1978). Genetic studies of the *lac* repressor. VII. On the molecular nature of spontaneous hotspots in the *lacI* gene of *Escherichia coli*. J. Mol. Biol. *126*, 847–857.

Fedoroff, N. V. (1979). Deletion mutants of Xenopus laevis 5S ribosomal DNA. Cell *16*, 551–563.

Foster, T. J., Lundblad, V., Hanley-Way, S., Halling, S. M. and Kleckner, N. (1981). Three Tn10-associated excision events: relationship to transposition and role of direct and inverted repeats. Cell *23*, 215–227.

Franklin, N. C. (1967). Extraordinary recombinational events in *Escherichia coli*: their independence of the rec$^+$ function. Genetics *55*, 699–707.

Gho, D. and Miller, J. H. (1974). Deletions fusing the *i* and *lac* regions of the chromosome in *E. coli*: isolation and mapping. Mol. Gen. Genet. *131*, 137–146.

Ghosal, D. and Saedler, H. (1979). IS2-61 and IS2-611 arise by illegitimate recombination from IS2-6. Mol. Gen. Genet. *176*, 233–238.

Kleckner, N., Steele D., Reichardt, K. and Botstein, D. (1979). Specificity of insertion by the translocatable tetracycline-resistance element Tn10. Genetics *92*, 1023–1040.

Lea, D. E. and Coulson, C. A. (1949). The distribution of the numbers of mutants in bacterial populations. J. Genet. *49*, 264–285.

Luria, S. E. and Delbrück, M. (1943). Mutations of bacteria from virus sensitivity to virus resistance. Genetics *28*, 491–511.

Marotta, C. A., Wilson, J. T., Forget, B. G. and Weissman, S. M. (1977). Human β-globin messenger RNA III. Nucleotide sequence derived from complementary DNA. J. Biol. Chem. *252*, 5040–5053.

Maxam, A. and Gilbert, W. (1980). Sequencing end-labelled DNA with base-specific chemical cleavages. Meth. Enzymol. *65*, 499–560.

Miller, J. H. (1972). Experiments in Molecular Genetics. (Cold Spring Harbor, New York: Cold Spring Harbor Laboratory).

Moore, C. W. and Sherman, F. (1975). Role of DNA sequences in genetic recombination in the iso-1-cytochrome c gene of yeast. I. Discrepancies between physical and genetic distances determined by fine mapping procedures. Genetics *79*, 397–418.

Müller-Hill, B. and Kania, J. (1974). *Lac* repressor can be fused to β-galactosidase. Nature *249*, 561–563.

Post, L. E., Arfsten, A. E., Davis, G. R. and Nomura, M. (1980). DNA sequence of the promoter region for the alpha ribosomal protein operon in *Escherichia coli*. J. Biol. Chem. *255*, 4653–4659.

Pribnow, D., Sigurdson, D. C., Gold, L., Singer, B. S., Napoli, C., Brosius, J., Dull, T. J. and Noller, H. F. (1981). rII cistrons of bacteriophage T4 DNA sequence around the intercistronic divide and positions of genetic landmarks. J. Mol. Biol. *149*, 337–376.

Radding, C. M. (1981). Recombination activities of E. coli RecA protein. Cell *25*, 3–4.

Ross, D. G., Swan, J. and Kleckner, N. (1979). Nearly precise excision: a new type of DNA alteration associated with the translocatable element Tn10. Cell *16*, 733–738.

Schmeissner, U., Ganem, D. and Miller, J. H. (1977). Genetic studies of the *lac* repressor II. Fine structure deletion map of the *lacI* gene, and its correlation with the physical map. J. Mol. Biol. *109*, 303–326.

Sommer, H., Schumacher, B. and Saedler, H. (1981). A new type of IS1-mediated deletion. Mol. Gen. Genet. *184*, 300–307.

Starlinger, P. (1980). IS elements and transposons. Plasmid *3*, 241–259.

Streisinger, G., Okada, Y., Emrich, J., Newton, J., Tsugita, A., Terzaghi, E. and Inouye, M. (1966). Frameshift mutations and the genetic code. Cold Spring Harbor Symp. Quant. Biol. *31*, 77–84.

Studier, F. W., Rosenberg, A. H., Simon, M. N. and Dunn, J. J. (1979). Genetic and physical mapping in the early region of the bacteriophage T7 DNA. J. Mol. Biol. *135*, 917–937.

Tanaka, T. and Weisblum, B. (1975). Construction of a colicin E1-R factor composite plasmid in vitro: means for amplification of deoxyribonucleic acid. J. Bacteriol. *121*, 354–362.

Witkin, E. (1976). Ultraviolet mutagenesis and inducible DNA repair in *Escherichia coli*. Bacteriol. Rev. *40*, 869–907.

Wu, A. M., Chapman, A. B., Platt, T., Guarente, L. and Beckwith, J. (1980). Deletions of distal sequence affect termination of transcription at the end of the tryptophan operon in E. coli. Cell *19*, 829–836.

Mutagenic Specificity :
Reversion of Iso-1-Cytochrome *c* Mutants of Yeast

Louise Prakash and Fred Sherman

Department of Radiation Biology and Biophysics
University of Rochester School of Medicine and Dentistry
Rochester, N.Y. 14642, U.S.A.

(*Received 10 April 1973*)

In previous studies the nucleotide sequences of numerous mutant codons in the *cy*1 gene have been identified from altered iso-1-cytochromes *c*. These studies not only revealed the mutant codons that caused the deficiencies but also experimentally determined which of the base pair changes allowed the formation of functional iso-1-cytochromes *c*. In this investigation we have quantitatively measured the reversion frequencies of eleven *cy*1 mutants which were treated with 12 mutagens. The *cy*1 mutants comprised nine mutants having single-base changes of the AUG initiation codon (Stewart *et al.*, 1971), an ochre mutant *cy*1-9 (Stewart *et al.*, 1972), and an amber mutant *cy*1-179 (Stewart & Sherman, 1972). In some cases the types of induced base changes could be inferred unambiguously from the pattern of reversion. Selective G·C to A·T transitions were induced by ethyl methanesulfonate, diethyl sulfate, *N*-methyl-*N*'-nitro-*N*-nitrosoguanidine, 1-nitrosoimidazolidone-2, nitrous acid, [5-³H]uridine and β-propiolactone. There was no apparent specificity with methyl methanesulfonate, dimethyl sulfate, nitrogen mustard and γ-rays. Ultraviolet light induced high rates of reversion of the ochre and amber mutants, but in these instances it appears as if the selective action is due to particular nucleotide sequences and not due to simple types of base pair changes.

1. Introduction

The most definitive procedures for establishing the specificities of mutagenic action require the analyses of amino acid sequences of mutationally altered proteins or of the base sequences of mutationally altered tRNAs. Since such procedures are tedious and impractical for investigating the mode of action of extensive numbers of mutagens, indirect genetic tests with micro-organisms or bacteriophage are commonly used for these purposes. The genetic assays are usually based on the assumed action of certain mutagens, and in some cases on the use of nonsense codons. For example, bacteriophage tester systems depend on the specific action of base analogs to induce only G·C → A·T and A·T → G·C transitions, of hydroxylamine to induce only G·C → A·T transitions, and of proflavin to induce frameshift mutations (see Drake, 1971). Lesser claims are usually made for the reliability of tester systems with bacteria, where at least some base-pair substitutions (transitions or transversions) and frameshift mutations are believed to be distinguished on the basis of reversion induced by such mutagens as nitrosoguanidine, base analogs and ICR-191 (see Hartman *et al.*, 1971). Determinations of mutagen specificities with fungi and other higher cells becomes even more dubious, although there have been suggested base-pair changes that were inferred from the rates of induced forward and reverse mutations (see Kilbey *et al.*, 1971).

The use of suppressors for recognizing the nonsense codons UAA, UAG and UGA has brought considerable refinement and flexibility to some tester systems. Nevertheless, even in well-characterized systems using bacteriophage, the base sequences of crucial mutant codons are often deduced only by indirect methods with a high degree of uncertainty. It is obvious that it would be desirable to have a tester system with established mutant codons which revert by known base changes. This goal has been achieved in part by the elucidation of numerous mutant codons in the tryptophan synthetase gene of *Escherichia coli*; however this system suffers from the limited numbers of revertants that have been analyzed in terms of amino acid substitutions that restore function (Yanofsky, 1971). In this paper we describe a simple tester system in yeast for determining mutagenic specificities with better precision than encountered in any other eucaryotic and most procaryotic systems.

Recently the nucleotide sequences of numerous mutant codons in the *cy1* gene have been identified from alterations of iso-1-cytochromes *c* in intragenic revertants. These studies not only revealed the mutant codons that caused the deficiencies but also experimentally determined which of the base changes allowed the formation of functional iso-1-cytochromes *c*. In this investigation we have quantitatively measured the reversion frequencies of a selected number of *cy1* mutants, which were treated with a variety of mutagens. This present study is restricted to tester strains that revert by base-pair substitutions and does not reveal the potential ability of the mutagens to cause base-pair additions and deletions. One major finding of this study was that numerous agents caused primarily $G \cdot C \rightarrow A \cdot T$ transitions, while other chemically-related agents showed no apparent specificity.

2. Experimental Design

The 11 mutants chosen for this study comprise *cy1-9*, which has an ochre codon corresponding to position 2 (Stewart *et al.*, 1972), *cy1-179*, which has an amber codon corresponding to position 9 (Stewart & Sherman, 1972), and the nine mutants that have single-base changes of the AUG initiation codon (Stewart *et al.*, 1971). These mutant sites occupy the region of the gene that determines the amino terminal sequence of the protein which is apparently dispensable for function (see Sherman & Stewart, 1973) and thus all expected revertant proteins should be recoverable. The advantages of these mutants include not only the knowledge of the nucleotide sequences of the mutant codons and the base changes associated with reversions, but also a knowledge of the nucleotide sequence of the entire region (Stewart & Sherman, unpublished data; Sherman & Stewart, 1973).

The mutant codons of the ochre and amber strains are presented in Figure 1 with the normal amino terminal sequence of iso-1-cytochrome *c*, and the amino acid replacements resulting from single base changes. In 59 revertant iso-1-cytochromes *c*, all amino acid replacements shown in Figure 1 for *cy1-9* revertants have been observed, as well as two instances of multiple base changes (Stewart *et al.*, 1972; Sherman & Stewart, unpublished data and 1973). Likewise, all expected replacements have been demonstrated in *cy1-179* revertants except for lysine, which is found at this position in normal iso-1-cytochrome *c*; included among the 52 revertant proteins

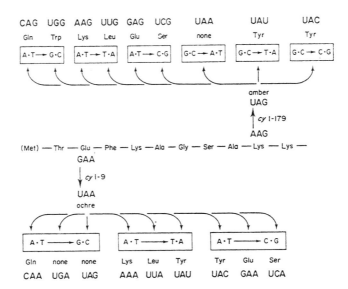

FIG. 1. A schematic representation of the mutational events and the amino acid replacements in iso-1-cytochromes *c* that are expected to occur in revertants of the *cy*1-9 ochre and the *cy*1-179 amber by single base-pair changes. All of these amino acid replacements have been observed except for residues of lysine in *cy*1-179 revertants (Stewart *et al.*, 1972; Stewart & Sherman, 1972; Sherman & Stewart, unpublished data). The sequence of the 10 amino terminal residues of normal iso-1-cytochrome *c* is shown in the middle of the Figure. The codons are presented either below or above the amino acid residues they specify. The base-pair changes associated with the amino acid replacements are circumscribed by boxes.

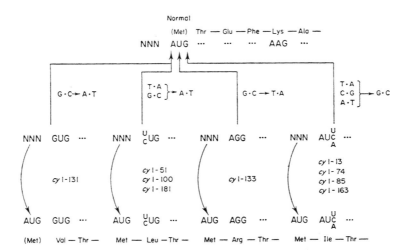

FIG. 2. A representation of the mutational events leading to reversion of initiation mutants. The codons of the 4 types of *cy*1 mutants that are defective in the AUG initiation codon are shown in the middle of the Figure; the mutational events leading to normal iso-1-cytochrome *c* are shown at the top of the Figure, while the mutational events leading to the 4 kinds of long forms of iso-1-cytochrome *c* are shown at the bottom. NNN designates an unknown codon that differs from AUG by a single base. The methionine residues, shown in parentheses, are excised from approximately 85% of the iso-1-cytochrome *c* in the *cy*1-131 revertant, and from all of the protein having the normal sequence (see Stewart *et al.*, 1971).

were four exceptional types that are most simply accounted for by concomitant two and three base-pair substitutions and by the deletion of six base-pairs (Stewart & Sherman, 1972; Sherman & Stewart, 1973).

Therefore, agents which induce any of the base-pair substitutions of A·T would be expected to revert cy1-9. These changes, as well as transversions of G·C base-pairs, would occur in revertants of cy1-179. Of all of the single base-pair substitutions, only G·C → A·T transitions would not cause the formation of functional iso-1-cytochromes c and, therefore, would not be detected since this change leads to the formation of the UAA ochre from the UAG amber codon.

Each of the nine initiator mutants contain codons for either valine, leucine, arginine or isoleucine that differ from AUG by one base, as presented schematically in Figure 2. It was impossible in the previous study (Stewart et al., 1971) to decide which of the leucine codons, UUG or CUG, are in the mutants cy1-51, cy1-100 and cy1-181, and whether or not any of these mutants are identical or different. Also the four mutants cy1-13, cy1-74, cy1-85 and cy1-163 may contain any one of the isoleucine codons AUU, AUC or AUA. Intragenic reversion of each of the initiation mutants can occur at three sites, which are presented schematically in Figure 3 for one of the

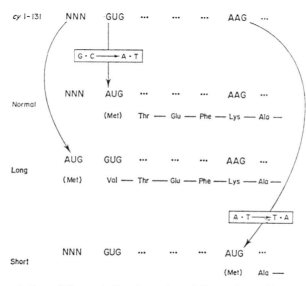

FIG. 3. A representation of the mutational events and the amino acid sequences of iso-1-cytochromes c in the 3 types of revertants of cy1-131. NNN designates an unknown codon that differs from AUG by a single base. The methionine residues, shown in parentheses, are excised from approximately 85% of the iso-1-cytochrome c from the long form and from all of the short form and of the normal protein (see Stewart et al., 1971).

mutants, cy1-131. First, the exact reversal of the mutant codon to the normal AUG initiation codon results in a normal iso-1-cytochrome c. Second, the mutation of the unknown codon NNN to AUG results in a longer protein with a residue of valine at the amino terminus. Mutation to an AUG initiation codon at a third location is possible by a single base change of the AAG codon determining lysine 4; this mutation causes the formation of a short protein that lacks the four normal amino terminal residues.

Thus all nine initiation mutants can be reverted by two common paths, which lead, respectively, to long and short proteins. In addition, these initiation mutants can revert exactly to the normal condition, but in this case the mutational pathway varies with the different mutants. The exact reversal to the normal AUG initiation codon can occur by at least three different types of base-pair substitutions, which are shown in Figure 2. The two mutants, cy1-131 and cy1-133, revert by a G·C → A·T transition and a G·C → T·A transversion, respectively. On the other hand, the group of cy1 mutants containing UUG or CUG codons reverts by either T·A → A·T or C·G → A·T transversions, while the other group containing AUU, AUC or AUA codons reverts either by an A·T → G·C transition or by a T·A → G·C or C·G → G·C transversion. While it may appear that the ambiguity of base changes associated with reverse mutations would make the initiation mutants ineffective for tester strains, it is clear that any difference in reversion frequencies must reflect the differences in reversal of the mutant codon to the normal AUG initiation codon. For example, if a mutagen was effective in inducing revertants with cy1-131, but not with the other initiation mutants, the simplest interpretation would be that this mutagen caused G·C → A·T transitions but not G·C → T·A transversions and not one of several other changes. Further restrictions of base pair changes are imposed if one considers reversion of the amber and ochre mutants. Excluding the two mutational changes common to all initiation mutants, the base changes associated with the formation of functional iso-1-cytochromes c are summarized in Table 1. It should be noted that reversion is indicative of which particular base changes are induced, and also that lack of reversion is indicative of which base changes are not induced. An example important in this study is that a mutagen would be inferred to cause only G·C → A·T transitions if cy1-131 was reverted and cy1-179 was not.

TABLE 1

Codon and single base-pair changes associated with reversion of cy1 mutants

Mutants		Codon changes	Base-pair changes
Initiation mutants	cy1-131	GUG → AUG	G·C → A·T
	cy1-51 cy1-100 cy1-181	^U_CUG → AUG	*or* T·A → A·T C·G → A·T
	cy1-133	AGG → AUG	G·C → T·A
	cy1-13 cy1-74 cy1-85 cy1-163	^U_A AUC → AUG	*or* T·A → G·C C·G → G·C *or* A·T → G·C
Ochre mutant	cy1-9	UAA → amino acid codons	*and* A·T → T·A A·T → G·C *and* A·T → C·G
Amber mutant	cy1-179	UAG → amino acid codons	All of the above plus *and* G·C → T·A G·C → C·G

3. Materials and Methods

(a) Strains

The cy1-9 and cy1-13 mutants were isolated by the benzidine procedure (Sherman *et al.*, 1968), while the remaining, independently derived mutants were isolated by the chlorolactate procedure (Sherman, Stewart, Jackson, Gilmore & Parker, unpublished work; see also Sherman & Stewart, 1973). All strains, except cy1-9 are direct isolates from strain D311-3A (**a** *lys2 his1 trp2*). The identification of the mutant codons in each of these eleven cy1 strains is discussed in the previous section and is summarized in Table 1. The mutagens used to induce the haploid mutants are presented in the last column of Table 2. The 11 haploid mutants were crossed to a strain (D234-10A) having the cy1-1 gene, which has been shown to contain an apparent deletion of at least the entire *CY1* locus, since cy1-1 strains do not revert nor recombine with any of the point mutants (Parker & Sherman, 1969; Sherman *et al.*, unpublished data). Such hemizygous diploids give clearer results in reversion studies than do haploids, probably because of the masking of recessive suppressors that cause growth on lactate medium. In addition, diploids are more resistant than haploids to the lethal effects of most mutagens and thus allow studies of reversion with populations having higher proportions of viable cells. For the sake of brevity, we have referred to the hemizygous diploids only by their cy1 point-mutations, i.e. cy1-9, cy1-13, cy1-51, etc., instead of the complete description, cy1-9/cy1-1, cy1-13/cy1-1, cy1-51/cy1-1, etc., which is given in Table 2 with the strain numbers.

TABLE 2

Tester strains

Diploid strain no.	Genotype		Inducing mutagen of haploid tester
	Haploid testers	cy1-1 deletion	
D-739	**a** cy1-9 *his1 his4 leu2* ×	α cy1-1 *trp1 ade1*	u.v.
D-576	**a** cy1-13 *his1 lys2 trp2* ×	α cy1-1 *trp1 ade1*	NIL†
D-557	**a** cy1-51 *his1 lys2 trp2* ×	α cy1-1 *trp1 ade1*	u.v.
D-558	**a** cy1-74 *his1 lys2 trp2* ×	α cy1-1 *trp1 ade1*	u.v.
D-577	**a** cy1-85 *his1 lys2 trp2* ×	α cy1-1 *trp1 ade1*	u.v.
D-578	**a** cy1-100 *his1 lys2 trp2* ×	α cy1-1 *trp1 ade1*	None
D-559	**a** cy1-131 *his1 lys2 trp2* ×	α cy1-1 *trp1 ade1*	u.v.
D-560	**a** cy1-133 *his1 lys2 trp2* ×	α cy1-1 *trp1 ade1*	u.v.
D-579	**a** cy1-163 *his1 lys2 trp2* ×	α cy1-1 *trp1 ade1*	None
D-740	**a** cy1-179 *his1 lys2 trp2* ×	α cy1-1 *trp1 ade1*	u.v.
D-580	**a** cy1-181 *his1 lys2 trp2* ×	α cy1-1 *trp1 ade1*	u.v.

† 1-nitrosoimidazolidone-2.

(b) Media

The general growth medium contained 1% Bacto-yeast extract, 2% Bacto-peptone and 2% dextrose. The lactate medium, which is used to select cy1 revertants, contained 0·67% Bacto-yeast nitrogen base without amino acids, 1% DL-lactate, 0·05% Bacto-yeast extract, 1·5% Ionagar no. 2 (Colab Laboratories, Chicago Heights, Ill., U.S.A.). Unless stated otherwise the lactate medium was adjusted to pH 5 with KOH. The glycerol medium used for assaying viability in reversion studies contained 1% Bacto-yeast extract, 2% Bacto-peptone, 3% (v/v) glycerol and 1% Ionagar. It should be pointed out that ρ^- strains (cytoplasmic "petites"), which may be induced by certain mutagens, do not grow on either glycerol medium or lactate medium, while the cy1 strains grow on glycerol medium but not on lactate medium.

(c) Source of chemical mutagens

The mutagens were obtained from the following sources; methyl methanesulfonate and ethyl methanesulfonate, Eastman Organic Chemicals; diethyl sulfate, Fisher Scientific Co.; dimethyl sulfate and *N*-methyl-*N'*-nitro-*N*-nitrosoguanidine, Aldrich Chemical

Co.; β-propiolactone, trade name "Betaprone", Fellows Medical Mfg. Co., Oak Park, Mich., 48237, U.S.A.; nitrogen mustard, trade name "Mustargen", Merck, Sharp and Dohme; 1-nitrosoimidazolidone-2, Drs F. K. Zimmermann (Technische Hochschule, Darmstade, Germany) and R. Preussman (Forschegruppe Präventivmedizin, Freiburg, Germany); [5-^{3}H]uridine, Schwarz–Mann.

Since commercially available preparations of the monofunctional alkylating agents EMS†, MMS, DES and DMS often contain impurities which increase toxicity but do not affect mutagenicity (Loppes, 1968; Strauss, personal communication), these chemical agents were repurified by vacuum distillation at 10 to 15 mm Hg before use.

(d) *Plate tests*

Reversion studies were carried out by seeding lactate medium with a lawn of approximately 10^6 to 10^7 cells and placing a small sample of the mutagen on a paper disc at the center of the plate. The following amounts of the various mutagens were used: 20 μl of undiluted EMS; 100 μl of undiluted β-propiolactone; 20 μl of 2% MMS in 0·05 M-potassium phosphate buffer, pH 7·0 (phosphate buffer); 50 μl of 0·5 mg NTG/ml in phosphate buffer; 50 μl of 0·5 mg HN2/ml in phosphate buffer. The plate test with [^{3}H]U consisted of mixing 250 μCi (30 Ci/mmol) with the medium of each plate. Standard lactate medium (pH 5) was used with all mutagens except NTG, where the pH was adjusted to 6·2, a condition that allows more effective mutagenic action of this agent.

(e) *Quantitative reversion frequencies*

Yeast was prepared for mutagenic studies by growth to stationary phase (2 to 3 days) in liquid general growth medium at 30°C. Cells were washed in sterile distilled water and resuspended in 0·05 M-potassium phosphate buffer, pH 7·0. The yeast suspensions, usually at 2 to 4×10^7 cells/ml, were treated with the mutagens as described below. Mutagenized and untreated cells were plated on lactate medium and the revertants were scored after 5 to 7 days of incubation at 30°C. Viability before and after mutagenic treatment was determined by plating cells on glycerol medium and scoring after 3 days of incubation at 30°C. A solution of filter-sterilized 5% sodium thiosulfate was used to inactivate the chemical mutagens at the end of the desired time, except in the cases described below.

(f) *Mutagenic treatments*

(i) *Ultraviolet light*

Cells spread on lactate and glycerol plates were irradiated with 900 ergs/mm^2 of u.v. light at a dose rate of 75 ergs/mm^2/s from a germicidal lamp.

(ii) *γ-ray irradiation*

Lactate and glycerol plates spread with cells were irradiated with 25,000 R, using a calibrated ^{60}Co γ source at a dose rate of 21·5 kR/min. (Model 109, J. L. Sheppard and Assoc., Glendale, Calif., kindly provided by Dr C. W. Lawrence.)

(iii) *Nitrogen mustard (di-(2-chloroethyl)methylamine)*

HN2 solutions were made just before use by dissolving the 10 mg content of a vial of "Mustargen" in phosphate buffer and diluting in the same buffer to the desired concentration. The standard condition consisted of treating cells for 1 h at 30°C in 0·2 mg HN2/ml.

(iv) *Methyl methanesulfonate*

Cells suspended in phosphate buffer were incubated for 40 min at 30°C with 0·4% MMS, which was prepared by adding 0·02 ml MMS to 5 ml of the cell suspension.

(v) *Ethyl methanesulfonate*

Cells suspended in phosphate buffer were incubated for 4 h at 30°C with 2% EMS, which was prepared by adding 0·05 ml EMS to 2·5 ml of the cell suspension.

† Abbreviations used: EMS, ethyl methanesulfonate; MMS, methyl methanesulfonate; DES, diethyl sulfate; DMS, dimethyl sulfate; NTG, *N*-methyl-*N'*-nitro-*N*-nitrosoguanidine; HN2, di-(2-chloroethyl)methylamine; [^{3}H]U, [5-^{3}H]uridine; NIL, 1-nitrosoimidazolidone-2.

(vi) *Diethyl sulfate*

Cells suspended in phosphate buffer were incubated for 20 min at 30°C with 2% DES, which was prepared by adding 0·05 ml DES to 2·5 ml of the cell suspension.

(vii) *Dimethyl sulfate*

Cells suspended in phosphate buffer were incubated for 10 min at 30°C with 0·1% DMS, which was prepared by adding 0·22 ml of 1% DMS, made just before use in phosphate buffer, to 2 ml of the cell suspension.

(viii) *β-propiolactone*

In order to obtain more reproducible results, the cells were starved by washing, resuspending in sterile distilled water and storing at 4°C for at least a day. Cells suspended in phosphate buffer were incubated at 30°C for 1 h with 0·02% β-propiolactone, which was prepared by adding 0·1 ml of a 1% β-propiolactone solution, in water, made just before use, to 5 ml of the cell suspension. The reaction was terminated by centrifugation and washing the cells with water.

(ix) N-*methyl*-N'-*nitro*-N-*nitrosoguanidine*

NTG was dissolved at 10 mg/ml in acetone just before use and diluted immediately to the desired concentration in phosphate buffer. NTG solutions were prepared in dim light and incubation of cells was carried out in the dark. Cells suspended in phosphate buffer were incubated at 30°C with 40 µg NTG/ml for 45 min.

(x) *1-nitrosoimidazolidone-2*

A solution of NIL was made as 3 mg/ml in phosphate buffer just before use. Cells suspended in phosphate buffer were incubated for 45 min at 30°C with 0·3 mg NIL/ml, which was prepared by adding 0·55 ml of the NIL solution to 5 ml of the cell suspension.

(xi) *Nitrous acid*

In order to obtain more reproducible results, the cells were starved by suspending in 0·05 M-KH_2PO_4 and storing at 4°C for 1 to 3 days. Starved cells were washed with sterile water and resuspended in 0·5 M-sodium acetate buffer, pH 4·8 (acetate buffer). HNO_2 was made just before use by dissolving sodium nitrite to make a 0·1 M-soln in acetate buffer. Cells suspended in acetate buffer were incubated with HNO_2 to yield a final concentration of 0·05 M-HNO_2. The reaction was terminated after 20 min of incubation by the addition of an equal volume of a solution of 2·7% $Na_2HPO_4 \cdot 7H_2O$/1% yeast extract.

(xii) [5-^3H]*uridine*

0·05 ml of a 2-day culture grown in synthetic medium (0·67% Bacto-yeast nitrogen base without amino acids, 2% dextrose) was added to 4·5 ml fresh synthetic medium. Cells were incubated for approximately 16 h at 30°C with 50 µCi [^3H]U/ml, which was prepared by adding 0·5 ml of 0·5 mCi/ml [^3H]U (30 Ci/mmol) to the 4·5-ml culture. The next day, cells were washed several times in distilled water, resuspended in 0·05 M-KH_2PO_4 and stored at 4°C. Cells were plated for study of viability and revertants both immediately and after 10 days of storage. Survival after ^3H decay was greater than 90% for all strains. A control culture was treated as described above, except that the [^3H]U was omitted from the medium.

4. Results

Seventeen mutagens were selected for investigation on the basis of their effective action on yeast (see Mortimer & Manney, 1971), their presumed ability to induce specific base changes in bacteriophage, or in the case of several alkylating agents, their similarities in chemical structures. Studies with one or more key tester *cyl* strains indicated that the following five mutagens were either completely ineffective or induced revertants at too low a frequency to be useful: 2-aminopurine, 2,6-diaminopurine, hydroxylamine, methoxylamine and sodium bisulfite. Lack of reversion

TABLE 3

Reversion frequencies (revertants per 10^7 survivors) of cy1 strains after treatment with various mutagens

Mutant	Altered codon	EMS	DES	NTG	NIL	HNO$_2$	[^{3}H]U	β-propiolactone	MMS	DMS	HN2	u.v. light	γ-rays
cy1-131	GUG	1226	240	1755	798	676	38	78	10	5	207	41	18
cy1-51	U UG	13	6	3	1	8	5	12	11	7	203	74	13
cy1-100	C	3	0	1	1	2	3	25	11	26	117	51	18
cy1-181		3	1	1	0	2	3	8	12	6	88	75	9
cy1-133	AGG	4	1	1	0	10	1	13	9	5	175	83	8
cy1-13		2	6	1	0	9	1	6	4	32	118	44	4
cy1-74	U AUC	3	5	2	0	2	2	8	23	10	305	85	9
cy1-85	A	2	0	4	1	5	1	11	18	29	293	60	5
cy1-163		1	1	0	1	2	1	15	4	32	125	76	8
cy1-9	UAA	8	8	1	0	5	6	10	18	9	257	2430	19
cy1-179	UAG	8	7	0	0	8	6	2	7	5	127	815	17

Reversion frequencies are expressed as the number of revertants obtained after treating cells, minus those that occurred spontaneously, except for treatments with [^{3}H]U. Reversion frequencies for cells grown in the presence of [^{3}H]U are expressed as the number of revertants obtained after 10 days of storage at 4°C, minus the number obtained after no storage. In most experiments, spontaneous reversion frequencies were less than 1 per 10^7 cells, except for β-propiolactone treatment of cy1-131, cy1-51, cy1-100 and cy1-74, HN2 treatment of cy1-133, and u.v. treatment of cy1-13, where the range was 4 to 15 per 10^7 cells. An entry of 0 indicates that no revertants were found out of 2 to 8×10^7 total cells plated, or that the difference between the induced and spontaneous reversion frequency was 0.

Survival after most treatments of the various mutants ranged from 50 to 100%, except for HN2 and u.v. light, where the range was 24 to 67% and 11 to 39%, respectively. The variation in survival observed for the different strains after treatment with a given mutagen is probably not significant.

of other $cy1$ strains treated with hydroxylamine was also reported by Parker & Sherman (1969). However, induced reversion of other yeast mutants have been reported to occur with 2-aminopurine, 2,6-diaminopurine (Jones, 1964; Hawthorne 1969a; Magni, personal communication) and hydroxylamine (Hawthorne, 1969b; Magni & Puglisi, 1966; Putrament & Baranowska, 1971).

The remaining 12 mutagens, listed in Table 3, were effective in reverting one or more of the tester strains. In some instances the strains were first tested by placing chemical mutagens on paper discs at the center of inoculated plates. Although this plate test suffers from being, at best, only semi-quantitative and by restricting the conditions of the mutagenic treatments, it is nevertheless rapid and convenient and it clearly distinguishes strains that give rise to extremely high frequencies of induced revertants. All eleven $cy1$ mutants were tested for revertibility with EMS and DES by using this plate method. In contrast with all of the other mutants, $cy1$-131 gave rise to high frequencies of induced revertants, a property that was previously noted for this mutant by Stewart $et\ al.$ (1971), Sherman & Stewart (1973), Sherman $et\ al.$ (unpublished data). This high revertibility was investigated further by comparing the two mutants, $cy1$-131 and $cy1$-133, for their response to the mutagens NTG, [^{3}H]U, β-propiolactone, MMS, and HN2 on paper discs. Some mutagens, NTG, [^{3}H]U, and β-propiolactone, induced higher frequencies of revertants in $cy1$-131 compared with $cy1$-133; however the other mutagens, MMS and HN2, had little effect on either $cy1$-131 or $cy1$-133. The differential response of $cy1$-131 and $cy1$-133 to several of the different mutagens is shown in Plate I.

While the plate test is convenient for the initial screening of mutagens and strains, procedures were developed to obtain quantitative results and to better control the conditions of treatments. In all cases, relatively short times of treatment were given

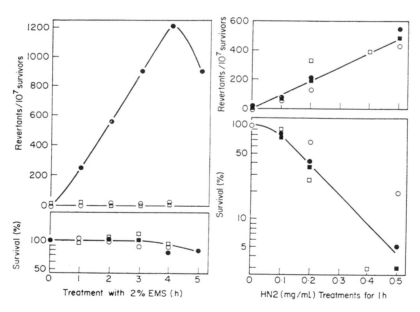

FIG. 4. Dose–response curves of various tester strains treated with EMS and HN2. (●) $cy1$-131; (□) $cy1$-9; (■) $cy1$-133; (○) $cy1$-179.

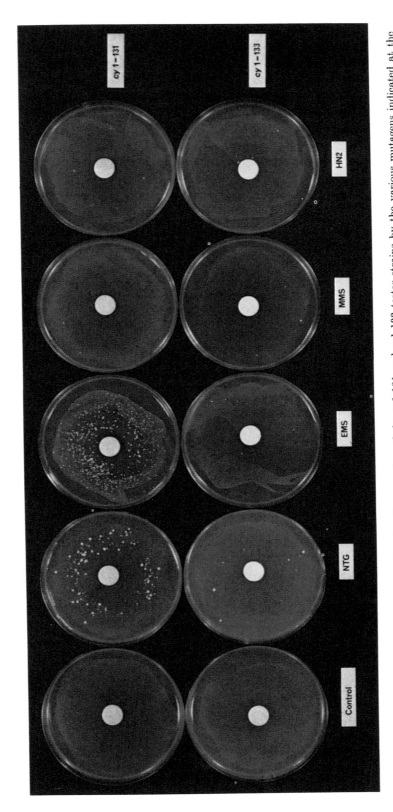

PLATE I. Photographs of the test plates, showing the reversion of the *cy1-131* and *cy1-133* tester strains by the various mutagens indicated at the bottom of the Plate. The mutagens were applied to paper discs at the center of lactate plates that were seeded with the tester strains.

to non-growing cells (except for [³H]U exposures), since it is believed that some mutagens may have less specificity if the treatments take place during growth of the cells.
Complete dose–response curves were obtained for several of the tester strains with
each of the 12 mutagens. The kinetic actions of most of the chemical mutagens were
studied by treating cells with single concentrations for various times as exemplified
in Figure 4 for EMS. In the case of the more labile agents, such as HN2 (Fig. 4) and
DMS, more reproducible curves could be obtained if cells were treated with various
concentrations of the mutagens for one fixed time. For each mutagen, one set of conditions was selected that resulted in the highest frequency of revertants per plate, a
condition that reflected a compromise between the lethal effect and the revertants
per survival. All of these treatments produced less than 50% lethality, except for the
u.v. treatment, which resulted in approximately 20% survival.

The results of reverting the eleven $cy1$ mutants with the 12 different mutagens
under the set conditions are presented in Table 3. The quantitative results are consistent with the results of the crude plate tests and establish that high rates of reversion of only $cy1$-131 are induced by EMS, DES, NTG, NIL, HNO₂, [³H]U and with
a lesser degree by β-propiolactone. In contradistinction, the mutagens MMS, DMS,
HN2, u.v. light and γ-rays show no preferential reversion of $cy1$-131. The only other
striking differences among the strains are the higher reversion of $cy1$-9 and $cy1$-179
by u.v. light.

It should be stressed that the differences in the rates of reversion are properties of
the $cy1$ alleles and not of variations in genetic backgrounds. Not only were the $cy1$
mutants, except for $cy1$-9, directly derived from a common strain, but the diploid
tester strains were made by crossing these haploid testers to the same deletion mutant
$cy1$-1 (Table 2). Also it cannot be argued that the high reversion rates are due to
dominant genetic factors fortuitously induced in the haploid tester strains, since the
high u.v.-induced reversion rate of $cy1$-9 and the high EMS-induced reversion rate
of $cy1$-131 have been observed in numerous segregants from various pedigrees. In
addition, all five of the independently-derived mutants that are identical to $cy1$-9
reverted at a high frequency after u.v.-irradiation (Sherman & Stewart, 1973).

Attempts were made to exclude possible systematic errors and to examine the
reproducibility of the values presented in Table 2. It should be pointed out that
many of the mutagenic treatments induced ρ⁻ mutants, which do not grow on lactate
medium. However, this effect was corrected for since "viabilities" were determined
on glycerol medium, which also does not permit growth of these mutants. In addition,
it has been shown previously that the colony-forming ability of normal cells on lactate medium is inhibited by an excess number of mutant cells (Parker & Sherman,
1969). While there is variation from strain to strain, usually there is a decreased efficiency of recovery with plating increasing cell concentrations of over 10⁸ cells per
plate. Conditions were selected to prevent this sensitivity to crowding with the strains
used in this study, both by plating various densities of treated cells and by plating
artificial mixtures of mutant and normal strains. It was also noted in the preliminary
experiments that an excessive variability occurred in the frequencies of revertants
induced with HNO₂ and β-propiolactone. More reproducible values were obtained
with these mutagens after starving the cells by the procedures described in Materials
and Methods.

It should be stressed that all or almost all of the large revertant colonies on lactate medium are the result of intragenic mutations and not the result of extragenic

suppressors. As previously shown in numerous studies (Sherman *et al.*, 1968, and unpublished data; Sherman & Stewart, 1971; Stewart *et al.*, 1971,1972; Stewart & Sherman, 1972,1973) intragenic and extragenic reversion of *cy*1 mutants can be differentiated on the basis of colony size and cytochrome *c* content. The vast majority of intragenic revertants have normal or near normal amounts of cytochrome *c* and have normal colony sizes on lactate medium, while nearly all of the extragenic revertants have below normal amounts of cytochrome *c* and form smaller colonies on lactate medium. The extragenic revertants can be due either to suppressors that usually cause increased levels of iso-2-cytochrome *c* or to nonsense suppressors that cause increased levels of iso-1-cytochrome *c* in amber and ochre *cy*1 mutants. The revertants having increased amounts of iso-2-cytochrome *c* can be distinguished clearly from intragenic revertants, since most of them still have far below the normal amounts of total cytochrome *c*. Even the rare revertants having normal amounts of cytochrome *c* that is entirely iso-2-cytochrome *c* can be conveniently identified by the slightly different spectral properties of the c_α-band. In addition, revertants containing nonsense suppressors, which are expected to act on the *cy*1-9 ochre and *cy*1-179 amber mutants, are easily distinguished from intragenic revertants by spectroscopic examination. In fact, the efficiency of suppression of *cy*1-9 is always so low that it is even difficult to distinguish the deficient mutant from the suppressed mutant (Gilmore *et al.*, 1971). In contrast, amber suppressors can cause the formation of from very low amounts to up to 50% of the normal amounts of iso-1-cytochrome *c* in *cy*1-179 and other *cy*1 amber mutants. However, for unknown reasons, amber suppressors rarely arise on lactate medium and the ones that do arise have a low efficiency of action (Sherman *et al.*, 1973). Numerous colonies from the experiments reported in Table 2 were picked and subcloned, and the resulting strains were examined for cytochrome *c* content and growth on lactate medium. From these results, we are confident that the colonies scored on lactate medium are truly the result of intragenic mutations.

5. Discussion

The 12 different mutagens (Table 3) could induce intragenic reversions of all eleven *cy*1 tester mutants. Even in the instances where values are listed as zero in Table 3, revertants could be induced by using more drastic treatments. However, the degree of reversion varied considerably and some mutagens caused over 1000-fold differences between certain strains. One striking pattern of the reversion frequencies can be interpreted unambiguously from the assumption given in Experimental Design (see Table 1). The seven mutagens, EMS, DES, NTG, NIL, HNO_2, [³H]U and to a lesser extent β-propiolactone, induce high rates of reversion of only *cy*1-131, while the remaining mutagens, MMS, DMS, HN2, u.v. light and γ-rays show no preferential action on this mutant. As can be seen in Table 1, of the eleven *cy*1 mutants, only *cy*1-131 can revert by a $G \cdot C \to A \cdot T$ transition. All other single base-pair substitutions can occur in the reversion of the *cy*1-179 amber mutant. Also the remaining nine mutants can revert by a variety of single base-substitutions but not by a $G \cdot C \to A \cdot T$ change. If one categorically accepts the assumptions concerning the base changes, it must be concluded that one group of mutagens preferentially causes only $G \cdot C \to A \cdot T$ changes, while the other group of mutagens does not. However, there are several qualifications and elaborations that should be considered.

While the simplest change that causes a selective reversion of cyl-131 is a $G \cdot C \rightarrow A \cdot T$ substitution, it is also possible that more complex changes could occur and still yield functional proteins. Such possibilities can be excluded almost unambiguously from the examinations of the primary structures of iso-1-cytochromes c. In this regard, four EMS-induced revertants of cyl-131 all contained the expected normal sequence (Stewart *et al.*, 1971). Even the EMS or DES-induced revertants of cyl-13 (Stewart *et al.*, 1971), cyl-9 (Stewart *et al.*, 1972), cyl-179 (Stewart & Sherman, 1972), cyl-76 (Stewart & Sherman, 1973), which arise at much lower frequencies, still took place by single base-substitutions, although without any obvious specificity. In the absence of evidence for any of these mutagens inducing multiple base changes, the high rate of cyl-131 reversion must be due to $G \cdot C \rightarrow A \cdot T$ transitions.

However, it is uncertain from these results whether this group of mutagens is highly capable of mutating every $G \cdot C$ base pair to an $A \cdot T$ base pair, or whether the specificity is restricted to $G \cdot C$ base pairs having particular neighboring bases that may be included in cyl-131. Extrinsic effects of adjacent base pairs has long been one explanation of "hot spots" and recently it was demonstrated that the frequencies of mutations induced with 2-aminopurine are influenced by nearby sequences (Koch, 1971; Salts & Ronen, 1971). In addition, it has been directly demonstrated with the iso-1-cytochrome c system that the position of the base pairs can play an important role not only in determining the rates of mutations but also in the types of base changes. Amino acid replacements in revertants of ochre and amber cyl mutants indicated that some $A \cdot T$ base pairs were more mutable than others in the same and in different codons. Numerous mutagens induce more mutations of the second $A \cdot T$ base pair than of the first $A \cdot T$ base pair in the two UAG mutants cyl-76 and cyl-179 (Stewart & Sherman, 1972, 1973). Also amino acid replacements in cyl-9 revertants indicated a strong specificity for $A \cdot T \rightarrow G \cdot C$ mutations with u.v. light (Stewart *et al.*, 1972), although this was not the case for the two UAG mutants cited above, not for another ochre mutant (Sherman *et al.*, 1969). In addition, the extremely high u.v.-induced rate of reversion of the cyl-9 ochre mutant (Parker & Sherman, 1969; Stewart *et al.*, 1971; Sherman & Stewart, 1973; see Table 3), is not observed for ochre mutants at other sites (Lawrence, Stewart & Sherman, unpublished results). Therefore, the generality of the findings from this study remains open to question, an uncertainty which is inherent to all assay systems that rely on reversion of tester strains. However, there is other evidence that the $G \cdot C \rightarrow A \cdot T$ specificity induced by the seven mutagens may be prevalent, or at least not unique to cyl-131. Another tester strain, cyl-115, that is currently under investigation also reverts by a $G \cdot C \rightarrow A \cdot T$ transition and also gives qualitatively the same pattern of reversion as cyl-131 (Prakash, Stewart & Sherman, unpublished results).

Whether or not the induced changes are general to all base pairs or whether or not the rates of reversion are strongly influenced by extraneous base sequences, it is still of interest to compare the base change assignments from this study to those deduced from other systems. Specific base changes have been reported in studies with bacteriophage T4, bacteriophage S13, which contains single-stranded DNA, *E. coli*, *Salmonella typhimurium* and *Neurospora crassa*, as well as RNA viruses. Some mutagens, such as u.v. light, EMS, NTG and HNO_2, have been the subject of numerous investigations involving various tester systems, while others, such as DES, [³H]U, β-propiolactone and HN2 have been used in only a few studies, and still others, such as NIL, MMS, DMS and γ-rays have not been previously used in studies where specific base changes were deduced. Most base change assignments were inferred indirectly from tests of forward and reverse mutations and, therefore, many of the conclusions are uncertain.

The results from genetic tests suggested that u.v. light induces different types of lesions in bacteriophage T4 (Folsome, 1962; Drake, 1963,1966a,b), bacteriophage S13 (Howard & Tessman, 1964), and possibly *E. coli* (Schwartz, 1963; Osborn et al., 1967), and *N. crassa* (Kilbey et al., 1971). More direct evidence for u.v. light causing a variety of changes comes from the analyses of forward mutations in tryptophan synthetase (Yanofsky, 1971) and iso-1-cytochrome c (Sherman & Stewart, 1973). The results from this study supplement this view and indicate that u.v. light does not produce $G \cdot C \to A \cdot T$ transitions at a particularly high rate, although other studies (Drake, 1963; Howard & Tessman, 1964; Osborn et al., 1967) indicated that this type of transition occurred at high frequencies. As noted above, the exceptionally high rate of u.v.-induced reversion of *cy*1-9 is the result of a specific $A \cdot T \to G \cdot C$ transition. However, neither the high rate of mutation nor the specific base change are observed for u.v.-revertants of ochre mutants at other sites. The *cy*1-9 strain is an interesting instance where its u.v.-induced reversion is dependent on unknown extraneous factors and its use as a tester strain may be deceptive if investigated only superficially.

The mutational specificity of EMS and a similar ethylating agent, ethyl ethane-sulfonate, has been extensively studied with the T4 bacteriophage system (Bautz & Freese, 1960; Bautz-Freese, 1961; Krieg, 1963a,b). It was concluded that the major base-pair substitution was $G \cdot C \to A \cdot T$, although a number of changes could not be assigned unambiguously (see Krieg, 1963a,b). Likewise, the analysis of mutations in bacteriophage S13 suggested that EMS induced mainly $G \to A$ and $C \to T$ transitions (Tessman et al., 1964). While the internal consistencies with bacteriophage systems give high credence to the base change assignments, the indirect nature of the method makes it difficult to assess the exceptional mutations and to quantitate the degree of specificity. Indirect genetic tests with *E. coli* also were consistent with the suggestion that EMS induced entirely or mainly $G \cdot C \to A \cdot T$ transitions (Schwartz, 1963; Osborn et al., 1967). However, the analysis of amino acid replacements in tryptophan synthetase mutants indicated that EMS did not induce any $G \cdot C \to A \cdot T$ transitions, while it did cause all other base-pair substitutions, $A \cdot T \to G \cdot C$, $A \cdot T \to T \cdot A$, and $G \cdot C \to C \cdot G$ (Yanofsky et al., 1966). In this particular case the conclusion of EMS specificity can be dismissed, since, as pointed out by the authors, the base pair changes were deduced from revertants of missense mutants that are expected to have restrictions in their amino acid replacements for functional proteins. In fact, $G \cdot C \to A \cdot T$ transitions of the extensively studied mutants, *trp*A23 and *trp*A46, lead to the replacement of a residue of lysine which probably would be incompatible with function since arginine at this position results in non-function. It has been concluded from reversion studies of the *ad-3A* mutants of *N. crassa* that EMS induces primarily $A \cdot T \to G \cdot C$ transitions and only a minor proportion (15%) of $G \cdot C \to A \cdot T$ transition (Malling & deSerres, 1968). However, as pointed out by Kilbey et al. (1971), these base-pair assignments should be considered only tentative, since the pathways of reversions are unknown and since the assignments were based largely on the assumed specificity of methoxylamine to induce $G \cdot C \to A \cdot T$ transitions. While hydroxyla-mine, whose action appears to be the same as methoxylamine (Malling, 1967), appears highly specific in bacteriophage, its specificity is lost if the mutagen is applied to phage inside their host cell (Tessman *et al.*, 1965) and there is no clear $G \cdot C \rightarrow A \cdot T$ specificity in *E. coli* (Osborn *et al.*, 1967; Mukai & Troll, 1969). We believe there is no convincing evidence invalidating the generalization that the main mutational event induced by EMS in all systems is $G \cdot C \rightarrow A \cdot T$ transition.

Apparently different actions of NTG are revealed with different tester systems. The transition $G \cdot C \rightarrow A \cdot T$ is almost exclusively seen to occur in bacteriophage T4, while all four types of transitions ($A \rightarrow T$, $T \rightarrow A$, $G \rightarrow C$ and $C \rightarrow G$) occur in bacteriophage S13 (Baker & Tessman, 1968). Perhaps the difference is due to the fact that T4 phage has a double-stranded DNA, whereas S13 phage has a single-stranded DNA. Indirect genetic analysis with less defined systems suggested that NTG induced at least two types of transitions, $A \cdot T \rightarrow G \cdot C$ and $G \cdot C \rightarrow A \cdot T$, in the bacteria *S. typhimurium* and *E. coli* (Eisenstark *et al.*, 1965; Zampieri & Greenberg, 1967) and probably $A \cdot T \rightarrow G \cdot C$ transitions in *N. crassa* (Malling & deSerres, 1970). However, direct analysis of primary structures of nine mutationally altered tRNAs established that NTG induced only $G \cdot C \rightarrow A \cdot T$ transitions in *E. coli* (Smith *et al.*, 1970). It is likely that NTG induces mainly $G \cdot C \rightarrow A \cdot T$ transitions in all systems that contain double-stranded DNA, including bacteriophage T4, bacteria and yeast.

It is surprising that HNO_2 appears to induce mainly $G \cdot C \rightarrow A \cdot T$ transitions in yeast while it induces both $G \cdot C \rightarrow A \cdot T$ and $A \cdot T \rightarrow G \cdot C$ transitions in bacteriophage, or the corresponding transitions in single-stranded viruses. HNO_2 induced *r*II mutants of bacteriophage T4 could be reverted with base analogs (Freese, 1959) and most mutants induced by base analogs and by HNO_2 also could be reverted by HNO_2 (Bautz-Freese & Freese, 1961; Champe & Benzer, 1962). Also, experiments with bacteriophage S13 suggested that HNO_2 can effectively induce $A \rightarrow G$, $C \rightarrow T$, and $G \rightarrow A$ transitions and to a lesser degree $T \rightarrow C$ transitions (Tessman *et al.*, 1964; Vanderbilt & Tessman, 1970). In addition, protein analysis of mutants of tobacco mosaic virus establish that HNO_2 induces mainly $A \rightarrow G$ and $C \rightarrow U$ transitions (see Sadgopal, 1968). However, there was no clear indication from the genetic work of Eisenstark & Rosner (1964) that HNO_2 produced mainly transitions in *E. coli*. If HNO_2 induced $A \cdot T \rightarrow G \cdot C$ transitions at approximately the same rate as $G \cdot C \rightarrow A \cdot T$ transitions in yeast, then the *cyl*-9 and *cyl*-179 tester strains (see Table 1) and possibly the *cyl*-13 tester strain should revert approximately the same way as the *cyl*-131 tester strain; the mutant codon in *cyl*-13 is probably AUA, since it was induced with NIL (Table 2), which appears to cause primarily $G \cdot C \rightarrow A \cdot T$ transitions (Table 3). More direct evidence for the lack of a highly specific $A \cdot T \rightarrow G \cdot C$ induction by HNO_2 comes from the amino acid replacements in ochre and amber revertants, which occur at a low rate compared to *cyl*-131 revertants. The amino acid replacements in revertants of *cyl*-9 (Stewart *et al.*, 1972), *cyl*-179 (Stewart & Sherman, 1972), and *cyl*-76 (Stewart & Sherman, 1973) indicated that, on the average, HNO_2 induced $A \cdot T \rightarrow G \cdot C$ transition only about twice as often as it induced transversions, and that the type of change may be dependent on the position of the base pair. The results from this study indicate that the action of HNO_2 may be more restrictive in yeast than in viruses.

The specific action of the mutagens [^{3}H]U, HN2 and β-propiolactone has been the subject of a limited number of studies. The $G \cdot C \rightarrow A \cdot T$ transition induced by [^{3}H]U in yeast is likewise found in *E. coli* (Osborn *et al.*, 1967) and is consistent with the $C \rightarrow T$ transition induced by [5-^{3}H]cytosine in bacteriophage S13 (Funk & Person, 1969). As observed with *E. coli*, we found that the related compound, [6-^{3}H]uridine did not exhibit a specificity for $G \cdot C \to A \cdot T$ transition. The genetic study by Corbett et al. (1970) indicated that while both HN2 and β-propiolactone induce various kinds of lesions in bacteriophage T4, the major base-pair substitutions are $G \cdot C \to A \cdot T$ transitions. Thus the action of β-propiolactone in bacteriophage T4 is in keeping with the results of our study with yeast, while the action of HN2 is not.

Whether or not the yeast tester system can definitively establish the types of base-pair substitution universally induced by agents, nevertheless it can be used in some cases to determine unequivocally whether these mutagens have a different mode of action. While it certainly cannot be inferred that all of the mutagens have the same mechanism of action if they are effective on cy1-131, it is clear that these mutagens differ from the mutagens that do not selectively revert this tester strain. As seen in Table 3, the monofunctional alkylating agents EMS, DES, NTG and NIL all have a striking specificity for inducing $G \cdot C \to A \cdot T$ transitions, while the chemically related agents MMS and DMS do not. In this regard, previous studies have revealed differences in the mutagenicity of monofunctional alkylating agents. It has been shown that NTG, EMS and DES are much more effective than MMS for mutating bacteriophage T2 or T4 (Loveless, 1959; Baker & Tessman, 1968). NTG is more mutagenic than MMS in N. crassa (Malling & deSerres, 1969) and Haemophilus influenzae (Kimball et al., 1971). This probably reflects the lack of ability of MMS to induce high rates of $G \cdot C \to A \cdot T$ transitions. However, MMS was reported to be more mutagenic than EMS using transforming DNA of Bacillus subtilis (Rhaese & Boetker, 1973).

The major products found in DNA after treatments of intact cells, bacteriophage, or purified DNA with either methylating or ethylating agents are 7-alkyl guanines, whether or not the agent is mutagenic. For example, the ethylating agents EMS and DES, and the methylating agent NTG are highly effective mutagens, while the methylating agents MMS and DMS are not. Because of such differences, it has recently been suggested that 7-alkyl guanine is not the major cause of mutation. Loveless (1969) proposed that mutagenicity is correlated with the formation of a relatively minor product O-6-alkyl guanine, which has been identified after treatment of DNA with N-methyl-N'-nitrosourea, N-ethyl-N'-nitrosourea and EMS, all of which are highly mutagenic for T2 phage (Loveless & Hampton, 1969). We would like to extend this hypothesis and suggest that the specificity as well as the mutagenicity of alkylating agents depends on the extent of formation of O-6-alkyl guanine. About ten times as much O-6-alkyl guanine is formed after the reaction of DNA or intact cells with EMS (Loveless, 1969) and NTG (Lawley & Orr, 1970; Lawley & Thatcher, 1970) as is found with DMS and MMS (Lawley & Thatcher, 1970; Lawley & Shah, 1972). Thus, the extent of formation of this product is much greater with EMS and NTG than with DMS and MMS, which correlates well with the mutagenic specificity of these agents. Also it should be pointed out that 7-methyl guanine is apparently not recognized by the repair system. There is no excision of methyl groups from the DNA of MMS-treated wild type or MMS-sensitive B. subtilis strains or from the DNA of MMS-treated E. coli B/r (Prakash & Strauss, 1970). After treatment of E. coli B/r with NTG, excision of methylation products other than 7-methyl guanine, namely, O-6-methyl guanine occurs (Lawley & Orr, 1970). Also, while the recA function in E. coli appears to be necessary for MMS-induced mutations, it is not required for EMS-induced mutation and it has only little effect on NTG-induced mutation (Kondo, et al., 1970). Thus it appears that at least part of the repair system that controls MMS mutability differs from the system that controls EMS and NTG mutability. It is

likely that errors in either repair or replication generate the high frequency of G·C →
A·T transitions in DNA that contains O-6-alkyl guanine.

This investigation was supported in part by U.S. Public Health Service fellowship
GM50480 and research grants GM19261 and GM12702 from the National Institutes of
Health and in part by the U.S. Atomic Energy Commission at the University of Rochester
Atomic Energy Project, Rochester, N.Y. and has been designated USAEC Report no.
UR-3490-296.

REFERENCES

Baker, R. & Tessman, I. (1968). *J. Mol. Biol.* **35**, 439–448.

Bautz, E. & Freese, E. (1960). *Proc. Nat. Acad. Sci., U.S.A.* **46**, 1585–1594.

Bautz-Freese, E. (1961). *Proc. Nat. Acad. Sci., U.S.A.* **47**, 540–545.

Bautz-Freese, E. & Freese, E. (1961). *Virology*, **13**, 19–30.

Champe, S. P. & Benzer, S. (1962). *Proc. Nat. Acad. Sci., U.S.A.* **48**, 532–546.

Corbett, T. H., Heidelberger, C. & Dove, W. F. (1970). *Mol. Pharmacol.* **6**, 667–679.

Drake, J. W. (1963). *J. Mol. Biol.* **6**, 268–283.

Drake, J. W. (1966a). *J. Bacteriol.* **91**, 1775–1780.

Drake, J. W. (1966b). *J. Bacteriol.* **92**, 144–147.

Drake, J. W. (1971). In *Chemical Mutagens* (Hollaender, A., ed.), vol. 1, pp. 219–233,
Plenum Press, New York.

Eisenstark, A. & Rosner, J. L. (1964). *Genetics*, **49**, 343–355.

Eisenstark, A., Eisenstark, R. & van Sickle, R. (1965). *Mutat. Res.* **2**, 1–10.

Folsome, C. (1962). *Genetics*, **47**, 611–622.

Freese, E. (1959). *Brookhaven Symp. Biol.* **12**, 63–73.

Funk, F. & Person, S. (1969). *Science*, **166**, 1629–1631.

Gilmore, R. A., Stewart, J. W. & Sherman, F. (1971). *J. Mol. Biol.* **61**, 157–173.

Hartman, P. E., Hartman, Z., Stahl, R. C. & Ames, B. N. (1971). *Advan. Genetics*, **16**,
1–34.

Hawthorne, D. C. (1969a). *Mutat. Res.* **7**, 185–197.

Hawthorne, D. C. (1969b). *J. Mol. Biol.* **43**, 71–75.

Howard, B. & Tessman, I. (1964). *J. Mol. Biol.* **9**, 372–375.

Jones, E. W. (1964). Ph.D. thesis, The University of Washington.

Kilbey, B. J., deSerres, F. J. & Malling, H. V. (1971). *Mutat. Res.* **12**, 47–56.

Kimball, R. F., Setlow, J. K. & Liu, M. (1971). *Mutat. Res.* **12**, 21–28.

Koch, R. (1971). *Proc. Nat. Acad. Sci., U.S.A.* **68**, 773–776.

Kondo, S., Ichikawa, H., Iwo, K. & Kato, T. (1970). *Genetics*, **66**, 187–217.

Krieg, D. R. (1963a). *Genetics*, **48**, 561–580.

Krieg, D. R. (1963b). *Prog. Nucleic Acid Res.* **2**, 125–168.

Lawley, P. D. & Orr, D. J. (1970). *Chem. Biol. Interactions*, **2**, 154–157.

Lawley, P. D. & Shah, S. A. (1972). *Chem. Biol. Interactions*, **5**, 286–288.

Lawley, P. D. & Thatcher, C. J. (1970). *Biochem. J.* **116**, 693–707.

Loppes, R. (1968). *Molec. Gen. Genet.* **102**, 229–231.

Loveless, A. (1959). *Proc. Roy. Soc., London* (Ser. B), **150**, 497–508.

Loveless, A. (1969). *Nature (London)*, **223**, 206–207.

Loveless, A. & Hampton, C. L. (1969). *Mutat. Res.* **7**, 1–12.

Magni, G. E. & Puglisi, P. P. (1966). *Cold Spring Harbor Symp. Quant. Biol.* **31**, 699–704.

Malling, H. V. (1967). *Mutat. Res.* **4**, 559–565.

Malling, H. V. & deSerres, F. J. (1968). *Mutat. Res.* **6**, 181–193.

Malling, H. V. & deSerres, F. J. (1969). *Ann. N.Y. Acad. Sci.* **163**, 789–800.

Malling, H. V. & deSerres, F. J. (1970). *Mol. Gen. Genetics*, **106**, 195–207.

Mortimer, R. K. & Manney, T. R. (1971). In *Chemical Mutagens* (Hollaender, A., ed.),
vol. 1, pp. 289–310, Plenum Press, New York.

Mukai, F. & Troll, W. (1969). *Ann. N.Y. Acad. Sci.* **163**, 828–847.

Osborn, M., Person, S., Phillips, S. & Funk, F. (1967). *J. Mol. Biol.* **26**, 437–447.

Parker, J. H. & Sherman, F. (1969). *Genetics*, **62**, 9–22.

Prakash, L. & Strauss, B. (1970). *J. Bacteriol.* **102**, 760–766.

Putrament, A. & Baranowska, H. (1971). *Mol. Gen. Genet.* **111**, 89–96.

Rhaese, H.-J. & Boetker, N. K. (1973). *Eur. J. Biochem.* **32**, 166–172.

Sadgopal, A. (1968). *Advan. Genetics*, **14**, 325–404.

Salts, Y. & Ronen, A. (1971). *Mutat. Res.* **13**, 109–113.

Schwartz, N. (1963). *Genetics*, **48**, 1357–1375.

Sherman, F. & Stewart, J. W. (1971). *Ann. Rev. Genet.* **5**, 257–296.

Sherman, F. & Stewart, J. W. (1973). In *The Biochemistry of Gene Expression in Higher Organisms* (Pollack, J. K. & Lee, J. W., eds), Reidel Publ. Co., Dordrecht. In the press.

Sherman, F., Stewart, J. W., Parker, J. H., Inhaber, E., Shipman, N. A., Putterman, G. J., Gardisky, R. L. & Margoliash, E. (1968). *J. Biol. Chem.* **243**, 5446–5456.

Sherman, F., Stewart, J. W., Cravens, M., Thomas, F. L. X. & Shipman, N. (1969). *Genetics*, **61**, s55.

Sherman, F., Liebman, S. W., Stewart, J. W. & Jackson, M. (1973). *J. Mol. Biol.* **78**, 157–168.

Smith, J. D., Barnett, L., Brenner, S. & Russell, R. L. (1970). *J. Mol. Biol.* **54**, 1–14.

Stewart, J. W. & Sherman, F. (1972). *J. Mol. Biol.* **68**, 429–443.

Stewart, J. W. & Sherman, F. (1973). *J. Mol. Biol.* **78**, 169–184.

Stewart, J. W., Sherman, F., Shipman, N. & Jackson, M. (1971). *J. Biol. Chem.* **246**, 7429–7445.

Stewart, J. W., Sherman, F., Jackson, M., Thomas, F. L. X. & Shipman, N. (1972). *J. Mol. Biol.* **68**, 83–96.

Tessman, I., Poddar, R. K. & Kumar, S. (1964). *J. Mol. Biol.* **9**, 352–363.

Tessman, I., Ishiwa, I. & Kumar, S. (1965). *Science*, **148**, 507–508.

Vanderbilt, A. S. & Tessman, I. (1970). *Genetics*, **66**, 1–10.

Yanofsky, C. (1971). In *Chemical Mutagens* (Hollaender, A., ed.), vol. 1, pp. 283–287, Plenum Press, New York.

Yanofsky, C., Ito, J. & Horn, V. (1966). *Cold Spring Harbor Symp. Quant. Biol.* **31**, 151–162.

Zampieri, A. & Greenberg, J. (1967). *Genetics*, **57**, 41–51.

An Improved Bacterial Test System for the Detection and Classification of Mutagens and Carcinogens

(*Salmonella typhimurium*/lipopolysaccharide/frameshift mutations)

BRUCE N. AMES, FRANK D. LEE, AND WILLIAM E. DURSTON

Biochemistry Department, University of California, Berkeley, Calif. 94720

Contributed by Bruce N. Ames, January 11, 1973

ABSTRACT We previously described a set of four strains of *Salmonella typhimurium* designed for detecting the various types of mutagens, and showed their utility in detecting a wide variety of carcinogens as mutagens. The lipopolysaccharide that normally coats these bacteria is a barrier to penetration of mutagens to the cell membrane. The set of tester strains has been improved by adding a mutation (*rfa*: deep rough) that results in a deficient lipopolysaccharide. The techniques for using these strains for detecting mutagens are presented and the tests are shown to be extremely sensitive and convenient. The specificity of frameshift mutagenesis is clarified. As adjuncts to the test with the four strains, we describe a test that compares mutagenic killing in deep rough strains with and without DNA excision repair, and a test using forward mutagenesis in a deep rough strain lacking excision repair.

We have described a set of four tester strains of *Salmonella typhimurium* designed for detecting and classifying mutagens (1–4). Each strain, which has been selected for its sensitivity and specificity, can be reverted back to the wild type by particular mutagens. In addition, the strains have a deleted excision repair system in and, consequently, are very much more sensitive to various mutagens. These strains are very valuable for detecting carcinogens as mutagens. The present paper describes a marked improvement in sensitivity obtained with new lipopolysaccharide (LPS)-defective derivatives of the strains, additional information as to specificity of frameshift mutagenesis, and methods for handling the strains.

MATERIALS AND METHODS

Compounds. We are indebted to H. J. Creech for ICR-191 and to J. A. Miller and H. Bartsch for nitrosobiphenyl and the fluorene compounds (4), except for 2-nitrofluorene (from Aldrich), 2,7-diaminofluorene (from Sigma), and 2,7-diacetyl-aminofluorene (from Schuchardt). 4-Nitroquinoline-*N*-oxide was purchased from Schuchardt, 9-aminoacridine was from Sigma, and methyl-nitro-nitroso-guanidine was from Aldrich.

Bacterial Strains. Each strain (Table 1) contains one of four mutations in the histidine operon resulting in a requirement for histidine. These four mutations are discussed in detail in *Results*. The deletion through the *uvrB* region of the chromosome eliminates the excision repair system for DNA. The *gal* and *rfa* (deep rough) mutations eliminate, to different extents, the polysaccharide side chain of the LPS that coats the bacterial surface, making the bacteria more

Abbreviation: LPS, lipopolysaccharide.

permeable and completely nonpathogenic. The TA1535 set (TA1535, TA1536, TA1537, TA1538), which is *rfa* and *uvrB*, is recommended for general testing for mutagens and carcinogens *in vitro*, as it is the most sensitive to mutagenesis. The TA1975 set is used for examining the effect of repair on mutagenesis and killing (in comparison to the TA1535 set). The TA1950 set and TA1530 set are less sensitive to mutagens *in vitro*, but may be required for use in the host-mediated assay in which *Salmonella* strains are incubated in the peritoneum of a mouse or rat (5). For good mutagenesis, especially with frameshift mutagens, there must be some bacterial multiplication in the peritoneum; this multiplication is influenced by the type of LPS. Which of the three sets to use must be determined for each type of animal. We also have constructed a set of auxotrophic derivatives of the TA1950 set of testers so that the four strains could be incubated as a set in the peritoneum of a single animal and sorted out afterward by plating on selective media.

Construction of Deep Rough Strains. The deep rough (*rfa*) derivatives of the tester strains were isolated from the TA1530 set of strains, which already carried deletions through the *gal–bio–uvrB* region of the chromosome (1, 2), by selection for bacteria resistant to C21 phage (6). Phage C21 will lyse *gal* deletion mutants, but not the deep rough strains or the wild type. The C21-resistant colonies were picked from confluent-lysis plates (nutrient agar) and purified. They were then screened for sensitivity to sodium deoxycholate (2 mg)

TABLE 1. *Genotype of the TA strains used for testing mutagens*

Additional mutations in:		Histidine mutation in strain			
LPS	Repair	*hisG46*	*hisC207*	*hisC3076*	*hisD3052*
+	+	*hisG46*	*hisC207*	*hisC3076*	*hisD3052*
+	Δ*uvrB*	TA1950	TA1951	TA1952	TA1534
Δ*gal*	Δ*uvrB*	TA1530	TA1531	RA1532	TA1964
rfa	Δ*uvrB*	TA1535	TA1536	TA1537	TA1538
rfa	+	TA1975	TA1976	TA1977	TA1978

All strains were originally derived from *S. typhimurium* LT-2. Wild-type genes are indicated by a +. The deletion (Δ) through *uvrB* also includes the nitrate reductase (*chl*) and biotin (*bio*) genes. The Δ*gal* strains (and the *rfa uvrB* strains) have a single deletion through *gal chl bio uvrB*. The *rfa*, repair⁺ strains (last row) have a mutation in *galE*.

and crystal violet (10 μg), which were applied to sterile filter paper discs (6 mm) placed in the center of nutrient agar pour plates containing 2×10^8 bacteria. After overnight incubation at 37°, a zone of inhibition could be seen around each disc, and the strains (TA1535, etc.) were chosen that had maximum sensitivity: 14 mm with crystal violet and 13 mm with deoxycholate. The wild type and the strains with the *gal* deletion show no zone of inhibition. The inhibition by the two compounds can be used as a simple test to confirm the properties of the deep rough strains.

Deep rough derivatives (TA1978, etc.) were constructed from the histidine-requiring mutants (*hisD3052*, etc.), which have a normal excision repair system. Mutations were first introduced in the galactose operon by selecting for resistance to deoxygalactose. Plates containing no carbon source were spread with 0.2 ml of 40% glycerol, 0.2 ml of 0.5 mM biotin, 0.06 ml of 100 mM histidine, 0.1 ml of 40% 2-deoxygalactose, 30 μl of 4% galactose, and 0.1 ml of a nutrient broth culture of *hisD3052*. Resistant colonies appeared after incubation for 2 days at 37°; these were picked and screened for sensitivity to C21 phage. The phage-sensitive strains (about 1/250 tested) were checked to make sure they were still resistant to ultraviolet light; from these, C21-resistant derivatives that were sensitive to crystal violet were then isolated as explained above.

Construction of gal⁺ uvrB⁻ Strains. The TA1950 set of strains were constructed from the four original histidine mutants, *hisG46*, etc., by introduction of a *chl bio uvrB* deletion. Each of the histidine mutants was put through an anaerobic selection (8) on glycerol–chlorate agar pour plates (minimal medium, 2% glycerol, 0.3% KClO$_3$, 6 μmol of histidine, 0.1 μmol of biotin, and 2×10^8 bacteria). The plates were incubated overnight at 37° inside of a dessicator under an atmosphere of N$_2$, then incubated aerobically for 2 more days. Chlorate-resistant colonies were picked and tested for sensitivity to ultraviolet light by streaking across a nutrient broth plate and exposing half of the plate to a 15-W G.E. germicidal lamp at 33 cm for 6 sec. After overnight incubation, the sensitive strains (about 1/200) were picked; they were also Gal⁺ and Bio⁻.

Quantitative Testing of Mutagens. A large number of suspected mutagens can be tested very simply by placing crystals or a few μl of the compound directly on a lawn of the tester strain (see below) (1). For quantitative testing and greater sensitivity, a known amount of the mutagen is incorporated in the form of a solution into the top agar of a pour plate. In this way the mutagen is spread uniformly over the plate along with the bacteria.

Pour plates are made by adding 0.1 ml of the tester strain culture to a small sterile test tube (13×100 mm) that contains 2 ml of molten (45°) *top agar* (which contains a trace of histidine and excess biotin). An appropriate volume of the mutagen in solution can be added to the tube with a sterile disposable capillary pipette. The tube is then mixed well by rotation between the palms of one's hands and poured onto the surface of a minimal agar plate with Vogel–Bonner E medium (7) (1.5% agar, 2% glucose). The plate can be tilted quickly to cover the surface with the top agar, then it is allowed to remain on a level surface several minutes for the agar to harden. A control plate for the spontaneous reversion rate should be done for each tester strain in which the

mutagen is omitted. A sterility check of the mutagen solution also should be done. All plates are incubated upside down at 37° for 2 days, after which the number of revertant colonies appearing can be counted. If too much of the compound is added so that the light lawn of the background and the spontaneous revertants are inhibited, then the experiment should be repeated with less compound.

The standard components of the pour plate assay do not have to be made each day. Bacterial cultures are grown up in nutrient broth for about 8 hr from a 1/100 inoculum and can be stored in a refrigerator for at least 1 week. Aqueous solutions of mutagen are prepared in sterile screw-cap tubes with sterile water or with dimethylsulfoxide (Schwarz–Mann, spectrophotometric grade, sterile as is). It is possible to add up to 0.5 ml of dimethylsulfoxide per plate without appreciably interfering with mutagenesis. *Top agar* (0.6% Difco agar, 0.6% NaCl) is autoclaved and stored in bottles in volumes of 100 ml at room temperature. Before use the agar is melted by placing the bottle in boiling water, and 10 ml of a sterile solution of 0.5 mM L-histidine·HCl–0.5 mM biotin is added; the bottle is mixed by gentle swirling. The agar is added to the tubes and allowed to equilibrate to 45° before addition of any bacteria.

The trace of histidine in the top agar allows all the bacteria on the plate to undergo several divisions; this growth is necessary in many cases for mutagenesis to occur. The slight background that grows up also allows any inhibition by the compound to be seen. Further increase of the histidine on the plate enhances mutagenesis, but it also gives a heavy background lawn that obscures the revertants.

The Repair Test: Comparison of Strains with and without Repair for Zones of Killing. Pour plates with a lawn of bacteria (TA1978/TA1538) are prepared as described for mutagen testing, except that an additional 3.0 μmol of L-histidine is added, thus allowing full growth of the bacterial lawn and giving more distinct zones of killing by test compounds. Up to 25 μl of the test solution is pipetted onto sterile filter paper discs (6 mm) with disposable glass capillary pipettes, and each loaded disc is placed on a plate. The plates are then inverted and placed in a 37° incubator for 24 hr, and the zone of killing is measured.

Forward Mutagenesis Test. We have discussed (1) a forward mutagenesis test using resistance to the proline analogue, azetidine carboxylic acid. The use of strain TA1538 increases the general sensitivity of this test, but with this strain an excess of histidine (3 μmol) should be added to the usual top agar, which has an excess of biotin. Addition of a trace of proline (0.02 μmol) also increases the sensitivity. The azetidine carboxylic acid can be L, or D,L (use 10 μmol of the L form per plate) and is available from Aldrich or Calbiochem. Mutagens can be added to the top agar for quantitative results or spotted for qualitative results.

RESULTS

Bacterial LPS is a barrier to mutagen penetration

We have made three sets of tester strains with different LPS coats (Table 1): TA1950, etc., have a normal LPS, TA1530, etc., have a partial LPS due to a deletion through the *gal* operon, and the newly constructed, and preferred, set, TA1535, etc., has a deep rough *rfa* mutation, which removes the LPS down to the ketodeoxyoctanoate–lipid core (6).

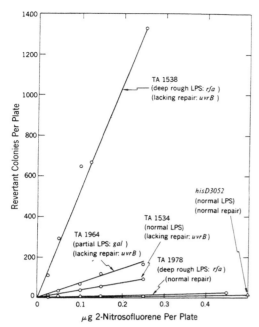

FIG. 1. Effect of repair and LPS mutations on sensitivity to mutagenesis by 2-nitrosofluorene. The spontaneous revertants, about 15 per plate, have been subtracted.

Fig. 1 shows quantitative data on the reversion by 2-nitrosofluorene of the same histidine mutation (*hisD3052*) in strains from each of these three sets that differ in their LPS. The advantage of the deep rough mutant, TA1538, is apparent. Comparison of various mutagens on strains with partial or no LPS is shown in Table 2. It can be seen that as the ring system increases in size the advantage of using the *rfa* derivatives becomes more pronounced.

Comparison of strains with and without excision repair

The difference in the number of revertant colonies between a strain with and without repair is useful in determining whether a frameshift mutagen is a simple or a reactive intercalator (1–4). This comparison was previously done with the pair TA1534/*hisD3052*, but we have now constructed a new pair, TA1538/TA1978, which is much more sensitive because both strains have the defective, deep-rough LPS. The differences between TA1538 and TA1978 or between TA1534 and *hisD3052* can be seen in Fig. 1, in which the sensitivity to reversion of the histidine mutation, *hisD3052*, by 2-nitrosofluorene, a reactive intercalator, is compared.

The new pair of deep rough strains is also much more sensitive in the *repair test*, a comparison of zones of killing by a compound. If the strain without repair (TA1538) is more sensitive to killing by a compound than the strain with repair (TA1978), then the compound is deduced to be killing because of a covalent reaction with DNA. This type of test has been studied in detail for the *polA* mutants in *E. coli* (9) and for the *rec* system in *B. subtilis* (10). We have used it for the *uvrB* excision repair system in our *Salmonella* strains (1, 2). The *repair test* for several compounds is shown in Table 3. Our *repair test* is well over 10-times more sensitive than the *polA* test, based on the reported zone of killing for 2-nitrosofluorene (9) compared to Table 3. One limitation of

the *repair test* is that it does not detect simple intercalating mutagens, as shown in Table 3 for 9-aminoacridine, ethidium bromide, quinacrine, and ICR 364-OH, which are equally inhibitory to both strains. Another limitation is that the *repair test* with *uvrB* does not detect a difference with methylating agents (and ethylating agents), as has been discussed in connection with the influence of *uvrB* on mutagenesis (2). The *polA* test (9) does detect methylating agents and the *polA* deep rough derivative of *hisG46* is being constructed.

Nature and specificity of the tester strains

The specificity of the most sensitive set (deep rough and lacking repair) of the four tester strains can be seen in Table 4. Some of the mutagens are fairly specific for reverting one of the strains and not the others, and these mutagens can be used as positive controls for checking out the strains when testing new compounds.

TA1535. This strain contains the histidine mutation *hisG46*, which is a missense mutation (11). It is reverted well by a wide variety of carcinogenic mutagens that cause base-pair substitutions (1, 2), but not by mutagens that cause

TABLE 2. *Comparison of mutagens on tester strains with different LPS*

	His⁺ revertants per plate		
Compound added	Normal LPS (TA1534)	galΔ LPS (TA1964)	Deep-rough LPS (TA1538)
2-Ring compounds			
4-Nitroquinoline-N-oxide (0.5 μg)	198	255	288
4-Hydroxylaminoquinoline-N-oxide (8 μg)	97	106	153
4-Nitrosobiphenyl (10 μg)	52	98	250
3-Ring compounds			
2-Nitrosofluorene (0.25 μg)	91	166	1327
2,7-Bis-(acetylamino)-fluorene (25 μg)	286	457	3900
2-Nitrofluorene (50 μg)	156	267	4200
2,7-Diaminofluorene (50 μg)	9	18	141
N-Hydroxy-2-amino-fluorene (1 μg)	288	1023	3800
N-Hydroxy-2-acetyl-aminofluorene (25 μg)	22	49	256
N-Acetoxy-2-acetyl-aminofluorene (10 μg)	47	58	1630
	(TA1952)	(TA1532)	(TA1537)
ICR-191 (1 μg)	31	170	955
4-Ring compounds			
ICR-312 (5 μg)	56	138	1706

The number of revertants caused by the mutagen on each plate is shown with the control subtracted: control plates never had more than 20 colonies. The mutagens were added to the top agar in dimethylsulfoxide, except for the ICR compounds, which were in sterile water, and 2-nitrosofluorene, which was in 95% ethanol. ICR-191 is a substituted acridine and ICR-312 is a substituted benzacridine (13).

frameshift mutations. It is not clear which base pair changes can revert the strain, but we suspect that most, if not all, of the six possible base pair substitutions can be detected with this strain.

TA1536. This strain contains the histidine mutation *hisC207*, a frameshift mutation (11, 12). It is reverted by various acridine half-mustards, the ICR compounds (12, 13), but not by any of the various other frameshift mutagens we have tried. This is the least useful of our tester strains, as ICR can also be detected easily with TA1537 (and TA1538) (Table 4). We are leaving it in the set as it is the most sensitive to ICR-191. It is not clear what the frameshift mutation is in this strain, but as ICR-191 is likely to react with a G, we suspect that a GC is involved. It does not appear to have the -GGGG- / -CCCC- sequence present in TA1537, or the alternating G-C sequence that is present in TA1538. In an experiment analogous to that described for TA1537, we have shown that the *hisC207* mutation is not suppressible by the *sufB*, -CCCC-, frameshift suppressor (TA1951, *hisC207 uvrB*, donor; TR944 recipient). Oeschger and Hartman suggest that frameshift mutations such as *hisC207* that do not revert at all with methyl-nitro-nitrosoguanidine (Table 4) are likely to be deletions of a base pair (14).

TA1537. This strain contains the histidine frameshift mutation *hisC3076* (14). The following evidence suggests that the frameshift mutation in this strain has an added -G- / -C- base pair resulting in -GGGG- / -CCCC-. It is suppressed by a frameshift

TABLE 3. *Repair test*

Test compound	Diameter of zone of killing (mm)	
	Repair +	Repair −
Crystal violet (10 μg)	19 (11)	20 (12)
Mitomycin C (1 μg)	<6	27
2-Nitrosofluorene (1 μg)	<6 (<6)	13 (<6)
(10 μg)	9 (<6)	32 (23)
4-Nitrosobiphenyl (100 μg)	12	24
4-Nitroquinoline-*N*-oxide (20 μg)	18	29
ICR-372 (100 μg)	14	19
ICR-372-OH (100 μg)	14	13
9-Aminoacridine (100 μg)	13	14
Ethidium bromide (50 μg)	15	16
Quinacrine (20 μg)	11	12
Diethylsulfate (10 μl)	14	15
N-Methyl-*N'*-nitro-*N*-nitroso-guanidine (100 μg)	28	28
Nitrogen mustard (100 μg)	11	16

The zones of killing produced by various test compounds are compared for the deep rough tester strains with (TA1978) and without (TA1538) excision repair. The data in parentheses are for a similar pair (*hisD3052*/TA1534) with a normal LPS. Diameters less than that of the disc (6 mm) cannot be measured. For a given test compound and strain, the diameter of the zone of killing is roughly proportional to (amount of compound)². ICR-372 is an alkylating and ICR 372-OH a nonalkylating derivative of aza-quinacrine (13).

TABLE 4. *Mutagen specificity for the four tester strains*

	Revertant colonies per plate on tester strains			
	TA1535	TA1536	TA1537	TA1538
Control (spontaneous)	18	0	5	12
N-Methyl-*N'*-nitro-*N*-nitrosoguanidine (10 μg)	40,000	0	36	15
ICR-191 (5 μg)	32	14,000	7500	2300
9-Aminoacridine (100 μg)	48	0	3800	15
2-Nitrosofluorene (0.5 μg)	32	0	36	3400
4-Nitroquinoline-*N*-oxide (1 μg)	107	0	30	380

The number of colonies per plate is shown: the spontaneous controls have not been subtracted.

suppressor *sufB* of Riddle and Roth (15), which they have shown to be a mutation in tRNA^Pro that suppresses +1 frameshift mutations of the -CCCC- type. This is likely to be caused by an added G in the normal -GGG- anticodon of the proline tRNA (15). We transduced TR944 (*sufB his01242 hisΔ2236*) (15) with P22 phage grown on *hisC3076* on a plate with no histidine, and found 5000 very small transductants (presumptive suppressed strains) and 250 large transductants (presumptive wild-type recombinants). Two of the small transductants were checked out by crossing with histidine deletions. We conclude they contain a suppressor, as they still contained the original histidine mutation. A control plate using the histidine deletion without the suppressor (TA462) as the recipient showed only 114 large, presumptive wild types. Another control plate with a known suppressible mutant (15) (*hisC3737* in TR970) transduced into TA944 gave about 3500 small colonies. TA1537 is reverted weakly by methyl-nitro-nitrosoguanidine (Table 4), a finding consistent with the properties of a +1 frameshift addition in a -GGGG- / -CCCC- sequence (14, 16). The TA1537 tester strain is reverted by 9-aminoacridine and ICR-191 (Table 4) and epoxides of polycyclic hydrocarbons (3), among other agents. It is reverted by various carcinogenic polycyclic hydrocarbons that have been activated by a mammalian microsomal system (manuscript in preparation).

TA1538. This strain contains the *hisD3052* frameshift mutation that was first used by Hartman *et al.* (17) to show that 4-nitroquinoline-*N*-oxide and hycanthone were frameshift mutagens. We have discussed (4) the evidence of Isono and Yourno that this strain contains a -CGCGCG- / -GCGCGC- sequence that is reverted by 2-nitrosofluorene with a −2 deletion of a -CG- / -GC-. This strain is reverted by various aromatic nitroso derivatives of amine carcinogens (4), and, in combination with a microsomal activation system, by the carcinogens aflatoxin B1 and benzpyrene and by a wide variety of aromatic amine carcinogens (manuscript in preparation).

DISCUSSION

The LPS that is normally present on the surface of *S. typhimurium* apparently acts as a partial barrier to the passage of mutagens to the membrane, as shown by the marked increase in the sensitivity to mutagens of LPS-defective strains. We first tried this approach when it was found that dibenz(*a,h*)anthracene epoxide did not work as a frameshift mutagen, although the closely related carcinogen benzanthracene epoxide did. We reasoned that the large size of the compound might prevent its entrance into the bacteria, and indeed we found that introducing the *rfa* mutation into the tester strain enabled us to detect the mutagen (3). This *rfa* mutation causing a shortened LPS has been put into all of our tester strains and gives a marked increase in sensitivity in detecting mutagens: the larger the ring system, the more pronounced the effect.

The genetics and biochemistry of the LPS of *Salmonella* have been investigated in detail (6). A deletion through the *gal* operon eliminates galactose synthesis from the cell and, therefore, the LPS loses the part of the polysaccharide chain that is distal to the first galactose unit. The *rfaF* and *rfaE* mutants (deep rough) are defective in enzymes that are responsible for the synthesis of the polysaccharide distal to the ketodeoxyoctanoate–lipid core and are particularly sensitive to deoxycholate and various antibiotics and other large compounds (6, 18). These mutations presumably cause the maximum permissible stripping of the LPS without lethality.

We have discussed the advantages of this *Salmonella* system for the detection of mutagens (1–4). We have screened many mutants to obtain those that were most sensitive to a wide variety of mutagens, then we increased the sensitivity by several orders of magnitude by introducing mutations in the repair system and the LPS. A comprehensive set of back-mutation tester strains has certain practical and theoretical advantages over a single forward mutagenesis assay (1, 2). The proof of the advantages of this set is its comprehensiveness in detecting the known classes of mutagens at very low concentrations (1–4) and its utility in making the correlation between carcinogenicity and mutagenicity (1–4, and manuscript in preparation).

Although our set of four strains appears to be able to detect almost all mutagens, it is clear that it is not yet completely comprehensive. We do not yet have a frameshift tester involving a repetition of A-T sequences. In addition, there are a few frameshift mutagens, such as activated aflatoxin B1 and activated benzpyrene that, although they work on our tester strains, are relatively inactive when compared to their activity in the *repair test*. The *repair test* compares zones of killing in strains with and without repair, and we recommend its use as an adjunct test until the back-mutation tester set is completed. The *repair test* by itself, however, can be much less sensitive than a specific back-mutation test, as can be seen with 2-nitrosofluorene (Fig. 1 versus Table 3). Another limitation of the *repair test* is that methylating agents, and simple intercalating mutagens that do not react with DNA

covalently, may not show an appreciable difference in zones of inhibition.

The forward mutagenesis test described also makes a useful adjunct to the set of back-mutation testers. It is not desirable as the sole test, however, as it is less sensitive than a specific back-mutation test (because of the many spontaneous mutants of various types) and it may, in particular cases, not work at all. We have found, for example, that 2-nitrosofluorene does not cause an increase in azetidine carboxylic acid resistance, even though it clearly is a very powerful mutagen for the G-C-G-C-G-C sequence. We calculate that this sequence is a rare one in DNA (it might occur in only about 25% of the genes) and, thus, it is reasonable that it may not occur in any one particular gene.

We have combined these test systems with a mammalian liver microsomal system (manuscript in preparation), and have shown that an extremely wide range of chemical carcinogens, become powerful mutagens through metabolic activation and can be detected with great sensitivity and simplicity.

We are indebted to E. G. Gurney for some of the earlier work on this project, and to J. R. Roth and P. E. Hartman for helpful discussions and strains. J. A. Miller, H. Bartsch, and H. J. Creech kindly furnished many carcinogens and mutagens. We are grateful to H. Nikaido for C21 phage and to him and B. D. Stocker for discussion about *Salmonella* LPS. This work was supported by A.E.C. Grant AT(04-3) 34, P.A. 156.

1. Ames, B. N. (1971) in *Chemical Mutagens*, ed. Hollaender, A. (Plenum Press, New York), Vol. 1, chap. 9.
2. Ames, B. N. (1972) in *Mutagenic Effects of Environmental Contaminants*, eds. Sutton, H. E. & Harris, M. I. (Academic Press, New York), pp. 57–66.
3. Ames, B. N., Sims, P. & Grover, P. L. (1972) *Science* **176**, 47–49.
4. Ames, B. N., Gurney, E. G. Miller, J. A. & Bartsch, H. (1972) *Proc. Nat. Acad. Sci. USA* **69**, 3128–3132.
5. Legator, M. S. & Malling, H. V. (1971) in *Chemical Mutagens*, ed. Hollaender, A. (Plenum Press, New York), Vol. II, chap. 22.
6. Wilkinson, R. G., Gemski, P., Jr. & Stocker, B. A. D. (1972) *J. Gen. Microbiol.* **70**, 527–554.
7. Vogel, H. J. & Bonner, D. M. (1956) *J. Biol. Chem.* **218**, 97–106.
8. Stouthamer, A. H. (1969) *Antonie Van Leeuwenhoek J. Microbiol. Serol.* **35**, 505–521.
9. Slater, E. E., Anderson, M. D. & Rosenkranz, H. S. (1971) *Cancer Res.* **31**, 970–973.
10. Kada, T., Tutikawa, K. & Sadaie, Y. (1972) *Mutat. Res.* **16**, 165–174.
11. Hartman, P. E., Hartman, Z., Stahl, R. C. & Ames, B. N. (1971) *Adv. Genet.* **16**, 1–34.
12. Ames, B. N. & Whitfield, H. J. Jr. (1966) *Cold Spring Harbor Symp. Quant. Biol.* **31**, 221–225.
13. Creech, H. J., Preston, R. K., Peck, R. M., O'Donnell, A. P. & Ames, B. N. (1972) *J. Med. Chem.* **15**, 739–746.
14. Oeschger, N. S. & Hartman, P. E. (1970) *J. Bacteriol.* **101**, 490–504.
15. Riddle, D. L. & Roth, J. R. (1972) *J. Mol. Biol.* **66**, 495–506.
16. Yourno, J. (1972) *Nature New Biol.* **239**, 219–221.
17. Hartman, P. E., Levine, K., Hartman, Z. & Berger, H. (1971) *Science* **172**, 1058–1060.
18. Roantree, R. J., Kuo, T., MacPhee, D. G. & Stocker, B. A. D. (1969) *Clin. Res.* **17**, 157.

Detection of Carcinogens as Mutagens: Bacterial Tester Strains with R Factor Plasmids

(error-prone recombinational repair/7,12-dimethylbenzanthracene/aflatoxin/nitrofurans)

JOYCE McCANN, NEIL E. SPINGARN, JOAN KOBORI, AND BRUCE N. AMES

Biochemistry Department, University of California, Berkeley, Calif. 94720

Contributed by Bruce N. Ames, December 23, 1974

ABSTRACT We described previously a simple test on petri plates for detecting chemical carcinogens as mutagens, using an especially sensitive set of bacterial strains to detect mutagenic activity and a mammalian liver extract for carcinogen activation. We now extend the utility of the method by introducing two new bacterial strains which can detect with great sensitivity many carcinogens which we did not detect before or detected with less sensitivity. Among these carcinogens are aflatoxin B₁, sterigmatocystin, benzyl chloride, benzo[a]pyrene, 7,12-dimethylbenzanthracene, 1′-acetoxysafrole, and the nitrofuran food additive furylfuramide (AF-2). The new strains TA100 and TA98 contain an R factor plasmid, pKM101, in our standard tester strains TA1535 and TA1538. The R factor increases mutagenesis with certain mutagens, but not others. We present evidence that the mutagens that become more effective work through an error-prone recombinational repair.

We have previously described a very sensitive and simple bacterial test for detecting chemical mutagens (1–4). The compounds are tested on petri plates with specially constructed mutants of *Salmonella typhimurium* as tester strains. Four tester strains have been selected, after screening hundreds of mutants, for sensitivity and specificity in being reverted from a histidine requirement back to prototrophy by a variety of mutagens. One strain (TA1535) can be used to detect mutagens causing base-pair substitutions and three (TA1536, TA1537, and TA1538) to detect various kinds of frameshift mutagens. In addition to the histidine mutation, we have added to the tester strains two additional mutations that greatly increase their sensitivity to mutagens: one causes loss of the excision repair system and the other loss of the lipopolysaccharide barrier that coats the surface of the bacteria (3).

We have shown that by adding a microsomal activation system from rat (or human) liver to the petri plates, a wide variety of carcinogens can be activated to mutagens and detected easily. Thus, an important aspect of mammalian metabolism can be duplicated in an *in vitro* test. A large group of carcinogens—aflatoxin B₁, benzo[a]pyrene, 2-acetylaminofluorene, etc., have been detected as reactive frameshift mutagens after liver activation (4). Each activated molecule contains a ring system capable of stacking interaction with DNA and an electrophilic group that can react with DNA (5–8). Other groups of carcinogens have been detected as mutagens causing base-pair substitutions: β-propiolactone, propane-

Abbreviations: MMS, methyl methanesulfonate; MNNG, *N*-methyl-*N*′-nitro-*N*-nitrosoguanidine; NQNO, 4-nitroquinoline-1-oxide; UV, ultraviolet.

sultone, etc. (1–4). Some carcinogens, such as nitroquinoline-1-oxide (NQNO), cause both types of mutations (3).

We report here the development of two new bacterial strains which contain an R factor (plasmids carrying antibiotic resistance genes) and which greatly extend the usefulness of the test system. This work stemmed from the observation of MacPhee (9) that methyl methanesulfonate (MMS) and trimethyl phosphate were more effective in reverting *hisG46* (the histidine mutation in TA1535) when another R factor, R-Utrecht, was present. Other reports had also indicated that certain plasmids increased ultraviolet- (UV) induced mutation rates (10–12).

MATERIALS AND METHODS

Chemicals were obtained as follows: Ampicillin trihydrate (Bristol Labs); methyl methanesulfonate (MMS), bis(2-chloroethyl)amine·HCl, *N*-methyl-*N*′-nitro-*N*-nitrosoguanidine (MNNG), sterigmatocystin, benzo[a]pyrene, benzyl chloride, and dimethylcarbamyl chloride (Aldrich); NQNO, and 2-aminoanthracene (Schuchardt/Munich); captan (Analabs); diethyl sulfate (Fisher); aflatoxin B₁ (Calbiochem); mitomycin C, ethyl methanesulfonate, and 7,12-dimethylbenz[a]anthracene (Sigma); trimethyl phosphate (British Drug Houses, Ltd.); furylfuramide [2-(2-furyl)-3-(5-nitro-2-furyl)acrylamide: trade name AF-2] (gift of T. Sugimura: National Cancer Research Institute, Tokyo); 1′-acetoxy-safrole, 1-phenyl-1-(3,4-xylyl)-2-propynyl-*N*-cyclohexyl carbamate, and 2-nitrosofluorene (gifts of J. and E. Miller); ICR-191 and ICR-191-OH (7, 8) (gifts of R. Peck and H. J. Creech); niridazole (gift of E. Bueding); dimethylsulfoxide (spectrophotometric grade) (Schwarz/Mann).

Bacterial Strains, some previously described (1, 3), are *Salmonella typhimurium* unless noted.

R Factor Transfer followed the procedure of K. Mortelmans and B. A. D. Stocker (12). Fully grown unshaken nutrient broth cultures of the R-factor-containing donor strain (0.1 ml) and the recipient strain (1.0 ml) were diluted in nutrient broth (9 ml) and incubated for 20 hr at 37° without shaking. Ampicillin-resistant recipients were selected on minimal-glucose petri plates containing ampicillin (0.8 mg per plate), and required supplements (usually histidine and biotin). Donor strains were SL1156 (*trpD1*/R-Utrecht), SL1127 (*pur pro*/R46), and TA2000 (*purF145*/pKM101) which we constructed by transferring pKM101 from *hisG46*/pKM101 (SL3379; = TA92) to *purF145*. SL strains were kindly provided by B. A. D. Stocker.

TABLE 1. *Reversion of TA100, TA98, and the standard tester strains with various mutagens and carcinogens*

		Revertant colonies/plate*			
Mutagen	μg	TA1535	TA100	TA1538	TA98
(*Spontaneous*)	—	11	160	25	39
MMS	570	5	3,244	0	5
NQNO	0.5	118	7,640	339	641
MNNG	2	1,511	18,701	0	22
Furylfuramide (AF-2)	0.02	0	1,674	0	169
Niridazole	0.2	3	1,636	180	468
Benzyl chloride	2,000	12	230	0	20
1′-Acetoxysafrole	50	7	556	46	57
1-Phenyl-1-(3,4-xylyl)-2-propynyl- *N*-cyclohexylcarbamate	100	5	2,087	0	589
Captan	10	150	820	30	184
Mitomycin C	1	0	100‡	0	—
Aflatoxin B₁†	0.1	0	2,260	80	1,940
Sterigmatocystin†	0.1	2	282	4	144
7,12-Dimethylbenz[a]anthracene†	20	0	1,458	72	714
Benzo[a]pyrene†	5	7	2,398	196	685
ICR-191	5	13	773	449	527
ICR-191-OH	100	0	0	44	18
2-Nitrosofluorene	0.5	0	462	3,936	3,841
2-Aminoanthracene†	10	333	8,835	7,725	6,801
Diethyl sulfate	5,000	14,762	2,123	0	9
Dimethylcarbamyl chloride	5,300	1,547	1,623	7	81
Bis(2-chloroethyl)-amine·HCl	50	2,708	2,306	0	0
Ethyl methanesulfonate	5,000	220	406	2	13

* Results are from linear dose–response curves after subtracting spontaneous revertants. Dose–response curves were nonlinear for diethyl sulfate, MNNG, and ethyl methanesulfonate.

† Activated by S-9 liver homogenate (4) from arochlor-induced (30) rats; one-third S-9 was used in the S-9 mix for aflatoxin, sterigmatocystin, and benzo[a]pyrene.

‡ TA100 was replaced by *hisG46*/pKM101 for mitomycin C (see *text*).

Storage of R Factor and Standard Tester Strains is at −80° after freezing a fresh nutrient broth culture (0.8 ml) with dimethylsulfoxide (0.07 ml) in small screw-capped vials on dry ice. Fresh cultures for mutagenesis testing are obtained by scraping a sterile wooden applicator stick over the surface of the frozen culture, inoculating nutrient broth (5 ml), and shaking overnight at 37°. The fresh culture can be kept in the refrigerator for a few days.

The new tester strains should be checked routinely, as R factors can be lost from bacteria. We recommend that this be done before freezing by confirming ampicillin resistance and increased mutagenesis (with aflatoxin B₁ and/or MMS) compared to TA1535 and TA1538 (see Table 1). We also routinely include such positive mutagenesis controls when using these strains.

RESULTS

Effect of R Factors on Mutagenesis. In MacPhee's original experiments (9) he put an R factor plasmid, R-Utrecht (= R205) into *hisG46* and observed a 2- to 3-fold increase, compared to *hisG46* alone, in the reversion of this histidine mutation by the mutagen MMS. Mortelmans and Stocker (12) have examined a number of R factors, among which were R-Utrecht, R46, and five derivatives of R46 that lack some of the original antibiotic resistance markers, for their effect in causing an increase in UV resistance and spontaneous and UV-induced reversion rates of *hisG46*, and they have kindly given us these strains. We have found that *hisG46* containing pKM101, a derivative of R46 with only the ampicillin resistance marker, is the most sensitive to MMS-induced reversion. We have also put pKM101, R46, and R-Utrecht into our tester strain TA1535, a derivative of *hisG46* which also lacks excision repair and the lipopolysaccharide barrier. Fig. 1 shows that TA100 (TA1535 with pKM101) is the most sensitive to MMS-induced reversion. A different plasmid, pSC101 (13), was inactive.

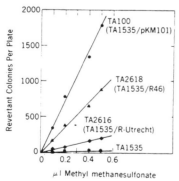

FIG. 1. Effect of R factors R-Utrecht, R46, and pKM101 on reversion of the standard tester strain TA1535 with MMS. Reversion was determined on petri plates, incorporating mutagen and bacteria directly into the top agar, as previously described (3). Revertants were scored after incubation of the petri plates for 48 hr at 37°. Spontaneous revertants have been subtracted.

TABLE 2. *The effect of the R factor pKM101 on reversion of hisG46 with different repair capacities*

Mutagen	μg	Revertant colonies*							
		hisG46		recA⁻		uvrB⁻		pol⁻	
		−R	+R	−R	+R	−R	+R	−R	+R
(Spontaneous)	—	*3*	*49*	*4*	*5*	*12*	*226*	*5*	*92*
MMS	2,300	32	2,007	0	2	6	1,627	2	171
NQNO	10	5	132	0	4	17	2,029	0	75
Bis(2-chloroethyl)amine	100	43	94	34	21	2,952	3,746	17	15
Furylfuramide	1	3	438	1	3				
Niridazole	10	4	155	3	3				
Trimethyl phosphate	10⁴	4	112	2	3				

* Revertants per plate after subtraction of the spontaneous revertant background. Paper discs (6 mm diameter) containing mutagens were applied to petri dishes with bacteria (10^8) and a trace of histidine in a thin overlay of agar (3). Histidine revertants were scored after 48 hr incubation at 37°. The strains are: hisG46, hisG46/pKM101, TA1950 (hisG46 uvrB), TA2410 (TA1950/pKM101), TA2322 (hisG46 pol-2 ara-9), TA2644 (TA2322/pKM101), TS24 (hisG46 recA) (from D. Straus), and TA2411 (TS24/pKM101). We thank H. Whitfield (23) for the pol strain AA3011, the parent of TA2322.

Effect of Various Mutagens on the Reversion of TA100 Compared to TA1535. We have surveyed a number of mutagens for their ability to revert the hisG46 mutation in TA100 and TA1535 (Table 1). The mutagens fall into two classes. Some mutagens, such as ethyl methanesulfonate, bis(2-chloroethyl)-amine and dimethylcarbamyl chloride, are about equally effective on the two strains (or in the case of diethyl sulfate even less effective on TA100), while others, such as the carcinogens benzyl chloride, NQNO, aflatoxin B₁, and the food additive furylfuramide, are enormously more effective on the new strain, TA100, which contains the R factor. Many of the reactive frameshift mutagens tested revert TA100 as well or better than they revert the standard frameshift tester strains TA1537 and TA1538. Mitomycin C, a carcinogen and a DNA cross-linking agent, does not revert TA100 (or hisG46) but does revert hisG46/pKM101 which has excision repair. Excision repair is required for mutagenesis with mitomycin C in *Escherichia coli* (14), and it has been suggested that mutation can only be detected if potentially lethal DNA crosslinks are broken by the excision repair system (14, 15).

Effect of pKM101 on the Frameshift Tester Strain TA1538. The tester strain TA1538 contains a well-characterized (16) histidine frameshift mutation and is reverted by a wide variety of aromatic carcinogens which can cause frameshift mutations. It is not reverted appreciably by simple alkylating agents which cause base-pair substitutions (2-4, 6). We have constructed the new strain TA98 by putting the R factor pKM101 into TA1538 and have examined a variety of mutagens (Table 1). Mutagens that revert TA1538 and TA98 fall into two classes: those that revert TA98 much better, such as aflatoxin, 7,12-dimethylbenzanthracene, and benzo-[a]pyrene, and those that do not, such as 2-aminoanthracene, 2-nitrosofluorene, and ICR-191.

Optimizing the Tester Strain: Other Test Mutations. We have attempted to construct a strain more sensitive than TA100 by putting the R factor pKM101 into many different histidine-requiring mutants. The mutations tested were (the numbers in parentheses are the corresponding strains containing pKM101): the missense mutations hisG52(TA2399), hisG499 (TA2398), hisD78(TA2628), hisD1714(TA2404), hisC201 (TA2620), hisC210(TA2621), hisC367(TA2622), hisC496 (TA2395), hisC899(TA2623); the amber mutations hisC31

(TA2630), hisC50(TA2624), hisC121(TA2625), hisC340(TA 2626); the ochre mutations: hisC117(TA2403), hisC354 (TA2396), hisC502(TA2627), hisC514(TA2629), hisO1242 hisG2101(TA2400); the UGA mutation hisG200(TA2397); and the unclassified mutations his-1743(TA2401) and his-1768(TA2402) (17, 18). These strains were tested for spontaneous, MMS-, and furylfuramide-induced reversion. None of the strains was superior to hisG46/pKM101. We have also done considerable work with the widely used tryptophan auxotroph *E. coli* B/r WP2 and its UV-sensitive derivative WP2 hcr, recently used by several groups for detecting mutagenicity of nitrofurans (19–21), a class of carcinogens that does not appreciably revert our standard set of tester strains (21). We first made and compared the gal uvrB deletion of WP2, TA85, with the WP2 hcr strain used by these other groups and found the deletion superior as a tester strain for reversion by the nitrofuran furylfuramide. We then put the pKM101 plasmid into TA85, to make the strain TA93. TA93 is 50 times more sensitive to furylfuramide reversion than the original TA85, and somewhat more sensitive than TA100, but because of its slow growth and the poor response of TA93 and its deep rough derivative to aflatoxin we have preferred TA100 as a general tester strain.

Effect of pKM101 on Reversion of hisG46 with Different Repair Capacities. MacPhee and Mortelmans have previously shown that increased UV mutagenesis and protection against UV killing by R-Utrecht and R46 do not occur in hisG46 containing a recA mutation (12, 22). Table 2 shows that mutagens which cause enhanced reversion (Table 1) of hisG46 strains containing the R factor (e.g., MMS, NQNO, furylfuramide) do not revert the recA strains. In contrast bis(2-chloroethyl)amine, which does not show significant enhanced mutagenesis (Table 1) in the R factor strains, is mostly rec-independent.

We have also looked at MNNG, diethyl sulfate, and ethyl methanesulfonate and the results are generally consistent with those in Table 2, but the interpretation is complicated by nonlinear dose–response curves (Table 1).

Table 2 also shows that uvrB and pol mutations do not abolish R factor enhancement of mutagenesis, although pol does appear to decrease the overall level of mutagenesis. The increase in reversion by certain mutagens in uvrB mutants has been previously reported (1, 3). Mortelmans and Stocker (12) have observed that R46 and pKM101 cause an increase in the number of spontaneous revertants of *hisG46* and this is shown for pKM101 in Table 2, along with a comparable increase in the *uvrB* and *pol-2* strains, but not in the *recA* strain.

DISCUSSION

We have previously described four histidine-requiring *Salmonella* tester strains for detecting carcinogens by means of their mutagenic activity (1–4). We describe here two new tester strains, TA100 and TA98, constructed by the addition of an R factor plasmid to the standard tester strains TA1535 and TA1538, and show that the new strains greatly increase the sensitivity of the test and the number of carcinogens detected. Among the many carcinogens previously detected as mutagens we show here that aflatoxin B_1, sterigmatocystin, benzo[a]pyrene, 7,12-dimethylbenzanthracene, and NQNO are much more easily detected with the new strains. The new strains can also detect a variety of carcinogens that do not appreciably revert our standard tester strains, such as 1'-acetoxysafrole, acetylenic carbamate derivatives, and furylfuramide (AF-2, a nitrofuran food additive that was widely used in Japan until recently). The carcinogenic nitrofurans had not previously reverted our tester set but were detected by the *E. coli* B/r strain WP2 (19–21). The new strain TA100, is considerably more sensitive than WP2 *hcr* for those nitrofurans that we have tested. Vinyl chloride is mutagenic in our system (24, 25) and we have shown the utility of TA100 in detecting chloroacetaldehyde, a possible active metabolic product of vinyl chloride. (J. McCann, V. Simmon, and B. N. Ames, in preparation).

The mechanism whereby the R factor enhances mutagenesis is not fully understood at present; however, recombinational repair does appear to be involved, as indicated by the following four points: (*1*) It is known that certain mutagens cause damage to the DNA that is not mutagenic directly, but that the mutations are caused by errors introduced when the damage is repaired by error-prone recombinational repair. This was first shown many years ago by Witkin, who found that UV light is not mutagenic in bacteria with a *rec* mutation, even though they are much more sensitive to killing by UV. This has also been shown for a variety of chemical mutagens, such as MMS and NQNO, by Kondo (14), and Table 2 shows the *recA* dependence of these, furylfuramide, niridazole, and trimethyl phosphate. (*2*) With all of these chemical mutagens the R factor causes a marked increase in mutagenesis (Tables 1 and 2). MacPhee (9, 11) has shown this with R-Utrecht for UV, MMS, and trimethyl phosphate. (*3*) The effect of the R factor on reversion of the *hisG46* mutation by these chemical mutagens (Table 2), by UV (22), or spontaneously, cannot be detected in a strain with a *recA* mutation but can when there is a *uvrB* or *pol* mutation. (*4*) Other mutagens, such as bis(2-chloroethyl)-amine or ethyl methanesulfonate, appear to be relatively independent of the *rec* system in causing mutation (Table 2; ref. 14), and these mutagens are not stimulated by the presence of the R factor (Table 1).

A postulated mechanism for R-factor-stimulated mutagenesis must then take into account *recA*-dependent repair. As recombinational repair needs a gap in one strand of the DNA to work (26), it seems likely that certain mutagenic events could lead to nicks, which then allow recombinational repair and base-pair substitutions or frameshift errors. The class of mutagens not showing an enhancement by the R factor would presumably be mutagenic directly. MacPhee (11, 22) has suggested that the role of the R factor is to enhance this error-prone repair system and has recently shown that a strain containing R-Utrecht has increased DNA polymerase activity (27). Mortelmans (12) has suggested that the R factor could supply a mistake-prone DNA polymerase. We have obtained evidence (in collaboration with D. Lackey and S. Linn) that the pKM101-containing strains have a new endonuclease which could play a role in nick and gap formation in the mutagenized DNA. At this point, however, the exact nature of the role of the R factor is not known.

Frameshift type errors are apparently caused by slippage of a repetitive sequence in the DNA, for example the C-G-C-G-C-G-C-G sequence in TA1538 (16). There is markedly increased frameshift mutagenesis by certain aromatic carcinogens, such as aflatoxin or dimethylbenzanthracene, in TA98 compared to TA1538. This may also be due to nick generation, with the additional factor of the mutagen stabilizing the mispairing by a stacking interaction with DNA (4). Frameshift mutations caused by some of the other reactive carcinogens, such as activated 2-aminoanthracene or 2-nitrosofluorene, are not increased by the presence of the R factor in TA98. Reversion by nonreactive frameshift mutagens, such as ICR-191-OH (and 9-aminoacridine on TA1537/pKM101), is also not increased by the R factor. We have not seen an effect of any repair system on nonreactive type frameshift mutagens.

Although the simple alkylating agents do not cause frameshift mutations, even in the strains carrying R factors, many of the reactive frameshift mutagens can revert the missense mutation *hisG46* (in the TA1535 tester strain) when the R factor is present, and this is presumably due to error-prone recombinational repair after DNA damage. It is still unclear, however, why some of the reactive frameshift mutagens such as activated 2-aminoanthracene and 2-nitrosofluorene are stimulated by the R factor in TA1535 but not in TA1538. Further work on the *rec* dependence of frameshift mutagens and the mechanism of frameshift mutagenesis is needed to clarify this point.

We recommend that TA98 (TA1538/pKM101) and TA100 (TA1535/pKM101) be added to the set of tester strains previously introduced. They can replace TA1535 and TA1538 for general screening for mutagenicity. Strains TA1535 and TA1538 will still be useful for classifying mutagens as to type, without the complications of the R factor, and, as they have a lower spontaneous mutation rate than TA98 and TA100, they will be more convenient and more sensitive in studying particular mutagens whose effectiveness is not increased by the R factor. One of the old frameshift tester strains, TA1536, can now be dropped from the set of tester strains, as extremely few mutagens revert it and those that do can be detected well with the other frameshift tester strains. The other frameshift tester strain in the set, TA1537, is still useful, though we are working on a somewhat more sensitive strain, TA90, with similar characteristics, that appears to have a run of 8 Cs in the DNA at the site of a +1 frameshift mutation. This strain and its pKM101 derivative (TA97) will be described in a separate communication. Another tester strain is also being developed for the detection of agents such as the carcinogenic antibiotic mitomycin C, which crosslinks DNA and is not active in the presence of a *uvrB* mutation (Table 1; ref. 14).

The *Salmonella*/liver test system is now in use in hundreds of laboratories throughout the world and large numbers of carcinogens and noncarcinogens have been tested. It is being used to examine mutagenic metabolites in urine (28, 29) and several groups are starting to screen the human population. It is also being used to detect mutagenic activity in complex mixtures such as cigarette smoke and its fractions (30). We are in the process of compiling the results for the many hundreds of carcinogens and noncarcinogens that have been tested in the system. The preliminary results indicate that over 70% of the carcinogens tested are detected as mutagens. In almost every case the test does not respond to known noncarcinogens. Some of the carcinogens previously missed can now be shown to be good mutagens with the new strains (Table 1) and we suspect that the test system will eventually detect over 80% of chemical carcinogens as mutagens.

We are living in a sea of chemicals that have not been tested for mutagenicity and carcinogenicity. It has been estimated that 80% of human cancer is due to environmental causes (31), yet only a very small percentage of the chemicals humans are exposed to can be tested in the extremely expensive and long-term cancer tests in rodents. Practically no tests are being done on mutagenicity of environmental chemicals in mammals. Microbial tests are rapid and inexpensive, and are being used as efficient screens to detect potentially hazardous chemicals. Compounds that give a positive test for mutagenicity in microbial tests should be considered potential hazards for man and should be scrutinized for benefit, risk, and need for further testing by other more time-consuming methods. A solution to the problem of cancer and birth defects is likely to be prevention.

We are indebted to B. A. D. Stocker and K. Mortelmans for strains, unpublished information, and discussion; to D. G. MacPhee, D. S. Straus, and W. E. Durston for strains; to J. Richards and V. Paulus for testing dimethylbenzanthracene and niridazole; to Edith Yamasaki for construction of TA98 and to S. Kondo for discussion. This work was supported by Atomic Energy Commission Grant AT(04-3)34 P.A.156 to B.N.A. J.McC. was supported by a postdoctoral fellowship from the California Division of the American Cancer Society.

1. Ames, B. N. (1971) in *Chemical Mutagens: Principles and Methods for their Detection*, ed. Hollaender, A. (Plenum Press, New York), Vol. 1, pp. 267–282.
2. Ames, B. N. (1972) in *Mutagenic Effects of Environmental Contaminants*, eds. Sutton, E. & Harris, M. (Academic Press, New York), pp. 57–66.
3. Ames, B. N., Lee, F. D. & Durston, W. E. (1973) *Proc. Nat. Acad. Sci. USA* 70, 782–786.
4. Ames, B. N., Durston, W. E., Yamasaki, E. & Lee, F. D. (1973) *Proc. Nat. Acad. Sci. USA* 70, 2281–2285.
5. Ames, B. N., Sims, P. & Grover, P. L. (1972) *Science* 176, 47–49.
6. Ames, B. N., Gurney, E. G., Miller, J. A. & Bartsch, H. (1972) *Proc. Nat. Acad. Sci. USA* 69, 3128–3132.
7. Ames, B. N. & Whitfield, H. J., Jr. (1966) *Cold Spring Harbor Symp. Quant. Biol.* 31, 221–225.
8. Creech, H. J., Preston, R. K., Peck, R. M., O'Connell, A. P. & Ames, B. N. (1972) *J. Med. Chem.* 15, 739–746.
9. MacPhee, D. G. (1973) *Appl. Microbiol.* 26, 1004–1005.
10. Howarth, S. (1966) *Mutat. Res.* 3, 129–134.
11. MacPhee, D. G. (1973) *Mutat. Res.* 18, 367–370.
12. Mortelmans, K. (1975) PhD Dissertation, Stanford University.
13. Cohen, S. N., Chang, A. C. Y., Boyer, H. W. & Helling, R. B. (1973) *Proc. Nat. Acad. Sci. USA* 70, 3240–3244.
14. Kondo, S., Ichikawa, H., Iwo, K. & Kato, T. (1970) *Genetics* 66, 187–217.
15. Murayama, I. & Otsuji, N. (1973) *Mutat. Res.* 18, 117–119.
16. Isono, K. & Yourno, J. (1974) *Proc. Nat. Acad. Sci. USA* 71, 1612–1617.
17. Whitfield, H. J., Jr., Martin, R. G. & Ames, B. N. (1966) *J. Mol. Biol.* 21, 335–355.
18. Hartman, P. E., Hartman, Z., Stahl, R. C. & Ames, B. N. (1971) *Advan. Genet.* 16, 1–34.
19. Kada, T. (1973) *Jap. J. Genet.* 48, 301–305.
20. McCalla, D. R. & Voutsinos, D. (1974) *Mutat. Res.* 26, 3–16.
21. Yahagi, T., Nagao, M., Hara, K., Matsushima, T., Sugimura, T. & Bryan, G. T. (1974) *Cancer Res.* 34, 2266–2273.
22. MacPhee, D. G. (1973) *Mutat. Res.* 19, 357–359.
23. Whitfield, H. J. & Levine, G. (1973) *J. Bacteriol.* 116, 54–58.
24. Rannug, U., Johansson, A., Ramel, C. & Wachtmeister, C. A. (1974) *Ambio* 3, 194–197.
25. Bartsch, H., Malaveille, C. & Montesano, R. (1975) *Int. J. Cancer*, in press.
26. Cooper, P. K. & Hanawalt, P. C. (1972) *Proc. Nat. Acad. Sci. USA* 69, 1156–1160.
27. MacPhee, D. G. (1974) *Nature* 251, 432–434.
28. Durston, W. E. & Ames, B. N. (1974) *Proc. Nat. Acad. Sci. USA* 71, 737–741.
29. Commoner, B., Vithayathil, A. J. & Henry, J. I. (1974) *Nature* 249, 850–852.
30. Kier, L. D., Yamasaki, E. & Ames, B. N. (1974) *Proc. Nat. Acad. Sci. USA* 71, 4159–4163.
31. Epstein, S. S. (1974) *Cancer Res.* 34, 2425–2435.

Genetic Studies of the *lac* Repressor

IV†. Mutagenic Specificity in the *lacI* Gene of *Escherichia coli*

Christine Coulondre and Jeffrey H. Miller

Département de Biologie Moléculaire
Université de Genève, Geneva, Switzerland

(Received 17 January 1977)

An extensive set of amber and ochre sites in the *lacI* gene has been characterized with respect to the base change required to generate the nonsense codon (Miller *et al.*, 1977; Coulondre & Miller, 1977). These mutations have been used to analyze the forward mutational spectrum of a series of mutagens in *Escherichia coli*. The sites induced by N'-methyl-N'-nitro-N-nitrosoguanidine, ethyl methanesulfonate, 4-nitroquinoline-1-oxide, and ultraviolet light, were examined, as well as those which arose spontaneously. Sites induced by the $G \cdot C \rightarrow A \cdot T$ transition were compared with those generated by 2-aminopurine mutagenesis. All together, more than 4000 independent occurrences of amber and ochre mutations were tabulated in order to define the respective mutagenic specificities. With the exception of the $A \cdot T \rightarrow G \cdot C$ change, all base substitutions lead to the generation of nonsense codons from wild-type. The $A \cdot T \rightarrow G \cdot C$ transition was monitored in a reversion system, in which the ochre to amber conversion (UAA $\rightarrow$ UAG) was scored, as well as the UAA $\rightarrow$ CAA reversion.

Both NG‡ and EMS were found to be highly specific for the $G \cdot C \rightarrow A \cdot T$ transition, less than 1% transversions appearing in either case. At between 1% and 5% the level of the $G \cdot C \rightarrow A \cdot T$ change, NG can stimulate the $A \cdot T \rightarrow G \cdot C$ transition. EMS stimulates the $A \cdot T \rightarrow G \cdot C$ transition at a significantly lower rate. NQO is also highly specific for $G \cdot C$ base-pairs, but approximately 10% of the changes found at these sites are transversions. Mutations found spontaneously or after irradiation with ultraviolet light showed none of the specificities found for EMS, NG or NQO. All transversions were detected in both cases. Moreover, a significant number of tandem double base changes were found to be induced by u.v. irradiation. Some of these have been verified directly by protein sequencing. The frequencies of occurrence of amber and ochre mutations arising from the $G \cdot C \rightarrow A \cdot T$ transition have been compared for different mutagens, revealing several striking hotspots. The implications of these findings with respect to the mechanism of mutagenesis and the application of different mutagens are discussed.

1. Introduction

The phenomenon of mutagenic specificity has been widely studied, both in prokaryotic and eukaryotic systems (Bautz & Freese, 1960; Bautz-Freese, 1961; Tessman *et al.*, 1964; Yanofsky *et al.*, 1966; Osborn *et al.*, 1967; Drake, 1970; Hartman *et al.*, 1971; Auerbach & Kilbey, 1971; Yanofsky, 1971; Prakash & Sherman, 1973; Drake &

† Paper III is Coulondre & Miller (1977).

‡ Abbreviations used: NG, N'-methyl-N'-nitro-N-nitrosoguanidine; EMS, ethyl methanesulfonate; NQO, 4-nitroquinoline-1-oxide; 2AP, 2-aminopurine.

Baltz, 1976). The knowledge of the molecular events preferentially induced by different mutagens has enabled workers to increase the variety of mutant phenotypes, and in some cases to identify specific base changes (see the first paper in this series, Miller *et al.*, 1977). Recently, a correlation between the mutagenic and carcinogenic properties of various compounds has been reported (Ames *et al.*, 1973; McCann *et al.*, 1975). As methods for analyzing specific base changes become more refined, it is relevant to attempt to determine more precisely the specificities of mutagens currently in use.

Most "tester" systems depend on the ability to detect reversion at certain sites, which have been characterized with respect to the changes required to produce a mutant phenotype. Thus, in the *his* operon of *Salmonella typhimurium* frameshifts and base substitutions can be recognized. Likewise, in the *trp* operon of *Escherichia coli* (Yanofsky, 1971), and the isocytochrome *c* system of yeast (Prakash & Sherman, 1973), a specific set of mutants can be used to identify transitions and transversions induced by particular mutagens. Almost all reversion systems, however, have the basic disadvantage of giving only a qualitative estimate of the general ability of a mutagen to induce a certain change, since the frequency of mutagen-induced reversion often varies from site to site. The use of one or only a few sites in a tester system could, therefore, give a misleading or incorrect result. Only by using many different sites can one construct a true picture of the specificity of a mutagen. A better method for this purpose is the use of a system in which forward mutations are analyzed, provided that enough sites are available to monitor each base change. In this type of experiment a large collection of independent mutations is examined and the relative frequencies of occurrence at each of many sites are compared. This kind of analysis requires a well-developed system in which forward mutations can be identified and classified with respect to the particular base change involved

In the *lacI* gene of *E. coli*, a large number of nonsense sites have been detected and assigned to various points in the gene normally specifying particular amino acids in the *lac* repressor (Miller *et al.*, 1977; Coulondre & Miller, 1977). Since all of these mutations result in a completely inactive repressor protein, there is no selection bias operating on any of these sites when the i⁻ phenotype is required. This system, described below, provides a ready assay for forward mutations and thus allows the determination of mutagenic specificity by the comparative analysis of many sites, thereby reducing the interference from genetic hotspots (Benzer, 1961). In this paper we analyze amber and ochre mutations derived spontaneously, and after mutagenesis with ethyl methanesulfonate, N'-methyl-N'-nitro-N-nitrosoguanidine, 4-nitroquino-line-1-oxide, and ultraviolet light. The base substitutions resulting from each mutagen are identified and tabulated. Genetic hotspots favored by these mutagens are compared with those found after treatment with 2-aminopurine, which have been previously analyzed (Miller *et al.*, 1977). In a forthcoming paper we will consider the effect of the surrounding nucleotide sequence on the mutation frequency at each site, since the entire DNA sequence of the I gene has recently been elucidated (P. J. Farabaugh, unpublished results).

2. Experimental Design

In a preceding study (Miller *et al.*, 1977; Coulondre & Miller, 1977) we characterized 90 nonsense sites in the *lacI* gene, and correlated most of them with specific codons. The determination of the *lacI* DNA sequence (P. J. Farabaugh, unpublished work)

has allowed us to verify virtually all of these assignments, as will be reported elsewhere. In these cases the conversion of the wild-type codon to amber or ochre (UAG or UAA) occurs by a known transition or transversion, as is depicted in Figure 1. Therefore we can use the distribution of amber and ochre sites as a measure of the mutations induced by different mutagens, and thus derive the respective mutagenic specificities. Figures 2 and 3 indicate how this is achieved. A total of 72 amber and ochre sites which arise from a single base change are used throughout this study. All four transversions and the $G \cdot C \to A \cdot T$ transition yield amber mutations, while the $G \cdot C \to T \cdot A$ and $A \cdot T \to T \cdot A$ transversions and the $G \cdot C \to A \cdot T$ transition yield ochre mutations from sense codons. Amongst base substitutions only the $A \cdot T \to G \cdot C$ transition fails to be detected in this forward mutagenesis system. However, reversion tests utilizing the amber and ochre sites can detect this base change, and these experiments are also reported here. It should be noted that only base substitutions are being measured in this study. Frameshifts, insertions and deletions are not monitored. However, base substitutions leading to nonsense mutations represent a significant fraction of the mutations induced by the mutagens used in this study (Coulondre & Miller, 1977). Only amongst the mutations arising spontaneously in this system do we find a low proportion of nonsense mutations (see Discussion).

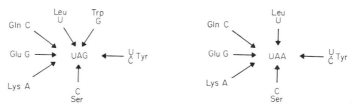

FIG. 1. The single base substitutions which can convert a wild-type codon to amber (UAG) or ochre (UAA) are depicted.

In order to deduce the specificity of a mutagen, we therefore analyze a large number of independently derived amber and ochre mutations and divide them into sites. Methods for achieving this are described in the preceding papers (Miller *et al.*, 1977; Coulondre & Miller, 1977). The total forward nonsense mutation spectrum can then be resolved into its component parts by arranging the nonsense sites according to the particular transition or transversion involved and indicating the frequency of occurrence at each site. The specificity of each mutagen becomes readily apparent, as shown in Figures 4 to 10 for the agents used in this study. Table 1 records the data used to construct Figures 4 to 13, and Tables 2 to 6 summarize the total occurrences of specific substitutions with each mutagen. The precision of this type of study depends on the accuracy of the assignments made in the preceding papers. As noted above, a comparison of the *lacI* nucleotide sequence (D. Steege, unpublished work; P. J. Farabaugh, unpublished work) with the genetic markers has shown that all of the mutations used in this study have been assigned to the correct base substitution. Moreover, several of the nonsense sites have been shown to arise from tandem double base changes (Coulondre & Miller, 1977). These are not included as sites in Figures 2 and 3, but are instead grouped together with other double mutations and considered in a subsequent section.

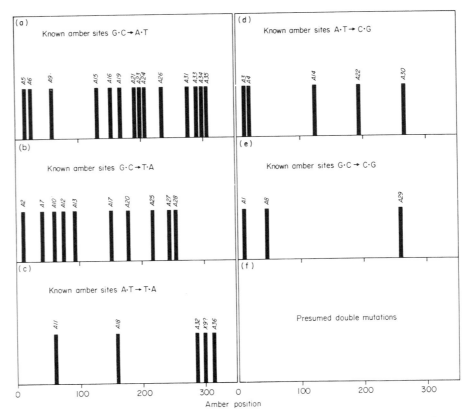

FIG. 2. The amber sites used in this study are shown, together with the particular base substitution required to generate each site. The bars depict sites, with the allele numbers corresponding to those given in the Tables of this and the accompanying paper (Coulondre & Miller, 1977). The horizontal axis represents the gene–protein map, expressed in amino acid position. The elucidation of the DNA sequence of the *lacI* gene (P. J. Farabaugh, unpublished results) has revealed the presence of additional codons in the *I* gene. As a result, all positions past residue 153 in these diagrams are 11 residues further than indicated here, and all positions after residue 232 are 13 residues further than shown in these Figures (see the accompanying paper, Coulondre & Miller, 1977). The sites have been assigned in preceding papers (Miller *et al.*, 1977; Coulondre & Miller, 1977), and most of the assignments have been indirectly verified by the elucidation of the nucleotide sequence of the *I* gene (D. Steege, unpublished results; P. J. Farabaugh, unpublished results). The codons affected by sites *A1, A3, A4, A6, A9, A10, A11, A21, A24, A28, A34* and *A36* have been directly verified by either protein or DNA sequencing (Weber *et al.*, 1975; Sommer, 1977; M. Lillis, 1977; A. Maxam, W. Gilbert & P. J. Farabaugh, unpublished results).

3. Materials and Methods

Unless otherwise indicated, all materials, methods, and bacterial strains are the same as those described in the accompanying paper (Coulondre & Miller, 1977).

(a) *Identification of independent mutations*

Each mutagenized suspension of cells was divided into a large number of different test-tubes immediately after mutagenesis and grown overnight in rich medium. Nonsense mutations were identified in the *lacI* gene after transfer of an F'*lacproB* episome into a set of suppressor strains. Between 25 and 50 clones from each mutagenized culture were tested, and only one amber and one ochre mutation from each culture was analyzed

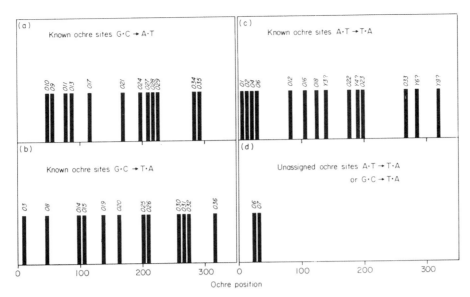

FIG. 3. The ochre sites resulting from different base substitutions are shown. See the legend to Fig. 2 for further details.

further. The mutation that was further tested always represented the first clone on a numbered grid to yield a nonsense mutation. (See the accompanying paper for further details.) Therefore, all of the mutations in the collections analyzed here were of independent origin, and were chosen without prejudice or selection bias.

(b) *Reversion tests*

Method A of the preceding paper was used (Coulondre & Miller, 1977). EMS† or NG was used in place of 2AP when the occasion arose. The amber derivative of each respective ochre mutation, carried on the *lacproB* episome, was used in the H3053 background to determine the plating efficiency for each reversion experiment.

4. Results

(a) *4-Nitroquinoline-1-oxide*

4-Nitroquinoline-1-oxide is both a potent carcinogen and mutagenic agent. Studies with *r*II mutants of bacteriophage T4 indicated that NQO acts on G·C base-pairs (Ishizawa & Endo, 1970,1971). More detailed work by Prakash *et al.* (1974) in yeast used a series of mutants with identified base changes in the iso-1-cytochrome *c* gene (Prakash & Sherman, 1973). This tester system demonstrated the specific induction of transitions and transversions of G·C base-pairs. The G·C → T·A transversion was clearly stimulated, although the G·C → C·G transition could not be unambiguously determined. Based on one transition site, the data of Prakash *et al.* suggest that transitions are induced at a higher rate than transversions.

We collected over 1000 nonsense mutations after treatment with NQO, each derived independently (see Materials and Methods). Because the induction of amber and ochre mutations was considerably greater than the spontaneous background

† See abbreviations on page 34.

(better than 500-fold), we would expect little interference from non-NQO-induced mutations, even in a collection of this size. The distribution of the 550 amber and 463 ochre mutations is shown in Figures 4 and 5 and in Tables 1 and 2. The virtual absence of $A \cdot T \to C \cdot G$ and $A \cdot T \to T \cdot A$ transversions is striking. The $G \cdot C \to T \cdot A$ transversion is clearly induced by NQO, although there is in general a tenfold higher preference for $G \cdot C \to A \cdot T$ transitions. However, this can be seen to vary from site to site. The highest $G \cdot C \to T \cdot A$ transversion peaks are on the same level as the lowest transition peaks. The $G \cdot C \to C \cdot G$ transversion is also induced, although at a low level relative to the $G \cdot C \to A \cdot T$ transition.

TABLE 1

Independent occurrences at each site

Site	Mutagen				
	None	EMS	NG	u.v.	NQO
A. Amber					
$G \cdot C \to A \cdot T$					
A5	0†	17	13†	19	23
A6	51	14	20	15	61
A9	8	30	34	1	61
A15	37	7	4	7	54
A16	9	14	21	20	29
A19	11	30	37	16	13
A21	8	12	22	5	16
A23	8	30	32	80	24
A24	10	39	34	9	51
A26	6	20	12	2	36
A31	1	19	18	2	20
A33	5	38	24	36	33
A34	12	15	12	1	55
A35	1	27	9	6	25
$G \cdot C \to T \cdot A$					
A2	2	0	0	5	3
A7	4	1	0	0	5
A10	2	0	0	3	3
A12	2	0	0	10	11
A13	4	0	0	3	3
A17	3	0	0	4	1
A20	3	0	0	4	2
A25	2	0	0	0	1
A27	13	1	0	3	6
A28	2	0	0	7	2
$A \cdot T \to T \cdot A$					
A11	1	0	0	12	0
A18	1	0	0	15	1
A32	0	0	0	12	0
X9	0	0	0	1	0
A36	2	0	0	8	1
$A \cdot T \to C \cdot G$					
A3	4	0	0	2	0
A4	3	0	0	4	0
A14	2	0	0	9	0
A22	2	1	1	10	0
A30	0	0	0	1	1

TABLE 1—*continued*

Site	None	EMS	NG	u.v.	NQO
			Mutagen		
G·C → C·G					
A1	2	0	0	0	4
A8	0	0	0	1	1
A29	0	0	0	1	3
C·G → T·A					
T·A → A·T					
X2	0	0	0	0	0
X3	0	0	0	1	0
X4	0	0	0	2	0
X5	0	0	0	1	1
X6	0	0	0	0	0
X7	0	0	0	1	0
X8	0	0	0	1	0
X10	0	0	0	0	0
X13	0	0	0	0	0
A·T → T·A					
C·G → A·T					
X1	0	0	0	1	0
T·A → A·T					
T·A → G·C?					
X15	0	0	0	0	0
B. Ochre					
G·C → A·T					
O10	7	17	10	4	31
O9	2	23	18	3	15
O11	2	56	28	2	11
O13	1	13	9	6	37
O17	3	27	26	3	28
O21	4	57	15	2	43
O24	0	16	16	61	22
O27	0	15	20	86	10
O28	2	13	12	4	24
O29	5	36	15	4	83
O34	2	46	19	2	47
O35	4	49	22	3	48
G·C → T·A					
O3	2	0	0	1	2
O8	1	0	0	2	4
O14	2	0	0	2	2
O15	2	0	0	4	5
O19	2	0	0	1	3
O20	0	0	0	3	10
O25	1	0	0	2	3
O26	4	0	0	6	8
O30	1	0	0	3	0
O31	1	0	0	0	10
O32	6	0	0	15	8
O36	6	0	0	10	3

TABLE 1—*continued*

Site	Mutagen				
	None	EMS	NG	u.v.	NQO
A·T → T·A					
O1	1	0	0	3	0
O2	0	0	0	5	0
O4	0	0	0	1	0
O5	0	0	0	4	0
O12	1	0	0	10	0
O16	0	0	0	6	0
O18	2	0	0	1	0
Y3	0	0	0	2	0
O22	8	0	0	12	1
Y4	0	0	0	1	0
O23	0	0	0	8	0
O33	0	0	0	2	0
Y6	0	0	0	1	0
Y8	0	0	0	1	1
Unassigned					
A·T → T·A or					
G·C → T·A					
O6	1	0	0	2	1
O7	3	0	0	1	2
C·G → T·A					
C·G → A·T					
Y1	0	0	0	1	0
G·C → A·T					
G·C → A·T					
Y5	0	0	0	1	0
T·A → A·T					
T·A → A·T?					
Y7	0	0	0	1	0

Independent occurrences of mutations at each site are shown. A, amber; B, ochre. The reference numbers for each site are given in the preceding paper (Coulondre & Miller, 1977).

† Sites which were determined in only half of the spontaneous or NG-induced collection.

Because of the clear preference of NQO for base substitutions at G·C pairs, we can assign one of the uncertain ochre sites to the C·C → T·A category. This site (*O19*) is significantly induced by NQO and all of the transition sites have been assigned. In subsequent analyses we consider *O19* as arising from the G·C → T·A transversion.

Table 2 summarizes the results depicted in Figures 4 and 5. The data for the ochre mutations are expressed with site *O19* as an unknown. The preference for G·C base-pairs is evident. Of the possible G·C transversion sites, 23 out of 24 (or 24 out of 25) are found in this collection and are represented by a total of 100 or (103) independent occurrences. For the A·T transversion sites, only 5 out of 24 sites are found, each represented by only a single occurrence. Since this is near the level of spontaneous background mutations, the actual number of mutations in this collection which are

TABLE 2

Mutations induced by 4-nitroquinoline-1-oxide

Substitutions	Amber (550 mutations)					Ochre (463 mutations)				
	Available sites	Sites found	Total occurrences	% of all mutations	% of assigned mutations	Available sites	Sites found	Total occurrences	% of all mutations	% of assigned mutations
G·C → A·T	14	14	501	91·1	91·3	12	12	399	86·2	87·5
G·C → T·A	10	10	37	6·7	6·7	11	10	55	11·9	12·1
A·T → T·A	5	2	2	0·4	0·4	14	2	2	0·4	0·4
A·T → C·G	5	1	1	0·2	0·2	0	—	—	—	—
G·C → C·G	3	3	8	1·4	1·4	0	—	—	—	—
Unassigned	—	—	—	—	—	3	3	6	1·3	—
Presumed double mutations	—	—	1†	0·2	—	—	—	1	0·2	—

The 1013 amber and ochre mutations induced by NQO are divided into different categories based on the base substitution required to generate each mutation.

† This represents a tandem double mutation. All other entries in this column in this and subsequent Tables are uncharacterized double mutations unless otherwise stated.

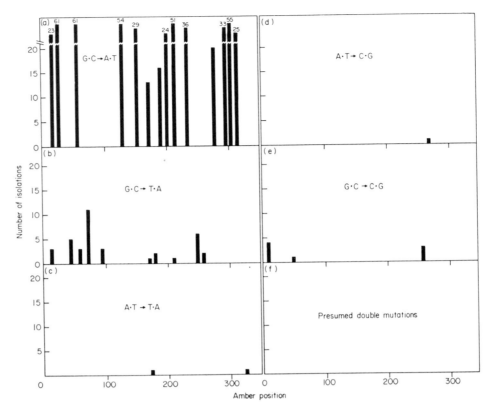

FIG. 4. The amber sites derived by NQO are shown, with the height of each bar representing the number of independent occurrences (see Table 1).

A·T base-pairs and are induced by NQO could be even lower. In any case, the totals of 99·4% and 99·6% for the mutations at G·C base-pairs amongst the amber and ochre sites, respectively, demonstrate the high degree of specificity in this system. (The A·T → G·C transition has not been measured.)

(b) Ethyl methanesulfonate

A number of studies have indicated that ethyl methanesulfonate causes principally G·C → A·T transitions (Bautz & Freese, 1960; Bautz-Freese, 1961; Krieg, 1963a,b; Schwartz, 1963; Tessman et al., 1964; Osborn et al., 1967; Prakash & Sherman, 1973), although it is difficult with these systems to determine quantitatively the degree of specificity. Other studies have suggested that EMS induces other base changes as well (Yanofsky et al., 1966; Malling & de Serres, 1968), but the restrictions of the tester systems used place doubt on the conclusions.

The results presented in Figures 6 and 7 show that of the base substitutions tested, EMS demonstrates a marked preference for the G·C → A·T transition. The degree of specificity is greater than 99%, as can be seen from Table 3. Tests for the A·T → G·C transition, described in a subsequent section, have also been carried out. Although EMS can induce A·T → G·C changes, these occur at a significantly reduced level compared to the G·C → A·T transition.

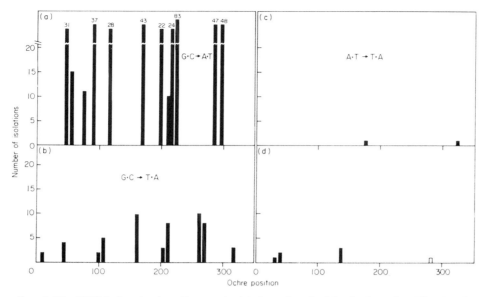

Fig. 5. The NQO-induced ochre sites are depicted, as described in the legend to Figs 2 and 4. The open bar in (d) refers to mutations derived from double events (see text and Materials and Methods). The site (*O19*) represented by the highest bar in (d) can now be assigned independently to the $G \cdot C \to T \cdot A$ transversion based on DNA sequencing results (P. J. Farabaugh, unpublished work).

(c) *Nitrosoguanidine*

N'-Methyl-N'-nitro-N-nitrosoguanidine has been reported to induce both the $A \cdot T \to G \cdot C$ and the $G \cdot C \to A \cdot T$ transitions (Eisenstark *et al.*, 1965; Zampieri & Greenberg, 1967; Malling & de Serres, 1970). However, studies in yeast (Prakash & Sherman, 1973) argue strongly that NG induces principally the $G \cdot C \to A \cdot T$ transition. This conclusion draws support from the sequence analysis of nine altered transfer RNA molecules (Smith *et al.*, 1970), and seven altered *lac* repressor proteins (Müller-Hill *et al.*, 1975).

It can be seen from Figure 8 that in the *lacI* system NG stimulates amber mutations at all of the 14 $G \cdot C \to A \cdot T$ transition sites and virtually none of the 23 transversion sites tested. As Table 4 demonstrates, this represents greater than 99% specificity. Of 210 ochre mutations attributed to a single base change, 100% were found to be $G \cdot C \to A \cdot T$ changes (Fig. 9, Table 4). All 12 of the $G \cdot C \to A \cdot T$ sites are well-induced by NG. Reversion studies described in a later section document the ability of NG to stimulate the $A \cdot T \to G \cdot C$ transition, but at a significantly lower rate than for the $G \cdot C \to A \cdot T$ transition (approx. 5%).

(d) *Ultraviolet light*

Several studies with ultraviolet light mutagenesis have argued that the $G \cdot C \to A \cdot T$ transition occurs at a high rate relative to other substitutions (Drake, 1963; Howard & Tessman, 1964; Osborn *et al.*, 1967), although more recent investigations on the nature of forward mutations (Yanofsky, 1971; Sherman & Stewart, 1973) and reverse mutations (Prakash & Sherman, 1973) indicate no such specificity.

The results of u.v. mutagenesis in the *lacI* systems are given in Figures 10 and 11,

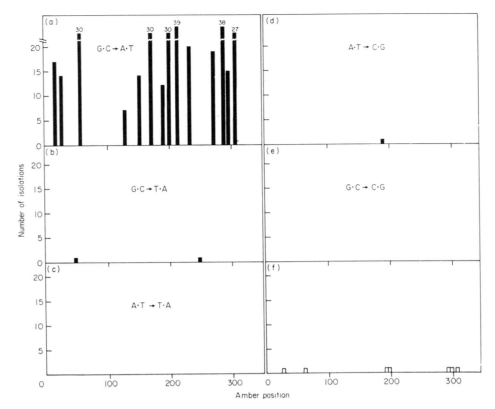

FIG. 6. The amber sites derived by EMS are shown. (f) Presumed double mutation.

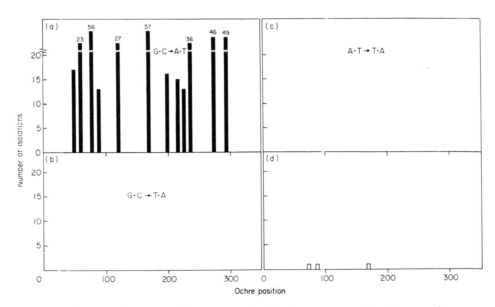

FIG. 7. The ochre sites derived by EMS are depicted. (d) Presumed double mutation.

TABLE 3

Mutations induced by ethyl methanesulfonate

Substitution	Amber (321 mutations)					Ochre (370 mutations)				
	Available sites	Sites found	Total occurrences	% of all mutations	% of assigned mutations	Available sites	Sites found	Total occurrences	% of all mutations	% of assigned mutations
G·C → A·T	14	14	312	97·2	99·0	12	12	368	99·4	100·0
G·C → T·A	10	2	2	0·6	0·6	12	0	0	0·0	0·0
A·T → T·A	5	0	0	0·0	0·0	14	0	0	0·0	0·0
A·T → C·G	5	1	1	0·3	0·3	0	—	—	—	—
G·C → C·G	3	0	0	0·0	0·0	0	—	—	—	—
Unassigned	—	—	—	—	—	2	0	0	0·0	—
Presumed double mutations	—	—	6	1·9	—		—	2	0·6	—

The 691 amber and ochre mutations induced by EMS are divided into different categories based on the base substitution required to generate each mutation.

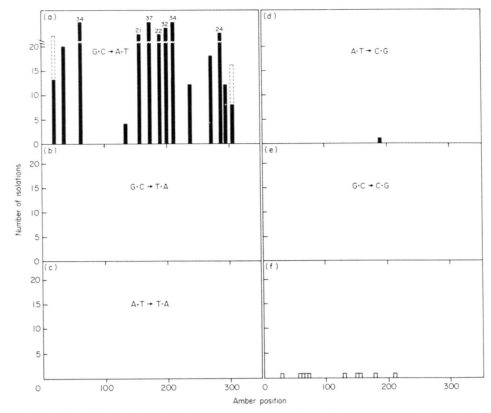

FIG. 8. The NG-induced amber sites are shown. Two sites (*A5* and *A35*) were determined in only half of the total NG-induced amber collection. The broken lines extend the bar height to twice the value found. (f) Presumed double mutation.

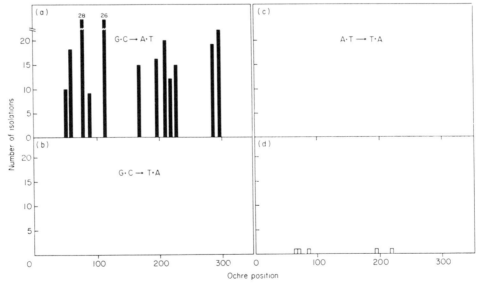

FIG. 9. The NG-induced ochre sites are depicted. (d) Presumed double mutation.

TABLE 4

Mutations induced by N'-methyl-N'-nitro-N-nitrosoguanidine

Substitution	Amber (303 mutations)					Ochre (215 mutations)				
	Available sites	Sites found	Total occurrences	% of all mutations	% of assigned mutations	Available sites	Sites found	Total occurrences	% of all mutations	% of assigned mutations
$G \cdot C \to A \cdot T$	14	14	292	96·4	99·7	12	12	210	97·7	100·0
$G \cdot C \to T \cdot A$	10	0	0	0·0	0·0	12	0	0	0·0	0·0
$A \cdot T \to T \cdot A$	5	0	0	0·0	0·0	14	0	0	0·0	0·0
$A \cdot T \to C \cdot G$	5	1	1	0·3	0·3	0	—	—	—	—
$G \cdot C \to C \cdot G$	3	0	0	0·0	0·0	0	—	—	—	—
Unassigned	—	—	—	—	—	2	0	0	0·0	—
Presumed double mutations	—	—	10	3·3	—	—	—	5	2·3	—

The 518 amber and ochre mutations induced by NG are divided into different categories based on the base substitution required to generate each mutation.

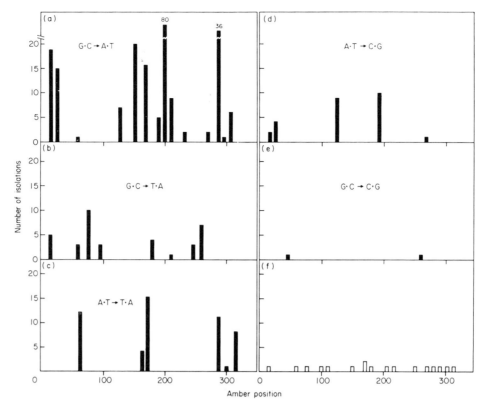

Fig. 10. The amber sites induced by u.v. are shown. (f) Presumed double mutations.

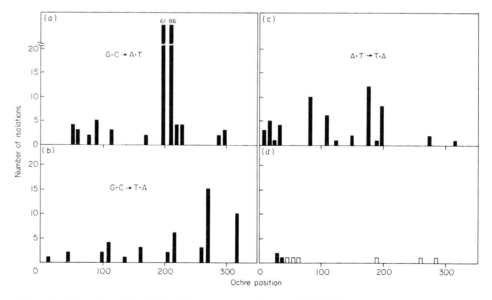

Fig. 11. The ochre sites induced by u.v. are shown. (d) Filled bars, unassigned; open bars, presumed double mutations.

TABLE 5

Mutations induced by ultraviolet light

Substitution	Amber (358 mutations)					Ochre (295) mutations				
	Available sites	Sites found	Total occurrences	% of all mutations	% of assigned mutations	Available sites	Sites found	Total occurrences	% of all mutations	% of assigned mutations
G·C → A·T	14	14	219	61·2	64·0	12	12	180	61·0	62·3
G·C → T·A	10	8	39	10·9	11·4	12	11	49	16·6	17·0
A·T → T·A	5	5	48	13·4	14·0	14	14	57	19·3	19·7
A·T → C·G	5	5	26	7·3	7·6	0	—	—	—	—
G·C → C·G	3	2	2	0·6	0·6	0	—	—	—	—
Tandem double mutations	14	7	8	2·2	2·3	3	3	3	1·0	1·0
Other double mutations	—	—	16	4·5	—	—	—	2	0·7	—
Unassigned	—	—	—	—	—	3†	3	4	1·4	—

The 653 amber and ochre mutations induced by u.v. are divided into different categories based on the base substitution required to generate each mutation.

† Site Y2 is listed as unassigned in this study.

and Table 5. The picture is considerably more complicated than for the other mutagens we have investigated, and can be ascertained best from a careful consideration of Figures 10 and 11. There are four transition sites which are significant hotspots with respect to all of the other sites. These four sites, from close to 90 possible sites, account for slightly more than 60% of all u.v.-induced amber and ochre mutations. The remainder of the mutations appear evenly distributed amongst both the $G \cdot C \rightarrow A \cdot T$ transition and three of the four transversions, for many of the available sites. Only the $G \cdot C \rightarrow C \cdot G$ transversion is not well-induced in this system, although with only three possible sites to screen for this transversion it is uncertain whether one can generalize from this result.

The double mutations shown in Figures 10 and 11 are of two types. One class, which occurs with virtually all mutagens, consists of nonsense mutations together with a secondary lesion somewhere else in the gene. A second and more interesting category involves tandem double base changes and has so far been found only after u.v. irradiation. Sequencing studies on the protein, messenger RNA, and DNA level (see the preceding paper, Coulondre & Miller, 1977) have established that between 15 and 17 of the nonsense sites in the *lacI* gene arise by tandem double base changes within the same codon. The changes detected are:

$$\text{Site } Y5: \begin{matrix} \text{G-G} \\ \bullet \ \bullet \\ \text{C-C} \end{matrix} \rightarrow \begin{matrix} \text{A-A} \\ \bullet \ \bullet \\ \text{T-T} \end{matrix}; \quad \text{Site } Y1: \begin{matrix} \text{C-C} \\ \bullet \ \bullet \\ \text{G-G} \end{matrix} \rightarrow \begin{matrix} \text{T-A} \\ \bullet \ \bullet \\ \text{A-T} \end{matrix};$$

$$\text{Sites } X2, X3, X4, X5, X6, X7, X8, X10 \text{ and } X13, \begin{matrix} \text{C-T} \\ \bullet \ \bullet \\ \text{G-A} \end{matrix} \rightarrow \begin{matrix} \text{T-A} \\ \bullet \ \bullet \\ \text{A-T} \end{matrix};$$

$$\text{Site } X1: \begin{matrix} \text{A-C} \\ \bullet \ \bullet \\ \text{T-G} \end{matrix} \rightarrow \begin{matrix} \text{T-A} \\ \bullet \ \bullet \\ \text{A-T} \end{matrix}; \quad \text{Site } X15 \text{ (probably)}: \begin{matrix} \text{T-T} \\ \bullet \ \bullet \\ \text{A-A} \end{matrix} \rightarrow \begin{matrix} \text{A-G} \\ \bullet \ \bullet \\ \text{T-C} \end{matrix};$$

$$\text{Site } Y7 \text{ (probably)}: \begin{matrix} \text{T-T} \\ \bullet \ \bullet \\ \text{A-A} \end{matrix} \rightarrow \begin{matrix} \text{A-A} \\ \bullet \ \bullet \\ \text{T-T} \end{matrix}.$$

These mutations are considered further in the Discussion.

(e) *Spontaneous mutations*

Nonsense mutations are rare (1 to 2%) amongst spontaneous I^- mutations, in contrast to the high proportion (20 to 30%) found with all of the mutagens used in this study. This stems from the fact that most of the spontaneous I^- mutations which occur in this system are not base substitutions, but rather deletions and insertions (P. J. Farabaugh, L. Johnsrud, M. P. Calos, U. Schmeissner & J. H. Miller, unpublished results). All possible base changes are found spontaneously, as can be seen from Figures 12 and 13, and Tables 1 and 6. Transitions predominate, but as in the case of u.v.-induced mutations, this is primarily due to the presence of several hotspots.

(f) *Genetic hotspots*

There are 26 nonsense sites in our collection which are generated by the $G \cdot C \rightarrow A \cdot T$ transition. Figure 14 shows the distribution of 3738 mutations found at these sites. It is evident that for each mutagen under study, the distribution is not random, but rather reveals several "hotspots", or preferred sites, as has been found in the *r*II

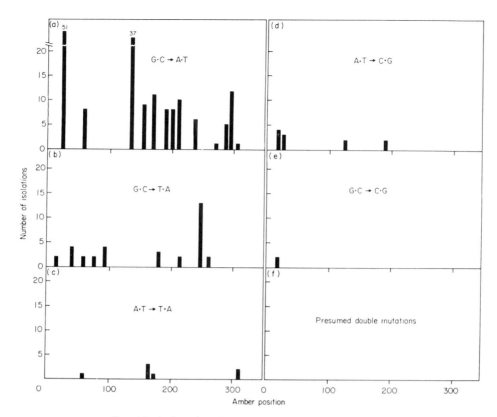

FIG. 12. Amber sites found spontaneously are depicted.

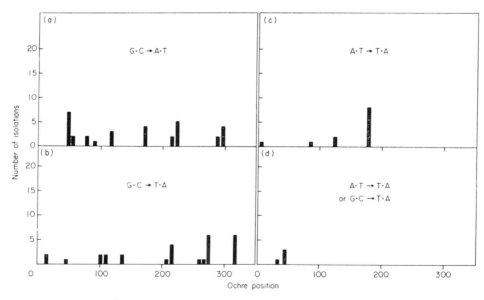

FIG. 13. Ochre sites found spontaneously are shown.

TABLE 6

Spontaneous mutations

Substitution	Amber (222 mutations)					Ochre (76 mutations)				
	Available sites	Sites found	Total occurrences	% of all mutations	% of assigned mutations	Available sites	Sites found	Total occurrences	% of all mutations	% of assigned mutations
G·C → A·T	14	13	167	75·2	75·6	12	10	32	42·1	44·4
G·C → T·A	10	10	37	16·7	16·7	12	11	28	36·8	38·9
A·T → T·A	5	3	4	1·8	1·8	14	4	12	15·8	16·7
A·T → C·G	5	4	11	5·0	5·0	0	—	—	—	—
G·C → C·G	3	1	2	0·9	0·9	0	—	—	—	—
Unassigned	—	—	—	—	—	2	2	4	5·3	—
Presumed double mutations	—	—	1	0·4	—	—	—	0	0·0	—

The 298 amber and ochre mutations arising spontaneously are divided into different categories based on the base substitution required to generate each mutation.

system of phage T4 (Benzer, 1961). This is particularly true for u.v.-induced, 2AP-induced, and spontaneously occurring nonsense sites. The 2AP and spontaneous amber hotspots are at the same sites, although this is not true for the 2AP hotspots at ochre sites. Further aspects of this phenomenon are considered in the Discussion.

(g) Reversion tests

Amongst the single base substitutions, only the $A \cdot T \to G \cdot C$ transition cannot generate a nonsense codon from a sense codon. Therefore, in order to detect this change, it is necessary to use a reversion system. We can specifically detect the $A \cdot T \to G \cdot C$ transition by monitoring the conversion of ochre mutations to amber mutations (UAA $\to$ UAG). In addition, we can also score for reversion of an ochre codon to a sense codon, at least for those mutagens which display a very low rate of transversions in the forward assay system. The frequency of revertants resulting from an $A \cdot T \to G \cdot C$ transition at an ochre site will be less than or equal to the frequency of all revertants having a base substitution in that codon. Since only the first base in the ochre codon (*UAA*) can be converted to sense (*CAA*) by a transition, we can compare this revertant frequency with the forward rate of appearance of the initial ochre mutant at that site. When ochre mutations are used which were originally derived from CAA codons, we have an opportunity to compare the frequencies of mutants arising from either the $G \cdot C \to A \cdot T$ transition, or the $A \cdot T \to G \cdot C$ transition at the *same site*.

At certain positions in the *lac* repressor, only specific amino acids restore the wild-type phenotype. In the cases where we utilize nonsense sites at the respective positions in the *lacI* message, we can identify the amino acid resulting from the reversion to a sense codon and thus the corresponding base substitution. For instance, only glutamine is acceptable at the position normally specified by ochre site *O9*. Therefore, all reversion at this site must be due to the TAA $\to$ CAA change.

(i) 2-Aminopurine

Tables 7 to 9 compare the $G \cdot C \to A \cdot T$ and the $A \cdot T \to G \cdot C$ transitions at a number of sites for 2AP, EMS and NG, respectively. The forward rates of 2AP mutagenesis are taken from a previous study (Miller *et al.*, 1977). For the 12 ochre sites derived from CAA codons (*O10,O9,O11,O13,O17,O21,O24,O27,O28,O29,O34* and *O35*), reversion to CAA restores glutamine (the wild-type residue) at the appropriate position in the repressor polypeptide chain, whereas conversion to UAG results in the insertion of tyrosine at this position. This requires a series of control experiments to determine the plating efficiency of the resulting amber mutant (see Materials and Methods). Also, the rates of 2AP-induced amber and ochre mutations fluctuate considerably from site to site (see Table 7 and Miller *et al.*, 1977). If we assume that this is a reflection of the differences in the surrounding base sequence, then the UAA $\to$ UAG conversion at position 3 in the codon is not as relevant to compare with the forward rate ($G \cdot C \to A \cdot T$) as is the reversion to CAA at position 1.

Normally, we would be concerned about the inability to distinguish the position 1 transition (UAA $\to$ CAA) from transversions at either positions 1, 2 or 3. However, in the case of 2AP, the forward assay system detected only $G \cdot C \to A \cdot T$ transitions and none of the four possible transversions (Miller *et al.*, 1977). Since over 1000 mutations were analyzed, it is unlikely that transversions could be induced by 2AP at more than a small fraction of the rate of $G \cdot C \to A \cdot T$ transitions and escape

TABLE 7

Induction and reversion of nonsense sites by 2-aminopurine

Site	$G \cdot C \to A \cdot T$ Position 1 (10^{-7})	$A \cdot T \to G \cdot C$ Position 1 (10^{-7})	$A \cdot T \to G \cdot C$ Position 3 (10^{-7})
O10	1·8		
O9	0·5	7·0	
O11	6·9	43·0	
O13	0·8	≤0·9	4·0
O17	7·4	40·4	2·6†
O21	4·4	67·5	7·5
O24	0·3		
O27	0·8	22·0	<0·5
O28	1·8		
O29	12·9		
O34	18·8	2·0	0·5
O35	13·6	11·0	3·0

The induction and reversion of ochre sites by 2AP is shown. The ochre sites (see Table 1) can revert *via* a transition ($A \cdot T \to G \cdot C$) only at position 1 in the codon, to a CAA, which specifies glutamine. Transversions can result in reversion at any of the 3 positions in the codon. The conversion of the ochre site to an amber site ($UAA \to UAG$) can occur only *via* the $A \cdot T \to G \cdot C$ transition. All numbers for the forward induction of the ochre site are derived from the 2 previous studies (Miller *et al.*, 1977; Coulondre & Miller, 1977). All numbers are given in revertants/10^7 cells.

† The amber derived from O17 has a plating efficiency of only 25% that of the wild-type, indicating that this value is a low estimate.

TABLE 8

Induction and reversions of nonsense sites by ethyl methylsulfonate

Site	$G \cdot C \to A \cdot T$ Position 1 (10^{-7})	$A \cdot T \to G \cdot C$ Position 1 (10^{-7})	$A \cdot T \to G \cdot C$ Position 3 (10^{-7})
O10	73·3		
O9	99·2	1·0	
O11	241·5	≤3·4	
O13	56·1	≤0·6	1·3
O17	116·4	≤0·8	0·8†
O21	245·8	≤4·8	1·6
O24	69·0		
O27	64·7	≤1·4	0·6
O28	56·1		
O29	155·3		
O34	198·4	0·7	
O35	211·3	3·3	

The induction and reversion of ochre sites by EMS. For details, see the legend to Table 7.
† See Table 7.

TABLE 9

N'-methyl-N'-nitro-N-nitrosoguanidine induction and reversion of nonsense sites

Site	$G \cdot C \to A \cdot T$ Position 1 (10^{-7})	$A \cdot T \to G \cdot C$ Position 1 (10^{-7})	$A \cdot T \to G \cdot C$ Position 3 (10^{-7})
O10	102·8		
O9	185·0	10·0	
O11	287·8	≤11·8	
O13	92·5	≤ 0·5	12·7
O17	267·3	≤23·6	9·0†
O21	154·2	≤13·9	0·9
O24	164·5		
O27	205·6	≤ 3·8	3·4
O28	123·4		
O29	154·2		
O34	195·3	17·0	1·0
O35	226·2	19·0	10·0

The induction and reversion of ochre sites by NG. For details see the legend to Table 7.
† See Table 7.

detection in this system. Because for 2AP the rates of reversion at position 1 of the UAA codon are 100% (or even considerably higher) those of the forward rates, we can safely conclude that reversion is due to the $A \cdot T \to G \cdot C$ transition. Site *O9* allows us to directly demonstrate the $A \cdot T \to G \cdot C$ transition, because only glutamine (which arises from this transition at position one in the codon) is acceptable as an amino acid in the corresponding position in the repressor (C. Coulondre & J. H. Miller, unpublished work). (All conversions from UAA → UAG result only from the $A \cdot T \to G \cdot C$ transition at the third position in the codon.)

It can be seen from Table 7 that, in general, 2AP induces the $A \cdot T \to G \cdot C$ transition better than the $G \cdot C \to A \cdot T$ transition. Although the most favourably induced $G \cdot C \to A \cdot T$ sites are equal to or greater than the lowest $A \cdot T \to G \cdot C$ sites, in most cases a comparison of the two transitions at the same site (forward and reverse rates at position 1 in the codon) shows a 10:1 preference for the $A \cdot T \to G \cdot C$ change.

(ii) *Ethyl methanesulfonate*

Table 8 records the results of EMS-stimulated reversion of the same set of ochre mutations as shown in Table 7 for 2AP. It is apparent that, unlike 2AP, EMS does not induce the $A \cdot T \to G \cdot C$ transition at anywhere near the rate of the $G \cdot C \to A \cdot T$ transition. With the same considerations mentioned in the preceding section in mind, at any given site EMS displays at least a 50 to 100-fold preference for the $G \cdot C \to A \cdot T$ transition over the $A \cdot T \to G \cdot C$ transition.

(iii) *Nitrosoguanidine*

The reversion tests with NG are shown in Table 9. A similar pattern to that found for EMS is evident, the $G \cdot C \to A \cdot T$ change being significantly favoured at any given site. The $A \cdot T \to G \cdot C$ change is better stimulated by NG than by EMS, although at any given site the $G \cdot C \rightarrow A \cdot T$ change is still favoured by at least $10:1$ (and in some cases $100:1$).

5. Discussion

We have described a system which allows the analysis of forward base substitution mutations in the *lacI* gene of *E. coli*. From a set of more than 80 possible nonsense mutation sites, 26 sites arising from the $G \cdot C \rightarrow A \cdot T$ transition have been identified, as well as 22 $G \cdot C \rightarrow T \cdot A$ sites, 19 $A \cdot T \rightarrow T \cdot A$ sites, 5 $A \cdot T \rightarrow C \cdot G$ sites, and 3 $G \cdot C \rightarrow C \cdot G$ sites (Miller *et al.*, 1977; Coulondre & Miller, 1977). By distributing amber and ochre mutations induced by a given mutagen amongst the identified sites, we can analyze the frequency of each base substitution (except for the $A \cdot T \rightarrow G \cdot C$ change) at each available site. The specificity of the mutagen can then be represented as a picture constructed from frequencies at many different sites, as is done in Figures 4 to 13. Therefore, this system offers a significant advantage over most reversion systems, since in the latter type of analysis only one or a few sites are considered, and the frequency of induced mutations often varies considerably from site to site.

The $A \cdot T \rightarrow G \cdot C$ transition cannot be detected in the forward assay system, although we can determine this substitution by monitoring the conversion of ochre to amber ($UAA \rightarrow UAG$), and also the reversion to wild-type of certain ochre and amber sites. Because the forward ($G \cdot C \rightarrow A \cdot T$) rates are known for each site, we have the advantage of being able to compare the relative rates of each transition at the same base-pair, the surrounding nucleotide sequence remaining unchanged (see Tables 7 to 9).

(a) *Specificity of mutagens*

Due to the presence of several frameshift hotspots (P. J. Farabaugh, U. Schmeissner & J. H. Miller, unpublished results), only a small fraction (1 to 2%) of spontaneous mutations in the *lacI* gene are nonsense mutations. Amongst these base substitution mutations no strict specificity is observed, since in addition to the $G \cdot C \rightarrow A \cdot T$ transition, all types of transversions are found. Numerous transversion sites are as well-induced as many of the transition sites.

In contrast to spontaneous mutations, base substitutions represent a major fraction of the mutations induced by the mutagens studied here. In these cases, nonsense mutations constitute 20 to 30% of the I^- mutations detected. NG and EMS prove to be highly specific for the $G \cdot C \rightarrow A \cdot T$ transition, with transversions representing less than 1% of the induced mutations. The $A \cdot T \rightarrow G \cdot C$ transition is also poorly induced by these mutagens, occurring at 1% or less of the rate of the $G \cdot C \rightarrow A \cdot T$ transition in the case of EMS, and between 1% and 5% of the $G \cdot C \rightarrow A \cdot T$ rate in the case of NG (on the average). On the other hand, 2AP clearly induces the $A \cdot T \rightarrow G \cdot C$ transition better than the $G \cdot C \rightarrow A \cdot T$ transition, by a factor of 10 to 20. Therefore, for the $A \cdot T \rightarrow G \cdot C$ change, 2AP is a better mutagen than NG at many sites (by a factor of 2 to 5; see Tables 7 and 9), and a much better mutagen than EMS (by a factor of 20 to 50; Tables 7 and 8).

NQO stimulates base substitutions only at $G \cdot C$ base-pairs, as can be seen in Figures 4 and 5. Both transversions and transitions occur, although transitions are clearly favoured. Ultraviolet light induces all types of base substitutions, without any apparent specificity for a particular class of substitution. In addition, tandem double mutations are found after u.v. irradiation (see below).

(b) *Double mutations*

Surprisingly, a significant proportion of ultraviolet light-induced mutations are tandem double base changes. An example of the $\begin{smallmatrix}C\text{-}C \\ \bullet\ \bullet \\ G\text{-}G\end{smallmatrix} \to \begin{smallmatrix}T\text{-}A \\ \bullet\ \bullet \\ A\text{-}T\end{smallmatrix}$ conversion has been verified by direct peptide analysis (A. Schmitz, unpublished results). Protein sequencing (Sommer, 1977) has also confirmed the assignment of one site ($Y5$) to a $\begin{smallmatrix}G\text{-}G \\ \bullet\ \bullet \\ C\text{-}C\end{smallmatrix} \to \begin{smallmatrix}A\text{-}A \\ \bullet\ \bullet \\ T\text{-}T\end{smallmatrix}$ substitution. We have detected three independent occurrences of this double mutation (Coulondre & Miller, 1977). With the aid of the wild-type DNA sequence (Farabaugh, unpublished work), as many as nine different sites can be attributed to the $\begin{smallmatrix}C\text{-}T \\ \bullet\ \bullet \\ G\text{-}A\end{smallmatrix} \to \begin{smallmatrix}T\text{-}A \\ \bullet\ \bullet \\ A\text{-}T\end{smallmatrix}$ change, and one example of an $\begin{smallmatrix}A\text{-}C \\ \bullet\ \bullet \\ T\text{-}G\end{smallmatrix} \to \begin{smallmatrix}T\text{-}A \\ \bullet\ \bullet \\ A\text{-}T\end{smallmatrix}$ change ($X1$) has been uncovered. Other probable double changes include the $\begin{smallmatrix}T\text{-}T \\ \bullet\ \bullet \\ A\text{-}A\end{smallmatrix} \to \begin{smallmatrix}A\text{-}A \\ \bullet\ \bullet \\ T\text{-}T\end{smallmatrix}$ and the $\begin{smallmatrix}T\text{-}T \\ \bullet\ \bullet \\ A\text{-}A\end{smallmatrix} \to \begin{smallmatrix}A\text{-}G \\ \bullet\ \bullet \\ T\text{-}C\end{smallmatrix}$ substitutions.

Although at least 2% of all nonsense mutations found after u.v. irradiation can be put into this category, the real percentage is probably much higher, since double changes cannot be recognized in many cases. For instance, amber and ochre mutations arising from CAG or CAA codons might carry an additional change in the third position of the preceding codon, which would be undetected by our methods. If we eliminate these sites and consider only those codons at which such double mutations can be discerned (i.e. using as examples of single base changes the sites generated by a change in the second position of the codon) then 10% of the u.v.-induced nonsense mutations arise *via* tandem double base changes. Since we have numerous examples of amber mutations derived from CUG and UUG codons, we can directly compare the respective frequencies of occurrence. From Table 3 it is apparent that the $\begin{smallmatrix}T \\ \bullet \\ A\end{smallmatrix} \to \begin{smallmatrix}A \\ \bullet \\ T\end{smallmatrix}$ change is seen 10 to 20 times more frequently than the $\begin{smallmatrix}C\text{-}T \\ \bullet\ \bullet \\ G\text{-}A\end{smallmatrix} \to \begin{smallmatrix}T\text{-}A \\ \bullet\ \bullet \\ A\text{-}T\end{smallmatrix}$ double change.

Because of possible differences in the rate of photodimer formation, excision and repair (see below), this can serve only as an approximation. However, at one site, the tryptophan codon at position 220, an amber (UAG; $A24$), an ochre (UAA; $Y5$) and a UGA mutation ($U6$) have been detected (see Table 3 of the preceding paper, Coulondre & Miller, 1977). Here we can compare the single base change $\begin{smallmatrix}G \\ \bullet \\ C\end{smallmatrix} \to \begin{smallmatrix}A \\ \bullet \\ T\end{smallmatrix}$ which generates the amber with the tandem double base change $\begin{smallmatrix}G\text{-}G \\ \bullet\ \bullet \\ C\text{-}C\end{smallmatrix} \to \begin{smallmatrix}A\text{-}A \\ \bullet\ \bullet \\ T\text{-}T\end{smallmatrix}$ which gives rise to the ochre. This reveals that approximately 10% of the time that the single $\begin{smallmatrix}G \\ \bullet \\ C\end{smallmatrix} \to \begin{smallmatrix}A \\ \bullet \\ T\end{smallmatrix}$ change is detected, an additional $\begin{smallmatrix}G \\ \bullet \\ C\end{smallmatrix} \to \begin{smallmatrix}A \\ \bullet \\ T\end{smallmatrix}$ substitution is seen in the neighbouring position. In these cases we can only detect one particular tandem double base change. We cannot score the other two base changes, since they do not result in a nonsense codon. Therefore, the percentage of total tandem double mutations might be even higher. As discussed below, the percentage of these double mutations might also depend on the action of different repair processes in the cell.

In our system only ultraviolet light stimulates tandem double base changes as a significant ($>0.2\%$) proportion of the induced base substitutions. (A single example of a tandem double base change has been detected in a collection of over 1000 NQO-induced mutations.) Such changes might be stimulated at a low rate by other mutagens, but these would have to be detected by direct selection methods. Sherman and co-workers have found tandem double mutations in yeast induced by u.v. light (J. W. Stewart & F. Sherman, unpublished work; Lawrence et al., 1974) and also by nitrous acid, X-rays, and alpha particles (Sherman & Stewart, 1973). u.v.-generated tandem double mutations have also been detected in E. coli by other workers (Yanofsky et al., 1966; J. Gralla, unpublished work; S. Adhya & B. de Crombrugghe, unpublished work).

(c) Mechanisms

Mutagenesis by ultraviolet light requires an inducible error-prone repair system in E. coli (Witkin, 1967,1976; Radman et al., 1977). Pyrimidine-pyrimidine photodimers which are not eliminated by error-free repair systems block replication, causing a gap in the complementary DNA strand. The inducible repair system, dependent on the recA and lexA gene products (see review by Witkin, 1976), allows DNA synthesis across from photodimers. However, this results in an increase in misincorporation, since pyrimidine dimers have presumably lost most or all of their base-pairing specificity. (Errors in incorporation may also occur at other points, due either to the error-prone system itself or to other u.v. photoproducts.) The high proportion of tandem double base changes found after u.v. irradiation is consistent with this interpretation. All but one of these double substitutions involve a pyrimidine-pyrimidine sequence. E. Witkin (personal communication) has pointed out that there are two types of u.v.-induced photoproducts involving adjacent pyrimidines: cyclobutane-type dimers, and oxetane pyrimidine adducts. The tandem double mutations might be caused by either one or the other, or both. This could be investigated by examining the effect of photoreactivation, which effectively eliminates the dimers, but not the adducts. On the other hand, in Uvr$^-$ strains photodimers cannot be excised (in the dark) and are the predominant photoproduct which leads to mutations. If tandem double mutations are caused by photodimers, they should be enhanced in a Uvr$^-$ background relative to a wild-type strain, in which 90 to 95% of the pyrimidine dimers are removed.

As reviewed by Drake & Baltz (1976), mutagenesis by alkylating agents such as EMS and NG could occur either by direct mispairing or by errors in repair. Although many different alkylation products can be formed after treatment with EMS or NG, only O-6-alkyl guanine (Loveless, 1969; Lawley & Shah, 1972) and to a lesser extent O-4-alkyl thymine (Lawley & Shah, 1972; Lawley et al., 1973) are believed to be mutagenic (Prakash & Sherman, 1973; Lawley, 1974; Drake & Baltz, 1976). It has been suggested by Prakash & Sherman (1973) that the specificity and high mutagenicity of alkylating agents depends on the extent of formation of O-6-alkyl guanine. This would account for the high preference for $G \cdot C \to A \cdot T$ changes. The data presented in this paper are in complete agreement with this idea.

In our system, NG induces the $A \cdot T \to G \cdot C$ transition significantly better than EMS, although at a low level relative to the G·C → A·T transition. It is possible that this difference between NG and EMS lies in an enhanced ability of NG to generate mutagenic methylation products at A·T base-pairs (such as O-4-alkyl thymine), although it is more likely to be due to a difference in the interaction with the error-prone repair system, as has been reported previously (Kondo et al., 1970). It is accepted that treatment with NG induces the recA, lexA-dependent error-prone repair system, whereas EMS does not (Witkin, 1976; Radman et al., 1977).

NQO also requires error-prone repair for mutagenesis, although the lesion responsible for the mutation is an addition product (NQO-guanine; Ikenaga et al., 1975) rather than a photodimer, as is the case with u.v. mutagenesis.

(d) Hotspots

Figure 14 shows the preferred sites amongst G·C → A·T transitions for a number of mutagens. For spontaneous, u.v.-induced and 2AP-induced mutations, a several hundred-fold variation can be seen for different sites, even though the same transition is involved. The "hotspots" found here are similar in appearance to those originally reported by Benzer (1961) for the rII system of bacteriophage T4, although the spontaneous hotspots found by Benzer have been shown to be frameshift mutations (in Roth, 1974). It was suggested at the time that the neighbouring base sequence might partly determine the rate of a particular base substitution. Now that the entire nucleotide sequence of the lacI gene has been elucidated (D. Steege, unpublished results; P. J. Farabaugh, unpublished results), the sequences surrounding different hotspots can be examined. This study will be reported elsewhere.

It is interesting to note that mutations found spontaneously prefer some of the same transition sites as those favoured by 2AP. On the other hand, u.v. light preferentially stimulates a different set of targets. For the sites tested here there are no predominant hotspots for NG or EMS, although there is still considerable variation from site to site. The nonsense spectra of NG and EMS appear almost identical, possibly suggesting that these two mutagens generate the G·C → A·T change by a similar mechanism.

(e) Considerations for obtaining mutants

Many investigators employ nitrosoguanidine (NG) or EMS for obtaining mutants in bacteria, because of the assumed high potency of these agents. However, both of these mutagens have the disadvantage of inducing only a limited number of mutational sites. As shown here, approximately 99% of the base substitutions found after NG mutagenesis are transitions, and at least 95% of these are G·C → A·T changes. EMS generates almost exclusively G·C → A·T changes. Therefore, at least in systems where it is possible to select directly for mutant phenotypes, other mutagens should be used.

2-Aminopurine stimulates the A·T → G·C change significantly better than EMS, and even better than NG at many sites. Many of the sites found after treatment with 2AP will be due to this substitution. The mutator gene mutT was used during the initial study with this system. Mutations induced by mutT are exclusively of the A·T → C·G type (Cox & Yanofsky, 1967). Since this transversion is not significantly induced (less than 1%) by either EMS, NG or 2AP, all mutational sites found by mutT will be different from those obtained by any of these three agents. u.v. light, because it stimulates all four transversions and both transitions, is the single most

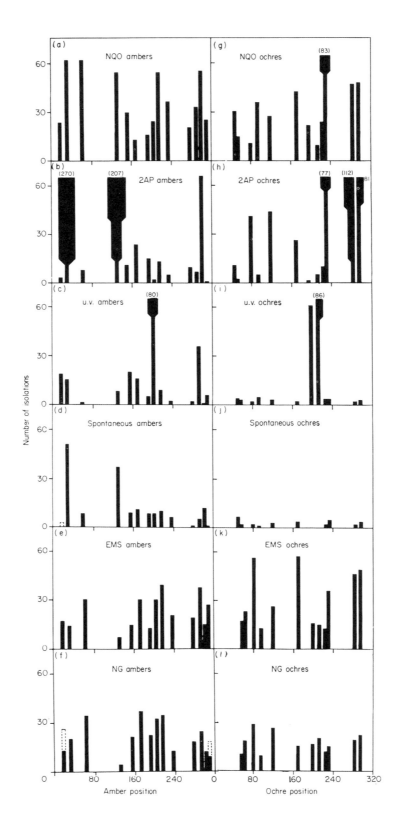

effective mutagen for generating a wide variety of mutant phenotypes. Moreover, u.v. also induces tandem double base changes. In situations where u.v. can be used, it should be the mutagen of choice, even though it does show a tendency to favour certain hotspots.

Clearly, it is advisable to collect mutants after treatment with several different mutagenic agents, rather than relying on one mutagen. This is particularly true when the purpose of the experiment is to find new mutants or to examine the distribution of a large number of mutations which cause a particular phenotype.

(f) *Future experiments*

The system described here allows the analysis of base substitution mutations at specific sites. The knowledge of the full *I* gene DNA sequence (P. J. Farabaugh, unpublished results) makes possible the comparison of the nucleotide sequence surrounding each site. Subsequent experiments will be aimed at uncovering the detailed specificity of additional mutagens, as well as examining mutagenesis at specific sites in repair-deficient strains. The molecular basis of genetic hotspots will also be explored.

We thank Drs S. Brenner, F. Sherman, J. Cairns, M. Radman, W. Gilbert, C. Yanofsky, D. Botstein, E. Witkin and J. Beckwith for helpful suggestions. Murielle Hofer provided excellent technical assistance. We also thank Dr S. Brenner for his generous gift of 4-nitroquinoline-1-oxide, and Otto Jenni for drawing the Figures. This work was supported by a grant from the Swiss National Fund (3.485.75) to one of us (J. H. M.).

REFERENCES

Ames, B. N., Durston, W. E., Yamasaki, E. & Lee, F. D. (1973). *Proc. Nat. Acad. Sci. U.S.A.* **70**, 2281–2285.
Auerbach, C. & Kilbey, B. (1971). *Annu. Rev. Genet.* **5**, 163–218.
Bautz-Freese, E. (1961). *Proc. Nat. Acad. Sci., U.S.A.* **47**, 540–545.
Bautz, E. & Freese, E. (1960). *Proc. Nat. Acad. Sci., U.S.A.* **46**, 1585–1594.
Benzer, S. (1961). *Proc. Nat. Acad. Sci., U.S.A.* **47**, 403–416.
Coulondre, C. & Miller, J. H. (1977). *J. Mol. Biol.* **117**, 525–567.
Cox, E. C. & Yanofsky, C. (1967). *Proc. Nat. Acad. Sci., U.S.A.* **59**, 1895–1902.
Drake, J. W. (1963). *J. Mol. Biol.* **6**, 268–283.
Drake, J. W. (1970). *The Molecular Basis of Mutation*, Holden-Day, San Francisco.
Drake, J. W. & Baltz, R. H. (1976). *Annu. Rev. Biochem.* **45**, 11–37.
Eisenstark, A., Eisenstark, R. & van Sickle, R. (1965). *Mutat. Res.* **2**, 1–10.
Hartman, P. E., Hartman, Z., Stahl, R. C. & Ames, B. N. (1971). *Advan. Genet.* **16**, 1–34.
Howard, B. & Tessman, I. (1964). *J. Mol. Biol.* **9**, 372–375.

FIG. 14. The distribution of 3738 mutations arising from the $G \cdot C \to A \cdot T$ transition is shown. The number of independent occurrences at each site is indicated by the bar height. One amber and one ochre mutation from each mutagenized culture were analyzed (see Materials and Methods). Therefore, hotspots can be directly identified by considering the frequency of induction of an amber site relative to the other amber sites, and of an ochre site relative to the other ochre sites. Large areas, instead of bar heights, indicate numbers of occurrences greater than 60. For instance, one of the 2AP-induced amber sites was detected 270 times in this collection, as indicated in the left part of (b). In order to consider amber and ochre mutations together, the relative frequency of each type of mutation, and the respective sample sizes, must be taken into account to produce a normalization factor. For instance, to compare spontaneous ochre sites directly with the spontaneous amber sites, the ochre bar heights must be multiplied by a factor of 3. For EMS and NG-induced mutations, the ochre bar heights should be multiplied by factors of 2·3 and 1·9, respectively. For 2AP, NQO and u.v.-induced ochres, the relevant factors are 0·9, 0·6 and 0·7, respectively.

Ikenaga, M., Ichikawa-Ryo, H. & Kondo, S. (1975). *J. Mol. Biol.* **92**, 341–356.

Ishizawa, M. & Endo, H. (1970). *Mutat. Res.* **9**, 134–137.

Ishizawa, M. & Endo, H. (1971). *Mutat. Res.* **12**, 1–8.

Kondo, S., Ichikawa, H., Iwo, K. & Kato, T. (1970). *Genetics*, **66**, 187–217.

Krieg, D. R. (1963a). *Genetics*, **48**, 561–580.

Krieg, D. R. (1963b). *Prog. Nucl. Acids Res.* **2**, 125–168.

Lawley, P. D. (1974). *Mutat. Res.* **23**, 283–295.

Lawley, P. D. & Shah, S. A. (1972). *Chem. Biol. Interact.* **5**, 286–288.

Lawley, P. D., Orr, D. J., Shah, S. A., Farmer, P. B. & Jarman, M. (1973). *Biochem. J.* **135**, 193–201.

Lawrence, C. W., Stewart, J. W., Sherman, F. & Christensen, R. (1974). *J. Mol. Biol.* **85**, 137–162.

Lillis, M. (1977). *J. Mol. Biol.* **117**, 568–571.

Loveless, A. (1969). *Nature (London)*, **223**, 206–207.

Malling, H. V. & deSerres, F. J. (1968). *Mutat. Res.* **6**, 181–193.

Malling, H. V. & deSerres, F. J. (1970). *Mol. Gen. Genet.* **106**, 195–207.

McCann, J., Spingarn, N., Kobori, J. & Ames, B. N. (1975). *Proc. Nat. Acad. Sci., U.S.A.* **72**, 979–983.

Miller, J. H., Ganem, D., Lu, P. & Schmitz, A. (1977). *J. Mol. Biol.* **109**, 275–302.

Müller-Hill, B., Fanning, T., Geisler, N., Gho, D., Kania, J., Kathmann, P., Meisner, H., Schlotmann, M., Schmitz, A., Triesch, I. & Beyreuther, K. (1975). In *Protein–Ligand Interactions* (Sund, H. & Blauer, G., eds), pp. 211–227, Walter de Gruyter, Berlin.

Osborn, M., Person, S., Phillips, S. & Funk, F. (1967). *J. Mol. Biol.* **26**, 437–447.

Prakash, L. & Sherman, F. (1973). *J. Mol. Biol.* **79**, 65–82.

Prakash, L., Stewart, J. W. & Sherman, F. (1974). *J. Mol. Biol.* **85**, 51–65.

Radman, M., Villani, G., Boiteux, S., Caillet-Fauquet, P., Defais, M. & Spadaris, S. (1977). In *Origins of Human Cancer* (Watson, J. D. & Hiatt, H., eds), Cold Spring Harbor Laboratory, in the press.

Roth, J. R. (1974). *Annu. Rev. Genet.* **8**, 319–346.

Schwartz, N. (1963). *Genetics*, **48**, 1357–1375.

Sherman, F. & Stewart, J. W. (1973). In *Biochemistry of Gene Expression in Higher Organisms* (Lee, J. W. & Pollak, J. K., eds), pp. 56–86, Sydney, Australian and New Zealand Book Co., Sydney.

Smith, J. D., Anderson, K., Cashmore, A., Hooper, M. L. & Russel, R. L. (1970). *Cold Spring Harbor Symp. Quant. Biol.* **35**, 21–27.

Sommer, H. (1977). *J. Mol. Biol.* **109**, 299–301.

Tessman, I., Poddar, R. K. & Kumar, S. (1964). *J. Mol. Biol.* **9**, 352–363.

Weber, K., Files, J. G., Platt, T., Ganem, D. & Miller, J. H. (1975). In *Protein–Ligand Interactions* (Sund, H. & Blauer, G., eds), pp. 228–237, Walter de Gruyter, Berlin.

Witkin, E. (1967). *Brookhaven Symp. Biol.* **20**, 17–55.

Witkin, E. (1976). *Bacteriol. Rev.* **40**, 869–907.

Yanofsky, C. (1971). In *Chemical Mutagens* (Hollaender, A., ed.), vol. 1, pp. 283–287, Plenum Press, New York.

Yanofsky, C., Ito, J. & Horn, V. (1966). *Cold Spring Harbor Symp. Quant. Biol.* **31**, 151–162.

Zampieri, A. & Greenberg, J. (1967). *Genetics*, **57**, 41–51.

Molecular basis of base substitution hotspots in *Escherichia coli*

Christine Coulondre & Jeffrey H. Miller
Département de Biologie Moléculaire, Université de Genève, Geneva, Switzerland

Philip J. Farabaugh & Walter Gilbert
Biological Laboratories, Harvard University, Cambridge, Massachusetts 02138

In the lacI *gene of* Escherichia coli *spontaneous base substitution hotspots occur at 5-methylcytosine residues. The hotspots disappear when the respective cytosines are not methylated. We suggest that the hotspots may result from the spontaneous deamination of 5-methylcytosine to thymine, which is not excised by the enzyme DNA-uracil glycosidase.*

IN 1961 Benzer demonstrated that all sites on DNA are not equally mutable, and termed highly mutable sites 'hotspots'[1]. We have studied base substitution mutations in the *lacI* gene of *E. coli*. Because deletions, insertions, and small frameshifts constitute ~90% of the mutations arising spontaneously in the *I* gene[2], we selected directly for base substitutions by focusing on nonsense mutations[3]. Over 80 of the characterised nonsense sites are correlated with specific codons[4,5]; thus in each of these cases the conversion to UAG or UAA occurs by a known base substitution. This system has been used to analyse the specificities of base substitutions detected spontaneously and after induction by various mutagens[3].

Several striking hotspots appear in this collection of mutations, particularly among spontaneous base substitutions, and among those generated by 2-aminopurine (2-AP) and ultraviolet light. The elucidation of the full nucleotide sequence of the *lacI* gene[6,7] now allows the examination of the DNA sequence surrounding each site of mutation. It is clear that 5-methylcytosine residues are associated with high mutability for the G:C→A:T change, and we describe here several experiments which demonstrate the direct involvement of 5-methylcytosine in causing base substitution hotspots.

Spontaneous hotspots

Figures 1 and 2 depict the nonsense mutations which arise through a single base change from wild-type, listing the sites according to the type of base substitution involved. In order to

Table 1 Spontaneous amber and ochre mutations

Site	No. of occurrences	Nucleotide sequence 5′ 3′					
A5	0	A	T	*C*	A	G	A
A6	51	A	C	*C**	A	G	G
A9	8	A	A	*C*	A	G	T
A15	37	A	C	*C**	A	G	G
A16	9	A	C	*C*	A	G	A
A19	11	A	C	*C*	A	G	C
A21	8	G	C	*T*	*G*	G	C
A23	8	T	T	*C*	A	G	C
A24	10	A	C	*T*	*G*	G	A
A26	6	A	T	*C*	A	G	A
A31	1	A	A	*C*	A	G	G
A33	5	C	T	*C*	A	G	G
A34	12	G	C	*C**	A	G	G
A35	1	A	T	*C*	A	G	C
O9	2	A	A	*C*	A	A	C
O10	7	C	A	*C*	A	A	C
O11	2	C	G	*C*	A	A	A
O13	1	A	T	*C*	A	A	C
O17	3	C	G	*C*	A	A	C
O21	4	A	G	*C*	A	A	A
O24	0	C	G	*C*	A	A	T
O27	0	T	T	*C*	A	A	C
O28	2	A	A	*C*	A	A	A
O29	5	T	G	*C*	A	A	A
O34	2	G	G	*C*	A	A	A
O35	4	T	G	*C*	A	A	C

The nucleotide sequence[5] surrounding each base (italic print) that generates a nonsense codon by a transition is shown. The anti-sense strand is depicted. Asterisks (*) indicate 5-methylcytosine. The number of occurrences refer to the amber and ochre mutations found spontaneously in a collection of 222 amber *I*⁻ and 76 ochre *I*⁻ mutations. The characterisation of these mutations has been described previously[2,3,12]. Only the transition sites are shown here. Table 2 lists the transversions found among the amber and ochre mutations from this collection.

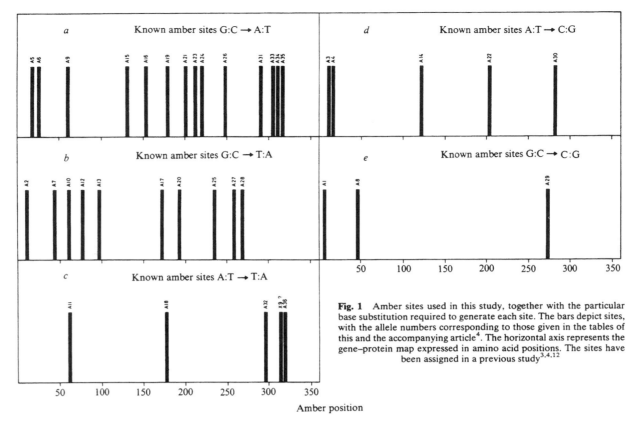

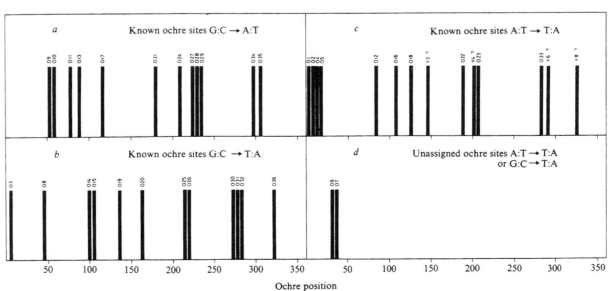

Fig. 1 Amber sites used in this study, together with the particular base substitution required to generate each site. The bars depict sites, with the allele numbers corresponding to those given in the tables of this and the accompanying article[4]. The horizontal axis represents the gene–protein map expressed in amino acid positions. The sites have been assigned in a previous study[3,4,12]

determine the frequency of mutations at each site, we picked independent occurrences of *I* mutations, without any selection bias, and assigned them to one of the known sites. Figure 3 shows the relative frequencies of spontaneous amber and ochre mutations. Although amber and ochre mutations arise at similar frequencies, more amber mutations (222) were analysed than ochre sites (76), so we have magnified the ochre scale by a factor of three to allow a direct comparison with the amber bar heights. The amber spectrum is dominated by two

hotspots, both involving a $G:C \rightarrow A:T$ transition. Out of approximately 70 single base substitutions that generate nonsense codons, 26 of which involve the $G:C \rightarrow A:T$ transition, mutations at these two sites are favoured by nearly a 10:1 ratio (over the average frequencies at the remaining transition sites).

Table 1 lists the sequences surrounding each $G:C \rightarrow A:T$ transition site. Both hotspots occur at the second C (cytosine) of a CCAGG sequence. One other CCAGG sequence appears

Fig. 2 Ochre sites resulting from different base substitutions. (See legend to Fig. 1).

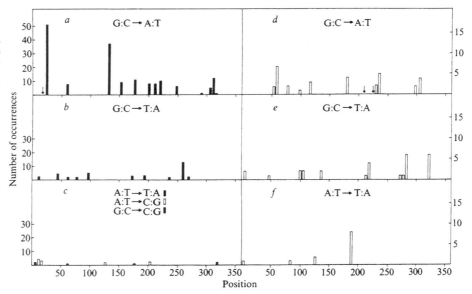

Fig. 3 The distribution of 222 spontaneous amber mutations (*a*, *b*, *c*) and 76 spontaneous ochre mutations (*d*, *e*, *f*). The mutations are of independent origin and have been characterised previously[2,3,12]. Although the ochre scale has been magnified to enable a direct comparison of amber and ochre mutations, hotspots can be detected with a greater degree of assurance by considering the amber and ochre distributions as separate groups. The arrows in *a* and *d* indicate transition sites not found in this collection. (Only half of the spontaneous collection was assayed for the missing site, *A*5.) Transition sites not represented in this collection can be recognised by consulting Figs 1 and 2.

among the remaining 24 transition sites, but mutations here are not as frequent. Because *E. coli* K12 carries the chromosomal *mec* gene[8], this sequence, the normal cutting site for the RII restriction endonuclease[9], should be methylated at the second C from the 5'-end of each strand, generating 5-methylcytosine (C-5meC-A- G -G-). This suggests that 5-methylcytosine
(G- G -T-5meC-C-) may be the cause of the spontaneous hotspots. The presence of 5-methylcytosine at these positions in the *I* gene DNA was verified directly by chemical DNA sequencing[7], as this substituted residue leaves a characteristic gap in the sequence, with a G (guanine) residue appearing at the corresponding position on the complimentary strand.

Creation of a new CCAGG sequence

To test whether the appearance of hotspots at two of the methylated bases was fortuitous, we introduced a new CCAGG sequence into the gene. The amber mutation *A*28 is derived from a codon normally specifying serine 269 (refs 4, 5) which lies in the sequence CTCGG, changed to CTAGG in *A*28. Reversion to a sense codon by a transition would generate either CCAGG or CTGGG, specifying glutamine or tryptophan, respectively. Tryptophan at this site should not produce an active repressor, as leucine and tyrosine, introduced in place of serine by nonsense suppressors produce i⁻ proteins[4]; while the replacement of serine by glutamine results in a temperature sensitive repressor[4]. We used 2-AP to induce i⁺ revertants. As all these revertants displayed temperature sensitive repression, they most probably represented the conversion of the amber UAG triplet to a CAG codon. We proved the construction by crossing the mutation onto a plasmid and sequencing the relevant region. We found a new 5-methylcytosine in the CCAGG sequence that replaced the original CTCGG. Figure 4 summarises the steps involved in this construction.

Amber mutations arising from the new CCAGG sequence

We collected spontaneous *I*⁻ amber mutations using an episome carrying the new CCAGG sequence at position 269, in our standard strain background[3]. Figure 5 presents the new distribution of amber mutations. In addition to the two original hotspots, a third hotspot appears at the new CCAGG sequence.

Table 2 Amber mutations detected in *E. coli* B and K12

Base substitution	Site	*E. coli* B	*E. coli* K12 a	b	c
G:C → A:T	A5	3	0	0	0
	A6	4	51	13	64
	A9	3	8	2	10
	A15	3	37	15	52
	A16	1	9	0	9
	A19	5	11	0	11
	A21	6	8	0	8
	A23	0	8	0	8
	A24	4	10	3	13
	A26	0	6	0	6
	A31	1	1	1	2
	A33	2	5	0	5
	A34	3	12	5	17
	A35	3	1	0	1
	A28*	—	—	11	—
G:C → T:A	A2	0	2	0	2
	A7	2	4	0	4
	A10	0	2	0	2
	A12	0	2	0	2
	A13	2	4	0	4
	A17	2	3	0	3
	A20	1	3	2	5
	A25	0	2	0	2
	A27	5	13	0	13
	A28	2	2	—	—
A:T → T:A	A11	0	1	0	1
	A18	4	1	0	1
	A32	0	0	0	0
	X9	0	0	0	0
	A36	3	2	0	2
A:T → C:G	A3	0	4	0	4
	A4	0	3	0	3
	A14	1	2	0	2
	A22	0	2	0	2
	A30	0	0	1	1
G:C → C:G	A1	0	2	0	2
	A8	1	0	0	0
	A29	2	0	0	0

The amber mutations found spontaneously in *E. coli* B are compared with those found in *E. coli* K12. *a*, The collection in K12 using the wild-type episome from strain GM1 (ref. 12); *b*, that for the episome carrying the additional CCAGG sequence; *c*, combined distribution showing both of these collections together (except for site *A*28, which is derived by a transition in *b* but by a transversion in *a*).

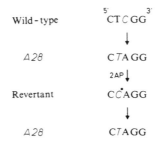

Fig. 4 The nucleotide sequence surrounding the codon at position 269. The amber mutation *A28* is generated by a C→A transversion from this sequence[3,4]. The resulting CTAGG sequence can be converted by 2-AP to a CCAGG sequence, which is methylated at the second cytosine (marked by asterisk; see text). This restores wild-type activity at 37 °C and allows the generation of *A28* by a C→T transition at the 5-methylcytosine.

Strains lacking methylation activity

E. coli B strains do not methylate the CCAGG sequence[10]. We crossed the *lacproB* deletion, XIII, into an *E. coli* B derivative in such a manner as to avoid transferring the region of the chromosome carrying the *mec* locus. We checked this by transforming this strain with a plasmid carrying the wild-type *I* gene[11] and sequencing one of the CCAGG sites in the *I* gene. It had unmethylated cytosines. After introducing the *lacpro* episome from strain GM1 (ref. 12) into this *E. coli* B strain, we derived and analysed amber mutations on the episome. Table 2 compares these results with those from the K12 strain. The two hotspots disappear when the *E. coli* B derivative is used. (This is particularly evident when the K12 results obtained with the altered sequence at position 269 are considered, see column *b*, since a similar sample size was analysed). Thus, the spontaneous hotspots are the result of methylation of cytosine at the 5 position.

2-Aminopurine induced mutations

The base analogue 2-AP specifically induces transitions at frequencies more than 100-fold above the spontaneous background[12–14]. Figure 6 shows the distribution of over 1,000 ochre and amber mutations induced by 2-AP (Fig. 6*a* and *b*, respectively), all arising by the G:C→A:T transition. There are significant hotspots at both amber and ochre sites. The three major amber hotspots are at the CCAGG sequences discussed above, and when we rederived the 2-AP spectrum

Fig. 5 The distribution of 50 spontaneous amber mutations derived from a G:C→A:T transition. This collection was obtained using a derivative carrying an F'*lacpro* episome with an additional CCAGG sequence in the *lacI* gene (see text). The asterisk marks the position of amber mutations derived from this sequence. In addition to the mutations shown above, three amber mutations generated by transversions were also found (see Table 2).

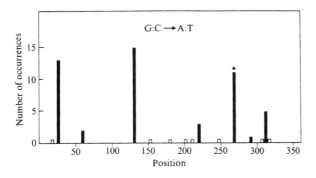

using the episome carrying the additional CCAGG sequence at 269, a fourth hotspot appeared at the new position (Fig. 6*c*). Therefore, 2-AP mutagenesis also favours the methylation CCAGG sequence. However, in the *E. coli* B derivative which lacks the *mec* system that methylates the CCAGG stretches, the 2-AP amber hotspots are reduced but not eliminated. In *E. coli.* K12 the two major hotspots are about 27 times more frequent than the average of the other sites; in *E. coli* B this ratio falls by a factor of 4 to 6.7:1. Both the methylation and the sequence seem to affect 2-AP mutability.

None of the ochre sites involves wild-type codons which are part of a methylation sequence, and yet there is still a wide

Table 3 Nucleotide sequence surrounding each mutational site

Site	Sequence (5'–3')								2-AP	EMS	NG	UV	NQO
A6	G	A	A	C	*C	A	G	G	C	270	14	20	15	61
	C	T	T	G	G	T	C	C	G					
A15	T	G	A	C	*C	A	G	G	A	207	7	4	7	54
	A	C	T	G	G	T	C	C	T					
A34	G	G	G	C	*C	A	G	G	C	66	15	12	1	55
	C	C	C	G	G	T	C	C	G					
A9	C	A	A	A	*C	A	G	T	C	8	30	34	1	61
	G	T	T	T	G	T	C	A	G					
A31	C	A	A	A	C	A	G	G	A	9	19	18	2	20
	G	T	T	T	G	T	C	C	T					
A16	T	G	A	C	C	A	G	A	C	11	14	21	20	29
	A	C	T	G	G	T	C	T	G					
A19	T	C	A	C	C	A	G	C	A	23	30	37	16	13
	A	G	T	G	G	T	C	G	T					
A21	A	T	G	C	C	A	G	C	C	15	12	22	5	16
	T	A	C	G	G	T	C	G	G					
A24	A	C	T	C	C	A	G	T	C	13	39	34	9	51
	T	G	A	G	G	T	C	A	G					
A5	T	T	A	T	C	A	G	A	C	3	17	13	19	23
	A	A	T	A	G	T	C	T	G					
A23	A	A	T	T	C	A	G	C	C	2	30	32	80	24
	T	T	A	A	G	T	C	G	G					
A26	C	G	C	T	C	A	G	A	T	5	20	12	2	36
	G	C	G	A	G	T	C	T	A					
A33	C	T	C	T	C	A	G	G	G	7	38	24	36	33
	G	A	G	A	G	T	C	C	C					
A35	C	A	A	T	C	A	G	C	T	1	27	9	6	25
	G	T	T	A	G	T	C	G	A					
O11	G	T	C	G	*C	A	A	A	T	41	56	28	2	11
	C	A	G	C	G	T	T	T	A					
O17	C	G	C	G	*C	A	C	A	G	44	27	26	3	28
	G	C	G	C	G	T	T	G	C					
O21	C	C	A	G	*C	A	A	A	T	26	57	15	2	43
	G	G	T	C	G	T	T	T	A					
O29	C	A	T	G	*C	A	A	A	T	77	36	14	4	83
	G	T	A	C	G	T	T	T	A					
O34	G	G	G	G	*C	A	A	A	C	112	46	19	2	47
	C	C	C	C	G	T	T	T	G					
O35	G	C	T	G	*C	A	A	C	T	81	49	22	3	48
	C	G	A	C	G	T	T	G	A					
O9	G	G	C	A	C	A	A	C	A	3	23	18	3	15
	C	C	G	T	G	T	T	G	T					
O10	A	C	A	A	*C	A	A	C	T	11	17	10	4	31
	T	G	T	T	G	T	T	G	A					
O28	T	C	A	C	A	A	A	A	A	11	13	12	4	24
	A	G	T	T	*G	T	T	T	G					
O13	C	A	A	T	C	A	A	A	T	5	13	9	6	37
	G	C	T	A	G	T	T	G	A					
O24	C	A	A	T	*C	A	A	A	T	2	16	16	61	22
	G	T	T	A	G	T	T	T	A					
O27	T	T	T	T	C	A	A	C	A	5	15	20	86	10
	A	A	A	A	G	T	T	G	T					

variation in the frequency of the $G:C \to A:T$ transition at these points. Table 3 shows the DNA sequence surrounding each mutational site. As described below, the C in a GCA sequence is more highly mutable with 2-AP.

Effect of neighbouring nucleotide sequence on mutagen-induced mutation rates

In Table 3 we present an analysis of the nucleotide sequence surrounding each mutational site which generates an amber (UAG) or ochre (UAA) codon by a $G:C \to A:T$ transition. The base involved in the transition is italicised. The columns give the relative frequencies of occurrence of each amber or ochre site in a collection of mutagen induced I^- mutations. One amber and one ochre mutation for each mutagenised culture was analysed[1,2], and therefore each mutation is of independent origin. A correction factor is necessary if amber and ochre mutations are to be considered together, as these two types of mutation did not always arise at identical frequencies, and different sample sizes were analysed. To compare 2-AP-induced ochres with the 2-AP-induced amber mutations, the ochre values should be multiplied by 0.9. For 4-nitroquinoline-1-oxide (NQO), ultraviolet light, ethyl methanesulphonate (EMS) and N'-methyl-N'-nitro-N-nitroso-guanidine (NG) ochres the respective factors are 0.6, 0.7, 2.3 and 1.9.

Even without placing too much emphasis on normalising amber and ochre frequencies, some patterns seem to emerge from these data. 2-aminopurine clearly prefers methylated cytosines for the $G:C \to A:T$ transition (see ref. 4). Otherwise,

Fig. 6 Distributions of 418 ochre (*a*) and 640 amber mutations (*b*) induced by 2-AP. These mutations were characterised in a previous study[12]. Fifty-two amber mutations were derived by 2-AP using the episome carrying an additional CCAGG sequence surrounding position 269 (see text). *c*, The distribution of these mutations. The asterisk (*) marks the position of site *A*28 which is derived by a $C \to T$ transition at the new CCAGG sequence. 2-AP-induced amber mutations derived in *E. coli* B are represented in *d*. The open bars in *c* and *d* refer to amber sites derived by $C \to T$ transitions which are not represented in these particular collections.

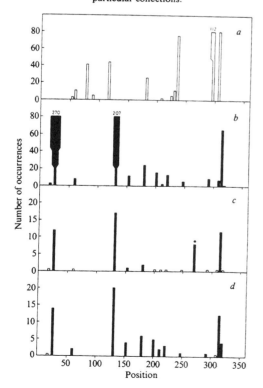

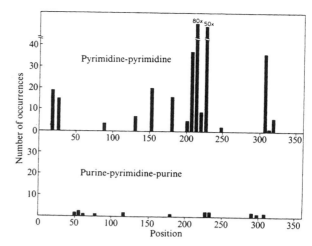

Fig. 7 Correlation of UV-induced mutations with the surrounding nucleotide sequence (see text).

the different frequencies of occurrence do follow the nature of the base on the 5' side of the cytosine residue, the tendency being $G > C > A > T$.

Figure 7 shows a strong correlation between being well induced by ultraviolet and being part of a pyrimidine–pyrimidine sequence (on one strand or the other), and a strong correlation for being poorly induced and not being part of such a sequence. All of the amber sites are in the pyrimidine–pyrimidine category except for *A*9 and *A*31, whereas only the ochre sites *O*13, *O*24, and *O*27 are part of a pyrimidine–pyrimidine sequence.

The EMS, NG and NQO data do not seem to allow any general rules to be deduced at this stage.

Hotspots involve methylated cytosines

By using a set of characterised nonsense mutations and the full nucleotide sequence of the *lacI* gene, we have demonstrated that base substitution hotspots occur at 5-methylcytosines. Two of the three methylated cytosines, which occur among 26 cytosines involved in the creation of amber and ochre codons, generate transitions at a 10-fold higher rate than the average. A new methylated cytosine introduced by creating an additional CCAGG sequence also results in a hotspot for the $G:C \to AT$ transition. The elimination of methylation at these sites, demonstrated in an *E. coli* B derivative lacking the methylating enzyme, results in the disappearance of the transition hotspots.

What mechanism could account for these results? 5-methylcytosine does not cause any direct mispairing[15], nor do *in vitro* measurements indicate a significant difference between cytosine and 5-methylcytosine in the tautomeric equilibria[16]. An attractive explanation is the deamination of cytosine to uracil, which occurs spontaneously at a high rate *in vitro* and presumably *in vivo*[17]. Uracil residues in DNA are rapidly excised by the enzyme uracil-DNA glycosidase[18]. Any uracil residues which are not removed would eventually result in $G:C \to A:T$ transitions, unless otherwise repaired. (Drake and coworkers have shown that spontaneous transition mutations occur in T4 DNA on extended storage in the cold, as a result of deamination of cytosine[17]. T4 DNA contains glucosylated 5-hydroxymethylcytosine instead of unsubstituted cytosine; after deamination, the resulting 5-hydroxymethyluracil residues are not subject to the action of uracil-DNA glycosidase, probably accounting for the high rate of transition mutations.) Although most spontaneous deaminations of cytosine to uracil would be efficiently repaired by uracil-DNA glycosidase, those occurring at 5-methylcytosine residues would yield thymine (5-methyluracil), which will not be released from DNA by this enzyme.

The G:T base pair would still be subject to various types of mismatch repair, as would any G:U base pairs which escape the action of the glycosidase. The greatly increased number of unexcised G:T base pairs which originated from G:5meC would then appear as a hotspot relative to other transition sites. This argues that deamination is a major cause of spontaneous transitions in *E. coli*, at least in the direction G:C → A:T. This model predicts that these hotspots should disappear in mutant strains lacking uracil-DNA glycosidase, since deaminations at all cytosines should then be immune to this excision repair. Such mutants, termed Ung⁻, have been described[20]. Hotspots among nitrous acid-induced amber mutations should also occur at 5-methylcytosines, since this mutagen preferentially stimulates deamination of cytosine[15].

Thus T is used in place of U in DNA to lower the mutation rate, the role of the methyl group being to distinguish one natural base from the deamination product of the other[18]. Possibly the structures of A and G are also selected to allow enzymatic repair of deamination.

The base analogue 2-AP shows a remarkable selectivity for certain sites. All three CCAGG sequences are hotspots for amber mutations, and a fourth CCAGG sequence introduced into the gene results in the appearance of a new hotspot. However, the elimination of methylation at these sites does not entirely remove the hotspots, although it does reduce their relative intensity by a factor of 4. One possibility is that a residual methylation exists in these strains, too low to detect by our methods. Alternatively, a different enzyme in the cell could be operating on these sites, or some subtle aspect of the base sequence may be responsible for the high mutability in the presence of 2-AP. The same situation is seen for the 2-AP-induced ochre mutations, where certain unmethylated sequences clearly result in significant hotspots. The elucidation of the mechanism that produces this phenomenon requires additional experiments. Other mutagens, such as ultraviolet light, NQO, NG, and EMS also result in considerable differences in mutation rate from site to site. The hotspots favoured by these mutagens, particularly ultraviolet light, are different from those described above. At least for 2-AP some rules are evident. Higher mutation rates occur when G is the adjacent base, in accordance with both predictions and *in vitro* findings of M. Bessman and coworkers (personal communication).

We thank S. Brenner, S. Hattman, W. Arber, J. D. Watson, M. Radman, T. Lindahl and A. Maxam for helpful discussions, and M. Hofer for technical assistance. This work was supported by a grant from the Swiss National Fund (3.179.77) to J.H.M. and an NIGMS grant to W.G. W.G. is an American Cancer Society Professor of Molecular Biology.

Note added in proof: Experiments with this system (B. K. Duncan and J. H. Miller, unpublished) show that G:C → A:T transitions occur at a high rate in an Ung⁻ strain, and that the 5-methylcytosine residues are no longer hotspots relative to the other cytosines.

Received 27 February; accepted 26 June, 1978.

1. Benzer, S. *Proc. natn. Acad. Sci. U.S.A.* **47**, 403–416 (1961).
2. Farabaugh, P. J., Schmeissner, U., Hofer, M. & Miller, J. H. *J. molec. Biol.* (in the press).
3. Coulondre, C. & Miller, J. H. *J. molec. Biol.* **117**, 577–606 (1977).
4. Coulondre, C. & Miller, J. H. *J. molec. Biol.* **117**, 525–575 (1977).
5. Miller, J. H., Coulondre, C. & Farabaugh, P. J. *Nature* **274**, 770–775 (1978).
6. Steege, D. A. *Proc. natn. Acad. Sci. U.S.A.* **74**, 4163–4167 (1977).
7. Farabaugh, P. J. *Nature* **274**, 765–769 (1978).
8. Gold, M., Gefter, R., Hausmann, R. & Hurwitz, J. in *Macromolecular Metabolism* 5–28 (Little Brown & Co., Boston, 1966).
9. Boyer, H. W., Chow, L. T., Dugaiczyk, A., Hedgpeth, J. & Goodman, H. M. *Nature new biol.* **244**, 40–48 (1973).
10. Lederberg, S. *J. molec. Biol.* **17**, 293–297 (1966).
11. Calos, M. *Nature* **274**, 762–765 (1978).
12. Miller, J. H., Ganem, D., Lu, P. & Schmitz, A. *J. molec. Biol.* **109**, 245–302 (1977).
13. Yanofsky, C., Ito, J. & Horn, V. *Cold Spring Harb. Symp. quant. Biol.* **31**, 151–162 (1966).
14. Osborn, M., Person, S., Phillips, S. & Funk, F. *J. molec. Biol.* **26**, 437–447 (1967).
15. Drake, J. W. & Baltz, R. H. *A. Rev. Biochem.* **45**, 11–37 (1976).
16. Jencks, W. P. & Regenstein, J. *CRC Handbook of Biochemistry* 5187–5226 (1976).
17. Shapiro, R. & Klein, R. S. *Biochemistry* **5**, 2358–2362 (1966).
18. Lindahl, T., Ljungquist, S., Siegert, W., Nyberg, B. & Sperens, B. *J. biol. Chem.* **252**, 3286–3294 (1977).
19. Baltz, R. H., Bingham, P. M. & Drake, J. W. *Proc. natn. Acad. Sci. U.S.A.* **73**, 1269–1273 (1976).
20. Duncan, B. K., Rockstroh, P. A. & Warner, H. R. *Fedn Proc.* **35**, 1493 (1977).

A set of *lacZ* mutations in *Escherichia coli* that allow rapid detection of each of the six base substitutions

CLAIRE G. CUPPLES* AND JEFFREY H. MILLER

Molecular Biology Institute and Department of Biology, University of California, 405 Hilgard Avenue, Los Angeles, CA 90024

Communicated by Bruce N. Ames, May 4, 1989 (received for review February 1989)

ABSTRACT We describe the construction of six strains of *Escherichia coli* with different mutations at the same coding position in the *lacZ* gene, which specifies the active site glutamic acid residue at position 461 in β-galactosidase. Each strain is Lac$^-$ and reverts to Lac$^+$ only by restoring the glutamic acid codon. The strains have been designed so that each reverts via one of the six base substitutions. The set of strains allows detection of each transition and transversion simply by monitoring the Lac$^-$ to Lac$^+$ frequency, as demonstrated here with characterized mutagens and mutator alleles. These strains are useful for rapidly determining the mutagenic specificity of mutagens at a single site, for detecting low levels of stimulation of certain base substitutions, for monitoring specific base changes in response to various experimental conditions or strain backgrounds, and for isolating new mutator strains.

One of the first steps toward elucidating mutagenic pathways is to determine the specificity of mutations generated spontaneously or by treatment with mutagens. In many cases, identifying the type of mutations produced yields important information on the nature of the premutagenic lesion, as well as the role of cellular systems in processing damaged DNA (reviewed in ref. 1). Toward this end, systems have been developed that allow the rapid determination of mutagenic specificity by genetic methods. For instance, reversion of *trpA* alleles was utilized by Yanofsky and coworkers (2) to examine mutagenic specificity in *Escherichia coli*. In yeast, Sherman and coworkers (3, 4) utilized the reversion of characterized mutations in the isocytochrome *c* system to deduce the base substitution specificity of different mutagens. Ames and colleagues (5, 6) monitored the reversion of specific mutations in the *his* operon of *Salmonella typhimurium* to allow the rapid screening of base substitution and frameshift activity of a large number of mutagens. This work was important because it established a strong correlation between carcinogens and mutagens (6). Levin and Ames (7) have modified this system to allow the determination of specific base substitutions, utilizing the reversion of nonsense codons, followed by analysis of the revertants, a principle first used by Person and coworkers (8). The *lacI* system (9, 10) provides a more detailed look at mutagenic specificity by examining the forward spectrum of nonsense mutations produced in the *lacI* gene of *E. coli*. Mutations at >80 sites can be monitored. In addition to these genetic methods, the direct DNA sequence determination (11–16) and colony hybridization with specific probes (17) have also been used for the determination of the nature of spontaneous and induced mutations.

All of the above systems require further analysis to determine the ability of a mutagen to produce each of the six possible base substitutions. A system that allows the determination of each base substitution, simply by measuring the number of revertant colonies that appear on a plate, would

greatly simplify the study of mutagenesis. Foster and coworkers (18) have described a strain that allows the unique determination of the G·C → T·A transversion by measuring reversion at a specific site in the plasmid-encoded *bla* gene in *E. coli*. We report here the design of six strains with different mutations at the same coding position in the *lacZ* gene, which detect, individually, all six types of base substitution mutations.

The *E. coli lacZ* gene encodes the enzyme β-galactosidase (19). Cells producing active enzyme can use lactose as a carbon source. One amino acid presumed to be in the active site (20), Glu-461, has been found to be essential for enzyme activity (21). We have shown that substitution of any other amino acid at this position lowers enzyme activity sufficiently to prevent growth on lactose minimal medium (21). We have constructed six strains that have point mutations in the Glu-461 codon and are therefore Lac$^-$. Only one specific base substitution will restore the glutamic acid codon in each strain and restore the Lac$^+$ phenotype. The set of strains provides a method of rapidly characterizing the mutagenic specificity of mutagens at a single site. The *lacZ* reversion system is capable of detecting extremely low rates of each of the base substitutions. In this paper, we outline the construction of the system and demonstrate its use on a set of known mutagens and mutator strains.

MATERIALS AND METHODS

Bacterial Strains. Strains CC101–CC106 (see also ref. 22) are derivatives of the strain P90C [*ara*Δ(*lac proB*)$_{XIII}$] carrying an F' *lacI$^-$ Z$^-$ proB$^+$* episome. Each strain carries a different *lacZ$^-$* mutation affecting residue 461 in β-galactosidase. The mutation carried in each strain is depicted in Fig. 1. The *mutY* strain is a *rpsL* (*strA*), *mutY* derivative of P90C, and the *mutT* strain (supplied by E. Eisenstadt, Harvard School of Public Health) is a *leu::*Tn*10, mutT* derivative of P90C. K. B. Low (Yale University Medical School) supplied the *mutH* strain (KL862: *his, leu, rpsL*). The *lac proB* deletion *XIII* was introduced into each of these last two strains by crossing with strain CSH63 (23), resulting in a Val^r Leu$^+$ Pro$^-$ derivative of each strain. The episomes from CC101–CC106 were introduced into the (*lac pro*) derivatives of each of the above-mentioned strains.

The methods used to introduce mutations into *lacZ*, and the procedures for transferring the mutant genes to the F' *lac proB* episome are described elsewhere (21).

Mutagenesis. Mutagenesis with 2-aminopurine (2AP), *N*-methyl-*N'*-nitro-*N*-nitrosoguanidine (MNNG), ethyl methanesulfonate (EMS), and UV is essentially as described by Coulondre and Miller (24), and ICR-191 mutagenesis was described by Calos and Miller (12). After mutagenesis, cul-

---

The publication costs of this article were defrayed in part by page charge payment. This article must therefore be hereby marked "*advertisement*" in accordance with 18 U.S.C. §1734 solely to indicate this fact.

Abbreviations: MNNG, *N*-methyl-*N'*-nitro-*N*-nitrosoguanidine; EMS, ethyl methanesulfonate; 2AP, 2-aminopurine; 5AZ, 5-azacytidine.
*Present address: Department of Biology, Concordia University, 1455 de Maisonneuve Boulevard West, Montreal, PQ H3G 1M8, Canada.

β-galactosidase

```
          -GGG AAT-GAG-TCA GGC
                  -GLU-
                  -461-

CCI0I   A·T -- C·G-TAG-AMBER-- GLU
                    ↓
                    G

CCI02   G·C -- A·T-GGG- GLY -- GLU
                       ↓
                       A

CCI03   G·C -- C·G-CAG- GLN -- GLU
                      ↓
                      G

CCI04   G·C -- T·A-GCG- ALA -- GLU
                      ↓
                      A

CCI05   A·T -- T·A-GTG- VAL -- GLU
                      ↓
                      A

CCI06   A·T -- G·C-AAG- LYS -- GLU
                     ↓
                     G
```

FIG. 1. Altered codon at position 461 in *lacZ*. Coding position 461 in *lacZ* has been altered in each of six different strains. The base substitution required to restore the codon to GAG is shown here, together with the amino acid change that results. Only glutamic acid at position 461 in β-galactosidase restores the wild-type phenotype.

tures were plated to determine survival and then grown in LB to allow expression and plated for Lac⁺ revertants and also for rifampicin-resistant (Rif^r) mutants to monitor the mutagenesis. Table 1 gives representative survival and Rif^r mutant data, which was similar in all strains, CC101–CC106. Table 2 shows the Lac⁺ revertant frequencies. Briefly, the protocols are as follows:

2AP. The strain to be treated was diluted so that 100–1000 cells were inoculated into separate tubes containing the desired concentration of 2AP in LB. These were grown for 20 hr at 37°C and plated for mutants and viable cells. The best results were obtained with 2AP at 700 μg/ml.

EMS. A fresh overnight culture was subcultured and grown until it reached a density of $2–3 \times 10^8$ cells per ml. The cells were chilled on ice, spun down, washed twice in A buffer, and then resuspended in half the original volume of A buffer (23). EMS was added in the cold by pipeting 0.07 ml of EMS into 5 ml of resuspended cells. The test tubes were closed with masking tape (or when glass screw-capped tubes were used, the tops were fastened tightly), mixed in a Vortex, and rotated on a roller drum at 30 rpm for different times at 37°C. After mutagenesis, the cells were spun down, washed twice in A buffer, and then resuspended in the same volume of A buffer and titered for viable cells. Samples (0.5 ml) were added to 10 ml of broth and the cultures were grown overnight and plated for mutants and viable cells.

MNNG. An overnight culture was subcultured and grown to a density of $2–3 \times 10^8$ cells per ml. The cells were spun down, washed twice in 0.1 M sodium citrate buffer (pH 5.5), and resuspended in the original volume of citrate buffer. The cells were chilled on ice for 10 min and then placed in a 37°C water bath; 0.5 ml of a 1 mg/ml solution of MNNG in distilled water was added to 4.5 ml of resuspended cells. (The stock solution can be prepared by dissolving 10 mg of MNNG per ml in acetone and then diluting 1:10 in distilled water.) The final concentration of MNNG was therefore 100 μg/ml. The cells were then spun down, after different times of exposure, washed twice in 0.1 M potassium phosphate buffer (pH 7.0), and resuspended in the original volume of phosphate buffer. The cultures were plated for viable cells at this point. Different overnight cultures were generated by adding 5 ml of

Table 1. Survival and Rif^r mutant frequency

Mutagen	Condition	% survival	Rif^r revertants per 10^8 cells
EMS	0 min	100	15
	15 min	71	16,100
	30 min	56	36,900
	45 min	44	85,200
	60 min	36	78,700
MNNG	0 min	100	61
	5 min	49	64,400
	10 min	45	91,800
	15 min	28	94,700
	30 min	5.2	106,000
UV	0 sec	100	9
	30 sec	14	2,150
	45 sec	2	3,100
	60 sec	0.75	5,140
	75 sec	0.025	1,960
5AZ	0 μg/ml	—	41
	1 μg/ml	—	105
	5 μg/ml	—	370
	10 μg/ml	—	1,223
	50 μg/ml	—	1,369
	70 μg/ml	—	2,340
	100 μg/ml	—	3,960
2AP	0 μg/ml	—	57
	10 μg/ml	—	72
	50 μg/ml	—	194
	100 μg/ml	—	361
	500 μg/ml	—	1,037
	700 μg/ml	—	1,380
	1000 μg/ml	—	2,033
mutT		—	350
mutY		—	150
mutH		—	500

Strains CC101–CC106 behaved identically in response to mutagens with respect to survival and the frequency of Rif^r mutants after treatment. Representative values are shown here. See Table 2 and *Materials and Methods* for further details.

washed suspension to 10 ml of broth. These were grown overnight at 37°C and plated for mutants and viable cells.

UV light. A fresh overnight culture was subcultured and grown to a density of 2×10^8 cells per ml. These were centrifuged and resuspended in half the original volume of 0.1 M MgSO₄ and placed on ice for 10 min. UV irradiation was carried out for different times with a Westinghouse Sterilamp fixture (type SB-30) using a glass Petri dish as a container set 86 cm from the lamp. Directly after irradiation, 0.5-ml samples were inoculated into separate 10-ml broth tubes and grown overnight, and samples were plated directly for survivors.

5-Azacytidine (5AZ). 5AZ was prepared directly before use by dissolving it in distilled water to a concentration of 1 mg/ml, filter-sterilizing, and then adding to bacterial medium at the appropriate concentration (see Table 2). As with 2AP treatment, 100–1000 cells were inoculated into LB + 5AZ and grown for ≈24 hr, until the density was between 10^8 and 10^9 cells per ml. Outgrowth cultures for each mutagenic treatment were plated on lactose minimal medium, and the number of colonies was counted after 36 and 48 hr and compared with the viable titer on glucose minimal medium or LB medium. Each value represents the average of several determinations.

Recovery and Sequencing of Lac⁺ Revertants. The region around coding position 461 of the *lacZ* gene from Lac⁺ revertants was transferred to an F1 bacteriophage by recombination with the *lacZ* region of the phage as a prelude for sequencing. Cells containing the mutant episome were grown

Table 2. Reversion of Lac⁻ strains in response to different mutagens

Mutagen	Condition	Strain (reversion event)					
		CC101 (A·T → C·G)	CC102 (G·C → A·T)	CC103 (G·C → C·G)	CC104 (G·C → T·A)	CC105 (A·T → T·A)	CC106 (A·T → G·C)
EMS	0 min	1.3	1.2	0.4	4.0	5.4	0.5
	15 min	0.8	242	—	13	3.9	4.3
	30 min	8.7	2,400	0.9	13	—	16
	45 min	29	5,200	2.3	25	19	34
	60 min	24	7,000	2.2	52	14	39
MNNG	0 min	3.8	3.0	<0.5	8.7	1.2	<0.5
	5 min	16	15,400	1.1	7.5	8.4	48
	10 min	38	23,000	5.7	—	20	87
	15 min	21	25,000	14	5.5	47	230
	30 min	130	—	23	5.1	28	130
UV	0 sec	<0.5	0.8	<0.5	2.4	1.0	<0.5
	30 sec	<0.5	15	1.7	14	11	8.3
	45 sec	3.2	46	0.8	31	13	150
	60 sec	20	67	1.3	12	33	240
	75 sec	8.7	47	1.3	7	—	130
5AZ	0 µg/ml	—	—	0	1	—	—
	1 µg/ml	—	—	20	1	—	—
	5 µg/ml	—	—	107	9	—	—
	10 µg/ml	—	—	313	15	—	—
	50 µg/ml	<0.5	<0.5	524	25	4	2
	70 µg/ml	—	—	731	40	—	—
	100 µg/ml	—	—	972	25	—	—
2AP	0 µg/ml	—	27	—	—	—	—
	10 µg/ml	—	31	—	—	—	—
	50 µg/ml	—	67	—	—	—	—
	100 µg/ml	—	88	—	—	—	—
	500 µg/ml	—	415	—	—	—	—
	700 µg/ml	<0.5	457	2	15	2	160
	1000 µg/ml	—	320	—	—	—	—
mutT		500	5	<0.5	<0.5	<0.5	<0.5
mutY		<0.5	4	<0.5	160	<0.5	<0.5
mutH		0	320	0	11	3	34

After EMS, UV, and MNNG (100 µg/mg) mutagenesis, cells were grown overnight in broth and titered on glucose minimal medium and lactose minimal medium, as described in *Materials and Methods*. Mutagenesis was monitored for survival and for the generation of Rif^r mutants (see Table 1). Results are expressed as Lac⁺ revertants per 10⁸ cells.

in rich medium to midlogarithmic phase. Cells (100 µl) were mixed with phage (100 µl), diluted to 10^{-6} in 1× minimal A salts. The phage is an F1 derivative that contains a *lacZ* gene with a missense mutation at the site encoding Glu-461 (21). Plaques from this phage are white on plates containing 5-bromo-4-chloro-3-indolyl β-D-galactoside (X-Gal). Phage and cells were incubated at 37°C for 10 min to allow attachment. LB (2 ml) was added, and the cultures were incubated overnight, with aeration, to allow recombination between the episomal and phage *lacZ* genes. The cells were pelleted, and the phage in the supernatant were used to infect JM801 [F⁺ *kan/ara*Δ(*lac proB*) *thi rpsL*]. Phage containing the *lacZ* gene from the episome produced bright blue plaques on plates containing X-Gal. Since the missense mutation, which specifies histidine at position 461, cannot revert to Lac⁺ by a single base change, blue plaques were the result of recombination with the episome that transferred the *lac*⁺ region to the phage and not the result of point mutations in the phage *lacZ* gene. Single-stranded DNA was recovered and sequenced by standard procedures.

RESULTS

Fig. 1 depicts the changes introduced at coding position 461 of *lacZ* in each of six strains. These changes were generated by oligonucleotide-directed, site-specific mutagenesis, as de-

scribed (21). Each strain can revert to Lac⁺ only by reverting the codon at position 461 to GAG, since this will specify the required glutamic acid at the corresponding position in β-galactosidase. Therefore, as shown in Fig. 1, each strain can revert to Lac⁺ via only one of the six base substitutions. This provides us with a valuable set of indicator strains for rapidly monitoring the base substitution specificity of different mutagens and mutators.

Reversion Tests. We have used strains CC101–CC106 to test a series of known mutators and mutagens in *E. coli*. Mutagenesis was monitored for resulting survival and for the generation of Rif^r mutants, as reported in Table 1 for a representative set of experiments. Rif^r mutants were induced at similar levels in each of the six strains CC101–CC106 with each mutagenic treatment. The Lac⁺ revertant frequencies are shown in Table 2.

Two transversion-specific mutators have been examined with this system. Strains that are *mutY* stimulate only the G·C → T·A transversion (22). As Table 1 shows, only CC104, which is diagnostic for the G·C → T·A transversion, reverts in response to the *mutY* background. The *mutT* allele specifically stimulates the A·T → G·C transversion (25). As anticipated, only CC101 responds to the *mutT* background (Table 1). Mutators lacking the mismatch repair system preferentially induce transitions among base substitutions (16, 26–28), and the *lacZ* system described here verifies this, since only CC102 and CC106 respond to a *mutH* strain (Table 1).

Mutagens known to favor the G·C → A·T transition, such as MNNG and EMS (10), stimulate preferentially CC102, the indicator of this transition. The *lacZ* system is sensitive enough to detect weaker stimulation of the other transition and all four transversions (Table 1) in most cases for these two mutagens, but the levels are 200 to 2000 times lower than for the G·C → A·T transition.

2AP, which has been shown to stimulate both A·T → G·C and G·C → A·T transitions (refs. 9 and 29 and references therein), reverts only CC102 and CC106, the strains that respond to these two events.

Levin and Ames (7) have reported that the base analog 5AZ specifically generates G·C → C·G transversions. CC103 should be the only strain that reverts strongly in response to 5AZ, a result borne out by the data shown in Table 2. We also detect a very low reversion over background of CC104 in response to 5AZ, indicating a slight stimulation of the G·C → T·A transversion. However, this is only 2–3% of the level of the G·C → C·G transversions.

We have also examined UV with the *lacZ* system. UV induces a variety of base substitutions. Although transitions are generally favored over transversions, both are induced, and a considerable variation is seen from site to site (see, for instance, ref. 13 and references therein). One determinant, at least for transitions, is the presence of adjacent pyrimidines on one strand or the other (13–15, 30). However, other aspects of the surrounding sequence clearly play a role in determining the UV mutability for any given site (13, 30), as first demonstrated for spontaneous and mutagen-induced mutations in the *rII* system of phage T4 by Benzer (31). Table 2 reveals that with the *lacZ* system, UV induces several transversions at low rates and the two transitions at higher rates. The A·T → G·C transition at the site present in strain CC106 is induced at approximately a 4-fold higher rate than the G·C → A·T transition in strain CC102.

Sequence Verification of Revertants. To verify the nature of some of the revertants to the Lac⁺ phenotype, the region surrounding coding position 461 in the *lacZ* gene was sequenced, as detailed in *Materials and Methods*. Table 3 depicts the results. In all cases examined, the revertants indeed resulted from mutations that restored the GAG codon at position 461.

DISCUSSION

We have described a system that will prove helpful for rapidly determining the base substitution specificity of different mutagens and mutators. The system is based on the use of a set of six isogenic strains that carry different mutations at coding position 461 in the *lacZ* gene. Only glutamic acid at the corresponding position in β-galactosidase results in the Lac⁺ phenotype. Therefore, each strain can only revert via a specific base substitution (Fig. 1). We have not encountered a single exception to this rule. Although one of the strains carries an amber mutation at position 461, only single step mutations that create an efficient glutamic acid inserting nonsense suppressor could result in the Lac⁺ phenotype by

a pathway other than restoring the GAG codon itself at position 461. Such nonsense suppressors have never been observed via a single base change.

The advantage of this system is that in each strain, the frequency of Lac⁺ cells is a direct measure of one specific base substitution. Determinations can be carried out without additional genetic or sequence analysis. Although the detailed spectrum of a mutagen ideally requires using numerous sites to monitor each specific event, reversion systems of the type described here can often outline the specificity of a mutagen. Reversion systems are valuable for screening a large number of mutagens (1–6) to pinpoint those that merit more detailed examination. Also, by being able to monitor a specific base substitution at one specific site, it is easy to test the effect of numerous variables on that mutational event. We have calibrated the system by testing a set of characterized mutagens and mutator strains. As revealed in Table 1 and *Results*, each of the six strains behaves as expected with each mutator and mutagen. This *lacZ* detection system is sensitive enough to detect relatively minor stimulation of base substitutions by different mutagens. For example, the low rate of transversions induced by MNNG and EMS is picked up by this system (Table 1). (The stimulation of transversions by these agents is, however, very small compared with the ≈1000-fold greater stimulation of G·C → A·T transitions.)

Of particular interest is the specificity of 5AZ, an analog of cytosine, which was first noted by Levin and Ames (7) to preferentially induce G·C → C·G transversions in *S. typhimurium*. As shown in Table 1, the same specificity is apparent in the *lacZ* system, with a low level of G·C → T·A transversions. At present, it is unclear how 5AZ induces such specific mutations among survivors.

In addition to its use in determining mutagenic specificity, the *lacZ* system described here is particularly useful in detecting new mutator strains. Mutators that induce specific transitions or transversions can be detected by using these strains as part of a papillation assay (22). Increased reversion from Lac⁻ to Lac⁺ is detected by increased incidence of blue (Lac⁺) papillae in a white (Lac⁻) colony. We have already detected four mutator loci specific for different transversion events (refs. 22 and 32; M. Michaels, C. Cruz, and J.H.M., unpublished results).

We thank Drs. K. B. Low and E. Eisenstadt for bacterial strains and Dr. P. L. Foster for helpful discussions. C. Cruz and M. Cabrera provided expert technical assistance. This work was supported by a grant from the National Institutes of Health (GM32184) to J.H.M. C.G.C. was supported during part of this work by a fellowship from the Natural Sciences and Engineering Research Council of Canada.

1. Eisenstadt, E. (1987) in *Escherichia coli and Salmonella typhimurium, Cellular and Molecular Biology*, eds. Ingraham, J. L., Low, K. B., Magasanik, B., Schaechter, M. & Umbarger, H. E. (Am. Soc. Microbiol., Washington, DC), Vol. 2, pp. 1016–1033.
2. Yanofsky, C., Ito, J. & Horn, V. (1966) *Cold Spring Harbor Symp. Quant. Biol.* **31**, 151–162.
3. Prakash, L. & Sherman, F. (1973) *J. Mol. Biol.* **79**, 65–82.
4. Prakash, L., Stewart, J. W. & Sherman, F. (1974) *J. Mol. Biol.* **85**, 51–65.
5. Ames, B. N., Durston, W. E., Yamasaki, E. & Lee, F. D. (1973) *Proc. Natl. Acad. Sci. USA* **70**, 2281–2285.
6. McCann, J., Spingarn, N., Kobori, J. & Ames, B. N. (1975) *Proc. Natl. Acad. Sci. USA* **72**, 979–983.
7. Levin, D. E. & Ames, B. N. (1986) *Environ. Mutagen.* **8**, 9–28.
8. Osborne, M., Person, S., Phillips, S. & Funk, F. (1967) *J. Mol. Biol.* **26**, 437–447.
9. Coulondre, C. & Miller, J. H. (1977) *J. Mol. Biol.* **117**, 577–606.
10. Miller, J. H. (1983) *Annu. Rev. Genet.* **17**, 215–238.
11. Farabaugh, P., Schmeissner, U., Hofer, M. & Miller, J. H. (1978) *J. Mol. Biol.* **126**, 847–863.
12. Calos, M. P. & Miller, J. H. (1981) *J. Mol. Biol.* **153**, 39–66.

Table 3. Sequences of selected Lac⁺ revertants

Strain	Codon 461	Mutagen	No. of revertants sequenced	Sequence at codon 461	Change
CC102	GGG	EMS	3	GAG	G·C → A·T
CC102	GGG	2AP	3	GAG	G·C → A·T
CC106	AAG	2AP	3	GAG	A·T → G·C
CC104	GCG	5AZ	3	GAG	G·C → T·A
CC103	CAG	5AZ	3	GAG	G·C → C·G

13. Miller, J. H. (1985) *J. Mol. Biol.* **182,** 45–68.
14. Wood, R. D., Skopek, T. R. & Hutchinson, F. (1984) *J. Mol. Biol.* **173,** 273–291.
15. LeClerc, J. E. & Istock, N. L. (1982) *Nature* **297,** 596–598.
16. Schaaper, R. M. & Dunn, R. L. (1987) *Proc. Natl. Acad. Sci. USA* **84,** 6220–6224.
17. Miller, J. K. & Barnes, W. M. (1986) *Proc. Natl. Acad. Sci. USA* **83,** 1026–1030.
18. Foster, P. L., Dalbadie-McFarland, G., Davis, E. F., Schultz, S. C. & Richards, J. H. (1987) *J. Bacteriol.* **169,** 2476–2481.
19. Jacob, F. & Monod, J. (1961) *J. Mol. Biol.* **3,** 318–356.
20. Herrchen, M. & Legler, G. (1984) *Eur. J. Biochem.* **138,** 527–531.
21. Cupples, C. G. & Miller, J. H. (1988) *Genetics* **120,** 637–644.
22. Nghiem, T., Cabrera, M., Cupples, C. G. & Miller, J. H. (1988) *Proc. Natl. Acad. Sci. USA* **85,** 2709–2713.
23. Miller, J. H. (1972) *Experiments in Molecular Genetics* (Cold Spring Harbor Lab., Cold Spring Harbor, NY).
24. Coulondre, C. & Miller, J. H. (1977) *J. Mol. Biol.* **117,** 525–567.
25. Yanofsky, C., Cox, E. C. & Horn, V. (1966) *Proc. Natl. Acad. Sci. USA* **55,** 274–281.
26. Choy, H. E. & Fowler, R. G. (1985) *Mutat. Res.* **142,** 93–97.
27. Glickman, B. W. (1979) *Mutat. Res.* **61,** 153–162.
28. Leong, P.-M., Hsia, H.-C. & Miller, J. H. (1986) *J. Bacteriol.* **168,** 412–416.
29. Drake, J. W. & Baltz, R. H. (1976) *Annu. Rev. Biochem.* **45,** 11–37.
30. Coulondre, C., Miller, J. H., Farabaugh, P. J. & Gilbert, W. (1978) *Nature (London)* **274,** 775–780.
31. Benzer, S. (1961) *Proc. Natl. Acad. Sci. USA* **47,** 403–416.
32. Cabrera, M., Nghiem, Y. & Miller, J. H. (1988) *J. Bacteriol.* **170,** 5405–5407.

The *mutY* gene: A mutator locus in *Escherichia coli* that generates G·C → T·A transversions

(*lacZ*/*lacI*/spontaneous mutations/repair)

Y. NGHIEM, M. CABRERA, C. G. CUPPLES, AND J. H. MILLER

Molecular Biology Institute and Department of Biology, University of California, 405 Hilgard Avenue, Los Angeles, CA 90024

Communicated by Jon Beckwith, January 11, 1988 (received for review October 6, 1987)

ABSTRACT   We have used a strain with an altered *lacZ* gene, which reverts to wild type via only certain transversions, to detect transversion-specific mutators in *Escherichia coli*. Detection relied on a papillation technique that uses a combination of β-galactosides to reveal blue Lac$^+$ papillae. One class of mutators is specific for the G·C → T·A transversion as determined by the reversion pattern of a set of *lacZ* mutations and by the distribution of forward nonsense mutations in the *lacI* gene. The locus responsible for the mutator phenotype is designated *mutY* and maps near 64 min on the genetic map of *E. coli*. The *mutY* locus may act in a similar but reciprocal fashion to the previously characterized *mutT* locus, which results in A·T → C·G transversions.

Mutants with higher than normal rates of spontaneous mutation have facilitated our understanding of mutational pathways. Some of the "mutator" strains have characterized defects in postreplication mismatch repair (1, 2), in specific glycosylases (3), or in the editing function provided by the ε subunit of DNA polymerase III (4). Characterization of additional mutators may reveal pathways of mutagenesis and repair. Toward this end, we have used a highly sensitive screening method to detect mutator strains that revert defined mutations in *lacZ* by a limited number of base substitutions. Here we report the characterization of a mutator locus, *mutY*, which results in the specific generation of G·C → T·A transversions.

MATERIALS AND METHODS

Bacterial Strains. All mutators were selected in strain CC503, which contains an F'*lacproB* episome carrying *lacI378*, *lacZ503*. The chromosome of CC503 is *ara*, Δ(*lacproB*)$_{XIII}$, *rpsL*. The series of strains CC101–106 is similar to CC503 but without the *rpsLA* mutation. Each strain carries a different *lacZ$^-$* allele (see Table 2). The Hfr strains PK191, KL16, and KL14 were a gift of K. B. Low (Yale University). The point of origin of each Hfr is shown in Fig. 5. Markers used for P1 mapping were carried in strains from the *Escherichia coli* genetic stock center, which were generously supplied by B. Bachmann (Yale University School of Medicine). The relevant mutation in each strain is as follows: *metK110*, CGSC6380 (EWH110); *galP*::Tn*10*, CGSC6902 (JM2071); *nupG511*::Tn*10*, CGSC6568 (SO1023); *metC69*, CGSC4524 (AT2699); Δ(*speC-glc*)63, CGSC4969 (PL8-31). Also, strain DF649 from D. Fraenkel was provided as KL472 by K. B. Low. This strain carries a Tn*10* insertion (*zgd*) between *metC* and *metK* (see Fig. 5).

Mutagenesis and Selection of Mutants. Strains were mutagenized with ethyl methanesulfonate as described by Coulondre and Miller (5). After mutagenesis and outgrowth in LB medium overnight, strain CC503 was plated on glucose minimal medium with phenyl β-D-galactoside (P-Gal) and 5-bromo-4-chloro-3-indolyl β-D-galactoside (X-Gal) (see below) to observe mutator colonies. Each mutagenesis was monitored for killing and for the generation of rifampicin-resistant (Rif^r) mutants.

Visualization of Mutators. The medium used to visualize blue papillae contained minimal A salts (6), 0.2% glucose, 0.05% P-Gal (500 μg/ml), and X-Gal (40 μg/ml). Plates were incubated 3–5 days and examined under a low-power stereo microscope to visualize mutator colonies.

Genetic Mapping. All Hfr crosses and P1 transductions were carried out as described (6). Selected markers in Hfr crosses were, for PK191 and KL16, *thyA* (introduced by trimethoprim selection; see ref. 6), and for KL14, *metB*, introduced by an Hfr cross with a Met$^-$ Hfr strain. Except for crosses involving *metC*, all P1 transductions used tetracycline resistance (Tet^r) as the selected marker. Purified colonies were subsequently scored for additional markers.

All media and genetic manipulations, unless otherwise stated, are as described (6).

RESULTS

Selection for Mutators. We have characterized an amber (UAG) mutation in *lacZ* at the position encoding tyrosine-503 in β-galactosidase (C.G.C. and J.H.M., unpublished data), which allows reversion to the full Lac$^+$ phenotype only if tyrosine is inserted at that position in the protein. As Fig. 1 shows, only G·C → T·A and G·C → C·G transversions will result in tyrosine insertion, whether the back mutation occurs at the amber site itself or in a tyrosine tRNA gene (resulting in a nonsense suppressor). To find transversion-specific mutators, we mutagenized CC503, a strain carrying the amber at position 503 on an F'*lacproB* episome, and we screened colonies for higher mutation rates by using indicator medium described below.

Detection of Mutators. Mutation rates can be estimated by exploiting the properties of papillae or microcolonies that grow out from the surface of a colony. Papillation, the formation of papillae, is frequently used with indicator plates such as MacConkey, eosin/methylene blue, or tetrazolium (7). We have developed a papillation test that uses glucose minimal plates containing X-Gal and P-Gal, which is often more sensitive than tests on rich media. On the supplemented minimal medium, constitutive Lac$^+$ revertants will form blue papillae growing out of white colonies, as shown in Fig. 2. The colonies grow until they exhaust the glucose in the medium. Then, only constitutive Lac$^+$ revertants, which can utilize the P-Gal in the medium, can continue to grow. The papillae are stained blue by the X-Gal. Colonies that generate papillae at higher rates than normal are readily detected (Fig. 2). After mutagenesis with ethyl methanesul-

Abbreviations: X-Gal, 5-bromo-4-chloro-3-indolyl β-D-galactoside; P-Gal, phenyl β-D-galactoside; Rif^r, rifampicin resistant.

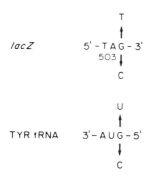

FIG. 1. Specific reversion of *lacZ503*. Effects of an amber mutation corresponding to position 503 in β-galactosidase can be reversed via the G·C → T·A or G·C → C·G transversion, which either recreates a wild-type tyrosine codon (*Upper*) or results in a tyrosine-inserting nonsense suppressor (*Lower*). The suppressor is generated by altering the portion of the tyrosine tRNA gene specifying the tRNA anticodon, as shown here.

fonate blue, we screened ≈50,000 colonies and found 13 strains with increased papillae formation.

Mutagenesis Tests. The 13 strains were retested for papillae formation on several different media and also for the generation of Lac⁺ and Rifʳ revertants in liquid culture. The putative mutators could be placed into four groups based on these tests. Results representative of each group are shown

A

B

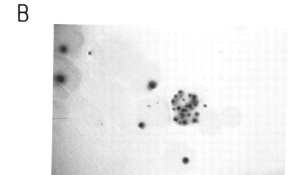

FIG. 2. Papillation tests. (*A*) Reversion to Lac⁺ results in the formation of blue papillae on medium with X-Gal, P-Gal, and glucose. (*B*) Mutator colonies display more papillae than wild-type colonies.

Table 1. Characteristics of different mutators

| Group | Number of mutants | Papillation | | Mutants per 10⁸ cells | |
		X-Gal, P-Gal	Lac Mac	Lac⁺	Rifʳ
I	6	+ +	+ +	150–200	150–200
II	1	+ +	+ +	500	4000
III	4	+	+	20	5–10
IV	2	+, w	−	5–10	5–10
Control (CC503)				1–2	5–10

The mutators selected from strain CC503 are grouped into four classes based on their papillation response on X-Gal, P-Gal and on lactose MacConkey (Lac Mac) medium and also the number of Lac⁺ and Rifʳ revertants. Papillation is indicated qualitatively. Strong, + +; moderate, +; weak, +, w; no increase over control, −.

in Table 1. The six members of group I and the single member of group II were selected for further study at this point. Initially, we tested the mutators against a series of *lacZ* mutations with alterations at codon 461, which revert to GAG (specifying glutamic acid) via a specific base substitution in each case. Only glutamic acid at position 461 results in the Lac⁺ phenotype (this system will be described in detail elsewhere; C.G.C. and J.H.M., unpublished data). All members of group I give an identical response in the six strains, and these mutators appear to be specific for the G·C → T·A transversion. Table 2 depicts the results for three representatives of this group. The group II mutator, on the other hand, promotes reversion of five of the six indicator strains at a relatively high rate. Genetic mapping studies (data not shown) indicate that this mutator results from an allele of *mutD*, affecting the ε subunit of DNA polymerase III. We have examined the group I mutators in detail by using the *lacI* system (see below).

Use of *lacI* Nonsense System. To determine the detailed mutagenic specificity of the group I mutators, we used the *lacI* nonsense system (8), which monitors the generation of 90 UAG (amber), UAA (ochre), and UGA mutations at 78 sites in the *lacI* gene. Fig. 3 shows the distribution of nonsense mutations in a wild-type strain. All types of mutations occur, although hot spots for the G·C → A·T transition are seen at 5-methylcytosine residues. The distribution of nonsense mutations in a representative of the group I mutators is markedly different, however, as diagrammed in Fig. 4. It can be seen from both Fig. 4 and Table 3 that only G·C → T·A transversions are stimulated. Of 436 mutations analyzed, 424 result from G·C → T·A transver-

Table 2. Mutational specificity of mutators

Strain donating F'*lacproB*	Base substitution	Lac⁺ colonies per 10⁸ cells				
		Control	Mutator strain			
			Group I			Group II
			a	b	c	
CC101	A·T → C·G	0	0	0	0	611
CC102	G·C → A·T	3	3	4	6	955
CC103	G·C → C·G	0	0	0	0	15
CC104	G·C → T·A	0	159	142	163	1103
CC105	A·T → T·A	0	0	0	0	902
CC106	A·T → G·C	0	0	0	1	527

Six strains (CC101–106) carrying different Z⁻ alleles on F'*lacproB* episomes. These episomes were donated to different mutator derivatives of CC503 cured of the original episome (Table 1). The number of Lac⁺ revertants in overnight cultures of each CC503 derivative was monitored. Three strains from group I and one strain from group II (Table 1) were examined. Each value represents the average of several determinations.

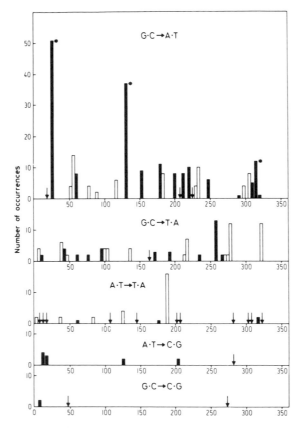

FIG. 3. Spontaneous amber (solid bars) and ochre (open bars) mutations occurring in a wild-type (*mutY⁺*) strain. The height of each bar represents the number of independent occurrences in a collection of 306 nonsense mutations. (The ochre bar heights have been normalized to account for a smaller sample size.) Arrows indicate the position of nonsense sites at which there were zero occurrences in this collection. Asterisks indicate 5-methylcytosine residues. The position of sites in the *lacI* gene is indicated on the horizontal axis by the number of the corresponding amino acid in the *lac* repressor. (Redrawn from ref. 8.)

sions. We consider these data further in the *Discussion*. A second member of group I gives similar results (data not shown).

At five sites we can monitor both G·C → T·A and G·C → C·G transversions at the same base pair; the former yields TAA in all five cases, and the latter yields TAG in the case of TAC tyrosine codons (third position) and TGA in the case of TCA serine codons (second position). As Table 4 shows, G·C → T·A transversions occurred a total of 49 times at these five sites, compared with zero occurrences of G·C → C·G transversions at the same sites.

Table 3. The distribution of nonsense mutations in a *mutY* strain

Substitution	Available sites	Sites found	Total occurrences	% of total occurrences
G·C → A·T	30	9	11	2.5
G·C → T·A	25	25	424	97.2
A·T → T·A	21	1	1	0.2
A·T → C·G	6	0	0	0
G·C → C·G	5	0	0	0
Total	87	35	436	

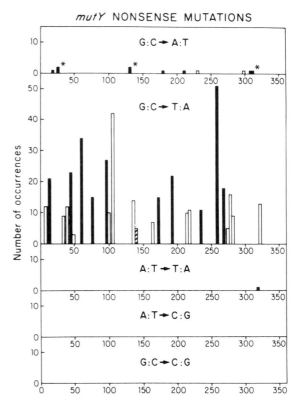

FIG. 4. Distribution of nonsense mutations in *lacI* in a *mutY* strain. Position and number of occurrences of 436 amber, ochre, and UGA mutations are shown. As in Fig. 3, solid bars represent amber mutations and open bars represent ochre mutations. Here, the single UGA site detected is indicated by a striped bar. All bar heights represent the exact number of mutations detected. Each mutation is of independent origin. The mutations have been analyzed as described (9). For further details, see legend to Fig. 3.

Genetic Mapping. We used a series of Hfr strains to determine the approximate position of the locus or loci responsible for the mutator phenotype described above. We selected for markers donated by each respective Hfr and then scored for the mutator character by papillation (see Fig. 2). All of these crosses indicated that the mutator locus mapped between 61 and 66 min on the *E. coli* genetic map (ref. 10; see Fig. 5 *Upper*). P1 cotransduction established

Table 4. Mutations occurring at the three TAC tyrosine and two TCA serine codons in the *lacI* gene

Site	Coding position	Independent occurrences	
		TAC → TAA (G·C → T·A)	TAC → TAG (G·C → C·G)
A1,O3	Tyr-7	12	0
A8,O8	Tyr-47	3	0
A29,O30	Tyr-273	5	0
		TCA → TAA	TCA → TGA
O31/U9	Ser-280	16	0
O36/U10	Ser-322	13	0
	Total	49	0

Both amber (*A*) and ochre (*O*) mutations can occur at the TAC codons and both ochre and UGA (*U*) mutations can occur at the TCA codons, allowing two different transversions to be monitored at each site (see text).

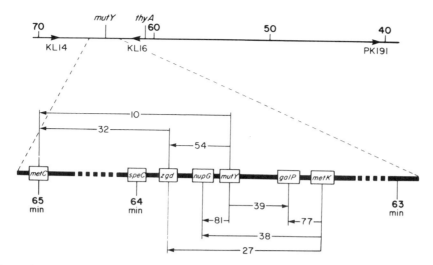

Fig. 5. Genetic mapping of *mutY*. (*Upper*) Point of origin of Hfr strains used to position *mutY*. (*Lower*) P1 cotransduction frequencies are given as percentage cotransduction with the arrow pointing to the selected marker. See *Materials and Methods* for a description of each mutation used. The cotransduction frequencies represent the average of several experiments. Most ordering was achieved by three-factor crosses. [The relative position of *speC* (10) is inferred from additional experiments; data not shown.] The map is not drawn to exact physical scale.

that the locus, which we designate *mutY*, maps very near *nupG*, between *metC* and *metK*, at ≈64 min. Fig. 5 (*Lower*) depicts the map location together with relevant surrounding loci.

DISCUSSION

We have developed a system that is capable of detecting mutators specific for certain base substitutions (C.G.C. and J.H.M., unpublished data). This system relies on the use of specific alleles of *lacZ* (Fig. 1) and also on a sensitive visualization assay involving histochemically stained papillae (Fig. 2). Here we report the characterization of a mutator locus, *mutY*, which maps at ≈64 min on the *E. coli* genetic map.

Strains that are *mutY* stimulate only G·C → T·A transversions (at least to the limits of our detection systems). This can be seen not only by examining the *lacZ* reversion system (Table 2) but also by using the *lacI* forward nonsense system (Fig. 4 and Table 3). The *lacI* system monitors 90-base substitutions at 78 different nonsense sites. Nonsense mutations constitute close to 30% of all *lacI* mutations generated by *mutY*. From 436 nonsense mutations, all but 12 were at one of the 25 nonsense sites arising from the G·C → T·A transversion. Moreover, a system capable of detecting frameshifts and deletions (23) indicates that *mutY* does not induce either of these types of mutations (data not shown).

mutY is highly specific compared to most mutators. The only other mutator that stimulates a specific transversion is *mutT*, which generates only A·T → C·G transversions (11, 12, 24). Both G·C → T·A and A·T → T·A transversions are stimulated by the SOS mutator effect (13). Among the G·C → T·A transversions in *lacI*, *mutY* displays a different site specificity than the SOS system (13). Strains defective in the mismatch repair system (*mutH*, *mutL*, *mutS*, *uvrD*, and *dam*) preferentially stimulate transitions and some frameshifts (9, 12, 14, 15), those lacking the editing function of DNA polymerase III (*mutD*) stimulate all types of base changes, although transitions predominate (12, 16) and cells lacking uracil DNA-glycosylase (*ung*) generate G·C → A·T transitions (17). It is not clear at this point whether an uncharacterized mutator locus, *mutB*, in *Salmonella typhi-*

murium, which maps between 62 and 72 min (18), is the counterpart of the *mutY* locus described here.

Several possible explanations for the specificity of *mutY* readily come to mind. The *mutY* locus might encode a glycosylase that excises spontaneously damaged guanine residues. Altered guanines might fail to pair properly and translesion synthesis could result in the preferential insertion of an adenine residue across from the damaged base, as appears to occur for a number of other lesions (19–21). However, the specificity appears far too tight to accommodate this type of mechanism. A second hypothesis is based on the presumed action of *mutT*, the one other transversion-specific mutator. Fresco and Topal (22) have proposed that replication errors that result in transversions might occur by the incorporation of the *syn* isomer of guanine or adenine across from either of the tautomers imino-adenine or *enol*-imino-guanine. The *mutT* locus might control a protein that normally prevents the incorporation of *syn*-guanine across from imino-adenine (12, 22), thus explaining its unidirectional action and predicting the existence of a similar protein that prevents the incorporation of *syn*-adenine (12). The *mutY* locus would be an excellent candidate to encode such a protein. (It is interesting to note that the levels of increased spontaneous mutations displayed by *mutT* and *mutY* are on the same order of magnitude.) One problem with this idea in its simplest form is that *mutT* might be expected to also cause G·C → C·G transversions if it were simply preventing the incorporation of *syn*-guanine (12), and *mutY* would be expected to also cause A·T → T·A transversions if it were just blocking the incorporation of *syn*-adenine. Perhaps additional complexities exist for this putative system. An exciting prospect would be to clone and sequence the *mutY* gene and compare it with the sequence of the *mutT* gene. Enzymes with functions as closely related as those postulated above might have recognizable homology.

A more straightforward model would involve a postreplication repair system specific for correcting mismatches leading to G·C → T·A transversions. Evidence for a repair pathway that corrects G·A mispairs to G·C base pairs in a reaction that is independent of *mutH*, *-L*, *-S* gene products has been observed in *E. coli* extracts (S.-S. Su, R. S. Lahue, G. Au, and P. Modrich, personal communication). There is as yet no evidence for such a pathway operating *in vivo*. A tantalizing possibility is that *mutY* affects one of the components of this putative pathway.

Of course, other mechanisms, such as effects on precursor pools, might be involved in the specific transversions seen with *mutY*.

We thank Drs. B. Bachmann and K. B. Low for bacterial strains, and Drs. P. Modrich, P. Foster, E. Eisenstadt, E. C. Cox, and J. R. Fresco for helpful discussions. This work was supported by a grant from the National Institutes of Health (GM32184) to J.H.M. C.G.C. was the recipient of a fellowship from the Natural Sciences and Engineering Research Council of Canada.

1. Radman, M., Wagner, R. E., Glickman, B. W. & Meselson, M. (1980) in *Progress in Environmental Mutagenesis*, ed. Alacevic, M. (Elsevier/North-Holland, Amsterdam), pp. 121–130.
2. Lu, A.-L., Welsh, K., Clark, S., Su, S.-S. & Modrich, P. (1984) *Cold Spring Harbor Symp. Quant. Biol.* **49**, 589–596.
3. Duncan, B. K., Rockstroh, P. A. & Warner, H. R. (1978) *J. Bacteriol.* **134**, 1039–1045.
4. Scheuermann, R., Tann, S., Burgers, P. M. J., Lu, C. & Echols, H. (1983) *Proc. Natl. Acad. Sci. USA* **80**, 7085–7089.
5. Coulondre, C. & Miller, J. H. (1977) *J. Mol. Biol.* **117**, 525–567.
6. Miller, J. H. (1972) *Experiments in Molecular Genetics* (Cold Spring Harbor Lab., Cold Spring Harbor, NY).
7. Konrad, E. B. (1978) *J. Bacteriol.* **133**, 1197–1202.
8. Coulondre, C. & Miller, J. H. (1977) *J. Mol. Biol.* **117**, 577–606.
9. Leong, P.-M., Hsia, H. C. & Miller, J. H. (1986) *J. Bacteriol.* **168**, 412–416.
10. Bachmann, B. J. (1983) *Microbiol. Rev.* **47**, 180–230.
11. Cox, E. C. (1973) *Genetics* **73**, Suppl., 67–80.
12. Cox, E. C. (1976) *Annu. Rev. Genet.* **10**, 135–156.
13. Miller, J. H. & Low, K. B. (1984) *Cell* **37**, 675–682.
14. Choy, H. E. & Fowler, R. G. (1985) *Mutat. Res.* **142**, 93–97.
15. Glickman, B. W. (1979) *Mutat. Res.* **61**, 153–162.
16. Fowler, R. G., Degnen, G. E. & Cox, E. C. (1974) *Mol. Gen. Genet.* **133**, 179–191.
17. Duncan, B. & Miller, J. H. (1980) *Nature (London)* **287**, 560–561.
18. Shanabruch, W. G., Behlau, I. & Walker, G. C. (1981) *J. Bacteriol.* **147**, 827–835.
19. Loeb, L. A. & Preston, B. D. (1986) *Annu. Rev. Genet.* **20**, 201–230.
20. Eisenstadt, E., Warren, A. J., Porter, J., Atkins, D. & Miller, J. H. (1982) *Proc. Natl. Acad. Sci. USA* **79**, 1945–1949.
21. Foster, P. L., Eisenstadt, E. & Miller, J. H. (1983) *Proc. Natl. Acad. Sci. USA* **80**, 2695–2698.
22. Fresco, J. R. & Topal, M. D. (1976) *Nature (London)* **263**, 285–293.
23. Miller, J. H. (1985) *J. Mol. Biol.* **182**, 45–68.
24. Yanofsky, C., Cox, E. C. & Horn, V. (1966) *Proc. Natl. Acad. Sci. USA* **55**, 274–281.

Evidence that MutY and MutM combine to prevent mutations by an oxidatively damaged form of guanine in DNA

(8-oxo-7,8-dihydroguanine/8-hydroxyguanine/DNA glycosylase/Fpg protein/mismatch repair)

Mark Leo Michaels*, Christina Cruz*, Arthur P. Grollman[†], and Jeffrey H. Miller*[‡]

*Department of Microbiology and Molecular Genetics and the Molecular Biology Institute, University of California, Los Angeles, CA 90024; and [†]Department of Pharmacological Sciences, State University of New York, Stony Brook, NY 11794-8651

Communicated by Charles Yanofsky, May 6, 1992 (received for review January 30, 1992)

ABSTRACT It has been previously shown both *in vivo* and *in vitro* that DNA synthesis past an oxidatively damaged form of guanine, 7,8-dihydro-8-oxoguanine (8-oxoG), can result in the misincorporation of adenine (A) opposite the 8-oxodG. In this study we show that MutY glycosylase is active on a site-specific, oxidatively damaged A/8-oxoG mispair and that it removes the undamaged adenine from this mispair. Strains that lack active MutY protein have elevated rates of G·C → T·A transversions. We find that the mutator phenotype of a *mutY* strain can be fully complemented by overexpressing MutM protein (Fpg protein) from a plasmid clone. The MutM protein removes 8-oxoG lesions from DNA. In addition, we have isolated a strain with a chromosomal mutation that suppresses the *mutY* phenotype and found that this suppressor also overexpresses MutM. Finally, a *mutY mutM* double mutant has a 25- to 75-fold higher mutation rate than either mutator alone. The data strongly suggest that MutY is part of an intricate repair system directed against 8-oxoG lesions in nucleic acids and that the primary function of MutY *in vivo* is the removal of adenines that are misincorporated opposite 8-oxoG lesions during DNA synthesis.

All organisms that use molecular oxygen need to defend themselves from the reactive byproducts of oxygen metabolism. Reactive oxygen species such as superoxide, hydrogen peroxide, and hydroxyl radical can be produced by the incomplete reduction of oxygen during aerobic metabolism (1). These oxidants can also be generated from lipid peroxidation, from phagocytic cells, and by exposure to radiation (1). Although organisms have developed systems to control active oxygen species, those that escape the primary defenses can damage nucleic acids and other cellular macromolecules.

Oxidative damage to DNA has been estimated at 10^4 lesions per cell per day in humans and an order of magnitude higher in rodents (2). Not surprisingly, organisms have developed a second line of defense to repair the oxidative damage to DNA. One of the lesions that is actively removed is 7,8-dihydro-8-oxoguanine (8-oxoG, also termed 8-hydroxyguanine). The lesion is removed by the glycosylase/apurinic endonuclease activity of the MutM protein [Fpg protein or 8-oxoG glycosylase] (3, 4). Recently, it has been shown that DNA synthesis past 8-oxoG can result in the misincorporation of adenine opposite the damaged guanine (5–7) and that inactivation of the *mutM* (*fpg*) gene leads specifically to G·C → T·A transversions (4, 8).

In this paper we present evidence that *Escherichia coli* has, at least in the case of the 8-oxoG lesion, a third line of defense against oxidative damage to DNA. Unlike the first two forms of protection, which target the active oxygen species or the damage it inflicts on nucleic acids, this activity leads to the correction of errors that are induced by replication of templates containing 8-oxoG lesions. We find that MutY protein, originally identified as an adenine glycosylase active on A/G mispairs (9), can also remove the undamaged adenine from A/8-oxoG mispairs. Strains that lack active MutY protein have elevated rates of G·C → T·A transversions (10). Overexpressing the MutM protein from a plasmid clone can completely complement the mutator phenotype of a *mutY* strain. We have isolated a strain with a chromosomal mutation that suppresses *mutY* and found that it has 15-fold greater MutM activity than the parental strain. Finally, a *mutM mutY* double mutant shows a 20-fold higher rate of G·C → T·A transversions than the sum of G·C → T·A transversions in either mutant alone. These observations suggest that the primary function of MutY glycosylase *in vivo* is the removal of adenines that have been misincorporated opposite 8-oxoG lesions during DNA replication, and that MutY and MutM are part of a multiple line of defenses against oxidative damage to DNA.

MATERIALS AND METHODS

Oligodeoxynucleotides. The 23-mer oligodeoxynucleotides, including the one containing the site-specific 8-oxoG lesion, were synthesized and purified as described (6, 11). The purified oligomers (4 pmol) were ^{32}P-labeled at the 5′ terminus with 10 units of T4 polynucleotide kinase in the presence of 7 pmol of [γ-^{32}P] ATP (6 Ci/μmol; New England Nuclear; 1 Ci = 37 GBq) for 10 min at 37°C. After heat inactivation at 90°C for 7 min, the labeled primers were annealed with an excess of unlabeled complementary oligodeoxynucleotide at 90°C in 50 mM NaCl for 2 min, cooled to room temperature, and then incubated on ice. The sequences of the oligodeoxynucleotides are shown below (nucleotides involved in mispair formation are underlined; GO, 8-oxoG).

(1) 5′-CTCTCCCTTC<u>GO</u>CTCCTTTCCTCT-3′

(2) 5′-CTCTCCCTTC<u>G</u>CTCCTTTCCTCT-3′

(3) 5′-AGAGGAAAGGAG<u>A</u>GAAGGGAGAG-3′

(4) 5′-AGAGGAAAGGAG<u>C</u>GAAGGGAGAG-3′

MutY Glycosylase Assay. Glycosylase reactions were carried out in a solution (10 μl) containing 20 mM Tris·HCl (pH 7.6), 0.5 μg of bovine serum albumin, 10 mM EDTA, 45 ng of MutY glycosylase [purified essentially as previously described (9)], and 20 fmol of 23-mer duplex with the indicated mispair. After incubation at 37°C for 30 min, reactions were terminated by the addition of 2 μl of 1 M NaOH and incubation

---

Abbreviation: 8-oxoG, 7,8-dihydro-8-oxoguanine.
[‡]To whom reprint requests should be addressed.

at 90°C for 4 min. This also served to cleave any apurinic/apyrimidinic sites generated by the glycosylase. Four microliters of loading dye (95% formamide/20 mM EDTA/0.05% bromophenol blue/0.05% xylene cylanol FF) was added to the mix and aliquots were run in denaturing (7 M urea) 15% polyacrylamide gels.

Strains and Plasmids. *E. coli* strain GT100 is *ara*, Δ(*gpt–lac*)5, *rpsL*, [F'*lacI^qL8*, *proA^+B^+*]. Strain CC104 is *ara*, Δ(*gpt–lac*)5, [F'*lacI378*, *lacZ461*, *proA^+B^+*] (12). CSH115 is *ara*, Δ(*gpt–lac*)5, *rpsL*, *mutS*::mini-Tn*10* and CSH116 is *ara*, Δ(*gpt–lac*)5, *rpsL*, *mutD5 zae502*::Tn*10*; these strains are further described by Miller (13). Plasmid pKK223-3 was purchased from Pharmacia, and pKK-Fapy2 carries a wild-type *mutM* (*fpg*) gene (4). All media and genetic manipulations, unless otherwise stated, were as described (14).

Complementation Tests. Eight independent cultures containing plasmid pKK223-3 or pKK-Fapy2 in strains GT100, GT100 *mutY*::mini-Tn*10*, GT100 *mutM*, or GT100 *mutS*::mini-Tn*10* were grown overnight in LB medium supplemented with ampicillin (100 μg/ml), and 50-μl samples were plated onto LB with rifampicin (200 μg/ml). After overnight incubation at 37°C, Rif^r colonies were counted.

MutM Protein Assay. Crude extracts were obtained by growing Sup17 [a strain carrying a suppressor of *mutY* (C.C., M.L.M., and J.H.M., unpublished work)] in LB medium. Cells (30 OD_600 units) were collected by centrifugation, resuspended in 2 ml 50 mM Tris·HCl, pH 7.5/20 mM β-mercaptoethanol/1 mM phenylmethylsulfonyl fluoride, and frozen at −70°C. The solution was thawed and sonicated on a Fisher Sonic Dismembrator model 300 on maximum output for two 30-sec bursts. The cell debris was removed by centrifugation (27,000 × g) for 20 min at 4°C. The supernatant was taken and glycerol was added to a concentration of 5% (vol/vol). The protein content of the extracts was measured with the BioRad protein assay kit using bovine serum albumin as the standard. Various amounts of extract were incubated with 20 fmol of 23-mer duplex containing a C/8-oxoG pair with a ^{32}P label in the 8-oxoG-containing strand (oligonucleotides 4 and 1; see above). The reaction was incubated at 37°C for 30 min in 10 μl of 20 mM Tris·HCl, pH 7.6/10 mM EDTA containing bovine serum albumin at 50 μg/ml. The reaction was stopped by the addition of 3 μl of loading dye and by heating at 100°C for 2 min. An aliquot of the reaction was loaded onto a denaturing 15% polyacrylamide gel. Autoradiographs were quantitated by measuring transmittance of substrate and product bands with a Bio-Rad 620 video densitometer.

Mutational Specificity Tests. Four or more independent cultures of CC104 and its derivatives were grown overnight, and 50 μl was plated onto LB with rifampicin (100 μg/ml) and 100 μl onto minimal lactose medium. After overnight incubation at 37°C, Rif^r colonies were counted. Lac^+ colonies were counted after 2 days of incubation at 37°C. For the double mutant (*mutY mutM*), 10^{-2} dilutions were done before plating. Lac^+ colonies were somewhat difficult to count for the double mutant due to Lac^+ colonies arising on the plate during incubation. Incubation times were reduced to combat this problem. This problem does not occur with the Rif^r mutants.

RESULTS

MutY Glycosylase Activity on A/8-oxoG Mispairs. Duplexes (23-mers) containing an undamaged A/G mispair or a site-specific A/8-oxoG mispair were tested as substrates for MutY glycosylase. The glycosylase was active on the duplex containing the A/8-oxoG mispair and removed the undamaged adenine from the duplex (Fig. 1, lane 7). MutY acted strictly as a glycosylase in this reaction—no endonuclease activity was detected. As previously observed (9), MutY was

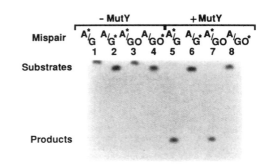

FIG. 1. Activity of MutY glycosylase on mispairs containing a site-specific 8-oxoG lesion. Glycosylase reactions were carried out as described in *Materials and Methods*. Blank reaction mixtures (lanes 1–4) contained everything except the glycosylase. Reactions were terminated by the addition of 2 μl of 1 M NaOH and incubation at 90°C for 4 min. This also served to cleave any apurinic sites generated by the glycosylase. The progress of the glycosylase reaction can therefore be monitored by a change in migration of the cleaved products. The A oligomer is sequence no. 3 (see *Materials and Methods*); the G and GO (8-oxoG) oligomers are nos. 2 and 1, respectively. The star indicates which strand in the duplex is ^{32}P-labeled.

also active on the undamaged adenine of an A/G mispair and did not cause strand cleavage at the apurinic site (lane 5).

All of the other possible combinations of mispairs with 8-oxoG were tested as potential substrates for MutY glycosylase. MutY does not remove cytosine, guanine, or thymine opposite 8-oxoG, nor does it remove 8-oxoG from any of the damaged duplexes (data not shown). MutY was active only on the A/8-oxoG and A/G mispairs.

The relative activity of MutY glycosylase on an A/8-oxoG or A/G mispair duplex substrate was determined. MutY removed the undamaged adenine from the A/G and A/8-oxoG mispairs at approximately the same rate (Fig. 2). The glycosylase specific activity on these substrates was >26 nmol/hr per mg of protein. This is comparable to the glycosylase specific activity observed for purified MutY glycosylase on a phage f1-derived heteroduplex containing an A/G mispair (1.35 nmol/hr per mg; ref. 9).

Complementation Tests. Previous work has shown that *mutY* (10) and *mutM* (*fpg*) (8) have nearly identical mutation spectra *in vivo* and that both specifically increase G·C → T·A transversions. Therefore, we suspected that the two proteins could be part of a common repair pathway. The above biochemical assay suggested that 8-oxoG might be common to both repair proteins. In the proposed scheme, the MutM protein would remove 8-oxoG lesions in DNA, and MutY

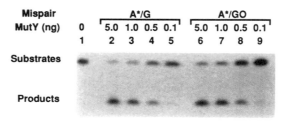

FIG. 2. Relative activity of MutY glycosylase on A/G and A/8-oxoG substrates. The blank reaction (lane 1) and glycosylase reactions (lanes 2–9) were performed on duplex 23-mers containing the indicated mismatch and analyzed as described in the legend to Fig. 1 except that the amount of MutY glycosylase was varied as shown in the figure. The A* oligomer in each duplex is no. 3 (*Materials and Methods*); the G and GO (8-oxoG) oligomers are nos. 2 and 1, respectively. The blank reaction (no glycosylase) was performed on A*/G.

Table 1. Complementation of a *mutY* strain with a MutM-overproducing plasmid

	No. of Rif^r colonies per 10^8 cells	
Strain	pKK223-3	pKK-Fapy2
GT100	1 ± 1	1 ± 1
GT100 *mutY*::mini-Tn*10*	57 ± 13	2 ± 1
GT100 *mutM*	13 ± 5	1 ± 1
GT100 *mutS*::mini-Tn*10*	71 ± 18	102 ± 21

Eight independent cultures were grown to saturation and plated onto LB medium with rifampicin. The average number of Rif^r colonies (±SD) per 10^8 cells is reported. Plasmid pKK223-3 is the vector and pKK-Fapy2 is a MutM overproducer (4).

glycosylase would remove any adenines that were misincorporated opposite 8-oxoG lesions that were not removed before replication.

The results of complementation tests support this theory. By overexpression of MutM protein in a *mutY* strain, the mutation rate of *mutY* was reduced to wild-type levels (Table 1). Overexpression of MutM protein in a mismatch repair-deficient strain (*mutS*) had no effect on its mutation rate. This control shows that the overproducer does not affect a mutator strain that causes mutations by an unrelated pathway. As expected, the clone complemented a *mutM* strain, and the vector alone had no effect on the mutation rate of any strain.

Characterization of a *mutM mutY* Double Mutant. Consistent with the idea that MutY glycosylase and the MutM protein protect the cell from the potentially mutagenic 8-oxoG lesion, a strain that lacks both defense systems has an extremely high rate of G·C → T·A transversions. We used P1 phage to transfer a *mutY*::mini-Tn*10* marker into a *mutM* strain and found that, like *mutM* and *mutY*, the double mutant was very specific for stimulating G·C → T·A transversions (Table 2). However, the mutation rate of the double mutant, as judged by both the generation of Rif^r colonies and the rate of G·C → T·A transversions in a Lac$^+$ reversion assay, is 20-fold higher than the sum of the separate mutators, suggesting that they are involved in a related repair system (Table 3).

The importance of the repair system is illustrated by comparing the mutation rate of a *mutM mutY* double mutant to the mutation rates obtained when other well-characterized error-avoidance systems are disabled. Strains lacking the polymerase III editing subunit (*mutD*) or the methyl-directed mismatch repair system (*mutS*) are the most potent mutator strains in *E. coli*. As judged by the formation of Rif^r colonies, the *mutM mutY* double mutant is just as strong a mutator as *mutD* and about an order of magnitude stronger than a strain lacking the mismatch repair system (Table 3).

Characterization of a Suppressor of *mutY*. We have characterized a suppressor of *mutY* that maps near to but distinct

Table 2. Mutational specificity of *mutM mutY* strains

Reversion event	Strain	No. of Lac$^+$ revertants	Strain	No. of Lac$^+$ revertants
A·T → C·G	CC101	1	CC101 *mutM mutY*	1
G·C → A·T	CC102	2	CC102 *mutM mutY*	2
G·C → C·G	CC103	<1	CC103 *mutM mutY*	<1
G·C → T·A	CC104	2	CC104 *mutM mutY*	5300
A·T → T·A	CC105	1	CC105 *mutM mutY*	1
A·T → G·C	CC106	<1	CC106 *mutM mutY*	3

Four or more independent cultures of each strain were grown to saturation in LB medium and plated onto minimal lactose medium. Average number of Lac$^+$ colonies per 10^8 cells is recorded above. Strains in this table are streptomycin-resistant (*rpsL*) versions of the CC101-106 series (12).

Table 3. Mutation frequency of *mutM*, *mutY*, and *mutM mutY* strains

Strain	No. of Lac$^+$ revertants	No. of Rif^r colonies
CC104	3	5–10
CC104 *mutM*	25	151
CC104 *mutY*	62	290
CC104 *mutM mutY*	1900	8200
CSH115 (*mutS*)	ND	760
CSH116 (*mutD*)	ND	4900

Mutation frequency of the double mutant is compared with those of the separate *mutM* and *mutY* mutants as well as with the mutation frequency of strains lacking the polymerase III editing function (*mutD*) or the mismatch repair system (*mutS*). Cultures were grown to saturation in LB medium and plated onto minimal lactose medium and LB with rifampicin. Average numbers of Lac$^+$ and Rif^r colonies per 10^8 cells are recorded. ND, not determined.

from the *mutM* gene (C.C., M.L.M., and J.H.M., unpublished work). We suspected that this antimutator candidate, Sup17, might overexpress MutM protein based upon our previous complementation results. In fact, when the extracts were tested for glycosylase/apurinic endonuclease activity on a 23-mer duplex containing a site-specific C/8-oxoG pair, the Sup17 extract had 15-fold greater activity than the parent strain. These results will be described in detail elsewhere.

DISCUSSION

The attack of reactive oxygen species on DNA poses a substantial threat to the cell. Endogenous oxidants generated by the incomplete reduction of oxygen or by lipid peroxidation can damage DNA and may be a major cause of the physiological changes associated with aging and cancer (2).

One of the products of oxidative attack on DNA is the 8-oxoG lesion. It has been determined that rat liver cells have a steady-state level of over 4×10^5 8-oxoG lesions per cell, yet it is estimated that 8-oxoG lesions may represent only 5% of the total oxidative damage to DNA (2). Even more significant is the finding that 8-oxoG lesions can lead to replication errors. *In vivo* and *in vitro* studies have shown that adenine is frequently misincorporated opposite oxidatively damaged guanine residues in DNA (5–7). In a *mutM* strain the protein that removes 8-oxoG lesions in DNA is not active (3, 4). The elevated level of G·C → T·A transversions in a *mutM* strain is thus due to the misinsertion of adenine residues opposite the accumulated 8-oxoG lesions in the parental strand during DNA replication. MutM (Fpg protein) can also excise formamidopyrimidine lesions in DNA (20).

The 8-oxoG lesion is not only present in chromosomal DNA but is also found in the nucleotide pool as 8-oxo-dGTP. This damaged nucleotide is potentially mutagenic, as 8-oxo-dGTP can be frequently misincorporated opposite template adenines (15). The MutT protein hydrolyzes 8-oxo-dGTP to 8-oxo-dGMP, thus eliminating the mutagenic substrate from the nucleotide pool (15). A strain that lacks active MutT protein has elevated levels of A·T → C·G transversions (16). These transversions are presumably due to the misincorporation of 8-oxo-dGTP opposite template adenines. Strains deficient in MutM or MutT protein have increased frequencies of opposite transversions. In a *mutM* strain, 8-oxoG lesions accumulate in the chromosome and lead to the misincorporation of adenine opposite template 8-oxoG lesions and produce G·C → T·A transversions, while in a *mutT* strain 8-oxo-dGTP nucleotides are misinserted opposite template adenines, resulting in A·T → C·G transversions.

Cells have multiple lines of defense against oxidative damage to DNA. The primary line of defense guards against the active oxygen species themselves. Oxidants can be

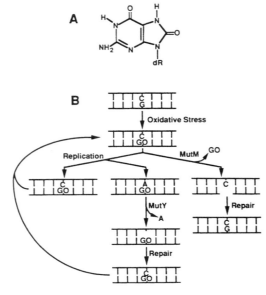

FIG. 3. Role of MutM and MutY in the 8-oxoG repair system. (A) Structure of the predominant tautomeric form of the 8-oxoG lesion. dR, deoxyribose. (B) Oxidative processes can lead to 8-oxoG lesions in DNA. The MutM protein removes 8-oxoG lesions and subsequent repair restores the original G·C base pair. If the 8-oxoG lesion (GO) is not removed before replication, translesion synthesis can be accurate or inaccurate. Accurate translesion synthesis results in a C·8-oxoG pair—a substrate for the MutM protein. However, inaccurate translesion synthesis leads to the misincorporation of dAMP opposite the 8-oxoG lesion (5–7). MutY glycosylase removes the misincorporated dA from the A/8-oxoG mispairs that result from error-prone replication past the 8-oxoG lesion. Repair polymerases are less error-prone during translesion synthesis (5) and can lead to a C·8-oxoG pair—a substrate for MutM.

eliminated by various enzymatic and nonenzymatic systems such as superoxide dismutase, catalase, ascorbic acid, and β-carotene (17). However, active oxygen species that escape these primary defenses can damage nucleic acids and other cellular macromolecules. The second line of defense works to remove the oxidative damage from nucleic acids. The MutM and MutT proteins are examples of this type of defense. Exonuclease III, endonuclease IV, and the excision nuclease and exonuclease activities associated with UvrAB are further examples of enzymes that can repair oxidized DNA (18–20).

The MutY protein represents a third level of protection against oxidative damage to DNA. Unlike the other defenses, which seek to neutralize the reactive oxygen species or repair the damage those species cause to nucleic acids, MutY glycosylase helps to correct the errors that result from the replication of DNA containing oxidative damage. It removes undamaged adenines that are misincorporated opposite template 8-oxoG lesions in DNA.

Although MutY glycosylase can remove the undamaged A from both an A/8-oxoG mispair or an undamaged A/G mispair duplex in DNA (Fig. 1), our results suggest that its primary function *in vivo* is the removal of the A from the oxidatively damaged mispair, A/8-oxoG. First, overexpression of MutM protein, which removes 8-oxoG lesions, completely complements a *mutY* strain (Table 1). Similarly, a

chromosomal suppressor of the mutator phenotype of *mutY* had 15-fold greater glycosylase/apurinic endonuclease activity on an 8-oxoG substrate than the parent strain. Finally, a *mutM mutY* double mutant has an extremely high G·C → T·A mutation rate (Tables 2 and 3). The mutation rate is about 20-fold higher than would be expected if the genes were involved in unrelated repair mechanisms. In fact, the mutation rate of the double mutant suggests that although the only mutagenic substrate this system handles is 8-oxoG, it is nonetheless one of the more important error-avoidance systems in *E. coli*.

The A/8-oxoG mispair represents an oxidatively damaged purine/purine mispair that is not efficiently removed by the proofreading function of polymerase III and appears to require a devoted repair system to prevent the oxidatively damaged guanine from introducing mutations into the chromosome. An intricate mechanism involving the MutM, MutT, and MutY proteins has evolved to protect the cell from the mutagenic effect of 8-oxoG (see Fig. 3).

We thank V. Bodepudi and R. Rieger for preparing the oligonucleotides containing the 8-oxoG lesion. We thank J. Tchou for helpful discussions and H. Hsiao for technical assistance. This work was supported by Grant GM32184 from the National Institutes of Health to J.H.M., Grant CA47995 from the National Cancer Institute to A.P.G., and a California Institute for Cancer Research Fellowship to M.L.M.

1. Halliwell, B. & Gutteridge, J. M. C. (1989) *Free Radicals in Biology and Medicine* (Clarendon, Oxford), 2nd Ed.
2. Fraga, C. G., Shigenaga, M. K., Park, J.-W., Degan, P. & Ames, B. N. (1990) *Proc. Natl. Acad. Sci. USA* **87**, 4533–4537.
3. Tchou, J., Kasai, H., Shibutani, S., Chung, M.-H., Grollman, A. P. & Nishimura, S. (1991) *Proc. Natl. Acad. Sci. USA* **88**, 4690–4694.
4. Michaels, M. L., Pham, L., Cruz, C. & Miller, J. H. (1991) *Nucleic Acids Res.* **19**, 3629–3632.
5. Shibutani, S., Takeshita, M. & Grollman, A. P. (1991) *Nature (London)* **349**, 431–434.
6. Moriya, M., Ou, C., Bodepudi, V., Johnson, F., Takeshita, M. & Grollman, A. P. (1991) *Mutat. Res.* **254**, 281–288.
7. Wood, M. L., Dizdaroglu, M., Gajewski, E. & Essigman, J. M. (1990) *Biochemistry* **29**, 7024–7032.
8. Cabrera, M., Nghiem, Y. & Miller, J. H. (1988) *J. Bacteriol.* **170**, 5405–5407.
9. Au, K. G., Clark, S., Miller, J. H. & Modrich, P. (1989) *Proc. Natl. Acad. Sci. USA* **86**, 8877–8881.
10. Nghiem, Y., Cabrera, M., Cupples, C. G. & Miller, J. H. (1988) *Proc. Natl. Acad. Sci. USA* **85**, 2709–2713.
11. Bodepudi, V., Iden, C. R. & Johnson, F. (1991) *Nucleotides Nucleosides* **10**, 755–761.
12. Cupples, C. G. & Miller, J. H. (1989) *Proc. Natl. Acad. Sci. USA* **86**, 5345–5349.
13. Miller, J. H. (1992) *A Short Course in Bacterial Genetics* (Cold Spring Harbor Lab., Cold Spring Harbor, NY).
14. Miller, J. H. (1972) *Experiments in Molecular Genetics* (Cold Spring Harbor Lab., Cold Spring Harbor, NY).
15. Maki, H. & Sekiguchi, M. (1992) *Nature (London)* **355**, 273–275.
16. Yanofsky, C., Cox, E. C. & Horn, V. (1966) *Proc. Natl. Acad. Sci. USA* **55**, 274–281.
17. Degan, P., Shigenaga, M. K., Park, E.-M., Alperin, P. E. & Ames, B. N. (1991) *Carcinogenesis* **12**, 865–871.
18. Demple, B., Johnson, A. & Fung, D. (1986) *Proc. Natl. Acad. Sci. USA* **83**, 7731–7735.
19. Lin, J. J. & Sancar, A. (1989) *Biochemistry* **28**, 7979–7984.
20. Czeczot, H., Tudek, B., Lambert, B., Laval, J. & Boiteux, S. (1991) *J. Bacteriol.* **173**, 3419–3424.

Unit 9 / Mutagenesis

Farabaugh et al. 1978

1. Describe the system the authors used to examine the distribution of spontaneous mutations.

2. Can you relate these authors' genetic findings to those of Benzer?

3. What is the sequence basis for the large hotspots?

4. What is the sequence basis for preferred deletions?

5. What mechanism(s) did the authors offer to account for the deletions?

Albertini et al. 1982

6. Explain the system constructed by the authors to detect deletions.

7. What did the authors find concerning the distribution of deletions? Were the endpoints randomly distributed?

8. What were the sequences at the deletion endpoints?

9. How did the authors alter the homology responsible for the largest deletion hotspot, and what were the results of this alteration?

10. What mechanism did the authors diagram?

11. What other factors did the authors propose as possibly playing a role in deletion rates?

Prakash and Sherman 1973

12. What is the basic object of this paper?

13. Describe the experimental design of the system used by Prakash and Sherman.

14. What were the authors' basic findings with a series of mutagens?

15. What was concluded about the specificity of the seven mutagens that gave a strong reaction on only one strain?

16. How did the authors rule out that complex changes other than G·C→ A·T transitions resulted in reversion of *cy*1-131?

17. How did the authors caution about generalizing from their results?

18. What model did the authors offer to account for the G·C→A·T specificity of the seven mutagens?

Ames et al. 1973

19. What is the *rfa* mutation and how is it relevant to the work described by the authors?

20. Explain Table 2 on page 369.

21. Which figure compares strains with and without excision repair, and what are the basic findings?

22. Describe the nature and specificity of each of the tester strains.

23. What type of mutation mentioned by the authors cannot be detected by their set of tester strains?

McCann et al. 1975

24. The tester strain TA1535 with the plasmid pKM101 is termed TA100. How does TA100 compare with TA1535 with regard to mutagenicity? Give some examples.

25. How does the presence of the plasmid pKM101 affect the frameshift tester strain TA1538?

26. How do the authors propose to utilize the set of tester strains?

Coulondre and Miller 1977

27. Describe the system used in this paper to determine mutagenic specificity.

28. What are the differences between this system and a reversion system such as used by Ames and co-workers to determine mutagenic specificity? What are the advantages and disadvantages of each type of system?

29. Describe the specificities for EMS and NG. Can you relate those specificities to the chemical properties of the respective mutagens?

30. Explain the specificity of UV irradiation.

31. What system was used to look for the $A \cdot T \rightarrow G \cdot C$ transition?

32. How were double mutations detected? Which mutagens induced these and why?

33. Explain Figure 14 on page 404. How does it relate to the work of Benzer discussed earlier in this course (see Unit 1)?

Coulondre et al. 1978

34. What aspect of the sequence was responsible for spontaneous hotspots due to base substitutions?

35. How was a new hotspot sequence created, and what was the result of it?

36. What was the explanation given for hotspots occurring spontaneously at the sites discussed in Question 35?

37. What aspect of the *lacI* sequence promoted more frequent UV-irradiation-induced transitions? Which figure shows this? Does this explain everything about UV hotspots?

Cupples and Miller 1989

38. Describe the system used to analyze mutations. What type of system is this? How was it built? What are its advantages and disadvantages?

39. What are the results, in detail, of using this system to analyze mutations induced by MNNG and EMS?

40. What is the specificity of 5-azacytidine (5AZ) and the mutator *mutT*?

41. How did the authors plan to use these strains for subsequent experiments?

Nghiem et al. 1988

42. What is a mutator strain?

43. How did the authors devise a papillation assay?

44. Describe exactly how the *mutY* locus was discovered? What were the steps involved in the isolation of this mutant?

45. Which systems were employed to determine the specificity of mutations occurring in a *mutY* strain? What were the results?

Michaels et al. 1992

46. What activities were found for the proteins encoded by the *mutY* and *mutM* genes?

47. What are some of the products of oxidative damage to the DNA?

48. Table 1 on page 425 gives complementation results. What are these results, and what do they signify?

49. What do Tables 2 and 3 on page 425 show?

50. How do the results in Tables 1, 2, and 3 on page 425 suggest a model for the concerted action of both *mutY* and *mutM*? Describe the model.

51. What does the *mutT*-encoded protein do, and how does it fit into the model described in Question 50?

Unit 10

Transposable Elements

Barbara McClintock's classic studies of maize, beginning in the 1930s, resulted in her discovery of mobile genetic elements. These DNA segments moved from one position to another on the same or a different chromosome, often interrupting genes. It was not until the late 1960s, however, that comparable phenomena were elucidated in bacteria. Working independently, Jim Shapiro and Peter Starlinger and co-workers, including Heinz Saedler, defined "insertion" (IS) elements in *Escherichia coli*. These consisted of a class of sequences ranging in size from approximately 750 base pairs to 1500 base pairs that were resident parts of the bacterial chromosome and moved from one position to another. Subsequently, more complex mobile elements were found in bacteria and later in other organisms, such as yeast and *Drosophila*. These elements have been termed "transposons." In bacteria, transposons play a large role in the rapid acquisition of multiple drug-resistance genes by transmissible R factors.

CHARACTERIZATION OF TRANSPOSITION

The paper from Naomi Datta's laboratory by **Hedges and Jacob** is one of the first detailed descriptions of transposition of elements conferring drug resistance (see also Datta et al. and Richmond and Sykes in Additional Readings). Here, the authors demonstrated transposition of the gene encoding ampicillin resistance, *amp*^{r}, from the conjugatable plasmid, the R factor RP4, to several other different plasmids. This indicated that rather than transposing by general recombination in a region of large homology with one specific plasmid, it might transfer indiscriminately to all plasmids. In addition, they showed that a plasmid that had received *amp*^{r} by transposition could itself act as a donor and transpose the *amp*^{r} to a third plasmid. Finally, the authors showed that the molecular weight of plasmids that were transposed to *amp*^{r} increased by about three to eight gene lengths and that the size of the transposed segment was the same in all cases examined.

USE OF TRANSPOSONS AS MUTAGENIC AGENTS

Further characterization of transposition and the use of transposons as mutagenic agents was described in an important paper from David Botstein's laboratory by Nancy **Kleckner** and co-workers. This study dealt with a transposon that carries the genes encoding tetracycline resistance (*tet*^{r}) and used phage P22 and its host *Salmonella typhimurium*. Previous work had characterized a P22 derivative with a DNA insertion of approximately 8.3 kb, which in heteroduplex mapping formed a 1.4-kb stem and a single-stranded loop, indicating a 1.4-kb inverted repeat flanking a unique sequence. The insertion was acquired during growth of the P22 phage on a strain carrying an R factor with a similar *tet*^{r}, leading to the idea that the *tet*^{r} element can transpose as a unit from one DNA molecule to another.

Kleckner and co-workers first characterized two independent *tet*^{r} insertions by heteroduplex mapping and showed that the inserts were at different positions in P22 but consisted of identical sequences. No loss of P22 DNA occurred as a result of the insertions. They then showed that the *tet*^{r} element could transpose from P22 into the *Salmonella* chromosome even when phage and bacterial recombination functions were inactivated and that the phage could not integrate into the chromosome or remain in the host cytoplasm. Some of the transpositions of *tet*^{r} resulted in recognizable mutations, such as auxotrophs requiring proline, methionine, histidine, arginine, or other supplements. Marker-rescue experiments revealed

that no P22 genes were transposed into the chromosome together with the *tet*^{r} element. When P22 generalized transduction was used to transduce the *tet*^{r} to another strain, the auxotrophy was also transduced. In addition, spontaneous revertants of the auxotrophs to prototrophs had lost the *tet*^{r} genes. Thus, the *tet*^{r} element had clearly integrated into specific genes in the *Salmonella* chromosome. Complementation tests with different His$^-$ auxotrophs resulting from *tet*^{r} insertion revealed four different patterns. Many of the *his* insertions exhibited "polar" effects in that the expression of downstream genes in the same operon was sharply reduced.

These experiments solidified the notion of **genetic elements** carrying drug resistance that could transpose from one DNA molecule to another. In addition to the *tet*^{r} element, other elements were described that encoded resistance to different antibiotics, including ampicillin, kanamycin, and chloramphenicol (see papers by Heffron et al., Kopecko and Cohen, Berg et al. [1975], and Gottesman and Rosner in Additional Readings as well as the paper by Hedges and Jacob reprinted here). The similarities of the properties of these transposons with the IS sequences defined by Shapiro and Starlinger and co-workers led to the realization by Kleckner and co-workers that the *tet*^{r} element consisted of two identical IS elements in opposite orientation that flank the *tet*^{r} genes.

MECHANISM OF TRANSPOSITION

Several different modes of transposition have been uncovered by genetic and biochemical analysis: replicative, conservative, and via an RNA intermediate. Let's review one key paper demonstrating each of these transpositional modes.

In the first paper presented here, **Heffron** and co-workers studied the transposon Tn3, which carries the *amp*^{r} gene. Previous work by this group had defined two apparent genes in Tn3 that encoded functions involved in transposition. Mutations in one locus abolish transposition, whereas those in a second locus result in an increase in transposition. In the paper reprinted here, the authors first determined the DNA sequence of the almost 5000 base pairs in the Tn3 transposon. They then determined the sequences of mutations in the *tnpA* gene, which are transposition-defective but can be complemented by a wild-type Tn3. All of the mutations affected the sequence encoding a 1021-amino-acid putative peptide, designated the "transposase." The authors also determined the sequence changes resulting from five mutations in the *tnpR* gene, all of which result in an increase in transposition frequency and are situated in a single coding region. Figure 7 on page 470 depicts the events involved in Tn3 transposition from one circular replicon to another. An intermediate structure, termed a **co-integrate,** is formed by a fusion of the two circular elements with two copies of the Tn3 element, one at each fusion juncture point. This step is catalyzed by the transposase, the product of the *tnpA* gene. Mutations in the *tnpA* gene prevent this structure from forming. Once formed, the co-integrate is resolved by a site-specific recombination event at a sequence in Tn3 termed the internal resolution site, or IRS. Mutations in the IRS prevent resolution of the co-integrate, thus allowing such structures to be recovered. These mutations act only in *cis*, which is as expected if they affect a recognition site on the DNA. Heffron and co-workers sequenced several mutations in the IRS and were able to delineate its boundaries. These authors also demonstrated that the *tnpR* gene encodes a repressor for the transposase. Mutations in *tnpR* result in a tenfold increase in transposase levels and, subsequently, higher transposition.

In the paper by **Bender and Kleckner**, elegant genetic techniques were used to show that Tn*10* transposes by a conservative (nonreplicative) mechanism. The authors used a marked Tn*10* molecule carrying both the *lacZ* gene and the *tet*[r] gene. First, identical elements were prepared, with the only differences being in silent restriction sites and in the *lacZ* gene. One element carried the wild-type *lacZ* gene, whereas the second element carried the Z gene with a single Z[−] point mutation. DNA was made from λ phage carrying each element, and heteroduplexes were prepared by denaturation and annealing. Due to inactivating mutations, the λ phage cannot replicate. After infection, Tet[r] colonies were selected. These result from transposition from the **heteroduplex Tn*10lacZ*** elements. Figure 1 on page 475 shows the products of replicative and nonreplicative transposition. In the replicative mode, only one strand of the donor transposon DNA contributes information, whereas in nonreplicative transposition, both strands contribute information. These two situations can be distinguished by looking for sectored colonies on medium containing Xgal indicator, which is converted to a blue stain by an active β-galactosidase, the product of the *lacZ* gene. Sectored colonies result from heteroduplexes, which give rise to both Lac[+] and Lac[−] cells in the same colony. The presence of such sectored colonies indicates the presence of a heteroduplex *lacZ* transposon. The result was that colonies with both blue and white sectors were observed frequently.

As reported in the paper by **Boeke et al.,** a third mechanism of transposition was revealed by experiments in Gerald Fink's laboratory with the Ty ele-

ment in yeast. Ty elements in yeast are 6 kb long and contain at each end identical 334-base-pair sequences called δ elements. There are about 30 Ty elements in a yeast cell, and they each transcribe a message beginning and ending within the δ elements. They are similar in structure to certain retroviral proviruses, raising the possibility that transposition from one site in the DNA to another might proceed via an **RNA intermediate**.

Boeke and co-workers engineered a high-copy-number plasmid to carry a single Ty element fused to the *GAL1* promoter of yeast, placing Ty transcription under galactose control. To monitor transposition of Ty, they also constructed a plasmid containing a deletion of the *HIS3* gene promoter. In a strain deleted for the chromosomal *HIS* genes, most of the revertants to His[+] are in fact due to Ty insertions upstream of the deleted promoter on the plasmid. Ty transposition was stimulated by turning on the *GAL1* promoter with the addition of galactose.

An **intron** was inserted into a Ty element on the plasmid, in this case the 398-nucleotide yeast ribosomal protein 51 gene intron together with extra flanking sequence. Galactose was added to turn on transposition, and the His[+] revertants in the assay strain were recovered and analyzed. Because the plasmid-derived Ty element had been marked with restriction-site differences, it was easy to determine which of the His[+] revertants were from the Ty element that had contained the intron. In these transposed elements, the intron had been precisely removed at the expected splice junction! In addition, because of a difference between the 5' and 3' δ sequences, it was possible to determine that in the transposed element, a part of the 5' δ sequence acted as a template for the corresponding part of the 3' δ sequence, as would be predicted if transposition occurred via an RNA molecule that was shorter than the whole element and as diagrammed in Figure 8 on page 494.

These experiments demonstrate that a Ty element transposes from one DNA location to another via an RNA intermediate.

CONCLUSIONS

Mobile DNA elements, first discovered by Barbara McClintock's pioneering studies in maize, are present in most organisms studied to date. In bacteria, transposable elements move from one position on the DNA to another by at least two different DNA-mediated modes. Such elements can cause different types of rearrangements, including the movement of other genes that can be incorporated into these elements. The rearrangement of different antibiotic-resistance determinants can be attributed to mobile DNA elements. In eukaryotes, some transposable elements also move via DNA-based mechanisms, although the majority are retrotransposons that transpose from one location to another via an RNA intermediate.

ADDITIONAL READINGS

Berg, C.M., D.E. Berg, and E.A. Groisman. 1989. Transposable elements and the genetic engineering of bacteria. In *Mobile DNA* (ed. D.E. Berg and M.M. Howe), pp. 879–925. American Society for Microbiology, Washington D.C.

Berg, D.E., J. Davies, B. Allet, and J.-D. Rochaix. 1975. Transposition of R factor genes to bacteriophage λ. *Proc. Natl. Acad. Sci.* **72:** 3628–3632.

Datta, N., R.W. Hedges, E.J. Shaw, R.B. Sykes, M.H. Rich-mond. 1971. Properties of an R factor from *Pseudomonas aeruginosa. J. Bacteriol.* **108:** 1244–1249.

Fink, G.R., J.D. Boeke, and D.J. Garfinkel. 1986. The mechanism and consequences of retrotransposition. *Trends Genet.* **2:** 118–123.

Gottesman, M.M. and J.L. Rosner. 1975. Acquisition of a determinant for chloramphenicol resistance by coliphage λ. *Proc. Natl. Acad. Sci.* **72:** 5041–5045.

Heffron, F., C. Rubens, and S. Falkow. 1975. Translocation of a plasmid DNA sequence which mediates ampicillin resistance: Molecular nature and specificity of insertion. *Proc. Natl. Acad. Sci.* **72:** 3623–3627.

Kopecko, D.J. and S.N. Cohen. 1975. Site-specific *recA*-independent recombination between bacterial plasmids: Involvement of palindromes at the recombinational loci. *Proc. Natl. Acad. Sci.* **72:** 1373–1377.

Richmond, M.H. and R.B. Sykes. 1972. The chromosomal integration of a β-lactamase gene derived from the P-type R-factor RP1 in *Escherichia coli. Genet. Res.* **20:** 231–237.

Transposition of Ampicillin Resistance from RP4 to Other Replicons

R. W. Hedges and A. E. Jacob

Bacteriology Department, Royal Postgraduate Medical School, London

Received May 1, 1974

Summary. The ampicillin resistance (β-lactamase) determinant of RP4 can be transposed onto various other replicons genetically unrelated to RP4 including several but not all R factors.

Plasmids which acquire this resistance show an increase in molecular weight. They also acquire the ability to transpose the ampicillin resistance to further replicons.

Introduction

RP4, a plasmid conferring resistance to ampicillin, tetracycline and kanamycin, is the prototype of compatibility group P (Datta, Hedges, Shaw, and Richmond, 1971). Numerous other R factors with identical resistance markers have been taken to be members of group P but the second proven P plasmid was R751, which determined resistance to trimethoprim (Jobanputra and Datta, 1974 and Table 2 lines 6, 7 and 8).

A third P plasmid, R702, conferring resistance to streptomycin, tetracycline, kanamycin, sulphonamides and mercury salts has recently been transferred into *Escherichia coli* K12 from a naturally occurring strain of *Proteus mirabilis* (Hedges, unpublished and Table 2, lines 10, 11, 12, 13 and 14). All three confer sensitivity to an RNA phage PRR1 (Olsen and Shipley, 1973) which adsorbs specifically to the sex pili determined by P group plasmids (Olsen, personal communication).

Datta *et al.* (1971) noted that conjugal transfer of RP4 was markedly reduced by the presence of R64, a plasmid of group Iα (Hedges and Datta, 1973), in the donor. The mechanism of this reduction is not understood. It is not due to inhibition of pilus synthesis (comparable with the inhibition of F pilus synthesis by fi^+ plasmids) since strains carrying RP4 and R64 are visibly lysed by phage PRR1. (Hedges, unpublished).

Transposition of the gene(s) determining ampicillin resistance from RP4 to R64 was reported by Datta *et al.* (1971). Analogous transfer of this determinant to the chromosome of *E. coli* K12 was reported by Richmond and Sykes (1972).

Materials and Methods

E.coli K12 strains:

J53	F⁻ *pro, met (λ)*	Clowes and Hayes (1968),
J62	F⁻ *pro, his, trp (λ)*	Clowes and Hayes (1968),
W677,	F⁻ *thr, leu, thi*	Clowes and Hayes (1968),
AB2487,	F⁻ *thr, leu, pro, trp, arg, thi, recA13*	Bachmann (1972),
AB2487T	F⁻ *thr, leu, pro, trp, arg, thi, recA13 thy*	P. T. Barth (unpublished),
LC173,	F⁻ *thr, leu, thy, ilv, thi, dnaAts* (T46)	Nishimura, Caro, Berg and Hirota (1971).

Table 1. Plasmids used in these experiments

No.	Compatibility	Resistance markers[a]	Origin or reference
RP4	P	A, T, K	Datta *et al.* (1971)
RP4-4	P	A, T	ICR 191 mutagenesis of RP4
RP4-8	P	A, K	ICR 191 mutagenesis of RP4
R702	P	S, T, K, Su	*P. mirabilis* from U.S.A.
R751	P	Tp	Jobanputra and Datta (1974)
R391	J	K	Coetzee, Datta and Hedges (1972)
Sa	W	S, C, K, Su	Hedges and Datta (1971)
R388	W	Su, Tp	Datta and Hedges (1972a)
R64	Iα	S, T	Hedges and Datta (1973)
JR66a	Iω	S, K	Hedges and Datta (1973)
R483	Iβ	S, Tp	Hedges and Datta (1973)

[a] A = ampicillin, S = streptomycin, T = tetracycline, K = kanamycin, C = chloramphenicol, Su = sulphonamides, Tp = trimethoprim.

Plasmids. Listed in Table 1.

Phages. PRR1 (Olsen and Shipley, 1973).

Plasmid Transfer and Compatibility. Techniques described by Datta *et al.* (1971) and Coetzee, Datta and Hedges (1972) *Radiolabelling and lysis of strains, isolation of R plasmid DNA by caesium chloride-ethidium bromide density gradient centrifugation, neutral sucrose gradient analysis and calculation of plasmid molecular weight* were as described by Jacob and Hobbs (1974), except that protoplasts were prepared by incubation with lysozyme for 10 minutes at 37° C before lysis with detergent.

Results

Mutants of RP4

Before the discovery of R702 and R751, it was not possible to test for incompatibility of any pair of naturally occurring R factors of group P, because all conferred identical resistance patterns. However, mutants of RP4 lacking resistance markers were obtained after treatment of J53(RP4) with the mutagen ICR191 (Ames and Whitfield, 1966). Three types of mutant strains were isolated: J53 (RP4-4) which had lost kanamycin resistance, J53(RP4-8) which had lost tetracycline resistance and several strains which had lost both kanamycin and tetracycline. No ampicillin sensitive mutants were observed.

RP4-4 and RP4-8 were self transmissible, mutually incompatible and excluded one another (Table 2, lines 1–5). Since both could revert to the wild type RP4 resistance pattern at low frequency ($<10^{-8}$ per cell) these were presumed to have suffered point mutations.

The other mutants were resistant only to ampicillin. This resistance was not transmissible and was not eliminable by acquisition of P group plasmids. Thus, we conclude that the ampicillin resistance gene(s) in these strains were carried on a replicon distinct from RP4 (presumably the *E. coli* chromosome). Resistance to kanamycin or tetracycline was never regained by mutation.

Table 2. Incompatibility properties of P group plasmids

Donor	Recipient	Drug used for selection	Transfer efficiency	Character of conjugatants
1. J53 (RP4)	J62	A, K, or T	1×10^{-3}	
2. J53 (RP4-4)	,,	T	1×10^{-3}	
3. ,,	J62 (RP4-8)	T	2×10^{-4}	$20/20\mathrm{T^r K^s}$
4. J62 (RP4-8)	J53	K	2×10^{-3}	
5. ,,	J53 (RP4-4)	K	9×10^{-5}	$20/20\mathrm{K^r T^s}$
6. J53 (RP4)	J62 (R751)	K	1×10^{-4}	$20/20\mathrm{K^r Tp^s}$
7. J62 (751)	J53	Tp	1×10^{-3}	
8. ,,	J53 (RP4)	Tp	5×10^{-6}	$10/10\mathrm{Tp^r K^s T^s A^r}$ [b]
9. ,,	W677 (RP4)	Tp	not measured	$10/10\mathrm{Tp^r K^s T^s A^s}$
10. ,,	J53 (R702)	Tp	2×10^{-6}	$20/20\mathrm{Tp^r K^s S^s T^s Su^s}$
11. J62 (R702)	J53	S	8×10^{-4}	
12. ,,	J53 (RP4)	S	7×10^{-5}	$20/20\mathrm{S^r T^r K^r Su^r A^r}$ [b]
13. J62 (R751)	J53 (R702-A^r)[a]	Tp	5×10^{-6}	$20/20\mathrm{Tp^r S^s T^s K^s Su^s A^r}$ [b]
14. J53 (R702)	J62 (R751)	S	5×10^{-6}	$20/20\mathrm{S^r T^r K^r Su^r Tp^s}$

[a] The recipient strain in mating No. 13 was one of the conjugatants from mating No. 12.— Abbreviations: as in Table 1.

[b] The ampicillin resistance was not transmissible.

Failure to Eliminate Ampicillin Resistance from Certain Strains

When R751 was transferred into J53(RP4) resistance to tetracycline and kanamycin was eliminated. Resistance to ampicillin was always retained but was nontransmissible from the conjugatants. Similarly acceptance of R702 never led to the loss of ampicillin resistance from J53(RP4) but the transmissibility of this resistance was lost. (Table 2 lines, 8, 12 and 13).

We conclude that in J53(RP4) the ampicillin resistance was determined by genes at two sites:

(i) On RP4 and hence transmissible and eliminable as part of that plasmid.

(ii) On some other replicon [presumably the bacterial chromosome as found by Richmond and Sykes (1972)] non transferable in these matings.

RP4 was transferred from J53 to a variety of nutritionally distinguishable strains of *E. coli* K12. Selection was made for kanamycin or tetracycline resistance but, among more than a thousand conjugatants tested, all were resistant to ampicillin. Thus, apparently the transposition of ampicillin resistance onto the *E. coli* chromosome did not involve loss of the resistance gene from the plasmid.

R751 was transferred by conjugation into a clone of W677(RP4). All the markers of RP4 (including ampicillin resistance) were eliminated: (Table 2, line 9). We conclude that, in this strain, the ampicillin resistance determinant exists only on the plasmid. Thus, the presence of RP4 in a strain of *E. coli* K12 does not always lead to insertion of the ampicillin resistance determinants into the chromosome.

Transfer of Ampicillin Resistance to Other Plasmids

The transfer of ampicillin resistance from RP4 to R64 (Datta *et al.*, 1971) could imply a homology between the two plasmids or might be a result of indiscriminate transfer of this marker to other replicons. That transposition is not specific for R64 was easily demonstrated by the results of transfer of ampicillin resistance from J53(RP4)(JR66a) to J62. Among ten conjugatants studied one was sensitive to tetracycline (and hence did not carry RP4). This clone J62 (JR66a-1) was tested further and found to be resistant to ampicillin, streptomycin and kanamycin only. Selection with any one of these drugs regularly lead to transfer of all three. The other clones (which could have carried a transposition product as well as RP4) were not tested further.

In order to examine the specificity of transposition, doubles (strains carrying two plasmids) were set up in J62 carrying RP4 and Sa in one case and RP4-4 and R391 in the other. Both doubles were mated with J53, selection being made for transfer of ampicillin resistance. In neither case was the efficiency of transfer of the P plasmid noticeably reduced by the presence of the other R factor.

Among twenty conjugatants from J62(Sa)(RP4) two were sensitive to tetracycline. These were found to show the typical resistances of Sa$^+$ cultures plus ampicillin resistance. One was chosen for further study. All resistances were nontransmissible (efficiency of transfer $< 10^{-9}$). Thus, apparently the insertion of the ampicillin resistance gene(s) had rendered the plasmid *tra*$^-$.

When R388 was transferred into the strain, all testable resistances (including ampicillin resistance) were eliminated. Thus, the ampicillin resistance gene had become part of a plasmid (designated Sa-1) with W compatibility properties. No transposition of ampicillin resistance from RP4-4 to R391 was observed amongst more than 100 conjugatants selected for having acquired ampicillin resistance.

Role of the Bacterial Recombination System

R$^+$ derivatives of 2487T$^-$ carrying RP4 or R64 transfer these plasmids at approximately the same rates as *rec*$^+$ strains and the inhibition of transfer of RP4 by R64 also occurs. When, however, 2487T$^-$(R64)(RP4) was mated with J53, selection being for ampicillin resistance, no conjugatants lacking kanamycin resistance were observed among 122 tested. Thus, apparently transposition of ampicillin resistance onto R64 requires a functional *rec*A product.

Transposition of Ampicillin Resistance from Sa-1

To test whether a plasmid to which ampicillin resistance has been transposed could act as a transposition donor, J53(Sa-1)(R64) was conjugated with J62. Conjugatants simultaneously resistant to tetracycline and ampicillin were selected. Transfer rate was about 10^{-5} per donor and all tested conjugatants (15/15) were resistant to streptomycin [but like R64 and unlike Sa, they were not simultaneously resistant to spectinomycin (Hedges, 1972)] tetracycline and ampicillin; that is they received the R64 determinants together with the ampicillin resistance determinant(s) of Sa-1. These R factors were indistinguishable from R64-1 (R64 carrying the transposed ampicillin resistance) in resistance, transfer and compatibility tests.

Table 3. Molecular weight of the transposition and parental plasmids

Plasmid	Molecular weight[a] (Megadaltons)	Molecular weight difference	cpm plasmid CCC DNA/ cpm chromo- somal DNA	No. of copies CCC DNA/ E. coli chromosome[b]
R64	72.3		0.010	0.4
R64-1	74.0	1.7	0.009	0.3
JR66a	57.4		0.011	0.5
JR66a-1	61.3	3.9	0.011	0.4
Sa	22.0		0.050	5.7
Sa-1	24.9	2.9	0.018	1.8

[a] Molecular weight determined with bacteriophage λ DNA (30.8 Mdal) as reference.
[b] Molecular weight of E. coli chromosome is 2500 Mdal (Cairns, 1963).

When J53(Sa-1)(R391) was tested as donor, no conjugatants resistant to ampicillin and kanamycin were detected although these would have been observed if they had been produced with a frequency of 10^{-8} per donor.

Molecular Weight of Plasmids which have Suffered Transposition

The molecular weight of three plasmids which had suffered transposition R64-1, JR66a-1 and Sa-1, was compared to that of the parental R plasmids, R64, JR66a and Sa respectively. The molecular weight of the parental R factors, each radiolabelled with ^{3}H, was determined by comparing their sedimentation rate through a neutral sucrose gradient with ^{14}C-labelled bacteriophage λ DNA as reference. The molecular weight of the transposition plasmids (labelled with ^{14}C) was then determined by direct comparison with the parental R plasmid. The results are presented in Fig. 1 and Table 3. Sedimentation of the DNA was from right to left in the gradients. The faster sedimenting bands in each gradient have been shown to be the covalently closed circular DNA form of each plasmid (data not shown) and the slower sedimenting bands are the open circular forms. It is clear that each of the transposition plasmids has a higher molecular weight than its parental plasmid. The increase in molecular weight of the transposition plasmids is, within experimental error, very similar and was calculated to be within 1.7 to 3.9 Megadaltons.

Failure of P Plasmids to Effect Integrative Suppression

Chromosomal integration of a plasmid capable of autonomous replication can restore ability to grow at 40–43° C to mutant strains of E. coli whose ability to initiate DNA synthesis had become thermolabile (Nishimura, Caro, Berg and Hirota, 1971). The presence of RP4, R702 or R751 in strain LC173 did not increase the efficiency of colony formation at 42° C. Thus, apparently, these plasmids rarely or never integrate in the E. coli K12 chromosome in such a way as to relieve the dependence of the host on the product of the dnaA gene.

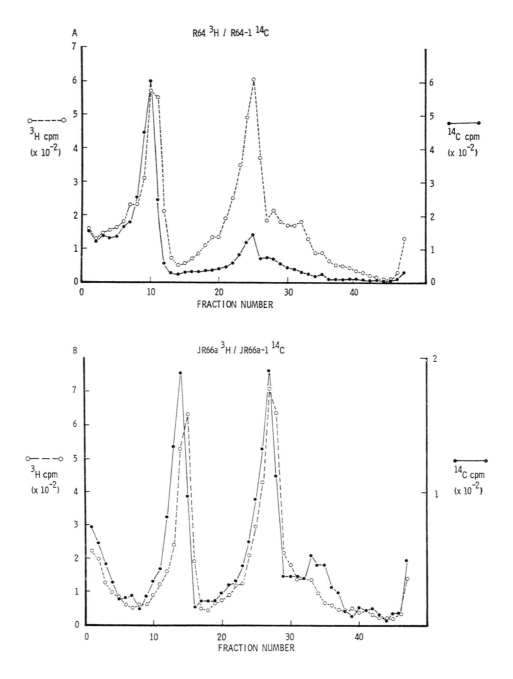

Fig. 1. Neutral sucrose gradient analysis of plasmid DNA carrying transposon A. Each
[14]C-labelled plasmid DNA carrying transposon A was mixed with the appropriate ^{3}H-labelled
parental plasmid and sedimented through a 5–20% sucrose gradient at $100\,000 \times g$, 20° C,
for 90 min. 0.1 ml fractions were collected directly onto glass fibre discs and, after drying
and washing, were assayed for ^{3}H and ^{14}C radioactivity

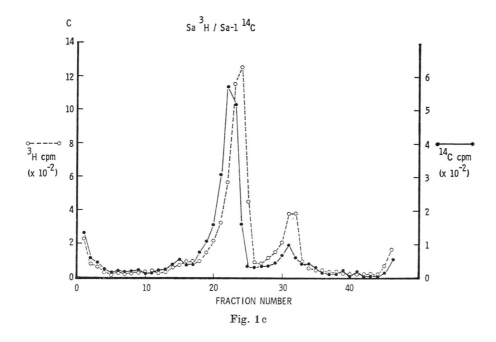

Fig. 1 c

Production of β-Lactamase by Strains Carrying R64-1, JR66a-1 and Sa-1

In *E. coli* J53 these three R factors all produced β-lactamase. According to the criteria of Hedges, Datta, Kontomichalou and Smith (1974) these R factors produce more than 500 units of enzyme activity per 10^9 cells.

Discussion

The ampicillin resistance of RP4 was shown by Datta *et al.* (1971) to be very readily transferred to R64. It was particularly easy to demonstrate transposition to R64 because the presence of R64 markedly reduced the rate of transfer of RP4. Thus a high proportion of ampicillin resistant conjugatants (from a mating in which an RP4+, R64+ double was donor) carried ampicillin resistance transposed onto R64 and only a small proportion carried complete RP4.

Transposibility was not limited to plasmids of the I complex. Transposition to the chromosome of *E. coli* K12 (Richmond and Sykes, 1972) and to Sa have been demonstrated. The latter plasmid is of particular interest since there is no significant homology between the DNA of Sa and that of either RP4 or Iα plasmids (Ingram, 1973; Falkow, Guerry, Hedges and Datta: in preparation). However, several attempts to transpose ampicillin resistance to R391 failed. Thus, not all replicons could act as transposition acceptors and there must be some degree of discrimination between potential receptor sequences. Transposibility was limited to the ampicillin resistance determinants. Neither the kanamycin and tetracycline resistances, the sensitivity to phage PRR1 (Olsen and Shipley,

1973), the compatibility properties of RP4 (Datta *et al.*, 1971), nor the capacity to transfer to the remarkable range of genera into which RP4, but not R64, can transfer (Datta and Hedges, 1972b; Olsen and Shipley, 1973) were transposed. However, genetic determinant(s) of transposability must have been themselves transposed since ampicillin resistance transposed onto Sa-1 could undergo a second transposition step onto R64.

The transposition of ampicillin resistance therefore seems to be by a specific mechanism. The alternative explanation in terms of conventional recombination mechanisms is implausible for the following reasons:

1. DNA homology tests show that plasmids of the I complex (R64 and JR66a), group P (RP4) and group W (Sa) have no significant homology (Falkow, Guerry Hedges and Datta, in preparation). Thus, the extremely efficient transfer of ampicillin resistance (but not other markers) between these R factors requires a special explanation.

2. In the three cases examined, plasmids which had received ampicillin resistance from RP4 increased their molecular weight by amounts calculated as between 1.7 and 3.9 Mdal. Allowing for the errors in the technique we can say that a similarly sized, perhaps identical, piece of DNA was transferred in each transposition event. Such uniformity would be an improbable consequence of random recombination, but seems to require a specific transposition mechanism. We designate DNA sequences with transposition potential as *transposons* (units of transposition) and the transposon marked by the ampicillin resistance gene(s) as transposon A. A transposon of this size is likely to be able to accommodate about 3–8 genes. At least one gene is required to determine β-lactamase production and Curtis, Richmond and Stanisich (1973) have suggested that the ampicillin resistance of RP4 involves two distinct mechanisms determined by separate genes. Thus, up to 7 genes may be available for the transposition determinants and any other functions. The failure to detect transposition from RP4 to R64 in a *rec*A mutant strain suggests that the chromosomally determined recombination enzymes are required for transposition but we have no evidence for the nature of the determinants located in the transposon.

The phenomena most closely analogous to the transposition of ampicillin resistance may be the insertion mutations described by Jordan, Saedler and Starlinger (1968) and Starlinger and Saedler (1972). These mutations are due to the insertion of DNA sequences into the continuity of a gene. Like transposon A the insertion sequences can integrate into the *E. coli* chromosome or into an autonomous plasmid (Saedler and Heiß, 1973). These sequences are shorter than transposon A (Hirsch, Starlinger and Brachet, 1972; Malamy, Fiandt and Szybalski, 1972; Fiandt, Szybalski and Malamy, 1972) and are not known to carry any active genetic determinants comparable with the ampicillin resistance gene(s) but in other respects seem analogous.

A question which remains to be answered is whether the transposon can dissociate from a plasmid and replicate autonomously before suffering transposition to some new replicon. However, we have found no evidence of any ability to replicate autonomously in three situations where such evidence might have been forthcoming:

1. Studies on the covalently closed circular DNA of plasmids including the transposon failed to show evidence for a species with a molecular weight of 1–4 megadaltons (Fig. 1).

2. The transfer of ampicillin resistance from J53 (Sa-1) (R64) might have been expected to include examples of the mobilization of autonomous copies of transposon A (rather than the transfer of this element integrated into R64). We observed no examples of this type of conjugatant.

3. Integration of plasmids capable of autonomous replication into chromosomes of mutant strains of *E. coli* in which the initiation of DNA synthesis is thermolabile permits colony formation at elevated temperatures (Nishimura *et al.*, 1971). We observed no increase in the efficiency of colony formation in such a mutant strain carrying RP4. Thus, apparently, integration of the transposon does not permit the chromosome to replicate from a replicator site in the transposon sequence. This suggests, but does not prove, that the DNA replicator and initiator genes of RP4 are not able to integrate into the *E. coli* chromosome.

This evidence also implies that the transposition mechanism is specific for the transposon as a separate unit; it cannot cause the integration of the whole RP4 sequence even though this is continuous with the transposon sequence.

Hedges *et al.* (1974) noted that ampicillin resistance determined by a diversity of unrelated plasmids was mediated by apparently identical β-lactamases. The ease with which the genetic determinant of this enzyme, as part of transposon A, can be transferred from one replicon to another may, in part, explain the promiscuity of the gene determining this enzyme.

Hedges *et al.* (1974) suggested that those plasmids, whose presence leads to the formation of large quantities of β-lactamase, might replicate under relaxed control *i.e.* a cell might contain numerous copies of such a plasmid. The ratio of plasmid to chromosomal DNA shows that R64-1, JR66-1 and Sa-1 probably replicate under stringent control (0.3–1.8 copies per chromosome). Since these R factors determine large amounts of β-lactamase, the notion that production of large amounts of β-lactamase implies multiple plasmid copies cannot be universally applied.

Acknowledgements. We are very grateful to Dr. J. T. Smith for penicillinase assays, to Dr. L. Caro for supplying *E. coli* strain LC173, to Dr. H. J. Creech for the gift of the mutagen ICR191, to Susan Hobbs, Peter Barth and Nigel Grinter for assistance in the characterization of plasmid DNAs and to Naomi Datta for advice and encouragement. A. E. Jacob was supported by a grant to Naomi Datta from the Medical Research Council of the United Kingdom.

References

Ames, B. N., Whitfield, H. J., Jr.: Frameshift mutagenesis in *Salmonella*. Cold Spr. Harb. Symp. quant. Biol. **31**, 221 (1966)

Bachmann, B. J.: Pedigrees of some mutant strains of *Escherichia coli* K12. Bact. Rev. **36**, 525 (1972)

Cairns, J.: The bacterial chromosome and its manner of replication as seen by autoradiography. J. molec. Biol. **6**, 208 (1963)

Clowes, R. C., Hayes, W.: Experiments in microbial genetics. Blackwell Oxford and Edinburgh: Scientific Publications 1968

Coetzee, J. N., Datta, N., Hedges, R. W.: R factors from *Proteus rettgeri*. J. gen. Microbiol. **72**, 543 (1972)

Curtis, N. A. C., Richmond, M. H., Stanisich, V.: R factor mediated resistance to penicillins which does not involve a β-lactamase. J. gen. Microbiol. **79**, 163 (1973)

Datta, N., Hedges, R. W.: Trimethoprim resistance conferred by W plasmids in Enterobacteriaceae. J. gen. Microbiol. **72**, 349 (1972a)

Datta, N., Hedges, R. W.: Host ranges of R factors. J. gen. Microbiol. **70**, 453 (1972b)

Datta, N., Hedges, R. W., Shaw, E. J., Sykes, R. B., Richmond, M. H.: Properties of an R factor from *Pseudomonas aeruginosa*. J. Bact. **108**, 1244 (1971)

Fiandt, M., Szybalski, W., Malamy, M. H.: Polar mutations in *lac*, *gal* and phage λ consist of a few IS-DNA sequences inserted with either orientation. Molec. gen. Genet. **119**, 223 (1972)

Hedges, R. W.: Resistance to spectinomycin determined by R factors of various compatibility groups. J. gen. Microbiol. **72**, 407 (1972)

Hedges, R. W., Datta, N.: *fi⁻* R factors giving chloramphenicol resistance. Nature (Lond.) **234**, 220 (1971)

Hedges, R. W., Datta, N.: Plasmids determining I pili constitute a compatibility complex. J. gen. Microbiol. **77**, 19 (1973)

Hedges, R. W., Datta, N., Kontomichalou, P., Smith, J. T.: Molecular specificities of R factor determined β-lactamases: correlation with plasmid compatibility. J. Bact. **117**, 56 (1974)

Hirsch, H. J., Starlinger, P., Brachet, P.: Two kinds of insertions in bacterial genes. Molec. gen. Genet. **119**, 191 (1972)

Ingram, L. C.: Deoxyribonucleic acid-deoxyribonucleic acid hybridization of R factors. J. Bact. **115**, 1130 (1973)

Jacob, A. E., Hobbs, S. J.: Conjugal transfer of plasmid-borne multiple antibiotic resistance in *Streptococcus faecalis* var *zymogenes*. J. Bact. **117**, 360 (1974)

Jobanputra, R. S., Datta, N.: Trimethoprim resistance factors in enterobacteria from clinical specimens. J. med. Microbiol. **7**, 169 (1974)

Jordan, E., Saedler, H., Starlinger, P.: 0°-and strong-polar mutations in the *gal* operon are insertions. Molec. gen. Genet. **102**, 353 (1968)

Malamy, M. H., Fiandt, M., Szybalski, W.: Electron microscopy of polar insertions in the *lac* operon of *Escherichia coli*. Molec. gen. Genet. **119**, 207 (1972)

Nishimura, Y., Caro, L., Berg, C. M., Hirota, Y.: Chromosome replication in *Escherichia coli* IV. Control of chromosome replication and cell division by an integrated episome. J. molec. Biol. **55**, 441 (1971)

Olsen, R. H., Shipley, P.: Host range and properties of the *Pseudomonas aeruginosa* R factor R1822. J. Bact. **113**, 772 (1973)

Richmond, M. H., Sykes, R. B.: The chromosomal integration of a β-lactamase gene derived from the P-type R factor RP1 in *Escherichia coli*. Genet. Res. **20**, 231 (1972)

Saedler, H., Heiß, B.: Multiple copies of the insertion—DNA sequences IS1 and IS2 in the chromosome of *E. coli* K-12. Molec. gen. Genet. **122**, 267 (1973)

Starlinger, P., Saedler, H.: Insertion mutations in micro-organisms. Biochimie **54**, 177 (1972)

Communicated by W. Maas

Dr. R. W. Hedges
Dr. A. E. Jacob
Bacteriology Department
Royal Postgraduate Medical School
Du Cane Road
London W12 OHS, England

Mutagenesis by Insertion of a Drug-resistance Element Carrying an Inverted Repetition

Nancy Kleckner, Russell K. Chan†, Bik-Kwoon Tye‡
and David Botstein

Department of Biology
Massachusetts Institute of Technology
Cambridge, Mass. 02139, U.S.A.

(Received 19 June 1975)

A novel genetic element, which carries genes conferring tetracycline resistance (flanked by a 1400 base-pair inverted repetition), is capable of translocation as a unit from one DNA molecule to another. The *tet*R element, which is found in nature on a variety of R-factors, was acquired by bacteriophage P22 (producing P22Tc-10 and P22Tc-106) and has now been observed to insert into a large number of different sites on the *Salmonella* chromosome. Insertion of the *tet*R element is mutagenic when it occurs within a structural gene, and polar when it occurs within an operon. Insertion of the element is usually precise, occurring without loss of information on the recipient DNA molecule. Excision, on the other hand, is usually *not* precise, although excisions precise enough to restore a gene function can always be detected at low frequencies. Both insertion and excision processes are independent of the *recA* function.

1. Introduction

Bacteriophage P22 is a temperate phage whose normal host is *Salmonella typhimurium*. We described previously an unusual variant of P22 (called P22Tc-10) which transduces resistance to tetracycline at high frequency (Watanabe *et al.*, 1972; Chan *et al.*, 1972). Examination of P22Tc-10 DNA in the electron microscope showed that this specialized transducing variant contains a large (8·3 kilobase) insertion which has an unusual structure: in heteroduplex DNA molecules, the insertion forms a lariat-like structure with a double-stranded stem (about 1·4 kilobases long) and a single-stranded loop (Tye *et al.*, 1974). This is interpreted to mean that the insertion consists of an inverted duplication separated by non-repeated DNA sequences.

The *tet*R insertion was acquired by P22 during a lytic cycle of growth in a *Salmonella* strain harboring a drug-resistance plasmid (R-factor) in whose DNA a similar non-tandem reverse duplication was found to be associated with the genetic determinant for tetracycline resistance (Watanabe *et al.*, 1972; Sharp *et al.*, 1973). Two independently-arising tetracycline-transducing P22 phages were examined in our previous studies and both had identical insertions (Watanabe *et al.*, 1972; Tye *et al.*,

---

† Present address: Department of Genetics, SK-50, University of Washington, Seattle, Wash. 98195, U.S.A.

‡ Present address: Department of Biochemistry, Stanford University School of Medicine, Stanford, Calif. 94305, U.S.A.

1974). In neither case was there any detectable (less than 100 bases) loss of P22 DNA accompanying the insertion.

More recently, we found that the site of the tet^R insertion in P22Tc-10 is not the phage attachment site: i.e. the insertion is not at the point at which the prophage is integrated by site-specific recombination into the *Salmonella* chromosome (Chan & Botstein, 1975). This made it unlikely that P22Tc-10 was formed by the mechanism normally associated with the production of specialized-transducing genomes of temperate phages (Campbell, 1962).

From these observations, and from other aspects of the genetic behavior of P22Tc-10, we formed the hypothesis that the tet^R element from the R-factor (with its inverted repeat) is capable of translocation, as a discrete unit, from one DNA molecule into any one of many different places on other DNA molecules. This paper describes both physical and genetic evidence in support of this idea.

Berg *et al.* (1975) have recently isolated coliphage λ-transducing variants carrying a kanamycin-resistant determinant which is associated with an inverted repetition. The structures of these phages is analogous to that of P22Tc-10. Heffron *et al.* (1975a,b) have recently shown that an ampicillin-resistance determinant, associated with a very small inverted repetition, is capable of translocation from one DNA molecule to another.

We suggest that genetic elements like the tet^R, amp^R and kan^R insertions play an important role in reassortment of drug-resistance determinants among resistance factors. The apparent ubiquity of inverted repetitions in both prokaryotic (Sharp *et al.*, 1972, 1973; Daniell *et al.*, 1973; Berg *et al.*, 1975; Heffron *et al.*, 1975b; Hsu & Davidson, 1975) and eukaryotic DNA (Garon *et al.*, 1972; Wolfson & Dressler, 1972; Locker *et al.*, 1974; Manning *et al.*, 1975; Wadsworth *et al.*, 1975) further suggests that such elements could play an important role in the mobilization and translocation of genetic information in many different biological systems.

2. Materials and Methods

(a) *Bacteriophage*

The P22Tc-10 and P22Tc-106 genomes are too long to fit into a single P22 phage head. The strains are therefore maintained as lysogens which, upon induction, give rise to particles which are defective on single infection (Chan *et al.*, 1972; Tye *et al.*, 1974). Tc-10 recombinants carrying the additional mutations c_2ts29 (heat-inducible repressor (Levine & Smith, 1964)); erf-$am12B$ (recombination-deficient (Botstein & Matz, 1970)); or int_3 (integration-deficient (Smith & Levine, 1967)) were constructed by crosses with induced lysates (Chan *et al.*, 1972) or rescue of tet^R from prophage deletions (Chan, 1974).

P22int_3 HT 12/4 was constructed in a standard phage cross between P22c^+int_3 and P22c_2^- HT 12/4 (Schmieger, 1972), a high-frequency generalized transducing derivative of P22.

(b) *Bacteria*

Strains of *S. typhimurium* used:

(i) In isolation of tet^R auxotrophs: DB7000 = LT2 $leuA414$ (Susskind *et al.*, 1974); NK80 = LT2 edd^- constructed for this work from two his^-edd^- strains obtained from J. Roth); and DB143 = LT7 $proAB47$ (deleted for P22 attachment site) $recA^-$ (Miyake & Demerec, 1960).

(ii) In complementation studies: the following strains were all the gift of John Roth: (1) derivatives of LT2 $trpA8$ $purE801$ $his612$ (BHAFIE deletion) carrying *Escherichia coli* F'hisbG2377, F'hisabD2381, and F'hisabD2382; (2) derivatives of LT2 $ser821$ $arg501$

*his*712 (DCBHAFIE deletion) carrying *E. coli* F′*his*⁺, F′*his*C2383, F′*his*C2385, F′*his* a(b)cdB2405, F′*his*abI2312 a(b)E, F′*his* bI2413, F′*his* a(b)E2414, and F′*his* a(b)cd B245. (The small letters denote deficiencies of the mutant with respect to intragenic complementation groups.)

(iii) In deletion mapping: for *his* deletion strains listed in Fig. 2, endpoints of deletions with respect to known *his* point mutations are shown in Hartman *et al.* (1971) and Scott & Roth (1975). Deletion strains were kindly supplied by J. Roth and P. Hartman.

(c) *Media*

Complete liquid medium: LB (Chan & Botstein, 1972); solid minimal medium: M9 + 1·5% agar (Smith & Levine, 1964); complete solid media: green plates (Chan & Botstein, 1972), trypticase plates (Stahl & Stahl, 1971). P22 phage stocks are stored and diluted in buffered saline (Chan & Botstein, 1972).

(d) *Visualization of DNA heteroduplexes in the electron microscope*

Procedures used for the isolation of phage DNA and for preparation and visualization of DNA in heteroduplex structures were as described by Tye *et al.* (1974).

(e) *Isolation of* tet^R *auxotrophs*

Stocks of P22Tc-10 derivatives were made by induction of corresponding lysogens (Chan *et al.*, 1972); lysates were purified once through discontinuous CsCl gradients and the concentration of particles determined from the A_{260} (Chan *et al.*, 1972). Exponentially growing recipient bacteria were mixed directly with phage at a multiplicity of 2 to 13 particles per cell, and after 10 to 30 min, were spread directly on green plates supplemented with 25 μg tetracycline hydrochloride (Calbiochem)/ml and 0·01 M-EGTA (Eastman). Plates were incubated at 37°C (experiment A) or 41°C (experiments B and C) and then replica plated onto M9 plates supplemented with glucose and any other nutrient required by the recipient strain (DB143 is *pro*⁻ and DB7000 is *leu*⁻). In accordance with the notation introduced by Bukhari & Metlay (1973) for mutations made by insertion of phage Mu, the symbol :: will be used here to indicate that the *tet*^R element is inserted at the locus preceding the symbol. For example, *his*::*tet*^R means that the *tet*^R element is inserted into the histidine operon.

(f) *Phage P22-mediated generalized transduction*

P22 is capable of mediating generalized transduction of bacterial DNA from one host strain to another (Zinder & Lederberg, 1952). For all generalized transduction experiments described here, the P22 derivative *int*₃ HT 12/4 was used. The HT 12/4 mutation, isolated and characterized by Schmieger (1972) and Raj *et al.* (1974), greatly increases the proportion of generalized transducing particles in a phage lysate. The *int*₃ mutation (Smith & Levine, 1967) prevents integration of normal P22 genomes into the host chromosome in the course of the transduction experiment.

Transducing lysates were made by putting a seed stock through a single cycle of growth on appropriate donor strains. For transducing lysates used in deletion mapping, the seed stock used to make single-cycle stocks was grown on a strain deleted for the entire histidine operon in order to prevent carry-over of *his*⁺ transducing particles from the seed stock to the transducing lysates.

For co-transduction experiments (Table 2), exponential cultures of the recipient strain were infected directly with the various transducing lysates at a multiplicity of 10. After 15 min adsorption at room temperature, the mixtures were diluted and spread on green plates +25 μg tetracycline/ml, and the plates were incubated at 37°C. Resulting *tet*^R colonies were then tested for growth in M9–glucose plates, and on either M9 glucose and leucine, M9–glucose and histidine, or M9–gluconate plates in order to detect the donor auxotrophy.

For deletion mapping (Fig. 2), recipient *his*-deletion strains were grown to 2×10^9 cells/ml in LB broth. 0·15 ml bacteria, 0·1 ml transducing lysate (at 1 to 3×10^{10} phage/ml), and 0·15 ml LB broth were then spread together directly on an M9–glucose plate (without prior pre-adsorption of phage and bacteria). Plates were incubated at 37°C for 2 days before scoring for the appearance of *his*⁺ recombinants. With this protocol, a positive result meant that *at least* 50 (and as many as 10⁴) *his*⁺ recombinants appeared on a single plate. A negative result meant that *no* (0) *his*⁺ recombinants appeared. As expected for deletion mutants, no *his*⁺ revertants of the recipient strains were ever observed.

(g) *Complementation of F'his strains by* his::tet^R *auxotrophs*

The histidine operons of *S. typhimurium* and *E. coli* can complement each other for all of the functions in the histidine biosynthesis pathway; however, recombinants between the two operons are almost never observed (Atkins & Loper, 1970). We asked which *his* functions can be provided by *his*::*tet*ᴿ auxotrophs by replica plating patches of *Salmonella* strains carrying F'*his* episomes (which themselves carried *his*⁻ mutations in various genes) onto minimal plates spread with cultures of the various *his*::*tet*ᴿ auxotrophs. The donor strain was counter-selected by omission of required nutrients (serine and arginine or tryptophan and purines). The F'*his* episome should mate into the *his*::*tet*ᴿ strain, but growth in the region of a patch will be seen only if the *his*::*tet*ᴿ recipient can supply the *his* function(s) not made by the F'*his*.

Cultures of donor F'*his* strains were spotted onto trypticase plates, and grown for 16 h at 37°C prior to replica plating. *His*::*tet*ᴿ auxotrophs were grown to late log phase and 0·15 ml was spread directly on M9 plates. After replica plating, plates were incubated for 48 h at 37°C prior to scoring.

Various F⁻*his*-deletion strains were included as control recipients to verify that the internal promoters detected by Atkins & Loper (1970) in such experiments were also detected here. A strain carrying an F'*his*⁺ episome was included among donors as a control for the ability of *his*::*tet*ᴿ auxotrophs to function as recipients and for the absence of negative complementation.

3. Results

(a) *DNA heteroduplexes between two independent P22* tet^R *transducing phage*

When a mixture of DNA from the two independent P22 *tet*ᴿ-transducing phages (P22Tc-10 and P22Tc-106) was denatured, slowly reannealed, and examined by electron microscopy, a number of unusual structures were seen. The structure shown in Plate I(a) is apparently a heteroduplex molecule containing one strand of Tc-10 and one strand of Tc-106, since the two complementary strands are not the same. From this structure, it is clear that Tc-10 and Tc-106 each contain a single insertion which is unaccompanied by any detectable loss of P22 DNA (less than 50 to 100 bases). The Tc-10 and Tc-106 insertions are indistinguishable; both are of the same total length and are bounded by inverted repetitions of similar size. The only difference between the two transducing phages appears to be the location of the insertion into the P22 genome. This indicates that there is more than one possible site for insertion of the *tet*ᴿ element.

Another structure which is seen in Tc-10/Tc-106 DNA heteroduplex preparations is shown in Plate I(b). This structure differs from that in Plate I(a) in that there has been partial pairing between the two single-strand "loops" of the inserted material. The pattern of paired and unpaired regions is reproducible among the many such structures we have seen. We interpret these structures to mean that the insertions carried by Tc-10 and Tc-106 are actually totally homologous, and that such structures represent instances in which intra-molecular pairing between the self-complementary portions of each strand preceded inter-molecular pairing between the complementary strands of the loop. Complete pairing in the loop region is apparently obstructed by by steric constraints imposed by the prior pairing of the self-complementary regions.

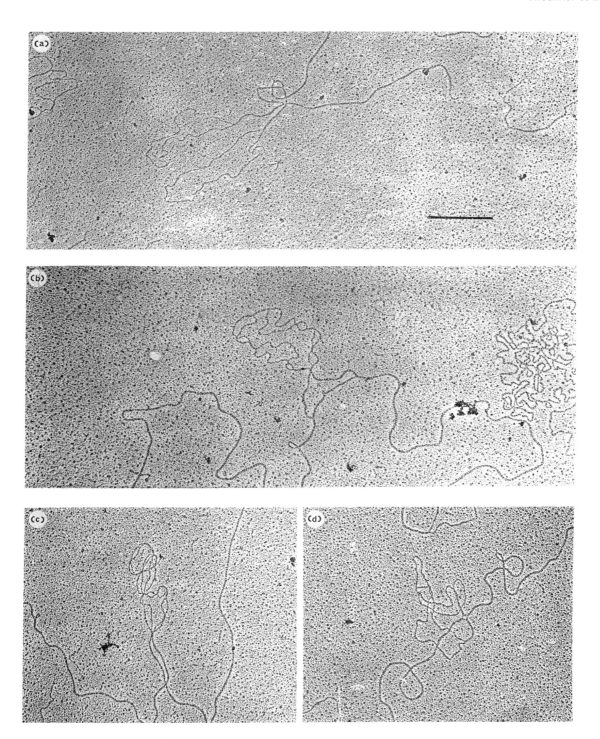

PLATE I. Heteroduplexes of Tc-10 and Tc-106.
(a) Tc-10/Tc-106 heteroduplex in which loops have not interacted.
(b) Tc-10/Tc-106 heteroduplex in which loops have interacted.
(c) Homoduplex (Tc-10/Tc-10 or Tc-106/Tc-106) in which loops have interacted.
(d) Homoduplex (Tc-10/Tc-10 or Tc-106/Tc-106) in which loops have not interacted but branch migration has occurred around the point of the insertions.
The bar represents 0·5 μm.

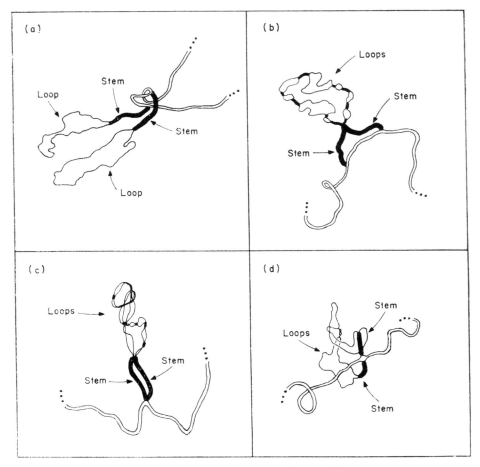

Fig. 1. Interpretation of heteroduplexes in Plate I.
(a) to (d) Correspond to micrographs (a) to (d) in Plate I. ■■■■■, Paired stems (double-stranded); ━━━━, paired regions within the loop (double-stranded); ─────, unpaired regions within the loop (single-stranded); ═════, P22 DNA (double-stranded).

Implicit in this interpretation is the idea that the insertions carried by P22Tc-10 and P22Tc-106 are not only homologous in base sequence but are also oriented in the same direction with respect to the P22 genome.

Alternative explanations for the structures in Plate I(b) involve partial homology within the loops. These alternative explanations are made less likely by the appearance of homoduplex molecules in the same experiment (Plate I(c)). In these structures, the stem and loop is seen emanating from the same point on the P22 genome; and here also the loops have interacted to give a partially paired structure whose pattern of paired and unpaired regions is very similar to that seen in heteroduplex molecules like the one shown in Plate I(b). Measurement of the lengths of the stems in these molecules indicates that "branch migration" (Lee *et al.*, 1970; Broker & Lehman, 1971) has occurred at the junction between the inserted DNA and the P22 DNA. For example, the lengths of both stems in Plate I(d) are about half the normal stem length measured for other stems in the same field. Observation of branch migration (in about half of the twenty homoduplexes examined) verifies that the two insertions are actually located at the same point. The slightly separated structure (resembling a square), at the point of the insertion in Plate I(d), is typical of double-stranded branch migrations of this sort (Broker, personal communication).

In summary, P22Tc-10 and P22Tc-106 apparently contain identical insertions (unaccompanied by detectable deletion of P22 DNA) of foreign material at different locations on the P22 genome.

(b) *Mutagenesis of* Salmonella *by insertion of the* tet^R *element carried by Tc-10*

The above physical evidence suggests that the integrity of the *tet*^{R} insertion (bounded by its inverted repetition) has been maintained during translocation of the material from the R-factor onto the P22 genome. The genetic evidence which follows shows that this *tet*^{R} element is capable of further translocation *out* of the P22 genome and *into* many different locations on the chromosome of *S. typhimurium*.

When P22 Tc-10 infects *Salmonella* under conditions where the phage DNA is unable to maintain itself in the host cell, transductants carrying the *tet*^{R} determinant are still obtained. As shown in Table 1, *tet*^{R} transductants are obtained at low frequencies after infection even in the absence of phage (*erf*$^-$) and bacterial (*recA*$^-$) recombination functions, and even though the infecting phage is unable to integrate (*int*$^-$/*ataA*$^-$), or repress (*c2*^{ts}) (Watanabe *et al.*, 1972; Chan *et al.*, 1972; Tye *et al.*, 1974).

Since it seemed possible that these *tet*^{R} transductants had arisen simply by translocation of the *tet*^{R} element out of the P22 genome and into the *Salmonella* chromosome we sought to identify instances in which the insertion into the host chromosome had resulted in an identifiable mutation. We screened *tet*^{R} transductants (isolated on rich medium) for ones which had simultaneously acquired an auxotrophic mutation making them unable to grow on minimal medium. As shown in Table 1, roughly 1% of all *tet*^{R} transductants were auxotrophs. A wide variety of nutritional requirements is represented: out of 142 independent auxotrophs, 27 required proline, 18 methionine, 17 histidine, 12 purines, 8 isoleucine, 8 arginine, 7 tryptophan, 5 cysteine, 3 leucine,

TABLE 1

Isolation of tet^R *auxotrophs*

Expt	Phage	Bacterium	Frequency *tet*^{R} transductants per infecting phage particle	Percentage of auxotrophs among *tet*^{R} transductants
A	P22Tc-10*erf*$^-$	*recA*$^-$ *ata*$^\triangledown_{P22}$	1×10^{-7}	~1 (14/~1500)
B	P22Tc-10*int*$^-$*c2ts*	*rec*$^+$ *ata*$^+_{P22}$	not measured	2 (7/362)
C	P22Tc-10*int*$^-$*c2ts*	*rec*$^+$ *ata*$^+_{P22}$	3×10^{-7}	1 (79/7892)

Bacteria were infected with derivatives of P22Tc-10 as indicated above and as described in Materials and Methods. *trt*^{R} transductants obtained from these infections were replica-plated directly onto minimal medium in order to identify auxotrophs. Candidate auxotrophs were then cloned and auxotrophy verified. In experiment C, 120 separate mixtures of phage and bacteria were made; transductants coming from different mixtures are assumed to be independent. In experiments B and C, different recipient strains were used (DB7000 and NK80, respectively).

3 thiamine, 2 alanine, 2 lysine, 1 phenylalanine, 1 tyrosine, 1 threonine, and 25 required nutrients as yet unidentified. This distribution, with its predominance of proline, methionine, purine, and histidine auxotrophs is similar to that obtained after standard chemical mutagenesis of *Salmonella*.

If these *tet*[R] auxotrophs indeed represent simple insertion of the *tet*[R] element alone into the *Salmonella* chromosome, these transductants should not carry an P22 genes. 18 of these *tet*[R] auxotrophs have been tested by marker rescue for the presence of alleles in any of 15 different P22 genes spanning the known genetic map; no rescue was observed.

Two types of experiments provide direct evidence that in these *tet*[R] auxotrophs the *tet*[R] element is intimately associated, both physically and functionally, with the simultaneously acquired auxotrophic mutations:

(1) When the *tet*[R] determinant from these auxotrophs is transferred to another *Salmonella* strain by P22-mediated generalized transduction, all of the recipient bacteria which have become *tet*[R] have also acquired the corresponding auxotrophic requirement (Table 2). Absolute co-transduction of the auxotrophy with the *tet*[R] suggests that the two determinants are physically very closely linked.

(2) A large number of independent *tet*[R] auxotrophs carrying a wide variety of auxotrophic mutations have been reverted to prototrophy. Revertants were obtained at frequencies of 10^{-9} to 3×10^{-7}, depending upon the strain. For 33/37 auxotrophs tested, reversion to prototrophy was always accompanied by loss of the *tet*[R] determinant (Table 3). Thus, not only have these *tet*[R] transductants simultaneously acquired a new auxotrophic mutation, but revertants of the new mutations have simultaneously lost *tet*[R].

These data strongly suggest that the acquisition of tetracycline resistance and of auxotrophy are the consequence of the same event, namely, the insertion of the *tet*[R] element into the affected gene. The wide distribution of auxotrophic requirements

TABLE 2

Co-transduction of auxotrophy with tetracycline resistance

Donor strain (*tet*[R] auxotroph)	Donor auxotrophy	Proportion of *tet*[R] transductants acquiring donor auxotrophy
NK144	*leu*	73/73
NK147	*leu*	82/82
NK120	*his*	64/64
NK127	*his*	82/82
NK219	*his*	71/71
NK231	*his*	78/78
NK114	*gnd*†	73/73
	Total	523/523

Seven independent *tet*[R] auxotrophs were used as donors in P22-mediated generalized transduction experiments. Lysates of P22*int*₃HT12/4 were grown on each donor and used to transduce recipient strain NK80 (*edd⁻leu⁺his⁺gnd⁺*) to tetracycline resistance on complete medium. *tet*[R] transductants were then tested for growth on appropriately supplemented minimal plates to determine how many had also acquired the donor auxotrophy.

† *gnd* = gluconate dehydrogenase; in the presence of an *edd⁻* mutation, a *gnd⁻* mutation renders *Salmonella* unable to use gluconate as a carbon source.

TABLE 3

Reversion of tet^R *auxotrophs to prototrophy*

	Expt A (recA^-)	Expt B (rec^+)	Expt C (rec^+)	Total
(a) Number of auxotrophs tested for reversion	10	6	34	50
Number yielding any revertants	6	5	34	45
(b) Tetracycline-resistance phenotypes of revertants				
Number of auxotrophs yielding:				
only *tet*^S revertants	6	5	22	33
only *tet*^R revertants	0	0	2	2
tet^R and *tet*^S revertants	0	0	2	2
Total	6	5	26	37

(a) Several colonies of each 50 *tet*^R auxotrophic strains were individually inoculated in LB broth, and grown to saturation; 0·1-ml samples were then spread directly on minimal plates. Revertants were obtained at frequencies of 3×10^{-9} to 5×10^{-7}, depending on the particular auxotrophic strain. No difference was seen in the frequencies or types of revertants obtained at temperatures from 28°C to 41°C.

(b) Many revertants were then directly tested for presence of the *tet*^R determinant (on minimal plates + 25 μg tetracycline/ml). A total of 397 revertants from 89 independent clones of 37 different auxotrophs were tested.

obtained means, therefore, that the *tet*^R element can insert into a large number of different sites on the *Salmonella* chromosome. The observation that nearly all of the *tet*^R auxotrophs can revert to prototrophy further suggests that, in most cases, insertion of the *tet*^R element is not accompanied by loss of genetic information on the bacterial chromosome. It seems most likely that the host nucleotide sequences on either side of the insertion are preserved exactly; although conceivably insertion could sometimes produce small alterations which do not preclude subsequent reversion to prototrophy.

(c) *Polarity of* tet^R *insertions in the* Salmonella *histidine operon*

In order to characterize some of the presumed *tet*^R insertions with respect to their precise locations and to ascertain their effects on gene expression, we chose to examine closely 16 independent *his*^- auxotrophs isolated in our experiments. The *his* operon of *Salmonella* is convenient because it has been extensively characterized both genetically and biochemically (Hartman *et al.*, 1971; Brenner & Ames, 1971); the only genes known to be required for biosynthesis of histidine are the nine structural genes which comprise this operon.

The *his*^- auxotrophs were first tested for their ability to complement a series of F′ factors (which carry heterologous *his* genes from *E. coli*), each of which was mutant in one of the *his* structural genes. This intergeneric complementation system, as described by Atkins & Loper (1970) allows the assessment of complementation in the virtual absence of recombination. Table 4 shows that the 16 histidine auxotrophs fall into only four categories on the basis of their complementation patterns. In three of these categories, the auxotrophs exhibit pleiotropic defects: they fail to complement with episomes carrying mutations in two or three contiguous genes in the operon.

TABLE 4

Complementation patterns of his⁻ tetᴿ *auxotrophs*

		his⁻ mutation on episome†									Inferred location of lesion
Promoters:‡		→G⁻	D⁻	C⁻	→B⁻	H⁻	A⁻	F⁻	→I⁻	E⁻	
his⁻-tetᴿ auxotrophs											
Class	Number of strains										
1	8	−	−	−	+	N.T.	+	+	+	+	G (or promoter)
2	3	+	−	−	+	N.T.	+	+	+	+	D
3	1	+	+	+	+	N.T.	+	+	−	−	I
4	4	+	+	+	+	N.T.	−/+	−/+	+	+	H or A?

16 independent his⁻-tetᴿ auxotrophs fell into only 4 classes on the basis of their ability to complement various his⁻ mutations carried on E. coli F'his episomes (see Materials and Methods). The locations of his⁻ lesions are inferred from the observed complementation patterns, the position of the promoters in the his operon, and the assumption that the lesions are polar. N.T. = not tested.

†His⁻ mutations are listed in the same order as the corresponding genes in the his operon. In this orientation, his operator/promoter region is just to the left of gene G.

‡ Positions of arrows indicate sites of primary promoter and two low-level internal promoters.

Auxotrophs in the fourth category (class 4) complement all *his*⁻ mutants tested, but complementation for genes *A* and *F* was quite poor. Complementation using episomes mutant in gene *H* was not done.

Since all of these *his*⁻ auxotrophs revert to prototrophy (data not shown), the pleiotropic effects of the *tet*ᴿ insertions are not attributable to a deletion. Using the same intergeneric complementation system, Atkins & Loper (1970) identified two internal secondary promoters in the *his* operon at the positions shown in Table 4. One of these promoters is in gene *C* and promotes transcription of distal genes, while the other is farther "downstream." The observation that *tet*ᴿ *his*⁻ auxotrophs of classes 1 and 2 are G⁻D⁻C⁻ and G⁺D⁻C⁻, respectively, but are still capable of expressing genes distal to gene *C*, suggested that the *tet*ᴿ insertion mutation is polar on distal genes and that this polarity extends only as far as the next downstream promoter. The complementation pattern of the class 3 auxotroph is consistent with such an hypothesis, as is that of the class 4 auxotrophs if the partial complementation seen for mutants in *A* and *F* is attributed to weak polarity.

If the polarity hypothesis is correct, each of the *tet*ᴿ insertions should map within the most operator–proximal of the genes it affects. Thus, class 1 mutants should map in the operator/promoter or in gene *G*; class 2 mutants in gene *D*; and the class 2 mutant in gene *I*. Deletion mapping (shown in Fig 2) places unambiguously all of these *tet*ᴿ auxotrophs in the expected genes.

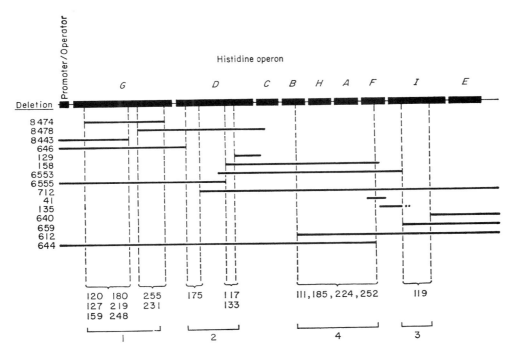

Fig. 2. Deletion mapping of *his*∷*tet*ᴿ auxotrophs.

Positions of 16 *his*∷*tet*ᴿ auxotrophs with respect to end points of known deletions in the histidine operon were determined by P22-mediated transductional crosses. Appearance of *his*⁺ recombinants was scored after infection of appropriate deletion strains with transducing lysates grown on each of the *his*∷*tet*ᴿ auxotrophs. Horizontal bars indicate extent of *his* material deleted. Map is not drawn to scale. Bracketed numbers denote *his*∷*tet*ᴿ strains mapping in the indicated interval. Complementation classes 1 to 4 (from Table 4) also indicated.

The locations of tet^R auxotrophs in classes 1 and 2 have been confirmed by an independent method. The final step in the pathway for histidine biosynthesis, the conversion of histidinol to histidine, is catalyzed by the product of the D gene, histidinol dehydrogenase. Bacteria able to express D function can grow on minimal medium supplemented with histidinol even if they are defective in any other his function. For tet^R auxotrophs located in gene D itself, all revertants selected on histidinol should also be his^+. For tet^R auxotrophs located nearer to the promoter (i.e. "upstream"), it should be possible to obtain revertants which grow on histidinol in which the polar effect of the tet^R insertion on the expression of D function has been alleviated, but total operon function has not been restored and the "revertants" remain his^-.

Revertants of class 2 auxotrophs (mapping in D) which are able to grow on histidinol arise at frequencies of 10^{-7} to 10^{-9}. All such revertants tested (a total of 459 revertants picked from 7 to 10 clones of each of the three class 2 strains) had also become his^+, confirming that these tet^R insertions are in fact located in gene D. Revertants of class 1 auxotrophs (mapping in G) which grow on histidinol occur at frequencies of up to 10^{-3} and fewer than 1% of these revertants have become his^+, confirming that these insertions do not lie in gene D.

All of the above observations are consistent with the notion that the tet^R insertions in the his operon exert polar effects on the expression of distal genes.

All of the revertants of class 1 auxotrophs (in G) which were selected for ability to grow on histidinol had simultaneously lost the tet^R determinant. The vast majority of these revertants had not regained full his^+ function, and thus must represent some imperfect and/or partial excision of the tet^R element. Thus, $excision$ of the tet^R element is usually not precise. This is in contrast to $insertion$ of the element which is seen to be precise enough to allow restoration of gene function (as discussed above).

4. Discussion

The above experiments substantiate the idea that a genetic element which carries genes conferring tetracycline-resistance (flanked by an inverted repetition about 1400 base-pairs long) is capable of translocation as a unit from one DNA molecule to another. The tet^R element is found in nature on a variety of R-factors (Sharp et al., 1973), was acquired by P22 (producing P22Tc-10 and P22Tc-106) and has now been observed to insert into a large number of different sites on the $Salmonella$ chromosome, including six different sites in the his operon. Translocation of the tet^R element has the following genetic properties:

(1) When the tet^R element is inserted into a structural gene, gene function is abolished.

(2) When the tet^R element is inserted into a group of genes forming a single transcription unit (operon), it exerts a polar effect on the expression of promoter-distal genes.

(3) Insertion is relatively non-specific; the distribution on the $Salmonella$ chromosome of tet^R insertion auxotrophs is similar to that obtained by chemical mutagenesis. On the other hand, there appears to be, within the his operon, some clustering of the sites of insertion.

(4) Insertion of the tet^R element virtually always occurs without loss of information from the molecule into which it inserts: most of the tet^R auxotrophs are capable of

reverting to prototrophy. Excision of the tet^R element, on the other hand, is usually not so precise: in the cases where we could test, there were hundreds of excisions which did *not* restore gene function for every excision that generated a prototrophic revertant.

(5) Insertion and excision of the tet^R element appears to be independent of the function of the *recA* gene of *Salmonella*.

Other laboratories have recently identified translocatable drug-resistance elements whose properties resemble those of the tet^R element. Heffron *et al.* (1975a,b) identified an ampicillin-resistance determinant which is flanked by a very short (150 base-pairs) inverted repetition. This element has been observed to translocate to at least a dozen sites within a 2800 base-pair segment of a small plasmid. Kopecko & Cohen (1975) report the *recA*-independent, apparently site-specific integration and translocation of a similar amp^R element. Most strikingly, Berg *et al.* (1975) describe two derivatives of coliphage λ which carry (as a simple insertion) a kanamycin-resistance element (derived from an R-factor) which is bounded by a 1400 base-pair inverted repetition. Thus, there appear to be many translocatable elements carrying drug-resistance determinants on R-factors which are associated with inverted repetitions.

However, Berg *et al.* also found derivatives of λ carrying a second type of kanamycin-resistance insertion (derived from a different R-factor) which do not have detectable inverted repetition; Gottesman & Rosner (1975) have also found a chloramphenicol-resistance determinant, which is translocatable into λ from coliphage P1, in which no reverse duplication was seen. These insertions may represent a different type of translocation element, or may be cases in which the inverted repetition is too short or too unstable to be detectable by standard visualization methods which depend on intra-molecular annealing.

In any case, it seems quite clear that translocatable genetic elements carrying drug-resistance determinants must make a substantial contribution to the reassortment of drug-resistant determinants which is seen among R-factors (Watanabe & Lyang, 1962; Clowes, 1972; Heffron *et al.*, 1975a).

In heteroduplex studies including the R-factor from which P22Tc-10 was made, Sharp *et al.* (1973) were able to correlate the tet^R determinant with a non-tandem inverted repetition having the same dimensions as the Tc-10 insertion. More recently, Ptashne & Cohen (1975) have shown that the inverted repetition associated with tet^R (on such an R-factor) is homologous with the IS3 insertion sequence of Malamy *et al.* (1972). The insertion sequences themselves were detected as individual insertion units which cause polar mutations (Shapiro, 1969; Jordan *et al.*, 1968; Malamy, 1970). In the cases of IS1 and IS2, polarity is attributable to the presence of transcription termination signals on the IS sequences themselves (Adhya *et al.*, 1974; Max Gottesman, personal communication). Thus, our tet^R element is bounded by two units which should be capable of functioning individually. This idea is supported by the preliminary observation that some of the his^-tet^S polarity relief revertants (obtained from class 1 *his*::tet^R insertions) can further revert to his^+ at high frequency. These could be instances in which excision of the tet^R determinant left behind a single IS sequence which can subsequently excise to restore $hisG^+$ function. (This explanation requires the additional assumption that the remaining IS sequence is non-polar or else can promote expression of *hisD* function; precedent exists for the idea that IS sequences might contain transcription termination signals when inserted in one orientation, but serve as new promoters when inserted in the other (Saedler *et al.*, 1974).)

The IS sequences, singly and as non-inverted duplications, have recently been associated with a large number of unusual (often "illegitimate" and *recA*-independent) recombination phenomena—deletions, fusions, integration of F-factors, and amplification of R-factors (Sharp *et al.*, 1972; Ptashne & Cohen, 1975; Lee *et al.*, 1974; Davidson *et al.*, 1975; Hu *et al.*, 1975). The precise relationship of these phenomena to the properties of the inverted duplications of an IS3 sequence in the *tet*[R] element remains to be worked out. We would like to suggest, based on our studies of the *tet*[R] element, that a pair of inverted IS sequences might be essential for efficient and relatively stable translocation of the DNA between them to many new sites.

There are other bacterial systems for translocation of particular genetic elements which may or may not be mechanistically related to insertion of the *tet*[R] element. The most striking example is bacteriophage Mu-1 which causes polar mutations by random insertion into the *E. coli* chromosome (for review, see Howe & Bade, 1975). Mutants of Mu which are capable of perfect excision much more frequently excise imperfectly (Bukhari, 1975), as is the case with the *tet*[R] element. Coliphage λ is also capable of integration into a large number of sites (many of them structural genes) on the *E. coli* chromosome when the normal λ attachment site is missing (Shimada *et al.*, 1973). This integration is still dependent on the phage enzyme involved in site-specific integration at the normal site. Unlike Mu integration, however, integration of λ in the absence of the normal attachment site still shows considerable preference for particular sites, and excision of λ from these sites is usually precise (Shimada *et al.*, 1975). Both Mu and λ integration are, like that of the *tet*[R] element, independent of *recA* function (Shimada *et al.*, 1975; Boram & Abelson, 1971).

Translocation of genetic material by such non-tandem inverted repetitions offers a powerful tool with which biological systems can perform substantial genetic rearrangements. Recombination between the inverted sequences themselves would generate an inversion of the material carried between them. Translocations by such elements could also result in duplications. Inverted repetitions (tandem and non-tandem) have been identified in the DNA of a large number of prokaryotic (Sharp *et al.*, 1972,1973; Berg *et al.*, 1975; Heffron *et al.*, 1975a,b; Daniell *et al.*, 1973) and eukaryotic (Wadsworth *et al.*, 1975; Wolfson & Dressler, 1972; Locker *et al.*, 1974; Manning *et al.*, 1975) organisms. In many of these cases, the inverted repetitions are associated with DNA rearrangements that can be explained in terms of translocatable segments. It seems possible therefore that a fundamental relationship may exist between translocatable segments of DNA and inverted repetitions.

We gratefully acknowledge the assistance of Elaine Lenk and the Massachusetts Institute of Technology, Department of Biology electron microscope facility; and the enthusiastic advice and ready access to strains from John Roth, Phil Anderson and John Scott. We also thank Norman Davidson, Tom Broker, Doug Berg, Fred Heffron, Stan Falkow, Lee Rosner and Stan Cohen for stimulating discussions and for access to unpublished results.

This work was supported in part by grant no. VC18D from the American Cancer Society, in part by grant no. GM21253 from the National Institutes of Health, and in part by grant no. GM18973 from the National Institutes of Health. One of us (D. B.) is supported by a Career Development award from the National Institutes of Health, no. GM70325.

Additionally, we thank Wanda Fischer for her help in preparing the manuscript.

REFERENCES

Adhya, S., Gottesman, M. & de Crombrugghe, B. (1974). *Proc. Nat Acad. Sci., U.S.A.* **71**, 2534–2538.

Atkins, J. F. & Loper, J. C. (1970). *Proc. Nat. Acad. Sci., U.S.A.* **65**, 925–932.

Berg, D. E., Davis, J., Allet, B. & Rochaix, J.-D. (1975). *Proc. Nat. Acad. Sci., U.S.A.* in the press.

Boram, W. & Abelson, J. (1971). *J. Mol. Biol.* **62**, 171–178.

Botstein, D. & Matz, M. J. (1970). *J. Mol. Biol.* **54**, 417–440.

Brenner, M. & Ames, B. N. (1971). In *Metabolic Regulation* (Vogel, H. J., ed.), pp. 349–387, Academic Press, New York.

Broker, T. R. & Lehman, I. R. (1971). *J. Mol. Biol.* **60**, 131–149.

Bukhari, A. (1975). *J. Mol. Biol.* **96**, 87–100.

Bukhari, A. & Metlay, M. (1973). *Virology*, **54**, 109–116.

Campbell, A. (1962). *Episomes Advan. Genet.* **11**, 101–145.

Chan, R. K. (1974). Ph.D. dissertation, Massachusetts Institute of Technology.

Chan, R. K. & Botstein, D. (1972). *Virology*, **49**, 257–267.

Chan, R. K. & Botstein, D. (1975). *Genetics*, in the press.

Chan, R. K., Botstein, D., Watanabe, T. & Ogata, Y. (1972). *Virology*, **60**, 833–898.

Clowes, R. C. (1972). *Bacteriol. Rev.* **36**, 361–405.

Daniell, E., Abelson, J., Kim, J. S. & Davidson, N. (1973). *Virology*, **51**, 237–239.

Davidson, N., Deonier, R. C., Hu, S. & Ohtsubo, E. (1975). *Microbiology*, **1**, in the press.

Garon, C. F., Berry, K. W. & Rose, J. (1972). *Proc. Nat. Acad. Sci., U.S.A.* **69**, 2391.

Gottesman, M. M. & Rosner, J. L. (1975). *Proc. Nat. Acad. Sci., U.S.A.*, in the press.

Hartman, P. E., Hartman, Z., Stahl, R. C. & Ames, B. N. (1971). *Advan. Genet.* **16**, 1–34.

Heffron, D., Sublett, R., Hedges, R. W., Jacob, A. & Falkow, S. (1975a). *J. Bacteriol.* **122**, 250–256.

Heffron, F., Reubens, C. & Falkow, S. (1975b). *Proc. Nat. Acad. Sci., U.S.A.*, in the press.

Howe, M. M. & Bade, E. G. (1975). *Science*, in the press.

Hsu, M.-T. & Davidson, N. (1975). *Virology*, **58**, 229–239.

Hu, S., Ohtsubo, E., Davidson, N. & Saedler, H. (1975). *J. Bacteriol.* **102**, 764–775.

Jordan, E., Saedler, H. & Starlinger, P. (1968). *Mol. Gen. Genet.* **102**, 353–364.

Kopecko, D. J. & Cohen, S. N. (1975). *Proc. Nat. Acad. Sci., U.S.A.* **72**, 1373–1377.

Lee, C. S., Davis, R. W. & Davidson, N. (1970). *J. Mol. Biol.* **48**, 1–22.

Lee, H. J., Ohtsubo, E., Deonier, K. & Davidson, N. (1974). *J. Mol. Biol.* **89**, 585–594.

Levine, M. & Smith, H. O. (1964). *Science*, **146**, 1581–1582.

Locker, J., Rabinowitz, M. & Getz, G. S. (1974). *Proc. Nat. Acad. Sci., U.S.A.* **71**, 1366–1370.

Malamy, M. (1970). In *The Lac Operon* (Beckwith, J. R. & Zipser, D., eds), pp. 359–373, Cold Spring Harbor Press, Cold Spring Harbor, New York.

Malamy, M. H., Fiandt, M. & Szybalski, W. (1972). *Mol. Gen. Genet.* **119**, 207–222.

Manning, J. E., Schmid, C. W. & Davidson, N. (1975). *Cell*, **4**, 141–155.

Miyake, T. & Demerec, M. (1960). *Genetics*, **45**, 755–762.

Ptashne, K. & Cohen, S. N. (1975). *J. Bacteriol.* **122**, 776–787.

Raj, A. S., Raj, A. Y. & Schmieger, H. (1974). *Mol. Gen. Genet.* **135**, 175–184.

Saedler, H., H., Reif, J., Hu, S. & Davidson, N. (1974). *Mol. Gen. Genet.* **132**, 265–289.

Schmieger, H. (1972). *Mol. Gen. Genet.* **119**, 75–88.

Scott, J. F. & Roth, J. R. (1975). *Proc. Nat. Acad. Sci., U.S.A.*, in the press.

Shapiro, J. A. (1969). *J. Mol. Biol.* **40**, 93–105.

Sharp, P. A., Hsu, M.-T., Ohtsubo, E. & Davidson, N. (1972). *J. Mol. Biol.* **71**, 471–497.

Sharp, P. A., Cohen, S. N. & Davidson, N. (1973). *J. Mol. Biol.* **75**, 235–255.

Shimada, K., Weisberg, R. A. & Gottesman, M. E. (1973). *J. Mol. Biol.* **80**, 297–314.

Shimada, K., Weisberg, R. A. & Gottesman, M. E. (1975). *J. Mol. Biol.* **93**, 415–430.

Smith, H. O. & Levine, M. (1964). *Virology*, **27**, 229–231.

Smith, H. O. & Levine, M. (1967). *Virology*, **31**, 207–216.

Stahl, M. M. & Stahl, F. W. (1971). In *The Bacteriophage Lambda* (Hershey, A. D., ed.), pp. 431–442, Cold Spring Harbor Press, Cold Spring Harbor, New York.

Susskind, M. M., Botstein, D. & Wright, A. (1974). *Virology*, **62**, 350–366.

Tye, B. K., Chan, R. K. & Botstein, D. (1974). *J. Mol. Biol.* **85**, 485–500.

Watanabe, T. & Lyang, K. W. (1962). *J. Bacteriol.* **84**, 422–430.

Watanabe, T., Ogata, Y., Chan, R. K. & Botstein, D. (1972). *Virology,* **50**, 874–882.

Wolfson, J. & Dressler, D. (1972). *Proc. Nat. Acad. Sci., U.S.A.* **69**, 3054–3057.

Zinder, N. & Lederberg, J. (1952). *J. Bacteriol.* **64**, 679–699.

DNA Sequence Analysis of the Transposon Tn3: Three Genes and Three Sites Involved in Transposition of Tn3

Fred Heffron and Brian J. McCarthy
Department of Biochemistry and Biophysics
University of California
San Francisco, California 94143
Hisako Ohtsubo and Eiichi Ohtsubo
Department of Microbiology
State University of New York
Stony Brook, New York 11794

Summary

The complete nucleotide sequence of the transposon Tn3 and of 20 mutations which affect its transposition are reported. The mutations, generated in vitro by random insertion of synthetic restriction sites, proved to contain small duplications or deletions immediately adjacent to the new restriction site. By determining the phenotype and DNA sequence of these mutations we were able to generate an overlapping phenotypic and nucleotide map. This 4957 bp transposon encodes three polypeptides which account for all but 350 bp of its total coding capacity. These proteins are the transposase, a high molecular weight polypeptide (1015 amino acids) encoded by the tnpA gene; the Tn3-specific repressor, a low molecular weight polypeptide (185 amino acids) encoded by the tnpR gene; and the 286 amino acid β–lactamase. The 38 bp inverted repeats flanking Tn3 appear to be absolutely required in cis for Tn3 to transpose. Genetic data suggest that Tn3 contains a third site (Gill et al., 1978), designated IRS (internal resolution site), whose absence results in the insertion of two complete copies of Tn3 as direct repeats into the recipient DNA. We suggest that these direct repeats of complete copies of Tn3 are intermediates in transposition, and that the IRS site is required for recombination and subsequent segregation of the direct repeats to leave a single copy of Tn3 (Gill et al., 1978). A 23 nucleotide sequence within the amino terminus of the transposase which shares strong sequence homology with the inverted repeat may be the internal resolution site.

Introduction

Genetic studies of the transposon Tn3 using deletions suggested the existence of two or more trans-acting transposition functions encoded by the transposon (Heffron et al., 1977; Gill et al., 1978). More recent studies in which Eco RI octamers were inserted as mutagens in vitro have provided a more extensive functional map of Tn3 (Heffron, So and McCarthy, 1978). Following cleavage with a nonspecific double-stranded endonuclease, a single synthetic Eco RI octamer$\binom{\text{GGAATTCC}}{\text{CCTTAAGG}}$ is introduced into the DNA and

the linear DNA is recircularized. This procedure has the obvious advantage that the location of mutations can be determined simply by cleavage with the Eco RI restriction enzyme. In vitro generated mutations of this type within a contiguous 3 kb region of Tn3 resulted in a transposition-negative phenotype, which could be complemented to transpose when a second Tn3 was placed in the same cell (Heffron et al., 1978). Gill, Heffron and Falkow (1979) have identified a high molecular weight polypeptide encoded at this region. Mutations affecting a second quite different function result in an increase in transposition frequency (Gill et al., 1978; Heffron et al., 1978). These mutations are recessive to wild-type (Gill et al., 1978) and affect a 20,000 dalton polypeptide encoded in this region (Dougan et al., 1979).

The ends of Tn3 are 38 bp inverted repeats (Ohtsubo, Ohmori and Ohtsubo, 1979). A second class of mutations is generated by deletions removing one 38 bp inverted repeat of Tn3. These are not recessive to wild-type but are cis-dominant transposition-negative (Heffron et al., 1977). Deletion data also suggest the existence of a second DNA site entirely contained within Tn3 and critical for transposition (Gill et al., 1978). Deletions which extend into this site invariably show insertion of two complete copies of the transposon as direct repeats when complemented by a second copy of Tn3 (Heffron et al., 1977; Gill et al., 1978). The structure of these repeats is identical to that of those generated by the transposition of non-mu DNA by mu (Toussaint and Faelen, 1973); similar structures have also been observed for transposition of Tn9, Tn1681, and Tn5 (MacHattie and Shapiro, 1978; Shapiro and MacHattie, 1979; Boch and Shapiro, 1979; So, Heffron and McCarthy, 1979; J. Miller, personal communication). It has been proposed that these direct repeats of two full copies of Tn3 are transposition intermediates (Gill et al., 1978; Shapiro, 1979). To help identify functions implicated by the above genetic data, we have determined the sequence of the 4957 nucleotides in the Tn3 transposon, including the precise location and nucleotide sequence of many of the mutations which affect its transposition.

Results

Overall Sequence Organization of the Transposon Tn3

The plasmid RSF1050 used in this study was originally made to demonstrate that there is a trans-acting function required for transposition which is encoded within the transposon itself (Heffron et al., 1977). This plasmid was constructed by transposition of Tn3 from R1drd, a derivative of R1 (Meynell and Datta, 1967), to pMB8 (Bolivar et al., 1977).

The isolation of a large number of Eco RI insertion

mutations within Tn3 (Heffron et al., 1978) and the determination of their phenotypes provided the basis for assembling an overlapping phenotypic and nucleotide map of the transposon. The new restriction sites were also extremely useful in the sequencing of many regions which were otherwise devoid of convenient restriction sites. Since DNA sequence changes may be introduced by the mutagenesis procedure, however, it was necessary to determine the same sequences from two adjacent Eco RI insertion mutations. In this way the wild-type sequence could be deduced from the overlapping sequences from at least two mutants. By these means we have determined that changes in base sequence are introduced immediately adjacent to the inserted Eco RI octamer by the mutagenesis procedure; these alterations can be either duplications or deletions, as will be discussed below.

Previous sequence studies of Tn3 have demonstrated a 5 bp direct repeat at either end of the transposon of a sequence originally found once in the recipient DNA (Ohtsubo et al., 1979). Similarly, in this pMB8 derivative, sequencing revealed that transposition has generated a 5 bp direct repeat of the sequence $\left(\begin{smallmatrix} ATTAA \\ TAATT \end{smallmatrix}\right)$ at both ends of the 38 bp repeat. Insertion of Tn3 in the sequenced derivative had occurred in a Hae III/Hinf I fragment corresponding to nucleotides 1948–2034 in the Sutcliffe sequence of pBR322 (Sutcliffe, 1979). The sequence duplicated corresponds to nucleotides 1972–1976 in that sequence; its origin and its possible relationship to sequences within the transposon have been discussed elsewhere (Grindley, 1978; Johnsrud, Calos and Miller, 1978; Ohtsubo et al., 1979).

Figure 1 summarizes the overall sequence organization of the transposon and shows the position and phenotype of the mutations used in this study. The location and direction of transcription of genes encoding proteins which have been deduced from the DNA sequence are also shown. [The sequence of the β–lactamase was determined by Sutcliffe (1978). We have not repeated the sequence determination between nucleotides 3900 and 4700, which encode the structural gene for β–lactamase, but we have reproduced it here with his permission to include the complete transposon base sequence.]

DNA Sequence Analysis of Mutations Which Are Recessive Transposition-Defective: Identification of the Transposase Encoded at tnpA

The DNA sequence for mutations 11, 31, 72, 34, 96, 23, 117, 88, 40, 76, 7, 120 and 33, all of which result in a transposition-negative phenotype, are listed in Table 1. The wild-type sequence for the portion of Tn3 containing these mutations is given in Figure 2. All of these mutants can be complemented to transpose by a second Tn3 (Heffron et al., 1978). According to the sequence determined, a single coding sequence begins to the right of mutation 11 and extends over 3000 bp into the left-hand inverted repeat. This region encodes an uninterrupted series of 1021 amino acids without stop codons. We refer to this high molecular weight polypeptide encoded by the tnpA gene as the "transposase" since this protein is absolutely required for transposition. Its molecular weight of

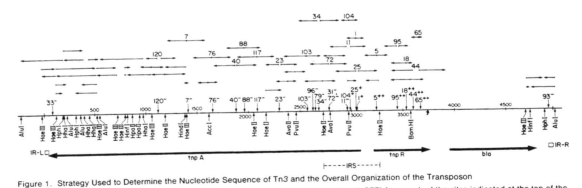

Figure 1. Strategy Used to Determine the Nucleotide Sequence of Tn3 and the Overall Organization of the Transposon

DNA sequencing was carried out by the Maxam-Gilbert chemical modification procedure (1977) from each of the sites indicated at the top of the figure. The length of the arrow corresponds to the number of nucleotides actually sequenced from each start. The gap (between arrows) adjacent to many of the mutations sequenced corresponds to the deletions present in these mutations. The middle line shows the position of the various mutations and restriction sites actually used in carrying out the DNA sequencing. Restriction sites not used in sequencing are not listed, although all Hae II and Pvu II sites are shown. The phenotype for each mutation is listed adjacent to the number which corresponds to the mutation; for example, mutation 33 is transposition-negative, while mutations 5, 95, 18, 44 and 65 show a higher transposition frequency than the wild-type. Marked at the bottom of the figure are the locations of the three genes and three sites deduced from this DNA sequence and previous genetic studies. The location of the genes tnpA and tnpR and the direction of their transcription corresponds closely to the location of the genes predicted from a complementary study by Gill et al. (1979) in which the corresponding prematurely terminated polypeptides using the sequence frameshift mutations shown in this figure have been identified. The bla gene which encodes β–lactamase has been described (Sutcliffe, 1978). IR-L and IR-R correspond to the left and right 38 bp inverted repeats which are located at either end of the transposon. IRS corresponds to the approximate location of the internal resolution site as deduced from previous genetic studies. [The Hind I site at position 1390 should read Hind II.]

Table 1. Location of Mutations in Tn*3* and Their Phenotypes

Mutation	Location (Nucleotide Number Preceding Eco RI Octamer)	Bases Deleted or Duplicated[a]	Alteration in bp (Excluding Eco RI Octamer)	Phenotype[b]
33	84	85–100 del	−16	rec Tnp⁻
120	1120	1121–1157 del	−37	rec Tnp⁻
7	1414	1412–1414 dup	+3	rec Tnp⁻
76	1654	1646–1654 dup	+9	rec Tnp⁻
40	1884	1885–1895 del	−11	rec Tnp⁻
88	1963	1962–1963 dup	+2	rec Tnp⁻
117	2088	2088 dup	+1	rec Tnp⁻
23	2298	2299–2317 del	−19	rec Tnp⁻
103	2572	2570–2572 dup	+3	rec Tnp⁻
96	2623	2624–2636 del	−13	rec Tnp⁻
79	2648	2648–2666 del	−19	rec Tnp⁻
34	2684	2685–2708 del	−24	rec Tnp⁻
31	2786	2787–2788 dup	+2	rec Tnp⁻
72	2789	2790–2805 del	−16	rec Tnp⁻
11	2960	2961–2997 del	−37	rec Tnp⁻
104	2988	2989–2990 del	−2	wt (?)
25	3045	3046–3068 del	−23	wt (?)
1	3051	3052–3053 dup	+2	wt (?)
5	3242	3243–3254 del	−12	Tnp⁺⁺
95	3444	3445–3466 del	−22	Tnp⁺⁺
18	3534	3537–3556 dup	+10	Tnp⁺⁺
44	3601	3602–3653 del	−52	Tnp⁺⁺
65	3672	3667–3672 dup	+6	Tnp⁺⁺
93	4918	4919–4943 del	+25	cis dom. Tnp⁻

[a] All the mutations sequenced which had additional DNA contained a duplication in which a sequence preceding the Eco RI octamer was duplicated after the Eco RI octamer. For example, in the wild-type the sequence starting at nucleotide 3533 reads CACCATCCTGTCGGC, whereas in mutant 18 the sequence is CACCATCCTGTC GGAATTCCCCATCCTGTCGGC. The two underlines mark the sequence which has been duplicated, and italics show the Eco RI octamer.

[b] Tnp refers to the transposition phenotype. Mutations 5, 95, 18, 44 and 65 show a 10 fold higher frequency of transposition than the wild-type transposon and are thus Tnp⁺⁺. Mutations 33–11 were all transposition-negative but could be complemented to transpose (Heffron et al., 1978). They are thus recessive, while mutation 93 could not be complemented. Mutations 1, 25 and 104 do not appear to be perfectly wild-type (Gill et al., 1979).

114,000 daltons corresponds to the molecular weight of a protein synthesized by Tn*3* in minicells (Gill et al., 1979).

The DNA sequences of several mutations within the apparent amino terminus of the transposase and the intercistronic region separating *tnpA* and *tnpR* are presented in Figure 3. The transposase probably begins translation in the region specified in Figure 3, an assumption based on the molecular weight of prematurely terminated polypeptides from the sequenced Eco RI frameshift mutations (Gill et al., 1979). A good candidate for the site of translational initiation is the ATG codon at position 3048, since it is preceded by the sequence GGAGG which matches the canonical Shine-Dalgarno sequence (1974). This conclusion is contradicted by the observation that mutation 25, which deletes both the ATG and the preceding Shine-Dalgarno sequence, is transposition-positive. We have provisionally designated the valine shown as the translational initiation site, since it is consistent with most of the genetic data and a GTG codon has been observed as the translational start of the *lacI* gene (Steege, 1977; Calos, 1978). This assignment is consistent with the fact that mutations 104 and 25 do not shift the reading frame and are both transposition-positive, while mutation 11 shifts the reading frame and does not transpose unless complemented. We cannot explain the transposition-positive phenotype for frameshift mutation 1, however. It is clear that the true start of translation cannot be distinguished without sequence information for the amino terminus of the transposase.

A sequence of 16 As and Ts precedes the amino terminus of the transposase and includes several possible −10 homology regions, such as the sequence TATAATA which has been reported for T5 promoters (H. Weiher and H. Schaller, unpublished observations). Assuming that transcriptional initiation takes place following this sequence, a possible −35 sequence is indicated in Figure 3.

DNA Sequence Analysis of Mutations with an Increased Frequency of Transposition: Identification of the Protein Encoded at *tnpR*

There are five mutations clustered in a relatively narrow region of the Tn*3* which show an increase in transposition frequency (5, 95, 18, 44 and 65) (Figure 1). Using DNA sequence analysis we have determined that all five of these mutations lie within a single uninterrupted coding sequence. As shown in Figure 3, this protein would initiate with a methionine at nucleotides 3210–3212. This methionine is preceded by an AT-rich region with several possible transcriptional initiation sites. One possible −10 homology region (Pribnow box) and a possible −35 sequence preceding it are bracketed in Figure 3. This 185 amino acid polypeptide, encoded by a gene designated *tnpR* in Figure 1, is unusual in its amino acid composition. The DNA sequence would suggest that it contains no Cys, Pro or Trp.

Regulation of the Transposase by the Tn*3*-Specific Repressor Encoded at *tnpR*

On the basis of insertion mapping of two antibiotic resistance genes (streptomycin and sulfonamide resistance) in a small plasmid (Heffron, Rubens and

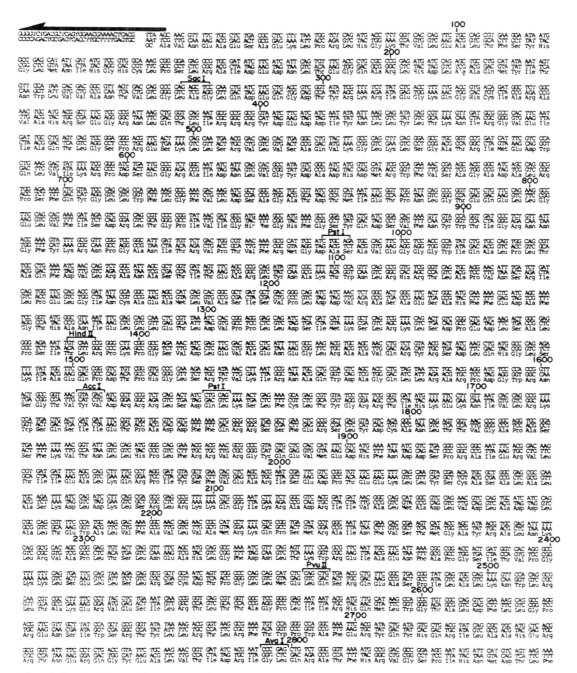

Figure 2. Complete Nucleotide Sequence of the Transposon Tn3

Included in this sequence are the translation of the three polypeptides, the location of the inverted repeats and the location of several restriction sites. A complete list of restriction sites may be obtained upon request.

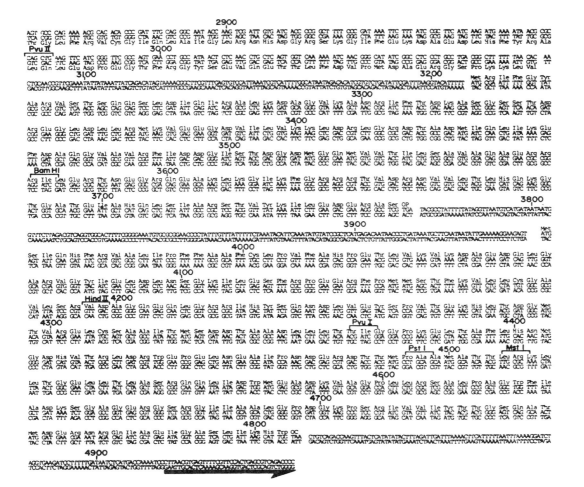

Falkow, 1975b; Rubens, Heffron and Falkow, 1976) it was concluded that these two genes lie in a single transcriptional unit with the gene for streptomycin resistance being distal to the promoter. Insertions of Tn3 within the sulfonamide resistance gene in one orientation were polar upon streptomycin resistance, reducing the level of streptomycin resistance at least 10 fold (Table 2). Restriction mapping of those insertions compared with the above sequence information reveals that in this orientation the transposase is transcribed in the same direction as the streptomycin resistance gene. A revertant which relieved the polarity on streptomycin resistance was selected and found to contain a deletion of a portion of the coding sequence for the 185 amino acid tnpR polypeptide (Heffron et al., 1977). We have recently found that supplying the product of the tnpR gene in trans decreases the level of streptomycin resistance (Table 2). It thus appears probable that a transcriptional fusion was created by inserting Tn3 into the sulfonamide resistance gene so that the streptomycin resistance gene

(streptomycin phosphotransferase) is transcribed from the transposase promoter. It is also probable that the initial deletion which restored streptomycin resistance was due to a release of repression by tnpR; supplying the repressor in trans decreases the level of streptomycin resistance by decreasing the level of transcription from the transposase promoter. Gill et al. (1979) have arrived at the same conclusion on the basis of the amount of transposase protein produced in the wild-type transposon, as compared with that produced by tnpR⁻ mutations. We conclude that the protein encoded by tnpR acts as a repressor to regulate expression of the transposase.

DNA Sequence of the Intercistronic Region between tnpR and tnpA

The region between the amino terminus of the two polypeptides tnpR and tnpA, like other regulatory regions, is AT-rich (70% A + T) (Rosenberg and Court, 1980). From genetic and biochemical data it has been established that the protein encoded at tnpR

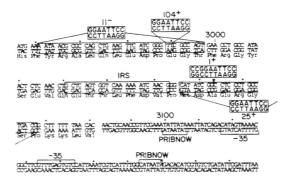

Figure 3. The Amino Terminus of the Transposase, Its Repressor and the Intercistronic Region between These Two Genes

This figure focuses on the regulatory region between *tnpR* and *tnpA*, and shows the sequence and phenotype for four mutations in the amino terminus of the transposase, as well as the internal resolution site.

(the repressor) represses both its own expression and that of the transposase (Gill et al., 1979), and that it probably acts by reducing transcription in both cases. This model would suggest the existence of two operators, or possibly one shared operator in the intercistronic region. In the absence of genetic and binding studies, however, it is impossible to predict the actual location of operator sequences. We have identified many sequences with 2 fold rotational symmetry by a computer search for repeated sequences, allowing for a predetermined number of deletions, insertions and mismatches. Examples of sequences having dyad symmetry are nucleotides 3110–3118 (also repeated at 3169–3177) and the inverse complement at 3180–3188; nucleotides 3144–3154 and the inverse complement at 3191–3200; and nucleotides 3140–3149 and the inverse complement at 3166–3175.

Essential Sites

Heffron et al. (1977) reported that the left-hand inverted repeat is required in cis for transposition. We have confirmed these results by carrying out more detailed mapping of the cis-dominant deletions reported earlier. By restriction mapping we have found that deletions 91 and 257 remove the entire left-hand inverted repeat and extend approximately 250 and 550 bp into the transposon, respectively (data not shown). In addition, one Eco RI insertion mutation which mapped within the right-hand inverted repeat also leads to a cis-dominant transposition-negative phenotype (Gill et al., 1979). The DNA sequence shown in Figure 4 establishes that this mutation did not remove the external terminus of the inverted repeat.

As previously discussed, genetic data imply the

Table 2. Effect of the Tn3-Specific Repressor on Expression of the Transposase

Plasmid(s)	Minimal Inhibitory Concentration (μg)[a] (Sm/ml)
RSF1010	100
A1M5 (Tn3 insertion into RSF1010)	10
RSF103	100
RSF103 + RSF1050	10
RSF103 + PFH5	100

[a] Minimal inhibitory concentration was determined by plating ~1000 cells on L agar plates containing the concentration of Sm indicated.

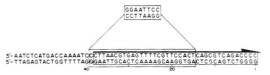

Figure 4. DNA Sequence for a Mutation (93) Which Lies within the Right-Hand Inverted Repeat

This mutation contains a 23 bp deletion. The 38 bp which are part of the terminal inverted repeat flanking Tn3 are indicated by the arrow.

existence of a site, contained entirely within the transposon, in the absence of which two complete copies of the transposon are invariably inserted into recipient DNA. Since direct repeats formed during complementation of deletions which lack that site are stable even in the presence of a wild-type Tn3 (Gill et al., 1978), it appears that this site is a DNA sequence which is recognized by whatever enzyme(s) acts to recombine out the extra Tn3 copy. We refer to this site, therefore, as the internal resolution site (IRS). Those mutations which result in co-integrates all remove a portion of a Hae II fragment (nucleotides 2726–3272). As shown in Figures 3 and 5, within this fragment is a sequence containing 19 out of 23 nucleotides identical to a sequence within the inverted repeats. This 19 nucleotide match requires two 1 bp frameshifts, as shown in Figure 5.

Discussion

Four transposons have been identified from different resistance plasmids which encode the TEM β-lactamase, Tn1, Tn2, Tn3 (at one time referred to collectively as TnA; Hedges and Jacob, 1974; Kopecko and Cohen, 1975; Heffron et al., 1975a) and Tn1701 (Yamada et al., 1979). Electron microscope heteroduplex studies have demonstrated overall homology of these sequences with one another, although sequence divergence of as much as 10% is revealed by DNA cross-annealing in solution (Heffron et al., 1975a; Rubens et al., 1976; Yamada et al., 1979). It can therefore be assumed that Tn1, 2, 3 and 1701

POSSIBLE INTERNAL RESOLUTION SITE

```
3021                    A 3043
    GCTCAGTGGTCAAAAAATCACG
GGGGTCTGACGCTCAGTGGACGAAAAACTCACGTTAG
1                   A                    38
```

INVERTED REPEAT

Figure 5. Comparison between a Sequence Located in the Amino Terminus of the Transposase and the Inverted Repeat

According to computer analysis, this sequence displays a higher degree of homology with the inverted repeat than any other in the transposon. The location of this sequence within an area of Tn3 which must contain the internal resolution site based on deletion mapping suggests that this sequence could be the internal resolution site.

have arisen from a common ancestor with third position substitutions, neutral amino acid changes and other alterations outside the actual coding sequence. The sequence for these other transposons should therefore be very similar to the sequence for Tn3 reported here.

Analysis of the Eco RI Insertion Mutations

DNA sequence analysis of has been carried out on Tn3 and 20 Eco RI insertion mutations contained within three genes and three sites essential for its transposition. The locations, phenotypes and alterations introduced by the insertions are shown in Table 1. The Eco RI insertion mutations always contain either deletions or duplications immediately adjacent to the Eco RI octamer. Several of the mutants used in this study contained deletions of up to 50 bp. While these deletions were valuable for the determination of both phenotypes and the direction of transcription (Gill et al., 1979), the changes are usually more complicated than the expected insertion of a single Eco RI octamer. It now appears that these substantial deletions were introduced by the E coli DNA polymerase I used to make flush ends in the initial study. More recently, mutants have been constructed in the same way but using T4 polymerase to make flush ends; these contain few deletions of over 20 bp (G. Swift and F. Heffron, unpublished observations). Mutations 65, 18, 1, 31, 103, 117, 88, 76 and 7 contain insertion of additional DNA beyond that of the Eco RI octamer. In all cases this additional DNA results from a duplication which flanks the inserted Eco RI octamer. Figure 6 shows the DNA sequences for mutation 18 and the wild-type sequence side by side in an autoradiogram of a DNA sequencing gel. This mutation contains a direct repeat of 10 bp in addition to the Eco RI octamer. The mutant has acquired a total of 18 additional bp. The most probable explanation for these duplications is that DNAase I made staggered breaks in the DNA, leaving a 5′ extension at both ends of the molecule. The DNA polymerase used in a subsequent step to make flush ends was able to fill in these staggered breaks to create a duplication.

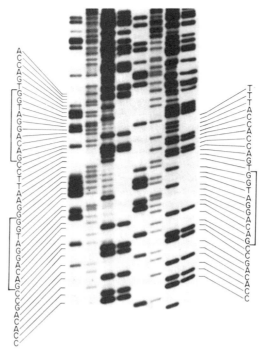

Figure 6. Autoradiogram of a Maxam-Gilbert Sequencing Gel for Mutation 18 Compared with Wild-type Sequence

This mutation contains a direct repeat of 10 bp which flanks the inserted Eco RI octamer. As described in the text, all other mutations which contain any additional DNA contain a similar direct repeat.

Functions Encoded by the Transposon

All those mutations within the coding sequence for a high molecular weight protein result in a transposition-negative but recessive phenotype consistent with the requirement of this polypeptide for transposition. We have called this protein the transposase. Gill et al. (1979) have identified a polypeptide which has the same molecular weight as that predicted from this sequence. Furthermore, using the sequenced frameshift mutations described in this paper, they have elucidated the direction of transcription and approximate initiation and termination sites of this protein. The molecular weights of prematurely terminated polypeptides they observed are in good agreement with those predicted from the sequence changes of the mutants listed in Table 1. Genetic data are also consistent with the encoding of a single polypeptide in this region. These invesitgators failed to observe complementation between several different transposition-negative mutations located within this region, a result consistent with there being only a single complementation group.

A single high molecular weight polypeptide encoded within Tn3 is necessary for transposition. This can be compared with another transposition system in which the genes for transposition have been identified. In the bacteriophage mu, transposition depends upon the products of the two genes A and B (Toussaint and Faelen, 1973; Faelen, Toussaint and de Lefontayne, 1975). In mutants of mu defective in gene B function (essential for mu replication), transposition takes place at a 10 fold lower frequency. In mutants missing gene A function, transposition is completely abolished. These two genes specify polypeptides whose combined molecular weight is smaller than that of the transposase encoded in Tn3. Perhaps the Tn3 transposase combines both of these activities into a single polypeptide. A mutation (33) within the carboxy terminal 20 amino acids of the transposase renders the transposase completely inactive within the limits of sensitivity of the assay. On the other hand, mutations 25, 104 and 1, all of which appear to be in the amino terminus of the transposase, have no more than a 5 fold effect on transposition frequency. Whether this means that the carboxy terminus is involved with DNA binding [in contrast to the arrangement in the *lac* repressor, in which the amino terminus binds to DNA (Adler et al., 1972)] can only be determined by more extensive genetic and biochemical studies. The arrangement of the transposase gene whereby the essential carboxy terminus of the protein is encoded within the inverted repeat, however, is quite reminiscent of the lambda *int* protein and the juxtaposition of its gene to its site of action, *att*.

By using computer programs we have determined that the transposase is unrelated (that is, shows no sequences of 25 amino acids with >25% homology) to the lambda *int* gene (R. Hoess, K. Bidwell, C. Foeher and A. Landy, unpublished observations); nor is the Tn3-specific repressor related to *lac* repressor (Farabaugh, 1978), *cro* (Roberts et al., 1977), CI (Ptashne, 1978) or the transposase. The transposase does not appear to contain repeated domains. According to a secondary structure program, however, it does contain an extremely long extended region (amino acids 239–386). This result may suggest that the protein contains two separate domains, a possibility that will be accessible to study once the protein has been purified and its activities determined.

Mutations within a contiguous 500 bp sequence adjacent to the amino terminus of the transposase all result in elevation of the frequency of transposition. Five mutations with this phenotype were sequenced and found to lie within the coding sequence for a single polypeptide. Four of these mutations, 5, 95, 44 and 65, shift the reading frame. We can predict that these mutations would generate prematurely terminated polypeptides of 2500, 9000 and 13,000, respectively, while in mutation 65 the frameshift would bypass the normal translational termination signal and lead to a polypeptide which has been extended from 185 amino acids to 197 (22,000). Polypeptides of corresponding molecular weight have been identified

in minicells from plasmids containing each of these mutants. Similarly, mutation 18, which adds six amino acids to the center of the polypeptide, would be expected to result in a protein slightly larger than the wild-type, and indeed such a protein is observed (Gill et al., 1979). The direction of transcription, molecular weight, initiation sites and termination site deduced from the properties of these prematurely terminated polypeptides are fully consistent with the DNA sequence presented here.

Sites Essential for Transposition

Tn3 contains three sites necessary for a complete transposition event. Both the right and left inverted repeats are absolutely required in cis for transposition, as demonstrated by the phenotype for a mutation illustrated in Figure 4. The inverted repeats may function as a recognition site for an enzyme required for transposition; presumably this would be the transposase itself.

The absence of a third site, which we have called IRS, results in a more subtle phenotype. Deletions which remove this site invariably (under rec⁻ conditions) result in the formation of co-integrates (Figure 7). Once formed, these direct repeats of Tn3 appear to be stable. These have the same structure as observed for the transposition of non-mu DNA by mu: two direct repeats of mu flank the non-mu DNA (Toussaint and Faelen, 1973). It has been proposed that

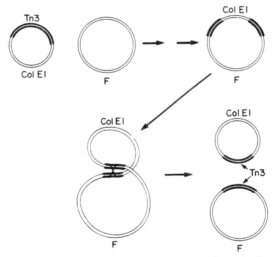

Figure 7. Resolution of Co-integrates by the Internal Resolution Site

In previous work it has been hypothesized that direct repeats of Tn3 are intermediates in transposition which are resolved by recombination through a site contained within the transposon (Gill et al., 1978). The first part of the figure shows the formation of direct repeats, leaving the mechanism undefined. The second part shows their resolution by recombination. A molecular model of transposition which generates co-integrates based on the observation of these direct repeats in several systems has been proposed by Shapiro (1979).

these repeats correspond to intermediates in transposition and that the normal function of the IRS sites is to resolve these direct repeats by recombination (Gill et al., 1978) (the last step in Figure 7). A molecular model for transposition has also been proposed in which direct repeats of the transposon are generated following insertion and DNA repair synthesis (Shapiro, 1979). A sequence which displays striking homology with the inverted repeat lies in a region of Tn3 which, according to deletion mapping, contains the IRS (Figure 5). Should this sequence prove to be the internal resolution site it might suggest that resolution is dependent upon the transposase.

Regulation of Transposase Expression by the Repressor Encoded at *tnpR*

Insertions 5, 95, 18, 44 and 65 show an increase in transposition frequency. These mutations, which lie within the repressor, lead to at least a 10 fold overproduction of the transposase (Gill et al., 1979). Given the low level at which the transposase is normally produced (< 0.001% of the total protein), it appears that this enzyme is limiting in transposition since even slight derepression results in an increase in transposition frequency; hence the increase of transposition observed for the tnpR⁻ mutants. Furthermore, the genetic data presented here suggest that the repressor regulates expression of the transposase transcriptionally. Transcription initiated at the beginning of the transposase gene reads through the entire 3000 bp of the transposase and can lead to expression of the gene for streptomycin resistance. The sequence data support this proposal since no transcriptional stop can be identified in the 33 bp extending from the translational stop at the end of the transposase gene to the end of the inverted repeat. An additional surprising result of the study performed by Gill et al. (1979) was their observation that each of the mutations in *tnpR* results in prematurely terminated polypeptides which are vastly overproduced as compared to the wild-type. This observation suggested that the repressor is autoregulatory (Gill et al., 1979). Similar findings have been reported by Chou et al. (1979).

What role does this repressor have in transposition? Current models such as that described by Shapiro (1979; see also Grindley and Sherratt, 1979) and recent experimental observations (Ljungquist and Bukhari, 1977; Bennett, Grinsted and Richmond, 1977; Waggoner and Pato, 1978) suggest that transposition involves replication of the transposon. If the transposon makes a second copy each time it moves, then clearly there must also be some process which eliminates transposons since otherwise an infinite number of copies would accumulate. Furthermore, Tn3 cannot be lost by precise excision since precise excision has not been observed for this transposon (Hedges and Jacob, 1974; G. Weinstock and D. Botstein, unpublished observations). Slight differential vi-

ability may be a sufficient explanation since cells containing a transposon may be less viable, either because of more rapid accumulation of mutations by insertion of the transposon or because of activities intrinsic to the transposase itself. The fine tuning of transposase expression provided by the autoregulated Tn3-specific repressor may account for the fine line between complete loss of the transposon (due to detrimental effects) and the successful survival of the transposon. In fact, cells containing a mutant transposon which lacks the repressor are noticeably less viable than wild-type cells.

The insertion of Tn3 into the sulfonamide and streptomycin resistance operon is normally strongly polar on the distal gene for streptomycin resistance. A second class of insertions identified in this study, however, were not polar (Rubens et al., 1976). These insertions occurred in the sulfonamide resistance gene in the opposite orientation. In this orientation the β–lactamase is transcribed in the same direction as streptomycin. It might be assumed that expression of the streptomycin phosphotransferase in this orientation resulted from read-through transcription from the β–lactamase promoter, although a stem and loop structure characteristic of transcription termination is located just distal to the translational stop codon of the β–lactamase gene. Calame et al. (1979) have identified a short transcript from this end of the transposon, the transcription of which originates beyond the stop codon and proceed in the same direction as the β–lactamase transcription. Perhaps transcription reinitiates in the short region between the end of the β–lactamase transcript and the end of the transposon and continues through to the streptomycin phosphotransferase gene in these nonpolar insertions of Tn3.

The finding that in repressorless derivatives of Tn3 transcription from either end of the transposon can influence expression of adjacent genes suggests a new use for this transposon as a movable regulated promoter. Indeed, insertions of Tn3 which generate transcriptional fusions could be directly selected in any gene in which a promoter-minus mutation is available.

Experimental Procedures

Bacterial Strains and Plasmids

E. coli C600 and SF800 have been described (Bolivar et al., 1977; Heffron et al., 1977). The plasmid RSF1050 is a 5.0 × 10⁶ dalton pMB8 derivative into which Tn3 has been transposed (Rodriguez et al., 1976; Heffron et al., 1977). Eco RI octamer insertion mutants have been described (Heffron et al., 1978). RSF2001, used for determining the transposition phenotype, is a kanamycin-resistant derivative of F. RSF103 is a derivative of RSF1010 (Heffron et al., 1977).

Determination of Transposition Phenotype

Transposition of Tn3 or mutant transposons to RSF2001 was detected by mating with a DNA polymerase I-deficient mutant (SF800) as described (Heffron et al., 1977). To determine whether the transposition-negative phenotype was recessive or dominant, we included an additional complementing plasmid (RSF103). The normal frequency of transposition for Tn3 is ~10^{-3} carbenicillin-resistant (Cb^R) nalidixic acid-resistant (Nx^R) transconjugant/kanamycin-resistant (Km^R) Nx^R transconjugant, while the frequency is at least 10 fold higher for each of the derepressed mutants. The transposition-defective mutants of Tn3 give 10^{-6} Cb^{R}Nx^R transconjugant/Km^R Nx^R transconjugant when uncomplemented, but 10^{-4} when complemented.

Isolation of Plasmid DNA

Plasmid DNA was isolated according to a modification (Kupersztock and Helinski, 1973) of a procedure reported by Clewell and Helinski (1969).

Digestion with Restriction Enzymes and DNA Kinase Labeling

All restriction enzymes used in this study were purchased from New England Biolabs, and digestions were carried out according to the conditions they have described. T4 polynucleotide kinase was purchased from Boehringer-Mannheim. Kinase and phosphatase conditions were the same as described by Ohtsubo et al. (1979). 200 μCi γ-^{32}P-ATP (New England Nuclear) were dried under vacuum and resuspended together with the restriction enzyme-digested, phosphatased DNA in 25 μl 70 mM Tris (pH 8.0), 10 mM MgCl$_2$, 10 mM dithiothreitol. 4 units of kinase were added and the kinase reaction was carried out for 30 min at 37°C.

DNA Sequencing

DNA sequencing was carried out using the chemical modification procedure developed by Maxam and Gilbert (1977). ^{32}P end-labeled fragments were obtained by cleavage with a second restriction, preparative purification on acrylamide gels and electrophoresis into dialysis tubing. Alternatively, labeled fragments were prepared by strand separation (Maxam and Gilbert, 1977).

Acknowledgments

We would particularly like to thank Hugo Martinez for the computer programming used in the analysis of this DNA sequence, and Ira Herskowitz for his enthusiasm and interest in this project. We would also like to thank Bruce Alberts and Magdelene So for their careful reading of the manuscript. This project was funded in part by grants from the NSF and the NIH, and by a fellowship to F. H. from Smith-Kline.

Received August 31, 1979

References

Adler, K., Beyreuther, K., Fanning, E., Geisler, N., Grovenborn, B., Klerr, A., Mueller-Hill, B., Pfahl, M. and Schnitz, A. (1972). How lac repressor binds to DNA. Nature 237, 322–327.

Bennett, P. M., Grinsted, J. and Richmond, M. H. (1977). Transposition of TnA does not generate deletions. Mol. Gen. Genet. 154, 205–211.

Bolivar, F., Rodriguez, R. L., Greene, P. J., Betlach, M. C., Heyneker, H. L. and Boyer, H. W. (1977). Construction and characterization of new cloning vehicles. I. Ampicillin-resistant derivatives of the plasmid pMB9. Gene 2, 95–107.

Calame, K. L., Yamada, Y., Shanblatt, S. H. and Nakada, D. (1979). Promoter sites on plasmid NTPI which contains the ampicillin resistance transposon Tn1701. J. Mol Biol. 127, 397–409.

Calos, M. P. (1978). DNA sequence for a low level promoter of the lac repressor gene and an "up" promoter mutation. Nature 274, 762–764.

Chou, J., Casadaban, M. J., Lemaux, P. and Cohen, S. N. (1979). Identification and characterization of a self-regulated repressor of translocation of the Tn3 element. Proc. Nat. Acad. Sci. USA 76, 4020–4024.

Clewell, D. B. and Helinski, D. R. (1969). Supercoiled circular DNA-protein complex in Escherichia coli: induced conversion to an open circular DNA form. Proc. Nat. Acad. Sci. USA 62, 1159–1166.

Dougan, G., Saul, M., Twigg, A., Gill, R. and Sherratt, D. (1979). Polypeptides expressed in Escherichia coli K-12 minicells by transposition elements Tn1 and Tn3. J. Bacteriol. 138, 48–54.

Faelen, M., Toussaint, A. and de Lefontayne, J. (1975). Model for the enhancement of lambda-gal integration into partially induced mu lysogens. J. Bacteriol. 121, 873–882.

Farabaugh, P. J. (1978). Sequence of the lacI gene. Nature 274, 765–769.

Gill, R., Heffron, F., and Falkow, S. (1979). Identification of the transposase and transposon-specific repressor encoded by Tn3. Nature, in press.

Gill, R., Heffron, F., Dougan, G. and Falkow, S. (1978). Analysis of sequences transposed by complementation of two classes of transposition-deficient mutants of Tn3. J. Bacteriol. 136, 742–756.

Grindley, N. D. F. (1978). IS1 insertion generates duplication of a nine base pair sequence at its target site. Cell 13, 419–426.

Grindley, N. D. F. and Sherratt, D. (1979). Sequence analysis at IS1 insertion sites: models for transposition. Cold Spring Harbor Symp. Quant. Biol. 43, 1257–1261.

Hedges, R. W. and Jacob, A. (1974). Transposition of ampicillin resistance from RP4 to other replicons. Mol. Gen. Genet. 132, 31–40.

Heffron, F., Sublett, R., Hedges, R. W., Jacob, A. and Falkow, S. (1975a). Origin of the TEM β-lactamase gene found on plasmids. J. Bacteriol. 122, 250–256.

Heffron, F., Rubens, C. and Falkow, S. (1975b). The translocation of a plasmid DNA sequence which mediates ampicillin resistance: molecular nature and specificity of insertion. Proc. Nat. Acad. Sci. USA 72, 3623–3627.

Heffron, F., Bedinger, P., Champoux, J. J. and Falkow, S. (1977). Deletions affecting the transposition of an antibiotic resistance gene. Proc. Nat. Acad. Sci. USA 74, 702–706.

Heffron, F., So, M. and McCarthy, B. J. (1978). In vitro mutagenesis using synthetic restriction sites. Proc. Nat. Acad. Sci. USA 75, 6012–6016.

Johnsrud, L., Calos, M. P. and Miller, J. H. (1978). The transposon Tn9 generates a 9 bp repeated sequence during integration. Cell 15, 1209–1219.

Kopecko, D. and Cohen, S. N. (1975). Site-specific recA-independent recombination between bacterial plasmids: involvement of palindromes at the recombinational loci. Proc. Nat. Acad. Sci. USA 72, 1373–1377.

Kupersztock, Y. M. and Helinski, D. (1973). Biochem. Biophys. Res. Commun. 54, 1451–1459.

Ljungquist, E. and Bukhari, A. E. (1977). State of prophage mu DNA upon induction. Proc. Nat. Acad. Sci. USA 74, 3143–3147.

MacHattie, L. A. and Shapiro, J. A. (1978). Chromosomal integration of phage lambda by means of a DNA insertion element. Proc. Nat. Acad. Sci. USA 75, 1490–1494.

Maxam, A. and Gilbert, W. (1977). A new method for sequencing DNA. Proc. Nat. Acad. Sci. USA 74, 560–564.

Meyer, R., Bock, G. and Shapiro, J. (1979). Transposition of DNA inserted into deletions of the Tn5 kanamycin resistance element. Mol. Gen. Genet. 171, 7–13.

Meynell, E. and Datta, N. (1967). Mutant drug resistant factors of high transmissibility. Nature 214, 885–887.

Ohtsubo, H., Ohmori, H. and Ohtsubo, E. (1979). Nucleotide sequence analysis of the ampicillin resistance transposon Tn3: implications for insertion and deletion. Cold Spring Harbor Symp. Quant. Biol. 43, 1269–1277.

Ptashne, M. (1978). A repressor function and structure. In The Operon, J. H. Miller and W. M. Resnikoff, eds. (New York: Cold

Spring Harbor Laboratory), pp. 325–343.

Roberts, T. M., Shimatake, H., Brady, C. and Rosenberg, M. (1977). The nucleotide sequence of the *cro* gene of bacteriophage lambda. Nature *270*, 274–275.

Rodriguez, R. L., Bolivar, F., Goodman, H. M., Boyer, H. W. and Betlach, M. (1976). Construction and characterization of cloning vehicles. In Molecular Mechanisms in the Control of Gene Expression, D. P. Nierlich, W. J. Rutter and C. F. Fox, eds. (New York: Academic Press), pp. 21–26.

Rosenberg, M. and Court, D. (1980). Regulatory sequences involved in the promotion and termination of RNA transcription. Ann. Rev. Genet., in press.

Rubens, C., Heffron, F. and Falkow, S. (1976). Transposition of a plasmid deoxyribonucleic acid sequence that mediates ampicillin resistance: independence from host *rec* functions and orientation of insertion. J. Bacteriol. *128*, 425–434.

Shapiro, J. A. (1979). Molecular model for the transposition and replication of bacteriophage mu and other transposable sequences. Proc. Nat. Acad. Sci. USA *76*, 1933–1937.

Shapiro, J. A. and MacHattie, L. A. (1979). Prophage insertion and excision mediated by IS*1*. Cold Spring Harbor Symp. Quant. Biol. *43*, 1135–1142.

Shine, J. and Dalgarno, L. (1974). The 3'-terminal sequence of E. coli 16S ribosomal RNA: complementarity to nonsense triplets and ribosome binding sites. Proc. Nat. Acad. Sci. USA *71*, 1342–1346.

So, M., Heffron, F. and McCarthy, B. (1979). The E. coli gene encoding heat-stable toxin is a bacterial transposon flanked by inverted repeats of IS*1*. Nature *277*, 453–456.

Steege, D. A. (1977). 5'-terminal nucleotide sequence of E. coli lactose repressor mRNA: features of translational initiation and reinitiation sites. Proc. Nat. Acad. Sci. USA *74*, 4163–4167.

Sutcliffe, G. (1978). Nucleotide sequence of the ampicillin resistance gene of E. coli plasmid pBR322. Proc. Nat. Acad. Sci. USA *75*, 3737–3741.

Sutcliffe, J. G. (1979). The DNA sequence of pBR322. Cold Spring Harbor Symp. Quant. Biol. *43*, 77–89.

Toussaint, A. and Faelen, M. (1973). Connecting two unrelated DNA sequences with a mu dimer. Nature New Biol. *242*, 1–4.

Waggoner, B. T. and Pato, M. L. (1978). Early events in the replication of mu prophage DNA. J. Virol. *27*, 587–594.

Yamada, Y., Calame, K. L., Grindley, J. N. and Nakada, D. (1979). Location of an ampicillin resistance transposon Tn*1701* in a group of small nontransferring plasmids. J. Bacteriol. *137*, 990–999.

Note Added in Proof

The orientation of Tn*3* and the designation of left and right ends are reversed from those used by Ohtsubo et al. (1979).

Genetic Evidence That Tn10 Transposes by a Nonreplicative Mechanism

Judith Bender and Nancy Kleckner
Department of Biochemistry and Molecular Biology
Harvard University
7 Divinity Avenue
Cambridge, Massachusetts 02138

Summary

We present genetic evidence that the tetracycline resistance element Tn10 transposes by a nonreplicative mechanism. Heteroduplex Tn10 elements containing three single base pair mismatches were constructed on λ phage genomes and allowed to transpose from λ into the bacterial chromosome. Analysis of TetR colonies resulting from such transpositions suggests that information from both strands of the transposing Tn10 element is transmitted faithfully to its transposition product. The simplest interpretation of these results is that the transposing element is excised from the donor molecule and inserted into the target molecule without being replicated. A mismatch 70 base pairs from one end of the transposon is preserved, suggesting that there is little or no replication, even at the termini of the element, during transposition in vivo.

Introduction

Tn10 is a composite tetracycline resistance transposon having inverted repeats of insertion sequence IS10 at its ends (Kleckner et al., 1975). IS10-Right (IS10R) is an intact, functional insertion sequence capable of independent transposition (Roberts et al., 1985); IS10-Left (IS10L) is functionally defective (Foster et al., 1981a). The transposase protein encoded by IS10R acts at the ends of Tn10 to promote transposition of the complete element (Foster et al., 1981a; Morisato et al., 1983).

For many prokaryotic moveable elements, transposition involves specific replication of the transposing segment, as evidenced by the ability of such elements to promote formation of structures called cointegrates, in which donor and target molecules are joined by duplicate copies of the element (for a review, see Grindley and Reed, 1985). The mechanism of IS10 and Tn10 transposition has not been clear. Neither the full element nor the IS10 module appears to promote formation of stable cointegrates (Harayama et al., 1984a; Weinert et al., 1984; and below). However, both nonreplicative transposition mechanisms and replicative mechanisms that do not lead to stable cointegrate formation can be considered. We present below strong genetic evidence that Tn10 transposes by a nonreplicative "cut-and-paste" mechanism.

The experiments described here were designed to examine how information on the two strands of a donor transposon is transmitted to the product of its transposition event. We monitored transposition of Tn10 elements carrying slightly different genetic information on their two

DNA strands due to the presence of three single base pair mismatches. As diagrammed in Figure 1, nonreplicative transposition of such elements should yield transposition products containing both strands of genetic information, while semiconservative replicative transposition should yield products containing information from only one strand.

Tn10 elements containing heteroduplex mismatches were generated on λ::Tn10 phage genomes. Tetracycline-resistant (TetR) colonies produced by transposition of single heteroduplex elements from λ into the bacterial chromosome were examined for the presence of relevant markers. The pattern of markers recovered is exactly that expected if both strands of the incoming transposon are excised from the donor molecule and integrated directly into the bacterial chromosome without concomitant replication. One of the marker sites analyzed is only 70 bp from one end of Tn10, suggesting that Tn10 transposition in vivo does not even involve replication of terminal transposon sequences lying only 70 bp into the element. Other possible transposition models are also considered. A low level of marker conversion is observed at all mismatched sites in both the experiment and the control and is attributable to host-directed mismatch correction. Several implications of a nonreplicative transposition mechanism are discussed.

Results

Experimental System

We have analyzed the products of transposition of single, genetically marked Tn10 elements from λ genomes into the bacterial chromosome following infection of E. coli with suitable heteroduplex λ::Tn10 phages.

The marked Tn10 transposon is 10 kb in length, approximately the same as a wild-type Tn10, and carries both tetR and lacZ genes. We constructed two isogenic derivatives of this transposon that differ at three separate positions within the element. One derivative contains two single base mutations that eliminate unique BamHI and HindIII restriction sites located 70 and 2272 bp, respectively, from opposite ends of the element; the second derivative contains a lacZam mutation located roughly in the middle of the element (Figure 2). Both marked elements were carried on otherwise isogenic λ phage genomes, λNK1212 (LacZ+ HindIII° BamHI°) and λNK1211 (LacZ− HindIII+ BamHI+), as seen in Figure 2. The λ::Tn10 genomes carrying heteroduplex Tn10 elements were made by denaturing, mixing, and reannealing equal amounts of DNA from the two phages and packaging the resulting molecules into complete phage particles in vitro (Experimental Procedures). This process yields a mixed phage population containing both types of homoduplex as well as both types of heteroduplex genomes (Figure 3).

The two phages contain λ mutations that eliminate expression of virtually all phage functions (Figure 2; Experimental Procedures). As a result, the λ::Tn10 genomes

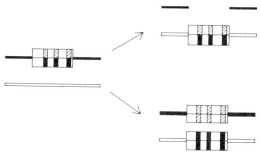

Figure 1. Products of Replicative and Nonreplicative Transposition Mechanisms

A heteroduplex transposon with three single base pair mismatches in the element is shown transposing into a target molecule by a nonreplicative mechanism (top) and by a semiconservative replicative mechanism (bottom). The nonreplicative mechanism integrates the transposon with all three mismatches intact and consequently integrates information from both strands of the original heteroduplex transposon DNA. In contrast, the replicative mechanism integrates information from only one strand of the original transposon DNA.

circularize and become supercoiled, but are otherwise essentially inert. They do not replicate, integrate, or kill the host; but they do serve effectively as donor molecules for Tn10 transposition events (Foster et al., 1981a). In addition, the phage mutations ensure that cells containing chromosomally integrated λ genomes are viable. Hence, if any Tn10-promoted cointegration events were to occur, they would be efficiently recovered.

Each selected TetR colony results from integration of the tetR genes from a single phage genome into the genome of the host, because infections were carried out at such a low multiplicity of infection that any cell receiving one phage particle had only an 0.1% chance of also receiving a second particle. More than one bacterial chromosome may be present in the infected cell at the time of the integration event. However, only the chromosome that receives a Tn10 insertion will be amplified into the selected colony. Analysis of the Tn10 markers present in descendant cells within the TetR colony will reveal which information was integrated into the target chromosome during transposition. More specifically, if both strands of a heteroduplex element are integrated, the resulting colony should be a mixture of two different types of cells, each containing different sets of transposon markers.

Transposition events were analyzed in two situations (Table 1). A small number of transposition events were obtained by self-driven transposition of the marked Tn10 element (Table 1, Situation 2). Larger numbers of Tn10 transposition events were obtained using a strain carrying a transposase overproducer plasmid (pNK972) whose presence increases the frequency of transposition 50-fold (Table 1, Situation 1). In both experiments, two types of TetR colonies were obtained: those containing insertions of Tn10 but no λ sequences and those containing both Tn10 and λ sequences (Table 1). Southern blot analysis de-

scribed below shows that the first class, whose frequency increased in the presence of the overproducer plasmid, were the products of single transpositions of Tn10. The latter class, whose frequency was not affected by the plasmid, resulted not from any Tn10-promoted process but from integration of the λ::Tn10 phage into homologous, cryptic prophage sequences present in the chromosomes of most E. coli strains (Kaiser and Murray, 1979).

As a control for the transposition experiments, we explicitly generated and analyzed TetR colonies that arose by homologous recombination between phages in the heteroduplex mixture and a wild-type λ prophage. When phages are introduced into cells lysogenic for λ, homologous recombination results in formation of TetR colonies at high frequency (Table 1, Situation 3). Since the prophage contains no transposon sequences, the selected recombination event primarily involves interactions among λ sequences and the majority of recombination events, at least, should not result in loss of heteroduplex information within the transposon itself (Figure 4). This control experiment is analogous in every way to the transposition experiment except for the nature of the integration event. Thus, it provides an independent assessment of how many heteroduplex λ::Tn10 genomes are present in the infecting phage population and survive the infection and selection procedure in the absence of transposition. A second, smaller control population was provided fortuitously by the subpopulation of TetR colonies arising by integration into cryptic prophage homologies, as discussed above.

Transposition Products Contain Information from Both Parental Strands

Colonies arising from Tn10 transposition events frequently contain information from both strands of the original transposing element. Colonies selected on X-Gal Tet plates, where LacZ⁻ colonies are white and LacZ⁺ colonies are blue, frequently contain sectors of both blue and white cells.

In fact, information from both strands of the original element must be preserved in virtually all (or at least the vast majority of) transposition events because the propo s and types of sectored colonies observed among transposition products are indistinguishable from those observed following integration of λ::Tn10 phages by homologous recombination into wild-type or cryptic prophages. Among TetR colonies arising in both transposition and homologous recombination experiments, approximately 42% of the TetR colonies were solid blue, an equal number were solid white, and the remaining 16% were sectored (Table 2, part A). In both experiments, approximately 30% of the sectored colonies contained approximately equal amounts of blue and white material, 20% contained one third blue and two thirds white material, 20% contained one third white and two thirds blue material, and 30% exhibited more complex patterns (Table 2, part B). Examples of different sectored colony types are provided in Figure 5.

The observed sector patterns can be understood as follows. Uncomplicated segregation and growth of descendants from a single heteroduplex bacterial chromosome

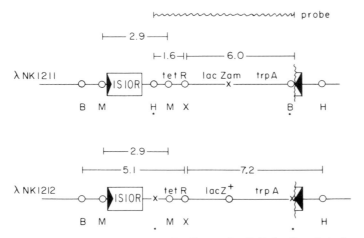

Figure 2. Structures of the Two Parental λ::Tn10 Elements Used in Making Heteroduplex Transposons

The marked Tn10 element consists of IS10R and adjacent tetR genes from wild-type Tn10, followed first by a segment containing E. coli lacZ and trpA genes and then by a short segment containing the outermost 70 bp of IS10R in the appropriate inverted orientation (Way et al., 1984). (Top) The lacZam HindIII⁺ BamHI⁺ transposon carried on λ NK1211. (Bottom) The lacZ⁺ HindIII° BamHI° transposon carried on λ NK1212. B indicates BamHI; H, HindIII; M, MspI; X, XbaI; (*) indicates HindIII and BamHI sites that differ in the two transposons. These sites are, respectively, 2272 and 70 bp from the left and right ends of the element as drawn here. Distances between sites are given in kb. Probe used for all Southern blots (internal HindIII–BamHI fragment) is shown at top of figure. Also shown are the 2.9 kb MspI fragment diagnostic of the parental λ–IS10R junction (λJ, Figure 6) and the four internal transposon fragments used to identify the presence or absence of the internal HindIII and BamHI sites (Figure 7). The complete genotype for both phages is λ b221 Nam7 Nam53 cI857 Pam80 nin::Tn10lacZtrpA.

will give rise to a colony containing one pure blue half and one pure white half. At the four cell stage, one of the descendants of the original cell may die (Zelle and Lederberg, 1951; M. Meselson, personal communication). In this case, the colony will grow up to have one third of its material of one color and two thirds of the other color. Our data suggest that cell death at this stage happens approximately 40% of the time in our strain background. Often, major white and blue sectors in ½:½ and ⅓:⅔ colonies contain small streaks of opposite color. Such variegation can be accounted for by the fact that the strain used in these experiments is fully motile and the descendants of each original TetR cell may change their spatial positions early in the growth of the colony. Most of the observed streaks appear to contain approximately 1/16 the total mass of the colony, suggesting that such changes usually occur before the fifth round of cell division.

Ideally half of the particles in the phage population would contain heteroduplex genomes, and hence in both transposition experiments and prophage integration experiments, half of the tetracycline-resistant colonies would be solid and half would be sectored. The lower proportion of sectored colonies actually observed is not due to efficient correction of the lacZ mismatch (see below); nor do any of the solid white colonies arise from nonspecific loss of lacZ information (see Experimental Procedures). We suggest that the paucity of sectored colonies is most likely explained by inefficient denaturation of homoduplex DNAs or inefficient formation or packaging of heteroduplex relative to homoduplex molecules during prepara-

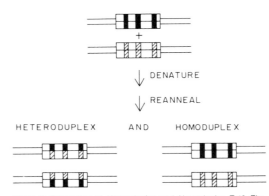

Figure 3. Generation of Heteroduplex and Homoduplex Tn10 Elements

Denaturation and reannealing of a mixture of two parental λ::Tn10 phages differing only at three single bases in the transposon yields a mixture of heteroduplex and homoduplex products.

tion of the heteroduplex λ::Tn10 phage mixture. In any case, this situation poses no problem for interpretation of the transposition results. Transposition and prophage integration experiments are both affected equally, and we assume that prophage integration usually occurs without replication of the prophage transposon sequences (previously discussed).

Table 1. Frequency and Genetic Analysis of TetR Colonies Arising from Heteroduplex λ::Tn10 Infection

| Situation | Host: NK7395 (= mutL103::Tn5 Δ lac U169 Δ (trpEA) su⁻) | Total TetR Colonies per Input Phage | TetR Colonies Without Rescuable λ Markers (Transposition Events) | | TetR Colonies With Rescuable λ Markers (Homologous Recombination Event) | |
			No. λ⁻ / Total TetR Tested	Frequency per Input Phage	No. λ⁺ / Total TetR Tested	Frequency per Input Phage
1. Complemented transposition	+ ptac-transposase⁺ Plasmid (pNK972)	5×10^{-4}	$\frac{141}{150}$ (94%)	5×10^{-4}	$\frac{9}{150}$ (6%)	3×10^{-5}
2. Self-driven transposition	+ ptac-transposase⁻ Plasmid (pNK1525)	4×10^{-5}	$\frac{8}{25}$ (32%)	10^{-5}	$\frac{17}{25}$ (68%)	3×10^{-5}
3. Homologous recombination	+ λ⁺ prophage (λNK112) + ptac-transposase⁻ Plasmid (pNK1525)	10^{-2}	NA	NA	NA	NA

A mixed population of heteroduplex and homoduplex λ::Tn10 phages made from λNK1211 and λNK1212 was used to infect three isogenic derivatives of NK7395. This strain is mutL to reduce host-directed correction of mismatched base pairs, is deleted for lacZ and trp genes to eliminate homology with the marked transposon, and is su⁻ so nonsense mutations in the phage are not suppressed. The strain used in Situation 1 carries a transposase (tpase) overproducer plasmid pNK972. The strain used in Situation 2 carries a deletion derivative of pNK972 that is defective for transposase (pNK1525). The strain used in Situation 3 is a lysogen for wild-type λ (λNK112) and also carries pNK1525 to make it as similar as possible to the strains used for isolating transposition events. Cells of each type were infected at low multiplicity with the heteroduplex phage mixture and plated on tetracycline medium as described in Experimental Procedures. The frequencies of TetR colonies per input phage were determined. TetR colonies from each experiment were then purified and further tested for the presence or absence of rescuable λ markers as described in Experimental Procedures. Each descendant colony analyzed had either all or none of the four λ markers tested (A, O, K, and cro). Southern blot analysis of all colony types is described in Results.

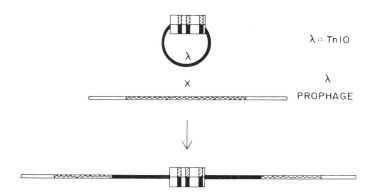

λ :: Tn10

λ
PROPHAGE

Figure 4. Integration of λ::Tn10 into a Prophage Leaves Transposon Information Intact

Integration of the λ::Tn10 phage via homologous recombination between phage sequences on the λ::Tn10 molecule and in the resident prophage does not alter the heteroduplex nature of Tn10 transposon sequences.

Blue and White Portions of Each Sectored Transposition Colony Contain the Same Tn10 Insertion

Southern blot analysis of solid and sectored colonies from transposition experiments shows directly that each TetR colony containing no λ markers resulted from a transposition event while each TetR colony containing λ markers arose by a non-Tn10-promoted event. Furthermore, the blue and white portions of each sectored colony lacking λ markers both contained the same new Tn10 insertion; that is, they arose from the same original Tn10 transposition event.

These conclusions derive from analysis in each TetR colony of the junction between the IS10R end of the marked transposon and adjacent sequences. Any Tn10- or

IS10-promoted event results in loss of the original joint between IS10 and λ sequences and formation of a new joint between IS10 and chromosomal sequences, which will be different for each different insertion. Changes in IS10R junction fragments were monitored by cleavage of DNAs with restriction enzyme MspI and Southern blot hybridization with probe specific to the IS10R end of the marked transposon (Figure 2; Figure 6).

All 58 TetR colonies derived from transposition experiments but not containing rescuable λ markers (Table 3) gave the fragment pattern expected for a single chromosomal Tn10 insertion: the DNA fragment containing the junction between IS10R and λ sequences in the parental λ::Tn10 phage genome was lost, and a single, new IS10-containing fragment was observed. The length of the new

Table 2. Proportions and Types of Sectored TetR Colonies Arising from Heteroduplex λ::Tn10 Infection

Situation:		1. Complemented Transposition		2. Self-Driven Transposition		3. Homologous Recombination	
Host:		NK7395 + pNK972		NK7395 + pNK1525		NK7395 (λNK112) + pNK1525	
		Number	%	Number	%	Number	%
A. Colony color morphology	Sectored	116	(14%)	8	(16%)	136	(16%)
	Solid blue (B)	331	(40%)	16	(33%)	358	(43%)
	Solid white (W)	387	(46%)	25	(51%)	334	(41%)
	Total analyzed:	834	(100%)	49	(100%)	838	(100%)
B. Sector types	1/2 B, 1/2 W	37	(32%)	2	(25%)	50	(38%)
	2/3 B, 1/3 W	22	(19%)	2	(25%)	27	(20%)
	1/3 B, 2/3 W	25	(21%)	1	(12%)	25	(18%)
	Other	32	(28%)	3	(38%)	34	(24%)
	Total analyzed:	116	(100%)	8	(100%)	136	(100%)

A mixed population of heteroduplex and homoduplex phages made from λNK1211 and λNK1212 was used to infect three bacterial strains, and infected cells were plated on tetracycline X-Gal medium as described in Table 1 and Experimental Procedures. LacZ⁺ colonies are blue, LacZ⁻ colonies are white, and mixed LacZ⁺/LacZ⁻ colonies are sectored blue and white. Colonies were first scored for color and presence of sectoring (A), and sectored colonies were further scored for individual sectoring patterns (B): half blue/half white, mostly (~2/3) blue, mostly (~2/3) white, and other. Colonies listed under Other contained fine streaks of color or star patterns rather than large discrete blocks of color (see Figure 5).

fragment was different in each colony, as expected for the Tn10–bacterial DNA junctions of insertions at different chromosomal sites. Most importantly, in 33/33 sectored colonies, both the blue and the white portions contained the same new junction fragment, which varied in size from one colony to another (Figure 6). This result excludes the possibility that the two sectors arose from different transposition events.

Similar analysis of 26/26 TetR colonies derived from transposition experiments and containing λ markers, including solid colonies and blue and white portions of sectored colonies (Table 3), exhibited the pattern expected for integration of the donor λ::Tn10 genome by a non-IS10-promoted event: the parental λ–IS10R junction fragment was retained and (with one exception described below) no new IS10-containing junction fragments were present (Figure 6). These colonies have presumably arisen by homologous recombination between the λ::Tn10 phage and cryptic prophage sequences. Consistent with this interpretation, no λ-containing TetR colonies (<0.1%) are obtained when the λ N⁻ P⁻ Tn10 phage is infected into a recA⁻ host lacking any transposase-overproducer plasmid (data not shown).

One solid white, λ-containing colony from the transposase-overproducer experiment contained both the parental λ::Tn10 fragment and a new Tn10 chromosomal junction band, which is the pattern expected for a Tn10- or IS10-promoted cointegrate. Further analysis shows that this colony does not contain a stable cointegrate structure, but instead contains a λ::Tn10 cryptic prophage recombinant plus an insertion of the Tn10 elsewhere in the chromosome (Experimental Procedures).

Analysis of colonies obtained in the lysogen control experiment confirmed that these too had arisen by homologous recombination. All 30 TetR lysogen control colonies retained the parental λ::Tn10 junction fragment and ex-

hibited no new IS10-containing junction fragment (Figure 6; also Figure 7 and Table 3).

Sectored Colonies Usually Retain All Six Markers Present on the Two Parental Transposon Strands

From the above results, we presume that each sectored colony arose by incorporation into a single chromosomal DNA molecule of a single heteroduplex Tn10 element or λ::Tn10 genome, each of which originally contained single base mismatches at the BamHI and HindIII sites as well as the lacZam site. Further analysis of DNAs from the blue and white portions of sectored colonies suggest that most transposition events occur without loss or rearrangement of the restriction site markers on either parental strand. A small amount of marker loss, attributable to host-promoted correction of base pair mismatches, is detected in both transposition and control samples. No additional alteration of markers specific to transposition is detected above this background.

The presence or absence of HindIII and BamHI sites within the Tn10 element was determined for the same set of DNAs analyzed for Tn10 junction fragments above (Table 3). DNAs were digested simultaneously with three enzymes—BamHI, HindIII, and XbaI—and then analyzed by Southern blots using the Tn10 HindIII–BamHI segment as probe (Figure 2). XbaI cleaves uniquely within the element, between the HindIII and BamHI sites. Thus presence or absence of the BamHI and/or the HindIII site is indicated by presence or absence of the specific internal BamHI–XbaI or HindIII–XbaI fragment. When a site is absent, the internal Tn10 fragment is replaced by a larger fragment containing the junction between transposon and adjacent chromosomal or λ sequences. The size of this junction fragment is variable for chromosomal insertions and constant for λ::Tn10 recombination products.

For most sectored transposition colonies, the blue and

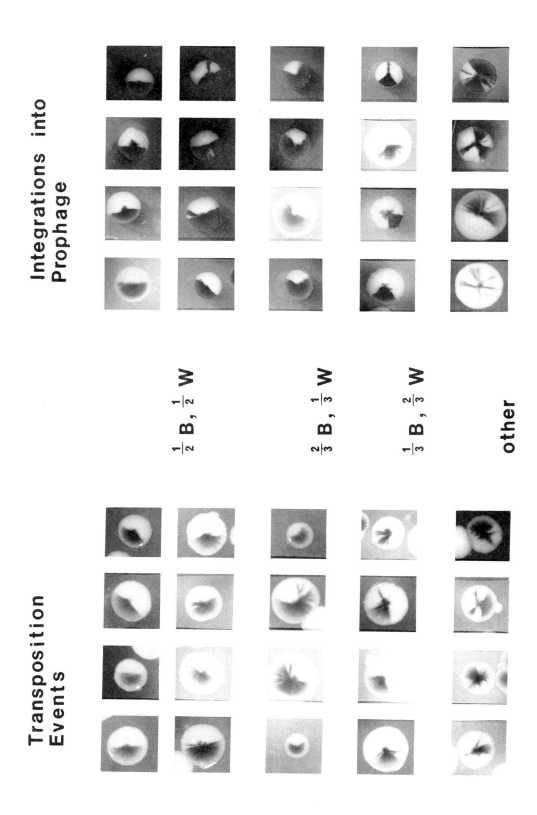

Figure 5. See page 480 for caption.

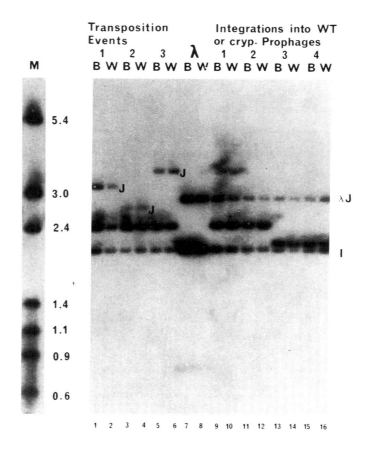

Transposition
Events
1   2   3   λ   Integrations into WT
                or cryp. Prophages
                1   2   3   4
B W B W B W B W B W B W B W B W

M
5.4
3.0
2.4
1.4
1.1
0.9
0.6

λ J
I

J
J
J

1 2 3 4 5 6 7 8 9 10 11 12 13 14 15 16

Figure 6. Southern Blot Analysis of IS10 Junction Fragments in Sectored TetR Colonies

DNAs described in Table 3 were digested with MspI and probed with the HindIII to BamHI fragment internal to the transposon to detect junction fragments containing the IS10R end of the transposon and adjacent sequences in the chromosome (see Figure 2). The MspI fragment containing the other end of the transposon does not have enough homology to the probe to be detectable. Pairs of samples from blue and white portions of different types of sectored TetR colonies are shown. Lanes 1–6 (Transposition Events) are colonies without λ markers obtained from the complemented transposition experiment in NK7395(pNK972). Lanes 9–16 (Integrations into WT or cryp. Prophages) are colonies from the same experiment that did contain λ markers (pairs 1 and 2) and colonies from the homologous recombination control experiment in NK7395(λNK112)-(pNK1525) (pairs 3 and 4). Lanes 7 and 8 (λ) contain λNK1212 and λNK1211 parental phage DNAs. Lane M (size markers) contains a mixture of PhiX174 DNAs digested singly with PstI, AccI, and HaeIII. J indicates fragments containing junction between IS10 and chromosomal sequences; λ J indicates a 2900 bp IS10-containing junction fragment from the parental λ::Tn10 phage (see Figure 2); and I indicates 2.0 kb fragment adjacent to the λJ fragment within the transposon (not shown in Figure 2). All unlabeled bands on the blot correspond to plasmid pNK972 or plasmid pNK1525 topoisomers. These plasmids are not cut by MspI and have homology to the TetR sequences on the probe. B denotes blue and W denotes white.

Table 3. Summary of Colonies Analyzed by Southern Blot

Situation	Host	Number of Transposition Events (TetR Colonies Without Rescuable λ Markers)			Number of Homologous Recombination Events (TetR Colonies with Rescuable λ Markers)		
		Sectored	Solid Blue	Solid White	Sectored	Solid Blue	Solid White
1. Complemented transposition	NK7395 + pNK972 (= tpase⁺)	30	10	10	2	3	4
2. Self-driven transposition	NK7395 + pNK1525 (+ tpase⁻)	3	3	2	2	7	8
3. Homologous recombination	NK7395 (λNK112) + pNK1525	NA	NA	NA	30	0	0

The indicated numbers of colonies, chosen from the experiments described in Table 2, were analyzed as described in Figures 6 and 7 and Table 4. Each colony was purified by restreaking on Tet X-Gal medium. For sectored colonies, sectors of each color were restreaked separately. Blue and/or white descendants of the original colony were then grown into cultures, and their DNA was extracted for blot analysis.

Figure 5. Photographs of Sectored Colonies

Under Transposition Events are TetR sectored colonies without rescuable λ markers from host strain NK7395(pNK972). Under Integrations into Prophage are TetR sectored colonies from host strain lysogen NK7395(λNK112)(pNK1525). All events are summarized in Table 2. In the complemented transposition experiment (Table 2, Situation 1) essentially all of the colonies arise from Tn10 transposition; in the self-driven transposition experiment (Table 2, Situation 2), approximately 1/3 of the colonies within each class arose from transposition and 2/3 arose from recombination into cryptic prophages, as expected from Table 1 (data not shown). B denotes blue; W denotes white.

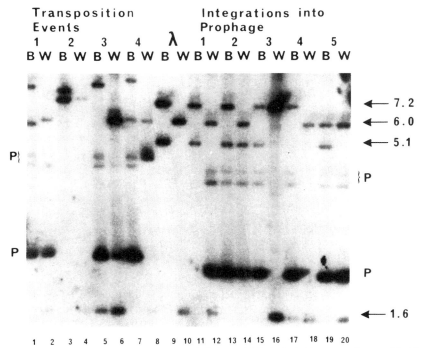

Figure 7. Southern Blot of Chromosomal DNA from TetR Sectored Colonies for the Presence or Absence of Restriction Enzyme Sites Near the Ends of Tn10 Insertions

DNAs were digested with BamHI, HindIII, and XbaI and were probed with the standard internal fragment (see Figure 2) to detect the presence or absence of HindIII and BamHI enzyme sites in the transposon. DNAs from blue and white portions of sectored colonies are paired as in Figure 6. Lanes 9 and 10 contain the parental λ::Tn10 phage DNAs. A chromosomal Tn10 insertion retaining the parental configuration of markers on its two strands would yield two internal fragments of 1.6 Kb and 6.0 Kb in the white (LacZ⁻ HindIII⁺ BamHI⁺) sector of its TetR colony and two junction fragments of variable size in the blue (LacZ⁺ HindIII° BamHI°) sector of the colony. If the white sector has lost either the HindIII or BamHI site(s), a variable junction fragment(s) will be present instead of the appropriate internal fragment(s); if the blue sector has gained either one or both of the two sites, the variable-sized junction fragment(s) will be absent and the appropriate internal fragment(s) will appear instead. Examples of these types in strain NK7395 (pNK972) are shown in lanes 1–8 (Transposition Events). Pair 1 has the parental pattern, pair 2 is missing the BamHI site in the white sector, pair 3 has acquired the HindIII site in the blue sector, and pair 4 has acquired the BamHI site in the blue sector. Lanes 11–20 (Integrations into Prophage) contain paired samples from the blue and white sectors of TetR sectored double lysogen colonies in NK7395(λNK112)(pNK1525). In this case, integration without loss of markers should result in blue and white sectors that yield the same sets of fragments as the corresponding LacZ⁺ and LacZ⁻ parental phages, 5.1 + 7.2 and 1.6 + 6.0 respectively. Gain or loss of a site should convert the affected fragment to the size observed in the parental phage of opposite color. Pair 1 has the parental configuration of enzyme sites, pair 2 is missing the HindIII site in the white sector, pair 3 is missing the BamHI site in the white sector, pair 4 has acquired the HindIII site in the blue sector, and pair 5 has acquired the BamHI site in the blue sector. Bands labeled P in all lanes correspond to plasmid pNK972 and pNK1525 topoisomers. These plasmids are not cut by HindIII, BamHI, and XbaI, and have homology to TetR sequences on the probe. Bands not explicitly labeled in lanes 1–8 are junction fragments of variable size. B denotes blue and W denotes white.

white portions contain the restriction site markers present in the corresponding *lacZ⁺* and *lacZ⁻* parental phages. In 21/33 (64%) colonies analyzed, both restriction sites were present in the LacZ⁻ portion and neither site was present in the LacZ⁺ portion (Table 4, Figure 7). Exactly the same result was obtained among sectored colonies derived by homologous recombination, of which 23/34 (68%) colonies contained the two parental marker configurations (Table 4; Figure 7).

The remaining third of sectored colonies resulting from either transposition or homologous recombination exhibited changes from the parental restriction marker configuration (Table 4; Figure 7). Among both types of integration products, the pattern of observed changes is that

expected if mismatch correction had occurred independently at each of the two heteroduplex sites. In 22/23 colonies containing changes, only one restriction site marker was converted; in one sector of the colony, one restriction site marker was converted to the marker of the parental phage having the opposite *lacZ* genotype. In 1/23 colonies (a cryptic prophage recombinant), one marker was converted in each sector, as if both markers had been corrected independently on the same molecule. In no case were two markers converted in the same sector.

There is no evidence for any difference between colonies arising from transposition and colonies arising from homologous recombination with respect to the frequency or the pattern of marker conversion. Within expected

Table 4. Analysis of HindIII and BamHI Markers in Blue and White Portions of Sectored Colonies

Marker Changes		Pattern of Restriction Enzyme Sites				Number of TetR Sectored Colonies Having This Pattern				
		Blue Sector		White Sector		Transposition		Homologous Recombination		
						Situation 1	2	1	2	3
Number	Site(s)	HindIII	BamHI	HindIII	BamHI	NK7395 + pNK972 (= tpase⁺)	NK7395 + pNK1525 (= tpase⁻)			NK7395 (λNK112) + pNK1525 (= tpase⁻)
0	(parental)	−	−	+	+	19	2	1	2	20
1	BamHI	−	−	+	−	5	0	0	0	2
		−	+	+	+	3	1	0	0	4
1	HindIII	−	−	−	+	0	0	0	0	2
		+	−	+	+	3	0	0	0	2
2	BamHI and HindIII	−	+	−	+	0	0	1	0	0
Total analyzed:						30	3	2	2	30

TetR sectored colonies were analyzed for the presence or absence of HindIII and BamHI sites in the transposon of each sector as described in Figure 7. The presence of a site is denoted by +; the absence of a site, by −.

statistical variation, the two markers are corrected at similar frequencies in colonies from both events: 9 BamHI and 3 HindIII conversions among 33 transposition colonies; 7 BamHI and 5 HindIII conversions among 34 homologous recombination colonies.

All of the bacterial strains used in these experiments, including those from which λ packaging extracts were prepared, contain a *mutL* mutation. *MutL* mutations eliminate one major pathway for host-directed correction of base pair mismatches but do not completely eliminate mismatch correction in vivo (Glickman and Radman, 1980; Pukkila et al., 1983). The overall frequency of correction in integrated Tn10 elements, approximately 15% at each mismatch, is somewhat high for a *mutL* strain. Correction might have occurred at any point or points after in vitro formation of heteroduplex DNA and before replication of the chromosomally integrated Tn10 element. We suggest that considerable mismatch correction is occurring during the in vitro packaging reactions and/or that the infected heteroduplex λ::Tn10 phage can persist in its unreplicated state within the infected cell for quite a long time, perhaps several cell generations, before giving rise to the selected transposition event.

Analysis of HindIII and BamHI sites in Tn10 DNAs from solid blue and solid white colonies obtained in transposition experiments shows that these colonies arose from integration of homoduplex Tn10 elements rather than integration of heteroduplex elements that had undergone mismatch correction at the *lacZ*am site. Twenty-five non-λ-containing and twenty-two λ-containing solid colored colonies exhibited the configuration of restriction sites appropriate to the corresponding *lacZ*⁺ or *lacZ*⁻ parent.

Tn10 Does Not Make Stable Cointegrates and Does Not Promote Resolution of an Artificially Made Cointegrate

A number of other transposable elements promote the formation of structures called cointegrates in which an entire circular donor molecule is integrated into a target molecule with directly repeated copies of the transposon at each newly created junction. Work in our own laboratory and published reports from other laboratories have indicated that Tn10 and IS10 fail to promote such events (M. Peifer and N. Kleckner, unpublished; Harayama et al., 1984a; Weinert et al., 1984). The results presented above provide further evidence against the occurrence of either Tn10-promoted cointegrates, in which the entire Tn10 element is duplicated, or IS10-promoted cointegrates, in which only the IS10R element is duplicated. Any colony containing a cointegrate structure would have contained λ markers and would have exhibited at least one new IS10R-containing MspI junction fragment (see above). In the complemented transposition experiment, colonies containing λ were very rare (6%, Table 1). Furthermore, none of the 26 λ-containing colonies analyzed (11 from complemented and 15 from noncomplemented transposition) exhibited the Southern blot pattern expected for a cointegrate (see above).

Some transposable elements that promote the formation of cointegrate structures also promote the resolution of such structures. Thus, conceivably, the failure to recover cointegrates might have been due to their relative instability. Analysis of an artificially reconstructed Tn10 cointegrate structure shows that such cointegrates are stable enough to be detected and that the low level of resolution which does occur results from host-promoted homologous recombination.

The structure of a (hypothetical) Tn10-promoted cointegrate is diagrammed in Figure 8. A colony carrying such a cointegrate would contain both a LacZ⁺ and a LacZ⁻ Tn10 element and hence should make a solid blue colony. A cointegrate of this structure was generated artificially by homologous recombination, and colonies containing such a cointegrate do in fact make solid blue colonies (see Figure 8 and below).

For the Tn10 cointegrate diagrammed, resolution would

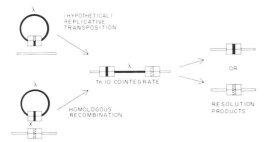

Figure 8. Predicted Structure and Genetic Construction of the Hypothetical Heteroduplex Tn10-Generated Cointegrate

The cointegrate structure that would be formed by a heteroduplex Tn10-promoted cointegration event analogous to those promoted by some other types of transposable elements is shown. A structure identical to this was reconstructed genetically and analyzed as follows. The *lacZ*+ phage λNK1212 was integrated by homologous recombination into a chromosomal insertion of the *lacZ* amber transposon by screening for *lacZ*+. The structure of the resulting construct was verified three ways. First, the chromosomal insertion chosen was an auxotrophic insertion mutant. Reversion of the cointegrate-containing strain to prototrophy resulted in loss of all cointegrate-specific genetic markers: TetR, *lacZ*+, and λ. Second, all the cointegrate genetic markers including auxotrophy could be cotransduced by P1 into a new strain. Third, Southern blot analysis of IS10 junction fragments, analogous to that in Figure 6, yielded the predicted pattern of one chromosomal junction fragment and one λ junction fragment. As expected from the structure shown, the resulting strain made blue (LacZ+) colonies on X-Gal Tet plates. The segregation properties of this strain are discussed in the text.

result in loss of λ sequences and one set of transposon sequences, as shown. Those resolution events resulting in loss of LacZ+ information can be identified as white (LacZ−) segregants in a population of cointegrate-containing cells. Resolution examined under conditions where the amount of IS10 transposase was either increased, decreased, or unchanged. The frequency of LacZ− segregants was measured in strains carrying plasmids that either overproduce transposase (pNK972), inhibit expression of transposase from IS10s in the cointegrate structure (pNK82, see Experimental Procedures), or are transposase− and noninhibiting (pNK1525). When restreaked on Tet X-Gal medium, colonies from strains containing each of these plasmids all behaved identically. Most of the resulting colonies were solid blue and none (<0.1%) were sectored. A few white colonies and a few blue colonies with white edges were observed. Blue colonies (with or without white edges) themselves contain about 7% LacZ− (resolved) cells as determined by suspension of single colonies in liquid and titration on X-Gal plates. These resolution events occur by host-promoted homologous recombination. Single colonies of *recA*− derivatives of the cointegrate-containing strains yield LacZ− segregants at a frequency of less than 10⁻⁴.

Discussion

Sectored Colonies in Transposition Experiments Arise from Nonreplicative Transposition

The results presented above can be explained very simply if Tn10 transposition occurs by excision of the element

from the donor molecule and insertion into the target molecule without replication of the element itself. The proportion of sectored colonies, the proportions of sector patterns in those colonies, and the distribution of parental restriction site markers in LacZ+ and LacZ− sectors observed among transposition products are indistinguishable from those observed among the products of a different event: integration of a λ::Tn10 phage into wild-type or cryptic prophage homology by homologous recombination, an event that should not usually involve replication of transposon sequences.

These data directly rule out the possibility that transposition occurs exclusively by semiconservative replication of the element followed by integration of a single replicated copy. The products of such a transposition event would have contained information from only one DNA strand, and no sectored colonies would have been observed. The results presented above also exclude the possibility that Tn10 or IS10 transposition involves the formation of either stable or unstable cointegrate structures containing two transposon copies flanking the donor λ replicon. No λ-containing colonies having the physical structure of a cointegrate were observed, and an artificially constructed Tn10 cointegrate was shown to resolve only at a low frequency by RecA-promoted recombination.

The results presented above also argue against a more complicated possibility: that transposition involves cointegrate formation followed by a very short, transient period during which cointegrates are very efficiently resolved. Such a model could give the observed proportions and types of sectored colonies, which are identical to those from the lysogen control experiment, only under very special conditions. Specifically, significant amounts of resolution cannot have occurred prior to the first round of chromosomal replication following formation of the cointegrate. Such events would have produced a single TetR chromosome carrying only a single type of information and hence would have reduced the proportion of sectored colonies in the transposition experiment relative to that in the lysogen control experiment. Resolution in either of the first two generations following the first round of chromosomal replication could conceivably result in sectored colonies with relatively simple sector patterns. However, to account for the observed results, the reduction scenario would have to generate sectored colonies in exactly the same proportions and with the same structures as was observed in the control experiment. Resolution of any significant proportion of cells after about the fourth round of replication is also excluded because mixed colonies resulting from such events would not have the observed simple sectoring patterns.

The results presented, while straightforwardly explained by nonreplicative transposition of Tn10, are formally compatible with two other types of transposition models that do involve replication. First, transposition might involve conservative rather than semiconservative DNA replication of the element. If replication resulted in conservation of the parental transposon molecule and generation of a replica in which both strands were newly synthesized off of the two parental strands, both the parental molecule and the replica would contain different information on the two strands. Second, as recently suggested to us by Howard Nash, transposition might involve semiconservative replication, generating a cointegrate, followed by a resolution reaction, producing stretches of heteroduplex DNA extending the entire length of the transposon.

Both of the above models are complex and therefore may be less likely than a nonreplicative mechanism. In addition, two other types of information provide independent evidence that Tn10 and IS10 transposition is nonreplicative. First, Tn10 promotes intrachromosomal deletion/inversions and intermolecular inverse transpositions which are not promoted by transposons known to carry out replicative transposition and which are most straightforwardly accounted for as the products of simple break–join events (Kleckner et al., 1979; Foster et al., 1981a; Chandler et al., 1979; Harayama et al., 1984b). IS10 transposase promotes the efficient occurrence of double strand breaks at the ends of Tn10 or IS10 in vivo (Morisato and Kleckner, 1984) and in vitro in the absence of high energy cofactors (D. Morisato and N. Kleckner, unpublished). Occurrence of such breaks is an essential feature of a "cut-and-paste" transposition model.

During Transposition, New DNA Synthesis Rarely if Ever Extends as Far as 70 bp into Tn10
DNA sequencing of Tn10 insertions shows that the element is flanked by 9 bp direct repeats that were present as a single 9 bp target site before insertion (Kleckner, 1979). These direct repeats are most likely generated by staggered 9 base cleavage of the target site followed by resynthesis of the 9 base segments at each end of the element that would be left single-stranded after Tn10 insertion. In a nonreplicative "cut-and-paste" transposition mechanism, such synthesis could be primed either by the single strand termini in flanking host sequences or by single strand termini within the transposon, depending upon the strand polarities of the cleavage and ligation events. In either case, sequences within the termini of the transposon might also be replicated during this final stage, either as a consequence of DNA degradation at those termini prior to resynthesis or, for target-primed synthesis, as a consequence of strand displacement or nick translation by DNA polymerase that continues into the element after filling the 9 bp gap. Significant tracts of such synthesis are in fact observed at the termini of bacteriophage Mu elements undergoing nonreplicative transposition in vitro (Mizuuchi, 1984).

The results presented above for Tn10 transposition in vivo are inconsistent with such replication extending as far as 70 bp into the element. Southern blot analysis of the transposon BamHI$^+$–BamHI$^\circ$ mismatch located 70 bp from one end shows that in 24/33 (73%) of cases, this mismatch remains intact after transposition. Correction of the BamHI$^+$–BamHI$^\circ$ mismatch observed in the remaining 27% of cases is largely, if not completely, accounted for by residual host-directed mismatch correction, since correction at this site was observed in 7/34 (21%) of the λ::Tn10 wild-type and cryptic prophage integrations.

Relationship of IS10 Transposition to That of Other Insertion Sequences
There is at least one other well-characterized insertion sequence whose transposition mechanism is probably closely analogous to that of IS10. IS50 does not promote cointegrate formation, and its composite transposon Tn5 promotes the same types of intrachromosomal deletion/inversion events as does Tn10 (Hirschel et al., 1982; Berg, 1983; Isberg and Syvanen, 1985). Other insertion sequences, notably IS1 and IS903, do have the capacity to transpose by a replicative cointegrate mechanism (Biel and Berg, 1984; Grindley and Joyce, 1980; Weinert et al., 1984). However, it has been suggested that these insertion sequences transpose by a cointegrate mechanism only 1%–5% of the time and by a nonreplicative, simple insertion mechanism the rest of the time (Grindley and Reed, 1985). Since relatively few IS elements have been analyzed in detail thus far, it is still possible that some insertion sequences may transpose exclusively by a cointegration mechanism. This range of transposition behaviors, from simple insertions to cointegrate formation, may all represent relatively minor variations on a similar mechanistic process (for reviews, see Kleckner, 1981, and Grindley and Reed, 1985).

Fate of the Donor Molecule during Transposition
The above experiments examine transposition of Tn10 from a nonreplicating λ chromosome into the bacterial chromosome. In this situation, it is not possible to determine what happens to the donor λ molecule as a consequence of the transposition event because it will be inevitably lost from the cell population due to its inability to replicate. In nature, however, a Tn10 or IS10 element may frequently transpose from one bacterial chromosomal site to another. In this case, the fate of the transposon donor molecule has important biological as well as mechanistic implications.

Genetic experiments strongly suggest that transposition does not result in precise excision of the element plus one copy of the 9 bp sequence to restore the original pretransposon wild-type DNA sequence (Kleckner et al., 1975; Foster et al., 1981b). Several other possible fates of the donor molecule following transposition are diagrammed in Figure 9. The donor chromosome might simply be lost. If transposon excision results in occurrence of a gap at the donor site, failure to repair this gap will result in loss of the chromosome from the cell. Such a loss can probably be tolerated by bacterial cells under reasonably rapid growth conditions when they contain more than a single copy of the chromosome. Alternatively, an interrupted donor molecule might be resealed, probably by nonspecific, host-encoded functions. The properties of genetic and physical events promoted by Tn10 argue against the possibility of transposon-promoted rejoining (Kleckner and Ross, 1979; Morisato and Kleckner, 1984). The resulting resealed molecule could retain both copies of the 9 bp direct repeats that flanked the Tn10 insertion, or it could contain a deletion of sequences around the insertion site if the gap produced by excision of the transposon is enlarged by exonucleolytic degradation prior to

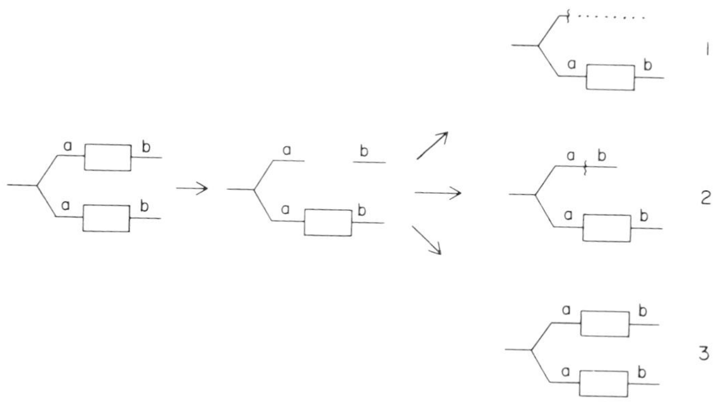

Figure 9. Possible Fates of the Donor Molecule Following Tn10 Transposition

Fate 1, "donor suicide," results in loss of the gapped donor molecule after transposition. Fate 2 involves resealing the gapped donor molecule, possibly after some degradation at the exposed ends of DNA. Fate 3 is double-strand-break repair of the gapped molecule to homologous sequences on its sister chromosome, restoring the original sequence including the transposon.

resealing. Finally, the gapped donor molecule could be repaired by interaction with homologous sequences of DNA present on a second (sister) chromosome in the cell, restoring the original donor molecule sequence including the transposon itself (double-strand-gap repair, for example see Szostak et al., 1983).

Evolutionary Implications of Nonreplicative Transposition

Transposable elements are highly evolved and must therefore possess strategies ensuring their long-term survival (Campbell, 1983). Two types of selective forces might individually or collectively be important. The element might confer some benefit—some direct phenotypic advantage—on an individual host cell or host cell population, or even on an individual gene. Alternatively, such elements might persist because they are replicated more frequently than the cellular genome, a property referred to as overreplication (Campbell, 1983).

For transposable elements that use a replicative transposition mechanism, overreplication occurs as a natural consequence of the transposition process. However, for elements that use a nonreplicative excision–insertion mechanism, overreplication can still occur in one of several ways. First, IS elements appear to be spread horizontally through bacterial populations on plasmids and phages and thus will be amplified passively as a consequence of overreplication of the transmitting vector. Second, overreplication of a chromosomally located element can occur if the donor molecule suffers either fate 1 or fate 3 of Figure 9, that is, either degradation or double-strand-gap repair off of a sister chromosome. The transposon to chromosome ratio is increased in either case: in the first case, by loss of the donor chromosome and survival of a single chromosome carrying two copies of the transposon and in the latter case, by duplication of the transposon as a consequence of the repair process subsequent to transposition. A nonreplicative transposition event will fail to result in overreplication only if the transposon-donor chromosome is efficiently resealed without restoration of the transposon sequences (Figure 9, fate 2), in which case

both the number of elements and the number of host chromosomes remain constant.

The above considerations suggest that for nonreplicative transposition mechanisms, it should be evolutionarily advantageous when the donor chromosome is not efficiently resealed as a direct (transposase-dependent) consequence of the transposition process per se. This consideration may in turn help to explain the striking mechanistic difference between transposition of elements like Tn10, which does not thus far appear to involve transposon-promoted resealing of the donor chromosome (Kleckner and Ross, 1979; Foster et al., 1981b), and site-specific recombination events such as excision of prophage λ from its usual bacterial attachment site, which is exquisitely reciprocal and always results in precise restoration of the host chromosome sequence.

Experimental Procedures

Bacterial Strains, Plasmids, and Phages

Strain NK7395 is a *mutL*103::Tn5 Δ*lac*U169 Δ(*trpEA*) *su⁻* derivative of E. coli K-12 strain W3110 constructed by P1*vir* transduction of *mutL*103::Tn5 (from strain RH302 of R. Hoess) into W3110 Δ*lac*U169 Δ(*trpEA*) *su⁻* (C. Yanofsky) performed according to Miller (1972).

Plasmid pNK972 is a multicopy, pBR322-derived plasmid carrying a fusion in which transcription of the transposase gene is driven by a *ptac* promoter. It is derived from pNK474 (Way et al., 1984) by deletion of the DNA between the XhoII site at the end of IS10R and the EcoRI site in the plasmid backbone. Plasmid pNK1525 is isogenic to pNK972 but contains an in-frame internal deletion between the two NcoI sites in the transposase gene of IS10R (Halling et al., 1982). Plasmid pNK82 is a multicopy, pBR322-derived plasmid carrying an intact IS10R element (Simons and Kleckner, 1983).

Phage λNK112 is wild-type λ. Phage λNK1211 is *b*221 *Nam*7*Nam*53 *c*I857 *Pam*80 *nin*::Tn10*lacZam*YA536*trpA*, and phage λNK1212 is *b*221 *Nam*7*Nam*53 *c*I857 *Pam*80 *nin*::Tn10*lacZtrpA*HindIII°BamHI° (Figure 2). Phage λNK1211 and phage λNK1212 are derived from λNK1045 (*b*221 *c*I857 *Pam*80 *nin*::Tn10*lacZtrpA*) (Way et al., 1984) by a phage cross with λNK70 (*b*221 *Nam*7*Nam*53 *c*I857) followed by screening for small (*N⁻*), blue (*lacZ⁺*) plaques on X-Gal top agar (described below). The *Nam*7*Nam*53 alleles were confirmed by standard complementation and recombination tests. The *b*221 deletion removes the λ attachment site and *int* gene, making these phages nonintegrating. The *Nam*7*Nam*53 mutations reduce expression of lytic gene functions and prevent the infecting phages from killing the host cell. The *c*I857 temperature-sensitive λ repressor is not active at 37°C, leaving these phages unrepressed under the conditions of our experiments. The Pam80 mutation eliminates phage DNA replication. In combination, the N⁻ and P⁻ amber mutations mean that bacterial strains containing the phage genome integrated into the chromosome but not repressed are still normally viable (Eisen et al., 1970).

Phage λNK1211 was made lacZamYA536 by growing the phage on strain LG75 (lacZamYA536, L. Guarante) and screening for white (lacZ⁻) plaques on X-Gal top agar. The lacZamYA536 allele was confirmed by suppression tests. The amber allele is efficiently suppressed to give blue plaques on an suIII indicator with X-Gal, but not on an suII indicator with X-Gal.

Unique HindIII and BamHI restriction enzyme sites in the Tn10-lacZtrpA insertion of λNK1212 were destroyed by bisulfite mutagenesis (Figure 2). Two plasmid clones were made from the unmutagenized lacZ⁺ parent phage. In the first, a BamHI fragment carrying the IS10R end of the transposon was inserted into a unique BamHI site on plasmid pNK313 (a derivative of pGL101 [Lauer et al., 1981] with a unique BamHI site and no HindIII sites). In the second, an EcoRI fragment extending from the tetR genes in the transposon to beyond the Q gene was inserted into a unique EcoRI site on plasmid pBR333 (a deletion derivative of pBR322 [Foster et al., 1981a] with a unique EcoRI site and no BamHI sites). The transposon HindIII site on the BamHI insert plasmid and the transposon BamHI site on the EcoRI insert plasmid were each mutagenized by bisulfite as described by Shortle and Nathans (1978).

The two restriction site mutations were crossed back onto the phage by homologous recombination. First, a new plasmid containing the entire transposon sequence and flanking λ sequences was constructed from the two mutagenized plasmids by ligating together the appropriate PstI (in the plasmid backbone ampR gene) to XbaI (in the transposon sequence) fragments from each plasmid. Phage λNK1211 (lacZ⁻) was grown on a lacZ-deleted strain transformed with this composite lacZ⁺ plasmid, and the phage stock obtained was then screened for blue (lacZ⁺) plaques on X-Gal top agar. LacZ⁺ phages purified from this screen were tested for the HindIII and BamHI mutations in the transposon by restriction mapping of phage DNA.

Media, Enzymes, and Chemicals

Luria broth (LB) and minimal medium (M9) were as described by Miller (1972); for solid media, 1.5% agar was added. λym broth, λ agar, and SM buffer were as described by Kleckner et al. (1978). When used, tetracycline was added to media at a concentration of 15 μg/ml, X-Gal at 40 μg/ml, amino acids at 40 μg/ml, thiamine at 0.5 μg/ml, and carbenicillin at 300 μg/ml. Bacteriological supplies were purchased from Difco; amino acids and drugs, from Sigma; and X-Gal, from Bachem, Inc.

Standard cloning techniques were used as described by Maniatis et al. (1982). Restriction enzymes, T4 DNA ligase, and DNA polymerase I were purchased from New England Biolabs.

Preparation of Heteroduplex Phage Particles

Large-scale lysates of λNK1211 and λNK1212 were grown and purified as described by Ross et al. (1979). For lysates, 300 ml batches of K broth supplemented with proline, arginine, methionine, and thiamine were inoculated with 0.5 ml of a fresh, saturated, overnight culture in λym broth of strain NK5898 (ΔlacproXIII, ara⁻, argEam, nalR, rifR, thi⁻, metB⁻, suII) and 2 × 10⁹ phages. Phages from these lysates were concentrated by PEG precipitation and purified by centrifugation through a CsCl step gradient followed by a CsCl equilibrium gradient and dialysis against SM buffer.

DNA was isolated from purified phage stocks by three extractions with an equal volume of phenol followed by four extractions with an equal volume of ether, and dialysis against TES (10 mM Tris base, 5 mM NaCl, 1 mM EDTA; pH 7.4). Heteroduplex phage genomes were prepared from λNK1129 and λNK1212 DNAs as described by Lichten and Fox (1983). Equal amounts of the two phage DNAs were mixed, denatured with 0.1 M NaOH, allowed to reanneal in the presence of formamide and neutralizing Tris buffer, ethanol precipitated, and resuspended in TES.

The resulting heteroduplex DNA mixture was packaged back into infective λ particles in vitro as described by Maniatis et al. (1982), except that the standard packaging extract bacterial strains BHB2688 and BHB2690 were made mutL⁻ to reduce the level of mismatch correc-

tion that could occur during the packaging reaction. The mutL⁻ extracts yielded about 10⁷ phages per microgram of the extracted parental λNK1211 or λNK1212 DNA and 10⁵ phages per microgram of the reannealed heteroduplex DNA. The 100-fold reduced efficiency of packaging of the heteroduplex DNA mixture is presumably due to incomplete renaturation or breakage of the λ DNAs during heteroduplex formation.

The mutL⁻ packaging extract strains NK7515 (BHB2688 mutL-103::Tn5) and NK7516 (BHB2690 mutL103::Tn5) were made by P1 transduction of mutL103::Tn5 into BHB2688 and BHB2690. Before P1 transduction, the two strains were made recA⁺ by transformation with a recA⁺ ampR plasmid (J. Salstrom). After P1 transduction, the plasmid was eliminated by growing the strains in the presence of 6 μg/ml trimethoprim and replica plating on carbenicillin medium for ampS colonies.

Isolation of TetR Transposition or Prophage Recombination Products

Cells were grown in λym broth to 5 × 10⁸ cells per milliliter. To each 0.1 ml of these cells, a 25 μl aliquot of packaged heteroduplex phage mixture (about 10⁵ infective phage particles) was added and allowed to adsorb for 30 min at room temperature. The sample was then spread directly (or with 10-fold dilution if necessary) on LB tetracycline X-Gal medium containing 1.25 mM sodium pyrophosphate, which inhibits the growth of any replication-proficient, revertant phages, and incubated at 37°C.

Genetic Analyses of Tetracycline-Resistant Colonies

All analyzed sectors and colonies were first restreaked on LB tetracycline X-Gal medium, and single colonies were chosen for genetic and physical tests.

Sectors and colonies from transposition experiments were tested for rescuable λ markers. Each colony from purification of the original sector or colony was grown in λym broth to 5 × 10⁸ cells per milliliter, and 0.1 ml of each culture was plated in 2.5 ml λ top agar (a 1 liter solution containing 10 g tryptone, 2.5 g NaCl, and 6.5 g agar), on λ medium. Phage λNK17 (imm434 0202), phage λNK587 (imm21 cI⁻ Aam32), and phage λNK588 (imm434 cIts Kam24) were each spotted on these lawns in three dilutions arranged so that a 10 μl spot contained either 10⁴, 10², or 10 phage particles. After 16 hr at 37°C, each lawn was scored for its ability to support phage growth. As an additional test for the presence of unrepressed λ in a colony, λNK112 (wild-type λ) was spotted on lawns, grown as described above, and scored for turbidity of the spot. We expect an integrated N⁻P⁻cI⁻ prophage to be in an "anti-immune" state (Eisen et al., 1970). Wild-type λ gives clear plaques on lawns of bacteria containing these prophages and gives turbid plaques on lawns of bacteria containing no prophage.

Solid white colonies and the white portions of sectored colonies do not result from nonspecific loss of lacZ information produced by the denaturation–renaturation protocol nor from spontaneous mutations in lacZ, which do occur at an elevated frequency in the mutL host strains. White (lacZ⁻) sectors and colonies from complemented transposition, self-driven transposition, and prophage recombination experiments were tested for presence of the correct lacZ amber allele. Eighty-five white colonies and ninety white colonies selected randomly from all three experiments contained the original lacZ⁻ amber allele (see below). Furthermore, a pure population of the LacZ⁺ parental phage subjected to denaturation, renaturation, and packaging without being mixed with LacZ⁻ phage DNA gave rise only to solid blue colonies upon infection into the control strain (data not shown).

The presence of the original lacZ amber mutation in white sectors and white colonies was determined using a lysogenizing, heteroimmune λ phage carrying the suIII amber suppressor tRNA gene (λNK1129 is to λB599 of S. Adhya). Lawns of each strain to be tested were prepared as for marker rescue with the addition of 100 μl of a 20 mg/ml solution of X-Gal to each 2.5 ml λ top agar. They were then spotted with aliquots of λNK1129 containing 10⁴ phages and grown for 24 hr at 37°C. Because the lacZamYA536 allele is specifically suppressed by the suIII suppressor, lawns derived from white colonies or from sectors that retain this allele give a blue (LacZ⁺) phage spot. Most of those containing a spontaneous lacZ mutation are not suppressed and give a white (LacZ⁻) phage spot.

Southern Hybridization

DNA was isolated from bacterial cultures (grown from the same restreaked colonies tested genetically above) as described by Raleigh and Kleckner (1984). DNA was digested with restriction enzymes and displayed on 1.2% agarose gels by standard procedures. About 5 µg of chromosomal DNA was loaded in each gel lane. DNA was transferred from gel to nitrocellulose filter and hybridized to a radioactive probe by the method of Southern (1975). The probe, a HindIII–BamHI fragment internal to our Tn10lacZ transposon (Figure 2), was purified by electroelution and ^{32}P-labeled by nick translation (Rigby et al., 1977). Filters were washed and exposed for 16–24 hr to Kodak XAR-5 film at −70°C with an intensifying screen.

Analysis of an Exceptional TetR Colony Containing Both a New and a Parental IS10 Junction Fragment

One solid white TetR colony from strain NK7395(pNK972) (the transposase overproducer strain) that contained rescuable λ markers was shown by MspI digest and Southern blot (described in Figure 6) to have a λ::Tn10 junction plus a new chromosomal Tn10 junction. These genetic and physical properties could correspond either to a stable cointegrate structure (Figure 8) or to a cryptic prophage recombinant of the λ::Tn10 phage plus an insertion of the Tn10 elsewhere in the chromosome. To distinguish between these two possibilities, the properties of this colony were compared with the properties of an explicitly reconstructed cointegrate (Figure 8).

Chromosomal DNA from the colony was analyzed by Southern blot to distinguish λ junctions at each end of a single transposon (a cryptic prophage structure) from a λ junction at only one end of each of two transposon copies (a cointegrate structure). The DNA was digested with PstI, an enzyme that cuts in λ and chromosomal sequences but not in the transposon, and then hybridized to a probe internal to the transposon (Figure 2). In this analysis, a cryptic prophage recombinant of λ::Tn10 shows one band the same size as the parental phage band, a true cointegrate shows two bands, neither of which is the same size as the parental phage band, and a chromosomal insertion of Tn10 shows one band that is not the same size as the parental phage band. The unusual colony showed one parental phage-sized band and one nonparental phage-sized band, while the reconstructed cointegrate showed two nonparental phage-sized bands. From this result we conclude that the unusual colony is not a stable cointegrate, but is instead a cryptic prophage λ::Tn10 recombinant with an insertion of Tn10 elsewhere in the chromosome.

This conclusion was confirmed by P1 transduction experiments that tested the genetic linkage of Tn10 (marked with TetR) to λ genes. In a colony containing a cryptic prophage λ::Tn10 recombinant with an insertion of Tn10 elsewhere in the chromosome, only the cryptic prophage-associated transposon is tightly linked to λ markers, so only about half of TetR transductants from this colony should have rescuable λ markers. Consistent with this prediction, 20/35 (57%) of TetR transductants made from a P1 lysate of the unusual colony contained rescuable λ markers. In contrast, both copies of the transposon in a cointegrate are tightly linked to λ markers, so most TetR transductants from a cointegrate should have rescuable λ markers. Analysis showed that 31/35 (89%) of TetR transductants made from a P1 lysate of the reconstructed cointegrate contained rescuable λ markers. Presumably, the remaining 4 transductants had lost the λ markers by homologous recombination between transposon direct repeats (Figure 8).

Acknowledgments

The work reported here was supported by grants to N. K. from the N. I. H. (5 R01 GM25326-08) and the N. S. F. (PCM-83-03415). We would like to thank Elisabeth Raleigh, Jeff Way, Michael Davis, Denise Roberts, and Donald Morisato for discussions and advice on this work and on this manuscript. We also appreciate discussions with Allan Campbell and John Roth, which helped us explore the evolutionary implications of nonreplicative transposition, and critical reading of the manuscript by Frank Stahl and Howard Nash. Finally, we would like to thank Greg Viglianti for his assistance and advice on photography of sectored colonies and Anna Ferri for help in preparation of the manuscript.

The costs of publication of this article were defrayed in part by the payment of page charges. This article must therefore be hereby marked "advertisement" in accordance with 18 U.S.C. Section 1734 solely to indicate this fact.

Received March 5, 1986; revised April 14, 1986.

References

Berg, D. E. (1983). Structural requirement for IS50-mediated gene transposition. Proc. Natl. Acad. Sci. USA 80, 792–796.

Biel, S. W., and Berg, D. E. (1984). Mechanism of IS1 transposition in E. coli: choice between simple insertion and cointegration. Genetics 108, 319–330.

Campbell, A. (1983). Transposons and their evolutionary significance. In Evolution of Genes and Proteins, M. Nei and R. K. Koehn, eds. (Sunderland, Massachusetts: Sinauer Association), pp. 258–279.

Chandler, M., Roulet, E., Silver, L., Boy de la Tour, E., and Caro, L. (1979). Tn10 mediated integration of the plasmid R100.1 into the bacterial chromosome: inverse transposition. Mol. Gen. Genet. 173, 23–30.

Eisen, H., Brachet, P., Pereira da Silva, L., and Jacob, F. (1970). Regulation of repressor expression in λ. Proc. Natl. Acad. Sci. USA 66, 855–862.

Foster, T. J., Davis, M. A., Roberts, D. E., Takeshita, K., and Kleckner, N. (1981a). Genetic organization of transposon Tn10. Cell 23, 201–213.

Foster, T. J., Lundblad, V., Hanley-Way, S., Halling, S. M., and Kleckner, N. (1981b). Three Tn10-associated excision events: relationship to transposition and role of direct and inverted repeats. Cell 23, 215–227.

Glickman, B. W., and Radman, M. (1980). Escherichia coli mutator mutants deficient in methylation-instructed DNA mismatch correction. Proc. Natl. Acad. Sci. USA 77, 1063–1067.

Grindley, N. D. F., and Joyce, C. M. (1980). Genetic and DNA sequence analysis of the kanamycin resistance transposon Tn903. Proc. Natl. Acad. Sci. USA 77, 7176–7180.

Grindley, N. D. F., and Reed, R. R. (1985). Transpositional recombination in prokaryotes. Ann. Rev. Biochem. 54, 863–896.

Halling, S., Simons, R., Way, J., Walsh, R., and Kleckner, N. (1982). DNA sequence organization of Tn10's IS10-Right and Comparison with IS10-Left. Proc. Natl. Acad. Sci. USA 79, 2608–2612.

Harayama, S., Oguchi, T., and Iino, T. (1984a). Does Tn10 transpose via the cointegrate molecule? Mol. Gen. Genet. 194, 444–450.

Harayama, S., Oguchi, T., and Iino, T. (1984b). The E. coli K-12 chromosome flanked by two IS10 sequences transposes. Mol. Gen. Genet. 197, 62–66.

Hirschel, B. J., Galas, D. J., and Chandler, M. (1982). Cointegrate formation by Tn5, but not transposition, is dependent on recA. Proc. Natl. Acad. Sci. USA 79, 4530–4534.

Isberg, R. R., and Syvanen, M. (1985). Tn5 transposes independently of cointegrate resolution: evidence for an alternative model for transposition. J. Mol. Biol. 182, 69–78.

Kaiser, K., and Murray, N. E. (1979). Physical characterization of the 'Rac prophage' in E. coli K12. Mol. Gen. Genet. 175, 159–174.

Kleckner, N. (1979). DNA sequence analysis of Tn10 insertions: origin and role of 9 bp flanking repetitions during Tn10 translocation. Cell 16, 711–720.

Kleckner, N. (1981). Transposable elements in prokaryotes. Ann. Rev. Genet. 15, 341–404.

Kleckner, N., and Ross, D. G. (1979). Translocation and other recombination events involving the tetracycline-resistance element Tn10. Cold Spring Harbor Symp. Quant. Biol. 43, 1233–1246.

Kleckner, N., Chan, R. K., Tye, B.-K., and Botstein, D. (1975). Mutagenesis by insertion of a drug-resistance element carrying an inverted repetition. J. Mol. Biol. 97, 561–575.

Kleckner, N., Barker, D. F., Ross, D. G., and Botstein, D. (1978). Properties of the translocatable tetracycline-resistance element Tn10 in Escherichia coli and bacteriophage lambda. Genetics 90, 427–461.

Kleckner, N., Reichardt, K., and Botstein, D. (1979). Inversions and deletions of the Salmonella chromosome generated by the translocatable tetracycline resistance element Tn10. J. Mol. Biol. 127, 89–115.

Lauer, G., Pastrana, R., Sherley, J., and Ptashne, M. (1981). Construction of overproducers of the bacteriophage 434 repressor and cro protein. J. Mol. Appl. Genet. *1*, 139–147.

Lichten, M. J., and Fox, M. S. (1983). Detection of non-homology-containing heteroduplex molecules. Nucl. Acids Res. *11*, 3959–3971.

Maniatis, T., Fritsch, E., and Sambrook, J. (1982). Molecular Cloning: A Laboratory Manual, (Cold Spring Harbor, New York: Cold Spring Harbor Laboratory).

Miller, J. (1972). Experiments in Molecular Genetics, (Cold Spring Harbor, New York: Cold Spring Harbor Laboratory).

Mizuuchi, K. (1984). Mechanism of transposition of bacteriophage Mu: polarity of the strand transfer reaction at the initiation of transposition. Cell *39*, 395–404.

Morisato, D., and Kleckner, N. (1984). Transposase promotes double strand breaks and single strand joints at Tn10 termini in vivo. Cell *39*, 181–190.

Morisato, D., Way, J. C., Kim, H.-J., and Kleckner, N. (1983). Tn10 transposase acts preferentially on nearby transposon ends in vivo. Cell *32*, 799–807.

Pukkila, P. J., Peterson, J., Herman, G., Modrich, P., and Meselson, M. (1983). Effects of high levels of DNA adenine methylation on methyl-directed mismatch repair in *Escherichia coli*. Genetics *104*, 571–582.

Raleigh, E. A., and Kleckner, N. (1984). Multiple IS10 rearrangements in *E. coli*. J. Mol. Biol. *173*, 437–461.

Rigby, P., Dieckmann, M., Rhodes, C., and Berg, P. (1977). Labeling deoxyribonucleic acid to high specific activity in vitro by nick translation with DNA polymerase I. J. Mol. Biol. *113*, 237–251.

Roberts, D., Hoopes, B. C., McClure, W. R., and Kleckner, N. (1985). IS10 transposition is regulated by DNA adenine methylation. Cell *43*, 117–130.

Ross, D. G., Swan, J., and Kleckner, N. (1979). Nearly precise excision: a new type of DNA alteration associated with the translocatable element Tn10. Cell *16*, 733–738.

Shortle, D., and Nathans, D. (1978). Local mutagenesis: a method for generating viral mutants with base substitutions in preselected regions of the viral genome. Proc. Natl. Acad. Sci. USA *75*, 2170–2174.

Simons, R. W., and Kleckner, N. (1983). Translational control of IS10 transposition. Cell *34*, 683–691.

Southern, E. (1975). Detection of specific sequences among DNA fragments separated by gel electrophoresis. J. Mol. Biol. *98*, 503–517.

Szostak, J. W., Orr-Weaver, T. L., Rothstein, R. J., and Stahl, F. W. (1983). The double-strand-break repair model for recombination. Cell *33*, 25–35.

Way, J. C., Davis, M. A., Morisato, D., Roberts, D. E., and Kleckner, N. (1984). New Tn10 derivatives for transposon mutagenesis and for construction of *lacZ* operon fusions by transposition. Gene *32*, 369–379.

Weinert, T. A., Derbyshire, K., Hughson, F. M., and Grindley, N. D. F. (1984). Replicative and conservative transpositional recombination of insertion sequences. Cold Spring Harbor Symp. Quant. Biol. *49*, 251–260.

Zelle, M. R., and Lederberg, J. (1951). Single-cell isolations of diploid heterozygous *Escherichia coli*. J. Bacteriol. *61*, 351–355.

Ty Elements Transpose through an RNA Intermediate

Jef D. Boeke, David J. Garfinkel,
Cora A. Styles, and Gerald R. Fink
The Whitehead Institute
9 Cambridge Center
Cambridge, Massachusetts 02142
and Department of Biology
Massachusetts Institute of Technology
Cambridge, Massachusetts 02139

Summary

We have followed Ty transposition with a donor Ty element, TyH3, whose expression is under the control of the GAL1 promoter. Sequence analysis reveals dramatic structural differences in TyH3 before and after transposition. If the donor TyH3 is marked with an intron-containing fragment, the intron is correctly spliced out of the Ty during transposition, suggesting that the Ty RNA is the intermediate for transposition. Furthermore, the pattern of sequence inheritance in progeny Ty insertions derived from the marked Ty follows the predictions of the model of retroviral reverse transcription. Comparison of marked Ty elements before and after movement shows that transposition is highly mutagenic to the Ty element. These results demonstrate that during transposition, Ty sequence information flows from DNA to RNA to DNA.

Introduction

The Ty elements of the yeast, Saccharomyces cerevisiae, are repeated about 30 times in the genome and constitute about 0.04% of the total DNA. These 6 kb elements contain a large central region, epsilon, flanked by direct repeats of 334 bp called delta (δ) elements. Although all Ty elements have this basic structure, they are polymorphic at certain sites (Cameron et al., 1979). The Ty message, which constitutes about 5%–10% of the total poly(A)$^+$ mRNA in a haploid yeast cell, is transcribed from δ to δ (Elder et al., 1983). However, since the initiation and termination sites are within the δ elements, the Ty message is shorter than a Ty at both the 5' and 3' ends; only 45 nucleotides of δ sequence is repeated in the Ty RNA. The recent sequencing of a complete Ty element, Ty912, revealed two large open reading frames that comprise most of the element (Clare and Farabaugh, 1985).

Ty elements move about the yeast genome by both homologous (i.e. recombinational) and nonhomologous (i.e. transpositional) events. Homologous events (10^{-4}–10^{-5}) are considerably more frequent than nonhomologous events (10^{-7}–10^{-8}). The homologous events involve reciprocal recombination and gene conversion between two Ty elements at different positions in the genome. These homologous recombination events can lead to chromosomal aberrations such as translocations, dele-

tions, and duplications. The nonhomologous events are transpositions in which a Ty element is inserted into a new chromosomal location unoccupied by a previously existing Ty or δ element. Transposition of a Ty element leads to insertion of a complete Ty flanked by a 5 bp duplication of the target sequence created during transposition (Farabaugh and Fink, 1980). Many Ty transpositions have been detected as insertions in the 5' noncoding regions of genes because they can activate or inactivate the adjacent gene (Roeder and Fink, 1983; Scherer et al., 1982). Activation of silent genes by Ty insertion can be used as a measure of Ty transposition frequency. Paquin and Williamson (1984) showed that the frequency of transpositional activation of ADH2 increases at low temperatures.

Ty elements are similar in overall structure to certain prokaryotic transposable elements, the copia elements of Drosophila (Finnegan et al., 1978), the TED element of Trichoplusia ni (Miller and Miller, 1982), and retroviral proviruses (Varmus, 1982). The similarity in structure and transcription pattern of Ty elements and retroviruses has encouraged speculation that these elements might share a common evolutionary origin (Temin, 1980). By this analogy Ty elements would be similar to the endogenous proviruses found as chromosomal components in vertebrates. Unfortunately, these comparisons of structure and sequence cannot settle the critical issue—the mechanism by which Ty elements transpose. Is the flow of information during transposition from DNA directly to DNA or from DNA through RNA to DNA? If transposition occurs by the former mechanism, then Tys are like bacterial transposons; if by the latter, then they are like retroviral proviruses, hepatitis B virus, and cauliflower mosaic virus (Baltimore, 1970; Temin and Mizutani, 1970; Summers and Mason, 1982; Pfeiffer and Hohn, 1983).

To determine the mechanism of Ty transposition we used a marked donor Ty element whose expression is under galactose control. When this promoter is induced, the marked Ty element and genomic Ty elements transpose at elevated frequencies. The data show that Ty elements transpose via an RNA intermediate. Ty transposition presumably involves reverse transcriptase and a mechanism similar to that used by retroviruses.

Results

An Assay for Ty Transposition

The success of an assay for Ty transposition depends upon a functional donor Ty element and a recipient target that yields a unique signal upon the insertion of the Ty element. The choice of the donor Ty is complicated by the possibility that a given element might be inactive. Since we did not know a priori whether a given element was active, we constructed a high copy plasmid containing a fusion of a single Ty element, TyH3, to the controllable GAL1 promoter of yeast (Figure 1a). This construction, called pGTyH3, bypassed the necessity for an active Ty promoter

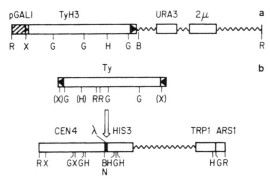

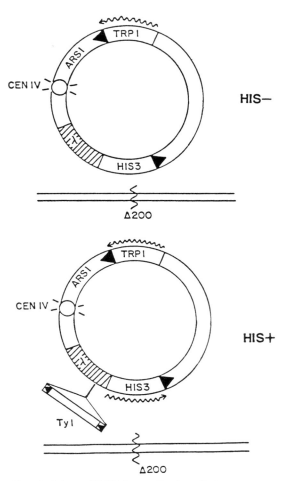

Figure 1. Restriction Maps of Donor Ty and Target Plasmids

Boxed segments represent yeast genes. Arrowheads represent δ elements; the arrows point in the direction of transcription of the Ty. It should be noted that in publications of the Davis group (e.g. Scherer et al., 1982) the arrows point in the *opposite* direction. The wavy lines represent pBR322 sequences. Restriction sites are abbreviated throughout as follows: B, Bam HI; G, Bgl II; H, Hind III; N, Nco I; R, Eco RI; S, Sal I; X, Xho I.

(a) Plasmid pGTyH3. The hatched box is the *GAL1* promoter sequence. Note that 97 nucleotides of 5' δ sequence remain in the construction. The TyH3 segment is derived from a Ty insertion into plasmid pNN162 (see Experimental Procedures). URA3 is the yeast *URA3* gene. 2μ is an origin-containing segment of the yeast 2 micron plasmid.

(b) Plasmid pAB100 (below) and insertion derivatives. CEN4 is the centromere segment from chromosome IV. The black box marked λ contains sequences from phage λ (see Figure 6). HIS3 is the yeast *HIS3* structural gene (lacking the 5' noncoding region). TRP1 is the yeast *TRP1* gene; ARS1 is a yeast autonomous replicator. Above the pAB100 map is a generalized map of the Tys that insert into the plasmid. Restriction sites in parentheses are found only in some Tys.

Figure 2. Scheme of *his3Δ4* Transposition Assay System

In a strain bearing the chromosomal *his3Δ200* allele, the presence of the *his3Δ4* plasmid pAB100 does not alter the his⁻ phenotype. Ty transposition as diagrammed results in a His⁺ phenotype.

and placed Ty transcription under galactose control. On galactose, the TyH3 fusion makes about as much Ty message as is made from the entire resident population of Ty elements, whereas on glucose it produces little or no Ty message (data not shown).

Our choice of the target for transposition in the assay is based on the observation of Scherer et al. (1982) that a large proportion of the His⁺ revertants obtained from a promoter deletion in the *HIS3* gene (*his3Δ4*) were Ty insertions in the region upstream of *his3Δ4*, which is composed of bacteriophage λ sequences. Ty-mediated His⁺ revertants were isolated using a *CEN* plasmid containing *his3Δ4*, pNN162. We also used a derivative of pNN162 that lacks the *URA3* gene, pAB100 (Figure 1b). In appropriate strains bearing a complete deletion of the *HIS3* gene on chromosome XV, the proportion of His⁺ revertants caused by Ty transposition into the target plasmid (pNN162 or pAB100) can be as high as 80% (Figure 2). Several hundred Ty transpositions into the *his3Δ4* locus were isolated in pNN162 and pAB100 (Figure 1b) in the absence of the pGTyH3 plasmid. These Ty elements are as heterogeneous in structure as random Ty elements from the genome.

Activation of the *GAL1* promoter on pGTyH3 stimulates Ty transposition into pAB100. The pGTyH3 plasmid and its marked derivatives (see below) were transformed into strain JB183, which contains pAB100. The frequency of His⁺ revertants increases from about 5 × 10⁻⁸ in JB183 to about 1 × 10⁻⁶ in the strains containing both plasmids.

Nearly all (37/39) of the revertants isolated from galactose-grown cells were Ty transpositions into pAB100, whereas only one of 33 His⁺ revertants from glucose-grown cells was caused by Ty transposition (Table 1).

A striking phenotype of cells containing pGTyH3 is that they grow very slowly on galactose (but normally on glucose) compared to control cells containing the vector alone or a *GAL1–β*-galactosidase fusion on the same vector (Figure 3). The high copy Ty fusion plasmid is lost rapidly, even from selectively grown cultures, only when galactose is the carbon source. One possible explanation for the slow growth phenotype is that the transposition frequency in such strains is abnormally high, resulting in an intolerably high mutation frequency.

To investigate this possibility, we examined Ty transposition into the *LYS2* gene on chromosome II (Simchen et al., 1984; Eibel and Philippsen, 1984). Transposition into the chromosomal *LYS2* locus is also increased significantly by overtranscription of the TyH3 element. In strains carrying the pGTyH3 plasmid, only 1/24 spontaneous *lys2* mutants

Table 1. Analysis of His[+] Revertants from Strain JB396, Which Contains Plasmids pAB100 and pGTyH3-*lacO*

Carbon Source	His[+] Revertants Analyzed	Ty Insertions[a]	Marked Ty Insertions	Other[b]
Galactose	39	37	8	2
Glucose	34	1	0	33

[a] Includes marked Ty insertions.
[b] Includes non-Ty-mediated plasmid duplications (Scherer et al., 1982) and aberrant recombinant plasmids derived from pGTyH3, which have presumably recombined with his3Δ4 as a result of the homologous bacteriophage λ and pBR322 sequences. None of these is the result of simple Ty insertion into pAB100 (see Experimental Procedures).

isolated on glucose are the result of Ty transposition, whereas 8/22 such mutants isolated on galactose are caused by Ty transposition events (Table 2). Only 1/22 mutants isolated on galactose in a cell bearing the control GAL1/β-galactosidase fusion plasmid pCGS286 are caused by Ty insertion. Our controls agree with previous studies showing that the fraction of spontaneous *lys2* mutants caused by Ty transposition is low (Simchen et al., 1984; Eibel and Philippsen, 1984).

An Intact 5′ Delta Sequence Is Not Required for Transposition; Marked TyS

Marking the pGTyH3 plasmid made it possible to determine whether the transposition events recovered came from the chromosome or from the pGTyH3 plasmid itself. One marker used was a 40 nucleotide synthetic *lacO* segment, derived from the plasmid pHOE101 (Sadler et al., 1980). The *lacO* marker was inserted at the Bgl II site near the 3′ end of the element (see Experimental Procedures for details). The marked plasmid, called pGTyH3-*lacO*, was transformed into the *his3Δ4* strain JB183, and His[+] revertants were obtained from glucose- and galactose-grown cultures (Table 1). Of 37 Ty-mediated His[+] revertants from the galactose-grown cells, eight contain the marked Ty element (Table 1). The marked transposed Ty plasmids were identified by the blue color of the E. coli transformants on indicator plates (see Experimental Procedures), by restriction enzyme digests with Bgl II (the insertion of the *lacO* fragment results in loss of the Bgl II site), and by DNA sequence analysis (see below). No transpositions of the marked element were obtained from the glucose-grown culture. Similar results were obtained with pGTyH3 derivatives marked by filling in the same Bgl II site (pGTyH3-*BglII⁰*), which results in a double restriction site polymorphism (see Experimental Procedures), and by inserting an intron-containing segment of the yeast rp51 gene (see below). Transposition of marked Tys lacking an intact 5′ δ sequence shows that an intact 5′ δ sequence is not required for transposition.

Transposition of the Marked Ty to Chromosomal DNA

We examined the chromosomal DNA of the strains in which the His[+] revertants were isolated to see if any additional marked Ty transpositions had occurred. In DNA from each of the His[+] revertants from galactose-grown

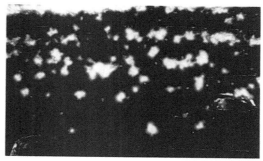
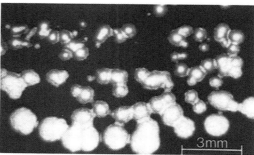

Figure 3. Growth Inhibition of Cells Overproducing Ty mRNA

Cells containing pGTyH3 (top) and pCGE329 (GAL1 promoter plasmid vector alone; bottom) were streaked for single colonies on SC-ura medium containing galactose and grown at 30°C for 14 days. Note the sectored morphology of the colonies overproducing Ty mRNA. This phenotype is slightly more pronounced in this strain background (GRF167) than in other backgrounds, but is noticeable in all GAL[+] strains we have tested.

Table 2. Effect of Ty mRNA Overproduction on Mutagenesis at *LYS2*

Strain[a]	Plasmid	Carbon Source	Ty Fraction[b]
JB282	pGTyH3	Galactose	8/22 (0.36)
JB282	pGTyH3	Glucose	1/24 (0.042)
JB314	pCGS286[c]	Galactose	1/22 (0.045)

[a] All strains are transformants of strain BWG1-7A.
[b] Determined as described in Experimental Procedures.
[c] pGAL1/lacZ fusion.

cells, multiple restriction fragments homologous to the *lacO* fragment are observed, whereas no such fragments are found in DNA from control cells grown on glucose (Figure 4). Even cells that have simply been plated on galactose-containing medium in the absence of selection for His[+] show evidence for multiple transpositions of the marked element. The overall Ty pattern (revealed by an epsilon-specific probe) in cells grown on galactose shows many new fragments, while the glucose-grown cells show few, if any, changes (not shown). These results suggest that transposition to many chromosomal loci occurs when the TyH3 mRNA is overproduced in these strains.

The Truncated 5′ Delta Is Healed by Transposition

To be sure that the transpositions of the *lacO* marked Ty elements were bona fide transposition events, we ana-

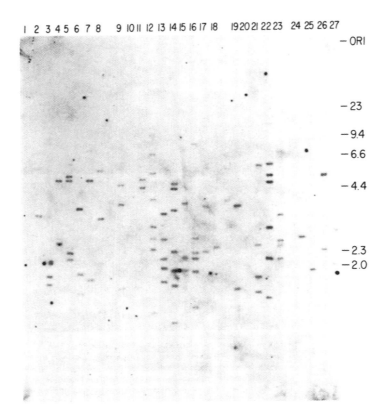

Figure 4. Genomic Southern Blots of Strain JB396 Grown on Galactose and Probed with a lacO-Specific Probe

Various derivatives of JB396 were cured of all plasmids and DNA was prepared. The DNA was cut with Hind III, electrophoresed on 0.6% agarose, and blotted. Not shown is an identical companion blot of 27 glucose-grown derivatives of JB396, which showed no hybridization at all (except to control plasmid).
Lanes 1–8: His⁺ revertants caused by insertion of lacO-marked Ty into pAB100.
Lanes 9–18: His⁺ revertants caused by insertion of an unmarked Ty into pAB100.
Lanes 19–27: Isolated colonies of JB396, not reverted to His⁺.

lyzed the structure of the transposed Ty and the target site in detail. Southern analysis using just that portion of the δ sequence deleted from the 5′ δ of pGTyH3 (i.e. nucleotides 1–237) as a hybridization probe demonstrates that this sequence is reconstructed during the transposition event (Figure 5). Two of the pAB100 derivatives containing the marked transposed Ty (pH1240 and pH1252) were sequenced in the junction regions between Ty and plasmid sequences. In both cases, the Ty is flanked by a 5 nucleotide duplication of the target sequence, as expected for a Ty transposition event (Farabaugh and Fink, 1980). Also, the point of insertion of each Ty is different from that of the "parental" TyH3 insertion (which had originally transposed into pNN162), ruling out the possibility that Ty movement is mediated by a homologous recombination event (Figure 6).

A 5′ Delta Polymorphism Transferred to the 3′ Delta

In retroviral proviruses, the U5 region of both LTR sequences is derived from the 5′ end of the genomic RNA. To determine whether the same is true of transpositions derived from the TyH3 mRNA, we sequenced the δ elements of the marked transposed Tys. The δ segment between nucleotides 237 and 334 (corresponding to the U5 region; Figure 8) is duplicated at the 5′ and 3′ ends of the pGTyH3 construction (Figure 1a), but the duplication is not perfect. Sequence comparison of the 5′ and 3′ δ elements shows that there is an A at position 328 in the remaining

segment of the 5′ δ and a T at the homologous position of the 3′ δ. In seven marked transposed Tys derived from this plasmid, the 3′ δ sequence is changed to A at position 328 (Figure 7). Therefore, we conclude that the donor of the U5 information is the 5′ δ.

Mutagenesis of Ty Elements during Transposition

Many of the marked transposed Ty elements are apparently mutagenized by transposition (Table 3). The parental Ty element has a Hind III site, but 2/21 progeny Ty elements have lost it (the other 19 elements are normal in their Hind III pattern). The parental element also contains four Hha I sites. Of the progeny elements, 2/17 lack one particular Hha I site, suggesting that certain sites are hotspots for mutagenesis (one of these progeny elements also lost the Hind III site). By these criteria, 3/17 marked transpositions show a mutation within a target of only 26 nucleotides. It should be noted that these enzymes were chosen because they are known to reveal heterogeneities in Ty elements; surveys with other enzymes revealed no differences.

The Xho I site found in many δ elements is present in the 5′ δ of pGTyH3 (it forms the boundary with the GAL1 sequences) but absent from the 3′ δ. In 20/21 marked transposition events, both δ's lack an Xho I site; in one (TyH1199), the 5′ δ has gained an Xho I site. The sequence of the TyH1240 δ sequences reveals a T to G transversion at position 240 (which is within what was the Xho I site)

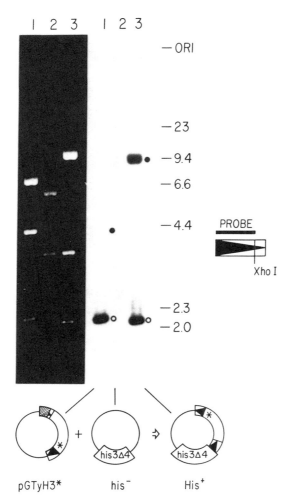

Figure 6. Target Sequence for Ty Transposition in pAB100

Sequence is derived from data of Struhl and Davis (1981) and Daniels et al. (1983). Shown are the Bam HI and Nco I sites, the initiator ATG of the *HIS3* gene, and the duplicated segments in the H3, TyH1240, and TyH1252 transpositions. Nucleotides 1–152 are derived from phage λ; nucleotides 148–end are derived from *HIS3*.

```
NcoI                                                                    H1252
------                                                                  -----
GGATCCATGG CATCACAGTA TCGTGATGAC AGAGGCAGGG AGTGGGACAA AATTGAAATC
------ 10           20         30         40         50         60
BamHI


AAATAATGAT TTTATTTTGA CTGATAGTGA CCTGTTCGTT GCAACAAATT GATAAGCAAT
        70         80         90        100        110        120

H1240
-----
GCTTTTTTAT AATGCCAACT TAGTATAAAA AAATGAGCAG GCAAGATAAA CGAAGGCAAG
-----             140        150        160        170        180
H3
                   START HIS3
                   ---
ATAAACGAAG GCAAAAGATG ACA
       190        200
```

Figure 5. Regeneration of the 5′ Delta Element in Transpositions from pGTyH3-*lacO*

Plasmids pGTyH3-*lacO* (lane 1), pAB100 (lane 2), and pH1240, a His⁺ derivative of pAB100 caused by insertion of a *lacO*-marked Ty (lane 3), were digested with Eco RI and Bam HI and electrophoresed on 0.6% agarose and stained with ethidium bromide (left). Such digestion produces (in pGTyH3-*lacO* and pH1240) 5′ fragments (filled circles) and 3′ fragments (open circles) of the Ty element. The Southern blot (right) was probed with an isolated fragment containing homology to the δ element as indicated (see Experimental Procedures).

of the 3′ δ. This position, near the boundary of the U3 and R regions of the δ element (Figure 8), may be a highly mutable part of the element.

Precise Removal of an Intron during Transposition

To determine whether Ty transposition occurs via an RNA intermediate, we followed the fate of an intron inserted into a Ty element used as a donor in a transposition experiment. For this experiment, the 398 nucleotide yeast ribosomal protein 51 gene (rp51) intron, along with 228 nucleotides of flanking sequences, was inserted into pGTyH3 (pGTyH3-RP51; Figure 9). His⁺ revertants were collected from cells grown on galactose and harboring

both pGTyH3-RP51 and pAB100. The structures of the resulting His⁺ pAB100 derivatives containing Ty insertions were determined.

The Ty elements in 4/19 His⁺ pAB100 derivatives selected from cells containing pGTyH3-RP51 are clearly derived from pGTyH3-RP51. These four elements lack the Bgl II site of Ty, which was destroyed during the construction of pGTyH3-RP51, and the Sal I site located in the rp51 intron, but they retain an Xho I and a Hind III site present in the flanking region of the rp51 segment (Figure 9). Further restriction enzyme analysis also indicates that although these four Ty elements originated from pGTyH3-RP51, they contain a precise deletion of the rp51 intron. Southern filter hybridizations support the conclusion that this deletion is the result of a splicing event (Figure 9). The transposed Ty elements marked with the rp51 segment hybridize only with the exon-containing probe, but not with the intron-specific probe. Furthermore, DNA sequence analysis shows the normal splice junction expected for the spliced rp51 gene in two independent transpositions.

Discussion

Our data show that a Ty element transposes from a DNA copy in one location to a DNA copy in another nonhomologous location via an RNA intermediate. The most compelling evidence for the involvement of an RNA intermediate in transposition is the correct splicing of an intron from a marked Ty element upon transposition. Ty elements do not have their own introns so we engineered an intron into a Ty element and followed the transposition of this modified element. Analysis of the DNA obtained from several independent transpositions of this marked element revealed that the intron was removed precisely.

Another remarkable aspect of Ty transposition is the regeneration upon transposition of a complete 5′ δ despite the fact that the parent element contains only the distal 97 nucleotides of the 5′ δ. Although the 5′ portion of the parental element is replaced by the *GAL1* promoter that we used to drive transcription, structural analysis of marked elements recovered after transposition shows that they have regenerated a wholly intact 5′ δ devoid of the galactose promoter. Since all but one of 21 regenerated 5′ δ ele-

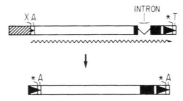

Figure 7. Features of Ty Transposition Events
This figure summarizes the structure of the marked *GAL1*-Ty fusions (upper segment), the corresponding RNA (wavy line), and the progeny Tys (lower segment). The hatched box is the *GAL1* promoter; the boxed arrows are δ sequences (note that about one-quarter of the 5' δ remains intact in the pGTyH3 construction); the large box is the epsilon segment; the black box symbolizes the rp51 segment. The letters A and T represent adenine and thymine residues at nucleotide 328 in the δ elements. The X marks the Xho I site. The asterisk shows the missing Xho I sites.

Table 3. Restriction Enzyme Cleavage Site Polymorphisms in Marked Transposed Ty Elements

Restriction Enzyme	No. Sites in TyH3	Total Tested	No. with Same No. of Sites as TyH3	No. with Extra Sites	No. Missing a Site
Hind III	1	21	19	0	2
Hha I	4[a]	17	15	0	2[b]
Xho I[c]	1	21	1	0	20

Ty elements were derived from pGTyH3-*lacO* and pGTyH3-*BglII°*. Only polymorphisms affecting the total number of sites are tabulated here. In addition to these, 2/17 elements underwent insertions (±0.1 and 0.9 kb) upon transposition.
[a] Assuming there are no sites closer together than 150 nucleotides.
[b] In both cases, the same Hha I site was missing.
[c] TyH3 has an Xho I site in the 5' δ, as does TyH1199; the other 20 marked Tys lack Xho I sites in both δ's.

Figure 8. The U3, R, and U5 Segments of Ty
The boxed arrows represent the 5' and 3' δ elements, the dashed box the epsilon segment (greatly shortened), and the wavy line the corresponding RNA.

ments lack an Xho I site, the template for regeneration of this region, which is at the border between the U3 and R regions, is probably the 3' δ.

In attempting to assess the mechanism by which δ regeneration occurs we were fortunate in finding that the parent element contains a sequence difference between the 5' and 3' δ's in the segment of the 5' δ that is present in our construction (the U5 region). In the marked transposed Tys, the 3' δ contains the information that was present in the 5' U5 of the donor Ty. It appears that upon transposition the sequence from the 5' δ acts as a template for the transfer of U5 sequences to the 3' δ. If the mRNA molecule diagrammed in Figure 8 is indeed the genetic material for Ty transposition, this is precisely the predicted pattern of sequence inheritance.

These observations, together with the finding that introns are spliced out of the Ty upon transposition, suggest that reverse transcription is a step in the transposition of Ty elements. By analogy with the LTR repeats flanking retroviral proviruses, the δ's can be divided into 5'-U3-R-U5-3' segments (Figure 8; Hsu et al., 1978; Shank et al., 1978). Ty elements are transcribed from the R region of the 5' δ to the R region of the 3' δ. The Ty RNA has the structure 5'-R-U5-epsilon-U3-R-3'. The Ty RNA would serve as a template for reverse transcription by a reverse transcriptase. Our data suggest that reverse transcription of Ty, like that of retroviruses, regenerates the 3' U5 from the 5' end of the message and the 5' U3 from the 3' end. We therefore propose the term *retrotransposon* for Ty and related elements.

An important implication of our work is that yeast cells contain reverse transcriptase. Shiba and Saigo (1983) have reported that *copia* RNA is found in ribonucleoprotein complexes that are associated with reverse transcriptase activity in cultured Drosophila cells. Clare and Farabaugh (1985) have found significant amino acid sequence homology between tyB protein of Ty and retroviral reverse transcriptases, suggesting that reverse transcriptase is encoded by the Ty element, just as reverse transcriptase is encoded by retroviral proviruses.

An unexpected finding is that transposition is extremely mutagenic to the Ty element. Many of the transposed elements have suffered alterations in their nucleotide se-

quence. These mutations do not result from the modifications we introduced to study the elements, since we also observed mutations in unmodified elements. The results show that the modified elements we constructed transpose normally. Like intact Tys, the modified element makes 5 bp repeats of the target DNA at the site of insertion and is capable of activating the promoterless *his3Δ4* gene. The high mutation rate of Ty elements upon transposition may explain the well documented but previously enigmatic structural heterogeneity of Ty elements. The phenomenally high mutation rate in transposed Ty elements is almost certainly a consequence of the reverse transcription step in the Ty transposition cycle, although high frequency recombination with chromosomal Tys immediately before, during, or after transposition is not ruled out. Transit through an RNA intermediate may be intrinsically mutagenic. However, we propose that Ty mutagenesis is due to the fact that Ty reverse transcriptase, like AMV reverse transcriptase, causes mutations at high frequency (Gopinathan et al., 1979).

Transposition is clearly controlled by genes within the Ty element. In our experiments with the marked Ty element in which transposition is promoted by the *GAL1* promoter, we find that overproduction of Ty mRNA by galactose induction allows the transposition of the marked element. In addition, the frequency of transposition of unmarked elements from the chromosome onto the target plasmid is greatly increased. We assume that increased levels of one or more of the gene products of the marked Ty, either the *tyA* or *tyB* proteins (Clare and Farabaugh, 1985), catalyze the increased transposition of these chromosomal elements. Ty elements also must contain sites

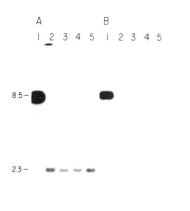

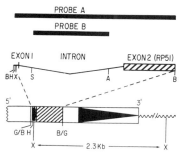

Figure 9. Removal of an Intron From a Marked Ty Element

The plasmids indicated were digested with Xho I and analyzed by gel electrophoresis on 0.7% agarose. Duplicate nitrocellulose filters were prepared from the gel and the filters were hybridized with two ³²P-labeled rp51-specific probes (see Experimental Procedures). (Lane 1) pGTyH3-RP51. Donor plasmid carrying the rp51 sequences. An 8.5 kb Xho I fragment that contains all but 18 nucleotides of the RP51 Bam HI fragment hybridizes with probes A and B. (Lanes 2–5) pH1542, pH1547, pH1551, and pH1552, His⁺ revertants of pAB100 caused by transpositions from pGTyH3-RP51. The map of these transpositions at the bottom shows the location of a 2.3 kb Xho I fragment that hybridizes with exon sequences (stippled box; probe A), but not with intron sequences (V-shaped line; probe B). The 3′ δ is shown (solid arrow) joined to pAB100 (wavy line). Refer to Figure 1b for a complete map. Additional restriction site abbreviations: A (Acc I), B/G and G/B (Bam HI/Bgl II hybrid, resistant to both enzymes).

that are required in *cis* for transposition. We have shown that no such site is present in the first 237 nucleotides of the element when a heterologous promoter is provided. Structures that are probably required in *cis* include homology to the methionine initiator tRNA (nucleotides 336–344; Taylor, 1977), a polypurine segment (nucleotides 5575–5584; Mitra et al., 1982), and the U3 and R regions of the 3′ δ element.

We know that overexpression of Ty RNA (and presumably, therefore, reverse transcriptase) in yeast cells leads to multiple transposition events, and also that the induced colonies grow very slowly on selective medium, suggesting a strong selection against cells overproducing Ty gene products. However, we do not know the exact cause of this negative selection. Several possible explanations for the slow growth phenotype can be imagined.

— The slow growth is due to the accumulation of sub-

lethal and lethal mutations caused by the many random transposition events in the selectively grown colonies.

— Overproduction of reverse transcriptase causes cellular mRNAs to be inactivated by reverse transcription.

— The reverse transcripts of the cellular mRNAs are themselves mutagenic to nuclear genes, as a result of the errors occurring during reverse transcription. The third hypothesis has been invoked as an origin of pseudogenes (Nishioka et al., 1980).

The frequency of transposition into *his3Δ4*, though elevated in the presence of high levels of TyH3 RNA, is still rather low (1 × 10⁻⁶). However, any estimate of overall transposition frequency based on this assay is misleading because it reveals only a very small proportion of the transpositions of the marked element. When we assay the total genome, rather than the limited target of the *his3Δ4* plasmid, we find that virtually every cell in the population has multiple transpositions of the marked element from the plasmid onto the chromosomes.

Why then does transposition occur at such a low frequency in cells that do not overproduce Ty mRNA? The amount of Ty mRNA produced by the induced marked element is about equal to that produced by the ensemble of chromosomal Ty elements. For this reason, we suspect that many of these chromosomal Ty elements are defective in some way. The process of transposition is so mutagenic to the element that it is reasonable to assume that many of the resident elements are defective as a result of transposition. Presumably, the overall viability of Ty elements in a cell is determined by the relative frequencies of mutation during transposition and repair of defective elements by gene conversion (Roeder and Fink, 1983).

Experimental Procedures

Strains and Plasmid Constructions

The strains used are described in Table 4. Plasmid pH3 is pNN162 (Scherer et al., 1982; kindly provided by R. Davis) containing the Ty insertion "H3"; it was selected as a His⁺ revertant in strain JB84A. TyH3 is identical in structure with Ty912 (Clare and Farabaugh, 1985) at all restriction sites shown in Figure 1b except that the 5′ δ contains an Xho I site. The 6.0 kb Xho I–Bam HI fragment from pH3 containing the Ty and 124 nucleotides of bacteriophage λ sequence was cloned into the pGAL1-Xho vector pCGE329 (kindly provided by J. Schaum and J. Mao, Collaborative Research, Waltham, Mass.). The GAL1 promoter segment contains nucleotides 2463-3204 of the GAL region (Citron and Donelson, 1984). The structure of the resulting plasmid, pGTyH3, is shown in Figure 1a. We have fused other Ty elements, such as Ty173 (Simchen et al., 1984), to the *GAL1* promoter in an analogous fashion. However, not all Ty elements are the same, and only some give the small colony phenotype on galactose mentioned for TyH3 (see Results). The *Gal1/lacZ* fusion plasmid pCGS 286 was kindly provided by J. Mao.

The *his3Δ4* plasmid pAB100 (Figure 1b) was constructed from pNN162 (Scherer et al., 1982) by the following steps. The *URA3* gene was removed by cutting at the unique Nru I site, addition of an Sma I linker, and digestion with Sma I (the only Sma I site in pNN162 is at the 3′ end of the *URA3* gene). These steps were followed by blunt-end ligation, transformation, and screening for Ura⁻ plasmids in bacterial strain DB6507 (*pyrF*::Tn5). We then removed 140 nucleotides of bacteriophage λ sequence by further digestion with Nco I and Bam HI. This was followed by filling-in with the Klenow fragment of DNA polymerase I and blunt-end ligation of the resultant molecules. Such ligation results in the sequence GGATCCATGG at the junction, which contains both an Nco I and a Bam HI site (see Figure 6). The presence of both sites was confirmed in pAB100.

Table 4. Strains

Strain	Genotype	Plasmid	Reference
Bacteria			
HB101	hsdS20, recA13, ara-14, proA2, lacY1, galK2, rpsL20, xyl-5, mtl-1, supE44		Maniatis et al., 1982
DB6507	HB101/pyrF74::Tn5		Silverman et al., 1982
Yeast			
GRF167	α, his3Δ200, ura3-167, GAL⁺		This work
JB84	a, ade2-1, rad52, rad50, his3Δ1, ura3-52, trp1-289, GAL⁺	pNN162	This work
JB84A	JB84 ADE⁺ revertant	pNN162	This work
JB183	a, his3Δ200, ura3-52, trp1-289, lys2, GAL⁺	pAB100	This work
JB396	Same as JB183	pAB100, pGTyH3-lacO	This work
BWG1-7A	a, ade1-100, ura3-52, leu2-3,112, his4-519, GAL⁺		Guarente et al., 1982

The marked pGTyH3 derivatives were made as follows. All markers were inserted at the 3′ Bgl II site of the element, because this is the only site that is outside the open reading frames (which we assume to be essential for transposition) and inside the epsilon segment. Plasmid pGTyH3 was partially cleaved with Bgl II by limited digestion and filled in with Klenow fragment if necessary. The appropriate marker fragment, lacO (EcoRI fragment from pHOE101, filled in) or rp51 (HZ18-B5 Bam HI fragment), was added and joined by ligation. Plasmids marked by the lacO fragment were identified by transformation into HB101 and selection of blue colonies on LB/ampicillin (50 μg/ml) plates containing X-gal (Miller, 1972). Plasmids marked by the rp51 intron-containing fragment were identified by colony hybridization. Plasmid pGTyH3-Bgl II° was made by filling in purified Bgl II partially digested, full-length linear molecules (isolated by electrophoresis on an 0.35% agarose gel) and blunt-end ligation. The presence of the correct junction was verified by showing loss of the Bgl II site and the presence of a new Cla I site at the same position, which was only revealed by growing the plasmid in a dam⁻ bacterial strain (see Backman, 1980). The origin of the lacO fragment was plasmid pHOE101 (Sadler et al., 1980; kindly provided by K. Arndt). The rp51 Bam HI fragment was excised from plasmid HZ18-B5, kindly provided by J. Teem. HZ18-B5 is identical with HZ18 (Teem and Rosbash, 1983) except that a Bam HI linker is inserted at nucleotide 592 (Ava II site) (Teem and Rosbash, 1983, and J. Teem, personal communication).

Selection of His⁺ Revertants
His⁺ revertants were selected by growing isolated colonies of the strain to be tested on agar plates containing SC medium lacking the appropriate nutrients (tryptophan and/or uracil) and containing the specified carbon source (glucose or galactose) at 2% final concentration. Such plates were incubated at low temperature (22°C unless otherwise specified; Paquin and Williamson, 1984) for 7–14 days and then replica-plated to SC (glucose) medium lacking histidine. The SC-his plates were incubated at 30°C until His⁺ colonies appeared. Only colonies arising from single colonies on the master plates were picked to ensure that all revertants were independent.

Isolation of His⁺ Plasmids from Revertants
His⁺ revertants selected on SC-his plates were grown overnight at 30°C in 10 ml YPD medium from a starting inoculum of 5–10 × 10⁶ cells. The cells were harvested by centrifugation, washed once with 1.0 M sorbitol, 100 mM EDTA (pH 7.5), transferred to a 1.5 ml Eppendorf tube, and resuspended in 0.4 ml sorbitol/EDTA. Zymolyase 60,000 (Kirin Breweries, Tokyo, Japan) was added (0.1 ml of a 2 mg/ml solution in sorbitol/EDTA) for 30 min at 37°C. The spheroplasts were resuspended in 0.5 ml TE (10 mM Tris-HCl, pH 7.6; 1 mM EDTA) on a mixer (Eppendorf 5432) and lysed by addition of 90 μl lysis solution (250 mM EDTA, pH 8.0; 0.4 M Tris base; 2% SDS, freshly prepared) for 30 min at 65°C. Potassium acetate (80 μl of 5 M solution) was added; the mixture was incubated on ice for 60 min or more. The precipitate was removed by centrifugation for 15 min at 4°C in a microcentrifuge (Eppendorf 5412). The supernatant was transferred to a new tube; a nucleic acid pellet was obtained by filling the tube with EtOH, inverting the tube several times, and centrifuging for 10 sec. The pellets were dried in air or in a Speed-Vac (Savant Instruments, Hicksville, NY; 15 min) vacuum concentrator and resuspended in 500 μl TE on the 5432 mixer. The samples were centrifuged for 15 min to remove insoluble material, and the

supernatants were saved (for blotting experiments, the DNA was further purified, see below). An aliquot of the nucleic acid solution (10 μl) was added to 300 μl competent HB101 (Mandel and Higa, 1970). The competent cells were incubated with the DNA at 0°C for 10 min, then at 37°C for 2.5 min. LB medium (1.5 ml) was added and incubation at 37°C continued for 60 min. The entire culture was concentrated by centrifugation and plated onto one LB + 50 μg/ml ampicillin plate and incubated overnight at 37°C.

Determining the Ty Fraction among His⁺ Revertants
His⁺ revertants from strains containing only pAB100 were analyzed by colony hybridization. Ten or more ampicillin-resistant HB101 transformants from each His⁺ revertant were patched onto LB + ampicillin plates. The patches were then probed by the Grunstein-Hogness (1975) procedure using a Ty-specific probe. In this case, the Ty fraction is defined as the fraction of His⁺ revertants whose plasmids hybridized to the Ty-specific probe. The colony hybridization procedure cannot be used on revertants from strains containing both pGTyH3 (or its derivatives) and pAB100 because HIS⁺ revertants with Ty homology can arise by recombination between the two plasmids. When two plasmids were present, the plasmid responsible for the His⁺ phenotype was purified by segregating the His⁻ plasmid (if necessary), followed by the plasmid isolation procedure outlined in the previous section. Rapid plasmid preparations were then analyzed by digestion with Bgl II and other enzymes in order to classify the plasmids. Simple Ty insertions give a characteristic band pattern with Bgl II.

Selection of α-Amino-Adipate-Resistant Mutants
Resistance to α-amino-adipate is a positive selection for lys2 mutations (Chattoo et al., 1979). Colonies of the strain to be tested were grown up at 30°C on SC-uracil medium containing the appropriate carbon source at 2%. The well-separated colonies were printed to α-amino-adipate medium (Chattoo et al., 1979) supplemented with all the nutritional requirements of the strain (including uracil). Only one α-amino-adipate-resistant mutant was picked from each colony on the master plate to ensure that the lys2 mutants were independent.

Determination of the Ty Fraction among lys2 Mutants
DNA was prepared from mutant strains as described above, except that RNAase was added to the nucleic acid sample (following removal of insoluble material) to a final concentration of 50 μg/ml for 30 min at 37°C, followed by precipitation with one volume of isopropanol. The resultant small precipitate was recovered on a small glass rod and air-dried. The DNA was resuspended in 50 μl of TE. Five-microliter samples were digested with Hind III and Xho I (separately) and analyzed by Southern blotting as described (Simchen et al., 1984). Those that showed a novel pattern (i.e. rearrangement) at the LYS2 locus were evicted and assayed for the presence of a Ty element by restriction enzyme digestion and hybridization with a Ty-specific probe. The Ty fraction was defined as those Lys⁻ mutants that were caused by Ty insertions, divided by the total number of mutants analyzed.

DNA Manipulations
Rapid isolations of plasmid DNA from E. coli was carried out as described by Holmes and Quigley (1981); restriction analysis, gel electrophoresis, Southern blot analysis, and DNA sequencing were as described by Maniatis et al. (1982). All nucleotide positions reported here

are based on the coordinates used by Clare and Farabaugh (1985). Yeast transformation was done by the LiAc procedure of Ito et al. (1983).

Hybridization Probes

The *lacO*-specific probe (Figure 4) was made as follows. Plasmid pHOE101 (2 μg) was digested to completion with Eco RI. The digest was labeled by filling in with α-³²P-dATP. Filters hybridized overnight with this 40 nucleotide probe were washed four times with 4× SSC at room temperature, then once at 55°C for 1 min. The δ-specific probe (Figure 5) was prepared as follows. DNA from the phage fKD7, a clone of the Sal I fragment containing Ty917δ (Roeder et al., 1980) cloned in the filamentous phage f1 (generously provided by K. Durbin), was digested with Xho I and labeled as above. The 364 nucleotide fragment containing the first 237 nucleotides of Ty917δ and 24 nucleotides of flanking *HIS4* homology was isolated from an agarose gel. Probe A in Figure 9 (rp51-specific) was made by nick-translating purified HZ18-B5 rp51 fragment. Probe B was made from an rp51 intron-specific M13 clone (Rodriguez et al., 1984; generously provided by N. Abovitch) by the method of Hu and Messing (1982).

Acknowledgments

We are particularly grateful to P. Farabaugh for supplying the Ty912 sequence prior to publication and to J. Teem for supplying the rp51 intron-containing fragment. D. Baltimore, K. Durbin, R. Gaber, R. Mann, R. Mulligan, M. Rose, S. Scherer, and F. Winston provided helpful discussion and comments on the manuscript.

This work was supported by grants GM35010 and CA34429 from the National Institutes of Health. G. R. F. is an American Cancer Society Research Professor of Genetics. J. D. B. is supported by a Helen Hay Whitney Foundation Fellowship; D. J. G. was supported by the Damon Runyon–Walter Winchell Cancer Fund Fellowship DRG 578.

The costs of publication of this article were defrayed in part by the payment of page charges. This article must therefore be hereby marked *"advertisement"* in accordance with 18 U.S.C. Section 1734 solely to indicate this fact.

Received December 18, 1984; revised December 31, 1984

References

Backman, K. (1980). A cautionary note on the use of certain restriction endonucleases with methylated substrates. Gene *11*, 167–171.

Baltimore, D. (1970). RNA-dependent DNA polymerase in virions of RNA tumour viruses. Nature *226*, 1209–1211.

Cameron, J. R., Loh, E. Y., and Davis, R. W. (1979). Evidence for transposition of dispersed repetitive DNA families in yeast. Cell *16*, 739–751.

Chattoo, B. B., Sherman, F., Azubalis, D. A., Fjellstedt, T. A., Mehvert, D., Ogur, M. (1979). Selection of *lys2* mutants in the yeast *Saccharomyces cerevisiae* by the utilization of α-amino-adipate. Genetics *93*, 51–65.

Citron, L. A., and Donelson, J. E. (1984). Sequence of the *Saccharomyces GAL* region and its transcription *in vivo*. J. Bacteriol. *158*, 269–278.

Clare, J., and Farabaugh, P. J. (1985). Nucleotide sequence of a Ty1 element: evidence for a novel mechanism of gene expression. Proc. Natl. Acad. Sci. USA, in press.

Daniels, D. L., Schroeder, J. L., Szybalski, W., Sanger, F., and Blattner, F. R. (1983). A molecular map of coliphage lambda. In Lambda II, R. W. Hendrix, J. W. Roberts, F. W. Stahl, R. A. Weisberg, eds. (Cold Spring Harbor, New York: Cold Spring Harbor Laboratory), pp. 469–676.

Eibel, H., and Philippsen, P. (1984). Preferential integration of yeast transposable element Ty into a promoter region. Nature *307*, 386–388.

Elder, R. T., Loh, E. Y., and Davis, R. W. (1983). RNA from the yeast transposable element Ty1 has both ends in the direct repeats, a structure similar to retrovirus RNA. Proc. Natl. Acad. Sci. USA *80*, 2432–2436.

Farabaugh, P. J., and Fink, G. R. (1980). Insertion of the eukaryotic transposable element Ty1 creates a 5-base pair duplication. Nature *286*, 352–356.

Finnegan, D. J., Rubin, G. M., Young, M. W., and Hogness, D. S. (1978). Repeated gene families in *Drosophila melanogaster*. Cold Spring Harbor Symp. Quant. Biol. *42*, 1053–1063.

Gopinathan, K. P., Weymouth, L. A., Kunkel, T. A., and Loeb, L. A. (1979). Mutagenesis *in vitro* by DNA polymerase from an RNA tumour virus. Nature *278*, 857–859.

Grunstein, M., and Hogness, D. (1975). Colony hybridization: a method for the isolation of cloned DNAs that contain a specific gene. Proc. Natl. Acad. Sci. USA *72*, 3961–3965.

Guarente, L., Yocum, R. R., and Gifford, P. (1982). A *GAL10-CYC1* hybrid yeast promoter identifies the *GAL4* regulatory region as an upstream site. Proc. Natl. Acad. Sci. USA *79*, 7410–7414.

Holmes, D. S., and Quigley, M. (1981). A rapid boiling method for the preparation of bacterial plasmids. Anal. Biochem. *114*, 193–197.

Hsu, T. W., Sabran, J. L., Mark, G. E., Guntaka, R. V., and Taylor, J. M. (1978). Analysis of unintegrated avian RNA tumor virus double-stranded DNA intermediates. J. Virol. *28*, 810–818.

Hu, N., and Messing, J. (1982). The making of strand-specific M13 probes. Gene *17*, 271–277.

Ito, H., Fukuda, Y., Murata, K., and Kimura, A. (1983). Transformation of intact yeast cells treated with alkali cations. J. Bacteriol. *153*, 163–168.

Luria, S. E., and Delbrück, M. (1943). Mutations of bacteria from virus sensitivity to virus resistance. Genetics *28*, 491–511.

Mandel, M., and Higa, A. (1970). Calcium-dependent bacteriophage DNA injection. J. Mol. Biol. *53*, 159–162.

Maniatis, T., Fritsch, E. F., and Sambrook, J. (1982). Molecular Cloning. (Cold Spring Harbor, New York: Cold Spring Harbor Laboratory).

Miller, D. W., and Miller, L. K. (1982). A virus mutant with an insertion of a *copia*-like transposable element. Nature *299*, 562–564.

Miller, J. H. (1972). Experiments in Molecular Genetics. (Cold Spring Harbor, New York: Cold Spring Harbor Laboratory).

Mitra, S. W., Chow, M., Champoux, J., and Baltimore, D. (1982). Synthesis of murine leukemia virus plus strand strong stop DNA initiates at a unique site. J. Biol. Chem. *257*, 5983–5986.

Nishioka, Y., Leder, A., and Leder, P. (1980). Unusual α-globin-like gene that has cleanly lost both globin intervening sequences. Proc. Natl. Acad. Sci. USA *77*, 2806–2809.

Paquin, C. E., and Williamson, V. M. (1984). Temperature effects on the rate of Ty transposition. Science *226*, 53–55.

Pfeiffer, P., and Hohn, T. (1983). Involvement of reverse transcription in the replication of cauliflower mosaic virus: a detailed model and test of some aspects. Cell *33*, 781–789.

Rodriguez, J., Pekielny, C., and Rosbash, M. (1984). In vivo characterization of yeast mRNA processing intermediates. Cell *39*, 603–610.

Roeder, G. S., and Fink, G. R. (1983). Transposable elements in yeast. In Mobile Genetic Elements, J. A. Shapiro, ed. (New York: Academic Press), pp. 299–326.

Roeder, G. S., Farabaugh, P. J., Chaleff, D. T., and Fink, G. R. (1980). The origins of gene instability in yeast. Science *209*, 1375–1380.

Sadler, J. R., Tecklenburg, M., and Betz, J. L. (1980). Plasmids containing many tandem copies of a synthetic lactose operator. Gene *8*, 279–800.

Scherer, S., Mann, C., and Davis, R. W. (1982). Reversion of a promoter deletion in yeast. Nature *298*, 815–819.

Shank, P. R., Hughes, S. H., Kung, H.-J., Majors, J. E., Quintrell, N., Guntake, R. V., Bishop, J. M., and Varmus, H. E. (1978). Mapping unintegrated avian sarcoma virus DNA: termini of linear DNA bear 300 nucleotides present once or twice in two species of circular DNA. Cell *15*, 1383–1395.

Shiba, T., and Saigo, K. (1983). Retrovirus-like particles containing RNA homologous to the transposable element *copia* in *Drosophila melanogaster*. Nature *302*, 119–124.

Silverman, S. J., Rose, M., Botstein, D., and Fink, G. R. (1982). Regulation of *HIS4 – lacZ* fusions in *Saccharomyces cerevisiae*. Mol. Cell. Biol. *2*, 1212–1219.

Simchen, G., Winston, F., Styles, C. A., and Fink, G. R. (1984). Ty-mediated expression of the *LYS2* and *HIS4* genes of *Saccharomyces cerevisiae* is controlled by the same *SPT* genes. Proc. Natl. Acad. Sci. USA *81*, 2431–2434.

Struhl, K., and Davis, R. W. (1981). Promoter mutants of the yeast *his3* gene. J. Mol. Biol. *152*, 553–568.

Summers, J., and Mason, W. S. (1982). Replication of the genome of a hepatitis B-like virus by reverse transcription of an RNA intermediate. Cell *29*, 403–415.

Taylor, J. M. (1977). An analysis of the role of tRNA species as primers for the transcription into DNA of RNA tumor virus genomes. Biochim. Biophys. Acta. *473*, 57–71.

Teem, J. L., and Rosbash, M. (1983). Expression of a β-galactosidase gene containing the ribosomal protein 51 intron is sensitive to the *rna2* mutation of yeast. Proc. Natl. Acad. Sci. USA *80*, 4403–4407.

Temin, H. M. (1980). Origin of retroviruses from cellular moveable genetic elements. Cell *21*, 599–600.

Temin, H. M., and Mizutani, S. (1970). RNA-directed DNA polymerase in virions from Rous sarcoma virus. Nature *226*, 1211–1213.

Varmus, H. E. (1982). Form and function of retroviral proviruses. Science *216*, 812–820.

Weinberg, R. A. (1980). Origins and roles of endogenous retroviruses. Cell *22*, 643–644.

Molecular model for the transposition and replication of bacteriophage Mu and other transposable elements

(DNA insertion elements/nonhomologous recombination/site-specific recombination/replicon fusion/topoisomerases)

JAMES A. SHAPIRO

Department of Microbiology, The University of Chicago, Chicago, Illinois 60637

Communicated by Hewson Swift, December 11, 1978

ABSTRACT   A series of molecular events will explain how genetic elements can transpose from one DNA site to another, generate a short oligonucleotide duplication at both ends of the new insertion site, and replicate in the transposition process. These events include the formation of recombinant molecules which have been postulated to be intermediates in the transposition process. The model explains how the replication of bacteriophage Mu is obligatorily associated with movement to new genetic sites. It postulates that all transposable elements replicate in the transposition process so that they remain at their original site while moving to new sites. According to this model, the mechanism of transposition is very different from the insertion and excision of bacteriophage λ.

Recent research on transposable elements in bacteria has provided important insights into the role of nonhomologous recombination in genetic rearrangements (1–4). These elements include small insertion sequences (IS elements), transposable resistance determinants (Tn elements), and bacteriophage Mu (3). There are detailed differences in the genetic behavior of these various elements (such as differences in specificity of site selection for insertion), but there is a consensus that they all share underlying recombination mechanisms (3, 5). Although this consensus originally included the bacteriophage λ (cf. refs. 3 and 4), the considerations elaborated below argue that phage Mu and other transposable elements differ radically from the elegant and simple λ model (6, 7).

The mechanisms by which transposable elements move from one genetic site to another are still unknown. However, there has been a rapid accumulation of information about the structural consequences of transposition events, the genetic control of transposition, and the replication of bacteriophage Mu from work in many laboratories. While some of this information is not yet based on completely unambiguous data, the outlines appear sufficiently clear to propose a partially detailed molecular model to explain the transposition process. This model also explains how phage Mu replicates. Its justification draws examples from work on various elements (particularly Mu, IS1, Tn3, and Tn5) on the assumption that they are all mechanistically equivalent as far as the details of the present model go. This proposal does not address the question of site selection for transposition events and specifically deals only with events that occur after an initial donor–target complex has been formed.

OBSERVATIONS TO BE EXPLAINED

A model for the mechanism of transposition and replication of phage Mu and the insertion of other transposable elements should be able to explain the following observations.

(*i*) Insertion of a transposable element into a genetic site

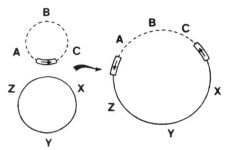

FIG. 1.   Replicon fusion. The boxes with an arrow indicate copies of a transposable element. The letters mark arbitrary regions of the two replicons to indicate the relative positions of the elements in the donor and cointegrate molecules.

results in the duplication of a short oligonucleotide sequence in the target. The duplicated sequence brackets the inserted element (8, 9). This characteristic of the insertion process has been detected in sequence data on insertions of IS1, Tn5, Tn9, and Tn10 [all having nine base pair (bp) duplications] and also insertions of IS2, Tn3, gamma-delta, and phage Mu (5 bp duplications) (summarized in ref. 10). Grindley and Sherratt have proposed a model to account for this phenomenon (10), and some features of their proposal are incorporated in the present model. Studies on the specificity of insertion and comparison of sibling Tn9 insertions indicate that there is no functional relationship between the sequences flanking the donor insertion and the repeat generated at the target site (11). A useful way to consider these observations is to think of insertion on *both* sides of the 5- or 9-bp sequence that is to be duplicated.

(*ii*) Transposable elements can serve to fuse two replicons, and replicon fusion occurs when only one of the parental molecules originally contained a transposable element (12–14). In all cases in which there is data on the structure of the cointegrate product, it contains a directly repeated copy of the transposable element at each juncture of the two replicons (Fig. 1; refs. 12, 15, and 16). In the case of phage Mu, replicon fusion requires expression of the *A* gene but not of the *B* gene (12). In the case of Tn3, replicon fusion is observed only when a specific internal region of the transposon has been deleted (13, 15). Absence of this region causes a *cis*-dominant change in recombination behavior so that deleted transposons catalyze replicon fusion in the presence of a normal Tn3 (15). There is preliminary genetic evidence that derivatives of Tn5 can catalyze replicon fusion. These derivatives are generated by substitution of the internal Tn5 *Hin*dIII fragment by a *trp* fragment, and in this case the fusion phenotype is recessive to a wild-type Tn5 element (17). It has been suggested that the cointegrate fused replicons represent intermediates in the transposition process (15–17).

Abbreviations: IS, insertion sequence; bp, base pair.

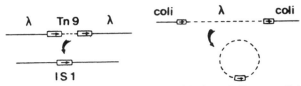

FIG. 2. Specific "cut-out" reactions. The boxes indicate parallel IS1 elements. (*Left*) The reaction observed in the formation of λ::IS1 phages from λ::Tn9 phages during vegetative growth (18). (*Right*) The reaction observed in the excision of an IS1-bounded prophage from the bacterial chromosome to yield λ::IS1 phage progeny (16). The dashed line indicates λ sequences.

(*iii*) DNA bracketed by direct repeats of the IS1 element is specifically excised under certain conditions. Growth of λ phages containing the chloramphenicol resistance transposon Tn9 results in a high rate of *rec-* and *red*-independent precise excision of material between homologous sites in the two IS1 elements (Fig. 2 *left*; ref 18). This "cam cut-out" reaction is not observed with Tn9 elements in the bacterial chromosome or in repressed prophages (14). An analogous IS1-specific excisive recombination event occurs after derepression of a λ prophage bracketed by direct repeats of IS1 (Fig. 2 *right*; ref. 16). These results suggest that the IS1 elements may serve as sites for a specific reciprocal recombination event. The observation that the excision of IS1-bounded prophages from the chromosome occurs efficiently in *rec⁻red⁻* conditions has led me to believe that a specific "cut-out" event plays a role in the transposition process (16).

(*iv*) Replication of phage Mu DNA shows several striking characteristics, two of which are especially significant. First, replication is associated with transposition of prophage DNA from site to site (19) and requires the activity of the Mu A gene product, the phage insertion function (20). Second, derepression of a Mu prophage leads quickly to the replication of Mu DNA but not to detectable replication of DNA immediately adjacent to the prophage (21). These results suggest that insertion of Mu in new sites may be essential to initiate phage replication and that replication begins or ends (or both) precisely at the prophage termini.

(*v*) Transposable elements appear to be able to move from one site to another without leaving the original site. This point is not yet firmly established in bacteria, but two lines of evidence suggest that it will prove to be correct. First, the experiments of Ljungquist and Bukhari indicate that a Mu prophage can replicate and transpose without leaving the original site (22). Second, transduction experiments with Tn5 indicate that a cell can harbor Tn5 both at an original site in the *lacZ* gene and also at a second site in the bacterial chromosome (23). Preliminary reversion and transduction data on the Tn7 element inserted into *Pseudomonas* plasmid *alk* genes also suggests that cells can harbor Tn7 at its original site as well as on the chromosome (M. Fennewald and J. Shapiro, unpublished results). In other words, these observations suggest that the donor element is retained or regenerated in the transposition event. A similar conclusion has been reached by Bennett *et al.* on the basis of quantitative measurements of transposition and excision events with the Tn1 element (24). It is worth noting that the appearance of an element at a new site without loss from the original site is precisely the behavior of the yeast mating-type "cassettes" (25).

(*vi*) Transposition will occur in *rec⁻* strains between intact replicons (1, 3, 5), within a single replicon (4, 5, 22, 26), and from an incomplete replicon (i.e., linear DNA molecule) to the bacterial chromosome (19, 27). Hence, homologous recombination functions, supercoiling of donor DNA (cf. ref. 7), and replication from an origin outside the transposable element are not necessary for transposition to occur.

THE MODEL

The model involves four steps (which can be further subdivided) and is schematized in Fig. 3:

Step I: Four single-strand cleavages occur. These are probably not simultaneous and almost certainly not independent events. The donor molecule is cleaved on either strand at the extremity of the transposable element. The cleavage is drawn at the 3'-hydroxyl end on each strand. The endonuclease responsible for this cleavage is probably an element-specific enzyme (e.g., Mu A gene product). The target molecule is cleaved at sites chosen with greater or lesser specificity (depending on the element) to yield 5- or 9-bp cohesive ends, as first postulated by Grindley and Sherratt (10). It is critical that the polarity of this cleavage be opposite that of the donor cleavage, so that this cleavage has been drawn at the 5'-phosphate ends of the oligonucleotide sequence on each strand. The endonuclease responsible for this cleavage is probably a cellular function that may be activated by the element-specific endonuclease, as first suggested by Grindley and Sherratt (10). Although the two pairs of cleavages

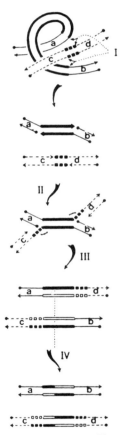

FIG. 3. Transposition and replication. The top cartoon illustrates how various DNA regions may be brought into close physical proximity for the subsequent cleavage and ligation events. The bottom four drawings show various steps in the transposition process as described in the text. Solid lines indicate donor DNA; dashed lines indicate target DNA; the heavy bars are parental DNA of the transposable element, and open bars are newly synthesized DNA; the small boxes indicate the oligonucleotide target sequence (filled, parental DNA; open, newly synthesized DNA). The arrowheads indicate 3'-hydroxyl ends of DNA chains and the dots indicate 5'-phosphate ends. The letters a, b, c, and d in the duplex arms flanking the transposable elements and target oligonucleotide serve to indicate the genetic structure of the various duplex products.

must have opposite polarities, there is no compelling reason now for choosing the particular ones depicted in Fig. 3.

Step II: The donor and target strands are ligated to generate a χ-shaped structure held together by the transposable element duplex as shown in Fig. 3. The ligation would almost certainly be catalyzed by a specific enzyme complex, perhaps including the same protein responsible for the original element-specific cleavages. Because both ends of the donor element have exposed 3'-hydroxyl groups and both ends of the target oligonucleotide have exposed 5'-phosphate groups, the joining can theoretically take place in either orientation. (The orientation may, however, be determined by the exact sequence of reaction.) Although there is probably some fraying at the ends of the transposable element duplex, this structure should be stable because the only regions that must be single-stranded are the 5- or 9-bp sequences from the target molecule.

I have described the reactions in steps I and II separately in order to clarify the sites of breaking and joining of DNA strands. This description is not meant to imply either a biochemical mechanism or a particular temporal sequence for these events. In order to guarantee maximal stability to the intermediate structures, for example, one could propose that there is initially only one cleavage of the target oligonucleotide followed by ligation to the donor element and then by a concerted cleavage–ligation reaction at the other target site. The types of biochemical reactions postulated are not unprecedented. T4 RNA ligase will join single DNA strands that are not held together by duplex regions (28). A number of topoisomerases will catalyze concerted cleavage–ligation (nicking–closing) reactions (29). In fact, the properties of one of these enzymes, DNA gyrase, are very similar to the postulated cellular function responsible for the staggered 5- or 9-bp cleavage of the target, for special conditions will induce gyrase to catalyze nonrandom DNA cleavages leaving a four-base cohesive end (ref. 30; A. Morrison and N. Cozzarelli, personal communication). The λ integrase complex will catalyze site-specific, concerted cleavage and ligation reactions involving different molecules to generate recombinant structures (7). And it has been proposed that the φX174 cisA protein carries out a nonconcerted cleavage and ligation reaction that has a protein-stabilized nicked DNA intermediate (31).

Step III: There is filling in of the unpaired oligonucleotide sequences at the ends and semiconservative replication of the transposable element. The ligation step actually results in formation of a replication fork at each end of the transposable element. Displacement synthesis from the unligated 3'-hydroxyl groups will result in the formation of large single-stranded regions adjacent to an unligated 5' end, and so seems unlikely to proceed very far without discontinuous replication on the opposite strand. (This situation will not be altered by reversing the polarities of the original cleavages.) The replication may proceed from both forks to the interior of the element, from one fork completely across the element, or (conceivably but not likely) bidirectionally from an internal site. The first two possibilities provide a very attractive explanation of why Mu must transpose in order to replicate. Polymerization and completion of this replication require no new biochemical activities, but in some cases specific proteins may be involved (e.g., Mu B gene product during vegetative phage growth). The result of this replication will be two recombinant duplexes each containing a semiconserved transposable element adjacent to the target 5- or 9-bp sequence. This oligonucleotide sequence has been duplicated in the process. Note that if the donor and target molecules are both intact replicons, the a and b duplex arms will be connected, and the c and d arms will also be connected. In other words, the recombinant products in Fig. 3 will constitute the join regions of a fused replicon (Fig. 1).

Step IV: Site-specific reciprocal recombination takes place between the two transposable elements to generate both the original donor molecule (with some newly synthesized material in the transposable element) and the target molecule containing an inserted element flanked by a 5- or 9-bp repeat. Although homologous recombination systems can catalyze this step, there must be some recA-independent process because transposition occurs normally in recA strains. This recombination probably involves specific proteins (e.g., the product lacking in Tn5–trp hybrids; ref. 17) acting on specific sites (e.g., the site deleted in certain Tn3 mutants that generate replicon fusions; ref. 13). It is possible, however, that there is a general cellular recombination function that recognizes particular sites when the DNA is replicating (cf. ref. 16). In this case, I would suggest that steps III and IV overlap in time, so that the reciprocal recombination event occurs between duplicated segments of the replicating element before the replication process is finished. This last step is not essential for Mu replication, and its efficiency may vary from element to element. In the case of λ::Tn9 infection of rec⁻ Escherichia coli cells, cointegrate formation (steps I–III) occurs approximately as often as transposition (steps I–IV) (16).

DISCUSSION

This model satisfactorily explains the six observations listed above and is not inconsistent with any of the other genetic phenomena [such as adjacent deletion formation (32)] that appear to be common to transposable elements. In fact, it is particularly instructive to consider the consequences of one simple alteration in the process just outlined: a failure to complete step IV. (A simple genetic formalism facilitates this kind of analysis because the net result of steps I–III is to generate two complete recombinant duplexes: a-element–oligonucleotide-d and c-oligonucleotide–element-b. Thus, it is not necessary to go through all the details of cleavage, ligation, and replication to work out recombinant structures.) If donor and target molecules are both intact circular replicons, the product will be a cointegrate replicon fusion with directly repeated elements, and it is certainly suggestive that Tn3 and Tn5 appear to generate fusions only when part of the transposon has been deleted (13, 15, 17). If the donor and target sites are both on the same replicon, the recombinant products of the replication step will depend on the orientation of the ligation step. If the duplex arms bracketing the transposable element (marked a and b in Fig. 3) and those bracketing the target site (c and d) are arranged as shown in the upper panel of Fig. 4, the products will be two circles. (a, b, c, and d in Fig. 3 are shown as A, B, C, and D in Fig. 4.) The larger one could represent an adjacent deletion mutant of the parental replicon. Both could represent the heterogeneous Mu-containing circles observed during Mu replication (19, 33). Thus, the model readily accounts for two observations that did not enter into the original formulation. If the duplex arms of the donor element and target site are arranged as depicted in the lower panel of Fig. 4, then the products will form an inversion bracketed by inverted repeats of the transposable element. It is tempting to speculate that such events might have given rise to structures like those of Tn5 and Tn10 (3). These hypothetical adjacent inversion events do not yield structures identical to those already observed by Kleckner and Ross (34). Although it is possible to generate their structures in the same four steps outlined above, I think the discrepancy provides an important test of the model. The model predicts that inversions such as those schematized in the lower panel of Fig. 4 will be the most common kind of adjacent inversion when there has been no selection for genetic fusion or loss of a particular transposon function. Although the data have not yet been published, Faelen and Toussaint refer to Mu-mediated inversions of the structure depicted in Fig. 4 (35).

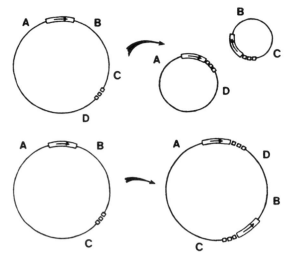

FIG. 4. Consequences of insertion and replication within a circular DNA molecule. The long boxes indicate copies of a transposable element, and the small boxes indicate the oligonucleotide target sequence. A, B, C, and D indicate the duplex regions similarly labeled in lower case in Fig. 3. The upper and lower panels illustrate the consequences of steps I–III, depending on the orientation of the ligation reaction.

A particularly appealing feature of the model is the intimate relationship it postulates between transposition and replication. This relationship has been proposed for phage Mu (19), and the model provides an explanation of many unusual facts of Mu replication. Furthermore, it makes clear predictions about the structure involved in the initiation of Mu-specific DNA synthesis.

The model makes several other genetic and biochemical predictions. Among these are the following:

(*i*) Transposition of an element to a new site does not remove the element from its original site. Thus, cells will accumulate multiple elements with time unless transposition is repressed. The discovery of a transposition repressor for Tn3 is particularly interesting in regard to this problem (13, 15).

(*ii*) Transposable element systems will code for three kinds of functions: a strand cleavage function for step I, a ligation function for step II, and a specific recombination function for step IV. As suggested above, one protein may participate in both element-specific cleavage and ligation reactions. The recombination function may be either a specific enzyme–site system (analogous to the integrase–*att* system of λ) or simply a site which makes use of some cellular *rec*-independent system for illegitimate recombination. Transposable elements that replicate, such as phage Mu, may also have specific proteins for step III.

(*iii*) The recombinant structures formed after step III are obligatory intermediates in transposition events. For two circular molecules this means a replicon fusion structure (Fig. 1). For genetically linear molecules (such as λ phages) this means that a transposable element will serve as a site for reciprocal recombination when the full process is aborted after step III. In such crosses, only one parental molecule will carry the transposable element, and recombination events will occur at various sites on the other parental molecule. Both recombinant products will carry the transposable element. These recombination events will not require DNA sequence homology nor homologous recombination systems and will differ from the postulated step IV reaction, which will occur at defined sites on both parental molecules.

(*iv*) The donor molecule in a transposition event will be regenerated with two segments of newly synthesized DNA on opposite strands, and the newly inserted transposon will contain parental DNA from the donor molecule in two segments on opposite strands. The transposable element in both donor and target molecules will consist of only hybrid (new-old) DNA.

There are four additional aspects of this model that merit emphasis. First, there is no autonomous existence of the transposable element. This is one of the striking features of phage Mu, in which even the virus particle contains an inserted prophage rather than an autonomous viral genome free of host DNA (19). Second, all reactions are limited to the local regions of the donor element and the target site. Thus, there is no requirement for physical circularity of either molecule. Third, the donor molecule is regenerated intact and does not have to commit suicide in order to donate its transposable element to a new site. Thus, it is possible to have transposition between sites in the same replicon. Fourth, the initial interactions between donor and target duplexes involve end-to-end joining of single DNA strands. Thus, there is no role for base-pairing (i.e., genetic homology) in the recombination process *at the site of insertion*. This feature distinguishes the present proposal from mechanisms based on the activity of restriction enzymes.

This model owes a great deal to the earlier proposal of Grindley and Sherratt (10). The ideas of staggered cleavages at the target site, of replicating the transposable element, and of regenerating the donor molecule were first explicitly stated by them. Thus, prediction *i* above is the same for both models and distinguishes them from models based on λ excision and insertion. There are, however, important differences between the two proposals. The model described above postulates that cleavages and ligations at both ends of the transposable element occur prior to DNA replication. The Grindley–Sherratt proposal postulates displacement synthesis across the transposable element between the first ligation at one of its ends and the subsequent ligation at the other end. Thus, the structure of transposition intermediates, the nature of cleavage and ligation reactions, and the functions of the element-specific enzymes are different. In particular, prediction *iii* of this model includes two potentially stable recombinant duplexes as intermediates. By postulating a strand switch during displacement synthesis across the transposable element, it is possible to generate recombinant duplex structures from the Grindley–Sherratt model. However, these are not intermediates for transposition, so that the presence of a *rec*-independent reciprocal recombination system for sibling elements is not a feature of their proposal. The nature of element-specific replication is also very different in the two models. According to Grindley and Sherratt, the transposable element is duplicated by two successive displacement reactions from free 3'-hydroxyl ends formed by separate cleavage events. These reactions can result in conservative replication of at least part of the transposable element. The model proposed here postulates strictly semiconservative replication of the transposable element. Thus, prediction *iv* about the presence of only hybrid DNA in final transposition products does not apply to the Grindley–Sherratt model. An additional (and more intriguing) difference is the possible role of a DNA replication termination function in transposition. To complete replication of the transposable element by the present model poses the same topological problems as finishing replication of any circular molecule that passes through a theta structure (36). Thus, the total process almost certainly requires the biochemical activities needed for normal termination and separation of daughter replicons. Without these, the two recombinant duplex products of step III would not be formed. Such an activity is not required by the Grindley and Sherratt replication scheme. The tests for many of the alternative predictions of these two models await development of *in vitro* transposition systems. Both models indicate that transposition is a more complex process than integrative λ recombination (7).

There are clearly many details to fill in. The mechanisms governing the formation of the initial donor–target complex remain to be elucidated. This is a particularly interesting question because both genetic and sequence data indicate that there are differences between the ways in which Tn9 and Tn10 choose insertion sites (11, 33). Steps III and IV are vague because the natures of both replication initiation and site-specific recombination events need to be specified. Nonetheless, this model has some original features, provides new explanations for previous observations, makes several testable predictions, and hopefully will aid in the design of both genetic and biochemical experiments for elucidation of the behavior of transposable elements.

Note Added in Proof. I thank Arianne Toussaint and Nigel Grindley for bringing some additional points about Mu replication and Mu-mediated chromosome rearrangements to my attention: (*i*) Mu DNA appears to replicate unidirectionally starting at the immunity (*c*) terminus [C. Wiffelman and P. van de Putte (1977), in ref. 3, pp. 329–333]. (*ii*) When a Mu prophage mediates deletion formation at a distant region of the genome, the resulting mutant cell contains two copies of Mu—one linked to the deletion and one at the original site (35). Thus, in this case transposition has occured without loss of the donor prophage. (*iii*) Both ends of the Mu prophage are required for the formation of an adjacent deletion (35). This is consistent with the model for adjacent deletion formation depicted in Fig. 4. (*iv*) Mu-mediated recombination events that require only one cycle of transposition and replication (e.g., adjacent deletion formation and integration of λ*gal* into the chromosome of a Mu lysogen) occur at the same frequencies in the presence or absence of Mu *B* function (12, 35). On the other hand, Mu-mediated recombination events that require two or more cycles of transposition and replication (e.g., deletion formation at sites distant from a prophage) occur at the frequency of a single event in presence of Mu *B* function but at the frequency of two successive independent events in the absence of Mu *B* function (35). This observation suggests a function for the Mu *B* gene product: the presence of Mu *B* product permits the Mu *A* function to catalyze repeated rounds of transposition (such as needed to initiate successive rounds of vegetative replication). In the absence of Mu *B* product, the Mu *A* function can catalyze only a single round of transposition and replication. This hypothesis predicts that density-labeled Mu A^+B^- phage will form hybrid density prophages after infection of sensitive bacteria.

I thank Lorne MacHattie for introducing me to the mysteries of Tn9, for long hours of invaluable discussions, and for making these figures understandable. I am grateful to Nicholas Cozzarelli, Alan Morrison, Pat Brown, Pat Higgins, and Ken Kreuzer for communicating unpublished results and helping me ensure the biochemical plausibility of the model; to Ahmad Bukhari, Martha Howe, and Arianne Toussaint for many helpful lessons on phage Mu biology; to Ron Gill and Jeff Miller for communicating unpublished results on replicon fusion experiments; and to Nigel Grindley for going over our respective models to clarify their similarities and differences. Research in my laboratory is supported by grants from the National Institute of General Medical Sciences (GM 24960), the University of Chicago Cancer Research Center (CA 14599-05-307), and the National Science Foundation (PCM 77-08591). I am the recipient of a Research Career Development Award (1-K04-AI00118-01) from the National Institute of Allergy and Infectious Diseases.

1. Cohen, S. N. (1976) *Nature* (*London*) **263**, 731–738.
2. Shapiro, J. A. (1977) *Trends Biochem. Sci.* **2**, 176–180.
3. Bukhari, A. I., Shapiro, J. A. & Adhya, S. L., eds. (1977) *DNA Insertion Elements, Plasmids and Episomes* (Cold Spring Harbor Laboratory, Cold Spring Harbor, NY).
4. Nevers, P. & Saedler, H. (1977) *Nature* (*London*) **268**, 109–115.
5. Kleckner, N. (1977) *Cell* **11**, 11–23.
6. Campbell, A. M. (1962) *Adv. Genet.* **11**, 101–145.
7. Nash, H. A., Mizuuchi, K., Weisberg, R. A., Kikuchi, Y. & Gellert, M. (1977) in *DNA Insertion Elements, Plasmids and Episomes*, eds. Bukhari, A. I., Shapiro, J. A. & Adhya, S. L. (Cold Spring Harbor Laboratory, Cold Spring Harbor, NY), pp. 363–373.
8. Grindley, N. D. F. (1978) *Cell* **13**, 419–427.
9. Calos, M. P., Johnsrud, L. & Miller, J. H. (1978) *Cell* **13**, 411–418.
10. Grindley, N. D. F. & Sherratt, D. (1978) *Cold Spring Harbor Symp. Quant. Biol.* **43**, in press.
11. Johnsrud, L., Calos, M. & Miller, J. H. (1978) *Cell* **15**, 1209–1219.
12. Faelen, M., Toussaint, A. & de la Fontayne, J. (1975) *J. Bacteriol.* **121**, 873–882.
13. Heffron, F., Bedinger, P., Champoux, J. & Falkow, S. (1977) in *DNA Insertion Elements, Plasmids and Episomes*, eds. Bukhari, A. I., Shapiro, J. A. & Adhya, S. L. (Cold Spring Harbor Laboratory, Cold Spring Harbor, NY), pp. 161–167.
14. MacHattie, L. A. & Shapiro, J. A. (1978) *Proc. Natl. Acad. Sci. USA* **75**, 1490–1494.
15. Gill, R., Heffron, F., Dougan, G. & Falkow, S. (1978) *J. Bacteriol.* **136**, 742–756.
16. Shapiro, J. A. & MacHattie, L. A. (1978) *Cold Spring Harbor Symp. Quant. Biol.* **43**, in press.
17. Meyer, R., Boch, G. & Shapiro, J. (1979) *Mol. Gen. Genet.*, in press.
18. MacHattie, L. A. & Jackowski, J. B. (1977) in *DNA Insertion Elements, Plasmids and Episomes*, eds. Bukhari, A. I., Shapiro, J. A. & Adhya, S. L. (Cold Spring Harbor Laboratory, Cold Spring Harbor, NY), pp. 219–228.
19. Bukhari, A. I. (1976) *Annu. Rev. Genet.* **10**, 389–412.
20. O'Day, K. J., Schultz, D. W. & Howe, M. M. (1978) in *Microbiology 1978*, ed. Schlessinger, D. (American Society for Microbiology, Washington, DC), pp. 48–51.
21. Waggoner, B. T. & Pato, M. C. (1978) *J. Virol.* **27**, 587–594.
22. Ljungquist, E. & Bukhari, A. I. (1977) *Proc. Natl. Acad. Sci. USA* **74**, 3143–3147.
23. Berg, D. (1977) in *DNA Insertion Elements, Plasmids and Episomes*, eds. Bukhari, A. I., Shapiro, J. A. & Adhya, S. L. (Cold Spring Harbor Laboratory, Cold Spring Harbor, NY), pp. 205–212.
24. Bennett, P. M., Grinsted, J. & Richmond, M. H. (1977) *Mol. Gen. Genet.* **154**, 205–211.
25. Hicks, J. B., Strathern, H. N. & Herskowitz, I. (1977) in *DNA Insertion Elements, Plasmids and Episomes*, eds. Bukhari, A. I., Shapiro, J. A. & Adhya, S. L. (Cold Spring Harbor Laboratory, Cold Spring Harbor, NY), pp. 457–462.
26. Botstein, D. & Kleckner, N. (1977) in *DNA Insertion Elements, Plasmids and Episomes*, eds. Bukhari, A. I., Shapiro, J. A. & Adhya, S. L. (Cold Spring Harbor Laboratory, Cold Spring Harbor, NY), pp. 185–203.
27. Kleckner, N., Chan, R. K., Tye, B. K. & Botstein, D. (1975) *J. Mol. Biol.* **97**, 561–575.
28. Snopek, T., Sugino, A., Agarwal, K. L. & Cozzarelli, N. R. (1976) *Biochem. Biophys. Res. Commun.* **68**, 417–424.
29. Wang, J. C. & Liu, F. (1978) in *Molecular Genetics*, ed. Taylor, J. H. (Academic, New York), Part III, in press.
30. Peebles, C. L., Higgins, N. P., Kreuzer, K. N., Morrison, A., Brown, P. O., Sugino, A. & Cozzarelli, N. R. (1978) *Cold Spring Harbor Symp. Quant. Biol.* **43**, 41–52.
31. Eisenberg, S., Griffith, J. & Kornberg, A. (1977) *Proc. Natl. Acad. Sci. USA* **74**, 3198–3202.
32. Reif, H. J. & Saedler, H. (1975) *Mol. Gen. Genet.* **137**, 17–28.
33. Waggoner, B., Pato, M. L. & Taylor, A. L. (1977) in *DNA Insertion Elements, Plasmids and Episomes*, eds. Bukhari, A. I., Shapiro, J. A. & Adhya, S. L. (Cold Spring Harbor Laboratory, Cold Spring Harbor, NY), pp. 263–274.
34. Kleckner, N. & Ross, D. G. (1978) *Cold Spring Harbor Symp. Quant. Biol.* **43**, in press.
35. Faelen, M. & Toussaint, A. (1978) *J. Bacteriol.* **136**, 477–483.
36. Gefter, M. (1978) *Annu. Rev. Biochem.* **44**, 45–78.

State of prophage Mu DNA upon induction

(bacteriophage Mu/bacteriophage λ/DNA insertion/DNA excision/transposable elements)

E. LJUNGQUIST AND A. I. BUKHARI

Cold Spring Harbor Laboratory, Cold Spring Harbor, New York 11724

Communicated by J. D. Watson, April 18, 1977

ABSTRACT We have compared the process of prophage λ induction with that of prophage Mu. According to the Campbell model, rescue of λ DNA from the host DNA involves reversal of λ integration such that the prophage DNA is excised from the host chromosome. We have monitored this event by locating the prophage DNA with a technique in which DNA of the lysogenic cells is cleaved with a restriction endonuclease and fractionated in agarose gels. The DNA fragments are denatured in gels, transferred to a nitrocellulose paper, and hybridized with ^{32}P-labeled mature phage DNA. The fragments containing prophage DNA become visible after autoradiography. Upon prophage λ induction, the phage–host junction fragments disappear and the fragment containing the λ *att* site appears. No such excision is seen in prophage Mu. The Mu–host junction fragments remain intact well into the lytic cycle, when Mu DNA has undergone many rounds of replication and apparently many copies of Mu DNA have been integrated into the host DNA. Therefore, we postulate that Mu DNA replicates *in situ* and that the replication generates a form of Mu DNA active in the integrative recombination between Mu DNA and host DNA. This type of mechanism may be common to many transposable elements.

Assimilation of one DNA molecule into another is a fundamental biological phenomenon spanning the whole range of prokaryotic and eukaryotic organisms. The insertion problem has been studied in its most clear-cut form in viral systems. The classic mode of integration of viral genomes involves recombination between the host DNA and a circular form of the inserting viral DNA. Specific sequences in the inserting circular genomes and in the host DNA are recognized for recombination, so that the process culminates in complete linear insertion of the circles (1). Rescue of the inserted DNA from the host is visualized as physical excision of the DNA in a manner that is a reversal of the insertion process. The question of whether or not the temperate bacteriophage Mu conforms to this classic mode of integration and excision has been the focus of the current work on Mu (2). This question has arisen because Mu is strikingly different from other temperate viruses of bacteria in several features.

Unlike other temperate phages, Mu inserts its DNA at randomly distributed sites on the genome of its host bacterium *Escherichia coli* (3, 4). As extracted from mature phage particles, Mu DNA, is a linear DNA duplex of 37–38 kilobases and has at its ends host DNA that differs in size and sequence from molecule to molecule (5, 6). Thus, Mu does not have terminally cohesive or repetitive sequences and lacks any obvious means of fusing its ends to form circular DNA molecules. The terminal host sequences are randomized during Mu growth, because Mu lysates grown from a single plaque still contain particles with different host sequences. Yet, a form of Mu DNA free of host DNA has remained undetected.

In its continuous association with host DNA, Mu resembles another class of insertion elements, referred to as the transposable elements. The transposable elements are specific stretches of DNA that can be translocated from one position to another in host DNA (7). Mu undergoes multiple rounds of transposition during its growth, far exceeding the transposition frequency of the *bona fide* transposable elements. When a Mu lysogen, carrying a single Mu prophage at a given site on the host chromosome, is induced, many copies of Mu DNA are rapidly integrated at different sites as the replication of Mu DNA proceeds.

We have sought to determine whether induction of a Mu prophage, with subsequent replication and transposition of Mu DNA, involves excision of the prophage DNA from the original site. To do this, we have examined the fate of prophage Mu DNA, and also of prophage λ DNA, *in situ* in the host chromosome after induction. This paper presents evidence that, unlike λ, prophage Mu DNA persists at its original site after induction.

MATERIALS AND METHODS

Bacterial Strains. The *E. coli* strains were all derivatives of *E. coli* K-12. The basic bacteriophages in the lysogenic cells were either Mu *cts*62, a temperature-inducible mutant of bacteriophage Mu carrying a mutation in the immunity gene *c* (8), or λ *c*I857S7, a temperature-inducible derivative of bacteriophage λ. The Mu *cts*62 lysogens were: BU563 (Mu *cts*62 located in one of the *pro* genes), BU568 (Mu *cts*62 located at the *thr* locus), BU575 (Mu *cts*62 located at the *trp* locus), BU8220 (Mu *cts*62 located in the *lacI* gene on an F′ *pro*⁺ *lac* episome). BU1216 carried the Mu A gene mutant Mu *cts*62 *A*ts5045. The λcI 857S7 lysogen was BU851.

Genetic Procedures. The media, growth, and induction conditions have been described in detail by Bukhari and Ljungquist (9).

Biochemical Procedures.

(i) *Extraction of DNA.* The bacterial cells were washed, resuspended in 0.01 M Tris·HCl/1 mM EDTA, pH 7.9, and lysed by the addition of 0.5% sodium dodecyl sulfate. The lysate was digested with Pronase (self-digested for 2 hr at 37° in 0.01 M Tris·HCl, pH 7.4) at a concentration of 1 mg/ml for 8 hr. The solution was then extracted twice with Tris buffer/EDTA/ saturated phenol. The aqueous phase was dialyzed against 0.01 M Tris·HCl/1 mM EDTA, pH 7.9, after which it was treated with RNase at a concentration of 100 μg/ml for 2 hr at 37° and then with Pronase at 100 μg/ml for 3 hr at 37°. The DNA was extracted with phenol again and dialyzed as above.

Abbreviations: *Eco*RI, *Bgl* II, and *Bal* I refer to restriction endonucleases from *E. coli* RY 13, *Bacillus globiggi*, and *Brevibacterium albidum*, respectively.

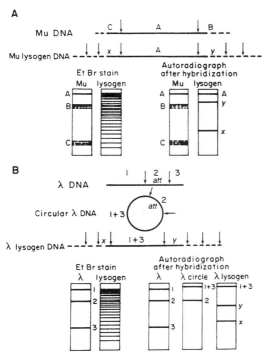

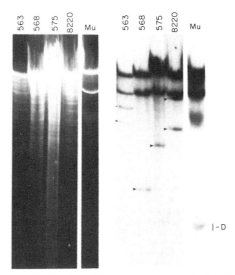

FIG. 2. Hybridization of fragments, generated by *Bal* I digestion of DNA extracted from different Mu lysogens, with ^{32}P-labeled Mu DNA. (*Left*) Ethidium bromide-stained gel; (*Right*) autoradiograph after blotting-hybridization. The lysogens show one or two new Mu-containing fragments, indicated by arrows.

FIG. 1. Scheme for identifying the prophage DNA. Phage DNA is indicated by solid lines and host DNA by broken lines. (*A*) A hypothetical restriction endonuclease cuts mature Mu DNA at two sites (arrows), generating one internal fragment, A, and the two end fragments, B and C, which are replaced in prophage Mu by two prophage–host junction fragments, *x* and *y*. The fragments A, *x*, and *y* will be visible in the autoradiograph after blotting-hybridization of the lysogen DNA fragments with ^{32}P-labeled Mu DNA as a probe. (*B*) A hypothetical restriction endonuclease cuts linear λ DNA at two sites, generating one internal fragment, 2, and the two end fragments, 1 and 3, which fuse to form one fragment (1 + 3) when λ DNA becomes circular (λ circle). Upon integration, fragment 2 (containing the λ *att* site) is split, giving rise to two host–phage junction fragments labeled *x* and *y* (λ lysogen). Blotting-hybridization with ^{32}P-labeled λ DNA as a probe will allow the visualization of λ DNA pattern in the λ lysogen DNA fragments.

(*ii*) *Fractionation, blotting, and hybridization of DNA fragments.* The DNA was digested with restriction endonucleases as described by Sharp *et al.* (10). The endonucleases used were *Eco*RI (from *E. coli* RY 13), *Bgl* II (from *Bacillus globiggi*), and *Bal* I (from *Brevibacterium albidum*). The fragments were resolved by electrophoresis in 1% agarose gels in the presence of ethidium bromide and photographed in ultraviolet light. The fragments were then denatured and transferred directly to a nitrocellulose paper (11) with a procedure referred to here as blotting. The nitrocellulose paper was then coated with Denhardt's solution and hybridized with ^{32}P-labeled denatured probe DNA by the DNA·DNA hybridization procedure described by Bukhari *et al.*(5). The nitrocellulose paper was then washed, dried, and autoradiographed.

RESULTS

Identification of Prophage Mu and Prophage λ DNA. To study the fate of prophage DNA upon induction, we wished to physically locate the DNA integrated in the host genome. The identification of prophage DNA was based on the following principle. When the total DNA of lysogenic cells is extracted and digested with a restriction endonuclease, the digest will contain fragments of host DNA and phage DNA and two fragments containing the right and left junctions of prophage

and host DNA. All the fragments will give rise to a complex pattern or a continuous smear after electrophoresis in agarose gels and staining with ethidium bromide. To identify the fragments containing phage DNA, the fragments in the gels are denatured and blotted onto a nitrocellulose paper and hybridized to ^{32}P-labeled denatured phage DNA. The bands containing phage DNA will become labeled and can be visualized after autoradiography. A schematic drawing of the expected results for prophage Mu and prophage λ is presented in Fig. 1.

For Mu, the prophage map and the phage map are collinear. Consequently, the internal phage DNA fragments obtained after digestion with any hypothetical restriction enzyme will be the same for the prophage and the mature phage DNA (fragment A in Fig. 1*A*). Since the ends of Mu are heterogeneous in size and sequence (5), the end fragments from mature phage DNA will appear diffuse or "fuzzy" if the cuts are close to the ends (fragments B and C in Fig. 1*A*). The junction fragments between prophage DNA and host DNA (labeled *x* and *y*) will be sharp bands with mobilities different from those obtained from the mature phage DNA. The junction fragments are expected to be different for prophages located at different sites on the host genome. The results of such an experiment are shown in Fig. 2. The total DNA from different lysogens was digested with *Bal* I. *Bal* I cuts mature Mu DNA at three sites (12), generating two larger internal fragments, A and B, and two smaller end fragments, C and D (see Fig. 4 for the *Bal* I cleavage map of Mu). The end fragments appeared fuzzy in this case because the cuts were close to the heterogeneous ends. The two internal fragments, A and B, were detected in all the lysogens but, as expected, new junction fragments were seen in each lysogen. In some cases, only one new fragment appeared; the other fragment was probably too large to be resolved from the largest internal fragment.

The schematic drawing in Fig. 1*B* shows the fragments expected from prophage λ as compared to circular and mature λ DNA. In λ, one of the internal fragments of the mature phage DNA contains the *att* site (fragment 2). Upon circularization, the end fragments will fuse and give rise to one new fragment

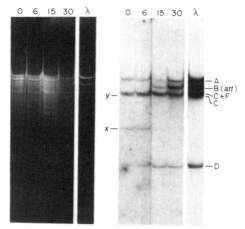

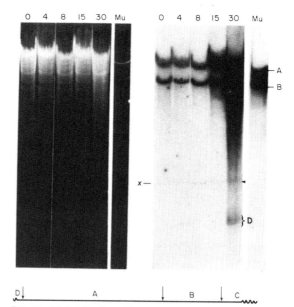

FIG. 3. Hybridization of fragments generated by *Bgl* II cleavage of the λ lysogen (BU851) DNA with ³²P-labeled λ DNA. The DNA was extracted before and after temperature-induction at the times indicated above each slot. Time 0 indicates time of shift to 44°. After 15 min at 44°, the culture was shifted to 37°. (*Left*) Ethidium bromide-stained gel; (*Right*) autoradiograph after blotting-hybridization. The *Bgl* II cleavage map of linear λ DNA is shown at the bottom. Fragment B contains the *att* site; the host–phage junction fragments are represented by x and y. Fragments E and F are not included.

(fragment 1 + 3). Upon integration, the fragment containing the *att* site will split and give rise to two new junction fragments (fragments x and y).

Excision of λ Prophage DNA. According to the well-established Campbell model, λ DNA is excised from the host chromosome upon induction of a normal λ prophage. To monitor this excision event, we extracted total DNA from a λ lysogen before and during temperature induction. The DNA was digested with restriction endonucleases, and after fractionation by gel electrophoresis the fragments were blotted and hybridized to ³²P-labeled λ DNA. As outlined (Fig. 1*B*), excision

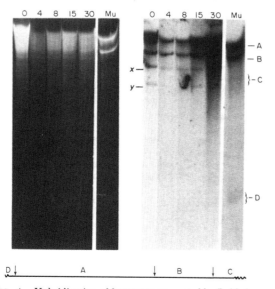

FIG. 4. Hybridization of fragments generated by *Bal* I cleavage of the Mu lysogen (BU563) DNA with ³²P-labeled Mu DNA. The DNA was extracted after temperature induction at the times indicated above each slot. Time 0 indicates time of shift to 44°. After 15 min, cultures were shifted to 37°. (*Left*) Ethidium bromide-stained gel; (*Right*) autoradiograph after blotting-hybridization.

FIG. 5. Hybridization of fragments generated by *Bal* I cleavage of the Mu lysogen (BU568) DNA with ³²P-labeled Mu DNA. The procedure was the same as described for Fig. 4. Only one host–phage junction fragment, x, is detected (arrow). (*Left*) Ethidium bromide-stained gel; (*Right*) autoradiograph.

of the prophage as a circular λ DNA molecule can be seen as the disappearance of the junction fragments and the appearance of the fragment containing the *att* site. Fig. 3 shows the results obtained after cleavage with the restriction enzyme *Bgl* II, which cuts mature linear λ into six fragments as indicated. Fragments C and F contain the cohesive or "sticky" ends, and fragment B contains the attachment site (13). Before induction, at time 0, the *att*-containing fragment B was absent and at least one new junction fragment, x, could be clearly seen. The other junction fragment, y, was probably the one just below the fusion fragment C + F. With time, the excision of λ DNA was observed as a disappearance of fragments x and y and the appearance of fragment B. Similar results were obtained with the restriction endonuclease *Eco*RI (data not shown). In both cases, disappearance of the junction fragments as well as appearance of the fragment containing the *att* site was seen 15 min after induction. This result is in agreement with the conclusions reached by Freifelder *et al.* with a different technique (14).

Fate of Prophage Mu DNA upon Induction. When a Mu *cts*62 lysogenic culture is temperature induced—i.e., the culture is transferred to 44° for 15 min and thereafter incubated at 37°—the phage begins to multiply and the cells are lysed. The total DNA was extracted from lysogenic cells before and at different times after induction. After digestion with the restriction endonuclease *Bal* I, the fragments were blotted and hybridized to denatured ³²P-labeled Mu DNA. Fig. 4 shows the ethidium bromide-stained gels and the corresponding autoradiographs of the fragments obtained after digestion of the DNA of induced cells. Fig. 5 shows the results obtained with another lysogen, BU568. As shown at the bottom of the figures, *Bal* I cut Mu DNA at three sites, giving rise to two larger internal fragments, A and B, and two smaller end fragments, C and D. The autoradiograph of strain BU563 before induction, time 0, showed two new fragments, labeled x and y (Fig. 4), but only one new fragment, x, was detectable in strain BU568 (Fig. 7). These fragments must be the junction fragments between prophage DNA and host DNA. It can be seen from Figs. 6 and

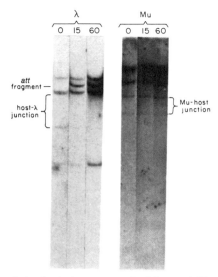

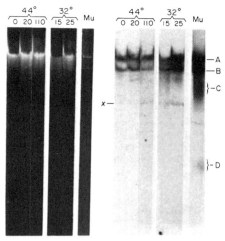

FIG. 7. Hybridization of fragments generated by *Bal* I cleavage of the Mu *cts Ats* lysogen (BU1216) DNA with ³²P-labeled Mu DNA. The procedure was the same as in Fig. 4, except that after 110 min at 44° one part of the culture was shifted to 32°. (*Left*) Ethidium bromide-stained gel; (*Right*) autoradiograph.

FIG. 6. Induction in the presence of nalidixic acid. The λ lysogen BU851 and the Mu lysogen BU563 were grown to a density of about 1×10^8 cells per ml. Nalidixic acid was added to a final concentration of 100 μg/ml, and the cultures were shifted to 44°; samples were taken at the times indicated and were treated as in Fig. 3 for λ and as in Fig. 4 for Mu. (*Left*) Autoradiograph of λ DNA samples after blotting-hybridization; (*Right*) autoradiograph of the Mu DNA samples after blotting-hybridization.

7 that the junction fragments remained intact after induction. Their intensity seemed to remain constant. When replication started, the internal fragments increased in intensity and a smear of hybridization appeared as a background. The junction fragments were seen distinctly at 15 min, when Mu DNA had certainly undergone a few rounds of replication. At later times, the fragments began to be covered by the hybridization background. However, the fragments were detectable at 30 min after induction. The background hybridization resulted from continuous integration of Mu DNA at different sites in the lytic cycle, giving rise to random new junction fragments. At the end of the lytic cycle, the mature fuzzy-end fragment D appeared as a consequence of the packaging of phage DNA (Fig. 5). The fact that the original junction fragments persist when replication is well under way can be interpreted to mean that the prophage genome is not excised upon induction. This interpretation would be complicated if the induction process of Mu were very asynchronous. In that case, a similar result might be obtained and the disappearance of the parental junction fragments might go undetected. The induction of prophage Mu, however, appeared to be highly the synchronous, as indicated by the rapid and complete lysis of the culture beginning at 45–50 min after the shift to 44° (data not shown). To further ensure against the possibility of asynchronous induction, we studied the fate of the junction fragments for long periods of time under inducing conditions when DNA synthesis is blocked.

The results obtained when a λ lysogen was temperature-induced in the presence of nalidixic acid (100 μg/ml, which inhibits DNA synthesis) are shown in Fig. 6 *left*. It can be seen that the fragment containing the λ *att* site (see above and Fig. 3) appeared 15 min after induction in the presence of nalidixic acid, and the host–λ junction fragments disappeared. In experiments with prophage Mu (Fig. 6 *right*), no change in the junction fragments was seen. The Mu–host junction fragments present in the uninduced lysogen persisted even after 1 hr at the inducing temperature. No indication of the appearance of

any new fragments or mature end fragments was seen under these conditions. Similar results were obtained when the Mu DNA replication was blocked by a phage mutation in gene *A*, which is required for Mu replication and integration (15, 16). The results obtained after induction of cells lysogenic for Mu *cts Ats* are shown in Fig. 7. This strain gave rise to one detectable junction fragment (labeled *x* in Fig. 7), which was distinguishable from the mature end fragments when digested with *Bal* I. This junction fragment persisted even 110 min after a temperature shift. When the culture was shifted to a permissive temperature, the junction fragment remained but an increase in the intensity of the internal fragments (A and B in Fig. 7) occurred about 25 min after the shift down.

DISCUSSION

The results presented in this paper indicate that bacteriophage Mu does not conform to the standard mode of integration-excision of temperate bacterial viruses. The behavior of prophage Mu upon induction is clearly different from that of prophage λ. According to the Campbell model, a seemingly simple recombinational event effectively reverses the process of λ integration, resulting in excision of λ DNA from the host chromosome (1).

We have shown here that excision of λ can be monitored *in vivo* by the DNA blotting–hybridization technique. In this technique, the viral DNA inserted in the host DNA is located by hybridization of ³²P-labeled viral DNA with the fragments generated from the total cellular DNA (5, 17). When prophage λ is derepressed, the junctions between phage and host sequences disappear and the original phage *att* site is restored. This process occurs even when DNA synthesis is inhibited. Our results are in agreement with the kinetics of λ excision reported by Freifelder *et al.* (14).

Our experiments on prophage Mu DNA show that the original junctions between prophage and host DNA persist after induction until late in the lytic cycle. The prophage–host junctions remain detectable at least up to 30 min after induction. These results imply that prophage DNA remains at its original location when the lytic cycle is well advanced and Mu DNA is actively replicating. When DNA synthesis is inhibited, the junctions of Mu prophage and host remain intact for long periods of incubation under conditions of prophage derepression. In the case of a Mu *cts Ats* mutant, no Mu replication is detected at the nonpermissive temperature. However, 25 min after a shift to permissive temperature, replication of Mu DNA is detected. These results confirm that the *A* gene product is required for normal Mu DNA replication.

Many copies of Mu DNA are known to be integrated at different sites in the host genome during the lytic cycle (2, 18). We find that by 30 min after prophage induction so many new junction fragments have been generated that a smear of hybridization activity is obtained on the autoradiographs. No Mu ends free of host sequences are detected. Toward the end of the lytic cycle the mature ends of Mu DNA begin to appear, indicating the beginning of the morphogenetic processes. If the original Mu–host junction fragments are cleaved after 30 min of induction, they would not be detectable because of the extensive hybridization background. A change in the junction fragments might occur if the prophage DNA is cut for packaging. Packaging of Mu DNA apparently occurs from maturation precursors that contain Mu DNA covalently linked to host DNA (19).

That Mu DNA does not appear to be excised upon prophage induction, and yet many copies of Mu DNA are inserted into the host genome, implies that prophage DNA remains at the original site. Therefore, we postulate that the Mu integrative precursor, the form of DNA that is inserted into the host DNA, is generated by replication of Mu DNA. This hypothesis is consistent with our observation that the parental Mu DNA after infection of host cells is not efficiently integrated into host DNA and thus must be replicated before integration (E. Ljungquist and A. I. Bukhari, unpublished data).

If Mu DNA replicates *in situ*, without having been excised, then the replication might be expected to proceed into the host sequences adjacent to the prophage DNA. In recent experiments by B. Waggoner and M. Pato (personal communication) and by us (unpublished data), no extensive amplification of the host sequences adjacent to the prophage could be detected after induction. These observations imply that a mechanism exists for the recognition of the specific Mu ends, such that replication does not penetrate the Mu–host junction. It should be noted that the heterogeneous host sequences at Mu ends are not inserted into the host chromosome during integration of Mu DNA after infection. Absence of replication of adjacent host sequences after prophage Mu induction suggests a mechanism by which the host sequences at the phage ends are left out during integration. If infecting phage DNA first replicates, leaving out the host sequences, the resulting integrative precursor will be a form devoid of host sequences. Such a form, however, has not been observed. It may be that the integrative precursor of Mu has a very short half-life and is quickly integrated or that the replication of Mu DNA is coupled to its integration.

We would like to point out that Mu integration after prophage induction is reminiscent of translocation of the transposable elements. The transposable elements can be excised at an apparently low frequency (10^{-5}–10^{-7}) from a specific site in a gene, and yet their transposition frequencies are higher by a factor of 10^3–10^4 (ref. 7). When reversion of mutations caused by the insertion of translocatable elements (or transposons) is examined, almost all of the revertants are found to have lost the transposon altogether (20, 21). Thus, excision of these elements does not generally lead to their in-

tegration. A similar phenomenon is seen in bacteriophage Mu. Prophage Mu under certain conditions (Mu *cts* prophages carrying the *X* mutation) can be excised at a frequency of 10^{-5}–10^{-7} and is lost from the cells (22, 23). As the experiments reported in this paper clearly indicate, this type of Mu excision does not occur efficiently upon induction. Thus, although a mechanism for prophage Mu excision exists, this mechanism does not appear to be involved during the normal Mu life cycle. In view of the mechanistic similarity, we propose that Mu is a representative of transposable elements. These elements constitute a class of insertion elements, different from most temperate phages, in which replication of the inserting molecule is a necessary step in the process of its integration.

We thank Linda Ambrosio for technical assistance. We also thank R. J. Roberts and Phyllis Myers for providing the enzymes *Eco*RI and *Bgl* II, and for helping in the preparation of *Bal* I. This work was supported by grants from the National Science Foundation (PCM 76-13460) and the National Cystic Fibrosis Foundation. A.I.B. holds a Career Development Award of the National Institutes of Health (5K04 GM 00127-01).

1. Campbell, A. (1976) *Sci. Am.* **235**, 102–113.
2. Bukhari, A. I. (1976) *Annu. Rev. Genet.* **10**, 389–411.
3. Bukhari, A. I. & Zipser, D. (1972) *Nature New Biol.* **236**, 240–243.
4. Daniell, E., Roberts, R. & Abelson, J. (1972) *J. Mol. Biol.* **69**, 1–8.
5. Bukhari, A. I., Froshauer, S. & Botchan, M. (1976) *Nature* **264**, 580–583.
6. Daniell, E., Kohne, D. & Abelson, J. (1975) *J. Virol.* **15**, 237–239.
7. Bukhari, A. I., Shapiro, J. & Adhya, S., eds. (1977) *DNA Insertion Elements, Plasmids and Episomes* (Cold Spring Harbor Laboratory, Cold Spring Harbor, NY).
8. Bukhari, A. I. & Allet, B. (1975) *Virology* **63**, 30–39.
9. Bukhari, A. I. & Ljungquist, E. (1977) in *DNA Insertion Elements, Plasmids and Episomes*, eds. Bukhari, A. I., Shapiro, J. & Adhya, S. (Cold Spring Harbor Laboratory, Cold Spring Harbor, NY), Appendix C8.
10. Sharp, P. A., Sugden, B. & Sambrook, J. (1973) *Biochemistry* **12**, 3055–3063.
11. Southern, E. M. (1975) *J. Mol. Biol.* **98**, 503–517.
12. Kahmann, R., Kamp, D. & Zipser, D. (1977) in *DNA Insertion Elements, Plasmids and Episomes*, eds. Bukhari, A. I., Shapiro, J. & Adhya, S. (Cold Spring Harbor Laboratory, Cold Spring Harbor, NY), 335–339.
13. Pirrotta, V. (1976) *Nucleic Acids Res.* **3**, 1747–1760.
14. Freifelder, D., Krischner, I., Goldstein, R. & Baron, N. (1973) *J. Mol. Biol.* **74**, 703–720.
15. Howe, M. M. & Bade, E. G. (1975) *Science* **190**, 624–632.
16. Wijffelman, C., Gassler, M., Stevens, W. F. & van de Putte, P. (1974) *Mol. Gen. Genet.* **131**, 85–96.
17. Botchan, M., Topp, W. & Sambrook, J. (1976) *Cell* **9**, 269–287.
18. Razzaki, T. & Bukhari, A. I. (1975) *J. Bacteriol.* **122**, 437–442.
19. Bukhari, A. I. & Taylor, A. L. (1975) *Proc. Natl. Acad. Sci. USA* **72**, 4399–4403.
20. Berg, D. E. (1977) in *DNA Insertion Elements, Plasmids and Episomes*, eds. Bukhari, A. I., Shapiro, J. & Adhya, S. (Cold Spring Harbor Laboratory, Cold Spring Harbor, NY), 205–212.
21. Botstein, D. & Kleckner, N. (1977) in *DNA Insertion Elements, Plasmids and Episomes*, eds. Bukhari, A. I., Shapiro, J. & Adhya, S. (Cold Spring Harbor Laboratory, Cold Spring Harbor, NY), 185–203.
22. Bukhari, A. I. (1975) *J. Mol. Biol.* **96**, 87–99.
23. Bukhari, A. I. & Froshauer, S. (1977) *Gene*, in press.

Bacteriophage Mu-1:
A Tool to Transpose and to Localize Bacterial Genes

Michel Faelen

UNAM, Instituto de Investigaciones Biomedicas
Apartado Postal 70228, Mexico 20 DF

AND

Ariane Toussaint

Département de Biologie Moléculaire, Laboratoire de Génétique
Université Libre de Bruxelles, 1640 Rhode-St-Genese, Belgium

(Received 27 October 1975, and in revised form 2 March 1976)

In a previous publication (Faelen *et al.*, 1975), it was predicted that the temperate phage Mu-1 would mediate transposition of bacterial genes. Here we show that this is indeed the case. By mating either induced F′ strains (which carry a thermoinducible Mu prophage in the bacterial chromosome), or sensitive F′ infected with Mu, with appropriate recipients, we were able to isolate new F′ episomes which carry various lengths of bacterial DNA. The frequency of transposition of a given marker can be as high as 10^{-4}. The episomes which carry the transposed DNA always carry Mu as well. When this is coupled with the fact that induction or infection with Mu is necessary for transposition to occur, it is probable that both Mu enzymes and Mu DNA are required by the transposition process. Episomes selected for the presence of a given marker were analyzed for the presence of unselected markers. It was found that: (1) only markers linked to the selected marker can be cotransposed with it; (2) when two markers are simultaneously transposed, all markers lying between them on the chromosome are also transposed; (3) the frequency at which an unselected marker is cotransposed is in some way related to the distance between that marker and the selected marker; (4) the transposition process occurs in both Rec⁺ and Rec⁻ strains. Mu-mediated transposition offers a new way to isolate F′ episomes and to localize and order bacterial genes as far apart as three minutes.

1. Introduction

The temperate phage Mu-1 can integrate at random into the chromosome of its host *Escherichia coli* K12 (Taylor, 1963; Bukhari & Zipser, 1972; Daniell *et al.*, 1972). The prophage is linearly inserted in the host DNA (Martuscelli *et al.*, 1971; Hsu & Davidson, 1972) such that the prophage and vegetative genetic maps are identical. Both possible orientations with respect to the Taylor–Trotter map are found to occur. A defined region of the Mu genome is used for integration (Boram & Abelson, 1973; Bukhari & Metalay, 1973; Howe, 1973; Wijffelman *et al.*, 1973; Faelen *et al.*, 1975). This attachment site might be generated by the association of two specific sequences lying near the extremities of Mu vegetative DNA near the variable ends.

These ends consist of short, random bacterial sequences (about 50 base-pairs on one end, ∼1000 base-pairs on the other) which are not present in the Mu prophage

(Bade *et al.*, 1973; Daniell *et al.*, 1975; Hsu & Davidson, 1974; Allet & Bukhari, 1975) and must therefore be lost at one step of the integration process. Synthesis of at least part of the integration enzymes is controlled by the phage.

It was previously shown that Mu can mediate integration of circular, non-Mu DNA (Faelen *et al.*, 1971; Van de Putte & Gruijthuijsen, 1972; Toussaint & Faelen, 1973; Faelen *et al.*, 1975). Both Mu gene expression and Mu DNA are required in this process. Circular DNA is integrated in any circular permutation and flanked by two entire Mu genomes of identical orientation. After integration by infection with Mu, the Mu–DNA–Mu structure is found at random in the bacterial chromosome. However, after induction of a Mu lysogen, the Mu–DNA–Mu structure is, in the large majority of cases, located at the site previously occupied by the original single Mu prophage. This suggests that upon *in situ* duplication, the prophage provides the site for integration of the non-Mu DNA (Faelen *et al.*, 1975).

It is also known that, after induction or infection with Mu, closed circles are formed which contain bacterial sequences covalently linked to complete Mu genome(s) (Schröder *et al.*, 1974; Waggoner *et al.*, 1974) .In addition, Mu can reintegrate at random during its lytic cycle (Schröder & Van de Putte, 1974; Razzaki & Bukhari, 1975). Since integrated Mu DNA can stimulate integration of circular, non-Mu DNA (Faelen *et al.*, 1975), one might expect the Mu–bacterial DNA circles to be able to integrate at random into the bacterial chromosome or into an episome; this would lead to transposition of the bacterial sequences carried by those circles to any location in either the chromosome or the episome.

In this paper, we show that (1) transposition of chromosomal genes to an F′ factor does indeed occur for all chromosomal markers tested, either after infection with Mu or after induction of a Mu prophage; (2) transposition is always accompanied by transfer of at least one and most probably two entire Mu genomes to the F′ episome; (3) cotransposition of genes linked to the selected marker occurs with frequencies correlated with the distances between the selected and unselected markers. This method provides a way to introduce any bacterial marker into any F or other transmissible episome. Moreover this method can be used to localize and order bacterial genes and possesses advantages compared to P1 transduction in that it allows mapping over distances of more than three minutes of the *E. coli* K12 map and occurs even in Rec⁻ strains.

2. Materials and Methods

(a) *Bacteriophages*

Muc⁺	Taylor (1963) *via* Starlinger
Muc*ts*62	Howe (1973)
Muc*ts*62 Sam*1004*	Howe (1973)
f₂	Loeb (1960)
φ80*vir*	Maurer-Richelle

(b) *Bacterial strains*

All strains are listed in Table 1.

(c) *Media*

Bacterial matings were performed in L-broth (10 g Tryptone, 5 g yeast extract, 5 g NaCl per litre double-distilled water; adjusted to pH 7·0). Phages were assayed on A medium (Fry, 1959). Minimal media were either 132 (Glansdorff, 1965: 7 g K₂HPO₄;

TABLE 1

Bacterial strains

Name	Genotype	Origin
C600	F⁻ thr⁻ leu⁻ tonA lacY supE gal⁻ thi⁻	Campbell (1961)
594	F⁻ gal1 gal2 Str^R	Appleyard (1954)
KMBL241	F⁻ thr⁻ leu⁻ tonA tsx lac⁻ cysB pyrF recA thyA argG ilv⁻ thi⁻	Van de Putte et al. (1966)
KMBL241(Muc⁺)	same as KMBL241 and (Muc⁺)	derived from KMBL241
KMBL241(Muc⁺) Spc^R Mu^R	same as KMBL241 and (Muc⁺) Spc^R and Mu^R	derived from KMBL241 (Muc⁺)
RH2603	lac⁻ gal⁻ trp : : (− Mucts62) recA argG ilv⁻ thi⁻/Flac	This work
RH2603(Muc⁺)	same as RH2603 and (Muc⁺)	derived from RH2603
594 recA glt : : (Mucts62S⁻)/Flac†	gal1 gal2 recA glt : : (−Mucts62 Sam1004)/Flac	Faelen et al. (1975)
PA3731 recA Rif^R (Muc⁺)	F⁻ thr⁻ leu⁻ gal6 recA argH Rif^R pur D (Muc⁺)	Toussaint & Lecocq (1972)
PA2004 recA (Muc⁺)	F⁻ thr⁻ leu⁻ gal6 recA pyrB (Muc⁺)	This work
KMBL1666	F⁻ lac⁻ tonB trp : : (−Muc⁺ ΔS-β) pyrF thyA thi⁻	Wijffelman et al. (1973)
N100 serA : : (Muc⁺)	F⁻ gal⁻ serA Str^R	This work
AB1181	F⁻ argA thi⁻	Maas
JM125 Val^R	F⁻ leu⁻ thyA lysA : : (Muc⁻) (λc⁺) Val^R	Martuscelli
RH3004	F⁻ cysC Val^R	This work
RH3023	Δlac pro, galE galX thi⁻ recA Val^R/FlacZΔM15 proA⁺, B⁺ ‡	This work

† Flac comes from 200PS/Flac (Cuzin & Jacob, 1967).

‡ FlacZΔM15 pro A⁺, B⁺ comes from CSH22 (Miller, 1972).

: : means that Mu is integrated within the gene that precedes the symbol (Howe & Bade, 1975).

− Mucts62 means that the c end of the Mu prophage is encountered first in the clockwise direction (0 min → 90 min) on the E. coli genetic map (Howe & Bade, 1975).

3 g KH_2PO_4; 1 g $(NH_4)_2SO_4$; 0·1 g $MgSO_4$; 0·5 g $C_6H_5Na_3O_7$; $MnSO_4$, 10^{-6} M; $Fe(SO_4)$· 3 H_2O, 10^{-6} M; thiamine hydrochloride, 1 ml of a 1 mg/ml solution; agar, 15 g per litre distilled water), or M9 (Miller, 1972: 5·8 g Na_2HPO_4; 3 g KH_2PO_4; 0·5 g NH_4Cl; 1 g NaCl; agar, 12 g per litre distilled water). The following were added as indicated: vitamin-free Casamino acids at a final concn of 0·2%, L-amino acids at 40 μg/ml, nucleosides and nucleotides at 50 μg/ml, carbon source at 0·2% or 1%, spectinomycin at 100 μg/ml. Lac types were tested on EMBlac (Lederberg, 1947) or McConkey lac plates.

Tryptone, yeast-extract, EMB agar, McConkey agar and agar were obtained from Difco.

(d) Mating procedure

Cultures of the donor and recipient strains were grown overnight at 30°C or 37°C in L-broth. They were diluted 100-fold in fresh L-broth, grown with aeration at 37°C to exponential growth ($\sim 2 \times 10^8$ cells/ml) and viable counts were determined on complete medium. Samples of each culture were mixed, and further incubated in a 25-ml Erlenmeyer flask, without shaking, for 2 h at 37°C or 42°C. Mating mixtures were centrifuged (5 min at 5000 revs/min), resuspended in 1 ml $MgSO_4$ (10 mM) and portions of them spread on selective media. As controls, 0·5 ml of each parent and 0·5 ml L-broth were treated in the same way. Plates were incubated for 48 h at 37°C. Under these conditions, the frequency of transfer of the Flac episome reaches 50%.

When a large number of episomes had to be transferred to the same recipient, plates of selective medium were seeded with 10^7 to 10^8 recipient cells, and log-phase cultures of the various donors were spotted on the F^- lawn.

This procedure was employed in the transfer of episomes to Rec^+ recipients.

(e) Analysis of sexductants

Sexductants were purified on the appropriate selective medium. Isolated colonies were tested for their Lac type by stabbing on EMBlac or McConkey lac. Sensitivity to phage f2 was determined by growing isolated colonies in L-broth, spreading samples on A medium and subsequently spotting with an f2 lysate (10^9 to 10^{10} phage/ml).

Episomes were examined for the presence of non-selected markers by replica plating, when the recipient strain carried the suitable markers, or by transferring the episome to a recipient auxotrophic for the marker to be tested.

Segregation of translocated markers was analyzed after transfer of the F' to a Rec^+ recipient. After purification on selective medium, auxotrophic segregants were isolated by stabbing on selective and non-selective media, and were subsequently checked for sensitivity to phage f2 and, when it was possible, for the retention of the lac genes on the episome.

The tonB character was tested by spotting with $\phi80$ vir; tonB were resistant to this phage while $tonB^+$ were sensitive.

3. Results

(a) Transposition after thermal induction of Mucts prophage

The occurrence of transposition was tested in the following way: F' strains, carrying a thermoinducible Mu prophage on the bacterial chromosome, were mated with polyauxotrophic recipients. Sexductants which had lost one of their auxotrophic requirements were selected. Such clones were expected to contain an F' episome which had gained the corresponding wild-type allele from the donor. The matings were performed at 37°C, a temperature which only partially induces the Mucts62 prophage and results in little bacterial death (Faelen et al., 1975).

In all these experiments, the donor and recipient strains were recA to avoid chromosome mobilization by the F', and the recipients were always lysogenic for Muc^+ to prevent zygotic induction when the F' DNA carried a Mu prophage.

(i) Transposition of markers adjacent to the Mucts prophage

We first looked for transposition of chromosomal genes lying close to a Mu*cts* prophage, into an F*lac* episome, in a partially induced lysogen. The donor, RH2603, was *recA*, *trp*::(-Mu*cts62*) *pyrF⁺*/F*lac*; the prophage in the *trp* operon was flanked by the *cysB⁺* and *pyrF⁺* genes on one side and by *tonB⁺* on the other (see Fig. 1). After growth at 37°C (as described in Material and Methods) RH2063 was mated with KMBL241 (Mu*c⁺*) whose relevant characters are *lac⁻*, *trp⁺*, *pyrF*, *recA*, *thyA*. Pyr⁺ Trp⁺ clones were selected by plating the mating mixture on minimal medium containing Casamino acids and thymine. A similar experiment was run in parallel, using RH2603 (Mu*c⁺*) as donor. This strain contained the Mu*cts62* prophage but was no longer thermoinducible due to the dominance of the *c⁺* allele. As shown in Table 2, Pyr⁺ Trp⁺ clones were indeed recovered but only when the prophage of the donor was thermoinducible, indicating that Mu functions were necessary for this process. Ten clones were purified and analyzed. All of them produced both Mu*c⁺* and Mu*cts62* phages. They were all sensitive to the male-specific phage, f2, as expected if they contained an episome; six were Lac⁺, and simultaneously transferred *lac⁺*, *pyrF⁺* and Mu*cts62* but not *tonB* to an F⁻ *lac⁻*, *pyrF*, *tonB* recipient. The other four, which were Lac⁻, transferred *pyrF⁺* and Mu*cts62* but not *tonB⁺* to the same recipient. In cases where it was tested, Pyr⁺ clones were always also *cysB⁺* (the marker located between *pyrF* and Mu*cts62* in the donor). Upon curing the episome (by selecting for resistance to f2), the simultaneous loss of *pyrF⁺*, *cysB⁺*, Mu*cts62* and *lac⁺* (when it was present) was observed.

These results are consistent with the idea that the Pyr⁺ clones contain an F*lac*

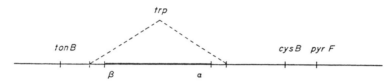

FIG. 1. Diagrammatic representation of the *tonB-pyrF* region of strain RH2603. α and β represent the α and β part of the Mu chromosome (see Howe & Bade, 1975).

TABLE 2

Transposition of pyrF⁺ *after partial induction of a* trp::(Mucts62)/Flac *strain*

Mating	Frequency of Pyr⁺ Trp⁺
KMBL241 (Mu*c⁺*)	3×10^{-8}
RH2603	$< 3.5 \times 10^{-8}$
RH2603 (Mu*c⁺*)	$< 1.5 \times 10^{-8}$
RH2603 × KMBL241 (Mu*c⁺*)	6.6×10^{-5}
RH2603 (Mu*c⁺*) × KMBL241 (Mu*c⁺*)	5×10^{-8}

Matings were performed as described in Materials and Methods. Pyr⁺ Trp⁺ clones were selected on glucose-containing minimal medium supplemented with Casamino acids and thymine.

Frequencies of transposition are given as the ratios of

$$\frac{\text{number of Pyr}^+\text{Trp}^+ \text{ clones/ml}}{\text{input F}'/\text{ml}}.$$

episome which carries the $pyrF^+$ gene, the $cysB^+$ gene and Mu$cts62$, but not $tonB^+$, and that the insertion of this new DNA into the episome sometimes inactivates its *lac* operon. The fact that the $tonB^+$ marker is not found on the episome suggests that markers lying on both sides of the induced prophage cannot be transposed at once. On the other hand, the fact that Pyr$^+$ clones were found to carry the $cysB^+$ gene shows that the whole region between the Mu prophage and the selected marker had been transposed. Five Pyr$^+$ episomes, three Lac$^+$ and two Lac$^-$, were transferred to a Rec$^+$, Pyr$^-$ recipient, where they were found to segregate, respectively, to Lac$^+$, Pyr$^-$, (Mu$cts62$) and Lac$^-$, Pyr$^-$, (Mu$cts62$) at frequencies of 1 to 10%. In those cases where it was tested, $cysB^+$ was found to segregate simultaneously with $pyrF^+$. All Pyr$^-$ segregants remained f2^s and when the episome was removed by curing, Mu$cts62$ and lac^+ (when it was present) were lost. These results are consistent with the hypothesis that the transposed piece of DNA is surrounded by two Mu$cts62$ genomes in the same orientation, thereby providing homology for Rec-mediated reciprocal recombination which can excise the transposed fragment and one Mu, leaving one Mu on the episome (see Fig. 2).

Transposition of other markers was investigated by using a different set of strains. The donor 594 *recA glt*::(-Mu$cts62$S$^-$)/*Flac* has its Mu prophage located between the $argH^+$-$purD^+$ region and that of $pyrB^+$ (see Fig. 3); it was mated at 37°C with an *argH purD* (Muc$^+$) (PA3731) and a *pyrB* (Muc$^+$) (PA2004) recipient and Arg$^+$ Glt$^+$,

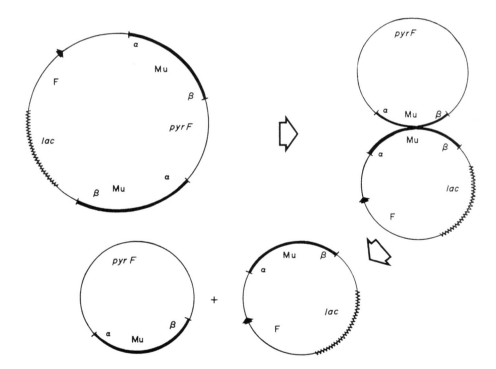

Fig. 2. A way to explain high segregation of the $pyrF^+$ marker from the *Flac* (Mu) $pyrF^+$ episomes in Rec$^+$ strains.

By Rec-mediated reciprocal recombination between the 2 Mu prophages which surround the $pyrF^+$ region, it is possible to generate an F'lac(Mu) and a Mu-$pyrF^+$ circle.

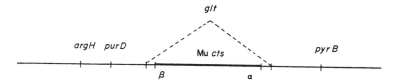

FIG. 3. Diagrammatic representation of the *argH-pyrB* region of strain 594 *recA glt* : : (Mu*cts62 S⁻*)/*Flac*.

TABLE 3

Transposition of argH⁺, purD⁺ *and* pyrB⁺ *after partial induction of 594*
recA glt : : *Mu*cts62 S⁻/*F*lac

	Frequency of transposition		
	Arg⁺	Pur⁺	Pyr⁺
594 *recA glt* : : (Mu*cts62 S⁻*)/*Flac*	$<7\times10^{-8}$	$<7\times10^{-8}$	—
PA3731 *recA* (Mu*c⁺*)	$<7\times10^{-8}$	$<7\times10^{-8}$	—
PA2004 *recA* (Mu*c⁺*)	—	—	2×10^{-6}
594 *recA glt* : : (Mu*cts62 S⁻*)/*Flac* × PA3731 *recA* (Mu*c⁺*)	$1\cdot7\times10^{-5}$	2×10^{-5}	—
594 *recA glt* : : (Mu*cts62 S⁻*)/*Flac* × PA2004 *recA* (Mu*c⁺*)	—	—	2×10^{-5}

The cultures were grown at 37°C as described in Materials and Methods to a cell density of $\sim 2\times10^8$ bacteria/ml. One sample of the donor was mated with PA3731 *recA* (Mu*c⁺*), a second sample with PA2004 *recA* (Mu*c⁺*).

Arg⁺ Glt⁺, Pur⁺ Glt⁺ and Pyr⁺ Glt⁺ were selected on minimal glucose medium containing threonine, leucine, purines and uracil; or threonine, leucine, arginine and uracil, or threonine, leucine and purines, respectively.

Frequencies of transposition are given as the ratio of:

$$\frac{\text{number of transposants/ml}}{\text{input F′/ml}}.$$

Pur⁺ Glt⁺ or Pyr⁺ Glt⁺ sexductants were selected. Those were recovered at frequencies of $1\cdot7\times10^{-5}$, 2×10^{-5} and 2×10^{-5}, respectively (see Table 3). This shows that markers lying on both sides of the Mu prophage can be independently transposed to the episome. Here again, all the episomes which carry a transposed DNA fragment carry at least one and probably two Mu*cts62S⁻*, and this can hardly result from infection of the F⁻ because the presence of the *S⁻* mutation prevents phage from being liberated by the donor.

(ii) *Transposition of markers distant from the* Mu*cts prophage*

Since Mu reintegrates at random during its lytic cycle, it was conceivable that even markers not located near the prophage could be transposed. The mating 594 *recA glt*::(Mu*cts62S⁻*)/*Flac* × KMBL241 (Mu*c⁺*), where KMBL241 (Mu*c⁺*) is *thr, leu, pyrF, his, thyA*, allowed us to select for Thr⁺ Glt⁺, Leu⁺ Glt⁺, Pur⁺ Glt⁺, His⁺ Glt⁺ or Thy⁺ Glt⁺ sexductants, respectively. As shown in Table 4, all these markers could be transposed, with frequencies ranging from 10^{-6} to 10^{-5}. Several clones of each type were purified and analyzed. Most of them (~90%) were Lac⁺. Among 14 Leu⁺ clones tested one was also Thr⁺ but none was either Pyr⁺, Thy⁺ or His⁺. Of 16 His⁺ clones tested for unselected markers, none was Thr⁺, Leu⁺, Pyr⁺ or Thy⁺. None of 13 Thy⁺ clones tested was Thr⁺, Leu⁺, Pyr⁺ or His⁺. This demonstrates

Table 4

Transposition of thr$^+$, leu$^+$, his$^+$, pyrF$^+$, *and* thyA$^+$ *after partial induction of*
594 recA glt::(Mucts62 S$^-$)/Flac

	Transposed marker	Frequency of transposition
594 *recA glt* :: (Mu*cts62 S$^-$*)/Flac × KMBL241 (Muc$^+$)	*pyrF$^+$*	$1\cdot2 \times 10^{-6}$
	thyA$^+$	2×10^{-5}
	his$^+$	$7\cdot4 \times 10^{-6}$
	thr$^+$†	$\sim 1\cdot3 \times 10^{-5}$
	leu$^+$	8×10^{-6}

Experimental conditions are those described in the legend to Table 3.

Selection medium was minimal glucose containing required amino acids and nucleotides except for uracil, thymine, histidine, threonine or leucine, respectively.

Frequencies of transposition of the various genes (except *thr*) are given by the ratio of

$$\frac{\text{number of transposants/ml}}{\text{input F}'/\text{ml}}.$$

† The frequency of reversion of the *thr$^-$* mutation in KMBL241 (Muc$^+$) is $\sim 2 \times 10^{-4}$. 16 Thr$^+$ Glt$^+$ clones isolated from the mating mixture were purified. Only one was found to have received the Flac. The frequency shown above was obtained by dividing the calculated frequency by 16.

that transposition of very long stretches of DNA does not occur frequently, or that when it does, physical limitations prevent its appearance. In addition it is clear that two or more short pieces (3 to 4 min) are not frequently transposed simultaneously to the episome.

The experiments described above were performed under conditions where the donor prophage is certainly not completely induced, since upon growth at 37°C approximately 50% of the cells survive and only about 10^{-2} phage per bacterium are liberated. The frequencies of transposition should increase under conditions where the donor is completely induced. Recently these experiments were repeated, growing the donors at 30°C or 37°C, and mating the cells at 42°C. We used Mu-resistant recipients or included 10^{-2} M-citrate in the selection medium to avoid killing of the F$^-$ by the large amount of phage produced by the induced donor. Under these conditions, the frequencies of transposition of markers either linked or unlinked to the prophage can be as high as 10^{-4} (results not shown).

(b) *Ordering bacterial genes by Mu-mediated transposition*

To estimate the maximal length of a DNA segment that can be transposed, we looked for cotransfer by Flac of several genes surrounding the *thyA* (54·3 min) locus; *cysC* (62·5 min), *argA* (53·6 min), *lysA* (54·7 min) and *serA* (56 min). RH2603 was mated with KMBL241 (Muc$^+$) at 37°C and Thy$^+$ Trp$^+$ sexductants were selected and purified. Out of 80 Thy$^+$ isolated, 55 which were still transferable were used as donors in further matings with *cysC*, *argA*, *lysA* and *serA* recipients, with subsequent testing for Cys$^+$, Arg$^+$, Lys$^+$ or Ser$^+$ transfer. As shown in Figure 4, the four genes tested are frequently cotransposed with *thyA$^+$*, and the two distal markers, *cysC$^+$* and *serA$^+$*, were jointly transposed on 16% of the episomes tested. Thus DNA pieces of more than 3·5 min of the chromosome can be transposed together. None of the 55 clones analyzed was *thyA$^+$* only, showing that very short DNA pieces are rarely transposed. Figure 4 also shows that there is a variation in the frequencies of co-transposition with $thyA^+$: $lysA^+$ (98%) > $argA^+$ (78%) > $serA^+$ (38%) > $cysC^+$ (32%). In Table 5 one can see that some $thyA^+$ are only $lysA^+$ or $argA^+$, but that all the $thyA^+$, $serA^+$ are $lysA^+$, all $thyA^+$, $cysC^+$ are also $argA^+$, and all $thyA^+$, $serA^+$, $cysC^+$ are also $lysA^+$ and $argA^+$. This shows that when two genes are cotransposed, all

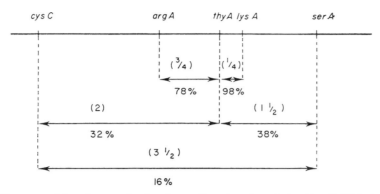

FIG. 4. Cotransposition frequencies in the *cysC-serA* region of the *E. coli* K12 chromosome, obtained upon partial induction of a Mu*cts* prophage inserted in the *trp* operon. Numbers in parentheses give the distances between the different markers (in min) of the *E. coli* K12 map, according to Taylor & Trotter (1972).

TABLE 5

Presence of the unselected markers cysC⁺, argA⁺, lysA⁺ and serA⁺ in the F′thyA⁺ transposants resulting from mating RH2603 with KMBL241 (Muc⁺)

Unselected markers present on the F′ *thy⁺* episomes					Number of transposants with that genotype	Length of the transposed DNA (min) of the *E. coli* K12 map
$cysC^+$	$argA^+$	$thyA^+$	$lysA^+$	$serA^+$		
		+			0	—
		+	+		7	$\frac{1}{4}$
		+	+	+	5	$1\frac{1}{2}$
	+	+			1	$\frac{3}{4}$
	+	+	+		17	1
	+	+	+	+	7	$2\frac{1}{4}$
+	+	+			0	2
+	+	+	+		9	$2\frac{1}{4}$
+	+	+	+	+	9	$3\frac{1}{2}$

% of cotransposition: $thyA$-$lysA$: $\dfrac{7+5+17+7+9+9}{55}$; 98%

$thyA$-$serA$: $\dfrac{5+7+9}{55}$; 38%

$thyA$-$argA$: $\dfrac{1+17+7+9+9}{55}$; 78%

$thyA$-$cysC$: $\dfrac{9+9}{55}$; 32%

Distances between the different markers were taken from Taylor & Trotter (1972).

55 Thy⁺ Trp⁺ clones isolated after mating RH2603 with KMBL241 (Muc⁺) were used for further matings with *cysC*, *argA*, *lysA* and *serA* recipients. + indicates the ability to transfer the mentioned marker, thus the presence of that marker on the F′*thy⁺* episome.

A blank indicates that the relevant marker is absent from the F′*thy⁺* episome.

genes lying between them are simultaneously translocated. Taking this into consideration, one can go backwards, and consider that since

(1) only $argA^+$ or $lysA^+$ can be found alone with $thyA^+$

(2) $thyA^+$, $serA^+$ are $lysA^+$ and sometimes $argA^+$ or $argA^+$, $cysC^+$

(3) $thyA^+$, $cysC^+$ are $argA^+$ and sometimes $lysA^+$ or $lysA^+$, $serA^+$,

the relative order of the markers on the chromosome must be cys-$argA$-$thyA$-$lysA$-$serA$, an order consistent with results obtained by other methods (Taylor & Trotter, 1972).

(c) *Transposition and mapping after infection of sensitive cells with Mu*

Since it is known that a marker need not reside near a Mu prophage as a prerequisite for its transposition, and that hybrid Mu–bacterial DNA circles are formed upon infection with Mu, investigations were conducted to see whether transposition occurs after Mu infection as well.

The donor RH3023 ($recA$/$Flac\varDelta Z$ pro^+) was infected with Muc$^+$ (m.o.i. ~ 0·5) and mated with KMBL241 (Muc$^+$), pyr, thy, $recA$, Spc^R, Mu^R (Mu^R to avoid killing of the recipient). As a control, the uninfected F′ was mated with the same recipient. Pyr$^+$ Spc^R and Thy$^+$ Spc^R sexductants were selected and purified for further analysis. Results summarized in Table 6 clearly show that transfer of either $pyrF^+$ or $thyA^+$ occurred only when the donor was infected before mating, and at frequencies similar to those observed upon partial induction of a Mu$cts62$ lysogen. Analysis of the Pyr$^+$ clones reveals that they propagate an $Flac\varDelta Z$ pro^+ that now carries $pyrF^+$ and in some cases $cysB^+$ (86%), or $cysB^+trp^+$ (41%), or $cysB^+$ trp^+ $tonB^+$ (34%) (see Fig. 5). All have also acquired Muc$^+$. The transposed regions are most likely always enclosed by Mu prophage on both sides and these prophages have similar orientations since upon transfer to a Rec$^+$ recipient it was found that a Pyr$^+$ Cys$^+$ Trp$^+$ (Muc$^+$) episome segregated to Pyr$^-$ Cys$^-$ Trp$^-$ TonB$^-$ (Muc$^+$) at a frequency of ~1%. Here again, the order of the genes which can be deduced from cotransposition data is consistent with the order found by other methods (Taylor & Trotter, 1972).

It should be mentioned that the analysis was limited to markers lying on one side of the $pyrF$ gene only, for technical reasons. The finding that cotransposition of $pyrF$ and $tonB$ occurs here, but not upon induction of a Mu$cts62$ inserted in the trp operon,

TABLE 6

Transposition of pyrF$^+$ *and* thyA$^+$ *to Flac after infection with Muc$^+$*

	Frequency of transposition	
	Pyr$^+$	Thy$^+$
RH3023	$<10^{-8}$	$<10^{-8}$
RH3023	$<10^{-7}$	$<10^{-7}$
KMBL241(Muc$^+$) Mu^R Spc^R	$1·2\times10^{-8}$	$<10^{-8}$
RH3023 × KMBL241(Muc$^+$) Mu^R Spc^R	$<10^{-8}$	$1·2\times10^{-8}$
(RH3023 + Muc$^+$) × KMBL241 (Muc$^+$) Mu^R Spc^R	5×10^{-5}	$1·4\times10^{-5}$

The donor and recipient were grown to ~ 2×10^8 bacteria/ml at 37°C as described in Materials and Methods. The donor was infected with Muc$^+$ (m.o.i. = 0·5) in L-broth + 50 mM·Ca^{2+}. After 15-min adsorption at 37°C, it was mated with the recipient for 2 h at 37°C.

Pyr$^+$ Spc^R and Thy$^+$ Spc^R clones were selected on minimum glucose medium containing Casamino acids, thymine and spectinomycin or Casamino acids, uracil and spectinomycin.

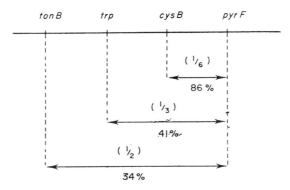

FIG. 5. Cotransposition frequencies in the *tonB-pyrF* region of *E. coli* K12 chromosome obtained upon infection with Mu*c*+.

Number in parentheses give the distances between the different markers (in min) according to the Taylor & Trotter map (1972).

is consistent with the idea that the presence of a Mu prophage between two markers prevents them from being cotransposed by the prophage.

4. Discussion

The experiments described in this paper clearly demonstrate that phage Mu efficiently mediates transposition of bacterial genes. Mu gene expression is required in this process since transposition occurs in induced Mu lysogens or after infection of sensitive cells but not in uninduced or uninfected bacteria. Mu DNA also directly participates in the transposition process since in all observed cases the transposed DNA fragment is linked to Mu DNA. Our results suggest that the transposed piece is probably surrounded by two entire prophages which have the same orientation. This has been confirmed recently by heteroduplex analysis of an RP4 plasmid which had received a bacterial DNA fragment including the structural gene for the *supIII* suppressor through Mu-mediated transposition (Van Montagu, unpublished data).

Two models, which we proposed previously to account for Mu-mediated integration of non-Mu DNA, provide alternative mechanisms for Mu-mediated transposition. In the first model (Toussaint & Faelen, 1973), a Mu dimer which carries two functional Mu attachment sites is formed by association of two vegetative genomes. If one assumes, as proposed by Waggoner *et al.* (1974), that pure bacterial DNA circles can be formed under the influence of Mu enzymes, the dimer could connect such a circle to an F*lac* episome, by recombination of one Mu attachment site with the circle, and the other attachment site with the F*lac*. This will generate the F*lac* (Mu-bacterial DNA-Mu) we observed (see Fig. 6). This mechanism does not involve formation of hybrid Mu-bacterial DNA rings. In the second model, which led us to predict the occurrence of Mu-mediated transposition (Faelen *et al.*, 1975) the Mu dimer is generated by duplication *in situ* of a Mu prophage; hybrid Mu-bacterial DNA circles are excised directly by recombination of one attachment site of the dimer with adjacent bacterial DNA. The hybrid circle, after one more duplication *in situ* of the integrated Mu, is reintegrated at a random location into the F*lac*, generating the F*lac* (Mu-bacterial DNA-Mu) structure (see Fig. 7). According to this model, hybrid Mu-bacterial DNA rings are involved. It is clear that more experimental data are needed to determine whether hybrid Mu-bacterial DNA circles are intermediates

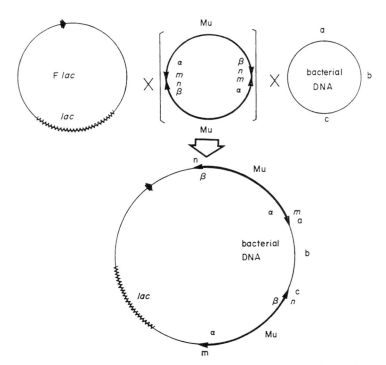

Fig. 6. The Mu dimer could be formed by association of 2 vegetative Mu DNA through their opposite ends. The dimer has been put in brackets because its exact structure cannot be inferred at this point. It could be a covalently closed circle, resulting from fusion of the m with the n sites and release of the variables ends; it could also be some kind of open circle if release of the variables ends, and connection of the m and n sequences with other random sequences (here the bacterial DNA circle on one hand, the F*lac* DNA on the other hand), occur at once. A new F′ episome which carries a Mu–bacterial DNA–Mu structure is formed through recombination of one Mu attachment site of the dimer with any site of the F*lac*, and the second attachment site with any site of the bacterial DNA ring. a, b, c are sequences in the bacterial chromosome.

in the transposition process, and whether transposition uses a normal step or a parallel pathway in Mu lytic cycle.

Mu-mediated transposition offers exciting possibilities in the construction and transference of novel genetic elements. We have successfully transposed the thr^+, leu^+, $pyrF^+$, $thyA^+$, his^+, $argH^+$, $purD^+$ and $pyrB^+$ genes onto an F*lac* episome. The process is, however, neither limited to the episome nor the markers used in this work; the method has also been used to move the $pyrF^+$ gene to the R64 plasmid (Faelen & Alfaro, unpublished results), the *aroE-cap* region on the KLF125 episome (Biemans & Cabezon, unpublished results) and the *supE* suppressor to the RP4 plasmid (Van Montagu, personal communication). As bacterial genes can be easily transposed onto plasmids which can then be transferred to other bacterial species, Mu-mediated transposition can be used to transfer *E. coli* genes into other species. On the other hand, it should be possible to extend the transposition method to other species in which Mu can integrate and establish immunity.

Selection of F′ episomes by Mu-mediated transposition has several advantages over methods described earlier (for a review see Low, 1972). An F′ carrying a given marker can be recovered at a frequency of $\sim 10^{-4}$, while by other methods it never exceeds 10^{-5}. Many F′s can be easily derived from the same F$^+$ strain, while other methods

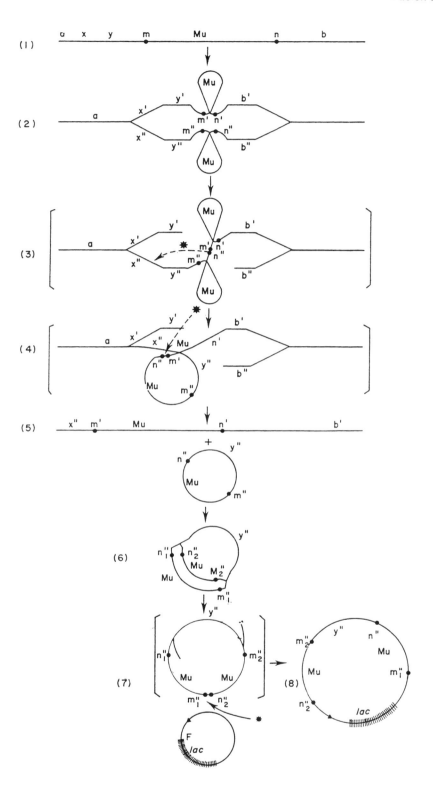

Figure 7. See page 522 for caption.

require a different Hfr for each F'. Any marker can be put on any F' episome, regardless of its location.

When first isolated, some of our episomes were unstable. Some of the selected sexductants are resistant to male-specific phage f2 and unable to further transfer their episome; part of the *Flac* DNA seems to be lost since many of these episomes are also Lac⁻, maybe as a result of Mu integration which can generate deletions (Howe & Bukhari, personal communication; Cabezon *et al.*, 1975). This situation is very similar to that described by Low (1968) who found that some of the sexductants isolated by mating Hfr strains with *recA* recipients are resistant to male-specific phage MS2, but also to female-specific phage ϕII, suggesting that they have received only part of the F genetic material.

The fact that all the episomes isolated by Mu-mediated transposition carry Mu, segregate and lose the transposed DNA piece in Rec⁺ hosts might be a handicap. However in many instances this problem can be overcome by using Mu lysogenic and Rec⁻ recipients (which will prevent both zygotic induction and segregation).

The procedure for genetic mapping which is being developed from this work presents several advantages over the method using a generalized transducing phage such as P1. It allows one to handle distances at least twice as long as those transduced by P1; this is obviously useful in the localization and ordering of genes in regions of the chromosome where there are only a few markers available. Moreover mapping can be performed in Rec⁻ as well as in Rec⁺ strains. The frequencies of cotransposition are in some way related to the distance between the cotransposed markers. Cotransposition frequency must depend on the frequencies at which Mu can integrate between two markers; the closer they are, the less chance there is to separate them by the prophage and consequently they exhibit a higher cotransposition frequency. The cotransposition frequency might also depend on the size distribution

---

FIG. 7. a, x, y, b: sequences in the bacterial chromosome; m, n: Mu sequences lying at the extremities of the prophage; *: sites of action for the Mu integration enzymes.

(1) Shows a Mu prophage inserted into the bacterial chromosomes between genes y and b. In (2) the region has been partially replicated (by either the bacterial or the phage replication functions) and 2 copies of the Mu genome now exist in *trans*. In (3) the Mu integration enzymes disconnect the prophage sequences m' and n" from the adjacent bacterial sequences y' and b", resulting in the appearance of a complete Mu attachment site m'n". Integrative recombination catalyzed by the Mu integration enzymes can now take place between this site and any other region of the bacterial chromosomes. In (4) this recombination occurs at a site between x" and y", and in (5) region y" is excised from the bacterial chromosome to form a Mu–y" circular DNA. Steps (1) to (4) may be the normal Mu excision pathway. In (6) replication originating within the prophage inserted in the Mu–y" ring again gives rise to 2 copies of the Mu genome in *trans*; and as in (3) the Mu integration enzymes disconnect the phage sequences m_1'' and n_2'' from the adjacent bacterial DNA to form a functional attachment site m_1'', n_2''. Integrative recombination between this site and a random site on an *Flac* episome leads in (8) to the formation of a hybrid *Flac*–Mu–y"–Mu episome.

This mechanism differs from our previous model (Faelen *et al.*, 1975) in that no enzymes are required for the transposition, apart from those responsible for the chromosomal insertion of the Mu prophage after infection. This modification was suggested by the finding (Allet & Bukhari, 1975) that a short variable DNA region is present at the immunity end of the Mu vegetative DNA, and that this extra fragment is lost upon integration. Thus during lysogenization by phage Mu, both extremities of the Mu genome (m and n in this Figure) are disconnected from the variable ends and become sealed to new bacterial sequences (as in steps (3), (4) and (7) of this Figure). Steps (3), (4) and (7) are put in brackets to indicate that m and n must not necessarily become covalently linked to each other; after disconnection from the bacterial chromosome (or from the variable ends during the lysogenization process) m and n may directly attach to new bacterial sequences. One implication of this hypothesis is that tandem Mu prophages or circles of pure Mu DNA would rarely if ever be formed.

of the bacterial DNA sequences in the hybrid Mu–bacterial DNA circles formed during the Mu lytic cycle. Waggoner *et al.* (1974) found that circles ranging from 61 to 82 kilobases somewhat predominate in the population of circles formed which ranged from ~37 kilobases (equivalent to one Mu length) to ~157 kilobases. At present the mapping function with regard to genetic distance cannot be defined since this must await a better understanding of the transposition mechanism.

We thank R. Thomas, J. Kuhn and C. Evans for their critical reading of this manuscript, and J. Martuscelli for giving Michel Faelen the opportunity to perform part of this work in his laboratory.

Work at Rhode St Genèse was carried out under a contract Euratom-ULB no. 099-72-1BIAB and under agreement between the Belgian Government and the Université libre de Bruxelles concerning priority action for collective basic research.

REFERENCES

Allet, B. & Bukhari, A. I. (1975). *J. Mol. Biol.* **92**, 529–540.

Appleyard, R. K. (1954), *Genetics*, **39**, 429–439.

Bade, E. G., Delius, H. & Schröder, W. (1973). *Fed. Proc. Fed. Amer. Soc. Exp. Biol.* **33**, 1487.

Boram, W. & Abelson, J. (1973). *Virology*, **54**, 102–108.

Bukhari, A. I. & Metlay M. (1973). *Virology*, **54**, 109–116.

Bukhari, A. I. & Zipser, D. (1972). *Nature New Biol.* **236**, 240–243.

Cabezon, T., Faelen, M., Dewilde, M., Bollen, A. & Thomas, R., (1975). *Mol. Gen. Genet.* **137**, 125–129.

Campbell, A. (1961). *Virology*, **14**, 22–32.

Cuzin, F. & Jacob, F. (1967). *Ann. Inst. Pasteur (Paris)*, **112**, 397–399.

Daniell, E., Roberts, R. & Abelson, J. (1972). *J. Mol. Biol.* **69**, 1–8.

Daniell, E., Kohne, D. E. & Abelson, J. (1975). *J. Virol.* **15**, 739–743.

Faelen, M. & Toussaint, A. (1973). *Virology*, **54**, 117–124.

Faelen, M., Toussaint, A. & Couturier, M. (1971). *Mol. Gen. Genet.* **113**, 367–370.

Faelen, M., Toussaint, A. & de LaFonteyne, J. (1975). *J. Bacteriol.* **121**, 873–882.

Fry, B. A. (1959). *J. Gen. Microbiol.* **21**, 676–689.

Glansdorff, N. (1965). *Genetics*, **51**, 167–179.

Howe, M. (1973). *Virology*, **54**, 93–101.

Howe, M. & Bade, E. G. (1975). *Science*, **190**, 624–632.

Hsu, M. T. & Davidson, N. (1972). *Proc. Nat. Acad. Sci., U.S.A.* **69**, 2823–2827.

Lederberg, J. (1947). *Genetics*, **32**, 505–525.

Loeb, T. (1960). *Science*, **131**, 932–933.

Low, B. (1968). *Proc. Nat. Acad. Sci., U.S.A.* **60**, 160–167.

Low, B. (1972). *Bacteriol. Rev.* **36**, 587–607.

Martuscelli, J. A., Taylor, A. L., Cummings, D. J., Chapman, V. A., De Long, S. S. & Canedo, L. (1971). *J. Virol.* **8**, 551–563.

Miller, J. H. (1972). *Experiments in Molecular Genetics*, Cold Spring Harbor Laboratory, New York.

Razzaki, T. & Bukhari, A. I. (1975). *J. Bacteriol.* **122**, 437–442.

Schröder, W. & Van de Putte, P. (1974). *Mol. Gen. Genet.* **130**, 99–104.

Schröder, W., Bade, E. G. & Delius, H. (1974). *Virology*, **60**, 534–542.

Taylor, A. L. (1963). *Proc. Nat. Acad. Sci., U.S.A.* **50**, 1043–1051.

Taylor, A. L. & Trotter, C. (1972). *Bacteriol. Rev.* **36**, 504–524.

Toussaint, A. & Faelen, M. (1973). *Nature New Biol.* **242**, 1–4.

Toussaint, A. & Lecocq, J. P. (1972). *Mol. Gen. Genet.* **129**, 185–186.

Van de Putte, P. & Gruijthuijsen, M. (1972). *Mol. Gen. Genet.* **118**, 173–183.

Van de Putte, P., Zwenk, H. & Rörsch, A. (1966). *Mutat. Res.* **3**, 381–393.

Waggoner, P. T., Gonzales, N. S. & Taylor, A. L. (1974). *Proc. Nat. Acad. Sci., U.S.A.* **71**, 1255–1259.

Wijffelman, K., Westmaas, G. & Van de Putte, P. (1973). *Virology*, **54**, 125–134.

Unit 10 / Transposable Elements

Hedges and Jacob 1974

1. What is meant by compatibility groups?

2. Previous work from the authors' group had shown that ampicillin resistance could be transferred from the plasmid RP4 to R64. To show the generality of this effect, they crossed ampicillin resistance from RP4 onto another plasmid. Describe this cross in detail and indicate the selections used.

3. What experiment showed that plasmids that had received ampicillin resistance through transposition could also donate it by transposition?

4. What physical experiment gave evidence of transposition?

Kleckner et al. 1975

5. Explain the meaning of the structures seen in Plate I on page 451. How were they generated? What do they reveal about the tet^r transposon?

6. Which experiment shows that the tet^r element, which was acquired by phage P22 from an R factor, can undergo further transposition out of the P22 genome?

7. Which experiments showed that in the Tet^r auxotrophs, the tet^r element appears to be inserted into the gene encoding the lost function?

8. Explain the polarity effect of insertion of the tet^r element.

Heffron et al. 1979

9. Explain the concept and utility of using *Eco*RI inserts into Tn*3*.

10. How was a transposase gene identified?

11. Describe the *tnpR* gene and the effects of mutations in it.

12. Describe the essential sites on the DNA of Tn*3*.

13. Explain the significance of the structure displayed in Figure 7 on page 470.

Bender and Kleckner 1986

14. How were the transposons used in the experiment marked?

15. What was the starting donor transposon, and how was it generated?

16. Describe the λ phage used as the vector in this experiment.

17. Explain the basic experiment that showed that transposition products contain information from both parental strands.

18. How did the authors show that the blue and white portions of each sectored colony arose from the same original Tn*10* transposition event?

Boeke et al. 1985

19. What are Ty elements of yeast?

20. Explain the nature of the donor vector and the recipient for the Ty transposition.

21. How could the authors tell whether addition of galactose increased transposition of the plasmid-borne Ty element?

22. How could the authors show that transposition occurred via an RNA intermediate?

23. The plasmid-borne Ty element contained a partial deletion of the 5′ δ sequence, which was replaced by the *GAL1* promoter. However, the transposed copy had regenerated both intact δs. How did this occur?

Section III

Questions, Answers, Problems, & Scenarios

Introduction

This section serves as a companion to the text and is in two parts. In the first part, "Unit Questions, Answers, & Problems," the questions posed at the end of each unit are restated and answered. At the end of each set of unit questions and answers, an additional set of problems based on the reading(s) is provided to challenge the student.

The second part of this section, "Scenarios," compiles more involved problems that also make use of the material in the units. Usually, these problems are in the form of interesting scenarios loosely based on different historic or mythological events, plots from classic and science fiction films, or quest themes of the "Mission Impossible" type. They require the students to transpose the concepts they learned from reading the papers into an analogous situation and then to solve the problem. For example, the students are asked to move genes around on a map where the loci have been named for characters and landmarks from the "Wizard of Oz" or to determine the identity of amino acids in a future "Star Wars" genetic code.

The solutions to both the Unit Problems and the Scenarios, along with methods for working them out, are provided in the companion *Solutions Manual and Workbook.*

Unit Questions, Answers, & Problems

Benzer 1961

1. Explain the *r*II system and the host range of *r*II mutants compared to wild-type T4 phage.

   Answer: The *r*II mutants of phage T4 cause rapid lysis that results in large plaques on *E. coli* B, as compared with the small, irregular plaques of the wild-type T4 phage. However, on *E. coli* K (short for *E. coli* K12 [λ]), *r*II mutants do not plate at all, whereas wild-type T4 phage still make small, irregular plaques. Therefore, we can recognize *r*II mutants by virtue of their large plaques on *E. coli* B and their failure to plate on *E. coli* K. In addition, we can select for wild-type phage by requiring plaques on *E. coli* K.

2. What does Benzer mean by topology and topography?

   Answer: The topology of a genetic region is the manner in which its parts are interconnected. The topography is the local differences in the properties of its parts. Thus, it was found that topologically, the gene consists of a linear array of subelements. Examining the topography is asking whether each of these subelements behaves the same in different tests, for example, mutability tests.

3. What is the concept behind deletion mapping?

   Answer: The key concept behind deletion mapping is that the wild-type allele for the mutation being mapped is either present in the partially deleted genetic segment or it is not. This allows recombination tests to be carried out as basic "yes–no" tests and avoids the comparison of different frequencies. Mutations are positioned as being on either one side or the other side of a deletion and can thus be assigned to a specific segment of a gene very rapidly. The only limit to the resolution of the mapping is the reversion rate of the mutation being mapped. If recombinants can be detected above the reversion rate of the mutation, then the corresponding wild-type allele has not been deleted.

4. What does Benzer mean when he says: "It is more meaningful to say that a mutation does recombine with a deletion or another mutation than to say that it does not."?

   Answer: This is really a restatement of the basic experimental principle that a positive result is more important than a negative result. Thus, if a recombination test gives a positive result, then the two mutations must be at different sites. However, if one fails to find recombination, it may mean that the two mutations are at different sites or it may mean that they are too close to yield recombinants at the level of resolution provided by the test. Perhaps if a test had a tenfold greater resolution, some of the mutations that appeared not to recombine would now show recombination. It should be pointed out here that Benzer was speaking generally. In his case, he had good experimental evidence that failure to recombine meant that two mutations were indeed at the same site. This is because the lowest level of recombination he ever saw was still three orders of magnitude above the detection level of his tests. This strongly indicated that the lowest observed level of recombination was that of neighboring nucleotides.

5. Why did Benzer choose mutations that reverted at very low levels (versus ones that did not revert at all) for his topography study?

   Answer: Benzer's objective was to look at the topography as revealed by the mutability of different sites. He wanted to examine point mutations. If he took mutations that did not revert at all, then he would expect to have many deletion mutations in his collection. By insisting on seeing some reversion rate, he could eliminate all but the tiniest of deletions. On the other hand, if the reversion rate was too high, then the resolution of his mapping tests would be insufficient to allow the separation of each mutation into a distinct site. Therefore, he chose to analyze mutations that reverted at low, but nonzero, rates.

6. Explain Figure 2 on page 20. Exactly how did Benzer perform this test? (You will have to understand the host range of *r*II mutants in order to answer this question.)

   Answer: The figure portrays the results of recombination tests with different point mutations and deletions. Recall that in order to cross mutations, one must use *E. coli* B, since *r*II mutants can grow on *E. coli* B and thus have an opportunity to recombine. Therefore, a drop of a lysate of each mutant phage to be tested is added to a sample of *E. coli* B in a test tube. After allowing a few minutes for adsorption to occur, a drop of the mixture is spotted with a paper strip onto a lawn of *E. coli* K spread over a nutrient plate. Wild-type recombinant phage will lyse the lawn of *E. coli* K and result in a darkening of the patch, as seen in the photograph. Look at the blanks at the bottom of the photograph, where no phage were seeded. In addition, the blank row at the far right, where individual mutants were plated, shows several isolated plaques. Note that the top horizontal row of labels designates the deletions that are mapped in Figure 1a and the left vertical row of labels designates the point mutations. The results of this test allow the easy placement of each mutation into a deletion segment. For example, mutation 548 fails to recombine with deletion PB242 but does recombine with deletion A105. Therefore, it is assigned to segment A5 on the map shown in Figure 1a.

7. What exactly is Benzer trying to show in Figure 5 on page 23?

   Answer: This figure compares the order of mutations deduced by traditional recombination tests with the order found by deletion mapping. Rows A and C give two different sets of results using point mutation x point mutation crosses, and the center row, B, gives the deletion map. It can be seen that the order of the mutations is the same in all cases. The distances between the mutations can only be estimated, but, considering this, the correlation between the distances shown in row A and row B is remarkably good. The estimates of distances for the point mutation x point mutation test are based on recombination frequency and for the deletion map on the size of the interval as estimated by the number of mutational sites within each interval.

8. Explain how the diagram in Figure 6 on page 25 was constructed. What does each square mean? What is the overall purpose of making this diagram?

   Answer: This figure represents an extraordinary amount of work. Each mutation was first mapped into one of 64 deletion segments and then tested for recombination with other mutations mapping in the same segment. This separated the collection of 1612 mutations into 251 distinct sites. Each occurrence of a mutation is indicated by a box. When more than one occurrence of a mutation was found at the same site, the boxes are drawn on top of one another. In some cases, when a very large number of occurrences are detected, as in the case of the two biggest hotspots, one has to draw a treelike structure to accommodate each box. The purpose of the figure is to represent the mutability of each site on a single diagram, which corresponds to a topographical map of the *r*II region.

9. What is a Poisson distribution? Give its formula and explain what each symbol means and when this formula is applicable.

   Answer: The Poisson distribution describes the distribution of random events. It can be expressed by the following formula:

   $$P_n = \frac{m^n e^{-m}}{n!}$$

   Here, P = the probability, or fraction, of events occurring n times and m = the mean number of events per interval. The formula is applicable when each event has an equal probability of occurring.

10. How did Benzer use the Poisson distribution to determine hotspots?

    Answer: First, Benzer calculated the Poisson distribution for all of the sites with 1 or 2 occurrences (see answer to Question 11 for details). Since these sites were the most frequent, he made the assumption that these sites were equally mutable and then determined the expected number of sites with 3, 4, 5, etc., occurrences. In other words, if all of the sites in this collection were equally mutable, then based on the number of sites with 1 and 2 occurrences, he would expect to find a certain number of sites with 3, 4, 5, etc., occurrences. After plotting this distribution, he designated any sites with more occurrences than expected (those falling outside the distribution) as being hotspots. This can be seen in Figure 7 on page 26.

11. Describe specifically how Benzer calculated the number of sites in the *r*II region with 0 occurrence of mutations. (Be careful, this is a little tricky.) Find the total number of sites that are part of the Poisson distribution.

Answer: Although Benzer had collected 1612 mutations, some of these were in hotspot sites. Therefore, he did not know the total number of sites in the Poisson distribution, since this covers only those sites with the same mutability. Specifically, he did not know the number of sites in this particular collection with 0 occurrence. However, by designating the sites with 1 and 2 occurrences as being part of the Poisson distribution, he could take the ratio of these sites. Let's look again at the Poisson formula and its expansion (see Unit 1, page 16). If we take the ratio of sites with 2 occurrences to those with 1 occurrence, we have:

$$\frac{\text{number of sites with 2 occurrences}}{\text{number of sites with 1 occurrence}} = \frac{P_2 \times \text{total sites}}{P_1 \times \text{total sites}} = \frac{P_2}{P_1}$$

We can also calculate from the Poisson formula that $P_2/P_1 = m/2$, since

$$\frac{m^2 e^{-m}/2!}{m e^{-m}} = \frac{m}{2}$$

In fact, you can see that $P_3/P_2 = m/3$ and, in general, $P_n/P_{n-1} = m/n$.

From Figure 7 on page 26, we can see that the number of sites with 1 occurrence is 117 and the number of sites with 2 occurrences is 53. Thus,

$$\frac{P_2}{P_1} = \frac{\text{sites with 2 occurrences}}{\text{sites with 1 occurrence}} = \frac{53}{117} = \frac{m}{2}$$

From this, $m/2 = .453$ and $m = \textbf{.906}$. Having m, one can calculate each point using the same ratio method. Thus, P_1/P_0 = sites with 1 occurrence/sites with 0 occurrence = m/n or 117/sites with 0 occurrence = .906/1 and, rearranging, 117/.906 = **sites with 0 occurrence = 129**. Using these ratios, see if you can calculate the number of sites with 3, 4, and 5 occurrences. Check your answer with the points on Figure 7.

There are several ways to calculate the total number of sites. The easiest is to use the formula $P_0 = e^{-m}$. Since in this case $m = .906$, then $P_0 = e^{-m} = .404$. Since $P_0 \times$ total number of sites = number of sites with 0 occurrence, then .404 × total number of sites = 129 and, rearranging, 129/.404 = **total number of sites = 319**.

12. How does Benzer, in the discussion, arrive at 14 different rates for base substitutions without even taking into account the effects of neighboring base pairs?

Answer: Benzer wanted to account for differences in apparent or observed mutation rates based on the different sensitivity of specific amino acids in the protein to replacement. Thus, as we shall see in detail in Unit 8, certain positions in a protein are more sensitive to substitution than others. Let's consider an A·T base pair. This can mutate in three different ways: A to G, A to C, and A to T. Let's pretend that at every A·T base pair, the three rates (call them x, y, and z) for each of these three changes are the same. For example, the rate x for the A to G change is the same everywhere. Thus, the total observed rate of mutation at each A·T base pair would be the sum of the rates x, y, and z, or rate $(r) = x + y + z$. However, at some of the A·T base pairs, only one of the three possible changes would result in an amino acid difference that would register as a mutant. At these sites, the rate would only be x or y or z. At other sites, only two of the changes would register as a mutant. At these sites, the rate would be $x + y$ or $x + z$ or $y + z$. With this in mind, we can ask how many combinations of different rates are there? This problem can be solved by assigning either a 0 or a 1 to x, y, and z and asking for the total number of different combinations. The actual number is 8 (see if you can list all of the combinations). However, one of the combinations is where x, y, and z have each been assigned a 0, which represents no change at all. Thus, we can arrive at 7 different rates of observed change at an A·T base pair and, by the same process, 7 different rates for a G·C base pair. The conclusion is that one can account for as many as 14 different observed rates of mutation.

It is interesting to note that these 14 rates are the observed rates of mutants with severely altered proteins. They do not represent 14 different rates of mutation on the DNA. In the strictest sense, if the above considerations were the only factors responsible for different observed rates of appearance of mutants, then Benzer would not have been measuring the topography of the gene (difference in mutability) at all, but rather the sensitivity of different parts of the rII protein to substitution!

SAMPLE PROBLEMS

To solve problems using the Poisson distribution there are two important distinctions to keep in mind. First, it is essential to understand what events or occurrences are being distributed among what intervals or sites. In Benzer's case, mutations were being distributed among mutational sites. Second, it is crucial to be able to distinguish between **probability (or fraction)** and the **expected number of events**. The formula for the Poisson distribution relates to the fraction of events, or the probability of a certain number of events, occurring within a specific interval. Thus, in Benzer's case, the Poisson distribution could predict the **fraction of the total sites** with 1 occurrence, 2 occurrences, etc. To find the expected **number of sites** with 1 occurrence, 2 occurrences, etc., it is necessary to multiply the fraction, or probability, by the total number of intervals or sites. If there are 300 mutational sites and the fraction of sites with 1 occurrence is 0.1, then we would expect to find 30 sites with 1 occurrence, since we would multiply the fraction, 0.1, by the total number of sites, 300. The following two solved problems illustrate some of these principles. Understanding the concepts in these sample problems should help you to solve the set of problems that follow, some of which provide challenging applications of the Poisson distribution.

Sample 1 A test tube contains a certain number of bacterial virus particles in a liquid buffer. Equal fractions of the liquid in the tube are pipetted into 200 smaller test tubes and the virus particles counted. No virus particles were found in 60 of the 200 test tubes. Using the Poisson distribution, calculate the number of test tubes that had exactly 2 virus particles.

Solution: First, let's establish what is being distributed among what intervals or sites. It is clear from the question that virus particles are being distributed among different test tubes. Since the distribution of virus particles among the tubes should be random, we can apply the Poisson distribution using the formula:

$$P_n = \frac{m^n e^{-m}}{n!}$$

where P = the probability that any interval will have n events and m = the mean number of events per interval. Because we are given the total number of intervals, or test tubes in this case, which is 200, and also the number of test tubes with 0 virus particles, 60, we can easily calculate the fraction, or P_0, of tubes that had 0 virus particles as $60/200 = 0.3$.

Having calculated that $P_0 = 0.3$ and knowing from the Poisson equation that $P_0 = e^{-m}$, then $e^{-m} = 0.3$. Since $\ln e^{-m} = -m$, then

$$\ln P_0 = -m = \ln(0.3) = -1.2, \text{ and } \textbf{m = 1.2}.$$

Having calculated m, we can easily find the number of tubes with only 2 virus particles. Since the fraction of tubes with only 2 particles is P_2, and $m = 1.2$ and $e^{-m} = 0.3$, then

$$P_2 = m^2 e^{-m}/2! = 1.44 \times 0.3/2 = \textbf{0.216 (= fraction of tubes)}$$

Note that 0.216 is the fraction of sites with 2 occurrences, or the fraction of test tubes with 2 virus particles. In order to find the number of test tubes with 2 particles, we have to multiply this fraction by the total number of test tubes, which is 200. Thus,

$$\text{Total tubes} \times P_2 = 200 \times .216 = 43.2, \text{ or rounded off} = \textbf{43 (= number of tubes)}$$

Sample 2 Suppose you analyzed a large number of mutations and found that out of a total of 900 possible sites, 50 sites had 3 occurrences of mutations and 150 had 2 occurrences. Using the Poisson distribution formula,

$$\textbf{\textit{P}}_n = \frac{m^n e^{-m}}{n!}$$

calculate:

a. the number of sites with 0 occurrence
b. the number of sites with 1 occurrence.

Solution: Here, we have a collection of mutations that are distributed among a group of sites, analogous to the situation that Benzer analyzed. The first step in solving this problem is to determine m for the distribution that has the sites with 0, 1, 2, and 3 occurrences. To do this, we employ the ratio of the number of sites with 3 occurrences to the number of sites with 2 occurrences, since we are given these numbers. Thus,

$$\frac{\text{number of sites with 3 occurrences}}{\text{number of sites with 2 occurrences}} = \frac{50}{150} = \frac{P_3 \times \text{total sites}}{P_2 \times \text{total sites}} = \frac{P_3}{P_2}$$

Since, as shown in the answer to Question 11 above, $P_3/P_2 = m/3$, then $50/150$ (or $1/3$) $= m/3$ and $\textbf{m = 1}$.

We note that by the same ratio as above, the number of sites with 2 occurrences divided by the number of sites with 1 occurrence $= P_2/P_1 = m/2$. Thus,

$$\frac{m}{2} = \frac{1}{2} = \frac{150}{\text{number of sites with 1 occurrence}}$$

and the **number of sites with 1 occurrence = 300.**

Since $P_1/P_0 = m$, the same process as described above yields the **number of sites with 0 occurrence = 300.** (Note, when $m = 1$, $P_0 = P_1$.)

This problem contains a trap that must be avoided. After we determined m, we could have calculated P_0 as $e^{-1} = .3678$ and then multiplied it by the total number of sites to get the number of sites with 0 occurrence. However, if we multiplied this number by 900, we would get 331 instead of the 300 calculated above! How can we explain this discrepancy? The trap is that although we make the assumption that the sites with a low number of occurrences are part of a random distribution, the total of 900 sites may include sites that are hotspots and thus not part of the random distribution. These sites cannot be included as part of the total number of sites for calculations of fractions for the Poisson distribution. In fact, even though we are given the total of 900 sites, we do not really know the number of sites that are part of the distribution. Thus, we need to rely on the ratio trick mentioned in the answer to Question 11 above, since taking a ratio of two points cancels out the exponential term and taking a ratio of two adjacent points results in a simple ratio of m. Thus,

$$\frac{P_n}{P_{n-1}} = \frac{m}{n}$$

For example, $P_3/P_2 = m/3$, $P_4/P_3 = m/4$, etc.

PROBLEMS

1. A tube contains a certain number of β-galactosidase molecules in a liquid buffer. Equal fractions of the liquid in the tube are pipetted into 1000 separate smaller test tubes and the number of β-galactosidase molecules determined by fluoroscopic methods. No β-galactosidase molecules were found in 400 of the test tubes. Assuming that the molecules were randomly distributed among the tubes, calculate the number of test tubes containing 1, 2, 3, and 4 molecules.

2. **(A)** Suppose you are determining the distribution of nonsense mutations in order to determine whether a particular group of sites are underrepresented (coldspots) or overrepresented (hotspots). You have 100 different nonsense sites in the gene you are studying and you have collected 400 mutations. You find that 15 sites have 6 occurrences of mutations and 15 other sites have 5 occurrences of mutations. You decide that these sites are part of the normal category of sites and that you will determine whether any of the other sites are hot or cold relative to these sites. Use the Poisson distribution to determine:

   a. m for the distribution
   b. the expected number of sites with 0 occurrence
   c. the expected number of sites with 9 occurrences.

   If you found a site with 14 occurrences of mutations in this collection, would you consider it a hotspot?

   (B) Suppose as in Problem 2A you are determining the distribution of nonsense mutations. You have 90 different nonsense sites in the gene you are studying and you have collected 360 mutations. You find that 14 sites have 5 occurrences of mutations and 14 other sites have 4 occurrences of mutations. You decide that these sites are part of the normal category of sites and that you will determine whether any of the other sites are hot or cold relative to these sites. Use the Poisson distribution to determine:

   a. m for the distribution
   b. the expected number of sites with 0 occurrence
   c. the expected number of sites with 10 occurrences.

If you found a site with 12 occurrences of mutations in this collection, would you consider it a hotspot?

(C) Suppose as in Problem 2A you are determining the distribution of nonsense mutations. You have 95 different nonsense sites in the gene you are studying and you have collected 380 mutations. You find that 16 sites have 5 occurrences of mutations and 16 other sites have 4 occurrences of mutations. You decide that these sites are part of the normal category of sites and that you will determine whether any of the other sites are hot or cold relative to these sites. Use the Poisson distribution to determine:

a. m for the distribution
b. the expected number of sites with 0 occurrence
c. the expected number of sites with 11 occurrences.

If you found a site with 13 occurrences of mutations in this collection, would you consider it a hotspot?

3. **(A)** Suppose you characterized a large number of independent deletions entering gene X from one side and ending somewhere within the gene. The gene consists of 1200 base pairs and has been divided into 15-base-pair intervals by a set of point mutations that occur at regular points in the sequence. After mapping 225 deletions, you find that one of the intervals contains 14 deletion endpoints. Does this represent a hotspot for deletion endpoints? Let's say that if the expectation of finding one interval in this gene with 14 or more deletions is less than 1 in 1000, then we would consider the observed interval a deletion endpoint hotspot. Calculate the mean, m, for the Poisson distribution that describes the deletions that end randomly in the gene. Show all work and logic.

(B) Suppose as in Problem 3A you characterized a large number of independent deletions entering gene X from one side and ending somewhere within the gene. After mapping 200 deletions, you find that one of the intervals contains 12 deletion endpoints. Does this represent a hotspot for deletion endpoints? Let's say that if the expectation of finding one interval in this gene with 12 or more deletions is less than 1 in 1000, then we would consider the observed interval a deletion endpoint hotspot. Calculate the mean, m, for the Poisson distribution that describes the deletions that end randomly in the gene. Show all work and logic.

(C) Suppose as in Problem 3A you characterized a large number of independent deletions entering gene X from one side and ending somewhere within the gene. After mapping 300 deletions, you find that one of the intervals contains 15 deletion endpoints. Does this represent a hotspot for deletion endpoints? Let's say that if the expectation of finding one interval in this gene with 15 or more deletions is less than 1 in 1000, then we would consider the observed interval a deletion endpoint hotspot. Calculate the mean, m, for the Poisson distribution that describes the deletions that end randomly in the gene. Show all work and logic.

4. **(A)** You have collected 700 mutations in the *lacI* gene, which you know has 350 mutational sites. You know that some of these sites are hotspots. You observe that 60 sites in the gene have 2 occurrences of mutations and 20 sites have 3 occurrences. You decide that these sites with 2 and 3 occurrences are part of the normal category of sites and will determine whether

any of the other sites are hotspots relative to these sites. Use the Poisson distribution to determine:

a. m for the distribution
b. the expected number of sites with 1 occurrence
c. the number of sites in the gene that are **not** hotspots (in other words, normal) based on the assumption that the sites with 2 and 3 occurrences are normal sites.

The formula for the Poisson distribution and several values of e^{-m} are given below.

$$P_n = \frac{m^n e^{-m}}{n!}$$

Values of m	Values of e^{-m}	Values of m	Values of e^{-m}
0.1	0.9	1.2	0.30
0.2	0.82	1.4	0.25
0.3	0.74	1.6	0.2
0.4	0.67	1.8	0.16
0.5	0.60	2.0	0.14
0.6	0.55	2.5	0.08
0.7	0.50	3.0	0.05
0.8	0.45	4.0	0.018
0.9	0.41	5.0	0.0067
1.0	0.37		

(B) Mu is a bacteriophage that inserts virtually at random into bacterial genes, inactivating them by splitting them into two parts. Suppose you use Mu phage to integrate into *E. coli*, which has 500 genes that can be inactivated and still allow *E. coli* to grow. You map the genes in which each of 350 different Mu phage insertions have occurred. In other words, there are 350 different experiments in which you save one Mu phage insertion per experiment. You want to determine whether there are any hotspots for Mu insertion among the 500 genes. You find that 5 different genes have 4 insertions each.

a. Calculate the Poisson distribution for this experiment by determining the number of genes that are expected to have:

0 Mu insertion
1 Mu insertion
2 Mu insertions
3 Mu insertions
4 Mu insertions.

b. Determine approximately how many of the 5 genes that have 4 insertions are "hotspots."

The formula for the Poisson distribution and several values of e^{-m} are given in Problem 4A above.

5. Suppose you have conditional mutants of phage T4 each containing a different mutation in gene X. Suppose that X mutants will grow and make normal plaques on *E. coli* strain A but not on strain B, whereas wild-type phage T4 will grow and make plaques on both strains.

Explain, with diagrams, how you would carry out crosses of X mutants to construct a map with recombination distances.

6. **(A)** It is now known that at least one gene in phage T4 contains an intron. Suppose Benzer had encountered an intron in the middle of the *r*II region.

How would his results for mutations in the *r*II coding sequences have been different for each of the following:

a. the order of genetic markers
b. complementation
c. two-factor-cross frequencies
d. definition of hotspots
e. occurrence of deletions?

How might Benzer have guessed that there was an intron present?

(B) Suppose Benzer had encountered the following gene structure:

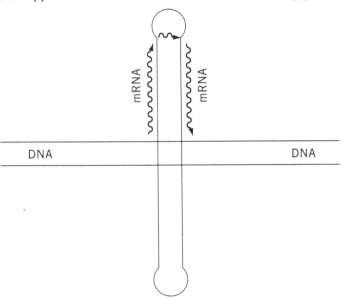

The coding region here consists of a cruciform structure where the mRNA is synthesized as indicated, following along certain parts of the coding sequence but not others. How would Benzer's results for mutations in the *r*II coding sequence have been different for each of the following:

a. the order of genetic markers
b. complementation
c. two-factor-cross frequencies
d. definition of hotspots
e. occurrence of deletions?

(C) Suppose Benzer had encountered the following gene structure:

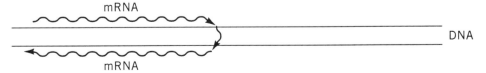

The coding region here consists of a gene that utilized both DNA strands where the mRNA is synthesized as indicated, following along one part of the coding sequence and then reading off of the complementary strand in the opposite direction. How would Benzer's results for mutations in the *r*II coding sequence have been different for each of the following:

a. the order of genetic markers
b. complementation
c. two-factor-cross frequencies
d. definition of hotspots
e. occurrence of deletions?

(D) Suppose Benzer had encountered the following gene structure:

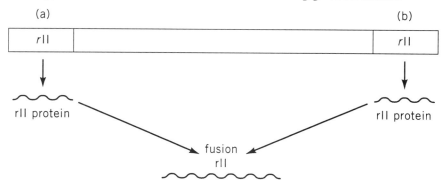

The coding region here consists of two genetic regions on different parts of the chromosome. Each codes for a portion of the protein: (a) for the first part and (b) for the second part. The protein is synthesized as two fragments that are then fused together by a cellular enzyme to create the final active single protein. How would Benzer's results for mutations in the *r*II coding sequence have been different for each of the following:

a. the order of genetic markers
b. complementation
c. two-factor-cross frequencies
d. definition of hotspots
e. occurrence of deletions?

(E) Suppose Benzer had encountered the following gene structure:

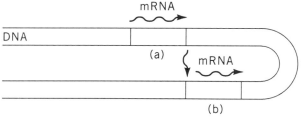

The coding region here consists of a bent gene structure, with DNA intervening between two parts of the coding sequence. If the gene is straightened out, then the mRNA can be considered to be read off of two different strands in two different segments of the gene. Here (a) and (b) refer to the first and second part of the same coding sequence and the first and second parts of the same respective final protein. How would Benzer's results for mutations in the *r*II coding sequence have been different for each of the following:

a. the order of genetic markers
b. complementation
c. two-factor-cross frequencies
d. definition of hotspots
e. occurrence of deletions?

How might Benzer have guessed the structure?

QUESTIONS AND ANSWERS

Crick et al. 1961

1. What is the difference between an overlapping and a nonoverlapping code?

   Answer: In an overlapping code, each base is part of several code words. In the case of an overlapping triplet, each base forms part of three different code words, as shown in the diagram on page 60. In a nonoverlapping code, each base is part of only one code word. Thus, for a nonoverlapping triplet code, each set of three consecutive bases forms a separate code word, also shown in the diagram on page 60.

2. What are the consequences of an overlapping code that can be tested by experiments and which experiments cited by the authors tested each prediction?

   Answer: There are two clear predictions of an overlapping code. First, since each base is part of more than one code word, many single-base-pair changes should result in the alteration of more than one amino acid in the corresponding protein. Second, in the case of an overlapping triplet code, the number of possible dipeptides is limited. For example, although there are 20 x 20 = 400 possible dipeptides, an overlapping triplet code will only be able to encode 256 dipeptides. This is because in an overlapping triplet code, four consecutive bases encode a dipeptide and there are only 256 possible quartets (4 x 4 x 4 x 4) of the four bases (A, G, T, C).

   The authors cited the work of Wittmann and of Tsugita and Fraenkel-Conrat (see page 64), who sequenced altered tobacco mosaic virus coat proteins resulting from mutagenesis with nitrous acid. All of the mutants had single amino acid changes (the rare exceptions having widely separated amino acid changes). In addition, they mentioned that all of the abnormal hemoglobins that had been analyzed had only single amino acid changes. Brenner's study of the known dipeptides (reprinted here on pages 73–80) was cited as having ruled out overlapping triplet codes. He had cataloged the known dipeptides and shown that there were too many to be accounted for by an overlapping triplet code.

3. What evidence led the authors to believe that acridines act as mutagens by adding or deleting a base?

   Answer: There were several lines of evidence.

   a. Mutants produced by acridines are seldom "leaky" and almost always result in the lack of function. Thus, only 6 of 126 acridine-yellow-induced *r*II mutants were leaky, whereas close to 50% of those generated by base analogs were leaky. The same was true of the lysozyme mutants analyzed by Streisinger and referred to by the authors.

   b. Other lines of evidence cited by the authors are presented in the paper by Brenner et al. (1961), which is provided here as Supplementary Reading (see pages 87–90). These reasons are given below.

      • The *o* locus of phage T4 encodes a head protein. Mutants resistant to osmotic shock require an alteration in this gene, but the head protein must still be present. These mutants are found only with base analogs and never with acridines.

• The *h* locus of phage T21 controls a protein involved in phage attachment to a host receptor. Mutants with an altered host range can be easily produced by base analogs but not by acridines. Again, the intact protein must be present in order to allow phage adsorption.

4. What is a suppressor? How many different types of suppressors can you imagine?

Answer: A suppressor is a mutation that counteracts the effects of another mutation. Suppressor mutations are at different sites from the mutations that they suppress and thus can be separated by mapping. Suppressors can be either in the same gene (internal) or in a different gene (external) from the mutation they are affecting. There are many types of suppressors. A few are mentioned below.

• Frameshift mutations of the type described by Crick et al. These mutations suppress other frameshift mutations by returning the altered reading frame to normal.

• Missense mutations that are in the same gene as the first mutation and that make compensating changes in the structure of the protein. Yanofsky and co-workers have studied these "second-site" revertants in the *trpA* gene, which encodes tryptophan synthetase. Some mutations affect residues that maintain the structure of the active site. Their suppressors change other amino acids, restoring the architecture of the active site.

• Nonsense suppressors alter tRNAs, usually at the anticodon, so that they can now read one of the nonsense codons and insert an amino acid at the corresponding position in the protein chain. Certain missense suppressors and frameshift suppressors also change the anticodon of specific tRNAs.

• Many mutations change the stability of proteins, which can be reversed by increasing the ionic strength. This can be accomplished by adding sucrose to the medium or by certain membrane mutations that affect the osmotic barrier, effectively increasing the ionic strength in the cell. These membrane mutations are suppressors for the first group of mutations, many of which result in temperature-sensitive proteins.

5. The authors selected suppressors of a mutation, *FC0*, and then found that "in all cases the suppressor was a nonleaky *r*." What does this mean? How could they determine this?

Answer: This means that they separated out the suppressor mutation and demonstrated that it alone generated the *r* phenotype. To do this, however, they had to "backcross" the suppressed mutation (the presumed double mutant) with wild-type phage to recover *r*II mutants. Operationally, they coinfected *E. coli* B with both the suppressed phage and the wild-type phage and then plated the progeny on *E. coli* B to look for large (*r*) plaques. Since two phenotypically wild-type phage were being crossed, the appearance of *r* phage over the spontaneous mutant background already indicated that the original mutation was still present. The *r* plaques could result from either the original mutation or the suppressor mutation, now separated from the original mutation. To distinguish between the two, a "test-cross" was performed in which a number of *r* phage recovered from this cross were crossed against the starting mutant carrying *FC0*. On the one hand, if the *r* phage being tested were simply ones containing only *FC0*, then they would fail to give wild-type recombinants. On the other hand, if the phage carrying the separated suppressor mutation were selected, then they would give wild-type recombinants with the test phage carrying *FC0*. Operationally, one first coinfects *E. coli* B with the two phage being crossed, but this time the progeny are plated on *E. coli* K, where wild-type recombinants can be selected.

6. Describe the sequence of experiments portrayed in Figure 2 on page 66.

Answer: The top panel of this figure shows the map positions of all of the suppressors to *FC0*. Each of these mutations was first separated out by the procedure outlined in the answer to Question 5 and then mapped in the *r*IIB gene. Several of the suppressors from this group (*FC1, 6, 10, 11, 9,* and 7) were then used to generate a second family of suppressors, which were in turn separated from the original mutation and mapped. These results are shown in panels *b* through *h*. Finally, two of the suppressors of a suppressor, *FC42* and *FC47*, both of which arose as suppressors of *FC7* in panel *g*, were used to produce a third generation of suppressors, which were in turn separated out and mapped, as shown in panels *i* and *j*.

7. What is "complementation" as mentioned in the second column of the paper on page 65? How could the authors test that a given pair of mutations was not exhibiting complementation?

Answer: Here, complementation refers to the tests performed by Benzer (see Unit 1) to distinguish the *r*IIA and *r*IIB cistrons. In complementation, there is a mixing of gene products in the cytoplasm. Mutations that complement will do so both in *cis* and in *trans*. In the *trans* configuration, each mutation is on a different phage. Crick, Brenner, and co-workers found that the mutations did not complement in *trans* at all, but in fact had to be in the *cis* configuration to display suppression. Operationally, one infects *E. coli* K simultaneously with two different phage, each containing one of the *r*II mutants, and looks for lysis and phage production within one cycle of growth. If the mutations complement, then they can produce phage and lyse *E. coli* K, otherwise they cannot.

8. Explain how the following combinations of mutations could be constructed and tested: a + + or a − −.

Answer: Let's examine how a + + phage is constructed.

Step 1: Infect *E. coli* B with each single + mutant. (Recall that since these are *r*II mutants, they must be crossed first in *E. coli* B to allow recombination to occur.) Plate the progeny on *E. coli* B, since *r* mutants cannot grow on *E. coli* K and the + + combination phage will still be an *r*II mutant.

Step 2: Pick large (*r*) plaques. If we diagram this cross, we can see that there are only four possible progeny. The two parentals, each single + phage, will be *r* mutants. The recombinants will be either wild-type or the double mutant + +. The wild-type phage will make small plaques on *E. coli* B, but the double mutant + + will make large (*r*) plaques like the parentals. Thus, by picking *r* plaques, we can only exclude the wild-type recombinants at this stage.

Step 3: Test-cross the *r*II phage from the cross against each parental. Here, we must test close to a hundred phage because the frequency of recombination may be only several percent. Most of the phage we are testing will be the parentals and will therefore give wild-type recombinants with one parental phage or the other. (Note that we cross in *E. coli* B and then plate on *E. coli* K to select for wild-type recombinants.) The double mutant + + will fail to give wild-type recombinants with either parental single + phage.

Step 4: When we find a phage that fails to recombine with either parental, we should still verify that it is really a + + and not a spontaneous deletion in *r*II that eliminates the wild-type alleles for both parental mutations. To do this, we could backcross against wild type, as described above, and find *r* mutants that now recombine with one of the two parental single + frameshift mutants.

9. Explain the concept of "barriers" that prevented certain + – and – + combinations from producing the wild-type phenotype.

   Answer: Barriers represented points that could not be crossed in one of the two incorrect reading frames. The authors were able to realize that, in fact, these barriers corresponded to nonsense mutations. Clearly, in each incorrect reading frame, a nonsense mutation will ultimately be encountered. When this happens, a compensating frameshift on the other side of the nonsense mutation will not be able to restore the correct protein sequence, since chain termination will have already occurred. The authors also reasoned that if there were very many different nonsense triplets, then one would expect barriers to occur very frequently. However, the infrequent occurrence of barriers argued that there were only a few nonsense codons, which in fact turned out to be true. The barrier concept was just the first example of the concept of open reading frames, which is so prevalent among DNA sequence analysis today.

10. Which experiment of the authors demonstrated best that the coding ratio was three or a multiple of three? How might they have constructed the mutant involved?

    Answer: Their most spectacular experiment was the construction of a triple mutant of the type + + +, which had a wild-type phenotype even though each individual + mutation resulted in the *r*II phenotype. The key to constructing this mutant is the ability to be sure that the final construct is correct. The route that the authors chose was to first make two overlapping double mutants of the type:

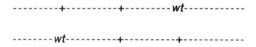

    Note that each of the two phage has a + frameshift at two positions and a wild-type (*wt*) allele at the third position. However, the positioning is such that the middle position has a + frameshift in each case. Therefore, no recombination event can produce a wild-type phage. However, a recombination event can produce a triple mutant + + +. Therefore, the two overlapping double mutants were crossed in *E. coli* B and the progeny plated on *E. coli* K to select for recombinants with the wild-type phenotype. The resulting wild-type or pseudo wild-type phage could then be tested by backcrosses to recover each of the three input frameshift mutations.

11. Which argument was used to say that the code was a triplet code, rather than one involving six or nine nucleotides to encode an amino acid?

Answer: In addition to being the simplest code, the triplet code, rather than one with six or nine nucleotides, made sense because mutations induced both by acridines and by hydrazine could be shown to be frameshifts with the identical properties of sign that were seen for the spontaneous revertants of *FC0*. Therefore, in order for the code to involve six bases, both acridines and hydrazine would have to add or delete exactly two bases every time. It seemed more likely that each of these agents was adding or deleting one base each time. Admittedly, this was not an airtight argument.

12. Explain the use of the 1589 deletion.

Answer: This deletion was first described by Benzer and Champe (see page 62) and represents the first example of gene fusions. In this case, the beginning of *r*IIB was removed, as was the end of *r*IIA. The resulting fused protein still retained B activity, although it was A⁻. All that the A portion of the fusion was needed for was to allow translation into B. However, acridine mutations in the A portion of the fusion destroyed B function, which could be restored by suppressor mutations, which turned out to be additional frameshifts in the A portion of the fusion.

13. What is meant by a degenerate code and how did the authors reason that the triplet code was likely to be degenerate?

Answer: If more than one code word is used for one amino acid, then the code is said to be degenerate. Since a triplet code has 64 code words and there are 20 amino acids, the code would have to be degenerate unless all of the other triplets were nonsense. As mentioned above, the authors showed that it was highly unlikely that only 20 of the 64 codons specified amino acids and that the remaining 44 stood for nonsense, since this would have resulted in many more barriers in incorrect reading frames. Therefore, the code was likely to be degenerate.

14. What direct experiment did the authors suggest to test their theory of frameshifts in the *r*II region?

Answer: They suggested that the phage T4 lysozyme system could be used to see whether a string of amino acids was altered. It is interesting to note that several years later George Streisinger succeeded in doing just this.

PROBLEMS

1. Suppose that the sequence below, which is read from the beginning as a triplet code, represents an mRNA molecule:

   A A T C A G U C G A G A U G G C G A A G U U U A A U A C U A A U G G G G

   a. Using the genetic code given on the next page, write out the amino acid sequence encoded by this mRNA.

   b. Suppose you add an -A- at the beginning of the sequence. Write out the new protein sequence.

   c. Suppose you delete the first base of the sequence. Write out the new protein sequence.

   d. If the mRNAs from parts *b* and *c* above were each translated in a strain with an *amber* suppressor, would it change their sequences? What if they were translated in an *ochre* suppressor strain?

The Genetic Code

Second letter

		U	C	A	G	
First letter	**U**	UUU ⎫ Phe UUC ⎭ UUA ⎫ Leu UUG ⎭	UCU ⎫ UCC ⎬ Ser UCA ⎮ UCG ⎭	UAU ⎫ Tyr UAC ⎭ UAA Stop UAG Stop	UGU ⎫ Cys UGC ⎭ UGA Stop UGG Trp	U C A G
	C	CUU ⎫ CUC ⎬ Leu CUA ⎮ CUG ⎭	CCU ⎫ CCC ⎬ Pro CCA ⎮ CCG ⎭	CAU ⎫ His CAC ⎭ CAA ⎫ Gln CAG ⎭	CGU ⎫ CGC ⎬ Arg CGA ⎮ CGG ⎭	U C A G
	A	AUU ⎫ AUC ⎬ Ile AUA ⎭ AUG Met	ACU ⎫ ACC ⎬ Thr ACA ⎮ ACG ⎭	AAU ⎫ Asn AAC ⎭ AAA ⎫ Lys AAG ⎭	AGU ⎫ Ser AGC ⎭ AGA ⎫ Arg AGG ⎭	U C A G
	G	GUU ⎫ GUC ⎬ Val GUA ⎮ GUG ⎭	GCU ⎫ GCC ⎬ Ala GCA ⎮ GCG ⎭	GAU ⎫ Asp GAC ⎭ GAA ⎫ Glu GAG ⎭	GGU ⎫ GGC ⎬ Gly GGA ⎮ GGG ⎭	U C A G

Third letter

2. **(A)** What are the consequences of the deletion of a single base from the coding sequence in an **overlapping** triplet code? In other words, how does the amino acid sequence past the point of the deletion change? Draw two different sequences of 8–10 base pairs, delete a base from the middle of each, and use the genetic code above to work out the resulting amino acid sequence changes. This should allow you to make a general statement.

   (B) Do the same as in Problem 2A, except now add a base to the middle of the sequences. What are the general consequences?

   (C) In one or two sentences, describe how the concept of frameshift relates to an overlapping code.

3. Suppose Crick, Brenner, and co-workers wanted to construct a double mutant containing both a +1 frameshift and a −1 frameshift in the *r*IIB gene of phage T4. They had the individual *r*II mutants (the +1 frameshift and the −1 frameshift), as well as *E. coli* B and *E. coli* K strains and the wild-type T4 phage. Describe how they could construct the double mutant, and then describe how they could verify the genotype of the double mutant, showing that it contained each of the input mutations. Diagram each cross and explain exactly how the cross would be carried out and how the products would be analyzed.

4. Suppose Crick, Brenner, and co-workers had constructed a double frameshift mutant with two −1 frameshifts in the *r*IIB cistron and this "− −" double mutant had the *r*II phenotype. Show how you would verify the genotype by separating out each of the "−" frameshift mutations. Let's call them −$_1$ and −$_2$ or −$_x$ and −$_y$. Show in detail the crosses you would carry out and how you would recognize and verify the correct mutants. The goal is to demonstrate

how you would separate and identify each of the two frameshifts starting with this double mutant. You can use any strains of *E. coli* and any single-mutant strains of *r*IIB. Be specific and use diagrams to show the procedure.

5. Suppose Crick, Brenner, and co-workers had an *r*II mutant that gave the *r*II phenotype. They wanted to determine whether this mutant had one mutation in the *r*IIB cistron or whether it was a double mutant with two mutations in the *r*IIB cistron, for example, two −1 frameshifts. Assume that either mutation alone would also give the *r*II phenotype. Assume also that they had only the following materials:

wild-type T4 phage
E. coli B
E. coli K

Show which crosses they could do to determine whether there were one or two different mutations. Explain the reason for doing each cross. Describe the conditions of the cross and how you would select and analyze the results. Give details.

6. Suppose you had an *r*II double mutant that had the wild-type phenotype and wanted to distinguish between a true wild type and a double mutant with a compensating + and − frameshift in *r*II. Show with crosses how you would:

a. demonstrate that the mutant was not a true wild-type
b. show that you actually had two different *r*II mutations.

Give details of all of the crosses.

QUESTIONS AND ANSWERS

Brenner et al. 1965

1. What property allowed mutants from different systems to be classified as *amber*?

   Answer: All of these mutants responded to the same set of suppressors. The mutants responding to a specific set of suppressors were termed *amber* and their suppressors were termed *amber* suppressors.

2. What is the evidence that *amber* mutants contain nonsense codons?

   Answer: There are several lines of evidence. *Amber* mutants of the alkaline phosphatase system contain no protein immunologically related to the enzyme. In *rII*, *amber* mutations show drastic effects. When combined with the 1589 deletion, *amber* mutations in the A cistron destroy activity of the B cistron in an *su⁻* strain. However, the activity of B is restored when a suppressor is added. In the T4 head protein system, *amber* mutations result in a fragment of the head protein, which is restored to a full-length protein upon the addition of a suppressor.

3. How are *ochre* mutants different from *amber* mutants?

   Answer: *Ochre* mutants are suppressed by a different set of suppressors.

4. On which mutations can *amber* and *ochre* suppressors act?

   Answer: *Amber* suppressors can only suppress *amber* mutations. However, *ochre* suppressors can suppress both *amber* and *ochre* mutations.

5. What evidence shows that chain termination occurs as part of protein synthesis?

   Answer: The best evidence presented by the authors is referred to as a manuscript in preparation. It is stated in the paper that both *amber* and *ochre* mutations vanish when the reading frame is altered. Thus, in the *rII* system, placing a + frameshift on one side of the *amber* mutation and a − frameshift on the other side of the mutation allows one to eliminate the effects of the nonsense mutation. Since it is presumed that only translation can recognize the reading frame, then *amber* and *ochre* mutations must exert their effects at the level of translation.

6. Show why only sense-strand changes created by hydroxylamine will result in phenotypic change before DNA replication.

   Answer: Hydroxylamine acts directly on the DNA, changing cytosine to a form that pairs like uracil not cytosine. Therefore, if the altered cytosine is on the sense strand, then the mRNA can already be altered before replication. It is the sense strand that specifies the mRNA. Cytosines that are changed on this strand will specify an adenine instead of a guanine on the mRNA. If this alteration of the mRNA results in a phenotypic change, then the phenotypic change will occur even before replication. If the altered cytosine is on the antisense strand, then the mRNA will not reflect any altered bases before replication, since the mRNA is not templated by the antisense strand. However, after replication, when a pure mutant segregates out from the heteroduplex, then there will be a phenotypic change regardless of whether the mutation occurred on the sense or the antisense strand.

7. Describe the experiment reported in Table 2 on page 104 and indicate how Table 2 was constructed.

Answer: This experiment asks whether or not *amber* and *ochre* mutants can revert to wild type with hydroxylamine. The phage were mutagenized and then passaged through *E. coli* B to allow replication before plating on *E. coli* K to select for revertants. The number of revertants on *E. coli* K divided by the titer on *E. coli* B provides the reversion index. As a control, a missense mutant, *UV256*, was used. It can be seen from the table that whereas *UV256* reverts several hundred times more frequently with hydroxylamine than the control (without hydroxylamine), none of the *amber* or *ochre* mutants revert significantly over the background spontaneous rate.

8. Describe the experiment that led to Table 3 on page 104 and indicate how Table 3 was compiled.

Answer: This experiment tests whether *ochre* mutants can be converted to *amber* mutants with 2AP. T4 *rII ochre* phage were used to infect *E. coli* B growing on 2AP (and without 2AP as a control). The progeny were then plated on *E. coli* K carrying an *amber* suppressor. The plaque-forming phage could either be revertants to wild type or represent actual conversions of the *ochre* mutants to *amber*. Therefore, a sample of the phage was tested on an *E. coli* K strain lacking an *amber* suppressor (*su⁻*) to determine the approximate percentage of true wild-type revertants. The ratio of revertants, and conversions to *amber*, to the titer on *E. coli* B is the reversion index shown in the table.

9. What does Table 4 on page 104 show?

Answer: Table 4 shows the same experiment as Table 3 except that hydroxylamine was used as the mutagen. The numbers in the table indicate that hydroxylamine does not stimulate the conversion of an *ochre* mutant to an *amber* mutant. This can be seen by comparing the values obtained with and without hydroxylamine.

10. Describe the experiment reported in Table 5 on page 105 and explain what each entry in Table 5 means.

Answer: The experiment reported in Table 5 represents an extraordinary amount of work and is similar to what Benzer did in his topography study (see Unit 1). Here, hydroxylamine was used to induce *amber* and *ochre* mutants from the wild type. After treatment with the mutagen, cells were divided into two groups. One, called set B, was first passaged through *E. coli* B, where all phage could grow regardless of whether or not an *rII* mutant was induced. They were then plated on *E. coli* B, where *r* mutants were collected. The second group, called set K, was first passaged through *E. coli* K before being plated on *E. coli* B. In this second set, hydroxylamine-induced changes on the sense strand that produced an *rII* mutant would register this phenotype immediately, and these mutants would not grow and thus would not be recovered as *r* plaques on *E. coli* B.

After finding *r* mutants (more than 7000 of which were picked), the *rII amber* and *ochre* mutants were found and then mapped and characterized with different suppressors to assign them to one of the known *amber* or *ochre* sites in *rII*. The number of occurrences of mutations at each *amber* and *ochre* site in each of the two groups was recorded. *Amber* mutations that appeared frequently in each of the two sets must have resulted from antisense changes, since these would not result in an *rII* phenotype before replication because the wild-type message would still be produced. Therefore, even a passage through *E. coli* K would not prevent the recovery of these *amber* mutants. However, *amber* mutations that appeared only in set B and not in set K must have resulted from sense-strand changes, since these would immediately register the *rII* phenotype and not survive the passage through *E. coli* K and thus not appear as plaques on *E. coli* B.

11. How does the experiment reported in Table 5 on page 105, together with previous experiments, establish the compositions of the *amber* and *ochre* codons?

Answer: The experiment recorded in Table 5 shows that there are two A·T base pairs in the *amber* codon and that these are in the opposite orientations. Thus, the composition of the codon must be (AUX), without regard to order. However, since *ochre* could be converted to *amber* by a transition (2AP causes transitions) but not by hydroxylamine, then the *amber* must have a G·C base pair at one site, the *ochre* must have an A·T base pair at the corresponding site, and the other two base pairs must be the same. Therefore, the *amber* codon must have the composition (UAG or UAC) and the corresponding *ochre* codon (UAA or UAU).

12. How could the authors determine whether the composition of the *amber* codon was (UAC) or (UAG)?

Answer: The authors could resolve the ambiguity by determining the amino acids to which the *amber* triplet is connected. The *amber* codon could be shown by protein chemistry to be connected by a transition to glutamine and tryptophan, as well as *ochre*. Since glutamine was clearly not (CAC) and (UGG) had been assigned to tryptophan, then (UAG) would have to be *amber*.

13. How did the authors assign the order of bases in the *amber* triplet?

Answer: Because Nirenberg and co-workers had recently assigned the CAG codon to glutamine, one could conclude that *amber* was indeed UAG and *ochre* UAA. In addition, assignments of UAC and UAU to tyrosine, known to be connected by a single base change to *amber*, confirmed the assignment.

14. What was the authors' proposed mechanism of chain termination and how accurate was their guess based on what we know today? What about their proposed mechanism of suppression?

Answer: The authors proposed that specific tRNAs recognize each nonsense triplet. Rather than carrying an amino acid, the tRNAs carry a special compound that results in termination of the polypeptide chain. We now know that chain termination is caused by protein factors R1 and R2, which themselves recognize the chain-terminating codons and stimulate release of the growing polypeptide chain from the ribosome. They also proposed that suppression could be achieved by altering the recognition of the special tRNA so that it now accepts an amino acid, which would then be inserted in response to the *amber* or *ochre* codon. In addition, the authors postulated that the anticodon of a normal tRNA might be altered so that it can now read the *amber* or *ochre* codon. In many cases, this is the correct mechanism of suppression of nonsense mutations.

PROBLEMS

1. Brenner and Crick originally worked with the *amber* UAG and *ochre* UAA codons. Shortly after their first paper, they worked with the third nonsense codon, *opal* UGA. Subsequently, suppressors were found that suppressed only *opal* codons. This allowed them to find *opal* mutations in the *r*II genes of phage T4. (As expected, neither *amber* or *ochre* suppressors operated on *opal* codons.)

   By using nonsense mutations in the *r*II genes of phage T4 and *opal, amber,* and *ochre* suppressor strains of *E. coli* K and the specificity of mutagens, describe a series of experiments that would allow you to determine the base composition (the bases in the triplet without respect to their order in the triplet) of the *opal* codon without knowing the identity of the bases in the *amber* or *ochre* triplets. Be as explicit as possible. Use diagrams and explain the strains you would use.

2. **(A)** Suppose you have an *r*II mutant in phage T4 that results from an isoleucine codon being mutated to a methionine codon (consult the genetic code, page 547). Would you be able to recover revertants of this mutant back to wild type if you treated with hydroxylamine and directly infected *E. coli* K?

   (B) Suppose you carried out the same experiments as in Problem 2A but with a different *r*II mutant that resulted from changing a serine codon to a proline codon. Could you recover wild-type revertants in which the serine codon was restored if you treated with hydroxylamine and directly infected *E. coli* K?

3. Suppose you have an *ochre* mutation in the *r*IIB gene and you want to convert it to an *amber* mutation using a mutagen that works directly on A residues and converts them to A*, which pairs like G. Suppose you are at the point in the analysis by Brenner and co-workers where you know the *ochre* codon on the mRNA is (UAU or UAA) and the *amber* codon is (UAG or UAC). You know that the two codons are connected by a single transition. You have access to strains of *E. coli* B and *E. coli* K both with and without *amber* and *ochre* suppressors. Describe how you would determine the mRNA codons for both *amber* and *ochre*. Use diagrams and be specific with regard to the experimental procedure.

4. Suppose you have a mutation in the *r*II region of phage T4 that results in the ATG codon at a particular point in the corresponding mRNA. You decide to revert this mutation using a mutagen that works on Ts (thymidine). After treating the mutant with the mutagen, you divide the culture into two parts. One part is first passaged through *E. coli* B and then plated on *E. coli* K to look for revertants. The second part is passaged through *E. coli* K and then plated on *E. coli* K to look for revertants.

   a. Show the codons that will be generated by the action of the mutagen. Assume that the mutagen makes only single-base-pair changes in any one virus particle.

b. Explain which codon(s) will be detected after treatment and passage through *E. coli* B (this may be any number of codons: none, one, two, or three). In addition, explain which codon(s), if any, will be detected after treatment and passage through *E. coli* K. Assume that each of the codons generated by the mutagen will result in wild-type revertants from the *r*II mutant. Use diagrams to explain your reasoning.

5. Suppose that a strain of *E. coli* had a fourth nonsense codon GAU. Suppose you have already determined that there is a G in the codon. Using the systems and principles of Brenner and co-workers, show how you could demonstrate that the other two bases in the codon were A and U (without regard to the order of the bases in the codon). You have the same materials as Brenner, and you also have a suppressor strain of *E. coli* that suppresses the GAU codon and restores the wild-type phenotype. Use diagrams if necessary.

6. Suppose that a nonsense codon in the *E. coli* strain you are using is UCG. Suppose you have a mutagen that works just like hydroxylamine except that it works on thymine residues (T), converting them to a derivative that pairs like cytosine. Using the *r*II system and following the principles of Brenner and co-workers, show how you could demonstrate that the nonsense codon contains a C and a G in opposite orientations (without regard to the order of the bases in the codon). Assume you also have a suppressor strain that suppresses the UCG codon and all of the tools that Brenner had. Give relevant details and draw a diagram if necessary.

7. Suppose you mutagenize wild-type T4 phage with hydroxylamine and attempt to recover *r*II mutants after first passaging through *E. coli* K before plating on *E. coli* B to look for *r*II plaques.

a. Would you be able to recover a mutant that resulted from a hydroxylamine-stimulated glycine to arginine change? (Consult the genetic code, page 547.) Explain your reasoning and use diagrams.

b. Would you be able to recover a mutant that resulted from a histidine to tyrosine change? Again, explain your reasoning and use diagrams.

Yanofsky et al. 1964

1. How were the A-protein mutants isolated?

   Answer: Most of the A-protein mutants were isolated following treatment with a mutagen, either ultraviolet irradiation or ethylmethanesulfonate, as pointed out in the Materials and Methods section of the paper. Two mutants were initially isolated as spontaneous second-site reversions and then separated from the original A mutants. However, one might ask "How do we find Trp⁻ mutants?" Even after mutagenesis, the frequency of Trp⁻ mutants in the population might be no higher than 1 in 10,000 to 1 in 1000 under the conditions employed. To delve further into this, we really need to consult one of the references cited in the introduction to the Yanofsky et al. paper that describes the use of penicillin enrichment to detect and isolate Trp⁻ mutants. The details of the penicillin method itself are given in a further reference cited in one of those papers. This presents a challenge to find the references and exact details and is an important exercise, since all too often we need to consult earlier references to find out everything we need to know about a question.

2. Describe the life cycle of P1 phage and show how generalized transduction occurs.

   Answer: The method used by Yanofsky and co-workers to order the *trp* mutations on the genetic map was P1 transduction. It may be helpful to consult an introductory genetics text to review the theory of generalized transduction. P1 is a virus that infects *E. coli* and can enter the lytic cycle. During phage production, an endonuclease cleaves P1 replicating intermediates and also *E. coli* DNA. Some fragments of the *E. coli* chromosome are incorporated into P1 phage heads. A lysate of P1 may contain 0.01% such particles, but since the titer of a lysate is often 10^{10} phage/ml, this amounts to a large number of particles. Every portion of the *E. coli* chromosome is represented in this population. When the P1 phage carrying a fragment of chromosomal DNA infects a recipient strain of *E. coli*, the chromosome fragment is injected into the cell. A portion of this fragment can be exchanged for a homologous region of the recipient chromosome by a double crossover. The fragment cannot be replicated and is diluted out during subsequent divisions of the cell.

3. How were the recombination experiments performed? How were recombination distances determined?

   Answer: The P1 transducing phage P1kc was used. P1 phage were grown on one TrpA strain and used to transduce a second strain carrying a different *trpA⁻* mutation. Trp⁺ recombinants were selected. To compare the frequencies of Trp⁺ from experiment to experiment, one has to devise some method of accounting for the variations in frequency due to experimental conditions, such as the efficiency of transduction. Therefore, the Trp⁺ values are normalized to the transduction frequencies for a second, completely unlinked marker. In this case, the authors chose the His marker. The recipient strain was always His⁻ and the donor strain His⁺. In addition to scoring Trp⁺ colonies from the transduction, the authors also selected for His⁺ colonies. The ratio of Trp⁺ to His⁺ colonies should not vary from experiment to experiment for the same transduction. This ratio allowed one to calculate relative recombination frequencies and to estimate distances, as shown in Figure 1 on page 118. As a minor adjustment, the values of each Trp⁺/His⁺ ratio were halved, since transduction in the *trp* region is more frequent than in the *his* region, and then these values could be compared to transductions in other genes.

4. Show how the mutations were ordered. Explain Table 2 on page 120.

    Answer: Although some ordering was done by deletion mapping, close markers were ordered by three-factor crosses. Consult the diagram on page 115. Crosses were set up utilizing the Anth marker. This marker is outside the *trp* region but closely linked to it. Each P1 donor carried one *trp⁻* mutation and the wild-type *anth⁺* allele. Each recipient carried a second *trp⁻* mutation and an *anth⁻* mutation. Depending on the order of the mutations, the resulting Trp⁺ colonies would be either about 80% Anth⁺ (20% Anth⁻) or about 50% Anth⁺. In this manner, each of the mutations used in these crosses could be ordered with respect to one another.

Yanofsky et al. 1967

5. Using the genetic code (see page 63), show the nucleotide changes that produced the altered proteins indicated in Figure 2 on page 126.

    Answer:
    A3 Glu to Val, GA-A/G to GU-A/G.
       Thus, the change was A to U, or A·T to T·A on the DNA.
    A33 Glu to Met, GA-A/G to AUG.
       Here we have a double change at the first two positions
       of the codon. GA goes to AU.
    A446 Tyr to Cys, UA-U/C to UG-U/C.
       Thus, the change was A to G, or A·T to G·C on the DNA.
    A487 Leu to Arg, CUX to CGX (where X is any base).
       Thus, the change was U to G, or T·A to G·C on the DNA.
    A223 Thr to Ile, ACX to AU-U,C,A.
       Thus, the change was C to U, or C·G to T·A on the DNA.
    A23 Gly to Arg, GGX to CGX.
       Thus, the change was G to C, or G·C to C·G on the DNA.
    A46 Gly to Glu, GGX to GA-A/G.
       Thus, the change was G to A, or G·C to A·T on the DNA.
    A187 Gly to Val, GGX to GUX.
       Thus, the change was G to U, or G·C to T·A on the DNA.
    A78 Gly to Cys, GGX to UG-U/C.
       Thus, the change was G to U, or G·C to T·A on the DNA.
    A58 Gly to Asp, GGX to GA-U/C.
       Thus, the change was G to A, or G·C to A·T on the DNA.
    A169 Ser to Leu, UCX to UU-A/G.
       Thus, the change was C to U, or C·G to T·A on the DNA.

6. What is odd about mutant A33 in Figure 2 on page 126? Do you have any ideas about how it was created?

    Answer: The *A33* mutation results in a Glu to Met change. Since Glu is encoded by GAA or GAG and Met is encoded by AUG, this means that a double change must have occurred that converted the GA to an AU. From the references, *A33* was detected after ultraviolet irradiation. The GA part of the codon has on the opposite strand a TC sequence at which different types of photodimers can form that occasionally lead to a tandem double base change. This might be the cause of the double mutation.

Sarabhai et al. 1964

7. What gene were the authors working with and what is its protein product?

   Answer: The authors were working with the phage T4 head protein gene, which controls the synthesis of the major head protein.

8. How did the authors order mutations? Explain Table 1 on page 130.

   Answer: They used a three-factor cross and compared the frequency of wild-type recombinants in that cross with the frequency in a related two-factor cross. For example, Table 1 shows that the cross of *B17* with *H11* gives a frequency of 0.80, but this is reduced to 0.14 if the T4 phage carrying *H11* also carries the third mutation *B278*. This is consistent with the order *H11*, *B17*, *B278*, as shown. (This does not completely rule out every other possibility, but they are eliminated by the total set of data, only part of which is shown here.)

9. Explain what complementation tests with T4 phage are.

   Answer: Two different phage mutants are used to infect *E. coli*. If the mutants carry mutations in different cistrons (genes), then all of the gene products will be present in cells that receive both phage, and these can mix in the cytoplasm and result in the synthesis of intact phage particles. This is complementation. If the mtuations are in the same cistron, then that gene product will be lacking and intact phage particles cannot be generated.

10. How did the authors produce the patterns shown in Figure 3 on page 129?

    Answer: Because such a high proportion of the protein synthesized late after infection is head protein, fragments of the head polypeptide could be detected by radioactive label without any prior purification. Autoradiographs of tryptic and chymotryptic peptides labeled with radioactive amino acids were used to anaylze the peptides synthesized in each mutant. In each *amber* mutant, certain peptides present in the wild type were absent. The pattern was characteristic for each *amber* mutant. The peptides present could be ordered with respect to the wild-type sequence of peptides, and this pattern is what is shown in Figure 3. Note that the mutants could be ordered on the basis of synthesizing more and more fragments, which extended in one direction based on the wild-type order. In other words, they formed a hierarchy.

11. Can you imagine any alternative explanations for the phenomenon described by the authors other than that they were seeing fragments produced during termination of polypeptide synthesis?

    Answer: One might hypothesize that the nonsense mutations actually represent degradation points on either the mRNA or the protein. The gene would still be colinear with the protein unless the degradation signals directed degradation at other points. The fact that nonsense mutations are the barriers (from the Crick et al. work on the triplet nature of the genetic code described in Unit 2) says that these mutations are operating at the level of translation, since they are sensitive to phase. Recall that barriers must be in the appropriate reading frame to be read or not read. Therefore, mRNA degradation signals could at least be ruled out. In any case, it is interesting that the fragments that the authors describe were not themselves degraded, as are many such fragments of bacterial proteins. It turns out that infection by T4 results in the synthesis of a phage-encoded inhibitor of the cellular proteases that degrade certain protein fragments. This piece of good fortune, unknown at the time, was what allowed the Sarabhai et al. experiment to work.

PROBLEMS

1. Suppose you wanted to use P1 generalized transduction to map a set of mutations in the *his* genes that rendered the cell His⁻ (unable to grow on minimal medium without histidine). Assuming that you could use various strains of *E. coli* with different mutations in either the *his* or any other gene, describe how you would map the mutations in the *his* genes with two-factor crosses and how you would obtain relative recombination frequencies between different *his* mutations.

2. Suppose you were mapping mutations in the *metB* gene that caused the Met⁻ phenotype (inability to grow without methionine). Explain how, using P1 phage, you would carry out:

   a. two-factor crosses to obtain relative frequencies of recombination between different *metB⁻* mutations
   b. three-factor crosses to determine the order of closely linked *metB⁻* mutations.

   Describe the steps you would take, the selective media you would use, and how you would calculate the required values. Assume you can exploit the properties of unlinked *trp⁻* mutations (which cause the inability to grow without added tryptophan) as well as very closely linked (95% cotransducible with the *metB* locus) *arg⁻* mutations (which cause the inability to grow without arginine).

3. Suppose you have two mutations in the *met* and *his* genes that prevent growth in the absence of methionine and histidine, respectively. These mutations are so close together that it is difficult to order them by two-factor-cross frequencies. You also have a linked marker, Arg⁻ (requirement for arginine), that is close to both markers but is not as close to Met and His as they are to each other. Diagram two types of crosses you might do to order the markers and give the conditions of the experiment (media used, selection, etc.).

4. Suppose you are studying mutations in the *xyl* locus, which controls growth on the sugar xylose. You have a series of *xyl⁻* mutations that result in failure to grow on xylose. Your goal is to map these mutations and order them within the *xyl* gene. You have at your disposal strains of *E. coli* that contain a

single mutation at the *proK* locus, which is 70% linked to the *xyl* locus by P1 cotransduction. You also have strains of *E. coli* that contain a single mutation in the unlinked locus *metB*. Thus, you can prepare any combination of strains that are either *xyl*+ or *xyl*−, *proK*+ or *proK*−, and *metB*+ or *metB*−. You also have a stock of the generalized transducing phage P1.

    a. Describe how you would first construct a two-factor-cross map of the *xyl* mutations. Show how you would carry out the relevant crosses and calculate the relative map distances. Use diagrams to clarify.

    b. Show how you would carry out three-factor crosses involving two different *xyl* mutations to order the mutations with respect to a third marker. Explain, with diagrams, how each possible order would yield different results.

5. Suppose you were studying the induction of mutations in the *x* gene of *E. coli* after treatment with a mutagen such as ultraviolet light (UV). Wild-type cells grow on medium without the x-compound, but X− mutants require the x-compound for growth. In addition, on complete medium with compound x and special indicator dyes, X− mutants are blue, whereas wild-type cells form white colonies. Using both selective and indicator media, outline the steps you would use to obtain UV-induced mutations in gene *x* and to determine whether there were hotspots for UV mutations in gene *x*. Outline the experimental details in addition to the concepts involved. Assume you already possess both point mutations and deletions in gene *x* from other experiments, as well as all of the genetic tools normally used in *E. coli*.

6. Suppose you are transducing a recipient strain from Gal− to Gal+ by either generalized transduction with phage P1 or by specialized transduction with the temperate phage λ. The donor strain is Gal+. Explain the effect of each of the following mutations on transduction by each of these phage and give reasons for your answers:

    a. a mutation in the recipient cell that causes a hyper Rec phenotype that results in increased generalized recombination at large homologies

    b. a mutation in the *malB* gene of the recipient that renders the cell resistant to infection by phage λ

    c. a deletion of the λ attachment site on the recipient chromosome

    d. a mutation in the recipient that causes rapid degradation of DNA fragments lacking an origin of replication

    e. a mutation in the donor cell that eliminates general recombination at large homologies (Rec−).

7. (A) We now know that many eukaryotic genes are split into introns and exons, with the introns providing intravening sequences that are removed from the initial RNA transcript to yield the final mRNA from which the protein is then synthesized as shown in the diagram on the next page. It is also known that at least one gene in phage T4 has an intron. Suppose both Yanofsky and co-workers and Sarabhai, Brenner, and co-workers in their respective colinearity studies had chosen to work with a T4 gene that had two introns, as also shown in the diagram. Describe which approach would yield more accurate results reflecting the possible intron structure of the

gene. How would each approach be affected by the presence of the introns compared to a situation where there were no introns?

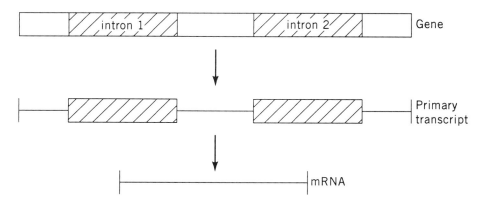

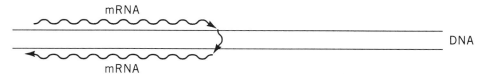

(B) Suppose Yanofsky and co-workers and Sarabhai, Brenner, and co-workers had encountered the following gene structure:

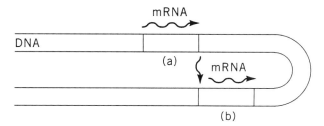

Here, the coding region consists of a DNA segment that encodes an mRNA on both strands. After transcribing the first portion of the mRNA, the mRNA synthesis changes strands and proceeds in the opposite direction on the complementary strand. How would the authors' results for colinearity have been different? Show how each of the experiments they did would have been affected. Would they have noticed this structure? How?

(C) Suppose Yanofsky and co-workers and Sarabhai, Brenner, and co-workers had encountered the following gene structure:

Here, the coding region consists of a bent gene structure, with DNA intervening between two parts of the coding sequence. If the gene is straightened out, then the mRNA can be considered to be read off of two different strands in two different segments of the gene. Here, (a) and (b) refer to the first and second parts of the same coding sequence and the first and second parts of the same respective final protein. How would the authors' results for colinearity have been different? Show how each of the experiments they did would have been affected. Would they have noticed this structure? How?

(D) Suppose Yanofsky and co-workers and Sarabhai, Brenner, and co-workers had encountered the gene structure shown on the next page:

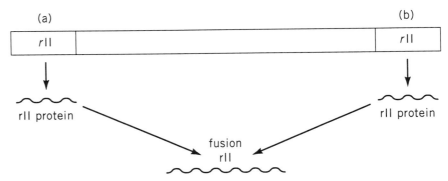

Here, the coding region consists of two genetic segments, each of which code for one part of the final protein. The protein is synthesized in two parts and an enzyme then fuses the two proteins together to make a final active enzyme. The two coding segments are separated by an inert DNA segment. In fact, the coding segments are at different ends of the chromosome. How would the authors' results for colinearity have been different? Show how each of the experiments they did would have been affected. Would they have noticed this structure? How?

(E) Suppose Yanofsky and co-workers and Sarabhai, Brenner, and co-workers had encountered the following gene structure:

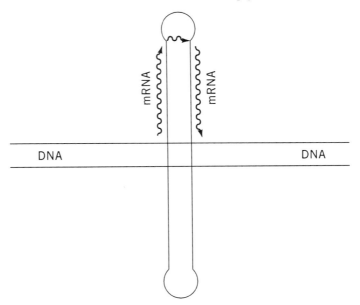

Here, the coding region consists of a cruciform structure where the mRNA is synthesized as indicated, following along certain parts of the coding sequence but not others. How would the authors' results for colinearity have been different? Show how each of the experiments they did would have been affected. Would they have noticed this structure? How?

Wollman et al. 1956

1. Why do Hfr strains display a higher rate of transfer and recombination of chromosomal markers in a cross with an F⁻ strain than an F⁺ strain does in a cross with an F⁻ strain?

    Answer: In an Hfr strain, every cell in the population has F integrated at a fixed point in the chromosome. Therefore, every cell donates chromosomal markers in a cross with an F⁻ strain. However, in a population of F⁺ cells, only a small fraction of the cells have F integrated into the chromosome. Only this fraction can donate chromosomal markers to an F⁻ cell in a conjugation experiment. Thus, the population as a whole displays a much lower frequency of transfer and subsequent recombination of chromosomal markers than an Hfr population.

2. What is the mechanism of transfer of chromosomal markers from an F⁺ strain to an F⁻ strain?

    Answer: As stated in the answer to Question 1 above, transfer of chromosomal markers from an F⁺ strain to an F⁻ strain only occurs by the small fraction of Hfr cells in a population of F⁺ cells. These Hfr cells transfer markers linked to the integrated F.

3. Describe the experiments pictured in Figure 2 on page 142.

    Answer: In Figure 2A, an Hfr carrying phage λ is crossed with an F⁻ strain that also carries λ. The frequencies of T^+L^+ and Gal^+ recombinants are monitored. It can be seen that these increase with time with the T^+L^+ markers entering before the Gal^+ marker. Figure 2B shows the same cross except that the recipient was not lysogenic for λ. Infective centers of λ phage were scored, as well as recombinants. Since the λ phage enters after T^+L^+ but very close to the same time as Gal^+, it can be seen that T^+L^+ recombinants occur but not Gal^+ recombinants. The increase in infective centers with time is also evident.

4. Describe the experiments pictured in Figures 3 and 4 on pages 143 and 144, respectively, and explain how they differ from the experiments pictured in Figure 2 on page 142.

    Answer: The key difference is that in the experiments shown in Figures 3 and 4 the matings are interrupted at different times by withdrawing samples and mixing in a Waring blendor. In Figure 3, the same markers are selected for as in Figure 2. However, in Figure 4, the recombinants are then tested for the inheritance of other markers from the donor as a function of time. In other words, the T^+L^+ recombinants from an interrupted mating are scored for *Az, T1, Lac,* and *Gal.*

5. Explain the experiment pictured in Figure 8 on page 151.

    Answer: In this experiment, an Hfr is crossed with a *Gal⁻* recipient and *Gal⁺* recombinants are selected and then examined for the inheritance of markers that entered before *Gal.* The intervals are numbered to show where different crossovers must have occurred to generate the observed genotypes.

6. What is meant by "segregation" and "phenotypic expression"?

Answer: Growing bacterial cells have as many as two to four copies of the chromosome. When an F⁻ recombines with a fragment of the Hfr chromosome that has been transferred, only one copy of the chromosome has been converted to the recombinant genotype. It is necessary for one or two cell divisions to occur before a completely pure haploid recombinant cell, with each copy of the chromosome having the recombinant genotype, will "segregate" out. Even after segregation of a pure recombinant, it may take additional time before the new phenotype is expressed. For example, in the case of recessive genes, it may take a few cell divisions before previously synthesized proteins are sufficiently diluted out to allow the new phenotype to be expressed. Thus, sensitivity to streptomycin is dominant to resistance, since the sensitive ribosomes will still result in cell death in the presence of streptomycin. When an Str^r recombinant is formed, it may take two or three cell divisions to dilute out all of the Str^s ribosomes.

PROBLEMS

1. Suppose you have a set of four Hfr strains and you carry out a series of crosses with a multiply marked recipient that is auxotrophic for many different nutritional markers. You do interrupted mating experiments and find the following results concerning which markers are transferred to the recipient from each of the Hfr strains at various times:

   Hfr 1: Lac at 5 min; Leu at 12 min; Pur at 14 min; Thr at 22 min; Ile at 30 min; Val at 45 min

   Hfr 2: Thr at 5 min; Pur at 13 min; Lac at 22 min; Cys at 30 min; Met at 40 min; Ala at 60 min

   Hfr 3: Val at 5 min; Ala at 20 min; Met at 40 min; Cys at 50 min

   Hfr 4: Ala at 5 min; Val at 20 min; Ile at 35 min; Thr at 43 min

   Determine the genetic map of the recipient and show the point of origin and direction of transfer of each Hfr strain.

2. If you have an Hfr with λ integrated at its attachment site near the *gal* genes, which of the following recipients will give more recombinants for markers that are transferred after the *gal* region and why:

   a. a recipient that also carries λ integrated at its attachment site *or*
   b. a recipient that does not carry λ at all?

3. You carry out an Hfr cross using an Hfr that transfers the *arg-rif(rpoB)* region early to a recipient that is Arg⁻Rif^s (sensitive to rifampicin). Here, you mate for 90 minutes and then plate on selective medium. When you select for Arg⁺ recombinants, you find that 98% of them have also brought in the Rif^r (resistance to rifampicin) marker from the Hfr strain. However, when you select for Rif^r directly, you find that there is a very low transfer of the Rif^r marker. How can you explain this?

Jacob and Monod 1961

1. Distinguish between "structural" and "regulatory" genes.

   Answer: Although this distinction between these types of genes is no longer used today, at the time Jacob and Monod wrote their paper the term "structural" gene referred to a gene that encoded a protein with specific function in the cell, whereas "regulatory" gene referred to a gene involved in the regulation of another gene. Thus, regulatory genes regulated the activity of structural genes.

2. What is "enzymatic adaptation"?

   Answer: Enzymatic adaptation is the ability of a cell to display an enzyme activity only in the presence of a substrate for that enzyme. The term was derived from the idea that cells adapted to their environment.

3. What was known about the induction phenomenon in the lactose system of *E. coli* at the start of the work described in the 1961 Jacob and Monod paper? What was known about the enzymology of the system?

   Answer: It was known that β-galactosidase was detected only in cells growing in the presence of certain galactosides. The levels were 1000 times higher than for cells grown in the absence of these galactosides. This was the induction phenomenon. In addition to β-galactosidase, a permease was required for growth on lactose. This permease and a third activity, transacetylase, also appeared only during growth in the presence of certain galactosides. Although it was thought that the same protein had both permease and transacetylase activities, it was later shown that these two activities reside in different proteins.

4. What was meant by negative control?

   Answer: Negative control referred to the fact that normal expression of a gene was blocked, and induction involved eliminating that block. A system in which a gene is not blocked but instead requires the presence of an activator to be expressed is termed "positive control."

5. What were cryptic mutants?

   Answer: Mutants that lacked the permease but were still able to synthesize β-galactosidase were termed "cryptic" mutants.

6. What was the evidence that galactosidase and acetylase activities were different proteins and not the same protein?

   Answer: Mutants could be found that had lost β-galactosidase activity but could still concentrate β-galactosides, and other mutants could be found that had lost the ability to concentrate galactosides but could still synthesize β-galactosidase.

7. Which experiments showed that "induction" caused the synthesis of new enzyme molecules?

   Answer: The experiments referred to in the paper showed first, that the enzyme formed upon induction is antigenically distinct from any protein present in uninduced cells and second, that little if any of the sulfur or carbon found in the induced protein is derived from preexisting proteins.

8. What conclusion could be drawn from studying the kinetics of induction? How was this conclusion reached?

Answer: The studies on the kinetics of induction allowed one to rule out the model that the inducer activated the synthesis of a stable intermediate able to accumulate in the cell. They concluded this because of the rapid onset of enzyme synthesis upon the addition of inducers and the rapid cessation of synthesis after the removal of inducers.

9. Describe the studies on the specificity of induction reported in Table 1 on page 198. What did they demonstrate?

Answer: In these studies, a variety of different compounds, including thio-β-D-galactosides (which replaced the oxygen of β-D-galactosides with sulfur and thus could not be cleaved), β-D-galactosides, and α-galactosides, were used as inducers. The levels of the lactose enzymes were measured, as well as the affinity of each compound for the enzymes and the ability of the enzymes to serve as substrates. Several things were demonstrated. First, both β-galactosidase and transacetylase responded to all of the inducers to the same degree. Thus, the respective genes were coordinately controlled. Second, it was clear that the recognition of inducers involved a stereospecificity that was different from that of β-galactosidase. Thus, on the one hand, some compounds that were potent inducers, such as isopropyl-β-D-thiogalactoside, were not substrates for β-galactosidase. (Other strong inducers, such as melibiose, could not even bind to β-galactosidase.) On the other hand, very effective substrates for β-galactosidase, such as phenyl-β-D-galactoside, were weak inducers for the lactose enzymes.

10. What is the distinction between the "induction" effect and the "repression" effect? What is "derepression"? Give an example.

Answer: The induction effect is the turning on of gene expression by the addition of a compound, the inducer. The repression effect is the blocking of gene expression by the addition of a compound or metabolite, the co-repressor. Derepression is simply the induction of enzyme synthesis provoked by the absence of co-repressor. An example is provided in the tryptophan biosynthetic pathway. The enzyme tryptophan synthetase is expressed at high levels in the absence of tryptophan and at low levels when tryptophan is present in excess. The removal of tryptophan from the medium results in derepression of tryptophan synthetase, just as the addition of β-galactosides results in the induction of the lactose enzymes.

11. What are Z⁻, Y⁻, and I⁻ mutants? What are "constitutive" mutants?

Answer: Z⁻ mutants lack β-galactosidase but can still synthesize permease. They result from mutations in the *lacZ* gene. Y⁻ mutants have a defective permease but still synthesize β-galactosidase. These mutants result from mutations in the *lacY* gene. I⁻ mutants are characterized by an uncontrolled synthesis of both β-galactosidase and permease. The mutations causing this phenotype map to a different gene, termed the *I* gene for inducibility. Constitutive mutants have an uncontrolled expression of genes. Therefore, I⁻ mutants are examples of constitutive mutants for the *lac* system.

12. Explain how stable partial diploids are formed and used.

Answer: Stable partial diploids are formed by the introduction of an F′ episome containing a segment of the bacterial genome. The F′ factors are formed by the aberrant excision of F from an Hfr strain. Thus, in the case of *lac,* the starting point was an Hfr strain that resulted from the integration of F very near the *lac* genes. In the case where the orientation of F is such that the *lac* genes are transferred very late, one can select for the transfer of the *lac* genes to F⁻ Lac⁻ cells in a short mating. Since the Hfr would normally require 90 minutes to transfer the *lac* genes, only cells that had received an F′ factor containing the *lac* genes would be Lac⁺. In the population of Hfr cells, only a few rare cells would have such an F′*lac* resulting from the abnormal excision of the integrated F. Once the F′*lac* is detected, it can be transferred to cells carrying a normal *lac* region, thus creating a partial diploid. These strains are often used for complementation tests, since one copy of *lac* can be wild-type and the second copy can carry different mutations.

13. Explain the complementation relationship between *Z, Y,* and *I* mutations as shown in Table 2 on page 205. What do the numbers indicate?

Answer: First, it can be seen that Z^+ is dominant to Z^- (line 4) and that Y^+ is dominant to Y^- (line 5). The numbers in the table indicate the level of each respective enzyme as a percentage of that observed with induced wild type. Notice that when the gene is on F, as in lines 4 and 5, it has a higher level of expression than when it is on the chromosome, as in lines 1 and 2 (for β-galactosidase). Lines 4 and 5 show that I^+ is dominant to I^-, since the resulting heterogenote is inducible and not constitutive.

14. What experiment determined that the *I* gene synthesized a cytoplasmic product? What are two interpretations of the result, and how did Jacob and Monod distinguish between them?

Answer: As presented in the paper, the complementation relationships between I^+ and I^- point to the fact that the *I* gene synthesizes a cytoplasmic product. This is because the *I* gene product can work in *trans* to shut off expression of a gene on a different chromosome, as shown in line 4 of Table 2 on page 205. The simplest model to account for these results is that the *I* gene product is a repressor that blocks the synthesis of the lactose enzymes. A second model that can also explain these results is that the *I* gene product is an enzyme that destroys an internal inducer for the *lac* genes. Jacob and Monod argued that the properties of the I^s mutant, including the result that the I^s mutation was dominant over the I^+, were inconsistent with the second model. (However, the second model can, in fact, also explain the I^s results.) In addition, on the basis of work done by others with the PaJaMo experiment, it appeared that the repressor could accumulate when protein synthesis was inhibited. Therefore, if the repressor was not a protein, then it could not be an enzyme that destroyed the inducer. (Of course, we now know that the repressor is a protein, so clearly the experimental data that said that repressor accumulated under conditions that inhibited protein synthesis were not reliable.)

15. Explain the experiment shown in Figure 4 on page 206. How was it carried out, and what was the interpretation of the experiment? Can you imagine any alternative explanation?

Answer: In this experiment, an Hfr was used to donate the I^+ and Z^+ genes to an F^- cell that is I^-Z^-. After mating, the Hfr was killed with T6 phage, and β-galactosidase synthesis was followed both with and without inducer. In the absence of inducer, the recipient cells synthesized β-galactosidase almost immediately after the entry of the *lac* genes, and this synthesis continued unchecked for about 60 minutes before it fell off considerably. However, at any time after this point, the addition of inducer restored the synthesis to its full level. The interpretation of this experiment was that when the Z gene first enters the F^- cell, there is no I gene product in the cytoplasm and synthesis can commence at the maximal rate. However, the introduction of the I gene also results in the synthesis of the I gene product, which finally accumulates in the cytoplasm of the F^- cell to the point where it blocks the synthesis of β-galactosidase. This experiment, performed before the construction of the stable diploids, was the crucial experiment that first convinced people that the I gene synthesized a product that could act in the cytoplasm to block enzyme synthesis.

Strictly speaking, this experiment does not represent a true *trans* test, since we are not looking at the ability of an I^+Z^- to repress an I^-Z^+. Therefore, despite the influence of the experiment at the time, it does not absolutely prove that a cytoplasmic product is involved. Because one is only observing the ability of an I^+Z^+ configuration to become inducible after a delay following transfer, one might argue that the I gene product makes a *cis*-acting factor that can only operate on a linked Z gene (particularly considering its direct proximity to the beginning of the Z gene). *Cis*-acting proteins are now known, and it would also have been possible to imagine that the I gene product was simply an RNA transcript that folds back and blocks Z gene expression, working in *cis* as an antimessage or to block the promoter. The delay in expressing this transcript could be ascribed to many things, such as slower transcription or a weaker promoter (which indeed it has).

16. It is now known that there are I^- mutations that are dominant to I^+ mutations. Can you provide an explanation for this?

    Answer: The *lac* repressor is a tetramer consisting of four identical subunits. Certain mutations in the I gene result in subunits with defective operator binding that can still aggregate normally. Therefore, wild-type subunits are incorporated into inactive tetramers. This negative complementation results in a partial dominance of the I^- mutation. This effect is very weak for most mutations that display it, although it can be enhanced if the defective repressor subunits are overproduced relative to the wild-type repressor subunits.

17. Which experiment mentioned by Jacob and Monod showed that the repressor was not a protein? What might the investigators have done wrong in this experiment?

    Answer: The experiment shown in Figure 4 on page 206 was modified so that an inhibitor of protein synthesis, 5-methyltryptophan, was added to the mated cells a few minutes before entry of the Z gene. The question was whether the repressor could be synthesized and accumulate during a 60-minute period of inhibition of protein synthesis. After 60 minutes, the inhibitor was washed out and the β-galactosidase measured. On the one hand, if the repressor could be synthesized during the 60 minutes, then one would expect no burst of β-galactosidase synthesis. On the other hand, if the repressor was not synthesized during this period, then there would be a burst of β-galactosidase synthesis, just as in the original experiment. The authors, quoting the results of Pardee and Prestidge that showed that the repressor does accumulate under these conditions, argued that the repressor was not a protein since apparently its synthesis was not blocked by the addition of a protein synthesis inhibitor. As we now know, the repressor is indeed a protein. Therefore, this experiment must have been wrong in some way. Probably, the inhibition by 5-methyltryptophan was not complete and this allowed some synthesis of the repressor to take place.

18. Describe the phage immunity system and point out the similarities between it and the *lac* system.

Answer: Phage λ can infect cells and either enter into the vegetative state, in which it replicates and then kills and lyses the host cell, or enter the lysogenic state, where it integrates into the host chromosome and represses its lytic functions. Cells harboring the prophage in the lysogenic state are immune to superinfection by other λ phage but not by other related phage. The prophage can be induced to enter the vegetative cycle by ultraviolet (UV) light. Immunity is conferred by a cytoplasmic entity, since immunity is dominant in *trans*. Mutants have been found that can no longer confer immunity or enter into the lysogenic state but always enter the vegetative state. These mutants are analogous to the I⁻ mutants in the *lac* system. The mutations responsible for this phenotype map in the λ *cI* gene. *cI⁺* is dominant to *cI⁻*, again indicating that a cytoplasmic molecule is responsible for conferring immunity and preventing the expression of lytic functions. In addition, a mutation, *ind⁻*, was detected that maps in the *cI* gene and renders the cell resistant to UV induction, much like the *I*^s mutation prevents *lac* expression even in the presence of inducer. The *ind⁻* mutation is dominant to *ind⁺*, just as the *I*^s mutation is dominant to *I⁺*.

19. Describe "zygotic induction" and provide an explanation for this phenomenon.

Answer: When an Hfr transfers part of the chromosome to an F⁻ recipient, the resulting strain is a temporary partial zygote. If the F⁻ carries λ as a prophage, then the transfer of a second λ prophage through conjugation does not result in phage production or killing of the zygote. However, if the F⁻ recipient is not lysogenic for λ, and thus does not carry a λ prophage, then upon entry of λ into the cell the λ prophage becomes induced. This is termed "zygotic induction." The explanation for this is that the nature of the cytoplasm in the F⁻ will determine whether induction occurs. When there is no prophage in the F⁻, there is no *cI* gene product in the cytoplasm, and thus nothing can block the expression of the lytic function of λ. However, if the F⁻ carries λ as a prophage, then the cytoplasm already contains *cI* gene product, which can block expression of the λ lytic functions and thus prevent entry into the vegetative state. The zygotic induction experiment is really a direct analog of the PaJaMo experiment. In the latter experiment, entry of an *I⁺Z⁺* segment into an F⁻ cell that does not contain any *I* gene product permits uncontrolled expression of *Z* until *I* gene product can be synthesized and accumulate in the cell. However, in the zygotic induction experiment, the uncontrolled expression of lytic functions results in phage growth and cell lysis before *cI* product can be synthesized and accumulate.

20. What are O^c mutants? How were they isolated?

Answer: O^c mutants have partly constitutive enzyme levels even in the presence of active repressor due to alterations in the operator region. O^c mutants were isolated by finding constitutive mutants from starting strains that were diploid for the wild-type *lac* region. (If a diploid that was I^s/I^s had been used, then one could have selected for Lac$^+$ cells directly.)

21. What does Table 3 on page 216 show? What were the key experiments and what were the conclusions from these experiments?

Answer: Table 3 shows that O^c mutants synthesize partially constitutive levels of the lactose enzymes (line 7) and that O^c is *cis*-dominant to O^+ but *trans*-recessive (lines 8 and 9). In addition, O^c is dominant to I^s (line 12). The conclusion was that the O^c mutations modify the specific repressor-accepting structure of the operator.

22. Briefly outline the Operon Model. Define "operon."

Answer: The Operon Model employs regulatory genes that encode repressors that act on controlling sites on the DNA, termed operators. When repressors bind to operators, they block expression of the genes under control, termed structural genes. The repressors show a stereospecific recognition of small-molecule inducers or co-repressors. Inducers inactivate repressors, and co-repressors activate repressors. The operator is defined as a set of linked, coordinately controlled genes and their controlling sites. In the *lac* system, the *IOZYA* segment (and later the *PIOZYA* segment) constitute an operon.

PROBLEMS

1. Suppose you were studying the operon in *E. coli* involved in the synthesis of the xylose-metabolizing enzymes. You have Xyl$^+$ strains and Xyl$^-$ mutants and can easily assay the xylose breakdown enzyme. You find that this enzyme is regulated by some type of control system that responds to xylose, since the breakdown enzyme is present in high amounts when xylose is present and in very low amounts when xylose is absent. You have detected regulatory mutations that are linked to the *xyl* genes and that result in the synthesis of high levels of the xylose breakdown enzymes even in the absence of xylose.

You decide to carry out an Hfr experiment in which the wild-type *xyl* region, with normal control genes, is introduced early into a recipient (F$^-$) that is deleted for the *xyl* region, including the regulatory genes. After the mating in the absence of xylose, you follow the levels of the xylose breakdown enzyme at intervals.

   a. Describe the kinetics of the production of the xylose breakdown enzyme (the level of enzyme measured at different times up to 2 hours after the mating) if the *xyl* genes are under the negative control of a repressor.

   b. Describe the kinetics of the production of the xylose breakdown enzyme if the *xyl* genes are under the positive control of an activator. Use diagrams to explain your answer.

2. Suppose you have three mutants with the Lac⁻ phenotype. One of these has a missense mutation in the *Z* gene, another has an *I*ˢ mutation, and the third has a *P*⁻ mutation (a mutation in the *lac* promoter that prevents transcription of the entire *lac* operon). How would you distinguish between each of the three mutants using only complementation tests with F′ factors? (You can employ any combination of mutations in the *lac* region.)

3. The genes shown in the table below (*K, L, M, N*) are from the *lac* operon system of *E. coli*. The symbols *K, L, M,* and *N* represent the repressor gene (*I*), the operator (*O*), the structural gene for β-galactosidase (*Z*), and the gene for permease (*Y*), although not necessarily in that order. Furthermore, the order in which the symbols are written in the genotypes is not necessarily the actual sequence in the *lac* operon.

   By looking at the relationships in the diploids, state which symbol represents each of the *lac* genes *I, O, Z,* and *Y*. (Here, all mutations in *I* are *I*⁻ and mutations in *O* are *O*ᶜ; in other words, there are no *I*ˢ mutations involved.) Show some of your logic.

Genotype	Activity of β-galactosidase		Activity of permease	
	no inducer	inducer	no inducer	inducer
K⁺*L*⁺*M*⁻*N*⁻	+	+	−	−
K⁻*L*⁻*M*⁺*N*⁺	−	−	+	+
K⁺*L*⁻*M*⁺*N*⁺	+	+	+	+
K⁻*L*⁻*M*⁺*N*⁺/*K*⁺*L*⁺*M*⁻*N*⁻	−	+	+	+
K⁺*L*⁺*M*⁺*N*⁺/*K*⁻*L*⁻*M*⁻*N*⁺	−	+	−	+

4. If Jacob and Monod had encountered the types of mutations listed below that might occur in the *lac* system, describe the behavior of each mutation in complementation tests with the wild type (dominant or recessive in *cis* or *trans*, etc.). Explain your reasoning.

   a. A mutation in the promoter for the *lac* operon that eliminates transcription initiation.

   b. A mutation in the *I* gene that causes the repressor to bind much more tightly to the operator. (In the presence of IPTG, which binds to repressor and lowers affinity for the operator, the mutant repressor still has enough residual affinity to bind to the operator normally.)

   c. A mutation in the *I* gene that results in repressors that can no longer bind to IPTG but can still form tetramers. (The repressor is composed of four identical subunits that can associate and disassociate in the cytoplasm.) The mutant subunits can still aggregate with wild-type subunits.

Beckwith and Signer 1966

1. Explain the difference between specialized and generalized transduction.

    Answer: Specialized transduction occurs by the integration into the chromosome of a phage that carries a specific set of genes. In the experiment reported in the Beckwith and Signer paper, the lambdoid phage ϕ80 integrates into a specific attachment site near the *try* (now called *trp*) region of the chromosome. When phage induction occurs, a small fraction of phage incorporate the nearby *try* genes into their genomes, usually leaving behind some segment of their own genomes. These phage can then integrate into the chromosome of an infected strain, which results in transduction of the *try* genes from the original host into the new host. Because the genes that can be transduced by any specific phage are usually limited to those "special" genes that are near the integration site of the phage, this method of transduction is termed "specialized transduction."

    Generalized transduction is so named because any gene can be transduced from one host to another. Phage P1, used by Yanofsky and coworkers for mapping (see Unit 4), is an example of a generalized transducing phage. In this case, the host chromosome is chopped up into fragments during phage growth. If some of these fragments are of similar size to the phage genome, they can be incorporated into phage heads and injected into a recipient strain upon subsequent infection. The incorporation of the new genes into the recipient must occur via a double crossover in an homologous region of the recipient chromosome, since these fragments can neither replicate nor integrate into a phage attachment site as in specialized transduction.

2. Describe the steps used to isolate the strain EC15.

    Answer: The aim of the method used by Beckwith and Signer was to select for the integration of an episome carrying the *lac* genes (or, ultimately, any gene) into a region of the chromosome near a prophage attachment site. The prophage could then be induced, allowing the selection of rare transducing phage carrying the *lac* genes. The first step was to utilize an F'*lac* in a strain deleted for the *lac* and *pro* regions so that there was no homology between the chromosomal region carried on the F' and the host chromosome. The F' also carried a temperature-sensitive mutation, *114*, which prevents replication at 42°C. At this temperature, the only way for the cell to maintain the F' was to have it integrated into the chromosome. Without homology, integrations would be rare, but they would be at many potential points on the chromosome. Integrations could be selected for by plating on minimal lactose medium at 42°C. In addition, Beckwith and Signer also selected for strains in which integration of the F' had occurred within the T1*rec* gene (now called *tonB*). This gene is near the attachment site of the lambdoid phage ϕ80 and encodes the synthesis of a protein needed for the receptor site of T1. In principle, one could seed the plates with a lysate of the virulent T1 phage, and the only colonies that would grow would be expected to have integrations of F'$_{ts}$*lac* into T1*rec*. In practice, one does not use T1 itself but instead a substitute consisting of a mixture of lysates of ϕ80*vir* and colicin V and B (see Question 3). In addition, instead of lactose minimal medium, the authors used indicator plates that score Lac$^+$ colonies as white and Lac$^-$ colonies as red. In summary, the strain EC0 was plated on lactose indicator plates seeded with lysates of φ80*vir* and colicin V and B and incubated at 42°C. White Lac⁺ colonies were chosen and analyzed.

3. Why were φ80*vir* and colicin V and B used to select for T1rec mutants, and how do these lysates select for T1rec mutants?

Answer: T1 is an air-stable, virulent phage that can destroy cultures of bacteria for a significant period of time after its introduction into a laboratory. Therefore, it is better to use other agents that utilize the same receptor for infection. The receptor for φ80 requires two genes, one of which is T1*rec* (*tonB*). Likewise, the receptor for the proteinaceous infecting agents colicin V and B also requires more than one gene, one of which is T1*rec*. The only single-step mutant that is resistant to both φ80*vir* (a derivative of φ80 that cannot lysogenize) and colicin V and B is generated by a mutation at the T1*rec* locus. Thus, a mixture of both lysates produces the desired result.

4. Describe the properties of strains EC8 and EC15.

Answer: Both strains are Hfr's in that they will donate chromosomal markers in an ordered fashion from a fixed starting point. Markers brought in early will be inherited at a high frequency relative to markers transferred late. Looking at the map in Figure 1 on page 243, we can see that EC8 should donate Su_c (*supC*) at high frequency and *try* (*trp*) at low frequency. EC15, on the other hand, has F integrated in the opposite orientation to that in EC8. Therefore, this strain should transfer *try* at high frequency and Su_c at low frequency.

5. Describe the steps in making a φ80d*lac* phage after the *lac* region has been transposed near the φ80 attachment site.

Answer: The first step involves infecting the strain with a φ80 phage and detecting lysogens. This is usually done by spotting a drop of a lysate of φ80 on a lawn of the strain on a broth plate, scraping bacteria from the center of the spot, and testing individual colonies for immunity to φ80. Then, UV irradiation is used to induce the φ80. A lysate is prepared and used to infect a strain that is deleted for the *lac* region. Lac⁺ colonies, which are rare, are then purified and tested for those that contain a φ80d*lac* transducing phage by UV-inducing these cells and testing the new lysate for the ability to transduce *lac*. Cells that carry a φ80d*lac* phage will yield lysates that transduce the *lac* genes with high frequency, since every cell in the population has the φ80d*lac* phage.

6. Since EC15 has the F'*lac* integrated into the T1*rec* locus, how could the authors infect EC15 with φ80 (see Question 5) to create a lysogen? The T1*rec* (*ton B*) locus is required for φ80 infection. (The answer to this is not actually given in the paper. See if you can work out a method for doing this. There are several possible ways.)

Answer: The method used by Beckwith and Signer involved first making a "mixed lysate" of λ and φ80 in a different strain. When both λ and φ80 infect a cell, some λ chromosomes are packaged into φ80 heads and some φ80 chromosomes are packaged into λ heads. These λ phage can now infect a T1rec strain, since the phage adsorbs to the λ receptors and injects the φ80 DNA.

A second method, which was used in subsequent experiments, involved making a mutant derivative of φ80, called φ80h (h for host range) that could infect T1rec cells. It would also be possible to introduce an episome carrying the T1*rec* locus, which would then complement the defect provided the episome was compatible with the F factor already in the chromosome in EC15.

7. Explain Table 2 on page 245.

   Answer: This table shows that *lac* can indeed be transduced by φ80 induced from lysogens of EC8 and EC15. Although *try* (now called *trp*) can be transduced, one cannot see the simultaneous transduction of *try* and *lac*, indicating that these two genes are too far apart to be carried on the same transducing particle.

8. What were the experiments reported in Table 3 on page 246 trying to show?

   Answer: The experiments reported in this table were designed simply to show that the φ80 transducing phage derived from EC8 and EC15 that carry *lac* also carry at least a part of F, since lysogens carrying these transducing phage can partially complement a defective F factor, which transfers chromosomal markers poorly.

9. How were φ80d*lacZ*$^+$*Y*$^-$ phage obtained?

   Answer: Phage that carry *Z* but not *Y* are rare, so a method was used to screen large numbers of *lac* transducing phage for those that were *Z*$^+$*Y*$^-$. The authors took advantage of a fusion described by Jacob and co-workers in which the *lacY* gene was under the control of the *purE* operon. In strains with an episome carrying this fusion, the *Y* gene was expressed when the concentration of adenine in the medium was low and not expressed when the adenine levels were high. In a strain otherwise deleted for *lac* but carrying this episome, Lac$^+$ transducing phage were selected under conditions of low adenine concentration. Since the *Y* gene was supplied by the episome, only the *Z* gene needed to be on the transducing phage. The Lac$^+$ colonies resulting from this selection were then transferred to medium containing high levels of adenine, shutting off the episomal *Y* gene. Under these conditions, Lac$^+$ colonies would indicate the presence of a Lac$^+$ transducing phage and Lac$^-$ colonies, which were Lac$^+$ in low adenine, would indicate *Z*$^+$*Y*$^-$ transducing phage.

10. Explain Figure 3 on page 247.

    Answer: This figure shows a map of the portions of the *Y* gene that are present and missing in the *Z*$^+$*Y*$^-$ transducing phage referred to in Question 9. When the transducing phage are integrated into a strain deleted for *lac*, the phage can be represented as having deletions extending into the *Y* gene, as shown in the figure.

11. Explain Table 4 and Figure 5 on page 249.

    Answer: The table and diagram portray the data from the experiment pictured in Figure 4 on page 248. Admittedly, this is a very complicated construction, but it does represent an elegant demonstration of the power of bacterial genetics. The goal was to demonstrate the orientation of the *lac* region when the φ80d*lac* transducing phage is integrated into the chromosome. Here, the Z^+Y^- phage derived from EC8 and EC15 were used in a strain carrying the *purE-lac* fusion. Since the integrated phage contain a deletion coming from one direction into *Y* and the episomes carry a deletion coming from the beginning of the *lac* operon and ending within *Z*, then the only homology within which a crossover can occur is in *lac*, as shown in Figure 4. This crossover is required for the F' carrying the fusion to be able to mobilize the chromosome. The order of markers transferred should reflect the orientation of *lac*, as pictured in Figure 4. Table 4 and Figure 5 show that in the strain carrying the phage derived from EC8, the *purB* locus, but not *try* (now called *trp*), is transferred early, whereas in the strain carrying the phage derived from EC15, *try*, but not *purB*, is transferred early.

Beckwith et al. 1966

12. How were fusions of the *lac* and *trp* (previously called *try*) operons isolated?

Answer: The object was to find strains in which the segment of the chromosome between *trp* and *lac* was deleted and in which the deletion ended within each operon. Such precise deletions would be very rare, and some method to select such rare events had to be employed. Fortunately, by putting the *lac* region into the chromosome at the att_{80} site via a transducing phage, one could select for T1rec mutants. Many of the spontaneous T1rec mutants result from deletions. Thus, by plating T1rec mutants on indicator plates and picking the Lac⁻ colonies, one could then screen those colonies for Trp⁻ colonies. These latter colonies could then be tested by recombination against point mutations within *lac* and *trp* to determine whether the deletion endpoint went past the operon or ended within it.

13. What are the properties of the *trp* (*try*)-*lac* fusions?

Answer: In these strains, the *lac* genes are expressed under the control of the *trp* operon. Thus, the *Y* gene, as measured by the ability to grow on melibiose at 42°C, is expressed when tryptophan is absent from the medium or when a mutation in the gene encoding the *trp* repressor is introduced but not when high levels of tryptophan are present.

Shimada et al. 1972

14. Describe the normal integration process of phage λ. Which genes and DNA segments are required?

Answer: Figure 1 on page 263 provides a detailed diagram of the insertion process. Insertion requires the product of the λ *int* gene, which acts on specific segments of DNA on both λ and the bacterial chromosome (termed attachment sites) to catalyze a site-specific recombination event.

15. How are the requirements for excision different from those for integration?

Answer: The excision process is the direct reverse of integration except that in addition to the *int* gene product, the product of the *xis* gene is also required.

16. How did the authors isolate lysogens with λ integrated at different sites?

Answer: The basic idea was to start with a strain deleted for the λ attachment site and then to select for rare integration events of λ into the bacterial chromosome. These integrations would have to be at sites other than the normal attachment site. The selection was achieved by spreading infected cells with a λ phage lacking the repressor gene that confers immunity. Only those cells with integrated λ or cells with mutations in the λ receptor gene could survive this challenge. The latter class was eliminated by testing against a λ virulent phage that could kill lysogens but not cells lacking the λ receptor gene.

17. Compare the frequency of λ integration at the normal attachment site with that at secondary attachment sites.

Answer: Table 4 on page 268 shows that the frequency of λ integration at the normal attachment site is close to 200 times higher than at secondary attachment sites. (Compare 0.88 with 0.0043.)

18. Is integration into secondary sites dependent on *int?* How do we know?

Answer: Yes, it is. Table 4 on page 268 shows that the frequency of integrations at secondary attachment sites (those occurring in the HfrH strain deleted for the attachment site) drops from 0.0043 to about 0.00001.

19. Explain auxotrophic lysogens and the experiments that characterized them.

Answer: Auxotrophic lysogens occur when λ integrates into the middle of a gene involved in synthesizing required nutrients. The authors found that some of the lysogens were either Pro⁻ or Leu⁻. All of the revertants to either Pro⁺ or Leu⁺ had lost the prophage. In addition, when the prophage was cured from the Pro⁻ lysogen, the resulting strain had become Pro⁺.

20. How were most of the prophage mapped? Describe these experiments in detail.

Answer: Some prophage were mapped by using the auxotrophic requirement as a genetic marker. Others were mapped by zygotic induction. (Recall that the starting strain was an Hfr [HfrH] with its origin near 0 minutes on the genetic map.) During conjugation experiments, samples were tested for the generation of λ phage at different times after the inception of mating. When the λ prophage is transferred into a recipient that has no immunity, the λ will be induced. Figure 2 on page 269 shows how measuring the phage (infective centers) can give a rough idea of the location of the integrated λ prophage with respect to other markers on the chromosome.

21. Explain how deletion mapping helps in finding prophage integration sites.

Answer: Some phage were mapped by heat-curing the λ and finding survivors with deletions of the prophage that extended into neighboring genes, sometimes creating auxotrophs or other recognizable mutants. The auxotrophic markers could then be mapped. Columns 4–6 in Table 5 on page 270 give an indication of the usefulness of this method.

22. How was prophage gene order determined?

Answer: Deletions extending into λ were generated by selecting for heat-resistant cells. To be heat-resistant, a cell must have deleted (by a spontaneous event in the population prior to the heat treatment) some of the phage genes involved in killing the host upon induction. The remaining genes can be determined by marker rescue or by their ability to recombine with point mutations in a superinfecting λ phage to generate wild-type phage. A series of deletions extending into any one lysogen can easily give the gene order (recall Benzer's work [see Unit 1]). Deletions that also extend into bacterial genes can give the order of prophage genes with respect to that gene. Table 6 on page 273 shows the order of genes found in secondary lysogens.

23. Describe how new transducing phage were obtained. Compare the strategy of Shimada et al. with that described by Beckwith and Signer.

    Answer: Heat-induced lysates were prepared and used to transduce auxotrophs. Numerous new transducing phage were obtained. In the Beckwith and Signer strategy, the gene of interest was moved to a position near the attachment site of a temperate phage. The phage was inserted and then transducing phage were sought. In the Shimada et al. method, the phage is moved to a position near the gene of interest. Although λ may only rarely integrate near certain genes, in some cases one can select for the integration of λ into a nearby site. Thus, the authors describe selecting for integration into the *tsx* gene by requiring T6-resistant lysogens.

24. What is the distribution of prophage among secondary sites?

    Answer: The distribution is not random; certain sites are favored over others.

25. How often did multiple lysogens occur?

    Answer: Nine of 17 lysogens were multiple.

PROBLEMS

1. The map of a strain, *E. coli* X, is given below.

leu	attC	pur				thr	V5rec	lys
tyr								
V1rec								
lac								ile
gal								attA
								ura
cys								
				E. coli X				mal
met								V4rec
V2rec								val
trp								
attD								
								attB
								cyt
gln								attE
		arg	ala	V3rec	glu			

Each box on the map of *E. coli* X represents one gene, whether it is labeled or not. In addition to sugar and auxotrophic markers such as *lac, gal, ala, glu,* etc., there are also genes (V1*rec,* V2*rec,* etc.) that encode receptor sites for the virulent phage V1, V2, V3, V4, and V5, respectively. The loci *attA, attB, attC,* etc., are attachment sites for the temperate phage A, B, C, D, and E. Each temperate phage will integrate only at its specific attachment site. These phage are induced at 42°C but remain uninduced at 37°C.

Using the method of Beckwith and Signer, show the steps you would use to isolate a specialized transducing phage carrying the *arg* genes. Give relevant details of the selections you would use. You have the following tools:

- a strain of *E. coli* X with the *arg* genes deleted (This strain is Arg⁻ and cannot grow on minimal medium without arginine.)
- the same strain as above, but with an F' factor (episome) carrying the *arg* genes (This F' factor replicates normally in all medium, except that when 0.1 M MgSO₄ is in the medium, the episome can no longer replicate.)
- all virulent phage (V1–V5) and all temperate phage (A–E) (The temperate phage are induced to enter the lytic cycle at 42°C. The temperate phage can transduce lengths of up to four bacterial genes.)
- minimal and rich medium.

2. Suppose you wanted to use the strain described in Problem 1 to isolate a transducing phage that carried the *ala* genes. Show how you would employ the method of Shimada et al. to isolate this phage. Assume you have all of the materials as in Problem 1 and you also have:

- a strain deleted for the *attD* locus
- a strain deleted for the *ala* locus
- derivatives of each temperate phage that have no immunity (C⁻) and that cannot integrate (Int⁻).

List the steps and give relevant details of the selections you would use.

3. Below is the map of a strain of bacteria, *E. coli* L, which is represented as a circle extending from 0 to 100 minutes.

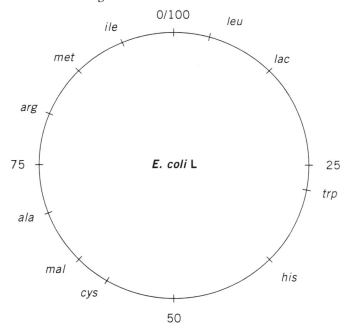

Suppose you wanted to clone the *cys* gene using the method of Beckwith and Signer. Describe the tools you would need to clone the *cys* gene (i.e., the strains and mutations in them). In addition, assume you have one virulent phage, V1, and one temperate phage, TP1. Assume you can place the genes for their receptor sites anywhere between 75 minutes (75′) and 100 minutes (100′) on the map. Assume also that the attachment site for TP1 can be placed anywhere between 75′ and 100′. Describe the steps you would use to clone the *cys* gene.

4. Assume you have a λ-like phage that is integrated into the chromosome at the *met* locus on the map of *E. coli* L (see Problem 3). Assume you have an Hfr that transfers the *mal* region first and transfers markers in a clockwise order (in other words, *mal* is the first marker and *cys* is the last marker to be transferred). Describe the inheritance of markers in the following recipients:

a. a recipient that has the same λ-like phage inserted in the *met* locus
b. a recipient that has no λ-like phage at all.

QUESTIONS AND ANSWERS

Perutz et al. 1965

1. What is hemoglobin? Where does it occur and what is its function?

   Answer: Hemoglobin is a protein that transports oxygen in red blood cells, carrying oxygen from the lungs to different tissues and then transporting H^+ and CO_2 from the tissues back to the lungs.

2. What is the basic structure of hemoglobin (subunits, lengths of chains, cofactors)?

   Answer: Hemoglobin consists of four subunits, containing two copies of the α chain and two copies of the β chain. The α chain consists of 141 residues and the β chain consists of 146 residues. Each chain has one oxygen binding site and binds one heme prosthetic group. The heme groups are made up of four pyrrole rings which bind an iron atom.

3. What is myoglobin? Where does it occur and how is it different from hemoglobin?

   Answer: Myoglobin is located in muscle and transports oxygen within muscle, acting as a reserve supply of oxygen. Unlike hemoglobin, myoglobin consists of a single polypeptide chain which binds a heme group.

4. What does a comparison of myoglobins and hemoglobins from different organisms show in terms of totally conserved or invariant residues?

   Answer: There are only nine totally invariant residues, which shows that they can have only a limited role in determining the secondary and tertiary structure of the globin chain.

5. What single general rule seems to emerge from considering the structures of all of the hemoglobins and myoglobins?

   Answer: There is almost complete exclusion of polar residues from interior sites.

6. What is the effect of proline on α helices? Where does proline usually occur in α helices?

   Answer: Prolines are found in either nonhelical regions or at the ends of helices, and in this way prolines limit the size of helices. When in helices, prolines often occupy the second site in the helix.

7. What would the effect of a replacement of a nonpolar residue on the surface of the hemoglobin molecule probably be on the function of the protein? Assume that a polar residue replaces the nonpolar residue. What would happen if the same type of replacement occurred in the interior of the protein?

   Answer: Most of the residues on the surface of the protein are interacting with water. Changing a residue from nonpolar to polar on the surface would be unlikely to cause a change in the protein's activity unless the residue was part of a contact with another subunit. However, if a polar residue replaces a nonpolar residue in the interior of the protein, then it would disrupt the internal contacts and cause loss of stability.

Perutz and Lehmann 1968

8. Find Hb Wien (the German word for Vienna) in the text and in Table 3 on page 305. Describe the change and explain why there are drastic effects.

   Answer: A tyrosine residue has been replaced by an aspartic acid residue at position 130 in the β chain. The ring of the tyrosine is in the internal cavity. The aspartic acid introduces a negative charge into the interior, and this negative charge is neutralized by drawing a positive charge near it, causing a displacement of helix A. The molecule is more unstable and this results in hemolytic anemia.

9. Find Hb Sogn in the text and in Table 3 on page 305. Explain the changes and consequences of this variant.

   Answer: This molecule has a change at position 14 in the β chain at which a leucine is replaced by an arginine. The leucine was in contact with several other hydrophobic residues, and the arginine introduces an extra positive charge. The protein denatures more rapidly, yielding free α chains. Despite this, there are no clinical symptoms.

10. What happens in Hb Santa Ana? Explain the effects of this mutation in terms of the replacement.

   Answer: Proline replaces leucine at position 44 in the β chain. This removes contacts with the heme group and no heme group is found in the β chain. This results in hemolytic anemia.

PROBLEMS

1. Explain why each of the following substitutions in a globular protein might result in a defective protein:

   a. substituting valine (nonpolar) for isoleucine (nonpolar) in the interior of the protein
   b. substituting glutamine (polar) for leucine (nonpolar) on the exterior
   c. substituting aspartic acid (polar) for glutamic acid (polar) in the crevice
   d. substituting proline (nonpolar) for leucine (nonpolar) on the exterior
   e. substituting arginine (polar) for leucine (nonpolar) in the interior.

2. Explain why each of the substitutions in Problem 1 might not result in a defective protein.

3. Suppose you are given the changes in hemoglobin listed below where the amino acids are encoded by the letters A through H:

   • a change from A to F in the interior
   • a change from F to D on the surface
   • a change from G to E in the crevice
   • a change from C to H in the interior
   • a change from A to B in the interior

   Eight amino acids are involved in this problem, and in each case, the mutants result from a single base change. You have the following eight amino acids: isoleucine, lysine, tryptophan, proline, cysteine, arginine, histidine, and serine. On the basis of the genetic code below (which gives the possible amino acid substitutions resulting from a single base change) and the principles described by Perutz and co-workers, assign each amino acid to one of the eight letters. Explain your reasoning. If there are several possibilities, explain them also.

The Genetic Code

Second letter

		U	C	A	G	
First letter	**U**	UUU ⎱Phe UUC ⎰ UUA ⎱Leu UUG ⎰	UCU ⎱ UCC ⎭Ser UCA ⎱ UCG ⎰	UAU ⎱Tyr UAC ⎰ UAA Stop UAG Stop	UGU ⎱Cys UGC ⎰ UGA Stop UGG Trp	U C A G
	C	CUU ⎱ CUC ⎭Leu CUA ⎱ CUG ⎰	CCU ⎱ CCC ⎭Pro CCA ⎱ CCG ⎰	CAU ⎱His CAC ⎰ CAA ⎱Gln CAG ⎰	CGU ⎱ CGC ⎭Arg CGA ⎱ CGG ⎰	U C A G
	A	AUU ⎱Ile AUC ⎭ AUA ⎰ AUG Met	ACU ⎱ ACC ⎭Thr ACA ⎱ ACG ⎰	AAU ⎱Asn AAC ⎰ AAA ⎱Lys AAG ⎰	AGU ⎱Ser AGC ⎰ AGA ⎱Arg AGG ⎰	U C A G
	G	GUU ⎱ GUC ⎭Val GUA ⎱ GUG ⎰	GCU ⎱ GCC ⎭Ala GCA ⎱ GCG ⎰	GAU ⎱Asp GAC ⎰ GAA ⎱Glu GAG ⎰	GGU ⎱ GGC ⎭Gly GGA ⎱ GGG ⎰	U C A G

Third letter

Farabaugh et al. 1978

1. Describe the system the authors used to examine the distribution of spontaneous mutations.

    Answer: The authors studied the distribution of spontaneous mutations in the *E. coli lacI* gene. Strains that can grow on phenyl-β-D-galactosidase (Pgal) have mutations in the *lacI* gene. A set of mutations (140) was treated in the same way that Benzer treated his mutations (see Unit 1). Namely, they were put into sites by deletion mapping and in some cases by pairwise crosses. Recurrences of mutations at the same site were cataloged.

2. Can you relate the authors' genetic findings to those of Benzer?

    Answer: Like Benzer, they found large hotspots. In fact, two hotspots at or near the same site in the gene accounted for close to 80% of all of the mutations. In addition, they detected deletions in the gene, some of which recurred at the same point.

3. What is the sequence basis for the large hotspots?

    Answer: Both large hotspots were at the same point. In the wild-type gene, there is a 4-base-pair sequence, CTGG, that is repeated in tandem three times. One of the two hotspots represents the loss of one unit of the CTGG sequence and the other hotspot represents the gain of one unit. In other words, one hotspot is the change from CTGGCTGGCTGG to CTGGCTGG and the other is the change to CTGGCTGGCTGGCTGG.

4. What is the sequence basis for preferred deletions?

    Answer: Seven of 12 deletions sequenced, including several recurring deletions, had occurred between short repeated sequences, in this case of 5 or 8 base pairs.

5. What mechanism(s) did the authors offer to account for the deletions?

    Answer: Deletions were proposed to occur either as recombination events between the short sequence repeats or as DNA synthesis (or replication) errors generated by slipped mispairing at the repeats. This is analogous to the mechanism proposed by Streisinger and co-workers for frameshifts.

Albertini et al. 1982

6. Explain the system constructed by the authors to detect deletions.

    Answer: The authors employed a fusion deletion that fused the end of *lacI* to the beginning of *lacZ* but still retained β-galactosidase activity. The fused repressor–β-galactosidase protein is synthesized from the *lacI* promoter. By placing two widely separated frameshifts in the *I*-encoded portion of the fusion, the authors interrupted the normal reading frame. To restore the correct reading frame, essential if the correct β-galactosidase protein is to be expressed, deletions of 700–1000 base pairs are required to remove the frameshifts. Lac⁺ colonies selected from this starting strain all contained deletions within the *lacI* gene that were 700–1000 base pairs long.

7. What did the authors find concerning the distribution of deletions? Were the endpoints randomly distributed?

   Answer: The deletion endpoints were not randomly distributed. There was one major hotspot and several minor hotspots at which deletion endpoints recurred.

8. What were the sequences at the deletion endpoints?

   Answer: Deletions occurred predominantly between short, sometimes broken, homologies. The largest hotspot occurred between the largest homologies in the system, two stretches, separated by 759 base pairs, where 14 of 17 base pairs were the same in the wild-type sequence. The minor hotspots also represented significant homologies, and even single-occurrence sites showed short homologies in the wild type before the deletion occurred.

9. How did the authors alter the homology responsible for the largest deletion hotspot, and what were the results of this alteration?

   Answer: Mutations at known positions were used in the starting strain. As shown in Figure 7 on page 342, two of these mutations interrupt part of the broken homology responsible for the hotspot. It can be seen from Table 4 on page 342 that a single-base-pair change in the region of homology can reduce the frequency of deletions at the hotspot by a factor of 20–40.

10. What mechanism did the authors diagram?

    Answer: Figure 9 on page 344 shows a slipped mispairing model for deletion formation.

11. What other factors did the authors propose as possibly playing a role in deletion rates?

    Answer: It is possible that secondary structures that allow hairpin loops to form, in analogy to certain transposable elements, can increase rates of deletion formation, as diagrammed in Figure 10 on page 344.

Prakash and Sherman 1973

12. What is the basic objective in this paper?

    Answer: The objective was to provide a reliable tester system for base pair substitutions.

13. Describe the experimental design of the system used by Prakash and Sherman.

    Answer: The system selected for revertants of iso-1-cytochrome *c* mutants of yeast by employing mutations at one of three positions in the gene. An *ochre* (UAA) site at codon 2 in the gene and message was used, as was an *amber* (UAG) mutation at position 9 and nine mutations affecting the starting (AUG) codon. Figures 1 and 2 on page 350 show the possible reversion events. Note that one could obtain intergenic revertants at any of three sites for the mutations in the starting (AUG) codon. Note also that for mutagens that are specific for the G·C→A·T transition, revertants could not be obtained for the mutants *cy*1-9 and *cy*1-179, which carried *ochre* or *amber* mutations at positions 2 and 9, respectively. After testing mutagens on each of the 11 strains, differences could be examined, as shown in Table 1 on page 352.

14. What were the authors' basic findings with a series of mutagens?

    Answer: Of 17 mutagens tested, 5 were very weak. Table 3 on page 356 shows that for the remaining 12, 7 had high rates of reversion of only *cy*1-131. These mutagens were EMS, DES, NTG, NIL, HNO_2, [^3H]U, and to a lesser extent, β-propiolactone. The four mutagens MMS, DMS, UV light, and γ-rays were not specific in their mutagenic action with this set of strains.

15. What was concluded about the specificity of the seven mutagens that gave a strong reaction on only one strain?

    Answer: Since of the 11 tester strains, only *cy*1-131 reverts via a G·C→A·T transition, it was concluded that these seven mutagens induced only this base substitution.

16. How did the authors rule out that complex changes other than G·C→A·T transitions resulted in reversion of *cy*1-131?

    Answer: Sequencing the protein produced by revertants showed that the normal sequence was present.

17. How did the authors caution about generalizing from their results?

    Answer: They noted that it was not established whether the seven mutagens generated exclusively G·C→A·T transitions at sites other than *cy*1-131, since the effects of neighboring base pairs might alter the specificity at other sites.

18. What model did the authors offer to account for the G·C→A·T specificity of the seven mutagens?

    Answer: They referred to work that suggested that the mutagenicity and specificity of alkylating agents depends on the extent of formation of *O*-6-alkyl guanine, which can mispair with thymine and result in G·C→A·T mutations.

Ames et al. 1973

19. What is the *rfa* mutation and how is it relevant to the work described by the authors?

    Answer: The *rfa* mutation removes the lipopolysaccharide (LPS) coat and makes the cell more permeable to certain compounds, including many mutagens. Its relevance is that many mutagens are more active on strains with the *rfa* mutation.

20. Explain Table 2 on page 369.

    Answer: Table 2 shows the effect of the *rfa* mutation on the mutability of certain His⁻ mutants (in an excision repair background). For example, in the normal LPS strain, ICR-191 gives 31 revertants per plate, which increases to 955 revertants per plate in the *rfa* (deep rough LPS) strain. Other mutagens show similar increases.

21. Which figure compares strains with and without excision repair, and what are the basic findings?

Answer: Figure 1 on page 369 shows the mutagenic effect of 2-nitrosofluorene. It can be seen that strains lacking excision repair are more mutable than normal strains. In addition, strains lacking the LPS coat are slightly more mutable than normal strains. However, the largest effect is seen by comparing an excision-repair-deficient *rfa* strain with a normal strain, or even an *rfa* strain with normal excision repair with a normal strain.

22. Describe the nature and specificity of each of the tester strains.

Answer: The strain TA1535 carries the *hisG46* mutation, which is a missense mutation that reverts via base substitutions. TA1536 carries *hisC207*, which is a frameshift mutation of unknown origin that reverts with some, but not all, frameshift mutagens. TA1537 carries *hisC3076*, which appears to carry an extra G·C pair that creates a run of four Gs (GGGG). This strain is reverted by agents that cause a −1 frameshift due to the loss of a base pair in the run of Gs or in a very nearby sequence. Strain TA1538 contains *hisD3052*, which appears to contain a CGCGCG sequence that is reverted by the loss of a CG sequence.

23. What type of mutation mentioned by the authors cannot be detected by their set of tester strains?

Answer: There is no frameshift tester strain that can detect frameshifts at a repetition of AT sequences.

McCann et al. 1975

24. The tester strain TA1535 with the plasmid pKM101 is termed TA100. How does TA100 compare with TA1535 with regard to mutagenicity? Give some examples.

Answer: Table 1 on page 373 shows that TA100 is much more mutable than TA1535 with certain mutagens. For example, we can see from Table 1 that MMS gives 5 revertants per plate with TA1535 but 3244 with TA100. MNNG increases from 1511 to 18,701 and AF-2 increases from 0 to 1674.

25. How does the presence of the plasmid pKM101 affect the frameshift tester strain TA1538?

Answer: Again, it is apparent from Table 1 on page 373 that some compounds revert the new strain TA98 better than they revert TA1538.

26. How do the authors propose to utilize the set of tester strains?

Answer: These strains, and those like them, can be used to quickly test a large number of chemicals in the environment for those that cause mutations and therefore are potentially dangerous to humans.

Coulondre and Miller 1977

27. Describe the system used in this paper to determine mutagenic specificity.

Answer: This system employs nonsense mutations in the *lacI* gene of *E. coli*. First, I⁻ mutants are selected on Pgal medium, and then the nonsense mutations (normally only *ambers* and *ochres* are dealt with) are identified by using suppressors. This fraction, which is often 20–30% of the I^- mutations, is then mapped and analyzed with a larger set of suppressors to identify each mutation as one of the known *amber* and *ochre* sites. Figures 2 and 3 on pages 380 and 381, respectively, show all of the possible sites resulting from single base changes. The number of occurrences at each site in the collection is then charted, and the specificity of the mutagen appears as a spectrum across as many as 80 different sites, as seen in the remaining figures in the paper.

28. What are the differences between this system and a reversion system such as used by Ames and co-workers to determine mutagenic specificity? What are the advantages and disadvantages of each type of system?

Answer: In a reversion system, a specific mutation is used to study the reversion to wild type. A set of mutations can be used in series. In the *lacI* nonsense system, one is analyzing a subset of all the forward mutations in *lacI*, namely, those causing nonsense mutations in the *I* gene. The advantage of a reversion system is that it is less work to obtain mutation rates for many different mutagens under a variety of conditions. In addition, one can directly measure mutation rates. The disadvantage is that in some reversion systems, it is not always clear which mutation is occurring to cause the revertant. In addition, one is only using one or a very few sites to score mutagenic activity. Forward mutation systems such as the *lacI* nonsense system are more laborious than reversion systems, but the mutations are scored at many different positions, so mutagenicity is scored as a spectrum of changes. If some sites are hotspots or coldspots, they do not distort the picture. In addition, these hotspots can be analyzed further. Forward systems are good at measuring relative mutation rates at different sites but not as accurate as reversion systems for measuring absolute mutation rates.

29. Describe the specificities for EMS and NG. Can you relate those specificities to the chemical properties of the respective mutagens?

Answer: In the *lacI* forward system, only $G \cdot C \rightarrow A \cdot T$ transitions are induced by these two mutagens, whereas in a nonsense reversion system, NG induced low, and EMS very low, levels of the $A \cdot T \rightarrow G \cdot C$ transition. The $G \cdot C \rightarrow A \cdot T$ specificity can be attributed to the generation of O-6-alkyl guanine by these agents, which then can mispair with T. The low levels of the $A \cdot T \rightarrow G \cdot C$ transition might be attributed to the generation of O-4-alkyl thymine, which can mispair with G.

30. Explain the specificity of UV irradiation.

Answer: UV irradiation causes all types of base substitutions, although $G \cdot C \rightarrow A \cdot T$ transitions are favored. Among the $G \cdot C \rightarrow A \cdot T$ transitions, certain hotspots are responsible for the majority of mutations.

31. What system was used to look for the $A \cdot T \rightarrow G \cdot C$ transition?

Answer: *Ochre* mutants were either reverted to wild type or converted to *amber* mutants. In some cases, direct comparisons could be made between $A \cdot T \rightarrow G \cdot C$ transitions and $G \cdot C \rightarrow A \cdot T$ transitions at the same exact site (base pair position).

32. How were double mutations detected? Which mutagens induced these and why?

Answer: A set of *amber* and *ochre* mutations had been previously shown to be due to tandem double base changes. The appearance of these mutations indicated the induction of tandem double base changes. UV light induced these changes in a number of cases, which can be correlated with the fact that two different types of pyrimidine-pyrimidine photodimers have been implicated in UV mutagenesis.

33. Explain Figure 14 on page 404. How does it relate to the work of Benzer discussed earlier in this course (see Unit 1)?

Answer: Like the classic figure from Benzer's work, this figure shows hotspots in a gene. Both spontaneous and mutagen-induced hotspots are shown here. However, Figure 14 goes a step beyond Benzer's work in that the base change is known in each case, since only G·C→A·T transitions are charted here. Thus, all of the differences in rates must be due to aspects of the surrounding base sequence.

Coulondre et al. 1978

34. What aspect of the sequence was responsible for spontaneous hotspots due to base substitutions?

Answer: The spontaneous base substitution hotspots occurred at 5-methylcytosine residues, which in turn occurred as part of a CCAGG (or CCTGG) sequence.

35. How was a new hotspot sequence created, and what was the result of it?

Answer: The object was to create a new CCAGG sequence in which the internal CAG would be in the correct reading frame so that it could mutate to UAG (TAG), thus creating an *amber* at a C which would be methylated at the 5 position. By scanning the sequence surrounding each *amber* site, one site was found where the wild-type sequence was CGAGG, and this mutated to CTAGG to create *amber* site *A28*. (Recall that this was before site-directed mutagenesis was invented.) 2AP-induced revertants of *amber* *A28* would result in the generation of either a CCAGG or a CTGGG sequence. These could be distinguished because of the properties of the pseudo revertant. The new strain, containing the extra CCAGG site, was then used to generate spontaneous *lacI amber* mutations. These were characterized, and as shown in Figure 5 on page 410, a hotspot occurred at the new position.

36. What was the explanation given for hotspots occurring spontaneously at the sites discussed in Question 35?

Answer: Spontaneous deaminations from cytosine to uracil would yield C→T transitions at the next round of replication. However, the enzyme uracil DNA glycosidase excises the uracils from the DNA. 5-Methylcytosine deaminates to yield 5-methyluracil, which is thymine and thus cannot be excised from the DNA. Therefore, deaminations at 5-methylcytosine escape the primary cellular defense mechanism and lead to a high mutability.

37. What aspect of the *lacI* sequence promoted more frequent UV-irradiation-induced transitions? Which figure shows this? Does this explain everything about UV hotspots?

Answer: Figure 7 on page 411 shows that sites that are part of a pyrimidine-pyrimidine sequence are much more prone to G·C→A·T transitions than sites that are not part of such a sequence. This does not explain everything about UV hotspots, however, since there is a great variation of mutation rates even among the sites that are part of a pyrimidine-pyrimidine sequence.

Cupples and Miller 1989

38. Describe the system used to analyze mutations. What type of system is this? How was it built? What are its advantages and disadvantages?

Answer: The system is a reversion system that depends on a set of six strains, each with a different base change in the codon for an essential glutamic acid residue of β-galactosidase at position 461. Each of the six strains reverts to wild type (on lactose minimal medium) by only one specific base change at one specific site. The set of six strains allows one to assay for each of the six base substitutions. It was built by introducing each mutation via site-directed mutagenesis in vitro. It has all of the advantages of a reversion system and offers a simple test of the specificity of a mutagen or mutator. The disadvantage is that one is only using one site to score each base substitution, so one must be cautious about generalizing from the results.

39. What are the results, in detail, of using this system to analyze mutations induced by MNNG and EMS?

Answer: It can be seen from Table 2 on page 415 that both of these agents induce the G·C→A·T transition very strongly and other base substitutions weakly. MNNG induces the A·T→G·C transition at 1% the level of G·C→A·T transitions at the sites examined. It induces most of the transversions at levels ranging from 0.1% to 0.5% of the G·C→A·T transition level. These low levels are real, however, as indicated by the dose-response data in the table. EMS follows the same pattern as MNNG, with A·T→G·C transitions at about 0.5% the G·C→A·T level and transversions ranging from 0.003% to 0.7% of this level.

40. What is the specificity of 5-azacytidine (5AZ) and the mutator *mutT?*

Answer: 5AZ causes G·C→C·G transversions and the mutator *mutT* induces only A·T→C·G transversions.

41. How did the authors plan to use these strains for subsequent experiments?

Answer: They planned to use these strains to detect new mutator strains.

Nghiem et al. 1988

42. What is a mutator strain?

Answer: A mutator strain is a strain that has a higher rate of spontaneous mutation.

43. How did the authors devise a papillation assay?

Answer: Papillation results from small microcolonies growing out of larger colonies that have stopped growing. One way to arrange this is to use two carbon sources. The colonies are grown up on one carbon source, and then only a small fraction of cells within the colony can use the second carbon source. These cells will continue to grow and form microcolonies, or papillae. The authors used Lac⁻ strains carrying one of the six *lacZ*⁻ mutations described in the paper by Cupples and Miller. The two sugars were glucose, on which all cells could grow, and Pgal (phenyl-β-D-galactosidase, an analog of lactose) on which only LacZ⁺ cells could grow. The cells form colonies and grow to a certain size, exhausting the glucose. Only rare LacZ⁺ revertants can grow on the second carbon source, Pgal. These cells form papillae, which are stained blue by the Xgal indicator dye in the medium.

44. Describe exactly how the *mutY* locus was discovered? What were the steps involved in the isolation of this mutant?

Answer: As shown in Figure 1 on page 419, an *amber* mutation was used that corresponds to a position in *lacZ* that normally encodes an essential tyrosine residue. Only tyrosine can function at this position in β-galactosidase. Therefore, revertants to Lac⁺ must be due to either a G·C→C·G or G·C→T·A transversion. These cells were mutagenized with EMS and then plated on medium to detect the blue papillae discussed in the answer to Question 43. Colonies with more papillae than normal were picked and analyzed, since these were likely to have a higher mutation rate.

45. Which systems were employed to determine the specificity of mutations occurring in a *mutY* strain? What were the results?

Answer: Both the *lacI amber* system of Coulondre and Miller and the *lacZ* reversion system of Cupples and Miller were used. Both systems showed that *mutY* strains had an increase in only the G·C→T·A transversion.

Michaels et al. 1992

46. What activities were found for the proteins encoded by the *mutY* and *mutM* genes?

Answer: The MutY protein is a glycosylase that excises adenine from a A/G or A/8-oxoG mispair. The MutM protein is a glycosylase that excises 8-oxoG, as well as certain other damaged guanines, from the DNA.

47. What are some of the products of oxidative damage to the DNA?

Answer: Oxidative damage results in 10,000 lesions per cell per day in humans. One lesion that can lead to mutagenesis is 7,8-dihydro-8-oxoguanine, or 8-oxoG.

48. Table 1 on page 425 gives complementation results. What are these results, and what do they signify?

Answer: These results show that a plasmid that overproduces the *mutM* gene product can suppress the effects of a *mutY* mutation.

49. What do Tables 2 and 3 on page 425 show?

Answer: Tables 2 and 3 show that the double mutation *mutM mutY* results in an enormously high mutation rate that is due to an increase in only the

G·C→T·A transversion. This increase in mutation rate also results in an increase in Rif^r mutants.

50. How do the results in Tables 1, 2, and 3 on page 425 suggest a model for the concerted action of both *mutY* and *mutM?* Describe the model.

Answer: In this model, the first line of defense is the MutM protein, which directly excises 8-oxoG lesions from the DNA. The gap is then filled in by repair synthesis. However, some of the lesions escape repair and result in the misincorporation of an A across from the 8-oxoG. This A is removed by the MutY protein. Repair synthesis incorporates a C across from the 8-oxodG most of the time, allowing the MutM protein another chance to remove the lesion. The results in Tables 1–3 suggest that if either of the glycosylases is not functioning, the other can remove 95% of the effects of 8-oxodG. However, when both glycosylases are inactive, the mutation rate goes way up.

51. What does the *mutT*-encoded protein do, and how does it fit into the model described in Question 50?

Answer: The MutT protein removes 8-oxo-dGTP from the pool of DNA precursors by hydrolyzing it to 8-oxo-dGMP, thus preventing its incorporation into DNA. In the absence of the MutT protein, the 8-oxo-dGTP could be misincorporated across from an A and result in A·T→C·G transversions.

PROBLEMS

1. The following continuous sequence, which is not necessarily translated, is from one of the two DNA strands in a genetic region. From the sequence, find the mutations that would be expected to occur most frequently at the DNA level spontaneously (without the aid of mutagens). Explain what each mutation is and why it would be frequent.

A A G G C T A G C T T T A G G A G A T C C C G A T C T C A A A G C T A T C T A G C
T T T A G G T A T A T A G A T C T A T G C T C T C T G A T C T A G C A T C C C T A
G C A T C A T A T C G G G A T C C T A C G A A T C T T T G A T C G G T A T C G G G
A T A C G T A T G A A G G C T A G C C T C A T C C A T C C A T C C A A G C T T
A A T A T C G A T C G G A T C C T G G A A T T G G A T T C C C A G A G
A T C T T T T T A G C T A G C T C C C G C C T A G C T T T C G G A G C T T A A T C
C T A A T G A G C A A C C A C C G G T A T A T A G C C A A T A C A A G C C G G A T
T C G G G A T C C T T A G G A T C C A A G A A T C T T C G A G A A A T C G G A T C
G G G A T C T T A T C G T C T C C A A G A A T C T C C T A G T T C C A A T C T T T
A T C G G A T C G G A A G G C T A T

2. Suppose you have a series of six *E. coli* strains that cannot metabolize the sugar maltose. These cells are therefore Mal⁻. They have a mutation in the *malA* gene that affects the amino acid at a position normally occupied by a histidine (HIS). (Consult the genetic code on page 580.) For the six Mal⁻ strains, the following substitutions are found in place of histidine:

Strain 1: TYR	**Strain 4:** LEU
Strain 2: ASN	**Strain 5:** PRO
Strain 3: ASP	**Strain 6:** ARG

Each results from a single base substitution at one of the **first two** positions in the HIS codon. All of the Mal⁻ mutants can grow on glucose minimal medium but not on maltose minimal medium. Only Mal⁺ revertants can grow on maltose minimal medium. On minimal medium, tetrazolium dye stains Mal⁺ colonies red in the presence of maltose.

a. Show which single base substitutions in double-stranded DNA would be required to restore each of the six strains to the wild type.

b. How would you isolate a mutator strain that specifically makes the A·T→ T·A transversion? Describe the steps, including the strain you would use, the procedures, and the materials.

3. Suppose that instead of using *amber* and *ochre* codons, Coulondre and co-workers had designed a forward system in *lacI* based on the induction (generation) of UGA codons from the wild type.

a. Show the codons that normally specify an amino acid (it is not necessary to say which one) and that are linked to the UGA codon by a single base change. In other words, which codons can go from wild type to UGA? Show the base change on double-stranded DNA involved in going from wild type to UGA in each case.

b. Suppose that the sequence below represents the *lacI* mRNA. Each codon position is numbered. Draw a chart, like the one in Coulondre and Miller (see Figure 2, page 380), that shows the expected UGA sites that can occur arranged by the base change that generates the UGA codon.

AUG AAA CCG UUA GCG GGG UGU GAA UGG AAC CGA UGC UCA AAA UUA
 1   2   3   4   5   6   7   8   9 10 11 12 13 14 15

AGA GGC UCA UGU GCU GGA UUA UGG UCA AGA CAG CAU GGA UCA CCG
16 17 18 19 20 21 22 23 24 25 26 27 28 29 30

c. Suppose that a mutagen only changed UCA codons to UGA. What would the chart look like for the analysis of a collection of about 50 UGA mutations induced in the *lacI* gene by this mutagen?

4. Adenine (A) can be oxidized, either in the DNA or as the DNA precursor ATP, to yield a product, A*, that mispairs frequently with either adenine (A) or guanine (G). If left uncorrected, these mispairs will lead to mutations. Suppose that three mutator loci, *mutA, mutB,* and *mutC,* have been found that have defects in a repair system that normally overcomes the effects of the oxidized adenine A*.

a. Which base substitution mutation(s) would result from the consequences of having unrepaired A* persist in the cell?

b. Describe a reasonable model for how the *mutA, mutB,* and *mutC* gene products might work to prevent mutations resulting from an oxidized adenine (A*). Show the postulated activities for each gene product.

5. Suppose you are working with a bacterial strain with a different triplet genetic code containing four bases B, D, X, and Y. In the double-stranded DNA, the coding rules are: B pairs with D and X pairs with Y. Suppose that the codon BYD is the only nonsense codon.

a. Show which sense codons could go to nonsense by a single base change. Arrange these in a table according to the category of base change in double-stranded DNA, in analogy with Coulondre and co-workers who listed categories as G·C→A·T, G·C→T·A, etc.

b. If a mutagen made B·D→D·B changes only, which sense codons in the sequence below would the mutagen convert to nonsense. Give the identity of the codon and its numbered position(s) in the sequence below. Here, the antisense strand (same as the message) is shown in triplets read in phase in the 5' to 3' direction.

5'   3'
 BBB BBD BYB XYD YXB XYD BYY DXD XXD BDD BYY DYD YXB BYX BXD YYY YYD
  1   2   3   4   5   6   7   8   9   10   11   12   13   14   15   16   17

c. If a mutagen only made the X·Y→D·B change, then which sense codons in the sequence would it convert to nonsense. Again, give the codon and its numbered position(s) in the sequence above.

d. The sequence 5' - YBX - 3' is methylated at the X, causing more frequent base changes of all types at this position. Therefore, mutations occurring at the X in a 5' - YBX -3' sequence are spontaneous hotspots. Are any of the sense codons spontaneous hotspots for the conversion to nonsense in the system you have just constructed? If so, list them and briefly point out why.

6. Using the same organism as in Problem 5, design a system like that of Cupples and co-workers by assuming that the BXX codon encodes an essential amino acid at position 20 in the gene encoding an enzyme needed for arabinose metabolism. (Arabinose is a sugar that, like glucose, can be used as a carbon source for this organism.) Cells growing on arabinose form red colonies in the presence of MacConkey dyes.

   a. Assume you can construct strains with specific mutations at the BXX codon. Show which mutations you would design and for which of the six possible base substitutions each mutation would test.

   b. Using the principles of Nghiem and co-workers, show how you would use the system you constructed to detect mutator strains and then to test their specificity.

7. Suppose that thymine (T) can be oxidized, either in the DNA or as a precursor, TTP, to yield a derivative, T*, that mispairs frequently with C during replication, leading to mutations. Let's say that the three mutator loci *mutJ*, *mutK*, and *mutN* have been characterized. Each locus encodes a repair gene involved in the repair or avoidance of mutations from the oxidized T, or T*.

   a. Show the base substitution(s) that would result from having no repair system for T* at all. Show briefly how these would occur.

   b. Describe a plausible model for how the *mutJ*, *mutK*, and *mutN* gene products might work to prevent mutations resulting from an oxidized thymine (T*). Show the postulated activities for each product.

8. The structures of adenine (A) and guanine (G) and also the structures of the normal Watson-Crick base pairs that they make in double-stranded DNA are shown on page 592. The spontaneous oxidative deamination of adenine produces hypoxanthine (HX), which is also shown. Because hypoxanthine can pair with cytosine, it will cause A→G transitions if not repaired. However, *E. coli* cells have a repair enzyme, hypoxanthine glycosylase, that recognizes HX in double-stranded DNA across from T and excises it from the DNA before replication. Repair synthesis then restores the normal A across from the T.

   2,6-Diaminopurine (DAP), also shown on page 592, can pair with T, just like adenine, and not with C. However, DAP can actually make three hydrogen bonds with T (as shown) instead of the two that adenine makes with T. Considering that the cell has evolved numerous glycosylases to remove unwanted products of oxidation and deamination, can you think of a possible explanation for why cells choose not to use 2,6-diaminopurine in DNA, despite its ability to make an extra hydrogen bond with T, but instead choose to use adenine?

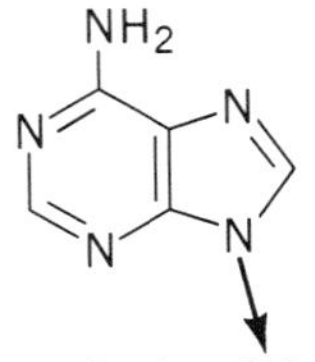

adenine (A)

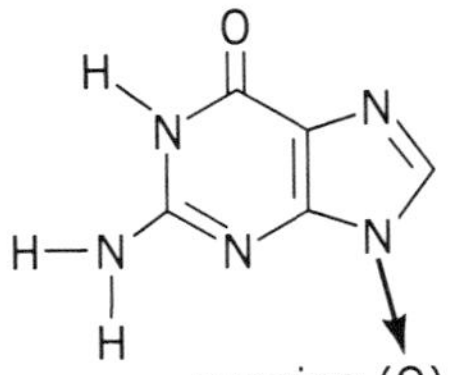

guanine (G)

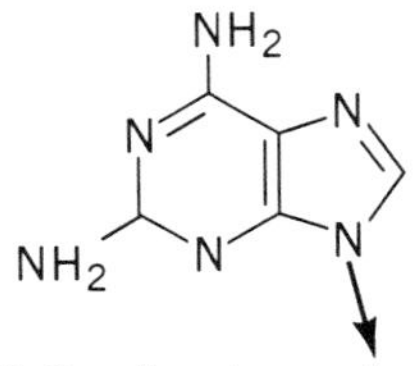

2,6 - diaminopurine (DAP)

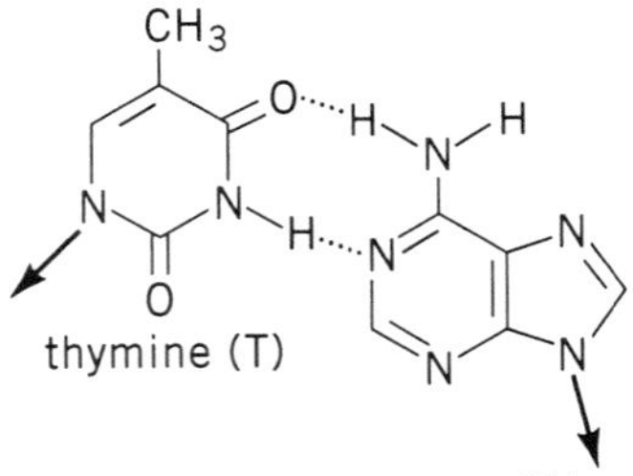

thymine (T)   (A)

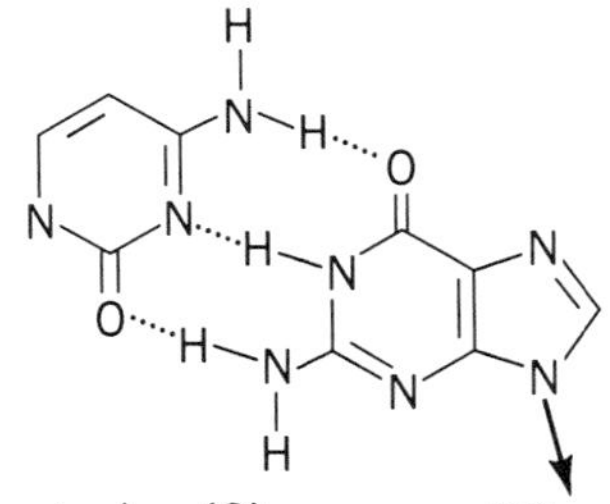

cytosine (C)   (G)

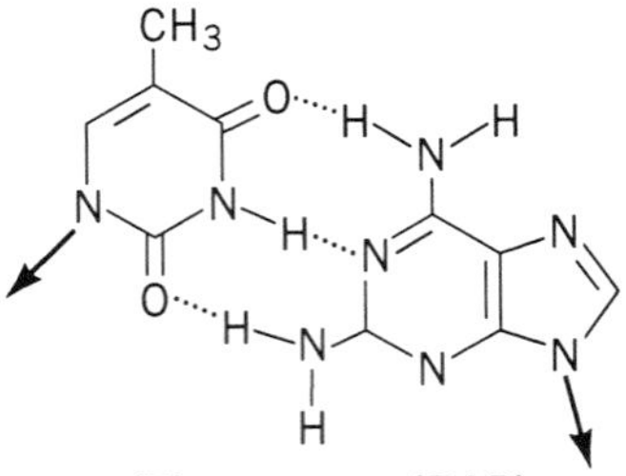

(T)   (DAP)

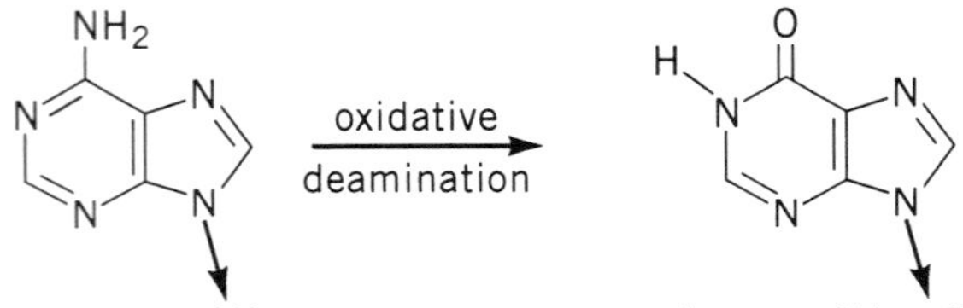

(A)   oxidative deamination   hypoxanthine (HX)

Hedges and Jacob 1974

1. What is meant by compatibility groups?

   Answer: Two plasmids in the same compatibility group cannot be maintained in the same cell. Thus, from Table 1 on page 438, RP4 and R751 cannot be maintained in the same cell but RP4 and R64 can.

2. Previous work from the authors' group had shown that ampicillin resistance could be transferred from the plasmid RP4 to R64. To show the generality of this effect, they crossed ampicillin resistance from RP4 onto another plasmid. Describe this cross in detail and indicate the selections used.

   Answer: The donor strain, J53, carried two plasmids, RP4 (encoding resistance to Amp, Tet, and Kan) and JR66a (encoding resistance to Str and Kan). These plasmids are in different compatability groups (see Table 1 on page 438). The donor is a methionine auxotroph, so the cross was probably plated on minimal medium with the supplements needed for the recipient, J62, but without methionine. The point of the cross was to select for the transfer of amp^r from RP4 to JR66a, which is Amp^s but Str^r. It appears that they selected only for Amp^r and then tested colonies for Tet^s. One of 10 colonies resulting from the transfer was Tet^s, Amp^r, Str^r, Kan^r. Thus, this colony did not carry RP4 but instead carried JR66a with the amp^r determinant transposed onto it.

3. What experiment showed that plasmids that had received ampicillin resistance through transposition could also donate it by transposition?

   Answer: The authors used a strain, J53, with the Sa-1 plasmid carrying a recently transposed amp^r gene and also the Amp^s plasmid R64. They showed that they could transpose amp^r to R64 in a conjugational cross with the recipient J62.

4. What physical experiment gave evidence of transposition?

   Answer: The molecular weights of the plasmids were determined both before and after transposition by examining their sedimentation rates in a sucrose gradient. As shown in Table 3 and Figure 1 on pages 441 and 442, respectively, the acquisition of amp^r by transposition brought about an increase in molecular weight from 1.7 to 3.9 megadaltons.

Kleckner et al. 1975

5. Explain the meaning of the structures seen in Plate I on page 451. How were they generated? What do they reveal about the tet^r transposon?

   Answer: The molecules examined in Plate I were heteroduplexes generated by denaturing and reannealing DNA from two independent tet^r transducing phage. Plate Ia shows two single-strand loops of equal size. Thus, each phage acquired the same transposable element, although at a different position. In Plate Ib, the single-stranded regions within the loops seen in Plate Ia have partly annealed themselves. This shows that the two insertions have the same sequence for at least much of their lengths. In addition, the two insertions must be oriented in the same direction, since complementary strands from the two phage also allow complementary pairing within the loops of the inserts. Plate Ic shows homoduplexes resulting from reannealing the same molecule. The fact that the same type of pairing within the loop is seen in Plate Ic reinforces the interpretation of Plate Ib. Plate Id shows another homoduplex that has undergone branch migration, since the paired stems are shorter.

6. Which experiment shows that the *tet*ʳ element, which was acquired by phage P22 from an R factor, can undergo further transposition out of the P22 genome?

   Answer: Table 1 on page 453 shows the results of an experiment in which P22*tet*ʳ was used to transduce *Salmonella typhimurium* under conditions where the P22 phage could not be maintained. In addition, some of the Tetʳ transductants were found to be auxotrophs for proline, methionine, histidine, isoleucine, arginine, or other identifiable markers. Thus, the *tet*ʳ element could integrate into many places, including known genes. Moreover, P22 functions were not present, as shown by marker-rescue experiments.

7. Which experiments showed that in the Tetʳ auxotrophs, the *tet*ʳ element appears to be inserted into the gene encoding the lost function?

   Answer: Table 2 on page 454 shows that when the Tetʳ phenotype is transferred from one strain to another by transduction, all of the recipients now acquire the associated auxotrophic requirement. For example, 73 of 73 Tetʳ transductants from a Leu⁻ strain (originally generated by transposition of the *tet*ʳ element into the *Salmonella* chromosome) are now Leu⁻ themselves. In addition, when the Tetʳ auxotrophs are reverted to prototrophy, the Tetʳ phenotype is lost, as can be seen in Table 3 on page 455.

8. Explain the polarity effect of insertion of the *tet*ʳ element.

   Answer: Detailed studies of insertions into the histidine operon show that insertions interfere with the expression of distal genes (or those downstream in the operon) within the same transcription unit.

Heffron et al. 1979

9. Explain the concept and utility of using *Eco*RI inserts into Tn3.

   Answer: *Eco*RI insertion mutations within Tn3 allowed the definition of functions involved in transposition, since, in many cases, inserts interrupt gene function. They also provided an aid to sequencing, since they placed a convenient restriction site at many points.

10. How was a transposase gene identified?

    Answer: A number of mutations had been characterized that eliminated transposition, but they were recessive in that they could be complemented in *trans* by a wild-type Tn3. The sequence change for each of these mutations was found to affect the same uninterrupted reading frame, which would encode a 1021-amino-acid protein, the presumed transposase. The molecular weight of 114,000 daltons corresponds to the molecular weight of a protein synthesized by Tn3 in minicells.

11. Describe the *tnpR* gene and the effects of mutations in it.

    Answer: Mutations in *tnpR* show an increase in transposition frequency. All of the mutations are in the coding sequence for a protein of 185 amino acids. Independent studies show that the TnpR protein is a repressor of the expression of the transposase.

12. Describe the essential sites on the DNA of Tn*3*.

    Answer: Mutational analysis, confirmed by sequencing reported here, shows that both the left- and right-hand inverted repeats are required for transposition. In addition, a site within the transposon is required to resolve the intermediate structure comprised of two copies of Tn*3* that is formed during transposition. This site is termed the internal resolution site (IRS). Sequencing of mutations indentified a site in which 19 of 23 base pairs match a sequence within the inverted repeats.

13. Explain the significance of the structure displayed in Figure 7 on page 470.

    Answer: This figure depicts a co-integrate intermediate in the transposition of Tn*3* from one plasmid to another. Transposition occurs by first replicating a copy of the transposon into the recipient circle. This fused circle is a co-integrate and is rapidly resolved by a site-specific recombination event at the internal resolution site (IRS) to yield the final products of the transposition. Note that the recipient has received a copy of the transposon but the donor still maintains a copy. Failure to resolve this structure, due to *cis*-acting mutations in the IRS, results in a stable co-integrate.

Bender and Kleckner 1986

14. How were the transposons used in the experiment marked?

    Answer: The λ phages carrying Tn*10* elements with the *lacZ* gene were marked with silent restriction changes. In addition, the *lacZ* gene on one element carried an *amber* mutation, whereas the *lacZ* gene on the other element was wild-type.

15. What was the starting donor transposon, and how was it generated.

    Answer: The transposon was generated by denaturing and reannealing a mixture of the two λ phages carrying the marked transposons. Heteroduplexes formed by this procedure will have one strand with the *lacZ* mutation and the other strand with the wild-type *lacZ* gene. The structures of the parents are shown in Figure 2 on page 476.

16. Describe the λ phage used as the vector in this experiment.

    Answer: The λ phage carried mutations that eliminate virtually all phage functions, including those involved in replication.

17. Explain the basic experiment that showed that transposition products contain information from both parental strands.

    Answer: Figure 1 on page 475 shows the results of replicative and non-replicative transposition mechanisms. If transposition does not involve replication, then the cell receiving a transposon will receive a heteroduplex containing all three mismatches. After subsequent rounds of replication, the mismatched *lacZ⁻/lacZ⁺* will yield pure Z⁺ and pure Z⁻ cells within the same colony. These sectored colonies can be observed using stains for β-galactosidase, in this case Xgal. Such colonies were in fact observed in significant numbers, as shown in Figure 5 on page 479.

18. How did the authors show that the blue and white portions of each sectored colony arose from the same original Tn*10* transposition event?

    Answer: Restriction enzyme cleavage and Southern blot hybridization with a probe specific to the IS*10* R end of the marked transposon allowed analysis of the new junctures created by the integration of the Tn*10* into the bacterial chromosome. Whereas the length of the new terminal junction fragment was different in each of 58 different Tet^r colonies generated during the experiment, in 33 of 33 sectored colonies both the blue and white portions of the colony contained the **same** new junction fragment.

Boeke et al. 1985

19. What are Ty elements of yeast?

    Answer: Ty elements are transposable elements that are 6 kb long and are present in about 30 copies in the yeast genome. They consist of a large central region, ε, and contain at each end a 334-base-pair direct repeat, termed δ elements. They are similar in structure to *copia* elements in *Drosophila* and to retroviruses.

20. Explain the nature of the donor vector and the recipient for the Ty transposition.

    Answer: The basic experiment involved using a marked donor Ty element. The element was placed under the control of an inducible promoter, in this case the *GAL1* promoter, which is induced by galactose. Upon induction, both the marked Ty element and the other resident Ty elements transpose at an elevated rate. Here, the marked element was on a high-copy-number plasmid and fused to the *GAL1* promoter. To assay for transposition, the authors employed a promoter deletion in the *His3* gene that reverts frequently via a transposition of Ty upstream of the promoter. In some cases, 80% of the His⁺ revertants are due to Ty transpositions.

21. How could the authors tell whether addition of galactose increased transposition of the plasmid-borne Ty element?

    Answer: The authors marked the plasmid-borne copy of Ty with a synthetic *lac* operator sequence that could be followed after transposition by the change in restriction sites and also by its ability to cause a blue colony when transformed into certain *E. coli* strains.

22. How could the authors show that transposition occurred via an RNA intermediate?

    Answer: The authors marked the plasmid-borne Ty element with an intron inserted into the sequence. His⁺ revertants were collected after galactose induction of transposition, and the structure of the Ty element that was now in the *His* region was determined. The authors could distinguish that the Ty element was derived from the plasmid copy since there are restriction sites specific to that copy. However, the intron, a 398-nucleotide yeast ribosomal protein 51 gene intron, was precisely excised.

23. The plasmid-borne Ty element contained a partial deletion of the 5′ δ sequence, which was replaced by the *GAL1* promoter. However, the transposed copy had regenerated both intact δs. How did this occur?

   Answer: The template for the regeneration of the missing region of the 5′ δ was clearly the 3′ δ sequence. In addition, during transposition, the 5′ δ sequence in the donor, or part of it, acts as a template for the 3′ δ sequence in the transposed element. This is as expected if transposition proceeds via an RNA intermediate that serves as a template for reverse transcriptase (see Figure 8 on page 494).

PROBLEMS

1. Suppose that one class of *lacZ* mutation results in no activity for either β-galactosidase (the *Z* gene product) or *lac* permease (the *Y* gene product). In addition, cells acquiring this type of mutation become resistant to tetracycline. These mutations revert spontaneously to yield Lac+ cells that are now Tet^s. Give an explanation for these mutations.

2. Suppose you have a new transposon in *E. coli*, Tn*400*, that confers resistance to rifampicin (Rif^r) and that can transpose from one plasmid to another. You routinely transpose Tn*400* from a Cam^r plasmid to a Kan^r plasmid, selecting for Rif^r Kan^r. However, one mutant yields a different result. Here, transposition generates a single plasmid that is both Cam^r and Kan^r. Describe how this might occur, what the structure of the plasmid might be, and what this suggests about the mechanism of transposition of Tn*400*.

3. Suppose you have a mutation in the *galK* gene of *E. coli* that confers the Gal^− phenotype to *E. coli* cells. On galactose MacConkey indicator plates, Gal+ strains are red and Gal^− strains are white. Gal+ revertants will form red papillae growing out of white Gal^− colonies. Suppose you wanted to use the Gal^− mutant to show that Tn*10* can transpose by a nonreplicative mechanism using the principles in the Bender and Kleckner paper. Assume you have the *gal* gene incorporated into Tn*10*. Explain what constructs you would need, and describe the experimental design and what results you would look for.

4. Suppose that in yeast you can select directly spontaneous resistance to a new antibiotic, komomycin. All komomycin-resistant (Kom^r) cells result from the transposition of the Ty element into the komomycin uptake gene, *kup*. Suppose you have a marked Ty element fused to the *GLY* promoter, which is activated by the addition of glycerol. Explain how you would design an experiment to show that Ty elements transpose via an RNA intermediate. Describe the experimental design and how you would analyze the results.

Scenarios

Scenario 1   Chances Are It's Poisson

A. Suppose that a large group of sky divers from the "Save the Garden Slug Sky Diving Club" parachuted over a sky diving target in Palm Springs. The target site was divided into a set of numbered squares, each of identical area (approximately one acre). After the divers landed, it was found that 2 different squares had 4 divers landing in them and 4 different squares had 3 divers landing in them. If the landing of the divers in the target area was completely at random, use the Poisson distribution to:

1. Determine the number of squares with 0 divers landing in them.

2. Set up the equation to show how you would calculate how many squares and how many divers there were. Explain the step or steps needed for this calculation. *Note:* The Poisson distribution is:

$$P_n = \frac{m^n e^{-m}}{n!}$$

B. Every month the *Wall Street Journal* asks a set of experts to pick 10 different stocks that they think will do well during the next month. They also have a blindfolded person throw darts at a dart board containing the names of different stocks on the New York Stock Exchange to randomly choose 10 stocks. The experts have to match the performance of the stocks they picked with those hit by darts. It is not uncommon for the dart board stocks to outperform the experts' stocks. Suppose we want to test whether the stocks hit by darts on the dart board are really random or whether there are "hotspots" on the board. Suppose we monitor the results of 200 darts thrown at a board containing 400 stocks. We note that 5 different stocks are hit 4 times. Calculate the Poisson distribution for the darts hitting the stocks on the dart board by determining the number of stocks that are expected to be hit by 0 darts, 1 dart, 2 darts, 3 darts, and 4 darts. Then determine about how many of the 5 stocks that are hit by 4 darts are "hotspots." The formula for the Poisson distribution, as well as some values for e^{-m} are given below.

$$P_n = \frac{m^n e^{-m}}{n!}$$

Values of m	Values of e^{-m}	Values of m	Values of e^{-m}
0.1	0.9	1.2	0.30
0.2	0.82	1.4	0.25
0.3	0.74	1.6	0.20
0.4	0.67	1.8	0.16
0.5	0.60	2.0	0.14
0.6	0.55	2.5	0.08
0.7	0.50	3.0	0.05
0.8	0.45	4.0	0.018
0.9	0.41	5.0	0.0067
1.0	0.37		

C. Suppose you go to Las Vegas and play roulette. You rapidly lose all of your money. However, you are suspicious that the roulette wheel may not be honest, so you remain to monitor the distribution of numbers that come up during subsequent spins of the wheel. You record the number that comes up for each of 360 spins of the wheel. Since there are 36 numbers (excluding 0 and 00), you can calculate how often, on average, numbers should come up. Suppose you find that one of the 36 numbers comes up 21 times.

Using the Poisson distribution, determine whether the roulette wheel is defective. Let's say that we will consider the wheel defective if the expected frequency of occurrence of one of the 36 numbers coming up 21 times is less than 1 out of 50 (.02). Specifically, determine the following:

1. The mean, m, for the distribution

2. The expected occurrences of numbers (how many of the 36 numbers) that will come up 10 times

3. The expected occurrences (among 36 numbers) of one number coming up 21 times.

To solve this problem, it is important to set it up correctly. In analogy with previous problems, be sure of which values are being applied to the distribution. Be careful to distinguish between the probability (or fraction) and the expected number of events or occurrences.

D. Suppose you play the daily double at Ups 'n Downs Race Track. You become suspicious that the results are not totally honest and that certain numbers come up more frequently than others. Therefore, you obtain the records of all daily double winners for the past several years. The daily double is the combination of the winners of the first and second race each day. There are 12 post positions for each race (in other words, 12 horses in each race with an assigned number for a post position). If the winner of the first race is horse number 6 and the winner of the second race is horse number 8, then the winning combination is number 6-8. (In the problems below, perhaps we might assume that the races are dishonest if the expectation of some combination coming up the stated number of times is less than 1 time out of 1000.)

1. Suppose that during the past two years, 710 daily doubles were run, and you find that the horse in post position 4 seemed to win more often than you would anticipate. In fact, the daily double winning combination of 4-4 came up 14 times. Does this mean that the races are fixed or would one

expect that some combination might come up 14 times in this sample size? Using the Poisson distribution, calculate the expected number of times some combination would appear 14 times out of 710 daily doubles. Show all work.

2. Suppose that during the past two years, 720 daily doubles were run, and you find that the horse in post position 5 seemed to win more often than you would anticipate. In fact, the daily double winning combination of 5-5 came up 18 times. Does this mean that the races are fixed or would one expect that some combination might come up 18 times in this sample size? Using the Poisson distribution, calculate the expected number of times some combination would appear 18 times out of 720 daily doubles. Show all work.

3. Suppose that during the past two years, 700 daily doubles were run, and you find that the horse in post position 8 seemed to win more often than you would anticipate. In fact, the daily double winning combination of 8-8 came up 17 times. Does this mean that the races are fixed or would one expect that some combination might come up 17 times in this sample size? Using the Poisson distribution, calculate the expected number of times some combination would appear 17 times out of 700 daily doubles. Show all work.

E. Suppose you go to Las Vegas and play electronic blackjack on a machine that claims to have an infinite number of decks of cards. (Assume normal playing decks with 52 cards.) Therefore, every card should have the same chance of being drawn as every other card in the deck each time a draw is made. (Let's say that if the observations in the problems below would happen less than 1 out of 1000 times by chance, then the machine is cheating you.)

1. Suppose you note the card drawn each time for 300 consecutive draws. You observe that one card, the five of diamonds, is drawn 18 times. Does this mean that the machine is cheating you? Use the Poisson distribution to calculate the expected number of occurrences of any card appearing 18 times out of 300 draws.

2. Suppose you note the card drawn each time for 200 consecutive draws. You observe that one card, the six of clubs, is drawn 15 times. Does this mean that the machine is cheating you? Use the Poisson distribution to calculate the expected number of occurrences of any card appearing 15 times.

F. Suppose you follow the lottery in which 6 numbers are picked each day out of a total of 49 numbers. Over the course of two years you follow the first number picked each time. Thus, there are 730 first numbers picked in total. (Let's say that if any of the observations in the problems below would occur less than 1 time out of 1000 by chance, then the lottery is fixed.)

1. You note that number 11 came up 1 time, whereas number 28 came up 31 times. Examine the probabilities and expected number of occurrences of each case independently. Determine whether either of these observations means the lottery is fixed.

2. You note that number 5 came up 3 times, whereas number 27 came up 35 times. Examine the probabilities and expected number of occurrences of each case independently. Determine whether either of these observations means the lottery is fixed.

3. You note that number 22 came up 2 times, whereas number 42 came up 34 times. Examine the probabilities and expected number of occurrences of each case independently. Determine whether either of these observations means the lottery is fixed.

G. Using the Poisson distribution, determine how many students would be expected to share the same birthday in each of the classes below. (Think carefully about your definition of terms here, since these problems are trickier than they seem at first glance.) Assume in each case that the students' birthdays are distributed randomly throughout the 365 days of the year.

1. A biology section in which there are 26 students.

2. A biology section in which there are 34 students.

3. A biology section in which there are 73 students.

H. In the "Big Spin" of the California lottery, each winner spins a giant wheel with a large number of slots, and his or her prize is determined by whichever slot the wheel ends up in. Let's say that there are 80 different slots in the wheel: 30 of these have $10,000 values, 20 have $20,000 values, 10 have $30,000 values, 8 have $40,000 values, 5 have $50,000 values, 4 have $100,000 values, 2 have $1,000,000 values, and 1 has a "grandprize" value. Suppose you are a lottery winner and spin the wheel and win only $10,000. You decide to chart the wheel to see whether the number of times that each of the larger prizes comes up is fairly represented. Think carefully before setting up these problems, and show all work.

1. Suppose you obtain the records for every Big Spin during a particular 5-year period in which there were 1120 spins of the wheel. You find that the $100,000 prize came up 24 times and the $1,000,000 prize came up 12 times. Use the Poisson distribution to calculate how rare each of these observations is. Calculate m for the relevant distribution and then the expected number of times (out of 1120 spins of the wheel) that the $100,000 prize would come up 24 times or less and the $1,000,000 prize would come up 12 times or less.

2. Suppose you obtain the records for every Big Spin during a particular 5-year period in which there were 1120 spins of the wheel. You find that the $100,000 prize came up 20 times and the $1,000,000 prize came up 14 times. Use the Poisson distribution to calculate how rare each of these observations is. Calculate m for the relevant distribution and then the expected number of times (out of 1120 spins of the wheel) that the $100,000 prize would come up 20 times or less and the $1,000,000 prize would come up 14 times or less.

3. Suppose you obtain the records for every Big Spin during a particular 5-year period in which there were 1200 spins of the wheel. You find that the $100,000 prize came up 40 times and the $1,000,000 prize came up 16 times. Use the Poisson distribution to calculate how rare each of these observations is. Calculate m for the relevant distribution and then the expected number of times (out of 1200 spins) that the $100,000 prize would come up 40 times or less and the $1,000,000 prize would come up 16 times or less.

4. Suppose you obtain the records for every Big Spin during a particular 5-year period in which there were 1360 spins of the wheel. You find that the $100,000 prize came up 36 times and the $1,000,000 prize came up 14 times. Use the Poisson distribution to calculate how rare each of these observations is. Calculate m for the relevant distribution and then the expected number of times (out of 1360 spins) that the $100,000 prize would come up 36 times or less and the $1,000,000 prize would come up 14 times or less.

Scenario 2   Munchkin Genetics

After 10 years as a successful high school teacher in Kansas, Dorothy decided to pack it in and return to the land of Oz and become a microbiologist. She obtained a teaching and research position at Emerald City University and proceeded to isolate a bacterial strain *Escherichia yellow brick*, which had many properties similar to *Escherichia coli*.

The map on the following page shows the position of markers starting from the Ozigin (the Oz version of the origin), which is at 0 min, and following along the *yellow brick* chromosome. The *crg* gene is deleted in this strain. Other strains available include any combinations of these markers in both the + and − form. Other tools include a cytoplasmic element similar to the F factor, the ruby red slippers (RRS), that can replicate and mediate gene transfer just like F. There is a temperature-sensitive RRS'-*crg* available. Two virulent phage, WWW (wicked witch of the west) and WWE (wicked witch of the east) are available. Each of these utilize receptors encoded by WWW-*rec* and WWE-*rec* genes, respectively. A temperate phage, the munchkin phage, which integrates at *att-munchk*, is also available.

A. Dorothy's first assignment was to conduct gene therapy on the cowardly lion by cloning the courage gene (*crg*), which encodes couragease, from the bacterial strain and then using it on the lion. (Use of a similar gene from other bacterial strains had shown promising results in clinical trials on panthers and jaguars, although it had never been tried on lions per se.) Dorothy's tools were similar to those available to Beckwith and Signer.

    1. How would you advise her to clone the *crg* locus in vivo onto a specialized transducing phage? You have selective medium for each marker. Explain each step.

    2. How could she use genetic crosses to prove the location of the *crg* genes in relation to other markers in the bacterial chromosome after she transposed it from its normal location to another site?

B. In her continuing genetic studies in Oz, Dorothy carried out a series of genetic crosses using an Hfr-like strain generated by integrating the RRS factor into the *E. yellow brick* chromosome between *kansas* and *wizard*. (Consult the map.) When these RRS⁺ strains were transferred to an RRS⁻ strain (not carrying the RRS factor at all), recombinants could be detected. She found that when the munchkin phage was integrated at the *att-munchk* site in the recipient, then inheritance of nearby markers was normal in conjugational crosses. However, different results were obtained when the donor carried the munchkin phage integrated at *att-munchk* and the recipient did not carry any munchkin phage. In this latter cross, among the viable recipient cells only the markers *wizard* and *scarecrow* were inherited from the donor. Explain these results and provide a mechanism for the events taking place.

Map of *Escherichia yellow brick* chromosome

Cornering the Market with *Escherichia monopoli*

Thornton Page, a Wall Street billionaire who was sent to prison for several years for illegal stock trading, went off the deep end while in jail. He was allowed to study bacterial genetics in the prison laboratory, where he discovered a bacterium similar to *Escherichia coli*. Page mapped all of the loci in this bacterium but named them according to the properties in the well-known Parker Brothers board game Monopoly®. His genetic map of this bacterium, *Escherichia monopoli*, is given on the next page. Page gave genes for Met, Trp, Lac, etc., names such as *Boardwalk, Park Place*, and *Marvin Gardens*. He named the receptor sites for virulent phages after the different railroads. Thus, the properties *Short Line, Reading Railroad, Pennsylvania Railroad*, and *B & O Railroad* are in fact the genes for the receptor sites for four different virulent phage. In addition, he named the specific attachment sites for different temperate phage after the utilities (*Water Works* and *Electric Company*) and the taxes (*Luxury Tax* and *Income Tax*). Under normal circumstances, these phage will only integrate at one unique site on the chromosome. Other loci were named after other Monopoly® game board items. For example, the bacterial origin of replication was placed at GO.

A. Suppose you have the bacterium *E. monopoli* and also the following tools:

- Each of the virulent phages Short Line, B & O Railroad, Pennsylvania Railroad, and Reading Railroad.

- Each of the temperate phages Luxury Tax, Income Tax, Water Works, and Electric Company. These phage are UV-inducible.

- An F' factor that carries the gene *Pennsylvania Avenue* and cannot replicate at high temperature.

- Selective "presidential" medium that allows Pennsylvania Avenue⁺ strains to grow but will not allow Pennsylvania Avenue⁻ strains to grow. You also have nonselective LB medium on which all strains grow.

Describe how you would:

1. Isolate a rare mutant that carries a deletion of the *Pennsylvania Avenue* gene.

2. Isolate a specialized transducing phage carrying the *Pennsylvania Avenue* gene by using the methods of Beckwith and Signer.

Outline each step in detail, indicating the materials used and the procedures involved. Use diagrams.

B. Suppose you want to isolate from *E. monopoli* a specialized transducing phage derived from the Water Works phage, which carries the *St. James Place* gene. Describe the steps you would use if you employed the Shimada, Weisberg, and Gottesman method. Assume you have Water Works phage mutants.

In addition to the tools described above in **A**, you also have an elitist medium that only allows St. James Place⁺ strains to grow, but not St. James Place⁻ strains, and each of the following strains:

- A strain carrying a deletion extending from *Boardwalk* to *Park Place*

- A strain carrying a deletion extending from *Virginia Avenue* to *St. Charles Place*

- A strain carrying a deletion extending from *Marvin Gardens* to *Atlantic Avenue*

- A strain carrying a deletion extending from *New York Avenue* to *St. James Place*.

Detail each step and use diagrams.

C. Suppose you have a strain of *E. monopoli* with the Water Works phage integrated at its normal attachment site. This strain is an Hfr with its origin at GO and transfers markers in the order: *Boardwalk, Park Place, Pennsylvania Avenue*, etc. Describe the inheritance of the markers *Pennsylvania Avenue, Pacific Avenue, Atlantic Avenue*, and *New York Avenue* in a cross with an F⁻ strain that is – for each of these four markers and that does not carry the Water Works phage in the chromosome.

Scenario 4   Cloning à la Bogie

Sy Waterman, a Hollywood movie mogul under intense pressure to increase film studio profits, has gone off the deep end and resorted to molecular biology to create movie addicts out of normal cinema patrons. This diabolical head of Polaris Films has detected a bacterial protein that when exposed to laser flashes of a certain frequency, breaks down in the human body to generate an endorphin (a brain peptide that acts like an opiate). He has cleverly seeded the popcorn and sodas at all movie theaters in the Los Angeles area with this protein. After ingesting the spiked refreshments, the movie goer is subjected to subliminal laser flashes of just the right frequency emitted only from movies turned out by his studio. The movie patron rapidly becomes addicted and returns to the same movie day after day for the laser-endorphin fix.

The bacterial source of the endorphin-generating protein is a strain related to *Escherichia coli* that Waterman has named *Escherichia bogie*, after his film hero Humphrey Bogart. Using a studio laboratory, he characterized numerous genes, virulent phage, and temperate phage. He named each gene after a Bogart movie (such as *Petrified Forest* or *Maltese Falcon*) or after a landmark from a Bogart movie (such as *Rick's Cafe* or *Blue Parrot*). All of the virulent phage are named after villains from Bogart movies (for example, Major Strasser or Señor Ferrari), and the temperate phage are named after heroes and heroines (for example, Sabrina, Ilsa Lund, or Victor Laszlo).

Fortunately, an impoverished grad student, Matilda Krump, who was moonlighting as an actress using the stage name Tania, uncovered Waterman's lab. She has furnished us with the map of the organism, shown on the next page. In addition, she has found that the endorphin-releasing gene is code-named "*Maltese Falcon*," "*African Queen*," or "*USS Caine*." The strain *E. bogie* cannot be cut with restriction enzymes in vitro or sequenced by normal DNA sequencing techniques. Therefore, in vivo methods similar to those employed by Beckwith and Signer must be used to clone these genes. Unfortunately, we have stopped receiving reports from Tania. We fear that she has been found out and made a prisoner in the studio and will be forced to make the same B movie over and over again.

To rescue Tania, we must start by cloning either the *Maltese Falcon, African Queen,* or *USS Caine*. The successful cloning of the correct gene will allow us to isolate sufficient quantities of the protein product to study the structure of the endorphin and will enable us to design counteracting drugs. The materials available to you are given below.

You have several strains of bacteria that contain the gene encoding the endorphin-generating protein. These strains behave very much like *E. coli* in genetic crosses. Each strain has the genetic map pictured on the next page. You also have a derivative with an F factor that is exactly like that described for *E. coli*. Also available is a wild-type and a Rec⁻ derivative of the strain without the F factor, which cannot undergo normal recombination, as well as derivatives of these strains that contain point mutations in each of the following genes: *China Clipper, San Quentin, Virginia City, Sahara, Seawitch, Blue Parrot, Dark Passage,* and *Sirocco*. Each of these genes gives a phenotype that requires a nutrient. For example, *Blue Parrot* mutations leave the cell Blue Parrot⁻, and these cells cannot grow on medium without Blue Parrot supplement.

You have a series of virulent phage—Canino, Major Stasser, Señor Ferrari, Ugarte, Dobbs, Johnny Rocco, Wilmer, and Captain Queeg—that infect cells via a cell wall receptor encoded by the respective genes Canino-*rec*, Major Strasser-*rec*, etc. You also have a set of temperate phage—Rick, Sam, Ilsa Lund, Victor

Laszlo, Rose Sayer, Charlie Allnut, and Sabrina—that integrate into the chromosome at specific attachment sites, *att-Rick, att-Sam,* etc.

Cells that make endorphin-generating protein form colonies that turn red when exposed to a 340-nm frequency laser beam.

A. Demonstrate how you would clone the *Maltese Falcon, African Queen,* or *USS Caine* gene onto a specialized transducing phage utilizing the selection methods of Beckwith and Signer. You will have to generate some of the genetic tools they used employing the strains provided. Some of these steps may require consulting the literature. Describe each step in detail, including how you would carry out each selection. You will have to do the following:

1. Generate a deletion of the gene encoding the endorphin-generating protein.

2. Put the gene onto the F' factor.

Escherichia bogie

3. Prove the structure or orientation of intermediates in the cloning construction.

Note: In order for genes to be incorporated into a specialized transducing phage, they must be adjacent to that phage on the chromosome (in other words, either at the adjacent position or within the gene that is adjacent to the prophage). However, F factors can incorporate genes within two gene lengths of their integration point. Deletions can be up to three gene lengths.

- **For the *Maltese Falcon:*** The F factor you are using can replicate normally at high temperature (42°C) but not at low temperature (30°C). Chromosomal replication is normal at both temperatures.

- **For the *African Queen:*** The F factor you are using can replicate normally at both high and low temperatures but it cannot replicate in the presence of 5 µg/ml nalidixic acid. Chromosomal replication is unaffected by the presence of nalidixic acid.

- **For the *USS Caine:*** The F factor you are using can replicate normally at both high and low temperatures but it cannot replicate in the presence of acridine orange. Chromosomal replication is unaffected by the presence of acridine orange.

B. Clone one of the following genes by the methods of Shimada et al. The same rules apply as for **A** above, and you have the same starting materials. Again, you will have to generate some of your own materials. Verify the structure or orientation of intermediates.

- **For the *Maltese Falcon:*** Clone the gene that encodes the endorphin-generating protein.

- **For the *African Queen:*** Clone the *Sirocco* gene (which is adjacent to the *African Queen* gene).

- **For the *USS Caine:*** Clone the gene that encodes the endorphin-generating protein.

C. Suppose that the endorphin-generating protein has been analyzed by finding mutant proteins that can no longer function. When the amino acid sequence of each mutation was determined, the changes listed below were found. Using the principles described by Perutz, explain why each amino acid exchange might result in a nonfunctional protein.

- **For the *Maltese Falcon:***
  1. a leucine to arginine change in the interior of the protein
  2. a leucine to valine change in the interior of the protein
  3. a histidine to tyrosine change in the crevice of the protein
  4. a serine to tyrosine on the surface of the protein
  5. a glutamine to proline on the surface of the protein

- **For the *African Queen:***
  1. a glycine to proline change on the surface of the protein
  2. a valine to alanine change in the interior of the protein
  3. a leucine to lysine change in the interior of the protein
  4. an aspartic acid to glutamic acid change in the crevice of the protein
  5. an asparagine to threonine change on the surface of the protein

- **For the *USS Caine:***
  1. an isoleucine to phenylalanine change in the interior of the protein
  2. a methionine to arginine change in the interior of the protein
  3. a cysteine to proline change on the surface of the protein
  4. a tyrosine to valine change in the crevice of the protein
  5. a tyrosine to glutamine change on the surface of the protein

D. Suppose you wanted to study the regulation of the gene encoding the endorphin-generating protein. You have found that it is regulated by a repressor-operator system not unlike the lactose system. Suppose that the repressor is encoded by an adjacent gene. Using the materials from **A–C** above, explain how you would isolate the equivalent of I^s mutants in this system. (You may have to consult the literature for help.)

E. Suppose you wanted to detect point mutations in the gene for Casablanca. Normally, these mutations are very rare in the population. In analogy with the methods used by Yanofsky and co-workers to enrich for Trp$^-$ mutants (you will have to consult the literature), describe how you would increase the frequency of, and enrich for, mutants that are Cas$^-$. Mutants unable to make the Casablanca protein (Cas$^-$) cannot grow in medium lacking the "Letters of Transit" supplement, whereas mutants that are Cas$^+$ can.

Scenario 5　　　　　　　　　Plantagenet Phage

A professor of medieval history took up the study of bacterial genetics and characterized a bacterial strain related to *Escherichia coli*, which he named *Escherichia plantagenet*. He worked out the genetic map of the bacterium but labeled the genetic loci after places and figures from the Hundred Years War between England and France in the 14th and 15th centuries (see Glossary on page 614 for *optional* reading). Nutritional markers, such as Trp, Lac, Met, His, etc., are encoded by genes named after events and places, such as *Orleans, Poitiers,* and *Agincourt*. Being a French sympathizer, he named the receptor sites for virulent phage (indicated by grey background in the genetic map on the next page) after English personages of the period. These include Edward III, Black Prince, John of Gaunt, Henry V, Henry VI, Earl of Salisbury, and Regent Bedford. He named the specific attachment sites for different temperate phage after French personages of the time. These include *att-Jean the Good, att-Duke of Orleans, att-Charles VI, att-The Dauphin,* and *att-Joan of Arc*.

Suppose you have the bacterium *E. plantagenet* and the following tools:

- Each of the virulent phage mentioned above.

- Each of the temperate phage mentioned above. These phage are UV-inducible.

- An F factor that can replicate at low temperature (30°C) but not at high temperature (42°C).

- Selective medium that allows strains to grow only if they have *all* of the nutritional requirements. In addition, you can add as a supplement any of the requirements. Thus, you can add "Calais" supplement, which allows Calais⁻ strains to grow. You also have rich medium on which all of the strains grow.

- Complete use of Rec⁻ and Str^r mutations, so that any strain you have or create can be easily rendered Rec⁻ or Str^r, or any combination thereof, without any description required.

- Deletions can only extend for four genes, including the gene in which the deletion begins and the gene in which the deletion ends. For example, a deletion that begins within *Poitiers* can extend into *Aquitaine* but cannot extend into *La Rochelle*. Lysogenic phage can only transduce markers of neighboring genes or insertions within neighboring genes. F can only incorporate two neighboring genes into an F'.

- For each temperate phage, you have derivatives that lack immunity and cannot integrate into the chromosome.

A. Using the methods of Beckwith and Signer, clone the *Agincourt* gene. To do this, you will have to carry out several steps, including:

　1. Isolate a complete deletion of the *Agincourt* gene.

　2. Isolate an F' derivative of the temperature-sensitive F that contains the *Agincourt* gene.

　3. Obtain a specialized transducing phage carrying the *Agincourt* gene.

Outline each step in detail, indicating the materials used and the procedures involved. Use diagrams.

B. Isolate a specialized transducing phage derived from The Dauphin temperate phage that carries the *Tours* gene by a selection that employs the Shimada, Weisberg, and Gottesman method. To isolate a Dauphin-*Tours* phage, you may have to first create certain mutant strain(s). Outline each step in detail, indicating the materials used and the procedures involved. Use diagrams.

C. Suppose you had an Hfr strain that had its origin at *Domrémy* and donated markers in a counterclockwise fashion. The temperate phage Jean the Good is integrated at its normal attachment site. Suppose you cross this Hfr with two different recipient strains, each of which contains auxotrophic mutations in the *Tours, Sluys, Calais, Poitiers, La Rochelle,* and *Bordeaux* genes and is Str^r. One strain carries the Jean the Good phage at its normal integration site, and the other phage does not carry any prophage. Describe the inheritance of the markers *Tours$^+$, Sluys$^+$, Calais$^+$, Poitiers$^+$, La Rochelle$^+$,* and *Bordeaux$^+$* from the Hfr in crosses with each of the recipients. Give a diagram.

D. Let's compare the processes of generalized and specialized transduction. Suppose we are comparing the transduction of the *Troyes* marker by generalized

Escherichia plantagenet

transducing phage such as P1 with that by a specialized transducing phage, in this case Joan of Arc-*Troyes* (a derivative of the Joan of Arc phage carrying the *Troyes* genes). Both the donor strain for P1 and the Joan of Arc phage carry the *Troyes*$^+$ marker. The recipient for each transduction is *Troyes*$^-$. In the case of the P1 experiment, the recipient carries a simple point mutation in the *Troyes* gene. In the case of the specialized transduction experiment, the recipient carries a complete deletion of the *Troyes* gene. What is the effect of each mutation listed below on the appearance of transductants in each case? Explain your reasoning.

- A mutation in each recipient that deletes the attachment site on the chromosome for the Joan of Arc phage.

- A mutation in each donor strain that renders the cell resistant to digestion of the DNA by DNA nucleases.

- A *recA* (Rec$^-$) mutation in each recipient that prevents generalized recombination.

GLOSSARY

The Hundred Years War	The Hundred Years War lasted from 1337, when Edward III formally claimed the throne of France, to 1453, when the last English stronghold in France fell.
Crecy	Site of important battle in which the English defeated the French in 1346.
Poitiers	The English, under the Black Prince, defeated the French in 1356. The French King Jean II was captured and brought to England, where he lived in exile until his death.
Edward III	English king who reigned from 1327–1377.
The Black Prince	Edward, Prince of Wales, son of Edward III. A fierce warrior of the Hundred Years War, he died one year before the end of his father's reign.
Agincourt	Site of crucial battle in 1415 in which 10,000 English troops under Henry V defeated a French army of 60,000 troops.
Henry V	Warrior king who defeated the French at Agincourt and married Catherine of France, daughter of King Charles VI.
Treaty of Troyes	Negotiated by Henry V and Charles VI in 1422, this made Henry V heir to the French throne and regent of France and arranged that his son, Henry VI, would be crowned King of France, as well as England.
Henry VI	The only English king to be crowned outside of England, the boy King served under a regent until he reached adulthood.
Charles VII	The crown prince, or Dauphin, was forbidden by the Treaty of Troyes to take part in the monarchy.
Domrémy	Birthplace in Lorraine of Joan of Arc in 1412.
Rheims	Charles the VII was crowned at the Cathedral.
Joan of Arc	She was thirteen when she first heard the voices, 17 when she took command of the armies of France, and 19 when she was captured by the British and burned at the stake as a witch in 1431. She had pushed the Dauphin to be crowned Charles the VII. In 1920, she was canonized a saint.
Rouen	City where Joan of Arc was burned at the stake in 1431.
Regent Bedford	Regent for Henry VI.
Orleans	Joan of Arc relieved the besieged garrison at Orleans in 1429.

Scenario 6 Globin Wars

Courtesy of Lucasfilm Ltd.

In a far off galaxy, many eons in the future, Darth Vader (shown in galactograph to left) decides to study the molecular biology of different space creatures in order to control their body chemistry. He studies galactoglobin (Gb), a ubiquitous protein that carries silicon molecules through the circulatory system to each cell. The protein consists of a globular globin polypeptide that binds to a large planar galactin molecule. The galactin molecule complexes with a rubidium atom that binds to the silicon. The chart below gives the 20 intergalactic amino acids that are found in all proteins in this future universe.

Intergalactic Amino Acids

With alkyl groups	Uncharged but can make hydrogen bonds with H_2O	Charged
dracodine*	virgosine	tritonic acid
mizarine	ursadine	galactic acid
camelopardaline	capricornidine	vulcanine
trafalmadine	aquaramine	pulsarine
α-centaurine	taurusine	
andromedine	canisine	
phobosine	fornaxine	
uranusine	polarisine	

*Similar to proline

A. Darth Vader carried out two types of studies. In one case, he examined galactoglobins from different species, and although he found that the three-dimensional structures of the proteins were very similar, the amino acids at corresponding positions were not always the same. His results are depicted in the chart below. For example, at amino acid 42, galactoglobin from Wookies contains phobosine, whereas that from Yoda is andromedine and from Jabba the Hutt trafalmadine (see galactographs of these latter species on page 616).

For each of the five positions shown on the chart (27, 42, 58, 68, 110), explain where the residue at that position is likely to be in the protein on the basis of the pattern of amino acids found at the site in different space creatures. Briefly explain your reasoning. Refer to the chart of Intergalactic Amino Acids above.

			Residue found at specific position		
Creature	27	42	58	68	110
Jabba the Hutt	andromedine	trafalmadine	uranusine	vulcanine	taurusine
Yoda	phobosine	andromedine	uranusine	galactic acid	taurusine
Wookie	uranusine	phobosine	uranusine	tritonic acid	taurusine
Android	uranusine	trafalmadine	uranusine	virgosine	taurusine
Jawas	phobosine	andromedine	uranusine	ursadine	taurusine
Ewok	andromedine	phobosine	phobosine	capricornidine	taurusine
R2D2	α-centaurine	trafalmadine	phobosine	vulcanine	taurusine

B. In a second study, Darth Vader looked at altered galactoglobins found in patients with galactonemia, a condition resulting from defective silicon transport. In mild cases, patients have a fogged-up glassy look, but in extreme cases they excrete plate glass fragments. The chart below lists the amino acid exchanges found in five different patients. In each case, explain why a defective Gb might be caused by the specific amino acid change given.

Altered galactoglobin (Gb)	Amino acid change	Location
Gb Aldebaran	polarisine to phobosine	crevice
Gb Endor	canisine to dracodine	exterior
Gb Tatooine	mizarine to pulsarine	interior
Gb Pit of Sarnak	fornaxine to ursadine	exterior
Gb Death Star	trafalmadine to camelo-pardaline	interior

Courtesy of Lucasfilm Ltd.

Yoda

Jabba the Hutt

Courtesy of Lucasfilm Ltd.

Scenario 7 The Lost Amino Acids of Atlantis

A joint UCLA-NATO expedition, working together with the team that located the resting place of the sunken luxury liner Titanic, has just discovered the long lost city of Atlantis. This ancient Greek city was a large island that had attempted to enslave the Mediterranean world but was destroyed in a tidal wave, possibly resulting from an eruption on the volcanic island of Santorini in 1450 B.C. Fortunately, numerous records of life in Atlantis were recovered intact from sealed pottery jars. These writings document a very sophisticated experimental molecular biology program in Atlantis, far beyond our wildest expectations. The scientists in Atlantis had actually studied hemoglobin more than 3000 years before Perutz and were capable of determining differences in amino acid sequences at certain positions in the molecule. Of course, they gave different names to each of the 20 amino acids that we know today. In fact, each amino acid was named after a character from Greek mythology or from the Greek Trojan War. Thus, instead of amino acids being named tyrosine, glutamine, serine, etc., we find that the amino acid residues were named Hermes, Aphrodite, Cassandra, Achilles, etc.

The Atlantis research group carried out two types of studies. In one project, they compared the amino acid sequence of the hemoglobins from different species. They focused on the residues occupying the same positions in each hemoglobin molecule at seven different places. The chart provided with each problem shows the residue appearing at each equivalent position. Position 1 is the same position for each hemoglobin, position 2 is also the same, etc. These positions are not necessarily the first seven residues in the protein, but they are seven positions, each one identical in each hemoglobin. The sources of the different hemoglobins were the creatures found in the ancient Greek world, such as Pegasus, the winged horse, or Cyclops, the one-eyed giants. (A description of the creatures is provided in a Glossary on page 620 for *optional* reading.)

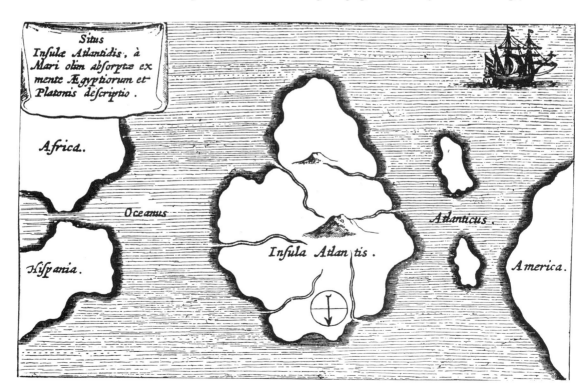

Centaur

In a second study, the ancient researchers looked at altered hemoglobins from people suffering from different types of anemia. The chart provided with each problem shows the name of each altered hemoglobin, based on the city where it was discovered, and the amino acid change detected, as well as the position in the molecule where the amino acid substitution occurred. The positions correspond to one of the seven positions on the first chart in each problem. Recall that each of these amino acid exchanges produces a defective protein that cannot carry out its function properly.

A. From the information given in the charts below, determine:

1. Which of the 20 amino acids named by the Atlantis team correspond to **polar** residues and which ones correspond to **nonpolar** residues.

2. Which of the amino acids corresponds to **proline**.

It is important to explain your logic and justify your conclusions as clearly as possible.

Creature	Residue found at specific position						
	1	2	3	4	5	6	7
Centaur	Hector	Adonis	Paris	Hecuba	Achilles	Apollo	Zeus
Triton	Hector	Patroclus	Paris	Ajax	Achilles	Poseidon	Zeus
Cyclops	Hector	Minerva	Paris	Priam	Achilles	Agamemnon	Achilles
Hydra	Zeus	Iphigenia	Calchas	Adonis	Odysseus	Hecuba	Helen
Scylla	Cassandra	Apollo	Hermes	Hecuba	Aphrodite	Patroclus	Achilles
Harpies	Zeus	Ajax	Calchas	Ajax	Odysseus	Poseidon	Helen
Stymphalian Birds	Cassandra	Minerva	Hermes	Priam	Aphrodite	Agamemnon	Cassandra
Gorgon	Hector	Iphigenia	Paris	Minerva	Achilles	Adonis	Cassandra
Satyrs	Zeus	Patroclus	Paris	Poseidon	Achilles	Minerva	Achilles
Pegasus	Zeus	Poseidon	Hermes	Iphigenia	Aphrodite	Ajax	Achilles
Chimaera	Cassandra	Hermes	Calchas	Hector	Aphrodite	Cassandra	Cassandra
Phoenix	Cassandra	Priam	Calchas	Odysseus	Odysseus	Aphrodite	Zeus
Laestrygones	Hector	Paris	Hermes	Zeus	Odysseus	Calchas	Zeus
Geryon	Cassandra	Adonis	Hermes	Iphigenia	Aphrodite	Zeus	Cassandra
Typhon	Zeus	Calchas	Paris	Hermes	Odysseus	Aphrodite	Helen

Triton

Altered hemoglobin	Amino acid change	Position in Hb
Hb Sparta	Cassandra to Iphigenia	1
Hb Charybdis	Achilles to Agamemnon	5
Hb Troy	Hector to Priam	1
Hb Syracuse	Paris to Minerva	3
Hb Sybaris	Iphigenia to Helen	2
Hb Delphi	Hermes to Poseidon	3
Hb Utica	Odysseus to Ajax	5
Hb Thrace	Priam to Helen	4
Hb Argos	Calchas to Patroclus	3
Hb Chalcis	Aphrodite to Apollo	5
Hb Styx	Zeus to Hecuba	7
Hb Tartarus	Poseidon to Helen	6
Hb Corinth	Hector to Adonis	1
Hb Naxos	Achilles to Iphigenia	7
Hb Rhodes	Calchas to Agamemnon	3

B. From the information given in the charts below, determine:

1. Which of the 20 amino acids named by the Atlantis team correspond to **polar** residues and which ones correspond to **nonpolar** residues.

2. Which of the amino acids corresponds to **proline**.

It is important to explain your logic and justify your conclusions as clearly as possible.

Creature	Residue found at specific position						
	1	2	3	4	5	6	7
Centaur	Hermes	Paris	Agamemnon	Calchas	Minerva	Aphrodite	Achilles
Triton	Aphrodite	Paris	Poseidon	Calchas	Adonis	Hecuba	Paris
Cyclops	Zeus	Helen	Priam	Calchas	Apollo	Minerva	Achilles
Hydra	Zeus	Helen	Hecuba	Hector	Patroclus	Ajax	Odysseus
Scylla	Zeus	Paris	Apollo	Aphrodite	Iphigenia	Poseidon	Odysseus
Harpies	Hermes	Cassandra	Minerva	Aphrodite	Hermes	Priam	Odysseus
Stymphalian Birds	Hermes	Cassandra	Iphigenia	Aphrodite	Aphrodite	Paris	Paris
Gorgon	Aphrodite	Cassandra	Ajax	Hector	Ajax	Apollo	Paris
Satyrs	Aphrodite	Helen	Zeus	Aphrodite	Hecuba	Hecuba	Achilles
Pegasus	Aphrodite	Helen	Paris	Hector	Zeus	Iphigenia	Achilles
Chimaera	Zeus	Paris	Hermes	Hector	Priam	Zeus	Achilles
Phoenix	Aphrodite	Cassandra	Apollo	Calchas	Adonis	Agamemnon	Paris
Laestrygones	Hermes	Helen	Adonis	Calchas	Poseidon	Patroclus	Odysseus
Geryon	Hermes	Cassandra	Hecuba	Aphrodite	Paris	Priam	Achilles
Typhon	Zeus	Paris	Helen	Hector	Patroclus	Minerva	Paris

Pegasus

Altered hemoglobin	Amino acid change	Position in Hb
Hb Sparta	Zeus to Apollo	1
Hb Charybdis	Cassandra to Hecuba	2
Hb Troy	Paris to Priam	7
Hb Syracuse	Ajax to Achilles	3
Hb Sybaris	Helen to Iphigenia	2
Hb Delphi	Calchas to Apollo	4
Hb Utica	Paris to Adonis	7
Hb Thrace	Hector to Minerva	4
Hb Argos	Adonis to Achilles	5
Hb Chalcis	Zeus to Poseidon	1
Hb Styx	Helen to Apollo	2
Hb Tartarus	Odysseus to Patroclus	7
Hb Corinth	Minerva to Achilles	6
Hb Naxos	Calchas to Priam	4
Hb Rhodes	Hermes to Adonis	1

GLOSSARY
Description of Species Used in Atlantis Study

Centaur	A tribe of wild creatures, half-human, half-horse, living on wooded mountains, particularly in Thessaly.
Triton	The merman of Greek myth and folklore, half-man, half-dolphin.
Cyclops	A race of one-eyed giants who lived in what is now Sicily.
Hydra	The many-headed monster living by Lake Lerna in the Peloponnese that Heracles had to destroy as his second labor. As one head was cut off, two others grew.
Scylla	A sea monster in the Straits of Messina, opposite Charybdis, with six heads and a ring of barking dogs around her belly.
Harpies	Winged monsters, which appear as large birds with women's faces.
Stymphalian Birds	Fabulous monsters that Heracles had to expel from Lake Stymphalus in Arcadia as his sixth labor.
Gorgon	One of three monstrous sisters. Medusa had the power to turn into stone anyone who looked at her. A winged female with snakes for hair and boar's tusks for teeth.
Satyrs	Half-bestial spirits of woods and hills, mischievous and amorous.
Pegasus	Winged horse of Bellerophon, born of the blood of Medusa.
Chimaera	Fire-breathing monster, often with a lion's head, a goat's body, and a serpent's tail.
Phoenix	A bird of Egypt that died on a funeral pyre and rose again, miraculously.
Laestrygones	A race of cannibal giants, who sank all but one of Odysseus' ships.
Geryon	A three-bodied giant, living in what is now Spain, whose marvelous cattle Heracles had to steal and drive back to Greece as his tenth labor.
Typhon	A hundred-headed monster, son of Taurus and Ge, and possibly the father of the Chimaera and the Hydra.

Phoenix

Scenario 8   The Hundred Years Hemoglobin War

When King Jean II (Jean the Good) of France was captured by the Black Prince at Poitiers in 1356, he was kept in exile in the court of King Edward III of England. To pass the time, we now know that Jean studied molecular biology and began an intense analysis of the hemoglobin molecule, 1600 years prior to Perutz. In order to please his captors, Jean named each of the 20 amino acids after the kings of England, up to that time, and their wives (a lineage chart is provided on page 623 for *optional* reading). Thus, instead of the amino acids being named serine, leucine, alanine, etc., they were named William I, Isabella of France, Richard I, etc.

Jean carried out two types of studies. In one study, he compared the hemoglobins from different vertebrates, concentrating on the residue occupying the same position in each hemoglobin molecule at seven different places. The first chart on page 622 shows the residue appearing at each equivalent position. Position 12 is the same for each hemoglobin, position 47 is the same, etc.

In a second study, Jean II examined the altered hemoglobins from patients in England suffering from severe anemias. The second chart on page 622 shows the name of each altered hemoglobin, which Jean II named after the city in England where it was discovered, and the amino acid change detected, as well as the position in the molecule where the amino acid substitution occurred. The positions correspond to one of the seven positions on the previous chart. Recall that each of these amino acid exchanges produces a defective protein that cannot carry out its function properly.

King Jean surrenders to the Black Prince at Poitiers.

From information given in the charts below, determine:

1. Which of the 20 amino acids named by Jean II correspond to **polar** residues and which ones correspond to **nonpolar** residues.

2. Which of the amino acids corresponds to **proline**.

It is important to explain your logic and justify your conclusions as clearly as possible.

Residue found at specific position

Vertebrate	12	25	47	56	92	108	138
Horse	Edward I	Richard I	Eleanor of Provence	Berengaria	Eleanor of Aquitaine	Henry I	Henry II
Cow	Philippa	Richard I	Edward II	Berengaria	Eleanor of Castille	Henry I	Henry II
Pig	William II	John	William II	Berengaria	Philippa	Hernry I	Edward II
Camel	Richard I	Richard I	John	John	Isabella of Angoulême	Isabella of Angoulême	Stephen
Whale	John	John	Edward III	John	Edward I	Isabella of Angoulême	Stephen
Lion	Henry III	John	Henry II	Berengaria	William II	Eleanor of Aquitaine	Stephen
Bear	Henry I	John	Henry I	William I	William I	Isabella of Angoulême	Edward II
Elephant	William I	John	Isabella of France	William I	Edward II	Eleanor of Aquitaine	Edward II
Badger	Matilda of Flanders	Richard I	Philippa	William I	Matilda of Flanders	Eleanor of Aquitaine	Henry II
Rat	Matilda of Scotland	John	Richard I	John	Henry II	Isabella of Angoulême	Edward II
Duck	Henry II	Richard I	Edward I	William I	Edward III	Henry I	Stephen
Rabbit	Stephen	Richard I	Stephen	John	Stephen	Eleanor of Aquitaine	Henry II

Altered hemoglobin	Amino acid change	Position in Hb
Hb Kent	Richard I to Eleanor of Castille	25
Hb York	Edward II to Matilda of Flanders	138
Hb Buckingham	Henry I to Matilda of Scotland	108
Hb Gloucester	Philippa to Berengaria	12
Hb Somerset	John to Edward I	56
Hb Wincester	Isabella of Angoulême to William II	108
Hb Exeter	William I to Edward III	56
Hb Lancaster	William II to Berengaria	92
Hb Wales	John to Eleanor of Provence	25
Hb Cambridge	Henry II to Isabella of France	138
Hb March	Eleanor of Provence to Berengaria	47
Hb Pembroke	Henry I to Philippa	108
Hb Bristol	Edward II to Edward I	138

LINEAGE CHART

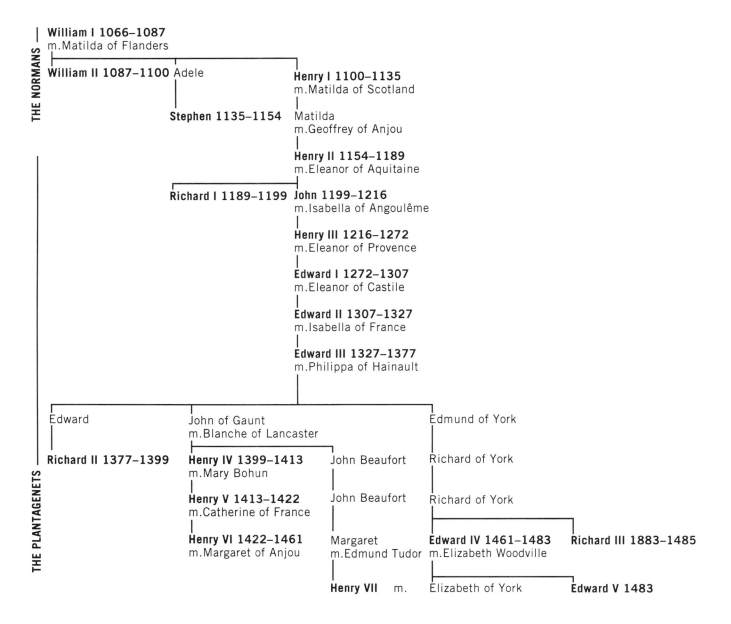

Scenario 9   Mission Impossible: To Decode "Deadly" Genotypes

A group of ex-Nazis based in South America has devised a scheme to raise money to establish a Fourth Reich. They have stolen nuclear weapons from a secret U.S. airbase and hidden a number of these bombs in the greater Los Angeles area. They have threatened to detonate the weapons in two weeks if the U.S. government does not pay a ransom of 10 billion dollars. Fortunately, one of our IMF (Impossible Mission Force) agents (see rare group photo on next page) was able to infiltrate this terrorist group and she found the secret location of each bomb and also the information required to deactivate those with a timing device. Unfortunately, she was captured, although she was able to pass a coded message out to a second agent by dabbing the sleeve of her velvet shirt with a set of bacterial strains. When this velvet is replicated onto predesigned media, the genotypes of each strain will be revealed. Thus, the seemingly invisible bacteria on the velvet will form a linear sequence of genotypes. Unfortunately, the code relating the sequence of these genotypes to letters in the alphabet has been lost, as has the exact number of genotypes that form each letter. Also, unfortunately, there are several sets of strains she could have been carrying and the code will need to be broken using each possibility.

Your mission, if you accept, is to decipher the linear code and determine where each bomb is hidden before it explodes. To do this, you will have to figure out how many strains in a row are required to form one letter (in other words, is it a singlet, doublet, triplet, quadruplet, etc., code). Then you will have to crack the code (which is actually a cipher) in a manner similar to solving a cryptogram. In other words, determine which genotype, or consecutive set of genotypes, encodes which letter of the alphabet. As an aid, a copy of Edgar Allen Poe's classic, "The Gold Bug," in which he solved a cryptogram that revealed the location of a buried treasure, is provided in the Appendix. The methods for solving such cryptograms today are remarkably similar to those explained by Poe in his story.

The solution of simple substitution ciphers is greatly aided by knowing the different frequencies of letters, initial letters, final letters, double letters, triple letters, etc. Poe used some of these rules in "The Gold Bug." The frequencies of letters in the English language are slightly different from what Poe indicated, the most accepted frequencies being, in order: **E T A O N I R S H** . . . . A chart of additional frequencies is given on the next page.

As always, if you or any of the IM force are caught or killed, the Secretary will disavow all knowledge of your action. Good luck!

FREQUENCIES OF LETTERS IN THE ENGLISH LANGUAGE

Single Letters	(*Valerio*) E T A O N I R S H D L C F U M P Y W G B V K X J Q Z
	(*Romanini*) E T A O N I R S H D L C W U, etc.
	(*Thomas*) E T A O N I R S H D L U C M P F Y W G B V K J X Z Q
	(*Thomas*) E T A I S O N H R D L U C M F W Y P G B V K J Q X Z
Initial Letters	T A O M S H W C I E P U R F, etc.
Final Letters	E T S D Y G N R M H C P, etc.
	(*Valerio*) E S D N T R Y O F A G L H I M W K U C X
Bigrams	(*Valerio*) TH HE AN ER ON RE IN ED ND AT OF OR HA EN NT EA TO TI ST IT
	(*Thomas*) TH ER ON AN RE HE IN ED ND HA
Trigrams	(*Valerio*) THE AND THA HET EDT ENT FOR ION TIO NDE HAS MEN NCE OFT STH
	(*Thomas*) THE AND THA ENT ION TIO FOR NDE HAS NCE
Double Letters	(*Valerio*) SS EE TT LL MM OO FF
Two-letter Words	OF TO IN IT IS BE AS AT SO HE BY AN OR ME MY
Three-letter Words	THE AND FOR ARE NOT BUT HAD HAS YOU WAS HIS
Four-letter Words	THAT WITH HAVE FROM THEY THEM THIS WHEN WILL OVER BOTH
Five-letter Words	THERE THESE THOSE THEIR BEING GOING, etc.

A. The agent possibly had a set of bacterial strains carrying different alleles at each of two loci. One locus, involved in lactose metabolism, was either wild-type (+), defective (–), or cold-sensitive (C); the second locus encoded resistance to the antibiotic trimethoprim, resulting in either sensitivity (S) or resistance (R) to the antibiotic. Thus, at the first locus, strains were +, –, or C, and at the second locus strains were either S or R. The genotype of each strain is then written with the lactose locus first and then the trimethoprim locus. For example, "+R" means Lac+, trimethoprim resistance, etc.

+S CR -S -R +S -R CR +R -R +S -S -S -R -R +S +S -S -S +R CR +S -S +R +S +R -R CR CR -S -R

CR -S CR CR +S +S -S -S CR +S -R +S CR -R -R +S +R CR +R -R -S -S -R +S -R +S +S -S +S -S

+R +S +R -R +S +R -S -R CR -R +R -R CR CR -S -R -R CR +R +R CR CR +S -R +S +R +S +S +R -R

+R CR +S -R -S -S +R CR +R -R +S +R +S -S +R +S +R -R -S +S -S -R -R +S +R +R CR +S -S -R

CR -R +S -S -R +S +S -S +S -S +R +S +R -R -S -S -S -R +S +R +S -S +R +S +R -R -S -S +R CR -S

-R -R -R +S -S +R +S +R -R -R -R +S +S +R -R +R +R +R CR +R CR +S +S CR -R CR +R -S -R -S

-S -S -S +R -R CR +R +S -S -R +S +R +R +R +R +S -S +R +S +S +R +R -R +R -R +R -R +R +R +R

-R CR +R +S -S +S +R +S +S CR +R CR +R -R +S CR CR +R +R +R -R CR -R

B. The agent perhaps possessed only two strains, which were either Arg+ or Arg–. Their genotypes can simply be written as either "+" or "–." The linear sequence of strains can then be given as a sequence of genotypes as shown below.

– + – + + – + – + – + + – – + – + – + – + – – + – + – + – + – + + – – + + – + – – – + + – – + – + – + – + – – + +

+ – + – – + + – – – – + – + – – – + + – – + – + – – + – – + + + – + – – + + + – + – + – + + – + – + – – + + + – – – +

– + – + – – + + + – + – + – + + + – + – + + – + + + – – + + – + – – + – + – + + + – + + – + – – + – + – – + + + – – + – + – –

+ + – – – – + – + – + + – – – + + + – – + + – – + – – + – – + + – + – + – + – + + – + + + – – – – +

– + – + – – + + + – + + + – – + – – + + – + + + + + – – + – + – + – – + + + – – + – + – + + + + + + + – + – – + + +

– + – + + + – + + + – – + – + – – + + + + – + – + – + – – + + – – + – + – + + – + – + – + – + – – + + + – + – + – + – + +

– + – – + + + – + – – + + – – – + – + – + – – – + – + – + – – + + – – + + – + + – + – + – + – + – + – + + – + –

– + + + – – + + + + + + + – – – + – + – + + – + + + – + + + + + – – + + + – – + + + – + – + – + + – + + + + +

– – + – – – – + + + – + – + – – + – + + – + – + – + – + + + – + – – – + – + + – – – + – + – – + + + + +

– – – – + + – + – – + – + – – + – + + – + + + + + – – + – + – – + – + – + – + – + – + – + + + + – + + + + –

+ – – + + + + + + – – + – + – – + – + – + – – + – + + – + – + + + – + + – + – – + – + – – + – + – + – + – + + – + + + – – + –

+ – + + + + + + – + – – + – + – – + – + + – + – + – + – – + + + – + – – + – – – + + + – – + – – + + – + – + – + – + –

+ + + + – + – – + + + + + + – – + – + – – + – + – – + – – + + + – – – + + – + + – + – + – + – + – + – + + + – + + + – +

+ +

C. The strains possibly available to the agent are either sensitive or resistant to the antibiotics kanamycin and ampicillin. Normally, one would write the wild type (sensitive) as + and resistance as "r." However, the genotypes are simplified by not indicating the wild type at all and just indicating the resistance. Kanamycin resistance is shortened to Kan^r, which is shortened to K; Ampicillin resistance is shortened to Amp^r, which is shortened to A. Thus, the designation "K" for a strain indicates + Kan^r; the designation "A" indicates + Amp^r; and the designation "KA" indicates Kan^r Amp^r.

```
KA KA K K KA KA K KA A K KA K A A K A A K A A KA KA A K A A K KA KA A KA A KA K KA A A K

K KA KA A A KA K A K K KA KA A A A K KA A KA A KA KA K KA A A KA K KA K K A A K A K A A A

A K KA KA A A KA A KA K A K K KA A KA K A K KA K K A KA A K KA A A KA K K KA KA A A K A A

A K KA K KA K KA KA A A KA KA K KA A A K KA KA KA K A A A K KA K K A K K A A K A K K KA K K KA

K K KA A A A A KA KA A KA A KA KA K KA A K A K K K A KA K KA KA A K A A A A KA A KA A KA KA

K KA A A K A KA KA K KA A A K A KA A KA KA K A K KA KA A A KA A KA K K KA KA K A K A A K

A A KA K KA A A K K KA A KA KA K KA A A K A KA KA A A K A A A K KA K KA K KA A KA KA A A

K KA .K KA K A K A K K A A KA K A KA K K A A A A A KA KA KA A KA A KA K KA A A K K A A K

KA KA A K A A K A K A KA KA A KA K KA K KA KA A A K KA KA KA A KA A KA A A A A KA K K KA KA A

A A A K K KA A KA KA A KA A A K A K K K A KA A A K KA A KA A A K K KA KA KA KA A KA A K A

A K KA KA A KA A KA A A A A K K A A KA KA A KA KA A K K KA A K A KA A A K KA A KA A A K K

KA KA KA KA A A K K K KA A K KA KA KA A KA KA K KA K KA A K A A KA A KA KA K KA A A K A

KA KA A A A K KA K K K K A A K A K KA K A K KA A KA
```

D. The strains perhaps at the agents disposal differ at each of three loci. Thus, each strain in the linear sequence could be either resistant or sensitive (+) to rifampicin, streptomycin, or nalidixic acid. Rif^r is indicated by "R," Str^r by "S," and Nal^r by "N." The genotype of each strain is indicated by either a "+" or one of these letters at each of the three loci. For simplicity, the "+" is not written. Thus, the designation "N" means Nal^r and implies "+" or sensitivity to the other antibiotics. Likewise, the designation "S" means Str^r; the designation "SN" means Str^r Nal^r; and the designation "RS" means Rif^r Str^r.

```
SN RS RS R S RS S R SN SN SN S S R R N N N RS R R N SN R SN R S RS N S R N N S RS SN R

RS N R N SN R N N N R RS N R N S SN R N S S RS N R RS N SN RS RS R S RS SN S N R SN RS

SN RS S RS RS N RS R SN SN RS N N S R N SN RS R N N N SN R R N N N N RS S SN R N N N S

RS SN R N R N N N R N N RS SN N R RS N S RS S R SN SN S R N N R RS S RS SN R N R N S SN

R R N N N N N RS S RS R S RS SN R S SN R RS S RS SN R SN RS SN SN S RS S N RS SN R RS

SN SN SN R S RS SN RS RS R RS N S RS S RS SN N S RS S RS S S N N RS RS RS N SN SN SN S

N SN S RS N N SN RS S RS RS N SN R N R N SN S RS R SN S RS N S R N N S N RS R N SN RS

RS S N R N S S R S RS SN R S RS RS RS S SN N N S RS SN R SN N R N SN RS RS R SN RS RS R

S RS RS S SN SN SN SN S S R R N N S N R SN RS R N SN SN N S SN RS RS R RS N S RS S RS RS N

R N N RS RS R SN RS SN RS SN N S RS N S SN RS N SN SN SN N S S RS R RS S RS RS RS SN RS

N N S RS R SN S RS N S SN RS S RS S RS N S RS N R N N RS RS R SN RS
```

E. The strains possibly available to the agent are either wild-type or mutationally altered at two loci, for the "Leu" and "Pro" pathways. They are thus either Leu⁺ or Leu⁻ and either Pro⁺ or Pro⁻. This is shortened to either "+" or "−." The Leu marker is indicated first and then the Pro marker. Thus, ++ always means Leu⁺ Pro⁺ and −+ indicates Leu⁻ Pro⁺, etc. When tested on the appropriate media, the linear sequence of strains indicates the following order of genotypes, which encodes the location of the nuclear weapon.

```
++ −+ ++ +− ++ +− +− −+ ++ +− ++ −− +− ++ +− +− +− −+ ++ +− +− +− −+ ++ ++ −− −− ++ −+
++ +− +− +− ++ +− ++ +− −+ ++ ++ −− +− ++ −+ ++ +− ++ +− +− −+ ++ ++ −− +− +− −+ ++ ++
+− +− ++ −+ +− ++ +− −+ +− −+ ++ ++ −+ +− +− ++ −+ ++ −+ ++ +− ++ +− +− −+ ++ ++ ++ −−
+− +− −+ ++ +− −− ++ +− ++ +− −+ ++ +− +− −+ ++ −+ ++ +− +− −+ ++ +− ++ +− −+ +− ++ −+
+− ++ −+ ++ ++ −− −− ++ −− +− ++ −+ +− ++ −− −− ++ ++ +− +− ++ ++ ++ −+ +− ++ −− −− +−
−+ ++ ++ −− +− +− +− −+ ++ −− −− +− +− −+ ++ −+ ++ +− ++ −− ++ +− ++ +− +− −+ +− ++ −+
+− ++ −+ +− +− +− ++ −− −− +− +− −+ +− ++ ++ ++ +− ++ +− ++ ++ ++ −− −− ++ +− ++ +− −+
++ ++ ++ ++ +− −+ +− +− ++ ++ ++ ++ −− ++ ++ −− +− +− ++ +− ++ ++ ++ −+ ++ ++ −+ ++ +−
++ +− +− −+ ++ ++ −+ ++ +− ++ +− ++ +− ++ +− −+ ++ +− −+ ++ ++ −+ ++ +− +− +− +− −+ +−
+− +− −− ++ +− ++ +− +− +− +− ++ −+ ++ −+ ++ ++ −+ ++ +− −+ ++ +− −+ ++ ++ −+ ++ +− ++
+− ++ −+ ++ +− +− +− ++ −+ +− +− ++ −+ +− +− −+ ++ +− −+ ++ −+ ++ ++ −+ +− ++ +− +− +−
+− −+ ++ −+ ++ +− −+ ++ ++ −+ ++ +− ++ +− +− −+ ++ +− −+ ++ ++ ++ ++ +− −+ +− ++ ++ −−
+− +− +− ++ −− −− ++ −+ +− ++ +− +− +− −+ ++ ++ −− −−
```

F. The strains possibly available to the agent included those with one of three alleles at each of three different loci (genes). The first locus encodes resistance, sensitivity, or dependence for the antibiotic streptomycin. R = resistance, S = sensitivity, and D = dependence. The second locus encodes ability to grow without arginine. Strains are either "+," "−," or "C" (cold-sensitive) at this locus. The third locus encodes phage resistance and is either "T" (T-phage), "M" (M13), or "F" (F2). Thus, each strain will have one allele at each of the three loci, as the entries in the linear sequence show.

```
D−F SCF S+T SCF S+T S−T S+F S−F D−M R−T S+T D−M D−T SCF R−T SCT S−M D−M D+M SCT S+F DCT
D−M R−T SCM D+F D−M S−M S+F S+T S−T S+F S−F R+F S+F S+F R−M D−M RCT RCT S−M SCF R−T S−M
S+F S−F S−F SCT SCF R−T RCT SCF SCF R+F S+T SCF S+T S−T S+F DCT SCT D−F S−T S+T D−M R−T SCM
S+M D−M RCT R+F D+F SCT D+F S+T S+F S+F R−T S−F S+T S+F D+M S−F SCF R−T S+T S−T S+F RCT S+F
D+F S+T S−F SCT SCM S+F S+T S−T S+F DCT S+F S+M SCT RCT RCT R−M S+F D−M D−F D−M DCT D−M
D−F S+F S+M SCT S+T S−T D−M DCT S+F SCM S−F SCT D−F R−T S+T S−T D−M S+T S−F D−M RCF S−F
SCM SCF R−T SCF S+T S+F R−T S+T S+F DCT S+T S−T S+F R−M SCF D−T R−M SCT S−F SCT R−T S−F SCT
SCM S+F S+T S−T S+F D−F D−M DCT D−M D−F S+F D−M R−T SCM S+T SCT D−T S+F SCM S+T SCF D−F SCF
SCF D+F D+F SCT R−T D+F SCF DCT S+T RCF S+F SCT D−F S−T S+T S−T SCF RCM DCT S−F SCT S+T S−M
D−M R−T R−M S+F SCT R−T D−M S−M S+T SCT R+T D−M S+T S+F SCM R−M RCF SCM SCT D−M RCT SCT
R−T D−F S+T S−T S+F R−T RCM D−T R−M S+F DCT S+T S+M SCF S−T RCM R−T SCM DCT S+F SCM S+T S−T
SCT DCT S+T RCF S+T S−T DCT S+F S+F D−M R−T SCM S+T S−T S+F R−T D+M DCT S+F S−F S−F SCT R−T
D−F S+T S−T S+F DCT S+F SCM R−M RCM S+T S+T SCF R−T
```

G. The strains possibly available to the agent have two different alleles at each of two loci. Thus, the strains are either chloramphenicol-resistant (C) or chloramphenicol-sensitive (wild type, indicated by the lack of a C) and either tetracycline-resistant (T) or tetracycline-sensitive (wild type, indicated by the lack of a T). For example, the genotypic designation "T" indicates tetracycline-resistant, chloramphenicol-sensitive, and the designation "TC" indicates tetracycline-resistant, chloramphenicol-resistant. The linear sequence of strain genotypes is shown below.

C TC T C TC C C TC TC T C TC C TC TC T TC TC TC T C T T C TC T T C C T T TC C TC C C T T C TC
T TC T TC TC C TC T C TC TC T C C C C T TC T T C T T T TC TC TC C C C C T T TC T T C T T T C C
C TC C C TC T T T T T C T C T C TC T C TC TC T T C TC T T C TC TC T TC TC C TC T C TC T C TC C
C TC TC T T TC T T C C TC C TC T T TC T C T TC TC T C T TC C C C T TC C TC TC C TC T C TC T TC
C TC C T T T C T T TC C C TC TC T C T C T T T C T TC T T T C C C TC TC T T T C TC T C TC C C
TC TC C T T T TC TC T T T T TC T TC C C C TC TC T TC T T TC TC T TC C C TC TC T T C C C TC C
TC T C TC C C TC TC T TC C C TC T T TC TC C TC T T C T C TC TC T T C C C TC C TC C C TC TC T T
T TC T TC T C T TC C C C TC TC T TC C TC T TC T C T C TC T C TC T C TC C C TC TC C T TC T T T
C TC TC C TC TC TC T T T C TC C C T T T T C TC TC

Scenario 10   Jurassic Engineering

Igor Karpak?

The person in the photograph to the left is thought to be Igor Karpak, an evil genius who has turned to a life of crime. This former high school of science graduate and university dropout has become demented and is threatening to use genetic engineering to terrorize the world. He and his sadistic cohorts have built a secret genetic engineering laboratory and are using it to construct deadly viruses and bacterial strains. We were able to infiltrate Karpak's group with a student, code-named "Tania," who pretended to share Karpak's goals of financial gain at any cost. Aided by a fake university transcript prepared by the registrar, Tania was able to join this secret genetic engineering unit.

Karpak has succeeded in cloning genes from the time of the dinosaurs, which roamed the earth 100 million years ago! Taking a page from Michael Crichton's recent thriller, "Jurassic Park," Karpak recovered ancient insects that had been embedded in amber. Reasoning that many of these insects had bitten and withdrawn blood from the large dinosaurs, Karpak and his cohorts isolated red blood cells from the insects and cloned out genetic segments. Their work has advanced to the point where they are able to identify different prehistoric viruses and bacterial cells. One virus, Tyrannosaur 4, infects each of two bacterial strains, *methanogen* B and *methanogen* K. One gene in the Tyrannosaur 4 virus is of particular interest in that it codes for a protein that causes severe toxic effects in humans. Because the protein is easily denatured, it must be synthesized in the digestive tract of a mammalian system and released into the blood stream in order to be dangerous. Karpak has incorporated the deadly viral gene into a hybrid *methanogen-coli* bacterium that can stably exist in the human digestive tract. He plans to introduce a sample of these bacteria into the food supply to infect scores of people. After these people become fatally ill, he will then announce his invention and demand an exorbitant bribe not to use it again. We have learned that Karpak plans to strike first at different university fast food centers, beginning in less than three weeks!

Karpak and his evil band must be stopped! Based on the information received from our informant, the only way we can buy time and protect students from the effects of the virus is to design an antisense RNA that will inactivate the mRNA for the deadly gene. In order to do this, we need to decode the message for the toxin gene.

The government is offering a research grant of 1 million dollars a year for life to anyone who can find the sequence of the toxin gene message, and also the genetic code of the age of the dinosaurs, since we now know that 6 bases were used in the DNA and 34 amino acids were used in the proteins. This will give the country a chance to weather the first assault from Karpak's deadly viral gene and allow the government enough time to find his laboratory and arrest his gang.

According to our informant, Tania, the world of 100 million years ago was different than the world of today and the genetic code was different than it is now. There were 6 bases in the DNA and 34 amino acids in proteins. (This is probably why the dinosaurs died out.) In addition to the 4 bases that we know (A, T, C, and G), two new bases, Stegosaurine and Dilophosaurine, both paired with each other. Let's call these bases X and Y. The pairing rules in the DNA were A pairs with T, G pairs with C, and X pairs with Y. The DNA sequence could be any sequence of 6 bases X, Y, A, T, C, G.

In addition to the normal 20 amino acids, there were 14 other amino acids that are no longer used. These are listed on the next page with their three letter symbols.

Selenocysteine   SCY
Phosphotyrosine   PTY
Hydroxyproline   HPR
Norleucine   NOR
Apatosauric acid   APA
Selenomethionine   SMT
Velociraptoric acid   VEL
Hypsilophodontidine   HYP
Pterosaurine   PTE
Carboxyglutamic acid   CGL
Brontosauric acid   BRO
Jurassic acid   JUR
Phosphothreonine   PTR
Phosphoserine   PSR

Tania attempted to sequence the DNA for the toxin gene, but unfortunately the composition of the archaic DNA does not permit DNA sequencing by the current set of techniques. Therefore, Tania carried out mutagenic specificity experiments and frameshift experiments, just like Brenner, Crick, and their colleagues. Because the Tyrannosaur 4 virus could attack and make plaques on the *methanogen* B and *methanogen* K bacteria, and because the toxin gene product was required before replication, there was a direct analogy between these experiments and those of Benzer in the *r*II system of bacteriophage T4. In summary, the Tyrannosaur 4 virus could make small plaques on both B and K, whereas mutants with a defective toxin gene made large plaques on B, but did not grow or make plaques on K. Armed with a set of different mutagens that act in different ways, causing both frameshifts and base substitutions, Tania set out to decode the toxin gene. Although DNA sequencing was not possible, sequencing the altered toxin proteins from different mutants was. The studies were so exhaustive that when a mutagen was used, every possible mutant protein (arising from a single base change) that could be found was in fact detected since hundreds of mutants were analyzed. Each chart on the following pages shows all of the altered proteins found under each of three mutagenic conditions. Thus, if an amino acid is not changed, then it cannot be affected by the respective base substitution caused by the particular mutagen. Row 1 depicts one set of mutagenic conditions, row 2 a second, and row 3 a third. Additional mutational data is also given. Finally, the protein resulting from a frameshift mutation at the beginning of the gene is shown. Since we have not heard from Tania after receiving these data (sent by long distance carrier pigeons), we have to presume that she has been captured. (She may have fallen into the hands of the infamous Karpak torturer, Mary Anne, shown at left in a computer-generated sketch provided by MI-6.) Therefore, our stopping Karpak and his mob depends on your being able to decode the toxin gene message using Tania's data.

Mary Anne

A. The arrows in level 1 point to changes made by a mutagen that specifically alkylates the *O*-4 position of thymidine, immediately changing it to a derivative that pairs like cytosine. Thus, this mutagen works exactly like hydroxylamine, except that here it changes T to C', where C' will pair with guanine. Any mRNA synthesized before replication will be affected by changes on the sense strand. Changes indicated in level 1 are made when these mutagenized viruses are passaged through strain B. The arrows in level 2 point to changes made by the same alkylating agent when the mutagenized viruses are passed through strain K before plating on B. Level 3 indicates changes made by the mutator locus *mutY*, which causes G·C→T·A changes during DNA replication. As an additional piece of information, it was found that when a mutagen was used that changed G→X, one of the altered proteins changed GLY→VEL. The protein sequence is continuous for the first two lines. The third and fourth lines indicate the protein sequence resulting from a deletion of the first base in the DNA sequence in the gene.

1. First determine how many bases encode one amino acid, and then decode the mRNA and make a chart of the genetic code. Show which codons are nonsense.

2. If there are still a few gaps in the code, describe what experiments you would do to resolve them.

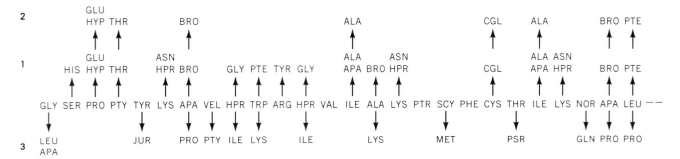

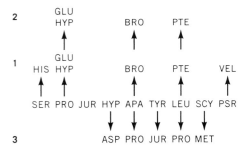

ASN JUR GLN CYS ASN HPR GLN ASN BRO SER LYS HIS ARG ASP TRP MET THR SMT PTY PHE TRP ASP HPR VEL PRO ASN — —

JUR CYS PRO PTE CYS APA BRO PTR

B. The arrows in level 1 point to changes made by hydroxylamine when the mutagenized viruses are passaged through strain B. The arrows in level 2 point to changes made by hydroxylamine when the mutagenized viruses are passaged through strain K before plating on B. Level 3 indicates changes made by 5-azacytosine, which causes G·C→C·G base changes during DNA replication. As an additional piece of information, it was found that when a mutagen was used that changed A→X, one of the altered proteins changed LEU→SER. The protein sequence is continuous for the first two lines. The very bottom line indicates the protein sequence resulting from a deletion of the first base in the DNA sequence in the gene.

1. First determine how many bases encode one amino acid, and then decode the mRNA and make a chart of the genetic code. Show which codons are nonsense.

2. If there are still a few gaps in the code, describe what experiments you would do to resolve them.

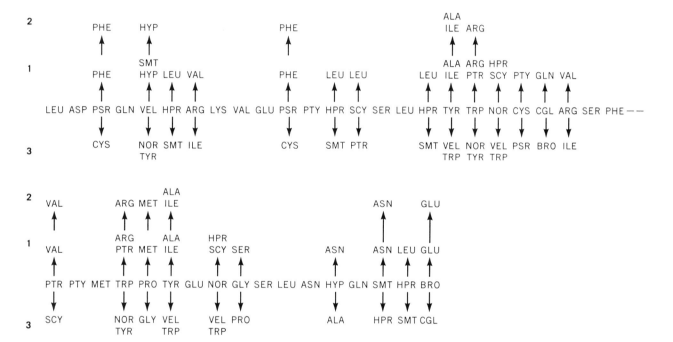

VAL PTE PRO PTR NOR SCY ASN PTY MET PTE HIS SCY LEU HPR GLN SCY PTR VEL VEL APA GLY NOR ASN

C. The arrows in level 1 point to changes made by hydroxylamine when the mutagenized viruses are passaged through strain B. The arrows in level 2 point to changes made by hydroxylamine when the mutagenized viruses are passaged through strain K before plating on B. Level 3 indicates changes made by the mutator locus *mutY*, which causes G·C→T·A base changes during DNA replication. As an additional piece of information, it was found that when a mutagen was used that changed X→C, one of the altered proteins changed LEU→HPR. The protein sequence is continuous for the first two lines. The bottom two lines indicate the protein sequence resulting from a deletion of the first base in the DNA sequence in the gene.

1. First determine how many bases encode one amino acid, and then decode the mRNA and make a chart of the genetic code. Show which codons are nonsense.

2. If there are still a few gaps in the code, describe what experiments you would do to resolve them.

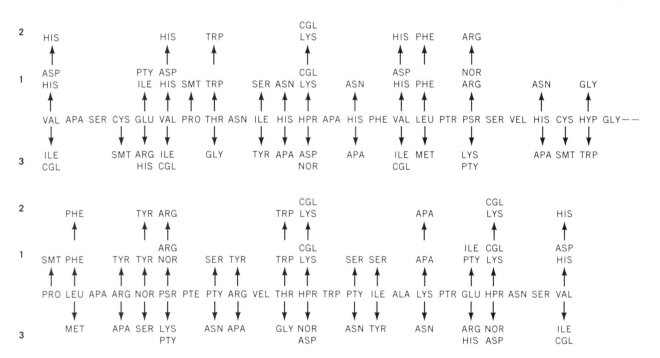

ARG ASN NOR SCY PSR GLU GLN PHE SER ARG PSR CGL APA HYP LYS HYP CYS SCY ASP GLY PHE PSR SCY MET BRO ——

ALA CGL HIS ASN VAL THR SCY ILE TRP LEU LEU CGL BRO SER PRO PHE CYS SCY PSR CGL SER NOR

D. The arrows in level 1 point to changes made by a mutagen that specifically alkylates the *O*-4 position of Y, immediately changing it to a derivative that pairs like X. Thus, this mutagen works exactly like hydroxylamine, except that here it changes Y to X', where X' will pair with Y. Any mRNA synthesized before replication will be affected by changes on the sense strand. Changes indicated in level 1 are made when these mutagenized viruses are passaged through strain B. The arrows in level 2 point to changes made by the same alkylating agent when the mutagenized viruses are passaged through strain K before plating on B. Level 3 indicates changes made by the mutator locus *mutY*, which causes G·C→T·A changes during DNA replication. As an additional piece of information, it was found that when a mutagen was used that changed Y→G, one of the altered proteins changed CYS→TYR and a second altered protein resulted from the change of CGL→ILE. The protein sequence is continuous for the first two lines. The third and fourth lines indicate the protein sequence resulting from a deletion of the first three bases in the DNA sequence in the gene. The framshifted sequence was translated in the presence of a nonsense suppressor that inserts tyrosine in response to particular nonsense codons. These tyrosines are indicated by parentheses.

1. First determine how many bases encode one amino acid, and then decode the mRNA and make a chart of the genetic code. Show which codons are nonsense.

2. If there are still a few gaps in the code, describe what experiments you would do to resolve them.

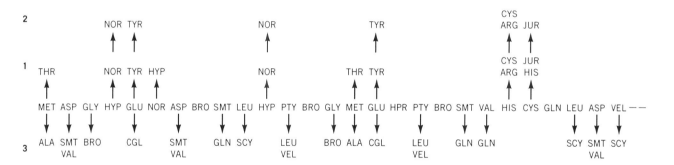

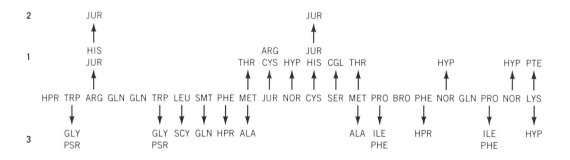

PRO GLN HIS ILE (TYR) ILE SCY GLY VAL ASN VAL SMT LEU CYS ILE PSR VAL SCY TRP HYP ARG PTR BRO PTY TRP GLN — —

PHE THR (TYR) BRO PHE VEL VEL ILE TRP JUR SER JUR ARG PSR TYR ILE GLN ILE (TYR) PHE ILE TYR

E. The arrows in level 1 point to changes made by a mutagen that specifically alkylates adenine, immediately changing it to a derivative that pairs like guanine. Thus, this mutagen works exactly like hydroxylamine, except that here it changes A to G', where G' will pair with cytosine. Any mRNA synthesized before replication will be affected by changes on the sense strand. Changes indicated in level 1 are made when these mutagenized viruses are passaged through strain B. The arrows in level 2 point to changes made by the same alkylating agent when the mutagenized viruses are passaged through strain K before plating on B. Level 3 indicates changes made by a mutator locus that causes A·T→X·Y changes during DNA replication. As an additional piece of information, it was found that when a mutagen was used that changed G→X, one of the altered proteins changed HYP→PHE. The protein sequence is continuous for the first two lines. The third and fourth lines indicate the protein sequence resulting from a deletion of the first base in the DNA sequence in the gene.

1. First determine how many bases encode one amino acid, and then decode the mRNA and make a chart of the genetic code. Show which codons are nonsense.

2. If there are still a few gaps in the code, describe what experiments you would do to resolve them.

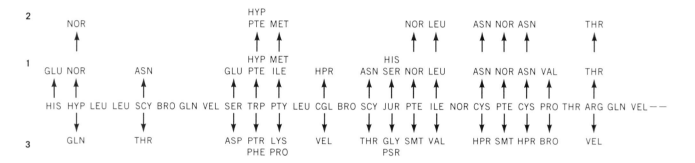

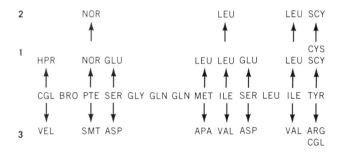

MET CYS ASN NOR GLY SMT ALA PSR ILE TYR CYS GLN GLY SMT JUR PTY ASN PTE HYP ILE HYP HIS SMT LYS APA ALA BRO — —

GLY PHE SCY HIS APA SMT CGL ASN TYR GLU ASN TRP

F. The arrows in level 1 point to changes made by a mutagen that specifically alkylates the *O*-6 position of guanine, immediately changing it to a derivative that pairs like adenine. Thus, this mutagen works exactly like hydroxylamine, except that here it changes G to A', where A' will pair with thymidine. Any mRNA synthesized before replication will be affected by changes on the sense strand. Changes indicated in level 1 are made when these mutagenized viruses are passaged through strain B. The arrows in level 2 point to changes made by the same alkylating agent when the mutagenized viruses are passaged through strain K before plating on B. Level 3 indicates changes made by the mutagen 5-azacytidine (5AZ), which causes G·C→C·G changes during DNA replication. As an additional piece of information, it was found that when a mutagen was used that changed G→X, one of the altered proteins changed GLU→NOR. The protein sequence is continuous for the first two lines. The third and fourth lines indicate the protein sequence resulting from a deletion of the first base in the DNA sequence in the gene. The frameshifted sequence is expressed in the presence of a nonsense suppressor that inserts tyrosine in response to nonsense codons. This tyrosine is indicated by parentheses.

1. First determine how many bases encode one amino acid, and then decode the mRNA and make a chart of the genetic code. Show which codons are nonsense.

2. If there are still a few gaps in the code, describe what experiments you would do to resolve them.

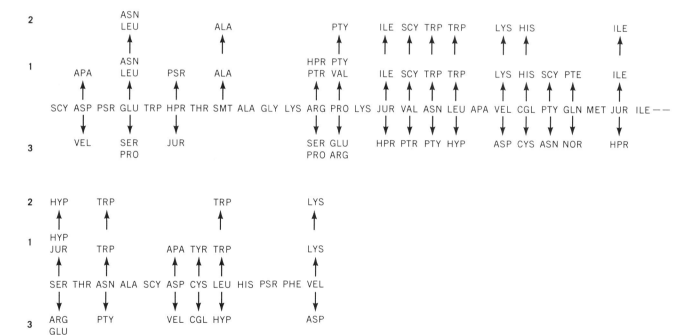

PTE PTR JUR LEU SCY HYP BRO CGL HIS MET PTY SER GLN SCY GLU ILE GLU THR PTE GLU ALA ARG BRO APA VAL PTY LEU — —

LYS CGL TRP PTE ARG SMT TRP (TYR) PTE PHE

G. The arrows in level 1 point to changes made by a mutagen that specifically alkylates adenine, immediately changing it to a derivative that pairs like guanine. Thus, this mutagen works exactly like hydroxylamine, except that here it changes A to G', where G' will pair with cytosine. Any mRNA synthesized before replication will be affected by changes on the sense strand. Changes indicated in level 1 are made when these mutagenized viruses are passaged through strain B. The arrows in level 2 point to changes made by the same alkylating agent when the mutagenized viruses are passaged through strain K before plating on B. Level 3 indicates changes made by a mutator locus that causes G·C→C·G changes during DNA replication. As an additional piece of information, it was found that when a mutagen was used that changed G→Y, one of the altered proteins changed PRO→PHE. The bottom line indicates the protein sequence resulting from a deletion of the first three bases in the DNA sequence in the gene. When the frameshifted sequence is expressed in the presence of a nonsense suppressor that inserts tyrosine in response to nonsense codons, the position of the new tyrosine is indicated by parentheses.

1. First determine how many bases encode one amino acid, and then decode the mRNA and make a chart of the genetic code. Show which codons are nonsense.

2. If there are still a few gaps in the code, describe what experiments you would do to resolve them.

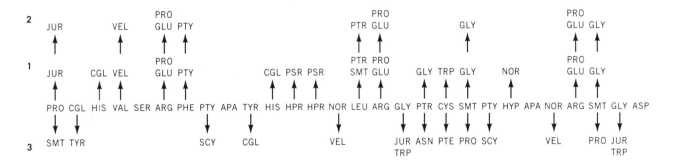

PSR (TYR) PHE GLN ARG VEL SER SER (TYR) THR HIS APA LYS ILE PRO BRO THR LYS BRO MET HPR MET LYS ARG BRO LYS

Scenario 11   America's Most Wanted: Against All Odds

We have uncovered an international cartel that sells high-technology weapons to terrorist groups. It is headed by Baron Pierre-Giscard St. Girons, who never allows himself to be photographed. St. Girons is a French nobleman who claims ancestry dating back to the 14th-century French knights who fought with King Jean II against Edward, the Black Prince, at Poitiers in 1356. We have long suspected that St. Girons' gambling casinos in Monte Carlo, Divonne, and Macao and his racetrack in Hong Kong are a front for illegal weapons sales.

Our best hope of nailing Pierre-Giscard St. Girons is when he pays off his suppliers of illegal weapons. Interpol has compiled an extensive dossier on two of the couriers for his suppliers. Gary "Geek" Cassidy carries money for the North American mob and travels to Monte Carlo once each month for payoffs. "Hong Kong" Maggie is a former UCLA student cafeteria worker who disappeared after being sought by the FBI for allegedly planting mind-altering memory loss drugs in pre-medical students' breakfasts just before the MCAT exams. She fronts for the Southeast Asian cartel and visits the Macao casino regularly. We have learned that St. Girons arranges to pay off his suppliers by letting these couriers win at various games of chance in his casinos. We intend to monitor his casino in Macao during a 3-day visit of Hong Kong Maggie and likewise his casino in Monte Carlo during a 2-day visit of Geek to see if we can catch them at their own game.

"Hong Kong" Maggie

A. On day 1 in Macao, Hong Kong Maggie (shown at left in a computer-generated sketch provided by the Japanese Secret Service) plays the "Wheel of Fortune" game. Here, they spin a wheel with 120 slots: 60 of the slots pay 2:1 (in other words, if you bet one dollar and win, you receive two dollars, including your own original dollar), 30 pay 4:1, 12 pay 9:1, 6 pay 18:1, 3 pay 35:1, 2 pay 50:1, 1 pays 100:1, and 6 have no payoff.

   You note that Hong Kong Maggie bets $2000 on the 35:1 slots each time. The wheel spins 180 times during the night, and she wins 16 times. Calculate how much money she won after subtracting her investment. Calculate the probability of this occurring by chance alone. In other words, what is the expected number of times that the 35:1 slots will come up 16 times during 180 spins? Is the wheel so obviously tilted in her favor that we can arrest her and St. Girons and claim it was a payoff? Let's say that if the expected number of times the 35:1 slots will come up 16 times out of 180 spins is less than 1 out of 1000, then we can arrest them.

B. On day 2, Hong Kong Maggie again plays the "Wheel of Fortune" game with the odds being the same as given in **A** above. This time she bets $2000 on the 50:1 slots each time. The wheel spins 100 times during the night, and she wins 10 times. Calculate how much money she won after subtracting her investment. Calculate the probability of this occurring by chance alone. In other words, what is the expected number of times that the 50:1 slots will come up 10 times during 100 spins? Is the wheel so obviously tilted in her favor that we can arrest her and St. Girons and claim it was a payoff? Let's say that if the expected number of times the 50:1 slots will come up 10 times out of 100 spins is less than 1 out of 1000, then we can arrest them.

C. On day 3, Hong Kong Maggie plays the Lotto-Deco game. Here a single card from a deck of 52 cards is used, and each time one card is drawn. Players bet on each card. The winning card pays 50:1. This time she bets on two cards each time, betting $2000 on each card each time. She played the game 150 times during the course of the evening and won 17 times. Calculate how much money she won after subtracting her investment. Calculate the probability of this occurring by chance alone. In other words, what is the expected number of times that one of her two numbers will come up 17 times during 150 draws? Is the deck so obviously stacked in her favor that we can arrest her and St. Girons and claim it was a payoff? Let's say that if the expected number of times that she will win 17 of 150 draws is less than 1 out of 1000, then we can arrest them.

Gary "Geek" Cassidy

D. Meanwhile, on day 1 in Monte Carlo, we note that Geek Cassidy (shown at left in a computer-generated sketch courtesy of Miami Vice) plays roulette all evening, each time betting $1000. He splits his bet between the same two numbers each time. There are a total of 36 numbers Each win pays 36:1 for any one number. During the entire night, the wheel spins 200 times. Cassidy wins 25 times. Calculate how much money he won after subtracting his investment. Calculate the probability of this occurring by chance alone. In other words, what is the expected number of times that one of the two numbers bet will come up 25 times during 200 spins? Is the wheel so obviously tilted in his favor that we can arrest St. Girons and Cassidy and claim it was a payoff? Let's say that if the expected number of times one of two numbers bet will come up 25 times out of 200 is less than 1 out of 1000, then we can arrest them.

E. On day 2, Geek Cassidy again plays roulette all evening, each time betting $1000. This time he splits his bet between the same three numbers each time. There are a total of 36 numbers, plus 0 and 00, to give a grand total of 38 numbers. Each win pays 36:1 for any one number. During the entire night, the wheel spins 200 times. Cassidy wins 34 times. Calculate how much money he won after subtracting his investment. Calculate the probability of this occurring by chance alone. In other words, what is the expected number of times that one of the three numbers bet will come up 34 times during 200 spins? Is the wheel so obviously tilted in his favor that we can arrest St. Girons and Cassidy and claim it was a payoff? Let's say that if the expected number of times one of three numbers bet will come up 34 times out of 200 spins is less than 1 out of 1000, then we can arrest them.

Scenario 12   Hitchhiker's Guide to the Galaxy: Follow That Sequence

While strolling drown Rodeo Drive you suddenly fall through a crack in the Universal Space-Time Continuum and are instantly transported to the planet Voltor in the 23rd Galaxy, in the fourth millennium in the year 3756. In order to return, you have to buy passage from Voltor back to Earth, back through the Space-Time Continuum. However, this would cost 2000 paralex credits, a price fixed by the Intergalactic League, of which Voltor is a member. Since you left home without your Andromeda Express Credit Card, you have to work off the debt by carrying out experiments in a biotech lab in Voltor's capital city, Paramador.

Your task is to identify the mutational spectrum of different space mutagens, using the *P* gene of the space moth *Pernicious galactocolis*, which infests one of Voltor's five moons, Traxor. The mutagen is applied to the eggs of the moth, and the *P* gene is then analyzed from developed moths. Each mutagen has a different mutagenic specificity. The moth's genetic code is of course different from that of 20th century Earthlings, although the DNA does consist of four bases that have distinct pairing rules and the code is read as a series of triplets, each of which codes for an amino acid, except for one nonsense codon.

A. You are given a stretch of DNA sequence. The single strand shown below is the nontemplate strand and is thus identical to the mRNA.

QQR RST QTT SRT QTS RRT RRQ SST RQT SSR TQT SRS QTS SRQ TTT SRQ SST
QTR SQT QQT RRS QTS QQT SRT SST QRS TQT SSS QQQ SRT QTR SRT QQT SSR
QTR SST STR RSR TRT STT QQT QQR TTT SSQ QST SST QTR SST RTQ TTT TSR
QRS QQT QQR TSR QTT SRT SSR QTR SST SQR SST QSS SRT QQT SSR TTR STQ
SSR TQT SSR QTR QQS QQR STQ TTQ SRT QQT SRQ RSR QTS RRQ STR SQT SSR
TTQ QTR TSQ TTS RQT SSR QQR TTQ SSR TQT SSR QST RSQ QTS TRT RSR QQT
SSS QQT SSR QSQ STT QQQ STT SRT SST QQR QST QTT SSR QTS QTQ SSR QTS
SSR TTR QTT SRQ SSS QTT QRS TTR QTS SSR QRR STQ SSQ TSR QQR SST SRQ
SST

Nonsense codon = QSR

Based on the specific pairing rules given below and the identity of the non-sense codon for that genetic code, describe the predicted experimental results you would obtain by using the provided mutagen and by following the principles of Coulondre and Miller.

- The four letter code you are analyzing has the bases T, Q, R, and S. In the DNA, T pairs with Q and R pairs with S.

- All base substitutions are possible spontaneously. The mutagen you are working with makes changes at T·Q base pairs and can make all possible changes at these bases.

- When T is part of a QRT sequence, with the orientation as written, it is methylated and, as a result, will frequently mutate spontaneously to any of the other bases.

1. Describe the system you would use. Namely, which codons can go to nonsense by a single base change in the stretch of DNA you are provided with?

    a. Draw a diagram of all of the possible sense codons that can go to nonsense by a single base change, just like Figure 1 in the Coulondre and Miller paper (see page 379). Then draw a figure showing these possible sites in your sequence, arranged by base change, as in Figure 2 of the same paper (see page 380).

    b. Draw a chart showing the expected results in your gene for the mutagen you are using. Explain the system and how it would show the mutagenic specificity. Be sure to provide a clear set of figures and an explanation for each figure.

    c. Considering the rules given to you above, draw a figure showing the expected results in your gene for spontaneous base substitutions.

2. Your goal is to develop a rapid mutagen and mutator tester system, based on the reversion of nonsense mutations, that will recognize base substitutions in the Traxor genetic code.

    a. Show what base changes would revert your nonsense codon from the preceding experiment to a sense codon. Let's assume that any change to a sense codon at that position will result in a wild-type protein.

    b. You have isolated a bacterium from Traxor, *Centauris polaris,* that grows on agar plates with minimal medium supplemented with

crushed Voltor rat liver as an energy source, making green colonies. Wild-type strains can also grow on minimal medium with only comet dust as a carbon source, making yellow colonies. However, mutants in the *K* gene cannot grow on comet dust, although they can grow on crushed Voltor rat liver. Assume you have K mutants of different types. Describe how you would devise a procedure using reversion of nonsense mutations to detect "mutators" in *C. polaris*. Give all of the technical details and use diagrams when relevant.

3. You have a phage that infects the Traxor bacteria *C. polaris* and can deliver a transposon, Tn*FX*, to the chromosome of *C. polaris*. You have integrated the *K* gene into the transposon. Assume you have strains deleted for the *K* gene and the same materials and conditions as for problem **A**2 above. Assume also that on medium with asteroid dust, K⁺ cells form blue colonies and K⁻ cells form red colonies. Design an experiment that will allow you to determine whether transposition occurs via a replicative or nonreplicative mechanism. Describe the constructions you would engineer, the experiment itself, and how you would interpret the results.

B. You are given a stretch of DNA sequence. The single strand shown below is the nontemplate strand and is thus identical to the mRNA.

DLD GGM DLD GGM LLM LMG GGM GLM DGG LMD LLM LLD GGM DGG GLM GGD
GLD GGL DML GLD GLD DGG GLL DLM DMD DMM GLD GGM DLL GGM DLL GMG
DDM GGM LDM GGL DDL LLG GMD GGL MMG LMD MLG DLD GGM DLM DLM GMG
DLM DDL GLG LDM GGM DLL GLD GMD LLG GMG DLD GML DDD GMG LLG GLM
DGL MGL DMG LDM GML DLD LLM DLL GMM DLL GMG DDL GMG MDL GMD LGD
GDL DDG LMD GLM DDM GGM GLG LDL GMG DLL GMG DMG LDM GGM LDD MDL
LMG GLL LMD DLM MLG GMM DLM GGL LDM DDG LDG GLD GML DLL LLG LMG
LLG DMG MDD GLM DMM MDD DMG

Nonsense codon = DLG

Based on the specific pairing rules given below and the identity of the nonsense codon for that genetic code, describe the predicted experimental results you would obtain by using the provided mutagen and by following the principles of Coulondre and Miller.

• The four letter code you are analyzing has the bases D, G, M, and L. In the DNA, D pairs with G and M pairs with L.

• All base substitutions are possible spontaneously. The mutagen you are working with makes changes at M·L base pairs and can make all possible base changes at these bases.

• When M is part of an MDD sequence, with the orientation as written, it is methylated and, as a result, will frequently mutate spontaneously to any of the other bases.

1. Describe the system you would use. Namely, which codons can go to nonsense by a single base change in the stretch of DNA you are provided with? Specifically, perform steps *a–c* detailed in problem **A**1 on page 642.

2. Your goal is to develop a rapid mutagen and mutator tester system, based on the reversion of nonsense mutations, that will recognize base substitutions in the Traxor genetic code.

a. Show what base changes would revert your nonsense codon from the preceding experiment to a sense codon. Let's assume that any change to a sense codon at that position will result in a wild-type protein.

b. You have isolated a bacterium from Traxor, *Centauris polaris*, that grows on agar plates with minimal medium supplemented with comet dust as an energy source, making orange colonies. Wild-type strains can also grow on minimal medium with only asteroid dust as a carbon source, making black colonies. However, mutants in the *R* gene cannot grow on asteroid dust, although they can grow on comet dust. Assume you have R mutants of different types. Describe how you would devise a procedure using reversion of nonsense mutations to detect "mutators" in *C. polaris*. Give all of the technical details and use diagrams when relevant.

3. You have a phage that infects the Traxor bacteria *C. polaris* and can deliver a transposon, Tn*FX*, to the chromosome of *C. polaris*. You have integrated the *R* gene into the transposon. Assume you have strains deleted for the *R* gene and the same materials and conditions as for problem **B**2 above. Assume also that on medium with Paramador rat liver, R⁺ cells form orange colonies and R⁻ cells form black colonies. Design an experiment that will allow you to determine whether transposition occurs via a replicative or nonreplicative mechanism. Describe the constructions you would engineer, the experiment itself, and how you would interpret the results.

C. You are given a stretch of DNA sequence. The single strand shown below is the nontemplate strand and is thus identical to the mRNA.

XXJ NJJ NXF NJX FNF XJX FNF XXX FNF XJF FNN XJF NNF XJX FFN XNF NXF XNF
XJF NXX FNF JJN FNF XJN FNJ NJJ FNF XXN FFN JNX FNX FJF FNX FJX FJF XNX
FFJ XJX FJF NXJ NFF FNN XNJ XFF NFF XJF XNJ FJN XJF FJX XNF JJN XXN FJF JJN
XNX JNJ XFF JFJ XNX FFN XNF XJF NXF NJX FNF XJF XXJ FNF FJX FNJ XJN NNJ XNJ
NNF JXN FJF NNJ XNF JXN NJJ FFX JNF NXF NJX FJJ XJN FNX JJN XXF NJX JNF
XNX FJF FJX FNJ XJJ NJX FJX FNF JJF FFN XJX FFF XNX FJF FFX NJJ JJF FNX
FJX FNF FNX FFX NFJ XJX FJF JJX FNF XJF XFJ FNX JFN XJF FNF XXJ FNF NJX FNF
NXF FFJ XNX JFN XJF NNX JFF JXJ NXX FFN JXJ FNX FJN XJN JJF FXJ

Nonsense codon = NJF

Based on the specific pairing rules given below and the identity of the nonsense codon for that genetic code, describe the predicted experimental results you would obtain by using the provided mutagen and by following the principles of Coulondre and Miller.

- The four letter code you are analyzing has the bases X, F, N, and J. In the DNA, X pairs with F and N pairs with J.

- All base substitutions are possible spontaneously. The mutagen you are working with makes changes at X·F base pairs and can make all possible base changes at these bases.

- When J is part of a JNX sequence, with the orientation as written, it is methylated and, as a result, will frequently mutate spontaneously to any of the other bases.

1. Describe the system you would use. Namely, which codons can go to nonsense by a single base change in the stretch of DNA you are provided with? Specifically, perform steps *a–c* detailed in problem **A**1 on page 642.

2. Your goal is to develop a rapid mutagen and mutator tester system, based on the reversion of nonsense mutations, that will recognize substitutions in the Traxor genetic code.

   a. Show what base changes would revert your nonsense codon from the preceding experiment to a sense codon. Let's assume that any change to a sense codon at that position will result in a wild-type protein.

   b. You have isolated a bacterium from Traxor, *Centauris polaris*, that grows on agar plates with minimal medium supplemented with Paramador bat extract as an energy source, making silver colored colonies. Wild-type strains can also grow on minimal medium with only Traxor soil mix as a carbon source, making gold colored colonies. However, mutants in the *Q* gene cannot grow on Traxor soil mix, although they can grow on Paramador bat extract. Assume you have Q mutants of different types. Describe how you would devise a procedure using reversion of nonsense mutations to detect "mutators" in *C. polaris*. Give all of the technical details and use diagrams when relevant.

3. You have a phage that infects the Traxor bacteria *C. polaris* and can deliver a transposon, Tn*FX*, to the chromosome of *C. polaris*. You have integrated the *Q* gene into the transposon. Assume you have strains deleted for the *Q* gene and the same materials and conditions as for problem **C**2 above. Assume also that on medium with comet dust, Q⁺ cells form white colonies and Q⁻ cells form purple colonies. Design an experiment that will allow you to determine whether transposition occurs via a replicative or non-replicative mechanism. Describe the constructions you would engineer, the experiment itself, and how you would interpret the results.

D. You are given a stretch of DNA sequence. The single strand shown below is the nontemplate strand and is thus identical to the mRNA.

CPL PGC CPL GGL CPL GGL PCL GPC PLG GLC GLP PLL GGL CPL GPL PLG CPL GGL
CPG GGC PLL GPL GPL CCL GPL PLG GLP CCL GLC GLC GLC GPC PPL PLP CLP GPL
CLP GLP CCL PGC PLG CLL GPC LPC GPL GLC GPL PLG GLG CCL GPP GLL CPP PPP
GLL CLG CCC GLC GPC GLG CPP GLC PPC GPC LGG PCL GPL CPL GLL LLC CCL GPL
CCL GPP PCL GGL PCC PPC GPC GPL CGC PLL PLG CCL CLC GGC PLG CLP PLP GGL
CPL GCC GCC GLC PLP GGL PPC GGL PLG GPC PLG CCP GGL CPG LCP GGL PPC
PPC GGG CLC PGL GGL CCP PGL CLL CCP GLP CPC GLP CLC GPL PLG GGC PLP
GLG CPP CCP GLL CPP PLG CPL GGC PLL GGC GLP CPC GLG

Nonsense codon = PLC

Based on the specific pairing rules given below and the identity of the nonsense codon for that genetic code, describe the predicted experimental results you would obtain by using the provided mutagen and by following the principles of Coulondre and Miller.

• The four letter code you are analyzing has the bases C, G, L, and P. In the DNA, C pairs with G and L pairs with P.

- All base substitutions are possible spontaneously. The mutagen you are working with makes changes at L·P base pairs and can make all possible base changes at these bases.

- When P is part of a PCL sequence, with the orientation as written, it is methylated and, as a result, will frequently mutate spontaneously to any of the other bases.

1. Describe the system you would use. Namely, which codons can go to nonsense by a single base change in the stretch of DNA you are provided with? Specifically, perform steps *a–c* detailed in problem **A**1 on page 642.

2. Your goal is to develop a rapid mutagen and mutator tester system, based on the reversion of nonsense mutations, that will recognize substitutions in the Traxor genetic code.

   a. Show what base changes would revert your nonsense codon from the preceding experiment to a sense codon. Let's assume that any change to a sense codon at that position will result in a wild-type protein.

   b. You have isolated a bacterium from Traxor, *Centauris polaris*, that grows on agar plates with minimal medium supplemented with Traxor soil mix as an energy source, making turquoise colored colonies. Wild-type strains can also grow on minimal medium with only silicon dioxide as a carbon source, making white colonies. However, mutants in the *T* gene cannot grow on silicon dioxide, although they can grow on Traxor soil mix. Assume you have T mutants of different types. Describe how you would devise a procedure using reversion of nonsense mutations to detect "mutators" in *C. polaris*. Give all of the technical details and use diagrams when relevant.

3. You have a phage that infects the Traxor bacteria *C. polaris* and can deliver a transposon, Tn*FX*, to the chromosome of *C. polaris*. You have integrated the *T* gene into the transposon. Assume you have strains deleted for the *T* gene and the same materials and conditions as for problem **D**2 above. Assume also that on medium with Paramador bat extract, T+ cells form blue colonies and T− cells form red colonies. Design an experiment that will allow you to determine whether transposition occurs via a replicative or nonreplicative mechanism. Describe the constructions you would engineer, the experiment itself, and how you would interpret the results.

E. You are given a stretch of DNA sequence. The single strand shown below is the nontemplate strand and is thus identical to the mRNA.

KLM MKL JLJ MMK JLL JJL JKM LLK JLM KJM LLJ MMM KKL MML JJL MKM LKM
JLJ LLL MML KMM JJK JLM KMM LLM LKK JLM KJM LLJ KLJ KKJ MLL KLJ MML
MKM LLL JMM JJM KKL JJL MMJ MML KKJ MML MKJ LLJ JMK KLM MML JJM JJL
KJM LLK MML JMM JLM KJL MLJ KMM JJL MKL LJK MLJ KJL MKL KKL MMK JJJ
MKM LJL MMM LKJ MML KKK JLJ MMJ KKL MKJ LLK JJL MKL MML JJK MLJ MMK
MKM LLJ KJM LLL KLL KKJ LKK KKJ LLL MJK MLJ MMK MML LKK LLL JJL MJM
KKK JJL MLJ MKJ MLL LLJ MKL JLM JJJ MKJ MML MKJ MLL KKL MML MMM KJM
LLK MMJ MKM LLJ KJM MML KLK JJL MKJ MKM JJL JLK MJL KJJ

Nonsense codon = KKM

Based on the specific pairing rules given below and the identity of the nonsense codon for that genetic code, describe the predicted experimental results you would obtain by using the provided mutagen and by following the principles of Coulondre and Miller.

- The four letter code you are analyzing has the bases J, K, L, and M. In the DNA, J pairs with K and L pairs with M.

- All base substitutions are possible spontaneously. The mutagen you are working with makes changes at J·K base pairs, changing J·K to L·M or to M·L pairs.

- When J is part of a JLK sequence, with the orientation as written, it is methylated and, as a result, will frequently mutate spontaneously to any of the other bases.

1. Describe the system you would use. Namely, which codons can go to nonsense by a single base change in the stretch of DNA you are provided with? Specifically, perform steps *a–c* detailed in problem **A**1 on page 642.

2. Your goal is to develop a rapid mutagen and mutator tester system, based on the reversion of nonsense mutations, that will recognize substitutions in the Traxor genetic code.

   a. Show what base changes would revert your nonsense codon from the preceding experiment to a sense codon. Let's assume that any change to a sense codon at that position will result in a wild-type protein.

   b. You have isolated a bacterium from Traxor, *Centauris polaris*, that grows on agar plates with minimal medium supplemented with meteor dust as an energy source, making black colonies. Wild-type strains can also grow on minimal medium with Traxor ring worn extract as a carbon source, making orange colonies. However, mutants in the *J* gene cannot grow on Traxor ring worm extract, although they can grow on meteor dust. Assume you have J mutants of different types. Describe how you would devise a procedure using reversion of nonsense mutations to detect "mutators" in *C. polaris*. Give all of the technical details and use diagrams when relevant.

3. You have a phage that infects the Traxor bacteria *C. polaris* and can deliver a transposon, Tn*FX*, to the chromosome of *C. polaris*. You have integrated the *J* gene into the transposon. Assume you have strains deleted for the *J* gene and the same materials and conditions as for problem **E**2 above. Assume also that on medium with traxor soil mix, J+ cells form green colonies and J− cells form yellow colonies. Design an experiment that will allow you to determine whether transposition occurs via a replicative or nonreplicative mechanism. Describe the constructions you would engineer, the experiment itself, and how you would interpret the results.

F. You are given a stretch of DNA sequence. The single strand shown below is the nontemplate strand and is thus identical to the mRNA.

VDD KDP PDK VVK PDK VKD DPD PDK VDP DPV VKV DPD VKV DPD KPD PDD KVV
VPD KDV KVP DPP DVD VKP DPK PKD DKK VPV KVD PDK VKD PDD KDP PDK VKV
VVV PDK VKD PDK VKV PDP VKV PDP VVP DPP VKV DKP VPV PKP PPP DKD VDD
PVK PVD DDK VPD DPD DDD VDP VVK PPK PKP DDD KKP DKV KVD PDP KKD VPD
VDP VVK DPK VPK KPP DKD KDP VKD PVD DDP VPD DPV VVK VPV PDD KPD VVV
PDK VVP PDD VKV DDP VPK DKV DDV KVV PDV DKK VPD VKD DPK VPD PKP VVV
PDD KVV DKP PDK VKV DDK VVK DPD PDK VKD PDP KVD DPV KPD PPD KPP PVD
PDK VVK VDP PKD KKV PDD VKP DPD DDK

Nonsense codon = VVD

Based on the specific pairing rules given below and the identity of the non-sense codon for that genetic code, describe the predicted experimental results you would obtain by using the provided mutagen and by following the principles of Coulondre and Miller.

- The four letter code you are analyzing has the bases D, V, K, and P. In the DNA, D pairs with V and K pairs with P.

- All base substitutions are possible spontaneously. The mutagen you are working with makes changes at D·V base pairs and can make all possible base changes at these bases.

- When K is part of a KVP sequence, with the orientation as written, it is methylated and, as a result, will frequently mutate spontaneously to any of the other bases.

1. Describe the system you would use. Namely, which codons can go to nonsense by a single base change in the stretch of DNA you are provided with? Specifically, perform steps *a–c* detailed in problem **A**1 on page 642.

2. Your goal is to develop a rapid mutagen and mutator tester system, based on the reversion of nonsense mutations, that will recognize substitutions in the Traxor genetic code.

    a. Show what base changes would revert your nonsense codon from the preceding experiment to a sense codon. Let's assume that any change to a sense codon at that position will result in a wild-type protein.

    b. You have isolated a bacterium from Traxor, *Centauris polaris*, that grows on agar plates with minimal medium supplemented with space ice as an energy source, making yellow colored colonies. Wild-type strains can also grow on minimal medium with Voltor insect extract as a carbon source, making brown colonies. However, mutants in the *V* gene cannot grow on Voltor insect extract, although they can grow on space ice. Assume you have V mutants of different types. Describe how you would devise a procedure using reversion of nonsense muta-tions to detect "mutators" in *C. polaris*. Give all of the technical details and use diagrams when relevant.

3. You have a phage that infects the Traxor bacteria *C. polaris* and can deliver a transposon, Tn*FX*, to the chromosome of *C. polaris*. You have integrated the *V* gene into the transposon. Assume you have strains deleted for the *V* gene and the same materials and conditions as for problem **F**2 above. As-sume also that on medium with silicon dioxide, V$^+$ cells form turquoise colonies and V$^-$ cells form gold-colored colonies. Design an experiment

that will allow you to determine whether transposition occurs via a replicative or nonreplicative mechanism. Describe the constructions you would engineer, the experiment itself, and how you would interpret the results.

Masterprints™ Silver Surfer™

Scenario 13   In Search of . . . Inhibitors

Our old friend Igor Karpak (see Jurassic Engineering) has escaped from a maximum security prison and has joined a secret laboratory operated by international drug barons somewhere in Central America. These evil people have devised a scheme to destroy the California wine industry for their own ends. They have cloned a gene from an obscure organism that encodes a protein that destroys the natural resistance of Cabernet Sauvignon grapes to infection from *Phylloxera*, which destroyed the French wine industry in the middle of the last century. Their goal is to secretly spray the wine-producing areas with plant-infecting bacteria that produce the "Phy" protein (which Karpak named *Escherichia phyllox*) and then to let the ever-present *Phylloxera* destroy the wine crop. They will then flood the market with their own cheap red wine spiked with small amounts of habit-forming drugs, which will create an increased demand for their illegal drugs. Karpak and his evil associates must be stopped!

Our agent, code-named Tania (of course), has infiltrated the secret laboratory and sent back a sample of the bacteria carrying the *phy* gene in its chromosome. Unfortunately, the DNA and chromosome of this bacterium does not permit conventional in vitro cloning and DNA sequencing. Therefore, genetic methods must be used to alter the protein and study its regulation. If we can examine the effects of different amino acid substitutions in the Phy protein, we hope to be able to design inhibitors that can be sprayed on the vines to protect them against the action of the Phy protein. We only have two weeks before Karpak and his crew will hit Napa Valley. His first target is the Mondavi vineyards! Your job is to clone the *phy* gene onto a specialized transducing phage, study its regulation, and examine the effects of different amino acid substitutions.

You have several strains of *E. phyllox* containing the *phy* gene. These strains behave very much like *Escherichia coli* in genetic crosses. Each strain has the genetic map shown on the next page. You also have a derivative with an F factor that is exactly like that described for *E. coli*. Also available is a Rec⁻ derivative of the strain without the F factor, which cannot undergo normal recombination, as well as derivatives of these strains that are Trp⁻, His⁻, PurG⁻, Met⁻, Thr⁻ Ilv⁻, PryC⁻, and Leu⁻. You have a series of virulent phage, W1, 2, 3, 4, etc., that infect cells via a cell wall receptor protein encoded by the respective genes W1-*rec*, W2-*rec*, etc. You also have a set of temperate phage, L10, 20, 30, 40, etc., that integrate into the chromosome at specific attachments sites, *att-L10*, *att-L20*, etc. Cells that make the PHY protein form red colonies on grape extract infusion medium containing Cabernet Sauvignon. Those that do not make PHY protein form white colonies on this medium.

A. Demonstrate how you would clone the *phy* gene onto a specialized transducing phage employing the methods of Beckwith and Signer. You will have to generate some of the genetic tools they used employing the strains provided. Describe each step in detail.

Note: The F factor can replicate normally at high temperature (42°C) but not at low temperature (30°C). Chromosomal replication is normal at both temperatures.

B. Describe the experiments you would perform to study the control of the *phy* gene. Suppose you know that the presence of certain tannins present in wine-producing grapes will induce the synthesis of the PHY protein when added to cultures of the bacteria carrying the *phy* gene. The *phy* gene is under the positive control of a gene that synthesizes an activator protein (similar to the *ara* operon). Show how your genetic experiments would lead to this model. Describe how you would isolate mutants in the structural and regulatory genes, and in the control region, and their properties and behavior in complementation tests. Assume you have the same type of genetic tools at your disposal as were available to Jacob and Monod. Recall that you can distinguish different colony colors on grape infusion medium with Cabernet Sauvignon (see above). You can also assay for the PHY protein quantitatively by following the change of color in a test tube.

C. Suppose that the PHY protein has been isolated and the structure determined by X-ray crystallography. A number of mutants have been characterized. Using the principles established by Perutz, describe why the following changes detected among mutants might have caused a defective protein:

1. a valine to arginine change in the interior of the protein
2. a serine to glycine change on the exterior of the protein
3. a glycine to proline change on the exterior of the protein
4. an arginine to lysine change in the crevice of the protein
5. an isoleucine to valine change in the interior of the protein.

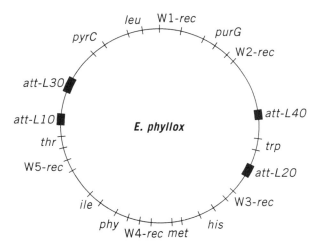

Scenario 14   Mission Impossible: Attack of the Oil-eating Clones

An enterprising researcher working for the EPA has decided to use bacteria to obtain enzymes that can digest oil spills off the California coast. These enzymes, as well as the bacteria that produce them, would be of great benefit for protecting the environment, as well as having enormous commercial value if they were controlled by certain private concerns. Reasoning that the capacity to produce such enzymes exists in certain bacteria, he screened UCLA students for those carrying intestinal bacteria with the desired properties. He found that students who frequent fast food centers have intestinal bacteria related to *E. coli* with greatly elevated levels of either the enzyme **slimase** or the enzyme **greasase**, which are extremely active in degrading oil slicks. Either of these enzymes enable bacteria to use crude oil as a carbon source. However, these bacteria do not grow in sea water. In order to be useful against oil slicks, the genes encoding slimase and greasase must be cloned and introduced into bacteria that can grow and propagate in the ocean.

Unfortunately, the researcher disappeared two weeks ago, leaving behind only the strain of bacteria, which he named *Escherichia oili*, and he has fallen into the hands of Columbian drug barons who will only release him and the cloned genes if the U.S. releases 20 drug lords currently serving time in Florida prisons. Otherwise, they will release an immense oil slick somewhere on the West Coast in exactly three weeks to demonstrate the need for this new antipollution clone.

Your mission, should you accept, is to clone the gene for slimase or greasase, study the regulation of the gene, and determine something about the structure of the respective protein.

As always, if you or any of the IM (Impossible Mission) force are caught or killed, the Secretary will disavow any knowledge of your actions. Good luck!

A. Suppose you have an F factor and wish ultimately to employ it as a tool to clone the gene with in vivo methods as used by Beckwith and Signer. Although you do not have a temperature-sensitive version of it, you do know that in the presence of the dye acridine orange, the F factor cannot replicate. Describe in a series of steps how you would isolate an F factor carrying the *grsE* gene (encoding greasase) and then use it to obtain a transducing phage carrying this gene. The genetic map of *E. oili* and the strains at your disposal are shown on the next page.

B. We can assay for the *grsE* gene because its product degrades crude oil. In addition, the enzyme activity is present in higher amounts in cells that have been exposed to small amounts of crude oil. Suppose that the *grsE* gene is actually under the control of a regulatory gene that makes an enzyme that destroys an internal inducer of the *grsE* gene (the alternative model of Jacob and Monod). In analogy with Jacob and Monod, detail the genetic experiments you would do to isolate mutants (both regulatory and structural) whose properties and complementation characteristics would enable you to zero in on the type of positive control that is occurring and would define the genetic loci involved, including the control region linked to the *grsE* gene. Assume you have the same types of materials at your disposal as were available to Jacob and Monod.

C. A number of Grease⁻ mutants have been characterized that no longer degrade crude oil. These have been related to the structure of the greasase protein, which has just been determined after being crystallized in outer space in the Space Shuttle. The changes below were noted among the mutant greasases. Employing the principles established by Perutz, describe why each change recorded here would register, in this specific case, as a Grease⁻ enzyme:

1. an alanine to leucine change in the interior of the protein
2. a lysine to arginine change on the exterior of the protein
3. a serine to tyrosine change on the exterior of the protein
4. a leucine to proline change on the exterior of the protein
5. an isoleucine to valine change in the crevice of the protein.

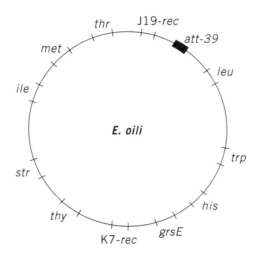

Strains

1. Wild type with F⁺ factor
2. Strain deleted for *grsE* gene (Grs⁻), which is also Thr⁻ Leu⁻ Trp⁻ His⁻ Thy⁻ Strʳ Ile⁻ Met⁻
3. Slm⁻ Strʳ Rec⁻
4. Slm⁻ strain, deleted for *slm* genes, Strˢ
5. Wild-type F⁻

Phage

1. K7 and J19 virulent phage
2. ɸ39, a temperate phage

Scenario 15   Mission Impossible: The Hunt for Red *mouR*

Wine connoisseurs pride themselves on being able to distinguish between average, good, and great wines, and even to be able to name the specific chateau that a wine is produced from. However, the average consumer or even the average wine merchant does not possess this capability. A misguided cartel of South American wine growers are seeking to undermine confidence in French wines, hoping to drive the wine-buying American public to lesser wines that they produce. They have decided to focus their assault on Chateaux Mouton Rothschild, a wine often costing between $100 and $200 per bottle. Their plan is to flood the market with a clever imitation of Chateau Mouton Rothschild that can only be distinguished from the real Mouton by wine experts. They will then reveal the hoax and precipitate a disastrous drop in French wine prices.

Fortunately, an enterprising researcher at UC Davis, where the world's greatest university wine-making program is, has isolated a strain of *Salmonella typhimurium* related to *Escherichia coli* that synthesizes a very small amount of an enzyme that modifies tannins, one of the components of wine. In searching for compounds that would induce the increased synthesis of this enzyme in a culture of the bacteria (which he named *Salmonella mouirium*), he tried adding samples of each of a variety of different red wines and was amazed to find that among hundreds of wines tested, only Mouton Rothschild could induce this enzyme. Apparently, one of the compounds resulting from the complex reactions in the production and aging of wine is unique to Mouton Rothschild and can be detected in this diagnostic induction test. Because of the nature of the bacteria, it cannot be shipped and used in every location for quick on the scene diagnostic tests. (One can imagine testing one bottle from a shipment by withdrawing a sample with a hypodermic needle and testing it on bacteria.) Therefore, the genes must be cloned into *E. coli.* Unfortunately, the UC Davis researcher has disappeared, leaving behind only the strain of bacteria, and we fear he has met an untimely end at the hands of the international cartel.

Your mission, if you accept, is to clone the gene (*mouR*) that encodes the enzyme (moutonase) induced by the component in Mouton Rothschild and to study its regulation and activity. Assume you can assay the activity of the gene product moutonase by monitoring the modification of tannins. Not only can you carry out these quantitative assays, but you can also distinguish colony phenotypes on "wine" media, containing agar, peptones, and Mouton Rothschild. On this media, colonies synthesizing large amounts of moutonase turn white, whereas those not synthesizing appreciable amounts of the enzyme turn red.

As always, if you or any of the IM (Impossible Mission) force is caught or killed, the Secretary will disavow any knowledge of your actions. Good luck!

A. Suppose you have a temperature-sensitive F factor. Describe the steps you would undertake to first isolate an F′ derivative carrying the *mouR* gene and then, in a manner analogous to that described by Beckwith and Signer, obtain by in vivo genetic engineering a specialized transducing phage carrying the *mouR* gene. The genetic map of *S. mouirium* and the strains at your disposal are shown on the next page. Depict the methodology in a clear and precise fashion, providing experimental details where necessary.

B. Describe the experiments you would perform to study the control of the *mouR* gene. Recall that Mouton Rothschild wine will induce the synthesis of the moutonase enzyme when added to cultures of bacteria. The *mouR* gene is under the **positive control** of the Mouton-activating protein. Show how your genetic experiments would demonstrate this. Describe how you would isolate mutants in the structural and regulatory genes, and in the control region, and their properties and behavior in complementation tests. Assume that you have the same types of genetic tools at your disposal as were available to Jacob and Monod.

C. The moutonase protein has been isolated and the structure determined by X-ray crystallography. In addition, mutants have been characterized that have a defective enzyme. The amino acid exchanges resulting in each defective protein are shown below. Employing the principles established by Perutz, explain in each case why the particular amino acid exchange could cause a defective enzyme:

1. a glutamic acid to aspartic acid change in the crevice of the protein
2. a glutamine to proline change on the exterior of the protein
3. a glutamine to tyrosine change on the exterior of the protein
4. a phenylalanine to asparagine change in the interior of the protein
5. an isoleucine to leucine change in the interior of the protein.

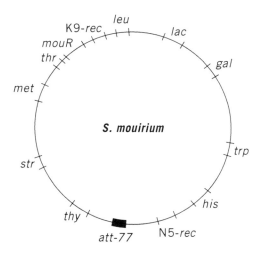

Strains

1. Wild type with F$^+_{ts}$ factor
2. Strain deleted for *mouR* gene, (MouR⁻), which is also Leu⁻ Gal⁻ His⁻ Thy⁻ Lac⁻ Trp⁻ Met⁻ Thr⁻ Str^r
3. MouR⁻ Str^r Rec⁻
4. MouR⁻ strain, deleted for *mouR* genes, Str^s

Phage

1. K9 and N5 virulent phage
2. φ77, a temperate phage

Scenario 16   The Swiss Connection: Trace the Mutants

About 15 years ago a graduate student at UCSF was hospitalized in serious condition after attending a small dinner party at which a certain type of Chinese mushrooms were served. Having recently returned from a trip to Switzerland, he had brought back a wedge of Vacherin cheese from a small village in the Swiss Rhone Valley. As it turns out, the Chinese mushrooms contained small amounts of a neurotoxin, which is normally harmless because it is destroyed by an enzyme in human cells. Unfortunately, the particular bacteria present in the processing of this Vacherin cheese synthesize an inhibitor for the enzyme that destroys the neurotoxin. In combination, something which rarely occurs due to the obscurity of the specific Vacherin cheese, the mushrooms and the cheese can be deadly. The student barely survived.

This deadly secret has now fallen into evil hands. An underworld international drug cartel has obtained the bacteria (which they have named *Escherichia vacheri*) and has succeeded in cloning the gene that encodes the enzyme synthesizing the inhibitor. We have learned that they are planning to seed Asian mushroom shipments with this compound to create panic in the American consumer markets, since eating mushrooms from one of these shipments will result in almost certain death. Their goal is to destroy the Asian mushroom market and force the farm owners to sell their farms at cut-rate prices, which the cartel will buy and convert to opium plantations. If they succeed, they will convert the entire Far East into one large farm for illegal drugs. They must be stopped!

Your job is to clone the gene for the inhibitor-producing enzyme to allow detailed molecular analysis so that drugs can be designed that will compete with the inhibitor binding site without inactivating the neurotoxin-destroying enzyme. We have obtained the bacterial strain that synthesizes the inhibitor (which we will call **neurotin**) of the enzyme that destroys the neurotoxin, from which you must clone the gene (which we will term *neuR*) and study its regulation. Assume that *E. vacheri* is related to *E. coli*. Also assume you can assay for the levels of the gene product, neurotin, by measuring the inhibition of the human neurotoxin destructase. In addition, on special indicator media, colonies synthesizing the inhibitor prevent a color reaction and are white, whereas colonies that do not synthesize appreciable levels of the inhibitor turn red.

A. You possess an F factor. Describe in steps how you would isolate a derivative of the F factor carrying the *neuR* gene and then employ it in a manner analogous to the work of Beckwith and Signer to clone it in vivo onto a specialized transducing phage. Although you do not have a temperature-sensitive version of the F factor, you do know that in the presence of acridine orange, the F factor cannot replicate. The genetic map of *S. vacheri* and the strains at your disposal are shown on the next page. Explain each step with sufficient clarity and detail.

B. Describe how, using methods analogous to those employed by Jacob and Monod, you would study the regulation of the *neuR* gene. Assume that it is already known that the levels of neurotin increase greatly when cells are grown in the presence of a compound that results from the splitting of the neurotoxin by the human enzyme. This split compound can be called "half-toxin" for simplicity. Show which experiments you would do, including the isolation of mutants and the examination of their properties and complementation characteristics, to demonstrate that the *neuR* gene is under the control of a regulatory protein that destroys an internal inducer of the operon (the alternative model of Jacob and Monod). Show how you might get mutants in the structural and regulatory genes, and in the control region.

C. Suppose that mutants in the NeuR protein have been characterized, and the three-dimensional structure of the protein has been determined by X-ray crystallography. Employing the principles established by Perutz, explain why each of the changes below might cause the inactivation of the protein in this particular case:

1. a serine to glycine change on the exterior of the protein
2. an alanine to glycine change in the interior of the protein
3. a tyrosine to histidine change in the interior of the protein
4. a phenylalanine to valine change in the crevice of the protein
5. a leucine to proline change on the exterior of the protein.

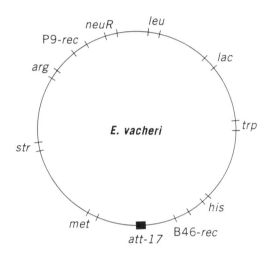

Strains

1. Wild type with F⁺ factor
2. Strain deleted for *neuR*, which is also Leu⁻ Lac⁻ Trp⁻ His⁻ Met⁻ Str^r Arg⁻
3. Str^r Rec⁻ NeuR⁻ (*neuR*⁻)
4. NeuR⁻ strain, deleted for *neuR* genes, also Str^s
5. Wild-type F⁻

Phage

1. P9 and B46 virulent phage
2. φ17, a temperate phage

Scenario 17

Outbreak

A killer virus has entered the United States, probably arriving from South America via illegally transported tropical birds, some of which have escaped and infected rodents, which are then bitten by fleas, which then transmit it to humans. Molecular analysis of postmortem tissue indicates that the virus destroys cells by disrupting their genes with inserts. However, when the DNA from these disrupted genes is sequenced, the 8000-bp inserts in the cellular genes do not correspond exactly to segments of the killer virus genome. In fact, on the virus genome, the first half of the 8000-bp segment is followed by a 2000-bp sequence that is not found in the inserts, and this is then followed by the second half of the 8000-bp segment.

Give a reasonable explanation for this, and explain what it suggests about a mechanism for these events. Suppose that you can engineer the virus in vitro and that it can infect strains of yeast. Design an experiment that would allow you to prove the mechanism you propose.

A Paradigm

The Purloined Letter
by Edgar Allen Poe

Nil sapientiæ odiosius acumine nimio.

Seneca

At Paris, just after dark one gusty evening in the autumn of 18—, I was enjoying the twofold luxury of meditation and a meerschaum, in company with my friend C. Auguste Dupin, in his little back library, or book-closet, *au troisème, No. 33, Rue Dunôt, Faubourg St. Germain*. For one hour at least we had maintained a profound silence; while each, to any casual observer, might have seemed intently and exclusively occupied with the curling eddies of smoke that oppressed the atmosphere of the chamber. For myself, however, I was mentally discussing certain topics which had formed matter for conversation between us at an earlier period of the evening; I mean the affair of the Rue Morgue, and the mystery attending the murder of Marie Rogêt. I looked upon it, therefore, as something of a coincidence, when the door of our apartment was thrown open and admitted our old acquaintance, Monsieur G——, the Prefect of the Parisian police.

We gave him a hearty welcome; for there was nearly half as much of the entertaining as of the contemptible about the man, and we had not seen him for several years. We had been sitting in the dark, and Dupin now arose for the purpose of lighting a lamp, but sat down again, without doing so, upon G.'s saying that he had called to consult us, or rather to ask the opinion of my friend, about some official business which had occasioned a great deal of trouble.

"If it is any point requiring reflection," observed Dupin, as he forbore to enkindle the wick, "we shall examine it to better purpose in the dark."

"That is another of your odd notions," said the Prefect, who had a fashion of calling everything "odd" that was beyond his comprehension, and thus lived amid an absolute legion of "oddities."

"Very true," said Dupin, as he supplied his visitor with a pipe, and rolled towards him a comfortable chair.

"And what is the difficulty now?" I asked. "Nothing more in the assassination way, I hope?"

"Oh no; nothing of that nature. The fact is, the business is *very* simple indeed, and I make no doubt that we can manage it sufficiently well ourselves; but then I thought Dupin would like to hear the details of it, because it is so excessively *odd*."

"Simple and odd," said Dupin.

"Why, yes; and not exactly that, either. The fact is, we have all been a good

659

deal puzzled because the affair *is* so simple, and yet baffles us altogether."

"Perhaps it is the very simplicity of the thing which puts you at fault," said my friend.

"What nonsense you *do* talk!" replied the Prefect, laughing heartily.

"Perhaps the mystery is a little *too* plain," said Dupin.

"Oh, good heavens! who ever heard of such an idea?"

"A little *too* self-evident."

"Ha! ha! ha!—ha! ha! ha!—ho! ho! ho!"—roared our visitor, profoundly amused. "Oh, Dupin, you will be the death of me yet!"

"And what, after all, *is* the matter on hand?" I asked.

"Why, I will tell you," replied the Prefect, as he gave a long, steady, and contemplative puff, and settled himself in his chair. "I will tell you in a few words; but, before I begin, let me caution you that this is an affair demanding the greatest secrecy, and that I should most probably lose the position I now hold, were it known that I confided it to anyone."

"Proceed," said I.

"Or not," said Dupin.

"Well, then; I have received personal information, from a very high quarter, that a certain document of the last importance has been purloined from the royal apartments. The individual who purloined it is known; this beyond a doubt; he was seen to take it. It is known, also, that it still remains in his possession."

"How is this known?" asked Dupin.

"It is clearly inferred," replied the Prefect, "from the nature of the document, and from the non-appearance of certain results which would at once arise from its passing *out* of the robber's possession;—that is to say, from his employing it as he must design in the end to employ it."

"Be a little more explicit," I said.

"Well, I may venture so far as to say that the paper gives its holder a certain power in a certain quarter where such power is immensely valuable." The Prefect was fond of the cant of diplomacy.

"Still I do not quite understand," said Dupin.

"No? Well; the disclosure of the document to a third person, who shall be nameless, would bring in question the honour of a personage of most exalted station; and this fact gives the holder of the document an ascendancy over the illustrious personage whose honour and peace are so jeopardized."

"But this ascendancy," I interposed, "would depend upon the robber's knowledge of the loser's knowledge of the robber. Who would dare—"

"The thief," said G., "is the Minister D——, who dares all things, those unbecoming as well as those becoming a man. The method of the theft was not less ingenious than bold. The document in question—a letter, to be frank—had been received by the personage robbed while alone in the royal boudoir. During its perusal she was suddenly interrupted by the entrance of the other exalted personage from whom especially it was her wish to conceal it. After a hurried and vain endeavour to thrust it in a drawer, she was forced to place it, open as it was, upon the table. The address, however, was uppermost, and, the contents thus unexposed, the letter escaped notice. At this juncture enters the Minister D——. His lynx eye immediately perceives the paper, recognizes the handwriting of the address, observes the confusion of the personage addressed, and fathoms her secret. After some business transactions, hurried through in his ordinary manner, he produces a letter somewhat similar to the one in question, opens it, pretends to read it, and then places it in close juxtaposition to the other. Again he converses, for some fifteen minutes, upon the public affairs. At length, in taking leave, he takes also from the table the letter to which he had no claim. Its rightful owner saw, but, of course, dared not call attention to the act, in the presence of the third personage who stood at her elbow. The minister decamped; leaving his own letter—one of no importance—upon the table."

"Here, then," said Dupin to me, "you have precisely what you demand to make the ascendancy complete—the robber's knowledge of the loser's knowledge of the robber."

"Yes," replied the Prefect; "and the power thus attained has, for some months past, been wielded, for political purposes, to a very dangerous extent. The personage robbed is more thoroughly convinced, every day, of the necessity of reclaiming her letter. But this, of course, cannot be done openly. In fine, driven to despair, she has committed the matter to me."

"Than whom," said Dupin, amid a perfect whirlwind of smoke, "no more sagacious agent could, I suppose, be desired, or even imagined."

"You flatter me," replied the Prefect; "but it is possible that some such opinion may have been entertained."

"It is clear," said I, "as you observe, that the letter is still in possession of the minister; since it is this possession, and not any employment of the letter, which bestows the power. With the employment the power departs."

"True," said G.; "and upon this conviction I proceeded. My first care was to make thorough search of the minister's hotel; and here my chief embarrassment lay in the necessity of searching without his knowledge. Beyond all things, I have been warned of the danger which would result from giving him reason to suspect our design."

"But," said I, "you are quite *au fait* in these investigations. The Parisian police have done this thing often before."

"Oh yes; and for this reason I did not despair. The habits of the minister gave me, too, a great advantage. He is frequently absent from home all night. His servants are by no means numerous. They sleep at a distance from their master's apartment, and, being chiefly Neapolitans, are readily made drunk. I have keys, as you know, with which I can open any chamber or cabinet in Paris. For three months, a night has not passed during the greater part of which I have not been engaged, personally, in ransacking the D—— Hôtel. My honour is interested, and, to mention a great secret, the reward is enormous. So I did not abandon the search until I had become fully satisfied that the thief is a more astute man than myself. I fancy that I have investigated every nook and corner of the premises in which it is possible that the paper can be concealed."

"But is it not possible," I suggested, "that although the letter may be in possession of the minister, as it unquestionably is, he may have concealed it elsewhere than upon his own premises?"

"This is barely possible," said Dupin. "The present peculiar condition of affairs at court, and especially of those intrigues in which D—— is known to be involved, would render the instant availability of the document—its susceptibility of being produced at a moment's notice—a point of nearly equal importance with its possession."

"Its susceptibility of being produced?" said I.

"That is to say, of being *destroyed*," said Dupin.

"True," I observed; "the paper is clearly then upon the premises. As for its being upon the person of the minister, we may consider that as out of the question."

"Entirely," said the Prefect. "He has been twice waylaid, as if by footpads, and his person rigorously searched under my own inspection."

"You might have spared yourself this trouble," said Dupin. "D——, I presume, is not altogether a fool, and, if not, must have anticipated these waylayings, as a matter of course."

"Not *altogether* a fool," said G.; "But then he's a poet, which I take to be only one remove from a fool."

"True," said Dupin, after a long and thoughtful whiff from his meerschaum, "although I have been guilty of certain doggerel myself."

"Suppose you detail," said I, "the particulars of your search."

"Why the fact is, we took our time, and we searched *everywhere*. I have had long experience in these affairs. I took the entire building, room by room; devoting the nights of a whole week to each. We examined, first, the furniture of each apartment. We opened every possible drawer; and I presume you know that, to a properly trained police agent, such a thing as a *secret* drawer is impossible. Any man is a dolt who permits a 'secret' drawer to escape him in a search of this kind. The thing is *so* plain. There is a certain amount of bulk—of space—to be accounted for in every cabinet. Then we have accurate rules. The fiftieth part of a line could not escape us. After the cabinets we took the chairs. The cushions we probed with the fine long needles you have seen me employ. From the tables we removed the tops."

"Why so?"

"Sometimes the top of a table, or other similarly arranged piece of furniture, is removed by the person wishing to conceal an article; then the leg is excavated, the article deposited within the cavity, and the top replaced. The bottoms and tops of bed-posts are employed in the same way."

"But could not the cavity be detected by sounding?" I asked.

"By no means, if, when the article is deposited, a sufficient wadding of cotton be placed around it. Besides, in our case, we were obliged to proceed without noise."

"But you could not have removed—you could not have taken to pieces *all* articles of furniture in which it would have been possible to make a deposit in the manner you mention. A letter may be compressed into a thin spiral roll, not differing much in shape or bulk from a large knitting-needle, and in this form it might be inserted into the rung of a chair, for example. You did not take to pieces all the chairs?"

"Certainly not; but we did better—we examined the rungs of every chair in the hotel, and, indeed, the jointings of every description of furniture, by the aid of a most powerful microscope. Had there been any traces of recent disturbance we should not have failed to detect it instantly. A single grain of gimlet-dust, for example, would have been as obvious as an apple. Any disorder in the gluing—any unusual gaping in the joints—would have sufficed to insure detection."

"I presume you looked to the mirrors, between the boards and the plates, and you probed the beds and the bed-clothes, as well as the curtains and carpets."

"That of course; and when we had absolutely completed every particle of the furniture in this way, then we examined the house itself. We divided its entire surface into compartments, which we numbered, so that none might be missed; then we scrutinized each individual square inch throughout the premises, including the two houses immediately adjoining, with the microscope, as before."

"The two houses adjoining!" I exclaimed; "you must have had a great deal of trouble."

"We had; but the reward is prodigious."

"You include the *grounds* about the houses?"

"All the grounds are paved with brick. They gave us comparatively little trouble. We examined the moss between the bricks and found it undisturbed."

"You looked among D——'s papers, of course, and into the books of the library?"

"Certainly; we opened every package and parcel; we not only opened every book, but we turned over every leaf of each volume, not contenting ourselves with a mere shake, according to the fashion of some of our police officers. We also measured the thickness of every book-*cover*, with the most accurate admeasurement, and applied to each the most jealous scrutiny of the microscope. Had any of the bindings been recently meddled with, it would have been utterly impossible that the fact should have escaped observation. Some five or six volumes, just from the hands of the binder, we carefully probed, longitudinally, with the needles."

"You explored the floors beneath the carpets?"

"Beyond doubt. We removed every carpet, and examined the boards with the microscope."

"And the paper on the walls?"

"Yes."

"You looked in the cellars?"

"We did."

"Then," I said, "you have been making a miscalculation, and the letter is *not* upon the premises, as you suppose."

"I fear you are right there," said the Prefect. "And now, Dupin, what would you advise me to do?"

"To make a thorough re-search of the premises."

"That is absolutely needless," replied G——. "I am not more sure that I breathe than I am that the letter is not at the Hôtel."

"I have no better advice to give you," said Dupin. "You have, of course, an accurate description of the letter?"

"Oh yes!"—And here the Prefect, producing a memorandum-book, proceeded to read aloud a minute account of the internal, and especially of the external appearance of the missing document. Soon after finishing the perusal of this description, he took his departure, more entirely depressed in spirits than I had ever known the good gentleman before.

In about a month afterwards he paid us another visit, and found us occupied very nearly as before. He took a pipe and a chair and entered into some ordinary conversation. At length I said,—

"Well, but G——, what of the purloined letter? I presume you have at last made up your mind that there is no such thing as overreaching the Minister?"

"Confound him, say I—yes; I made the re-examination, however, as Dupin suggested—but it was all labour lost, as I knew it would be."

"How much was the reward offered, did you say?" asked Dupin.

"Why, a very great deal—a *very* liberal reward—I don't like to say how much, precisely; but one thing I *will* say, that I wouldn't mind giving my individual cheque for fifty thousand francs to anyone who could obtain me that letter. The fact is, it is becoming of more and more importance every day; the reward has been lately doubled. If it were trebled, however, I could do no more than I have done."

"Why, yes," said Dupin, drawlingly, between the whiffs of his meerschaum, "I really—think, G——, you have not exerted yourself—to the utmost in this matter. You might—do a little more, I think, eh?"

"How?—in what way?"

"Why—puff, puff—you might—puff, puff—employ counsel in the matter, eh?—puff, puff, puff. Do you remember the story they tell of Abernethy?"

"No; hang Abernethy!"

"To be sure! hang him and welcome. But, once upon a time, a certain rich miser conceived the design of sponging upon this Abernethy for a medical opinion. Getting up, for this purpose, an ordinary conversation in a private company, he insinuated his case to the physician, as that of an imaginary individual."

"'We will suppose,' said the miser, 'that his symptoms are such and such; now doctor, what would *you* have directed him to take?'

"'Take!' said Abernethy, 'why, take *advice*, to be sure.'"

"But," said the Prefect, a little discomposed, "I am *perfectly* willing to take advice, and to pay for it. I would *really* give fifty thousand francs to anyone who would aid me in this matter."

"In that case," replied Dupin, opening a drawer, and producing a cheque-book, "you may as well fill me up a cheque for the amount mentioned. When you have signed it, I will hand you the letter."

I was astounded. The Prefect appeared absolutely thunderstruck. For some minutes he remained speechless and motionless, looking incredulously at my friend with open mouth, and eyes that seemed starting from their sockets; then, apparently recovering himself in some measure, he seized a pen, and after several pauses and vacant stares, finally filled up and signed a cheque for fifty thousand francs, and handed it across the table to Dupin. The latter examined it carefully and deposited it in his pocket-book; then, unlocking an escritoire, took thence a letter and gave it to the Prefect. This functionary grasped it in a perfect agony of joy, opened it with a trembling hand, cast a rapid glance at its contents, and then, scrambling and struggling to the door, rushed at length unceremoniously from the room and from the house, without having uttered a syllable since Dupin had requested him to fill up the cheque.

When he was gone, my friend entered into some explanations.

"The Parisian police," he said, "are exceedingly able in their way. They are persevering, ingenious, cunning, and thoroughly versed in the knowledge which their duties seem chiefly to demand. Thus, when G—— detailed to us his mode of searching the premises at the Hôtel D——, I felt entire confidence in his having made a satisfactory investigation—so far as his labours extended."

"So far as his labours extended!" said I.

"Yes," said Dupin. "The measures adopted were not only the best of their kind, but carried out to absolute perfection. Had the letter been deposited within the range of their search, these fellows would, beyond a question, have found it."

I merely laughed—but he seemed quite serious in all that he said.

"The measures, then," he continued, "were good in their kind, and well executed; their defect lay in their being inapplicable to the case, and to the man. A certain set of highly ingenious resources are, with the Prefect, a sort of Procrustean bed, to which he forcibly adapts his designs. But he perpetually errs by being too deep or too shallow, for the matter at hand; and many a schoolboy is a better reasoner than he. I knew one about eight years of age, whose success at guessing in the game of 'even and odd' attracted universal admiration. This game is simple, and is played with marbles. One player holds in his hand a number of these toys, and demands of another whether that number is even or odd. If the guess is right, the guesser wins one; if wrong, he loses one. the boy to whom I allude won all the marbles of the school. Of course he had some principle of guessing; and this lay in mere observation and admeasurement of the astuteness of his opponents. For example, an arrant simpleton is his opponent, and, holding up his closed hand, asks 'are they even or odd?' Our schoolboy replies, 'odd,' and loses; but upon the second trial he wins, for he then says to himself, 'the simpleton had them even upon the first trial, and his amount of cunning is just sufficient to make him have them odd upon the second; I will therefore guess odd';—he guesses odd, and wins. Now, with a simpleton a degree above the first, he would have reasoned thus: 'This fellow finds that in the first instance I guessed odd, and, in the second, he will propose to himself upon the first impulse, a simple variation from even to odd, as did the first simpleton; but then a second thought will suggest that this is too simple a variation, and finally he will decide upon putting it even as before. I will therefore guess even';—he guesses even, and wins. Now, this mode of reasoning in the schoolboy, whom his fellows termed 'lucky,'—what, in its last analysis, is it?"

"It is merely," I said, "an identification of the reasoner's intellect with that of his opponent."

"It is," said Dupin; "and, upon inquiring of the boy by what means he effected the *thorough* identification in which his success consisted, I received answer as follows: 'When I wish to find out how wise, or how stupid, or how good, or how wicked is anyone, or what are his thoughts at the moment, I fashion the expression of my face, as accurately as possible, in accordance with the expression of his, and then wait to see what thoughts or sentiments arise in my mind or heart, as if to match or correspond with the expression.' This response of the schoolboy lies at the bottom of all the spurious profundity which has been attributed to Rochefoucauld, to La Bougive, to Machiavelli, and to Campanella."

"And the identification," I said, "of the reasoner's intellect with that of his opponent depends, if I understand you aright, upon the accuracy with which the opponent's intellect is admeasured."

"For its practical value it depends upon this," replied Dupin; "and the Prefect and his cohort fail so frequently, first, by default of this identification, and, secondly, by ill-admeasurement, or rather through non-admeasurement, of the intellect with which they are engaged. They consider only their *own* ideas of ingenuity; and, in searching for anything hidden, advert only to the modes in which *they* would have hidden it. They are right in this much—that their own ingenuity is a faithful representative of that of *the mass*; but when the cunning of the individual felon is diverse in character from their own, the felon foils them, of course. This always happens when it is above their own, and very usually when it is below. They have no variation of principle in their investigations; at best, when urged by some unusual emergency—by some extraordinary reward—they extend or exaggerate their old modes of *practice*, without touching their principles. What, for example, in this case of D——, has been done to vary the principle of action? What is all this boring, and probing, and sounding, and scrutinizing with the microscope, and dividing the surface of the building into registered square inches—what is it all but an exaggeration *of the application* of the one principle or set of principles of search, which are based upon the one set of notions regarding human ingenuity, to which the Prefect, in the long routine of his duty, has been accustomed? Do you not see he has taken it for granted that *all* men proceed to conceal a letter,—not exactly in a gimlet-hole bored in a chair leg—but, at least, in *some* out-of-the-way hole or corner suggested by the same tenor of thought which would urge a man to secrete a letter in a gimlet-hole bored in a chair-leg? And do you not see also, that such recheché nooks for concealment are adapted only for ordinary occasions, and would be adopted by ordinary intellects; for, in all cases of concealment, a disposal of the article concealed—a disposal of it in this recheché manner,—is, in the very first instance, presumable and presumed; and thus its discovery depends, not at all upon the acumen, but altogether upon the mere care, patience, and determination of the seekers; and where the case is of importance—or, what amounts to the same thing in the political eyes, when the reward is of magnitude,—the qualities in question have *never* been known to fail. You will now understand what I meant in suggesting that, had the purloined letter been hidden anywhere within the limits of the Prefect's examination—in other words, had the principle of its concealment been comprehended within the principles of the Prefect—its discovery would have been a matter altogether beyond question. This functionary, however, has been thoroughly mystified; and the remote source of his defeat lies in the supposition that the Minister is a fool, because he has acquired renown as a poet. All fools are poets; this the Prefects *feels*; and he is merely guilty of a *non distributio medii* in thence inferring that all poets are fools."

"But is this really the poet?" I asked. "There are two brothers, I know; and both have attained reputation in letters. The Minister I beleve has written learnedly on the Differential Calculus. He is a mathematician, and no poet."

"You are mistaken; I know him well; he is both. As poet *and* mathematician, he would reason well; as mere mathematician, he could not have reasoned at all, and thus would have been at the mercy of the Prefect."

"You surprise me," I said, "by these opinions, which have been contradicted by the voice of the world. You do not mean to set at naught the well-digested idea of centuries. The mathematical reason has long been regarded as *the* reason par excellence."

"'*Il y a à parier*,'" replied Dupin, quoting from Chamfort, "'*que toute idée publique, toute convention reçue, est une sottise, car elle a convenu au plus grand nombre.*' The mathematicians, I grant you, have done their best to promulgate the popular error to which you allude, and which is none the less an error for this promulgation as truth. With an art worthy of better cause, for example, they have insinuated the term 'analysis' into application to algebra. The French are the originators of this particular deception; but if a term is of any importance—if words derive any value from applicability—then 'analysis' conveys 'algebra' about as much as, in Latin, '*ambitus*' implies 'ambition;' '*religio*,' 'religion;' or '*homines honesti*,' a set of *honourable* men."

"You have a quarrel on hand, I see," said I, "with some of the algebraists of Paris; but proceed."

"I dispute the availability, and thus the value, of that reason which is cultivated in any especial form other than the abstractly logical. I dispute, in particular, the reason educed by mathematical study. The mathematics are the science of form and quantity; mathematical reasoning is merely logic applied to observation upon form and quantity. The great error lies in supposing that even the truths of what is called *pure* algebra are abstract or general truths. And this error is so egregious that I am confounded at the universality with which it has been received. Mathematical axioms are *not* axioms of general truth. What is true of *relation*—of form and quantity—is often grossly false in regard to morals, for example. In this latter science it is very usually *un*true that the aggregated parts are equal to the whole. In chemistry also the axiom fails. In the consideration of motive it fails; for two motives, each of a given value, have not, necessarily, a value when united, equal to the sum of their values apart. There are numerous other mathematical truths which are only truths within the limits of *relation*. But the mathematician argues, from his *finite truths*, through habit, as if they were of an absolutely general applicability—as the world indeed imagines them to be. Bryant, in his very learned *Mythology*, mentions an analogous source of error, when he says that 'although the Pagan fables are not believed, yet we forget ourselves continually, and make inferences from them as existing realities.' With the algebraists, however, who are Pagans themselves, the 'Pagan fables' *are* believed, and the inferences are made, not so much through lapse of memory, as through an unaccountable addling of the brains. In short, I never yet encountered the mere mathematician who could be trusted out of equal roots, or one who did not clandestinely hold it as a point of his faith that $x^2 + px$ was absolutely and unconditionally equal to q. Say to one of these gentlemen, by way of experiment, if you please, that you believe occasions may occur where $x^2 + px$ is *not* altogether equal to q, and, having made him understand what you mean, get out of his reach as speedily as convenient, for, beyond doubt, he will endeavour to knock you down.

"I mean to say," continued Dupin, while I merely laughed at his last observations, "that if the Minister had been no more than a mathematician, the Prefect would have been under no necessity of giving me this cheque. I knew him, however, as both mathematician and poet, and my measures were adapted to his capacity, with reference to the circumstances by which he was surrounded. I knew him as a courtier, too, and as a bold intriguant. Such a man, I considered, could not fail to be aware of the ordinary policial modes of action. He could not have failed to anticipate—and events have proved that he did not fail to anticipate—the waylayings to which he was subjected. He must have foreseen, I reflected, the secret investigations of his premises. His frequent absences from home at night, which were hailed by the Prefect as certain aids to his success, I regarded only as *ruses*, to afford opportunity for thorough search to the police, and thus the sooner to impress them with the conviction to which G——, in fact, did finally arrive—the conclusion that the letter was not upon the premises. I felt, also, that the whole train of thought, which I was at some pains in detailing to you just now, concerning the invariable principle of police action in searches for articles concealed—I felt that this whole train of thought would necessarily pass through the mind of the Minister. It would imperatively lead him to despise all the ordinary *nooks* of concealment. *He* could not, I reflected, be so weak as not to see that the most intricate and remote recess of his hotel would be as open as his commonest closets to the eyes, to the probes, to the gimlets, and to the microscopes of the Prefect. I saw, in fine, that he would be driven, as a matter of course, to *simplicity*, if not deliberately induced to it as a matter of choice. You will remember, perhaps, how desperately the Prefect laughed when I suggested, upon our first interview, that it was just possible this mystery troubled him so much on account of its being so *very* self-evident."

"Yes," said I, "I remember his merriment well. I really thought he would have fallen into convulsions."

"The material world," continued Dupin, "abounds with very strict analogies to the immaterial; and thus some colour of truth has been given to the rhetorical dogma, that metaphor, or simile, may be made to strengthen an argument, as well as to embellish a description. The principle of the *vis inertiae*, for example, seems to be identical in physics and metaphysics. It is not more true in the former, that a large body is with more difficult set in motion than a smaller one, and that its subsequent momentum is commensurate with this difficulty, than it is, in the latter, that intellects of the vaster capacity, while more forcible, more constant, and more eventful in their movements than those of inferior grade, are yet the less readily moved, and more embarrassed and full of hesitation in the first few steps of their progress. Again: have you ever noticed which of the street signs, over the shop doors, are the most attractive of attention?"

"I have never given the matter a thought," I said.

"There is a game of puzzles," he resumed, "which is played upon a map. One party playing requires another to find a given word—the name of town, river, state or empire—any word, in short, upon the motley and perplexed surface of the chart. A novice in the game generally seeks to embarrass his opponents by giving them the most minutely lettered names; but the adept selects such words as stretch, in large characters, from one end of the chart to the other. These, like the over-largely lettered signs and placards of the street, escape observation by dint of being excessively obvious; and here the physical oversight is precisely analogous with the moral inapprehension by which the intellect suffers to pass unnoticed those considerations which are too obtrusively and too palpably self-evident. But this is a point, it appears, somewhat above or beneath the understanding of the Prefect. He never once thought it probable, or possible, that the Minister had deposited the letter immediately beneath the nose of the whole world, by way of best preventing any portion of that world perceiving it.

"But the more I reflected upon the daring, dashing, and discriminating ingenuity of D——; upon the fact that the document must always have been *at hand*, if he intended to use it to good purpose; and upon the decisive evidence, obtained by the Prefect, that it was not hidden within the limits of that dignitary's ordinary search—the more satisfied I became that, to conceal this letter, the Minister had resorted to the comprehensive and sagacious expedient of not attempting to conceal it at all.

"Full of these ideas, I prepared myself with a pair of green spectacles, and called one fine morning, quite by accident, at the Ministerial hotel. I found D—— at home, yawning, lounging, and dawdling, as usual, and pretending to be in the last extremity of ennui. He is, perhaps, the most really energetic human being now alive—but that is only when nobody sees him.

"To be even with him, I complained of my weak eyes, and lamented the necessity of the spectacles, under cover of which I cautiously and thoroughly surveyed the apartment, while seemingly intent only upon the conversation of my host.

"I paid special attention to a large writing-table near which he sat, and upon which lay, confusedly, some miscellaneous letters and other papers, with one or two musical instruments and a few books. Here, however, after a long and very deliberate scrutiny, I saw nothing to excite particular suspicion.

"At length my eyes, in going the circuit of the room, fell upon a trumpery filigree card-rack of paste-board, that hung dangling by a dirty blue ribbon, from a little brass knob just beneath the middle of the mantelpiece. In this rack, which had three or four compartments, were five or six visiting cards and a solitary letter. This last was much soiled and crumpled. It was torn nearly in two, across the middle—as if a design, in the first instance, to tear it entirely up as worthless, had been altered, or stayed, in the second. It had a large black seal, bearing the D—— cipher *very* conspicuously, and was addressed in a diminutive female hand, to D——, the Minister, himself. It was thrust carelessly, and even, as it seemed, contemptuously, into one of the upper divisions of the rack.

"No sooner had I glanced at this letter, than I concluded it to be that of which I was in search. To be sure, it was, to all appearance, radically different from the one of which the Prefect had read us so minute a description. Here the seal was large and black, with the D—— cipher; there it was small and red, with the ducal arms of the S—— family. Here the address, to the Minister, was diminutive and feminine; there the superscription, to a certain royal personage, was markedly bold and decided; the size alone formed a point of correspondence. But, then, the *radicalness* of these differences, which was excessive; the dirt; the soiled and torn condition of the paper, so inconsistent with the *true* methodical habits of D——, and so suggestive of a design to delude the beholder into an idea of the worthlessness of the document; these things, together with the hyperobtrusive situation of this document, full in the view of every visitor, and thus exactly in accordance with the conclusions to which I had previously arrived; these things, I say, were strongly corroborative of suspicion, in one who came with the intention to suspect.

"I protracted my visit as long as possible, and, while I maintained a most animated discussion with the Minister, on a topic which I knew well had never failed to interest and excite him, I kept my attention really riveted upon the letter. In this examination, I committed to memory its external appearance and arrangement in the rack; and also fell, at length, upon a discovery which set at rest whatever trivial doubt I might have entertained. In scrutinizing the edges of the paper, I observed them to be more *chafed* than seem necessary. They presented the *broken* appearance which is manifested when a stiff paper, having been once folded and pressed with a folder, is refolded in the reverse direction, in the same creases or edges which had formed the original fold. This discovery was sufficient. It was clear to me that the letter had been turned, as a glove, inside out, re-directed, and re-sealed. I bade the Minister good morning, and took my departure at once, leaving a gold snuff-box on the table.

"The next morning I called for the snuff-box, when we resumed, quite eagerly, the conversation of the preceding day. While thus engaged, however, a loud report as if of a pistol, was heard immediately beneath the windows of the hotel, and was succeeded by a series of fearful screams, and the shouting of a mob. D—— rushed to the casement, threw it open, and looked out. In the meantime, I stepped to the card-rack, took the letter, put it in my pocket, and replaced it by a facsimile, (so far regards externals), which I had carefully prepared at my lodgings; imitating the D—— cipher, very readily, by means of a seal formed of bread.

"The disturbance in the street had been occasioned by the frantic behaviour of a man with a musket. He had fired it among a crowd of women and children. It proved, however, to have been without ball, and the fellow was suffered to go his way as a lunatic or a drunkard. When he had gone, D—— came from the window, whither I had followed immediately upon securing the object in view. Soon afterwards I bade him farewell. The pretended lunatic was a man in my own pay."

"But what purpose had you," I asked, "in replacing the letter by a *facsimile*? Would it not have been better, at the first visit, to have seized it openly, and departed?"

"D——," replied Dupin, "is a desperate man, and a man of nerve. His hotel, too, is not without attendants devoted to his interests. Had I made the wild attempt you suggest, I might never have left the Ministerial presence alive. The good people of Paris might have heard of me no more. But I had an object apart from these considerations. You know my political prepossessions. In this matter, I act as a partisan of the lady concerned. For eighteen months the Minister has had her in his power. She has now him in hers; since, being unaware that the letter is not in his possession, he will proceed with his exactions as if it was. Thus will he inevitably commit himself, at once, to his political destruction. His downfall, too, will not be more precipitate than awkward. It is all very well to talk about the *facilis descensus Averni*; but in all kinds of climbing, as Catalani said of singing, it is far more easy to get up than to come down. In the present instance I have no sympathy—at least no pity—for him who descends. He is that *monstrum horrendum*, an unprincipled man of genius. I confess, however, that I should like very well to know the precise character of his thoughts, when, being defied by her whom the Prefect terms 'a certain personage,' he is reduced to opening the letter which I left for him the card-rack."

"How? did you put anthing particular in it?"

"Why—it did not seem altogether right to leave the interior blank—that would have been insulting. D——, at Vienna once, did me an evil turn, which I told him, quite good-humouredly, that I should remember. So, as I knew he would feel some curiosity in regard to the identity of the person who had outwitted him, I thought it a pity not to give him a clue. He is well acquainted with my MS., and I just copied into the middle of the blank sheet the words—

——Un dessein si funeste,
S'il n'est dignne d'Atrée, est digne de Thyeste.

They are to be found in Crébillon's *Atrée*."

Appendix

The Gold Bug
by Edgar Allen Poe

> What ho! what ho! this fellow is dancing mad!
> He hath been bitten by the Tarantula
> *All in the Wrong*

Many years ago, I contracted an intimacy with a Mr. William Legrand. He was of an ancient Huguenot family and had once been wealthy; but a series of misfortunes had reduced him to want. To avoid the mortification consequent upon his disasters, he left New Orleans, the city of his forefathers, and took up his residence at Sullivan's Island, near Charleston, South Carolina.

This island is a very singular one. It consists of little else than the sea and sand, and is about three miles long. Its breadth at no point exceeds a quarter of a mile. It is separated from the mainland by a scarcely perceptible creek, oozing its way through a wilderness of reeds and slime, a favourite resort of the marsh-hen. The vegetation, as might be supposed, is scant, or at least dwarfish. No trees of any magnitude are to be seen. Near the western extremity, where Fort Moultrie stands, and where are some miserable frame buildings, tenanted, during summer, by the fugitives from Charleston dust and fever, may be found, indeed, the bristly palmetto; but the whole island, with the exception of this western point, and a line of hard, white beach on the sea-coast, is covered with a dense undergrowth of the sweet myrtle so much prized by the horticulturist of England. The shrub here often attains the height of fifteen or twenty feet, and forms an almost impenetrable coppice, burthening the air with its fragrance.

In the inmost recesses of this coppice, not far from the eastern or more remote end of the island, Legrand had built himself a small hut, which he occupied when I first, by mere accident, made his acquaintance. This soon ripened into friendship—for there was much in the recluse to excite interest and esteem. I found him well educated, with unusual powers of mind, but infected with misanthropy, and subject to perverse moods of alternate enthusiasm and melancholy. He had with him many books, but rarely employed them. His chief amusements were gunning and fishing, or sauntering along the beach and through the myrtles, in quest of shells or entomological specimens—his collection of the latter might have been envied by a Swammerdamm. In these excursions he was usually accompanied by an old negro, called Jupiter, who had been manumitted before the reverses of the family, but who could be induced, neither by threats nor by promises, to abandon what he considered his right of attendance upon the footsteps of his young "Massa Will." It is not improbable that the relatives of Legrand, conceiving him to be somewhat unsettled in intellect, had contrived to instil this obstinacy into Jupiter, with a view to the supervision and guardianship of the wanderer.

The winters in the latitude of Sullivan's Island are seldom very severe, and in the fall of the year it is a rare event indeed when a fire is considered necessary. About the middle of October, 18—, there occurred, however, a day of remarkable chilliness. Just before sunset I scrambled my way through the evergreens to the hut of my friend, whom I had not visited for several weeks—my residence being, at that time, in Charleston, a distance of nine miles from the island, while the facilities of passage and re-passage were very far behind those of the present day. Upon reaching the hut I rapped, as was my custom, and getting no reply, sought for the key where I knew it was secreted, unlocked the door, and went in. A fine fire was blazing upon the hearth. It was a novelty, and by no means an ungrateful one. I threw off an overcoat, took an arm-chair by the crackling logs, and awaited patiently the arrival of my hosts.

Soon after dark they arrived, and gave me a most cordial welcome. Jupiter, grinning from ear to ear, bustled about to prepare some marsh-hen for supper. Legrand was in one of his fits—how else shall I term them?—of enthusiasm. He had found an unknown bivalve, forming a new genus, and, more than this, he had hunted down and secured, with Jupiter's assistance, a scarabaeus which he believed to be totally new, but in respect to which he wished to have my opinion on the morrow.

"And why not tonight?" I asked, rubbing my hands over the blaze, and wishing the whole tribe of scarabaei at the devil.

"Ah, if I had only known you were here!" said Legrand, "but it's so long since I saw you; and how could I foresee that you would pay a me a visit this very night of all others? As I was coming home, I met Lieutenant G——, from the fort, and, very foolishly, I lent him the bug; so it will be impossible for you to see it until the morning. Stay here tonight, and I will send Jup down for it at sunrise. It is the loveliest thing in creation!"

"What?—sunrise?"

"Nonsense! no!—the bug. It is of a brilliant gold colour—about the size of a large hickory-nut—with two jet-black spots near one extremity of the back, and another somewhat longer, at the other. The antennae are—"

"Dey ain't *no* tin in him, Massa Will, I keep a tellin' on you," here interrupted Jupiter; "de bug is a goole-bug, solid, ebery bit of him, inside and all, sep him wing—neber feel half so hebby a bug in my life."

"Well, suppose it is, Jup," replied Legrand, somewhat more earnestly, it seemed to me, than the case demanded; "is that any reason for your letting the birds burn? The colour"—here he turned to me—"is really almost enough to warrant Jupiter's idea. You never saw a more brilliant metallic lustre than the scales emit—but of this you cannot judge till tomorrow. In the meantime, I can give you some idea of the shape." Saying this, he seated himself at a small table, on which were a pen and ink, but no paper. He looked for some in the drawer, but found none.

"Never mind," he said at length, "this will answer"; and he drew from his waistcoat pocket a scrap of what I took to be very dirty foolscap, and made upon it a rough drawing with the pen. While he did this, I retained my seat by the fire, for I was still chilly. When the design was complete, he handed it to me without rising. As I received it, a loud growl was heard, succeeded by scratching at the door. Jupiter opened it, and a large Newfoundland, belonging to Legrand, rushed in, leaped upon my shoulders, and loaded me with caresses; for I had shown him much attention during previous visits. When his gambols were over, I looked at the paper, and, to speak the truth, found myself not a little puzzled at what my friend had depicted.

"Well!" I said, after contemplating it for some minutes; "this *is* a strange scarabaeus, I must confess; new to me; never saw anything like it before—unless it was a skull, or a death's-head, which it more nearly resembles than anything else that has come under *my* observation."

"A death's-head!" echoed Legrand. "Oh—yes—well, it has something of that appearance upon paper, no doubt. The two upper black spots look like eyes, eh? and the longer one at the bottom like a mouth—and then the shape of the whole is oval."

"Perhaps so," said I; "but, Legrand, I fear you are no artist. I must wait until I see the beetle itself, if I am to form any idea of its personal appearance."

"Well, I don't know," said he, a little nettled, "I draw tolerably—*should* do it at least—have had good masters, and flatter myself that I am not quite a block-head."

"But, my dear fellow, you are joking then," said I, "this is a very passable *skull*—indeed, I may say that it is a very *excellent* skull, according to the vulgar notions about such specimens of physiology—and your scarabaeus must be the queerest scarabaeus in the world if it resembles it. Why, we may get up a very thrilling bit of superstition upon this hint. I presume that you will call the bug *scarabaeus caput hominis*, or something of that kind—there are may similar titles in the Natural Histories. But where are the antennae you spoke of?"

"The antennae!" said Legrand, who seemed to be getting unaccountably warm upon the subject; "I am sure you must see the antennae. I made them as distinct as they are in the original insect, and I presume that is sufficient."

"Well, well," I said, "perhaps you have—still I don't see them"; and I handed him the paper without additional remark, not wishing to ruffle his temper; but I was much surprised at the turn affairs had taken; his ill-humour puzzled me—and, as for the drawing of the beetle, there were positively no antennae visible, and the whole *did* bear a very close resemblance to the ordinary cuts of a death's-head.

He received the paper very peevishly, and was about to crumple it, apparently to throw it in the fire, when a casual glance at the design seemed suddenly to rivet his attention. In an instant his face grew violently red—in another as excessively pale. For some minutes he continued to scrutinize the drawing minutely where he sat. At length he arose, took a candle from the table, and proceeded to seat himself upon a sea-chest in the farthest corner of the room. Here again he made an anxious examination of the paper; turning it in all directions. He said nothing, however, and his conduct greatly astonished me; yet I thought it prudent not to exacerbate the growing moodiness of his temper by any comment. Presently he took from his coat-pocket a wallet, placed the paper carefully in it, and deposited both in a writing desk, which he locked. He now grew more composed in his demeanor; but his original air of enthusiasm had quite disappeared. Yet he seemed not so much sulky as abstracted. As the evening wore away he became more and more absorbed in reverie, from which no sallies of mine could arouse him. It had been my intention to pass the night at the hut, as I had frequently done before, but, seeing my host in this mood, I deemed it proper to take leave. He did not press me to remain, but, as I departed, he shook my hand with even more than his usual cordiality.

It was about a month after this (and during the interval I had seen nothing of Legrand) when I received a visit at Charleston from his man, Jupiter. I had never seen the good old negro look so dispirited, and I feared that some serious disaster had befallen my friend.

"Well, Jup," said, I, "what is the matter now?—how is your master?"

"Why, to speak de troof, massa, him not so berry well as mought be."

"Not well! I am truly sorry to hear it. What does he complain of?"

"Dar! da't it!—he never 'plain ob nothin'—but him berry sick for all dat."

"*Very* sick, Jupiter!—why didn't you say so at once? Is he confined to bed?"

"No, dat he ain't—he ain't 'fin'd nowhar—dat's just whar de shoe pinch—my mind is got to be berry hebby 'bout poor Massa Will."

"Jupiter, I should like to understand what it is you are talking about. You say your master is sick. Hasn't he told you what ails him?"

"Why, massa, 'tain't worf while for to git mad about de matter—Massa Will say noffin at all ain't de matter wid him—but den what make him go about looking dis here way, wid he head down and he soldiers up, and as white as a gose? And den he keep a syphon all de time—"

"Keeps a what, Jupiter?"

"Keeps a syphon wid de figgurs on de slate—de queerest figgurs I ebber did see. Ise gettin' to be skeered, I tell you. Hab for to keep mighty tight eye 'pon him 'noovers. Todder day he gib me slip 'fore de sun up and was gone de whole ob de blessed day. I had a big stick ready cut for to gib him deuced good beating when he did come—but Ise sich a fool dat I hadn't de heart arter all—he looked so berry poorly."

"Eh?—what?—ah yes!—upon the whole I think you had better not be too severe with the poor fellow—don't flog him, Jupiter—he can't very well stand it—but can you form no idea of what has occasioned this illness, or rather this change of conduct? Has anything unpleasant happened since I saw you?"

"No, massa, dey ain't bin noffin' onpleasant *since* den—'twas 'fore den I'm feared—'twas de berry day you was dare."

"How? What do you mean?"

"Why, massa, I mean de bug—dare now."

"The what?"

"De bug—I'm berry sartain dat Massa Will bin bit somewhere 'bout de head by dat goole-bug."

"And what cause have you, Jupiter, for such a supposition?"

"Claws, enuff, massa, and mouff too. I nebber did see sich a deuced bug—he kick and he bite ebery ting what cum near him. Massa Will cotch him fuss, but had for to let him go 'gin mighty quick, I tell you—den was de time he must ha' got de bite. I didn't like de look ob de bug mouff, myself, nohow, so I wouldn't take hold ob him wid my finger, but I cotch him wid a piece ob paper dat I found. I rap him up in de paper and stuff a piece of it in he mouff—dat was de way."

"And you think, then, that your master was really bitten by the beetle, and that the bite made him sick?"

"I don't think noffin' about it—I nose it. What make him dream 'bout de goole so much, if'tain't 'cause he bit by de goole-bug? Ise heerd 'bout dem goole-bugs 'fore dis."

"But how do you know he dreams about gold?"

"How I know? why, 'cause he talk about it in he sleep—dat's how I nose."

"Well, Jup, perhaps you are right; but to what fortunate circumstances am I to attribute the honour of a visit from you today?"

"What de matter, massa?"

"Did you bring any message from Mr. Legrand?"

"No, Massa, I bring dis here pissel"; and here Jupiter handed me a note which ran thus:

My dear——,

Why have I not seen you for so long a time? I hope you have not been so foolish as to take offence at any little brusquerie of mine; but no, that is improbable.

Since I saw you I have had great cause for anxiety. I have something to tell you, yet scarcely know how to tell it, or whether I should tell it at all.

I have not been quite well for some days past, and poor old Jup annoys me, almost beyond endurance, by his well-meant attentions. Would you believe it?—he had prepared a huge stick, the other day, with which to chastise me for giving him the slip, and spending the day, *solus*, among the hills on the mainland. I verily believe that my ill looks alone saved me a flogging.

I have made no addition to my cabinet since we met.

If you can, in any way, make it convenient, come over with Jupiter. *Do* come. I wish to see you *tonight*, upon business of importance. I assure you that it is of the *highest* importance.

Ever yours,

WILLIAM LEGRAND

There was something in the tone of this note which gave me a great uneasiness. Its whole style differed materially from that of Legrand. What could he be dreaming of? What new crotchet possessed his excitable brain? What "business of the highest importance" could *he* possibly have to transact? Jupiter's account of him boded no good. I dreaded lest the continued pressure of misfortune had, at length, fairly unsettled the reason of my friend. Without a moment's hesitation, therefore, I prepared to accompany the negro.

Upon reaching the wharf, I noticed a scythe and three spades, all apparently new, lying in the bottom of the boat in which we were to embark.

"What is the meaning of all this, Jup?" I inquired.

"Him syfe, massa, and spade."

"Very true; but what are they doing here?"

"Him de syfe and de spade what Massa Will sis 'pon my buying for him in de town, and de debbil's own lot of money I had to gib for 'em."

"But what, in the name of all that is mysterious, is your 'Massa Will' going to do with scythes and spades?"

"Dat's more dan I know, and debbil take me if I don't b'lieve 'tis more dan he know too. But it's all cum ob de bug."

Finding that no satisfaction was to be obtained of Jupiter, whose whole intellect seemed to be absorbed by "de bug," I now stepped into the boat, and made sail. With a fair and strong breeze we soon ran into the little cove to the northward of Fort Moultrie, and a walk of some two miles brought us to the hut. It was about three in the afternoon when we arrived. Legrand had been awaiting us in eager expectation. He grasped my hand with a nervous empressement which alarmed me and strengthened the suspicions already entertained. His countenance was pale even to ghastliness, and his deepset eyes glared with unnatural lustre. After some inquiries respecting his health, I asked him, not knowing what better to say, if he had yet obtained the scarabaeus from Lieutenant G——.

"Oh, yes," he replied, colouring violently, "I got it from him the next morning. Nothing should tempt me to part with that scarabaeus. Do you know that Jupiter is quite right about it?"

"In what way?" I asked him, with a sad foreboding at heart.

"In supposing it to be a bug of *real gold*." He said this with an air of profound seriousness, and I felt inexpressibly shocked.

"This bug is to make my fortune," he continued, with a triumphant smile; "to reinstate me in my family possessions. Is it any wonder, then, that I prize it?

Since Fortune has thought fit to bestow it upon me, I have only to use it proper-ly, and I shall arrive at the gold of which it is the index. Jupiter, bring me that scarabaeus!"

"What! de bug, massa? I'd rudder not go fer trubble dat bug; you mus' git him for your own self." Hereupon Legrand arose, with a grave and stately air, and brought me the beetle from a glass case in which it was enclosed. It was a beautiful scarabaeus, and, at that time, unknown to naturalists—of course a great prize from a scientific point of view. There were two round black spots near one extremity of the back, and a long one near the other. The scales were exceedingly hard and glossy, with all the appearance of burnished gold. The weight of the insect was very remarkable, and, taking all things into considera-tion, I could hardly blame Jupiter for his opinion respecting it; but what to make of Legrand's concordance with that opinion I could not, for the life of me, tell.

"I sent for you," said he, in a grandiloquent tone, when I had completed my examination of the beetle, "I sent for you that I might have your counsel and assistance in furthering the views of Fate and of the bug—"

"My dear Legrand," I cried, interrupting him, "you are certainly unwell, and had better use some little precautions. You should go to bed, and I will remain with you for a few days, until you get over this. You are feverish and—"

"Feel my pulse," said he.

I felt it, and to say the truth, found not the slightest indication of fever.

"But you may be ill and yet have no fever. Allow me this once to prescribe for you. In the first place go to bed. In the next—"

"You are mistaken," he interposed, "I am as well as I can expect to be under the excitement which I suffer. If you really wish me well you will relieve this excitement."

"And how is this to be done?"

"Very easily. Jupiter and myself are going upon an expedition into the hills, upon the mainland, and, in this expedition, we shall need the aid of some per-son in whom we can confide. You are the only one we can trust. Whether we succeed or fail, the excitement which you now perceive in me will be equally al-layed."

"I am anxious to oblige you in any way," I replied; "but do you mean to say that this infernal beetle has any connexion with your expedition to the hills?"

"It has."

"Then, Legrand, I can become a party to no such absurd proceeding."

"I am sorry—very sorry—for we shall have to try it by ourselves."

"Try it by yourselves! The man is surely mad!—but stay!—how long do you propose to be absent?"

"Probably all night. We shall start immediately, and be back, at all events, by sunrise."

"And you will promise me, upon your honour, that when this freak of yours is over, and the bug business (good God!) settled to your satisfaction, you will then return home and follow my advice implicitly, as that of your physician."

"Yes; I promise; and now let us be off, for we have no time to lose."

With a heavy heart I accompanied my friend. We started about four o'clock—Legrand, Jupiter, the dog, and myself. Jupiter had with him the scythe and spades—the whole of which he insisted upon carrying—more through fear, it seemed to me, of trusting either of the implements within reach of his master, than from any excess of industry or complaisance. His demeanour was dogged in the extreme, and "dat deuced bug" were the sole words which escaped his lips during the journey. For my own part, I had charge of a couple of dark lanterns, while Legrand contented himself with the scarabaeus, which he carried attached to the end of a bit of whipcord; twirling it to and fro, with the air of a conjurer, as he went. When I observed this last, plain evidence of my friend's aberration of mind, I could scarcely refrain from tears. I thought it best, however, to humour his fancy, at least for the present, or until I could adopt some more energetic measures with a chance of success. In the meantime, I endeavoured, but all in vain, to sound him in regard to the object of the expedition. Having succeeded in inducing me to accompany him, he seemed unwilling to hold conversation upon any topic of minor importance, and to all my questions vouchsafed no other reply than "we shall see!"

We crossed the creek at the head of the island by means of a skiff, and, ascending the high grounds on the shore of the mainland, proceeded in a north-westerly direction, through a tract of country excessively wild and desolate, where no trace of a human footstep was to be seen. Legrand led the way with decision; pausing only for an instant, here and there, to consult what appeared to be certain landmarks of his own contrivance upon a former occasion.

In this manner we journeyed for about two hours, and the sun was just setting when we entered a region infinitely more dreary than any yet seen. It was a species of tableland, near the summit of an almost inaccessible hill, densely wooded from base to pinnacle, and interspersed with huge crags that appeared to lie loosely upon the soil, and in many cases were prevented from precipitating themselves into the valleys below merely by the support of the trees against which they reclined. Deep ravines, in various directions, gave an air of still sterner solemnity to the scene.

The natural platform to which we had clambered was thickly overgrown with brambles, through which we soon discovered that it would have been impossible to force our way but for the scythe; and Jupiter, by direction of his master, proceeded to clear for us a path to the foot of an enormously tall tulip-tree, which stood, with some eight or ten oaks, upon the level, and far surpassed them all, and all other trees which I had then ever seen, in the beauty of its foliage and form, in the wide spread of its branches, and in the general majesty of its appearance. When we reached this tree, Legrand turned to Jupiter, and asked him if he thought he could climb it. The old man seemed a little staggered by the question, and for some moments made no reply. At length he approached the huge trunk, walked slowly around it, and examined it with minute attention. When he had completed his scrutiny, he merely said:

"Yes, massa, Jup climb any tree he ebber see in he life."

"Then up with you as soon as possible, for it will soon be too dark to see what we are about."

"How far mus' go up, massa?" inquired Jupiter.

"Get up the main trunk first, and then I will tell you which way to go—and here—stop! take this beetle with you."

"De bug, Massa Will!—de goole-bug!" cried the negro, drawing back in dismay—"what for mus' tote de bug way up de tree?—d——n if I do!"

"If you are afraid, Jup, a great big negro like you, to take hold of a harmless little dead beetle, why you can carry it up by this string—but, if you do not take it up with you in some way, I shall be under the necessity of breaking your head with this shovel."

"What de matter now, massa?" said, Jup, evidently shamed into compliance; "always want for to raise fuss wid old nigger. Was only funnin' anyhow. *Me* feered de bug! what I keer for de bug?" Here he took cautiously hold of the extreme end of the string, and, maintaining the insect as far from his person as circumstances would permit, prepared to ascend the tree.

In youth, the tulip-tree, or *Liriodendron tulipifera*, the most magnificent of American foresters, has a trunk peculiarly smooth, and often rises to a great height without lateral branches; but, in its riper age, the bark becomes gnarled and uneven, while many short limbs make their appearance on the stem. Thus, the difficulty of ascension, in the present case, lay more in semblance than in reality. Embracing the huge cylinder, as closely as possible, with his arms and knees, seizing with his hands some projections, and resting his naked toes upon others, Jupiter, after one or two narrow escapes from falling, at length wriggled himself into the first great fork, and seemed to consider the whole business as virtually accomplished. The risk of the achievement was, in fact, now over, although the climber was some sixty or seventy feet from the ground.

"Which way mus' go now, Massa Will?" he asked.

"Keep up the largest branch—the one on this side," said Legrand. The negro obeyed him promptly, and apparently with but little trouble; ascending higher and higher, until no glimpse of his squat figure could be obtained through the dense foliage which enveloped it. Presently his voice was heard in a sort of halloo.

"How much fudder is got for go?"

"How high up are you?" asked Legrand.

"Ebber so fur," replied the negro; "can see de sky fru de top ob de tree."

"Never mind the sky, but attend to what I say. Look down the trunk and count the limbs below you on this side. How many limbs have you passed?"

"One, two, tree, four, fibe—I done pass fibe big limb, massa, pon dis side."

"Then go one limb higher."

In a few minutes the voice was heard again, announcing that the seventh limb was attained.

"Now, Jup," cried Legrand, evidently much excited, "I want you to work your way out upon that limb as far as you can. If you see anything strange let me know."

By this time what little doubt I might have entertained of my poor friend's insanity was put finally at rest. I had no alternative but to conclude him stricken with lunacy, and I became seriously anxious about getting him home. While I was pondering upon what was best to be done, Jupiter's voice was again heard.

"Mos' feerd for to venture pon dis limb berry far—'tis dead limb putty much all de way."

"Did you say it was a *dead* limb, Jupiter?" cried Legrand in a quavering voice.

"Yes, massa, him dead as de door-nail—done up for sartain—done departed dis here life."

"What in the name of heaven shall I do?" asked Legrand, seemingly in the greatest distress.

"Do!" said I, glad of an opportunity to interpose a word, "why come home and go to bed. Come now!—that's a fine fellow. It's getting late, and, besides, you remember your promise."

"Jupiter," cried he, without heeding me in the least, "do you hear me?"

"Yes, Massa Will, hear you ebber so plain."

"Try the wood well, then, with your knife, and see if you think it *very* rotten."

"Him rotten, massa, sure nuff," replied the negro in a few moments, "but not so berry rotten as mought be. Mought venture out leetle way pon de limb by myself, dat's true."

"By yourself!—what do you mean?"

"Why, I mean de bug. 'Tis *berry* hebby bug. S'pose I drop him down fuss, and den de limb won't break wid just de weight ob one nigger."

"You infernal scoundrel!" cried Legrand, apparently much relieved, "what do you mean by telling me such nonsense as that? As sure as you drop that beetle I'll break your neck. Look here, Jupiter, do you hear me?"

"Yes, massa, needn't hollo at poor nigger dat style."

"Well! now listen!—if you will venture out on the limb as far as you think safe, and not let go the beetle, I'll make you a present of a silver dollar as soon as you get down."

"I'm gwine, Massa Will—deed I is," replied the negro very promptly—"mos' out to the end now."

"*Out to the end!*" here fairly screamed Legrand; "do you say you are out to the end of the limb?"

"Soon be to de end, massa—o-o-o-o-oh! Lor-gol-a-marcy! what *is* dis here pon de tree?"

"Well!" cried Legrand, highly delighted, "what is it?"

"Why, 'tain't noffin but a skull—somebody bin lef him head up de tree, and de crows done gobble ebery bit of de meat off."

"A skull, you say!—very well—how is it fastened to the limb?—what holds it on?"

"Sure nuff, massa; mus' look. Why di berry curous sarcumstance, pon my word—dare's a great big nail in de skull, what fastens ob it on to de tree."

"Well now, Jupiter, do exactly as I tell you—do you hear?"

"Yes, massa."

"Pay attention, then—find the left eye of the skull."

"Hum! hoo! dat's good! why dey ain't no eye lef at all."

"Curse your stupidity! Do you know your right hand from your left?"

"Yes, I knows dat—knows all bout dat—it's my lef hand what I chops de wood wid."

"To be sure! you are left-handed; and your left eye is on the same side as your left hand. Now, I suppose, you can find the left eye of the skull, or the place where the left eye has been. Have you found it?"

Here was a long pause. At length the negro asked:

"Is de lef eye ob de skull pon de same side as de lef hand side of de skull too?—cause de skull ain't got not a bit of a hand at all—neber mind! I got de lef eye now—here de lef eye! what mus' do wid it?"

"Let the beetle drop through it, as far as the string will reach—but be careful and not let go of your hold on the string."

"All dat done, Massa Will; mighty easy ting for to put de bug fru de hole—look out for him dare below!"

During this colloquy no portions of Jupiter's person could be seen; but the beetle, which he had suffered to descend, was now visible at the end of the string, and glistened, like a globe of burnished gold, in the last rays of the setting sun, some of which still faintly illumined the eminence upon which we stood. The scarabaeus hung quite clear of any branches, and, if allowed to fall, would have fallen at our feet. Legrand immediately took the scythe, and cleared with it a circular space, three or four yards in diameter, just beneath the insect, and, having accomplished this, ordered Jupiter to let go the string and come down from the tree.

Driving a peg, with great nicety, into the ground, at the precise spot where the beetle fell, my friend now produced from his pocket a tape-measure. Fastening one end of this at the point of the trunk of the tree which was nearest the peg, he unrolled it till it reached the peg and thence further unrolled it, in the direction already established by the two points of the tree and the peg, for the distance of fifty feet—Jupiter clearing away the brambles with the scythe. At the spot thus attained a second peg was driven, and about this time, as a centre, a rude circle, about four feet in diameter, described. Taking now a spade himself, and giving one to Jupiter and one to me, Legrand begged us to set about digging as quickly as possible.

To speak the truth, I had no especial relish for such amusement at any time, and, at that particular moment, would most willingly have declined it; for the night was coming on, and I felt much fatigued with the exercise already taken; but I saw no mode of escape, and was fearful of disturbing my poor friend's equanimity by a refusal. Could I have depended, indeed, upon Jupiter's aid, I would have had no hesitation in attempting to get the lunatic home by force; but I was too well assured of the old negro's disposition to hope that he would assist me, under any circumstances, in a personal contest with his master. I made no doubt that the latter had been infected with some of the innumerable Southern superstitions about money buried, and that his phantasy had received confirmation by the finding of the scarabaeus, or, perhaps, by Jupiter's obstinacy in maintaining it to be "a bug of real gold." A mind disposed to lunacy would readily be led away by such suggestions—especially if chiming in with favourite preconceived ideas—and then I called to mind the poor fellow's speech about the beetle's being "the index of his fortune." Upon the whole, I was sadly vexed and puzzled, but, at length, I concluded to make a virtue of necessity—to dig with a good will, and thus the sooner to convince the visionary, by ocular demonstration, of the fallacy of the opinions he entertained.

The lanterns having been lit, we all fell to work with a zeal worthy of a more rationale cause; and, as the glare fell upon our persons and implements, I could not help thinking how picturesque a group we composed, and how strange and suspicious our labours must have appeared to any interloper who, by chance, might have stumbled upon our whereabouts.

We dug very steadily for two hours. Little was said; and our chief embarrassment lay in the yelpings of the dog, who took exceeding interest in our proceedings. He, at length, became so obstreperous that we grew fearful of his giving the alarm to some stragglers in the vicinity,—or, rather, this was the apprehension of Legrand;—for myself, I would have rejoiced at any interruption which might have enabled me to get the wanderer home. The noise was, at length, very effectually silenced by Jupiter, who, getting out of the hole with a dogged air of deliberation, tied the brute's mouth up with one of his suspenders, and then returned, with a grave chuckle, to his task.

When the time mentioned had expired, we had reached a depth of five feet, and yet no signs of any treasure became manifest. A general pause ensued, and I began to hope that the farce was at an end. Legrand, however, although evidently much disconcerted, wiped his brow thoughtfully and recommenced. We had excavated the entire circle of four feet diameter, and now we slightly enlarged the limit, and went to the farther depth of two feet. Still nothing appeared. The gold-seeker, whom I sincerely pitied, at length clambered from the pit, with the bitterest disappointment imprinted upon every feature, and proceeded, slowly and reluctantly, to put on his coat, which he had thrown off at the beginning of his labour. In the meantime I made no remark. Jupiter, at a signal from his master, began to gather up his tools. This done, and the dog having been unmuzzled, we turned in profound silence toward home.

We had taken, perhaps, a dozen steps in this direction, when, with a loud oath, Legrand strode up to Jupiter, and seized him by the collar. The astonished negro opened his eyes and mouth to the fullest extent, let fall the spades, and fell upon his knees.

"You scoundrel!" said Legrand, hissing out the syllables from between his clenched teeth—"you infernal black villain!—speak, I tell you!—answer me this instant, without prevarication!—which—which is your left eye?"

"Oh, my golly, Massa Will! ain't dis here my lef eye for sartain?" roared the terrified Jupiter, placing his hand upon his *right* organ of vision, and holding it there with a desperate pertinacity, as if in immediate dread of his master's attempt at a gouge.

"I thought so!—I knew it! hurrah!" vociferated Legrand, letting the negro go, and executing a series of curvets and caracoles, much to the astonishment of his valet, who, arising from his knees, looked, mutely, from his master to myself, and then from myself to his master.

"Come! we must go back," said the latter, "the game's not up yet"; and he again led the way to the tulip-tree.

"Jupiter," said he, when we reached its foot, "come here! was the skull nailed to the limb with the face outward, or was the face to the limb?"

"De face was out, massa, so dat de crows could get at de eyes good, widout any trouble."

"Well, then was it this eye or that through which you dropped the beetle?"—here Legrand touched each of Jupiter's eyes.

"'Twas dis eye, massa—de lef eye—jis as you tell me,"—and here it was his right eye that the negro indicated.

"That will do—we must try it again."

Here my friend, about whose madness I now saw, or fancied that I saw, certain indications of method, removed the peg which marked the spot where the beetle fell to a spot about three inches to the westward of its former position. Taking, now, the tape-measure from the nearest point of the trunk to the peg, as before, and continuing the extension in a straight line to the distance of fifty feet, a spot was indicated, removed, by several yards, from the point at which we had been digging.

Around the new position a circle, somewhat larger than in the former instance, was now described, and we again set to work with the spade. I was dreadfully weary, but, scarcely understanding what had occasioned the change in my thoughts, I felt no longer any great aversion from the labour imposed. I had become most unaccountably interested—nay, even excited. Perhaps there was something, amid all the extravagant demeanour of Legrand—some air of forethought, or of deliberation, which impressed me. I dug eagerly, and now and then caught myself actually looking, with something that very much resembled expectation, for the fancied treasure, the vision of which had demented my unfortunate companion. At a period when such vagaries of thought most fully possessed me, and when we had been at work perhaps an hour and a half, we were again interrupted by the violent howlings of the dog. His uneasiness, in the first instance, had been, evidently, but the result of playfulness or caprice, but he now assumed a bitter and serious tone. Upon Jupiter's again attempting to muzzle him, he made furious resistance, and, leaping into the hole, tore up the mould frantically with his claws. In a few seconds he had uncovered a mass of human bones, forming two complete skeletons, intermingled with several buttons of metal, and what appeared to be the dust of decayed woollen. One or two strokes of a spade upturned the blade of a large Spanish knife, and, as we dug farther, three or four loose pieces of gold and silver coin came to light.

At sight of these the joy of Jupiter could scarcely be restrained, but the countenance of his master wore an air of extreme disappointment. He urged us, however, to continue our exertions, and the words were hardly uttered when I stumbled and fell forward, having caught the toe of my boot in a large ring of iron that lay half buried in the loose earth.

We now worked in earnest, and never did I pass ten minutes of more intense excitement. During this interval we had fairly unearthed an oblong chest of wood, which, from its perfect preservation and wonderful hardness, had plainly been subjected to some mineralizing process—perhaps that of the bichloride of mercury. This box was three and a half feet long, three feet broad, and two and a half feet deep. It was firmly secured by bands of wrought iron, riveted, and forming a kind of open trellis-work over the whole. On each side of the chest, near the top, were three rings of iron—six in all—by means of which a firm hold could be obtained by six persons. Our utmost united endeavours served only to disturb the coffer very slightly in its bed. We at once saw the impossibility of removing so great a weight. Luckily, the sole fastenings of the lid consisted of two sliding bolts. These we drew back—trembling and panting with anxiety. In an instant, a treasure of incalculable value lay gleaming before us. As the rays of the lanterns fell within the pit, there flashed upward a glow and a glare, from a confused heap of gold and of jewels, that absolutely dazzled our eyes.

I shall not pretend to describe the feelings with which I gazed. Amazement was, of course, predominant. Legrand appeared exhausted with excitement, and spoke very few words. Jupiter's countenance wore, for some minutes, as deadly a pallor as it is possible, in the nature of things, for any negro's visage to assume. He seemed stupefied—thunderstricken. Presently he fell upon his knees in the pit, and burying his naked arms up to the elbows in gold, let them there remain, as if enjoying the luxury of a bath. At length, with a deep sigh, he exclaimed, as if in a soliloquy:

"And dis all com ob de goole-bug! de putty goole-bug! de poor little goole-bug, what I boosed in dat sabage kind ob style! Ain't you shamed ob yourself, nigger!—answer me dat!"

It became necessary, at last, that I should arouse both master and valet to the expediency of removing the treasure. It was growing late, and it behooved us to make exertion, that we might get everything housed before daylight. It was difficult to say what should be done, and much time was spent in deliberation—so confused were the ideas of all. We finally lightened the box by removing two-thirds of its contents, when we were enabled, with some trouble, to raise it from the hole. The articles taken out were deposited among the brambles, and the dog left to guard them, with strict orders from Jupiter, neither, upon any pretence, to stir from the spot, nor to open his mouth until our return. We then hurriedly made for home with the chest; reaching the hut in safety, but after excessive toil, at one o'clock in the morning. Worn out as we were, it was not in human nature to do more immediately. We rested until two, and had supper: starting for the hills immediately afterward, armed with three stout sacks, which by good luck, were upon the premises. A little before four we arrived at the pit, divided the remainder of the booty, as equally as might be, among us, and, leaving the holes unfilled, again set our for the hut, at which, for the second time, we deposited our golden burdens, just as the first faint streaks of the dawn gleamed from over the tree-tops in the east.

We were now thoroughly broken down; but the intense excitement of the time denied us repose. After an unquiet slumber of some three or four hours' duration, we arose, as if by preconcert, to make examination of our treasure.

The chest had been full to the brim, and we spend the whole day, and the greater part of the next night, in a scrutiny of its contents. There had been nothing like order or arrangement. Everything had been heaped in promiscuously. Having assorted all with care, we found ourselves possessed of even vaster wealth than we had at first supposed. In coin there was rather more than four hundred and fifty thousand dollars—estimating the value of the pieces, as accurately as we could, by the tables of the period. There was not a particle of silver. All was gold of antique date and of great variety—French, Spanish, and German money, with a few English guineas, and some counters, of which we had never seen specimens before. There were several very large and heavy coins, so worn that we could make nothing of their inscriptions. There was no American money. The value of the jewels we found more difficult in estimating. There were diamonds—some of them exceedingly large and fine—a hundred and ten in all, and not one of them small; eighteen rubies of remarkable brilliancy; three hundred and ten emeralds, all very beautiful; and twenty-one sapphires, with an opal. These stones had been broken from their settings and thrown loose in the chest. The settings themselves, which we picked out from among the other gold, appeared to have been beaten up with hammers, as if to prevent identification. Besides all this, there was a vast quantity of solid gold ornaments: nearly two hundred massive finger- and ear-rings; rich chains—thirty of these, if I remember; eighty-three very large and heavy crucifixes; five gold censers of great value; a prodigious gold punch-bowl, ornamented with richly chased vine-leaves and Bacchanalian figures; with two sword-handles exquisitely embossed, and many other smaller articles which I cannot recollect. The weight of these valuables exceeded three hundred and fifty pounds avoirdupois; and in this estimate I have not included one hundred and ninety-seven superb gold watches; three of the number being worth each five hundred dollars, if one. Many of them were very old, and as timekeepers valueless; the works having suffered more or less from corrosion—but all were richly jewelled and in cases of great worth. We estimated the entire contents of the chest, that night, at a million and a half of dollars; and upon the subsequent disposal of the trinkets and jewels (a few being retained for our own use), it was found that we had greatly undervalued the treasure.

When, at length, we had concluded our examination, and the intense excitement of the time had, in some measure, subsided, Legrand, who saw that I was dying with impatience for a solution of this most extraordinary riddle, entered into a full detail of all the circumstances connected with it.

"You remember," said he, "the night when I handed you the rough sketch I had made of the scarabaeus. You recollect also that I became quite vexed at you for insisting that my drawing resembled a death's-head. When you first made this assertion, I thought you were jesting; but afterward I called to mind the peculiar spots on the back of the insect, and admitted to myself that your remark had some little foundation in fact. Still, the sneer at my graphic powers irritated me—for I am considered a good artist—and, therefore, when you handed me the scrap of parchment, I was about to crumple it up and throw it angrily into the fire."

"The scrap of paper, you mean," said I.

"No; it had much of the appearance of paper, and at first I supposed it to be such, but when I came to draw upon it I discovered it at once to be a piece of very thin parchment. It was quite dirty, you remember. Well, as I was in the very act of crumpling it up, my glance fell upon the sketch at which you had been looking, and you may imagine my astonishment when I perceived, in fact, the figure of a death's-head just where, it seemed to me, I had made the drawing of the beetle. For a moment I was too much amazed to think with accuracy. I knew that my design was very different in detail from this—although there was a certain similarity in general outline. Presently I took a candle, and seating myself at the other end of the room, proceeded to scrutinize the parchment more closely. Upon turning it over, I saw my own sketch upon the reverse, just as I had made it. My first idea, now, was mere surprise at the really remarkable similarity of outline—at the singular coincidence involved in the fact that, unknown to me, there should have been a skull upon the other side of the parchment, immediately beneath my figure of the scarabaeus, and that this skull, not only in outline, but in size, should so closely resemble my drawing. I say the singularity of this coincidence absolutely stupefied me for a time. This is the usual effect of such coincidences. The mind struggles to establish a connexion—a sequence of cause and effect—and, being unable to do so, suffers a species of temporary paralysis. But, when I recovered from this stupor, there dawned upon me gradually a conviction which startled me even far more than the coincidence. I began distinctly, positively, to remember that there had been *no* drawing upon the parchment when I made my sketch of the scarabaeus. I became perfectly certain of this; for I recollected turning up first one side and then the other, in search of the cleanest spot. Had the skull been then there, of course I could not have failed to notice it. Here was indeed a mystery which I felt it impossible to explain; but, even at that early moment, there seemed to glimmer, faintly, with the most remote and secret chambers of my intellect, a glow-worm-like conception of that truth which last night's adventure brought to so magnificent a demonstration. I arose at once, and putting the parchment securely away, dismissed all further reflection until I should be alone.

"When you had gone, and when Jupiter was fast asleep, I betook myself to a more methodical investigation of the affair. In the first place I considered the manner in which the parchment had come into my possession. The spot where we discovered a scarabaeus was on the coast of the mainland, about a mile eastward of the island, and but a short distance above high-water mark. Upon my taking hold of it, it gave me a sharp bite, which caused me to let it drop. Jupiter, with his accustomed caution, before seizing the insect, which had flown toward him, look about him for a leaf, or something of that nature, by which to take hold of it. It was at this moment that his eyes, and mine also, fell upon the scrap of parchment, which I then supposed to be paper. It was lying half buried in the sand, a corner sticking up. Near the spot where we found it, I observed the remnants of the hull of what appeared to have been a ship's longboat. The wreck seemed to have been there for a great while; for the resemblance to boat timbers could scarcely be traced.

"Well, Jupiter picked up the parchment, wrapped the beetle in it, and gave it to me. Soon afterward we turned to go home, and on the way met Lieutenant G——. I showed him the insect, and he begged me to let him take it to the fort. Upon my consenting, he thrust it forthwith into his waistcoat pocket, without the parchment in which it had been wrapped, and which I had continued to hold in my hand during his inspection. Perhaps he dreaded my changing my mind, and thought it best to make sure of the prize at once—you know how enthusiastic he is on all subjects connected with Natural History. At the same time, without being conscious of it, I must have deposited the parchment in my own pocket.

"You remember that when I went to the table, for the purpose of making a sketch of the beetle, I found no paper where it was usually kept. I looked in the drawer, and found none there. I searched my pockets, hoping to find an old letter, when my hand fell upon the parchment. I thus detail the precise mode in which it came into my possession; for the circumstances impressed me with peculiar force.

"No doubt you will think me fanciful—but I had already established a kind of *connexion*. I had put together two links of a great chain. There was a boat lying upon a sea-coast, and not far from the boat was a parchment—*not a paper*—with a skull depicted upon it. You will, of course, ask, 'Where is the connexion?' I reply that the skull, or death's-head, is the well-known emblem of the pirate. The flag of the death's-head is hoisted in all engagements.

"I have said that the scrap was parchment, and not paper. Parchment is durable—almost imperishable. Matters of little moment are rarely consigned to parchment; since, for the mere ordinary purposes of drawing or writing, it is not nearly so well adapted as paper. This reflection suggested some meaning—some relevancy—in the death's-head. I did not fail to observe, also, the *form* of the parchment. Although one of its corners had been, by some accident, destroyed, it could be seen that the original form was oblong. It was just such a slip, indeed, as might have been chosen for a memorandum—for a record of something to be long remembered and carefully preserved."

"But," I interposed, "you say that the skull was *not* upon the parchment when you made the drawing of the beetle. How then do you trace any connexion between the boat and the skull—since this latter, according to your own admission, must have been designed (God only knows how or by whom) at some period subsequent to your sketching the scarabaeus."

"Ah, hereupon turns the whole mystery; although the secret, at this point, I had comparatively little difficulty in solving. My steps were sure, and could afford but a single result. I reasoned, for example thus: when I drew the scarabaeus, there was not skull apparent upon the parchment. When I completed the drawing I gave it to you and observed you narrowly until you returned it. *You*, therefore, did not design the skull, and no one else was present to do it. Then it was not done by human agency. And nevertheless it was done.

"At this stage of my reflections I endeavoured to remember, and *did* remember, with entire distinctness, every incident which occurred about the period in question. The weather was chilly (oh, rare and happy accident!), and a fire was blazing upon the hearth. I was heated with exercise and sat near the table. You, however, had drawn a chair close to the chimney. Just as I had placed the parchment in your hand, and as you were in the act of inspecting it, Wolf, the Newfoundland, entered, and leaped upon your shoulders. With you left hand you caressed him and kept him off, while your right, holding the parchment, was permitted to fall listlessly between your knees, and in close proximity to the fire. At one moment I thought the blaze had caught it, and was about to caution you, but, before I could speak, you had withdrawn it, and were engaged in its examination. When I considered all these particulars, I doubted not for a moment that *heat* had been the agent in bringing to light, upon the parchment, the skull which I saw designed upon it. You are well aware that chemical preparations exist, and have existed time out of mind, by means of which it is possible to write upon either paper or vellum so that the characters shall become visible only when subjected to the action of fire. Zaffre, digested in aqua regia, and diluted with four times its weight of water, is sometimes employed; a green tint results. The regulus of cobalt, dissolved in spirit of nitre, gives a red. These colours disappear at longer or shorter intervals after the material written upon cools, but again become apparent upon the reapplication of heat.

"I now scrutinized the death's-head with care. Its outer edges—the edges of the drawing nearest the edge of the vellum—were far more *distinct* than the others. It was clear that the action of the caloric had been imperfect or unequal. I immediately kindled a fire, and subjected every portion of the parchment to a glowing heat. At first, the only effect was the strengthening of the faint lines in the skull; but, upon persevering in the experiment, there became visible, at the corner of the slip, diagonally opposite to the spot in which the death's-head was delineated, the figure of what I at first supposed to be a goat. A closer scrutiny, however, satisfied me that it was intended for a kid."

"Ha! ha!" said I, "to be sure I have no right to laugh at you—a million and a half of money is too serious a matter for mirth—but you are not about to establish a third link in your chain—you will not find any especial connexion between your pirates and a goat—pirates, you know, have nothing to do with goats; they appertain to the farming interest."

"But I have just said that the figure was *not* that of a goat."

"Well, a kid then—pretty much the same thing."

"Pretty much, but not altogether," said Legrand. "You may have heard of one *Captain* Kidd. I at once looked upon the figure of the animal as a kind of punning or hieroglyphical signature. I say signature; because its position upon the vellum suggested this idea. The death's-head at the corner diagonally opposite, had, in the same manner, the air of a stamp, or seal. But I was sorely put out by the absence of all else—of the body to my imagined instrument—of the text for my context."

"I presume you expected to find a letter between the stamp and the signature."

"Something of that kind. The fact is, I felt irresistibly impressed with a presentiment of some vast good fortune impending. I can scarcely say why. Perhaps, after all, it was rather a desire than an actual belief;—but do you know that Jupiter's silly words, about the bug being of solid gold, had a remarkable effect upon my fancy? And then the series of accidents and coincidences—these were so *very* extraordinary. Do you observe how mere an accident it was that these events should have occurred upon the *sole* day of all the year in which it has been or may be sufficiently cool for fire, and that without the fire, or without the intervention of the dog at the precise moment in which he appeared, I should never have become aware of the death's-head, and so never the possessor of the treasure."

"But proceed—I am all impatience."

"Well; you have heard, of course, the many stories current—the thousand vague rumours afloat about money buried, somewhere upon the Atlantic coast, by Kidd and his associates. These rumours must have had some foundation in fact. And that the rumours have existed so long and so continuous could have resulted, it appeared to me, only from the circumstance of the buried treasure still *remaining* entombed. Had Kidd concealed his plunder for a time, and afterwards reclaimed it, the rumours would scarcely have reached us in their present unvarying form. You will observe that the stories told are all about money-seekers, not about money-finders. Had the pirate recovered his money, there the affair would have dropped. It seemed to me that some accident—say the loss of a memorandum indicating its locality—had deprived him of the means of recovering it, and that this accident had become known to his followers, who otherwise might never have heard that treasure had been concealed at all, and who, busying themselves in vain, because unguided, attempts to regain it, had first given birth, and then universal currency, to the reports which are now so common. Have you ever heard of any important treasure being unearthed along the coast?"

"Never."

"But that Kidd's accumulations were immense is well known. I took it for granted, therefore, that the earth still held them; and you will scarcely be surprised when I tell you that I felt a hope, nearly amounting to certainty, that the parchment so strangely found involved a lost record of the place of deposit."

"But how did you proceed?"

"I held the vellum again to the fire, after increasing the heat, but nothing appeared. I now thought it possible that the coating of dirt might have something to do with the failure: so I carefully rinsed the parchment by pouring warm water over it, and, having done this, I placed it in a tin pan, with the skull downward, and put the pan upon a furnace of lighted charcoal. In a few minutes, the pan having become thoroughly heated, I removed the slip, and, to my inexpressible joy, found it spotted, in several places, with what appeared to be figures arranged in lines. Again I placed it in the pan, and suffered it to remain another minute. Upon taking it off, the whole was just as you see it now."

Here Legrand, having reheated the parchment, submitted it to my inspection.

The following characters were rudely traced, in a red tint, between the death's-head and the goat:

```
53‡‡†305))6*;4826)4‡.)4‡);806*;48†8¶ 60))85;1‡(;:
‡*8†83(88)5*†;46(;88*96*?;8)*‡(;485 );5*†2:*‡(;4956*2(5
*—4)8¶8*;4069285);)6†8)4‡‡;1(‡9;48081;8:8‡1;48†85;
4)485†528806*81(‡9;48;(88;4(‡?34;48)4‡;161;:188;‡?;
```

"But," said I, returning him the slip, "I am as much in the dark as ever. Were all the jewels of Golconda awaiting me upon my solution of this enigma, I am quite sure that I should be unable to earn them."

"And yet," said Legrand, "the solution is by no means so difficult as you might be led to imagine from the first hasty inspection of the characters. These characters, as anyone might readily guess, form a cipher—that is to say, they convey a meaning; but then from what is known of Kidd, I could not suppose him capable of constructing any of the more abstruse cryptographs. I made up my mind, at once, that this was of a simple species—such, however, as would appear, to the crude intellect of the sailor, absolutely insoluble without the key."

"And you really solved it?"

"Readily; I have solved others of an abstruseness ten thousand times greater. Circumstances, and a certain bias of mind, have led me to take interest in such riddles, and it may well be doubted whether human ingenuity can construct an enigma of the kind of which human ingenuity may not, by proper application, resolve. In fact, having once established connected and legible characters, I scarcely gave a thought to the mere difficulty of developing their import.

"In the present case—indeed in all cases of secret writing—the first question regards the *language* of the cipher; for the principles of solution, so far, especially, as the more simple ciphers are concerned, depend upon, and are varied by, the genius of the particular idiom. In general, there is no alternative but experiment (directed by probabilities) of every tongue known to him who attempts the solution, until the true one be attained. But with the cipher now before us all difficulty was removed by the signature. The pun upon the word 'Kidd' is appreciable in no other language than the English. But for this consideration I should have begun my attempts with the Spanish and French, as the tongues in which a secret of this kind would most naturally have been written by a pirate of the Spanish main. As it was, I assumed the cryptograph to be English.

"You observe there are no divisions between the words. Had there been divisions the task would have been comparatively easy. In such cases I should have commenced with a collation and analysis of the shorter words, and, had a word of a single letter occurred, as is most likely, (*a* or *I*, for example,) I should have considered the solution as assured. But, there being no division, my first step was to ascertain the predominant letters, as well as the least frequent. Counting all, I constructed a table thus:

Of the character 8	there are 33	†1	there are 8
;	" 26	0	" 6
4	" 19	92	" 5
‡)	" 16	:3	" 4
*	" 13	?	" 3
5	" 12	¶	" 2
6	" 11	—.	" 1

"Now, in English, the letter which most frequently occurs is *e*. Afterward, the succession runs thus: *a o i d h n r s t u y c f g l m w b k p q x z*. *E* predominates so remarkably that an individual sentence of any length is rarely seen in which it is not the prevailing character.

"Here, then, we have, in the very beginning, the groundwork for something more than a mere guess. The general use which may be made of the table is obvious—but, in this particular cipher, we shall only very partially require its aid. As our predominant character is 8, we will commence by assuming it as the *e* of the natural alphabet. To verify the supposition, let us observe if the 8 be seen often in couples—for *e* is doubled with great frequency in English—in such words, for example, as 'meet,' 'fleet,' 'speed,' 'seen,' 'been,' 'agree,' etc. In the present instance we see it doubled no less than five times, although the cryptograph is brief.

"Let us assume 8, then is *e*. Now, of all *words* in the language; 'the' is most usual; let us see, therefore, whether there are not repetitions of any three characters, in the same order of collocation, the last of them being 8. If we discover repetitions of such letters, so arranged, they will most probably represent the word 'the.' Upon inspection, we find no less than seven such arrangements, the characters being ;48. We may, therefore, assume that ; represents *t*, 4 represents *h*, and 8 represents *e*—the last being now well confirmed. Thus a great step has been taken.

"But, having established a single word, we are enabled to establish a vastly important point; that is to say, several comments and terminations of other words. Let us refer, for example, to the last instance but one in which the combination ;48 occurs—not far from the end of the cipher. We know that the ; immediately ensuing is the commencement of a word, and, of the six characters succeeding this 'the,' we are cognizant of no less than five. Let us set these characters down, thus, by the letters we know them to represent, leaving a space for the unknown—

t eeth

"Here we are enabled, at once, to discard the '*th*,' as forming no portion of the word commencing with the first *t*; since, by experiment of the entire alphabet for a letter adapted to the vacancy, we perceive that no word can be formed of which this *th* can be a part. We are thus narrowed into

t ee

and, going through the alphabet, if necessary, as before, we arrive at the word 'tree' as the sole possible reading. We thus gain another letter, *r*, represented by (, with the words 'the tree' in juxtaposition.

"Looking beyond these words, for a short distance, we again see the combination ;48, and employ it by way of *termination* to what immediately precedes. We have thus this arrangement:

the tree ;4(‡?34 the

or, substituting the natural letters, where known, it reads thus:

the three thr‡?3h the

"Now, if, in place of the unknown characters, we leave blank spaces, or substitute dots, we read thus:

the three thr. . .h the

when the word 'through' makes itself evident at once. But this discovery gives us three new letters, *o*, *u*, and *g*, represented by ‡, ?, and 3.

"Looking now, narrowly, through the cipher for combinations of known characters, we find, not very far from the beginning, this arrangement:

83(88

or

egree

which, plainly, is the conclusion of the word 'degree,' and gives us another letter, *d*, represented by †.

"Four letters beyond the word 'degree' we perceive the combination

;46(;88*

"Translating the known characters, and representing the unknown by dots, as before, we read thus:

th.rtee.

an arrangement immediately suggestive of the word 'thirteen,' and again furnishing us with two new characters, *i* and *n* represented by 6 and *.

"Referring, now to the beginning of the cryptograph, we find the combination

53‡‡†

"Translating as before, we obtain

.good

which assures us that the first letter is *A*, and that the first two words are 'A good.'

"It is now time that we arrange our key, as far as discovered, in a tabular form, to avoid confusion. It will stand thus:

5	represents	a
†	"	d
8	"	e
3	"	g
4	"	h
6	"	i
*	"	n
‡	"	o
(	"	r
;	"	t
?	"	u

"We have, therefore, no less than eleven of the most important letters represented, and it will be unnecessary to proceed with the details of the solution. I have said enough to convince you that ciphers of this nature are readily soluble, and to give you some insight into the *rationale* of their development. But be assured the specimen before us appertains to the very simplest species of cryptograph. It now only remains to give you the full translation of the characters upon the parchment, as unriddled. Here it is:

> "*A good glass in the bishop's hostel in the devil's seat forty-one degrees and thirteen minutes northeast and by north main branch seventh limb east side shoot from the left eye of the death's-head a bee-line from the tree through the shot fifty feet out.*"

"But," said I, "the enigma seems still in as bad a condition as ever. How is it possible to extort a meaning from all this jargon about 'devil's seats,' 'death's-heads,' and 'bishop's hotels'?"

"I confess," replied Legrand, "that the matter still wears a serious aspect, when regarded with a casual glance. My first endeavour was to divide the sentence into the natural division intended by the cryptographist."

"You mean, to punctuate it?"

"Something of that kind."

"But how was it possible to effect this?"

"I reflected that it had been a *point* with the writer to run his words together without division, so as to increase the difficulty of solution. Now, a not over-acute man, in pursuing such an object, would be nearly certain to overdo the matter. When, in the course of his composition, he arrived at a break in his subject which would naturally require a pause, or a point, he would be exceedingly apt to run his characters, at this place, more than usually close together. If you will observe the MS., in the present instance, you will easily detect five such cases of unusual crowding. Acting upon this hint, I made the division thus:

> "*A good glass in the bishop's hostel in the devil's seat—forty-one degrees and thirteen minutes—northeast and by north—main branch seventh limb east side—shoot from the left eye of the death's-head—a bee-line from the tree through the shot fifty feet out.*"

"Even this division," said I, "leaves me still in the dark."

"It left me also in the dark," replied Legrand, "for a few days; during which I made diligent inquiry, in the neighbourhood of Sullivan's Island, for any building which went by the name of the 'Bishop's Hotel'; for, of course, I dropped the obsolete word 'hostel.' Gaining no information on the subject I was on the point of extending my sphere of search and proceeding in a more systematic manner, when, one morning, it entered my head, quite suddenly, that this 'Bishop's Hostel' might have some reference to an old family, of the name of Bessop, which time out of mind, had held possession of an ancient manorhouse, about four miles to the northward of the island. I accordingly went over to the plantation, and reinstituted my inquiries among the older negros of the place. At length, one of the most aged of the women said that she had heard of such a place as Bessop's Castle, and thought that she could guide me to it, but that it was not a castle, nor a tavern, but a high rock.

"I offered to pay her well for her trouble, and, after some demur, she consented to accompany me to the spot. We found it without much difficulty, when, dismissing her, I proceeded to examine the place. The 'castle' consisted of an irregular assemblage of cliffs and rocks—one of the latter being quite remarkable for its height as well as for its insulated and artificial appearance. I clambered to its apex, and then felt much at a loss as to what should be done next.

"While I was busied in reflection, my eyes fell upon a narrow ledge in the eastern face of the rock, perhaps a yard below the summit upon which I stood. This ledge projected about eighteen inches, and was not more than a foot wide, while a niche in the cliff just above it gave it a rude resemblance to one of the hollow-backed chairs used by our ancestors. I made no doubt that here was the 'devil's seat' alluded to in the MS., and now I seemed to grasp the full secret of the riddle.

"The 'good glass,' I knew, could have reference to nothing but a telescope; for the word 'glass' is rarely employed in any other sense by seamen. Now here, I at once saw, was a telescope to be used, and a definite point of view, *admitting no variation*, from which to use it. Nor did I hesitate to believe that the phrases, 'forty-one degrees and thirteen minutes,' and 'northeast and by north,' were intended as directions for the levelling of the glass. Greatly excited by these discoveries, I hurried home, procured a telescope, and returned to the rock.

"I let myself down to the ledge, and found that it was impossible to retain a seat upon it except in one particular position. This fact confirmed my preconceived idea. I proceeded to use the glass. Of course, the 'forty-one degrees and thirteen minutes' could allude to nothing but elevation above the visible horizon, since the horizontal direction was clearly indicated by the words, 'northeast and by north.' This latter direction I at once established by means of a pocket-compass; then, pointing the glass as nearly at an angle of forty-one degrees of elevation as I could do it by guess, I moved it cautiously up or down, until my attention was arrested by a circular rift or opening in the foliage of a large tree that overtopped its fellows in the distance. In the centre of this rift I perceived a white spot, but could not, at first, distinguish what it was. Adjusting the focus of the telescope, I again looked, and now made it out to be a human skull.

"Upon this discovery I was so sanguine as to consider the enigma solved; for the phrase 'main branch seventh limb east side' could refer only to the position of the skull upon the tree, while 'shoot from the left eye of the death's-head' admitted, also, of but one interpretation, in regard to a search for buried treasure. I perceived that the design was to drop a bullet from the left eye of the skull, and that a bee-line, or, in other words, a straight line, drawn from the nearest point of the trunk through 'the shot' (or the spot where the bullet fell), and thence extended to a distance of fifty feet, would indicate a definite point—and beneath this point I thought it at least *possible* that a deposit of value lay concealed."

"All this," I said, "is exceedingly clear, and, although ingenious, still simple and explicit. When you left the Bishop's Hotel, what then?"

"Why, having carefully taken the bearings of the three, I turned homeward. The instant that I left 'the devil's seat,' however, the circular rift vanished; nor could I get a glimpse of it afterward, turn as I would. What seems to me the chief ingenuity in this whole business, is the fact (for repeated experiment has convinced me it *is* a fact) that the circular opening in question is visible from no other attainable point of view than that afforded by the narrow ledge upon the face of the rock.

"In this expedition to the 'Bishop's Hotel' I had been attended by Jupiter, who had, no doubt, observed, for some weeks past, the abstraction of my demeanour, and took especial care not to leave me alone. But, on the next day, getting up very early, I contrived to give him the slip, and went into the hills in search of the tree. After much toil I found it. When I came home at night my valet proposed to give me a flogging. With the rest of the adventure I believe you are as well acquainted as myself."

"I suppose," said I, "you missed the spot, in the first attempt at digging, through Jupiter's stupidity in letting the bug fall through the right instead of through the left eye of the skull."

"Precisely. This mistake made a difference of about two inches and a half in the 'shot'—that is to say, in the position of the peg nearest the tree; and had the treasure been *beneath* the 'shot' the error would have been of little moment; but the 'shot,' together with the nearest point of the tree, were merely two points for the establishment of a line of direction; of course the error, however trivial in the beginning, increased as we proceeded with the line, and by the time we had gone fifty feet threw us quite off the scent. But for my deep-seated impressions that treasure was here somewhere actually buried, we might have had all our labour in vain."

"But your grandiloquence, and your conduct in swinging the beetle—how excessively odd! I was sure you were mad. And why did you insist upon letting fall the bug, instead of a bullet, from the skull?"

"Why, to be frank, I felt somewhat annoyed by your evident suspicions touching my sanity, and so resolved to punish you quietly, in my own way, by a little bit of sober mystification. For this reason I swung the beetle, and for this reason I let it fall from the tree. An observation of yours about its great weight suggested the latter idea."

"Yes, I perceive; and now there is only one point which puzzles me. What are we to make of the skeletons found in the hole?"

"That is a question I am no more able to answer than yourself. There seems, however, only one plausible way of accounting for them—and yet it is dreadful to believe in such atrocity as my suggestion would imply. It is clear that Kidd—if Kidd indeed secreted this treasure, which I doubt not—it is clear that he must have had assistance in the labour. But this labour concluded, he may have thought it expedient to remove all participants in his secret. Perhaps a couple of blows with a mattock were sufficient, while his coadjutors were busy in the pit; perhaps it required a dozen—who shall tell?"

Author Index

Unit Index